Key to Road Maps

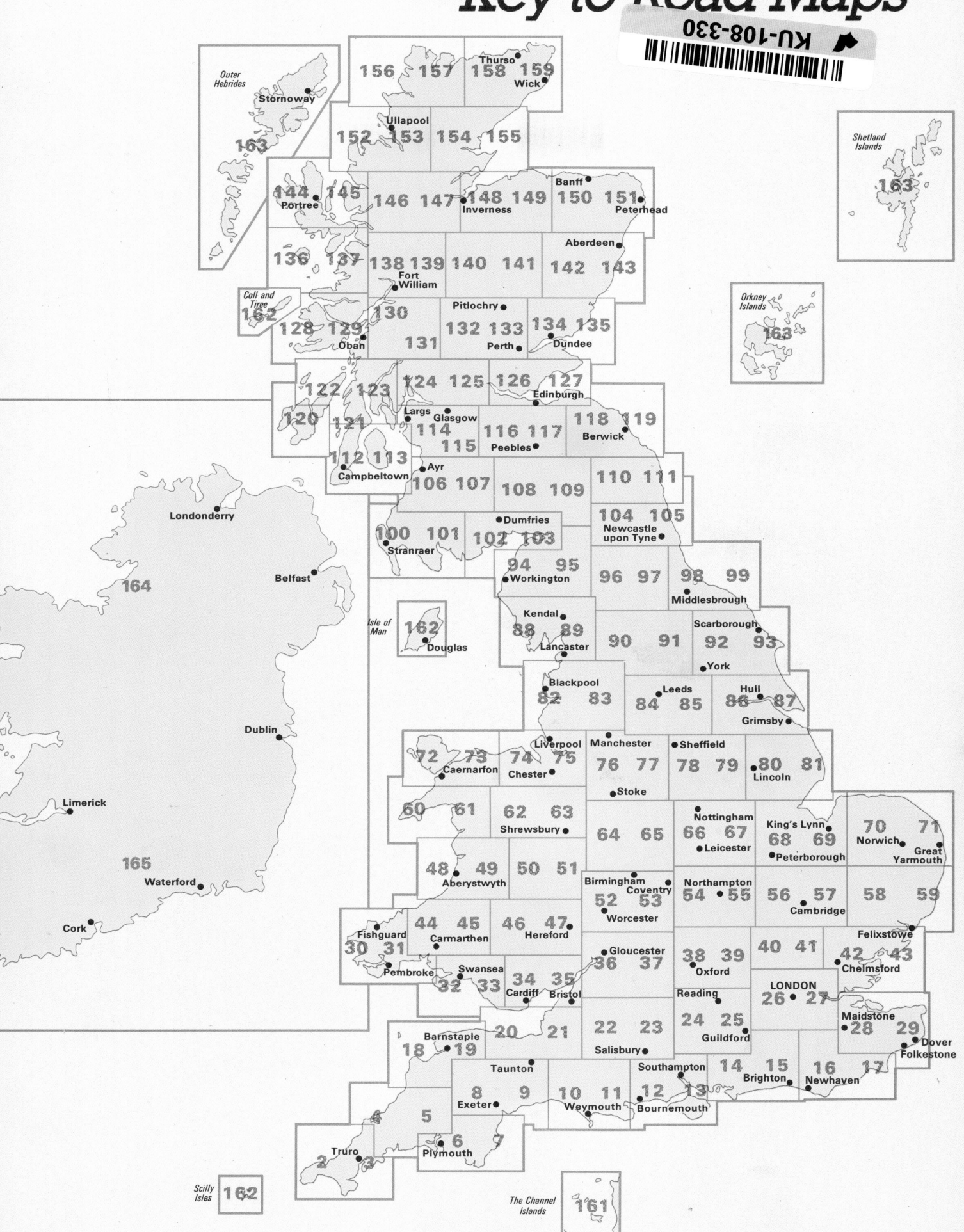

Outer Hebrides
Stornoway
163
156
157
158
159
Thurso
Wick
Ullapool
152
153
154
155
144
145
Portree
146
147
148
149
150
151
Inverness
Banff
Peterhead
Aberdeen
136
137
138
139
140
141
142
143
Fort William
Coll and Tiree
162
128
129
Oban
130
131
Pitlochry
132
133
Perth
134
135
Dundee
122
123
124
125
126
127
Edinburgh
120
121
Largs
Glasgow
114
115
116
117
Peebles
118
119
Berwick
112
113
Campbeltown
Ayr
106
107
108
109
110
111
104
105
Newcastle upon Tyne
Dumfries
100
101
Stranraer
102
103
94
95
Workington
96
97
98
99
Middlesbrough
Kendal
88
89
Lancaster
90
91
Scarborough
92
93
York
Blackpool
82
83
Leeds
84
85
Hull
86
87
Grimsby
Liverpool
72
73
Caernarfon
74
75
Chester
Manchester
76
77
Stoke
Sheffield
78
79
80
81
Lincoln
60
61
62
63
Shrewsbury
64
65
Nottingham
66
67
Leicester
King's Lynn
68
69
Peterborough
70
71
Norwich
Great Yarmouth
48
49
Aberystwyth
50
51
Birmingham
Coventry
52
53
Worcester
Northampton
54
55
56
57
Cambridge
58
59
Fishguard
30
31
Pembroke
44
45
Carmarthen
46
47
Hereford
Gloucester
36
37
38
39
Oxford
40
41
Felixstowe
42
43
Chelmsford
Swansea
32
33
34
35
Cardiff
Bristol
Reading
24
25
Guildford
LONDON
26
27
Maidstone
28
29
Dover
Folkestone
Barnstaple
18
19
20
21
22
23
Salisbury
Taunton
Southampton
14
15
Brighton
16
17
Newhaven
8
9
Exeter
10
11
Weymouth
12
13
Bournemouth
4
5
6
7
Plymouth
Truro
2
3
Scilly Isles
162
The Channel Islands
161
Shetland Islands
163
Orkney Islands
163
Isle of Man
162
Douglas
Londonderry
Belfast
164
Dublin
Limerick
165
Waterford
Cork

CONTENTS

Watching the Weather

The British climate is extreme in one respect only: the obsessive hold it has over us. The climate itself, compared to other parts of the world, is kind. Variation in temperature between summer and winter is not great, partly because of the moderating effect of the seas around us.

British weather is, whatever one may feel in a sudden downpour, temperate. Not for us the great extremes experienced in the USA's Mid-West, or Central Russia, where they bake in summer and freeze in winter. Our temperatures rarely rise above 32 degrees C (90 degrees F) or fall below −10 degrees C (14 degrees F).

Although the range of climatic conditions is not great, the patterns are constantly shifting. Britain's weather, in that sense, is unpredictable.

Day-to-day (even hour to hour) variations, often very localised, create a hotchpotch of seemingly unreliable weather conditions which test the Meteorological Office's most sophisticated techniques.

Yet when we complain and joke about our weather, we tend to forget that our mild-mannered, dampish climate has produced a lush, green landscape that is envied and admired the world over.

It is no surprise that the umbrella has become almost a part of our national identity. Even in these days of casual wear, many Englishmen feel undressed without one; it is, perhaps, a symbol of their indulgent attitude to extremes in other people's behaviour and thought.

NOAA-8 (left) of the National Oceanic and Atmospheric Administration series, launched to take swathes of pictures in its orbit, now one of space's 'dead' satellites

Keeping pace with the Earth, METEOSTAT-2 (below) takes half-hourly shots of the whole hemisphere. Studied in sequence they reveal weather movements

EYES IN THE SKIES

Facts, not folklore, are used in predicting the weather. High technology information-gathering systems and computer analysis have consigned the theories about aching joints to the dustbin.

The technology is, quite literally, space age. Satellites, rockets and aircraft carry sophisticated instruments which feed a network of land-based computers with data on atmospheric pressure, temperature and cloud patterns.

The age of the meteorological satellite, a development from the manned balloons of previous centuries, began on 1 April 1960 with the launching of TIROS-1. Many weather satellites now monitor the earth's climate, filling the gaps in the ground observatory network and providing up-to-the minute information.

Weather satellites operate in either a polar orbit or maintain a geostationary position, about 22,500 miles (36,000 km) above the equator (see diagram). This latter type orbits in such a way that it always maintains a position which appears motionless above the same point on the earth's surface, providing a constant monitoring service. Polar orbiting satellites, by comparison, travel at relatively low altitudes — normally from around 430 to 940 miles (700 to 1,500

km). They circle the earth once every 100 minutes at right angles to the direction of the earth's rotation, providing complete global coverage every 12 hours.

Most of the satellite data used by the Meteorological Office is supplied by the geostationary METEOSTAT-2, launched 19 June 1981, and NOAA-7 and NOAA-6, launched 23 June 1981 and 27 June 1979 respectively, which orbit at an average altitude of 530 miles (850 km).

A nose for rain — No. 15 Hercules (below) of the Meteorological Research Flight collects cloud data

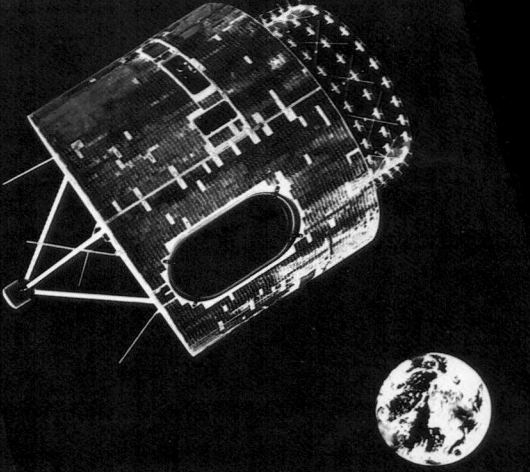

AA

3 MILE
ROAD
ATLAS
OF BRITAIN

Published by the Automobile Association,
Fanum House, Basingstoke, Hampshire RG21 2EA.

A Closer Look at Britain

This is a 3 mile atlas with a difference. Imagine looking down on Britain from one of the satellites that circles hundreds of miles above us, beaming down its images of this green and blue planet. Imagine making the journey from that satellite, coming closer and watching Britain's details take shape and grow until a richly colourful country appears, small in size but big in its history and wonderful countryside, with a dense network of roads linking great cities and remote villages the length and breadth of the land.

As a foretaste of what's revealed in the 3 miles to the inch detail of this atlas, the pages that follow make that journey, closing in on Britain from 530 miles, 440 miles, 1500 ft – and coming right down to travel its roads and explore its many different kinds of landscape. They arrive finally at an overview of some of its finest scenery with a look at the AA's Viewpoints – and a look from the top of nine of them.

Each step of this journey reveals something more of Britain: its climate, its intricate system of roads, its scenery – from lowlands to mountains and ever-changing coast – and its historic towns and villages.

Practical information is given on leisure activities for every type of countryside, together with essential advice on dealing with some of Britain's trickier road conditions.

And once the journey of discovery has been made through these early pages – what better than to turn to the clarity and detail of the three-miles-to-the-inch atlas that follows and discover the real thing. The atlas itself comes with local radio maps, a detailed London street map, 61 town plans (with area plan and street index) and 12 town plans marked out for tourists. It is preceded by 10 pages of route planning maps. These are designed to help you plan long distance journeys quickly and easily – for a full explanation of how to use them, start reading at page 42.

3rd edition Oct 1986, reprinted December 1986, reprinted March 1987
2nd edition Sept 1985, reprinted April 1986
1st edition Feb 1985

Produced by the Cartographic Department, Publishing Division of the Automobile Association

Based on the Ordnance Survey maps, with the permission of the Controller of Her Majesty's Stationery Office.
Crown Copyright Reserved

Typeset by Petty & Sons Ltd., Leeds, member of the BPCC Group

Colour separation by Mullis Morgan Ltd., 12-24 Brunswick Centre, London WC1N 1BX

Printed and bound in Spain by
Graficromo SA, Spain

The contents of this book are believed correct at the time of printing. Nevertheless, the publisher can accept no responsibility for errors or omissions, or for changes in the details given.

Published by the Automobile Association, Fanum House, Basing View, Basingstoke, Hampshire RG21 2EA

ISBN 0 86145 394 8   AA Ref 54014M

Picture: The Atlantic from Greenland to the United Kingdom - an image taken by satellite TIROS N, 530 miles (850 km) out in space

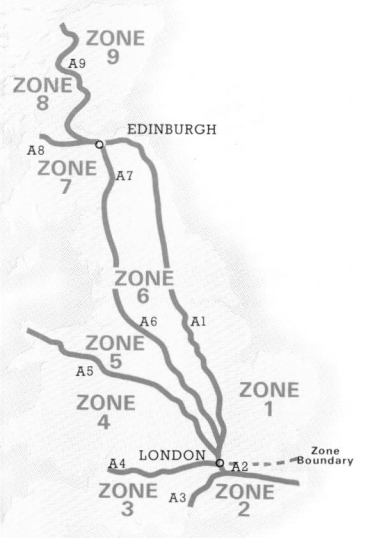

THE ROAD ZONES

London is the hub for the spokes of roads numbered A1 to A6, Edinburgh for the A7, A8 and A9. This system has made the numbering of other roads very simple. The lower the subsequent numbers, the closer the road's starting point to London — similarly to Edinburgh. Broadly speaking, motorway numbers also follow a similar pattern.

Britain's Road Pattern

Good communications are the life-blood of any organised society. The Romans were probably the first to realise this fact over 2,000 years ago. Many of the roads they built in Britain — improved, of course, over the centuries — have been in constant use ever since. Yet, apart from occasional innovation, there was precious little in the way of real change until the turn of this century.

The catalyst was the motor car. In the 1890s, Henry Ford pioneered mass car construction. In 1896, the car was emancipated from the red flag. Britain was poised on the brink of a new era.

To cope with a now vast traffic flow, Great Britain's road network continues to grow. At the last count there were 214,575 miles (343,320 km) of road, 1,711 miles (2,754 km) of which are motorways built in the last 25 years.

Making sense of the system

Navigation along the complex maze of roads which covered Britain in the early 20th century — none of which was classified or numbered — was often a nightmare. In 1919, the Ministry of Transport was established and soon introduced a classification and numbering system which began to make sense of the chaos by forming a three-tier network of Class 1, Class 2 and Class 3 roads.

The classification system was based on the function of the road rather than its standard of construction.

Class I roads were deemed to be the more important through-traffic routes, connecting large

Below: a model for success — Ford Motor Co's entire London staff, 1911, at 55 Shaftesbury Ave, with Model T: the first mass-made car

Above: the Montego gets the robot touch for front and rear screens at Austin Rover's automated Cowley works

Check on road conditions

The "Traveline" service gives information by recorded message — roads affected by bad weather, roadworks, etc — on areas in a 50-mile radius of major towns and cities. The preface to the telephone directory lists the relevant numbers.

For road and weather conditions see also local radio maps, pages 52 and 53.

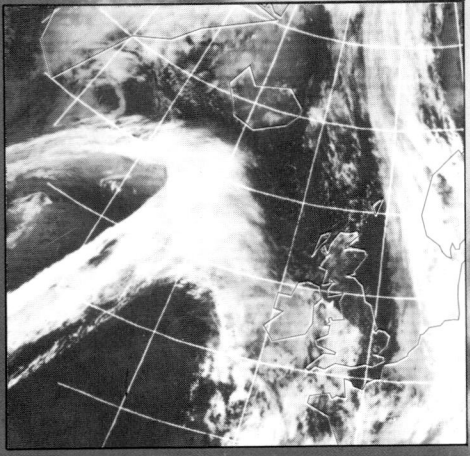

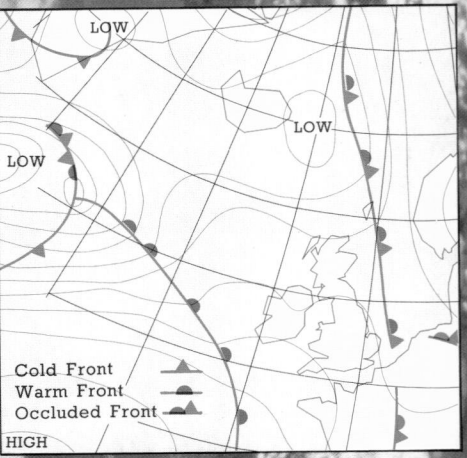

Cold Front
Warm Front
Occluded Front

HIGH

HIGHS AND LOWS

'Highs' and 'Lows' hold the answer to Britain's weather — 'lows' in particular, for weather patterns are mainly influenced by areas of low pressure called depressions.

These depressions are usually formed in the Western Atlantic. Depressions, or 'lows', are aptly named, for they generally bring periods of disturbed, wet weather (possibly with snow in winter).

They can travel, uninterrupted, across thousands of miles of ocean, gathering moisture along the way. Prevailing westerly winds meet the land mass of the British Isles, and in rising over the mountains, cool and condense to bring cloud and rain.

They are easily recognised by the close, concentrated pattern of their isobars — lines which link up places of equal pressure. Winds blow in an anticlockwise direction and, because the isobars are close together, are normally quite strong. Britain's mild, moist, westerly climate is associated with the passage of such depressions.

Of course, it is not quite as simple as that. These depressions suck in air from the regions of high pressure and normally arrive with adjacent areas of warm and cold air, the leading edges of which are called warm and cold fronts. They bring with them a mixed bag of weather which can include rain and bright spells, with windy conditions along the coast.

To complicate matters even further, 'lows' can be slowed down or stopped by belts of high pressure over the Continent. Under such circumstances, their influence may be limited to the western half of Britain. Poor Wales might be suffering a downpour while East Anglians are basking under blue skies.

Areas of prolonged high pressure in the summer are much better news, bringing bright, warm weather with long spells of sunshine. In winter, a 'high' over northern Europe can bring very cold east winds across Britain; also fog and frost. Winds, which blow clockwise around the high pressure centres, are generally light since the isobars are further apart.

Above: the photo (left) on which the weather chart (right) was based. A swirl of cloud north-west of Britain is a low pressure centre. South is high pressure (cloud free), south-east a warm front (cloud belt). An occluded front (cloud belt) runs from north to south

Main picture: Britain from the satellite's point of view — an image from NOAA-6, polar orbiting 530 miles above the Earth

THE FACTS

Once in a while, our reliably moderate climate is affected by freak, bizarre or extreme conditions. Here are some of the least typical in the record book:

HIGHEST RECORDED (SHADE) TEMPERATURE: 36.7 degrees C (98 degrees F) at Epsom, 9 August 1911. Lowest (screen) −27.2 degrees C (−17 degrees F) at Braemar in 1895 and again 10 January 1982.

HIGHEST RECORDED MONTHLY SUNSHINE TOTAL: 383.9 hours (over 10 hours a day) at Eastbourne, July 1911. Lowest: 0.0 hours (none!) in Westminster, December 1890.

WETTEST PLACE ON RECORD: Sprinkling Tarn, Cumbria, with 257 inches of rain (6,527.8 mm) in 1954.

WINDIEST LOCATIONS, AS MEASURED BY EXTREME GUSTS: Lowland — Kirkwall with 118 knots in February 1969; Highland — Cairngorm, with 125 knots in March 1967.

Summer motoring

For many motorists, the summer holiday months usually involve the longest drive of the year. Hot weather, traffic jams and sustained use will test your car (especially its cooling system) to the full. Before a long journey, treat your car to a full service. Minor faults en route can often be easily repaired if you carry a small spares kit containing a fan belt, radiator hoses, bulbs, points, a condenser, spark plugs and insulating tape.

Pack your luggage sensibly Loads should be balanced, with heavy articles as near the centre of the car as possible. Roof racks should be firmly fixed and loaded to a low profile to minimise wind resistance. Check tyre pressures — they may have to be increased.

Driver fatigue can be a killer Keep the car well ventilated. Keep your driving down to three hours at a time without a break, and certainly no more than eight hours in one day. If you feel tired, stop at the nearest lay-by or motorway service area (not the hard shoulder) and stretch your legs.

Keep calm in a traffic jam (You are trapped, and there is nothing you can do about it). Switch off the engine if the congestion looks like lasting.

Read the road And don't forget that warm sunshine can melt the surface, making it slippery. So can rain at the end of a long, dry period; the water mixes with dust, oil and tyre rubber to produce very slippery surfaces.

Winter motoring

Snow and ice, rain and slush, fog and frost . . . these are all part of a typical British winter.

Car check list Make sure that the antifreeze solution in the car's cooling system is up to strength.

Add a de-icing solution to the windscreen washing fluid.

Carry a de-icing aerosol spray to free frozen locks.

Carry an aerosol water dispellant for damp starting.

Make sure that the battery is topped up and in good condition.

If you must travel in difficult conditions carry a simple "survival" kit of a torch, blankets, boots, gloves and a set of jump-leads for starting a car with a flat battery.

Driving techniques It's a case of "softly, softly" in winter weather. Look out for potential skid traps — wet leaves, shady spots, bridges (cold air above and below the road surface can cause ice to linger). Stick to the well-gritted main roads and motorways wherever possible. Use the highest gears to prevent sudden surges of power which can cause wheelspin.

Do nothing suddenly If you spot skid traps in time, reduce speed gradually. Do not brake abruptly or turn the steering wheel quickly. Do not brake during a skid. When visibility is severely reduced, use dipped headlights, windscreen wipers and rear fog-warning lights; even in daylight. Slow right down and keep a safe distance. Do not hang on to someone else's tail lights. Make sure you can stop within your range of vision.

The figures

Calling the experts: Local area forecasts for most parts of the country are available on the recorded message "Weatherline". Telephone numbers appear in the preface to the telephone directory.

In addition to "Weatherline's" standard information, the Meteorological Office's regional Weather Centres can usually answer individual queries and give personal advice to callers. (N.B. at particularly busy times, they may switch to a standard answering service).

Centres: Telephone Aberdeen (0224) 722334; Birmingham 021-743 4747; Bristol (0272) 279298; Cardiff (0222) 397020; Glasgow 041-248 3451; Leeds (0532) 451990; London 01-836 4311; Manchester 061-832 6701; Newcastle-upon-Tyne (0632) 326453; Norwich (0603) 660779; Nottingham (0602) 384092; Southampton (0703) 28844.

Main picture: 9.30 am — the south coast and Isle of Wight as seen by LANDSAT-4's thematic mapper, 440 miles up. Red shows vegetation, with green-brown for moor!and and built-up areas (and M27) picked out in pale blue — providing invaluable data for cartographers and planners. Image supplied by NRSC Farnborough

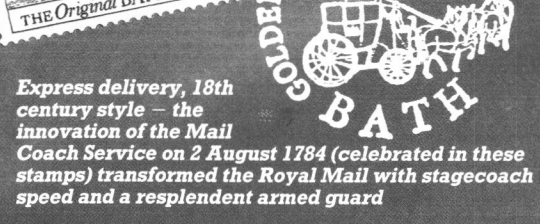

Express delivery, 18th century style — the innovation of the Mail Coach Service on 2 August 1784 (celebrated in these stamps) transformed the Royal Mail with stagecoach speed and a resplendent armed guard

The age of the stage

The habit of coach travel was introduced into Britain in the 1560s by a Dutchman, Guylliam Boonen, who became Queen Elizabeth's coachman. Soon, the streets of London were becoming congested creating traffic jams which we are all too familiar with today.

With the spread of turnpike routes (see page 12) and the improvements in road construction and maintenance, out-of-town stagecoach travel became faster and less arduous. By the 18th century, coaches were able to travel 80 miles in a good day, averaging ten miles an hour, with a change of horses every 12 miles.

As was reported in 1771: "Now a country fellow, 100 miles from London, jumps on a coach box in the morning and gets to town by night."

The Roman road at Blackstone Edge near Littleborough, Lancashire, is generally regarded as the best preserved in Britain. Part of the trans-Pennine route which ran from Manchester to Ilkley, its 16ft wide surface is paved with flat stone blocks which incorporate a centre groove.

Below, Hardknott Pass

Thomas Telford

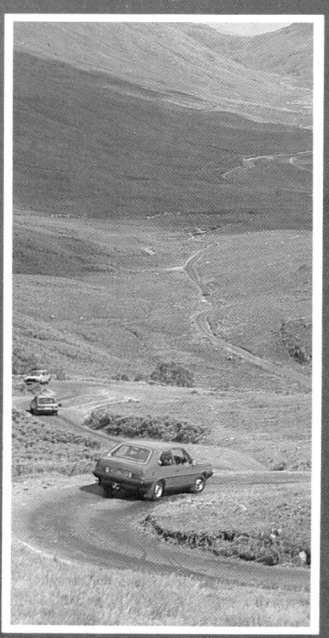

Thomas Telford (1757–1835) was a Scots engineer who transformed communications in Britain. He built bridges, canals, a spectacular aqueduct, docks and harbours — and, of course, roads.

His road building skills are legendary. He pioneered design and engineering techniques which led to the construction of direct, efficient and durable roads the length and breadth of Britain.

Telford's genius was that he was able to tame the mountainous areas of Britain, and make them accessible to fast and reliable coach travel. The legacy he left in North Wales stands as his shining example. In 1811, he surveyed a route from Shrewsbury to the port of Holyhead which has become today's A5. The mountains of Snowdonia posed a formidable barrier, yet nowhere along the road he subsequently built was the gradient allowed to impede speedy communications.

He worked on the basis that the gradient, wherever possible, should not exceed 1 in 20. The measure of his engineering feat was that in his ascent of the Nant Ffrancon Pass, south of Bangor, Telford cut the road into the hillside, starting his climb two miles down the valley, to minimise the slope. For the first time, proper foundations were laid down, and camber and drainage channels were used to protect the surface against rain damage.

Telford's achievements can still be admired along the A5 and on many other stretches of roads in Britain, which faithfully follow his finely-engineered gradients through the mountains of Snowdonia.

---

centres of population. These Class I routes were made 'A' roads and were numbered according to a radiating zone principle. The country was divided into nine zones, the divisions being the nine single-number A routes, A1 to A9.

Class II roads, our B roads, were those which formed an important link between Class I roads and smaller centres of population.

Class III roads — the C roads — are less used but vital transport links within local areas. The road number is rarely shown on traffic signs.

This classification principle — a system based on function — still applies today to our "A", "B" and "C" roads. Some of the A roads, subsequently including motorways, were given a special status, based again on their traffic use. These were designated Trunk roads — strategic routes of national importance dedicated to the through movement of long-distance traffic. They are under the control of the Department of Transport.

Since then, certain A roads which act as routes between places of major traffic importance and are of distinct significance, were given Primary Routes status, creating an additional network within the A-route category. These are identified by direction signs, introduced in 1969, with the familiar green background.

In 1968, the authorities introduced different names for the classes of roads. Now Class I roads are known as principal roads, Class II roads are classified numbered roads, Class III roads are classified un-numbered roads, and other roads are still referred to as "unclassified".

Roman Roadbuilders

Britain had its roads and trackways long before the Roman invasion in AD 43. Contrary to popular belief, prehistoric man was extremely mobile. Traces of our oldest paths are probably over 10,000 years old. Neolithic highways, such as Norfolk's Icknield Way (now partly the busy A11) and the famous Ridgeway, are fortunately still with us.

But this ancient system was patchy and haphazard, the product of spontaneous growth. It took the coming of the Romans, with proven experience as road engineers, to give Britain its first coherent, planned system of routeways providing fast, reliable communications between their key forts, camps and towns, and penetrating every corner of their conquered territories.

It is a testament to their skills that Britain's road network, right up to the coming of the motorways, was based on foundations laid nearly 2,000 years ago.

Hardknott — the hard way

The ascent and descent of the Hardknott Pass in the Lake District is, even in a modern motor car, a memorable driving experience (see right).

Roman engineers, undaunted by 1 in 3 gradients, established a steep, zigzag climb, to a 1,291 ft col, which modern road builders have found impossible to improve.

Just beyond the summit stands the ruin of an ancient fort which must have represented the worst posting for a Roman garrison.

Bridges

Bridges come in all shapes and sizes, depending on when they were built and what purpose they were intended to serve.

The *Iron Bridge at Coalbrookdale*, in Shropshire, is a symbol of Britain's Industrial Revolution. Built in 1779, it was the first of several, notably Thomas Telford's cast-iron bridge over the River Spey at Craigellachie, in Grampian Region, Scotland, in 1814, and his design of the Waterloo Bridge over the River Conwy at Betws-y-Coed in Wales in 1815.

Another notable example is at Coalport, Shropshire, over the River Severn, dating back to 1818.

The design of the Coalbrookdale Iron Bridge harks back to some of the earlier *medieval stone bridges* which, with their elegant arches, still grace many parts of the country.

These stone bridges are one of the great glories of the period — strangely enough, since the roads were usually no more than muddy pathways.

You can find them at St Ives in Cambridgeshire (dating back to c.1415), at Bakewell over the River Wye in Derbyshire (13th century), Holme Bridge over the River Dart west of Ashburton, Devon, the Exeter Old Bridge (between new gyratory bridges), and the Bideford Bridge, now widened, in Devon.

The packhorse bridges built from the 14th century to the early 19th century, were smaller, simpler single-span constructions, usually found in difficult terrain. They can be seen at Birstwith, in North Yorkshire, over the River Nidd, at Allerford near Porlock, in Somerset and at Bakewell over the River Wye in Derbyshire, built in 1664.

Clapper bridges, the most primitive type of stone bridge, consisted of boulders topped by flat stone slabs. Easy to make, they continued to be built until the 18th century. Examples are at Postbridge, over the East Dart River on Dartmoor and at Tarr Steps near Liscombe over the River Barle in Somerset.

Devil's Bridge in Mid Wales is a unique site. Three bridges, one piled on top of the next, span a deep rocky gorge. The first, a simple stone structure, is medieval. The next, a wider bridge, was put up in 1708 to take horsedrawn vehicles. An iron bridge, built in 1901, sits over the two, carrying today's road traffic.

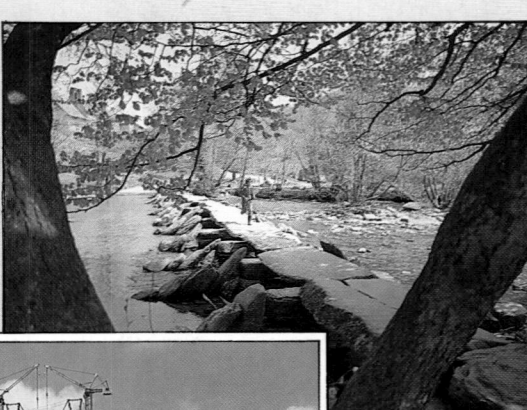

Two ways to bridge a gap — the slab and boulder Tarr Steps clapper bridge on Exmoor (above) may date back to prehistoric times; the £96 million Humber Estuary Bridge was opened 17 July 1981 by HM The Queen. At 1.38 miles (2.2km) long, with a 4,626ft (1,410m) main span (the world's longest), its 510ft (155.5m) towers were designed off-parallel, due to the earth's curve. The cables contain 44,000 miles (71,000km) of wire

Where Roads Meet

Junctions can test the motorist's road sense to the utmost. From the straight-forward "T" configuration to the complexities of the notorious Spaghetti Junction, they demand from drivers a keen sense of observation and often instant decisions. Crossroads, roundabouts, flyovers, underpasses, staggered-junctions and Y junctions, the huge variety of meeting places where traffic merges are a potential hazard requiring a high level of driver discipline and anticipation.

Main picture: the road ahead — Britain's newest motorway, the M25 London Orbital, meets the M3 (seen here from the west) at Chertsey. Due to make a complete ring around the capital, the M25 could be the world's biggest roundabout at 122 miles (195km) long. For M25 London Orbital map, turn to the inside back cover.

M-way loving kestrel

Life by the hard shoulder

A busy, noisy, traffic-laden motorway is a unique type of nature reserve, largely undisturbed by man, inhabited by hundreds of species of wild plants, insects and larger animals.

Flora Motorways are hardly conducive to the close examination of their flora. But, in slow-moving traffic, or a hold-up, flowers such as dandelions and Oxford ragwort can be picked out among the grass. The latter escaped from Oxford's Botanic Gardens nearly 200 years ago and has spread widely, attracted to the stony ground beside the road.

Unruly patches of gorse, broom, hawthorn and willow also make an appearance. The alder, a deciduous, narrow tree with a dark trunk, was planted because of its ability to survive in poor soils.

Fauna Slugs, snails and insects in the rough ground beside the hard shoulder attract hedgehogs. Rabbits — spotted at dawn and dusk — often build their warrens right on the verges.

The verges are also full of mice, voles and shrews — which explains the presence of the kestrel.

Many other birds can also be spotted, including the jackdaw (a gregarious creature, often seen around service stations), magpie (an indiscriminate scavenger), lapwing (usually in open spaces), black-headed gull and rook (feeding off worms on the edge of the carriageway, and most common in the North of England).

Red campion and ragwort (below) thrive on the motorway verge

The motorway map Great Britain, at the last count, had 1,711 miles (2,754 km) of motorway. The network, built since the 1950s, comprises in essence four long-distance arterial routes which link London with the cities of the Midlands, the North, North-West and South-West. This basic framework is supplemented by over 30 shorter motorways, mainly around London and Manchester. Motorway numbers usually follow the radiating zone principle.

Main picture: looking north up the M23 at Junction 9, near Horley

Britain is getting smaller all the time. Speed and convenience of travel is changing our attitudes to time and distance. Two hundred years ago, an overland journey from London to Glasgow would have taken days — a daunting prospect indeed. Today, it can be accomplished in a handful of hours thanks to the influences of advanced car technology and a rapid modern road system.

The spread of motorways, like the coming of the canals and railways before them, has revolutionised patterns of travel throughout Britain. Motorways represent less than one per cent of our total road mileage, yet they carry ten per cent of all traffic. Nearly a quarter of all heavy goods vehicles use them.

They were built to aid economic recovery and development by speeding up traffic flow, and to take through traffic away from heavily populated areas. Goods can now be whisked swiftly and inexpensively from one corner of the country to the other. Personal mobility has improved enormously. And, as a happy spin-off, scenic areas such as the Lake District, parts of Scotland and Wales and the West Country are now within easy reach of most urban centres.

Miles of millions

Motorway construction techniques have come a long way since the early days of the Preston Bypass, Britain's first stretch of motorway, opened on 5 December, 1958. An early section of the M6, it had dual two-lane carriageways and was eight miles (12.8km) long. A year later, the first part of the M1 was opened.

Living with Motorways

Better design has meant safer, more comfortable driving conditions on motorways, and a more harmonious blend of road and the environment on which it has been imposed. Improvements in construction standards have meant fewer stretches requiring periodic repair — these maintenance problems have given older motorways a bad name.

Building costs have rocketed. Motorways are exceedingly expensive. Approximate average costs per mile for new motorways in 1983 were £3 million (two-lane rural), £8 million (two-lane urban) and £11 million (three-lane urban).

Final costs are even greater — between 20 and 25 per cent has to be added to these figures to take into account land acquisition and other items of expenditure.

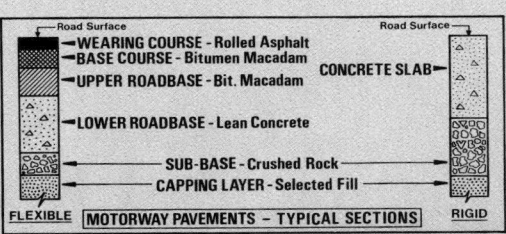

Flexible surfaces are more often chosen for 'unstable' ground, but both types of roadway are widely used in Britain

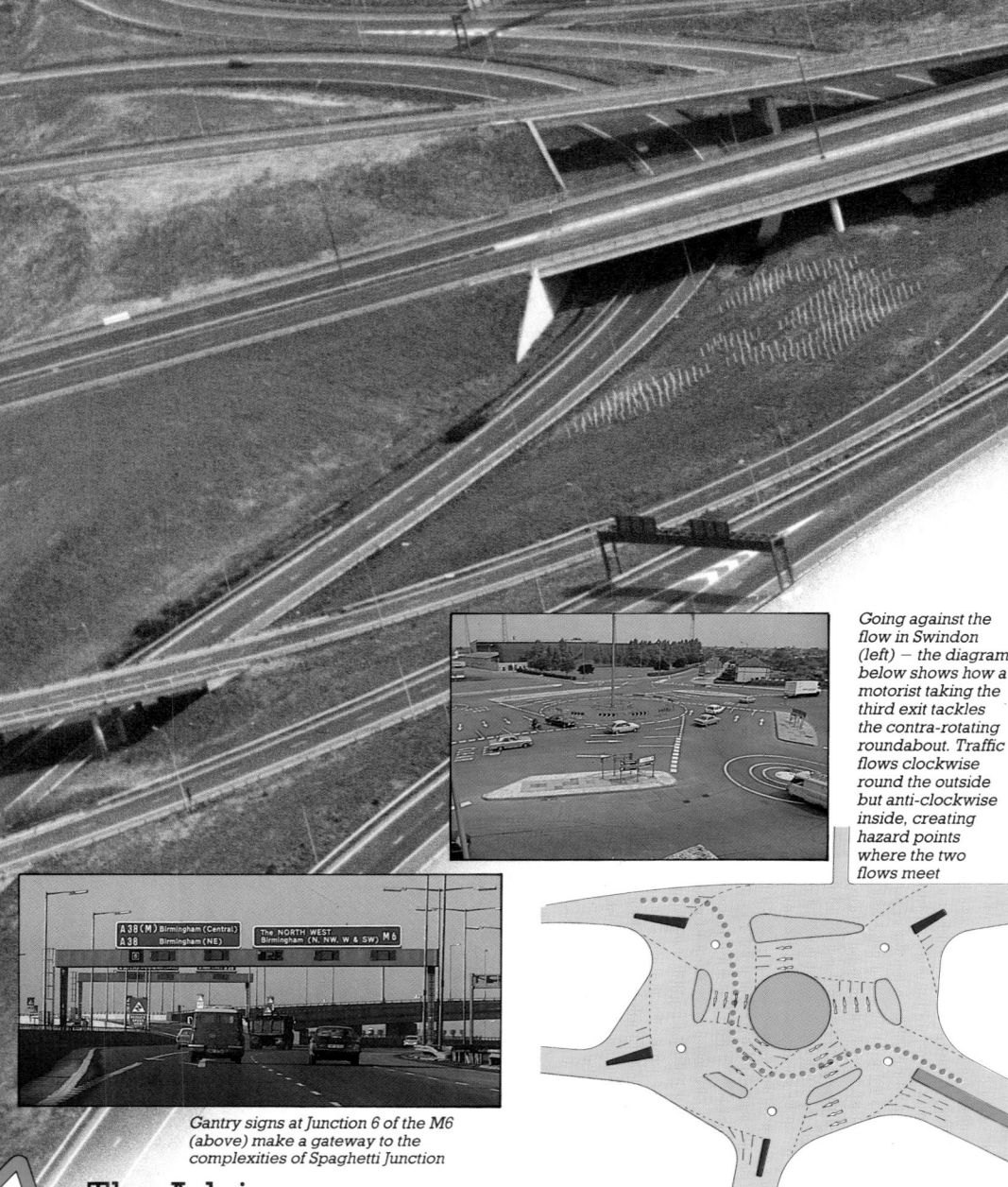

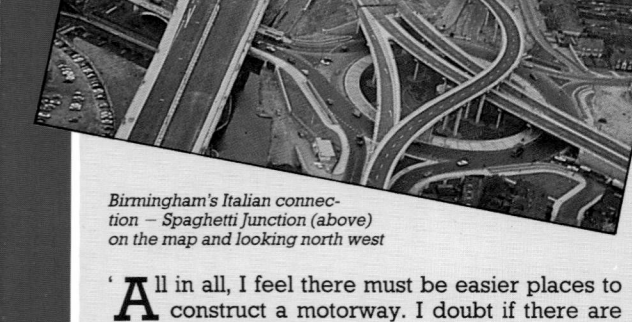

Pasta Junction

Birmingham's Italian connection — Spaghetti Junction (above) on the map and looking north west

Going against the flow in Swindon (left) — the diagram below shows how a motorist taking the third exit tackles the contra-rotating roundabout. Traffic flows clockwise round the outside but anti-clockwise inside, creating hazard points where the two flows meet

Gantry signs at Junction 6 of the M6 (above) make a gateway to the complexities of Spaghetti Junction

The Advice

Whether it's a complex junction or a simple merging of two roads, approach with care, and always follow the drill, especially on…

… **Motorway interchanges** Plan your journey and be guided by the signs. When motorways join or separate, plenty of advance warning is given. Get into the correct lane in good time by paying attention to the signs.

… **Roundabouts** These, the archetypal road junctions, sometimes cause the most confusion. Their very function — to mix several streams of traffic together — demands special care and attention. Remember the *Give Way* rule (traffic from the immediate right has priority), but keep moving if the way is clear. In exceptional circumstances traffic may even go the 'wrong' way round, as in the multi-roundabouts of Hemel Hempstead, Herts and Swindon, Wilts. Alternatively, priority may be given to traffic entering a roundabout, a situation clearly indicated by double broken white lines across the road and Give Way signs.

When turning left at a roundabout, approach and keep to the left — and signal left — throughout. When going straight on, approach in the left- or right-hand lane (depending on circumstances) and stay in that lane on the roundabout itself (though if it is clear of traffic, you can take the most convenient lane). Give a left signal when you have passed the exit prior to the one you need, and leave in the left lane unless conditions dictate otherwise.

When turning right, approach and keep to the right. Leave by the left lane, conditions permitting. Use the right signal until the exit before the one you need, then change to the left signal.

THE FIGURES

Spaghetti Junction was officially opened on 24 May 1972. It took over 3½ years to complete at the cost of £9.06 million, using in the course of construction 170,000 cubic yards of concrete and 300,000 cubic yards of fill (for the embankments).

At a recent count, there were 7,975 traffic signals (and 6,925 pelican crossings) in the United Kingdom. London alone has some 1,200 sets of lights.

THE FACTS

Traffic lights could legally be ignored until the 1930 Road Traffic Act was passed.

The Gravelly Hill Interchange qualifies as Britain's most complex junction, but the busiest junction must be London's Hyde Park Corner, which has Britain's heaviest traffic: an approximate average of 149 vehicles a minute measured over 24 hours in 1982.

Britain's two biggest traffic jams were both 35 miles (56km) long: between Torquay and Yarcombe on 15 July 1964, and on the A30 from Egham to Micheldever on 23 May 1970.

The City of London's first hand-operated traffic lights (below) installed at Ludgate Circus, 1930

Ready, Steady, Go

Traffic light technology has come a long way since the time, in 1868, when the world's first traffic signals were installed in Westminster. It was an inauspicious start, for this system of semaphore arms and gas lamps, mounted on a 20ft high column, soon exploded.

In 1918, the first manually operated three-colour lights were used in New York. A similar system was used in Piccadilly, London, in 1926.

The first attempts at vehicular control of signals came in the 1930s, when drivers in the USA were asked to sound their horns into microphones placed at the side of lights. This cacophonous system was, not surprisingly, soon dropped. In Britain, a more discreet method was chosen at the junction of Gracechurch Street and Cornhill in the City of London. This, Europe's first vehicle-actuated system, used electric contacts placed in the road. Unfortunately, history repeated itself when the lights exploded soon after their inauguration on 14 March 1932.

In 1931, the first linked systems based entirely on vehicle-actuated lights were installed in London and Glasgow. Britain's traffic lights still operate on this principle. Until the late sixties they were controlled by vehicles passing over a pneumatic tube. More sophisticated electronic systems, using cables buried beneath the road, are now in use.

Computers also arrived in the sixties. Computerised systems are amazingly flexible and can be programmed to deal with a wide range of traffic conditions. Not only that: the co-ordinated programmes can themselves be continually and automatically revised by information fed in by traffic sensors.

'**A**ll in all, I feel there must be easier places to construct a motorway. I doubt if there are any more difficult.'

These words appear in the conclusion of a report by the contractors A Monk and Company, who constructed the Gravelly Hill Interchange, Birmingham, better known to the world perhaps as Spaghetti Junction.

Spaghetti Junction — number six along the M6 as it runs a few miles north of Birmingham's city centre — looks innocuous enough on the map. Anyone who has seen this concrete knot of interconnecting road systems, its different layers linked by serpentine, elevated slipways, will instantly recognise the reason it took its name from a famous dish of pasta.

Basically, the interchange consists of two separate junctions. Primarily, it is a meeting place for the two-thirds of a mile stretch of elevated M6 Motorway and the A38(M) Aston Expressway, which is also partly elevated, and which leads into the city centre.

Beneath lies a second major junction, a large ground-level traffic island with a sunken concourse. This connects two busy main roads, the A5127 (Gravelly Hill) and the A38 (Tyburn Road) and a number of lesser routes.

The complications set in when connections between the two different tiers have to be made.

The traffic island is crossed by five elevated roadways, a complex system of viaducted slip roads (total length of viaduct here is 2.6 miles/4.2km). The M6 itself, also elevated, crosses the A38 on a series of 13 steel box girders, each 150ft long. The welding together, in situ, of these giant sections posed one of the most formidable challenges faced by the contractors.

Problem piled on problem during the course of construction. The difficulties in building such a complicated road junction were compounded by the nature of the site itself. Covering 30 acres, the Spaghetti Junction site is extremely congested. It is either surrounded or intersected by a maze of rivers, tributaries, canals, and a railway line — and to complicate matters just a little further, a major system of underground electric cables (part of the national grid), a trunk sewer and a high-pressure gas main.

How long, how fast

The impact of the motorways on speed and mobility is reflected in these figures based on comparative journeys between London (Oxford Circus), and three major regional destinations: Manchester, Cardiff and Edinburgh.

	Manchester	Cardiff	Edinburgh
Time taken in hours: Average speed mph in brackets			
1966	4¼ (44)	4½ (37)	8¾ (42)
1983	3½ (56)	2¾ (56)	7¼ (56)

Percentage of journey on motorways:			
1966	62%	14%	38%
1983	91%	91%	75%

The spectacular cut in journey time between London and Cardiff is a reflection of the growth of the motorway mileage between the two capital cities since 1966.

ORBITAL RECORD
Britain does not possess the largest motorway system in the world, but the M25, relieving London of through traffic, should be the world's largest orbital motorway.

THE FACTS
Though motorway mileages in Britain have increased dramatically over the years there is still only one mile of motorway for every hundred miles of other roads. Yet the 1,711 miles (2,754 km) of existing motorway carry a tenth of all our traffic.

THE FIGURES
Building costs per mile: *
Two lane rural stretch: £3,000,000
Three lane rural stretch: £5,000,000
Two lane urban stretch: £8,000,000
Three lane urban stretch: £11,000,000
* 1983 construction figures

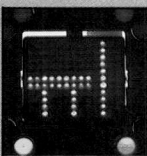  

Light warnings for motorists (above): motorway control rooms remote-operate these computer-monitored signals. Left: two lanes closed. Centre: road closed — red lights flash for STOP. Right: restrictions end (70mph limit)

Knowing the regulations

Speed limit: cars: 70mph; heavy lorries: 60mph; trailers and caravans: towing limits 50mph.

Pedestrians and horses (and all other animals) are banned. So, too, are learner-drivers (except in heavy goods vehicles), motorcycles of less than 50cc, certain invalid cars and carriages, agricultural vehicles and slow-moving vehicles (unless special police permission is obtained).

Parking and reversing, both on the hard shoulder and central reservation, are not allowed (but the hard shoulder can be used in emergencies).

Vehicles of over three tons laden weight, or those towing a trailer, are not allowed to use the right-hand lane of a three-lane motorway (unless there are exceptional circumstances).

Above: a numbered marker post at every 100 yd shows nearest phone — whatever the phone looks like, it's always within half a mile

RUBBISH ON THE ROAD
A massive amount of rubbish is thrown or dumped on our motorways, creating sudden and sometimes unavoidable hazards.

Debris which has accidentally fallen from lorries is another peril; not to mention the nuts, bolts, metal plates, petrol caps, plugs and ball bearings which become parted from cars.

Some of the items found on our motorways — everything from newspapers and tin cans to ancient washing machines, antique tables, old carpets, bedsteads, even a fairground organ — might raise a wry smile were it not for the fact that such motorway debris can be a killer. In fast-moving traffic even a plastic bag can be lethal if it blows on to a windscreen.

Hundreds of accidents a year, some fatal, are attributed to rubbish on the motorway. And hundreds of tons of it are collected every week from the carriageways. A survey in the 1970s of a 16 mile (26km) section of the M5 produced 530 different items in one day.

STAY SAFE
If anything falls off either your vehicle or the one ahead, or if you notice any dangerous debris on the motorway *do not* attempt to retrieve anything yourself. Stop at the next roadside telephone and inform the police.

Motorway signs

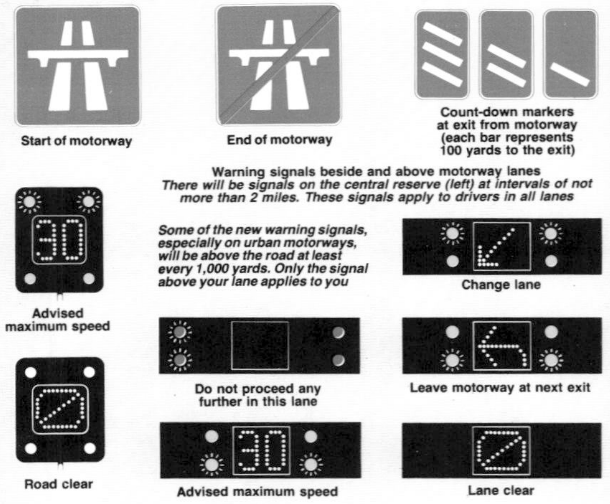

Start of motorway

End of motorway

Count-down markers at exit from motorway (each bar represents 100 yards to the exit)

Warning signals beside and above motorway lanes
There will be signals on the central reserve (left) at intervals of not more than 2 miles. These signals apply to drivers in all lanes.

Advised maximum speed

Some of the new warning signals, especially on urban motorways, will be above the road at least every 1,000 yards. Only the signal above your lane applies to you

Change lane

Road clear

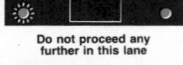
Do not proceed any further in this lane

Leave motorway at next exit

Advised maximum speed

Lane clear

Emergency diversion signs

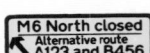
M6 North closed
Alternative route
A123 and B456

Sometimes there are too many route numbers to show on the diversion sign, or the alternative route may not have a route number. When this happens, the diversion route will be indicated by symbols of various shapes shown on the diversion sign and along the recommended route. The symbols may be a rectangle, a circle, a triangle or a diamond, and each of these may be either all black or yellow with a thick black border.

Warning signs

Roundabout

Two-way traffic crosses one-way road

Road narrows on right (left if symbol reversed)

Road narrows on both sides

Dual carriageway ends

Traffic joins from right

Traffic merges from left

Two-way traffic straight ahead

Distance to STOP sign ahead

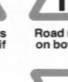
Distance to GIVE WAY sign ahead

Slippery road

Pedestrian crossing

Falling or fallen rocks

Right-hand lane closed (symbols may be varied)

Road works

Flashing amber lights used at school times at some sites; be prepared to stop

Headroom at hazard ahead (eg low bridge)

Steep hill downwards

Steep hill upwards

Change to opposite carriageway (may be reversed)

Uneven road

Hump bridge

Cattle

Low-flying aircraft or sudden aircraft noise

Level crossing without gate or barrier ahead

Level crossing with barrier or gate ahead

Count-down markers approaching concealed level crossing

AUTOMATIC BARRIERS
STOP when lights show

When amber light shows, STOP unless unsafe to do so; when red lights flash, STOP close to white line

Sharp deviation of route to left (or right if chevrons reversed)

Location of level crossing without gate or barrier

Accident
Other danger (plate indicates nature of danger)

Humps for ½ mile
Road humps ahead

Loose chippings

Max speed 20
Advisory speed limit at surface dressing site

The Main Road

Britain's road network, such as it existed at the end of the Middle Ages, was in a shocking state. Daniel Defoe, writing as recently as the 1720s, remarked that a 'Lady of very good Quality' who lived in Sussex was forced to use oxen to draw her coach, 'the way being so stiff and deep that no Horses could go on it'.

No such trials and tribulations await the modern traveller. Today, we enjoy a comprehensive, far-reaching system of main roads which make the going far easier.

THE FACTS
STOPPERS AND STARTERS

In 1923, the AA's 650-strong patrol force (274 with motorbike and sidecar) was called out 3,700 times. In the 1980s, 3,000 patrols go to the rescue approximately two million times a year. Top of the problems are ignition and electrical faults, causing about half of all call-outs, with engine trouble (oil leaks, starter faults, etc) accounting for about a fifth. Running out of petrol and other fuel system problems come third, while losing a key or getting locked out of the car results in about 100,000 calls a year.

Taking its toll on the driver (below right), London's Hyde Park Corner features typical tollgate architecture in the Gentleman's Magazine, 1792. Below: the tolls charged at Oxenton, Gloucestershire

Trusting the turnpikes

An attempt at establishing a properly maintained 'main road' system in Britain was made as far back as 1663 when the horse-drawn carriage and the cart were a long way from being superseded by our modern, motorised wheeled road traffic. An Act of Parliament in that year gave the responsibility to turnpike companies, so called because they originally used a pivoted bar, resembling a spear or pike, which swung on a central pillar to open and close the road (these were later replaced by gates).

The companies, known as turnpike trusts, were entitled to collect tolls in return for which they undertook the upkeep and maintenance of the road. By the 1750s, the growth in such trusts had reached proportions of 'road mania'; by the early 19th century, 1,100 trusts had been established to administer 23,000 miles (36,800km) of road.

Although prone to corrupt practices, the turnpikes undoubtedly brought a genuine improvement to Britain's neglected road network, as many vital stretches of road were straightened, surfaced, levelled and graded. New road legislation and competition from the railways brought further changes, and the last remaining trust was wound up in 1895. Many of the little roadside toll houses used by the pikemen still survive. Their distinctive architectural features and compact dimensions make them quite easy to identify.

Main picture: a fast-moving fraction of the main road system — the A322, Bagshot, Surrey

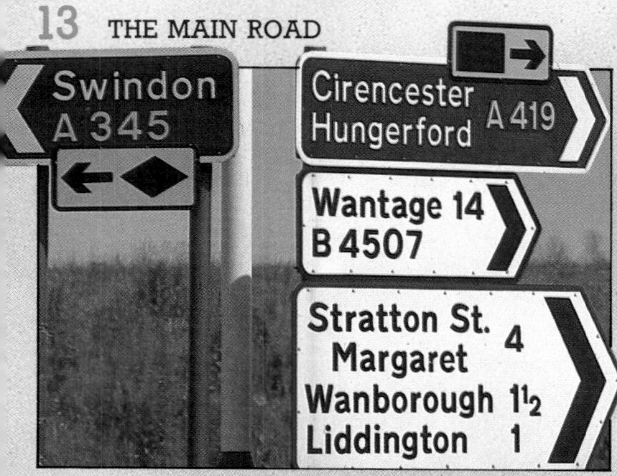
Swindon
A 345
Cirencester
Hungerford A 419
Wantage 14
B 4507
Stratton St. Margaret 4
Wanborough 1½
Liddington 1

Sign language for motorists (above) — green backgrounds point the way along the primary routes; black on white is used for B roads. Diversion routes for traffic taken off motorways are shown with geometric symbols on yellow with a black border

The A's have it

Our 'A' roads come in many guises, from a fast dual-carriageway to a winding tortuous country road.

Those who have been puzzled why a narrow, bumpy, single-track road with passing places in the Scottish Highlands, enjoys an 'A' road designation, will understand that it is not the width, the condition or the location that determines its classification, but its role in carrying through traffic, and its importance as a route linking vital centres. The A roads link up major towns and cities; B roads connect A roads with smaller centres and C roads (seldom numbered on signs) make the local connections.

Primary routes form another network: usually running along A roads, they are second only in importance to motorways for long distance travellers who want to find their way easily across country.

The system may be complex, but it's certainly well-used. In 1982, people travelling in Britain's 15 million plus cars clocked up 283 billion miles (452 billion km) — 85 per cent of all passenger travel. As well as the cars, there were 1,000,702 goods vehicles, over a million motorbikes and 111,000 public transport vehicles on the roads.

Over a third of car-owning households in the UK have two cars or more — and in Scotland, two thirds of the cars owned in 1982 were less than five years old. The climate could be responsible: in the balmy south-west of England a healthy 7.8 per cent of cars had been on the road since before 1969.

Read all about it

Too many motorists, having successfully coped with heavy traffic on their driving tests and answered the questions on the Highway Code, consign the book to the dustbin along with their L-plates. Admittedly, it may not be the most exciting read in the world; yet it should remain the road-user's Bible.

Familiarity with the Highway Code brings important road safety benefits. It is full of useful advice and guidance. Drivers in the habit of switching on their rear fog lamps at the slightest provocation, for example, would do well to read what the Code has to say (they are to be used only when visibility is *seriously* reduced). The eight point 'Fog Code' is illuminating enough. Look out also for the three-page section on approaching railway level crossings — another little-known morsel of information in its compact pages.

In the regular revision, the Highway Code is constantly being up-dated, so make sure you always have the latest edition.

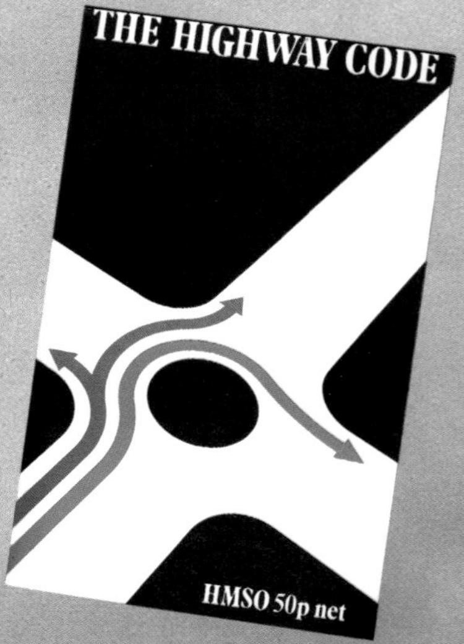
THE HIGHWAY CODE
HMSO 50p net

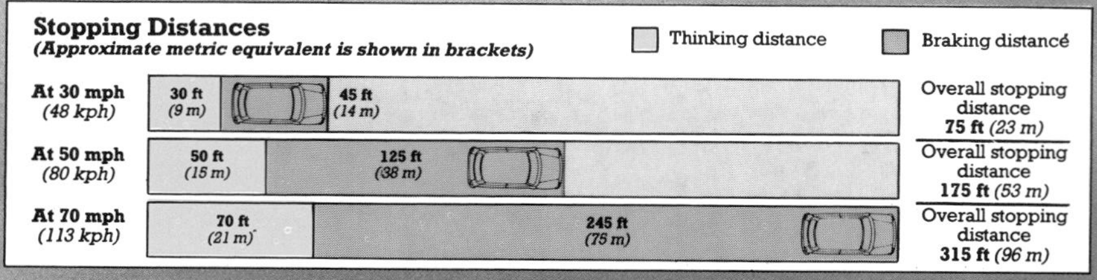
Stopping Distances
(Approximate metric equivalent is shown in brackets)
Thinking distance
Braking distance
At 30 mph (48 kph)
30 ft (9 m)
45 ft (14 m)
Overall stopping distance 75 ft (23 m)
At 50 mph (80 kph)
50 ft (15 m)
125 ft (38 m)
Overall stopping distance 175 ft (53 m)
At 70 mph (113 kph)
70 ft (21 m)
245 ft (75 m)
Overall stopping distance 315 ft (96 m)

Keep us safe

Even though Britain has one of the busiest road networks in the world, with extremely high traffic densities, our accident record is markedly better than that of many other countries.

This is attributed to a number of factors, including the seat belt legislation introduced in January 1983, the segregation of vehicles from pedestrians, and successful road safety campaigns which focus on particularly vulnerable groups — child pedestrians, cyclists and motor-cyclists, for example.

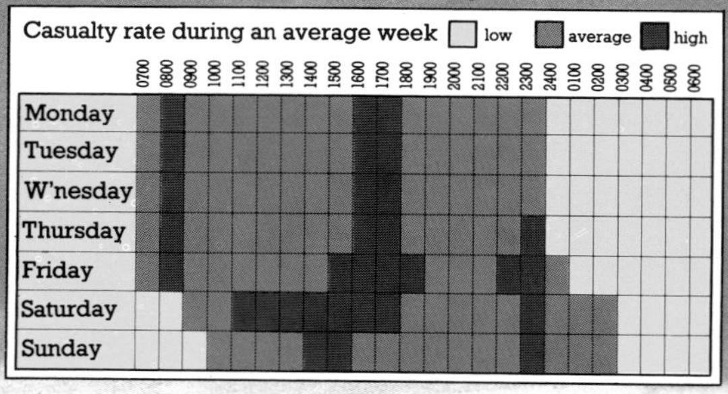
Casualty rate during an average week
low
average
high
0700 0800 0900 1000 1100 1200 1300 1400 1500 1600 1700 1800 1900 2000 2100 2200 2300 2400 0100 0200 0300 0400 0500 0600
Monday
Tuesday
W'nesday
Thursday
Friday
Saturday
Sunday

THE FACTS

STOPPING DISTANCES

At 30mph, 75ft; 50mph, 175ft; 70mph, 315ft (distance based on a dry road, alert driver and car in good condition in poor conditions, these distances may be doubled).

THE FIGURES

Great Britain has more than 29,000 miles (46,400km) of 'A' or Principal Roads. As the longest designated road in Britain, the A1 from London to Edinburgh accounts for 404 miles (650km).

SPEED LIMITS

(unless signed to the contrary): Dual Carriageway — 70mph: Single Carriageway — 60mph; Roads normally designated urban — 30mph. On September 28 1901, Richard Moffat Ford was timed driving at over 12mph by a plain clothes policeman — and later fined £5.

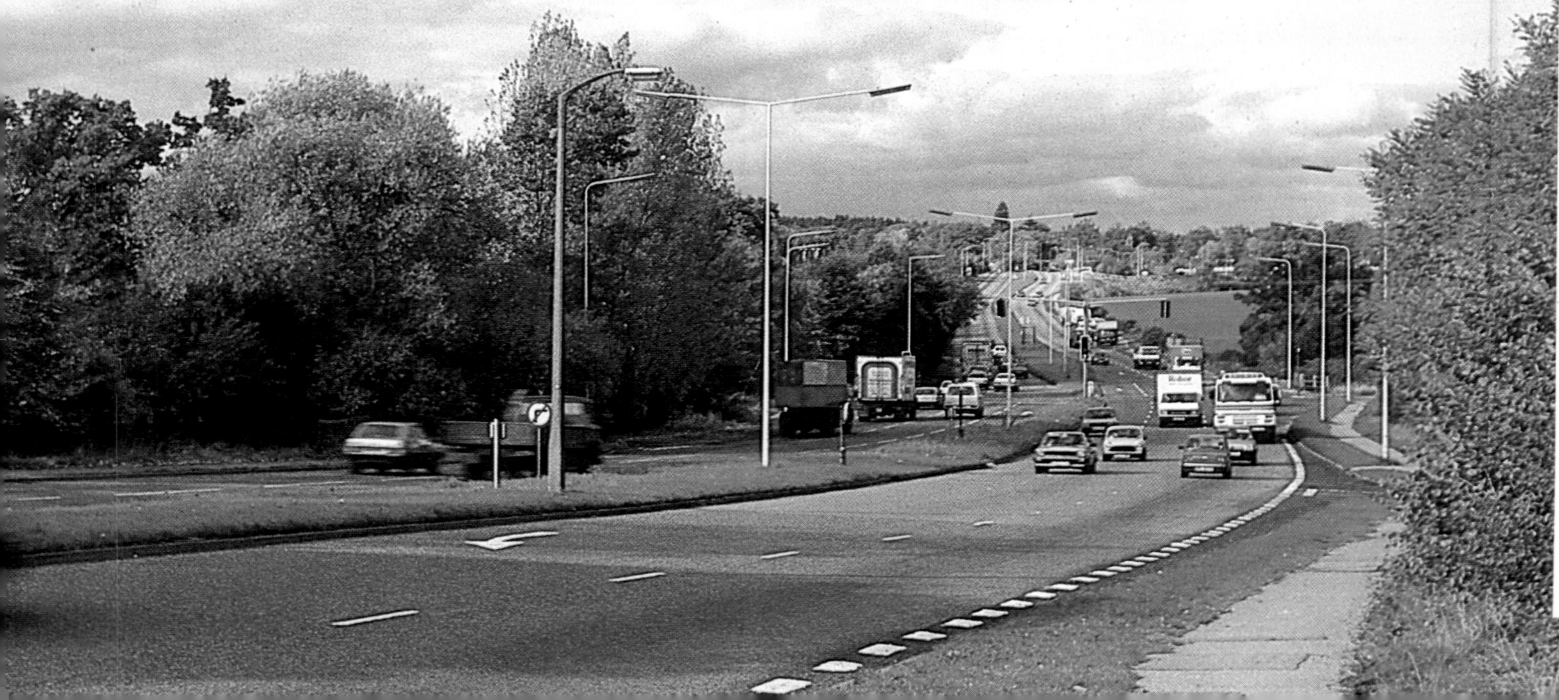

Direction signs

Direction signs with a blue background are used on motorways. Signs with a green background are used on primary routes: those with a white background on other routes.

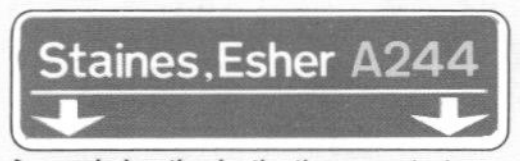
Staines, Esher A244

Arrows below the destination mean 'select your destination, and get in lane'

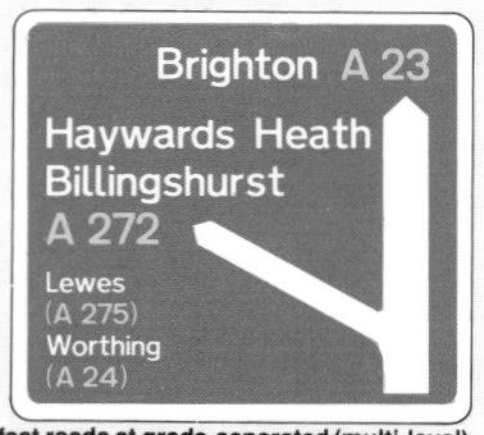
Brighton A 23
Haywards Heath
Billingshurst
A 272
Lewes
(A 275)
Worthing
(A 24)

On fast roads at grade-separated (multi-level) junctions, information about the junction is usually given at least half a mile in advance and repeated at the beginning of the deceleration lane which leads to the exit slip road.

Signs giving orders

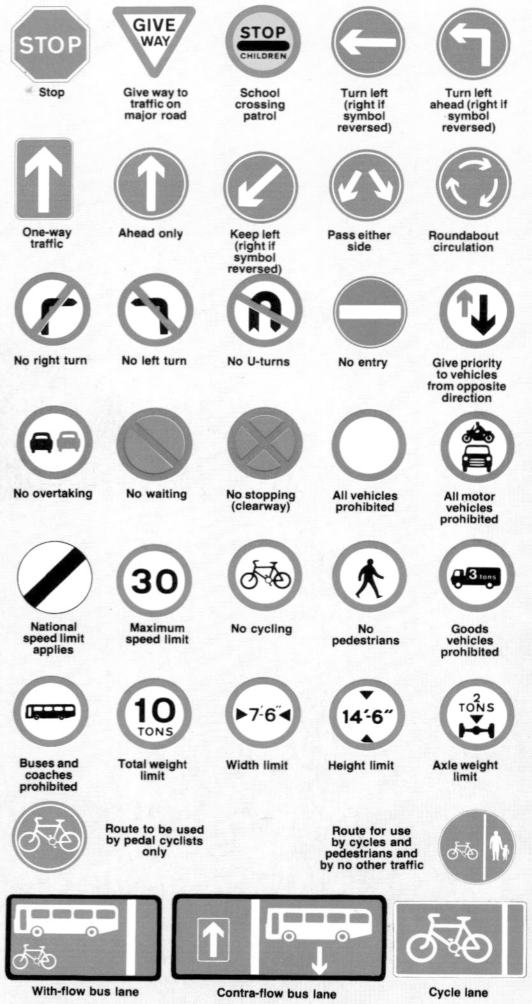
STOP
Stop
GIVE WAY
Give way to traffic on major road
STOP CHILDREN
School crossing patrol
Turn left (right if symbol reversed)
Turn left ahead (right if symbol reversed)
One-way traffic
Ahead only
Keep left (right if symbol reversed)
Pass either side
Roundabout circulation
No right turn
No left turn
No U-turns
No entry
Give priority to vehicles from opposite direction
No overtaking
No waiting
No stopping (clearway)
All vehicles prohibited
All motor vehicles prohibited
National speed limit applies
30
Maximum speed limit
No cycling
No pedestrians
3 tons
Goods vehicles prohibited
Buses and coaches prohibited
10 TONS
Total weight limit
7'6"
Width limit
14'-6"
Height limit
2 TONS
Axle weight limit
Route to be used by pedal cyclists only
Route for use by cycles and pedestrians and by no other traffic
With-flow bus lane
Contra-flow bus lane
Cycle lane

Information signs

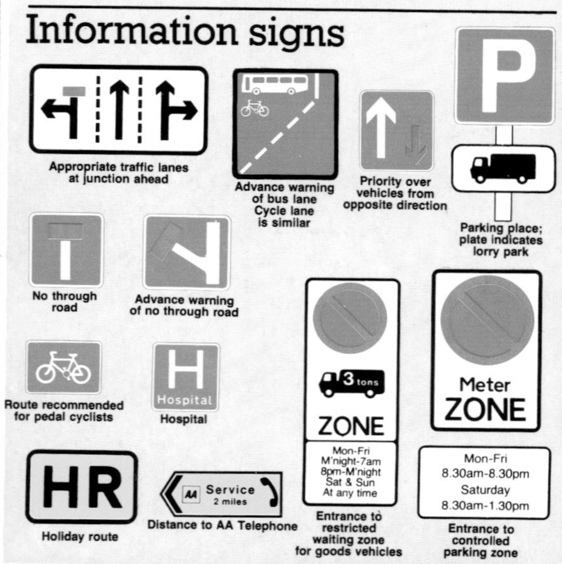
Appropriate traffic lanes at junction ahead
Advance warning of bus lane Cycle lane is similar
Priority over vehicles from opposite direction
P
Parking place; plate indicates lorry park
No through road
Advance warning of no through road
Route recommended for pedal cyclists
H
Hospital
Hospital
3 tons
ZONE
Mon-Fri
M'night-7am
8pm-M'night
Sat & Sun
At any time
Entrance to restricted waiting zone for goods vehicles
Meter ZONE
Mon-Fri
8.30am-8.30pm
Saturday
8.30am-1.30pm
Entrance to controlled parking zone
HR
Holiday route
AA Service 2 miles
Distance to AA Telephone

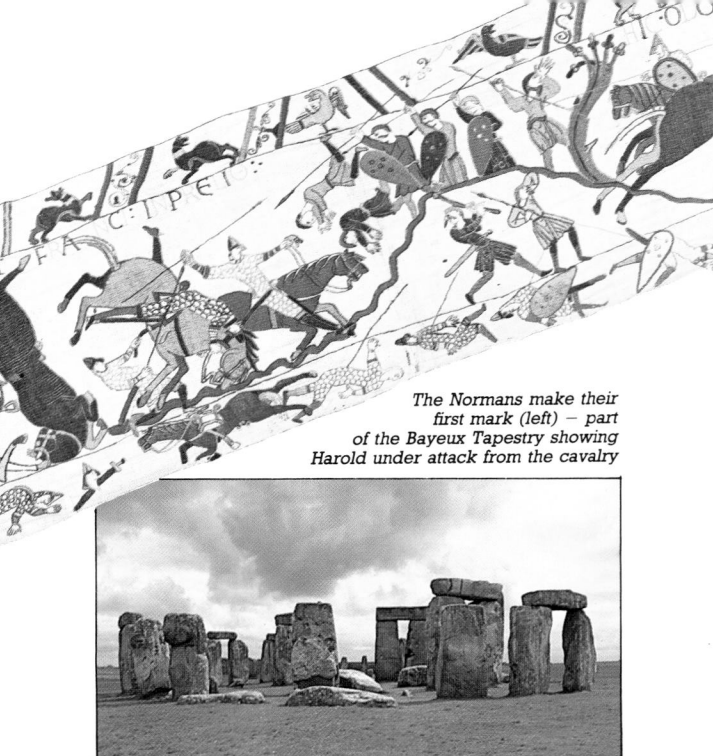

The Normans make their first mark (left) — part of the Bayeux Tapestry showing Harold under attack from the cavalry

Remote and mysterious, Stonehenge was begun in the Neolithic and completed in the Bronze Age — but no one knows its purpose

Who are the British?

This question is almost impossible to answer accurately. It is difficult to know just where we can start tracing our genealogical roots. Recorded history began to emerge more or less with Britain's Celtic civilisation (the name Britain probably has Celtic origins); yet we also know something of prehistoric man by the artefacts and monuments — an obvious example is Stonehenge — which he left.

Our island status has never given us complete immunity from the outside world. The Romans, who arrived in the first century AD, left an indelible mark on Celtic Britain. Following their withdrawal, our shores were exposed to influences brought in by the Angles, Saxons and Jutes, invaders from Europe (it is from the Angles that England derives its name).

Later — in the ninth and tenth centuries — came the Danes, prior to a monumental event etched on every schoolchild's memory. In 1066, England suffered its last successful invasion. The Norman conquerors from France soon became Anglo-Normans, further adding to the mixed bag of influences from which the modern British have emerged.

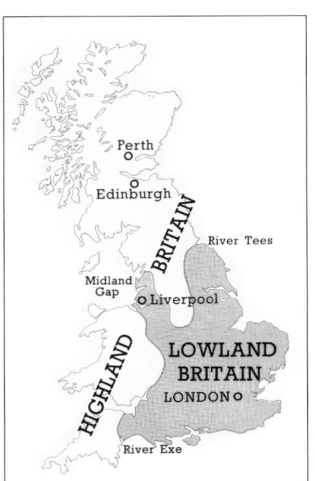

HIGHLAND & LOWLAND

Britain's two contrasting halves are separated by an imaginary line, running from the mouths of the Rivers Exe and Tees. This is a zone of transition between land below and above 1,000ft (305m), not a sharp frontier.

England is predominantly lowland country of soft limestone, chalk and clay, undulating or flat, and crossed by low ranges of hills such as the Cotswolds and Sussex Downs. The Scottish Highlands, Southern Uplands and Welsh Mountains are, in comparison, rugged areas made up of tough, ancient rocks over 250 million years old.

Illustrations ① – ㉒

1 cow parsley, 2 thyme, 3 ling, 4 tormentil, 5 nightjar, 6 Dartford warbler, 7 emperor moth, 8 common lizard, 9 yellowhammer, 10 burnet rose, 11 harebell, 12 bee orchid, 13 Southdown sheep, 14 chalkhill blue butterfly, 15 common knapweed, 16 white horse cut in chalk, 17 kestrel, 18 small scabious, 19 ox eye daisy, 20 six spot burnet moth, 21 stemless thistle, 22 shrew

The facts and the figures

Nearly 56 million people live in Britain. This compares with two million at the end of the eleventh century and a projected 60 million by the early 21st century.

Although only the 14th most crowded country in the world, Britain's population density — at 591 people per square mile — is predictably proportioned to give England 951 people per square mile, Wales 343, Northern Ireland 284 and Scotland 168.

Greater London is way above the rest of the cities with 10,977 people per square mile. But London is shrinking, its population slipping from third in the world (in the mid-1960s) to a current 11th.

The greatest concentrations of population in Britain are to be found in the areas of the Thames estuary and Channel coast, the industrial cities of West Yorkshire and north-west England, and the conurbations around Birmingham and the Tyne and Tees. But the 1981 census found a growing population (over 20 per cent of England and Wales, 11 per cent for Scotland) in rural areas.

Down among the rocks

The downlands of southern England are a classic landscape feature. Their gentle, rounded profiles can be seen from Kent to Dorset, most noticeably along the North and South Downs and on Salisbury Plain.

Their characteristically curving, rolling profiles come from chalk, the soft underlying rock which has folded to produce a smooth landscape with not a rough edge in sight. The chalk also determines a lack of surface water, for the rock is extremely permeable and porous.

These were among the first areas in Britain to be cleared and cultivated by prehistoric man. Later they were used as grazing lands. Arable farming has now taken over, and much of the old downlands have been ploughed to grow corn. Enough of the traditional grass and turf downs remain to support a distinctive plant and animal life. Unploughed downland is a prolific breeding ground: it can contain as many as 40 different types of flowering plant per square yard. Downland flowers include round headed rampion, harebell, common centaury, salad burnet and bird's foot trefoil. Most beautiful of all are the orchids. The common spotted orchid flowers May to August; but look out especially for the bee orchid, named after its uncanny likeness to a bumble bee. Wild thyme and marjoram scent the grasslands July to September.

The open downlands do not attract great numbers of birds or mammals. Kestrels (drawn to the easy hunting in this open countryside), skylarks, brown hares and rabbits are among the exceptions.

Butterflies are abundant: the chalkhill blue is seen in July and August, together with three species — the marbled white, dark green fritillary and silver-spotted skipper — attracted to flowering thistles.

Around Britain

Britain is one of the world's most complete geological museums. Rocks from almost every era in the Earth's evolution make an appearance here, creating a landscape of unusual variety and striking contrasts. Our network of highways and byways gives us the opportunity to discover, explore and enjoy an incomparable, constantly changing vista.

Ours is not a big country. Its area is only a modest 94,200 square miles (244,100 sq km) but size alone is no guarantee of variety — as anyone who has driven across the endlessly monotonous Great Plains of the USA will testify.

Such tedium is hard to find for long in Britain, where scenic variety comes around almost every corner. Chalk downlands rise into high, windswept mountain ranges; sandy coves lie sheltered among towering sea-cliff scenery; traditional country villages cluster near historic market towns. Roman remains and medieval castles stand as monuments to a fascinating history. Britain's role as a great maritime nation is remembered all along the coast.

Carved into Wiltshire's chalk downland, the 1778 Westbury White Horse (below) may have replaced a 9th century version

A national asset

Large tracts of Britain's land, much of it still in private hands, are being preserved as national parks. As such, they are something of a misnomer, for they are neither national nor parks.

The parks exist to conserve and protect areas of special scenic beauty. The parks also provide opportunities for outdoor recreation and enjoyment. This dual responsibility is sometimes challenged, but no one can dispute that the parks have created a greater awareness of — and respect for — the tremendous scenic diversity and natural beauty of Britain.

The world's first national park was founded at Yellowstone in the USA over a hundred years ago, but Britain had to wait until April 1951 for its first national park. It was created in the Peak District. Six years later the tenth to be designated was the Brecon Beacons.

Brecon Beacons A 519 square mile (1,344 sq km) swathe of green Welsh uplands, stretching from the west to the Black Mountains along the Welsh border. Pen-y-Fan, its highest peak at 2,907ft (889m), is in the middle. Pony trekking is popular in the Black Mountains; caving along the limestone band in the south. National Park Office, 6 Glamorgan Street, Brecon, Powys LD3 7DP. Tel: Brecon (0874) 4437.

Dartmoor Its 365 square miles (746 sq km) are often described as the last wilderness in southern Britain. This desolate moorland, the setting for many classic stories, has changed little since it was inhabited by prehistoric man. Dartmoor's characteristic features are the weatherbeaten granite rocks, or tors, which outcrop among the heather and bogs. National Park Office, "Parke", Bovey Tracey, Newton Abbot, Devon, TQ13 9JQ. Tel: Bovey Tracey (0626) 832093.

Exmoor This park is famous for its heather moorland and red deer (the park's symbol), the largest herds outside the Scottish Highlands. Exmoor is a small park (265 square miles — 686 sq km) full of contrasts: high moor, prosperous farmlands and spectacular cliff-backed coast. This is gentle walking country: follow the "Lorna Doone Trail" or the 20 mile (32km) North Devon Coast Path. National Park Office, Exmoor House,

Dulverton, Somerset TA22 9HL. Tel: Dulverton (0398) 23665.

Lake District The biggest (880 square miles — 2,280 sq km) and best known park. Eight major lakes spread long, thin fingers of water amongst fells and mountains to create an unforgettable landscape. National Park Office, Busher Walk, Kendal, Cumbria LA9 4RH. Tel: Kendal (0539) 24555.

Northumberland This bleakly beautiful wilderness has never really been tamed. Hadrian's Wall marked the boundary of the mighty Roman Empire. The 398 square mile (1,030 sq km) park stretches from the Wall to the Cheviot Hills. National Park Office, Eastburn, South Park, Hexham NE46 1BS. Tel: Hexham (0434) 605555.

North York Moors One of the quietest parks, with vast areas of heather moorland. The park's 553 square miles (1,432 sq km) contain the upland mass of the Cleveland Hills, rising to nearly 1,500ft (457m). National Park Office, The Old Vicarage, Bondgate, Helmsley YO6 5BP. Tel: Helmsley (0439) 70657.

Peak District The most visited park, located within a 50 mile (80km) drive of nearly 20 million people. Yet its 542 square miles (1,403 sq km) contain areas of true wilderness. National Park Office, Aldern House, Baslow Road, Bakewell, Derbyshire DE4 1AE. Tel: Bakewell (062981) 4321.

Pembrokeshire Coast At 225 square miles (583 sq km), this is the smallest park — and the odd one out, for the focus here is on coastline. Its 230 mile (370km) seashore is rated as one of Europe's finest. National Park Office, County Offices, Haverfordwest, Dyfed SA61 1QZ. Tel: Haverfordwest (0437) 4591.

Snowdonia This park packs a tremendous variety into its 840 square miles (2,171 sq km): rugged mountains (the highest in England and Wales), wooded valleys, moorlands, forests, lakes and sandy estuaries. Park Information Office, Penrhyndeudraeth, Gwynedd LL4 6LS. Tel: Penrhyndeudraeth (0766) 770274.

Yorkshire Dales This 680 square mile (1,761 sq km) park takes its name from the idyllic, green dales which wind in amongst the Pennines. National Park Office, "Colvend", Hebden Road, Grassington, Skipton BD23 5LB. Tel: Grassington (0756) 752002.

NATIONAL PARKS
Britain's ten national parks cover 5,250 square miles (13,600 sq km). They represent nine per cent of the area of England and Wales. Scotland has no national parks as such, but has identified 40 'natural scenic areas'.

Illustrations (23) – (56)
23 chalkhill blue butterfly, 24 ox eye daisy, 25 knapweed, 26 brown hare, 27 cowslip, 28 salad burnet, 29 mole, 30 wild marjoram, 31 dark mullein, 32 nettle, 33 violet, 34 badger, 35 corn marigold, 36 cock pheasant, 37 poppy, 38 silverweed, 39 field bindweed, 40 meadow brown butterfly, 41 wheat, 42 oats, 43 ribwort plantain, 44 dandelion, 45 early purple orchid, 46 hoary plantain, 47 creeping thistle, 48 silver studded blue butterfly, 49 goldfinches, 50 great green bush cricket, 51 buttercup, 52 orange tip butterfly, 53 buff-tailed bumblebee, 54 hedge bindweed, 55 stitchwort, 56 red clover

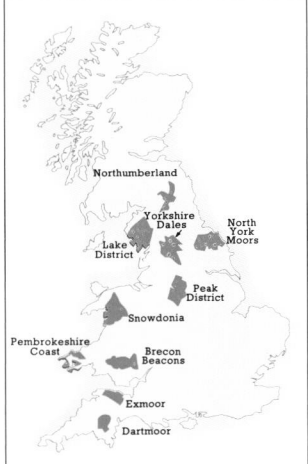

Doone Country (above): Exmoor's Hoccombe Combe area, known to the world through R D Blackmore's Lorna Doone

The Lake District's Wast Water (above), England's deepest lake at 250ft (76m)

The Yorkshire Dales (above), with Pennine Way and Pen-y-ghent's 2,273ft (694m) peak

Heathland tracts

These areas of sandy, gravelly, acidic soil are scattered over southern England, from East Anglia to the far tip of Cornwall. Their coverings of gorse, heather and bracken, shallow-rooted plants suited to poor soils, give them an appearance of uncultivated wilderness. Yet the heathlands are largely man-made.

Before the land was cleared centuries ago to grow crops for Neolithic man, they were covered with woods. Without continued grazing and man's control, these heaths would slowly return to their true wilderness. As it is, small clumps of Scots birch and pine trees, both well suited to sandy soils, can often be seen.

Flora The plant populations most at home here are those which can survive constant grazing and acidic soils: the pink and purple heaths and heathers (look out for the distinctive bell heather which flowers June to September on drier heaths), the gorse bushes which bring a vibrant splash of yellow to the scene and the impenetrable seas of bracken.

Fauna Birds attracted to this habitat include the pretty black-headed stonechat (often seen perched on a gorse branch), the linnet, woodlark (rare), yellowhammer and nightjar (a summer visitor). Pinewoods on the heath are breeding grounds for the hobby, a bird which resembles a peregrine falcon.

Butterflies are a familiar sight: the small heath butterfly, the silver-studded blue (June to August), and the grayling (June to September). Moths are also plentiful, particularly the common heath moth (May to August), the emperor moth (April to May) and the fox moth (May to June). At ground level, heathlands attract the common lizard and — take note — the adder, Britain's only poisonous snake.

Heathlands — the lowland equivalent to moorlands — are spread far and wide, though each has its own characteristics. East Anglia's Breckland, for example, is unique dry heath with sandy soil and dunes. The heaths in Dorset contain the rarest reptiles in Britain — the sand lizard and 1½ft long smooth snake. Other areas with distinctive heathland habitats include the New Forest, land around Bournemouth and Swanage, and Cornwall's Lizard Peninsula.

MINI-MOUSE
Although it lives throughout lowland Britain, the harvest mouse is not often seen. With a body of only two and a half inches, and a tail two inches or so, it is the smallest rodent in Britain. It breeds amongst cornfields and reed beds in ball-like nests made from woven grass attached to standing stalks.

Looking at the Lowlands

Britain's image as a 'green and pleasant land' springs from the grassy, low-lying countryside which fills much of England. Around one-half of the English landscape is lowland of one type or another — river meadows, gentle hills and escarpments, open heath, green fields and broad vales.

Soft underlying rocks create rounded profiles and sweeping horizons dominated by the sky. Nothing high or mighty interrupts the view.

But Britain's lowland stretches change mile by mile. As in other parts of the country, contrasts abound, for the lowlands are a patchwork made up of many and diverse parts — including the billiard-table landscape of the Fens, the undulating Cotswolds, ancient woods in the New Forest and the enchanting rural heartlands of Wessex and Thomas Hardy country.

Slow boat through Britain

At the end of the Canal Age, in the 1840s, 4,250 miles (6,800km) of navigable rivers and canals carried 13 million tons of freight per annum. 'Canal mania', encouraged by the Industrial Revolution, gave Britain its first transportation system

While larger rivers and canals continue to carry freight, most of the system is now used principally for leisure and recreation — cruising, canoeing and angling. The network spreads its watery web across much of lowland England, though it also occasionally ventures into the hills and mountains (most notably along the Leeds and Liverpool Canal, which climbs the Pennines with the aid of such engineering feats as the 'Five Rise' staircase of locks at Bingley).

Canals are full of contrasts. Stretches of still water thread their way through secluded, forgotten corners of England. Other sections offer the novelty of a journey into the centre of a busy Midlands city by boat. There are locks to negotiate, aqueducts to cross, tunnels to travel through — all at a sedate average speed of 3mph. Many travellers insist this is the *only* way to see Britain.

Canal holidays are easy to arrange. Boats, sleeping from two to twelve, can be hired throughout the country (no previous experience is necessary). Do not be ambitious when planning your routes. In a typical day with around seven hours of cruising and ten locks (at around ten minutes each) you will cover only 16 miles.

The quiet waters of the canals are ideal for canoeing, especially for beginners. Navigable rivers — the Severn and the Trent, for example — offer excellent conditions. Canal fishing is also an increasingly popular activity, as is towpath walking. Many people now use canal towpaths for rambling and nature study. The wide selection of water-bank nature trails now available reflects the demand, and gives access to a wealth of flora, even in industrial areas such as Birmingham.

At 1,007ft (307m), Telford's Pontcystyllte Aqueduct for the Shropshire Union Canal at Trevor is the longest in Britain

Illustrations (35) – (65)

35 corn marigold, 36 cock pheasant, 37 poppy, 38 silverweed, 39 field bindweed, 40 meadow brown butterfly, 41 wheat, 42 oats, 43 ribwort plantain, 44 dandelion, 45 early purple orchid, 46 hoary plantain, 47 creeping thistle, 48 silver studded blue butterfly, 49 goldfinches, 50 great green bush cricket 51 buttercup, 52 orange tip butterfly, 53 buff-tailed bumblebee, 54 hedge bindweed, 55 stitchwort, 56 red clover, 57 fieldmouse, 58 meadow-sweet, 59 great spotted woodpecker, 60 wild angelica, 61 kingfisher, 62 bullrush, 63 emperor dragonfly, 64 kingcup, 65 ducks

For further information on all aspects of inland waterways, particularly boat hire and canal holidays, contact: British Waterways Board, Information Centre, Melbury House, Melbury Terrace, London NW1 6JX. Tel: 01-262 6711. The Inland Waterways Association is for everyone using rivers and canals and has more than 20,000 members: 114 Regents Park Road, London NW1 8UQ. Tel: 01-586 2510.

Reclaiming the Fens

Flood walls are part of the unusual pattern of the Fenland area, thanks to the ravages wreaked by rivers such as the Ouse, Welland and Nene when they overflowed, regularly flooding vast areas of low-lying landscape around the Wash.

In the 17th century, Dutchman Cornelius Vermuyden was called in to reclaim this fertile marshland, with its peaty, silty soils. The network of blue lines which now criss-cross the map are a testament to his skills as a

CANAL ART
Traditional narrowboats are floating works of art. They come in all colours — deep blues, striking reds, vibrant greens — decorated with ornate, intricate signwriting (usually the name of the bargee or his company) and flower-patterned designs. These florid, hand-painted motifs are carried through to the utensils — the pots, mugs and plates — used in the narrowboat itself and much sought-after today.

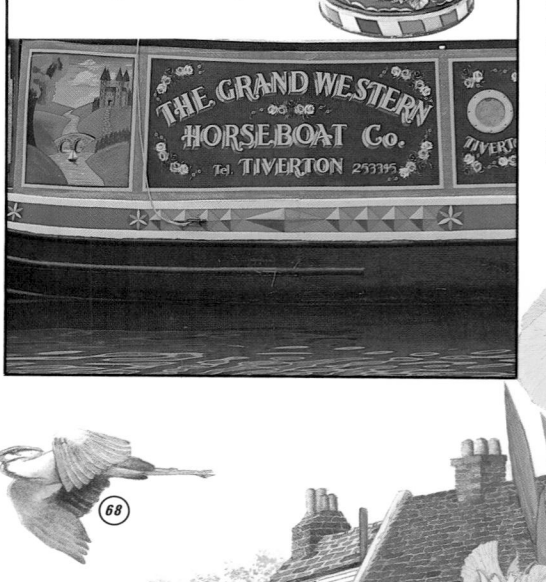

Drainage has transformed the Fens (right) but the windmill on Wicken Fen (below) is part of a complex system to pump water **in** — and preserve this habitat. Several feet higher than surrounding fields (because undrained) this National Trust nature reserve has numerous birds, over 300 types of flowering plant and 5,000 insect species, including 700 butterflies and moths

drainage engineer. They are part of his vast, complex system of dykes, sluices and channels which carry surface water into the Wash.

The construction of this system, long before the days of heavy earth moving equipment, was a gigantic operation. The Bedford River, for example, an artificial channel 21 miles (34km) long, was dug with just spades. Water was pumped into these channels by windmill (a typical Fenland sight) and, later, steam engine.

The Fens, reclaimed by man, have changed forever. Old basket and paper-making industries which once thrived in a watery landscape, have been replaced by productive farmlands, some of the richest and most fertile in the world.

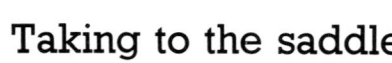

Taking a Dip

Roads in lowland areas — and low-lying roads in the hills and mountains — are prone to flooding. Follow this simple procedure when the road is well and truly submerged.

1. Stop and try to estimate how deep the water is. If you decide to proceed, make use of the camber on the road to drive through the shallowest of the water.

2. Drive as slowly as you can, in first gear, to avoid creating a large wave in front of the car which might flood the engine.

3. Try your brakes as soon as you reach dry land.

4. Drive slowly with your left foot pressing lightly on the brake pedal to dry the brakes out.

THE FACTS
Britain's inland waterways are used by 250,000 anglers and 60,000 boats (4,000 of them for hire — the world's biggest hire fleet). 3,000 miles (4,830km) of rivers and canals are navigable. 990 miles (1,590km) used commercially carry 40 million tons of cargo.

Illustrations ⓺⓺ – ⑨⑤

66 water vole, 67 swan, 68 heron, 69 moorhen, 70 coot, 71 newt, 72 frog, 73 arrowhead, 74 yellow flag, 75 sedge warbler, 76 common reed, 77 elm, 78 water mint, 79 farmland, 80 long tailed tit, 81 blackberry, 82 wasp, 83 red admiral butterfly, 84 marbled white butterfly, 85 bullfinch, 86 bryony, 87 small tortoiseshell butterfly, 88 small tortoiseshell (underside of wing), 89 elder, 90 northern eggar moth, 91 chanterelle, 92 dryad's saddle fungi, 93 barn owl, 94 oak, 95 harts tongue fern

Taking to the saddle

Britain may well have been purpose-built for pony trekkers. Trekking is a relaxing, leisurely activity which takes riders into remote and beautiful areas otherwise accessible only on foot. Apart from the rocky and difficult terrain of the true high country, a wide variety of regions can be explored on an organised trek. Since trekking started at Llanwrtyd Wells, a village tucked away in the Welsh hills, in the 1950s, approved centres have spread through the country.

These have been approved by such bodies as:
Ponies of Britain, Ascot Race Course, Ascot, Berkshire.
British Horse Society, British Equestrian Centre, Stoneleigh, Kenilworth, Warwickshire.
Other contacts are available from the English, Scottish and Wales Tourist Boards. Full addresses appear on page 23.

What's hiding in that hedge?

Hedgerows are hundreds of years old. Some, originally planted by our Saxon ancestors, are over a thousand years old. Hedgerows are much more than boundary lines. Natural historians look upon them as miniature woodlands, inhabited by countless species of wild plants and animals.

Estimating the approximate age of a hedge is fascinating. The key is to count the number of different shrub and tree species (hawthorn, elder, hazel, for example) growing in every 30 yard stretch, allowing one species for every hundred years of the hedge's life.

Although under threat, hedgerows are still a common sight in the countryside. They are not confined to lowland Britain, but tend to give way to dry stone walls in the northern and western uplands. Around 600,000 miles (966,000km) of hedgerows still exist, regarded as the longest unofficial nature reserve in the world.

Scots Pine   Alder   Elm   Oak
Holly   Hawthorn

30 yards   400 years

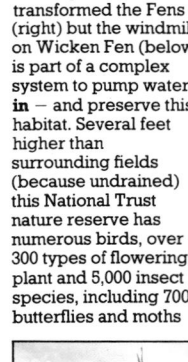

Sharing the highway

Horses While accidents involving horses and motor vehicles are naturally more likely to happen in areas of high population and traffic density, the horse as a means of transport comes into its own in Britain's country and uplands. It is a particularly common sight since pony trekking and riding make such popular pastimes.

The unaccustomed presence of a horse on the road can be disconcerting to motorists. First remember that a horse, being not just another piece of road traffic, is unpredictable in movement and temperament. A speeding vehicle can frighten the animal if it shies; and so never pass it at more than 15mph. Make plenty of space between your vehicle and the horse as you overtake so that the rider can control the animal if it shies; and do not cut in too sharply afterwards. Horses can also be scared by the sight of flashing lights, waving passengers − even flapping luggage-rack covers − and most of all, by the noise of a revving engine, loud horn or worn silencer, especially on noisy motorbikes.

Sheep As anyone who lives in the country will tell you, sheep are even more unpredictable than horses. In hilly country they often wander freely beside, and even on, the road. Treat such situations with extreme caution.

Cattle Normally encountered when a farmer is herding them along the road. Please be patient and do not attempt to pass. If the herd is coming towards you, switch off your engine until they pass.

Use your horn sparingly, so as not to startle animals, but do sound it on narrow, winding country roads when coming up to 'blind' bends, to warn approaching drivers and pedestrians who cannot see or hear you coming.

Follow the Country Code

Enjoy the countryside and respect its life and work.

Leave livestock, crops and machinery alone.

Guard against all risk of fire.

Fasten all gates.

Take your litter home.

Keep your dogs under close control.

Help to keep all water clean.

Keep to public paths across farmland.

Protect wildlife, plants and trees.

Use gates and stiles to cross fences, hedges and walls.

Take special care on country roads.

Make no unnecessary noise.

The wildcat (above top) − like but far bigger than the domestic tabby with record measured length of 3ft 9in. Above, the ptarmigan, brown in spring and summer but snow white in winter

Illustrations 76 − 111
76 common reed, 77 elm, 78 water mint, 79 hawthorn, 81 blackberry, 82 wasp, 83 red admiral butterfly, 84 marbled white butterfly, 85 bullfinch, 86 bryony, 87 small tortoiseshell butterfly, 88 small tortoiseshell (underside of wing), 89 elder, 90 northern eggar moth, 91 chanterelle, 92 dryad's saddle fungi, 93 barn owl, 94 oak, 95 harts tongue fern, 96 bracken, 97 curlew, 98 wheatear, 99 cotton grass, 100 large heath butterfly, 101 gorse, 102 birch, 103 short eared owl, 104 starry saxifrage, 105 butterwort, 106 sundew, 107 small mountain ringlet, 108 heather, 109 moss campion, 110 heather, 111 birch

Life among the Peaks

Moors and mountains are havens for some of the rarest birds, animals and plants in Britain.

Still to be seen (but you have to be very lucky) are:

The golden eagle Around 200 pairs survive, breeding only in parts of Scotland and the Lake District. With a wingspan of up to seven feet, the golden eagle is Britain's largest bird of prey, nesting among ledges in huge piles of sticks and heather. Their powerful talons allow them to carry off grouse, ptarmigan, rabbits and hares − even small lambs.

Wildcats These fierce-looking, bushy-tailed cats are now largely confined to the Scottish Highlands. Although they have a passing resemblance to the humble domestic cat, they are not related in any way.

Red deer The largest mammal living wild in Britain today (a fully-grown Highland stag weighs in at over 200lbs). They inhabit the Scottish Highlands in their greatest numbers, spending the summer in the high country and descending for winter. Herds also live in the Lake District, Exmoor and the New Forest.

Ptarmigan This distinctive member of the grouse family changes colour, chameleon-fashion, to blend with its habitat. The bird lives high in the Scottish mountains, where snow lingers for a large part of the year.

Other birds Buzzards (often seen soaring and gliding − listen out for their characteristic mewing call), ravens (the largest British crow), golden plovers (which breed on upland moors and winter on farmlands in the lowlands), merlins (the smallest falcon in Britain), dippers (seen beside fast-flowing highland streams) and red grouse.

Arctic-alpine plants The Snowdon lily, a white-petalled member of the arctic-alpine species, is now to be found in Britain only among the high crags of Snowdonia. The starry saxifrage is a more widespread member of this hardy species of wild mountain flower which is specially adapted for survival in difficult habitats. This type of saxifrage can be seen on the summit of Ben Nevis, and as far south as the slopes above 2,000ft (610m) on Cader Idris, Mid Wales.

The High Country

Upland Britain begins at 1,000ft (305m) and ends at over four times that height among the summits of our loftiest peaks.

The hand of man, a common and confident presence in lowland areas, becomes increasingly hesitant and ineffectual as the landscape rises. In some parts of the country, it is still virtually non-existent, making nonsense of our reputation as an overcrowded island.

This unchanging timeless face of Britain resides in the north and west, among the windswept plateaux of Plynlimon, the 'roof of Wales', in the high peaks of the Pennines, around Cumbria's deep lakes and steepsided fells; and in the wilderness of Scotland's mountain ranges.

On the steep side

With its fiendish combination of hairpin bends and 1 in 3 gradients, the 1,291ft (394m) Hardknott Pass between Eskdale and Ambleside qualifies as one of Britain's trickiest roads. The six mile rise from sea level to 2,054ft (626m) between Lochcarron and Applecross in Scotland (to Bealach Na Ba') is certainly Britain's longest steep hill. Less dramatic but still steep hills are not uncommon in Britain. Gradient signs give advance warning. The figures show the pitch − 1 in 4 (or 25%) means that the road rises or falls 1ft for every 4ft horizontally. The lower the figure (or higher the percentage), the tougher the hill.
Upwards Change down as soon as the engine begins to slow. Don't try to maintain speed in a high gear: the car will climb more happily in a low one. Change down *before* bends − turning and climbing puts extra strain on the engine.

Left: the long steep rise to Bealach Na Ba' (maximum gradient 1 in 4) – and an AA Viewpoint

Downwards Change down in advance (Gradient signs may carry a warning to use a low gear). Declutching will speed the car up, while keeping the brakes on instead of using low gears will 'polish' and make them ineffective.
Hairpin bends Approach in low gear and stick to the nearside.
Always keep a good distance from traffic ahead, so as not to have to stop suddenly.

Three of the best

Introducing Britain's numerous long-distance footpaths . . . a daunting prospect to all but the most dedicated. Beginners should tackle short sections only, of about eight miles (13km).

Pennine Way Those who have completed its 250 miles (402km) remember a combination of bad dream and euphoria. The long, hard slog runs from Edale in the Peak District to Kirk Yetholm.

Offa's Dyke Path This 168 mile (270km) walk follows the earthern dyke put up by King Offa of Mercia in the eighth century and runs from Chepstow to Prestatyn through countryside which varies from tough moorlands to wooded vales.

Cleveland Way Its 93 miles (150km) are split into the high-level Moors Path, running through the Cleveland Hills, and a slightly easier Coast Path. In use since at least Roman times – but some moorland sections are extremely arduous and poorly defined.

WALKING HIGH

Upland weather is extremely fickle. Check local forecasts first and avoid mountain walks in mist or rain. Go in a group of four to six – not more and not alone. Wear stout comfortable footwear, two pairs of socks – one thick, one thin – and a thigh length anorak. Avoid denims – uncomfortable when wet. Carry a cagoule, extra sweater, Ordnance Survey map(s), compass, food and drink, first aid kit and torch and whistle (for emergencies – six long blasts or torch flashes repeated after one minute). Leave word of the route and try to stick to it: 1¾mph is a good average to aim for. Respect those who live and work on the land and always follow the Country Code.

THE FACTS AND THE FIGURES

THE HIGHEST MOUNTAINS:
Scotland: Ben Nevis, at 4,406ft (1,343m), the highest in Britain.

Wales: Snowdon, at 3,560ft (1,085m).

England: Scafell Pike in the Lake District, at 3,206ft (977m).

THE LONGEST WATERFALLS:
Scotland: Falls of Glomach, in the Western Highlands above Glen Elchaig, 370ft (113m).

Wales: Pistyll Rhaedr, in the hills east of Bala, 240ft (72m).

England: Cauldron Snout, Upper Teesdale, 200ft (60m).

THE HIGHEST ROADS (CLASSIFIED):
Scotland: A93, Cairnwell Pass, 2,199ft (670m).

England: A689, Killhope Cross, 2,056ft (626m).

Wales: A4107, east of Abergwynfi 1,750ft (533m).

Illustrations 112 – 133
112 buzzard, 113 bracken, 114 crowberry, 115 red grouse, 116 hard fern, 117 cowberry, 118 stoat, 119 blackfaced sheep, 120 rooks, 121 conifer plantation, 122 hooded crow, 123 mountain hare, 124 mountain fern, 125 garden tiger moth, 126 white dead nettle, 127 ladybird, 129 bank vole, 130 scarlet pimpernel, 131 red valerian, 133 toad

The foot-sure climber

There is a world of difference between a scramble up a roadside slope and the ascent of a sheer rock face. Experience, skill and technique can not be acquired overnight; and in addition to the pure climbing element, novice mountaineers who want to graduate from low-level slopes must also be well versed in mountaincraft such as route planning and navigation, bivouacking and coping with emergency situations.

Those who want to learn climbing should first enrol in a climbing course. The national Sports Council can provide information on availability and location. Contact the British Mountaineering Council for information on local clubs.

USEFUL ADDRESSES
Sports Council, 16 Upper Woburn Place, London WC1H 0QP. Tel: 01-388 1277.
Sports Council for Wales, Sophia Gardens, Cardiff CF1 9SW. Tel: Cardiff (0222) 397571.
Sports Council for Scotland, 1 St Colme Street, Edinburgh EH3 6AA. Tel: 031-225 8411.
British Mountaineering Council, Crawford House, Precinct Centre, Booth Street East, Manchester M13 9RZ.

The highest pub?

The crossroads at Tan Hill, County Durham, have been busy since the 13th century with cattle drovers and pack-horse drivers – even colliers – who worked the ancient, now-deserted mines nearby. But this is no ordinary meeting place: it stands at a height of 1,758ft (536m) in remote uplands north of Wensleydale, a junction of minor mountain routes which link the trans-Pennine A66 with the B6270 Upper Swaledale road. This lonely spot has had its own pub for centuries, the Tan Hill Inn, which claims to be the highest in the country.

A welcome halt on the Pennine Way – the Tan Hill Inn

USEFUL ADDRESSES FOR WALKERS
Backpackers' Club, 20 St Michael's Road, Tilehurst, Reading RG3 4RP.
Countryside Commission, John Dower House, Crescent Place, Cheltenham, Glos GL50 3RA.
Offa's Dyke Association, Old Primary School, West Street, Knighton, Powys LD7 1EW.
Pennine Way Council, c/o Mr C Sainty, 89 Radford Road, Lewisham, London SE13 6SB.
Ramblers' Association, 1-5 Wandsworth Road, London SW8 2LJ.
Youth Hostels Association, Trevelyan House, 8 St Stephen's Hill, St Albans, Herts AL1 2DY.

Understanding place names

Signposts can give us far more than just directional information. The place names they carry will usually have their roots in the distant past, some even over a thousand years ago.

Scandinavians and Saxons
Scandinavian influences, mainly confined to northern and central England, are still with us in suffixes such as **by** and **thorpe** (meaning village, settlement or farmstead) and **thwaite** (clearing or meadow).

The Saxons left abundant evidence of their thorough colonisation of lowland England. The suffixes **ham**, **ton** and **ing** are a common sight on signposts, the first two denoting a settlement (an enclosure, farmstead or village), the last referring to 'the people of a tribal leader.

Here are other examples of Norse and Saxon place names:
ley, field, hurst, holt, hey = land cleared from forest
wich, wick = dwelling, farm
stead = place, religious site
burgh, bury, borough = fortified place (burgh can also mean hill, mound or tumulus)
worth = enclosure
bourne = stream, spring
hampton = home farm
beck = stream

Wales and Scotland
Place names, based on the ancient Welsh and Gaelic languages, are often very poetic and descriptive in translation.

WALES

aber = mouth of river	**glyn** = deep valley
afon = river	**hafod** = summer dwelling
bach, fach = small, little	**hendre** = winter dwelling
betws, bettws = chapel	**llan** = church, enclosure
bryn = hill	**llyn** = lake
bwlch = pass, gap	**mawr, fawr** = great, big
cefn = ridge	**mynydd** = mountain
coed = woods, trees	**nant** = brook
cwm = valley, corrie	**ystrad** = valley floor
dyffryn = valley	

SCOTLAND

aber = mouth, confluence	**inch** = island, pasture
ach, auch = field	**kil** = church, grave
ard = high	**kyle** = strait
car = rock	**mull** = headland
craig = crag, rock, cliff	**strath** = valley
dum, dun = fort, hill	

Biddenden's Maids (on village sign) were Siamese twins who set up a yearly 'dole' of bread

FANCY THAT

Barnstaple, Devon, claims to have the oldest town charter in Britain — over 1,000 years old.

The oldest village is thought to be Thatcham, Berkshire — artefacts have been found there from the Mesolithic period, 7,720 years ago.

Illustrations (120) – (142)
120 rooks, 121 conifer plantation, 122 hooded crow, 123 mountain hare, 124 mountain fern, 125 garden tiger moth, 126 white dead nettle, 127 ladybird, 128 buddleia, 129 bank vole, 130 scarlet pimpernel, 131 red valerian, 132 honeysuckle, 133 toad, 134 feverfew, 135 rooster 136 garden snail, 137 rosebay willow-herb, 138 jay, 139 horse chestnut, 140 geese, 141 fox, 142 rosebay willow-herb

From Village to Town

Two hundred years ago, a traveller passing through the placid, predominantly rural British landscape would only infrequently come across anything approaching the size of a town or city.

The change has taken place in only a comparatively few short years. The imperatives of a new industrial economy, born on the black coalface and in the white heat of the blast furnace, irrevocably altered our way of life and where we lived.

Hamlets grew, almost overnight, into villages; villages expanded into teeming towns and cities. Cardiff, Wales's capital, is a good example. In 1801 it was an obscure village of 1,000 forgotten souls; one hundred years later, it had become a fully-fledged seaport with around 180,000 inhabitants.

In 1086, when England's first 'official census' was complete, the Domesday Book showed that 90 per cent of the population lived in villages, hamlets or individual farms. Towns as we know them — busy, bustling, sprawling places at the mercy of commercial development and the motor car — were created by the demands of a new industrial era.

Some towns, though, have been around for considerably longer. These are our market towns, many of which have flourished, serving the needs of both industrial and agricultural Britain. Some have charters stretching back to early medieval times. All provide a free spectacle when the country comes to town during weekly livestock sales, and market traders set up their stalls.

Hundreds of these attractive towns hold markets every week — places like Barnard Castle, Durham (Wednesdays); Brecon, Powys (Tuesdays and Fridays) and Ledbury, Hereford and Worcester (Tuesdays).

Customs of the land

Colourful old customs and celebrations still thrive throughout Britain. Here are some of those which a visitor may enjoy. Check with local post office or tourist office before visiting — and remember that sometimes a degree of participation is expected, even if it's just a matter of moving aside.

DANCING Morris dancers can be seen on the traditional date of Whit Monday (nowadays Spring Bank Holiday) at **Bampton** and **Headington**. The **Abington Morris Men** hold a mock Election of the Mayor of Ock Street on the Saturday nearest 19 June. All these are in **Oxfordshire**.

North West or Processional ('Cloggies') Morris traditionally accompanied Wakes Week rushcart processions: two of great interest can be seen at **Saddleworth, Lancashire** and at **Sowerby Bridge, Yorkshire**, in late August.

At **Abbots Bromley, Staffordshire**, Horn Dancers carrying sets of reindeer horns perambulate the village and farms on the first Monday after the first Sunday after 4 September.

MAY FESTIVALS Padstow, Cornwall celebrates 1 May with singing, dancing and its vibrant 'Obby 'Oss. A slightly quieter event but with a vigorous horse takes place in **Minehead, Somerset**, on 1, 2 and 3 May. On 8 May, the people of **Helston, Cornwall**, dance in and out of houses, streets and gardens for Floral (or Furry) Dance Day.

WELL DRESSING From May to September, villagers in **Derbyshire** 'dress' wells with an elaborate, usually biblical, mosaic of flower petals on a base of wet clay. Notable are **Tissington, Youlgreave, Bakewell** and **Tideswell**: check with Peak District Tourist Board in Bakewell, Derbyshire, for dates.

BEATING THE BOUNDS Predating accurate written records, this can be seen on Ascension Day at **St Michael's, Oxford** (annually) and the **Tower of London** (in 1987 and every 3 years). Boundary Riding is more elaborate in the Borders, and at **Peebles** lasts a week.

GAMES AND RACES The Shrove Tuesday Pancake Race has been run at **Olney, Buckinghamshire** since 1445. On the same day at **Ashbourne, Derbyshire**, an unruly football game is played by hundreds with goals miles apart. Similar Shrovetide games are played at **Atherstone, Warwickshire** and **Alnwick, Northumberland**. On Shrove Tuesday, the people of **Scarborough, Yorkshire**, skip with ropes on the seashore.

The **Hallaton (Leicestershire)** Hare Pie Scramble and Bottle Kicking takes place on Easter Monday; on Spring Bank Holiday Monday competitors at **Coopers Hill, Gloucestershire**, chase a Double Gloucester cheese down a 1 in 5 incline for the annual Cheese Rolling.

NOVEMBER 5 Lewes, Sussex has torchlight processions by fantastically dressed Bonfire Societies and the burning of large effigies. **Ottery St Mary, Devon**, has hand-held cannon and blazing tar barrels.

NEW YEAR'S EVE Allendale, Northumberland is the place to be, with elaborately dressed 'guyzers' carrying blazing tar barrels on their heads, an enormous bonfire in the square, the singing of Auld Lang Syne and first footing to complete the occasion.

Below: the Horn Dancers of Abbots Bromley, Staffordshire

Thatchers at work (above) at Corton, Wylye Valley. The decoration 'trademarks' and also secures the thatch

Quintessentially English

The thatched cottage, more than any other building, symbolises an idyllic vision of life in an English village; so much so that the tradition-starved Americans are now importing the skills and artistry of the English thatcher to create a piece of the historic old home country for themselves.

Americans notwithstanding, around 750 thatchers are still kept busy, looking after roofing requirements of cottages from East Anglia across to the south and west of England. East Anglia's steep-pitched roofs will probably be made of local Norfolk reed, the best raw material in the world for this type of work. The softer, more rounded roof profiles further west are created with wheat straw, the most widely used base material. The skill — or art — of the thatcher is long-established. This is the oldest building craft in Britain. And, in the traditions of the artisan, each thatcher will have a trademark in the form of the personal touches brought to roof ridges, eaves, gables and small decorative features such as crosses or birds..

In the drier eastern counties, a good thatched roof will last around 80 years. In wetter climates further west they do well to survive 30 years.

Top: burr-covered 'Burryman' of South Queensferry's Ferry Fair. Above: Druids greet Midsummer

Illustrations (143) – (167)
143 cotoneaster horizontalis, 144 privet hawk moth caterpillar, 145 germander speedwell, 146 privet, 147 whitebeam, 148 privet hawk moth, 149 blackbird, 150 house sparrow, 151 house mouse, 152 Oxford ragwort, 153 hoverfly, 154 stock dove, 155 small tortoiseshell butterfly, 156 hedgehog, 157 blue tit, 158 starling, 159 robin, 160 tree mallow, 161 large white butterfly, 162 grey squirrel, 163 sea holly, 164 sea campion, 165 marram grass, 166 turnstone, 167 bar-tailed godwit

Driving hints

The AA's three-point town driving plan is summarised here:

1. Anticipation and consideration
Pedestrians may step out unexpectedly into the road. Motorists should, wherever possible, drive some distance from the kerb. Turning into a side street calls for particular care: pedestrians often cross side roads without looking.

Buses should be treated with the utmost consideration.

A roadsign which displays the traffic light symbol with a red diagonal bar means that the lights ahead are not working. In such circumstances, police or traffic wardens may be directing the flow. The driver must clearly signal any intentions.

2. Driving regulations
Special regulations have been applied to urban centres.

Bus lane There are two types, the with-flow and the contra-flow. Cyclists can use the first; the second allows buses to proceed against traffic in one-way streets. Restrictions for private cars are posted at the start of the stretch.

Box junctions Drivers should not enter the box unless their exits are clear. This rule does not apply to those making a right turn. If the road they want to enter is clear, drivers can wait in the box.

Pedestrian crossings Zebra crossings speak for themselves. The Pelican type is controlled by red, amber and green lights. Amber flashes tell the motorist to give way to pedestrians already crossing, though the driver can proceed if the crossing is clear. Parking and overtaking are prohibited in the zones indicated by zig-zag lines before a Zebra crossing; also within the studs surrounding a Pelican crossing.

At night, dipped headlights should be used. Where street lights are good, sidelights alone can be used, but dipped headlights are advised whatever the standard of lighting. **Always** use them in conditions of seriously reduced visibility.

3. Parking regulations
Controlled parking zones are identified by yellow lines. Consult the plates or signs which indicate restriction times.

Parking-meter zones have signs which identify times of operation. They allow two types of parking: for residents (permits must be displayed) and by meter.

Those using parking-disc zones must display the disc (available from local authorities and the police) on the vehicle.

Urban clearways apply only during specified hours. Stopping for up to two minutes for passengers is permitted.

The Hungry Sea

King Canute's ill-fated attempt to turn back the sea is a telling little cameo. All along the coast, waves and tides are eating away at the fragile cliffs and headlands. In a complex game of give-and-take, the land is also gaining from the sea, as silts are deposited and estuaries reclaimed.

The soft clay cliffs at Holderness on the Yorkshire coast are disappearing by as much as six feet a year. Owners of doomed cliff-top bungalows live on possibly the fastest eroding coastline in the world.

The converse is happening on the opposite side of Britain. Harlech Castle, North Wales, is the classic example. When Edward I came to build this mighty fortress in 1283, he constructed it on a rocky sea-cliff for strategic reasons. The town's railway station now occupies the place where waves lapped beneath the castle walls, for the sea has receded by almost one mile.

Doomed bungalows on Holderness cliff-top (below)

Britain's changing shape (above): coastal erosion and deposition

THE FACTS

Chesil Beach, its barrier of pebbles stretching for over 15 miles (25km) of Dorset coast from Bridport to Portuneswell, is unique in Britain, if not in the world. The tides have 'sorted' its millions of pebbles, which increase in size from north-west to south-east. Locals can tell where they are by the size of the stones.

Illustrations (154) – (175)

154 stock dove, 156 hedgehog, 159 robin, 163 sea holly, 164 sea campion, 165 marram grass, 166 turnstone, 167 bar-tailed godwit, 168 dunlin, 169 shrubby sea blite, 170 sea beet, 171 scallop shell, 172 great black-backed gull, 173 black-headed gull, 174 sanderling, 175 sea sandwort

Our maritime heritage

Britain's history has been influenced, possibly more so than that of any other nation, by the sea.

Portsmouth's two warships The whole world looked on when the **Mary Rose** was rescued from her watery grave in the Solent on 11 October 1982. The surviving hull and outstanding collection of Tudor weapons and artefacts it contained are on view at Portsmouth harbour; also **HMS Victory**, Admiral Lord Nelson's flagship during the Battle of Trafalgar in 1805.

Drake's Plymouth Sir Francis Drake's insouciance in finishing his game of bowls before dealing with the Spanish Armada is now part of our folklore. Plymouth became the base for this great Elizabethan adventurer — and, by no coincidence, that of the English navy. His statue stands at the Hoe. The Pilgrim Fathers set off on their voyage to the New World from here in 1620.

"All ship-shape and Bristol fashion" This saying came from Bristol's League of Merchant Venturers, formed 1552. They turned Bristol into one of the world's leading trading ports, dealing in wine, tobacco, wool, sugar — even slaves. Brunel's **SS Great Britain**, first ocean-going screw-propelled iron ship in the world, was launched from here in 1843; her rotting hulk, recovered from the Falkland Islands in 1970, is now being restored.

Bamburgh's heroine Grace Darling's rescue of nine survivors from a shipwreck off the wild Northumbrian coast on 7 September 1838 captured the hearts of a nation. The boat which this 23-year-old and her father used is now in a local museum dedicated to her memory. An elaborate memorial to her stands in Bamburgh churchyard.

Father Thames London grew up around the Thames, a busy waterway and gateway to the world. The National Maritime Museum at Greenwich is vast, its three-and-a-half miles of galleries full of items relating to British seafaring. **Cutty Sark** (19th century tea clipper) and **Gypsy Moth IV** (Sir Francis Chichester's around-the-world ketch) are also at Greenwich.

HMS Belfast, a World War Two cruiser, is permanently moored in the Thames (opposite the Tower of London) as a floating naval museum. St Katherine's Dock nearby has a collection of historic ships, including Captain Scott's **Discovery**.

A Coastal Journey

Nowhere in Britain is more than a few hours' drive from the sea. The implications of this elementary truth are profound.

Britain's past is embodied in its coastline. Prehistoric man, Roman invader, Christian saint and medieval warlord all left their mark along its headlands and bays. In later centuries, Britannia went out and ruled the waves, both in a military and commercial sense.

The seaside holiday was born along Britain's coast 200 years ago. Those first tentative journeys to the sea have multiplied by millions and in all directions, creating a whole new leisure industry.

Britain's coast has everything from mountain-backed sea lochs to sand and dune. Seven thousand miles of seashore surround us.

Beside the seaside

It all started in the 1750s in an insignificant little fishing village in Sussex when a local doctor, Richard Russell, proclaimed the therapeutic benefits of sea bathing. Brightelmstone soon reduced its name to Brighton and never looked back.

George III added the royal seal of approval in the late 18th century by enjoying the waters at Weymouth. The privileged few became the milling masses, thanks to the coming of the railways and new purpose-built resorts — such as Llandudno and Southend — in the 19th century.

Blackpool, the epitome of the old-style resort, continues to attract 16 million visitors annually.

Brighton, where it all began, now provides a vision of the future: a massive new marina and leisure complex, the largest in Europe, which is almost a resort in itself.

Parking places

It's the end of the journey — and time to find somewhere to park. A variety of parking control systems is in use; familiarity with them will make life easier and it could avoid a fine.

Road markings No waiting (except for loading or unloading) during time shown on nearby plates or at entrance to controlled parking zone

during any period other than those shown on the right | during every working day | during every working day plus additional times

Kerb markings No loading or unloading at times shown on nearby plates

during any period other than those shown on the right | during every working day | during every working day plus additional times

General parking tips Do not park in dangerous places, especially junctions or corners. At night, parked vehicles must display lights unless within a 30mph (or less) area, or designated parking place. Vehicles must be parked with the nearside close to the kerb, and at least 10 metres away from any road junction.

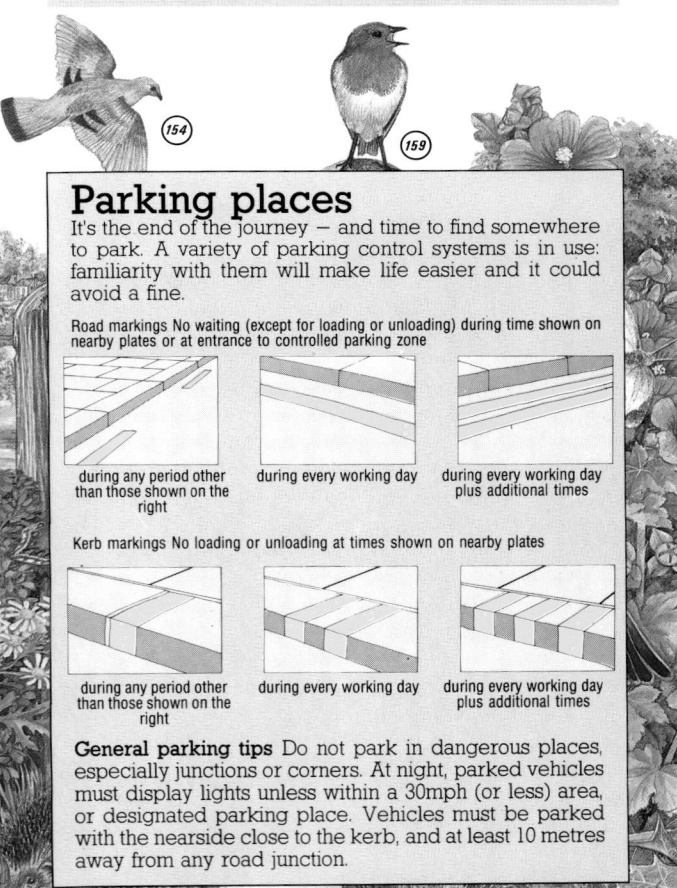

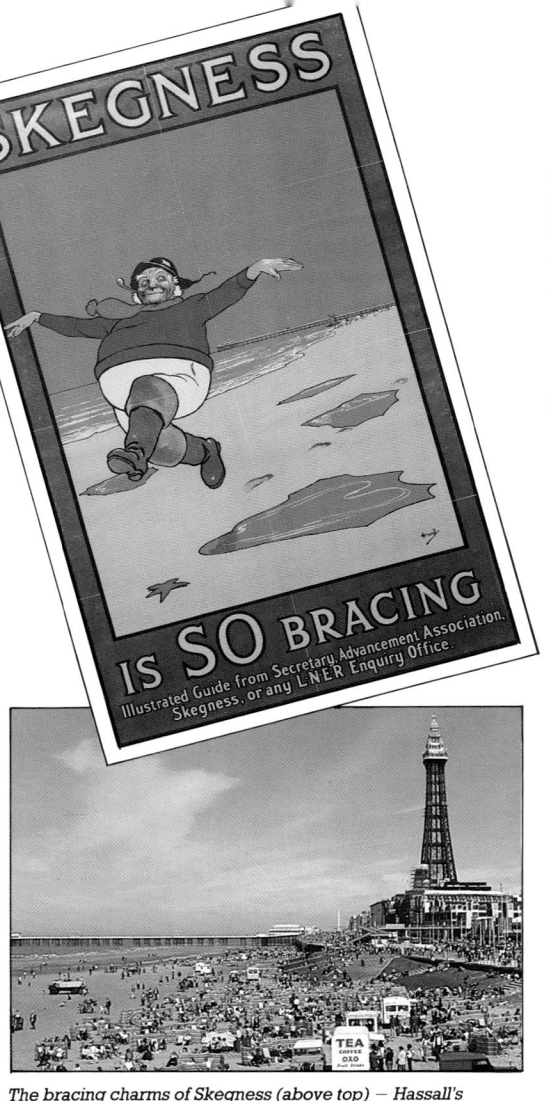

Taking to the waters

The use of the first bathing machine, to protect the modesty of those pioneering seaside pleasure-seekers, marked the birth of a new era. Soon, the British were flocking to the sea *en masse* in search of leisure and recreation. In the last twenty years, the simple pleasures of a stay-beside-the-sea side have been superseded by all kinds of aquatic recreations, from riding the Atlantic surf on our west-facing beaches to fishing for porbeagle shark above the deep-water reefs and wrecks off the Cornish coast.

Sailing, fishing and water sporting holidays are now big business. Here are some useful addresses:

English Tourist Board, 4 Grosvenor Gardens, London SW1W 0DU. Tel. 01-730 3400.

Scottish Tourist Board, 23 Ravelston Terrace, Edinburgh EH4 3EU. Tel. 031-332 2433.

Wales Tourist Board, PO Box 1, Cardiff CF1 2XN. Tel. Cardiff (0222) 27281.

Sports Council, 70 Brompton Road, London SW3 1EX. Tel. 01-589 3411.

Royal Yachting Association, Victoria Way, Woking Surrey. Tel. Woking (0483) 5022.

National Yacht Harbour Association, Harleyford, Marlow, Bucks. Tel. Marlow (06284) 71361.

British Canoe Union, 45 High Street, Addlestone, Weybridge, Surrey. Tel. (0932) 41341.

Life by the sea

Sea-cliffs are the last refuge for flora and fauna which rely on wild, impregnable surroundings. Plants grow in relation to the saltiness of the cliff-face. At the base of the cliff, constantly splashed by the sea, only specially adapted lichens can survive. A little higher, plants such as rock samphire and wild cabbage maintain a foothold. The most attractive of all are to be found amongst the cliff-top turf: pretty pink sea thrift (flowering March to October) and white-petalled sea campion (June to September).

Cliffs are also colonised by a variety of sea birds — shags, fulmars, razorbills, puffins, guillemots, kittiwakes, herring gulls, and cormorants amongst them. Many have specific preferences. Puffins, for example, nest in cliff-top burrows.

The bracing charms of Skegness (above top) — Hassall's classic railway poster. Above: Blackpool — the tower, pier and kiss-me-quick style still draw 16 million visitors a year

Rough riders at the Sea side.

THE FIGURES

Great Britain (England, Wales and Scotland) is a small island with a big coastline. The distance from the South Coast to the extreme North of Scotland is not even 600 miles (1,960km); its widest point is under 300 miles (500km) across.

The length of its coastline — around 7,000 miles (11,200km) — is much more impressive.

No place in Britain is more than about 80 miles (128km) from saltwater.

There are no fewer than 1,040 islands off the coast. The most remote of all is Rockall, a tiny 70ft pinnacle of granite, around 200 miles (320km) west of the Outer Hebrides.

Illustrations (176) – (194)
176 death's head hawk moth, 177 painted lady, 178 oystercatcher, 179 yellow horned poppy, 180 edible crab, 181 barnacle goose, 182 star fish, 183 mussels, 184 saw wrack, 185 sea anemone, 186 limpet, 187 winkles, 188 common tern, 189 cormorant, 190 thrift, 191 puffin, 192 lichen, 193 kittiwake, 194 grey seals

Drive to an Island

Lindisfarne (above) — an area of outstanding natural beauty

Many of our islands — Anglesey, Foulness and Sheppey, for example — are regarded as almost part of mainland Britain because of their long-standing road bridge connections. One island, off the empty Northumbrian coast a few miles from the Scottish border, really lives up to its description — and it can be visited by car.

Holy Island, or Lindisfarne, is completely cut off from the mainland twice daily by a rapid tide. At other times, motorists can drive across a well-surfaced, three-mile causeway to this peaceful island, renowned as the birthplace of Christianity in England. A lovely ruined priory stands on the site of the first Christian settlement, close to a small but romantic looking 16th-century castle.

St Michael's Mount in Cornwall (below), is also accessible by causeway at low tide, though only on foot.

AA Viewpoints – Where distance lends enchantment

On 18 May 1951, a group of people stood on a patch of high ground in Shropshire and ceremoniously declared it a perfect spot – for standing and staring. The place was Clee Hills, near Ludlow, and the occasion was the inauguration of the very first AA Viewpoint: a site offering outstanding panoramic scenery, which people could reach by car.

Since that day in early summer, the AA has sought out many more Viewpoints, and today the total stands at around 40. They range from Bealach Na Ba' in the north of Scotland to southern Cornwall's Pendennis Head, and from wild rural landscapes to a decidedly urban, reclaimed wasteland in Stoke-on-Trent – but each one commands a

stunning view. The chief criterion for a Viewpoint is a vista of at least 180 degrees. Some, such as Cockleroy in Lothian, stand in the centre of a spectacular panorama, and have views all the way round 360 degrees. Every Viewpoint has landmarks to look for: towns and villages, rivers and mountains – all pointed out on the engraved plaque embedded in the Viewpoint plinth. And good car parking facilities near at hand are a must if a Viewpoint is to meet the standards required.

The AA is constantly on the lookout for more Viewpoints. They are becoming harder to find, but Clent Hills in Worcestershire is an exciting addition: its approach has been specially designed for easy

access by the disabled. On the following pages, Clent Hills and other outstanding AA Viewpoints are captured in breathtaking photographs: rare places for pausing in peaceful contemplation in a world of rush and change.

What is this life if, full of care,
We have no time to stand and stare?

(W. H. DAVIES)

Sugar Loaf, Abergavenny, GWENT

The two-mile detour off the A40 along a sometimes steep and narrow country lane to this Viewpoint is well worth while. It stands in a lofty spot, 1,132ft (345m) above sea level on the western shoulder of the Sugar Loaf mountain near Abergavenny, and commands views far and wide across a huge slice of South Wales.

Spectacular vistas are only part of the story. This viewpoint also gives a dramatic insight into the two very different faces of South Wales. In the distance, the A465 'Heads of the Valley' road snakes its way up the

Clydach Gorge into the old iron and coal producing areas. Yet immediately below, in the bottom of the valley, the River Usk flows in a lazy loop through pastoral countryside.

Gilwern, a pretty village near the river, spreads itself out amongst a patchwork of green fields. Higher up, these fields peter out into open mountain pasture, domain of the hardy hill sheep. Higher still stands the 1,833ft (589m) summit of Blorenge, one of the many mountains identified by the AA plinth.

South of Abergavenny, the hills subside to luxuriant, rich farmlands, while the horizon to the west is filled

with the wide open spaces of 1,735ft (529m) high Mynydd Llangattock, signalling the start of the Brecon Beacons National Park.

The plinth points the eye past Mynydd Llangattock to the peak of Waen-Rydd, 12½ miles (20km) distant, near the mountainous heart of the park. The 1,955ft (596m) summit of the Sugar Loaf itself is only a three-and-a-half mile walk there and back, on a well-defined footpath.

This viewpoint, the first in Wales, was unveiled in 1970, and stands next to a good-sized car park.

HOW TO GET THERE

From Abergavenny: Leave by the A40 Brecon road. After passing Nevill Hall Hospital on left, in ½ mile at crossroads turn right, then follow signs along narrow unclassified road. From Cardiff: A48 and A48(M) to M4. At J26 take A4042 to Abergavenny — then as above. From Gloucester: A40 past Ross, Monmouth and Raglan to Abergavenny — then as above. From Swansea: A483 and A465 past Merthyr Tydfil and along Heads of the Valley road to Abergavenny — then as above.

The Viewpoint and the view – looking west to the village of Gilwern, nestling in the valley of the Usk

Main picture: from the slopes of Mynydd Llangattock, the bare summits of the Black Mountains loom on the horizon

AA Viewpoints

Atlas Page No.	Name	Map Ref.
35	Portishead	ST 4676
3	Pendennis Head	SW 8231
78	Highoredish	SK 3559
11	Bulbarrow	ST 7805
36	Robinswood Hill	SO 8415
47	Symonds Yat	SO 5615
14	Portsdown Hill	SU 6606
52	Windmill Hill	SO 9776
13	Bembridge Down	SZ 6285
28	Farthing Corner	TQ 8163
66	Beacon Hill	SK 5114
38	Wittenham Clumps	SU 5692
51	Clee Hills	SO 5975
20	Dunkery Beacon	SS 8941
9	Wellington Monument	ST 1317
76	Central Forest Park	SJ 8848
14	Duncton Hill	SU 9516
54	Magpie Hill	SP 3952
23	Barbury Castle	SU 1576
92	Sutton Bank	SE 5182
84	Holme Moss	SE 0903
72	South Stack	SH 2082
30	Foel Eryr	SN 0632
34	Sugar Loaf	SO 2616
73	Great Orme's Head	SH 7583
118	Scott's View	NT 5934
125	David Marshall Lodge	NN 5201
124	Queen's View	NS 5080
145	Bealach Na Ba'	NG 7741
153	Knockan Cliff	NC 1909
154	Struie Hill	NH 6585
126	Cockleroy	NS 9974
133	Queen's View	NN 8659
27	One Tree Hill	TQ 6986
50	Montgomery	SO 2195
139	Glengarry	NH 2102
52	Clent Hills	SO 9380
124	Lyle Hill	NS 2577

Route Planning

The *3 Mile Road Atlas of Britain* has been specially designed by AA experts to make the exploration and navigation of Britain's roads as easy and pleasurable as possilbe.

The route planning maps on this and the following pages can be used to help with journey planning. If you know the name of the village or town of your destination but not its location, look the name up in the index at the back of this atlas. Next to the name will be the atlas page number on which it appears and its National Grid reference. (An explanation of the National Grid is given on page 54) Once you have located the place, note the name of the nearest large conurbation to it shown on the route planning maps. By locating the nearest marked conurbation to your start point, it is then possible to plot a basic route between the two large places. More detailed routes can be planned by consulting the main atlas. A special feature of these maps is that a key to the atlas pages is superimposed –making at-a-glance place location much easier.

As a general rule, motorways are the quickest and most efficient means of travelling across the country; primary routes are usually the next-best thing. The shortest route is not necessarily the quickest, whereas motorways and primary routes usually avoid the centres of towns, other roads may lead you into a maze of side streets and an endless succession of traffic lights, one-way systems etc. Radio stations often give invaluable information about road conditions in areas that you may be passing through; maps of the areas covered by BBC and Independent local radio stations can be found on pages 52 and 53.

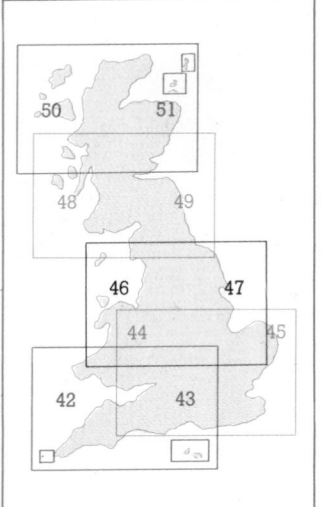

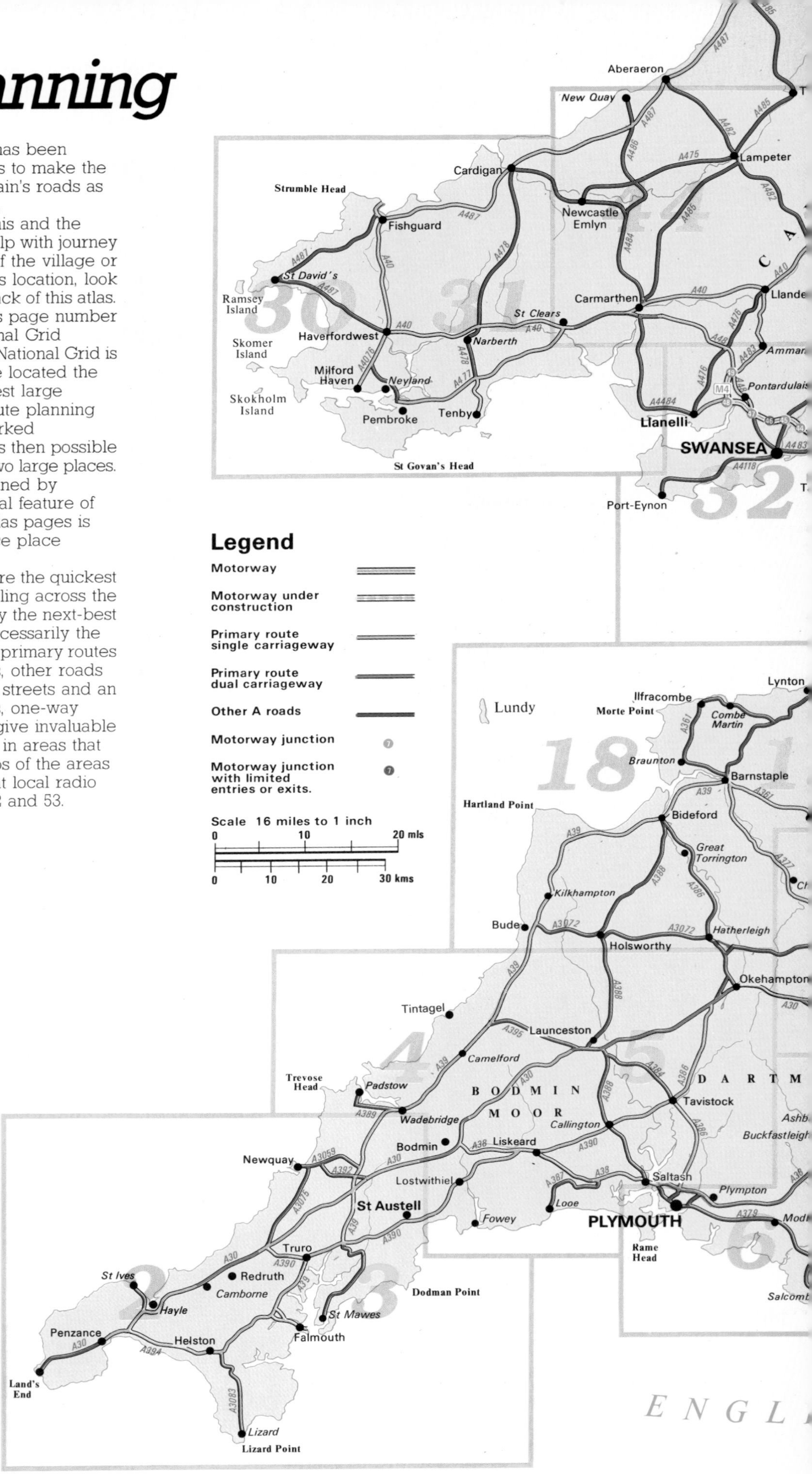

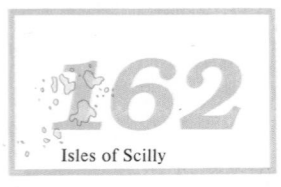

162 Isles of Scilly

Legend

Motorway	
Motorway under construction	
Primary route single carriageway	
Primary route dual carriageway	
Other A roads	
Motorway junction	⑦
Motorway junction with limited entries or exits.	⑦

Scale 16 miles to 1 inch

0   10   20 mls

0   10   20   30 kms

Knighton
Ludlow
Kidderminster
Bewdley
COVENTRY
Rugby
Kettering
Rhayader
Presteigne
Tenbury Wells
Stourport-on-Severn
Bromsgrove
Henley in Arden
Redditch
Leamington Spa
Warwick
Daventry
Wellingborough
Llandrindod Wells
Leominster
Droitwich
Southam
NORTHAMPTON
Kington
Builth Wells
Bromyard
Worcester
Alcester
Stratford-upon-Avon
Llanwrtyd Wells
Great Malvern
Pershore
Newbold-upon-Stour
Towcester
Hay-on-Wye
Hereford
Ledbury
Upton on Severn
Evesham
Shipston-on-Stour
Banbury
Llyswen
Talgarth
Fownhope
Tewkesbury
Broadway
Moreton-in-Marsh
Brackley
Milton Keynes
Brecon
Deddington
Buckingham
Pontrilas
Bishop's Cleeve
Stow-on-the-Wold
Chipping Norton
Leighton Buzzard
BLACK MTS
Ross-on-Wye
Cheltenham
Bicester
BRECON BEACONS
Gloucester
Bourton-on-the-Water
Abergavenny
Monmouth
COTSWOLDS
Northleach
Woodstock
Burford
Aylesbury
Ebbw Vale
Tredegar
Witney
Hirwaun
Merthyr Tydfil
Raglan
Stroud
Wendover
Aberdare
Usk
Lydney
Cirencester
OXFORD
Thame
Pontypool
Nailsworth
Treorchy
Cwmbran
Chepstow
Lechlade
Farringdon
Abingdon
High Wycombe
Pontypridd
Tetbury
Cricklade
Didcot
Wallingford
Caerphilly
NEWPORT
Malmesbury
Swindon
Wantage
Marlow
Bridgend
Henley-on-Thames
CARDIFF
Cowbridge
Chippenham
READING
Barry
Clevedon
BRISTOL
Calne
Hungerford
Marlborough
Newbury
Bracknell
Weston-super-Mare
Congresbury
Melksham
BATH
Bradford-on-Avon
Devizes
Camberley
Channel
Churchill
Trowbridge
Kingsclere
Cheddar
Radstock
Basingstoke
Minehead
Burnham-on-Sea
Wookey Hole
Westbury
Whitchurch
Watchet
Wells
Frome
SALISBURY PLAIN
Andover
Farnham
Williton
Glastonbury
Shepton Mallet
Warminster
Amesbury
Bridgwater
Alton
Street
Othery
Wiveliscombe
Langport
Wilton
Stockbridge
Liphook
Salisbury
Alresford
Winchester
Taunton
Wincanton
Bampton
Ilchester
Wellington
Shaftesbury
Romsey
Eastleigh
Petersfield
Midhurst
Ilminster
Yeovil
Sturminster Newton
Tiverton
Sherborne
Crewkerne
SOUTHAMPTON
Chard
Blandford Forum
Lyndhurst
Fareham
Havant
Honiton
Wimborne Minster
Ringwood
Fawley
Beaminster
Cerne Abbas
Axminster
Cowes
Gosport
PORTSMOUTH
Clyst Honiton
Lymington
Ryde
Seaton
Lyme Regis
Bridport
Dorchester
Poole
BOURNEMOUTH
Christchurch
Yarmouth
Newport
Sidmouth
Wareham
Sandown
Exmouth
Isle of Wight
Budleigh Salterton
Godshill
Shanklin
Lyme Bay
Weymouth
Swanage
Chale
Ventnor
Dawlish
Niton
Teignmouth
St Alban's Head
St Catherine's Point
Fortuneswell
Bill of Portland
Torquay
Paignton
Brixham
Dartmouth
CHANNEL
ENGLAND
ENGLISH CHANNEL
Guernsey
Jersey
FRANCE
161

Betws-y-Coed
Ruthin
Wrexham
Crewe
Biddulph
Kidsgrove
Leek
Alfreton
Kirby-in-Ashfield
Wirksworth
Hucknall
Nantwich
Newcastle-under-Lyme
Stoke-on-Trent
Belper
Blaenau Ffestiniog
Ffestiniog
Corwen
Ruabon
Llangollen
Whitchurch
Cheadle
Ashbourne
NOTTIN
DERBY
Bala
Ellesmere
Market Drayton
Stone
Uttoxeter
Oswestry
Burton upon Trent
Stafford
Loughborou
Dolgellau
Newport
Rugeley
Ashby-de-la-Zouch
Coalville
Mallwyd
Welshpool
Shrewsbury
Cannock
Lichfield
Telford
Tamworth
LEICES
Llanbrynmair
Brownhills
Machynlleth
Montgomery
Much Wenlock
WOLVERHAMPTON
Walsall
Sutton Coldfield
Atherstone
Hinckley
Wigston
Caersws
Church Stretton
Bridgnorth
West Bromwich
Nuneaton
Coleshill
Newtown
Dudley
Stourbridge
Bedworth
BIRMINGHAM
Halesowen
Lutterworth
Llanidloes
Solihull
COVENTRY
Llangurig
Kidderminster
Bewdley
Rugby
Knighton
Ludlow
Stourport-on-Severn
Bromsgrove
Leamington Spa
Rhayader
Presteigne
Tenbury Wells
Redditch
Henley in Arden
Warwick
Daventry
Llandrindod Wells
Droitwich
Southam
Tregaron
Leominster
Alcester
Kington
Bromyard
Stratford-upon-Avon
Builth Wells
Worcester
Pershore
Towcester
Llanwrtyd Wells
Great Malvern
Newbold-upon-Stour
Banbury
Hay-on-Wye
Evesham
Shipston-on-Stour
Hereford
Ledbury
Upton on Severn
Broadway
Brackley
Llyswen
Moreton-in-Marsh
Deddington
Llandovery
Talgarth
Fownhope
Tewkesbury
Buckingham
Brecon
Bishop's Cleeve
Pontrilas
Stow-on-the-Wold
Chipping Norton
BLACK MTS
Llandeilo
Ross-on-Wye
Cheltenham
Bicester
BRECON BEACONS
Abergavenny
Gloucester
Bourton-on-the-Water
Northleach
Burford
Woodstock
Monmouth
Ebbw Vale
Tredegar
Witney
OXFORD
Hirwaun
Merthyr Tydfil
Raglan
Lydney
Stroud
Cirencester
Aberdare
Pontypool
Usk
Nailsworth
Lechlade
Abingdon
Neath
Treorchy
Cwmbran
Chepstow
Tetbury
Cricklade
Farringdon
Didcot
Wallingfo
Port Talbot
Pontypridd
Caerphilly
NEWPORT
Malmesbury
Wantage
Swindon
Bridgend
Porthcawl
CARDIFF
Cowbridge
Chippenham
READIN
Barry
Clevedon
BRISTOL
Calne
Hungerford
Congresbury
Marlborough
Newbury
Weston-super-Mare
BATH
Bradford-on-Avon
Melksham
Devizes
Bristol Channel
Churchill
Cheddar
Trowbridge
Kingsclere
Basingstoke
Foreland Point
Radstock
Westbury
Wookey Hole
Lynmouth
Minehead
Burnham-on-Sea
Frome
Warminster
SALISBURY PLAIN
Whitchurch
Watchet
Wells
Andover
Williton
Glastonbury
Shepton Mallet
Amesbury
Alton
Street
Bridgwater
Othery
Stockbridge
Alresford
EXMOOR
Wiveliscombe
Wilton
Salisbury
Langport
Winchester
South Molton
Taunton
Wincanton
Ilchester
Bampton
Wellington
Shaftesbury
Romsey
Eastleigh
Peters
Sturminster Newton
Ilminster
Yeovil
Sherborne
Chulmleigh
Tiverton
SOUTHAMPTON
Blandford Forum
Chard
Crewkerne
Lyndhurst
Fareham
Fawley
Wimborne Minster
Ringwood
Cerne Abbas
Beaminster
Crediton
Honiton
Gosport
Cowes
Axminster
EXETER
Clyst Honiton
Lymington
Ryde
Seaton
Lyme Regis
Bridport
Dorchester
Poole
BOURNEMOUTH
Christchurch
Yarmouth
Newport
Sidmouth
Wareham
Sandown
Exmouth
Isle of Wight
Chudleigh
Budleigh Salterton
Shanklin
Godshill
Lyme Bay
Weymouth
Swanage
Chale
Ventnor
Niton
Dawlish
St Alban's Head
St Catherine's Point
Newton Abbot
Teignmouth
Fortuneswell
Ashburton
Bill of Portland
Torquay
Paignton
CAMBRIAN MOUNTAINS
COTSWOLDS
M1
M5
M6
M4
M50
M42
M45
M69
M54
M3
M27
M32
A48(M)
A38(M)
52
53
54
36
37
38
22
23
24
12
13
44

The Wash
Sleaford
Boston
Grantham
Swineshead
Hunstanton
Wells-next-the-Sea
Sheringham
Cromer
Holbeach
Fakenham
North Walsham
Aylsham
Spalding
King's Lynn
Bourne
Mowbray
Wroxham
East Dereham
Caistor-on-Sea
Acle
Great Yarmouth
NORWICH
Wisbech
Stamford
Downham Market
Swaffam
Watton
Wymondham
March
Peterborough
Attleborough
Lowestoft
Corby
Oundle
Chatteris
Littleport
Brandon
Beccles
Bungay
Thetford
Diss
Thrapston
Ely
Southwold
Halesworth
Huntingdon
Stretham
Soham
Eye
Godmanchester
Rushden
Waterbeach
Newmarket
Bury St Edmunds
Stowmarket
Saxmundham
St Neots
Cambridge
Aldeburgh
THAMPTON
Coddenham
Sandy
Bedford
Woodbridge
Orford Ness
Newport Pagnell
Haverhill
IPSWICH
Ampthill
Royston
Sudbury
Saffron Walden
Felixstowe
East Bergholt
Harwich
Letchworth
Baldock
Halstead
Hitchin
Stevenage
The Naze
Braintree
Colchester
Dunstable
Luton
Bishop's Stortford
Brightlingsea
Harpenden
Hertford
Ware
Witham
West Mersea
Clacton-on-Sea
Tring
Colne Point
Berkhamsted
St Albans
Harlow
Hemel Hempstead
Hoddesdon
Chelmsford
Potters Bar
Maldon
CHILTERNS
Amersham
Rettendon
Watford
Chigwell
Brentwood
Beaconsfield
Rayleigh
Foulness Island
Romford
Basildon
Maidenhead
LONDON
Hadleigh
Southend-on-Sea
Slough
Grays
Tilbury
Windsor
Woolwich
Dartford
Sheerness
Staines
Gravesend
Isle of Sheppey
Margate
Rochester
Herne Bay
North Foreland
Gillingham
Orpington
Sittingbourne
Whitstable
Croydon
Faversham
Ramsgate
Woking
Epsom
NORTH DOWNS
Caterham
Canterbury
Sandwich
Aldershot
Leatherhead
Sevenoaks
Maidstone
Dorking
Godstone
Deal
Guildford
Reigate
Tonbridge
Milford
Gatwick
Ashford
Dover
East Grinstead
Crawley
Tunbridge Wells
Biddenden
Hythe
Folkestone
Haslemere
Lamberhurst
Tenterden
Horsham
Hawkhurst
Billingshurst
Haywards Heath
New Romney
Uckfield
Rye
Pulborough
Hurstpierpoint
Battle
Winchelsea
Dungeness
SOUTH DOWNS
Hailsham
Arundel
Lewes
Hastings
Bexhill
Chichester
Bognor Regis
Littlehampton
Worthing
Shoreham-by-Sea
BRIGHTON
Newhaven
Seaford
Eastbourne
Beachy Head
Strait of Dover

Mull of Galloway
ISLE OF MAN
Point of Ayre
Bride
Andreas
Ballaugh
Ramsey
Maughold Head
Peel
Laxey
Douglas
Craigneish
Castletown
Calf of Man
Dreswick Point
IRISH SEA
Workington
Keswick
Whitehaven
Egremont
Appleby-in-Westmorland
Ambleside
Windermere
Coniston
Kendal
Sedbergh
Millom
Ulverston
Grange-over-Sands
Kirkby Lonsdale
Ingleton
Barrow-in-Furness
Carnforth
Isle of Walney
Morecambe
Heysham
Lancaster
Fleetwood
Garstang
Clitheroe
BLACKPOOL
Kirkham
Lytham St. Annes
PRESTON
Southport
Leyland
Chorley
Ormskirk
Skelmersdale
Formby
Wigan
Crosby
Bootle
Salford
Wallasey
LIVERPOOL
St Helens
Hoylake
Birkenhead
Widnes
Warrington
Bebington
Runcorn
Carmel Head
Amlwch
ANGLESEY
Puffin Island
Great Ormes Head
Point of Ayr
Holyhead
Holy Island
Beaumaris
Llandudno
Colwyn Bay
Rhyl
Prestatyn
Conwy
Abergele
St Asaph
Holywell
Flint
Frodsham
Northwich
Bangor
Llanfairfechan
Connah's Quay
Bethesda
Denbigh
Chester
Middlewich
Caernarfon
Llanrwst
Mold
Llanberis
Betws-y-Coed
Ruthin
Sandbach
Crewe
Nantwich
Wrexham
Beddgelert
Blaenau Ffestiniog
Ffestiniog
Newcastle-under
Porthmadog
Corwen
Ruabon
Llangollen
Whitchurch
Criccieth
Pwllheli
Bala
Ellesmere
Market Drayton
Harlech
Oswestry
Abersoch
Bardsey Island
Barmouth
Dolgellau
Newport
Mallwyd
Welshpool
Shrewsbury
Telford
Llanbrynmair
Tywyn
Aberdovey
Machynlleth
Montgomery
Much Wenlock
Cardigan Bay
Caersws
Church Stretton
Bridgnorth
Newtown
Llanidloes
Aberystwyth
Llangurig
Knighton
Ludlow
Rhayader
Presteigne
Tenbury Wells
Aberaeron
Llandrindod Wells
Leominster
New Quay
Tregaron
Kington
Bromyard
Builth Wells
Great Malvern
Cardigan
Lampeter
Llanwrtyd Wells
Strumble Head
Hay-on-Wye
Newcastle Emlyn
Hereford
Ledbury
Fishguard
Llyswen
Llandovery
Talgarth
Fownhope
CAMBRIAN MOUNTAINS

Bishop Auckland
West Auckland
Newton Aycliffe
Stockton on Tees
Middlesbrough
Redcar
Saltburn-by-the-Sea
Barnard Castle
Darlington
Guisborough
Stokesley
Whitby
Richmond
Catterick
NORTH YORKS MOORS
Leyburn
Northallerton
Kirkby Moorside
Pickering
Scalby
Scarborough
NORTH SEA
Masham
Thirsk
Seamer
Filey
Sherburn
Humanby
THE WOLDS
Ripon
Boroughbridge
Easingwold
Malton
Flamborough Head
Bridlington
Great Driffield
Knaresborough
Skipton
Harrogate
YORK
Pocklington
Ilkley
Otley
Wetherby
Tadcaster
Market Weighton
Keighley
Bingley
Yeadon
Beverley
Shipley
LEEDS
BRADFORD
Garforth
Selby
Halifax
Castleford
Brighouse
Knottingley
North Ferriby
HULL
Withernsea
Goole
Wakefield
Pontefract
Dewsbury
Barton-upon-Humber
Patrington
HUDDERSFIELD
Hemsworth
Thorne
Ulceby
Immingham Dock
Spurn Head
Scunthorpe
Grimsby
Barnsley
Brigg
Cleethorpes
Oldham
Penistone
Doncaster
Caister
CHESTER
Ashton-under-Lyne
Glossop
Rotherham
Bawtry
LINCOLN WOLDS
Gainsborough
Market Rasen
STOCKPORT
SHEFFIELD
Maltby
Louth
Hazel Grove
Mablethorpe
Whaley Bridge
Worksop
Retford
Dronfield
Wragby
Alford
Macclesfield
Buxton
Staveley
Tuxford
Lincoln
Horncastle
Bakewell
Chesterfield
Warsop
Ollerton
Spilsby
Skegness
Leek
Matlock
Mansfield
Alfreton
Kirkby-in-Ashfield
Wirksworth
Newark-on-Trent
Hucknall
Belper
Stoke-on-Trent
Ashbourne
Sleaford
Boston
The Wash
Cheadle
NOTTINGHAM
Swineshead
Hunstanton
DERBY
Grantham
Stone
Uttoxeter
Holbeach
Burton upon Trent
Stafford
Spalding
King's Lynn
Loughborough
Rugeley
Ashby-de-la-Zouch
Melton Mowbray
Bourne
Coalville
Cannock
Lichfield
Oakham
Wisbech
Stamford
Swaffam
Downham Market
Tamworth
Brownhills
LEICESTER
Walsall
Sutton Coldfield
Uppingham
March
Atherstone
Hinckley
Wigston
Peterborough
West Bromwich
Nuneaton
Coleshill
Market Harborough
Corby
Oundle
Chatteris
Bedworth
Littleport
Brandon
BIRMINGHAM
Lutterworth
Husbands Bosworth
Rothwell
Thetford
Solihull
Ely
COVENTRY
Kettering
Thrapston
Rugby
Huntingdon
Stretham
Soham
Bromsgrove
Henley in Arden
Leamington Spa
Godmanchester
Redditch
Warwick
Daventry
Wellingborough
Rushden
Waterbeach
Droitwich
Southam
Newmarket
Bury St Edmunds
Alcester
NORTHAMPTON
St Neots
Cambridge
Stratford-upon-Avon
Pershore
Towcester
Bedford
Sandy
Newbold-upon-Stour
Newport Pagnell
Haverhill
Evesham
Shipston-on-Stour
Banbury
Ampthill
Royston
Sudbury
Broadway
Moreton-in-Marsh
Brackley
Milton Keynes
Saffron Walden
Baldock

Sound of Arisaig
Spean Bridge
Corpach
Fort William
Kinlochmoidart
Salen
Blair Atholl
Tobermory
Drimnin
COLL
Glencoe
South Ballachulish
Aberfeldy
TIREE
Lochaline
Portnacroish
Salen
Lismore
ISLAND OF MULL
Connel
Taynuilt
Killin
Oban
Kerrera
Dalmally
Crianlarich
Lochearnhead
Comrie
Crieff
Firth of Lorn
Sound of Mull
128
129
130
131
132
Luing
Kilmelford
Inveraray
Callander
Scarba
Ford
Strachur
Arrochar
Aberfoyle
Doune
Dunblane
Alva
Dollar
Colonsay
Luss
Kippen
Stirling
Drymen
Lochgilphead
122
123
124
125
Helensburgh
JURA
Sound of Jura
Dunoon
Gourock
Dumbarton
Kilsyth
Falkirk
Tighnabruaich
Colintraive
Greenock
Kirkintillock
Cumbernauld
Linlithgow
Tarbert
Wemyss Bay
Rothesay
Airdrie
Rubhana Traille
Kennacraig
Bute
Paisley
GLASGOW
Motherwell
Shotts
ISLAY
Clachan
Largs
East Kilbride
Hamilton
Port Mor
Sound of Bute
Millport
Kilbirnie
Larkhall
Carluke
120
Gigha
Sound of Gigha
Tayinloan
114
115
Stewarton
Strathaven
Island of Arran
Ardrossan
Saltcoats
Lanark
Brodick
Irvine
Lesmahagow
Kilbrannan Sound
Troon
Kilmarnock
Bellochantuy
112
113
Holy Island
Mauchline
Prestwick
Muirkirk
Kilchenzie
Campbeltown
Ayr
Cumnock
Maybole
Sanquhar
Dalmellington
Kirkoswald
106
107
Mull of Kintyre
Ailsa Craig
Girvan
Thornhill
Carsphairn
Ballantrae
NORTH CHANNEL
SOUTHERN
New Galloway
Cairnryan
Loch Ryan
Newton Stewart
100
101
NORTHERN IRELAND
Stranraer
Castle Douglas
Dalbeattie
Gatehouse of Fleet
Wigtown
Portpatrick
Glenluce
Auchencairn
Kirkcudbright
Port William
Whithorn
Abbey Head
Port Logan
Solway
Drummore
Isle of Whitown
Burrow Head
Mull of Galloway
Workington
Whitehaven
Point of Ayre
ISLE OF MAN
Bride
Andreas
Ramsey
Ballaugh
Maughold Head
Peel

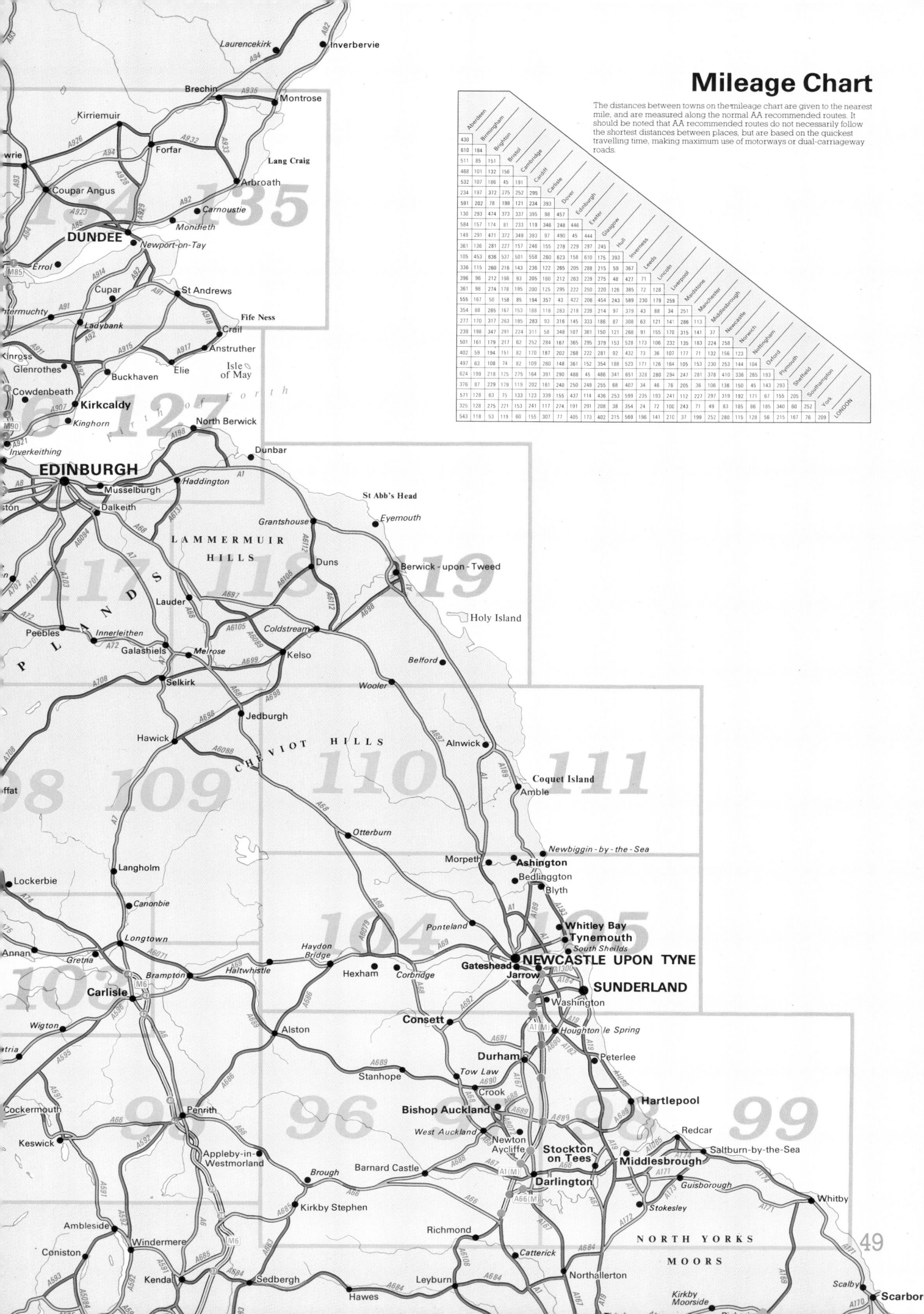

Mileage Chart

The distances between towns on the mileage chart are given to the nearest mile, and are measured along the normal AA recommended routes. It should be noted that AA recommended routes do not necessarily follow the shortest distances between places, but are based on the quickest travelling time, making maximum use of motorways or dual-carriageway roads.

Aberdeen	Birmingham	Brighton	Bristol	Cambridge	Cardiff	Carlisle	Dover	Edinburgh	Exeter	Glasgow	Hull	Inverness	Leeds	Lincoln	Liverpool	London	Maidstone	Manchester	Middlesbrough	Newcastle	Norwich	Nottingham	Oxford	Plymouth	Sheffield	Southampton	York	LONDON
430																												
610	184																											
511	85	151																										
468	101	132	156																									
532	107	186	45	191																								
234	197	372	252	295																								
591	202	78	198	121	234	393																						
130	293	474	373	337	395	98	457																					
584	157	174	81	233	119	346	248	446																				
149	291	471	372	349	393	97	490	45	444																			
361	136	281	227	157	246	155	278	229	297	245																		
105	453	636	537	501	558	260	623	158	610	175	393																	
336	115	260	216	143	236	122	265	205	288	215	59	367																
396	96	212	166	93	205	180	212	263	239	275	48	427	71															
361	98	274	178	195	200	125	295	222	250	220	126	385	72	128														
555	167	50	158	85	194	357	43	422	206	454	243	589	230	179	259													
354	88	285	167	153	188	118	283	218	239	214	97	379	43	88	34	251												
277	170	317	263	195	283	93	316	145	333	186	87	308	63	121	141	286	113											
239	198	347	291	224	311	58	368	107	361	150	121	268	91	155	170	315	141	37										
501	161	179	217	62	252	284	187	365	295	379	153	528	173	106	232	135	183	224	258									
402	59	194	151	82	170	187	202	268	222	281	92	432	73	36	107	177	71	132	156	123								
497	63	108	74	82	109	260	148	361	152	354	188	523	171	126	164	105	153	253	144	104								
624	199	218	125	275	164	391	290	488	45	486	341	651	328	280	294	247	281	378	410	336	265	193						
376	87	229	179	119	202	161	240	250	248	255	68	407	34	46	76	205	36	106	136	150	45	143	293					
571	128	61	75	133	123	339	155	437	114	436	253	599	235	193	241	112	227	319	192	171	67	155	205					
325	128	275	221	153	241	117	274	191	291	208	38	354	24	72	100	243	71	49	83	185	86	185	340	60	252			
543	118	53	119	60	155	307	77	405	170	402	215	569	196	141	210	37	199	252	280	115	128	56	215	167	76	208		

49

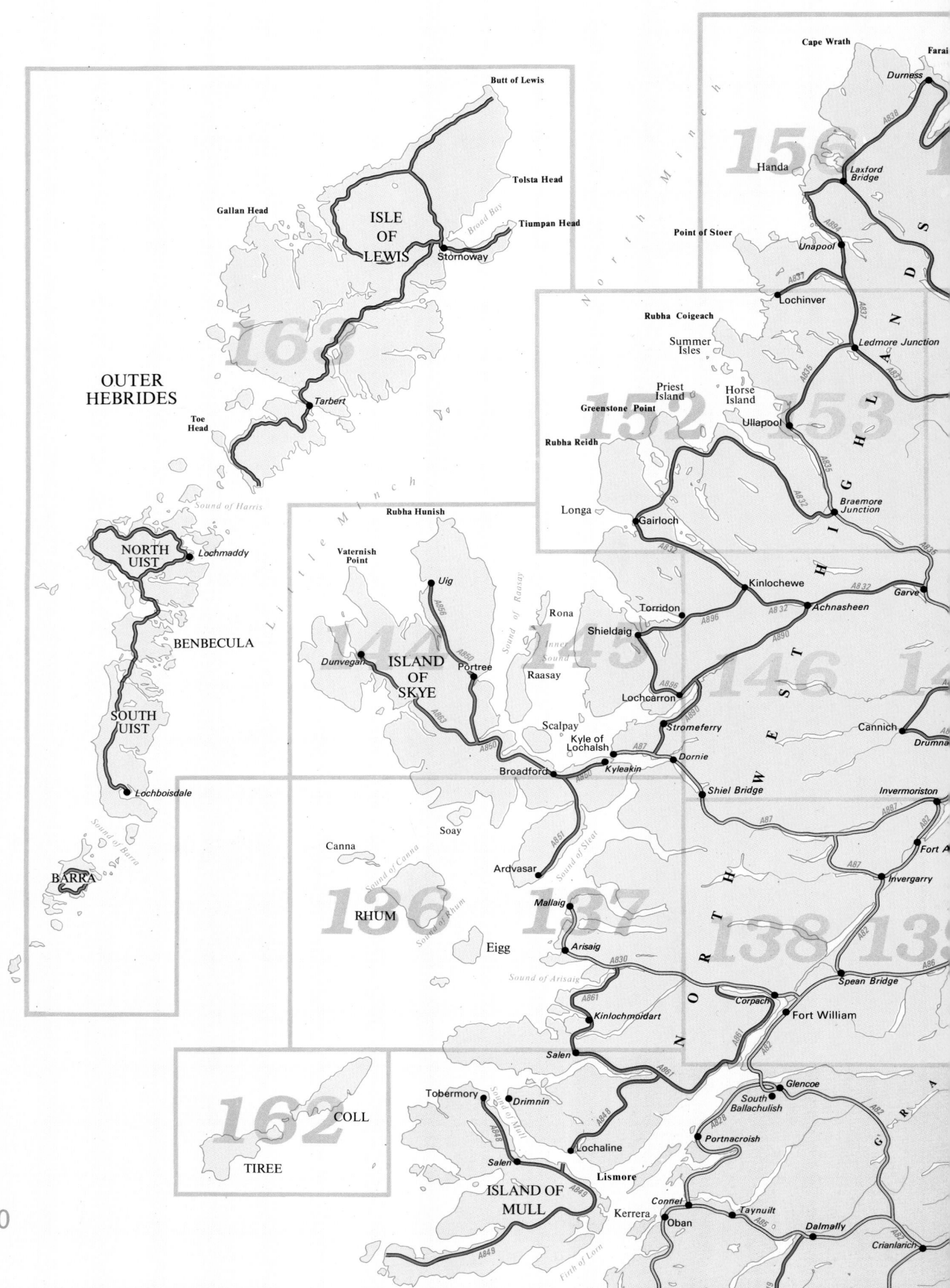

OUTER
HEBRIDES

ISLE
OF
LEWIS

Butt of Lewis

Tolsta Head

Tiumpan Head

Broad Bay

Stornoway

Gallan Head

Tarbert

Toe
Head

163

Sound of Harris

NORTH
UIST

Lochmaddy

BENBECULA

SOUTH
UIST

Lochboisdale

Sound of Barra

BARRA

162

COLL

TIREE

Rubha Hunish

Vaternish
Point

Uig

A866

Dunvegan

ISLAND
OF
SKYE

A850

Portree

144

Rona

143

Raasay

Scalpay

A851

Kyle of
Lochalsh

Broadford

Kyleakin

A850

A861

Soay

Ardvasar

Canna

RHUM

136

Sound of Conna

Eigg

Sound of Rhum

137

Mallaig

Arisaig

A830

Sound of Arisaig

A861

Kinlochmoidart

Salen

A861

Tobermory

Drimnin

Sound of Mull

A848

Lochaline

Salen

A849

ISLAND
OF
MULL

Lismore

Connel

Kerrera

Oban

Firth of Lorn

A849

North Minch

Cape Wrath

Farai

Durness

A838

156

Handa

Laxford
Bridge

A894

Point of Stoer

Unapool

A837

Lochinver

Rubha Coigeach

Summer
Isles

Ledmore Junction

A835

A837

Priest
Island

Horse
Island

153

Greenstone Point

Ullapool

152

Rubha Reidh

Braemore
Junction

A832

A835

Longa

Gairloch

A832

Kinlochewe

A832

Garve

Torridon

A896

Achnasheen

A890

Shieldaig

146

A896

Lochcarron

Stromeferry

A890

Cannich

Drumna

Dornie

A87

Shiel Bridge

Invermoriston

A887

A87

Fort A

A87

Invergarry

NORTH

A861

Spean Bridge

138

139

Corpach

Fort William

A82

Glencoe

A82

South
Ballachulish

A828

Portnacroish

Taynuilt

Dalmally

Crianlarich

A819

50

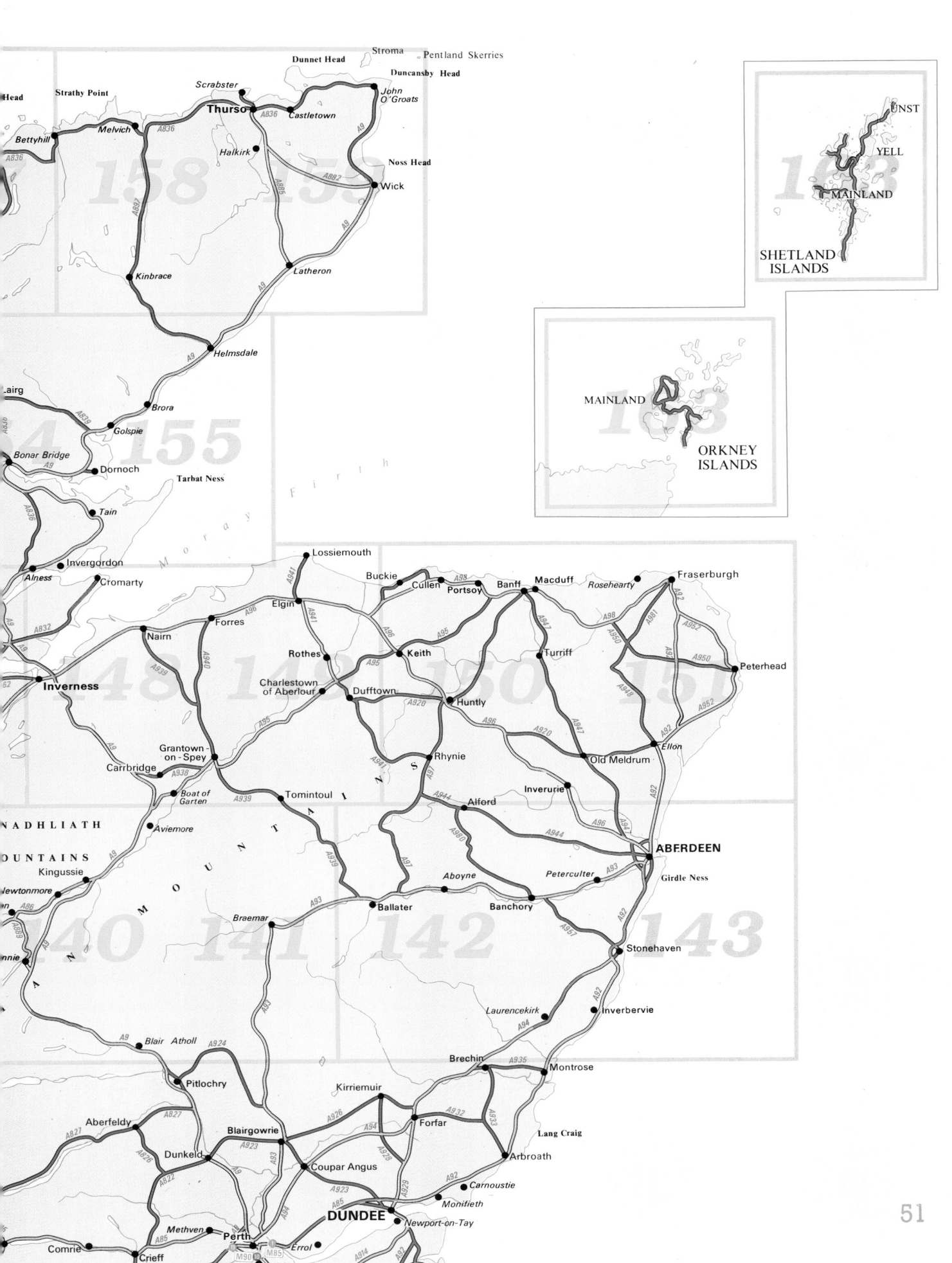

Head

Strathy Point

Scrabster
Thurso
Melvich

Stroma Pentland Skerries

Dunnet Head

Duncansby Head

John O'Groats

A836
Castletown

Bettyhill

158

Halkirk

Noss Head

A882
Wick

A9

A887

A885

A9

Kinbrace

Latheron

A9

Helmsdale

Lairg

Brora

A839

Golspie

155

Bonar Bridge

A9

Dornoch

Tarbat Ness

Tain

A836

Invergordon

Alness

Cromarty

A832

A9

Inverness

148

Forres

A96

Elgin

A941

Nairn

A940

Rothes

Charlestown of Aberlour

A95

A95

Lossiemouth

Buckie

A98

Cullen

Portsoy

Banff

Macduff

Rosehearty

Fraserburgh

A92

A98

A947

Keith

Turriff

A950

A981

A952

A91

Dufftown

A920

Huntly

150

A96

A920

A947

151

Peterhead

A948

A952

A92

A839

Grantown-on-Spey

Carrbridge

A938

Boat of Garten

A939

Rhynie

A941

Old Meldrum

Ellon

A92

Tomintoul

Inverurie

A944

Alford

Inverurie

Aviemore

A9

NADHLIATH

OUNTAINS

Kingussie

Newtonmore

A86

A889

140

141

A93

Braemar

A939

A97

Aboyne

Peterculter

A93

Ballater

Banchory

A96

A944

A94

ABERDEEN

Girdle Ness

A957

142

143

A960

A97

A93

Stonehaven

A957

A92

Laurencekirk

A94

Inverbervie

A9

Blair Atholl

A924

A93

Brechin

A935

Montrose

Pitlochry

Kirriemuir

A926

Lang Craig

Aberfeldy

A827

A932

A933

Forfar

A94

Blairgowrie

A923

A928

Arbroath

Dunkeld

A876

Coupar Angus

A822

A923

A92

Carnoustie

A85

A94

Monifieth

A930

Methven

DUNDEE

Newport-on-Tay

Comrie

A85

Perth

Errol

A914

Crieff

M90 M85

Bridge of Earn

Cupar

A91

St Andrews

51

Moray

Firth

FIRTH

SHETLAND ISLANDS

163

UNST

YELL

MAINLAND

MAINLAND

163

ORKNEY ISLANDS

Local Radio Broadcasting

All BBC & IBA local radio stations, including three of the BBC national networks, give up to date information on road and weather conditions in their programmes. Under normal circumstances any car radio should be able to receive local radio broadcasts within the reception areas shown on these maps. In some parts of the country reception areas overlap.

The VHF/FM signal can sometimes vary over a very small area, depending on local topography, and MW reception coverage is considerably reduced at night. In fringe areas, either the VHF, or the MW signal, may prove stronger.

Where no frequency or wavelength is given, this indicates that there is usually poor reception coverage from a main transmission area, or no reception coverage at all.

In the list below the name of each station is followed by its Wavelength (Mtrs), and Frequency (KHz) on Medium Wave, followed by the Frequency (MHz) on VHF/FM.

NB Frequency changes

Some VHF frequencies are likely to change during the currency of this publication, in accordance with a new international frequency plan. The current situation may be checked with the BBC Engineering Information Department on 01-927 5040 (and in relevant editions of Radio Times) and/or the IBA Engineering Information Service on Winchester (0962) 822444.

TBA – To be announced

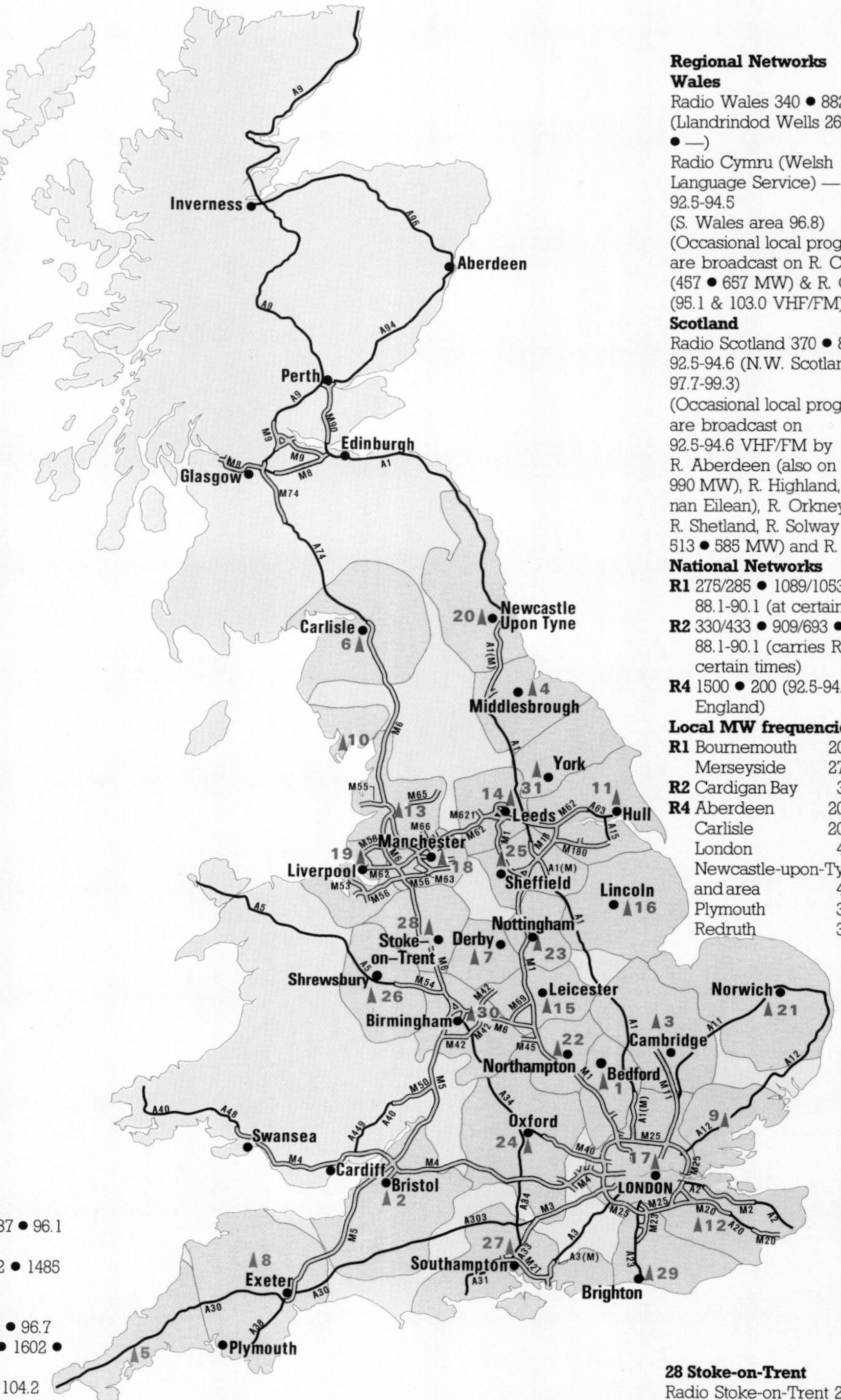

BBC Local Radio

1 Bedfordshire
Radio Bedfordshire
Bedford area 258 ● 1161 ● 95.5
Luton area 476 ● 630 ● 103.7

2 Bristol
Radio Bristol 194 ● 1548 ● 95.5
Bristol area 194 ● 1548 ● 104.4
Taunton area 227 ● 1323 ● 95.5

3 Cambridgeshire
Radio Cambridgeshire 292 ● 1026 ● 96.0
Peterborough and
N. Cambridgeshire area 207 ● 1449 ● 94.8

4 Cleveland
Radio Cleveland 194 ● 1548 ● 96.6
Whitby area 194 ● 1548 ● 95.9

5 Cornwall
Radio Cornwall
East Cornwall 457 ● 657 ● 95.2
West Cornwall 476 ● 630 ● 96.4
Isles of Scilly area 476 ● 630 ● 97.3

6 Cumbria
Radio Cumbria 397 ● 756 ● 95.6
Whitehaven area 206 ● 1458 ● 95.6

7 Derby
Radio Derby 269 ● 1116 ● 96.5
Derby only 269 ● 1116 ● 94.2

8 Devon
Radio Devon
Exeter area 303 ● 990 ● 97.0
Torbay area 206 ● 1458 ● 97.5
Plymouth area 351 ● 855 ● 97.5
Barnstaple & N. Devon area 375 ● 801 ● 94.8
Okehampton area — ● — ● 96.2

9 Essex
Radio Essex TBA ● TBA ● 103.5
Southend & Basildon area 1530 ● 196 ● 95.3
N.E. Essex TBA ● TBA ● 104.9

10 Furness
Radio Furness 358 ● 837 ● 96.1

11 Humberside
Radio Humberside 202 ● 1485 ● 95.9

12 Kent
Radio Kent 290 ● 1035 ● 96.7
Tunbridge Wells 187 ● 1602 ● 96.7
East Kent 388 ● 774 ● 104.2

13 Lancashire
Radio Lancashire 351 ● 855 ● 96.4
Lancaster area 193 ● 1557 ● 104.5

14 Leeds
Radio Leeds 388 ● 774 ● 92.4
Wharfedale area 388 ● 774 ● 95.3

15 Leicester
Radio Leicester 358 ● 837 ● 95.1

16 Lincolnshire
Radio Lincolnshire 219 ● 1368 ● 94.9

17 London
Radio London 206 ● 1458 ● 94.9

18 Manchester
Radio Manchester 206 ● 1458 ● 95.1

19 Merseyside
Radio Merseyside 202 ● 1485 ● 95.8

20 Newcastle
Radio Newcastle 206 ● 1458 ● 95.4
NE Northumberland 206 ● 1458 ● 96.0
Newcastle & Gateshead 206 ● 1458 ● 104.4

21 Norfolk
Radio Norfolk 351 ● 855 ● 95.1
King's Lynn area 344 ● 873 ● 96.7

22 Northampton
Radio Northampton 271 ● 1107 ● 104.2
Corby area 271 ● 1107 ● 103.6

23 Nottingham
Radio Nottingham 197 ● 1521 ● 103.8
Central Nottinghamshire area 189 ● 1584 ● —

24 Oxford
Radio Oxford 202 ● 1485 ● 95.2

25 Sheffield
Radio Sheffield 290 ● 1035 ● 104.1
Sheffield city 290 ● 1035 ● 88.6

26 Shropshire
Radio Shropshire
N. Shropshire 397 ● 756 ● 96.0
S. Shropshire 189 ● 1584 ● 95.0

27 Solent
Radio Solent 300 ● 999 ● 96.1
Bournemouth area 221 ● 1359 ● 96.1

28 Stoke-on-Trent
Radio Stoke-on-Trent 200 ● 1503 ● 94.6

29 Sussex
Radio Sussex
Brighton area 202 ● 1485 ● 95.3
East Sussex area 258 ● 1161 ● 104.5
Reigate/Crawley area 219 ● 1368 ● 104.0

30 West Midlands
Radio WM 206 ● 1458 ● 95.6
Wolverhampton area 362 ● 828 ● 95.6

31 York
Radio York 450 ● 666 ● 103.7
Scarborough area 238 ● 1260 ● 95.2

Channel Islands
Radio Guernsey 269 ● 1116 ● 93.2
Radio Jersey 292 ● 1026 ● 88.8

Regional Networks

Wales
Radio Wales 340 ● 882 ● — (Llandrindod Wells 267 ● 1125 ● —)
Radio Cymru (Welsh Language Service) — ● — ● 92.5-94.5 (S. Wales area 96.8) (Occasional local programmes are broadcast on R. Clwyd (457 ● 657 MW) & R. Gwent (95.1 & 103.0 VHF/FM)

Scotland
Radio Scotland 370 ● 810 ● 92.5-94.6 (N.W. Scotland 97.7-99.3) (Occasional local programmes are broadcast on 92.5-94.6 VHF/FM by R. Aberdeen (also on 303 ● 990 MW), R. Highland, (with R. nan Eilean), R. Orkney, R. Shetland, R. Solway (also on 513 ● 585 MW) and R. Tweed)

National Networks
R1 275/285 ● 1089/1053 ● 88.1-90.1 (at certain times)
R2 330/433 ● 909/693 ● 88.1-90.1 (carries R1 at certain times)
R4 1500 ● 200 (92.5-94.7 – England)

Local MW frequencies

R1	Bournemouth	202 ● 1485
	Merseyside	271 ● 1107
R2	Cardigan Bay	303 ● 990
R4	Aberdeen	207 ● 1449
	Carlisle	202 ● 1485
	London	417 ● 720
	Newcastle-upon-Tyne and area	498 ● 603
	Plymouth	388 ● 774
	Redruth	397 ● 756

Local Radio Broadcasting

Independent Local Radio

1 Aberdeen
North Sound 290 ● 1035 ● 96.9

2 Ayr
West Sound 290 ● 1035 ● 96.2
Girvan area 290 ● 1035 ● 97.1

3 Birmingham
BRMB Radio 261 ● 1152 ● 94.8

4 Bournemouth
2CR (Two Counties Radio) 362 ● 828 ● 97.2

5 Bradford/Halifax/Huddersfield
Pennine Radio
Bradford area 235 ● 1278 ● 97.5
Halifax/Huddersfield area 196 ● 1530 ● 102.5

6 Brighton
Southern Sound 227 ● 1323 ● 103.4

7 Bristol
GWR
Avon & N. Somerset 238 ● 1260 ● 96.3
W. Wiltshire 321 ● 936 ● 97.4
Swindon area 258 ● 1161 ● 96.4

8 Bury St Edmunds
Saxon Radio 240 ● 1251 ● 96.4

9 Cardiff/Newport
Red Dragon Radio
Cardiff 221 ● 1359 ● 96.0
Newport 230 ● 1305 ● 104.0

10 Coventry
Mercia Sound 220 ● 1359 ● 95.9

11 Dundee/Perth
Radio Tay
Dundee area 258 ● 1161 ● 95.8
Perth area 189 ● 1584 ● 96.4

12 Edinburgh
Radio Forth 194 ● 1548 ● 96.8

13 Exeter/Torbay
DevonAir Radio
Exeter area 450 ● 666 ● 95.8
Torbay area 314 ● 954 ● 95.1

14 Glasgow
Radio Clyde 261 ● 1152 ● 95.1

15 Gloucester & Cheltenham
Severn Sound 388 ● 774 ● 95.0

16 Great Yarmouth & Norwich
Radio Broadland 260 ● 1152 ● 97.6

17 Guildford
County Sound 203 ● 1476 ● 96.6

18 Hereford/Worcester
Radio Wyvern
Hereford area 314 ● 954 ● 95.8
Worcester area 196 ● 1530 ● 96.2

19 Humberside
Viking Radio 258 ● 1161 ● 102.7

20 Inverness
Moray Firth Radio 271 ● 1107 ● 95.9

21 Ipswich
Radio Orwell 257 ● 1170 ● 97.1

22 Leeds
Radio Aire 362 ● 828 ● 94.6

23 Leicester
Leicester Sound 238 ● 1260 ● 97.1

24 Liverpool
Radio City 194 ● 1548 ● 96.7

25 London
Capital Radio (General) 194 ● 1548 ● 95.8
LBC (News & Information) 261 ● 1152 ● 97.3

26 Luton/Bedford
Chiltern Radio
Luton area 362 ● 828 ● 97.6
Bedford area 378 ● 792 ● 95.5

27 Maidstone & Medway/East Kent
Invicta Radio 242 ● 1242 ● 103.1
East Kent 497 ● 603 ● 102.8
Thanet area 497 ● 603 ● 95.9
Dover/Folkestone 497 ● 603 ● 97.0
Ashford area 497 ● 603 ● 96.1

28 Manchester
Piccadilly Radio 261 ● 1152 ● 103.0

29 Nottingham
Radio Trent 301 ● 999 ● 96.2

30 Peterborough/Northampton
Hereward Radio
Peterborough area 225 ● 1332 ● 95.7
Northampton area 193 ● 1557 ● 102.8

31 Plymouth
Plymouth Sound 261 ● 1152 ● 96.0
Tavistock — ● — ● 96.6

32 Preston & Blackpool
Red Rose Radio 301 ● 999 ● 97.3

33 Reading
Radio 210 210 ● 1431 ● 97.0

34 Reigate & Crawley
Radio Mercury 197 ● 1521 ● 102.7
Horsham — ● — ● 97.5

35 Sheffield/Rotherham/Barnsley/Doncaster
Radio Hallam
Sheffield area 194 ● 1548 ● 97.4
Rotherham area 194 ● 1548 ● 96.1
Barnsley area 230 ● 1305 ● 102.9
Doncaster area 302 ● 990 ● 103.4

36 Southampton/Portsmouth
Ocean Sound (from late '86)
South Hampshire and Isle of Wight 193 ● 1557 ● TBA
Portsmouth† 257 ● 1170 ● 95.0
†Radio Victory until late '86

37 Southend/Chelmsford
Essex Radio
Southend area 210 ● 1431 ● 96.3
Chelmsford area 220 ● 1359 ● 102.6

38 Stoke-on-Trent
Signal Radio 256 ● 1170 ● 102.6

39 Swansea
Swansea Sound 257 ● 1170 ● 95.1

40 Teesside
Radio Tees 257 ● 1170 ● 95.0

41 Tyne & Wear
Metro Radio 261 ● 1152 ● 97.0

42 Wolverhampton & Black Country
Beacon Radio 303 ● 990 ● 97.2

43 Wrexham & Deeside
Marcher Sound/Sain-Y-Gororau 238 ● 1260 ● 95.4

Isle of Man
Manx Radio (Not run by IBA) 219 ● 1368 ● 96.9/89.0

The National Grid

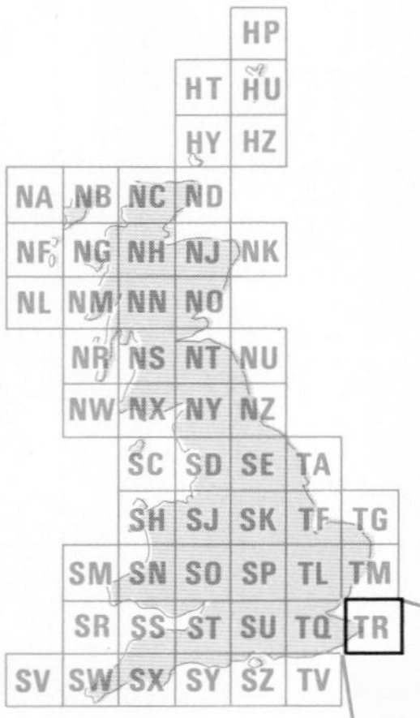

To locate a place in this atlas, first look up the name of the town or village required in the index, which starts on page 210. Each entry is followed by the page number on which the place can be found and its National Grid reference.

eg:
Hyssington	50	SO 3194
Hythe (Hants)	13	SU 4207
Hythe (Kent)	29	TR 1635

Hythe (Kent) is on page 29 with National Grid reference TR 1635.

When the required place name and its reference have been found in the index:

a) turn to the page number indicated

b) find the location using the last four numbers.

Taking Hythe (Kent) as our example: the first figure of the reference – 1, refers to the numbered grid line running along the bottom of the page. Having found this line, the second figure – 6, tells you the distance to move in tenths to the right of this line. A vertical line through this point is the first half of the reference.

The third figure – 3, refers to the numbered grid lines on the left hand side of the page. Finally the fourth figure – 5, indicates the distance to move in tenths above this line. A horizontal line drawn through this point to intersect with the first line gives the precise location of the place in question. See example below.

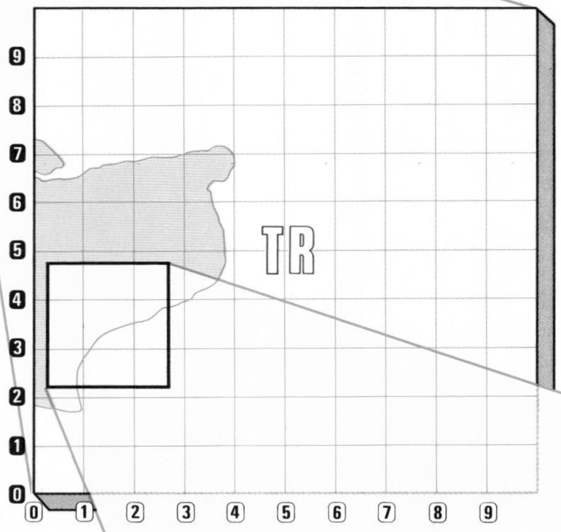

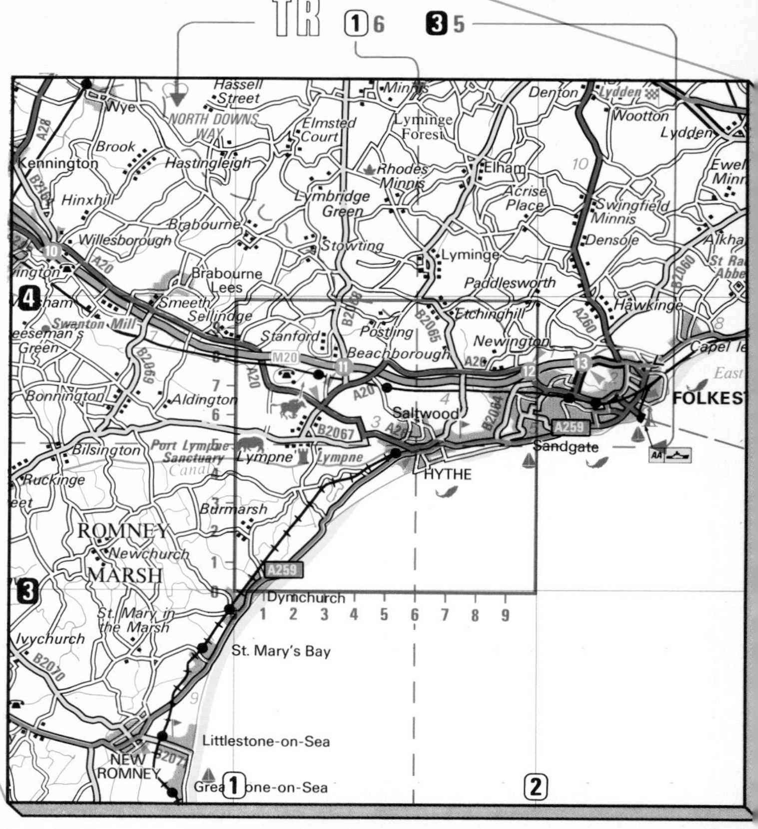

THE NATIONAL GRID

The National Grid provides a system of reference common to maps of all scales. The grid covers Britain with an imaginary network of 100 kilometre squares. Each square is identified by two letters, *eg* TR. Every 100 kilometre square is then subdivided into 10 kilometre squares which appear as a network of blue lines on the map pages. These blue lines are numbered left to right 0-9 and bottom to top 0-9 These 10 kilometre squares can be further divided into tenths to give a place reference to the nearest kilometre.

3 MILE ROAD ATLAS OF BRITAIN

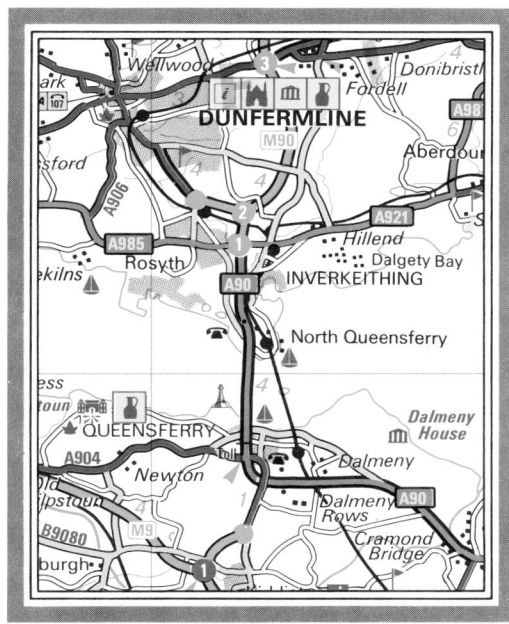

Wellwood
Fordell
DUNFERMLINE
M90
A906
A921
A985
Hillend
Rosyth
Dalgety Bay
A90
INVERKEITHING
North Queensferry
QUEENSFERRY
Dalmeny House
A904
Newton
Dalmeny
Dalmeny Rows
Cramond Bridge
B9080
M9

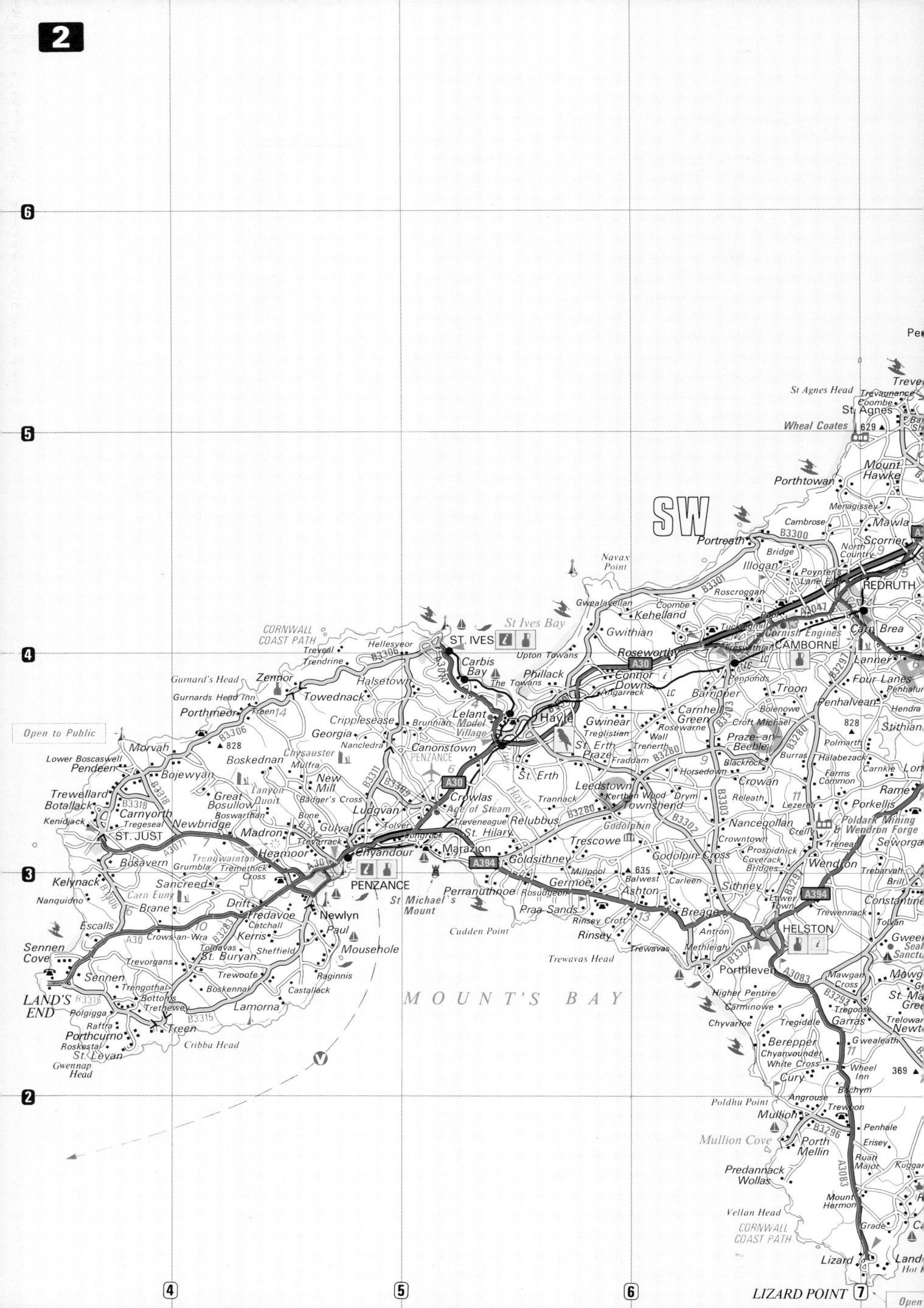
6
5
4
3
2
4
5
6
7
SW
LIZARD POINT
Open to Public
St Agnes Head
Trevaunance Coombe
St. Agnes
Wheal Coates
629
Mount Hawke
Porthtowan
Menagissey
Cambrose
Mawla
Portreath
B3300
Scorrier
North Country
Bridge
Illogan
Poynter's Lane End
REDRUTH
Navax Point
Gwealavellan
Coombe
Kehelland
B3301
Roscroggan
Pool
A3047
Tuckingmill
Cornish Engines
Carn Brea
St Ives Bay
CORNWALL COAST PATH
ST. IVES
Gwithian
Roseworthy
Treswithian
CAMBORNE
Lanner
Hellesveor
Treveal
Trendrine
B3306
Carbis Bay
Upton Towans
A30
Connor Downs
Pengegon
Four Lanes
Phillack
The Towans
Angarrack
Barripper
Troon
Penhalvean
Gurnard's Head
Zennor
Halsetown
Towednack
Gurnards Head Inn
Lelant
Model Village
Hayle
Gwinear
Carnhell Green
Bolenowe
Hendra
Porthmeor
Treen
Cripplesease
Brunnian
Treglistian
Rosewarne
Croft Michael
Stithians
Georgia
Nancledra
Canonstown
St. Erth Praze
Wall
Praze-an-Beeble
828
Open to Public
B3306
828
Chysauster
PENZANCE
Trenerth
B3280
Polmarth
Morvah
Lower Boscaswell
Pendeen
Boskednan
Mulfra
Fraddam
Blackrock
Burras
Halabezack
Bojewyan
New Mill
St. Erth
Horsedown
Carnkie
Farms Common
Trewellard
Botallack
Great Bosullow
Lanyon Quoit
Badger's Cross
Crowlas
Leedstown
Crowan
Rame
B3318
Carnyorth
Boswarthan
Ludgvan
Age of Steam
Trannack
Kerthen Wood
Drym
Releath
Lezerea
Porkellis
Kenidjack
Tregeseal
Newbridge
Bone
Gulval
Tolver
Treveneague
Relubbus
Townshend
Nancegollan
Poldark Mining & Wendron Forge
ST. JUST
Madron
Trevarrack
Longrock
St. Hilary
Godolphin
Crelly
Crowntown
Treneal
Sevorgan
Bosavern
Trengwainton
Heamoor
Chyandour
Marazion
Trescowe
Godolphin Cross
Prospidnick
Coverack Bridges
Wendron
Kelynack
Grumbla
Tremethick Cross
A394
Goldsithney
Millpool
635
Balwest
Carleen
Trebarvah
Brill
Sancreed
PENZANCE
Perranuthnoe
Germoe
Ashton
Sithney
Nanquidno
Carn Euny
St Michael's Mount
Rosudgeon
Lower Town
Constantine
Brane
Drift
Fredavoe
Newlyn
Praa Sands
Breage
Trewennack
Escalls
Catchall
Cudden Point
Rinsey Croft
Tolvan
Kerris
Paul
Rinsey
Antron
HELSTON
Sennen Cove
A30
Crows-an-Wra
Toldavas
Sheffield
Mousehole
Trewavas
Methleigh
St. Buryan
Trevorgans
Trewavas Head
Porthleven
B3304
Mawgan Cross
A3083
Sennen
Trewoofe
Raginnis
Trengothal
Boskennal
Castallack
Higher Pentire
B3293
Tregoose
LAND'S END
B3315
Bottoms
Lamorna
MOUNT'S BAY
Carminowe
Polgigga
Trethewey
Garras
Trelowarren
Raftra
Treen
Chyvarloe
Tregiddle
Porthcurno
Cribba Head
Gwealeath
Roskestal
Berepper
St. Levan
Chyanvounder
White Cross
Gwennap Head
Wheel Inn
369
Cury
Bochym
Angrouse
Poldhu Point
Mullion
Trewoon
B3296
Penhale
Mullion Cove
Porth Mellin
Erisey
Ruan Major
Kuggar
Predannack Wollas
A3083
Mount Hermon
Vellan Head
Grade
CORNWALL COAST PATH
Lizard
Landewednack

3
4
COAST PATH
Downhill
Trevengenow
Cannalidgey
Berryl's Point
Trenance
Trevilledor
Mawgan Porth
Denzell
Trevarrian
St. Mawgan
Rosenannon
Watergate Bay
Trembleath
Talskiddy
Tregurrian
Carloggas
Gluvian
NEWQUAY
St. Columb Major
Trebelzue
Towan Head
Newquay Bay
St. Columb Minor
Tregaswith
Fistral Bay
Porth
Colan
Trevithick
Trebudannon
Pentire
NEWQUAY
Penpol
Mountjoy
Trevarren
Ruthvoes
Crantock
Rosecliston
Trevemper
Quintrell Downs
Lane
Kestle Mill
Carines
Tresean
St. Columb Road
Trerice
Indian Queens
Enniscaven
Toldish
Polgreen
Lappa Valley Railway
Fraddon
Treveal
Cubert
Blue Anchor
St. Enoder
Penhale
Retew
Newlyn East
Mount
Cargoll
Rejerrah
Trevilson
Summercourt
Treamble
Fiddlers Green
Burthy
Treviscoe
Meledon
Burgotha
Rose
Goenrounsen
Brighton
490
Mitchell
Shepherds
Rosehill
Goonhavern
Carland Cross
Trelassick
St. Stephen
Carnkief
Perranwell
Ennis
New Mills
Killiserth
Treveale
Trelion
Gwindra
Perranzabuloe
Zelah
Ladock
Hay
Coombe
Halezy
Penhallow
Little Callestock
Pengelly
Grampound Road
Callestick
St. Allen
Trispen
Bissick
Tregear
Tresawsen
Treworgan
Nantellan
Killivose
St. Erme
Grampound
Treverbyn
Gwarnick
Probus
Shortlanesend
Bodrean
Treheveras
Idless
Tresillian
County Demonstration Garden & Arboretum
Creed
Treworder
Buckshead
Kenwyn
Higher Town
Penair
Pencalenick
Tresawle
Merther
Trewirgie
Newbridge
TRURO
St. Clement
Tregenna
Baldhu
Newham
Kea
St. Michael Penkivil
Gare
Ruan Lanihorne
Cregoe
Malpas
Twelveheads
Killiow
Playing Place
Bissoe
Cusgarne
Coombe
Lamorran
Carnon Downs
Old Kea
Ardevora
Treworga
Penelewey
Lanes
Penpol
Trelissick
Philleigh
Devoran
Perran Wharf
Treworlas
274
Treworthal
Carclew
Feock
Stockdale
Messack
Trewithian
Mylor Bridge
Enys
Trelew
PENRYN
St. Just
Mylor
Flushing
Vosk
Pendennis Castle
Pendennis Head
FALMOUTH
Budock Water
Kergilliack
Penjerrick
Falmouth Bay
Maenporth
Carlidnack
Mawnan Smith
Glendurgan
Rosemullion Head
Mawnan
Helford River
St. Anthony
Nare Point
Manaccan
Lestowder
Roskorwell
Porthallow
Tregarne
Treleague
Trenance
Porthoustock
Manacle Point
Lanarth
St. Keverne
Coverack
Trewillis
Treleaver
Black Head
Gerrans Bay
Rosevine
Portscatho
Gerrans
Greeb Point
Trewince
St. Mawes
Bohortha
Zone Point
Veryan
Gwendra
Carne
Treluggan
Nare Head
Portloe
Veryan Bay
Calendra
Portholland
Treviskey
St. Michael Caerhays
Rescassa
Treveor
Boswinger
Penare
373
Dodman Point
Tregony
Tregonhayne
Goviley Major
Trevarrick
Trewarthenick
Hay
Polmassick
Trevithick
Tregarton
Gorran High Lanes
Gorran Churchtown
Gorran Haven
Chapel Point
Portmellon
Mevagissey
Mevagissey Bay
Tregiskey
Corran
Kestle
Pengrugla
Pentewan
St. Ewe
Tucoyse
Tregideo
Carwinnick
Bosue
Trevissick
Black Head
Trenarren
Towan
London Apprentice
Levalsa Meor
Hewas Water
Rescorla
Sticker
Polgooth
Trelowth
St. Mewan
Trewoon
Lanjeth
High Street
ST. AUSTELL
Charlestown
Porthpean
St Austell Bay
Carlyon Bay
Boscoppa
Par
Polkerris
St Catherine's
Menabilly
Gribbin Head
FOWEY
Polruan
Bodinnick
Lombard
Lanteglos Highway
Golant
Penpoll
St Veep
Tywardreath
Tywardreath Highway
Torfrey
Cliff
St. Blazey
St Blazey Gate
Biscovey
Carclaze
Mills
Tregrehan
Trethurgy
Stents
Penwithick
Wheal Martyn Museum
Carthew
Foxhole
Trethosa
Carpalla
Nanpean
Yondertown
Whitemoor
St. Dennis
Carne
Gothers
Roche
Tregoss
Victoria
Higher Town
Bilberry
Carbis
Bugle
Carnsmerry
Stenalees
Treverbyn
Rosevean
Molinnis
Bodiggo
Luxulyan
Lanlivery
Tredennick
Bodwen
Redmoor
Lockengate
Trevellion
Bokiddick
Sweetshouse
Trebyan
Penpillick
Penhale
Castle
Trewether
Milltown
LOSTWITHIEL
Polscoe
Restormel
Brooks
Sandylake
Couch's Mill
Bottallick
Langunnett
Lerryn
Braddock
Fairy Cross
St. Ingunger
Maudlin
Lanhydrock
Cutmadoc
West Taphouse
East Taphouse
Middledrift
Glynn
Fletchersbridge
Tredinnick
Kirland
Lidcutt
Tregullon
St. Nicholas
Lanivet
Retire
Lamorick
Tremore
Withielgoose
Withiel
St. Lawrence
Nanstallon
Tregawne
Ruthernbridge
Tregustick
Treliver
Trewallack
St. Wenn
Demelza
744
Tregonetha
Belowda
Boscarne
Dunmere
Bridge
BODMIN
Penbugle
Cooksland
Welltown
Cardinham
Brocton
Lane End
Norton
River Camel
River Fowey
River Fal
A30
A39
A390
A3059
A392
A3075
A3076
A3058
A391
A3082
A3078
A3078
A389
A38
B3274
B3276
B3279
B3285
B3284
B3287
B3289
B3268
B3269
B3273
B3293
B3294
LC
PS
AA 24 hour
SX
SCALE
0 1 2 3 4 5 miles
0 1 2 3 4 5 kilometres
8
9
0
1

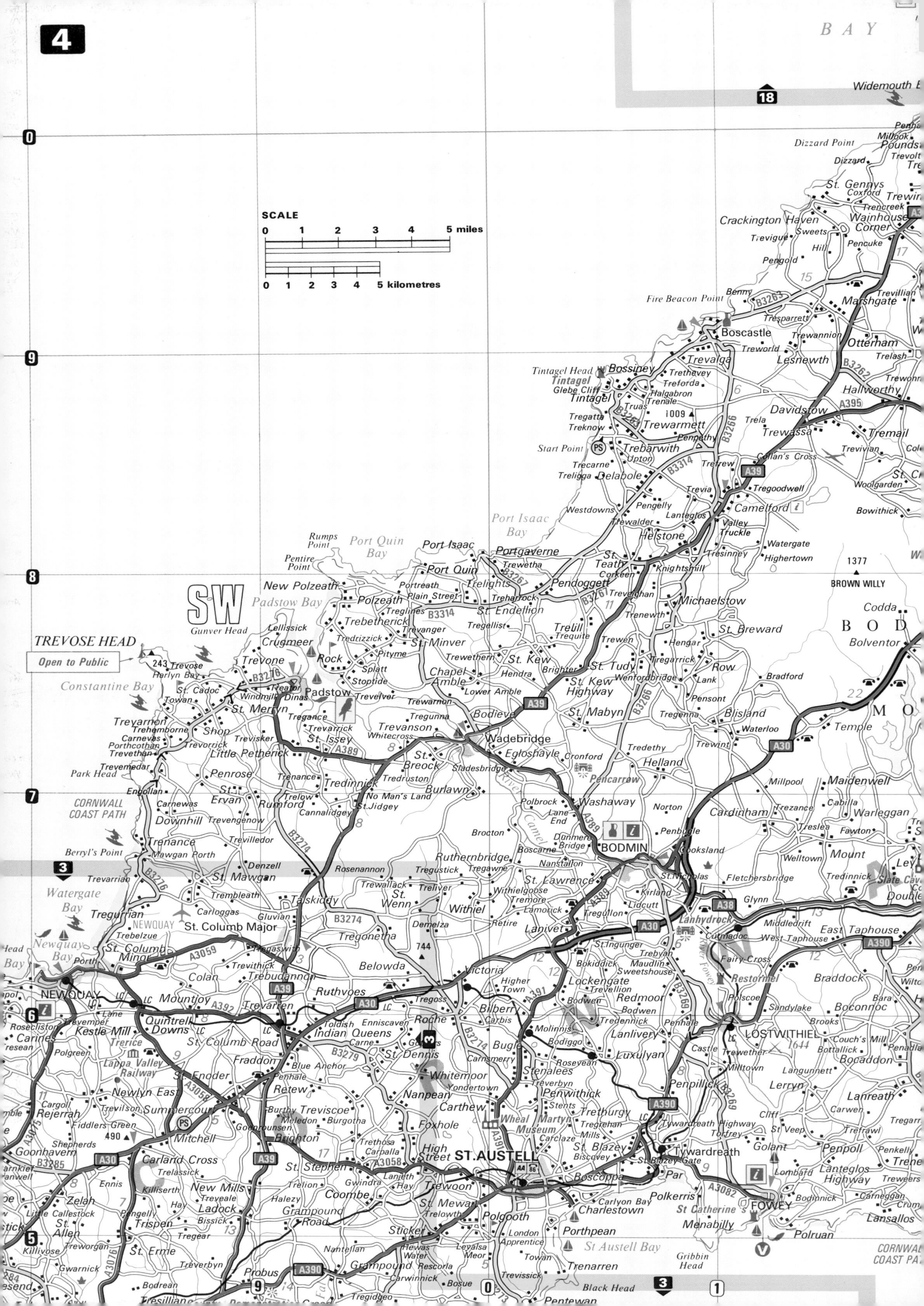

BAY

SCALE

0 1 2 3 4 5 miles

0 1 2 3 4 5 kilometres

TREVOSE HEAD
Open to Public

CORNWALL COAST PATH

SW

Padstow Bay
Gunver Head
Constantine Bay
Watergate Bay
Newquay Bay

Port Quin Bay
Port Isaac Bay
Rumps Point
Pentire Point

BROWN WILLY
BOD...
BODMIN MOOR
Bolventor
Codda

NEWQUAY
BODMIN
ST. AUSTELL
LOSTWITHIEL
FOWEY

St Austell Bay
Gribbin Head
Black Head

Widemouth B...
Dizzard Point
St. Gennys
Crackington Haven
Wainhouse Corner
Boscastle
Tintagel
Trebarwith
Delabole
Camelford
Davidstow
Tremail
Hallworthy
Lesnewth
Otterham
Marshgate

Port Isaac
Port Quin
New Polzeath
Polzeath
Trebetherick
Rock
Trevone
Padstow
St. Merryn
St. Issey
Wadebridge
Egloshayle
St. Kew
St. Mabyn
St. Tudy
Blisland
Temple
St. Breward
Row
Michaelstow
St. Teath
Pendoggett

Trevose
Harlyn Bay
St. Cadoc
Towan
Treyarnon
Trevemedar
Park Head
Berry's Point
Mawgan Porth
St. Mawgan
Denzell
Talskiddy
St. Columb Major
St. Columb Minor
Colan
Mountjoy
Quintrell Downs
St. Columb Road
Fraddon
Indian Queens
Roche
Bugle
Luxulyan
Lanlivery
Lostwithiel
Restormel

Trelissick
Little Petherick
Penrose
Rumford
Tredinnick
St. Breock
Sladesbridge
Burlawn
Ruthernbridge
Tregawne
Withiel
Lanivet
Nanstallon
St. Lawrence
Glynn
East Taphouse
West Taphouse
Braddock
Boconnoc
Lanreath
Lerryn

Newlyn East
Mitchell
Summercourt
Fiddlers Green
Goonhavern
Rejerrah
Zelah
St. Allen
St. Erme
Probus
Grampound Road
Grampound
New Mills
St. Stephen
St. Dennis
Nanpean
Foxhole
High Street
Charlestown
Porthpean
Pentewan

Wheal Martyn Museum
Carthew
Penwithick
Stenalees
Bugle
Carbis
Roseyean
Tregrehan
Par
Polkerris
St. Blazey
Tywardreath
Golant
Polruan
Menabilly
St Catherine's

Lappa Valley Railway
Trerice
Kestle Mill
Carland Cross

A30 A39 A389 A390 A391 A38 A3058 A3059 A3082 A3083
B3276 B3274 B3279 B3314 B3266 B3267 B3262 B3263 B3265

243 Trevose
1009
1377
744
490
1644

6 17 18 3

CORNWALL COAST PATH

5
Launcells
Pancrasweek
South Arscott
Halsdon
Holemoor
Black Torrington
Monkokehampton
Broadwood-Kelly
Marsh
HOLSWORTHY
Cookbury Wick
Strawbridge
Trew
Highampton
A3072
B3254
Marhamchurch
Derril
Derriton
Anvil Corner
Whimble
Brandis Corner
Hatherleigh
Upcott
Cadham
Woodhall
Odham
Lydacott
Passaford
Kerswell
Bridgerule
Hapworthy
Pyworthy
Chasty
Hollacombe
Chilla
Lake
Headon
Bounds Cross
18
19
Esworthy
Exbourne
Budd's Titson
Langford Barton
B3218
Jacobstowe
Narracott
Sampford Courtenay
Yeomaden
Leworthy
Clawford
Statfold
Halwill Junction
Whiddon
Worth
Norley
South Yeo
Westacott
Norleigh
Kitsham
Froxton
Kitleigh
Corfcott Green
Churchtown
Whitstone
Venton
East Balsdon
West Balsdon
Buckhorn
Clawton
Halwill
Langaford
Crowden
Beaworthy
Northlew
Oak Cross
Inwardleigh
Risdon
Sellick
Higher Horslett
Prestacott
East Kimber
Ashbury
Westacombe
Great Stewardstone
Week St. Mary
Boot
Landhill
Stowford
Patchacott
Folly Gate
Brightley
North Tamerton
Trebarrow
Tetcott
Quoditch
West Yenn
Foxhole
Bogtown
Hook
Week Green
Goscott
Foxhole
Wilsworthy
Lana
Nethercott
Higher Prestacott
Metherell
Croft
Widefield
Ellmead
Pudson
Chichacott
OKEHAMPTON
Creddacott
Ashwater
Ashmill
Northcombe
916
Lurchardon
Weeks-in-the-Moor
Southcott
Maddaford
Ditchen
Mountlane
Moor
Eworthy
Langworthy
543
Higher Whiteleigh
West Curry
Luffincott
Henford
Westmanton
Germansweek
Voulsdon Cross
B3218
Boasley Cross
Thorndon Cross
A30
8
Okehampton Camp
South Wheatley
Maxworthy
East Curry
Chapmans Well
Middlecott
Bradaford
Virginstow
Southweek
Voaden
Boasley
Thorndon
Meldon
Clubworthy
Beardon
Northcott
Woodleypark
Breazle
Eversfield
Copthorne
North Beer
Bennacott
Grinacombe
Canworthy Water
Troswell
Winsdon
Boyton
East Panson
Sitcott
Frankaborough
Grinacombe Moor
Bratton Clovelly
Week
Ebsworthy Town
YES TOR 2030
Billacott
Brazacott
South Beer
Dunns
West Panson
St. Giles-on-the-Heath
Ellacott
Forda
Sourton
Forda
Gridley Corner
Bridgetown
Upcott
Combepark
Trussell
Trillacott
North Petherwin
Polapit Tamar
Wannacott
Way
2038 HIGH WILLHAYS
Penrose
River Ottery
Eggbear
Coombe
Rextor
Broadwoodwidger
Orchard
Churndon
Bridestowe
Three Hammers
Petherwin Gate
Hellescott
Ladycross
Pool
Kellacott
Rexon Cross
Combebow
Axworthy
Bidlake
A386
Trebeath
Yeolmbridge
Werrington
Cross Green
Rexon
Thrushelton
Lobhillcross
Tresmeer
Egloskerry
Rockwell
Lower Cookworthy
Stowford
Foxcombe
B3278
Langore
St. Stephens
Higher Cookworthy
Hayne
Lewdown
Cross Roads
Kersford
Shortacombe
Tregeare
Badharlick
Liftondown
Lifton
Portgate
Lewtrenchard
Waddlestone
Downtown
Dutson
Tinhay
Dippertown
Eastcott
Lydford
Pipers Pool
LAUNCESTON
Lowertown
Beardon
Trespearne
Tregadillett
Treburself Oak
Lydford Gorge
Laneast
A395
Router
Coryton
Trewen
Kennards House
Daw's House
PS
Liddaton Green
Woodmanswell
Tregunnon
Tregaller
Hurdon
Lawhitton
Marystow
Burnville
North Brentor
A30
South Petherwin
Cleave
Treween
Treguddick
Meadwell
Higher Chillaton
Chillaton
Quither
Willsworthy
Polyphant
Kelly
DARTM
Tredaule
Tregillis
Trelinnoe
Hilltown
Fivelanes
A384
Week
Lewannick
Hexworthy
Bradstone
Narracott
Uppaton
Horndon
Trecrogo
Trewarlett
Trekelland
Pollinick
Lezant
B3257
Eastcott
Blackdown
Mary Tavy
Wapsworthy
Plusha
B3254
Landue
Trevague
Trekelland
Milton Abbot
Trevadlock
Trecarrel Manor
Hardstone
Dunterton
Tuelldown
Great Haye
Cudliptown
Illand
Trekenner
Congdon's Shop
Larrick
Milton Green
Grendon
Stonaford
Coad's Green
Trebullett
Rezare
Willestrew
A386
Peter Tavy
1768 GREAT MIS TOR
Trebartha
Tuell
Chaddlehanger
Hanford
Godsworthy
Culverhill
Treburley
Lamerton
North Hill
Tregoiffe
Bealsmill
River Tamar
Sydenham Damerel
Wilminstone
Goosewell
A384
Cholwell
Rushford
Collaton
Merrivale
1280 KILMAR TOR
SX
Berriow Bridge
Bray Shop
Kingston
Chipshop
Hurdwick
Rendlestone
Bathpool
Pengelly
Rillaton
B3257
Venterdon
Horsebridge
Old Clims
Moorshop
B3357
North Darley
Stoke Climsland
Townlake
TAVISTOCK
Moortown
Linkinhorne
Oldmill
Hampt
Rubbytown
Henwood
Luckett
Latchley
Chollacott Estate
Princetown
Sharptor
Upton
South Hill
Coxpark
Chilsworthy
Gulworthy
Sampford Spiney
Rilla Mill
Plushabridge
Downgate
Middlemoor
Siblyback
Upton Cross
Mornick
Buctor
Whitchurch
Caradon Town
Kelly Bray
St. Ann's Chapel
1094 KIT HILL
Gunnislake
Grenofen
Eggworthy
Minions
1216
Golberdon
Trewoodloe
A390
Drakewalls
Sortridge
Higher Walreddon
Peat Cot
Gonamena
Downgate
CARADON HILL
Haye
Harrowbarrow
Albaston
Dittisham
Stone Circle
Holy Well
PS
Grimstone
Common Moor
Darite
Trevigro
Metherell
Norris Green
Horrabridge
Walkhampton
Charaton
Callington
Cotehele
Buckland Monachorum
Trethevy Quoit
Crow's Nest
Pensilva
A386
Dousland
9
Woolston
Gang
Frogwell
Ashton
Calstock
St. Cleer
Westcott
Bohetherick
Crapstone
Sheepstor
Trethinnick
Tremar
Keason
Newbridge
St. Dominick
Buckland Abbey
Yelverton
Meavy
Miniature Railway
Tremabe
Merrymeet
St. Ive
Parkfield
Burraton
Amytree
Bere Alston
Lovaton
Bealbury
Crocadon
Milton Combe
Hoo Meavy
Crift
Treweatha
Halton Quay
Cotts
Sowton
Brisworthy
Newton Ferrers
St. Mellion
A390
Pengover Green
Weir Quay
Maristow
Clearbrook
Polborder
LISKEARD
Quethiock
A388
Goodameavy
1557 SHELL TOP
Tencreek
Trehane
Pillaton
Gnatham
Tregrill
Trewint
Trehunist
Pillatonmill
Sillaton
Tinnel
Bere Ferrers
Lower Upperton
Shaugh Prior
Lamellion
Blunts
Cargreen
Menheniot
Blaxton
Wotter
A38
Cuttivett
Trethawle
Doddycross
Tilland
Wotton Cross
Hatt
Landulph
Tamerton Foliot
Bickleigh
Lee Moor
St. Keyne
Brighton
Tideford Cross
Botusfleming
Hartstone
Landrake
Trewidland
Cutmere
Notter
Carkeel
Dartmoor Wild Life Park
Benoak
Tideford
A38
B3373
Trematon
A386
Cornwood
B3251
South Pill
Penimble
Budge's Shop
St. Erney
SALTASH
Trevallard
Trehan
Drakeland Corner
Lutton
Trerulefoot
Crownhill
Vondertown
Widegates
Markwell
St. Budeaux
St. Stephens
6
PS
Wringworthy
Rosedale
Egg Buckland
Sparkwell
A387
St. Germans
A388
Fardel
Colebrook
Hemerdon
Moryal
PLYMOUTH
B3416
Venton
No Man's Land
Hessenford
Ivybridge
Sandplace
Narkurs
Polbathic
Antony House
Devonport
Plympton
B3253
Maryfield
Lee Mill
Sheviock
PS
St. Martin
B3247
Deviock
A374
TORPOINT
Seaton
Trifle
Crafthole
Saltram
A38
Shutta
Antony
Billacombe
East Sherford
Westlake
Trelawne
A387
EAST LOOE
Downderry
Lower Tregantle
Stonehouse
Cremyll
A379
Elburton
Monkey Sanctuary
Portwrinkle
St. John
Insworke
Yeo Park
WEST LOOE
Looe Bay
Goosewell
Brixton
Worston
Porthallow
WHITSAND BAY
Higher Tregantle
Withnoe
Hooe
Plymstock
Freathy
Mount Edgcumbe Park
The Sound
Dunstone
Millbrook
Wiggle
B3247
Staddiscombe
Spriddlestone
Yealmpton
Puslinch
Torr
Kingsand
Cawsand
Raneleigh
379
Kitley Caves
Down Thomas
Knighton
Holbeton
CORNWALL COAST PATH
Rame
Penlee Point
Heybrook Bay
West Wembury
Wembury
Newton Ferrers
Bridgend
Poole
B3186
Battisborough
Rame Head
Open to Public
Worswell
Noss
3
4
5
6

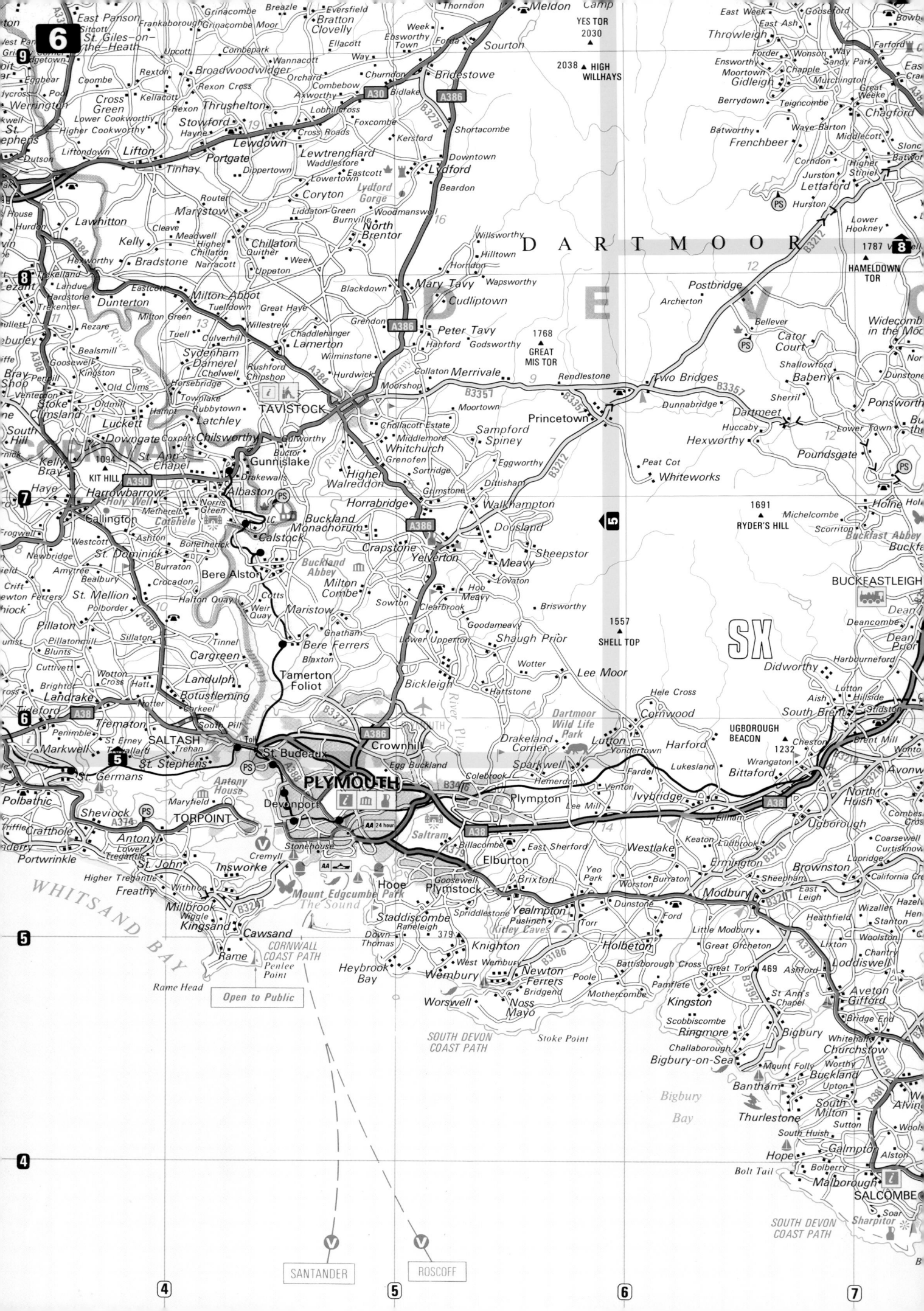
6
DARTMOOR
DEVON
CORNWALL
SX
PLYMOUTH
TAVISTOCK
SALTASH
TORPOINT
BUCKFASTLEIGH
SALCOMBE
YES TOR 2030
2038 HIGH WILLHAYS
1768 GREAT MIS TOR
1787 HAMELDOWN TOR
1691 RYDER'S HILL
1557 SHELL TOP
1094 KIT HILL
UGBOROUGH BEACON 1232
WHITSAND BAY
Bigbury Bay
CORNWALL COAST PATH
SOUTH DEVON COAST PATH
Open to Public
SANTANDER
ROSCOFF
The Sound
Rame Head
Penlee Point
Stoke Point
Bolt Tail
A30
A38
A386
A384
A388
A390
A374
A379
A3121
A381
B3357
B3212
B3351
B3278
B3373
B3396
B3247
B3186
B3210
B3392
Okehampton
Meldon
Sourton
Bridestowe
Lydford
Lydford Gorge
Lewdown
Lifton
Portgate
Lewtrenchard
Coryton
Mary Tavy
Peter Tavy
Cudliptown
North Brentor
Milton Abbot
Lamerton
Chillaton
Marystow
Lawhitton
Kelly
Bradstone
Dunterton
Sydenham Damerel
Gunnislake
Calstock
Callington
Harrowbarrow
Albaston
St. Ann's Chapel
Luckett
Latchley
Stoke Climsland
Bere Alston
Bere Ferrers
Tamerton Foliot
Buckland Monachorum
Buckland Abbey
Milton Combe
Yelverton
Crapstone
Horrabridge
Walkhampton
Dousland
Sheepstor
Meavy
Princetown
Two Bridges
Postbridge
Merrivale
Dartmeet
Hexworthy
Poundsgate
Whiteworks
Sampford Spiney
Whitchurch
Shaugh Prior
Lee Moor
Bickleigh
Cornwood
Harford
Ivybridge
Bittaford
Plympton
Crownhill
St. Budeaux
Devonport
Saltram
Plymstock
Hooe
Elburton
Yealmpton
Brixton
Staddiscombe
Wembury
Heybrook Bay
Newton Ferrers
Noss Mayo
Holbeton
Modbury
Kingston
Ringmore
Bigbury
Bigbury-on-Sea
Bantham
Thurlestone
Aveton Gifford
Loddiswell
Churchstow
South Milton
Hope
Malborough
Galmpton
South Brent
Ugborough
Ermington
St. Germans
Landrake
St. Dominick
St. Mellion
Pillaton
Cargreen
Landulph
Botusfleming
Antony
Antony House
St. John
Millbrook
Kingsand
Cawsand
Rame
Crafthole
Sheviock
Portwrinkle
Polbathic
Mount Edgcumbe Park
Cotehele
Chagford
Gidleigh
Throwleigh
Lettaford
Widecombe in the Moor
Holne
Chilsworthy
Stowford
Thrushelton
Broadwoodwidger
St. Giles-on-the-Heath
Bratton Clovelly
Dartmoor Wild Life Park
Kitley Caves
Sharpitor
4
5
6
7
8
9

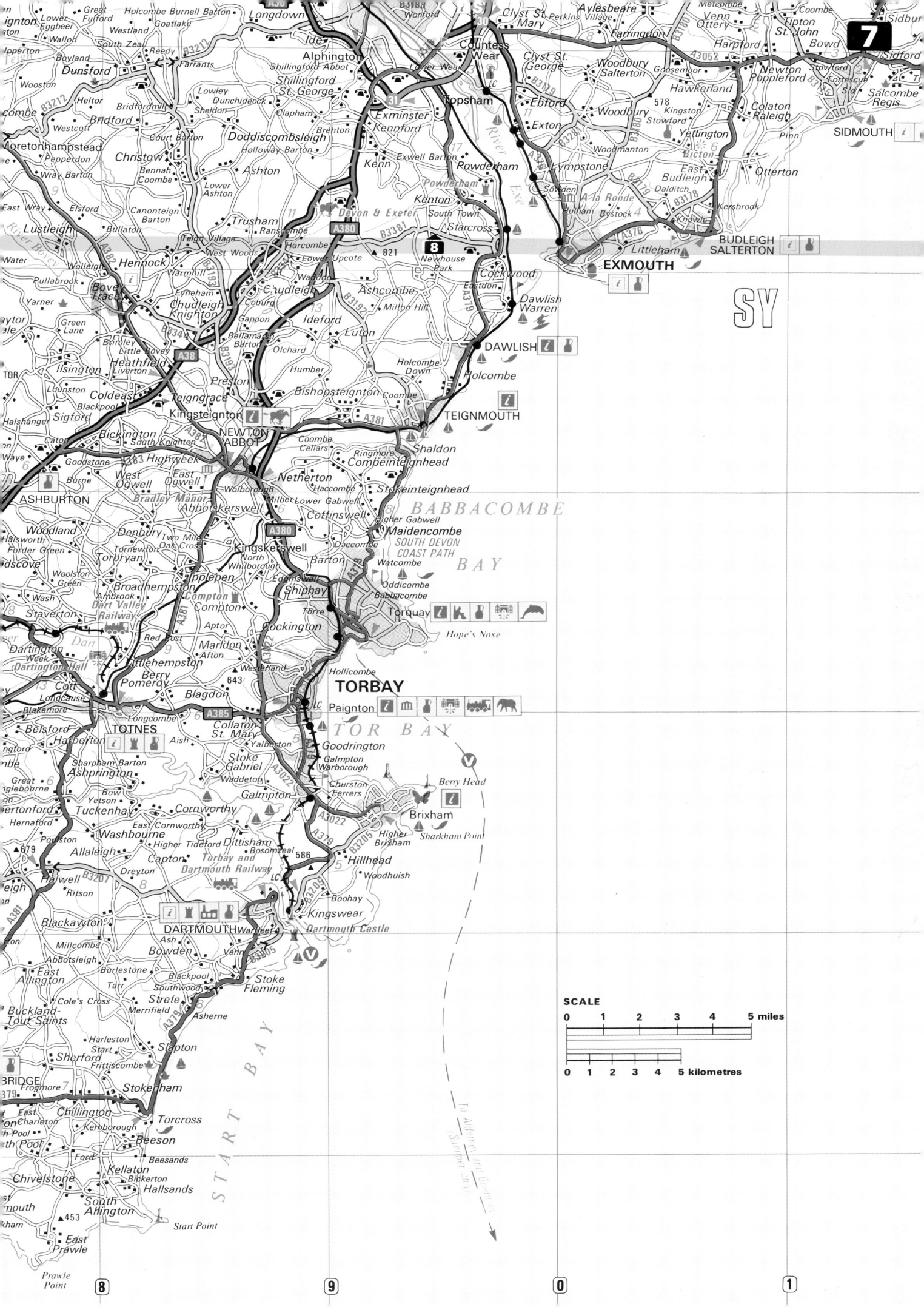
7
Longdown
Ide
Alphington
Shillingford Abbot
Shillingford St. George
Countess Wear
Topsham
Clyst St. Mary
Aylesbeare
Farringdon
Venn Ottery
Tipton St. John
Harpford
Newton Poppleford
Sidford
Clyst St. George
Woodbury Salterton
Hawkerland
Colaton Raleigh
Salcombe Regis
SIDMOUTH
Ebford
Exton
Woodbury
Yettington
Bicton
East Budleigh
Otterton
Lympstone
A la Ronde
Exminster
Kennford
Kenn
Powderham
Kenton
Starcross
Doddiscombsleigh
Christow
Dunsford
Bridford
Moretonhampstead
Ashton
Trusham
Lustleigh
Bovey Tracey
Hennock
Chudleigh
Chudleigh Knighton
Heathfield
Ilsington
Coldeast
Teigngrace
Kingsteignton
NEWTON ABBOT
Preston
Bishopsteignton
Ideford
Luton
Ashcombe
Cockwood
Dawlish Warren
DAWLISH
Holcombe
TEIGNMOUTH
Shaldon
Combeinteignhead
Stokeinteignhead
Netherton
Littleham
EXMOUTH
BUDLEIGH SALTERTON
SY
BABBACOMBE BAY
SOUTH DEVON COAST PATH
Maidencombe
Watcombe
Oddicombe
Babbacombe
Torquay
Hope's Nose
Cockington
Kingskerswell
Abbotskerswell
Ipplepen
Denbury
Torbryan
Broadhempston
Compton
Marldon
Littlehempston
Berry Pomeroy
Blagdon
Staverton
Dart Valley Railway
Dartington
Dartington Hall
ASHBURTON
Bickington
Highweek
West Ogwell
East Ogwell
Woodland
TORBAY
Paignton
TOR BAY
Goodrington
Galmpton Warborough
Churston Ferrers
Berry Head
Brixham
Sharkham Point
Higher Brixham
Hillhead
Woodhuish
Kingswear
Dartmouth Castle
Torbay and Dartmouth Railway
Dittisham
Galmpton
Cornworthy
Tuckenhay
Ashprington
TOTNES
Harberton
Collaton St. Mary
Stoke Gabriel
Washbourne
Allaleigh
Capton
Halwell
Blackawton
DARTMOUTH
Stoke Fleming
Strete
Slapton
Stokenham
Torcross
Chillington
Beeson
Kellaton
Hallsands
South Allington
Start Point
East Prawle
Prawle Point
Chivelstone
Sherford
East Allington
Buckland-Tout-Saints
START BAY
To Alderney and Guernsey (Summer only)
SCALE
0 1 2 3 4 5 miles
0 1 2 3 4 5 kilometres
8
9
0
1

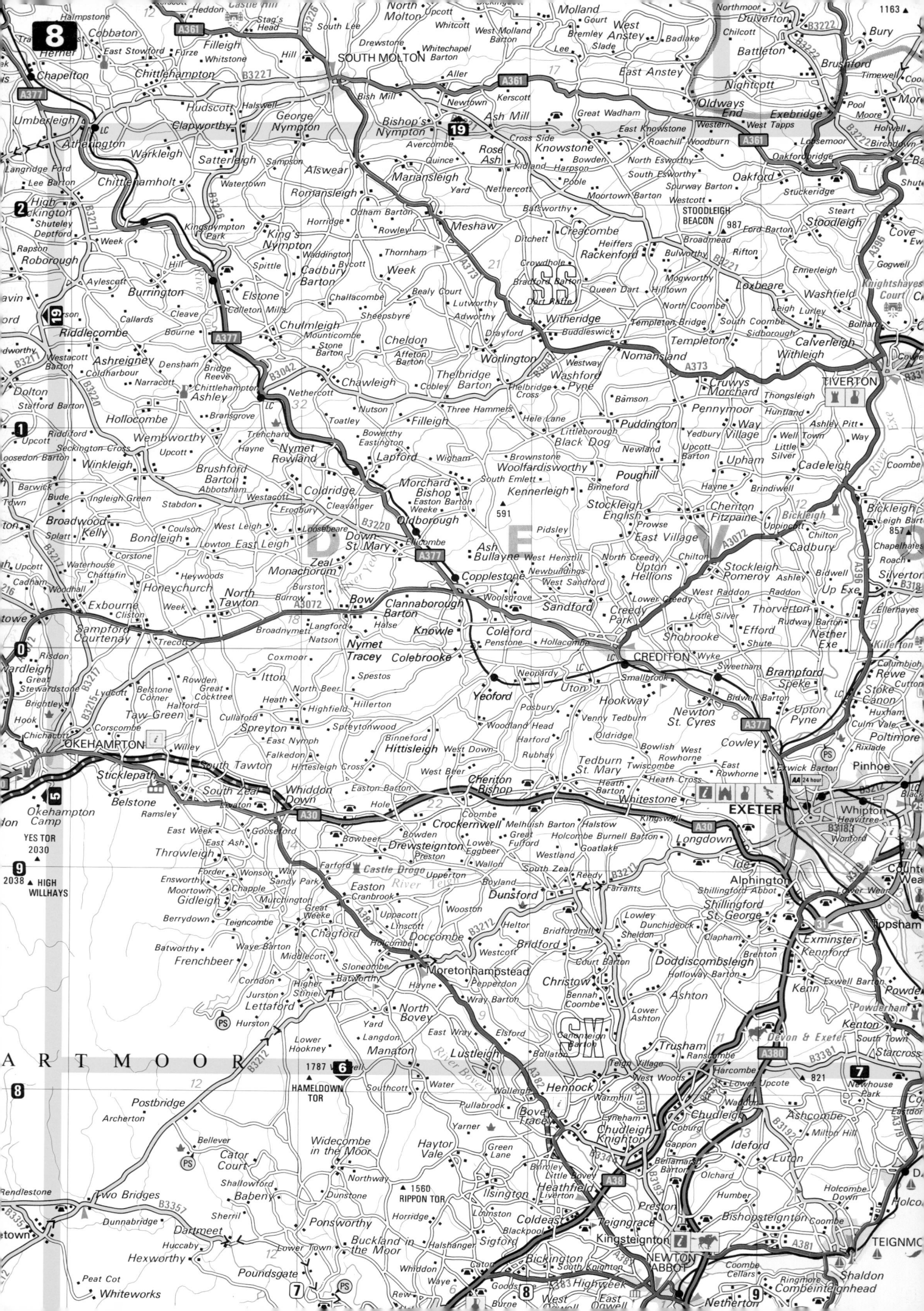

9
Wiveliscombe
Fitzhead
Halse
Hestercombe
Monkton
Athelney
Stathe
Chipstable
Milverton
Heathfield
Staplegrove
Cheddon Fitzpaine
Monkton Heathfield
Creech St. Michael
Durston
Stoke St. Gregory
Mare Green
Curry Rivel
Waterrow
Oake
Norton Fitzwarren
Bathpool
Knapp
North Curry
Petton
Bathealton
Hillfarrance
TAUNTON
Ruishton
Thornfalcon
Clayhanger
Langford Budville
Nynehead
Bradford-on-Tone
Stoke St. Mary
Wrantage
Fivehead
Ashbrittle
Appley
Runnington
WELLINGTON
Trull
Orchard Portman
Curry Mallet
Isle Brewers
Thorne St. Margaret
West Buckland
Poundisford Park
West Hatch
Isle Abbotts
Hockworthy
Holywell Lake
Sampford Arundel
Pitminster
Corfe
Hatch Beauchamp
Beercrocombe
Holcombe Rogus
Wrangway
Angersleigh
Blagdon Hill
Bickenhall
Puckington
Westleigh
Burlescombe
Wellington Monument
Ford Street
Staple Fitzpaine
Ashill
Ilton
Whitnage
BLACKDOWN HILLS
STAPLE HILL
1035
Curland
Windmill Hill
Shepton Beauchamp
Nicholashayne
Clayhidon
Appledore
Rosemary Lane
Churchstanton
Fyfett
Broadway
ILMINSTER
Sampford Peverell
Culmstock
Stapley
Buckland St. Mary
Donyatt
Kingstone
Uffculme
Hemyock
Bolham Water
Churchinford
Bishopswood
Combe St. Nicholas
Dowlish Wake
Smithincott
Ashill
Abbey
Smeatharpe
Marsh
Wadeford
Cudworth
Willand
Blackborough
Newcott
Whitestaunton
Chaffcombe
Sheldon
Dunkeswell
Yarcombe
CHARD
Forton
Kentisbeare
Upottery
Wambrook
Cricket St. Thomas
929
BLACK DOWN
Rawridge
Winsham
Dulford
Kerswell
Luppitt
South Chard
Mutterton
Beacon
Stockland
Chardstock
Forde Abbey
Westcott
Norman's Green
Broadhembury
Shelvin
Monkton
Membury
Thorncombe
Tytherleigh
Langford
Plymtree
Payhembury
Combe Raleigh
Cotleigh
Hawkchurch
Clyst Hydon
Higher Tale
Awliscombe
Buckerell
HONITON
Smallridge
Wilmington
Dalwood
Loughwood Meeting House
Marshwood
Clyst St. Lawrence
Talaton
Feniton
Offwell
Kilmington
Axminster
Fenny Bridges
Whimple
Gittisham
Alfington
Shute
DORSET
Fairmile
Church Green
Northleigh
Rockbeare
Cadhay
OTTERY ST. MARY
Farway
Musbury
Wootton Fitzpaine
West Hill
Wiggaton
Southleigh
Colyton
Uplyme
Charmouth
Marsh Green
Colyford
LYME REGIS
Aylesbeare
Venn Ottery
Tipton St. John
Sidbury
SEATON
Axmouth
Rousdon
Farringdon
Harpford
Bowd
Sidford
Woodbury Salterton
Newton Poppleford
Beer
Hawkerland
Salcombe Regis
Branscombe
Vicarage
SOUTH DEVON COAST PATH
Beer Head
Woodbury
Colaton Raleigh
SIDMOUTH
SY
LYME
Yettington
Otterton
East Budleigh
A-la Ronde
Knowle
BUDLEIGH SALTERTON
Littleham
EXMOUTH
SCALE
0 1 2 3 4 5 miles
0 1 2 3 4 5 kilometres
7
10
0
1
2
3

10
Huntham
Curry
Curry Rivel
Episcopi
Muchelney
Muchelney Abbey
Knole
Long Sutton
Downhead
Weston Bampfylde
South Cadbury
Compton Pauncefoot
Blackford
Lower Knapp
Upper Fivehead
Willtown
Drayton
Northover
21
Podimore
West Camel
Queen Camel
Sutton Montis
Charlton Horethorne
Fivehead
Isle
Long Load
Ilchester
Fleet Air Arm Museum
Yeovilton
Marston Magna
Corton Denham
Stowell
Curry Mallet
Isle Brewers
Hambridge
Thorney
Milton
Limington
Chilton Cantelo
Rimpton
Kingsbury Episcopi
Stapleton
Ashington
Parkway
Milborne Wick
Lower Street
Isle Abbotts
Stembridge
Coat
Ash
Tintinhull
West Mudford
Adber
Holway
Sandford Orcas
Poyntington
Hatch Beauchamp
Beercrocombe
Westport
West Lambrook
East Lambrook
Martock
Chilthorne Domer
Yeovil Marsh
Mudford
Henstridge Ash
Puckington
Barrington
Hurst
Stoke sub Hamdon
Upper Mudford
Trent
Oborne
Milborne
Ashill
Ilton
Ilford
Compton Durville
Bower Hinton
Vagg
Thorne
Over Compton
Nether Compton
Goathill
Stocklinch
YEOVIL
Stallen
Rapps
Southtown
Horton Cross
Shepton Beauchamp
South Petherton
Montacute
Preston Plucknett
Butterfly Farm
SHERBORNE
Haydon
Whitelackington
Seavington St. Michael
Norton sub Hamdon
Odcombe
Little Norton
Brympton d'Evercy
A303
A30
A37
ILMINSTER
Kingstone
Seavington St. Mary
Over Stratton
Lopen
Chiselborough
West Coker
Bradford Abbas
North Wootton
Allweston
Donyatt
Allowenshay
West Chinnock
Middle Chinnock
Barwick
Thornford
Folke
Crock Street
Dinnington
Hardington Moor
Coker
Stoford
Coundle Marsh
Longburton
Combe St. Nicholas
Dowlish Ford
Dowlish Wake
Ludney
Hinton St. George
Merriott
East Chinnock
Ryme Intrinseca
Lillington
Leweston
Knowle St Giles
Cudworth
Chillington
Puddle Town
Haselbury Plucknett
Hardington Mandeville
Sutton Bingham
Beer Hackett
Bishop's Down
Wadeford
Higher Chillington
CREWKERNE
North Perrott
Pendomer
Closworth
Yetminster
Boys Hill
Sandhills
Chaffcombe
Roundham
781
Hardington Marsh
Holnest
Crouch
Purtington
Hewish
Woolminstone
Misterton
Higher Halstock
Leigh
Lower Halstock Leigh
Melbury Osmond
Hamlet
Drive End
Leigh
Totnell
Glanvilles Wootton
CHARD
Forton
Cricket St. Thomas
Halstock
Chetnole
Three Gates
West P
Whatley
Clapton
South Perrott
Lewcombe
Hermitage
Middlemarsh
Winsham
Wayford
Stockwood
Tatworth
Perry Street
Seaborough
Netherhay
Greenham
East Chelborough
Melbury Sampford
Melbury Bubb
Castle Hill
Lyon's Gate
Forde Abbey
Chedington
Corscombe
Grexy Cross
Hilfield
871
Chard Junction
Drimpton
West Chelborough
Mosterton
Holywell
Thorncombe
Gribb
Laymore
Horn Ash
Benville
Evershot
Minterne Magna
Burstock
Batcombe
Tytherleigh
Hewood
Blackdown
Broadwindsor
Newtown
Uphall
Holditch
School House
Frome St Quintin
Up Cerne
Beaminster
Rampisham
Hawkchurch
Birdsmoorgate
Stoke Abbott
Toller Whelme
Higher Wraxhall
Chalmington
Up Sydling
Cerne Abbas
Hill Figure
DEVON
Bettiscombe
Hooke
Parnham
Cattistock
Netherbury
Higher Kingcombe
Sydling St. Nicholas
Marshwood
South Bowood
Mapperton
Axminster
839
Pilsdon
Melplash
North Poorton
Lower Kingcombe
Chilfrome
Maiden Newton
Nether Cerne
Sector
Fishpond Bottom
Shave Cross
Waytown
Oxbridge
Toller Porcorum
The Mount
West Milton
South Poorton
Toller Fratrum
Raymond's Hill
Broadoak
Wynford Eagle
Godmanstone
Whitchurch Canonicorum
Salwayash
Powerstock
Moorbath
Dottery
Mangerton
Nettlecombe
Forston
Wootton Fitzpaine
Ryall
Pymore
Bradpole
Harcombe Bottom
North Chideock
Loders
West Compton
Frampton
Southover
Symondsbury
Uploders
827
Spyway
Grimstone
Stratton
Sodern
Charmouth
Morcombelake
St Andrews Well
Askerswell
Charminster
Chideock
BRIDPORT
Walditch
Compton Valence
Muckleford
Seatown
Watton
Shipton Gorge
Kingston Russell
Bradford Peverell
LYME REGIS
Eype
Chilcombe
Winterbourne Abbas
DORCHESTER
DORSET COAST PATH
Bothenhampton
Long Bredy
Litton Cheney
West Bay
Victoria Park
Martinstown
Burton Bradstock
White Cross
Littlebredy
Winterbourne Steepleton
Puncknowle
Maiden Castle
Swyre
SY
Winterborne Monkton
LYME BAY
West Bexington
Friar Waddon
Abbotsbury
Portesham
Waddon
Coryates
Well
Swannery
Upwey
Rodden
Shilvinghampton
Broadway
Preston
Langton Herring
Buckland Ripers
Nottington
Chickerell
Fleet
East Fleet
Charlestown
Chesil Beach
Westham
WEY
Wyke Regis
Portland Castle
Castleton
Chesil
West Bay
424
Weston
Southwell
BILL OF PORTLAND
A35
A354
A353
A356
A352
A3066
A358
A3070
A3052
B3162
B3165
B3164
B3163
B3157
B3159
SCALE
0 1 2 3 4 5 miles
0 1 2 3 4 5 kilometres
4
5
6
7

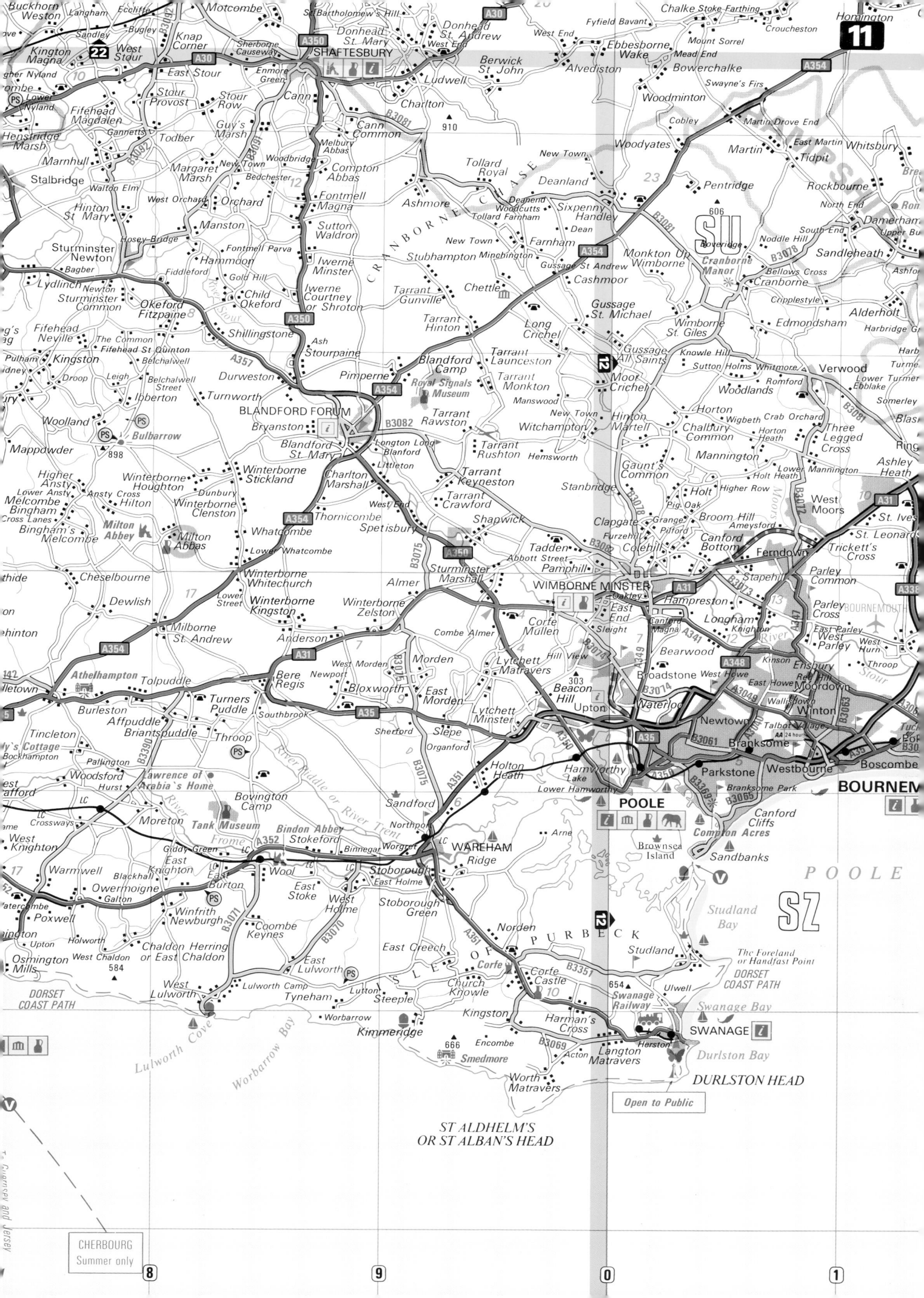

11
Buckhorn Weston
Langham
Ecclitte
Motcombe
St Bartholomew's Hill
A30
Chalke
Stoke Farthing
Homington
Kington Magna
Sandley
Bugley
Knap Corner
Donhead St. Mary
Donhead St. Andrew
West End
Fyfield Bavant
Ebbesborne Wake
Croucheston
Mount Sorrel
22
West Stour
Sherborne Causeway
A350
SHAFTESBURY
Mead End
Bowerchalke
Berwick St John
Alvediston
A354
Nyland
East Stour
Enmore Green
Ludwell
Swayne's Firs
Lower Nyland
Stour Provost
Stour Row
Cann
Charlton
Woodminton
Fifehead Magdalen
Gannetts
Guy's Marsh
Cann Common
B3081
910
Cobley
Martin Drove End
Henstridge Marsh
Todber
B3092
B3091
Melbury Abbas
Woodyates
East Martin
Whitsbury
Marnhull
New Town
Woodbridge
Compton Abbas
Tollard Royal
New Town
Martin
Tidpit
Stalbridge
Margaret Marsh
Bedchester
Fontmell Magna
Deanland
Pentridge
Rockbourne
Walton Elm
West Orchard
Orchard
Ashmore
Deanend
Woodcutts
Sixpenny Handley
606
North End
Hinton St Mary
Tollard Farnham
Dean
Damerham
Manston
Sutton Waldron
CRANBORNE CHASE
Noddle Hill
South End
Upper Bu
Sturminster Newton
Hosey Bridge
Fontmell Parva
New Town
Farnham
Monkton Up Wimborne
Boveridge
B3078
Sandleheath
Bagber
Hammoon
Stubhampton
Minchington
Gussage St Andrew
Cranborne Manor
Bellows Cross
Ashfor
Lydlinch
Newton
Fiddleford
Iwerne Minster
Cashmoor
Cranborne
Sturminster Common
Gold Hill
Child Okeford
Iwerne Courtney or Shroton
Tarrant Gunville
Chettle
Cripplestyle
Okeford Fitzpaine
River Stour
Gussage St. Michael
Wimborne St. Giles
Alderholt
Fifehead Neville
The Common
Fifehead St Quinton
Shillingstone
Tarrant Hinton
Long Crichel
Edmondsham
Harbridge
Kingston
Belchalwell
A357
Ash
Stourpaine
Tarrant Launceston
Gussage All Saints
Knowle Hill
Verwood
Pulham
Droop
Leigh
Belchalwell Street
Durweston
Blandford Camp
Pimperne
Royal Signals Museum
Tarrant Monkton
Moor Crichel
Sutton Holms
Whitmore
Romford
Lower Turmer
Ebblake
Woodlands
Ibberton
Turnworth
Manswood
Somerley
Woolland
BLANDFORD FORUM
Tarrant Rawston
New Town
Horton
B3081
Bulbarrow
Bryanston
B3082
Witchampton
Hinton Martell
Wigbeth
Crab Orchard
Chalbury Common
Horton Heath
Three Legged Cross
Mappowder
898
Blandford St. Mary
Longton Long Blanford
Tarrant Rushton
Hemsworth
Littleton
Gaunt's Common
Mannington
Lower Mannington
Ashley Heath
Higher Ansty
Winterborne Houghton
Winterborne Stickland
Charlton Marshall
Tarrant Keyneston
Holt Heath
Lower Ansty
Melcombe Bingham
Ansty Cross
Hilton
Dunbury
Winterborne Clenston
West End
Tarrant Crawford
Stanbridge
Holt
Higher Row
West Moors
A31
Cross Lanes
Milton Abbey
Thornicombe
Shapwick
Pig Oak
Broom Hill
St. Ives
Bingham's Melcombe
Milton Abbas
Whatcombe
A354
Spetisbury
Clapgate
Grange
Pilford
Ameysford
St. Leonards
Lower Whatcombe
B3075
A350
Tadden
Furzehill
Colehill
Canford Bottom
Ferndown
Trickett's Cross
Abbott Street
Cheselbourne
Winterborne Whitechurch
Sturminster Marshall
Pamphill
Stapehill
Parley Common
Dewlish
17
Lower Street
Almer
WIMBORNE MINSTER
Oakley
A31
B3073
Winterborne Kingston
Winterborne Zelston
East End
Hampreston
Parley Cross
BOURNEMOUTH
Milborne St. Andrew
Corfe Mullen
Longham
Knighton
East Parley
West Parley
Sleight
Anderson
Combe Almer
Canford Magna
A341
A347
River
West Hurn
A354
A31
Lytchett Matravers
Hill View
B3074
A349
Bearwood
Kinson
Ensbury
Throop
Athelhampton
Tolpuddle
West Morden
Morden
Newport
Bere Regis
A348
Broadstone
West Howe
East Howe
Red Hill
Moordown
Stour
Burleston
Turners Puddle
Bloxworth
East Morden
303
Beacon Hill
B3074
A3049
Wallisdown
Winton
Affpuddle
Southbrook
A35
Lytchett Minster
Upton
Waterloo
Tincleton
Briantspuddle
Throop
Sherford
Slepe
Newtown
Talbot Village
B3063
Cottage
Bockhampton
River Piddle or River Trent
Organford
A35
B3061
Branksome
Pallington
B3390
Holton Heath
Hamworthy
Parkstone
Westbourne
Boscombe
Woodsford
Lawrence of Arabia's Home
Lake
Branksome Park
BOURNEM
Hurst
A351
Lower Hamworthy
B3369
B3065
Bovington Camp
Sandford
POOLE
Canford Cliffs
Crossways
Moreton
Tank Museum
River
Bindon Abbey
Northport
Arne
Compton Acres
West Knighton
Frome
A352
Stokeford
Worgret
WAREHAM
Brownsea Island
Sandbanks
Giddy Green
Binnegar
Ridge
East Knighton
Wool
Stoborough
POOLE
Warmwell
Blackhall
East Burton
East Holme
Owermoigne
East Stoke
Galton
Winfrith Newburgh
West Holme
Stoborough Green
Studland Bay
SZ
Poxwell
B3071
B3070
Coombe Keynes
Norden
Holworth
Upton
Chaldon Herring or East Chaldon
East Creech
ISLE OF PURBECK
Studland
The Foreland or Handfast Point
Osmington Mills
West Chaldon
584
East Lulworth
Corfe
Corfe Castle
B3351
DORSET COAST PATH
West Lulworth
Lulworth Camp
Lutton
Church Knowle
654
Swanage Railway
Ulwell
DORSET COAST PATH
Tyneham
Steeple
Swanage Bay
Worbarrow
Kingston
Harman's Cross
SWANAGE
Lulworth Cove
Worbarrow Bay
Kimmeridge
666
Encombe
B3069
Langton Matravers
Herston
Acton
Durlston Bay
Smedmore
Worth Matravers
DURLSTON HEAD
Open to Public
ST ALDHELM'S OR ST ALBAN'S HEAD
To Guernsey and Jersey
CHERBOURG
Summer only
8
9
0
1

12
Fonthill Gifford
Ridge
Teffont Evias
Lower Chicksgrove
Dinton
B3089
Burcombe
A30
Quidhampton
Paul's Dene
Laverstock
Pitton
Winterslow
Compton Chamberlayne
Bulbridge
Wilton
Bemerton
SALISBURY
Farley
Tisbury
Tuckingmill
River Nadder
Netherhampton
Newtown
Sutton Mandeville
West Harnham
East Harnham
A36
Alderbury
East Grimstead
Hatch
West Hatch
Wardour Old Castle
Fovant
Salisbury
Britford
Hill Figures
Coombe Bissett
Stratford Tony
A338
WILTSHIRE
Semley
Swallowcliffe
Broad Chalke
Stoke Farthing
Bishopstone
Bodenham
Whaddon
West Grimstead
Dean Hill
Ansty
A30
St Bartholomew's Hill
Fyfield Bavant
Homington
Odstock
Nunton
513
Croucheston
Donhead St. Andrew
West End
Donhead St. Mary
West End
Whiteparish
A350
SHAFTESBURY
Ebbesborne Wake
Mount Sorrel
Mead End
23
A354
Charlton
15
Berwick St. John
Alvediston
Bowerchalke
17
Newton
Ludwell
Swayne's Firs
Downton
Woodminton
Morgan's Vale
Charlton
Wick
Redlynch
B3081
910
ST
Cobley
Martin Drove End
Cann Common
Lover
Melbury Abbas
Woodyates
Martin
East Martin
Whitsbury
SU
Upper Street
Woodfalls
North Charford
Tidpit
Breamore
Hale
Hamptworth
Compton Abbas
New Town
Tollard Royal
North Street
Deanland
23
Pentridge
Rockbourne
Breamore
Woodgreen
B3080
Nomansland
418
Fontmell Magna
Ashmore
Deanend
Woodcutts
Tollard Farnham
Sixpenny Handley
606
North End
Roman Villa
Damerham
B3078
Dean
South End
Upper Burgate
Lower Burgate
Sutton Waldron
CRANBORNE CHASE
B3081
Noddle Hill
Bramshaw
New Town
Farnham
Boveridge
Fordingbridge
Godshill
Iwerne Minster
Stubhampton
Minchington
A354
Monkton Up Wimborne
Cranborne Manor
B3078
Sandleheath
Gussage St Andrew
Bellows Cross
Ashford
Stuckton
Blissford
Fritham
Iwerne Courtney or Shroton
Tarrant Gunville
Chettle
Cashmoor
Cranborne
Cripplestyle
Frogham
Hyde
Stoney Cross
Gussage St. Michael
Alderholt
Bickton
Hungerford
A350
Tarrant Hinton
Long Crichel
Wimborne St. Giles
Edmondsham
Harbridge Green
North Gorley
Gorley
Ash
Harbridge
A338
South Gorley
Newton
Stourpaine
Tarrant Launceston
Gussage All Saints
Knowle Hill
Sutton Holms
Whitmore
Verwood
Turmer
Ibsley
Mockbeggar
Linwood
Blandford Camp
Tarrant Monkton
Moor Crichel
Romford
Lower Turmer
Ebblake
Ellingham
Moyles Court
Emery Down
Pimperne
Royal Signals Museum
Woodlands
Somerley
Rockford
A354
Manswood
Horton
B3081
Blashford
Linford
A31
BLANDFORD FORUM
Tarrant Rawston
New Town
Hinton Martell
Wigbeth
Crab Orchard
Three Legged Cross
North Poulner
B3082
Witchampton
Chalbury Common
Horton Heath
Shobley
NEW FOREST
Blandford St. Mary
Langton Long Blandford
Tarrant Rushton
Ringwood
Poulner
Littleton
Hemsworth
Mannington
Ashley Heath
Picket Post
Burley Street
Charlton Marshall
Tarrant Keyneston
Gaunt's Common
Lower Mannington
Holt Heath
Ashley
Hightown
Crow
Stanbridge
Holt
Higher Row
West Moors
A31
Burley Lawn
West End
Tarrant Crawford
Moortown
Burley
Bisterne Close
Thornicombe
Shapwick
Pig Oak
Broom Hill
St. Ives
North Kingston
A35
Spetisbury
Clapgate
Grange
Pilford
Ameysford
St. Leonards
Sandford
B3075
Furzehill
Colehill
Canford Bottom
Trickett's Cross
B3347
Kingston
15
A350
Tadden
Abbott Street
B3082
Pamphill
Ferndown
DORSET
Sturminster Marshall
Stapehill
Parley Common
Thorney Hill
Almer
WIMBORNE MINSTER
Oakley
A31
North Ripley
Ripley
A338
Winterborne Zelston
East End
Hampreston
Parley Cross
BOURNEMOUTH
Bransgore
Wootton
B3058
Corfe Mullen
Canford Magna
Longham
Knighton
A347
East Parley
Avon
Tiptoe
Combe
Almer
Sleight
A341
River Stour
West Parley
Sopley
Bashley
Beckley
B3055
B3074
West Hurn
Hurn
Neacroft
Morden
Lytchett Matravers
Hill View
Bearwood
A348
Kinson
Ensbury
Throop
Godwinscroft
Hinton Admiral
New Milton
West Morden
Newport
Broadstone
West Howe
Red Hill
Winkton
Hinton
Bloxworth
303
Beacon Hill
B3074
East Howe
Moordown
Burton
A35
Old Milton
East Morden
Upton
A3049
Wallisdown
B3063
Highcliffe
Lytchett Minster
Waterloo
Winton
A3060
Iford
Barton on Sea
A35
Newtown
Talbot Village
Tuckton
Somerford
Sherford
Slepe
A35
B3061
Branksome
Pokesdown
CHRISTCHURCH
Organford
A350
B3059
Tuckton
Wick
Mudeford
B3075
Holton Heath
Hamworthy
Parkstone
Westbourne
A35
Boscombe
Christchurch Bay
Lake
A350
Southbourne
HENGISTBURY HEAD
B3369
Branksome Park
BOURNEMOUTH
River Piddle or River Trent
Lower Hamworthy
POOLE
B3065
Sandford
Canford Cliffs
SY
SZ
Bindon Abbey
Stokeford
Northport
Arne
Compton Acres
Binnegar
Worgret
WAREHAM
Brownsea Island
Sandbanks
Ridge
Stoborough
POOLE BAY
East Holme
East Stoke
West Holme
Stoborough Green
Studland Bay
B3070
A351
Norden
PURBECK
East Creech
Studland
The Foreland or Handfast Point
East Lulworth
ISLE OF PURBECK
Corfe
Corfe Castle
B3351
DORSET COAST PATH
Church Knowle
654
Ulwell
Lutton
Steeple
Swanage Railway
Swanage Bay
Tyneham
Worbarrow
Kingston
Harman's Cross
SWANAGE
Kimmeridge
666
Encombe
B3069
Herston
Smedmore
Acton
Langton Matravers
Durlston Bay
Worth Matravers
DURLSTON HEAD
Open to Public
ST ALDHELM'S OR ST ALBAN'S HEAD
9
0
1
2

WINCHESTER
SOUTHAMPTON
EASTLEIGH
FAREHAM
GOSPORT
PORTSMOUTH
LYMINGTON
COWES
RYDE
NEWPORT
SANDOWN
SHANKLIN
VENTNOR
ROMSEY
ISLE OF WIGHT
THE SOLENT
Alresford
Headbourne Worthy
Sparsholt
Ashley
Horsebridge
King's Somborne
East Tytherley
Brook
Lower Brook
Mottisfont
Mottisfont Abbey
Michelmersh
Standon
Oliver's Battery
Compton
Shawford
Twyford
Morestead
Chilcomb
Cheriton
Hinton Marsh
Tichborne
Ovington
Avington
Easton
Bishop's Sutton
Ropley
Ropley Dean
West Tisted
Bramdean
Hinton Ampner
Kilmeston
Beauworth
Brockwood Park
West Meon
Warnford
Privett
Froxfield Green
East Meon
Exton
Corhampton
Meonstoke
Droxford
Brockbridge
Chidden
Clanfield
Hambledon
Catherington
Soberton
Soberton Heath
Vineyard & Winepress
Anthill Common
Horndean
Lovedean
Denmead
Hoe Gate
Worlds End
North Boarhunt
Purbrook
Southwick
Wymering
Portsdown Hill
Bedhampton
Drayton
Cosham
Hilsea
North End
Portsea
Portsea Island
Fratton
Southsea
Eastney
Portsmouth Harbour
Braishfield
Hillier Arboretum
Hursley
Timsbury
Kent's Oak
Awbridge
Ampfield
Otterbourne
Abbotswood
Colden Common
Owslebury
Marwell Zoo
Upham
Lower Upham
Fisher's Pond
Crowdhill
Bishopstoke
Fair Oak
Horton Heath
Durley
Durley Street
Bishop's Waltham
Waltham Chase
Swanmore
Shirrell Heath
Shedfield
Curdridge
Botley
Hedge End
Wickham
Newtown
Hundred Acres
Boarhunt
Funtley
Wallington
Titchfield
Titchfield Abbey
Stubbington
Hill Head
Bridgemary
Lee-on-the-Solent
Alverstoke
Stokes Bay
Gilkicker Point
Portchester
East Wellow
West Wellow
Broadlands
North Baddesley
Chandler's Ford
Chilworth
Toot Hill
Rownhams
Bassett
Nursling
Totton
Testwood
Shirley
Portswood
Bitterne
Swaythling
West End
Millbrook
Northam
Sholing
Woolston
Netley
Bursledon
Lower Swanwick
Sarisbury
Locks Heath
Park Gate
Warsash
Hamble
Fleetend
Little Posbrook
Calmore
Copythorne
Cadnam
Bartley
Netley Marsh
Woodlands
Ashurst
Lyndhurst
Pooksgreen
Marchwood
Dibden
Hythe
Dibden Purlieu
Langdown
Butts Ash
Hardley
Holbury
Fawley
Blackfield
Calshot
Langley
Exbury
Lepe
Beaulieu
Beaulieu Heath
Hill Top
East Boldre
Bucklers Hard
Balmerlawn
Setley
Battramsley
Boldre
Norleywood
Portmore
East End
South Baddesley
Walhampton
New Forest Butterfly Farm
Stansore Point
Needs Ore Point
Thorns Beach
Lower Pennington
Keyhaven
Hurst
Sconce Point
Yarmouth
Norton
Norton Green
Totland
Freshwater
Freshwater Bay
Cranmore
Hamstead
Newtown
Shalfleet
Ningwood
Wellow
Newbridge
Calbourne
Shalcombe
Brook
Mottistone
Brighstone
Brighstone Bay
Chilton Chine
Atherfield Point
Little Atherfield
Shorwell
Yafford
Kingston
Chale
Chale Green
Blackgang Chine
Blackgang
Niton
St. Lawrence
The Undercliff
ST CATHERINE'S POINT
Whitwell
Bierley
Godshill
Rookley
Chillerton
Gatcombe
Carisbrooke
Gurnard
Northwood
Parkhurst
East Cowes
Norris Castle
Osborne
Whippingham
Wootton Bridge
Fishbourne
Binstead
Havenstreet
Isle of Wight Steam Railway
Arreton
Arreton Manor
Newchurch
Alverstone
Brading
Bembridge
FORELAND
Bembridge Point
Bembridge Down
Culver Cliff
Yaverland
St Helens
Nettlestone
Seaview
Sandown Bay
Wroxall
Appuldurcombe
Luccombe Village
DUNNOSE
Open to Public

14
Winslade
Tunworth
South Warnborough
Crondall
Upper Hale
Badshot Lea
Tongham
A31
Farleigh Wallop
Ellisfield
Weston Corbett
Weston Patrick
Herriard
Long Sutton
Well
FARNHAM
Runfold
Seale
Puttenham
Compton
Littleton
Loseley
Farncombe
Upper Common
Lower Common
Bagmore
Nash's Green
Southrope
Lower Froyle
Bentley
The Sands
Shackleford
Peper Harow
Elstead
Wrecclesham
Waverley Abbey
Birdworld
Rowledge
Shalden Green
Golden Pot
Upper Froyle
Bucks Horn Oak
Isington
Old Kiln
Tilford
Eashing
GODALMING
Busbridge
Axford
Lasham
Shalden
Shortfield Common
Millbridge
Milford
Spreakley
Cuckoo's Corner
Blacknest
Bradley
Holybourne
Frensham
Rushmoor
Wheelerstreet
Tuesley
Lower Wield
Binsted
Neatham
Batt's Corner
A286
Hydestile
ALTON
Anstey
Wyck
Wheatley
Thursley
Witley
Culmer
Bentworth
Halt End
Thedden Grange
Wilsom
East Worldham
The Straits
Frithend
Pitch Place
Hydons Ball
Upper Wield
The Butts
Wormley
Hambledon
Wivelrod
Beech
B3004
Kingsley
Sleaford
Green Cross
Place
Churt
Brook
Sandhills
Medstead
Chawton
B3006
West Worldham
Hearn
Bowlhead Green
Combe Common
Hattingley
Jane Austen's House
Hartley Mauditt
Bordon
Artford
Headley Down
Beacon Hill
Chiddingfold
South Town
Lower Farringdon
Shortheath
Lindford
Hindhead
894
GIBBET HILL
West End
Oakhanger
Headley
B3002
Grayshott
Upper Farringdon
Bordon
Soldridge
Four Marks
Standford
Sydenhurst
Highstreet Green
North Street
Gilbert White Museum
Selborne
Grayswood
Hawthorn
Whitehill
Bramshott
A283
Kitwood
Blackmoor
Catchmere
HASLEMERE
Mid Hants Railway
Shottermill
Ramsnest Common
Conford
Gilbert Street
Newton Valence
Longmoor Camp
Griggs Green
Liphook
Hammer
Camelsdale
Anstead Brook
The Buildings
East Tisted
Haste Hill
Ropley
Charlwood
B3006
Bohunt Manor
B2131
Gospel Green
Fisherstreet
Bishop's Sutton
Ropley Dean
Colemore
Empshott
Linchmere
Kingsley Green
Monkwood
Greatham
West Tisted
Hawkley
Liss Forest
25
Langley
Hollycombe Steam Museum
Northchapel
Plaistow
Bramdean
Burgates
Milland
Hillgrove
Filmore Hill
Bailey Green
Privett
Oakshott
Liss
East Liss
Fernhurst
Lurgashall
High Cross
Woodmansgreen
Dial Green
Hinton Ampner
West Meon Woodlands
Steep Marsh
Rake
Milland Marsh
A272
Brockwood Park
West Meon Hut
Froxfield Green
Stoner Hill
Hill Brow
Redford
Henley
Lickfold
Steep
Borden
Bexleyhill
West Meon
East End
Lower Bordean
Tote Hill
Terwick Common
Rogate
Eastshaw
Keyfox
Warnford
Stroud
Bell Hill
Sheet
SU
Iping
Lodsworth
Petworth
Langrish
A32
Ripplington
PETERSFIELD
Chithurst
Woolbeding
Upperton
River
Exton
East Meon
Weston
Habin
Trotton
Halfway Bridge
Easebourne
Coombe Cross
Ramsdean
Causeway
Nursted
West Harting
Stedham
Tillington
889
BUTSER HILL
Nyewood
Minsted
Midhurst
West Lavington
South Ambersham
Selham
Meonstoke
Coombe
South Mill
Buriton
Elsted
Lower Elsted
Cocking Causeway
Heyshott Green
Coultershaw Bridge
Fittleworth
Brockbridge
South Harting
East Harting
Treyford
Heyshott
Upper Norwood
Lower Fittleworth
Chidden
Uppark
Didling
Bepton
Duncton
Lower Hornc
B2150
Clanfield
Chalton
North Marden
Cocking
Graffham
Soberton
13
Vineyard & Winepress
Hambledon
A3
East Lavington
Duncton Hill
Barlavington
Catherington
Compton
Chilgrove
Sutton
Soberton Heath
East Marden
Bignor
Blendworth
West Marden
Up Marden
Singleton
Upwaltham
Anthill Common
Finchdean
West Burton
Horndean
Hoe Gate
Worlds End
Lovedean
Forestside
West Dean
Charlton
East Dean
SOUTH DOWNS WAY
Deanlane End
Rowland's Castle
Open Air Museum
North Boarhunt
Denmead
Soake
A3(M)
Stoughton
Madehurst
Furzeley Corner
Cowplain
Lordington
Walderton
Earlham
Waterlooville
Purbrook
B2146
Woodend
West Stoke
Lavant
Goodwood
Slindon
A29
Aldsworth
Funtington
Halnaker
HAVANT
Westbourne
Southwick
Stakes
Portsdown Hill
Purbrook Park
Wymering
Bedhampton
New Brighton
West Ashling
East Ashling
GOODWOOD AERODROME
Strettington
Westerton
Boxgrove
Crockerhill
Fontwell
Tangmere
Boxgrove Priory
Fontwell Park
Drayton
Woodmancote
Hermitage
Breach
Hambrook
Westhampnett
Norton
Nyton
Walberton
Binstead
Cosham
Emsworth
Southbourne
Langstone
Prinsted
Roman Palace
CHICHESTER
Aldingbourne
Eastergate
Portchester
Hilsea
Portsmouth Harbour
Northney
Broadbridge
Walton
Bosham
Fishbourne
Oving
Westergate
Woodgate
Barnham
North End
THORNEY ISLAND
Chidham
Apuldram
Dell Quay
Merston
Colworth
Yapton
Langstone Harbour
North Hayling
Tye
Bosham Hoe
Donnington
North Mundham
Elbridge
Shripney
Hardway
Stoke
West Thorney
Crouchers
Hunston
Runcton
North Bersted
Flansham
Climping
Portsea
PORTSEA ISLAND
Fleet
HAYLING ISLAND
West Itchenor
South Mundham
Chichester Harbour
Ancton
Fratton
Birdham
Sidlesham Common
Fisher
Bersted
South Bersted
Middleton-on-Sea
Elmer
Gosport
Southsea
Eastney
West Town
South Hayling
Eastoke
Shipton Green
Street End
Rose Green
Felpham
Sandy Beach Estate
West Wittering
Somerley
Nyetimber
Sidlesham
Aldwick
Bay Estate
BOGNOR REGIS
PORTSMOUTH
Hayling Bay
Highleigh
Almodington
Pagham Beach Estate
Pagham
Earnley
Bracklesham
East Wittering
Norton
Church Norton
SZ
East Beach
RYDE
Puckpool Point
Nettlestone Point
Selsey
To Jersey and Guernsey
Seaview
LE HAVRE
ST MALO CHERBOURG CAEN LE HAVRE
SELSEY BILL
7
8
9

Shere
Gomshall
Westcott
Brockham
26
Doversgreen
South Nutfield
Ridge Green
Godstone Station
Crowhurst Lane End
Albury
Abinger Hammer
Wotton
Bushbury
North Holmwood
Strood Green
Dawesgreen
Leigh
Salfords
South Godstone
Crouch House Green
Blackheath
Brook
Albury Heath
Sutton
Abinger Common
Sidlowbridge
Blindley Heath
Watermill Museum
Farley Green
Peaslake
Abinger Bottom
Coldharbour
South Holmwood
Holmwood Corner
Nalderswood
Old Mill
Outwood
Lingfield Common
Waterside
Feldav
Norwood Hill
M23
Horne
Lingfield
Plaistow Street
Shamley Green
Holmbury St. Mary
Leith Hill Tower
Holmwood Station
Beare Green
Parkgate
Hookwood
Weatherhill
Smallfield
Horley
Povey Cross
Forest Green
Newdigate
Newchapel
Lingfield
Dormans Land
Rowly
Thorn's Flush
Charlwood
GATWICK AIRPORT LONDON
Burstow
Marmon Temple
Felcourt
Ewhurst
Ockley
Capel
Gatwick Garden
Fernhill
Black Corner
Felbridge
Dormans Park
Baldwins Hill
Cranleigh
Ewhurst Green
Clark's Green
Russ Hill
Lowfield Heath
Shipley Bridge
Copthorne
Old Bonnetts
Tinsley Green
North End
EAST GRINSTEAD
Walliswood
Oakwoodhill
Ifieldwood
Three Bridges
Crawley Down
Sunnyside
Rusper
Ifield
Pound Hill
Standen
Baynard's Park
Kingsfold
Lambs Green
Worth
CRAWLEY
Turner's Hill
Saint Hill
Laker's Green
Alfold Crossways
Ellen's Green
Tilgate
War Museum
Faygate
Selsfield Common
Forest Row
Cox Green
Rowhook
Warnham
Colgate
Worth Abbey
Priests House
Rudgwick
Pease Pottage
Sharpthorne
Tisman's Common
Cricketers Inn
Loxwood
Bucks Green
Broadbridge Heath
Roffey
ST LEONARDS FOREST
Tilgate Forest Row
Balcombe Lane
Wakehurst Place
West Hoathly
Tyes Cross
Park Street
Slinfold
The Haven
HORSHAM
TQ
Handcross
Balcombe
Highbrook
Tanyard
Doomsday Green
Ardingly
Horsted Keynes
Birchgrove
Five Oaks
Itchingfield
Buckman Corner
Ashfold Crossways
Nymans
Staplefield
Ardingly Reservoir
Chelwood Common
Newpound Common
Manning's Heath
Slaugham
Southwater Street
Barns Green
New Bridge
Monk's Gate
Nuthurst
Lower Beeding
Bluebell Railway
Danehill
Billingshurst
Southwater
Whitemans Green
Brook Street
Borde Hill
Wisborough Green
Parbrook
Brooks Green
Copsale
Leonardslee
Crabtree
Warninglid
Slough Green
Furner's Green
Coneyhurst Common
Maplehurst
CUCKFIELD
Lindfield
Sheffield Green
HAYWARDS HEATH
Adversane
Dragons Green
Green Street
Coolham
A272
Bolney
Ansty
Bolney Common
Fletching
Fletching Common
North Heath
Shipley
Belloc's Mill
Broadford Bridge
Cowfold
Crosspost
Legh Manor
Scayne's Hill
Gay Street
Whitehall
Kent Street
Twineham Green
North Common
Broomer's Corner
West Grinstead
Butcher's Row
Wineham
Hickstead
Goddards Green
Wivelsfield Station
Wivelsfield
Newick
Sharps Bridge
Pulborough
Broomershill
Woods Hill
Nutbourne
West Chiltington
Littleworth
Shermanbury
Twineham
Wivelsfield Green
Chailey
Marehill
Thakeham
Dial Post
Partridge Green
Sayers Common
BURGESS HILL
South Common
South Street
Town Littleworth
Nutbourne Common
Wiggonholt
West Chiltington Common
Spear Hill
Bines Green
High Cross
Albourne Green
Hurstpierpoint
Plumpton Green
South Chailey
Gallybird Hall
Greatham
Ashington
Ashurst
Henfield
West End
Blackstone
Albourne
Ditchling
Plumpton
Northpark Wood
Cootham
Storrington
Hole Street
Horsebridge Common
Nep Town
Oreham Common
Woodmancote
Hassocks
Keymer
Streat
East Chiltington
Chiltington
Parham Park
Rackham
Sullington
Rock
Buncton
Newtimber Place
Clayton
Westmeston
Cooksbridge
Newtimber Place
700
The Chantry
Washington
Wiston
Small Dole
Pyecombe
813
DITCHLING BEACON
Plumpton
Hamsey
KITHURST HILL
639
MOUNT HARRY
Offham
Edburton
Poynings
Saddlescombe
North Stoke
South Stoke
549
HARROW HILL
North End
Steyning
Bramber
Fulking
Stanmer
1264
South Malling
LEWES
Burpham
Wepham
Findon
Upper Beeding
Botolphs
Patcham
Coldean
Falmer
Kingston near Lewes
Coombes
Hollingbury
Iford
Warningcamp
The Vale
SHOREHAM-BY-SEA
Mile Oak
West Blatchington
Hangleton
Moulsecoomb
Patching
Hammerpot
Clapham
High Salvington
Upper Cokeham
SHOREHAM AIRPORT
Portslade
Preston
Rodmell
Kingston by Sea
SOUTHWICK
BRIGHTON
Bevendean
Poling Corner
Salvington
Durrington
Old Shoreham
Woodingdean
Poling
Highdown
Sompting
Lancing
Southease
Angmering
Hangleton
Broadwater
PORTSLADE-BY-SEA
HOVE
Brighton
Red Hill
Telscombe
Ovingdean
Deans
Saltdean
Piddinghoe
Rustington
East Preston
Kingston
Ferring
West Worthing
WORTHING
Kemp Town
Goring-by-Sea
Rottingdean
Telscombe Cliffs
Peacehaven
LITTLEHAMPTON
Kingston Gorse
NEWHAVEN
TV
16
1
2
3
4

16
Oxted
Tandridge
Hurst Green
Chartwell
Crockham Hill
Toy's Hill
Long Barn
Sevenoaks Weald
Shipbourne
Four Wents
Goose Green
Nettlestead Green
Yalding
Hadlow
The Bush
East Peckham
Hale Street
Benover
Godstone Station
Crowhurst Lane End
Marlpit Hill
Four Elms
Bough Beech Res
27
Hildenborough
Higham Wood
Cage Green
Golden Green
Barnes Street
Laddingford
Chiddingstone Causeway
Hall Place
The Stair
R Medway
Beltring
South Godstone
Blindley Heath
Crowhurst
Crouch House Green
Mowshurst
Edenbridge
Bough Beech
Penshurst Station
Barden Park
TONBRIDGE
Whetsted
Fowlhall
Rhoden Green
Gain Hill
Old Mill
Watermill Museum
Haxted
Lingfield Common
Waterside
Stanford's End
Hever
Chiddingstone
Ensfield
Leigh
Haysden
Tudeley Hale
Tudeley
Queen Street
Paddock Wood
Lingfield
Plaistow Street
Marsh Green
Cowden Pound
Penshurst Place
Upper Haysden
Crockhurst Street
Five Oak Green
Colt's Hill
Badsell
Pearson's Green
Mile Oak
Matfield
Penshurst
Printstile
Chiddingstone Heath
Bidborough
SOUTHBOROUGH
Castle Hill
Lower Green
Brenchley
The Corner
Newchapel
Mormon Temple
Dormans Land
Markbeech
Smart's Hill
Swale Land
Stockland Green
Cowden Station
Glover's Hawes
Cowden
Poundsbridge
Fordcombe
Speldhurst
High Brooms
Burr's Hill
Winchet
Felcourt
Dormans Park
Felbridge
Baldwins Hill
Rusthall
Pembury
Petteridge
Kipping's Cross
Horsmonden
Grovehurst
North End
Hammerwood
Holtye
Ashurst
Langton Green
ROYAL TUNBRIDGE WELLS
Broad Ford
EAST GRINSTEAD
Little Cansiron
Great
Blackham
Crawley Down
Sunnyside
Ashurstwood
Balls Green
Groombridge
Owl House
Lamberhurst
Spelmonden
Hartfield
Standen
Saint Hill
Upper Hartfield
Withyham
Eridge Green
Frant
Bells Yew Green
Bayham Abbey
Hook Green
Lamberhurst Down
Scotney Castle
Risedown
28
Selsfield Common
Forest Row
Lye Green
Matt's Mill
Eridge Station
Platt
Bewlbridge
Kilndown
Priests House
Coleman's Hatch
Boarshead
Danegate
Wood's Green
Cousley Wood
Stonecrouch
Sharpthorne
Friar's Gate
Chuck Hatch
Jumper's Town
Pell Green
West Hoathly
Tyes Cross
Wych Cross
Mardens Hill
Mark Cross
Bestbeech Hill
Beggars Bush
Wadhurst
Whiligh
Three Leg Cross
Crowborough Town
Steel Cross
Bewl Bridge Reservoir
WEST
Highbrook
ASHDOWN FOREST
Crowborough
Town Row
Riseden
Shover's Green
Dale Hill
Union Street
Tanyard
Beacon Hill
Tidebrook
Wallcrouch
Ticehurst
Horsted Keynes
Birchgrove
Chelwood Gate
Camp Hill
Poundgates
Jarvis Brook
Rotherfield
Bardown
Chelwood Common
Marlpits
Sweethaws
Nutley
Duddleswell
Stone Cross
SUSSEX
Argos Hill
Rusher's Cross
Stonegate
Cooper's Corner
Bluebell Railway
Danehill
Fairwarp
Burnt Oak
Mayfield
Woolbridge
Coggins Mill
Witherenden
Burgh Hill
Lindfield
Ford Green
Cackle Street
High Hurstwood
Etchingham
Witherenden Hill
Furner's Green
River Rother
Holmshurst
Southover
Holton Hill
Robertsbridge Aeronautical Museum
HAYWARDS HEATH
Sheffield Green
Splayne's Green
Maresfield
Butcher's Cross
Pound Green
Five Ashes
Burwash Common
Copper's Green
Burwash
Five Ash Down
Hadlow Down
Batemans
Robertsbridge
Scayne's Hill
Fletching
Fletching Common
Down Street
Piltdown
Budletts Common
Potter's Green
Buxted
Street End
Uckfield
Etchingwood
Heathfield
Burwash Weald
R Dudwell
Oxley's Green
North Common
Grisling Common
Blackboys
Broadoak
Cade Street
Wivelsfield
Newick
Sharps Bridge
Beeches Farm
New Town
Cross in Hand
Three Cups Corner
Hollingrove
Brightling
Twelve Oaks
Mountfield
Wivelsfield Green
Newick Rough
Chailey
Ridgewood
Framfield
Little London
Heathfield
Old Punnett's Town
Wood's Corner
Darwell Hole
Waldron
Maynard's Green
Turner's Green
Rushlake Green
Dallington
South Common
Town Littleworth
Hawkhurst Common
Lions Green
Wayside
Netherfield
South Street
Spithurst
Isfield
Little Horsted
Foxhunt Green
Horam
Warbleton
Plumpton Green
Mount Pleasant
South Chailey
Gallybird Hall
Barcombe Cross
Halland
Davis's Town
East Hoathly
Vine's Cross
Penhurst
Ditchling
Plumpton
Rose Hill
Bentley Wildfowl
Burlow
Marle Green
Foul Mile
Ponts Green
Steven's Crouch
Streat
East Chiltington
Chiltington
Barcombe
Shortgate
Park Corner
North Street
Chiddingly
Broadbread Street
Bodle Street Green
Laughton Common
Whitesmith
Cowbeech
Ashburnham Place
Westmeston
Upper Wellingham
Cooksbridge
Chilsham
Marlpits
DITCHLING BEACON
Norlington
Hamsey
Laughton
Golden Cross
Muddles Green
Ginger Green
Herstmonceux
Windmill Hill
Ninfield
MOUNT HARRY
Offham
Ringmer
Hellingly
Chapel Row
Lower Street
Mark Cross
Lower Dicker
Flowers Green
Russell's Green
South Malling
Glyndebourne
Horsebridge
Magham Down
Boreham Street
Royal Observatory
LEWES
CLIFFE HILL
Ripe
Upper Dicker
Leap Cross
Hoe Common
Falmer
Glynde Place
Michelham Priory
Hailsham
Hooe
Kingston near Lewes
Glynde
Chalvington
Wartling
Hamlins
Downash
Moulsecoomb
Iford
Beddingham
West Firle
Firle Place
Selmeston
Wickstreet
Little Common
Cooden
Rodmell
Alciston
Arlington
Bevendean
SOUTH DOWNS WAY
Tilton
FIRLE BEACON
Hankham
Mill Hill
Pevensey
Norman's Bay
Woodingdean
Southease
Berwick
Drusilla
Polegate
Brighton
Tarring Neville
Alfriston
Clergy House
Wilmington
Stone Cross
Westham
Pevensey Bay
Ovingdean
Telscombe
Deans
South Heighton
Folkington
Wannock
Lower Willingdon
Friday Street
Kemp Town
Saltdean
Piddinghoe
Denton
Alfriston
Litlington
Willingdon
Langney
Norton
Jevington
Ratton Village
Hampden Park
Rottingdean
Telscombe Cliffs
Peacehaven
Bishopstone
St Anthony's Hill
Langney Point
NEWHAVEN
East Blatchington
Sutton
Exceat
Westdean
WILLINGDON HILL
Old Town
SEAFORD
East Dean
EASTBOURNE
Friston
Birling Gap
BEACHY HEAD
DIEPPE
TV
TQ

17
Langley
Kingswood
Lenham
Lenham Heath
Charing
Charing Heath
Challock Lees
Molash
Godmersham
Petham
Bilting
Boughton Aluph
Boughton Malherbe
Chartway Street
Sutton Valence
Chart Sutton
Headcorn
Staplehurst
Pluckley
Egerton
Little Chart
Hothfield
Westwell
Boughton Lees
Wye
Crundale
Waltham
Kennington
Hastingleigh
Brook
Elmsted Court
Lymbridge Green
ASHFORD
Godinton Park
Intelligence Corps Museum
Great Chart
South Ashford
Willesborough
Hinxhill
Brabourne
Brabourne Lees
Stowting
Smarden
Bethersden
Kingsnorth
Sevington
Mersham
Swanton Mill
Smeeth
Sellindge
Stanford
Postling
Beachborough
Frittenden
Cranbrook Common
Sissinghurst
Biddenden
High Halden
Tenterden
Tiffenden
Shadoxhurst
Woodchurch
Orlestone
Aldington
Bonnington
Bilsington
Lympne
Port Lympne Sanctuary
Cranbrook
St. Michaels
TENTERDEN
Benenden
Leigh Green
Kenardington
Hamstreet
Ruckinge
Burmarsh
ROMNEY MARSH
Newchurch
Dymchurch
Martello Tower
St. Mary's Bay
Kent & East Sussex Railway
Rolvenden
Great Maytham Hall
Rolvenden Layne
Small Hythe
Smallhythe Place
Reading Street
28
Appledore
Warehorne
Snave
Snargate
Brenzett
Ivychurch
St. Mary in the Marsh
ISLE OF OXNEY
Stone
Wittersham
Newenden
Sandhurst
Bodiam
Northiam
Great Dixter
Brookland
Old Romney
NEW ROMNEY
Littlestone-on-Sea
Greatstone-on-Sea
Peasmarsh
Iden
Beckley
Ewhurst
Rye Foreign
Playden
WALLAND MARSH
East Guldeford
Romney Hythe & Dymchurch Light Railway
LYDD
Camber
Lydd-on-Sea
Denge Marsh
RYE
Udimore
Broad Oak
Sedlescombe
Brede
Rye Harbour
Rye Bay
Winchelsea
DUNGENESS
Westfield
Icklesham
Winchelsea Beach
Guestling Green
Pett
Fairlight
Cliff End
Ore
HASTINGS
St. Leonards
Hollington
Crowhurst
A20
M20
A28
A259
A21
A268
A2070
B2067
B2080
B2082
B2089
SCALE
0 1 2 3 4 5 miles
0 1 2 3 4 5 kilometres
TW
8
9
0
1

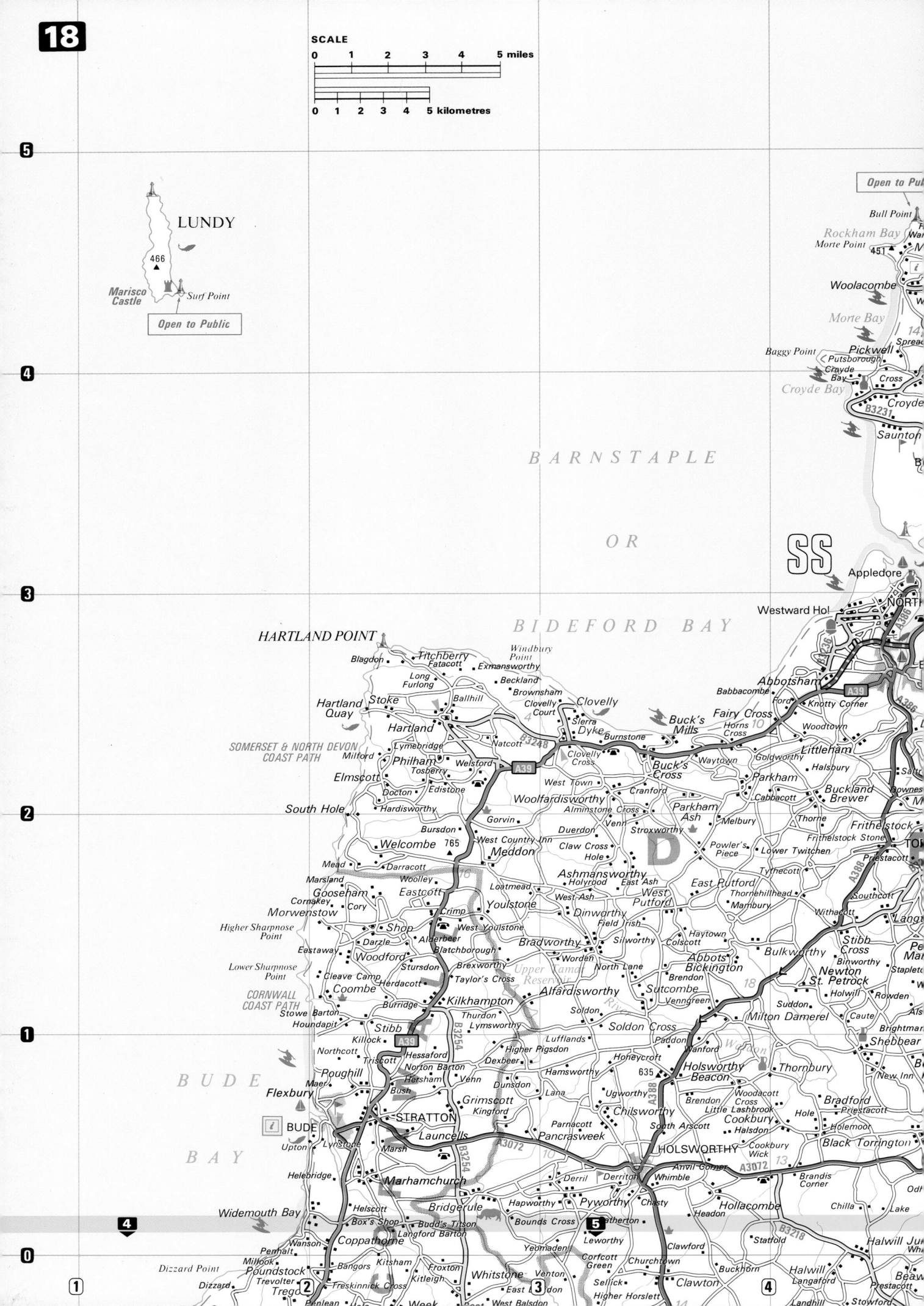

18
SCALE
0 1 2 3 4 5 miles
0 1 2 3 4 5 kilometres
LUNDY
466
Marisco Castle
Surf Point
Open to Public
Open to Public
Bull Point
Rockham Bay
Morte Point
451
Woolacombe
Morte Bay
Baggy Point
Pickwell
Putsborough
Croyde Bay
Cross
Croyde Bay
Croyde
B3231
Saunton
BARNSTAPLE
OR
BIDEFORD BAY
SS
Appledore
Westward Ho!
HARTLAND POINT
Windbury Point
Blagdon
Titchberry
Fatacott
Exmansworthy
Long Furlong
Beckland
Brownsham
Clovelly Court
Clovelly
Hartland Quay
Stoke
Ballhill
Hartland
Sierra
Dyke
Burnstone
Buck's Mills
Fairy Cross
Horns Cross
Abbotsham
Babbacombe
Ford
A39
Knotty Corner
Woodtown
Littleham
SOMERSET & NORTH DEVON COAST PATH
Lymebridge
Natcott
B3248
Milford
Philham
Welsford
Tosberry
Clovelly Cross
Buck's Cross
Waytown
Goldworthy
Halsbury
Elmscott
Docton
Edistone
West Town
Cranford
Parkham
Cabbacott
Buckland Brewer
South Hole
Hardisworthy
Woolfardisworthy
Alminstone Cross
Parkham Ash
Venn
Melbury
Thorne
Frithelstock
Bursdon
Gorvin
Durdon
Stroxworthy
Frithelstock Stone
Welcombe
765
West Country Inn
Meddon
Claw Cross
Hole
D
Powler's Piece
Lower Twitchen
Priestacott
Mead
Darracott
Marsland
Woolley
Ashmansworthy
Holyrood
East Ash
East Putford
Tythecott
Gooseham
Eastcott
Loatmead
West Putford
Thornehillhead
Cornakey
Cory
Youlstone
West Ash
Mambury
Southcott
Morwenstow
Crimp
Dinworthy
Field Irish
Withacott
Higher Sharpnose Point
Shop
West Youlstone
Haytown
Stibb Cross
Darzle
Alderbeer
Bradworthy
Silworthy
Colscott
Eastaway
Blatchborough
Worden
Abbots Bickington
Bulkworthy
Binworthy
Woodford
Sturdson
Brexworthy
Upper Tamar Reservoir
North Lane
Brendon
Newton St. Petrock
Lower Sharpnose Point
Cleave Camp
Herdacott
Taylor's Cross
Alfardisworthy
Sutcombe
Holwill
Rowden
CORNWALL COAST PATH
Coombe
Burridge
Kilkhampton
Venngreen
Suddon
Stowe Barton
Thurdon
Soldon
Milton Damerel
Caute
Houndapit
Lymsworthy
Soldon Cross
B3254
Stibb
Lufflands
Brightmar
Killock
A39
Paddon
Shebbear
Northcott
Higher Pigsdon
Honeycroft
Wanford
Hessaford
Triscott
Dexbeer
Holsworthy Beacon
Thornbury
Norton Barton
635
Poughill
Hamsworthy
BUDE
Maer
Hersham
Venn
New Inn
Flexbury
Dunsdon
Bush
Woodacott Cross
Ugworthy
Brendon
Lana
Grimscott
Bradford
Little Lashbrook
Priestacott
Kingford
Chilsworthy
A388
Hole
STRATTON
Cookbury
BUDE
Parnacott
South Arscott
Holemoor
Upton
Lynstone
Launcells
Halsdon
Pancrasweek
Cookbury Wick
Black Torrington
BAY
Marsh
A3072
HOLSWORTHY
Anvil Corner
A3072
Helebridge
Derril
Derriton
Whimble
Brandis Corner
Marhamchurch
Widemouth Bay
Helscott
Bridgerule
Hapworthy
Pyworthy
Chasty
Hollacombe
Chilla
Lake
Box's Shop
Budd's Titson
Bounds Cross
Headon
Langford Barton
Wanson
Coppathorne
Leworthy
B3218
Statfold
Halwill Junction
Penhalt
Yeomadon
Clawford
Millook
Corfcott Green
Churchtown
Dizzard Point
Poundstock
Bangors
Kitsham
Froxton
Whitstone
Venton
Buckhorn
Halwill
Langaford
Prestacott
Dizzard
Trevolter
Kitleigh
Freskinnick Cross
East Bowdon
Sellick
Clawton
Tregole
Penlean
Week
West Balsdon
Higher Horslett
Landhill
Stowford
5
4
3
2
1
0
1
2
3
4
4
5

Open to Public
Foreland Point
SOMERSET & NORTH DEVON
COAST PATH
LYNTON
Countisbury
Lynmouth
Combe Martin
Bay
Combe Martin
Trentishoe
Martinhoe
Brendon
Broomstreet
Culbone
Porlock
Bay
Porlock
Oare
Malmsmead
Watermouth
Hele
Berrynarbor
Chambercombe
Manor
Heale
Parracombe
Kentisbury
Blackmoor Gate
Barbrook
Cheriton
Shallowford
EXMOOR
SOMERSET
River Exe
1598
Dunkery
Beacon
West
Down
Bittadon
East
Down
Arlington
Arlington Court
Challacombe
Simonsbath
Exford
Withypool
Lucott
Muddiford
Loxhore
Marwood
Pippacott
Heanton
Ashford
Bratton
Fleming
Lydcott
Leworthy
Shirwell
Stoke
Rivers
Goodleigh
BARNSTAPLE
Newport
Landkey
Swimbridge
Bishop's
Tawton
Brayford
Charles
North
Heasley
South
Radworthy
Longstone
Wells
Twitchen
Liscombe
Hawkridge
Castle Hill
Filleigh
SOUTH MOLTON
North
Molton
Molland
West
Anstey
East Anstey
Chittlehampton
Chapelton
Umberleigh
Atherington
George
Nympton
Bishop's
Nympton
Knowstone
Oldways
End
Newton
Tracey
Horwood
Bickleton
Alverdiscott
Yarnscombe
Warkleigh
Satterleigh
Alswear
Romansleigh
Mariansleigh
Meshaw
Rackenford
Creacombe
Chittlehamholt
High
Bickington
St. Giles in
the Wood
Kingscott
Roborough
King's
Nympton
Cadbury
Barton
Burrington
Elstone
Chulmleigh
Cheldon
Witheridge
Templeton
Nomansland
Cruwys
Morchard
Rosemoor
Beaford
Riddlecombe
Ashreigney
Ashley
Chawleigh
Worlington
Thelbridge
Barton
Washford
Pyne
Puddington
Black Dog
Pennymoor
Merton
Huish
Dolton
Dowland
Hollocombe
Wembworthy
Nymet
Rowland
Lapford
Woolfardisworthy
Poughill
Petrockstow
Meeth
Iddesleigh
Winkleigh
Brushford
Barton
Coldridge
Morchard
Bishop
Kennerleigh
Stockleigh
English
Cheriton
Fitzpaine
Monkokehampton
Broadwood
Kelly
Bondleigh
East Leigh
Down
St. Mary
Copplestone
Zeal
Monachorum
Oldborough
Ash
Bullayne
Upton
Hellions
Hatherleigh
Jacobstowe
Exbourne
North
Tawton
Bow
Clannaborough
Barton
Sandford
Creedy
Park
Shobrooke
Sampford
Courtenay
Nymet
Tracey
Colebrooke
Knowle
Coleford
CREDITON
Inwardleigh
Yeoford
Uton
Hookway
Folly Gate
A39
A361
A377
A373
A386
A3072
B3358
B3223
B3226
B3227
B3217
B3220
B3230
B3343
B3232
B3042
20
8
6
7

CARDIFF
PENARTH
BARRY
BARRY ISLAND
FLAT HOLM
STEEP HOLM
WESTON
COWBRIDGE
Llantwit Major
Open to Public
SCALE
0 1 2 3 4 5 miles
0 1 2 3 4 5 kilometres
SS
B R I D G W A T E R
B A Y
SOMERSET & NORTH DEVON COAST PATH
MINEHEAD
WATCHET
Dunster Castle
Cleeve Abbey
West Somerset Railway
B R E N D O N   H I L L S
Combe Sydenham Hall
Gaulden Manor
Hestercombe
TAUNTON
WELLINGTON
Wiveliscombe
Dulverton
Wimbleball Reservoir

Avonmouth
Kings Weston
Henbury
Filton
Stoke Gifford
Kendleshire
Henfield
MANGOTSFIELD
Shirehampton
Hambrook
Frenchay
Westbury-on-Trym
Stapleton
Downend
Blackhorse
Pucklechurch
Shortwood
Redland
Soundwell
Battery Point
PORTISHEAD
Portishead
Sheepway
Easton-in-Gordano
Pill
Redcliff Bay
Weston-in-Gordano
North Weston
Portbury
Ham Green
Abbots Leigh
Clifton
BRISTOL
KINGSWOOD
Warmley
Webb's Bridge
Walton-in-Gordano
Clapton-in-Gordano
Clifton Suspension Bridge
Leigh Woods
Walton Park
Middletown
Wraxall
Failand
Long Ashton
Hanham
CLEVEDON
Tickenham
Nailsea
Flax Bourton
Bedminster
Brislington
Hanham Green
Oldland
Willsbridge
Wain's Hill
West End
Stone-edge Batch
Grove
East End
Farleigh
Knowle
Bedminster Down
Bishopsworth
West Town
Bitton
Swineford
River Avon
Kenn
Chelvey
Backwell
Barrow Common
Withywood
Whitchurch Green
Stockwood
Queen Charlton
KEYNSHAM
North End
Claverham
West Town
588
Barrow Gurney
Dial
Dundry
East Dundry
Whitchurch
Kingston Seymour
Brockley
Potters Hill
Upper Town
Maiden Head
North Wick
Chewton Keynsham
Saltford
Wick St. Lawrence
Sand Point
Horsecastle
Yatton
Cleeve
Lulsgate Bottom
Felton
Winford
Norton Hawkfield
Compton Dando
Corston
Sand Bay
Ebdon
Icelton
East Hewish
Frost Hill
Hewish
Congresbury
BRISTOL
Norton Malreward
Publow
Burnett
Kewstoke
Sand Bay
Norton
Worle
West Hewish
Puxton
Kingdown
Chew Magna
Stanton Drew
Woollard
Pensford
Stanton Prior
Bourton
356
Milton
Ashcombe
Rolstone
East Rolstone
Redhill
Ridgehill
Hunstrete
Marksbury
Brinsea
Wrington
Lye Cross
Lye Hole
Chew Stoke
Stanton Wick
Priston
West Wick
Stock
Blackmoor
Lower Langford
Cowslip Green
Butcombe
Lower Strode
Chelwood
Woolvers Hill
Churchill Green
Churchill
Bourne
Blagdon Lake
Plaster's Green
Nempnett Thrubwell
Chew Valley Lake
Clutton Hill
680
Farmborough
Sandford
Upper Langford
Rickford
Banwell
Stowey
Clutton
Timsbury
Meadgate
Uphill
Locking
Hillend
Lower Canada
Upper Canada
Sandford Batch
Star
Burrington
Blagdon
North Widcombe
Bishop Sutton
Temple Cloud
High Littleton
Hutton
Oldmixon
Rowberrow
Ubley
Cameley
Bleadon
Yarborough
Winscombe
Shipham
1065
Compton Martin
South Widcombe
Hinton Blewett
Hallatrow
Camerton
Christon
Shiplate
Loxton
Barton
Sidcot
West Harptree
Keighton Hill
Paulton
Compton Bishop
Charterhouse
East Harptree
Coley
Farrington Gurney
Batch
Eastertown
Webbington
Rackley
Cross
Axbridge
Cheddar Gorge & Caves
MENDIP
MIDSOMER NORTON
Litton
Lympsham
Biddesham
Lower Weare
Edingworth
Tarnock
Cheddar
Chewton Mendip
Ston Easton
Clapton
Westfield
Norton Hill
Kilmersdon
Downside Abbey
East Brent
Weare
Brinscombe
Badgworth
Rooks Bridge
Draycott
Townsend
B3135
Bathway
Chilcompton
HILLS
1000
East Water
Hunters Lodge Inn
Green Ore
Emborough
Brent Knoll
Battleborough
Edithmead
Stone Allerton
Chapel Allerton
Clewer
Priddy
Charlton
Stratton-on-the-Fosse
Holcombe
Cocklake
Rodney Stoke
Old Ditch
The Batch
Binegar
Ashton
Westbury-sub-Mendip
Wookey Hole Caves
Gurney Slade
Nettlebridge
West Stoughton
Mark Causeway
Mark
Blackford
Wedmore
Wookey Hole
West Horrington
Upper Milton
Ashwick
Coleford
Walrow
Watchfield
Yarrow
Latcham
Theale
Easton
Wattles Hill
Haybridge
Walcombe
East Horrington
Oakhill
Oakhill Manor
Hackness
Bason Bridge
Westham
Heath House
Sand
Mudgley
Wookey
WELLS
Thrupe
Stoke St. Michael
East End
East Huntspill
Henton
Panborough
Bleadney
Yarley
Worth
Dulcote
Croscombe
Downside
Waterlip
Dean
Leigh
Cote
Stretcholt
Edington Burtle
Burtle Hill
Catcott Burtle
Coxley
Woodford
Dinder
Darshill
SHEPTON MALLET
Cranmore
Polsham
Lower Godney
Upper Godney
West Compton
Charlton
Doulting
East Somerset Railway
Puriton
Woolavington
Westhay
Worminster
Wootton Vines
North Town
Godney
Southway
North Wootton
East Compton
Chesterblade
Oxenpill
Meare
Pilton
Royal Bath & West Showground
Prestleigh
Higher Alham
Cossington
Bawdrip
Stileway
Brindham
Street on the Fosse
Westcombe
Knowle
Chilton Polden
Edington
Ashcott Corner
Northload Bridge
West Pennard
Steanbow
Evercreech
Horsey
Catcott
GLASTONBURY
Edmund Hill
520
Pylle
Stoney Stratton
Bradney
Stawell
Shapwick
Buscott
Havyatt
Piltdown
East Pennard
Pye Hill
East Bower
Parchey
Ashcott
Edgarley
Milton Clevedon
Chedzoy
Moorlinch
STREET
Northover
West Bradley
Hambridge
Ditcheat
1685
Sutton Mallet
Greinton
Pedwell
Butleigh Wootton
Cobridge
Parbrook
Wraxall
Lamyatt
Bussex
Liney
Berhill
Walton
Overleigh
West Town
Tilham Street
Westonzoyland
Ham St
Alhampton
Bruton
Nythe
Baltonsborough
Catsham
Wyke Champflower
Huntworth
Andersea
Middlezoy
Butleigh
Stone
Hornblotton Green
Sutton Clanville
Pitcombe
Ansford
Cole
Park Corner
Thorngrove
Henley
Compton Dundon
Silver Street
Southwood
Four Foot
Castle Cary
Stoney
Northmoor Green or Moorland
Othery
Dundon
391
Barton St. David
Lydford
Alford
Shepton Montague
Stout
Kingweston
North Newton
Pathe
Beer
High Ham
Littleton
Hurcot
Keinton Mandeville
East Lydford
Wheathill
Lovington
Galhampton
Bratton Seymour
St. Michael Church
Lyng
Burrow Bridge
Aller
Low Ham
Bramwell
Somerton
North Barrow
Foddington
Hedging
Athelney
Babcary
Yarlington
Wincanton
West Lyng
Stathe
Wearne
Pitney
Charlton Mackrell
Charlton Adam
South Barrow
North Cadbury
Woolston
River Tone
Woodhill
Langport
Stoke St. Gregory
Oath
Wick
Upton
Lytes Cary
Sparkford
Holton
Maperton
Mare Green
Heale
Huish Episcopi
Kingsdon
Weston Bampfylde
South Cadbury
Compton Pauncefoot
Blackford
Huntham
Curry Rivel
Catsgore
Downhead
Lower Knapp
North Curry
Muchelney
Muchelney Abbey
Knole
Long Sutton
Queen Camel
Charlton Horethorne
Greenway
Upper Fivehead
Wiltown
Drayton
Northover
Podimore
West Camel
Sutton Montis
Fivehead
Long Load
Ilchester
Fleet Air Arm Museum
Yeovilton
Marston Magna
Corton Denham
Stowell
Curry Mallet
Isle Brewers
Thorney
Ilambridge
Kingsbury
Milton
Stapleton
Limington
Chilton Cantelo
Rimpton
Milborne
OF THE SEVERN
AVON
M5
M32
A4
A38
A39
A37
A303
A361
A367
A368
A369
A370
A371
A372
A378
B3114
B3124
B3128
B3130
B3133
B3134
B3135
B3139
B3140
B3141
B3151
B3153
B3165
B3168
B3371
3
4
5
6
10
22
35

23
37
12
13
24
1
2
3
4
Chiseldon
Wroughton
Uffcott
Barbury Castle
Lambourn
Baydon
Aldbourne
Ramsbury
Hungerford
MARLBOROUGH
Avebury
Beckhampton
East Kennett
West Overton
Lockeridge
Savernake Forest
Great Bedwyn
Little Bedwyn
Shalbourne
Burbage
Pewsey
Wilcot
Upavon
Collingbourne Kingston
Collingbourne Ducis
Ludgershall
Tidworth
North Tidworth
South Tidworth
Netheravon
Figheldean
Durrington
Larkhill
Bulford Barracks
Amesbury
Stonehenge
Woodhenge
Shrewton
Orcheston
Tilshead
Andover
Weyhill
Thruxton
Quarley
Amport
Monxton
Abbotts Ann
Grateley
Cholderton
Newton Toney
Palestine
Over Wallop
Middle Wallop
Nether Wallop
Longstock
Leckford
Stockbridge
Broughton
Houghton
King's Somborne
Mottisfont
Michelmersh
Timsbury
Braishfield
Hillier Arboretum
Ampfield
Hursley
Abbotswood
ROMSEY
WINCH
Lockerley
East Dean
West Dean
East Tytherley
West Tytherley
Whiteparish
Landford
Newtown
Awbridge
Pitton
Farley
Alderbury
Whaddon
West Grimstead
Downton
Charlton
Odstock
Nunton
Bodenham
Britford
SALISBURY
Laverstock
Old Sarum
Wilton
WILTON
Netherhampton
Coombe Bissett
Stratford Tony
Homington
Bishopstone
Salisbury
Barford St. Martin
Burcombe
Compton Chamberlayne
Quidhampton
Bemerton
Stapleford
Steeple Langford
Little Langford
Great Wishford
South Newton
Lower Woodford
Middle Woodford
Upper Woodford
Great Durnford
Lake
Wilsford
Winterbourne Stoke
Berwick St. James
Porton
Idmiston
Boscombe
Allington
Winterbourne Gunner
Winterbourne Dauntsey
Winterbourne Earls
West Winterslow
Middle Winterslow
The Common
Lopcombe Corner
Fyfield
Penton Mewsey
Enham-Alamein
Hatherden
Tangley
Wildhern
Hurstbourne Tarrant
Vernham Dean
Linkenholt
Faccombe
Ashmansworth
Upton
Ibthorpe
Inkpen
Kintbury
Combe
Buttermere
Oxenwood
Fosbury
Chute
Kimpton
Appleshaw
Clanville
Upper Clatford
Goodworth Clatford
Wherwell
Chilbolton
Fullerton
Harewood Forest
Everleigh
Enford
Compton
Rushall
Chirton
Urchfont
Marden
Wilsford
North Newton
Woodborough
Alton Priors
All Cannings
Stanton St. Bernard
Allington
Horton
Coate
Etchilhampton
Beechingstoke
Patney
Wedhampton
Manningford Bruce
Manningford Bohune
Milton Lilbourne
Easton Royal
East Grafton
West Grafton
Wexcombe
Tidcombe
Brunton
Marten
Wilton
Oare
Huish
Wootton Rivers
Clench Common
Cadley
Durley
Chisbury
Froxfield
Mildenhall
Axford
Ogbourne Maizey
Ogbourne St. Andrew
Ogbourne St. George
Rockley
Fyfield
West Kennet
Yatesbury
Cherhill
Winterbourne Monkton
Berwick Bassett
Winterbourne Bassett
Broad Hinton
Clyffe Pypard
Bushton
Compton Bassett
Highway
Woodsend
Upper Upham
Whittonditch
Chilton Foliat
Eastbury
East Garston
Great Shefford
Weston
Welford
Wickham
Avington
Kintbury
Hill Figure
TAN HILL
964
892
950
735
974
513
584
SU
SALISBURY PLAIN
A4
A36
A30
A303
A338
A342
A343
A345
A346
A354
A361
A3057
A272
A27
B4192
B3087
B3084
B3086
B3083
B390
B3089

24
Letcombe Bassett
Upper Lambourn
Lambourn
Fawley
South Fawley
Farnborough
West Ilsley
Chilton
Blewbury
East Ilsley
Catmore
Compton
Brightwalton
Lilley
Stanmore
Chaddleworth
Beedon
World's End
East Garston
Eastbury
Great Shefford
East Shefford
Leckhampstead
Peasemore
Hampstead Norreys
Ashampstead
Aldworth
Streatley
Moulsford
South Stoke
Goring
Woodcote
Checkendon
Basildon
Whitchurch Hill
Upper Basildon
Pangbourne
Purley
Mapledurham
Tilehurst
Yattendon
Frilsham
Hermitage
Chieveley
Downend
Welford
Weston
Wickham
Winterbourne
Boxford
Hungerford Newton
Hungerford
Kintbury
Avington
Halfway
Stockcross
Donnington
Cold Ash
Bucklebury
Upper Bucklebury
Thatcham
Midgham
Woolhampton
Bradfield
Stanford Dingley
Englefield
Theale
Calcot
Sulhamstead
Burghfield
Aldermaston
Aldermaston Wharf
Brimpton
Wasing
NEWBURY
Speen
Shaw
Enborne
Greenham
Crookham
Inkpen
Bagshot
Upper Green
North End
Ball Hill
Newtown
Headley
Heath End
Ashford Hill
Tadley
Baughurst
Silchester
Mortimer
Stratfield Mortimer
West Woodhay
Combe
East Woodhay
Woolton Hill
Burghclere
Highclere
Old Burghclere
Ecchinswell
Kingsclere
Plastow Green
Wolverton
Ramsdell
Monk Sherborne
Sherborne St. John
Pamber Heath
Pamber Green
Little London
Bramley
Sherfield on Loddon
Buttermere
Oxenwood
Linkenholt
Faccombe
Vernham Dean
Vernham Street
Ashmansworth
Crux Easton
Sydmonton
Litchfield
Hannington
North Oakley
Ibworth
Wootton St. Lawrence
BASINGSTOKE
Chineham
Old Basing
Upton
Ibthorpe
Lower Chute
Tangley
Hurstbourne Tarrant
Stoke
Binley
St. Mary Bourne
Quidhampton
Deane
Oakley
East Oakley
Overton
Laverstoke
Whitchurch
Hatherden
Wildhern
Little London
Enham Alamein
Penton Mewsey
Picket Piece
Andover Down
Weyhill
ANDOVER
Monxton
Abbotts Ann
Upper Clatford
Harewood Forest
Hurstbourne Priors
Longparish
Middleton Army Camp
Steventon
North Waltham
Dummer
Cliddesden
Winslade
Farleigh Wallop
Ellisfield
Popham
Woodmancott
Preston Candover
Axford
Micheldever Station
MICHELDEVER FOREST
East Stratton
Bury Hill
Goodworth Clatford
Wherwell
Newton Stacey
Barton Stacey
Wonston
Sutton Scotney
Stoke Charity
Micheldever
Northington
Brown Candover
Upper Wield
Lower Wield
Bentworth
Fullerton
Chilbolton
Leckford
Longstock
Nether Wallop
Stockbridge
Crawley
South Wonston
Kings Worthy
Itchen Abbas
Itchen Stoke
Old Alresford
New Alresford
Bighton
Medstead
Ropley
Broughton
Houghton
Up Somborne
Sparsholt
Littleton
Headbourne Worthy
Ashley
Avington
Ovington
Horsebridge
King's Somborne
WINCHESTER
Tichborne
Cheriton
Hinton Marsh
Bramdean
West Tisted
Mottisfont
Brook
Easton
Bishop's Sutton
Ropley Dean
Mid Hants Railway
Four Marks
M4
A4
A34
A339
A303
A30
A33
M3
A31
A343
A338
A272

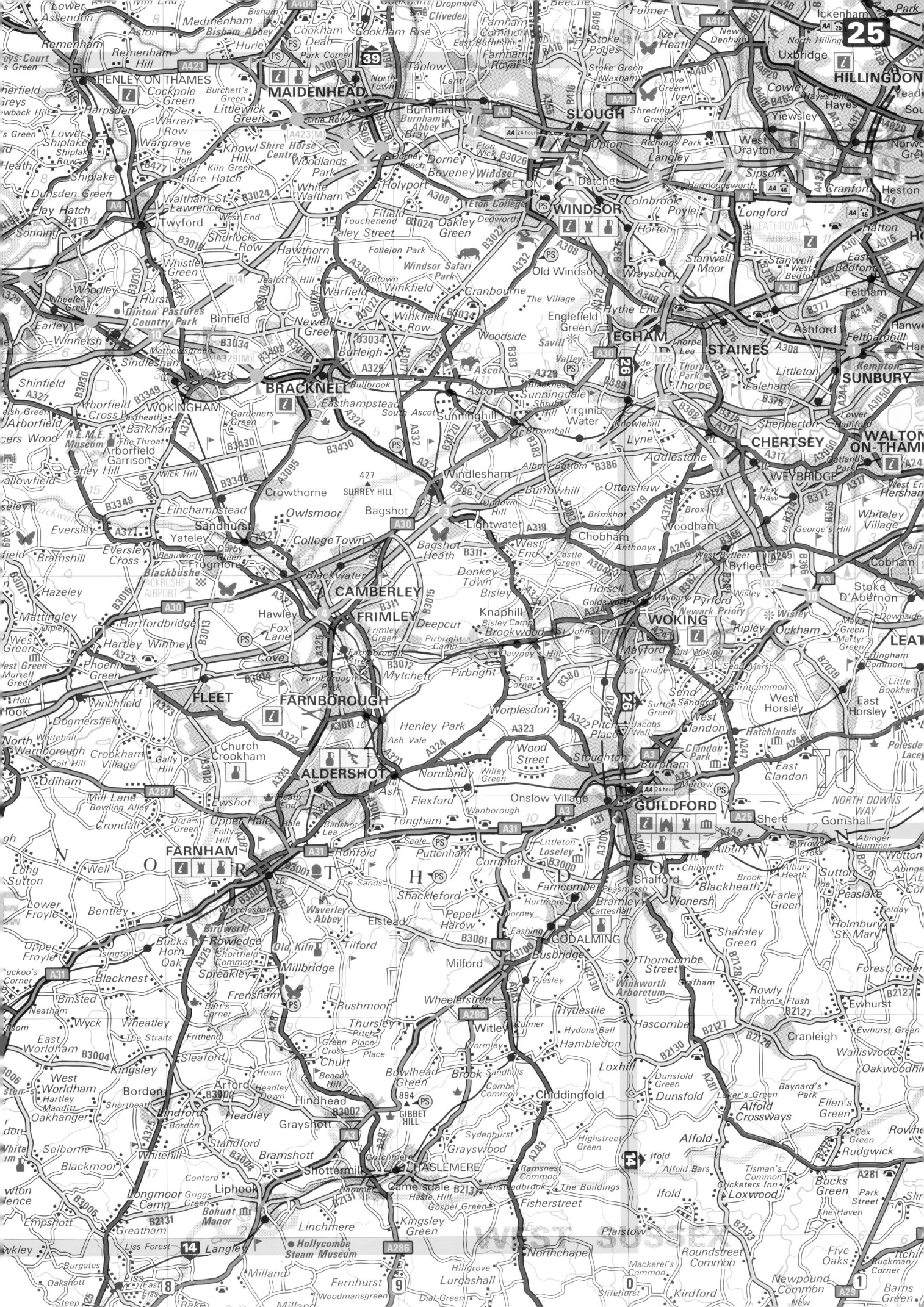
25
Lower Assendon
Medmenham
Bisham Abbey
Cookham Dean
Cookham Rise
Cliveden
Dropmore
Farnham Common
Fulmer
Iver Heath
Ickenham
Remenham
Remenham Hill
Hurley
Bisham
Stoke Poges
Farnham Royal
Uxbridge
HILLINGDON
HENLEY ON THAMES
Cockpole Green
MAIDENHEAD
Taplow
Burnham
SLOUGH
Iver
Cowley
Yiewsley
Hayes
Harpsden
Littlewick Green
Burnham Abbey
Bray
Langley
West Drayton
Wargrave
Shire Horse Centre
Knowl Hill
Woodlands Park
Dorney
Eton Wick
Upton
Sipson
Shiplake
Hare Hatch
White Waltham
Holyport
Boveney
Windsor
ETON
Datchet
Colnbrook
Poyle
Harmondsworth
Cranford
Heston
Dunsden Green
Waltham St Lawrence
Eton College
WINDSOR
Longford
Play Hatch
Sonning
Twyford
Fifield
Oakley Green
Dedworth
Horton
HEATHROW AIRPORT LONDON
Hatton
Shurlock Row
Paley Street
Foliejon Park
Stanwell Moor
Stanwell
East Bedfont
Hawthorn Hill
Windsor Safari Park
Old Windsor
Wraysbury
Feltham
Woodley
Whistley Green
Jealott's Hill
Naptown
Winkfield
Cranbourne
The Village
Hurst
Warfield
Dinton Pastures Country Park
Binfield
Newell Green
Winkfield Row
Englefield Green
Hythe End
Ashford
Earley
Winnersh
Woodside
Savill
EGHAM
Thorpe Lea
STAINES
Feltham Hill
Sindlesham
Burleigh
Ascot
Valley
Kempton
SUNBURY
Shinfield
WOKINGHAM
BRACKNELL
Bullbrook
Sunningdale
Virginia Water
Thorpe
Littleton
Laleham
Arborfield Cross
Arborfield
Gardeners Green
Easthampstead
South Ascot
Sunninghill
Shrubs Hill
Lyne
Shepperton
Lower Halliford
Barkham
R.E.M.E. Museum
The Throat
Arborfield Garrison
Broomhall
CHERTSEY
WALTON-ON-THAMES
Farley Hill
Wick Hill
Crowthorne
427 SURREY HILL
Windlesham
Albury Bottom
Addlestone
Oatlands Park
WEYBRIDGE
Finchampstead
Owlsmoor
Bagshot
Burrowhill
Updown Hill
Ottershaw
Brimshot
New Haw
Whiteley Village
Eversley
Sandhurst
Yateley
Lightwater
Brox
Woodham
Chobham
St George's Hill
Bramshill
Eversley Cross
Frogmore
College Town
Bagshot Heath
West End
Castle Green
Anthonys
West Byfleet
Byfleet
Cobham
Blackbushe
BLACKBUSHE AIRPORT
Blackwater
Donkey Town
Bisley
Horsell
Pyrford
Wisley
Stoke D'Abernon
Hazeley
CAMBERLEY
FRIMLEY
Deepcut
Knaphill
Bisley Camp
Goldsworth
Maybury
Newark Priory
WOKING
Mattingley
Hawley
Hartfordbridge
Fox Lane
Frimley Green
Pirbright Camp
Brookwood
St Johns
Ripley
Ockham
Downside
Hartley Wintney
Cove
Farnborough Street
Mytchett
Pirbright
Dawney's Hill
Mayford
Old Woking
Send Marsh
Effingham Common
Phoenix Green
Farnborough Park
Fox Corner
Cartbridge
Send
Burntcommon
Little Bookham
FLEET
FARNBOROUGH
Winchfield
Dogmersfield
Henley Park
Ash Vale
Worplesdon
Sutton Green
Jacobs Well
Sendgrove
West Clandon
West Horsley
East Horsley
North Warnborough
Crookham Village
Church Crookham
Gally Hill
Colt Hill
Pitch Place
Wood Street
Stoughton
Hatchlands
Clandon Park
Polesden Lacey
Odiham
ALDERSHOT
Normandy
Willey Green
Burpham
East Clandon
Mill Lane
Bowling Alley
Heath End
Ash
Flexford
Onslow Village
Merrow
NORTH DOWNS WAY
Crondall
Ewshot
Dora's Green
Upper Hale
Hale
Badshot Lea
Tongham
Wanborough
GUILDFORD
Shere
Gomshall
Folly Hill
Seale
Puttenham
Littleton
Loseley
Abinger Hammer
FARNHAM
Runfold
Compton
Chilworth
Albury
Wotton
Long Sutton
Well
Shalford
Albury Heath
Sutton
The Sands
Farncombe
Pegsmarsh
Blackheath
Brook
Lower Froyle
Bentley
Wrecclesham
Waverley Abbey
Shackleford
Hurtmore
Bramley
Catteshall
Wonersh
Farley Green
Peaslake
Birdworld
Elstead
Peper Harow
Norney
Eashing
GODALMING
Shamley Green
Holmbury St Mary
Upper Froyle
Isington
Bucks Horn Oak
Rowledge
Shortfield Common
Old Kiln
Tilford
Milford
Busbridge
Thorncombe Street
Forest Green
Spreakley
Millbridge
Tuesley
Winkworth Arboretum
Grafham
Rowly
Thorn's Flush
Blacknest
Binsted
Frensham
Rushmoor
Wheelerstreet
Hydestile
Ewhurst
Neatham
Batt's Corner
Witley
Culmer
Wyck
Wheatley
The Straits
Frithend
Thursley
Pitch Place
Wormley
Hydons Ball
Hambledon
Hascombe
Cranleigh
East Worldham
Green Cross
Sleaford
Churt
Ewhurst Green
Walliswood
Kingsley
Beacon Hill
Bowlhead Green
Brook
Sandhills
Loxhill
Oakwoodhill
West Worldham
Hartley Mauditt
Arford
Hearn
Headley Down
Combe Common
Dunsfold Green
Dunsfold
Laker's Green
Baynard's Park
Oakhanger
Bordon
Shortheath
Hindhead
894
GIBBET HILL
Chiddingfold
Alfold Crossways
Ellen's Green
Lindford
Headley
Grayshott
Sydenhurst
Highstreet Green
Cox Green
Selborne
Whitehill
Standford
Bramshott
Grayswood
Alfold
Rudgwick
Blackmoor
Crutchmere
HASLEMERE
Ifold
Alfold Bars
Tisman's Common
Conford
Liphook
Shottermill
Camelsdale
Ramsnest Common
Anstead Brook
The Buildings
Ifold
Cricketers Inn
Loxwood
Bucks Green
Park Street
Longmoor Camp
Griggs Green
Bohunt Manor
Hammer
Haste Hill
Gospel Green
Fisherstreet
The Haven
Empshott
Greatham
Linchmere
Kingsley Green
Plaistow
Liss Forest
Langley
Hollycombe Steam Museum
WEST SUSSEX
Northchapel
Roundstreet Common
Five Oaks
Buckman Corner
Burgates
Milland
Fernhurst
Hillgrove
Lurgashall
Mackerel's Common
Newpound Common
Oakshott
Liss
East Liss
Woodmansgreen
Dial Green
Slifehurst
Kirdford
Barns Green
Steep
Rake
Milland
8
9
0
1
14
26
39
A4
A30
A3
A31
A287
A325
A286
A283
A281
A29
A323
A322
A320
A329
A412
A404
B3004
B3006
B2131
B2127
B2130
M3
M4
M25
AA 24 hour

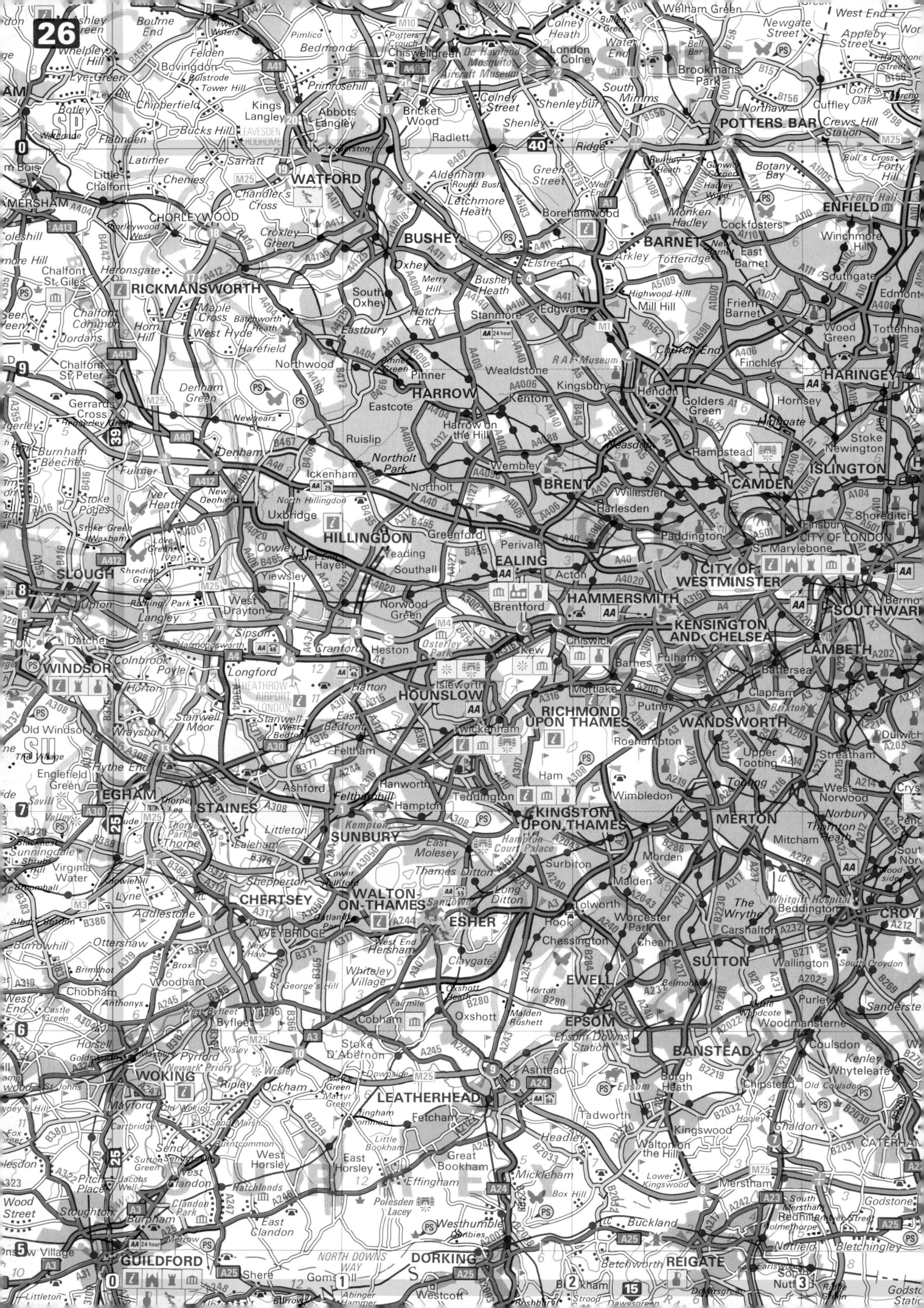
26
Bourne End
Felden
Bovingdon
Chipperfield
Kings Langley
Abbots Langley
Bedmond
Chiswellgreen
Bricket Wood
Radlett
Colney Heath
London Colney
Colney Street
Shenleybury
Shenley
South Mimms
Welham Green
Brookmans Park
Newgate Street
Northaw
Cuffley
Potters Bar
Crews Hill
Watford
Aldenham
Letchmore Heath
Borehamwood
Elstree
Bushey
Bushey Heath
Oxhey
South Oxhey
Chorleywood
Croxley Green
Rickmansworth
Chenies
Sarratt
Latimer
Little Chalfont
Amersham
Chalfont St. Giles
Chalfont Common
Chalfont St. Peter
Maple Cross
West Hyde
Harefield
Northwood
Pinner
Eastcote
Harrow
Stanmore
Edgware
Mill Hill
Barnet
Arkley
Totteridge
Monken Hadley
Cockfosters
East Barnet
Friern Barnet
Enfield
Winchmore Hill
Southgate
Edmonton
Wood Green
Tottenham
Finchley
Haringey
Hornsey
Highgate
Hendon
Golders Green
Hampstead
Stoke Newington
Islington
Camden
Kingsbury
Kenton
Wealdstone
Harrow on the Hill
Wembley
Neasden
Brent
Willesden
Harlesden
Paddington
St. Marylebone
Finsbury
City of London
Shoreditch
City of Westminster
Southwark
Kensington and Chelsea
Hammersmith
Lambeth
Denham
Gerrards Cross
Fulmer
Burnham Beeches
Stoke Poges
Iver Heath
Iver
Uxbridge
Ickenham
Ruislip
Northolt
Hillingdon
Cowley
Hayes
Yeading
Southall
Greenford
Perivale
Ealing
Acton
Yiewsley
West Drayton
Norwood Green
Brentford
Chiswick
Kew
Barnes
Fulham
Battersea
Slough
Langley
Datchet
Windsor
Old Windsor
Colnbrook
Poyle
Sipson
Harmondsworth
Heathrow Airport London
Longford
Stanwell
Stanwell Moor
Wraysbury
Cranford
Heston
Hounslow
Isleworth
Hatton
East Bedfont
Feltham
Twickenham
Richmond upon Thames
Mortlake
Putney
Roehampton
Wandsworth
Clapham
Brixton
Streatham
Tooting
Upper Tooting
Wimbledon
Merton
Ham
Teddington
Hanworth
Hampton
Ashford
Staines
Egham
Englefield Green
Thorpe
Laleham
Littleton
Sunbury
Kingston upon Thames
Hampton Court Palace
East Molesey
Thames Ditton
Surbiton
Long Ditton
Tolworth
Malden
Morden
Mitcham
Thornton Heath
West Norwood
Croydon
Sutton
Carshalton
Cheam
Worcester Park
Chessington
Hook
Esher
Claygate
Walton-on-Thames
Shepperton
Chertsey
Addlestone
Weybridge
Hersham
Whiteley Village
Oxshott
Cobham
Stoke D'Abernon
Ewell
Epsom
Banstead
Belmont
Wallington
Purley
Coulsdon
Kenley
Whyteleafe
Caterham
Chaldon
Chipstead
Kingswood
Burgh Heath
Tadworth
Walton on the Hill
Headley
Ashtead
Leatherhead
Fetcham
Great Bookham
Little Bookham
Effingham
East Horsley
West Horsley
Ockham
Ripley
Wisley
Byfleet
West Byfleet
Pyrford
Woking
Chobham
Ottershaw
Woodham
Virginia Water
Sunningdale
Send
West Clandon
East Clandon
Merrow
Guildford
Shere
Gomshall
Dorking
Westhumble
Mickleham
Box Hill
Polesden Lacey
Betchworth
Buckland
Reigate
Redhill
Merstham
South Merstham
Nutfield
Bletchingley
Godstone
Westcott
Brockham
Dawesgreen

Nazeing
Lower Nazeing
Nazeing Gate
Bumble's Green
Epping Green
Thornwood Common
Tyler's Green
Bovinger
Fyfield
Bobbingworth
Norton Mandeville
Norton Heath
Writtle
Widford
Great Baddow
Galleyend
Holyfield
Epping Upland
Woodside
North Weald Basset
Shelley
High Ongar
Loves Green
Highlands
Howe Green
Bicknacre
Cheshunt
Upshire
Epping
Coopersale Common
Coopersale Street
Greensted
Chipping Ongar
King Street
Nine Ashes
Blackmore
Handley Green
Galleywood
Waltham Abbey
Copthall Green
Fiddlers Hamlet
Toot Hill
Marden Ash
Colliers Hatch
Stanford Rivers
Paslow Wood Common
Stondon Massey
Mill Green
Fryerning
Margaretting
Margaretting Tye
West Hanningfield
Theydon Bois
Hobbs Cross
Stapleford Tawney
Passingford Bridge
Little End
Hare Street
Kelvedon Hatch
Navestock
Fox Hatch
Doddinghurst
Wyatt's Green
Ingatestone
Stock
Hanningfield Reservoir
South Hanningfield
Ramsden Heath
Heybridge
Mountnessing
High Beach
Debden Green
Abridge
Loughton
Epping Forest Museum
Stapleford Abbotts
Navestock Side
Bentley
Pilgrims Hatch
Crow Green
Coxtie Green
Horseman Side
Bournebridge
Lambourne End
Havering's Grove
Downham
Runwell
Billericay
Ramsden Bellhouse
Hutton
Shenfield
South Weald
Noak Hill
Buckhurst Hill
Chigwell
Chigwell Row
Woodford Green
Grange Hill
Hainault
Havering-atte-Bower
Harrold Hill
Brentwood
Brook Street
Ingrave
Little Burstead
South Green
Crays Hill
Wickford
Shotgate
Great Burstead
Nevendon
Woodford Bridge
Collier Row
Herongate
Dunton Wayletts
Great Warley
Little Warley
Harold Wood
Gidea Park
North Benfleet
Barkingside
Redbridge
Romford
Squirrel's Heath
Havering
Hornchurch
Cranham
Basildon
Laindon
Pitsea
Vange
Bowers Gifford
Hope's Green
Seven Kings
Wanstead
Becontree
Ilford
Rush Green
Upminster
West Horndon
East Horndon
Dunton Hall
Landon Hills
Lee Chapel
Westley Heights
Garlesters
Bulphan
Great Malgraves
One Tree Hill
Barking
Elm Park
Hacton
South Hornchurch
North Ockendon
Horndon on the Hill
Fobbing
Corringham
Dutch Cottage
Canvey
Northwick
Forest Gate
West Ham
Eastbury Manor
Dagenham
Plaistow
East Ham
Newham
Creekmouth
Beckton
Rainham
South Ockendon
Baker Street
Orsett
Stanford le Hope
Coryton
River Thames
Thames Barrier
Thamesmead
Erith Marshes
Wennington
North Stifford
Mucking
Thames Haven
Aveley
Little Thurrock
Chadwell St. Mary
Linford
Mucking Ford
Woolwich
Charlton
Abbey Wood
Lesnes Abbey
Belvedere
Purfleet
West Thurrock
Grays
West Tilbury
Halstow Marshes
East Tilbury
Low Street
Tilbury
Cliffe
Cooling
Kidbrooke
East Wickham
Welling
Erith
Slade Green
Tunnel
Crayford
Greenhithe
Church Street
Cooling Street
Lewisham
Eltham
Bexley
Stone
Swanscombe
Knockhall
Northfleet
Milton
Denton
Gravesend
Cliffe Woods
Eltham Palace
New Eltham
Catford
Dartford
Coldblow
Lower Higham
Mottingham
Sidcup
Wilmington
Bean
Singlewell or Ifield
Chalk
Shorne
Wainscott
Grove Park
Foots Cray
North Cray
Stonehill Green
Hawley
Darenth
Betsham
Southfleet
Thong
Higham
Frindsbury
Upnor
Chislehurst
Ruxley Corner
Hextable
Clement Street
Swanley Street
Sutton at Hone
Green Street Green
Longfield
Istead Rise
Nash Street
Owletts
Cobham
Shorne Ridgeway
Strood
Rochester
Bromley
Widmore
St. Pauls Cray
South Darenth
St. Johns
Swanley
Dean Bottom
New Barn
Bickley
Petts Wood
St. Mary Cray
Horton Kirby
Hartley
Hartley Green
Fawkham Green
Longfield Hill
Meopham Station
Henley Street
Cuxton
Borstal
Chatham
Bromley Common
Orpington
Crockenhill
Farningham
Luddesdown
Luton
Hayes
Wested
Hulberry
Eynsford
Meopham
North Halling
Halling
Wayfield
Capstone
Keston
Farnborough
Chelsfield
Roman Villa
Brands Hatch
West Yoke
Ash
Meopham Green
Priestwood Green
Harvel
Upper Halling
Wouldham
Walderslade
Nash
Green Street Green
Well Hill
Lullingstone
Hever Place
Ridley
South Street
Culverstone Green
New Addington
Farthing Street
Badgers Mount
West Kingsdown
Stansted
Hodsall Street
North Downs Way
Holborough
Snodland
Burham
Blue Bell Hill
Leaves Green
Pratt's Bottom
Downe
Shoreham
Romney Street
Vigo
Fairseat
Trottiscliffe
Birling
Fickleshole
Cudham
Knockholt Pound
Halstead
Knockholt
Woodlands
Ryarsh
New Hythe
Priory
Eccles
Biggin Hill Airport
Biggin Hill
Otford
Heaverham
Crowdleham
Wrotham
Addington
Leybourne
Larkfield
Aylesford
Berry's Green
Knockholt
Dunton Green
Kemsing
Borough Green
Offham
West Malling
Ditton
Sandling
Allington
Tatsfield
Chevening
Longford
Seal
Noah's Ark
Fuller Street
Ightham
Wrotham Heath
British Legion Village
Chipstead
Riverhead
Platt
Great Comp
St Leonards Tower
East Malling
Barming Heath
Brasted
Sundridge
Sevenoaks
Hatch
Basted
Claygate Cross
Old Soar
Herne Pound
East Malling Heath
East Barming
Tovil
Titsey
Brasted Chart
Knole
Stone Street
Plaxtol
Mereworth
Wateringbury
Teston
Maidstone
Westerham
Quebec
The Chart
Whitley Row
Undet River
Old Soar Roughway
West Peckham
East Farleigh
Loose
Limpsfield
Squerryes Court
Ide Hill
Emmetts
Goathurst Common
Black Charles
Shipbourne
Dunk's Green
Nettlestead
West Farleigh
Oxted
Hurst Green
Crockham Hill
Chartwell
Toy's Hill
Long Barn
Four Wents
Goose Green
Nettlestead Green
Yalding
Coxheath
Boughton Monchelsea
Cooper's Corner
Sevenoaks Weald
Oakhurst
Hadlow
The Bush
East Peckham
Hunton
Linton
Marlpit Hill
Pootings
Four Elms
Winkhurst Green
Hildenborough
Pitt's Wood
Hale Street
Benover
Chainhurst
Golden Green
Barnes Street
Chiddingstone
Laddingford
TL
TQ
KENT

28
Linford
Mucking
St Tilbury
East Tilbury
Low Street
TILBURY
Halstow Marshes
Allhallows-on-Sea
St. Mary's Hoo
Allhallows
Cuckold's Green
Stoke
High Halstow
Cooling
Cliffe
Church Street
ISLE OF GRAIN
Grain
Wallend
SHEERNESS
Marine Town
Mile Town
Halfway Houses
West Minster
Minster
Warden
Mud Row
Eastchurch
Queenborough
Rushenden
Chetney
ISLE OF SHEPPEY
ELMLEY ISLAND
ISLE OF HARTY
The Swale
GRAVESEND
Milton
Denton
Singlewell or Ifield
Chalk
Shorne
Lower Higham
Higham
Cliffe Woods
Lee Green
Wainscott
Cooling Street
Fenn Street
Sharnal Street
North Street
Broad Street
Hoo
Chattenden
Lower Upnor
Upnor
Frindsbury
Strood
Thong
Shorne Ridgeway
Henhurst
Cobham
Owletts
ROCHESTER
Borstal
Brompton
GILLINGHAM
CHATHAM
Luton
Bayford
Ham Green
Wetham Green
Iwade
Upchurch
Lower Halstow
East Rainham
Otterham Quay
Breach
Bobbing
Howt Green
Kemsley
Milton Regis
Tonge Corner
Blacketts
Conyer
Teynham Street
Uplees
Luddenham Court
Moor Street
Rainham
Key Street
SITTINGBOURNE
Sailing Barge Museum
Bapchild
Teynham
Deerton Street
Oare
FAVERSHAM
Davington Hill
Preston
Henley Street
Cuxton
Luddesdown
Foxendown
Meopham
Meopham Green
North Halling
Halling
Priestwood Green
Harvel
Upper Halling
Wouldham
Wayfield
Capstone
Hempstead
Walderslade
Wigmore
Farthing Corner
Hartlip
Newington
Lidsing
Blue Bell Hill
Bredhurst
Hill Green
Borden
Tunstall
Rodmersham
Rodmersham Green
Lewson Street
Lynsted
Highsted
Rawling Street
Newbury
Erriottwood
Dungate
Hansletts Forstal
Ospringe
NORTH DOWNS WAY
Holborough
Snodland
Burham
Birling
Ryarsh
Priory
Eccles
Westfield Sole
Dunn Street
Stockbury
Oad Street
Bredgar
South Green
Lower Cox Street
Pollyfield
Boxley
Addington
Leybourne
New Hythe
Aylesford
Hucking
Swanton Street
Bicknor
Milsted
Baxon
Painter's Forstal
Whitehill
Offham
West Malling
Ditton
Sandling
Allington
Detling
Thurnham
Broad Street
Wormshill
Doddington
Newnham
North Street
Sheldwich
Hogben's Hill
Selling
Sheldwich Lees
St Leonards Tower
East Malling
British Legion Village
Eyhorne Manor
Ringlestone
Frinsted
Seed
Tong
Eastling
Throwley
Herne Pound
East Malling Heath
East Barming
Barming Heath
Grove Green
Bearsted
Hollingbourne
Wichling
Tong Green
Leaveland
Badlesmere
Wateringbury
Teston
Livesey Street
Tovil
MAIDSTONE
Otham
Eyhorne Street
Woodside Green
Harrietsham
West Street
Stalisfield Green
Bell's Forstal
Shepway
Caring
Leeds
Otham Hole
Broomfield
Warren Street
East Lenham
Lenham
Pested
Nettlestead
Nettlestead Green
West Farleigh
East Farleigh
Loose
Boughton Green
Langley
Kingswood
Lenham Heath
Stocker's Head
Charing Hill
Challock Lees
Yalding
Coxheath
Boughton Monchelsea
Cock Street
Boughton Monchelsea Place
Five Wents
Chartway Street
Boughton Malherbe
Warmlake
East Sutton Park
Liverton Street
Ulcombe
Charing
Hunton
Linton
Chart Sutton
Sutton Valence
Grafty Green
Bush
East Peckham
Hale Street
Benover
Chainhurst
Rabbit's Cross
Charing Heath
Westwell Leacon
Coppins Corner
Westwell
Boughton Aluph
Barnes Street
Beltring
Laddingford
Medway
Stile Bridge
Cross-at-Hand
Farthing Green
Jubilee Corner
Potter's Forstal
Egerton
Pivington
Little Chart
Boughton Lees
Mockbeggar
Collier Street
Underling Green
Milebush
Sweetlands Corner
Plumtree Green
The Forstal
Southernden
Ram Lane
Goat Lees
Fowlhall
Rhoden Green
Gain Hill
Queen Street
Great Pattenden
Little Pattenden
Hawkenbury
Headcorn
Bedlam Lane
Pluckley
Pluckley Thorne
Hothfield
Badsell
Paddock Wood
Claygate
Marden
Wanshurst Green
Waterlane Farm
Wheeler's Street
Swift's Green
The Quarter
Chambers Green
Pluckley Station
Godinton Park
ASHFORD
Mile Oak
Pearson's Green
Marden Beech
Marden Thorn
Staplehurst
Sinkhurst Green
Smarden Bell
Smarden
Biddenden Green
Maltman's Hill
Intelligence Corps Museum
Great Chart
Matfield
Castle Hill
The Corner
Romden Castle
Pimphurst
Snoadhill
Daniel's Water
Bethersden
Beaver Green
South Ashford
Brenchley
Burr's Hill
Winchet Hill
Curtisden Green
Knox Bridge
Lashenden
Frittenden
Haffenden Quarter
Gilliam
Standen
Chilmington Green
Woolreeds Estate
Sevington
Petteridge
Kipping's Cross
Horsmonden
Grovehurst
Broad Ford
Cranbrook Common
Sissinghurst
Three Chimneys
Curteis Corner
Stede Quarter
High Halden
Further Quarter
Tanden
Kingsnorth
Shipley Hatch
Mersham
Cheeselands
Goudhurst
Flishinghurst
Biddenden
Goose Green
Woolpack
Brissenden Green
Great Engeham
Plurenden
Owl House
Iden Green
Wilsley Green
Glassenbury
Sissinghurst
Forest Green
Arcadia
Redbrook Street
Henghurst
Bromley Green
Shadoxhurst
Hoathly
Lamberhurst
Spelmonden
Smugley
Scotney Castle
Bisedown
Hook Green
Golford Green
East End
London Beach
St. Michaels
Tiffenden
Shirkoak
Coldblow
Bayham Abbey
Kilndown
Hartley
Cranbrook
TENTERDEN
Brook Street
Woodchurch
Orlestone
Down
Bewlbridge
Pinetum Bedgebury Forest
Stonecrouch
Goddard's Green
Benenden
Beacon Hill
Leigh Green
Kenardington
The Leacon
Hamstreet
Cousley Wood
Pell Green
Primrose Hill
Strood
Kent & East Sussex Railway
Wadhurst
Whiligh
Three Leg Cross
Flimwell
High Street
Gill's Green
Iden Green
Rolvenden
Warehorne
Reading Street
Dale Hill
Union Street
Gun Green
Historic Vehicles Collection
Great Maytham Hall
Small Hythe
Appledore Heath
Snave
Wallcrouch
Ticehurst
Hawkhurst
The Horns
The Moor
Four Throws
Kensham Green
Rolvenden Layne
Smallhythe Place
Appledore
Bardown
Stonegate
Cooper's Corner
Burgh Hill
Little Conghurst
Conghurst
Sandhurst
Sandhurst Cross
Peening Quarter
ISLE OF OXNEY
The Stocks
Stone
Snargate
Brenzett Green
Ivychurch
Hurst Green
Newenden
Wittersham
Brenzett
Etchingham
Bodiam
Northiam
Brookland
Southover
Holton Hill
Robertsbridge Aeronautical Museum
Salehurst
Bodiam
Great Dixter
Four Oaks
Old Romney
Copper's Green Hill
Burwash
Batemans
Northbridge Street
Ewhurst
Brickwall
Peasmarsh
Iden
Lower Bosney
Robertsbridge
Staple Cross
Millcorner
Collier's Green
Cackle Hill
Beckley
WALLAND MARSH
Guldeford Lane Corner
Burwash Weald
Vinehall Street
John's Cross
Rye Foreign
Houghton Green
Playden
Rye Hill
East Guldeford
LYDD

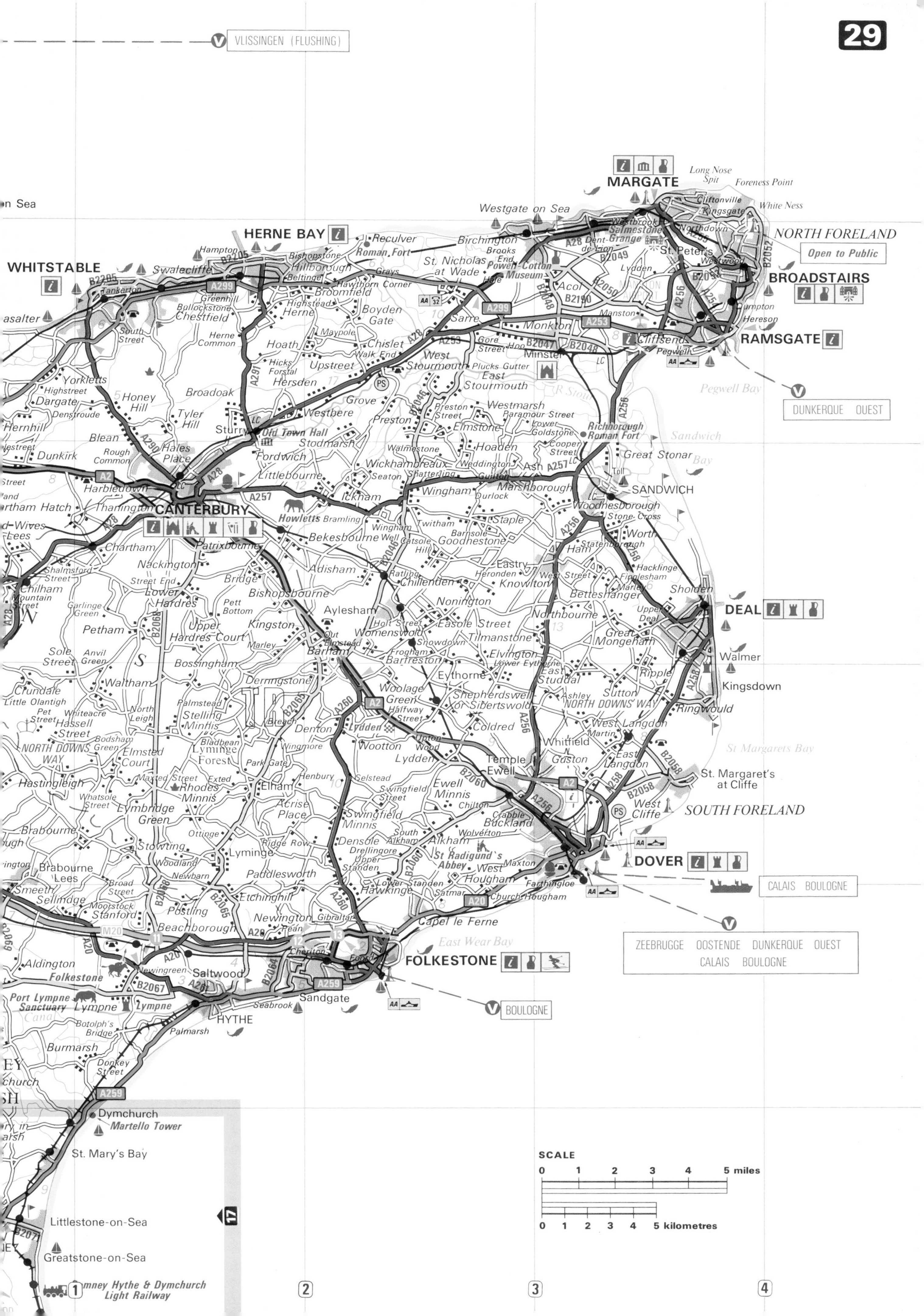

VLISSINGEN (FLUSHING)

MARGATE
Long Nose Spit
Foreness Point
Westgate on Sea
Cliftonville
Kingsgate
White Ness
NORTH FORELAND
Open to Public
HERNE BAY
Reculver
Roman Fort
Birchington
Brooks End
Dent-de-Lion
Salmestone
Northdown
St. Peters
Westwood
BROADSTAIRS
Hampton
Bishopstone
Hillborough
Beltinge
St. Nicholas at Wade
Hale
Powell-Cotton Museum
Acol
Lydden
Manston
RAMSGATE
WHITSTABLE
Swalecliffe
Tankerton
Greenhill
Bullockstone
Chestfield
Herne
Broomfield
Highstead
Hawthorn Corner
Boyden Gate
Sarre
Monkton
Minster
Cliffsend
Pegwell
Salcoats
Grays
Maypole
Chislet
Walk End
West Stourmouth
Plucks Gutter
East Stourmouth
Hoo
Gore Street
Pegwell Bay
DUNKERQUE OUEST
Yorkletts
Highstreet
Dargate
Denstroude
Honey Hill
Broadoak
Tyler Hill
Hoath
Upstreet
Hersden
Grove
Westbere
Preston
Elmstone
Westmarsh
Paramour Street
Lower Goldstone
Cooper Street
Richborough Roman Fort
Sandwich Bay
Hernhill
Dunkirk
Blean
Rough Common
Hales Place
Sturry
Old Town Hall
Stodmarsh
Fordwich
Littlebourne
Wickhambreaux
Seaton
Shatterling
Weddington
Guilton
Ash
Marshborough
Woodnesborough
Stone Cross
Great Stonar
SANDWICH
Toll
Harbledown
Thanington
CANTERBURY
Howletts
Bramling
Ickham
Wingham
Durlock
Staple
Worth
Statenborough
Chartham
Patrixbourne
Bekesbourne
Well
Catsole
Barnsole
Goodnestone
Ham
Hacklinge
Fleppesham
Sholden
DEAL
Shalmsford Street
Nackington
Bridge
Bishopsbourne
Adisham
Ratling
Chillenden
Heronden
Knowlton
West Street
Betteshanger
Upper Deal
Chilham
Lower Hardres
Pett Bottom
Aylesham
Holt Street
Easole Street
Nonington
Tilmanstone
Northbourne
Great Mongeham
Walmer
Garlinge Green
Kingston
Marley
Elmstead
Barham
Womenswold
Snowdown
Elvington
East Studdal
Ripple
Kingsdown
Petham
Bossingham
Derringstone
Woolage Green
Halfway Houses
Shepherdswell or Sibertswold
Lower Eythorne
Ashley
Sutton
Ringwould
Waltham
Anvil Green
North Leigh
Breach
Denton
Upton
Coldred
West Langdon
Martin
NORTH DOWNS WAY
Crundale
Little Olantigh
Pet Street
Whiteacre
Hassell Street
Bodsham Green
Elmsted Court
Palmstead
Stelling Minnis
Bladbean
Lyminge Forest
Winmore
Wootton
Lydden
Temple Ewell
Whitfield
Guston
East Langdon
St. Margaret's at Cliffe
St Margarets Bay
Hastingleigh
Whatsole Street
Masted Street
Rhodes Minnis
Park Gate
Gelstead
Swingfield Street
Chilton
Wolverton
Buckland
West Cliffe
SOUTH FORELAND
Brabourne
Lymbridge Green
Ottinge
Elham
Henbury
Ewell Minnis
Densole
South Alkham
Alkham
Crabble
Maxton
St Radigund's Abbey
West Hougham
Smeeth
Sellindge
Stowting
Lyminge
Ridge Row
Swingfield Minnis
Drellingore
Upper Standen
Farthingloe
DOVER
CALAIS BOULOGNE
Brabourne Lees
Broad Street
Postling
Newbarn
Paddlesworth
Lower Standen
Satmar
Church Hougham
Moorstock
Stanford
Etchinghill
Newington
Gibraltar
Hawkinge
Capel le Ferne
Aldington
Beachborough
Pean
Cheriton
East Wear Bay
ZEEBRUGGE OOSTENDE DUNKERQUE OUEST CALAIS BOULOGNE
Newingreen
Saltwood
Folkestone
FOLKESTONE
Port Lympne Sanctuary
Lympne
Seabrook
Sandgate
Palmarsh
HYTHE
BOULOGNE
Botolph's Bridge
Burmarsh
Donkey Street
Dymchurch
Martello Tower
St. Mary's Bay
SCALE
0 1 2 3 4 5 miles
0 1 2 3 4 5 kilometres
Littlestone-on-Sea
Greatstone-on-Sea
Romney Hythe & Dymchurch Light Railway

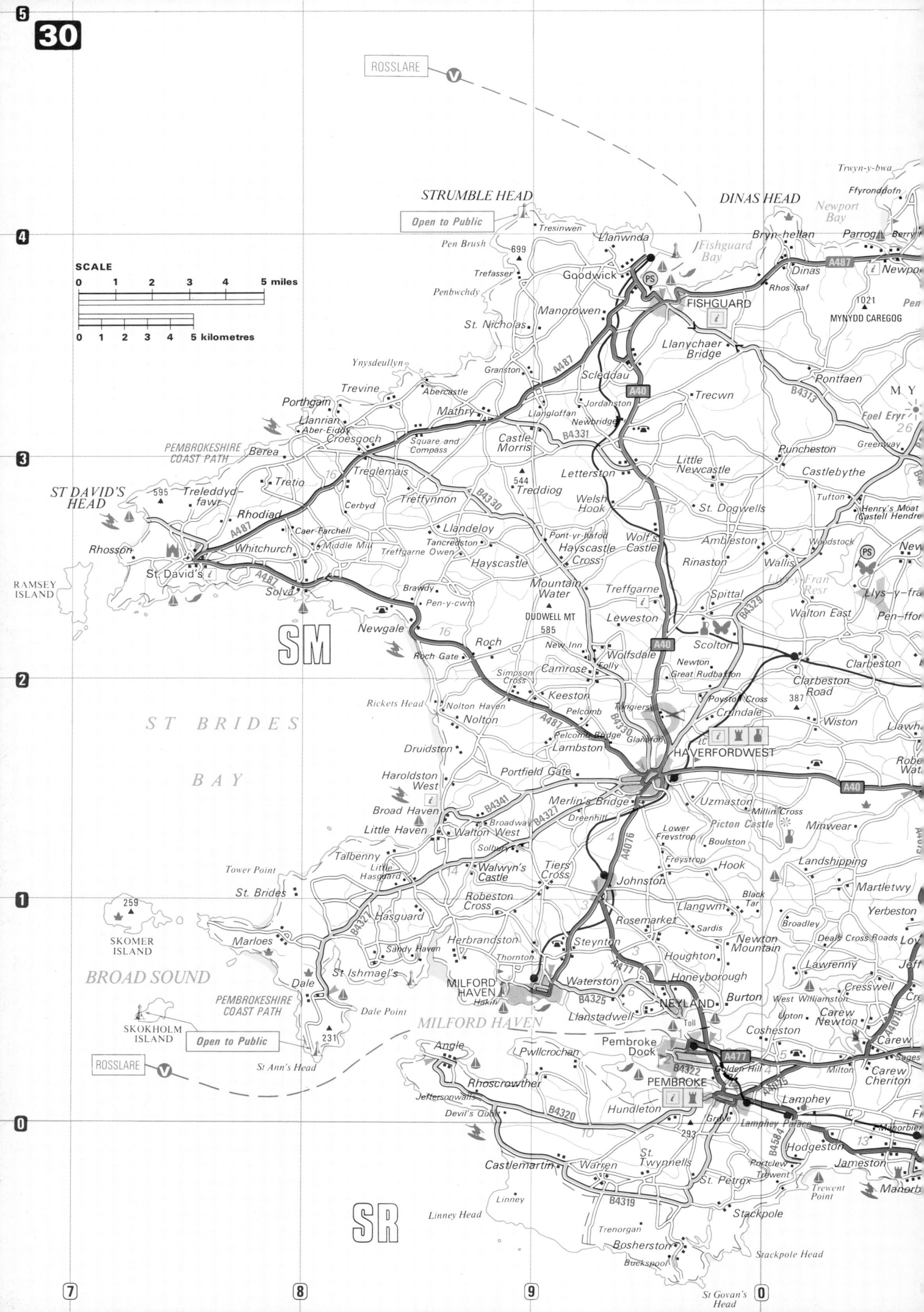

ROSSLARE
STRUMBLE HEAD
Open to Public
DINAS HEAD
Newport Bay
Fishguard Bay
SCALE
5 miles
5 kilometres
Goodwick
FISHGUARD
Llanwnda
Dinas
Newport
Manorowen
St. Nicholas
Llanychaer Bridge
MYNYDD CAREGOG
Trevine
Porthgain
Mathry
Scleddau
Trecwn
Pontfaen
PEMBROKESHIRE COAST PATH
Berea
Croesgoch
Castle Morris
Letterston
Puncheston
Castlebythe
ST DAVID'S HEAD
Tretio
Treglemais
Treddiog
Welsh Hook
Little Newcastle
St. Dogwells
Rhodiad
Cerbyd
Treffynnon
Llandeloy
Wolf's Castle
Ambleston
Whitchurch
Hayscastle Cross
Rinaston
Rhosson
St. David's
Solva
Hayscastle
RAMSEY ISLAND
Mountain Water
Treffgarne
Spittal
Walton East
Newgale
DUDWELL MT
Leweston
Scolton
Roch
Wolfsdale
Camrose
Clarbeston
Clarbeston Road
Keeston
SM
ST BRIDES BAY
Nolton Haven
Nolton
Crundale
Wiston
Druidston
Lambston
HAVERFORDWEST
Haroldston West
Portfield Gate
Broad Haven
Merlin's Bridge
Uzmaston
Little Haven
Walton West
Picton Castle
Minwear
Talbenny
Walwyn's Castle
Tiers Cross
Landshipping
Tower Point
St. Brides
Johnston
Martletwy
SKOMER ISLAND
Hasguard
Langwm
Yerbeston
BROAD SOUND
Marloes
Herbrandston
Steynton
Houghton
Rosemarket
Newton Mountain
Lawrenny
Dale
St Ishmael's
MILFORD HAVEN
Honeyborough
Cresswell
SKOKHOLM ISLAND
PEMBROKESHIRE COAST PATH
Dale Point
Waterston
NEYLAND
Burton
Llanstadwell
Carew Newton
Cosheston
St Ann's Head
Angle
Pwllcrochan
Pembroke Dock
Carew
Rhoscrowther
PEMBROKE
Carew Cheriton
Lamphey
Hundleton
Lamphey Palace
Hodgeston
Castlemartin
Warren
St. Twynnells
St. Petrox
Jameston
Stackpole
Linney Head
SR
Bosherston
Stackpole Head
St Govan's Head

31
Gwbert-on-Sea
Verwig
Blaenannerch
Tan-y-groes
Capel Cynon
Bwlchyfadfa
1062
Tre-cwn
Granant
Yr Hendre
St Dogmaels
St Dogmaels
Cwnconell
Tremain
A487
Glynarthen
Aber
Castell-Howell
Penparc
CARDIGAN
Blaenporth
Bettws Evan
Hawen
Rhydlewis
A486
Ffostrasol
B4459
Pontshaen
Cwmsychpant
B4546
B4548
Pantgwyn
Beulah
Penrhiwpal
Llangoedmor
B4570
608
Brongest
B4333
B4334
Troedyraur
Croes-lan
Tre-groes
A475
Llanwenog
A487
Afon
Cilgerran
A484
Ponthirwaun
Blaengwenllan Cross
Llangynllo
Maesllyn
Rhydowen
Monington
Cross-way
Cilgerran
Llechryd
Llandygwydd
Felin Geri Mill
Cwmcoy
B4571
Aber-banc
Horeb
Pren-gwyn
B4459
Rhyddlan
Glanrhyd
Pen-y-bryn
PS
B4476
Capel Dewi
Bridell
Teifi
Penrhiwllan
Afon
B4582
Pont-garreg
Trewilym
A478
Abercych
Cenarth
A475
Llandyfriog
Llanllwni
Cwmbettws
Penrhiw
Henllan
Llandysul
Llanfihangel ar-Arth
44
Pentre-cagal
Pontwelly
B4336
Velindre
NEWCASTLE EMLYN
A484
Llangeler
Llanllwni
Eglwyswrw
Llanfair-Nant-Gwyn
B4332
Newchapel
Shiral
Drefach
Pentre-cwrt
B4336
Gilwendeg
Boncath
Penrherber
Velindre
Museum of Woolen Industry
A486
Banc-y-ffordd
B4459
B4332
Glynteg
Pontgynon
Saron
Pencader
New Inn
Crosswell
Blaenffos
1100
Whitechurch
Clydey
Capel Iwan
MOELFRE
Cwmpengraig
A478
Bwlch-y-groes
Star
Rhôs
Gwyddgrug
Brynberian
Pen-y-bwlch
Llwyn-drain
Cilrhedyn
B4333
Dol-gran
PRESELI
Crymmych
Tegryn
B4299
A485
1173
Pen-y-ffin
Mynachlog-ddu
Pentre-golar
Hermon
Waun-deg
Cwmduad
Alltwalis
Llanfyrnach
Trelech
Maenieuan
Hermon
Dinas
Llanpumsaint
Glandwr
Mynachlog-ddu
Ffynnon-wen
SN
Esgair
Pontarsais
Hebron
Blaenwaun
Trelech a'r Betws
Blaen-y-coed
Llanglydwen
Cynwyl Elfed
Plâs
Llangolman
Llanwinio
A484
Rhydargaeau
Pantymenyn
Cwmfelin Mynach
Talog
B4301
Efailwen
Cefn-y-pant
Cwmbach
Blaen-pant
Sarnau
Pant-teg
A478
B4299
Newchurch
Maesgwynne
Bwlchnewydd
Peniel
Bronwydd Arms
Login
Abernant
Llanfihangel uwch-Gwili
622
Crosshands
Llanboidy
Gellywen
Pandy
Gwili Railway
Portis-Bach
Capel Gwyn
White Mill
Llandissilio
Dyffryn
Ffynnonddrain
Rickett's Mill
Meidrim
Henllan Amgoed
Tre-Vaughan
Llanfallteg
Llangynin
Merther
Abergwili
Nantgaredig
CARMARTHEN
Johnstown
B4298
Capel Dewi
Cwmfelin Boeth
Sarnau
A40
B4300
Llangunnor
Llanfallteg West
Bron-y-gaer
Llanllwch
Whitland Abbey
Pensarn
Nant-y-caws
Penblewan Cross
B4299
Whitland
LC
LC
LC
Bancyfelin
A48
Commercial
A40
LC
Pwll Trap
A484
Cwmffrwd
Llanddewi Velfrey
19
502
Oaklands
St. Clears
Llangain
Trevaughan
Backe
Llangynog
Idole
Croesyceiliog
Cwmisfael
Crinow
Llanddowror
Llwyn-y-brain
Bancycapel
Lampeter Velfrey
Cwmllyfri
Pen-y-bont
Llangendeirne
B4328
B4306
Melinau
Pilgrim's Rest
Llanybri
B4312
Crwbin
B4315
B4314
Tavernspite
Red Roses
A477
22
44
Pontantwn
Velindre
Cold Blow
Princes Gate
Llandawke
Llandefaelog
B4309
Bancffosfelen
Crunwear
Llanstephan
Ludchurch
Meinciau
Ferryside
Four Roads
B4317
Longstone
Llanteg
Llansadurnen
Laugharne
Llanstephan
Broadway
A478
609
Marros
Llanmiloe
Broadlay
Broadway
A484
Pontyates
Trelessy
A4066
Thomas Chapel
Kilgetty
Pendine
Ginst Point
Llansaint
Mynyddygarreg
Stepaside
Tanylan
Llangadog
Amroth
B4317
Cynheidre
KIDWELLY
Carway
Wiseman's Bridge
PEMBROKESHIRE COAST PATH
Woodside
B4308
Pentlepoir
East Williamston
Saundersfoot
Trimsaran
Pinged
Warm Boglan
B4308
Broadfield
Monkstone Point
B4317
Cwm Capel
B4309
New Hedges
BURRY PORT
Cwm-bach
Achddu
Pembrey
TENBY
Dyfatty
Pwll
CARMARTHEN
BAY
LLANELLI
Whitford Point
CALDEY ISLAND
SS
32
Llanmadoc
Landimore
Weobley
Cheriton
Burrygreen
2
3
4

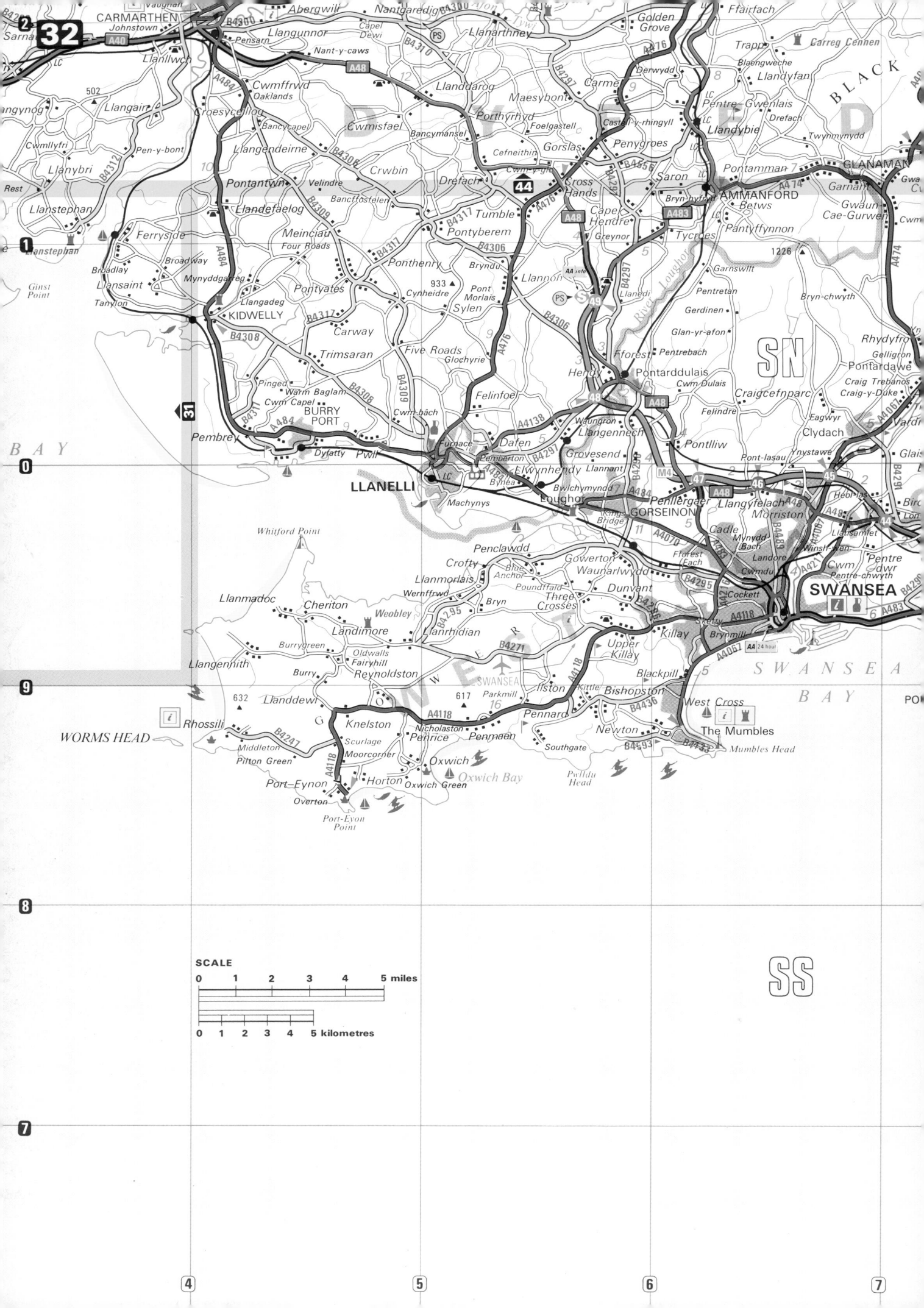

CARMARTHEN
Johnstown

Abergwili   Nantgaredig   Ffairfach

Llangunnor   Capel Dewi   Llanarthney   Golden Grove   Trapp   Carreg Cennen

B4300   PS   Derwydd   B L A C K

Pensarn   B4310   Llanddarog   Carme   Blaengweche   Llandyfan

Nant-y-caws   Maesybont   Pentre-Gwenlais   Drefach   Twynmynydd

Cwmffrwd   Oaklands   Porthyrhyd   Foelgastell   Castell-y-rhingyll   Llandybie

Groesyceiling   Bancycapel   Cwmisfael   Bancymansel   Cefneithin   Gorslas   Penygroes   Pontamman   GLANAMAN   Garnant

Llangendeirne   Crwbin   Drefach   Cross Hands   Saron   AMMANFORD   Gwaun Cae-Gurwen

Pontantwn   Velindre   Tumble   Capel Hendre   Bryn-hyfryd   Betws   Pantyffynnon   Cwm

Llandefaelog   Bancffosfelen   Pontyberem   Greynor   Tycroes

Meinciau   Four Roads   Ponthenry   Bryndu   Llannôn   Garnswllt   Bryn-chwyth

Ferryside   Pont Morlais   Pentretan   Gerdinen   Rhydyfro

Broadlay   Broadway   Mynyddgarreg   Pontyates   Cynheidre   Sylen   Llanedi   Glan-yr-afon   Pentrebach   Gelligron   Pontardawe

Llansaint   Llangadeg   1226   Fforest   Craig Trebanos

Tanylon   KIDWELLY   Carway   Five Roads   Hendy   Pontarddulais   Cwm Dulais   Craigcefnparc   Craig-y-Duke

Trimsaran   Glochyrie   Felindre   Eagwyr   Clydach

Pinged   Warm Baglam   Cwm Capel   Felinfoel   Waungron   Llangennech   Pontlliw   Ynystawe   Glais

BURRY PORT   Cwm-bâch   Daren   Grovesend   Pont-lasau

Pembrey   Furnace   Llanelli   Loughor   GORSEINON   Penllergaer   Llangyfelach   Morriston

Dyfatty   Pwll   Machynys   Bwlchymynydd   Kings Bridge   Cadle   Mynydd-Bach   Landore   Winsh-wen

B A Y   Penclawdd   Gowerton   Waunarlwydd   Fforest fach   SWANSEA

Whitford Point   Crofty   Blue Anchor   Three Crosses   Dunvant   Cockett

Llanmorlais   Wernffrwd   Bryn   Killay   Brynmill

Llanmadoc   Cheriton   Weobley   Poundffald   Upper Killay   Blackpill

Landimore   Llanrhidian   Bishopston   West Cross

Burrygreen   Oldwalls   Fairyhill   Parkmill   Ilston   Kittle   Newton   The Mumbles

Llangennith   Burry   Reynoldston   Pennard   Southgate   Mumbles Head

Rhossili   Llanddewi   Knelston   Nicholaston   Penmaen

WORMS HEAD   Middleton   Scurlage   Moorcorner   Penrice   Oxwich   Pwlldu Head

Pilton Green   Oxwich Green   Oxwich Bay

Port-Eynon   Horton

Overton

Port-Eyon Point

SN

WEST   SWANSEA BAY

SCALE

0   1   2   3   4   5 miles

0   1   2   3   4   5 kilometres

SS

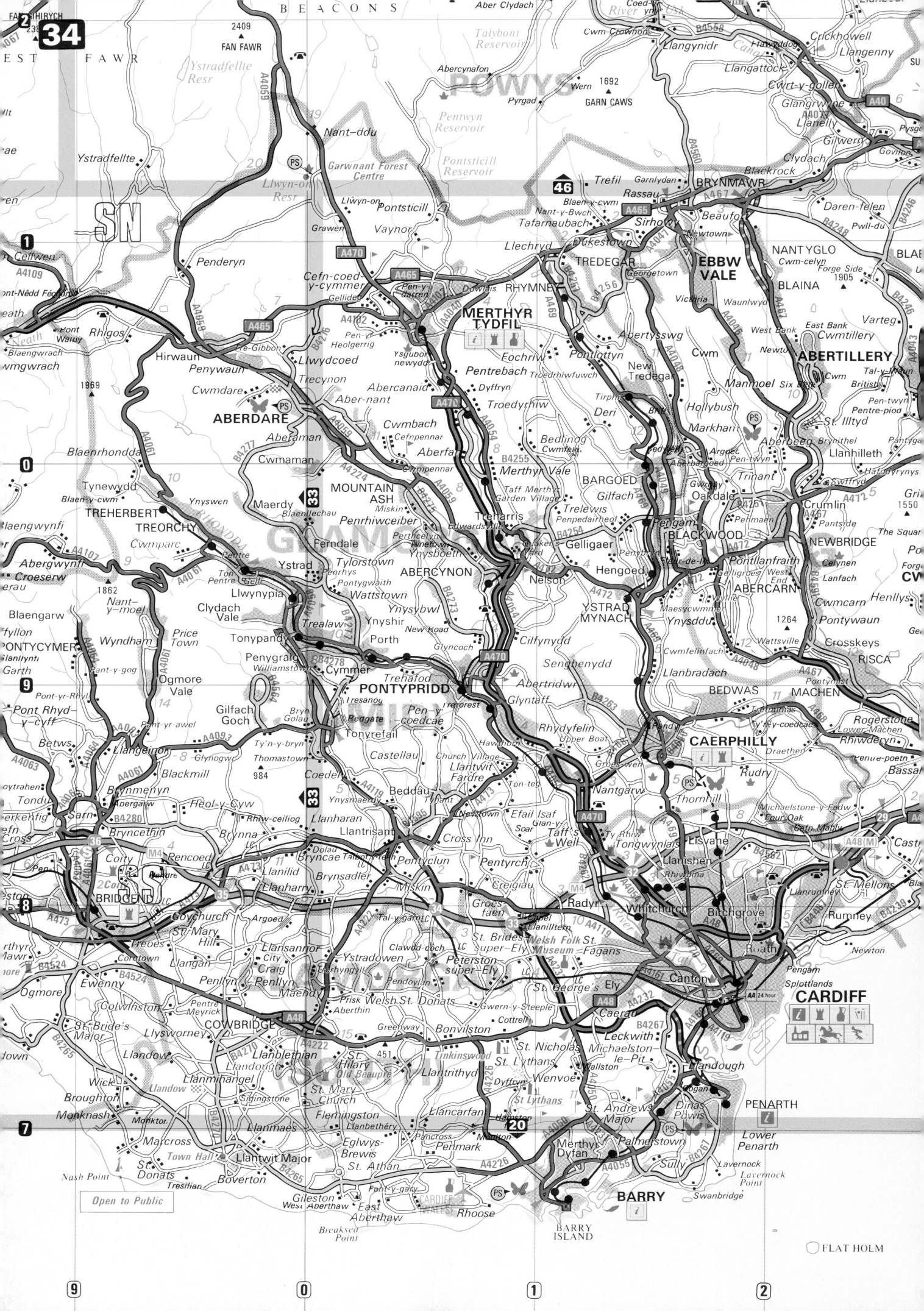
BEACONS
FAWR
FAN FAWR
Ystradfellte Resr
Aber Clydach
Talybont Reservoir
Cwm-Crownon
Llangynidr
Crickhowell
Llangenny
Llangattock
Abercynafon
POWYS
Wern
GARN CAWS
Pyrgad
Cwrt-y-gollen
Glangrwyne
Llanelly
Gilwern
Govilon
Clydach
Blackrock
Nant-ddu
Pentwyn Reservoir
Pontsticill Reservoir
Ystradfellte
Garwnant Forest Centre
Llwyn-on Resr
SN
Trefil
Garnlydan
BRYNMAWR
Rassau
Blaen-y-cwm
Nant-y-Bwch
Tafarnaubach
Sirhowy
Beaufort
Daren-felen
Pwll-du
Llwyn-on
Pontsticill
Grawen
Vaynor
Llechryd
Dukestown
Newtown
TREDEGAR
EBBW VALE
NANTYGLO
Cwm-celyn
Forge Side
BLAINA
Cellwen
Penderyn
Cefn-coed-y-cymmer
Gellideg
Pen-y-darren
Dowlais
RHYMNEY
Georgetown
Victoria
Waunlwyd
Varteg
Pont Walby
Rhigos
Neath
Blaengwrach
Cwmgwrach
Hirwaun
Tre-Gibbon
Llwydcoed
Penywaun
Pen-y-Heolgerrig
Ysgubor-newydd
MERTHYR TYDFIL
Abertysswg
Pontlottyn
New Tredegar
Cwm
West Bank
East Bank
Cwmtillery
ABERTILLERY
Tal-y-Waun
British
Eochriw
Pentrebach
Troedrhiwfuwch
Trecynon
Cwmdare
Abercanaid
Aber-nant
Dyffryn
Troedyrhiw
Tirphil
Deri
Manmoel
Six Bells
Hollybush
Markham
Pen-twyn
Pentre-piod
St. Illtyd
ABERDARE
Aberaman
Cwmbach
Cefnpennar
Aberfan
Bedlinog
Cwmfelin
Bedwellty
Aberbeeg
Brynithel
Llanhilleth
Blaenrhondda
Cwmaman
Cwmpennar
Merthyr Vale
BARGOED
Argoed
Aberbargoed
Pen-twyn
Trinant
Hafodyrynys
Tynewydd
Blaen-y-cwm
MOUNTAIN ASH
Miskin
Taff Merthyr Garden Village
Gilfach
Gwrhay
Oakdale
Swffryd
Crumlin
Ynyswen
Maerdy
Blaenllechau
TREHERBERT
TREORCHY
Penrhiwceiber
Treharris
Trelewis
Penpedairheol
Penmaen
Pantside
The Square
Blaengwynfi
RHONDDA
Cwmparc
GLAMORGAN
Ferndale
Perthcelyn
Edwardsville
Quakers Yard
Gelligaer
Pengam
BLACKWOOD
NEWBRIDGE
Abergwynfi
Croeserw
Pentre
Ton Pentre
Gelli
Ystrad
Tylorstown
Penrhys
Pontygwaith
Ynysboeth
ABERCYNON
Nelson
Hengoed
Penybryn
Fleur-de-lis
Pontllanfraith
Gelligroes
West End
Celynen
Lanfach
Nant-y-moel
Llwynypia
Clydach Vale
Wattstown
Ynysybwl
YSTRAD MYNACH
Maesycwmmer
Ynysddu
ABERCARN
Cwmcarn
Henllys
Blaengarw
PONTYCYMER
Garth
Wyndham
Price Town
Tonypandy
Trealaw
Ynyshir
New Road
Porth
Glyncoch
Cilfynydd
Cwmfelinfach
Wattsville
Pontywaun
Crosskeys
RISCA
Pant-y-gog
Penygraig
Williamstown
Cymmer
Trehafod
Senghenydd
Llanbradach
Ogmore Vale
PONTYPRIDD
Abertridwr
Pontymister
Pont-yr-Rhyl
Pont Rhyd-y-cyff
Gilfach Goch
Tresanog
Bryn Golau
Treforest
Glyntaff
BEDWAS
MACHEN
Trethomas
Ty'n-y-coedcae
Rogerstone
Lower Machen
Rhiwderyn
Betws
Llangeinor
Pant-yr-awel
Ty'n-y-bryn
Redgate
Tonyrefail
Pen-y-coedcae
Rhydyfelin
Upper Boat
Pandy
CAERPHILLY
Draethen
Pentre-poeth
Bassaleg
Glynogwr
Blackmill
Thomastown
Castellau
Church Village
Llantwit Fardre
Hawthorn
Groes-wen
Rudry
Coytrahen
Tondu
Brynmenyn
Abergarw
Coedely
Ynysmaerdy
Beddau
Tynant
Ton-teg
Nantgarw
Thornhill
Michaelstone-y-Fedw
Pound Oak
Cefn Mably
Sarn
Bryncethin
Heol-y-Cyw
Rhiw-ceiling
Llanharan
Llantrisant
Newtown
Efail Isaf
Glan-y-llyn
Soar
Taff's Well
Ty Rhiw
Tongwynlais
Lisvane
Castleton
Coity
Pencoed
Dolau
Bryncae
Talbot Green
Pontyclun
Cross Inn
Pentyrch
Llanishen
Rhiwbina
St. Mellons
Llanrumney
BRIDGEND
Llanilid
Llanharry
Brynsadler
Miskin
Creigiau
Radyr
Whitchurch
Birchgrove
Rumney
Coychurch
Argoed
Tal-y-garn
Groes-faen
Capel Llanilltern
St. Brides-super-Ely
Welsh Folk Museum
St. Fagans
Roath
Newton
Treoes
St. Mary Hill
Corntown
Llansannor
City
Craig
Penllyn
Clawdd-coch
Ystradowen
Peterston-super-Ely
Canton
Pengam
Splottlands
CARDIFF
Ogmore
Ewenny
Llangan
Frerhyngyll
Pendoylan
Maendy
Prisk
Aberthin
Welsh St. Donats
Gwern-y-Steeple
St. George's
Ely
Caerau
Colwinston
Pentre Meyrick
COWBRIDGE
Cottrell
St. Bride's Major
Llysworney
Greenway
Bonvilston
Leckwith
Michaelston-le-Pit
Llandow
Llanblethian
Llandough
St. Hilary
Old Beaupre
Tinkinswood
St. Nicholas
St. Lythans
Wallston
Llandough
Wick
Llandow
Llanmihangel
Llantrithyd
Dyffryn
Wenvoe
Cogan
Broughton
Sigingstone
St. Mary Church
St Lythans
PENARTH
Monknash
Monkton
Flemingston
Llancarfan
Hamston
St. Andrews Major
Dinas Powis
Llanmaes
Llanbethery
Marcross
Pancross
Penmark
Moulton
Merthyr Dyfan
Palmerstown
Lower Penarth
Town Hall
Llantwit Major
Eglwys-Brewis
St. Athan
Nash Point
St. Donats
Tresilian
Boverton
Sully
Lavernock
Lavernock Point
Open to Public
Gileston
West Aberthaw
East Aberthaw
Font-y-gary
CARDIFF (WALES)
Rhoose
BARRY
Swanbridge
Breaksea Point
BARRY ISLAND
FLAT HOLM
9
0
1
2
7
8
SS
Cardiff Bay
Rhymney River
River Usk
River Taff
A470
A465
A4059
A48
A48(M)
A4232
A4119
A473
A4061
A4063
A4067
A4109
A40
A467
A469
A472
A4048
A4046
A4054
A4058
M4
B4265
B4270
B4267
B4280
B4524
1969
1862
1264
1550
1905
984
451
2409
1692

35
MONMOUTH
ABERGAVENNY
CHEPSTOW
NEWPORT
CAERLEON
USK
PORTISHEAD
CLEVEDON
BRISTOL
KINGSWOOD
MANGOTSFIELD
KEYNSHAM
MOUTH OF THE SEVERN
SO
ST
46
47
36
21

36
Lower Buckenhill
Chandos
Sollers Hope
Bounds
Much Marcle
Donnington
Bromsberrow Heath
Greenway
Broome Green
Ryton
52
M50
Portway
Green
White End
Pendock
Long Green
Hardwick Green
Eldersfield
TEWKESBURY
A38
Walton Cardiff
Ashchurch
Pamington
53
Ladyridge
Ballingham
Crossway
Falcon
Lyne Down
Stocking
B4024
Dymock
Redmarley D'Abitot
Playley Green
Lowbands
A417
Forthampton
Linkend
Lime Street
Chaceley
Odda's Chapel
Fiddington
How Caple
Yatton
Kempley
Kempley Green
Poolhill
Hethelpit Cross
Staunton
Pillows Green
Corse Lawn
Town Street
Deerhurst
Apperley
Tredington
Stoke Orchard
3
Fawley Chapel
Kings Caple
A449
Fishpool
Hole-in-the-Wall
Foy
Four Oaks
B4215
Botloe's Green
Brand Green
Oridge Green
Snig's End
B4211
Tirley
B4213
River Severn
Deerhurst Walton
Coombe Hill
Hardwick
Baysham
Brampton Abbotts
Hill of Eaton
Crow Hill
Upton Crews
Upton Bishop
Shaw Common
Oxenhall
Upleadon
The Haw
Piff's Elm
Elmstone Hardwicke
A435
Phocle Green
B4221
Gorsley
Gorsley Common
Hasfield
Lower Apperley
The Stream
Leigh
Corse
Tithe Barn
Blackwellsend Green
Hartpury
Ashleworth
288
Boddington
Swindon
Bridstow
ROSS-ON-WYE
Rudhall
47
Linton
Newent
Kilcot
Little Gorsley
Anthony's Green
Kent's Green
Highleadon
Bishop's Norton
Barrow
Prior's Norton
Uckington
A40
Ashfield
Tudorville
PS
Weston under Penyard
665
Bromsash
Ryeford
Aston Crews
Aston Ingham
Crews Hill
Lea
Glasshouse
Clifford's Mesne
Taynton
Tibberton
Rudford
Woolridge
Sandhurst
Norton
Down Hatherley
Staverton
Staverton Bridge
Golden Valley
Arle
B4228
Coughton
Pontshill
Howle Hill
Goodrich
Boxbush
Glasshouse Hill
Bright's Hill
Highnam Green
Maisemore
A417
Twigworth
GLOUCESTER CHELTENHAM
A38
Up Hatherley
The Reddings
2
Walford
Kerne Bridge
Kiln Green
Hope Mansell
East Dean
B4224
Dursley Cross
Little London
Huntley
Woodgreen
Highnam
Bulley
Over
Longford
A40
Churchdown
Badgeworth
Chargrove
Bentham
Leckhampton
Shurdington
Ruardean
Mitcheldean
Crooked End
A4136
Longhope
Abenhall
Birdwood
Nottswood Hill
Oakle Street
Churcham
Linton
Calcott's Green
Barnwood
Hucclecote
GLOUCESTER
Ullenwood
Lower Lydbrook
Ruardean Woodside
Drybrook
Blaisdon
Upper Ley
A48
Minsterworth
Brockworth
The Butts
A417
A46
Symonds Yat
English Bicknor
Upper Lydbrook
Broadmoor
Nailbridge
Ruardean Hill
Flaxley
Northwood Green
Elmore Back
Hempsted
Elmore
Tuffley
Robinswood Hill
Roman Villa
Little Witcombe
Birdlip
Brierley
Bilson Green
Cinderford
Elton
Westbury Court
Parleys End
Chaxhill
Stantway
Waterend
Quedgeley
Bondend
Upton St. Leonards
Great Witcombe
Stockwell
A417
B4228
Edge End
Dean Hall
A4151
Littledean
Westbury-on-Severn
Hardwicke
Whaddon
Prinknash
Cranham
A4136
B4226
FOREST
Broadoak
Newnham
Boxbush
Four Mile Elm
Brookthorpe
Prinknash Bird Park
Brimpsfield
Five Acres
Cannop
Ruspidge
Longney
Epney
A4173
OF
Mile End
Ruddle
Upper Soudley
Rodley
Milton End
Paradise
Edge
Sheepscombe
Whiteway
Caudle Green
Syde
Broadwell
DEAN
Arlingham
207
Upper Framilode
A38
12
Haresfield
Harescombe
Painswick
Wishanger
Miserden
1
Milkwall
Ancient Iron Mines
B4234
Lower Soudley
B4431
Aylesford
Northington
Saul
Moreton Valence
M5
B4008
Pitchcombe
B4070
The Camp
Winstone
Duntisbourne
Marsh Lane
Parkend
Bran's Green
Awre
Standish
Stroud Green
Slad
Througham
881
Ellwood
Yorkley
Blakeney Hill
Blakeney
Frampton on Severn
B4071
Whitminster
Randwick
Sudgrove
Duntisbourne Abbots
Bream's Meend
Nibley
Ducky
Oldcroft
Etloe
Claypits
13
Westend
Nastend
Whiteshill
A46
Bisley
Edgeworth
Whitecroft
A4419
Alkerton
Stonehouse
Ebley
STROUD
Nashend
Eastcombe
Bournes Green
B4231
Dean Forest Railway Society
Bream
Allaston
A48
Purton
River Severn
Wildfowl Trust
Middle Street
Shepherd's Patch
Eastington
Dudbridge
King's Stanley
Selsley
Bussage
Far Oakridge
Sapperton
St. Briavels
Lydney
Primrose Hill
Purton
Slimbridge
Cambridge
Thrupp
Chalford
Oakridge
Aylburton Common
Newerne
Sharpness
Brookend
Moorend
Frocester
Leonard Stanley
B4066
Woodchester
Brimscombe
Frampton Mansell
Hewelsfield
Tutnalls
Halmore
Gossington
Coaley
St Chloe
Burleigh
Hyde
Woolaston Common
Aylburton
Newtown
Wanswell
PS
Far Green
Amberley
Minchinhampton
Alvington
B4066
Breadstone
A38
Lower Cam
Ashmead Green
Windsoredge
Nympsfield
Crackstone
Cherington
Woolaston
Hook Street
35
Berkeley
B4066
The Quarry
Berkeley Road
Cam
Uley Bury
Crawley
NAILSWORTH
Box
Ball's Green
Tarlton
Ham
Berkeley Heath
Stinchcombe
Uley
Owlpen
B4058
Downend
B4014
Stroat
Dursley
B4066
Woodmancote
Horsley
Avening
Nag's Head
Rodmarton
Barton End
Widdon
Bevington
Newport
Lower Wick
Nibley Green
A4135
812
Tiltups End
Millend
Nupdown
Hystfield
Woodford
Pitt Court
Culkerton
Upper Hill
North Nibley
B4060
Kingscote
Chavenage
Tetbury Upton
Ashley
Shepperdine
Hill
Stone
B4058
Bournstream
A4135
Lower Stone
Damery
Newington Bagpath
Beverston
Chelworth
Oldbury Naite
Rockhampton
Tortworth
Wotton-under-Edge
Lasborough
Tetbury
Crudwell
14
Falfield
B4509
B4058
Kingswood
Boxwell
A46
Long Newnton
Oldbury-on-Severn
Lower Morton
Wortley
B4014
Pullens Green
Whitfield
Bibstone
Charfield
Leighterton
Murcott
Cowhill
Littleton-on-Severn
Milbury Heath
Townwell
Talbot's End
B4060
Alderley
Tresham
A433
Doughton
Hankerton
Morton
9
Kington
Cromhall
Cromhall Common
Hillesley
Westonbirt Arboretum
Lower Kilcott
Brokenborough
Filands
21
Thornbury
B4061
Gravesend
Westonbirt
Shipton Moyne
Charlton
Elberton
A38
West End
Upper Kilcott
Oldbury on the Hill
Starveall
Willesley
MALMESBURY
B4461
Olveston
Old Down
Alveston
Wickwar
Hawkesbury Upton
Knockdown
Tytherington
Didmarton
Easton Grey
Milbourne
Ingst
Northwick
M4
Green Hill
Itchington
B4060
Hawkesbury
Foxley
Lea
Awkley
Rudgeway
Bagstone
Rangeworthy
Dunkirk
Sopworth
Sherston
B4042
Tockington
Woodhouse Down
Earthcott Green
Horton Court
657
Foxley Green
Almondsbury
M5
B4059
B4058
Horton
B4040
A429
Little Somerford
Latteridge
Gaunt's Earthcott
Engine Common
A46
Petty France
Luckington
Corston
Over
20
16
Iron Acton
Little Sodbury
Little Badminton
Little Sodbury End
Badminton
Norton
Alderton
B4427
B4058
Nibley
Chipping Sodbury
Great Badminton
New Town
Rodbourne
Frampton Cotterell
Yate
Old Sodbury
Hullavington
Startley
Lower Seagry
Patchway
Watley's End
Great Stoke
35
Coalpit Heath
A432
Dodington
Lower Stanton St. Quintin
17
Catbrain
B4057
Winterbourne
Rodford
Acton Turville
B4040
Littleton Drew
Grittleton
Upper Seagry
8
Cribb's Causeway
A38
Stoke Gifford
Ram Hill
Wapley
Doddington
Leigh Delamere
Stanton St. Quintin
17
Filton
Westerleigh
Kendleshire
B4465
Burton
B4039
Sutton Benger
B4056
19
Moorend
Codrington
Tormarton
Nettleton
Sevington
AA info
Upper Draycot
A4174
1
Hambrook
M4
A420
Horfield
M32
MANGOTSFIELD
18
Hinton
22
Castle Combe
Kington St. Michael
A429
Foxham
Frenchay
Lockleaze
B4058
Blackhorse
Pucklechurch
West Kington
Castle Combe
Kington Langley
Stapleton
Downend
Dyrham Park
8
Yatton Keynell
6
Redland
Soundwell
B4465
7
Dyrham
A46
West Littleton
North Wraxall
Ford
West Yatton
Allington
9
PS

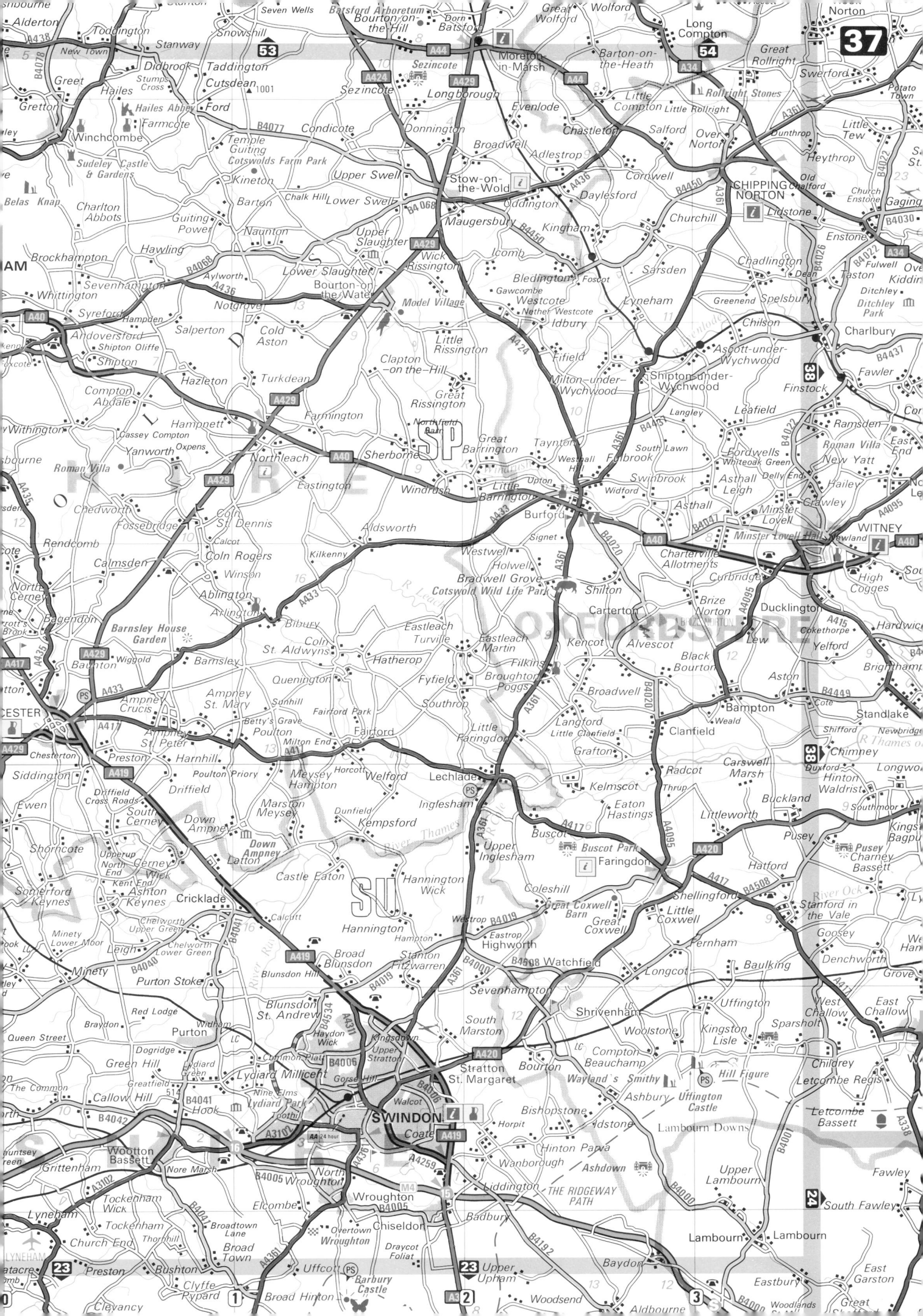
Alderton
Toddington
Snowshill
Seven Wells
Batsford Arboretum
Bourton-on-the-Hill
Dorn
Batsford
Great Wolford
Wolford
Long Compton
Norton
Stanway
New Town
Didbrook
Taddington
Cutsdean
Sezincote
Moreton-in-Marsh
Barton-on-the-Heath
Great Rollright
Swerford
Greet
Hailes
Gretton
Stumps Cross
Longborough
Little Compton
Little Rollright
Rollright Stones
Hailes Abbey
Ford
Farmcote
Evenlode
Chastleton
Salford
Over Norton
Little Tew
Winchcombe
Temple Guiting
Cotswolds Farm Park
Condicote
Donnington
Broadwell
Adlestrop
Dunthrop
Heythrop
Sudeley Castle & Gardens
Kineton
Upper Swell
Stow-on-the-Wold
Cornwell
Daylesford
CHIPPING NORTON
Old Chalford
Church Enstone
Belas Knap
Charlton Abbots
Barton
Chalk Hill
Lower Swell
Oddington
Churchill
Lidstone
Guiting Power
Naunton
Upper Slaughter
Maugersbury
Kingham
Enstone
Brockhampton
Hawling
Wick Rissington
Icomb
Chadlington
Fulwell
Lower Slaughter
Bledington
Foscot
Sarsden
Dean
Taston
Sevenhampton
Aylworth
Bourton-on-the-Water
Gawcombe
Westcote
Nether Westcote
Ditchley
Whittington
Notgrove
Model Village
Lyneham
Greenend
Spelsbury
Ditchley Park
Syreford
Hampden
Idbury
Chilson
Charlbury
Andoversford
Shipton Oliffe
Salperton
Cold Aston
Little Rissington
Ascott-under-Wychwood
Shipton
Fifield
Shipton-under-Wychwood
Fawler
Hazleton
Turkdean
Clapton-on-the-Hill
Milton-under-Wychwood
Finstock
Compton Abdale
Great Rissington
Leafield
Withington
Hampnett
Cassey Compton
Farmington
Northfield Barn
Langley
Ramsden
Yanworth
Oxpens
Great Barrington
Taynton
South Lawn
Roman Villa
East End
Roman Villa
Northleach
Sherborne
Westhall Hill
Fulbrook
Fordwells
Whiteoak Green
New Yatt
Eastington
Windrush
Little Barrington
Upton
Swinbrook
Widford
Asthall Leigh
Delly End
Hailey
Chedworth
Coln St. Dennis
Burford
Asthall
Crawley
Fossebridge
Minster Lovell
Aldsworth
Signet
Minster Lovell Hall
Newland
WITNEY
Rendcomb
Calcot
Coln Rogers
Kilkenny
Westwell
Charterville Allotments
Calmsden
Winson
Holwell
Curbridge
High Cogges
North Cerney
Ablington
Bradwell Grove
Cotswold Wild Life Park
Shilton
Brize Norton
Ducklington
Arlington
Carterton
Bagendon
Bibury
OXFORDSHIRE
Barnsley House Garden
Eastleach Turville
Eastleach Martin
Hardwick
Cokethorpe
Coln St. Aldwyns
Kencot
Alvescot
Lew
Yelford
Baunton
Wiggold
Barnsley
Hatherop
Filkins
Black Bourton
Brighthampton
Quenington
Fyfield
Broughton Poggs
Aston
Ampney St. Mary
Sunhill
Southrop
Broadwell
Cote
Standlake
CIRENCESTER
Ampney Crucis
Fairford Park
Bampton
Betty's Grave
Langford
Little Clanfield
Weald
Poulton
Fairford
Little Faringdon
Clanfield
Shifford
Newbridge
Ampney St. Peter
Milton End
Grafton
Chesterton
Harnhill
Chimney
Preston
Siddington
Poulton Priory
Horcott
Welford
Lechlade
Radcot
Carswell Marsh
Duxford
Longworth
Driffield
Meysey Hampton
Kelmscott
Hinton Waldrist
Driffield Cross Roads
Thrup
Eaton Hastings
Ewen
South Cerney
Marston Meysey
Dunfield
Inglesham
Buckland
Southmoor
Down Ampney
Kempsford
Littleworth
Down Ampney
Buscot
Buscot Park
Pusey
Kingston Bagpuize
Shorncote
Upperup
River Thames
Upper Inglesham
Pusey
Charney Bassett
North End
Cerney Wick
Latton
Faringdon
Hatford
Kent End
Castle Eaton
Hannington Wick
Somerford Keynes
Ashton Keynes
Coleshill
Shellingford
Stanford in the Vale
Cricklade
Great Coxwell Barn
Little Coxwell
Chelworth Upper Green
Calcutt
Great Coxwell
Minety Lower Moor
Westrop
Hannington
Eastrop
Highworth
Goosey
Chelworth Lower Green
Hampton
Fernham
Leigh
Broad Blunsdon
Stanton Fitzwarren
Watchfield
Denchworth
Minety
Baulking
Grove
Purton Stoke
Blunsdon Hill
Longcot
Sevenhampton
Blunsdon St. Andrew
Uffington
East Challow
West Challow
Red Lodge
Shrivenham
Braydon
South Marston
Sparsholt
Woolstone
Widham
Kingston Lisle
Queen Street
Purton
Haydon Wick
Kingsdown
Upper Stratton
Dogridge
Common Platt
Compton Beauchamp
Childrey
Green Hill
Lydiard Green
Stratton St. Margaret
Bourton
Lydiard Millicent
Gorse Hill
Wayland's Smithy
Hill Figure
Letcombe Regis
The Common
Greatfield
Nine Elms
Ashbury
Uffington Castle
Callow Hill
Lydiard Park
Walcot
Hook
Toothill
Bishopstone
Letcombe Bassett
SWINDON
Horpit
Idstone
Lambourn Downs
Coate
Wootton Bassett
Hinton Parva
Grittenham
Nore Marsh
North Wroughton
Wanborough
Ashdown
Upper Lambourn
Fawley
Wroughton
Liddington
THE RIDGEWAY PATH
Tockenham Wick
Elcombe
South Fawley
Lyneham
Tockenham
Broadtown Lane
Badbury
Overtown
Chiseldon
Lambourn
Lambourn
Church End
Thornhill
Wroughton
Draycot Foliat
Broad Town
Baydon
East Garston
Preston
Bushton
Uffcott
Barbury Castle
Upper Upham
Eastbury
Clyffe Pypard
Broad Hinton
Woodsend
Aldbourne
Woodlands
Clevancy
SP
SU

38
Brailes
Sibford Gower
Swalcliffe
Broughton
Sutton-under-Brailes
Stourton
Tadmarton
Sibford Ferris
Bloxham
Whichford
Ascott
Hook Norton
Milcombe
Long Compton
Wigginton
Great Rollright
Swerford
Nether Worton
Potato Town
Little Tew
Great Tew
Over Worton
Dunthrop
Heythrop
Sandford St. Martin
Over Norton
CHIPPING NORTON
Old Chalford
Church Enstone
Gagingwell
Lidstone
Enstone
Chadlington
Dean
Taston
Greenend
Spelsbury
Ditchley Park
Chilson
Charlbury
Ascott-under-Wychwood
Shipton-under-Wychwood
Fawler
Finstock
Leafield
Ramsden
Whiteoak Green
Field Assarts
Delly End
Asthall Leigh
Hailey
Crawley
Minster Lovell
Minster Lovell Hall
WITNEY
Curbridge
Brize Norton
Ducklington
Lew
Yelford
Aston
Bampton
Weald
Clanfield
Carswell Marsh
Buckland
Pusey
Hatford
Shellingford
Baulking
Uffington
Kingston Lisle
Sparsholt
Childrey
Letcombe Regis
Letcombe Bassett
Hill Figure
Lambourn Downs
Upper Lambourn
Fawley
Farnborough
WANTAGE
West Challow
East Challow
Charlton
Grove
Denchworth
Goosey
Stanford in the Vale
River Ock
Charney Bassett
Kingston Bagpuize
Southmoor
Hinton Waldrist
Longworth
Duxford
Chimney
Shifford
Standlake
Brighthampton
Hardwick
Cokethorpe
Sutton
Stanton Harcourt
High Cogges
South Leigh
Eynsham
Barnard Gate
Freeland
North Leigh
New Yatt
East End
Combe
Stonesfield
Long Hanborough
Church Hanborough
Begbroke
Cassington
Yarnton
WOODSTOCK
Old Woodstock
Blenheim Palace
Bladon
Wootton
Kiddington
Over Kiddington
Ditchley
Glympton
Tackley
Rousham
Steeple Barton
Westcott Barton
Middle Barton
Ledwell
Duns Tew
North Aston
Deddington
Hempton
South Newington
Barford St John
Barford St. Michael
Clifton
Milton
Adderbury
Bodicote
Twyford Gardens
Newington
Upper Astrop
King's Sutton
Astrop
Charlton
Walton Grounds
Newbottle
Rowler
Aynho
Souldern
Croughton
Farthinghoe
Steane
NORTHAMPTONSHIRE
BRACKLEY
Whitfield
Turweston
Hinton-in-the-Hedges
Evenley
Dadford
Shalstone
Westbury
Chackmore
Stowe
Water Stratford
Finmere
Mixbury
Radclive
Tingewick
Little Tingewick
Cottisford
Newton Purcell
Barton Hartshorn
Preston Bissett
Chetwode
Hethe
Fringford
Godington
Cowley
Twyford
Hardwick
Baynard's Green
Stoke Lyne
Fritwell
Fewcott
Ardley
Somerton
Middle Aston
Steeple Aston
Upper Heyford
Lower Heyford
Caulcott
Bucknell
Bainton
Stratton Audley
Caversfield
Poundon
Charndon
BICESTER
Woodfield
Highfield
Launton
Marsh Gibbon
Edgcott
Calvert
Middleton Stoney
Northbrook
Chesterton
Kirtlington
Wendlebury
Blackthorn
Ambrosden
Ludgershall
Bletchingdon
Weston-on-the-Green
Merton
Arncott
Piddington
Shipton-on-Cherwell
Thrupp
Hampton Poyle
Charlton-on-Otmoor
Fencott
Murcott
Boarstall Duck Decoy
Boarstall
Nature Reserve
Dorton
Brill
Upper Pollicott
Lower Pollicott
Little London
Oxford Airport
Kidlington
Islip
Oddington
Noke
Studley
Beckley
Studley Priory Hotel
Oakley
Water Eaton
Woodeaton
Elsfield
Woodperry
Stanton St. John
Easington
Forest Hill
Worminghall
Peppershill
Ickford
Lower End
Shabbington
Waterperry
Holton
Draycot
Waterstock
Albury
Tiddington
Rycote Chapel
Sunnymead
Wolvercote
Summertown
Binsey
Marston
New Marston
Barton
Headington
Wytham
Swinford
Farmoor
Farmoor Reservoir
Botley
Dean Court
North Hinksey
Osney
West End
Cumnor
Eaton
Cutts End
OXFORD
Iffley
Cowley
Horspath
Wheatley
Cuddesdon
Denton
Blenheim
Littlemore
Garsington
Southend
Great Milton
Great Haseley
Milton Common
Latchford
Little Haseley
Tetsworth
Adwell
Stoke Talmage
Wheatfield
South Weston
Little Milton
Toot Baldon
Marsh Baldon
Chislehampton
Stadhampton
Golden Balls
Berinsfield
Easington
Chalgrove
1643
Pyrton
Newington
Drayton St. Leonard
Cuxham
Berrick Prior
Berrick Salome
Brightwell Baldwin
Warborough
Shillingford
Britwell Salome
Ewelme
Benson
Preston Crowmarsh
WALLINGFORD
Cookley Green
Park Corner
Crowmarsh Gifford
Nuffield
Nettlebed
Highmoor
Wellplace Bird Farm
Hailey
Ipsden
Stoke Row
Checkendon
Exlade Street
Rotherfield Peppard
Greenmoor Hill
Woodcote
Cray's Pond
South Stoke
North Stoke
Moulsford
Streatley
Cholsey
Winterbrook
West End
Aston Tirrold
Aston Upthorpe
South Moreton
North Moreton
Mackney
Brightwell
Blewbury
Upton
East Hagbourne
West Hagbourne
Harwell
Chilton
West Ilsley
East Ilsley
THE RIDGEWAY PATH
871
BERKSHIRE
Catmore
Didcot
Milton
Milton Manor
Railway Museum
Long Wittenham
Little Wittenham
Wittenham Clumps
Pendon
Appleford
Sutton Courtenay
Culham
Dorchester
Burcot
Clifton Hampden
Nuneham Courtenay
Nuneham
Radley
ABINGDON
Caldecott
Sutton Wick
Drayton
Steventon
Priory Cottages
Milton Hill
East Hanney
West Hanney
Ardington
Ardington Wick
West Hendred
East Hendred
West Lockinge
East Lockinge
West Ginge
East Ginge
Marcham
Frilford
Fyfield Wick
Garford
Lyford
Fyfield
Tubney
Shippon
Cothill
Dry Sandford
Sunningwell
Appleton
Bessels Leigh
Wootton
Boars Hill
Sandleigh
Kennington
Sandford-on-Thames
Northmoor
Rock End
Cote
Newbridge
R Thames or Isis
Toll
OXFORDSHIRE
R Cherwell
R Dorn
R Glyme
R Swere
R Great Ouse
R Ray
Roman Villa
Hillesden
Mount
Gawcott
Akeley
SU

39
40
MILTON KEYNES
Passenham
Calverton
Leckhampstead
Upper Weald
Loughton
Shenley Church End
Beachampton
Wavendon
Woburn Sands
Walton
Simpson
Bow Brickhill
Shenley Brook End
Thornton
Thornborough
Nash
Whaddon
BLETCHLEY
Far Bletchley
Fenny Stratford
Little Brickhill
Great Horwood
Singleborough
Little Horwood
Newton Longville
Great Brickhill
Adstock
Winslow
Mursley
Drayton Parslow
Stoke Hammond
Addington
Shipton
North End
Swanbourne
Soulbury
East Claydon
Hoggeston
Stewkley
Stewkley South End
LINSLADE
Granborough
Dunton
Burcott
Wing
Littleworth
North Marston
Ascott
Cublington
Oving
Ledburn
Whitchurch
Quainton
Pitchcott
Aston Abbotts
Nup End
Mentmore
Crafton
Wingrave
Quainton Railway Society
Hardwick
Waddesdon
Weedon
Rowsham
Cheddington
Long Marston
Hulcott
Bierton
AYLESBURY
Upper Winchendon
Burcott
Astrope
Puttenham
Lower Hartwell
Lower Winchendon
Stone
Hartwell
Aston Clinton
Wilstone
Wilstone Green
Buckland
Weston Turville
Upton
Southcourt
Stoke Mandeville
Westlington
Bishopstone
Halton
Ford
Haddenham
North Lee
Kimble Wick
Aston Sandford
Nash Lee
Kimble
Owlswick
Meadle
Kingsey
Ilmer
Ellesborough
Askett
Cadsden
Dunsmore
Longwick
Towersey
The Ford
Pitch Green
Princes Risborough
Henton
Bledlow
Parkfield
Saunderton
Chinnor
Oakley
Crowell
Loosley Row
Lacey Green
Speen
Kingston Blount
Bledlow Ridge
Upper North Dean
Saunderton
Radnage
The City
Bradenham
Stokenchurch
Beacon's Bottom
West Wycombe
West Wycombe Park
Ibstone
Ibstone Common
Cadmore End
HIGH WYCOMBE
Turville
Bolter End
Fingest
Lane End
Summer Heath
Skirmett
Stonor Park
Stonor
Frieth
Chisbridge Cross
Parmoor
Marlow Bottom
Rockwell End
Pheasant's Hill
Fawley
Lower Woodend
Bovingdon Green
Hambleden
MARLOW
Mill End
Lower Assendon
Medmenham
Bisham
Bisham Abbey
Aston
Remenham
Remenham Hill
Hurley
HENLEY ON THAMES
Cockpole Green
Burchett's Green
Littlewick
Harpsden
MAIDENHEAD
Cookham
Cookham Dean
Cookham Rise
Park Corner
Taplow
Burnham
Hedsor
Bourne End
Wooburn
Wooburn Green
Wooburn Moor
Flackwell Heath
Little Marlow
Booker
Loudwater
Wycombe Marsh
Downley
Hazlemere
Naphill
Hughenden Manor
Hughenden Valley
Tylers Green
Penn
Penn Street
Holmer Green
Little Missenden
Great Kingshill
Heath End
Little Kingshill
Prestwood
Bryant's Bottom
Great Missenden
Hampden Row
Hampden
Ballinger Common
Lee Common
Lee Clump
The Lee
Lee Gate
Kingsash
Buckland Common
Chartridge
Bellingdon
South Heath
Hyde Heath
CHESHAM
Chesham Bois
AMERSHAM
Coleshill
Winchmore Hill
Beaconsfield
BEACONSFIELD
Seer Green
Bekonscot Model Village
Chalfont St Giles
Chalfont Common
Jordans
Chalfont St Peter
Gerrards Cross
Hedgerley
Burnham Beeches
Farnham Common
Farnham Royal
Stoke Poges
Stoke Green
Wexham
SLOUGH
Fulmer
Iver Heath
Iver
Denham
Denham Green
New Denham
Uxbridge
North Hillingdon
HILLINGDON
Ickenham
Ruislip
Northolt Park
Eastcote
Northwood
Harefield
West Hyde
Maple Cross
Ratsworth Heath
RICKMANSWORTH
Heronsgate
Chorleywood West
CHORLEYWOOD
Chenies
Latimer
Little Chalfont
Flaunden
Bucks Hill
Chipperfield
Botley
Ley Hill
Lye Green
Whelpley Hill
Ashley Green
Bovingdon
Bulstrode
Tower Hill
Felden
Bourne End
BERKHAMSTED
Northchurch
Cholesbury
Shootersway
HEMEL HEMPSTEAD
Boxmoor
Two Waters
Kings Langley
Abbots Langley
Bedmond
Pimlico
Primrose Hill
WATFORD
Sarratt
Chandler's Cross
Croxley Green
South Oxhey
Oxhey
Eastbury
Wendover
Hastoe
Wigginton
THE RIDGEWAY PATH
THE THREE HUNDREDS OF AYLESBURY
St. Leonards
TRING
Tring Wharf
New Mill
Bulbourne
Marsworth
Pitstone
Ivinghoe
Ivinghoe Aston
Horton
Slapton
Billington
Edlesborough
Northall
Eaton Bray
Eaton Green
Totternhoe
Stanbridge
Eggington
Ledburn
LEIGHTON BUZZARD
The Heath
Heath and Reach
Hockliffe
Potsgrove
Battlesden
Woburn
Woburn Abbey
Aspley Guise
Husborne Crawley
Birchmoor Green
Eversholt
Tingrith
Harlington
Westoning
Flitwick
Toddington
Tebworth
Wingfield
Chalton
Tilsworth
Puddlehill
Houghton Regis
DUNSTABLE
Dunstable Downs
Whipsnade
Kensworth
Kensworth Common
Caddington
Slip End
Studham
Dagnall
Ringshall
Little Gaddesden
Ashridge Management College
Aldbury
Dudswell
Nettleden
Frithsden
Great Gaddesden
Water End
Potten End
Piccotts End
Markyate
Flamstead
Redbourn
Gaddesden Row
Jockey End
Clement's End
Leagrave
Sundon Park
Lower Sundon
Upper Sundon
Streatley
Sharpenhoe
Barton in the Clay
Pulloxhill
Greenfield
Flitton
Silsoe
AMPTHILL
Maulden
Clophill
Millbrook
Lidlington
Brogborough
Ridgmont
Holcot
Steppingley
Hexton
Lilley
LUTON
HARPENDEN
Gorhambury
Verulamium Theatre
Stopsley
Limbury
Eastcote

40
MILTON KEYNES
Wavendon
Woburn Sands
Holcot
Lidlington
Brogborough
Millbrook
Clophill
Beadlow
Shefford
Henlow
Hall End
Maulden
Upper Gravenhurst
Campton
Meppershall
AMPTHILL
Ridgmont
Husborne Crawley
Aspley Guise
Walton
Simpson
Bow Brickhill
BLETCHLEY
Fenny Stratford
Little Brickhill
Woburn
Woburn Abbey
Eversholt
Steppingley
Flitwick
Flitton
Greenfield
Silsoe
Wrest Park
56
Lower Gravenhurst
Shillington
Upper Stondon
Arlesey
Higham Gobion
Pulloxhill
Westoning
Harlington
Tingrith
Milton Bryan
Potsgrove
Great Brickhill
Newton Longville
Barton in the Clay
Apsley End
Holwell
Ickleford
Pirton
Hexton
Pegsdon
HITCHIN
Wellbury
Little Offley
Sharpenhoe
Streatley
Upper Sundon
Lower Sundon
Sundon Park
Toddington
Battlesden
Heath and Reach
Stoke Hammond
Drayton Parslow
Soulbury
Hockliffe
Tebworth
LEIGHTON BUZZARD
LINSLADE
Stewkley
Wing
Dunton
Wingfield
Chalton
Fancott
Eggington
Tilsworth
Stanbridge
Houghton Regis
Leagrave
Limbury
Stopsley
LUTON
LUTON AIRPORT
Lilley
Great Offley
Preston
Gosmore
King's Walden
Cockernhoe Green
Breachwood Green
Ascott
Cublington
Ledburn
Billington
Totternhoe
Eaton Bray
DUNSTABLE
Church End
Caddington
Kensworth
Slip End
Luton Hoo
Kimpton
Whitwell
Codicote
Mentmore
Wingrave
Aston Abbotts
Rowsham
Cheddington
Horton
Edlesborough
Dunstable Downs
Whipsnade
Ivinghoe
Ivinghoe Aston
Kensworth Common
Markyate
East Hyde
HARPENDEN
Weedon
Long Marston
Hulcott
Bierton
Pitstone
Dagnall
Studham
Flamstead
Marsworth
Puttenham
Wilstone
Aston Clinton
Buckland
TRING
New Mill
Aldbury
Ringshall
Little Gaddesden
Great Gaddesden
Redbourn
Wheathampstead
Weston Turville
Halton
Wendover
Wigginton
Hastoe
THE RIDGEWAY PATH
Northchurch
Berkhamsted
Nettleden
Potten End
Piccotts End
HEMEL HEMPSTEAD
ST. ALBANS
Verulamium Theatre
Gorhambury
Sandridge
THE THREE HUNDREDS OF AYLESBURY
St. Leonards
Cholesbury
BERKHAMSTED
Ellesborough
Dunsmore
Buckland Common
Lee Clump
The Lee
Hampden
Princes Risborough
Bellingdon
Chartridge
Ashley Green
Whelpley Hill
Bourne End
Bovingdon
Felden
Chiswellgreen
London Colney
De Havilland Mosquito Aircraft Museum
Great Missenden
CHESHAM
South Heath
Botley
Chipperfield
Kings Langley
Abbots Langley
Bricket Wood
Shenleybury
Shenley
Radlett
26
Prestwood
Little Kingshill
Hyde Heath
Flaunden
Latimer
Sarratt
Chenies
WATFORD
Aldenham
Great Kingshill
Chesham Bois
Little Missenden
AMERSHAM
Little Chalfont
CHORLEYWOOD
Chandler's Cross
Letchmore Heath
Borehamwood
Naphill
Hughenden Valley
Holmer Green
Coleshill
Penn Street
Croxley Green
BUSHEY
Elstree
Hazlemere
Winchmore Hill
Chalfont St. Giles
Heronsgate
RICKMANSWORTH
Oxhey
Bushey Heath
HIGH WYCOMBE
Downley
Tylers Green
Penn
Bekonscot Model Village
Seer Green
Chalfont Common
Maple Cross
West Hyde
Harefield
Stanmore
Edgware
Loudwater
Wycombe Marsh
Jordans
BEACONSFIELD
Northwood
Pinner
HARROW
Wealdstone
Kenton
Kingsbury
Flackwell Heath
Wooburn Green
Chalfont St. Peter
Gerrards Cross
Denham Green
Eastcote
Ruislip
Harrow on the Hill
Wembley
Little Marlow
MARLOW
Bourne End
Hedsor
Hedgerley
Burnham Beeches
Denham
Ickenham
Northolt
BRENT
Cookham
Cliveden
Farnham Common
Fulmer
Iver Heath
Uxbridge
Cookham Dean
Cookham Rise
Farnham Royal
Stoke Poges
HILLINGDON
Greenford
Perivale
Hurley
Taplow
MAIDENHEAD
Burnham
SLOUGH
Cowley
Yeading
EALING
Southall

The Thrift
Newnham
Odsey
Therfield
Barley
Smith's End
Chrishall
Shaftenhoe End
Little Chishill
Bridge Green
Wendens Ambo
Audley End
Radwinter
Sewards End
Wimbish
Cole End
Tye Green
Upper Green
Wimbish Green
Reed
Kelshall
Slip End
Bygrave
56
57
Chapel Green
Reed End
Barkway
Nuthampstead
Duddenhoe End
Langley
Audley End Station
Arkesden
Elder Street
Debden
Howlett End
Wallington
Roe Green
Sandon
Green End
Buckland
Lower Green
Anstey
Bird Green
Stickling Green
Hill Green
Newport
BALDOCK
Quickswood
Redhill
Mill End
Shaw Green
Chipping
Rushden
Roast Green
Clavering
Wicken Bonhunt
Debden Green
Debden Cross
Boyton End
Thaxted
Clothall
Green End
Weston
Snow End
Meesden
Cole Green
Wyddial
Blackhall
Brent Pelham
Rickling
Starling's Green
Mole Hall
Widdington
Cutler's Green
Hamperden End
Bardfield End Green
Throcking
Buntingford
Great Hormead
Borley Green
Berden
Quendon
Little London
Rickling Green
Woodend Green
Luffenhall
Warren's Green
Hall's Green
Cottered
Hare Street
Little Hormead
Stocking Pelham
Maggots End
Monk Street
Sibley's Green
Cromer
Stonebury
Furneux Pelham
Barleycroft End
Pinchpools
Ugley
Henham
Aspenden
Ardeley
Muncher's Green
Westmill
Patient End
East End
Ugley Green
Broxted
Duton Hill
Lindsell
Bassus Green
Hay Street
Patmore Heath
Manuden
Gallow Green
Walkern
Wood End
Farnham Green
Bentfield
Elsenham
Tilty
Great Easton
Duck End
STEVENAGE
Clay End
Braughing
Chatter End
Gaunt's End
Brick End
Aston End
Rush Green
Nasty
Hamels
Braughing Friars
Albury
Clapgate
Farnham
Fuller's End
Stansted Mountfitchet
Molehill Green
Butcher's Pasture
Benington
Great Munden
Puckeridge
Albury End
Level's Green
Hazeland
Burton End
Little Easton
Shephall
Levens Green
Little Hadham
Birchanger
Bamber's Green
Great Dunmow
Aston
Hebing End
Haultwick
Green End
Westland Green
Stansted Airport
Takeley
Canfield End
Broadwater
Bragbury End
Standon
Wellpond Green
Hadham Ford
Cradle End
Bury Green
Takeley Street
Old Hall Green
Whempstead
Dane End
Collier's End
BISHOP'S STORTFORD
Brewers End
Hope End Green
Bacon End
Knebworth
Watton-at-Stone
Potter's Green
Latchford
Thorley Houses
Thorley
Puttock's End
Barnston
Sacombe
Standon Green End
Much Hadham
Great Hallingbury
Great Canfield
Philpot End
Bishop's Green
Datchworth
Barwick
Woolmer Green
High Cross
Kettle Green
Hadham Cross
Spellbrook
Little Hallingbury
Taverners
High Roding
Tonwell
Baker's End
Trims Green
Allen's Green
Perry Green
Wright's Green
Broad Green
Street
Rodingbury
Stapleford
Burnham Green
Wadesmill
Hatfield Heath
Hatfield Broad Oak
Aythorpe Roding
Bramfield
Chapmore End
WARE
Babbs Green
SAWBRIDGEWORTH
Gaston Green
High Easter
Harmer Green
Widford
White Roding
Roundbush Green
Tewin
Waterford
Wareside
Hunsdon
Lower Sheering
Ardley End
Leaden Roding
Clatterford End
HERTFORD
Panshanger
Great Amwell
Gilston
High Wych
Sheering
Good Easter
WELWYN GARDEN CITY
Little Amwell
Stanstead Abbots
Eastwick
Pye Corner
Churchgate Street
Newman's End
Matching
Margaret Roding
Cole Green
Hertingfordbury
Matching Tye
Abbess Roding
Fambridge End
Chalk End
St. Margarets
Matching Green
Hertford Heath
Hailey
HARLOW
Woodend
Pepper's Green
Letty Green
Woollensbrook
Eastend
Hobbs Cross
Potter Street
High Laver
Little Laver
Beauchamp Roding
Boyton Cross
Roxwell
Essendon
West End
HODDESDON
Roydon
Foster Street
Loyter's Green
THE RODINGS
Hatfield
Bayford
Hacketts
Broxbourne
Great Parndon
Magdalen Laver
Norwood End
Shellow Bowells
Birds Green
Little Berkhamsted
Epping Green
Broadley Common
Rye Hill
Hastingwood
Miller's Green
Willingale
Broxbourne
Moreton
Fyfield
West End
Nazeing
Keysers Estate
Lower Nazeing
Nazeing Gate
Epping Green
Thornwood Common
Tyler's Green
Bovinger
Bobbingworth
Norton Mandeville
Norton Heath
Newgate Street
Wormley
Appleby Street
Nazeing Long Green
Bumble's Green
Shelley
High Ongar
North Weald Basset
Hammond Street
Turnford
Epping Upland
Woodside
Greensted
Brookmans Park
Goff's Oak
Holyfield
Coopersale Common
Chipping Ongar
King Street
Nine Ashes
Cuffley
Churchgate
CHESHUNT
Coopersale Street
Toot Hill
Marden Ash
Blackmore
Northaw
Waltham Abbey
Upshire
EPPING
Colliers Hatch
Paslow Wood Common
POTTERS BAR
Crews Hill Station
Copthall Green
Fiddlers Hamlet
Stanford Rivers
Mill Green
Stondon Massey
Fryerning
Waltham Cross
Theydon Bois
27
Little End
Hare Street
Wyatt's Green
Bull's Cross
Forty Hill
Enfield Lock
Debden Green
Stapleford Tawney
Kelvedon Hatch
Botany Bay
Ganwick Corner
Hadley Wood
Enfield Wash
High Beach
Hobbs Cross
Passingford Bridge
Navestock
Fox Hatch
Doddinghurst
Forty Hall
ENFIELD
Abridge
Mountnessing
Cockfosters
Ponders End
Sewardstonebury
Loughton
Stapleford Abbotts
Navestock Side
Bentley
Crow Green
Pilgrims Hatch
New Barnet
East Barnet
Winchmore Hill
Epping Forest Museum
Lambourne End
Horseman Side
Coxtie Green
Bournebridge
Southgate
Chingford
Shenfield
Hutton
South Weald
Edmonton
Buckhurst Hill
Chigwell
Chigwell Row
Noak Hill
BRENTWOOD
Friern Barnet
Wood Green
Tottenham
Woodford Green
Grange Hill
Hainault
Havering-atte-Bower
Harrold Hill
Brook Street
Ingrave
Herongate
WALTHAM FOREST
Woodford Bridge
Collier Row
Gidea Park
Harold Wood
Great Warley
Little Warley
Finchley
HARINGEY
Barkingside
REDBRIDGE
Romford
Squirrel's Heath
Hornsey
Walthamstow
Seven Kings
Hornchurch
HAVERING
Cranham
West Horndon
Golders Green
Highgate
Stoke Newington
Wanstead
Leyton
Rush Green
Bulphan
Hampstead
ISLINGTON
HACKNEY
Ilford
Becontree
BARKING
Upminster
Elm Park
Hacton
North Ockendon
CAMDEN
Forest Gate
West Ham
Bethnal Green
Dagenham
South Hornchurch
Shoreditch
Eastbury Manor
East Ham
Finsbury
CITY OF LONDON
TOWER HAMLETS
Plaistow
NEWHAM
Creekmouth
Rainham
South Ockendon
Baker Street
St. Marylebone
Poplar
Canning Town
Beckton
River Thames
Thamesmead
Orsett
CITY OF WESTMINSTER

Radwinter
Hempstead
Chapelend Way
Dyer's End
Stambourne
Stambourne Green
Robinhood End
Gestingthorpe
Bulmer Tye
Little Cornard
Great Henny
Henny Street
Assington
Spain's End
Great Sampford
Toppesfield
Le Hurst
Cornish Hall End
Pool Street
Audley End
Colne Valley
Wickham St. Paul
Twinstead
Workhouse Green
Rose Green
King Tye
Wimbish
Cole End
River Pant
Gainsford End
Delvin Green
Delvin End
Castle Hedingham
Twinstead Green
Great Maplestead
Lucking Street
Alphamstone
Lamarsh
Honey Tye
Bures Green
Tye Green
Upper Green
Wimbish Green
Little London
Highstreet Green
Elder Street
Debden
Howlett End
Howe Street
Morris Green
Sible Hedingham
A604
Little Maplestead
Cross End
Bures
Wissington
Spain's Hall
Doe's Corner
Pebmarsh
Debden Green
Debden Cross
Little Sampford
Boyton End
Hawkspur Green
Guildhall and Museum
Finchingfield
Daw Street
Forry's Green
Southey Cross
Mount Bures
Mole Hall
Cutler's Green
Thaxted
Little Bardfield
Bardfield End Green
Bridge End
Wethersfield
Whiteash Green
A131
Colne Engaine
Wakes Colne Green
Wormingford
Hamperden End
Great Bardfield
Waltham's Cross
Blackmore End
HALSTEAD
Countess Cross
Bardfield Cottage
Gosfield
White Colne
Wakes Colne
Chappel & Wakes Colne Station
Monk Street
Sibley's Green
Holder's Green
Oxen End
Shalford Church End
Beazley End
Earls Colne
Rose Green
Chappel
Fordham
Henham
Lindsell
Bardfield Saling
Shalford Green
Greenstead Green
Burton's Green
Swan Street
Fordstreet
Duton Hill
Broxted
Tilty
Gallow Green
Duck End
Great Easton
Crow's Green
Jasper's Green
High Garrett
Folly Green
Tumbler's Green
Great Tey
Dowsland Green
Eight Ash Green
Brick End
Bran End
Great Saling
Bocking Churchstreet
Markshall
Aldham
Gaunt's End
Butcher's Pasture
Stebbing Park
Stebbing
Panfield
Stisted
Pattiswick Green
Little Tey
Marks Tey
Molehill Green
Little Easton
Bocking
Bradwell
Coggeshall
Broad Green
Tilkey
Stanway
Bamber's Green
Great Dunmow
Church End
Stebbing Green
Blake End
Rayne
BRAINTREE
Stockstreet
Paycocke's
Surrex
Copford Green
A120
Takeley
Canfield End
Bannister Green
Molehill Green
White Court
Beddall's End
Perry Green
Blackwater
Skye Green
Langley Green
Pott's Green
Heckfordbridge
Hope Green
Little Dunmow
Row Green
Black Notley
Tye Green
Cressing
Coggeshall Hamlet
Feering
Easthorpe
Pledgdon Green
Willows Green
The Green
Hawbush Green
Silver End
Gore Pit
Hardy's Green
Bacon End
Barnston
North End
Felsted
Young's End
Messing
Birch Green
Philpot End
Causeway End
Cock Green
White Notley
Kelvedon
Haynes Green
Great Canfield
Wellstye Green
Hartford End
Littley Green
Great Leighs
Rank's Green
Faulkbourne
Inworth
Smythe's Green
Taverners Green
Bishop's Green
Little Leighs
Fairstead
Layer Marney
Layer Marney Tower
Broad Street Green
High Roding
Hounslow Green
Rivenhall End
Tiptree
High Rodingbury
Hatfield Broad Oak
Aythorpe Roding
High Easter
Ford End
Fuller Street
Chipping Hill
Powershall End
Little Braxted
Tiptree Heath
Tolleshunt Knights
White Roding
Roundbush Green
Stagden Cross
Howe Street
R Ter
Terling
WITHAM
Great Braxted
Oxley Green
Leaden Roding
Clatterford End
Pleshey
Chatham Green
Great Totham
Great Waltham
Broad's Green
Little Waltham
Russell Green
Wickham Bishops
Margaret Roding
Good Easter
Chignall Smealy
Hatfield Peverel
Little Totham
Tollesbury
Abbess Roding
Pembridge End
Mashbury
Great Totham
Nounsley
Tolleshunt Major
Woodend
Chalk End
Pepper's Green
THE RODINGS
Broomfield
Tolleshunt D'Arcy
Beauchamp Roding
Boyton Cross
Roxwell
Chignall St. James
Boreham
Ulting
Wick
Langford
Goldhanger
Norwood End
Shellow Bowells
Birds Green
Miller's Green
Little Baddow
Beeleigh Abbey
Heybridge
River Blackwater
Canal
Springfield
CHELMSFORD
Woodham Walter
Heybridge Basin
OSEA IS
The Stone
Fyfield
Willingale
Cooksmill Green
Great Oxney Green
Elm Green
Danbury
MALDON
NORTHEY IS
Norton Mandeville
Norton Heath
Writtle
Widford
Great Baddow
Sandon
Woodham Mortimer
Shelley
High Ongar
Gay Bowers
Hazeleigh
Loves Green
Hylands
Galleyend
Howe Green
Butt's Green
Rudley Green
Mundon Hill
Lower Mayland
Chipping Ongar
King Street
Nine Ashes
Bicknacre
Cock Clarks
Purleigh
Roundbush
Mayland
Maylandsea
Paslow Wood Common
Blackmore
Handley Green
Galleywood
Farther Howegreen
Stondon Massey
Mill Green
Margaretting
Margaretting Tye
West Hanningfield
East Hanningfield
Chapel Row
Stow Maries
Latchingdon
Snoreham
Fryerning
Woodham Ferrers
Cold Norton
Althorne
Ingatestone
Stock
Wyatt's Green
Hanningfield Reservoir
South Hanningfield
Doddinghurst
Fox Hatch
Heybridge
South Hanningfield Tye
Rettendon
Fambridge Station
Ostend
North Fambridge
South Woodham Ferrers
Mountnessing
Ramsden Heath
Coalhill
Rettendon Place
Bentley
Crow Green
Pilgrims Hatch
Downham
South Fambridge
Coxtie Green
Havering's Grove
BILLERICAY
Ramsden Bellhouse
Runwell
R Crouch
Hullbridge
Canewdon
South Weald
Shenfield
Hutton
South Green
Battlesbridge
Rawreth
Hockley Hall
Hockley
Ashingdon
Paglesham
BRENTWOOD
Little Burstead
Crays Hill
Wickford
Mill Hill
Ballards Gore
Brook Street
Ingrave
Shotgate
Hawkwell
Great Stambridge
Herongate
Great Burstead
Nevendon
Rochford
Stroud Green
Great Warley
Dunton Wayletts
North Benfleet
RAYLEIGH
Barling
Little Warley
SOUTHEND AIRPORT
Aircraft
R Roach
BASILDON
Laindon
Pitsea
Thundersley
Stonebridge
Burton
Little Wakering
HAVERING
Cranham
East Horndon
Dunton Hall
West Horndon
Langdon Hills
Lee Chapel
Vange
Bowers Gifford
Daws Heath
Eastwood
Jordons
Westley Heights
SOUTH BENFLEET
Hadleigh
Prittlewell
Bournes Green
Great Wakering
Upminster
Garlesters
Bulphan
Great Malgraves
One Tree Hill
Moat's Green
Hadleigh
Leigh-on-Sea
Southchurch
North Shoebury
Thorpe Bay
Westcliff-on-Sea
Dutch Cottage
North Ockendon
Horndon on the Hill
Fobbing
Winter Gardens
CANVEY ISLAND
SOUTHEND-ON-SEA
Corringham
Northwick
Balstonia
Baker Street
Stanford le Hope
Coryton
Leigh Beck
South Ockendon
Orsett
Mucking
North Stifford
Thames Haven
TL
TQ
M25
A12
A127
A13
A130
A414
A131
A604
A120
A1017
A128
A129
A132
A176
A1235
A1321
A1159
B1053
B1054
B1051
B1057
B1256
B184
B1008
B1018
B1019
B1022
B1023
B1024
B1026
B1389
B1137
B1417
B1418
B1010
B1012
B1013
B1014
B1015
B1016
B1017
B1020
B1002
B1007
B1009
B1148
B1464
B1420
B1421
B1186
B1335
B1058
B1059

58
59
Shelley
Polstead
Raydon
Wenham
Bentley
Capel St.Mary
Woolverstone
Tattingstone White Horse
Pinmill
River Orwell
Chelmondiston
Thorpe Common
Falkenham
Lower Falkenham
Trimley Heath
Felixstowe Ferry
Mill Street
Lower Raydon
Holton St. Mary
Thorington Street
Higham
East Bergholt
Tattingstone
Alton Water
Holbrook
Lower Street
Trimley
Shotley Street
Walton
Old Felixstowe
Nayland
Stratford St. Mary
Flatford Mill & Lock
East End
Upper Street
Brantham
Stutton
Lower Holbrook
Harkstead
Shop Corner
Erwarton
Shotley Gate
Walton Lower Street
A45
FELIXSTOWE
Boxted
Langham
Boxted Cross
Dedham
Cattawade
Holbrook Bay
River Stour
Wrabness
Bath Side
HARWICH
Parkeston
Manningtree
New Mistley
Mistley
Mistley Towers
B1352
A120
Harwich Harbour
Dovercourt
ZEEBRUGGE
KRISTIANSAND Summer Only
ESBJERG GOTEBORG
HAMBURG HOEK VAN HOLLAND
HIRTSHALLS OSLO
Great Horkesley
Langham Wick
Castle
Ardleigh Heath
Langham Moor
A12
A137
Lawford
Foxash Estate
Ardleigh
Little Bromley
B1035
Bradfield
Bradfield Heath
Ramsey
Upper Dovercourt
Horsleycross Street
Wix
Wix Green
Little Oakley
B1414
TM
COLCHESTER
Parson's Heath
Burnt Heath
Horsley Cross
Goose Green
Stones Green
Great Oakley
Cabbage Row
Mile End
A120
B1029
Great Bromley
Tendring Heath
Tendring Green
Crockleford Heath
Little Bentley
Goose Green
Beaumont
Greenstead
A133
Elmstead Market
Hare Green
Tendring
B1035
Old Heath
Frating Green
Thorpe Green
The Naze
Naze Park
Wivenhoe Cross
Weeley
Thorpe-le-Soken
Kirby le Soken
Walton Ashes
Elmstead Heath
Frating
Great Bentley
B1033
B1034
Upper Kirby
WALTON ON THE NAZE
Rowhedge
Maypole Green
WIVENHOE
Blackheath
B1027
Weeley Heath
Kirby Cross
Malting Green
Alresford
High Park Corner
Tenpenny Heath
Aingers Green
Fingringhoe
Langenhoe
Thorrington
South Green
Row Heath
Cook's Green
Great Holland
Little Clacton
FRINTON-ON-SEA
Abberton
South Heath
Samson's Corner
St Osyth Heath
Great Clacton
B1032
BRIGHTLINGSEA
Hurst Green
St Osyth Priory
B1027
St. Osyth
A133
Holland-on-Sea
B1025
Rush Green
MERSEA ISLAND
East Mersea
Point Clear
St Osyth Marsh
CLACTON-ON-SEA
Seawick Sands
Jaywick
WEST MERSEA
Colne Point
Bradwell Waterside
Sales Point
Bradwell-on-Sea
B1021
Tillingham
Dengie
Old Montsale
Deal Hall
Holliwell Point
East Wick
Foulness Point
Courtsend
Churchend
FOULNESS ISLAND
TR
SCALE
0 1 2 3 4 5 miles
0 1 2 3 4 5 kilometres
0
1
2
3

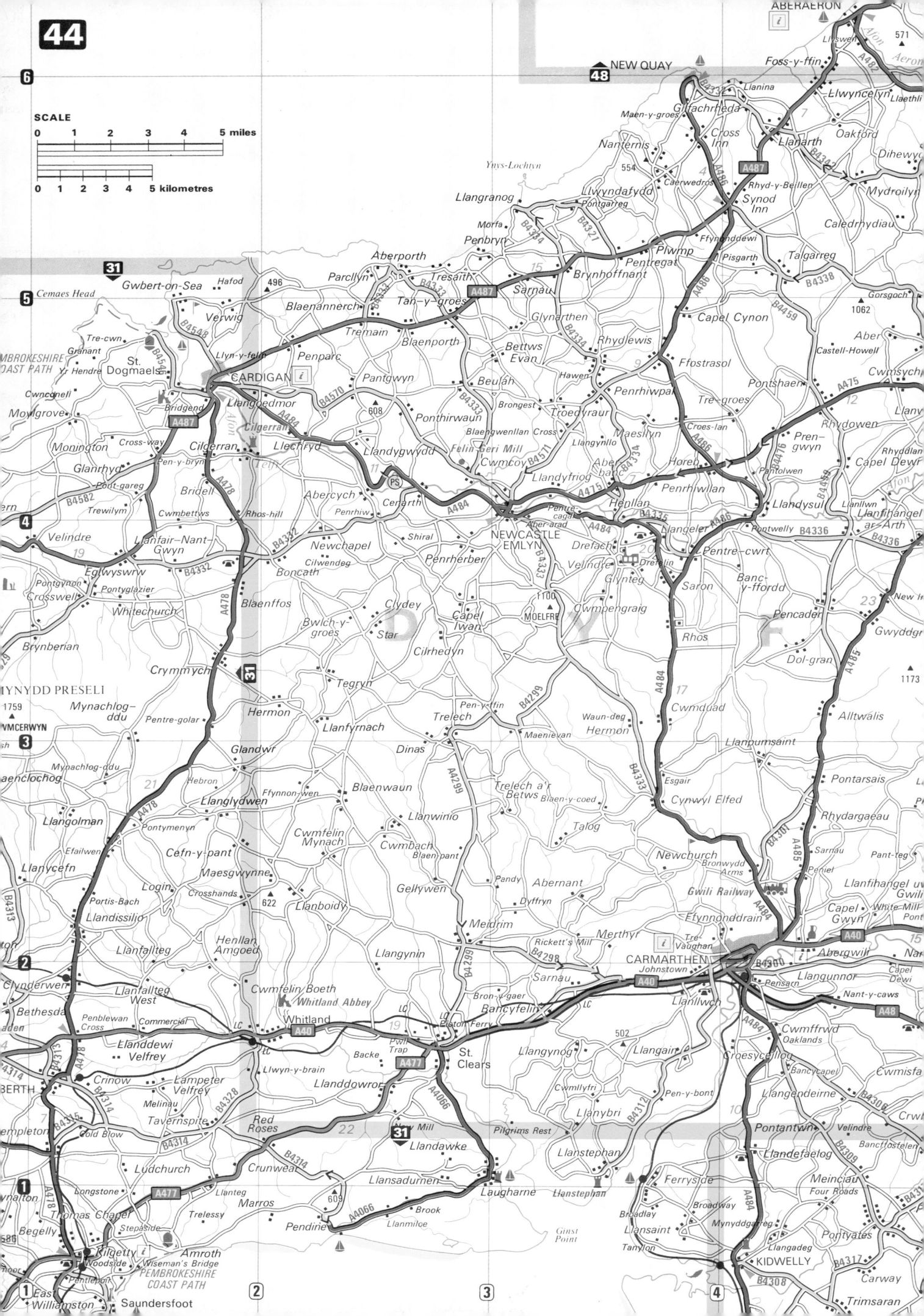

44
6
SCALE
0 1 2 3 4 5 miles
0 1 2 3 4 5 kilometres
ABERAERON
NEW QUAY
48
Llanina
Foss-y-ffin
Llwyncelyn
Gilfachrheda
Maen-y-groes
Cross Inn
Llanarth
Oakford
Nanternis
554
Caerwedros
A487
Rhyd-y-Beillen
Mydroilyn
Dihewyd
Ynys-Lochtyn
Llangranog
Llwyndafydd
Pontgarreg
Synod Inn
Caledrhydiau
Morfa
Penbryn
B4334
B4321
Ffynnonddewi
Plwmp
Pentregat
Pisgarth
Talgarreg
Aberporth
Parcllyn
Tresaith
Brynhoffnant
B4338
31
Gwbert-on-Sea
Hafod
496
Tan-y-groes
Sarnau
Gorsgoch
1062
5
Cemaes Head
Verwig
Blaenannerch
Glynarthen
Capel Cynon
B4459
Tre-cwn
Granant
B4548
Tremain
Blaenporth
Bettws Evan
Rhydlewis
Aber
Castell-Howell
PEMBROKESHIRE COAST PATH
Yr Hendre
St. Dogmaels
Llyn-y-felin
Penparc
CARDIGAN
Pantgwyn
Beulah
Hawen
Ffostrasol
Pontshaen
Cwmsychpant
Cwnconeli
Moylgrove
Bridgend
Llangoedmor
B4570
608
Brongest
Penrhiwpal
Tre-groes
A475
Llanwnen
A487
Cilgerran
A484
Ponthirwaun
Troedyraur
Croes-lan
Rhydowen
Monington
Cross-way
Cilgerran
Llechryd
Blaengwenllan Cross
Maesllyn
Prengwyn
Rhyddlan
Llandygwydd
Felin Geri Mill
Llangynllo
B4476
Capel Dewi
Pen-y-bryn
Teifi
Cwmcoy
B4571
Aberbanc
B4334
Horeb
Glanrhyd
A478
Llandyfriog
A486
Pantolwen
Pont-gareg
Bridell
PS
Penrhiwllan
Afon
B4582
Abercych
A475
Henllan
Llandysul
Llanllwni
Trewilym
Cwmbettws
Rhos-hill
Penrhiw
Cenarth
A484
Pentre-cagal
B4335
Llanfihangel-ar-Arth
Aber-arad
Llangeler
Pontwelly
B4336
4
Velindre
Llanfair-Nant-Gwyn
B4332
Newchapel
Shiral
NEWCASTLE EMLYN
A484
Drefach
Pentre-cwrt
19
Cilwendeg
Penrherber
Velindre
Drefelin
Eglwyswrw
B4332
Boncath
B4333
Glynteg
Saron
Banc-y-ffordd
Pontgynon
Pontyglazier
Crosswell
Blaenffos
Clydey
F100
MOELFRE
Cwmpengraig
23
New Inn
Pencader
Whitechurch
A478
Bwlch-y-groes
Capel Iwan
Star
Rhos
Gwyddgrug
Brynberian
Cilrhedyn
A484
Dol-gran
A485
Crymmych
31
MYNYDD PRESELI
Tegryn
1173
1759
Mynachlog-ddu
17
Pentre-golar
Hermon
Pen-y-ffin
B4299
Cwmduad
Alltwalis
Llanfyrnach
Trelech
Waun-deg
Hermon
Maenievan
3
Glandwr
Dinas
Llanpumsaint
Mynachlog-ddu
Maenclochog
A4299
B4333
Hebron
Ffynnon-wen
Blaenwaun
Trelech a'r Betws
Blaen-y-coed
Esgair
Pontarsais
21
Llanglydwen
Cynwyl Elfed
Llangolman
A478
Llanwinio
Rhydargaeau
Pontymenyn
Talog
B4301
Cwmfelin Mynach
Cwmbach
Newchurch
A485
Sarnau
Pant-teg
Efailwen
Blaen-pant
Bronwydd Arms
Llanycefn
Cefn-y-pant
Maesgwynne
Pandy
Abernant
Peniel
Llanfihangel uwch Gwili
Login
Gellywen
Gwili Railway
Crosshands
622
Dyffryn
B4313
Portis-Bach
Llanboidy
A484
Capel Gwyn
White Mill
Llandissilio
Meidrim
Efynnonddrain
Henllan Amgoed
Merthyr
Tre-Vaughan
A40
Llanfallteg
Llangynin
Rickett's Mill
CARMARTHEN
Abergwili
2
B4298
Johnstown
B4300
Llangunnor
Capel Dewi
Clynderwen
Llanfallteg West
Cwmfelin Boeth
Sarnau
A40
Pensarn
Whitland Abbey
Bron-y-gaer
Nant-y-caws
Bethesda
Bancyfelin
Llanllwch
A48
Penblewan Cross
Commercial
Whitland
A40
Piston Ferry
502
A484
Cwmffrwd
Oaklands
Llanddewi Velfrey
Pwll Trap
St. Clears
Llangynog
Llangain
Croesyceiliog
Backe
A477
Bancycapel
Cwmisfael
B4314
Crinow
Llwyn-y-brain
NARBERTH
Lampeter Velfrey
Llanddowror
A4066
Cwmllyfri
Llangendeirne
B4314
Melinau
B4328
Pen-y-bont
B4306
B4315
Tavernspite
Llanybri
B4312
Templeton
Cold Blow
Red Roses
22
New Mill
31
Pilgrims Rest
Pontantwn
Velindre
Llandawke
B4309
B4314
Llanstephan
Bancffosfelen
Ludchurch
Crunwear
B4314
Llandefaelog
Llansadurnen
Ferryside
1
Longstone
A477
Llanteg
Laugharne
Llanstephan
Meinciau
Four Roads
A478
Marros
609
Broadway
Broadlay
Thomas Chapel
Trelessy
A4066
Brook
Mynyddgarreg
A484
Begelly
Stepaside
Pendine
Llanmiloe
Llansaint
Pontyates
Ginst Point
Tanylan
Kilgetty
Amroth
Llangadeg
Woodside
Wiseman's Bridge
KIDWELLY
PEMBROKESHIRE COAST PATH
Pentlepoir
B4317
East Williamston
Saundersfoot
B4308
Carway
Trimsaran
1
2
3
4

45
48
49
46
32
33
6
7
8
9
SN
POWYS
BLACK MOUNTAIN
FFOREST FAWR
Tregaron
Camer-fawr
Glan-yr-afon uchaf
Tyn-y-swydd
Penuwch
Crynfryn
Bethania
Llangeitho
Bwlchllan
Trefilan
Talsarn
Felin Fach
Capel Betws Lleucu
Llwyn-y-groes
Gartheli
Garthenor
Aber-meurig
Olmarch
Temple Bar
Llangybi
Garth
Aber-coed
Aber-Carfan
Llanddewi Brefi
Bettws Bledrws
Pont Creuddyn
Cribyn
Llanfair Clydogau
Silian
Maestir
Olwen
Cellan
Falcondale
Lampeter
Llanwnen
Pentre-bach
Cwmann
Treherbert
Ram
Pencarreg
Glan-Duar
Llanybydder
Llanycrwys
Ffald-y-Brenin
Farmers
Bryn-gwyn
1588
BRYN BRAWD
1497
PEN Y GURNOS
1827
BRYN GARW
1732
BRYN CRWN
Abergwesyn
Afon Irfon
Beulah
Cwm Irfon
1695
MYNYDD TRAWSNANT
Llanwrtyd
LLANWRTYD WELLS
Cefngorwydd
1515
Rhandirmwyn
Llandulas
Tirabad
Cynghordy
1361
Esgerdawe
Pumsaint
Dolaucothi
Llandre
Caeo
Neuadd Fawr
Cilycwm
Llanfair-ar-y-bryn
Albert Mount
Aber-Bowlan
Porthyrhyd
Rhydcymerau
Crugybar
Llansawel
Talog
Pentre ty gwyn
Babel
1449
Edwinsford
Abergorlech
Talley Abbey
1079
Talley
Cwm-byr
LLANDOVERY
Llandeilo'r Fan
Pentre-bach
Halfway
Pentre-bâch
Pen-y-garn
Waun-clyn-da
Cwm-dwr
Llanwrda
Llansadwrn
Brechfa
Cwmdu
Halfway
Felindre
Myddfai
Cilgwyn
Usk Reservoir
Llywel
Trecastle
Llanfynydd
Pant-Soar
Capel Isaac
Maerdy
Llangadog
Felindre
Salem
Pont-ar Hydfer
Pantglas Hall
Cwm-Ifor
Caledfwlch
Pant-Gwyn
Bethlehem
Dyffryn Ceidrych
Twynllanan
Cross Inn
Llanddeusant
Crai
Ffynnon-y-gwyddau
Penybanc
Court Henry
Rhosmaen
1360
Pont-ar-llechau
TRICHRUG
Pont-Newydd
LLANDEILO
Capel Gwynfe
2630
Cilsan
Llangathen
Dryslwyn
Neuadd
Crai Resr
Golden Grove
Ffairfach
FAN GIHIRYCH
2381
Llanarthney
Trapp
Carreg Cennen
Blaengweche
Derwydd
Llandyfan
Carmel
Maesybont
Pentre-Gwenlais
Dan-yr-Ogof Caves
Glyntawe
Penwyllt
Craig-y-nos
Porthyrhyd
Drefach
Foelgastell
Castell-y-rhingyll
Llandybie
Twynmynydd
Brynamman
Rhosaman
Pen-y-cae
Cefneithin
Gorslas
Penygroes
Ystradfellte
Pontamman
GLANAMAN
Cwmgwili
Saron
Gwaun-Leision
Cwmllynfell
Ystradowen
Abercraf
Ynyswen
Caehopkin
Coelbren
Cross Hands
Garnant
AMMANFORD
Bryn-hyfryd
Betws
Gwaun-Cae-Gurwen
Cwmgorse
Pen Rhiwfawr
Upper Cwmtwrch
Cwmgiedd
Cae'r-bont
Penrhos
Tumble
Capel Hendre
Greynor
Tycroes
Pantyffynnon
Lower Cwmtwrch
Ystradgynlais
Onllwyn
Pontyberem
1226
Gurnos
Penywern
Ystalyfera
Glan-rhyd
Dyffryn Cellwen
Bryndu
Garnswllt
Llannon
Gwrhyd
Seven Sisters
Pont Morlais
Llanedi
Pentretan
Bryn-chwyth
Godre'r-graig
Mynydd Allt-y-grug
Nant-y-cafn
Pont-Nêdd Fechan
Gerdinen
Glyn-Neath
Cilmaengwyn
Ynysmeudwy
Morfa Glas
Pont Walby
Rhigos
Glan-yr-afon
Rhydyfro
Gelligron
Blaengwrach
Fforest
Pentrebach
Cilybebyll
Cwmgwrach
Afon Tywi
River Tawe
Neath
A485
A482
A475
A483
A40
A4069
A474
A4068
A476
A48
A4067
A4221
A4109
A465
B4577
B4578
B4576
B4337
B4342
B4343
B4310
B4302
B4300
B4297
B4556
B4306
B4599

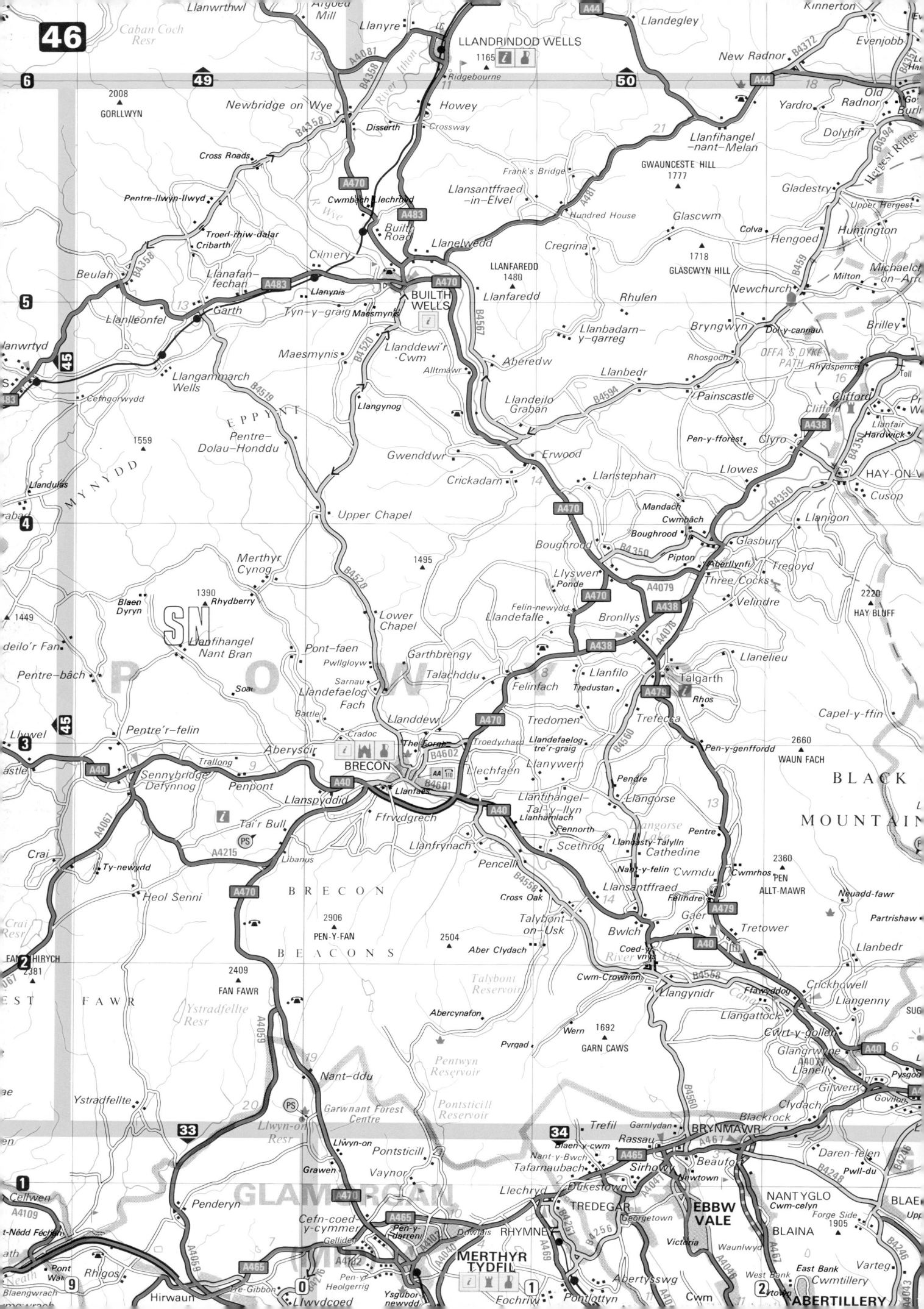

Llanwrthwl
Argoed Mill
Caban Coch Resr
Llanyre
LLANDRINDOD WELLS
1165
A44
Llandegley
Kinnerton
New Radnor
B4372
Evenjobb
6
49
50
Ridgebourne
A4081
B4358
River Ithon
A44
18
Old Radnor
Yardro
2008
GORLLWYN
Newbridge on Wye
Howey
Disserth
Crossway
B4358
21
Llanfihangel -nant-Melan
Dolyhir
Hergest Ridge
Cross Roads
GWAUNCESTE HILL
1777
Frank's Bridge
A470
Llansantffraed -in-Elvel
A481
Gladestry
Pentre-llwyn-llwyd
Cwmbach Llechryd
R. Wye
A483
Hundred House
Glascwm
Upper Hergest
Builth Road
Colva
Hengoed
Huntington
Troed-rhiw-dalar
Cribarth
Llanelwedd
Cregrina
1718
Cilmery
GLASCWYN HILL
Beulah
B4358
Llanafan-fechan
A483
LLANFAREDD
1480
A470
Llanynis
BUILTH WELLS
Llanfaredd
Rhulen
Newchurch
Michaelchurch-on-Arrow
Milton
B459
5
13
Garth
Llanlleonfel
Tyn-y-graig
Maesmynis
B4567
Llanbadarn-y-garreg
Bryngwyn
Dol-y-cannau
Brilley
Llanwrtyd
45
Maesmynis
B4520
Llanddewi'r Cwm
Aberedw
Rhosgoch
OFFA'S DYKE PATH
Rhydspence
Alltmawr
A483
Llangammarch Wells
Llanbedr
16
Cefngorwydd
Llangynog
Llandeilo Graban
B4594
Painscastle
Clifford
B4519
EPPYNT
A438
Llanfair
Hardwick
1559
Pentre-Dolau-Honddu
Gwenddwr
Erwood
Pen-y-fforest
Clyro
MYNYDD
Crickadarn
14
Llanstephan
Llowes
B4350
HAY-ON-WYE
Llandulas
Cusop
4
A470
Mandach
Upper Chapel
Cwmbach
Llanigon
B4350
Boughrood
Glasbury
Boughrood
B4350
Pipton
1495
Merthyr Cynog
Aberllynfi
Tregoyd
B4520
Llyswen
Ponde
Three Cocks
A4079
A470
Velindre
2220
HAY BLUFF
1390
Rhydberry
Blaen Dyryn
SN
A438
Lower Chapel
Felin-newydd
Llandefalle
Bronllys
1449
Llanfihangel Nant Bran
A4078
A438
Llandeilo'r Fan
Pont-faen
Pwllgloyw
Garthbrengy
Llanfilo
Llanelieu
Talgarth
Pentre-bâch
Talachddu
POWYS
Sarnau
Felinfach
Tredustan
A479
Soar
Llandefaelog Fach
Rhos
45
Battle
Tredomen
Trefecca
Capel-y-ffin
Pentre'r-felin
Llanddew
Llywel
Cradoc
A470
Troedyrharn
B4560
Pen-y-genffordd
2660
WAUN FACH
3
Aberyscir
The Forge
Llandefaelog-tre'r-graig
A40
Trallong
9
BRECON
B4602
Llanywern
Llechfaen
BLACK MOUNTAINS
Sennybridge Defynnog
Penpont
A40
AA
B4601
Pendre
Llanspyddid
Llanfaes
Llanfihangel-Tal-y-llyn
Llangorse
13
A4067
A40
Llanhamlach
Tai'r Bull
PS
Ffrwdgrech
Pennorth
Llangorse Lake
Pentre
Scethrog
Llangasty-Talyllin
Llanfrynach
Cathedine
A4215
Crai
Libanus
Pencelli
2360
Ty-newydd
Nant-y-felin
Cwmdu
PEN ALLT-MAWR
B4558
Cwmrhos
Llansantffraed
BRECON
A470
Heol Senni
Cross Oak
14
Felindre
Neuadd-fawr
A479
Gaer
2906
Talybont-on-Usk
Partrishaw
PEN-Y-FAN
Tretower
Crai Resr
2504
Bwlch
A40
Aber Clydach
Llanbedr
BEACONS
Coed-yr-ynys
FAN HIRYCH
River Usk
2
2381
2409
Talybont Reservoir
B4558
Cwm-Crawnon
FAN FAWR
Llangynidr
Crickhowell
Ffawyddog
Canal
Llangenny
FOREST FAWR
Ystradfellte Resr
A4059
Abercynafon
Llangattock
1692
Wern
Cwrt-y-gollen
Pyrgad
GARN CAWS
A40
Glangrwyne
A4077
19
Pentwyn Reservoir
Llanelly
Nant-ddu
Gilwern
B4560
Govilon
Ystradfellte
20
PS
Garwnant Forest Centre
Pontsticill Reservoir
Clydach
Blackrock
33
Llwyn-on Resr
34
Trefil
Garnlydan
BRYNMAWR
A467
Rassau
Daren-felen
Blaen-y-cwm
A465
Llwyn-on
Pontsticill
Nant-y-Bwch
Beaufort
B4248
Pwll-du
Tafarnaubach
Sirhowy
Newtown
Grawen
Vaynor
1
Cellwen
GLAMORGAN
A470
Llechryd
Dukestown
NANTYGLO
A4109
Penderyn
TREDEGAR
EBBW VALE
Cwm-celyn
Forge Side
A465
Cefn-coed-y-cymmer
Pen-y-darren
B4256
Georgetown
1905
Blaina
Gellideg
A4102
Dowlais
RHYMNEY
A4047
Victoria
A467
B4246
A4102
A469
Waunlwyd
Pont Walby
Rhigos
A4059
A465
MERTHYR TYDFIL
Varteg
9
Pen-yr-Heolgerrig
A4046
East Bank
Cwmtillery
Blaengwrach
Tre-Gibbon
0
1
West Bank
2
Hirwaun
Llwydcoed
Ysgubor-newydd
Fochriw
Pontlottyn
Abertysswg
Cwm
ABERTILLERY

47
Combe
Combe Moor
Nash
Stansbatch
Shobdon
Little Brampton
Burcher
Titley
Mowley
Staunton Green
Staunton on Arrow
Broom
Shirl Heath
Ledicot
Kingsland
Luston
Aston
Bicton
Eyton
Cobnash
Cholstrey
Stockton Cross
The Broad
Kimbolton
Stockton
Berrington Hall
Woonton
Whyle
Kyre Green
Grafton
Bank Street
Pie Corner
Pudleston
Bockleton
Collington
High Lane
Lower Sapey
Wolferlow
50
51
Shawl
The Forge
Pembridge
Lawton
Ebnall
Grantsfield
LEOMINSTER
Hatfield
Thornbury
Tedstone Wafre
Lewis Wych
Cabal
Eardisland
Baron's Cross
Marston
Monkland
Stoke Prior
Stretford
Steen's Bridge
Docklow
Bilfield
Edwyn Ralph
Edvin Loach
Sandy Cross
Nextend
New Street
Lower Barewood
Barewood
Burton Court
Sollers Dilwyn
Ivington Green
Newtown
Ivington
Southfield
Humber Court
Grendon Green
Great Wacton
Bredenbury
Bromyard Downs
Lyonshall
Weston
Moorcot
Luntley
Dilwyn Common
Stretford Court
Brierley
Wharton
Marston Stannett
Elsdon
Stockmoor
Haven
Aulden
Marlbrook
Newton
Risbury
Hegdon Hill
The Green
Birchyfield
Bromyard
Holme Marsh
Upper Spond
Broxwood
Dilwyn
Little Dilwyn
Birley
Upper Hill
Pencombe
Wootton
Almeley Wooton
Upper Broxwood
Woonton
Hope under Dinmore
Bowley Town
Bowley
Almeley
Weobley
Knapton Green
Crowels Ash
Munderfield Row
Saffron's Cross
Little Cowarne
Ferny Common
Weobley Marsh
Bush Bank
Westhope
Maund Bryan
Stoke Cross
Stanford Bishop
Upcott
Newchurch
Sarnesfield
Dinmore Manor
Bodenham
Bodenham Moor
Munderfield Stocks
Acton Beauchamp
Kinnersley
Ledgemoor
King's Pyon
Highway
Urdimarsh
The Vauld
Cornett
Upper Town
Ullingswick
Stoke Lacy
Norton Wood
Canon Pyon
Felton
Moreton Jeffries
Panks Bridge
Bishop's Frome
Evesbatch
Ailey
Eccles Green
Wellington Marsh
Walker's Green
Burley Gate
Wynne's Green
Much Cowarne
Halmond's Frome
Parton
Willersley
Calver Hill
Norton Canon
Yarsop
Wormsley
Wellington
Paradise Green
Preston Wynne
Hillhampton
Ocle Pychard
Five Bridges
Castle Frome
Foxley
Yazor
Tillington Common
Marden
Sutton
Moorhampton
Mansell Lacy
Ellington
Sutton St Michael
Sutton St Nicholas
Letton
Staunton on Wye
HEREFORD
Burghill
Moreton on Lugg
Withington Marsh
Westhide
Newtown
Stretton Grandison
Fromes Hill
52
Mansell Gamage
Brinsop
Upper Lyde
Sutton Marsh
Monkhide
Canon Frome
Monnington on Wye
Credenhill
Pipe and Lyde
Nunnington
Shelwick
Withington
Yarkhill
Bosbury
Byford
Bishopstone
Stretton Sugwas
Westfields
Withies
Shucknall
Cold Green
The Bage
Moccas
Preston on Wye
Kenchester
Sugwas Pool
Holmer
Lower Town
Ashperton
Blakemere
Holywell
Bridge Sollers
The Weir
Hereford
Kings Acre
White Stone
Weston Beggard
Swinmore Common
Staplow
Swainshill
Lugwardine
Hagley
Wood End
Ploughfield
Lulham
Canon Bridge
Upper Breinton
Tupsley
Bartestree
Tarrington
Munsley
Bellimoor
White Cross
Warham
Perton
Stoke Edith
Trumpet
Tyberton
Madley
Wormhill
Ruckhall Common
Eaton Bishop
Breinton
Dormington
Plaistow
Stockley Hill
Hinton
Peterchurch
The Crossways
Blackmarstone
Durlow Common
Waller's Green
Shenmore
Gorsty Common
Clehonger
Lower Bullingham
Hampton Bishop
Aylton
LEDBURY
Sufton Court
Mordiford
Vowchurch
Webton
Grafton
Bullinghope
Dinedor
Putley
Putley Green
Turnastone
Blackhole
Coldwell
Goose Pool
Cobhall Common
Allensmore
Dinedor Cross
Holme Lacy
Woolhope
Little Marcle
Upper Maes-coed
Kingstone
Portway
Twyford Common
Kynaston
Ledbury
Preston
St. Margarets
Hungerstone
Thruxton
Winnal Common
Haywood
Callow
Fownhope
Rushall
Chandos
Cockyard
Dewsall Court
Bogmarsh
Lower Buckenhill
Sollers Hope
Donnington
Middle Maes-coed
Kerry's Gate
The Rhydd
Aconbury
Bounds
Much Marcle
Newton
Bacton
Crizeley
Kingsthorne
904
Newtown
Belstone
Brockhampton
Greenway
St Devereux
Wormbridge
Didley
Little Dewchurch
Ladyridge
Falcon
Lyne Down
Lower Maes-coed
Little Birch
Ballingham
Carey
Crossway
Stocking
Dymock
Abbey Dore
Much Dewchurch
Kilpeck
Wormelow Tump
The Mynde
Much Birch
How Caple
Yatton
Kempley
The Cleaver
Hoarwithy
Penalt
Fawley Chapel
Kempley Green
Howton
Orcop Hill
Kings Caple
Fishpool
Longtown
Ewyas Harold
Llandinabo
Foy
Hole-in-the-Wall
Pontrilas Road
Strangford
Rowlstone
Bagwy Llydiart
Llanwarne
Harewood End
Sellack
Baysham
Hill of Eaton
Crow Crews Hill
Upton Bishop
Clodock
Pontrilas
Netherton
Pencoyd
Upper Grove Common
Pict's Cross
Brampton Abbotts
Phocle Green
Walterstone Common
Llancillo
Llangua
Kentchurch
1202
Orcop
Michaelchurch
Lower Grove Common
Bridstow
Rudhall
Walterstone
Grosmont
Garway Hill
St. Weonards
St. Owen's Cross
Poolmill
ROSS-ON-WYE
36
Linton
Oldcastle
Grosmont
Maerdy
Little Garway
Tretire
Peterstow
Wilton
Bromsash
Cwmyoy
Hoaldalbert
Cross
Garway Common
Old Furnace
Three Ashes
Wilson
Ashfield
Tudorville
Ryeford
Aston Crews
Tre-wyn
Pandy
Garway
Broad Oak
Glewstone
665
Weston under Penyard
Aston Ingham
Great Campston
Hom Green
Coughton
Crews Hill
Lea
Stanton
OFFA'S DYKE PATH
1389
Llangarron
Pontshill
Llangattock Lingoed
Skenfrith
Whitfield
Goodrich
Howle Hill
Hope Mansell
East Dean
Cross Ash
Llancloudy
Pencraig
Walford
Kiln Green
Dursley Cross
Llanfair-green
Norton
Skenfrith
Goodrich Cross
Kerne Bridge
Bont
Crossway
Hilston Park
Llangrove
791
Marstow
Ruardean
Mitcheldean
Crooked End
Longhope
Abenhall
1595
Upper Green
Llanrothal
Whitchurch
Welsh Newton
Blaisdon
Caggle Street
Newcastle
St Maughans
Drybrook
Llantilio Pertholey
Llanvetherine
St Maughans Green
Little Doward
Great Doward
Lower Lydbrook
Ruardean Woodside
Ruardean Hill
Llanfaenor
Maypole
Crocker's Ash
Symonds Yat
Nailbridge
Flaxley
White
Hen Gwrt
Llangattock-Vibon-Avel
Ganarew
Symonds Yat
English Bicknor
Brierley
Broadmoor
Cinderford
ABERGAVENNY
Llanvapley
Llantilio-Crossenny
Onen
Rockfield
Hillersland
Upper Lydbrook
Bilson Green
Dean Hall
Littledean
Dixton
The Hendre
Fiddler Elbow
Christchurch
Edge End
Llanddewi Rhydderch
Llanvihangel-Ystern-Llewern
MONMOUTH
Kymin
35
Berry Hill
Five Acres
FOREST
Broadoak
34
Wernrheolydd
Wyesham
Staunton
Ruspidge
Penrhos
Coed Morgan
Wonastow
Mile End
Cannop
OF
Ruddle
Upper Soudley
Llanvihangel Gobion
Llanarth
Pen-yr-Heol
Tregare
Jingle Street
Penallt
Coleford
Whitecliffe
Broadwell
DEAN
Lower Soudley
Great Oak
Dingestow
Redbrook
The Bryn
Mitchel Troy
Milkwall
Ancient Iron Mines
Aylburton
Llanover
Bryngwyn
Raglan
Mitcheltroy Common
Newland
Millend
Iron Mines
Marsh Lane
Parkend
Brain's Green
Pen-twyn
Clearwell
Ellwood
Yorkley
Blakeney
Llanfair Kilgeddin
Raglan
Pen-y-clawdd
Caer Llan
Tregagle
Newmills
Blakeney Hill
Nibley
Goetre
Bettws-Newydd
Cwmcarvan
Whitebrook
Trow Green
Bream's Meend
Oldcroft
Etloe
Twyn-y-Sheriff
Llangovan
The Narth
Stowe
Whitecroft
Purton
Ton
4
Kingcoed
Trelleck
5
1005
The Fence
6
Bream
Dean Forest
Gwehelog
A44
A49
A4112
A4110
A480
A4103
A438
A465
A417
A4137
A40
A466
A449
A48
A4136
A4151
A4172
B4362
B4355
B4352
B4230
B4349
B4348
B4347
B4399
B4224
B4214
B4203
B4215
B4221
B4222
B4227
B4228
B4229
B4234
B4226
B4231
B4233
B4293
B4431
B4521
B4598
B4024
SO

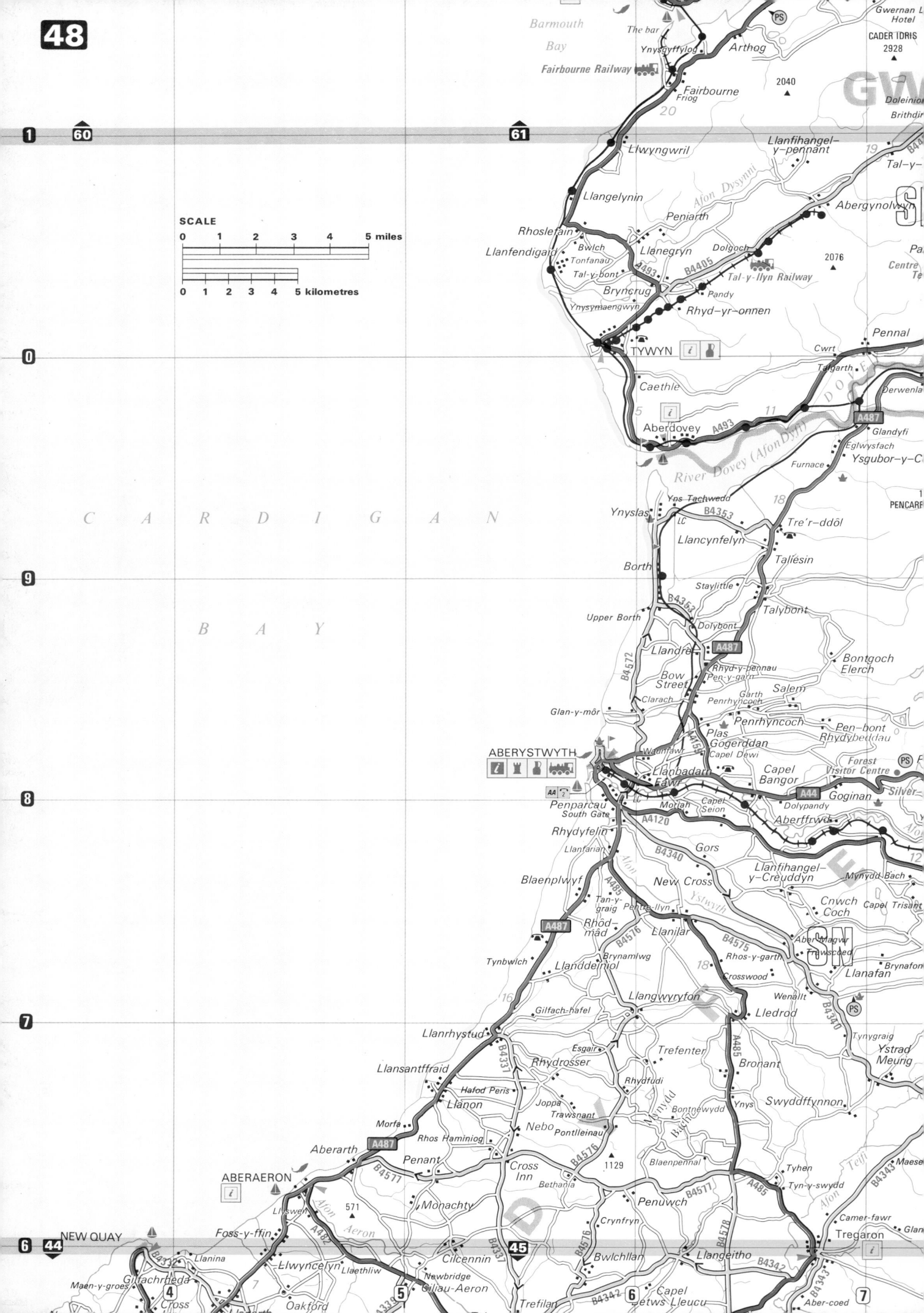

SCALE
0 1 2 3 4 5 miles
0 1 2 3 4 5 kilometres
CARDIGAN
BAY
Barmouth Bay
Fairbourne Railway
Arthog
Fairbourne
Friog
CADER IDRIS 2928
Llwyngwril
Llanfihangel-y-pennant
Llangelynin
Afon Dysynni
Abergynolwyn
Rhoslefain
Peniarth
Llanfendigaid
Bwlch
Tonfanau
Tal-y-bont
Llanegryn
Dolgoch
Tal-y-llyn Railway
Bryncrug
Pandy
Ynysymaengwyn
Rhyd-yr-onnen
TYWYN
Pennal
Caethle
Aberdovey
Glandyfi
Eglwysfach
Furnace
River Dovey (Afon Dyfi)
Ynyslas
Yns Tachwedd
Tre'r-ddôl
Llancynfelyn
Taliesin
Borth
Staylittle
Talybont
Upper Borth
Dolybont
Llandre
Bontgoch Elerch
Bow Street
Rhyd-y-pennau
Pen-y-garn
Salem
Clarach
Garth
Penrhyncoch
Glan-y-môr
Plas Gogerddan
Pen-bont Rhydybeddau
ABERYSTWYTH
Waunfawr
Capel Dewi
Forest Visitor Centre
Llanbadarn Fawr
Capel Bangor
Goginan
Penparcau
South Gate
Moriah
Capel Seion
Dolypandy
Aberffrwd
Rhydyfelin
Llanfarian
Gors
Llanfihangel-y-Creuddyn
Blaenplwyf
New Cross
Mynydd Bach
Cnwch Coch
Capel Trisant
Tan-y-graig
Pentre-llyn
Rhôd-mâd
Llanilar
Abermagwr
Trawscoed
Tynbwlch
Brynamlwg
Rhos-y-garth
Llanddeiniol
Crosswood
Llanafan
Llangwyryfon
Wenallt
Gilfach-hafel
Lledrod
Llanrhystud
Tynygraig
Esgair
Trefenter
Ystrad Meurig
Rhydrosser
Bronant
Llansantffraid
Rhydfudi
Hafod Peris
Llanon
Joppa
Ynys
Swyddffynnon
Trawsnant
Morfa
Nebo
Pontllleinau
Rhos Haminiog
Aberarth
Penant
Cross Inn
1129
Blaenpennal
Tyhen
ABERAERON
Bethania
Tyn-y-swydd
Monachty
Penuwch
Llwswen
Crynfryn
Camer-fawr
Aeron
Tregaron
NEW QUAY
Foss-y-ffin
Llanina
Llwyncelyn
Cilcennin
Bwlchllan
Llangeitho
Gilfachreda
Llaethliw
Maen-y-groes
Newbridge
Ciliau-Aeron
Cross
Oakford
Trefilan
Capel Betws Lleucu
Aber-coed

49
Dinas-Mawddwy
Minllyn
Cwm-Cewydd
Mallwyd
A458
Wern
Foel
Llangadfan
Llwydiarth
Pontrobert
Dolanog
B4382
B4395
Plas Coch
New Bridge
Heniarth
Llanerfyl
Llysun
Aberangell
Clipiau
Aberllefenni
A470
1715
61
62
Four Crosses
A495
Railway Museum
Cwm-Llinau
Dolwen
Neuadd
Melin-y-ddôl
Cyfronydd
Welshpool & Llanfair Light Railway
Esgairgeiliog
Dol-fôr
Cemmaes
Pentre-celyn
Sychtyn
Melin-y-grug
SJ
Llanfair Caereinion
B4385
Cil-haul
Brynmelyn
Plas Llwyngwern
Mathafarn
Cemmaes Road
Pandy
Bryn-penarth
1193
Coed-ddôl
Pentre-Maw
Llanwrin
Commins Coch
Llanbrynmair
Llanllugan
Manafon
B4389
B4404
Abergwydol
Abercegir
Tafolwern
Dolfach
B4390
Pant-y-ffridd
Darowen
Llanwyddelan
A489
Penegoes
Llan
Bont-Dolgadfan
B4518
Talerddig
Rhyd
Glan-yr-afon
Adfa
New Mills
Talywern
Machynlleth
Melin-byrhedyn
1537
Moelfre
Tregynon
Brooks
Pentre Llifior
Pantglas
Aberhosan
1602
Brynamlwg
Sarn
Plas Llysyn
50
Bettws Cedewain
Pennant
Pont Crugnant
Carno
Afon Garno
Bwlch-y-ffridd
Dylife
Clatter
Derfferwd
Highgate
Abermule
847
Llanwnog
B4568
Rhydlydan
1909
Pontdolgoch
Caersws
Llanllwchaiarn
A483
Staylittle
Llawryglyn
B4569
LC
Milford
Newtown
Gwernafon
Trefeglwys
Mochdre
Kerry
Llyn Clywedog
1580
Fan Hill
Cerist
Little London
Pentre
Llandinam
Glascoed
Dolfor
Plynlimon (Pumlumon Fawr)
2468
PS
Y Fan
Oakleypark
River Severn
B4518
Geufron
Glan-y-nant
Lower Penrhuddlan
Upper Penrhuddlan
B4355
Eisteddfa Gurig
Llanidloes
Newchapel
Dyffryn Castell
A44
Pant Mawr
Cwmergyr
Rhos-y-pentref
Cwmbelan
1849
Tyncwm
1915
Felindre
B4343
Llangurig
Tylwch
Llaithddu
Upper Llaithddu
River Ithon
SO
Dolfach
Sychnant
Llanbadarn Fynydd
1618
Red Lion Hill
Nantgwyn
Blaenycwm
Neuadd-ddu
Pant-y-dwr
Rhydmoelddu
Bryn
Cwmystwyth
Dernol
Dolhelfa
The Pound
Bwlch-y-sarnau
B4356
1873
Geifas
River Elan
River Wye
St. Harmon
Llanbister
Abbeycwmhir
Craig Goch Resr
Hirnant
Llanddewi Ystradenni
Pen-y-garreg Resr
Llansantffraed-Cwmdeuddwr
Rhayader
Dolau
Strata Florida Abbey
1738
Dibyn Du
1633
Lower Llanfadog
Garreg-ddu Resr
Gaufron
Ddau
Nantmel
Gwystre
Fron
Elan Village
Nant-glâs
Nantymynach
Crossgates
Penybont
Claerwen Reservoir
Llanwrthwl
Argoed Mill
Llanyre
Caban Coch Resr
Llandrindod Wells
1827
Bryn Garw
A4081
B4358
1165
Ridgebourne
46
2008
Gorllwyn
Newbridge on Wye
Howey
8
1732
Bryn Crwn
9
0
Disserth
Crossway
1
21

Llwydiarth
Trefnannau
Pontysgawrhyd
Sarnau
Pentrebeirdd
Pontrobert
Meifod
Geuffordd
Guilsfield
Dolanog
Llangadfan
Foel
Wern
Llanerfyl
Llysun
Four Crosses
Plas Coch
New Bridge
Maesgwyn-Isaf
Groesllwyd
Moel-y-Garth
Cloddiau
Heniarth
WELSHPOOL
Buttington
Hope
Leighton
Dolwen
Sychtyn
Melin-y-grug
Neuadd
Melin-y-ddôl
Llanfair Caereinion
Castle Caereinion
Welshpool & Llanfair Light Railway
Powys Castle
Cil-haul
Pentre-celyn
Pandy
Bryn-penarth
1193
Manafon
Llwynderw
Llanbrynmair
Dolfach
Llanllugan
Llanwyddelan
Pant-y-ffridd
Cross Lane
Kingswood
Marton
Bont-Dolgadfan
Talerddig
Rhyd
Glan-yr-afon
Adfa
New Mills
Berriew
Forden
Brooks
Garthmyl
Tregynon
Chirbury
1602
BRYNAMLWG
Sarn
Plas Llysyn
Pentre Llifior
Bettws Cedewain
Fron
Panney
Carno
Crugnant
Bwlch-y-ffridd
MONTGOMERY
Clatter
Derffrwd
Llanwnog
Highgate
847
Abermule
Llandyssil
Town Hill
Llanmerewig
1158
Church Stoke
Pontdolgoch
Caersws
Rhydlydan
Llanllwchaiarn
Llawryglyn
Gwernafon
Trefeglwys
Milford
Newtown
Glan-Mule
Sarn
City
Bacheldre
1580
FAN HILL
Cerist
Mochdre
Kerry
Pentre
Little London
Llandinam
Glascoed
Oakleypark
Y Fan
Dolfor
Mainstone
Pentre
Lower Penrhuddlan
Upper Penrhuddlan
Glan-y-nant
LLANIDLOES
Newchapel
Rhos-y-pentref
Cwmbelan
Anchor
Hall of the Forest
Newcastle
Whitcott Keysett
1915
Felindre
Crug-y-byddar
Lower Spoad
Llangurig
Tylwch
Llaithddu
Quabbs
Upper Llaithddu
Beguildy
SN
Dutlas
Llanbadarn Fynydd
Sychnant
Nantgwyn
1618
RED LION HILL
1796
BEACON HILL
Llanfair Waterdine
Dolfach
Neuadd-ddu
Pant-y-dwr
Rhydmoelddu
Lloiney
Five Turnings
Dernol
Dolhelfa
Bwlch-y-sarnau
The Pound
Knucklas
Skyborry Green
St. Harmon
Llanbister
Crûg
Abbeycwmhir
Gravel
Llangunllo
SO
Cwm-y-geist
Pen-y-garreg Resr
Llansantffraed-Cwmdeuddwr
Rhayader
Llanddewi Ystradenni
Tynwain
Bleddfa
Pilleth
Rhos-y-meirch
1633
Lower Llanfadog
Gaufron
Ddau
Nantmel
Nantywylan
Dolau
Fish Pools
Whitton
Garreg-ddu Resr
Elan Village
Nant-glâs
Nantymynach
Gwystre
Fron
Llanfihangel Rhydithon
Pentre
Bridge End
Crossgates
RADNOR FOREST
2166
Maes-Treylow
Llanwrthwl
Argoed Mill
Penybont
Beggar's Bush
Kinnerton
Caban Coch Resr
Llanyre
Llandegley
Evancoyd
LLANDRINDOD WELLS
1165
Evenjobb
New Radnor
Lower Harpton
Ridgebourne
2008
GORLLWYN
Newbridge on Wye
Howey
Yardro
Old Radnor
Walton
Burlingjobb
Disserth
Crossway
Llanfihangel
Dolyhir
River Severn
River Ithon
River Wye
Afon Banwy
Afon Rhiw
Afon Garno
Teme
OFFA'S DYKE PATH
SH
SJ
A458
A470
A483
A489
A495
A490
A44
A488
A4081
B4395
B4382
B4392
B4390
B4389
B4385
B4386
B4388
B4518
B4569
B4568
B4368
B4355
B4356
B4358
B4357
B4372

62
49
46

51
Crew Green
Coedway
Alberbury
Montford Bridge
Montford
Eyton
Ford
Calcott
Bicton
Rosehill
Coton Hill
Shelton
Battlefield
Uffington
Somerwood
Rodington
Abbey
Upton
Tern
Lane
Sleapford
Weald Moors
Eyton upon Weald Moors
Marsh Green
Admaston
Bratton
Allscott
Withington
Underdale
Wollaston
Halfway House
Rowton
Shoot Hill
SHREWSBURY
Stretton Heath
Cardeston
Meole Brace
Preston
Upton Magna
Walcot
Wrockwardine
Hadley
Trench
Wellington
Donnington
Charlton
Smethcott
Ford Heath
Nox
Cruckton
Sutton
Weeping Cross
Yockleton
Cruckmeole
Nobold
Attingham Park
Atcham
Norton
Uppington
Aston
Arleston
Lawley
Oldpark
Oakengates
Westbury
Stoney Stretton
Lea
Great Hanwood
Betton Strange
Bayston Hill
Roman Town (Viroconium)
Rushton
Farley
Edge
Upper Pulley
Lower Bayston
Wroxeter
Little Wenlock
Huntington
TELFORD
Dawley
Westley
Asterley
Hinton
Annscroft
Great Lyth
Berrington
Cross Houses
Donnington
Longwood
Aston Rogers
Horsebridge
Plealey
Pontesford
Boreton
Condover
Eyton on Severn
Eaton Constantine
Garmston
Coalmoor
Horsehay
Stirchley
Minsterley
Pontesbury
Longden
Exfordsgreen
Leighton
Coalbrookdale Museum
Buildwas
Worthen
Pontesbury Hill
Oaks
Longden Common
Condover Green
Great Ryton
Cantlop
Upper Cound
Cound
Coundlane
Buildwas Abbey
Coalbrookdale
Madeley
Blists Hill
Stapleton
Wrentnall
Pitchford
Golding
Leigh
Ploxgreen
Habberley
Wagbeach
Church Pulverbatch
Dorrington
Cressage
Sheinton
Iron Bridge
Coalport
China Museum
Broseley
Tar Tunnel
Snailbeach
Crowsnest
Castle Pulverbatch
Acton Burnell
Acton Pigott
Acton Burnell Castle
Frodesley
Harley
Homer
Wyke
Benthall
Posenhall
Barrow
Hope
Perkins Beach
Longnor
Wigwig
Priory
Willey
Gravels
Pennerley
Picklescott
Betchcott
Ruckley
Kenley
The Bank
Stretton Westwood
MUCH WENLOCK
Linleygreen
Apley Park
Shelve
Leebotwood
Hughley
The Smithies
Shirlett
Nordley
Woolstaston
Church Preen
Presthope
Atterley
Callaughton
The Bog
Kinnerton
Ratlinghope
Enchmarsh
Plaish
Bourton
Haughton
Muckleycross
All Stretton
Bridges
Cardington
Gretton
Easthope
Acton Round
Muckley
Aston Eyre
Cross Lane Head
Morville
1349
1694
Church Stretton
The Long Mynd
Hope Bowdler
Wall Bank
East Wall
Longville in the Dale
Brockton
Astonlane
Tasley
Linley
Norbury
Wentnor
Little Stretton
Hazler
Ragdon
Heywood
Wilderhope Manor
Shipton Hall
Shipton
Weston
Monkhopton
The Lye
Morville Heath
Upton Cressett Hall
Upton Cressett
Oldbury
More
Whitcot
Asterton
Hatton
Ticklerton
Rushbury
Wenlock Edge
Netchwood
Derrington
Stanton Long
Middleton Priors
Cross Houses
Minton
Hardwick
Myndtown
Marshbrook
Eaton
Broadstone
Brockhampton
Ditton Priors
Chetton
Eardington
Severn Valley Railway
Lea
Eaton
Choulton
Whittingslow
Working Farm Museum
Acton Scott
Holloway
Holdgate
Eudon George
Glazeley
Eyton
Plowden
Henley
Harton
Wolverton
Middlehope
White House
Neenton
Oldfield
Lower Faintree
Lydbury North
Horderley
Woolston
Alcaston
Munslow Aston
Tugford
Abdon
1770
Cleobury North
Middleton Scriven
Upper Affcot
Westhorpe
Munslow
Broncroft
Overton
Billingsley
Brockton
Edgton
Wistanstow
Diddlebury
Bouldon
Upper Heath
Wrickton
Walcot
Brunslow
Basford
Cheney Longville
Strefford
Burwarton
Sidbury
Hawkswood
Lower Down
Grove
Dinchope
Corfton
Peaton
Clee St Margaret
Aston Botterell
Chorley
New England
Hopesay
Sibdon Carwood
Halford
Pedlar's Rest
Sieflon
Sutton
Cold Weston
Duddlewick
Kempton
Aston on Clun
Craven Arms
Norton
Little Sutton
Hinton
High Green
Little Brampton
Stokesay Castle
Vernolds Common
Culmington
Stoke St. Milborough
Loughton
Norton
Stottesdon
759
Long Meadowend
Stokesay
Upper Hayton
The Green
Farlow
Bagginswood
Kinlet
Purslow
Clunbury
Broome
Hayton's Bent
Bromdon
Prescott
Oreton
Cwm
Twitchen
Clungunford
Aldon
Onibury
Stanton Lacy
Hoptongate
Hopton Cangeford
Cleestanton
Cleedownton
Silvington
TITTERSTONE CLEE HILL 1750
Baveney Wood
Catherton
Obley
Hopton Castle
Hoptonheath
Shelderton
Duxmoor
Wooton
Ludlow
Middleton
Bitterley
Cleeton St. Mary
Neen Savage
Chapel Lawn
1004
Marlow
Bromfield
Foxwood
Doddington
Silligrove
Hopton Wafers
Wyre Common
Bedstone
Henley
Angelbank
Clee Hill
Farden
Cleobury Mortimer
Todding
Rockgreen
Snitton
Hints
Clee Hills
Dudnill
Bransley
Bucknell
Coxall
Kinton
Leintwardine
LUDLOW
The Sheet
Knowbury
Cleehill
Southwood
Weston
Buckton
Knowle
Milson
Bayton
Downton on the Rock
Ludford
Hope Bagot
Coreley
Neens Hill
Bayton Common
Lilebrook
Brampton Bryan
Walford
Burrington
Overton
Caynham
Whitton
Nash
Mamble
Paytoe
Aston
Ashford Carbonel
Bleathwood Common
Whatmore
Neen Sollars
Clows Top
Adforton
Ashford Bowdler
Greet
Villa
Boraston
Bickley
Elton
Greete
Aston Bank
Frith Common
Letton
Richards Castle
Woofferton
Middleton
Newnham Bridge
Birtley
Newton
Wigmore
Leinthall Starkes
Wylde
Lindridge
Eardiston
Ongar Street
Leinthall Earls
Brimfield
Little Hereford
Burford
Tenbury Wells
Upper Rochford
Rochford
Rochford Mount
Orleton
Orleton
Lingen
Lower Lye
Yatton
Bircher
Stony Cross
Burford House
Hanley William
Stanford on Teme
Elms Green
Stapleton
Limebrook
Upper Lye
Croft Castle
Lower Upton
St. Michaels
Callows Grave
Kinsham
Aymestrey
Ashton
Middleton on the Hill
Nineveh
Broadheath
PRESTEIGNE
Water Mill
Byton
Yarpole
Eye
The Hundred
Miles Hope
Kyre Park
Sapey Common
Mortimer's Cross
1461
Lucton
Bicton
Berrington Hall
Laysters Pole
Stoke Bliss
Upper Sapey
Shelsley Walsh
Combe
HEREFORD AND WORCESTER
Kyre Green
Combe Moor
Ledicot
Luston
Aston
Kingsland
Kimbolton
Woonton
Whyle
Grafton
Bank Street
Pie Corner
Wolferlow
Three Gates
Harpley
Stansbatch
Shobdon
Eyton
Stockton Cross
Stockton
Collington
High Lane
Clifton upon Teme
Mowley
Staunton Green
Staunton on Arrow
Broom
Shirl Heath
Cobnash
The Broad
Cholstrey
Bockleton
Pudleston
Lower Sapey
The Forge
Ebnall
LEOMINSTER
Thornbury
Tedstone Wafre
Tedstone Delamere
Shawl
Cabal
Pembridge
Lawton
Hatfield
Lewis Wych
Eardisland
Baron's Cross
Steen's Bridge
Docklow
Edvin Loach
Marston
Burton Court
Monkland
Stoke Prior
Stretford
Edwyn Ralph
Sandy Cross
Whitbourne
Newtown
Great Wacton
A5
A49
A442
A5223
B5062
B5063
B4473
A458
B4393
B4386
A488
B4394
B4380
B4373
M54
B4387
B4499
B4371
B4378
B4376
B4368
A4169
B4370
B4364
B4363
B4383
A489
B4385
B4367
B4365
A4117
A4113
B4202
A4110
B4361
B4214
A456
A443
B4204
B4362
A4112
B4360
A44
B4203

52
SHROPSHIRE
HEREFORD AND WORCESTER
WYRE FOREST
SO
Neenton
Glazeley
Chelmarsh
Quatt
Six Ashes
Kingswinford
Brierley Hill
Quarry Bank
Abdon
Cleobury North
Middleton Scriven
Sutton
Hampton
Hampton Loade
Enville
Wordsley
Amblecote
Stourton
Burwarton
Aston Botterell
Sidbury
Billingsley
Woodhill
Birdsgreen
Potter's Cross
Lye
Cradley
Chorley
Highley
Alveley
Romsley
Kinver
STOURBRIDGE
Pedmore
Loughton
Stottesdon
Farlow
Kinlet
Upper Arley
Shatterford
Kingsford
Whittington
Hagley
Cleedowntown
TITTERSTONE CLEE HILL
1750
Oreton
Cleeton St. Mary
Catherton
Buttonoak
Trimpley
Wolverley
Blakeshall
Cookley
Churchill
Broome
Clent Hills
Holy Cross
Doddington
Neen Savage
Habberley
Franche
Blakedown
KIDDERMINSTER
Belbroughton
Farden
Hopton Wafers
Cleobury Mortimer
Far Forest
Lem Hill
BEWDLEY
Blakebrook
West Midlands Safari Park
Wribbenhall
Stone
Drayton
Fairfield
Cleehill
Clee Hills
Hints
Milson
Coreley
Bayton
Pound Bank
Callow Hill
Ribbesford
Mustow Green
Harvington Hall
Chaddesley Corbett
Bournheath
Hope Bagot
Nash
Neen Sollars
Mamble
Bliss Gate
STOURPORT-ON-SEVERN
Shenstone
Dodford
Boraston
Newnham Bridge
Frith Common
Clows Top
Rock
Areley Kings
Hartlebury
Rushock
Tenbury Wells
Rochford
Lindridge
Eardiston
Pensax
Abberley
Dunley
Astley Cross
Elmley Lovett
Crossway Green
Cutnall Green
Upton Warren
Stoke Prior
Orleton
Hanley William
Stanford on Teme
Stockton on Teme
Astley
Lincomb
Noutard's Green
Dunhampton
Elmbridge
Callows Grave
Broadheath
Stanford Bridge
Great Witley
Sytchampton
Doverdale
Hampton Lovett
Wychbold
Kyre Park
Stoke Bliss
Upper Sapey
Sapey Common
Shrawley
Little Witley
Oldfield
DROITWICH
Ombersley
Holt Heath
Holt
Salwarpe
Hadzor
Bank Street
Wolferlow
Shelsley Walsh
Shelsley Beauchamp
Wichenford
Sinton Green
Hawford
Martin Hussingtree
Grafton
Collington
Harpley
Clifton upon Teme
High Lane
Martley
Moseley
Grimley
Fernhill Heath
Oddingley
Hatfield
Thornbury
Tedstone Wafre
Tedstone Delamere
Shoulton
Hallow
Hindlip
Himbleton
Docklow
Edwyn Ralph
Berrow Green
Horsham
Peachley
Warndon
Tibberton
Grendon Green
Bromyard Downs
Whitbourne
Broad Green
Broadheath
Huddington
Bredenbury
Brockhampton
Knightwick
Lulsley
Henwick
WORCESTER
Broughton Hackett
Hegdon Hill
Bromyard
Broadwas
Rushwick
St John's
Whittington
Upton Snodsbury
Pencombe
Linley Green
Alfrick
Leigh
Spetchley
Little Cowarne
Munderfield Row
Suckley
Bransford
Bowling Green
Powick
Norton
White Ladies Aston
Stanford Bishop
Longley Green
Leigh Sinton
Stoulton
Acton Green
Acton Beauchamp
Stifford's Bridge
Newland
Callow End
Littleworth
Drake's Broughton
Peopleton
Moreton Jeffries
Stoke Lacy
Bishop's Frome
Much Cowarne
Evesbatch
Storridge
Malvern Link
Madresfield
Kempsey
Pirton
Wadborough
Ocle Pychard
Castle Frome
Fromes Hill
Cradley
Ridgeway Cross
GREAT MALVERN
Clifton
Kerswell Green
Pershore
Newtown
Stretton Grandison
Mathon
West Malvern
Guarlford
Severn Stoke
Besford
Yarkhill
Canon Frome
Bosbury
Wyche
Hanley Swan
Rhydd
Kinnersley
Defford
Birlingham
Ashperton
Coddington
Colwall Stone
Malvern Wells
Hanley Castle
Eckington
Weston Beggard
Munsley
Colwall Green
Upton upon Severn
Earl's Croome
Strensham
Bartestree
Tarrington
Trumpet
Wellington Heath
Little Malvern
Welland
Naunton
Bredon's Norton
Dormington
Aylton
LEDBURY
Castlemorton
Ripple
Overbury
Twyning Green
Mordiford
Putley
Little Marcle
Eastnor
Hollybush
Birts Street
Longdon
Bredon
Kemerton
Woolhope
Ludstock
Preston
Shuthonger
Twyning
Northway
Fownhope
Rushall
Donnington
Sledge Green
Bushley
Much Marcle
Pendock
TEWKESBURY
Ashchurch
Ryton
Eldersfield
Forthampton
Walton Cardiff
Dymock
Redmarley D'Abitot
Chaceley
Fiddington
A4101
A461
A458
A451
A491
A456
A442
A449
A450
A448
A443
A4117
A451
A4133
A38
A44
A4103
A422
A465
A417
A438
A4104
A4209
A4211
A4105
M5
M50
B4363
B4364
B4555
B4194
B4202
B4190
B4195
B4196
B4197
B4203
B4204
B4214
B4220
B4219
B4503
B4208
B4232
B4216
B4215
B4224
B4024
B4211
B4084
B4082
B4080
B4090
B4079
B4188
A4110
A4112
64
51
47
36
1770
759
1034
886

53
BIRMINGHAM
COVENTRY
SOLIHULL
REDDITCH
KENILWORTH
ROYAL LEAMINGTON SPA
WARWICK
WARWICKSHIRE
STRATFORD-UPON-AVON
EVESHAM
Castle Bromwich
Coleshill
Astley
Arbury Hall
Maxstoke
Fillongley
Corley Ash
Goodyers End
Bedworth Woodlands
Bulkington
Smethwick
Tile Cross
Chelmsley Wood
Stechford
Marston Green
Yardley
Small Heath
Chad Valley
Harborne
Edgbaston
Balsall Heath
Sparkhill
Moseley
Sheldon
National Exhibition Centre
Little Packington
Outwoods
Corley Moor
Keresley
Hawkes End
Longford
Foleshill
Acock's Green
Elmdon
Elmdon Heath
Bickenhill
Meriden
Stonebridge
Selly Oak
Bournville
Springfield
King's Heath
Olton
Hall Green
King's Norton
Northfield
West Heath
Longbridge
Shirley
Hampton in Arden
Eastcote
Berkswell
Balsall Common
Tile Hill
Earlsdon
Stoke
Binley
Willenhall
Baginton
Stoneleigh
Bubbenhall
Knowle
Dorridge
Bentley Heath
Barston
Temple Balsall
Fen End
Burton Green
Hopwood
Wythall
Cheswick Green
Cofton Hackett
Alvechurch
Hockley Heath
Packwood
Chadwick End
Wroxall
Meer End
Honiley
Beausale
Kingswood
Lapworth
Rowington
Haseley
Leek Wootton
Hatton
Lowsonford
Shrewley
Tardebigge
Beoley
Tanworth in Arden
Ullenhall
Oldberrow
Henley-in-Arden
Mappleborough Green
Preston Bagot
Claverdon
Budbrooke
Hampton on the Hill
Langley
Norton Lindsey
Wootton Wawen
Studley
Sambourne
Coughton
Great Alne
Aston Cantlow
Bearley
Snitterfield
Wilmcote
Alcester
Arrow
Ragley Hall
Exhall
Temple Grafton
Binton
Billesley
Haselor
Ardens Grafton
Shottery
Anne Hathaway's Cottage
Bidford-on-Avon
Welford-on-Avon
Clifford Chambers
Atherstone on Stour
Barford
Sherbourne
Wasperton
Charlecote Park
Hampton Lucy
Charlecote
Wellesbourne
Tiddington
Alveston
Newbold Pacey
Moreton Morrell
Ashorne
Harbury
Bishop's Tachbrook
Whitnash
Radford Semele
Offchurch
Cubbington
Lighthorne
Chesterton Green
Gaydon
Chadshunt
Kineton
Butlers Marston
Pillerton Hersey
Pillerton Priors
Ettington
Alderminster
Preston on Stour
Long Marston
Dorsington
Marlcliff
Cleeve Prior
Salford Priors
Harvington
Norton
Offenham
Middle Littleton
South Littleton
Honeybourne
Badsey
Wickhamford
Mickleton
Hidcote Manor
Kiftsgate Court
Ilmington
Admington
Quinton
Newbold on Stour
Armscote
Tredington
Halford
Oxhill
Whatcote
Idlicote
Honington
Shipston on Stour
Darlingscott
Ebrington
Chipping Campden
Broad Campden
Willersey
Saintbury
Weston Subedge
Broadway
Broadway Tower
Buckland
Laverton
Stanton
Snowshill
Stanway
Toddington
Didbrook
Blockley
Batsford Arboretum
Bourton-on-the-Hill
Moreton-in-Marsh
Sezincote
Paxford
Draycott
Aston Magna
Stretton on Fosse
Todenham
Tidmington
Barcheston
Cherington
Long Compton
Little Wolford
Great Wolford
Barton-on-the-Heath
Whichford
Stourton
Sutton-under-Brailes
Lower Brailes
Upper Brailes
Shenington
Sibford Ferris
Sibford Gower
Swalcliffe
Hook Norton
Wigginton
Great Rollright
Swerford
Epwell
Shutford
Lower Tysoe
Middle Tysoe
Upper Tysoe
Radway
Ratley
Sedgeberrow
Hinton Cross
Childswickham
Aston Somerville
Wormington
Alderton

NUNEATON
Attleborough
Stockingford
Chilvers Coton
Burton Hastings
Marston Jabbet
Griff
BEDWORTH
Bramcote
Shelford
Smockington
Copston Magna
Wibtoft
Wolvey
Cloudesley Bush
Arbury Hall
How Green
Bedworth Woodlands
Goodyers End
Coalpit Field
Ryton
Bulkington
Hawkesbury
Corley Ash
Neal's Green
Rowley's Green
Little Bayton
Barnacle
Longford
Shilton
Withybrook
Hopsford
Sowe Common
Keresley
Little Heath
Hall Green
Ansty
Foleshill
COVENTRY
Walsgrave on Sowe
Stoke
Binley
Binley Common
Brinklow
Earlsdon
Pinley
Bretford
Brandon
Stivichall
Willenhall
Tollbar End
Wolston
Baginton
Lunt Roman Fort
COVENTRY AIRPORT
Ryton-on-Dunsmore
Stoneleigh
KENILWORTH
Stareton
Bubbenhall
Princethorpe
National Agricultural Centre
Wappenbury
Weston under Wetherley
Cubbington
Eathorpe
Hunningham
ROYAL LEAMINGTON SPA
Offchurch
Radford Semele
Whitnash
Bishop's Tachbrook
Ufton
Harbury
Ashorne
Chesterton Green
Cross Green
Bishop's Itchington
Moreton Morrell
Lighthorne
Gaydon
Knightcote
Chadshunt
Northend
Magpie Hill
Kineton
Little Kineton
Butlers Marston
Avon Dassett
Fenny Compton
Radway
Arlescote
Farnborough Hall
Warmington
Pillerton Hersey
Ratley
Oxhill
Lower Tysoe
Upton
Whatcote
Middle Tysoe
Upper Tysoe
Hornton
Horley
Alkerton
Shenington
Wroxton
Balscote
Winderton
Epwell
Shutford
North Newington
Lower Brailes
Sibford Gower
Sutton-under-Brailes
Broughton
Swalcliffe
Stourton
Sibford Ferris
Tadmarton
Whichford
Ascott
Hook Norton
Milcombe
Bloxham
Barford St John
Barford
OXFORDSHIRE
Drayton
BANBURY
Hanwell
Bodicote
Twyford Gardens
Adderbury
Milton
Middleton Cheney
Chacombe
Little Bourton
Great Bourton
Williamscot
Shotteswell
Mollington
Cropredy
Hays Bridge
Wardington
Upper Wardington
Chipping Warden
Edgcote
Appletree
Claydon
Farnborough
Lower Boddington
Upper Boddington
Aston le Walls
Wormleighton
Priors Hardwick
Priors Marston
Marston Doles
Ladbroke
Southam
Napton on the Hill
Napton
Stockton
Tomlow
Lower Shuckburgh
Upper Shuckburgh
Long Itchington
Cuttle
Bascote
Bascote Heath
Leamington Hastings
Broadwell
Grandborough
Marton
Birdingbury
Frankton
Draycote
Kites Hardwick
Woolscott
Willoughby
Bourton on Dunsmore
Thurlaston
Stretton-on-Dunsmore
RUGBY
Cawston
Bilton
Dunchurch
Long Lawford
New Bilton
Newbold on Avon
Church Lawford
Cathiron
Easenhall
Harborough Magna
Stretton under Fosse
Pailton
Street Ashton
Monks Kirby
Brockhurst
Willey
Churchover
Cotesbach
Lutterworth
Bitteswell
Ullesthorpe
Claybrooke Magna
Frolesworth
Sharnford
Leire
Dunton Bassett
Ashby Parva
Ashby Magna
Peatling Parva
Shearsby
Bruntingthorpe
Gilmorton
Walton
Kimcote
Misterton
Walcote
North Kilworth
South Kilworth
Swinford
Stanford Hall
Stanford on Avon
Shawell
Newton
Catthorpe
Lilbourne
Clifton upon Dunsmore
Dunsmore
Hillmorton
Clay Coton
Yelvertoft
Crick
Winwick
Kilsby
Barby
Ashby St Ledgers
Braunston
Welton
Sawbridge
Wolfhampcote
Nethercote
Flecknoe
Staverton
DAVENTRY
Norton
Catesby
Badby
Newnham
Dodford
Hellidon
Everdon
Fawsley
Charwelton
Church Charwelton
Preston Capes
Little Preston
Farthingstone
Hinton
Byfield
Woodford Halse
West Farndon
Eydon
Canons Ashby
Moreton Pinkney
Culworth
Thorpe Mandeville
Sulgrave Manor
Sulgrave
Weston
Marston St Lawrence
Stuchbury
Helmdon
Falcut
Greatworth
Thenford
Lower Middleton Cheney
Great Purston
Farthinghoe
Halse
Steane
BRACKLEY
Radstone
Upper Astrop
Astrop
Newbottle
King's Sutton
Charlton
Walton Grounds
Rowler
Hinton-in-the-Hedges
Evenley
Mixbury
Westbury
Finmere
Turweston
Shalstone
Whitfield
Dadford
Syresham
Crowfield
Biddlesden
Silverstone
Wappenham
Slapton
Abthorpe
Foscote
Towcester
Bradden
Weedon Lois
Plumpton
Woodend
Blakesley
Adstone
Maidford
Litchborough
Grimscote
Cold Higham
Duncote
Greens Norton
Pattishall
Upper Stowe
Church Stowe
Weedon
Upper Weedon
Flore
Upper Heyford
Nether Heyford
Brockhall
Harpole
Little Brington
Great Brington
Whilton
Long Buckby
Watford
West Haddon
Coton Manor
Guilsborough
Ravensthorpe
East Haddon
Thornby
Cold Ashby
Naseby
Welford
Sulby Reservoir
Husbands Bosworth
Theddingworth
Lubenham
Laughton
Mowsley
Saddington
Gumley
LEICESTERSHIRE
WARWICKSHIRE
NORTHAMPTONSHIRE
SP
R Avon
R Leam
R Nene
R Swift
R Cherwell
R Great Ouse
Canal

55
Langton
Weston by Welland
Rockingham
Rockingham Castle
Deenethorpe
Southwick
Tansor
Warmington
Ashley
Middleton
Cottingham
Weldon
Sutton Bassett
East Carlton
Wilbarston
Glapthorn
Cotterstock
Upper Benefield
Lower Benefield
OUNDLE
Ashton
Dingley
Little Bowden
MARKET HARBOROUGH
Brampton Ash
Stoke Albany
CORBY
Little Oakley
Stanion
ROCKINGHAM FOREST
Lyveden New Bield
Stoke Doyle
Polebrook
Lutton
Barnwell St. Andrew
Hemington
Pipewell
Great Oakley
Brigstock
Pilton
Lilford Park
Barnwell All Saints
Luddington in the Brook
Braybrooke
Great Oxendon
DESBOROUGH
Geddington
Wadenhoe
Thurning
Triangular Lodge
Newton
Eleanor Cross
Rushton
Achurch
Wigsthorpe
Arthingworth
Sudborough
Weekley
Grafton Underwood
Aldwincle
Thorpe Waterville
Winwick
Thorpe Underwood
ROTHWELL
Lowick
Clopton
Orton
Harrington
Warkton
Slipton
Islip
Titchmarsh
KETTERING
Cranford St. Andrew
Twywell
Loddington
Thorpe Malsor
Maidwell
Barton Seagrave
Woodford
Thrapston
Old Weston
Great Cransley
Little Cransley
Draughton
Broughton
Cranford St. John
Denford
Molesworth
Brington
BURTON LATIMER
Great Addington
Ringstead
Keyston
Leighton Bromswold
Lamport
Lamport Hall
Pytchley
Bottom End
Isham
Bythorn
Church End
Catworth
Brook End
Old
Orlingbury
Finedon
Little Addington
RAUNDS
Little Catworth
Scaldwell
Walgrave
Great Harrowden
Stanwick
Hannington
Little Harrowden
Hargrave
Covington
Stow
Tilbrook
IRTHLINGBOROUGH
Chelveston
Holcot
Hardwick
WELLINGBOROUGH
HIGHAM FERRERS
Caldecott
Shelton
Lower Dean
Upper Dean
Kimbolton
Newtown
Pitsford
Sywell
Mears Ashby
RUSHDEN
Yielden
River Til
Wood End
Swineshead
Moulton
Knuston
Overstone
Wilby
Little Irchester
Irchester
London End
Little Wymington
Wymington
Newton Bromswold
Melchbourne
Chadwell End
Pertenhall
Staughton Green
Boughton
Overstone Solarium
Great Doddington
Green End
Great Staughton
Boothville
New Barton
Earls Barton
Farndish
Knotting
Riseley
Brook End
Green End
Little Staughton
Kingsthorpe
Ecton
Wollaston
Podington
Knotting Green
Keysoe
West End
Weston Favell
Great Billing
Little Billing
Souldrop
Top End
Hardwick End
Hatch End
NORTHAMPTON
Abington
Strixton
Whiston
Lower End
Hinwick
Keysoe Row
Cogenhoe
Grendon
Bourne End
Little Houghton
Brafield-on-the-Green
Castle Ashby
Santa Pod
Sharnbrook
Church End
Bletsoe
Cross End
Bolnhurst
Delapré Abbey
Great Houghton
Castle Ashby
Eleanor Cross
Far Cotton
Easton Maudit
Bozeat
Odell
Coffle End
Felmersham
Radwell
Thurleigh
Chapel End
Colmworth
Little Odell
Scald End
Hardingstone
Denton
Harrold
Duck's Cross
Wootton
Yardley Hastings
Chellington
Milton Ernest
The Grange
Wood End
Wilden
Hackleton
Collingtree
Milton Malsor
Carlton
Pavenham
Stafford Bridge
Oakley
Ravensden
East End
Quinton
Horton
Lavendon
Sevicks End
Piddington
Quinton Green
Warrington
Cold Brayfield
West End
Clapham
Renhold
Courteenhall
Stevington
Salph End
Roade
Olney
Turvey
Bromham
Village Green
Weston Underwood
Eakley Lanes
Waterways Museum
Hartwell
Clifton Reynes
Newton Blossomville
Goldington
Ravenstone
Water End
Willington
BEDFORD
Emberton
Stagsden Bird Gardens
Stagsden
Biddenham
Queen's Park
Ashton
Petsoe End
Cople
Stoke Goldington
Filgrave
Hardmead
KEMPSTON
Cardington
Long Street
Stocking Green
Tyringham
Astwood
Moot Hall
Harrowden
Grafton Regis
Hungate End
Sherington
Wood End
Keeley Green
Elstow
Hanslope
Tathall End
Gayhurst
Chicheley
Chicheley Hall
Bourne End
Wootton
Cotton End
Yardley Gobion
Castlethorpe
North Crawley
Kempston Hardwick
Herring's Green
Wilshamstead
Moor End
Lathbury
Brook End
Upper Shelton
Little Linford
Haversham
NEWPORT PAGNELL
Gossard's Green
Wootton Broadmead
Stewartby
Cosgrove
Wharley End
Lower Shelton
Potterspury
New Bradwell
Great Linford
Chapel End
Silver End
Cranfield
East End
Caulcott
Puxley
Old Wolverton
Moulsoe
Marston Moretaine
Old Stratford
Wolverton
Willen
How End
Houghton Conquest
Haynes
Deanshanger
Stony Stratford
Broughton
Little Woolstone
Escheat
Millbrook Station
Haynes West End
Houghton
Salford
Bradwell
Calverton
Holcot
Passenham
MILTON KEYNES
Lidlington
Millbrook
Clophill
Beadlow
Leckhampstead
Brogborough
Boughton End
Hall End
Upper Weald
Shenley Church End
Loughton
Wavendon
Lower End
Woburn Sands
Ridgmont
AMPTHILL
Maulden
Upper Gravenhurst
Wrest Park
Beachampton
Shenley Brook End
Simpson
Walton
Bow Brickhill
Denel End
Flitton
Wardhedges
Silsoe
Thornton
Aspley Guise
Husborne Crawley
Steppingley
Greenfield
Lower Gravenhurst
Thornborough
Whaddon
BLETCHLEY
Far Bletchley
Birchmoor Green
Higher Berry End
Church End
Eversholt
Flitwick
Pulloxhill
Hanscombe End
Nash
Fenny

Tansor
Warmington
Morborne
Norman Cross
Whittlesey Mere
Ramsey Mereside
R Nene (Old Course)
B1093
Corner
Benwick
Primrose Hill
North End
68
Folksworth
Caldecote
Stilton
Holme
Ramsey St. Mary's
Middle Moor
B1096
A141
Ashton
A427
A605
PS
Chapel End
Lutton
Denton
Polebrook
Glatton
B660
B1040
Ramsey Forty Foot
Slade Field
West moor
B1098
CHATTE
Barnwell St. Andrew
Lilford Park
Hemington
Conington
A1
RAMSEY
Ramsey Heights
Sawtry
Bury
Tick Fen
A142
B1050
Mill End
Horseley Fen
Barnwell All Saints
Luddington in the Brook
Great Gidding
Chapel End
Green End
Little Gidding
Thurning
Church End
Upwood
Great Raveley
Wistow Fen
Turf Fen
Chapel Head
Wigsthorpe
B662
B1090
Wistow
Warboys
Little End
Pidley Fen
Thorpe Waterville
Winwick
Clopton
Steeple Gidding
Wood Walton
Mill End
Fenton
Chatteris Fen
8
Titchmarsh
Coppingford
Upton
Hamerton
Wennington
Little Raveley
Abbots Ripton
Broughton
Church End
Pidley
Somersham
Old Weston
55
Alconbury Weston
B1089
Oldhurst
B1086
Molesworth
A604
Buckworth
Little Stukeley
Kings Ripton
Colne
Brington
Alconbury
B1043
Wood End
Earith
Keyston
Bythorn
Leighton Bromswold
Barham
Great Stukeley
A14
Woodhurst
Bluntisham
B663
Church End
Catworth
Woolley
Sapley
Hartford
A141
B1090
A1123
Brook End
Spaldwick
HUNTINGDON
St. Peter's Hill
Houghton
ST. IVES
Green End
Little Catworth
Huntingdon
Stanton Butts
Easton
Ellington
Wyton
Hemingford Abbots
Needingworth
Church End
Holywell
Over
Covington
Stow Longa
Ellington Thorpe
Brampton
GODMANCHESTER
Hemingford Grey
West End
Fen Drayton
Tilbrook
7
Shelton
Grafham
Grafham Water
Newtown
Kimbolton
Buckden
Fenstanton
Church End
Swavesey
Middle Watch
Lower Dean
Upper Dean
River Til
Stonely
East Perry
Buckden Palace
Offord Cluny
Offord Darcy
Littleworth End
Hilton
Conington
Boxworth End
Swineshead
Wood End
West Perry
B661
Stirtloe
Melchbourne
Chadwell End
Staughton Green
Dillington
Staughton Highway
Pertenhall
Diddington
Boughton
Papworth St. Agnes
Elsworth
Boxworth
Oakington
Green End
Riseley
Brook End
Great Staughton
Southoe
Duck End
Great Paxton
Graveley
Kisby's Hut
Papworth Village
Papworth Everard
Lolworth
Bar Hill
Keysoe
West End
Little Staughton
Hail Weston
A45
Little Paxton
Toseland
Yelling
Knapwell
High Street
Girton
Top End
Hardwick End
Hatch End
Duloe
ST. NEOTS
Dry Drayton
Keysoe Row
Eaton Ford
Madingley
Bourne End
6
Staploe
Bushmead
Upper Staploe
Green End
Weald
Eltisley
Caxton Gibbet
A1303
Bolnhurst
Church End
Eaton Socon
Eynesbury
Croxton
Caxton End
Caxton
Highfields
Coton
Bletsoe
Church End
Cross End
Colmworth
B1428
B1046
Bourn
Hardwick
Thurleigh
Chapel End
Channel's End
Wyboston
Little Barford
Abbotsley
Great Gransden
Caxton End
Caldecote
Comberton
Scald End
Duck's Cross
Green End
B1046
Milton Ernest
Wood End
Wilden
Chawston
Bourn
Toft
Barton
The Grange
Colesden
Waresley
Little Gransden
Longstowe
Kingston
Claypit Hill
Church End
Ravensden
East End
Roxton
Langford End
Sevicks End
A428
Great Eversden
Haslingfield
Clapham
Renhold
Green End
Tempsford
Gamlingay Cinques
B1046
Little Eversden
Salph End
Great Barford
Gamlingay
Hatley St. George
Harlton
A6
Goldington
AA 24 hour
Water End
Willington
Blunham
Everton
Gamlingay Great Heath
Wimpole Hall
Orwell
Harston
5
BEDFORD
Mogerhanger
Cockayne Hatley
East Hatley
Arrington
Queen's Park
A603
Cople
St. Johns
SANDY
Croydon
New Wimpole
Barrington
Cardington
Hatch
Potton
Wrestlingworth
B1042
Wendy
Shepreth
Moot Hall
Harrowden
Thorncote Green
Beeston
The Lodge
Stratford
Tadlow
Foxton
Elstow
BEDFORDSHIRE
Northill
Sutton
Whaddon
Frog End
A421
Cotton End
Ickwell Green
Swiss Garden
Upper Caldecote
Eyeworth
Shingay
Bassingbourn
R Cam or Rhee
Meldreth
Kempston Hardwick
Herring's Green
Abington Pigotts
Kneesworth
Chiswick End
Fowlmere
Wilshamstead
New Town
North End
A6
Old Warden
Shuttleworth Collection
Dunton
Guilden Morden
North Brook End
Melbourn
BIGGLESWADE
South End
Bassingbourn
Stewartby
Broom
Steeple Morden
Litlington
Chapel End
Silver End
Southill
Haynes
Langford
Edworth
Ashwell End
ROYSTON
A505
Houghton Conquest
Ireland
Stanford
Hinxworth
B1039
B1368
Haynes West End
B658
4
Houghton
Shefford
Clifton
Ashwell
The Thrift
Henlow
Clophill
Beadlow
Caldecote
Barley
Hall End
Campton
Astwick
Odsey
Therfield
A507
Maulden
Upper Gravenhurst
Newnham
A10
Smith's End
Church End
Reed
Wrest Park
Meppershall
Brook End
Slip End
Kelshall
Wardhedges
Flitton
40
Henlow Camp
Arlesey
Bygrave
41
Reed End
Silsoe
Bury End
Stotfold
Radwell
A505
Chapel Green
Barkway
Nuthampstead
Greenfield
Lower Gravenhurst
Upton End
Upper Stondon
Wallington
Sandon
Norton
Roe Green
Pulloxhill
Hanscombe End
Shillington
Higham Gobion
Apsley
Lower Green
BALDOCK
Redhill
Green End
Buckland
1
2
3
4

Boot's Bridge
Manea
The Biggins
Purls Bridge
Welches Dam
Oxlode
Pymore
Black Bank
Downham
Apes Hall
Mare Fen
Littleport Bridge
Littleport
Burnt Fen
Brandon Creek
Brandon Bank
Feltwell Anchor
Feltwell
Hockwold cum Wilton
Hockwold Fens
Weeting
Grimes Graves
Santon Downham
Brandon
Town Street
Little Ouse River
Lakenheath Halt
Wangford Fen
Warren Lodge
Thetford Warren
Lakenheath
Undley
Little Erlswell
Shippea Hill Halt
Mile End
Prickwillow
Chettisham
West Fen
Coveney
Witcham
ELY
Queen Adelaide
Middle Fen
Stuntney
Great Fen
Kennyhill
Holmsey Green
Mildenhall Fen
River Lark
Beck Row
Eriswell
Elveden
Wentworth
Witchford
Little Thetford
Broad Hill
Thistley Green
West Row
Mildenhall
Holywell Row
Wilburton
Stretham
Barway
Soham Cotes
Isleham
Worlington
Barton Mills
Icklingham
Aldreth
Green End
Elford Closes
Soham Mere
Soham
Green Hills
Fordham
Freckenham
Tuddenham
West Stow
Brockley
Smithey Fen
Chittering
Upware
Wicken
New River
Redlodge Warren
Herringswell
Lackford
Flempton
Cottenham
Green End
Denny Abbey
River Bank
Adventurers' Fen
North Street
Landwade
Chippenham
Cavenham
Hengrave
Waterbeach
Reach
Burwell
Snailwell
Kennett
Tuddenham Corner
Fornham All Saints
Landbeach
Kennett End
Kentford
Risby
Lower Green
Higham
Swaffham Prior
Exning
Moulton
Needham Street
Gazeley
Upper Green
Barrow
Burthorpe Green
Westley
Little Saxham
Clayhithe
Commercial End
Newmarket Heath
NEWMARKET
Horningsea
Anglesey Abbey
Lode
Swaffham Bulbeck
Stow cum Quy
Bottisham
Ashley
Dalham
Denham End
Great Saxham
Denham
Horringer
Ickworth
Cheveley
Broad Green
Dunstall Green
Hargrave
Lady's Green
Hargrave Green
Chevington
Fen Ditton
Saxon Street
Stetchworth
Wood Ditton
Upend
Ousden
Back Street
Tan Office Green
Frog End
Little Wilbraham
Teversham
Dullingham
Ditton Green
Kirtling
Lidgate
Stonecross Green
Church End
Great Wilbraham
Six Mile Bottom
Burrough End
Baxter's Green
Depden Green
Chedburgh
Rede
Cherry Hinton
Fulbourn
Holme End
Westley Waterless
Burrough Green
Kirtling Green
Boyden End
Thorns
Ashfield Green
Gulling Green
Trumpington
Wickhambrook
Brockley Green
Wandlebury Ring
Gog Magog Hills
Willingham Green
Brinkley
Sharp's Corner
Great Bradley
Lambfair Green
Attleton Green
Pound Green
Wickham Street
Clopton Green
Great Shelford
Weston Colville
Cowlinge
Denston
Hawkedon
Carlton
Little Bradley
Cock & End
Farley Green
Stradishall
Stansfield
Somerton
Stapleford
West Wratting
Carlton Green
Weston Green
Little Thurlow Green
Assington Green
Upper Street
Thurston End
Boxted
Fenstead End
Fishers
R Granta
Little Shelford
Babraham
Balsham
Thurlow
Sowley Green
Little Abington
Temple End
West Wickham
Great Wratting
Hundon
Babel Green
Sawston
Pampisford
Hildersham
Barnardiston
Poslingford
The Spike
Great Abington
Linton
Horseheath
Streetly End
Mount Pleasant
Chilton Street
Nether Hall
Glemsford
Vineyards
Withersfield
Hanchet End
Little Wratting
Brockley Green
Cavendish
Cardinal's Green
Bartlow
Mill Green
HAVERHILL
Burton End
Kedington
Clare
Pentlow Street
Foxearth
Duxford
Duxford Airfield
Zoological Gardens
Nosterfield End
Hazel Stub
Boyton End
Pentlow
Hickford Hill
Hinxton
Hadstock
Shudy Camps
Sturmer
Wixoe
Stoke by Clare
Belchamp St. Paul
Borley
Stump Cross
Great Chesterford
Castle Camps
Ickleton
Steventon End
Wiggens Green
New England
Baythorne End
Ovington
Borley Green
Little Chesterford
Ashdon
Camps End
Pale Green
Birdbrook
Ashen
Little Walden
Olmstead Green
Helions Bumpstead
Belchamp Otten
Belchamp Walter
Elmdon
Strethall
Church End
Littlebury
Water End
Smith's Green
Steeple Bumpstead
Moyns Park
Ridgewell
Knowl Green
Tilbury Green
Puttock End
Belchamp Hall
SAFFRON WALDEN
Radwinter End
Great Yeldham
Little Yeldham
Bulmer Tye
Littlebury Green
Audley End
Millfield
Chrishall
Radwinter
Hempstead
Chapel End Way
Dyer's End
Stambourne
Grass Green
Gestingthorpe
Bridge Green
Sewards End
Robinhood End
Toppesfield
Pool Street
Audley End
Wickham St. Paul
Wendens Ambo
Wimbish
Spain's End
Cornish Hall End
Le Hurst
Colne Valley
Castle Hedingham
Cole End
Tye Green
Great Sampford
River Pant
Gainsford End
Delvin Green
Audley End Station
Arkesden
Upper Green
Wimbish Green
Elder Street
Debden
Little London
Delvin End
Highstreet Green
Great Maplestead
Lucking Street
Langley
Bird Green
Howlett End
Howe Street
Little Maplestead
Stickling Green
Hill Green
Newport
Little Sampford
Spain's Hall
Morris Green
Sible Hedingham
Doe's

Lynford Cottages
East Wretham
Hockham
Stonebridge
Snetterton
Eccles Road
South End
Larling
Wilby
Stacksford
Cake Street
New Buckenham
Hargate
Aslacton
Tibenham
70
Weeting
Grimes Graves
Santon Downham
Croxton
A1075
Quidenham
Hunt's Corner
Banham
B1134
Pristow Green
N
O
R
F
O
Harling Road Station
A11
Brandon
Town Street
Bridgham
East Harling
River Thet
Middle Harling
International Motor Museum
Kenninghall
Winfarthing
Gissing
Dam Green
Shelfanger
Mill Green
Warren Lodge
Thetford Warren
Priory
"Latin American" Wildlife Park
Shadwell
A1066
Brettenham
North Lopham
South Lopham
Fersfield
Bressingham Common
Bressingham
Burston
Garboldisham
THETFORD
Rushford
Gasthorpe
Snow Street
Walcot Green
Thelveton
A1088
A134
Smallworth
Blo Norton
Live Steam Museum
Roydon
DISS
Scole
Palgrave
Waterloo
Knettishall
Elveden
Euston
Barnham
Euston Hall
Coney Weston
Hopton
Redgrave
Thelnetham
Wortham
Stuston
Oakley
A11
Barningham
Market Weston
Hinderclay
Thrandeston
A143
Fakenham Magna
Sapiston
Rickinghall Inferior
Botesdale
Mellis
Brome
Honington
Hepworth
B1111
B1112
B1106
Bardwell
Rickinghall Superior
Yaxley
EYE
Icklingham
Stanton
Wattisfield
A1101
Troston
Ixworth Thorpe
Bangrove
Upthorpe
Allwood Green
Thornham Parva
B1117
Braiseworth
West Stow
Brockley
Ingham
Ampton
Great Livermere
Walsham le Willows
Cranmer Green
Gislingham
Thornham Magna
Lackford
Culford
Ixworth Abbey
Ixworth
West Street
Langham
Four Ashes
Finningham
Wickham Street
Stoke Ash
Standwell Green
Flempton
Timworth Green
Grimstone End
Badwell Ash
Badwell Green
Westhorpe
Thorndon
Hengrave
B1106
Conyer's Green
Upper Town
Stowlangtoft
Long Thurlow
Wyverstone
Wickham Skeith
A140
Thwaite
Fornham All Saints
Fornham St. Martin
Hunston
Hestley Green
Risby
Great Barton
Pakenham
Stanton Street
Great Ashfield
Wyverstone Street
Bacton
Cotton
Brockford Street
Wetheringsett
A143
East Barton
Thurston
Norton
Bird Gardens
Earl's Green
Cow Green
Ford's Green
Mendlesham
Burthorpe Green
Westley
Cattishall
BURY ST. EDMUNDS
Thurston Planch
Tostock
Elmswell
Haughley Green
Ward Green
Brockford Green
Little Saxham
A45
Beyton Green
Gipping
Mendlesham Green
Park Green
Great Saxham
Horringer
Blackthorpe
Kingshall Street
Beyton
Woolpit
Wetherden
Brown Street
Old Newton
Mickfield
A134
Rushbrooke
Hessett
Drinkstone
Haughley
Saxham Street
Middlewood Green
Denham
Low Green
Ickworth
Sicklesmere
Rougham Green
Bradfield St. George
Drinkstone Green
Haughley Park
Harleston
Stowupland
Little Stonham
Chevington
Hawstead
Little Welnetham
Clopton Green
Hargrave Green
Tan Office Green
Great Welnetham
Maypole Green
Rattlesden
STOWMARKET
Forward Green
Stonham Aspel
Hawstead Green
Stonecross Green
Bradfield St. Clare
Gedding
Poystreet Green
Earl Stonham
Whepstead
Bradfield Combust
Buxhall
Great Finborough
Creeting Bottoms
Depden Green
Chedburgh
Melon Green
Bush Green
Felsham
Hightown Green
Combs Ford
Creeting St. Mary
Crowfield
Rede
Stanningfield
Oldhall Green
Combs
Coddenham Green
Ashfield Green
Gulling Green
Harrow Green
Hart's Green
Cross Green
Great Green
High Street Green
Needham Market
Jack's Green
Gosbeck
Brockley Green
World's End
Moats Tye
Lawshall
Brettenham
Battisford Tye
Battisford
Coddenham
Clopton Green
Cockfield
Thorpe Green
Denston
Hawkedon
Cross Green
Audley End
Lawshall Green
Shimpling Street
Thorpe Morieux
Cross Green
Charles Tye
Ringshall
B1078
Barking
Hemingstone
Stansfield
Somerton
Hartest
Hitcham
Hitcham Causeway
Wattisham
Barking Tye
Baylham
Barham
Thurston End
Boxted
Fenstead End
Upper Street
Fishers
Shimpling
Alpheton
Preston
Hitcham Street
Nedging Tye
Ringshall Stocks
Upper Street
Willisham Tye
Great Blakenham
Claydon
Stanstead
A134
Lavenham
Guildhall
Kettlebaston
Great Bricett
Offton
Akenham
Poslingford
Bridge Street
Whelp Street
Chelsworth
Bildeston
Naughton
Somersham
Little Blakenham
B1066
Glemsford
Kentwell Hall
Brent Eleigh
Nedging
Nether Hall
Chilton Street
Vineyards
High Street
Ash Street
Elmsett
Bramford
Cavendish
A1092
B1115
Monks Eleigh
Flowton
Little Waldingfield
Milden
Semer
Whatfield
Melford Hall
Long Melford
Drakestone Green
Pentlow Street
Foxearth
Lindsey Tye
Sproughton
Clare
Pentlow
Acton
Lindsey
St. James Chapel
Aldham
Hickford Hill
Newman's Green
Great Waldingfield
Rose Green
Burstall
Belchamp St. Paul
Borley
Rodbridge Corner
Castling's Heath
Kersey
Stone Street
A1071
Hintlesham
Ovington
Borley Green
B1115
Kersey Tye
Coram Street
Duke Street
Mill Green
Hadleigh
Chantry
SUDBURY
Chilton
Edwardstone
Groton
Kersey Upland
Guildhall
Washbrook
Belchamp Otten
Belchamp Walter
Cornard Tye
Sherbourne Street
Wicker Street Green
Chattisham
Knowl Green
Ballingdon
Boxford
Layham
California
Mace Green
Copdock
Bulmer
Newton
A1071
Bower House Tye
Hadleigh Heath
A45
Puttock End
Belchamp Hall
A131
Great Cornard
Belstead
Little Yeldham
Bulmer Tye
Middleton
Stone Street
Polstead Heath
B1070
Little Wenham
A12
Little Cornard
Calais Street
Whitestreet Green
Great Wenham
Gestingthorpe
Great Henny
Polstead
Shelley
Raydon
Bentley
Assington
Henny Street
Capel St. Mary
Pool Street
Audley End
Wickham St. Paul
Leavenheath
Mill Street
Lower Raydon
Holton St. Mary
ESSEX
Colne Valley
B1058
Twinstead
Workhouse Green
Rose Green
Stoke-by-Nayland
Thorington Street
Four Sisters
Tattingstone
Castle Hedingham
Twinstead Green
42
Honey Tye
Higham
East Bergholt
43
Alton Water
Great Maplestead
Alphamstone
Lamarsh
Bures Green
B1068
East End
Lucking Street
Nayland
Stratford St. Mary
Flatford Mill & Lock
Upper Street
Sible Hedingham
A604
Little Maplestead
Cross End
Bures
Dedham
Brantham
Cattawade
Stutton
Pebmarsh
Wissington

Shelton
Shelton Green
Ditchingham
Broome
Geldeston
Kirkley
Hardwick
Great Green
BUNGAY
Wainford
Shipmeadow
Worlingham
River Waveney
Barnby
Transport Museum
North Cove
Carlton Colville
North Green
Otter Trust
Mettingham
Barsham
BECCLES
Mutford
Gisleham
Earsham
Ringsfield
Denton
Rushmere
Colegate End
Bush Green
Alburgh
Ellough
Black Street
Kessingland
Pulham Market
Flixton
Ilketshall St. Margaret
Ilketshall St. Andrew
Ringsfield Corner
Hulver Street
Pulham St. Mary
Wortwell
Homersfield
Henstead
Suffolk Wildlife Park
Kessingland Beach
Redenhall
St. Margaret South Elmham
Redisham
Shadingfield
Sotterly
Starston
Benacre
Garlic Street
St. Michael South Elmham
Long Cottages
Church Street
Harleston
St. Cross South Elmham
All Saints South Elmham
Cox Common
Brampton Station
Wrentham
Mendham
Stone Street
Stoven
Clay Common
Covehithe
Needham
Withersdale Street
Rumburgh
Brampton
Frostenden
St. James South Elmham
Mill Common
South Cove
Weybread
Spexhall
Westhall
Barnaby Green
Cove Bottom
Metfield
Uggeshall
Brockdish
Wissett
Wangford
Chediston Green
Syleham
Broadway
Holton
Mount Pleasant
Fressingfield
Wingfield
Chediston
Blyford
Reydon
Wingfield Green
Little Whittingham Green
Linstead Parva
Blackwater
Cross Street
HALESWORTH
Broad Road
Mells
Heckfield Green
Pixey Green
Silverley's Green
Rackham's Corner
Cratfield
Cookley
Wenhaston
Blackheath
Blythburgh
SOUTHWOLD
Stradbroke
Walpole
Walberswick
Denham
Huntingfield
Walpolelane
Thorington
Denham Green
Bramfield
Horham
Wootten Green
Ashfield Green
Laxfield
Owl's Green
Heveningham
Athelington
Wilby
Ubbeston Green
High Street
Dunwich
Stanway Green
Brundish Street
Fingal Street
Crown Corner
Poys Street
Darsham
Grey Friars
Brundish
Southolt
Worlingworth
Peasenhall
Sibton
Westleton
Badingham
Goddard's Corner
Yoxford
Shop Street
Capon's Green
Tannington
Maypole Green
Rotten End
Middleton
Bedfield Long Green
Middleton Moor
Bedfield
Saxtead
Dennington
Bruisyard
Bruisyard Street
Theberton
North Green
Eastbridge
Kelsale
Saxtead Little Green
Brabling Green
Cransford
East Green
Poplar Street
Monk Soham
Carlton
Leiston Abbey
Framlingham
Rendham
Saxtead Green
Swefling
LEISTON
Sizewell
Ashfield
Earl Soham
North Green
SAXMUNDHAM
Knodishall
Bigsby Corner
Sternfield
Lampardbrook
Great Glemham
Benhall Street
Aldringham
Brandeston
Kettleburgh
Mill Green
Silverlace Green
Farnham
Benhall Green
Coldfair Green
Framsden
Parham
Stratford St. Andrew
Friston
Thorpeness
Cretingham
Hoo Green
Hacheston
Snape
Glemham Hall
Little Glemham
Snape Street
Monewden
Easton Farm Park
Easton
Magpie Street
Letheringham
Marlesford
Blaxhall
Lower Hacheston
Campsea Ashe
ALDEBURGH
Charsfield
Otley Green
Wickham Market
Iken
Otley
Clopton Corner
Dallinghoo
Tunstall
High Street
Aldeburgh Bay
Ashbocking Green
Debach
Pettistree
Tunstall Forest
Sudbourne
Upper Street
Ufford
Bredfield
River Alde
Swilland
Boulge
Lower Street
Chillesford
Friday Street
Clopton
Burgh
Eyke
Hasketon
Butley
Grundisburgh
Melton
Bromeswell
Orford
Tuddenham
Rendlesham Forest
Orford Ness
WOODBRIDGE
Boot Street
Bealings
Capel Green
Butley Corner
Capel St Andrew
Kingston
Playford
Methersgate
Rushmere St. Andrew
Martlesham
Sutton
Boyton
Kesgrave
Stores Corner
Oak Hill
Shottisham
Waldringfield
Duck Corner
IPSWICH
Hollesley
Hollesley Bay Colony
Brightwell
Newbourn
Warren Heath
Hollesley Bay
Newbourn Estate
Hemley
Shingle Street
Bucklesham
Ramsholt
Alderton
River Deben
Nacton
Alnesbourn Priory
Bawdsey
Levington
Kirton
Falkenham
Lower Falkenham
River Orwell
Thorpe Common
Trimley Heath
Pinmill
Chelmondiston
Felixstoweferry
Trimley Lower Street
Trimley
Shotley Street
Walton
Old Felixstowe
Harkstead
Walton Lower Street
Shotley Gate
Erwarton
FELIXSTOWE
SCALE
0 1 2 3 4 5 miles
0 1 2 3 4 5 kilometres

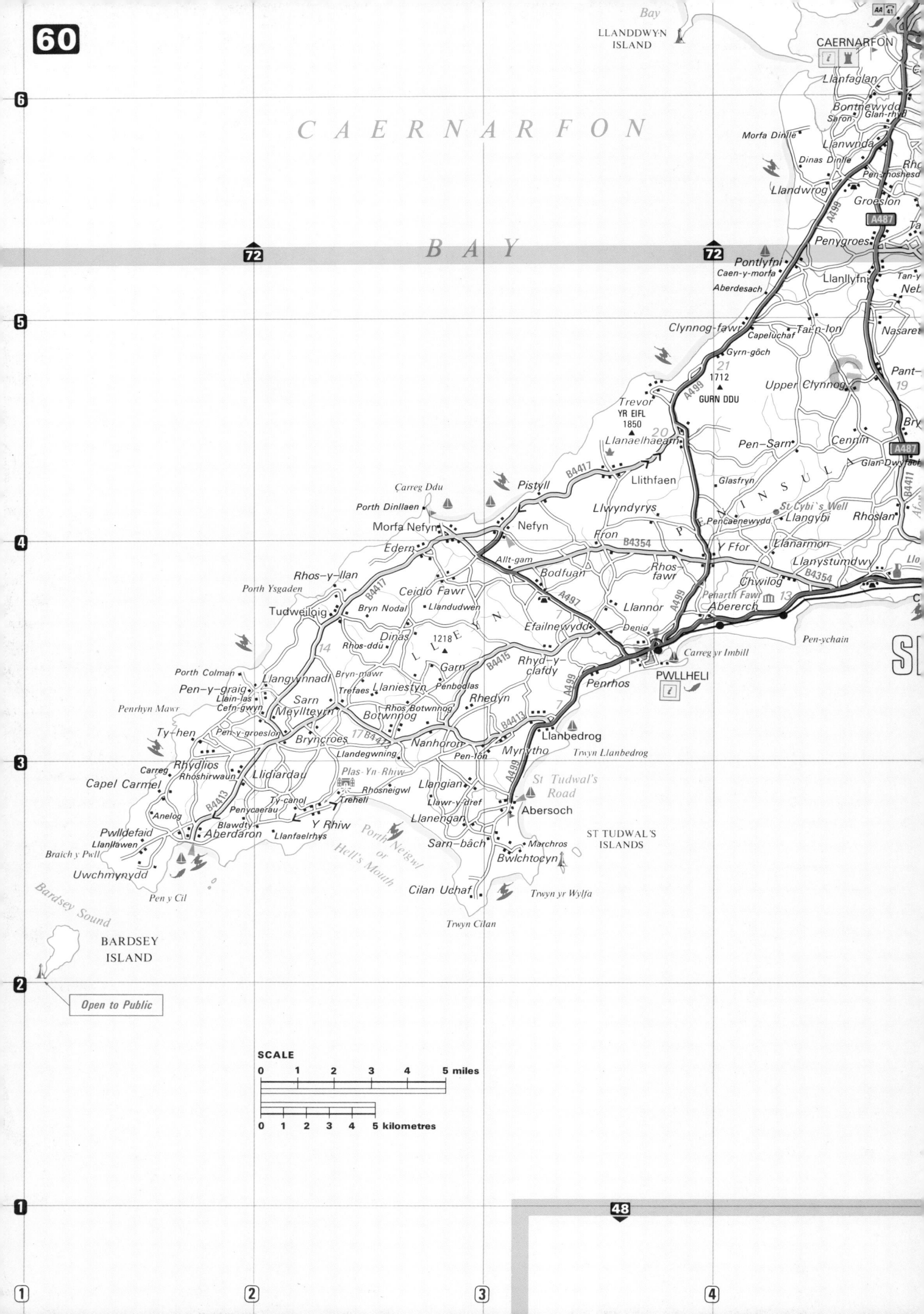

C A E R N A R F O N
B A Y
72
LLANDDWYN ISLAND
CAERNARFON
Llanfaglan
Bontnewydd
Saron
Glan-rhyd
Morfa Dinlle
Llanwnda
Dinas Dinlle
Pen-rhoshesd
Llandwrog
Groeslon
A499
A487
Penygroes
Pontlyfni
Caen-y-morfa
Llanllyfni
Aberdesach
Clynnog-fawr
Capeluchaf
Tai-n-lon
Nasareth
Gyrn-gôch
1712
GURN DDU
Upper Clynnog
Trevor
YR EIFL
1850
Llanaelhaearn
Pen-Sarn
Cennin
Glan-Dwyfach
B4417
Pistyll
Llithfaen
Glasfryn
Carreg Ddu
Porth Dinllaen
Morfa Nefyn
Nefyn
Llwyndyrys
St Cybi's Well
Pencaenewydd
Llangybi
Rhoslan
Edern
Fron
B4354
Y Ffor
Llanarmon
Allt-gam
Bodfuan
Rhos-fawr
Llanystumdwy
Rhos-y-llan
Porth Ysgaden
Ceidio Fawr
A497
Chwilog
Penarth Fawr
Abererch
Tudweiliog
Bryn Nodal
Llandudwen
Llannor
Efailnewydd
Denio
Pen-ychain
Dinas
1218
Rhos-ddu
Carreg yr Imbill
PWLLHELI
Porth Colman
Llangwnnadl
Bryn-mawr
Garn
B4415
Rhyd-y-clafdy
Penrhos
Pen-y-graig
Llain-las
Cefn-gwyn
Trefaes
Llaniestyn
Penbodlas
Rhedyn
Penrhyn Mawr
Sarn Meyllteyrn
Rhos Botwnnog
Botwnnog
B4413
Ty-hen
Pen-y-groeslon
Bryncroes
Llandegwning
Nanhoron
Pen-lôn
Llanbedrog
Mynytho
Trwyn Llanbedrog
Carreg
Rhydlios
Rhoshirwaun
Llidiardau
Plas-Yn-Rhiw
Capel Carmel
Llangian
St Tudwal's Road
Rhosneigwl
Ty-canol
Treheli
Llawr-y-dref
Anelog
Penycaerau
Abersoch
Blawdty
Y Rhiw
Llanengan
Pwlldefaid
Aberdaron
Llanfaelrhys
Porth Neigwl or Hell's Mouth
Llanllawen
Sarn-bâch
Marchros
ST TUDWAL'S ISLANDS
Braich y Pwll
Bwlchtocyn
Uwchmynydd
Cilan Uchaf
Trwyn yr Wylfa
Pen y Cil
Bardsey Sound
Trwyn Cilan
BARDSEY ISLAND
Open to Public
SCALE
0 1 2 3 4 5 miles
0 1 2 3 4 5 kilometres
48

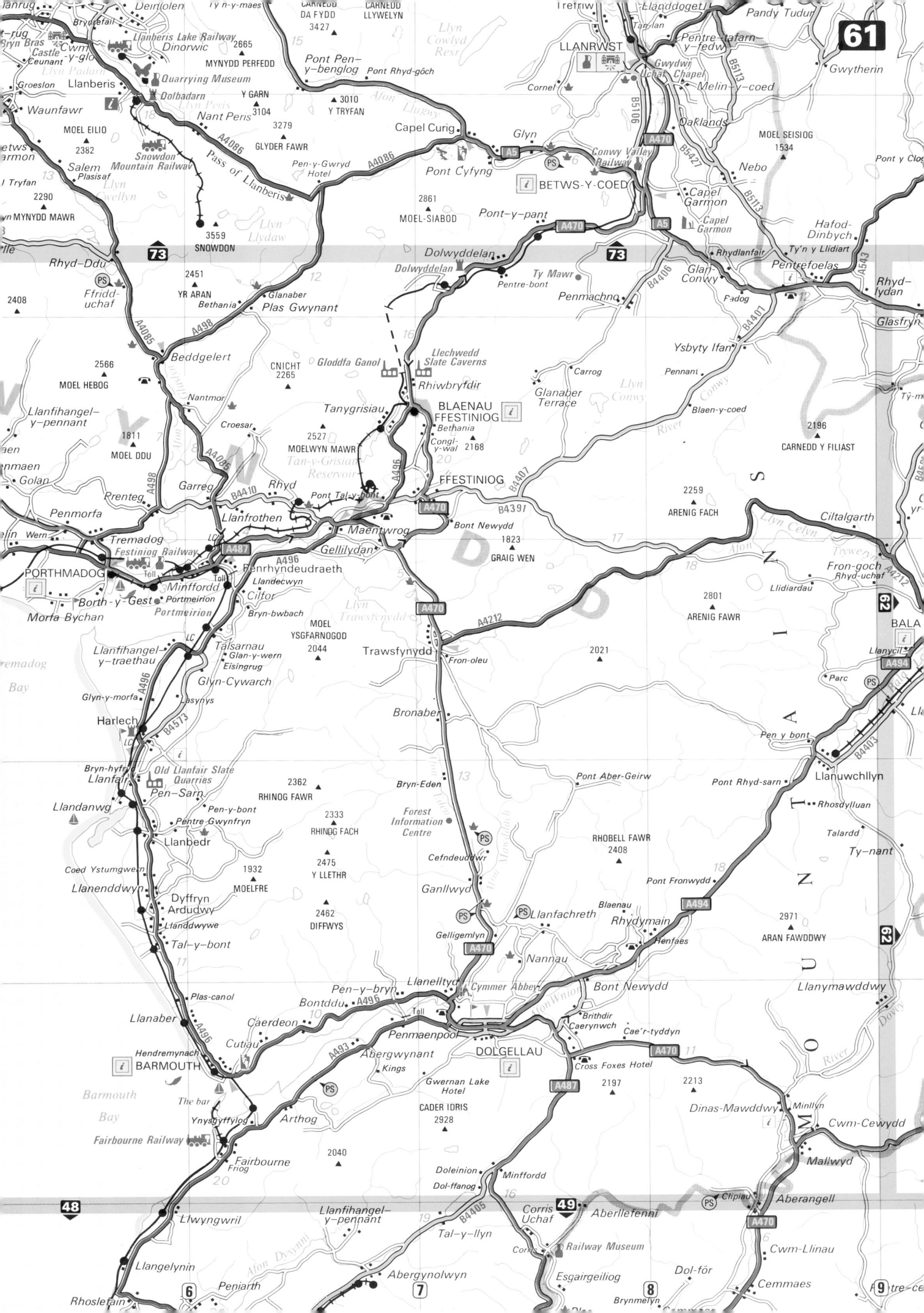
LLANRWST
BETWS-Y-COED
Capel Curig
Llanberis
Snowdon Mountain Railway
SNOWDON
3559
Pass of Llanberis
Beddgelert
BLAENAU FFESTINIOG
Llechwedd Slate Caverns
Gloddfa Ganol
FFESTINIOG
Maentwrog
PORTHMADOG
Tremadog
Festiniog Railway
Penrhyndeudraeth
Minffordd
Portmeirion
Borth-y-Gest
Morfa Bychan
Harlech
Old Llanfair Slate Quarries
Llanbedr
Trawsfynydd
Dolwyddelan
Pentrefoelas
Ysbyty Ifan
Llanuwchllyn
BALA
Cymmer Abbey
Llanelltyd
DOLGELLAU
Penmaenpool
CADER IDRIS
2928
BARMOUTH
Barmouth Bay
Fairbourne Railway
Fairbourne
Arthog
Dinas-Mawddwy
Mallwyd
Corris Uchaf
Railway Museum
Abergynolwyn
Tal-y-llyn
Llwyngwril
Llangelynin
Rhoslefain
Llanymawddwy
ARENIG FAWR
2801
RHOBELL FAWR
2408
ARAN FAWDDWY
2971
RHINOG FAWR
2362
MOELWYN MAWR
2527
MOEL HEBOG
2566
CNICHT
2265
GLYDER FAWR
3279
Y TRYFAN
3010
MOEL-SIABOD
2861
Conwy Valley Railway
Llanberis Lake Railway
Quarrying Museum
Dolbadarn
Forest Information Centre
Gwernan Lake Hotel
Cross Foxes Hotel
73
48
49
62
6
7
8
9

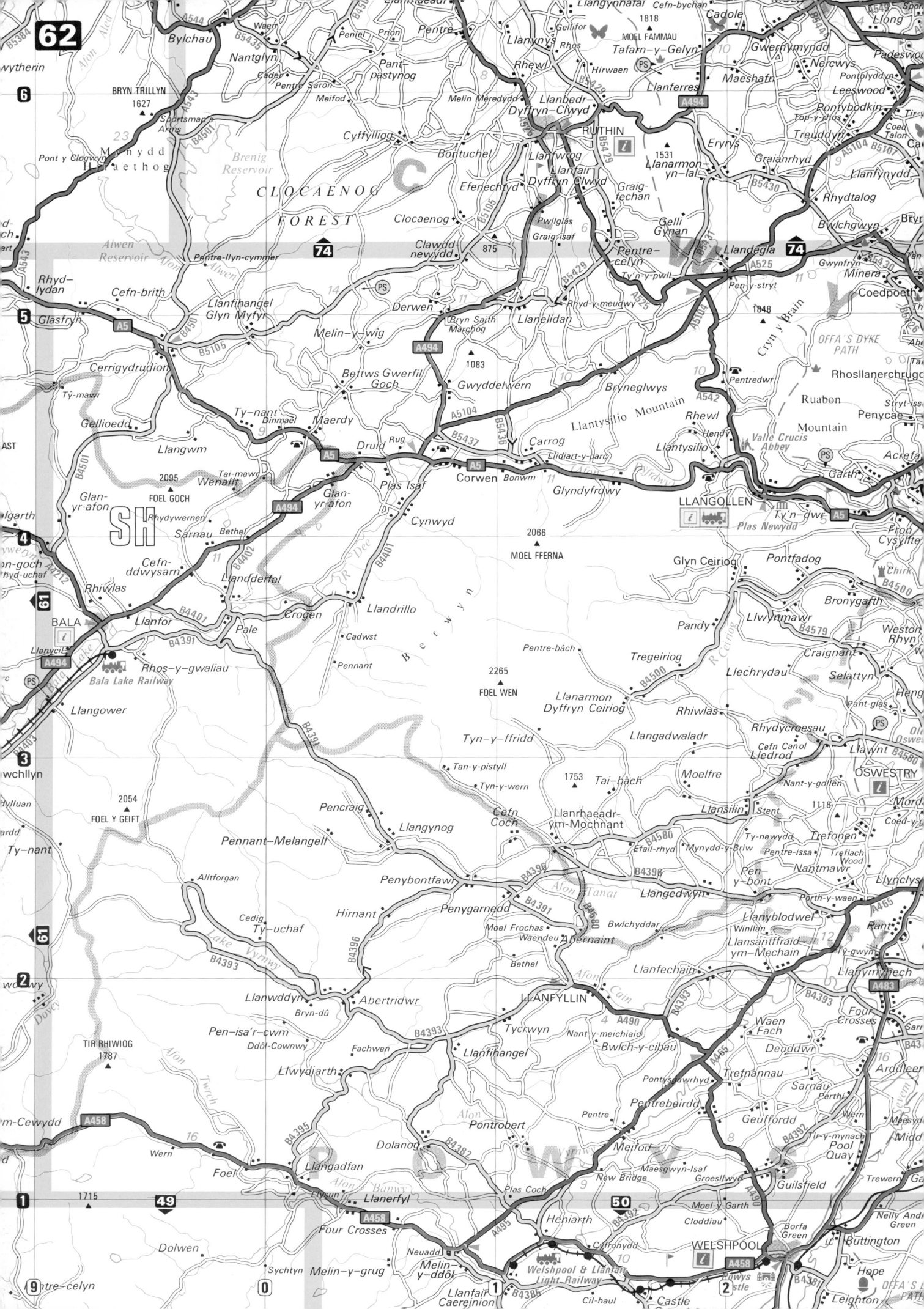
62
Bylchau
Nantglyn
BRYN TRILLYN
Mynydd Hiraethog
Brenig Reservoir
CLOCAENOG FOREST
Alwen Reservoir
Cyffylliog
Bontuchel
Clocaenog
Clawdd-newydd
Pentre
Llanynys
Rhewl
MOEL FAMMAU
Tafarn-y-Gelyn
Cadole
Gwernymynydd
Nercwys
Maeshafn
Llanferres
Llanbedr-Dyffryn-Clwyd
RUTHIN
Llanfwrog
Llanfair Dyffryn Clwyd
Efenechtyd
Llanarmon-yn-Ial
Eryrys
Graianrhyd
Treuddyn
Llanfynydd
Rhydtalog
Bwlchgwyn
Minera
Coedpoeth
Llandegla
Pentre-celyn
Graig-fechan
Gelli Gynan
Pwllglâs
Pentre-llyn-cymmer
Rhyd-lydan
Cefn-brith
Glasfryn
Llanfihangel Glyn Myfyr
Derwen
Llanelidan
Melin-y-wig
Cerrigydrudion
Bettws Gwerfil Goch
Gwyddelwern
Bryneglwys
Cryn y Brain
OFFA'S DYKE PATH
Rhosllanerchrugog
Ruabon Mountain
Penycae
Llantysilio Mountain
Rhewl
Llantysilio
Valle Crucis Abbey
Acrefair
Garth
Ty-nant
Maerdy
Gellioedd
Llangwm
Druid
Carrog
Corwen
Bonwm
Glyndyfrdwy
LLANGOLLEN
Plas Newydd
Ty'n-dwr
Froncysyllte
FOEL GOCH
Wenallt
Glan-yr-afon
Plas Isaf
Cynwyd
Sarnau
Cefn-ddwysarn
Llandderfel
MOEL FFERNA
Glyn Ceiriog
Pontfadog
Chirk
Rhiwlas
BALA
Llanfor
Pale
Crogen
Llandrillo
Berwyn
Bronygarth
Llwynmawr
Pandy
Weston Rhyn
Craignant
Selattyn
Llechrydau
Tregeiriog
Pentre-bâch
Cadwst
Pennant
Rhos-y-gwaliau
Bala Lake Railway
Llangower
FOEL WEN
Llanarmon Dyffryn Ceiriog
Rhiwlas
Rhydycroesau
Llangadwaladr
Tyn-y-ffridd
Cefn Canol
Lledrod
OSWESTRY
Moelfre
Tai-bâch
Tan-y-pistyll
Tyn-y-wern
FOEL Y GEIFT
Pencraig
Llangynog
Cefn Coch
Llanrhaeadr-ym-Mochnant
Llansilin
Trefonen
Nantmawr
Pen-y-bont
Llangedwyn
Pennant-Melangell
Alltforgan
Penybontfawr
Penygarnedd
Hirnant
Moel Frochas
Abernaint
Bwlchyddar
Llanyblodwel
Llansantffraid-ym-Mechain
Llanymynech
Cedig
Ty-uchaf
Lake Vyrnwy
Llanwddyn
Abertridwr
LLANFYLLIN
Llanfechain
Four Crosses
Waen Fach
Deuddwr
Arddleen
TIR RHIWIOG
Pen-isa'r-cwm
Ddôl-Cownwy
Fachwen
Tycrwyn
Llanfihangel
Nant-y-meichiaid
Bwlch-y-cibau
Llwydiarth
Trefnannau
Pontysgawrhyd
Pentrebeirdd
Sarnau
Geufordd
Pool Quay
Pontrobert
Dolanog
Meifod
Wern
Foel
Llangadfan
Llanerfyl
Four Crosses
Plas Coch
New Bridge
Maesgwyn-Isaf
Groesllwyd
Guilsfield
Trewern
Heniarth
Moel-y-Garth
Cloddiau
Dolwen
Neuadd
Melin-y-ddôl
Melin-y-grug
Sychtyn
Cyfronydd
Welshpool & Llanfair Light Railway
WELSHPOOL
Powys Castle
Buttington
Hope
Leighton
Llanfair Caereinion
Cil-haul
Castle
Pentre-celyn
CLWYD
POWYS
SH
74
61
49
50

CHESHIRE
WREXHAM
CREWE
NANTWICH
Whitchurch
Wem
MARKET DRAYTON
SHREWSBURY
TELFORD
Wellington
Ellesmere
Overton
Malpas
Bangor-on-Dee
Hodnet
Newport
SJ
75
76
64
51

Royal's Green
A51
A525
76
Shutlanehead
UNDER-LYME
Clayton
Longton
Normacot
Meir
Cookshill
Caverswall
Buerton
A525
Lightwood Green
Kinsey Heath
Woore
Onneley
Hanford
Dresden
Lightwood
Wilkesley
Coxbank
Dorrington
Pipe Gate
Aston
Whitmore
Butterton
A53
A5182
Hem Heath
Trentham
Blythe Bridge
Broughall
Knighton
Willoughbridge
Baldwin's Gate
Hanchurch
Wedgwood Museum
Stallington
Ash Magna
Adderley
Norton in Hales
Bearstone
A51
Elds Wood
Hill Chorlton
Tittensor
A34
Rough Close
Saverley Green
Ash Parva
Ightfield
Blackbrook
Stableford
Fulford
Maer
Chapel Chorlton
Beech
Barlaston
Knenhall
Crossgate
Prees Higher Heath
Calverhall
Mucklestone
Upper Hatton
A520
Moddershall
Betton
Ashley
Cranberry
Oulton
Loggerheads
Podmore
Bowers
Standon
Swynnerton
Sharpley
Hilderstone
Longslow
Sandylane
A53
Almington
Hookgate
Chatcull
Walford
Cotes
A34
Cotwalton
STONE
Moreton Say
Longford
Sandford
MARKET DRAYTON
Broughton
Hales
Wetwood
Aspley
Millmeece
Walton
Dayhills
Darliston
Bletchley
Croxtonbank
Slindon
Fairoak
Coldmeece
Yarnfield
Little Stoke
Milwich
Fauls
Ternhill
Sutton
The Fouralls
Chipnall
Little Sugnall
Brockton
Butterhill Bank
Marchamley Wood
Lostford
Croxton
Sturbridge
Aston
Burston
A442
Wollerton
Woodseaves
Woodwall Green
Bishop's Offley
Sugnall
Norton Bridge
Yarlet
Marchamley
Rosehill
Cheswardine
Lipley
Pershall
Chebsey
Izaak Walton's Cottage
Sandon
Hawkstone
Wistanswick
Heathcote
Sweet Appletree
Copmere End
Eccleshall
Enson
A51
Hodnet
Hodnet Hall
Great Soudley
Doley
Offleymarsh
Adbaston
Whitgreave
Millgreen
Lockleywood
Tunstall
Wootton
Salt
Hopton
A53
Weobly
Stoke upon Tern
Hinstock
Hungryhatton
Knighton
High Offley
Whitley Heath
Ellenhall
Great Bridgeford
A34
Marston
Booley
A442
Ashfields
Ellerton
A518
High Hatton
Shebdon
Woodseaves
Knightley
Lawnhead
Seighford
Holmcroft
Hopton
Stanton upon Hine Heath
Child's Ercall
Standford Bridge
Grub Street
Five Lanes Ends
Doxley
Ollerton
Howle
Weston Jones
B5405
Ranton
Coton Clanford
STAFFORD
Peplow
Sambrook
Knightley Dale
Aston
Moreton Corbet
Moretonmill
Ellerdine Heath
Eaton upon Tern
Puleston
Norbury
Norbury Junction
Long Compton
Derrington
Forebridge
Weeping Cross
Great Bolas
Oulton
Whitecross
Shut Heath
Edgebolton
Lane End
Chetwynd
Sutton
Audmore
Haughton
Castle Bank
Walton-on-the-Hill
Muckleton
Meeson
Tibberton
Edgmond Marsh
Forton
Aqualate Mere
Gnosall
Hyde Lea
Cold Hatton Heath
Cherrington
Meretown
Gnosall Heath
A518
A34
Rowton
Waters Upton
Edgmond
Islington
A518
Coton
Four Lanes End
Walton
Moortown
B5062
NEWPORT
Bromstead Heath
Upper Cowley
Allimore Green
Coppenhall
Bednall
B5063
B5062
Adeney
Lower Cowley
Little Heath
High Ercall
Cotwall
Crudgington
Longford
A41
Wood Eaton
Apeton
Dunston
Acton Trussell
Tern
Kynnersley
Cheswell
A518
Chetwynd Aston
Moreton
High Onn
Bradley
Church Eaton
Church Eaton Common
Roden
Longdon upon Tern
Long Lane
Sleapford
Preston upon the Weald Moors
Pave Lane
Woodcote
Stockton
Lynn
Great Chatwell
Orslow
Mitton
Levedale
Honnington
Lilleshall
Little Onn
Penkridge
Eyton upon the Weald Moors
A442
Muxton
Marston
Longridge
Marsh Green
Admaston
Bratton
Lilleshall Abbey
Heath Hill
Chadwell
Bickford
Boscomoor
Allscott
Donnington
Weston Heath
Brineton
Whiston
Congreve
Pillaton
Huntington
Trench
Lilyhurst
Lapley
Lyne Hill
Wrockwardine
Sheriffhales
Blymhill
Wheaton Aston
Stretton
A449
Walcot
Hadley
Donnington Wood
Burlington
Weston-under-Lizard
Charlton
Wellington
A5
A5
Gailey
Hatherton
Aston
M54
Oakengates
Crackleybank
Weston Park
Bishop's Wood
Uppington
Arleston
Lawley
Oldpark
Hollinswood
Decker Hill
Horsebrook
Fourcrosses
Roman Town (Viroconium)
Rushton
TELFORD
Haughton
Shifnal
Tong Norton
Boscobel
Royal Oak
Kiddemore Green
Brewood
Great Saredon
Little Wenlock
Huntington
Dawley
The Wyke
Standeford
Four Ashes
Donnington
Longwood
Coalmoor
Horsehay
A442
Tong
Whiteladies Priory
Chillington Hall
Shareshill
Wroxeter
Eyton on Severn
Garmston
Stirchley
Upton
Slade Heath
Eaton Constantine
Leighton
Coalbrookdale Museum
Buildwas
Evelith
A464
Cosford
Codsall Wood
Coven
Cross Green
Featherstone
Coundlane
Buildwas Abbey
Coalbrookdale
Madeley
Aerospace Museum (R.A.F. Cosford)
Donnington
Codsall
M54
Cressage
Sheinton
Iron Bridge
Blists Hill
Kemberton
Grindle
Whiston Cross
Albrighton
Bilbrook
Moseley Old Hall
Essington
Ironbridge
Coalport
China Works
Brockton
Oaken
Lane Green
Bushbury
Homer
Wyke
Benthall
Broseley
Tar Tunnel
Ryton
A41
Oxley
Wood Hayes
Posenhall
Barrow
Sutton Maddock
Beckbury
Boningale
Kingswood Common
A41
Wergs
Wolverhampton
Tettenhall
Wood End
Harley
Wigwig
B4376
Burnhill Green
Priory
Norton
WOLVERHAMPTON
Wednesfield
Stretton Westwood
MUCH WENLOCK
Willey
Stockton
Astol
Badger
Nurton
A454
Heath Town
The Bank
Linleygreen
Apley Park
Stableford
Kingslow
Perton
Pattingham
Moseley
Atterley
The Smithies
Shirlett
Nordley
Ewdness
Ackleton
Great Moors
A454
Presthope
Callaughton
Trescott
Castlecroft
Blakenhall
Bilston
Bourton
Haughton
Muckleycross
Astley Abbotts
Worfield
Chesterton
Shipley
Seisdon
Lower Penn
Cross Lane Head
Allscott
Rindleford
Orton
Coseley
Easthope
Acton Round
Muckley
Aston Eyre
A458
Bromley
Hilton
Upper Ludstone
Earlswood
Sedgley
Bradley
Morville
Tasley
Swancote
Burcote
Wyken
Hopstone
Trysull
Astonlane
A442
A449
Brockton
Roughton
Claverley
The Bratch
Ounsdale
Gospel End
Monkhopton
The Lye
Morville Heath
Hoccum
BRIDGNORTH
Draycott
Wombourne
The Straits
Tipton
Lower Gornal
Weston
Upton Cressett Hall
Upton Cressett
Oldbury
Midland Motor Museum
Heathton
Himley
Himley Hall
Shipton
Netchwood
Cross Houses
Danesford
Lower Beobridge
Halfpenny Green
Stanton Long
Derrington
Middleton Priors
A458
Quatford
Bobbington
Oakfarm
Ditton Priors
Chetton
Eardington
Swindon
DUDLEY
Severn Valley Railway
A442
Mose
Wootton
Quatt
Shut End
Udgate
Neenton
Eudon George
Glazeley
Chelmarsh
Broad Oak
Six Ashes
Hinksford
A4101
Oldbury
Lower Faintree
Oldfield
Kingswinford
Pensnett
Abdon
1770
Cleobury North
Middleton Scriven
Sutton
Hampton
Tuckhill
Four Ashes
Enville
Ashwood
Brockmoor
Brierley Hill
Overton
Wrickton
Billingsley
Hampton Loade
Birdsgreen
Coxgreen
52
Prestwood
Wordsley
Audnam
Amblecote
Quarry Bank
Upper Heath
Sidbury
Woodhill
Potter's
Stourton
Dennis Park
Lye

76
77
Cheadle
Alton Towers
Alton
Norbury
Edalston
Mugginton
Mercaston
Weston Underwood
Duffield
Coxbench
Rokeway
Threapwood Head
Lower Ellastone
Snelston Common
Wyaston
Shirley
Ednaston
Quarndon Hill
Flaxholme
Bradley in the Moors
Tithebarn
Darley Moor
Brailsford
Quarndon
Mobberley
Gallows Green
Quixhall
Roston
Denstone
Ednaston Manor
Brailsford Green
Kedleston
Teanford
Winnothdale
Rodsley
Windy Arbour
Upper Tean
Croxden
Croxden Abbey
Greatgate
Yeaveley
Over Burrows
Kedleston Hall
Allestree
Breadsall
Lower Tean
Rocester
Thurvaon
Hollington
Kirk Langley
Langley Green
Breadsall Hilltop
Darley Abbey
Hollington Grove
Longlane
Lees Green
Mackworth
Markeaton
Chaddesden
Fole
Checkley
Hollington
Combridge
Marston Montgomery
Great Cubley
Alkmonton
DERBYSHIRE
Lees
Langley Common
Longford
Thurvaston
Churchbalk
New Zealand
Leigh
Church Leigh
Beamhurst
Stramshall
Somersal Herbert
Potter Somersal
Boylestone
Longford lane
Radbourne
DERBY
Lower Leigh
Withington
Spath
Harebill
Trusley
Cropper
California
Lane Ends
Littleover
UTTOXETER
Doveridge
Church Broughton
Dalbury
Sutton on the Hill
Mickleover
Crewton
Field
Painleyhill
Bramshall
Oaks Green
Normanton
Alvaston
Fradswell Heath
Gratwich
Blounts Green
Uttoxeter
R. Dove
Sudbury
Sudbury Hall
The Bent
Burnaston
Sunny Hill
Elvaston
Highwood
Marchington
Foston
Hilton
Etwall
Allenton
Loxley Green
Hatton
Findern
Shelton Lock
Chellaston
Leese Hill
Netherland Green
Scounslow Green
Birch Cross
Scropton
Marston on Dove
Kingstone
Moreton
Tutbury
Willington
Barrow upon Trent
Swarkeston
Gorsty Hill
Marchington Woodlands
Draycott in the Clay
Fauld
Hanbury
Rolleston on Dove
Egginton
Twyford
Repton
Ingleby
Stanton by Bridge
King's Newton
Blythebridge
Stowe
Booth
Heatley
Drointon
Lea Heath
Dapple Heath
Woodend
Rolleston
Beam Hill
Parson's Hill
Milton
Foremark
Dunstal
Newborough
Anslow Gate
Anslow
Stretton
Newton Solney
Melbourne
Melbourne Hall
Hixon
Newton
Abbots Bromley
Needwood
Needwood Forest
Horninglow
Foremark Reservoir
Bretby
Blithfield Reservoir
Tolldish
Admaston
Newchurch
Callingwood
BURTON UPON TRENT
Winshill
Ticknall
Breedon on the Hill
Hoar Cross Hall
Mill Green
Hoar Cross
Rangemore
Stanhope Bretby
Calke
Little Haywood
Stapenhill
Newhall
Stockwell Heath
Hadley End
Tatenhill
Southwood
Heath End
Colwich
Rowley
SK
Dunstall
Hartshorne
Colton
Wolseley
Hamstall Ridware
Woodne
Branston
SWADLINCOTE
Weaverslake
Morrey
Yoxall
Barton-under-Needwood
Church Gresley
Woodville
Smisby
Lount
The Beeches
Blithbury
Stanton
Etchinghill
Hill Ridware
Olive Green
Nethertown
Bond End
Castle Gresley
Blackfordby
Coleorton
Roke End
Barton Green
RUGELEY
Mavesyn Ridware
Yoxall Bridge
King's Bromley
Efflinch
Walton-on-Trent
Cauldwell
Coton Park
High Cross Bank
Norris Hill
ASHBY-DE-LA-ZOUCH
Brereton
A513
Orgreave
Wychnor
Rosliston
Linton
Moira
Farm Town
Armitage
Handsacre
Alrewas
Linton Heath
Overseal
Stone Rows
Brereton Cross
Upper Longdon
Brook End
Longdon
Rileyhill
Coton in the Elms
Short Heath
Packington
Brindley Heath
Fradley
Croxall
Acresford
Donisthorpe
Ravenstone
Hazelslade
Longdon Green
Hilliard's Cross
Lullington
Oakthorpe
Measham
Gentleshaw
Edingale
Netherseal
Cannock Wood
Elmhurst
Stretton en le Field
Wimblebury
Heath Hayes
Chase Terrace
Farewell
Chorley
Netherstowe
Stowe
Streethay
Elford
Haunton
Chilcote
Swepstone
Burntwood
Creswell Green
Harlaston
Clifton Campville
Appleby Magna
Snarestone
Heather
Norton East
Chasetown
Leamonsley
LICHFIELD
Whittington
Hademore
Thorpe Constantine
No Man's Heath
Appleby Parva
Newton Burgoland
Odstone
Little Norton
Chasewater Light Railway
Hammerwich
Staffordshire Regiment Museum
Comberford
Shackerstone
Shackerstone Station
Great Wyrley
Roman Remains
Wall
Wigginton
Seckington
Newton Regis
Norton-Juxta-Twycross
Little Wyrley
Chesterfield
Austrey
Twycross
Little Twycross
Congerstone
Springhill
Coton
Alvecote
Shuttington
Clayhanger
BROWNHILLS
Shenstone
Weeford
Hopwas
Amington
Warton
Twycross
Bilstone
Carlton
Pelsall
Pelsall Wood
Shire Oak
Lower Stonnall
Glascote
Orton-on-the-Hill
Market Bosworth
Walsall Wood
Stonnall
Footherley
Hints
TAMWORTH
Kettlebrook
Belgrove
Wilnecote
Polesworth
Bloxwich
Shelfield
Vigo
Little Hay
Bonehill
Sheepy Parva
Wellsborough
Stubbers Green
ALDRIDGE
Shenstone Woodend
Fazeley
Birchmoor
St. Helena
Sheepy Magna
Sibson
Rushall
Daw End
Drayton Manor
Hockley
Two Gates
Freasley
Dordon
Shenton
Coal Pool
Barr Common
Little Aston
Roughley
Drayton Bassett
Dosthill
Grendon Common
Grendon
Ratcliffe Culey
Upton
Hardwick
Mere Green
Bassetts Pole
Atherstone
Atterton
WALSALL
Four Oaks
Whitehouse Common
Middleton
Wood End
Baddesley Ensor
Merevale
Witherley
Stoke Golding
Palfrey
Streetly
Doe Bank
SUTTON COLDFIELD
Allen End
Hurley Common
Baxterley
Fenny Drayton
Daisy Bank
Kingsbury
Bentley Common
Bentley
Mancetter
Higham on the Hill
Great Barr
Queslett
Langley Heath
Thimble End
Wishaw
Marston
Hurley
Birchley Heath
Ridge Lane
Oldbury
Caldecote
Kingstanding
Wylde Green
Over Green
Lea Marston
Foul End
Nether Whitacre
Church End
Ansley Common
Hartshill
Caldecote Hill
Weddington
Short Heath
Hamstead
Walmley
Curdworth
Whiteacre Heath
Botts Green
Chapel End
Galley Common
Perry
Erdington
Hogrill's End
Furnace End
Over Whitacre
Ansley
Stockingford
WEST BROMWICH
Perry Barr
Gravelly Hill
Minworth
Tyburn
Water Orton
Blyth End
Cole End
Shustoke
Church End
Arley
Chilvers Coton
NUNEATON
Attleborough
Birchfield
Aston
Handsworth
West Smethwick
Castle Bromwich
Coleshill
SP
Gun Hill
Astley
Arbury Hall
Griff
Marston Jabbet
Hasty
Smethwick
Stechford
Tile Cross
Maxstoke
Fillongley
Wood End
Bedworth Woodlands
BEDWORTH
Bearwood
Saltley
Ward End
Corley Ash
Goodyers End
Coalpit Field
Bulkington
BIRMINGHAM
Chelmsley Wood
Marston Green
Green End
Corley
Ash Green
Hayes Green
Barnacle
Chad Valley
Small Heath
Yardley
Outwoods
Chapel Green
53
M6
M42
M5
A38
A50
A5
A51
A444
A453

BELPER
Denby
EASTWOOD
HEANOR
Watnall Chaworth
Bulwell
Leapool
Lowdham
Kilburn
Horsley Woodhouse
Marlpool
Nuthall
ARNOLD
Lambley
Milford
Makeney
Holbrook
Horsley
Smalley
Awsworth
Kimberley
Daybrook
Burton Joyce
Gunthorpe
Duffield
Coxbench
Mapperley
78
Cossall Marsh
Cossall
Gedling
79
Shelford
Weston Underwood
Flaxholme
Stanley Common
CARLTON
Quarndon Hill
Little Eaton
Morley
Strelley
Bilborough
Quarndon
Morleymoor
West Hallam
ILKESTON
NOTTINGHAM
Stoke Bardolph
Newton
Kedleston
Stanley
Allestree
Breadsall
Dale Moor
Kirk Hallam
Hallam Fields
New Stanton
Holme Pierrepont Hall
Saxondale
Kedleston Hall
Dale
Stanton by Dale
Adbolton
Nottingham
Radcliffe on Trent
Mackworth
Chaddesden
Dale Abbey
Sandiacre
Bramcote
Wilford
Gamston
Bassingfield
DERBY
New Zealand
Spondon
Ockbrook
Risley
STAPLEFORD
BEESTON
Rylands
Clifton Bridge
WEST BRIDGFORD
Edwalton
Cotgrave
Littleover
Borrowash
Shacklecross
Breaston
Chilwell
Toton
Clifton
Tollerton
Normanton
Crewton
Attenborough
Owthorpe
Clipston
Sunny Hill
Alvaston
Wilsthorpe
Barton in Fabis
Normanton on the Wolds
Burnaston
Elvaston
Draycott
LONG EATON
Ruddington
Plumtree
Allenton
Elvaston
Church Wilne
Trentlock
Bradmore
Keyworth
Stanton-Old Houses
Sinfin
Shelton Lock
Thulston
Aston Moor
Shardlow
Sawley
Thrumpton
New Barns
Findern
Chellaston
Gotham
Stanton on the Wolds
Barrow upon Trent
Swarkestone
Aston-on-Trent
Bunny
Lockington
Ratcliffe on Soar
SK
Widmerpool
Hickling
Hickling Pastures
Willington
Twyford
Weston-on-Trent
Bridge Fields
Kingston on Soar
West Leake
East Leake
Wysall
Ingleby
Stanton by Bridge
Castle Donington
Milton
Kegworth
Repton
Foremark
King's Newton
Donington Park
EAST MIDLANDS AIRPORT
Costock
Willoughby-on-the-Wolds
Cokhay Green
Melbourne
Sutton Bonington
West Thorpe
Upper Broughton
Foremark Reservoir
Melbourne Hall
Wilson
Isley Walton
Diseworth
Rempstone
Ticknall
Whatton
Bretby
Breedon on the Hill
Tonge
Normanton on Soar
Long Whatton
Hoton
Wymeswold
Old Dalby
Zouch
Hathern
Stanford on Soar
Burton on the Wolds
Calke
Cotes
Hartshorne
Southwood
Worthington
Belton
Heath End
Thorpe Acre
Midway
SWADLINCOTE
Lount
Walton on the Wolds
Woodville
Smisby
Newbold
Osgathorpe
Griffydam
SHEPSHED
LOUGHBOROUGH
Ragdale
Blackfordby
Coleorton
Grace Dieu
Seagrave
High Cross Bank
ASHBY-DE-LA-ZOUCH
Thringstone
Nanpantan
Barrow upon Soar
Hoby
Norris Hill
Woodthorpe
Quorndon
Thrussington
Moira
Farm Town
Mount St Bernard's Abbey
CHARNWOOD FOREST
Main Line Steam Trust
Sileby
Stone Rows
Swannington
New Swannington
Woodhouse
Ratcliffe on the Wreake
Brooksby
Rearsby
Short Heath
Packington
Whitwick
Beacon Hill
Mountsorrel
Donisthorpe
Ravenstone
COALVILLE
Woodhouse Eaves
Rothley Plain
Cossington
Acresford
Snibston
East Goscote
Oakthorpe
Measham
Normanton le Heath
Donington-le-Heath Manor
Bardon
Copt Oak
Swithland
Rothley
Queniborough
Stretton en la Field
Ellistown
Wanlip
Syston
Swepstone
Newtown Linford
Cropston
Thurcaston
Appleby Magna
Heather
Ibstock
Stanton under Bardon
Barkby
South Croxton
Snarestone
Belcher's Bar
Markfield
Birstall
Mowmacre Hill
Barkby Thorpe
Appleby Parva
Newton Burgoland
Anstey
Field Head
Beeby
Odstone
Bagworth
Thurmaston
Shackerstone
Shackerstone Station
Barton in the Beans
Nailstone
Thornton
LEICESTER
Norton-Juxta-Twycross
Groby
Austrey
Little Twycross
Barlestone
Merry Lees
Ratby
Glenfield
Congerstone
Scraptoft
Twycross Zoo
Twycross
Bilstone
Carlton
Carlton Gate
Botcheston
Dane Hills
Humberstone
Tropical Bird Garden
Newtown Unthank
Bushby
Orton-on-the-Hill
Market Bosworth
Osbaston
Kirby Muxloe
Evington
Thurnby
Newbold Verdon
Desford
Sheepy Parva
Wellsborough
Cadeby
Leicester Forest East
Braunstone
Stoneygate
Sheepy Magna
Cadeby Light Railway
Knighton
Stoughton
Sibson
Sutton Cheney
Peckleton
Leicester Forest West
Aylestone
University Gardens
OADBY
Mallory Park
Enderby
Kirkby Mallory
Ratcliffe Culey
Shenton
Thurlaston
Leicester
Glen Parva
Little Stretton
Upton
Whittington
Witherley
Dadlington
Stapleton
Narborough
WIGSTON
Harper's Hill
Stoke Golding
Earl Shilton
Blaby
South Wigston
Great Glen
Barwell
Fenny Drayton
Potters Marston
Huncote
Whetstone
Ward's Hill
Mancetter
Newton Harcourt
Higham on the Hill
Stoney Stanton
Croft
Ridge Lane
Caldecote
Littlethorpe
Wistow
Elmesthorpe
Cosby
Oldbury
Kilby
Countesthorpe
Kibworth Harcourt
Sutton in the Elms
HINCKLEY
Foston
Hartshill
Ansley Common
Primethorpe
Fleckney
Caldecote Hill
Weddington
Willoughby Waterleys
Peatling Magna
Galley Common
Chapel End
Burbage
Sapcote
Arnesby
Broughton Astley
Aston Flamville
Stockingford
NUNEATON
SP
Chilvers Coton
Sharnford
Attleborough
Ashby Magna
Shearsby
Saddington
Robinson's End
Leire
Frolesworth
54
Dunton Bassett
Burton Hastings
Smockington
Shelford
Copston Magna
Wibtoft
Peatling Parva
Bruntingthorpe
Mowsley
Arbury Hall
Marston Jabbet
Ashby
Astley
NOTTINGHAMSHIRE
LEICESTERSHIRE
DERBYSHIRE
A6
A38
A52
A453
A60
A606
A46
A6006
A50
A512
A47
A444
A5
A447
A426
A5070
M1
M69
B5010
B6540
B5401
B5324
B676
B591
B5327
B5328
B582
B585
B586
B4116
B4114
B4112
B581
B578
B4069
AA 24 hour
AA info

67
Syerston
Dry Doddington
Hough-on-the-Hill
Normanton
Holdingham
Kirkby Thorpe
Flintham
Sibthorpe
Top Green
Long Bennington
Gelston
Carlton Scroop
Rauceby
SLEAFORD
Screveton
Shelton
Hougham
Westborough
Sudbrook
Ancaster
Quarrington
Heckington
Hawksworth
Marston
A153
Town End
LC
Little Green
Flawborough
Kilvington
79
A1
Foston
Honington
Wilsford
80
Thoroton
Alverton
Barkston
Silk Willoughby
Burton Pedwardine
Northbeck
Aslockton
Orston
Allington
Syston
Kelby
Swarby
Culverthorpe
Aswarby
Normanton
Great Gonerby
Heydour
Whatton
Allington Manor
Belton
Welby
Oasby
Aunsby
Scredington
A52
Elton
Bottesford
Aisby
Scott Willoughby
Osbournby
Sutton
Sedgebrook
Muston
B1174
A607
B6403
Londonthorpe
Dembleby
Manthorpe
Granby
Redmile
Green Hill
Haceby
Newton
Threekingham
Barrowby
Earle's Fields
GRANTHAM
New Somerby
Braceby
Barnstone
Langar
Barkestone-le-Vale
Belvoir
Woolsthorpe
Ropsley
Sapperton
Walcot
Stow
Plungar
Belvoir Castle
Old Somerby
Pickworth
Birthorpe
Denton
Harston
Harlaxton
Little Ponton
Humby
Hanby
Folkingham
Stathern
Laughton
Harby
Knipton
Stroxton
Boothby Pagnell
TF
Lenton
Hungerton
Great Ponton
Scotland
Little Dowsby
Branston
Lower Bassingthorpe
B1176
Ingoldsby
Aslackby
Eaton
Hose
Croxton Kerrial
Graby
Keisby
A15
Wyville
Bitchfield
Rippingale
Eastwell
Stoke Rochford
Bassingthorpe
Kirkby Underwood
Irnham
Long Clawson
Easton
Bescaby
Saltby
Dunsby
Goadby Marwood
Waltham on the Wolds
Bulby
Skillington
Wycomb
B6403
Burton Coggles
Corby Glen
Scalford
Stainfield
Hacconby
Colsterworth
Sproxton
Chadwell
Holwell
Stonesby
Birkholme
A151
Elsthorpe
Hanthorpe
Morton
Woolsthorpe
Buckminster
Stainby
Twyford
Ab Kettleby
Woolsthorpe Manor
Grimsthorpe
Dyke
Coston
B676
Swayfield
Swinstead
Thorpe Arnold
Sewstern
Gunby
North Witham
Edenham
Freeby
Scottlethorpe
The Spinney
Garthorpe
Creeton
Asfordby Hill
B676
South Witham
Saxby
A6121
Bourne
Eastgate
Wymondham
Brentingby
Wyfordby
Lound
Castle Bytham
Little Bytham
Northorpe
A607
MELTON MOWBRAY
Stapleford
Thistleton
R. Glen
Toft
Careby
Bellars
Edmondthorpe
Witham on the Hill
Thurlby
Eye Kettleby
Burton Lazars
Market Overton
Clipsham
Manthorpe
Great Dalby
Teigh
Stretton
A606
Whissendine
Aunby
Carlby
B6047
Barrow
Obthorpe
Upper End
Little Dalby
Greetham
Pickworth
Wilsthorpe
Ashwell
B1176
Cottesmore
Braceborough
Leesthorpe
Essendine
Thorpe Satchville
Pickwell
Langham
B668
Ryhall
Greatford
Ranksborough
Exton
Towngate
Burrough on the Hill
Cold Overton
Great Casterton
Barholm
Somerby
Barleythorpe
Burley
Belmesthorpe
A6121
Whitwell
Empingham
Little Casterton
West Deeping
OAKHAM
Marefield
Knossington
Tickencote
Newtown
B1081
STAMFORD
Uffington
Upper Hambleton
A606
A16
Tallington
Lowesby
Owston
Egleton
Normanton
Tinwell
Burghley
Bainton
Braunston
Rutland Water
Halstead
Brooke
Gunthorpe
Ketton
Pilsgate
B1443
Ashton
Manton
Edith Weston
Barnack
Tilton on the Hill
The Green
River Chater
A6003
Lyndon
North Luffenham
A6121
Aldgate
A43
Easton on the Hill
Ufford
Skeffington
Loddington
Ridlington
Wing
Collyweston
Southorpe
Pilton
Preston
South Luffenham
Tugby
Belton
Ayston
Morcott
Wittering
Glaston
Thornhaugh
Rolleston
PS
A47
East Norton
Allexton
Uppingham
Barrowden
Duddington
Upton
Wardley
Tixover
B664
Bisbrooke
B672
Wansford
Stibbington
Goadby
Wakerley
Noseley
Stockerston
Lyddington
Bede
Seaton
King's Cliffe
Nene Valley Railway
Sutton
Hallaton
Horninghold
Harringworth
Yarwell
Sibson
Shangton
Glooston
Stoke Dry
Thorpe by Water
Laxton
Blatherwycke
Nassington
Chesterton
Cranoe
Blaston
Eyebrook Reservoir
Apethorpe
B671
Stonton Wyville
Slawston
Great Easton
B672
Gretton
Woodnewton
NORTHAMPTONSHIRE
Bulwick
Church Langton
Medbourne
Nevill Holt
Caldecott
Deene
Fotheringhay
Elton
Over End
Welham
Drayton
Kirby Hall
Deene Park
East Langton
Thorpe Langton
Weston by Welland
Bringhurst
Rockingham
Deenethorpe
Eaglethorpe
Warmington
Rockingham Castle
Southwick
TL
Tansor
Ashley
Middleton
Cottingham
Sutton Bassett
Weldon
55
East Carlton
Glapthorn
Cotterstock
B670
A427
A427
8
9
0
1
OUNDLE
Wilbarston
A43
Upper Benefield
Ashton

68
LINCOLNSHIRE
CAMBRIDGESHIRE
BEDFORD LEVEL
TL
BOSTON
SPALDING
BOURNE
STAMFORD
PETERBOROUGH
WHITTLESEY
OLD FLETTON
Heckington
Great Hale
Little Hale
Helpringham
Swineshead
Kirton
Donington
Gosberton
Surfleet
Pinchbeck
Moulton
Whaplode
Holbeach
Crowland
Thorney
Market Deeping
Deeping St. James
Eye
Yaxley
Wildfowl Trust
Lowlands Farm
Springfields
Nene Valley Railway
80
67
56

69
THE WASH
NORFOLK
HUNTANTON
KING'S LYNN
WISBECH
DOWNHAM MARKET
SWAFFHAM
Holme next the Sea
Old Hunstanton
New Hunstanton
Brancaster
Brancaster Staithe
Burnham Norton
Burnham Deepdale
Burnham Market
Thornham
Titchwell
Choseley Farm
Ringstead
Norfolk Lavender
Heacham
Summerfield
Docking
Stanhoe
Littleport
Sedgeford
Snettisham
Fring
Bircham Newton
Bircham Tofts
Barmer
Southgate
Shernborne
Great Bircham
Bagthorpe
Ingoldisthorpe
Dersingham
Anmer
Doddshill
Wolferton Station
Wolferton
Sandringham
West Newton
Houghton Hall
New Houghton
Tattersett
Flitcham
West Rudham
Castle Rising
Hillington
Harpley
Little Massingham
North Wootton
South Wootton
Congham
Roydon
Great Massingham
Grimston
Pott Row
Gaywood
Massingham Heath
Weasenham All Saints
Rougham
Brow-of-the-Hill
Ashwicken
Gayton
Gayton Thorpe
East Winch
East Walton
Castle Acre
West Bilney
Middleton
Blackborough End
Pentney
West Acre
Narborough
South Acre
Great Palgrave
Wormegay
River Nar
Marham
Shouldham
Shouldham Thorpe
Beachamwell Warren
Barton Bendish
Beachamwell
Cockley Cley
Iceni Village
Fincham
Stradsett
Eastmoor
Crimplesham
Boughton
Bexwell
Wereham
Oxborough
Gooderstone
Oxburgh Hall
Hillborough
Stoke Ferry
Wretton
West Dereham
Whittington
Foulden
Beckett End
Bodney
Northwold
Cranwich
Brookville
Methwold
Methwold Hythe
Ickburgh
Methwold Fens
Queens Ground
Mundford
Feltwell
Lynford
Hockwold cum Wilton
Weeting
Feltwell Anchor
Brandon Bank
Brandon Creek
Southery
Southery Fens
Hilgay
Hilgay Fen
Ten Mile Bank
Fordham
Denver
Denver Mill
Salters Lode
Nordelph
Apes Hall
Mare
Upwell Fen
Three Holes
Euximoor Fen
Euximoor Drove
Iron Bridge
Christchurch
Lakesend
Upwell Fen
Tipp's End
Welney
Wildfowl Trust
Suspension Bridge
Gold Hill
Boot's Bridge
Manea
The Biggins
Laddus Fen
Upwell
Outwell
Friday Bridge
Collett's Bridge
Elm
Gaultree
Holly End
Emneth
Emneth Hungate
Chequers Corner
New Walsoken
Walsoken
The Smeeth
Marshland Fen
Stowbridge
West Head
Wimbotsham
Stow Bardolph
Stow Bardolph Fen
Downham Bridge
Barroway Drove
Runcton Holme
South Runcton
Tottenhill
Watlington
Wiggenhall St. Mary Magdalen
Wiggenhall St. Germans
Lordsbridge
St. John's Fen End
Tilney St. Lawrence
Walpole Highway
Walton Highway
West Walton
Rattan Row
Ingleborough
Walpole St. Peter
St. John's Highway
Wiggenhall St. Mary the Virgin
Saddle Bow
West Winch
North Runcton
Setchey
Tilney High End
Terrington St. John
Hay Green
Walpole St. Andrew
Walpole Marsh
Four Gotes
Tilney All Saints
West Lynn
Walpole Cross Keys
Terrington St. Clement
Bellmount
Clenchwarton
Terrington
Ongar Hill
Sutton Bridge
Guy's Head
Gedney Drove End
River Great Ouse
River Nene
Middle Level
R Wissey
Hundred Foot Drain
A149
A148
A47
A17
A10
A134
A1122
A1065
A1101
A1078
B1454
B1155
B1153
B1439
B1440
B1145
B1160
B1106
B1112
B1386
B1507
B1094
B1098
B1100
B1093
B1411
B1198
B1101
70
81
57
5
6
7
8

Blakeney Point
Brancaster Staithe
Brancaster
Burnham Norton
Overy Staithe
Holkham
WELLS-NEXT-THE-SEA
Salt Marshes
Morston
Blakeney
Cley next the Sea
Salthouse
Weybourne
SHERINGHAM
Burnham Deepdale
Burnham Market
Burnham Overy
Carmelite Friary
Holkham Hall
Golden Gates
B1155
A149
Warham St. Mary
Stiffkey
Cockthorpe
B1388
Greencroft
Wiveton
Newgate
Glandford
Kelling
Kelling Park
Sheringham Hall
Upper Sheringham
Shell Museum
Langham
Warham All Saints
Burnham Thorpe
New Holkham
B1153
B1155
B1355
B1105
Wighton
Westgate
Field Dalling
Saxlingham
B1156
Bodham Street
High Kelling
Holt
A148
West Beckham
Creak Abbey
Copy's Green
Binham
Letheringsett
Little Thornage
Baconsthorpe
Baconsthorpe
Hempstead
North Creake
Great Walsingham
B1388
Lower Green
Bale
Sharrington
B1110
B1149
Docking
Stanhoe
B1155
Little Walsingham
Walsingham Abbey
Waterden
Hindringham
Shirehall Museum
Thornage
TF
South Creake
Southgate
North Barsham
Houghton St. Giles
Great Snoring
Brinton
North Street
Plumstead
Edgefield Green
Edgefield
Hunworth
Stody
Gunthorpe
Thursford Collection
Thursford
B1354
Briningham
Barmer
Bircham Tofts
West Barsham
East Barsham
Edgefield Street
Little Barningham
Melton Constable
Briston
B1354
Barney
Little Snoring
A148
Bagthorpe
Syderstone
Sculthorpe
Swanton Novers
Croxton
Kettlestone
Mannington Hall
Saxthorpe
Craymere Beck
Corpusty
Fulmodestone
B1454
Dunton
Nethergate
Tattersett
Coxford
Shereford
Fakenham
A1067
Stibbard
Hindolveston
Thurning
Norton Corner
Houghton Hall
New Houghton
Hempton
Little Ryburgh
Wood Norton
Tyby
Guestwick
Oulton
East Rudham
Tatterford
Fakenham
A148
Toftrees
B1146
Heydon
West Rudham
Helhoughton
Great Ryburgh
East Raynham
Wood Dalling
Colkirk
Guist
Harpley
Foulsham
Southgate
West Raynham
Oxwick
Broom Green
Sall
B1149
Little Massingham
West Raynham
Whissonsett
Gateley
Twyford
Themelthorpe
Weasenham St. Peter
A1065
South Raynham
Bintree
Reepham
Cawston
Great Massingham
Horningtoft
Potthorpe
B1110
North Elmham
Foxley
Eastgate
Whitwell Street
B1145
Weasenham All Saints
Wellingham
Billingford
Bawdeswell
Brandiston
Rougham
Tittleshall
Stanfield
Brisley
Sparham
Norfolk Wildlife Park
Worthing
B1145
Mileham
East Bilney
B1147
A1067
Sparhamhill
Alderford
Mill Street
Mill Street
Lyng
Swannington
Upgate
West Lexham
Litcham
Bittering
Beetley
Walton
Norfolk Rural Life
Swanton Morley
Lenwade
Felthorpe
Castle Acre
East Lexham
Longham
Hoe
Morton
Attlebridge
Gressenhall Green
Primrose Green
Weston Longville
Newton
Beeston
Elsing
Woodgate
West Acre
Castle Acre
Woodgate
Drury Square
Sparrow Green
Gressenhall
Northall Green
North Tuddenham
Greensgate
Ringland
Great Dunham
Great Fransham
Etling Green
South Acre
B1146
A47
Narborough
Great Palgrave
Little Dunham
Crane's Corner
EAST DEREHAM
Mattishall Burgh
Hockering
Wendling
Honingham
Scarning
Dumpling Green
Clint Green
Sporle
Little Fransham
Toftwood
Mattishall
East Tuddenham
A1065
A47
Westfield
Mattishall South Green
Colton
Easton
SWAFFHAM
Necton
West Bradenham
Daffy Green
Yaxham
Welborne
Brandon Parva
Marlingford
Bawburgh
Beachamwell Warren
Holme Hale
East Bradenham
Shipdham
Whinburgh
B1135
Runhall
Barford
Garvestone
Thuxton
Barnham Broom
Little Melton
North Pickenham
Coston
B1077
Crowshill
Reymerston
Lings
Wramplingham
Danemoor Green
Carleton Forehoe
Lynch Green
Beachamwell
Ashill
High Common
Low Street
B1108
High Green
Cockley Cley
Cranworth
Southburgh
Hethersett
Kimberley
Iceni Village
South Pickenham
Kidd's Moor
Woodrising
Hardingham
Crownthorpe
A1075
Saham Hills
B1135
Wicklewood
Saham Toney
Kettering
Great Cressingham
Carbrooke
Northfield
Gooderstone
Ovington
Hingham
Hackford
WYMONDHAM
Watton Green
Hillborough
Little Cressingham
Scoulton
Highoak
Watton
B1108
Deopham
B1077
Silfield
Griston
Little Ellingham
Deopham Green
Wreningham
Merton
Beckett End
Morley St. Botolph
Northacre
Suton
Bodney
B1108
Rockland St. Peter
Ashwellthorpe
The Arms
Caston
Baw Street
Great Ellingham
Spooner Row
Northwold
B1135
A1065
Thompson
Fundenhall
Stow Bedon
Rockland All Saints
Besthorpe
Baconsthorpe
Cranwich
MILITARY TRAINING AREA
Ickburgh
Attleborough
B1111
Fen Street
Tacolneston
Black Car
Lower Stow Bedon
Mount Pleasant
Breckles
Bunwell
Forncett End
Shropham
B1077
TL
Mundford
North End
A11
Carleton Rode
Old Buckenham
Puddledock
Great Hockham
Pottergate Street
Upgate Street
PS
East Wretham
Snetterton
Lynford Cottages
Cake Street
Aslacton
Eccles Road
Stonebridge
South End
Hargate
Larling
Wilby
Tibenham
Stacksford
New Buckenham
Weeting
Grimes Graves
PS
PS
58
Snetterton
Hunt's
Pristow Green
B1106
A1075
A134
B1134
69
69
69
4
3
2
1
0
9
8
9
0
1
17
10
12
13
11
14
12
10
9
11
14
16
21
30
8

SCALE
0 1 2 3 4 5 miles
0 1 2 3 4 5 kilometres
Open to Public
East Runton
CROMER
Overstrand
Sidestrand
Felbrigg
Felbrigg Hall
Crossdale Street
Northrepps
Trimingham
Gimingham
Roughton
Metton
Mundesley
Thorpe Market
Southrepps
Lower Street
Trunch
Paston
Bacton Green
Bacton
Stow Mill
Knapton
Old Hall Street
Keswick
Bradfield
Antingham
Alby Hill
Erpingham
Suffield
Swafield
Edingthorpe
Pollard Street
Walcott
Edingthorpe Green
Colby
Ridlington
Happisburgh
Witton
Spa Common
Ingworth
Felmingham
Tungate
NORTH WALSHAM
Crostwight
Ridlington Street
Whimpwell Green
Banningham
Happisburgh Common
Eccles on Sea
Hempstead
Meeting House Hill
Aylsham
Honing
Lessingham
Sea Palling
Tuttington
Bengates
Briggate
East Ruston
Ingham Corner
Westwick
Worstead
Waxham
Burgh next Aylsham
Swanton Abbot
Dilham
Stalham
Ingham
Calthorpe Street
Skeyton
Smallburgh
Brampton
Stalham Green
Hickling
Oxnead
Lamas
Scottow
Sloley
Low Street
Sutton
Hickling Green
Horsey Corner
Horsey
Fairstead
Pennygate
Hill Common
Buxton
Little Hautbois
Tunstead
Market Street
Barton Turf
Wood Street
Hickling Heath
Drainage Windmill
Beeston Hall
Catfield
Stratton Strawless
Sco Ruston
St. James
Neatishead
Irstead
Potter Heigham
Somerton
Winterton-on-Sea
Waterloo
Horstead
Coltishall
Threehammer Common
Ludham
Hainford
Belaugh
Hoveton
Horning
Bastwick
Martham
Cess
Hemsby
Hembsy Hole
St. Helena
Frettenham
Johnson's Street
Repps
Newport
Newton St. Faith
Wroxham
Upper Street
Ludham Bridge
Rollesby
Scratby
Upper Street
Thurne
Ormesby St. Margaret
California
Crostwick
Woodbastwick
Burgh St. Margaret
East End
Horsham St. Faith
Spixworth
Rackheath
Ranworth
Salhouse
Clippesby
Filby
Ormesby St. Michael
Panxworth
Pilson Green
Billockby
Roman Town
Caister-on-Sea
NORWICH AIRPORT
New Rackheath
Little Plumstead
Fairhaven
Thrigby
Catton
South Walsham
Mautby
Caister
Sprowston
Hemblington
Upton
Stokesby
Thorpe End Garden Village
North Burlingham
West Caister
NORWICH
Blofield Heath
Acle
West End
Runham
Great Yarmouth
Great Plumstead
Lingwood
Damgate
Blofield
Stracey Arms Wind Pump
Runham
Thorpe St. Andrew
Brundall
Beighton
Tunstall
Halvergate
Postwick
South Burlingham
Moulton St. Mary
Cobholm Island
Trowse Newton
Strumpshaw
Surlingham
Steam Museum
Berney Arms Station
Southtown
GREAT YARMOUTH
Eaton
Buckenham
Southwood
Freethorpe
Lakenham
Kirby Bedon
Burgh Castle
Hassingham
Wickhampton
Arminghall
Framingham Pigot
Bramerton
Berney Arms
Burgh
Freethorpe Common
Bradwell
Rockland St. Mary
Cantley
Gorleston on Sea
Caistor St. Edmund
Framingham Earl
Hellington
Limpenhoe
Claxton
Pettitts Rural Industries
Langley Street
Witton Green
Belton
Elm Grove
Browston Green
Dunston
Yelverton
Ashby St. Mary
Reedham
Alpington
Hardley Street
Hobland Hall
Stoke Holy Cross
Upper Stoke
East Poringland
Bergh Apton
Thurton
Fritton
St Olaves Priory
Hopton on Sea
Swainsthorpe
Howe
Chedgrave
Nogdam End
Lower Thurlton
Lound
Bracon Ash
Hawe's Green
High Green
Brooke
Norton Subcourse
St Olaves
Shotesham
Mundham
Loddon
Thorpe
Herringfleet
Somerleyton Hall
Blundeston
Newton Flotman
The Ling
Hales
Thurlton
Corton
Saxlingham Nethergate
Kirstead Green
Seething
Haddiscoe
Somerleyton
Gunton
Tasburgh
Hales Hall
Raveningham
Saxlingham Green
Maypole Green
Lowestoft End
Upper Tasburgh
Hempnall
Thwaite St. Mary
Kirby Cane
Toft Monks
Oulton
Woodton
Wheatacre
Stratton St Michael
Hempnall Green
Hedenham
Stockton
Bull's Green
LOWESTOFT
Fritton
Topcroft
Ellingham
Kirby Row
Aldeby
Burgh St. Peter
Oulton Broad
Roman Hill
Long Stratton
Lundy Green
Morningthorpe
Topcroft Street
Gillingham
Kirkley
Geldeston
River Waveney
Shelton
Shelton Green
Ditchingham
Broome
Wainford
Shipmeadow
Pakefield
Great Green
BUNGAY
Worlingham
Barnby
Transport Museum
Hardwick
Otter Trust
Mettingham
Barsham
BECCLES
North Cove
Carlton Colville
A148
A140
A149
B1159
B1145
B1150
A1151
A1062
B1152
A1064
A47
A146
A143
A12
A1117
B1074
B1136
B1332
B1135
B1140
B1062
B1354
B1354
A1067
B1149
B1113
AA 24 hour
AA 54
TG
TM
59
2
3
4
5

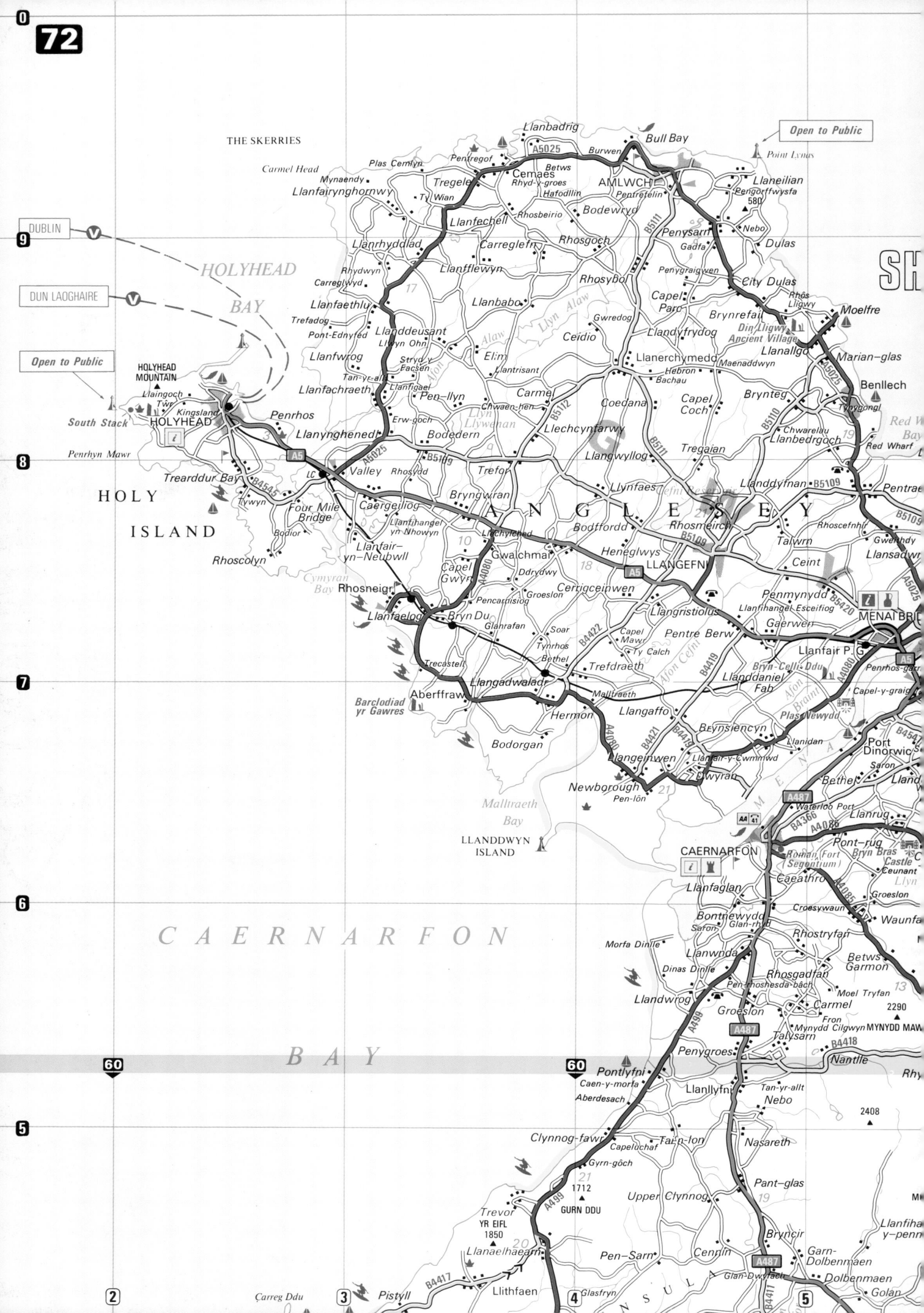
THE SKERRIES
Carmel Head
Llanbadrig
Bull Bay
Open to Public
Point Lynas
Plas Cemlyn
Pentregof
A5025
Burwen
Mynaendy
Cemaes
Betws
Rhyd-y-groes
AMLWCH
Llaneilian
Pengorffwysfa
580
Llanfairynghornwy
Tregele
Ty Wian
Hafodllin
Pentrefelin
Llanfechell
Rhosbeirio
Bodewryd
Nebo
DUBLIN
Llanrhyddlad
Carreglefn
Rhosgoch
B5111
Penysarn
Gadfa
Dulas
HOLYHEAD
BAY
Rhydwyn
Carreglwyd
Llanfflewyn
Penygraigwen
Rhosybol
City Dulas
Rhôs Lligwy
DUN LAOGHAIRE
Llanfaethlu
Llanbabo
Capel Parc
Brynrefail
Moelfre
Trefadog
Pont-Ednyfed
Llanddeusant
Llywyn Ohn
Alaw
Llyn Alaw
Gwredog
Ceidio
Llandyfrydog
Din Lligwy Ancient Village
Llanallgo
Marian-glas
Open to Public
HOLYHEAD MOUNTAIN
Llanfwrog
Stryd y Facsen
Afon
Elim
Llantrisant
Llanerchymedd
Maenaddwyn
A5025
Llaingoch
Twr
Kingsland
South Stack
HOLYHEAD
Tan-yr-allt
Llanfachraeth
Llanfigael
Pen-llyn
Carmel
Hebron
Bachau
Capel Coch
Brynteg
Benllech
Tynygongl
Penrhos
Erw-goch
Chwaen-hen
B5112
Coedana
Llyn Llywenan
Llanynghenedl
Bodedern
Llechcynfarwy
B5110
Chwarelau
Llanbedrgoch
Red Wharf Bay
Red Wharf
Penrhyn Mawr
A5
A5025
B5109
B5111
Llangwyllog
Tregaian
Trearddur Bay
Valley
Rhosydd
Trefor
Llanddyfnan
B5109
Pentraeth
LC
HOLY ISLAND
B4545
Tywyn
Four Mile Bridge
Bodior
Caergeiliog
Llanfihangel yn Nhowyn
Bryngwran
Llynfaes
Cefni Reservoir
ANGLESEY
Bodffordd
Rhosmeirch
Rhoscefnhir
B5109
Talwrn
Gwenrhdy
Llansadwrn
Rhoscolyn
Llanfair-yn-Neubwll
Llechylched
Gwalchmai
Heneglwys
LLANGEFNI
Ceint
Cymyran Bay
Rhosneigr
Capel Gwyn
A4080
Ddrydwy
A5
Cerrigceinwen
Penmynydd
Groeslon
Pencarnisiog
Llangristiolus
Llanfihangel Esceifiog
B5420
MENAI BRIDGE
Llanfaelog
Bryn Du
Glanrafan
Soar
Capel Mawr
Pentre Berw
Gaerwen
Tynrhos
Ty Calch
B4422
B4419
Llanfair P.G.
A5
Bethel
Afon Cefni
Trecastell
Trefdraeth
Bryn-Celli-Ddu
Llanddaniel Fab
A4080
Penrhos-garnedd
Capel-y-graig
Llangadwaladr
Aberffraw
Malltraeth
Barclodiad yr Gawres
Hermon
Llangaffo
Afon Braint
Plas Newydd
A4080
B4421
B4419
Brynsiencyn
Llanidan
Port Dinorwic
Bodorgan
Llangeinwen
Llanfair-y-Cwmmwd
MENAI
Saron
Bethel
Newborough
Dwyran
Pen-lôn
Malltraeth Bay
A487
Waterloo Port
Llanrug
B4366
A4086
LLANDDWYN ISLAND
CAERNARFON
Pont-rug
Bryn Bras Castle
Roman Fort (Segontium)
Caeathro
Ceunant
Llanfaglan
A4085
Groeslon
CAERNARFON
Bontnewydd
Saron
Glan-rhyd
Croesywaun
Waunfawr
Morfa Dinlle
Rhostryfan
Llanwnda
Dinas Dinlle
Betws Garmon
Rhosgadfan
Pen-rhoshesda-bâch
Moel Tryfan
Llandwrog
Carmel
2290
A499
Groeslon
Fron
Mynydd Cilgwyn
MYNYDD MAWR
A487
Talysarn
B4418
BAY
Penygroes
Nantlle
Pontlyfni
Caen-y-morfa
Llanllyfni
Tan-yr-allt
Aberdesach
Nebo
2408
Clynnog-fawr
Capeluchaf
Tai-n-lon
Nasareth
Gyrn-gôch
1712
Pant-glas
A499
GURN DDU
Upper Clynnog
Trevor
YR EIFL
1850
Llanaelhaearn
Bryncir
Garn-Dolbenmaen
Pen-Sarn
Cennin
A487
B4417
Glan-Dwyfach
Dolbenmaen
Llithfaen
Glasfryn
B4411
Golan
Carreg Ddu
Pistyll
60
60
2
3
4
5
0
9
8
7
6
5

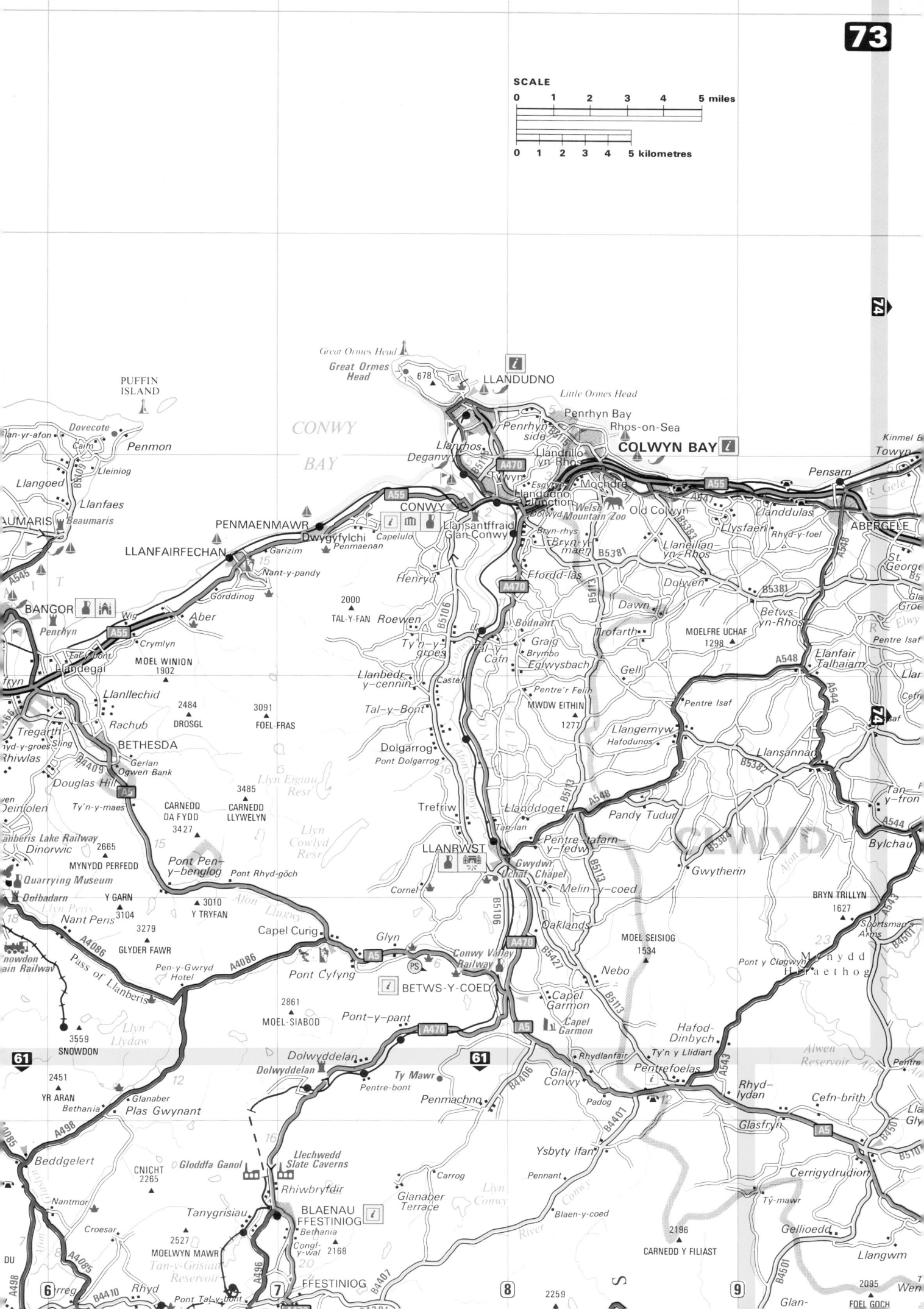
SCALE
0 1 2 3 4 5 miles
0 1 2 3 4 5 kilometres
74
PUFFIN ISLAND
Great Ormes Head
LLANDUDNO
Little Ormes Head
Penrhyn Bay
Rhos-on-Sea
COLWYN BAY
CONWY BAY
Penmon
Llangoed
Llanfaes
Beaumaris
PENMAENMAWR
Dwygyfylchi
LLANFAIRFECHAN
CONWY
Llansantffraid Glan Conwy
Llandudno Junction
Welsh Mountain Zoo
Old Colwyn
Llanddulas
ABERGELE
Pensarn
Towyn
BANGOR
Aber
Llandegai
MOEL WINION 1902
TAL-Y-FAN
Roewen
Henryd
Llanbedr-y-cennin
Tal-y-Bont
Dolgarrog
Trefriw
LLANRWST
Llanllechid
BETHESDA
Tregarth
Rachub
DROSGL
FOEL-FRAS
CARNEDD DAFYDD 3427
CARNEDD LLYWELYN
Llyn Eigiau Resr
Llyn Cowlyd Resr
Llanberis Lake Railway
Dinorwic
MYNYDD PERFEDD
Quarrying Museum
Dolbadarn
Y GARN
Nant Peris
Y TRYFAN
GLYDER FAWR
Capel Curig
Pass of Llanberis
Pen-y-Gwryd Hotel
Snowdon Mountain Railway
SNOWDON 3559
Pont Cyfyng
BETWS-Y-COED
Conwy Valley Railway
MOEL-SIABOD
Pont-y-pant
Dolwyddelan
Ty Mawr
Penmachno
YR ARAN
Plas Gwynant
Beddgelert
CNICHT
Gloddfa Ganol
Llechwedd Slate Caverns
Rhiwbryfdir
Tanygrisiau
BLAENAU FFESTINIOG
MOELWYN MAWR
Tan-y-Grisiau Reservoir
FFESTINIOG
Carrog
Glanaber Terrace
Ysbyty Ifan
Pennant
Blaen-y-coed
CARNEDD Y FILIAST
Glan-Conwy
Pentrefoelas
Rhydlanfair
Hafod-Dinbych
Capel Garmon
Nebo
Oaklands
Melin-y-coed
Gwytherin
Pandy Tudur
Llanddoget
Llangernyw
Llansannan
Llanfair Talhaiarn
Betws-yn-Rhos
MOELFRE UCHAF 1298
Trofarth
Gell
Dawn
Dolwen
Llaneilian-yn-Rhos
Llysfaen
Bryn-y-maen
Eglwysbach
Bodnant
Tal-y-Cafn
MWDW EITHIN 1277
MOEL SEISIOG 1534
BRYN TRILLYN 1627
Mynydd Hiraethog
Alwen Reservoir
Rhyd-lydan
Cefn-brith
Glasfryn
Cerrigydrudion
Gelliodd
Llangwm
Bylchau
CLWYD
61
A55
A470
A5
A548
A543
A4086
A498
B5106
B5113
B5381
6
7
8
9

74
SCALE
0 1 2 3 4 5 miles
0 1 2 3 4 5 kilometres
82
73
62
LIVERPOOL
BAY
BELFAST
DOUGLAS
DUBLIN
CROSBY
Brighton le Sands
Waterloo
Seaforth
BOOTLE
New Brighton
WALLASEY
Liscard
Egremont
Tunnel
Toll
Poulton
Seacombe
Great Meols
HOYLAKE
Moreton
Bidston
Upton
BIRKENHEAD
Greasby
Woodchurch
Frankby
WEST KIRBY
Grange
Prenton
Caldy
WIRRAL
Irby
Storeton
Thurstaston
Pensby
Barnston
Brimstage
HESWALL
Gayton
Thornton Hough
Raby
Parkgate
Willaston
NESTON
Little Neston
Ness
Liverpool Botanic Gardens
Burton
Puddington
Shotwick
RIVER DEE (AFON DYFRDWY)
Point of Ayr
Talacre
Llawndy
Gwespyr
Ffynnongroew
PRESTATYN
y-Ffrith
RHYL
Gronant
Picton
Glan-yr-afon
Llanasa
Rhewl-fawr
Gwaenysgor
Meliden
Trelogan
Mostyn
Tre-Mostyn
Glan-y-don
Llannerch-y-mor
Kinmel Bay
Towyn
Rhuddlan
Plâs Llwyd
Dyserth
Trelawnyd
Walwen
Berthengam
Gwibnant
Sarn
Whitford
Downing
Bychton
Tai-Trevor
Greenfield
Bodrhyddan Hall
OFFA'S DYKE PATH
Pant-y-Wacco
Carmel
Wal-Wen
Whelston
R Gele
ABERGELE
Pengwern
Cwm
Gorsedd
Holway
HOLYWELL
Bagillt
Pentre Bagillt
St. George
Bodelwyddan
Rhuallt
Pen-y-cefn
Pant
Calcot
Milwr
SJ
Flint
FLINT
Pentre Ffwrndan
Oakenholt
The Roe
St. Asaph
950
Glascoed
Groesffordd Marli
Pen-rhewl
Babell
Brynford
Pentre Halkyn
Mynydd-llan
Pen-Ucha'r Plwyf
R Elwy
Tremeirchion
Caerwys
Ysceifiog
Lixwm
Walwen
Plas-yn-Cefn
Graig
Sodom
Pentre Isaf
Afon-wen
Ddôl
Flint Mountain
Halkyn
Catch
Trefnant
Llanfair Talhaiarn
Llannefydd
Bodfari
Geinas
Pen-y-felin
Nannerch
Rhes-y-cae
Wern-y-gaer
Rhosesmor
Northop
CONNAH'S QUAY
Shotton
Queensferry
Garden City
Cefn Berain
Henllan
Green
SH
DENBIGH
Frondeg
Brookhouse
Kilford
Llandyrnog
Waen
Llangwyfan
Rhiwbebyll
Glan-yr-afon
Rhydymwyn
Llyn-y-pandy
Soughton
Northop Hall
Ewloe
Ewloe Green
Fawnog
Mancot
Hawarden
Groes
Lawnt
Tan-y-fron
Rhydgaled
Llwyn
Llanrhaeadr
Penbre'r felin
Ffordd-las
Cilcain
Gwernaffield
Cefn-bychan
New Brighton
Alltami
MOLD
BUCKLEY
Spon Green
Drury
Llong
Bylchau
Waen
Peniel
Prion
Pentre
Llanynys
Gellifor
Rhos
Llangynhafal
1818
MOEL FAMMAU
Tafarn-y-Gelyn
Cadole
Gwernymynydd
Padeswood
Nantglyn
Cader
Pentre Saron
Pant-pastynog
Rhewl
Hirwaen
Llanferres
Maeshafn
Nercwys
Pontblyddyn
Leeswood
Penyffordd
Pen-y-mynydd
1627
Sportsman's Arms
Meifod
Melin Meredydd
Llanbedr-Dyffryn-Clwyd
RUTHIN
Pontybodkin
Top-y-rhos
Tir-y-fron
Hope
Cyffylliog
Treuddyn
Coed Talon
Caergwrle
Brenig Reservoir
Bontuchel
Llanfwrog
1531
Llanarmon-yn-Iâl
Eryrys
Graianrhyd
Llanfynydd
Cymau
Cefn-y-bedd
CLOCAENOG FOREST
Llanfair Dyffryn Clwyd
Efenechtyd
Graig-fechan
Rhydtalog
Ffrith
Ffrwd
Clocaenog
Pwllglas
Graig-isaf
Gelli Gynan
Bwlchgwyn
Brymbo
Clawdd-newydd
875
Pentre-celyn
Ty'n-y-pwll
Llandegla
Tan-y-fron
Moss
Southsea
Pentre-llyn-cymmer
Alwen
Gwynfryn
Minera
Coedpoeth
Llanfihangel Glyn Myfyr
Derwen
Rhyd-y-meudwy
Pen-y-stryt
1848
Cryn y Brain
The Nant
Bersham
Melin-y-wig
Bryn Saith Marchog
Llanelidan
OFFA'S DYKE PATH
Aber-oer
Rhostyllen
Talwrn
1083
Erddig House
Bettws Gwerfil Goch
Gwyddelwern
Bryneglwys
Pentredwr
Rhosllanerchrugog
Ruabon Mountain
Stryt-issa
Penycae
Johnstown
Pont-Afon-goch
Ty-nant
Dinmael
Maerdy
Llantysilio Mountain
Rhewl
Hendy
Llantysilio
Valle Crucis Abbey
Llangwm
Druid
Rug
Carrog
Lidiart-y-parc
Acrefair
Ruabon
Rhosymedre
Cefn Mawr
2095
Tai-mawr
Wenallt
Plas Isaf
Corwen
Bonwm
Glyndyfrdwy
Garth
FOEL GOCH
Glan-
A565 A551 A553 A5027 A552 A5139 A540 M53 A5137 A541 A548 A547 A5151 A525 A55 B5119 B5381 B5429 B5122 B5121 A5026 A5119 B5126 A550 B5428 B5382 A543 A494 A5118 A5104 B5107 B5430 A525 B5105 B5429 B5437 A5104 A542 A5 A483 B5436 B4501 B5435 A544 B5430 B5426 B4401
0 1 2 3
5 6 7 8 9 0

75
Melling
RAINFORD
BILLINGE
ASHTON-IN-MAKERFIELD
LEIGH
Pennington
Astley Green
Lower Green
ECCLES
Aintree
Waddicar
KIRKBY
Crank
Leyland Green
Garswood
Chadwick Green
Haydock Park
GOLBORNE
Lowton Common
Lowton St Mary's
Lowton
Lately Common
Moss Bank
HAYDOCK
Carr Mill
ST HELENS
NEWTON-LE-WILLOWS
Lane Head
Twiss Green
Glazebury
Higher Irlam
Fazakerley
Knowsley
Eccleston
Broad Oak
Kenyon
Newchurch
Culcheth
IRLAM
URMSTON
Flixton
Croxteth Hall
Knowsley Safari Park
West Derby
Pilkington Glass
Collins Green
Earlestown
Vulcan Village
Croft
Little Town
The Rowe
Lower Irlam
LIVERPOOL
Sutton
Thatto Heath
Winwick
Eaves Brow
PRESCOT
B5204
Burtonwood
Risley
Cadishead
Carrington
Whiston
Clock Face
Fearnhead
Hollins Green
Partington
Carrington Moss
ROBY
HUYTON
Rainhill
Whiston Lane Ends
Rainhill Stoops
WARRINGTON
Orford
Woolston
Lane End
Sinderland Green
Broadheath
Paddington
Mossbrow
Childwall
Cronton
Bold Heath
Lingley Green
Great Sankey
Martinscroft
Warburton
Dunham Town
Thelwall
Statham
Heatley
Tarbock Green
Upton
Farnworth
Penketh
Sankey Bridges
Woolton
Halewood Green
Appleton
Aigburth
Allerton
Hunt's Cross
Hough Green
Ditton
WIDNES
Lower Walton
Higher Walton
Grappenhall
LYMM
Broomedge
BOWDON
Grassendale
Halewood
Lugsdale
Stockton Heath
Bollington
Spodegreen
Booth Bank
Garston
West Bank
Moore
High Legh
Norton Priory
Appleton Thorn
Swineyard
Swarton Heath
Hoo Green
Bucklow Hill
Rostherne
Tatton Dale
Tatton Park
TON
LIVERPOOL
Speke
Hale Bank
Keckwick
Hatton
Stretton
Speke Hall
Hale Cliff
Oglet
Hale
RUNCORN
Norton
Halton
Daresbury
Lower Stretton
Arley Hall
Mere
borough
Weston Point
Weston
Preston Brook
Higher Whitley
Arley
Polelane Ends
Tabley Hill
stham
RIVER MERSEY
Bate Heath
Antrobus
Sutton Weaver
Aston Heath
Dutton
Lower Whitley
Whitley
Frandley
Kilrie
Aston
Comberbach
Great Budworth
ELLESMERE PORT
Frodsham
Overton
Willow Green
Danes Green
Little Leigh
Pickmere
Toft
Ince
Boat Museum
Bradley
Acton Bridge
Anderton
Wincham
Plumley
Elton
Fivecrosses
Lostock Gralam
Whitby
Thornton-le-Moors
Helsby
Kingsley
Barnton
Marston
Lower Peover
Whitby heath
Elton Green
Hapsford
Newton
Commonside
NORTHWICH
Little Stanney
Stoak
Thornton Green
Alvanley
Crowton
Onston
Ruloe
Weaverham
Lower Shurlach
Lostock Green
Swan Green
Backford
Bridge Trafford
Dunham-on-the-Hill
Gorstage
Broken Cross
Dunkirk
Hatchmere
Norley
Hartford
Leftwich
Wervin
Manley
Cuddington
Lach Dennis
Picton
Long Green
Mouldsworth
Blakemere
Davenham
Mere Heath
Shipbrookhill
Rudheath
Mollington
Chester Zoo
Mickle Trafford
Plemstall
Little Barrow
Guilden Sutton
Ashton
EDDISBURY HILL
Sandiway
Byley
Whitegate
Moulton
Cranage
Upton
Hollowmoor Heath
Great Barrow
Tarvin Sands
Stamford Bridge
Kelsall
Boothdale
Nova Scotia
Delamere
Marton Green
Foxwist Green
Marton
Little
Bostock Green
Sproston Green
Blacon
Hoole
Littleton
Oscroft
Willington Corner
Salterswall
Wharton
Kilnhouses
Tarvin
Westwood Common
Quarrybank
Cotebrook
Little Budworth
CHESTER
Christleton
Handbridge
Over
WINSFORD
MIDDLEWICH
Huntington
Brown Heath
Saltney
Rowton
Duddon
Eaton
Oulton Park
Hebden Green
Clive Green
School Green
Church Hill
Bradwall Green
Burton
Rushton
Waverton
Occlestone Green
Lee Green
Moston Green
Hargrave
Clotton
Eccleston
Rhuddall Heath
SANDBACH
Tarporley
Wettenhall
Walley's Green
Eaton Hall
Saighton
Hatton Heath
Brassey Green
Four Lane Ends
Huxley
Tiverton
Tilstone Fearnall
Town Green
Church Minshull
Cross Lane
Warmingham
Elworth
Bruera
Wettenhall Green
Alpraham
Gatesheath
Newton
Beeston
Tilstone Bank
Barratts Green
Calveley
Wades Green
Bradfield Green
Coppenhall Moss
Aldford
Milton Green
Newtown
Beeston
Wheelock
Barrow's Green
Wheelock Heath
Lavister
Rossett
Tattenhall
Bunbury Heath
Bunbury
Aston juxta Mondrum
Winterley
Handley
Burwardsley
Spurstow
Wardle
CREWE
Maw Green
Churton
Aldersey Green
Coddington
Chowley
Higher Burwardsley
Peckforton
Barbridge
Poole Green
Worleston
Haslington
Farndon
Harthill
Haughton Moss
Wistaston Green
Oakhanger
Clutton
Broxton
Reaseheath
Crewe Green
Holt
Barton
Ridley Green
Burland
Wistaston
Wells Green
Smith's Green
Borras Head
Cowleyhill
Stretton
Fuller's Moor
Bulkeley
Gallantry Bank
Barford
Acton
Gresty Green
Barthomley
Crewe
Stretton Mill
Bickerton
Croxton Green
Cholmondeley Castle
Faddiley
Gradeley Green
Hollin Green
Dorfold Hall
Willaston
Shavington
Weston
Hugmore
Chorley
NANTWICH
Hough
Englesea brook
Castletown
Tilston
Duckington
Larden Green
Ravensmoor
Stoneley Green
Butt Green
Haymoor Green
Wybunbury
Chorlton
Edge Green
Horton Green
Hetherson Green
Bickley Moss
Stapeley
Walgherton
Shrale
Shocklach
Hampton Heath
Buddileigh
Betley
Bowling Bank
Simmonds Green
Shockloch Green
Bickley Town
Sound Heath
Newtown
Talwrn
Chorlton Lane
Malpas
Cat Hill
Ebnal
Bickley
No Man's Heath
Wrenbury
Sutton Green
Tushingham cum Grindley
Norbury
Pinsley Green
Hatherton
Blakenhall
Bangor-is-y-coed
Bradley Common
Gaunton's Bank
Aston
Parrah Green
Hunterston
Cross Lanes
Cuddington Heath
Bell o' th' Hill
Marley Green
Hankelow
Checkley Green
Checkley
Middle Madele
Worthenbury
Upper Threapwood
Marbury
Newhall
Threapwood
Hollyhurst
Dodd's Green
Audlem
Madeley
Bangor-on-Dee
Tallarn Green
Higher Wych
Grindley Brook
Wheel Green
Wirswall
Brynhovah Bank
Royal's Green
Buerton
Overton
Iscoud
Lightwood Green
Kinsey Heath
Woore
Whitchurch
Burleydam
Coxbank
CHESHIRE

76
LEIGH
SWINTON
MANCHESTER
ASHTON-UNDER-LYNE
ECCLES
SALFORD
DROYLSDEN
STALYBRIDGE
DUKINFIELD
AUDENSHAW
Lowton Common
Lately Common
Glazebury
Higher Irlam
IRLAM
URMSTON
Flixton
STRETFORD
Trafford Park
Old Trafford
Hulme
Gorton
Rusholme
Levenshulme
DENTON
HYDE
Haughton Green
Kenyon
Culcheth
Croft
The Rowe
Lower Irlam
Chorlton cum Hardy
Withington
Reddish
Ashton upon Mersey
Carrington
Partington
Carrington Moss
SALE
Brooklands
Didsbury
Burnage
Cadishead
Hollins Green
Fearnhead
Orford
Woolston
Martinscroft
Warburton
Thelwall
Sinderland Green
Broadheath
Dunham Town
Timperley
GATLEY
CHEADLE
STOCKPORT
Bredbury
ROMILEY
Compstall
Marple Bridge
MARPLE
HAZEL GROVE
Stepping Hill
Heaviley
Heatley
Statham
ALTRINCHAM
BOWDON
HALE
Halebarns
Heald Green
Cheadle Hulme
BRAMHALL
Norbury Moor
High Lane
Disley
Grappenhall
Stockton Heath
Appleton Thorn
Stretton
Lower Stretton
LYMM
Broomedge
Bollington
Spodegreen
High Legh
Swinton Heath
Ashley
Styal
Heyhead
Hollinlane
Handforth
Poynton
Hockley
Lyme Park
Rostherne
Tatton Dale
Tatton Park
Mere
Morley Green
WILMSLOW
Woodford
Wardsend
Dean Row
Adlington
Arley Hall
Arley
Higher Whitley
Whitley
Antrobus
Bate Heath
Tabley hill
The Oaks
Knolls Green
Fulham Park
ALDERLEY EDGE
Adlington Hall
Pott Shrigley
Kettleshulme
Comberbach
Great Budworth
Mobberley
Cross Town
KNUTSFORD
Lindow End
Hough
Kirkleyditch
Prestbury
BOLLINGTON
Kerridge
Little Leigh
Anderton
Wincham
Pickmere
Lostock Gralam
Plumley
Toft
Ollerton
Marthall
Nether Alderley
Tytherington
Rainow
Barnton
Marston
NORTHWICH
Lower Peover
Parkgate
Monks Heath
Hurdsfield
MACCLESFIELD
Hartford
Broken Cross
Lostock Green
Lach Dennis
Peover Heath
Chelford
Capesthorne Hall
Henbury
Langley
Macclesfield Forest
Davenham
Shipbrookhill
Blackden Heath
Goostrey
Jodrell Bank
Withington Green
Siddington
Sutton Lane Ends
Moulton
Byley
Cranage
Gawsworth
Gawsworth Hall
Oakgrove
Wildboarclough
Foxwist Green
Bostock Green
Sproston Green
Holmes Chapel
Swettenham
Marton
Rode Heath
Wharton
Allgreave
WINSFORD
MIDDLEWICH
Brereton Green
Hulme Walfield
North Rode
Wincle
Bosley
Danebridge
Over
Clive Green
Church Hill
Bradwall Green
Brereton Heath
CONGLETON
Key Green
Lee Green
Occlestone Green
Arclid Green
Buglawton
Timbersbrook
Heaton
Wettenhall
SANDBACH
Brookhouse Green
Astbury
Hightown
Rushton Spencer
Church Minshull
Warmingham
Elworth
Overton Green
Congleton Edge
Newtown
Meerbrook
Bradfield Green
Wheelock
Hassall Green
Fourlanes End
Brownlow Heath
Gillow Heath
Biddulph Moor
Rudyard
LEEK
Aston juxta Mondrum
CREWE
Winterley
Hassall
Rode Heath
Little Moreton Hall
Mow Cop
BIDDULPH
Horton
Poole Green
Worleston
Haslington
ALSAGER
Church Lawton
Harriseahead
Knypersley
Blackwood Hill
Longsdon
Rease Heath
Wistaston
Crewe Green
Radway Green
Hardings Wood
KIDSGROVE
Brindley Ford
Endon
Acton
Willaston
Barthomley
Weston
Talke
Newchapel
Goldenhill
Brown Edge
Cheddleton
NANTWICH
Shavington
Hough
Balterley
Bed Street
Tunstall
Baddeley Green
Stanley
Butt Green
Wybunbury
Chorlton
Audley
Chesterton
Burslem
Milton
Abbey Hulton
Wetley Rocks
Stapeley
Walgherton
Betley
Alsagers Bank
Hanley
Werrington
Newtown
Hatherton
Blakenhall
Wrinehill
Leycett
Silverdale
Bucknall
Cellarhead
Aston
Newhall
Hankelow
Checkley
Madeley
Keele
STOKE-ON-TRENT
Fenton
Audlem
Wheel Green
NEWCASTLE-UNDER-LYME
Clayton
Caverswall
Dilhorne
Buerton
Woore
Onneley
Hanford
Meir
Forsbrook

77
Crowden
Woodhead
A628
Langsett Reservoir
A616
Midhopestones
Green Moor
Wortley
Pilley
Tankersley
Elsecar
Wentworth
THE PENNINE WAY
STOCKSBRIDGE
Garden Village
Bolsterstone
Midhope Moors
Deepcar
Bromley
Howbrook
High Green
A629
A61
Thorpe Hesley
Nether Haugh
Chapeltown
Burn Cross
B6088
B6086
B6090
Braken Hill
2060
84
Dinting Railway Centre
A57
GLOSSOP
Ewden Village
Wigtwizzle
Brightholmlee
Wharncliffe Side
Grenoside
Whitley
Ecclesfield
Scholes
Greasbrough
Dropping Well
A629
Oughtibridge
Agden Reservoir
Bradfield Moors
Bradfield
Shiregreen
Hill Top
Chunal
Derwent Reservoir
Low Bradfield
Worrall
Parson Cross
Wincobank
A6178
Tinsley
Snake Inn
Uphill
Stacey Bank
Wadsley Bridge
HIGH PEAK
Strines Reservoir
Dungworth
Owlerton
Carbrook
Brinsworth
Brookhouses
Ladybower Reservoir
Load Brook
Stopes
B6077
B6076
Catcliffe
Stannington
Attercliffe
2088
Hayfield
Walkley
Crookes
SHEFFIELD
Highgate Head
Edale
1504
HIGH NEB
Nether Booth
A6013
Handsworth
Barber Booth
78
Fulwood
Ecclesall
Woodhouse
Treak Cliff Cavern
Blue John Caverns
Hope
Aston
Bamford
Redmires Reservoir
Ringinglow
Abbeydale Industrial Hamlet
Hackenthorpe
A624
Chinley
Malcoff
Slackhall
A625
Castleton
Thornhill
Shepherd Wheel
Oakes Park
Speedwell Cavern
Peveril
Smalldale
Brough
Hathersage
Hathersage Booths
Fox House Inn
Brick Houses
Dore
Beauchief
Gleadless Townend
Highlane
Ridgeway
Mosborough
Sparrowpit
Bradwell
Totley
Greenhill
Norton
Townend
Lower Crossings
Cockyard
Old Dam
Peak Forest
Abney
Upper Padley
Northern Common
Dronfield Woodhouse
Mickley
Coal Aston
Troway
DRONFIELD
Eckington
Bramley
A623
Coplow Dale
Leam
B6001
Owler Bar
Hallsteads Top
Dove Holes
Little Hucklow
Great Hucklow
Bretton
Grindlow
Grindleford
Nether Padley
B6054
Stubley
Apperknowle
Smalldale
West Handley
Unstone
1662
A6
Peak Dale
Wheston
Lane Head
Foolow
Housley
Eyam
B6521
Froggatt
Holmesfield
Cowley
Nether Handley
Upper End
1322
Tunstead
Tideswell
Hargatewell
Town End
Litton
Stoney Middleton
Calver Sough
Curbar
A621
Common Side
Wilday Green
Bolehill
Crowhole
Barlow
Whittington
Borrow Hill
Revolution House
A5002
Wormhill
Wardlow
Moorhall
Overgreen
Newgate
Newbold
A616
Middlecroft
Brimington
Fairfield
Miller's Dale
Cressbrook
SK
Calver
Baslow
Hare Edge
Cutthorpe
Four Lane Ends
B6049
Little Longstone
Rowland
Linacre Reservoir
Old Brampton
CHESTERFIELD
Calow
Canhole
Staden
Blackwell
Cowdale
King Sterndale
Priestcliffe Ditch
Great Longstone
Hassop
Nether End
A619
West End
New Brampton
Cock Alley
A53
Harpur Hill
A515
Taddington
PS
Ashford
B6465
Pilsley
Chatsworth
Wadshelf
Fairfield
Belmont
Walton
Boythorpe
Bolehill
Dunsa
Edensor
Holymoorside
Nether Lands
Chelmorton
Sheldon
Hasland
Hasland Green
Calow Green
Brand Top
Hindlow
Hollow
Flagg
BAKEWELL
B6012
Beeley
Gamball's Green
Earl Sterndale
Hurdlow Town
B5055
Haddon Hall
Wingerworth
Grassmoor
B5057
Belfit Hill
Hollinsclough
Sparklow
Monyash
Over Hadden
Rowsley
Little Rowsley
Nether Moor
New Tupton
High Needham
Morridge Top
Crowdicote
Alport
Stanton in Peak
Uppertown
Northedge
Old Tupton
North Wingfield
Longnor
Youlgreave
Northwood
Brockhurst
Alton
Fawfieldhead
Arbor Low Stone Circle
Nine Ladies Stone Circle
Kelstedge
CLAY CROSS
Littlemoor
Two Dales
Pilsbury
B5053
Middleton
B5056
Darley Dale
Upper Hackney
Ashover
Fallgate
Stretton
Pilsley
Sheen
Darley Bridge
Handley
Hartington
Friden
Dale End
Upper Town
Birchover
Winster
Dimple
Milltown
Morton
Brund
Newhaven Hotel
Elton
Market
Wensley
MATLOCK
B6014
Woolley
Higham
Upper Elkstone
Warslow
Heathcote
A5012
Brightgate
Riber Castle Fauna Reserve
Tansley
Butterley
Highoredish
Stonebroom
Lower Elkstone
Hulme End
Biggin
Pikehall
Grangemill
Heights of Abraham
Matlock Bath
Brackenfield
Ecton
1272
Bonsall
Slaley
Lea
Wessington
Shirland
Aldwark
Cromford
Willersley
B5053
Butterton
Wetton
Alstonefield
Alsop en le Dale
Longcliffe
Ible
Middleton
Bolehill
Holloway
South Wingfield
Wakebridge Tramway
ALFRETON
Ballidon
Hope
Milldale
Stanshope
Parwich
WIRKSWORTH
Whatstandwell
Wirksworth Moor
Oakerthorpe
Crich
Crich Common
Fritchley
Swanwick
Ford
Grindon
Tissington
Brassington
Carsington
Warmbrook
B5023
Alderwasley
Somercotes
Oldfield
Millers Green
Carsington Reservoir
Pentrich
Riddings
Ironville
Waterfall
Bradbourne
Knockerdown
Winkhill
Back o' th' Brook
Ilam
Fenny Bentley
B5033
Upper Town
Beighton Hill
Ambergate
Toadmoor
Nether Heage
A610
Ridgeway
Butterley
RIPLEY
Golden Valley
Waterhouses
Calton
Calton Green
Thorpe
Rowfield
Kniveton
Hognaston
Kirk Ireton
Irdinghay Green
Shottle
Mount Pleasant
Heage
Broadholm
Peasehill
Blore
Mapleton
Blackwall
Biggin
Idridgehay
White Moor
Street Lane
Greenhillocks
Cauldon Lowe
Cauldon
Atlow
Ashbourne Green
Hulland Ward
Ireton Wood
Blackbrook
Shottlegate
Loscoe
Upper Cotton
Near Cotton
A52
Swinscoe
ASHBOURNE
Turnditch
Hazelwood
BELPER
Smithy Houses
Denby Common
Denby
B6179
Mayfield
Hulland
Hulland Moss
Cross o' th' hands
Kilburn
Stanton
Ramshorn
A517
Bradley
Milford
Horsley Woodhouse
A608
Whiston
Whiston Eaves
Middle Mayfield
Spitalhill
Clifton
Windley
Dakamoor
Farley
Wootton
Smalley
Ellastone
B5032
Church Mayfield
Snelston
Osmaston
Muggintonlane End
Holbrook
Horsley
Duffield
Mugginton
Coxbench
Mapperley
B5032
Alton Towers
Alton
Lower Ellastone
Norbury
Snelston Common
Edlaston
Wyaston
65
Ednaston
Mercaston
Shirley
Weston Underwood
Quarndon Hill
Flaxholme
Little Eaton
Stanley Common
Threapwood Head
Tithebarn
1
2
3
4

STOCKSBRIDGE
Midhope Moors
Bolsterstone
Deepcar
Tankersley
HOYLAND NETHER
Elsecar
Wentworth
MEXBOROUGH
WATH UPON DEARNE
SWINTON
Denaby
CONISBROUGH
New Edlington
Old Edlington
Cadeby
Chapeltown
Kilnhurst
RAWMARSH
Thrybergh
Hooton Roberts
Braithwell
Stainton
Wigtwizzle
Ewden Village
Wharncliffe Side
Grenoside
Ecclesfield
Greasbrough
Ravenfield
Dalton
Bramley
ROTHERHAM
MALTBY
Bradfield Moors
Oughtibridge
Bradfield
Low Bradfield
Worrall
Wincobank
Tinsley
Wickersley
Whiston
Brinsworth
Hooton Levitt
Loxley
Stannington
Owlerton
Walkley
Attercliffe
Catcliffe
Treeton
Thurcroft
Firbeck
Crookes
SHEFFIELD
Aughton
Ulley
Laughton-en-le-Morthen
Dinnington
Letwell
Ladybower Reservoir
HIGH NEB
Greystones
Fulwood
Ecclesall
Handsworth
Woodhouse
Hackenthorpe
Beighton
Wales
Todwick
Kiveton Park
Anston
Woodsetts
Aston
Bamford
Hathersage
Brough
Bradwell
Redmires Reservoir
Ringinglow
Beauchief
Gleadless Townend
Norton
Mosborough
Killamarsh
Harthill
Thorpe Salvin
Dore
Totley
Greenhill
Coal Aston
Eckington
Rhodesia
Great Hucklow
Grindleford
Nether Padley
Dronfield Woodhouse
DRONFIELD
Apperknowle
Renishaw
Barlborough
Eyam
Holmesfield
Unstone
West Handley
Clowne
Hodthorpe
Froggatt
Curbar
Stoney Middleton
Common Side
Whittington
Mastin Moor
Whitwell
Creswell
Wardlow
Calver
Baslow
Moorhall
Barlow
Newbold
Brimington
STAVELEY
Elmton
Welbeck Abbey
Rowland
Hassop
Cutthorpe
CHESTERFIELD
Long Duckmanton
Shuttlewood
Holbeck
Whaley
Great Longstone
Pilsley
Chatsworth
Brampton
Wadshelf
Calow
BOLSOVER
Nether Langwith
Ashford
Edensor
Holymoorside
Walton
Hasland
Arkwright Town
Carr Vale
Langwith
Church Warsop
BAKEWELL
Beeley
Grassmoor
Temple Normanton
Scarcliffe
Palterton
Upper Langwith
Haddon Hall
Rowsley
Wingerworth
Heath
Glapwell
Shirebrook
Over Haddon
Alport
Stanton in Peak
Tupton
Holmewood
North Wingfield
New Houghton
MANSFIELD WOODHOUSE
Youlgreave
Nine Ladies Stone Circle
Two Dales
Ashover
CLAY CROSS
Hardstoft
Pleasley
Forest Town
Birchover
Darley Dale
Upper Hackney
Stretton
Pilsley
Tibshelf
Teversal
MANSFIELD
Middleton
Winster
Elton
Wensley
MATLOCK
Milltown
Morton
Stanton Hill
Skegby
Higham
Stonebroom
SUTTON IN ASHFIELD
Tansley
Heights of Abraham
Bonsall
Matlock Bath
Brackenfield
Shirland
Huthwaite
Aldwark
Cromford
Lea
Wessington
Westhouses
South Normanton
KIRKBY IN ASHFIELD
Longcliffe
Ible
Holloway
South Wingfield
ALFRETON
Middleton
Brassington
WIRKSWORTH
Whatstandwell
Crich
Pinxton
Selston
Annesley Woodhouse
Carsington
Bradbourne
Alderwasley
Fritchley
Swanwick
Somercotes
Bagthorpe
New Annesley
Newstead Abbey
Pentrich
Ripley
Ironville
Underwood
Newstead
Kniveton
Ambergate
Codnor
Brinsley
Linby
Papplewick
Hognaston
Kirk Ireton
Shottle
Heage
Idridgehay
Hucknall
HUCKNALL
Biggin
Turnditch
BELPER
Loscoe
EASTWOOD
ASHBOURNE
Hulland
Hazelwood
Kilburn
Denby
HEANOR
Watnall
Bulwell
Bradley
Windley
Milford
Horsley Woodhouse
Holbrook
Smalley
Awsworth
Nuthall
Osmaston
Mugginton
Duffield
Horsley
Coxbench
Mapperley
Kimberley
66

79
Blaxton
Finningley
Rossington
Austerfield
Bawtry
Scaftworth
Bircotes
Harworth
Scrooby
Serlby
Ranskill
Blyth
Torworth
Misson
Newington
Everton
Drakeholes
Mattersey
Mattersey Thorpe
Wiseton
Gringley on the Hill
Misterton
Walkeringham
Stockwith
Walkerith
Haxey
Upperthorpe
Westwoodside
East Lound
Graizelound
Broomston
Gunthorpe
River Idle
Owston Ferry
East Ferry
Wildsworth
Laughton
Scotton
Northorpe
Kirton in Lindsey
Redbourne
Blyton
Grayingham
Blyborough
Pilham
Aisby
Willoughton
Yawthorpe
Corringham
Hemswell
Morton
Beckingham
Clayworth
Saundby
GAINSBOROUGH
Springthorpe
Sturgate
Harpswell
Heapham
Glentworth
Upton
Knaith Park
Kexby
Fillingham
Lea
Bole
Wheatley
Hayton
Lound
Sutton
Barnby Moor
Tiln
Clarborough
Sturton le Steeple
North Leverton with Habblesthorpe
Fenton
Littleborough
Knaith
Gate Burton
Willingham by Stow
Coates
Ingham
Stow
Cammeringham
Marton
Trent Port
Cottam
Sturton by Stow
Thorpe in the Fallows
Brattleby
Aisthorpe
Scampton
RETFORD
Welham
South Leverton
West Retford
Babworth
Ranby
Scofton
Morton
Thrumpton
Ordsall
Grove
Treswell
Sundown Pets Garden
Rampton
Brampton
Torksey
Bransby
North Carlton
South Carlton
Eaton
Nether Headon
Headon
Woodbeck
Stokeham
Laneham
Fenton
Saxilby
Hardwick
Gamston
Upton
East Drayton
Laughterton
Kettlethorpe
Drinsey Nook
Burton
Elkesley
West Drayton
Askham
Dunham
Lound Hall
Bothamsall
Carburton
Haughton
Beverotes
Milton
West Markham
East Markham
Darlton
Ragnall
Newton on Trent
Thorney
Broadholme
Skellingthorpe
Jerusalem
LINCOLN
Riseholme
Thoresby
Thoresby Hall
Walesby
Budby
Tuxford
Normanton on Trent
South Clifton
North Clifton
Harby
Doddington
Doddington Hall
Wigsley
Boughton
New Ollerton
Ollerton
Edwinstowe
Kirton
Egmanton
Low Marnham
Grassthorpe
Spalford
Eagle Moor
Eagle
North Scarle
Whisby
Hykeham Moor
North Hykeham
Bracebridge Heath
Weston
Sutton on Trent
Weecar
Girton
Wellow
Grimston Hill
Laxton
Moorhouse
Ompton
Kneesall
Ossington
Besthorpe
South Scarle
Thorpe on the Hill
Eagle Barnsdale
Morton Hall
Carlton-on-Trent
Norwell Woodhouse
Norwell
Swinderby
Haddington
Harmston
Aubourn
Aubourn Hall
Thurlby
Waddington
Kersall
Eakring
Caunton
Cromwell
Collingham
Coleby
Bilsthorpe
Bilsthorpe Moor
Belle Eau Park
Maplebeck
Norton Disney
Bassingham
Boothby Graffoe
Winkburn
Knapthorpe
Bathley
North Muskham
Holme
Brough
Langford
Stapleford
Carlton-le-Moorland
Farnsfield
Kirklington
Hockerton
South Muskham
Winthorpe
Wellingore
White Post Inn
Edingley
Normanton
Kelham
Upton
NEWARK-ON-TRENT
Air Museum
Halam
Averham
Southwell
Staythorpe
Brant Broughton
Welbourn
Easthorpe
Rolleston
Brinkley
Parkhill
Coddington
Beckingham
Leadenham
Farndon
Balderton
New Balderton
Barnby in the Willows
Stragglethorpe
Oxton
Halloughton
Fiskerton
Hawton
Fenton
Thurgarton
East Stoke
Thorpe
Epperstone
Bleasby
Fulbeck
Gonalston
Elston
Claypole
Stubton
Brandon
Caythorpe
Friesthorpe
Lowdham
Hoveringham
Syerston
Cotham
Dry Doddington
Normanton
Lambley
Kneeton
Flintham
Sibthorpe
Top Green
Long Bennington
Hough-on-the-Hill
Gelston
Carlton Scroop
Caythorpe
East Bridgford
Shelton
Hougham
Westborough
Sudbrook
Burton Joyce
Gunthorpe
Screveton
Hawksworth
Marston
Ancaster
Shelford
Car Colston
Little Green
Flawborough
Thoroton
Kilvington
Alverton
Foston
Honington
Wilsford
Gedling
RETFORD
Worksop
Hodsock
Spital Hill
Spital in the Street
Caenby Corner
Normanby
Owmby
Saxby
West Firsby
Hackthorn
Snitterby
Atterby
Bishop Norton
Waddingham
Dunholme
86
80
66
67
7
8
9

80
Scotter
Kirton in Lindsey
Redbourne
North Kelsey
Caistor
Hatcliffe
West Ravendale
East Ravendale
Scotton
Northorpe
Moortown
North End
South Kelsey
Nettleton
Rothwell
Brandy Wharf
Waddingham
Holton le Moor
Croxby
Thoresway
Thorganby
Grayingham
Thornton le Moor
Normanby le Wold
Stainton le Vale
Swinhope
Blyborough
North Owersby
Pilham
Snitterby
Claxby
Aisby
Willoughton
South Owersby
Kirkby
Usselby
Kirmond le Mire
Binbrook
Atterby
Bishop Norton
Yawthorpe
Kingerby
Osgodby
Walesby
Corringham
Hemswell
Bishopbridge
Great Tows
Spital in the Street
Middle Rasen
Tealby
Glentham
Caenby Corner
Caenby
West Rasen
MARKET RASEN
Ludford
North Willingham
Springthorpe
Sturgate
Harpswell
GAINSBOROUGH
Heapham
Glentworth
Normanby
Toft next Newton
Newton by Toft
Market Rasen
Upton
Owmby
Burgh on Bain
Saxby
Linwood
Sixhills
Kexby
Fillingham
East Firsby
Buslingthorpe
Legsby
Faldingworth
West Firsby
Spridlington
Bleasby
Hainton
South Willingham
Willingham by Stow
Coates
Ingham
Cold Hanworth
Friesthorpe
Lissington
East Torrington
Gate Burton
Stow
Cammeringham
Hackthorn
Snarford
Wickenby
Holton cum Beckering
West Torrington
Beckering
East Barkwith
Benniworth
Sturton by Stow
Thorpe in the Fallows
Brattleby
Welton Hill
Snelland
West Barkwith
Brampton
Aisthorpe
Welton
Ryland
Fulnetby
Scampton
Dunholme
Stainton by Langworth
Rand
Panton
Sotby
Torksey
Bransby
North Carlton
Scothern
Wire Hill
Wragby
Fenton
Bullington
Hatton
South Carlton
Sudbrooke
Langworth
Langton by Wragby
Low Langton
Great Sturton
Hardwick
Saxilby
Apley
Kettlethorpe
Drinsey Nook
Burton
Riseholme
Nettleham
Barlings
Kingthorpe
Baumber
Broadholme
Cherry Willingham
Reepham
Minting
Thorney
Skellingthorpe
Low Barlings
Stainfield
Fiskerton
Gautby
Jerusalem
Harby
Washingborough
Wispington
Edlington
Doddington
LINCOLN
Wigsley
Doddington Hall
New Boultham
Canwick
Heighington
Branston Booths
Bardney
Bucknall
Thimbleby
Horsington
Swanpool Garden Suburb
Boultham
Swallow Beck
Branston
Langton
Eagle Moor
North Scarle
Eagle
Whisby
Bracebridge Heath
Potterhanworth Booths
Southrey
Woodhall
Hykeham Moor
Bracebridge Low Fields
Potterhanworth
Martin
Thorpe on the Hill
Eagle Barnsdale
Stixwould
Reeds Beck
Roughton
North Hykeham
Wasps Nest
Sots Hole
Nocton
WOODHALL SPA
Morton Hall
Waddington
Martin Dales
Swinderby
Haddington
Aubourn
Aubourn Hall
Harmston
Dunston
Kirkstead Bridge
Kirkby on Bain
Thurlby
Metheringham
Kirkstead Abbey
Coleby
Blankney
Martin
Timberland Delph
Norton Disney
Bassingham
Boothby Graffoe
Timberland
Tattershall Thorpe
Brough
Stapleford
Scopwick
Kirkby Green
Tattershall
Carlton-le-Moorland
Navenby
Wellingore
Walcot
Tattershall Bridge
Ashby de la Launde
Rowston
NEWARK-ON-TRENT
Welbourn
Dogdyke
Brant Broughton
Billinghay
Hawthorn Hill
Scrub Hill
Bloxholm
Digby
Chapel Hill
Hundle Houses
Haven Bank
Coddington
Beckingham
Leadenham
North Kyme
Dorrington
Barnby in the Willows
Stragglethorpe
Anwick
River Witham
Fenton
RAF College
Cranwell
Ruskington
South Kyme
Fulbeck
Leasingham
Claypole
Stubton
Brandon
Caythorpe
South Kyme Fen
Frieston
Evedon
Ewerby Thorpe
Ewerby
Amber Hill
Dry Doddington
Normanton
Holdingham
Kirkby la Thorpe
Howell
Long Bennington
Hough-on-the-Hill
Rauceby
SLEAFORD
Carlton Scroop
Gelston
Sudbrook
Asgarby
East Heckington
Houghan
Westborough
Ancaster
Quarrington
Heckington
Marston
Town End
Foston
Honington
Wilsford
Silk Willoughby
Burton Pedwardine
Great Hale
Swineshead Bridge
R Eau
R Till
R Witham
R Brant
R Slea
SK
LINCOLN
87
79
67
68

SCALE
0 1 2 3 4 5 miles
0 1 2 3 4 5 kilometres
Tetney
North Coates
North Thoresby
Marshchapel
Donna Nook
Eskham
Fulstow
Grainthorpe
North Somercotes
Church End
Covenham St Bartholomew
Conisholme
Toby's Hill
Saltfleet
South Somercotes
Covenham St. Mary
Utterby
Yarburgh
Skidbrooke
Fotherby
Alvingham
Saltfleetby St. Clements
North Elkington
Cockerington
North End
Saltfleetby St. Peter
Saltfleetby All Saints
Keddington
LOUTH
River Head
Stewton
Grimoldby
Theddlethorpe St. Helen
Theddlethorpe All Saints
Manby
Little Carlton
Great Carlton
Meers Bridge
Legbourne
MABLETHORPE
Trusthorpe
Raithby
Little Cawthorpe
North Reston
Gayton le Marsh
Strubby
Thorpe
Sutton-on-Sea
South Reston
Withern
Maltby le Marsh
Tathwell
Haugham
Muckton
Authorpe
Sandilands
Cadwell Park
Beesby
Sutton le Marsh
Burwell
Belleau
Markby
Swaby
Claythorpe
Aby
Saleby
Asserby
Ruckland
Huttoft
Scamblesby
Worlaby
South Thoresby
ALFORD
Bilsby
Anderby Creek
Belchford
Tetford
South Ormsby
Calceby
Rigsby
Thurlby
Anderby
Farlesthorpe
Mumby
Fulletby
Brinkhill
Driby
Well
Cumberworth
Authorpe Row
Salmonby
Ulceby
Willoughby
Mawthorpe Collection
Helsey
Hogsthorpe
Chapel St. Leonards
Somersby
Harrington
Greetham
Aswardby
Langton
Claxby
Sloothby
Slackholme End
Hagworthingham
Dalby
Skendleby
Hasthorpe
Addlethorpe
Ingoldmells
Ingoldmells Point
Lusby
Partney
Welton le Marsh
Sausthorpe
Scremby
Orby
Hameringham
Mavis Enderby
Raithby
Candlesby
Spilsby
Gunby Hall
Winthorpe
Asgarby
Hundleby
Halton Holegate
Bratoft
Burgh le Marsh
Seathorne
Hareby
Old Bolingbroke
Great Steeping
Moorby
Keal
Toynton All Saints
Irby in the Marsh
Miningsby
Firsby
SKEGNESS
Wilksby
East Kirkby
Toynton Fen Side
Toynton St. Peter
Little Steeping
Croft
Revesby
Keal Cotes
Thorpe St. Peter
Seacroft
Mareham le Fen
Fendike Corner
Havenhouse Station
Stickford
Wainfleet Bank
Wainfleet All Saints
New Bolingbroke
Gibraltar
New Leake
Midville
Eastville
Key's Toft
Stickney
Friskney
Medlam
Friskney Eaudike
Small End
Carrington
West Houses
Lade Bank
Northlands
Snowden's Bridge
Sibsey Fen Side
Sibsey
Wrangle Lowgate
Frithville
Leake Common Side
Wrangle
Old Leake
Hall End
High Ferry
Fishtoft Drove
Leake Hurn's End
Frith Bank
Hill Dyke
Leverton
Leverton Lucasgate
Brothertoft
Cowbridge
Benington
Halltoft End
Benington Sea End
BOSTON
Butterwick
Boston West
Brand End
Freiston
Skirbeck
Fishtoft
Old Hu...

88 89

FLEETWOOD
CLEVELEYS
BLACKPOOL
LYTHAM ST ANNE'S
SOUTHPORT
ORMSKIRK
FORMBY
SKELMERSDALE
KIRKBY
CROSBY
PRESTON
LEYLAND
Garstang
Poulton-le-Fylde
Thornton
Preesall
Kirkham
Fulwood
Walton-le-Dale
Standish
Rainford
Orrell
Maghull
River Wyre
River Ribble
To Belfast
To Douglas
DUBLIN

2 74 3 4 75 5

Forest of Bowland
WHINS BROW
Sykes
Hareden
Slaidburn
Newton
Dunsop Bridge
EASINGTON FELL
Holden
Bolton by Bowland
Hellifield
Halton West
Coniston Cold
Gargrave
Embsay
Nappa
Paythorne
Newsholme
West Marton
Gisburn
Sawley
Rimington
Whitewell
Browsholm Hall
Grindleton
West Bradford
Bashall Eaves
Waddington
Chatburn
Downham
Worston
CLITHEROE
BARNOLDSWICK
Salterforth
EARBY
Lothersdale
Kelbrook
Thornton-in-Craven
Elslack
Carleton
Cononley
Glusburn
Cowling
Foulridge
COLNE
Laneshaw Bridge
Wycoller
TRAWDEN
The Forest of Trawden
KEIGHLEY MOOR
THE PENNINE WAY
Barley
Roughlee
Blacko
Newchurch in Pendle
BARROWFORD
NELSON
BRIERFIELD
Sabden
Pendleton
Barrow
Wiswell
Great Mitton
Hurst Green
Longridge Fell
Ribchester
Whalley
Billington
Read
Higham
Fence
PADIHAM
Habergham
BURNLEY
Worsthorne
Hurstwood
Towneley Hall
Mereclough
Simonstone
GREAT HARWOOD
CLAYTON-LE-MOORS
Altham
Hapton
Huncoat
Wilpshire
Salesbury
Osbaldeston
Mellor
RISHTON
BLACKBURN
CHURCH
ACCRINGTON
OSWALDTWISTLE
HAMELDON HILL
Dunnockshaw
Love Clough
Crawshawbooth
Forest of Rossendale
Holme Chapel
Heptonstall
Mytholm
Cornholme
Eastwood
TODMORDEN
Lydgate
Cragg
Mankinholes
Walsden
Pleasington
Feniscowles
Darwen
DARWEN
Withnell
Brinscall
Belthorn
Haslingden Grane
HASLINGDEN
RAWTENSTALL
BACUP
Stacksteads
Waterfoot
Helmshore
Edenfield
Shawforth
WHITWORTH
Calderbrook
WARDLE
LITTLEBOROUGH
Summit
Belmont
EDGWORTH
RAMSBOTTOM
Rivington
WINTER HILL
ADLINGTON
HORWICH
Egerton
Turton Bottoms
Greenmount
TOTTINGTON
Summerseat
Walmersley
BURY
ROCHDALE
MILNROW
HEYWOOD
Norden
BOLTON
Ainsworth
Radcliffe
RADCLIFFE
LITTLE LEVER
FARNWORTH
Kearsley
WHITEFIELD
PRESTWICH
MIDDLETON
CHADDERTON
OLDHAM
ROYTON
SHAW
ASPULL
WESTHOUGHTON
HINDLEY
ATHERTON
Walkden
TYLDESLEY
PENDLEBURY
Little Hulton
LEIGH
WORSLEY
SWINTON
ECCLES
SALFORD
MANCHESTER
FAILSWORTH
ASHTON-UNDER-LYNE
MOSSLEY
STALYBRIDGE
DUKINFIELD
LEES
Delph
Denshaw
SD
M65
M66
M62
M61
M60
M602
A59
A56
A58
A666
A671
A682
A646
A6068
A677
A678
A680
A681
A673
A675
A580
B6478
B6243
B6246
B6232
B6231
B6214
B6222
B6138
90
84
75
76

90
91
83
77
NORTH YORKSHIRE
GREATER MANCHESTER
DERBYSHIRE
LANCASHIRE
SD
SK
Marton
Elslack
Carleton
Low Bradley
High Bradley
Cringles
Low Cringles
ILKLEY
Middleton
Denton
Askwith
Lindley Green
Braythorn
West Side
North Rigton
Stainburn
Huby
Weeton
Thornton-in-Craven
EARBY
Wedding Hall Fold
Dale End
Cononley
Kildwick
Town Head
SILSDEN
Bruntwaite
Ben Rhydding
Ilkley Moor
Stead
Clifton
Farnley
Weston
Newall Carr Side
OTLEY
Newall
Leathley
Lothersdale
Glusburn
Cross Hills
Becks
Silsden Br.
Steeton
Burley in Wharfedale
Castley
Pool
Kelbrook
Lane Ends
New Road Side
Ickornshaw
Ellers
Sutton-in-Craven
Eastburn
Whitley Head
Riddlesden
West Morton
Burley Woodhead
Menston
Westbourne
East Carlton
Kelcliffe
GUISELEY
Bramhope
Arthington
Black Lane Ends
Cowling
Cliffe
Utley
East Riddlesden Hall
Stockbridge
East Morton
Puritan Chapel
Eccup
Laycock
Braithwaite
Thwaites
Thwaites Brow
Micklethwaite
Hawksworth
Park Gate
YEADON
LEEDS AND BRADFORD
Tinshill
Alwoodley
Laneshaw Bridge
Winewall
Wycoller
KEIGHLEY
Eldwick
Cross Flatts
Gilstead Moor
BAILDON
Esholt
Little London
Rawdon
Canada
West End
HORSFORTH
Moortown
TRAWDEN
Lane End
Oakworth
Hainworth
Harden
BINGLEY
Gilstead
Baildon Green
Tarn
Charlestown
Wood End
Thackley
Simpson Grn.
Weetwood
Oldfield
KEIGHLEY MOOR
Scar Top
Stanbury
Scholes
Lees
Barcroft
Cullingworth
Cottingley
Saltaire
Moor Head
Idle
SHIPLEY
Apperley Br.
Cragg Hill
Kirkstall Abbey
Meanwood
The Forest of Trawden
Bronte Parsonage
Haworth
Flappit Spring
Wilsden
Sandy Lane
Frizinghall
Wrose
Eccleshill
Greengates
Calverley
Rodley
Headingley
Kirkstall
THE PENNINE WAY
Keighley and Worth Valley Railway
Hewenden
Lingbob
Heaton
Woodhall Hill
Bagley
Moorside
Bramley
Thursden
Leeming
Harecroft
Allerton
Manningham
Girlington
Farsley
Swinnow
Stanningley
Walshaw Dean Reservoir
Oxenhope
DENHOLME
Egypt
Thornbury
Upper Moor
Troy
Hough End
Armley
Widdop
Sawood
Well Heads
Thornton
School Green
Laisterdyke
Tyersal
Fartown
PUDSEY
Wortley
Whiddop Res
Alcomden
Denholme Clough
Keelham
Warley Moor Reservoir
Clews Moor
Clayton
Great Horton
Little Horton
Fulneck
Farnley
Walshaw
Ogden
Yews Green
QUEENSBURY
West Bowling
Bowling
BRADFORD
Upper Moor Side
New Farnley
Beeston
Widdop Gate
Pecket Well
Bradshaw
Beggarington
Mountain
Buttershaw
Slack Side
Wibsey
Westgate Hill
Tong
Cockersdale
Moor Head
Gildersome
Colden
Slack
Old Town
HEBDEN BRIDGE
Wainstalls
Mixenden
Holdsworth
Ambler Thorn
Odsal
East Bierley
Drighlington
Daisy Hill
Heptonstall
Illingworth
Shibden Head
SHELF
Stone Chair
Birkenshaw
Adwalton
Churwell
Booth
Moor End
Holmfield
Oakenshaw
Morley
Shore
Cornholme
Blackshaw Head
Mytholm
Charlestown
Midgley
Mt. Tabor
Luddenden
Wheatley
Ovenden
Booth Town
Norwood Green
Wyke
Swincliffe
Birstall
Smithies
Bruntcliffe
Birks
Eastwood
Northowram
Priestley Gr.
Lower Wyke
Scholes
Mytholmroyd
Luddenden Foot
HALIFAX
Hipperholme
Lightcliffe
CLECKHEATON
Gomersal
Tingley
Lydgate
Hough Foot
Shade
TODMORDEN
Lumbutts
Cragg
Boulder Clough
Steep Lane
Friendly
Piece Hall
Bank Top
Hove Edge
Shaw Hill
Stoney Royd
Southowram
Thornhills
Clifton
LIVERSEDGE
Well Fold
HECKMONDWIKE
BATLEY
Upper Batley
Beggarington Hill
Mankinholes
Butcher Hill
Walsden
Sowerby
SOWERBY BRIDGE
Copley
BRIGHOUSE
Exley
Norristhorpe
Roberttown
Lower Soothill
Chidswell
DEWSBURY
Triangle
Lumb
Longley
Greetland
Elland Lower Edge
Rastrick
Hartshead
Dewsbury Moor
Gawthorpe
Flushdyke
Bottoms
Warland Reservoir
Mill Bank
Lighthazles
Soyland Town
Greetland Wall Nook
Barkisland
Broad Carr
ELLAND
Bradley
Battye Ford
Crossley
Northorpe
Ravensthorpe
Savile Town
Earlsheaton
Warland
RIPPONDEN
Deighton
Colne Br.
Thornhill Lees
OSSETT
South Ossett
Calderbrook
Summit
Stainland
Krumlin
Holywell Gn
Netheroyd Hill
Birchencliffe
Sheepridge
Fartown
MIRFIELD
Upper Heaton
Thornhill
Healey
HORBURY
Sowood
Mount
Lindley
HUDDERSFIELD
Upper Hopton
Whitley Lower
Middlestown
WARDLE
Rishworth
Pike End
Roadside
Outlane
Scapegoat Hill
Hill Side
Kirkheaton
Falhouse
Houses Hill
Grange Moor
Coxley
Caldermoor
Durn
Lydgate
Deanhead
Gawmes
Lepton
Overton
Netherton
Dearnley
LITTLEBOROUGH
Smithy Bridge
Scammonden
Pole Moor
Golcar
Bolster Moor
Crosland Hill
Fenay Bridge
Rowley Hill
Almondbury
Flockton Green
Great Cliff
Midgley
Smallbridge
Rakewood
Bradshaw
SLAITHWAITE
Dogley Lane
High Green
Highburton
Flockton
Firgrove
Lowhouse Fold
Blackmoorfoot
Linthwaite
Hill Top
South Crosland
Berry Brow
Kaye La.
Farnley Tyas
Emley Moor
West Bretton
MILNROW
Newhey
Higher Ogden
Helme
Crosland Edge
Netherton
KIRKBURTON
Roydhouse
Emley
Clayton West
Lower Place
Haugh
MARSDEN
Shelley
Park Mill
Balderstone
Burnedge
Crompton Fold
Denshaw
MELTHAM
Meltham Mills
Honley
Brockholes
Shelley Far Bank
Scissett
High Hoyland
Summit
Thongsbridge
Thurstonland
Skelmanthorpe
Clough
Grains Bar
Wessenden
Wilshaw
Netherthong
Woodlands
Lane End
Lower Cumberworth
Upper Cumberworth
Kexbrough
SHAW
Slackcote
Harrop Dale
Upperthong
New Mill
Shepley
DENBY DALE
Cannon Hall
Besom Hill
Delph
Diggle
Birds Edge
High Flats
Lower Denby
Gawthorpe
ROYTON
Heyside
New Delph
Dobcross
Austonley
HOLMFIRTH
Scholes
Park Head
Jackson Bridge
Upper Denby
Hay Dale
Long Sight
Moorside
Holmbridge
Paris
Hepworth
Silkstone
OLDHAM
Scouthead
Holme
Longley
Victoria
Ingbirchworth
DODWORTH
Grasscroft
Uppermill
Hade Edge
Thurlstone
Noblethorpe
Hoyland Swaine
LEES
Lydgate
Alt
Pitses
Greenfield
BLACK HILL
Holme Moss
Snittlegate
Crow Edge
Millhouse Green
Spring Vale
Wentworth
MANCHESTER
Winscar Reservoir
Townhead
Carlecotes
PENISTONE
Four Lane End
FAILSWORTH
Park Bridge
Hurst
Luzley
Heyheads
Carrbrook
MOSSLEY
Dunford Bridge
Flouch Inn
Oxspring
Cubley
Bardsley
Woodhouses
Langsett
Thurgoland
ASHTON-UNDER-LYNE
Hazelhurst
Heyrod
Millbrook
Crowden
Woodhead
Langsett Reservoir
Upper Midhope
Snowden Hill
Dean Head
Green Moor
STALYBRIDGE
Copley
Midhopestones
Arnfield
Tintwistle
Garden Village
STOCKSBRIDGE
DUKINFIELD
Bower Fold
Stalyhill
Roe Cross
Mottram-in-Longdendale
Hadfield
Padfield
Bolsterstone
Ewden Village
DENTON
Hollingworth
Dinting Railway Centre
BLEAKLOW HILL
Wharncliffe Side
HYDE
Godley
Gamesley
Woolley Bridge
Simmondley
Shire Hill
GLOSSOP
Oughtibridge
Haughton Green
Reddish
Castle Hill
Broadbottom
Hodgefold
Charlesworth
Charlestown
Bradfield
Gee Cross
Werneth Low
Woodley
Holehouse
Chisworth
Chunal
Derwent Reservoir
Low Bradfield
Greave
ROMILEY
Compstall
Higher
Snake Inn
Bredbury
AA 24 hour
1273
1320
1699
1479
1573
1530
1641
1908
1009
2060
1791
A629
A6034
A65
A659
A660
A658
A650
A6068
A6033
A629
A6038
A657
A6037
A658
A6177
B6157
B6144
B6141
B6145
A647
A6177
A641
A6036
M606
A650
A58
A621
M621
A646
A58
A643
A638
A653
A6025
A629
A58
B6138
B6113
A62
A644
B6117
A58
A672
A640
M62
B6114
A629
A642
A637
A62
A640
A616
A629
A663
A664
B6194
A62
B6107
B6108
A635
A670
A671
A62
A669
A635
B6194
A6024
B6106
A616
A628
A616
B6462
A628
B6105
A635
A627
M67
A57
A57
M66
A560
A626

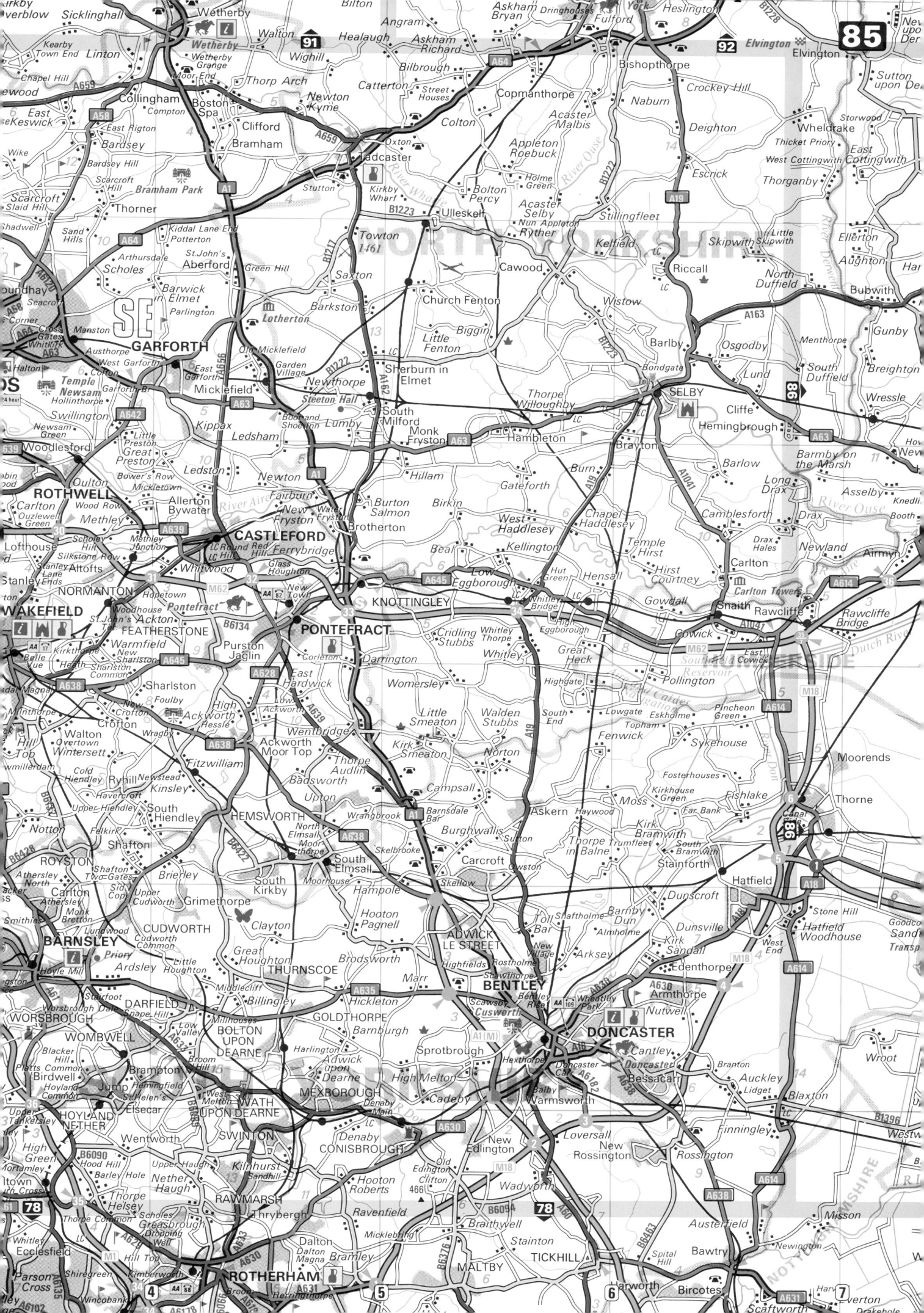
85
Wetherby
Sicklinghall
Kearby Town End
Linton
Walton
Wighill
Healaugh
Angram
Askham Richard
Askham Bryan
Dringhouses
York
Heslington
Fulford
Elvington
Bishopthorpe
Wetherby Grange
Moor End
Chapel Hill
Collingham
Compton
Boston Spa
Thorp Arch
Newton Kyme
Bilbrough
Catterton
Street Houses
Copmanthorpe
Naburn
Crockey Hill
Sutton upon Derwent
East Keswick
East Rigton
Bardsey
Clifford
Bramham
Oxton
Tadcaster
Colton
Acaster Malbis
Deighton
Wheldrake
Storwood
Thicket Priory
West Cottingwith
East Cottingwith
Wike
Bardsey Hill
Scarcroft Hill
Bramham Park
Stutton
Kirkby Wharf
River Wharfe
Bolton Percy
Appleton Roebuck
Holme Green
River Ouse
Escrick
Thorganby
Scarcroft
Slaid Hill
Thorner
Shadwell
Sand Hills
Kiddal Lane End
Potterton
Ulleskelf
Acaster Selby
Nun Appleton
Ryther
Stillingfleet
Kelfield
Skipwith
Little Skipwith
Ellerton
Aughton
Towton 1461
NORTH YORKSHIRE
Arthursdale
St.John's
Aberford
Scholes
Green Hill
Saxton
Cawood
Riccall
North Duffield
Bubwith
Barwick in Elmet
Parlington
Lotherton
Barkston
Church Fenton
Wistow
Seacroft
Manston
Austhorpe
West Garforth
GARFORTH
Old Micklefield
East Garforth
Garden Village
Newthorpe
Sherburn in Elmet
Little Fenton
Biggin
Barlby
Osgodby
Menthorpe
Gunby
Bondgate
Lund
South Duffield
Breighton
Halton
Colton
Temple Newsam
Hollinthorpe
Micklefield
Steeton Hall
South Milford
Lumby
Booth and Shoe Inn
Thorpe Willoughby
SELBY
Cliffe
Wressle
Hemingbrough
Swillington
Newsam Green
Kippax
Ledsham
Monk Fryston
Hambleton
Brayton
Little Preston
Great Preston
Woodlesford
Bower's Row
Mickletown
Ledston
Newton
Hillam
Burn
Barlow
Barmby on the Marsh
Long Drax
Asselby
ROTHWELL
Oulton
Carlton
Wood Row
Ouzlewell Green
Methley
Allerton Bywater
River Aire
Fairburn
New Fryston
Water Fryston
Burton Salmon
Brotherton
Birkin
Gateforth
West Haddlesey
Chapel Haddlesey
Camblesforth
Drax
Knedlington
Booth
Lofthouse
Scholey Hill
Methley Junction
Silkstone Row
CASTLEFORD
Round Hill
Red Hill
Ferrybridge
Beal
Kellington
Temple Hirst
Drax Hales
Newland
Airmyn
Stanley
Stanley Lane Ends
Altofts
Whitwood
Glass Houghton
Low Eggborough
Hut Green
Hensall
Hirst Courtney
Carlton
Carlton Towers
NORMANTON
Hopetown
New Town
KNOTTINGLEY
Whitley Bridge
Gowdall
Snaith
Rawcliffe
Rawcliffe Bridge
WAKEFIELD
Woodhouse
Pontefract
St.John's
Ackton
FEATHERSTONE
PONTEFRACT
Cridling Stubbs
Whitley Thorpe
High Eggborough
Cowick
Dutch River
Kirkthorpe
Warmfield
New Sharlston
Heath
Sharlston Common
Belle Vue
Purston Jaglin
Corleton
Darrington
Whitley
Great Heck
East Cowick
Southfield Reservoir
HUMBERSIDE
Sandal Magna
Sharlston
East Hardwick
Womersley
Highgate
Pollington
Aire and Calder Navigation
New Crofton
Foulby
Crofton
Ackworth
High Ackworth
Low Ackworth
Hessle
Little Smeaton
Walden Stubbs
South End
Lowgate
Eskholme
Pincheon Green
Topham
Milnthorpe
Walton
Overtown
Wintersett
Wragby
Wentbridge
Ackworth Moor Top
Kirk Smeaton
Norton
Fenwick
Sykehouse
Hill Top
Thorpe Audlin
Moorends
Cold Hiendley
Ryhill
Newstead
Kinsley
Fitzwilliam
Badsworth
Campsall
Fosterhouses
Kirkhouse Green
Fishlake
Thorne
Havercroft
Upper Hiendley
South Hiendley
HEMSWORTH
Upton
Wrangbrook
Barnsdale Bar
Askern
Haywood
Moss
Far Bank
Notton
Felkirk
North Elmsall
Moorthorpe
Burghwallis
Sutton
Kirk Bramwith
South Bramwith
Canal
Shafton
ROYSTON
Shafton Two Gates
South Elmsall
Skelbrooke
Carcroft
Owston
Thorpe in Balne
Trumfleet
Stainforth
Hatfield
Athersley North
Brierley
South Kirkby
Moorhouse
Hampole
Skellow
Dunscroft
Carlton
Athersley
Monk Bretton
Sid Cop
Upper Cudworth
Grimethorpe
Hooton Pagnell
Toll Bar
Shaftholme
Barnby Dun
Stone Hill
Hatfield Woodhouse
Smithies
Lundwood
CUDWORTH
Clayton
ADWICK LE STREET
Almholme
Dunsville
BARNSLEY
Cudworth Common
Priory
Great Houghton
Brodsworth
New Village
Kirk Sandall
West End
Ardsley
Little Houghton
THURNSCOE
Highfields
Rostholme
Arksey
Edenthorpe
Hoyle Mill
Stairfoot
Middlecliff
Marr
Scawthorpe
BENTLEY
Armthorpe
DARFIELD
Billingley
Hickleton
Scawsby
Bentley Rise
Wheatley Park
Nutwell
WORSBROUGH
Worsbrough Dale
Snape Hill
Low Valley
Millhouses
GOLDTHORPE
Barnburgh
Cusworth
DONCASTER
WOMBWELL
BOLTON UPON DEARNE
Harlington
Adwick upon Dearne
Sprotbrough
Hexthorpe
Cantley
Wroot
Blacker Hill
Platts Common
Birdwell
Brampton
Broom Hill
Doncaster Carr
Doncaster
Branton
Hoyland Common
Jump
Hemingfield
West Melton
WATH UPON DEARNE
MEXBOROUGH
High Melton
Cadeby
Balby
Warmsworth
Bessacarr
Auckley
Lidget
Blaxton
St.Helen's
Elsecar
HOYLAND NETHER
Denaby Main
Loversall
New Rossington
Finningley
Wentworth
SWINTON
Denaby
CONISBROUGH
New Edlington
Rossington
High Green
Hood Hill
Upper Haugh
Kilnhurst
Sandhill
Old Edlington
Clifton
Mortamley
Barley Hole
Nether Haugh
Hooton Roberts
Wadworth
Thorpe Hesley
RAWMARSH
Ravenfield
Thorpe Common
Scholes
Greasbrough
Thrybergh
Braithwell
Austerfield
Misson
Dropping Well
Micklebring
Whitley
Ecclesfield
Dalton
Dalton Magna
Bramley
Stainton
TICKHILL
Spital Hill
Bawtry
Newington
Hill Top
Kimberworth
ROTHERHAM
MALTBY
Parson Cross
Shiregreen
Wincobank
Broom
Herringthorpe
Harworth
Bircotes
Everton
Scaftworth
NOTTINGHAMSHIRE
A1
A19
A64
A63
A645
A639
A638
A628
A642
A58
A659
A656
A162
A163
A1041
A614
A18
A630
A635
A633
A631
A6182
A638
A61
A6123
A629
A6135
A6102
A6178
A60
A1(M)
M1
M18
M62
B1223
B1222
B1217
B1228
B6134
B6422
B6428
B6090
B6089
B6094
B6376
B6463
B1396
91
92
78
98

87
SCALE
0 1 2 3 4 5 miles
0 1 2 3 4 5 kilometres
93
HORNSEA
North Cliff
South Cliff
Hornsea Mere
Hornsea Pottery
Nunkeeling
Burshill
Little Burton
Brandesburton
Seaton
Leven
B1244
Sigglesthorne
Rolston
Catwick
Goxhill
Mappleton
Routh
Long Riston
Arnold
Tickton
A1035
B1243
Little Hatfield
Great Hatfield
Rise
North End
Great Cowden
Withernwick
North Skirlaugh
New Ellerby
South End
Marton
West Carlton
East Carlton
Meaux
South Skirlaugh
West Newton
Aldbrough
East Newton
Woodmansey
Plaxton Bridge
A165
Old Ellerby
Etherdwick
Wawne
Flinton
B1242
Thearne
Burton Constable Hall
Garton
Grimston
Swine
Coniston
Dunswell
Ganstead
Thirtleby
B1238
Sproatley
Humbleton
Fitling
Hilston
83
New Village
B1237
Wyton
Lelley
Owstwick
Tunstall
Sutton-on-Hull
Sutton Ings
Bilton
B1239
B1240
Elstronwick
Danthorpe
North End
B1233
A1165
Newland
Stoneferry
Marfleet
Preston
West End
East End
Burton Pidsea
Roos
A165
AA 24 hour
A1033
HEDON
TA
Waxholme
Rimswell
B1362
Owthorne
WITHERNSEA
Haven Side
Burstwick
West End
Halsham
East End
Batty's Corner
KINGSTON UPON HULL
Thorngumbald
Paull
Hollym
Ryehill
Keyingham
Goxhill Haven
Little Humber
Ottringham
Winestead
A1033
New Holland
LC
North End
Thorney Crofts
Patrington
Holmpton
Barrow Haven
Barrow upon Humber
Goxhill
Patrington Haven
B1445
Out Newton
Welwick
Weeton
Skeffling
South End
RIVER HUMBER
A1077
East Halton
Sunk Island
17
Easington
Thornton Curtis
Stone Creek Ho.
South End
North Killingholme
Wootton
A160
A1173
Immingham Dock
Kilnsea
Ulceby Skitter
South Killingholme
54
Immingham
Ulceby
Habrough
LC
A180
Croxton
B1211
B1210
Stallingborough
GRIMSBY
AA
Kirmington
Melton Ross
Brocklesby
HUMBERSIDE
Healing
Pyewipe
West Marsh
A1136
A180
SPURN HEAD
New Barnetby
Barnetby le Wold
Keelby
Great Coates
A18
Great Limber
Little Coates
Old Clee
CLEETHORPES
ROTTERDAM (EUROPOORT)
ZEEBRUGGE
Aylesby
A46
Bigby
Nunsthorpe
Thrunscoe
A1084
Riby
A46
Laceby
A1098
Searby
Bradley
Scartho
Owmby
Humberston
Irby upon Humber
A16
Clixby
A1173
Waltham
B1203
New Waltham
Grasby
Barnoldby le Beck
Holton le Clay
Swallow
A1031
Cabourne
Brigsley
Tetney Lock
314
North End
Beelsby
Caistor
Cuxwold
Ashby cum Fenby
Tetney
North Cotes
Waithe
B1205
Hatcliffe
A18
A46
Nettleton
West Ravendale
Grainsby
Marshchapel
Moortown
Rothwell
East Ravendale
B1201
Eskham
Church-thorpe
Fulstow
West End
Grainthorpe
Holton le Moor
LC
Croxby
Thorganby
North Thoresby
North Somercotes
Wold Newton
550
TF
Thoresway
29
LINCOLNSHIRE
80
Swinhope
Ludborough
Covenham St Bartholomew
81
Church End
Conisholme
Claxby
Normanby le Wold
Stainton le Vale
Wyham
Covenham St Mary
South Somercotes
Saltfleet
Binbrook
Bank Lane
North Ormsby
Utterby
Osgodby
Walesby
Yarburgh
Skidbrook
A16
Fotherby
Kirkby
Kirmond le Mire
Alvingham
1
2
3
4
A1103
North Elkington
Little Grimsby
Saltfleetby All Saints

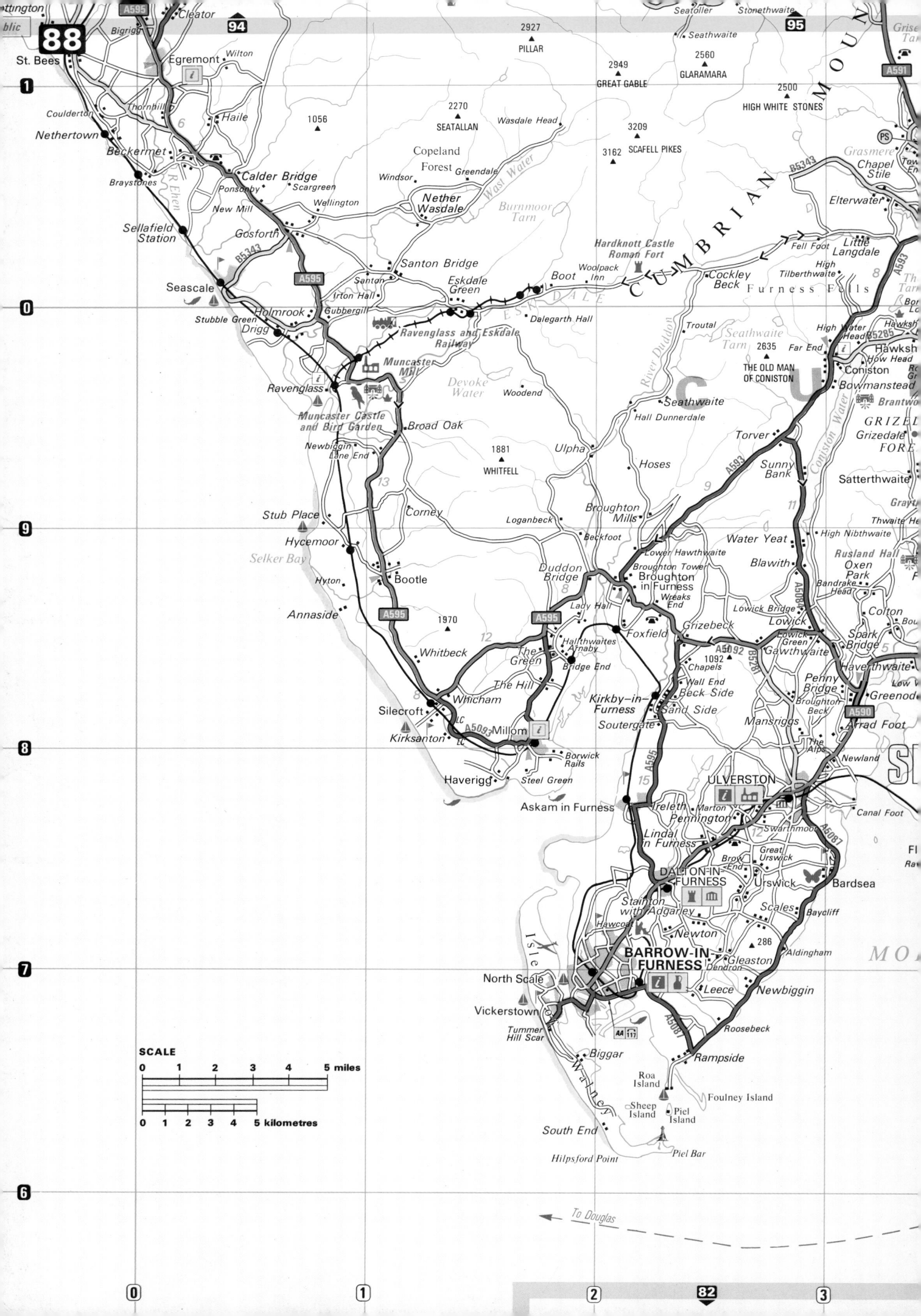
94
95
St. Bees
Egremont
Cleator
Bigrigg
Wilton
Coulderton
Thornhill
Haile
Nethertown
Beckermet
Braystones
Calder Bridge
Ponsonby
Scargreen
New Mill
Wellington
Sellafield Station
Gosforth
Seascale
Stubble Green
Holmrook
Drigg
Santon Bridge
Santon
Irton Hall
Cubbergill
Eskdale Green
Boot
Woolpack Inn
Dalegarth Hall
Ravenglass and Eskdale Railway
Ravenglass
Muncaster Mill
Muncaster Castle and Bird Garden
Broad Oak
Newbiggin
Lane End
Devoke Water
Woodend
Stub Place
Hycemoor
Selker Bay
Corney
Bootle
Hyton
Annaside
Whitbeck
Silecroft
Kirksanton
Whicham
Millom
Haverigg
Steel Green
Borwick Rails
Askam in Furness
PILLAR
GREAT GABLE
GLARAMARA
SEATALLAN
Wasdale Head
Copeland Forest
Greendale
Windsor
Nether Wasdale
Wast Water
Burnmoor Tarn
SCAFELL PIKES
HIGH WHITE STONES
Seatoller
Stonethwaite
Seathwaite
Hardknott Castle Roman Fort
CUMBRIAN MOUNTAINS
Cockley Beck
Furness Fells
Troutal
Seathwaite Tarn
THE OLD MAN OF CONISTON
River Duddon
Seathwaite
Hall Dunnerdale
Ulpha
WHITFELL
Hoses
Broughton Mills
Loganbeck
Beckfoot
Duddon Bridge
Lady Hall
The Green
The Hill
Hallthwaites
Arnaby
Bridge End
Foxfield
Kirkby-in-Furness
Soutergate
Sand Side
Beck Side
Wall End
Chapels
Grizebeck
Lower Hawthwaite
Broughton Tower
Broughton in Furness
Wreaks End
Water Yeat
Blawith
Lowick Bridge
Lowick
Lowick Green
Gawthwaite
Mansriggs
Torver
Sunny Bank
Coniston Water
Coniston
Bowmanstead
Far End
High Water Head
Hawkshead
How Head
Satterthwaite
Grizedale
Grizedale Forest
High Nibthwaite
Thwaite Head
Rusland Hall
Oxen Park
Bandrake Head
Colton
Spark Bridge
Haverthwaite
Penny Bridge
Broughton Beck
Greenodd
Arrad Foot
The Alps
Newland
ULVERSTON
Ireleth
Marton
Pennington
Lindal in Furness
Swarthmoor
Canal Foot
Great Urswick
Brow End
Urswick
Bardsea
DALTON-IN-FURNESS
Stainton with Adgarley
Scales
Baycliff
Hawcoat
Newton
Aldingham
BARROW-IN-FURNESS
Gleaston
Dendron
Leece
Newbiggin
North Scale
Vickerstown
Isle of Walney
Tummer Hill Scar
Biggar
Roosebeck
Rampside
Roa Island
Foulney Island
Sheep Island
Piel Island
South End
Hilpsford Point
Piel Bar
To Douglas
Grasmere
Chapel Stile
Elterwater
Little Langdale
Fell Foot
High Tilberthwaite
Elterwater
SCALE
0 1 2 3 4 5 miles
0 1 2 3 4 5 kilometres
82

89
95
96
90
83
Hartsop
Brothers Water
Hayeswater
Blea Water
Wet Sleddale Reservoir
2547
2539
HARTER FELL
Kentmere Reservoir
Kirkstone Pass Inn
A592
NORTHBOUND TRAFFIC ONLY
M6
B6261
B6260
Orton
1353
Raisbeck
Sunbiggin
Little Asby
Crosby Garrett
Waitby
Smardale
Soulby
Bleatarn
Sadgill
Greenholme
Bretherdale Head
Old Tebay
Kelleth
Brownber
Newbiggin-on-Lune
Coldbeck
A685
1264
Gaisgill
Weasdale
Tebay
Ravenstonedale
1739
AMBLESIDE
Waterhead
High Green
Town Head
Kentmere
Green Quarter
Troutbeck
A591
High Borrans
Troutbeck Bridge
Lowbridge Ho.
Forest Hall
A6
Low Borrowbridge
Studfold
A683
High Wray
Ings
Staveley
Garnett Bridge
Watchgate
WINDERMERE
2219
THE CALF
Aisgill
Garth Row
Grayrigg
Lowgill
Beck Foot
Bowness-on-Windermere
Far Sawrey
Crook
Burneside
Meal Bank
B5284
Plumgarths
A5284
KENDAL
1040
1109
LAMBRIGG FELL
B6257
Firbank
Cautley
Sedbergh
National Park Centre
2217
Storrs Hall Hotel
Winster
Gill Head
Underbarrow
Castle Green
A684
New Hutton
Ingmire Hall
Millthrop
Crosthwaite
752
Grigghall
Church Town
Tarnside
Oxenholme
Garths
Millholme
SOUTHBOUND TRAFFIC ONLY
Garsdale
River Dee
Bowland Bridge
1054
Brigsteer
A5074
Row
Howe
Middleshaw
Natland
Old Hutton
Killington
Beckside
Gawthrop
Cowgill
A592
Lake Side
Cartmel Fell
Sizergh
Cotes
Halfpenny
A65
Holmescales
Staveley
Witherslack Hall
Levens
Sedgwick
Crosslands
Summerlands
Middleton
Dent
1999
CALF TOP
Stone House
High Tarn Green
Askew Green
Sampool Br.
Causeway End
Stainton
Gatebeck
B6254
Rigmaden Park
Low Tarn Green
Witherslack
Mill Side
Hincaster
A590
Leasgill
Endmoor
Deepdale
Ayside
Holme
Town End
Crooklands
Mansergh
High Newton
Latterbarrow
Heversham
Milness
933
Old Town
Barber Green
Nether Newton
SCOUT HILL
Nook
Barbon
2419
WHERNSIDE
Milnthorpe
Overthwaite
Lupton
Bullpot
Ulpha
Ackenthwaite
Whasset
B5282
Storth
Meathop
Farleton
Kearstwick
Underley Hall
Hampsfield
727
Eden Mount
Lindale
Beetham
Casterton
High Casterton
Cartmel
Slack Head
Arnside
Holme
Hutton Roof
High Biggins
Low Biggins
Kirkby Lonsdale
Holme Island
Hale
Clawthorpe
GRANGE-OVER-SANDS
Allithwaite
Yealand Redmayne
Yealand Storrs
Burton-in-Kendal
Whittington
A683
Overtown
Cowan Bridge
Leck
Ireby
Chapel le Dale
Kents Bank
Yealand Conyers
A6070
Dalton Hall
Nether Burrow
Masongill
Silverdale
Priest Hutton
Newton
Docker
Westhouse
Thornton in Lonsdale
B6255
2373
INGLEBOROUGH
Silverdale Green
Leighton Hall
Tunstall
Skirwith
Head Point
Warton
Cantsfield
NORTH YORKSHIRE
Ingleton
Borwick
Arkholme
Capernwray Hall
466
A681
Burton in Lonsdale
Yarlsber
Millhead
Capernwray
B6254
Wrayton
Cold Cotes
MORECAMBE BAY
Melling
Wennington
Lower Bentham
High Bentham
A65
Newby
CARNFORTH
Over Kellet
Tatham
Gressingham
B6480
National Centre
Clapham
Bolton le Sands
Hornby
Wray
Nether Kellet
Bolton Town End
Farleton
Lawkland
Hest Bank
Aughton
Keasden
Slyne
Halton Park
Claughton
MORECAMBE
Halton
Halton Green
Caton Green
Eldroth
Brookhouse
Lowgill
Torrisholme
A683
Caton
Quernmore Park Hall
Skerton
Sandylands
Salter
A589
B5273
Crossgill
Thrushgill
LANCASTER
High Salter
Lower Heysham
HEYSHAM
Higher Heysham
Heaton
1595
CATLOW FELL
Aldcliffe
Quernmore
1786
WHITE HILL
LANCASHIRE
Scotforth
Upper Brow Top
Lee Fell
Middleton
Stodday
Overton
Heysham Lake
R. Lune
Ellel
A588
Conder Green
Sunderland
Glasson
Galgate
Lee
Dunkinshaw
Tarnbrook
Stocks Reservoir
Tosside
Sunderland Point
Thurnham Hall
Lower Greenbank
Ortner
Wyresdale
B6478
4
5
6
7

90
96
97
89
83
84
Coldbeck
A685
1264
Stonedale
Outhgill
2328
B6270
West Stonesdale
1914
GREAT PINSEAT
Whaw
Langthwaite
Booze
Arkle Town
Washfold
Helwith
Hurst
Skelton
Marske
Keld
Angram
Thwaite
Muker
Ivelet
Gunnerside
Satron
Feetham
Kearton
Healaugh
Reeth
Fremington
Grinton
Marrick
Low Row
Crackpot
Studfold
A683
B6259
Aisgill
2349
GREAT SHUNNER FELL
Cotterdale
Garsdale Head
Moorcock Inn
2217
High Shaw
Simonstone
Sedbusk
Hardrow
Appersett
Hawes
Gayle
National Park Centre
Bainbridge
A684
Burtersett
Askrigg
Newbiggin
Woodhall
Worton
Castle Bolton
Preston-under-Scar
Redmire
Bolton Hall
Carperby
Swinithwaite
Thornton Rust
Countersett
Aysgarth
Thoralby
West Witton
Agglethorpe
West Burton
Melmerby
Carlton
Garsdale
Cowgill
Lea Yeat
Stone House
Deepdale
B6255
2192
Marsett
Stalling Busk
B6160
Walden
Gammersgill
West Scrafton
2419
WHERNSIDE
Oughtershaw
Kidstones
Horsehouse
Walden Head
Bradley
LANGSTROTHDALE CHASE
Deepdale
Yockenthwaite
Cray
2302
BUCKDEN PIKE
Woodale
1984
LITTLE WHERNSIDE
Scar House Reservoir
Hubberholme
Kirk Gill
Buckden
Angram Res
Chapel le Dale
Foxup
Halton Gill
High Birkwith
B6479
Selside
2373
INGLEBOROUGH HILL
2731
Starbotton
Skirwith
THE PENNINE WAY
Hesleden
Litton
River Skirfare
New Houses
2273
PEN-Y-GHENT
New Inn
Horton in Ribblesdale
SD
R Wharfe
2308
GREAT WHERNSIDE
Middlesmoor
Stean
Yarlsber
Cold Cotes
Arncliffe
Kettlewell
Newby
Higher Studfold
Studfold
Arncliffe Cote
Hawkswick
Clapham
Wharfe
National Park Centre
Helwith Bridge
Austwick
YORK
Kilnsey
Conistone
Feizor
Little Stainforth
Malham Tarn
Stainforth
Keasden
Lawkland
Eldroth
Lawkland Green
Stackhouse
Langcliffe
1815
Bordley
Grimwith Reservoir
National Park Centre
Grassington
Greenhow
Giggleswick
Settle
Threshfield
Hebden
B6265
Wham
Malham
National Park Centre
Linton
Burnsall
Parcevall
Hanlith
Threapland
Thorpe
A65
Mearbeck
Kirkby Malham
Cracoe
Appletreewick
Skyreholme
Calton
Rathmell
Town Head
Long Preston
Airton
Hetton
Rylstone
Drebley
Otterburn
Winterburn
Wigglesworth
Lunds
Bell Busk
Tosside
Stocks Reservoir
Eshton
Flasby
Hellifield
Park Ho.
B6478
Coniston Cold
Halton West
Swinden
Little Stainton
Gargrave
Embsay
Kirk
Eastby
Halton East
Bolton Abbey
Hill End
Slaidburn
New Brighton
Bank Newton
Stirton
Nappa
719
A682
River Ribble
Thorlby
Bolton Bridge
Beamsley
Paythorne
Newsholme
Broughton
SKIPTON
Draughton
Forest Becks
West Marton
Horton
A59
Horse Close Estate
Addingham
Langbar
Newton
Lane Ends
Bay Gate
East Marton
Monk Bridge
Elslack
Carleton
Low Snaygill
High Bradley
Low Bradley
1300
EASINGTON FELL
Holden
Bolton by Bowland
Bracewell
Bolton Hall
Gisburn
Thornton-in-Craven
Cringles
Low Cringles
A6034
Lane End
1273
Sawley
Coates
BARNOLDSWICK
EARBY
Wedding Hall Fold
Dale End
Cononley
A629
Kidwick
Town Head
SILSDEN
Newby
Grindleton
WEST YORKSHIRE
LANCASHIRE
CUMBRIA
NORTH

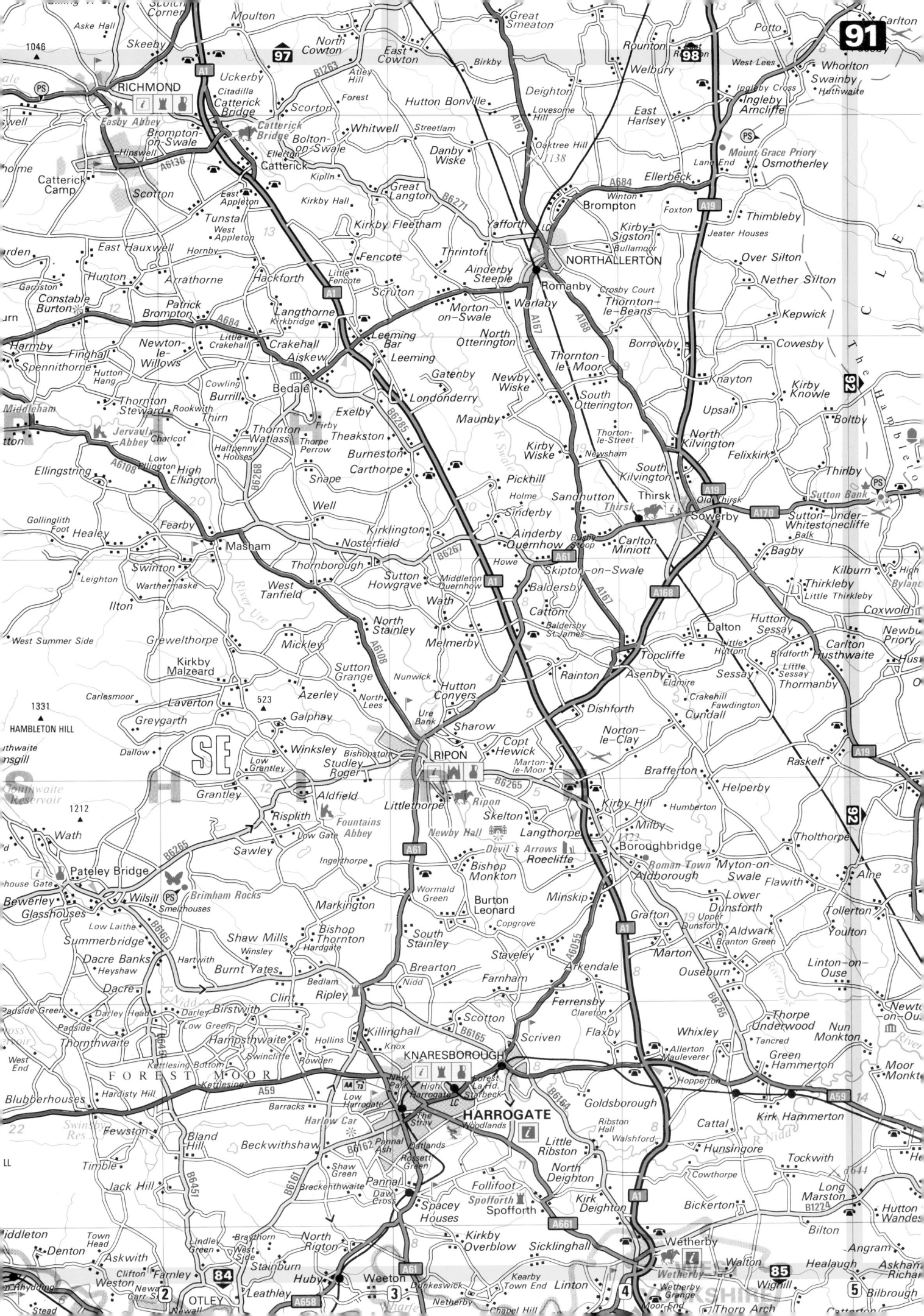
RICHMOND
NORTHALLERTON
Thirsk
RIPON
KNARESBOROUGH
HARROGATE
Wetherby
Boroughbridge
Bedale
Masham
Pateley Bridge
Catterick
Catterick Camp
Sowerby
Ripley
OTLEY
Spofforth
Fountains Abbey
Newby Hall
Ripon
Brimham Rocks
Jervaulx Abbey
Easby Abbey
Mount Grace Priory
Devil's Arrows
Roman Town
FOREST MOOR
HAMBLETON HILL
WEST YORKSHIRE
SE
97
98
92
84
85

92
99
91
85
86
Broughton
Carlton
Clay Bank
1427
1422
1490
Urra
Whorlton
Swainby
Huthwaite
Seave Green
Chop Gate
1326
Danby Botton
Street
Egton Bridge
Esk Valley
Green End
Ralph Cross
Beck Hole
Goathland
Blakey House
Cockayne
CLEVELAND HILLS
NORTH YORK MOORS
Hill Cottages
Low Bell End
North Yorkshire Moors Railway
Hunt Ho.
Church Houses
Thorgill
Rosedale Abbey
Grange
1132
Saltergate Inn
Fangdale Beck
Low Mill
BRANSDALE
River Seven
Stape
Hartoft End
NEWTON DALE
B1257
Laskill
Lowna
Gillamoor
Lastingham
Lower Askew
Levisham
Newton-on-Rawcliffe
Lockton
Kepwick
Cowesby
Hawnby
Wether Cote
Fadmoor
Hutton-le-Hole
Spaunton
Cropton
Cawthorn
Appleton-le-Moors
Ravenswick
Keldholme
Kirby Knowle
The Hambleton Hills
Old Byland
Carlton
Kirkbymoorside
Pockley
Sinnington
Wrelton
Aislaby
Middleton
Boltby
CLEVELAND WAY
Rievaulx
Rievaulx Abbey and Terrace
Beadlam
Nawton
A170
Kirkby Mills
Gallow Heads
Keld Head
Pickering
Thornton Dale
Wilton
Cold Kirby
Thirlby
Helmsley
Wombleton
Little Edstone
River Dove
Great Edstone
PICKERING
Sutton Bank
Scawton
Helmsley
R Rye
Harome
Marton
Allerston
Sutton-under-Whitestonecliffe
Balk
A170
Sproxton
Summerfield
Low North Holme
Low Riseborough
Normanby
Brignam Park
A169
Oldstead
Muscoates
Little Barugh
Flamingo Land
Kilburn
High Kilburn
Wass
Oswaldkirk
West Ness
Salton
Thirkleby
Little Thirkleby
Byland Abbey
Shandy Hall
East Newton
Nunnington
Ness
Brawby
Great Barugh
Kirby Misperton
High Marishes
Coxwold
Ampleforth
B1257
Stonegrave
Butterwick
Low Marishes
River Derwent
Water Gate
SE
Little Habton
Gilling
Gilling East
Cawton
Great Habton
Newburgh Priory
Thorpe Hall
Newburgh Priory
Carlton Husthwaite
Husthwaite
B1363
Hovingham
Slingsby
Ryton
Wykeham
Scampston
West Knapton
Barton-le-Street
Little Sessay
Thormanby
Oulston
River Rye
Yearsley
Coulton
Fryton
B1257
Amotherby
Broughton
Old Malton
Rillington
24
Brandsby
Scackleton
Appleton-le-Street
Swinton
A64
Howardian Hills
MALTON
Stearsby
Dalby
Scagglethorpe
Mill Green
Crayke
Skewsby
Terrington
Ganthorpe
Coneysthorpe
Castle Howard
NORTON
Settrington
Raskelf
A19
Auburn Hill
Easingwold
Marton Abbey
Whenby
Castle Howard
Whitewall Corner
B1248
A64
North Grimston
High Hutton
Welburn
Welham Wold
Farlington
High Stittenham
Bulmer
Hutton
Menethorpe
B1253
Tholthorpe
Stillington
Sheriff Hutton
Firby
Langton
Whitwell-on-the-Hill
Sheriff Hutton
Kirkham
Alne
23
Huby
Kennythorpe
Birdsall
Cross Lanes
Sutton-on-the-Forest
Thornton-le-Clay
Foston
Kirkham Priory
Westow
Tollerton
West Lilling
Crambe
Burythorpe
WOLDS WAY
Sutton Park
Youlton
15
Barton-le-Willows
Howsham
Leavening
Burdale
New Parks
Flaxton
Linton-on-Ouse
Harton
Raisthorpe
Thixendale
Acklam
Bossall
Leppington
A19
B1363
Plainville
Strensall
Newton-on-Ouse
Claxton
Scrayingham
Nun Monkton
Towthorpe
A64
Goman Castle
Kirby Underdale
Shipton
Sand Hutton
Buttercrambe
River Ouse
Wigginton
Earswick
Bugthorpe
Painsthorpe
Moor Monkton
Haxby
Haxby Gates
Huntington
Upper Helmsley
Skirpenbeck
Garrowby Hall
29
Nether Poppleton
Skelton
East Huntington
Stockton on the Forest
Stamford Bridge
A166
A59
14
Rawcliffe
New Earswick
Warthill
1066
Full Sutton
Youlthorpe
Bishop Wilton
Hammerton
Upper Poppleton
Gate Helmsley
Gowthorpe
Great Givendale
Holtby
Low Catton
Fangfoss
A1036
Murton
High Catton
Spittal
Tockwith
Hessay
1644
Dunnington
Meltonby
Knapton
YORK
Bolton
Millington
Long Marston
Osbaldwick
A1079
B1224
Holgate
Acomb
A64
Wilberfoss
Yapham
Warter
Rufforth
AA 24 hour
Kexby
Hutton Wandesley
Barmby New Inn
Barmby Moor
Kilnwick Percy
B1246
Bilton
York
Heslington
B1228
Askham Bryan
Dringhouses
Fulford
8
Newton upon Derwent
Warter Priory
Angram
Pocklington
Healaugh
Askham Richard
Elvington
18
Burnby Hall
Nunburnholme
Elvington
A64
Bilbrough
Bishopthorpe
Allerthorpe
Burnby
Sutton upon Derwent

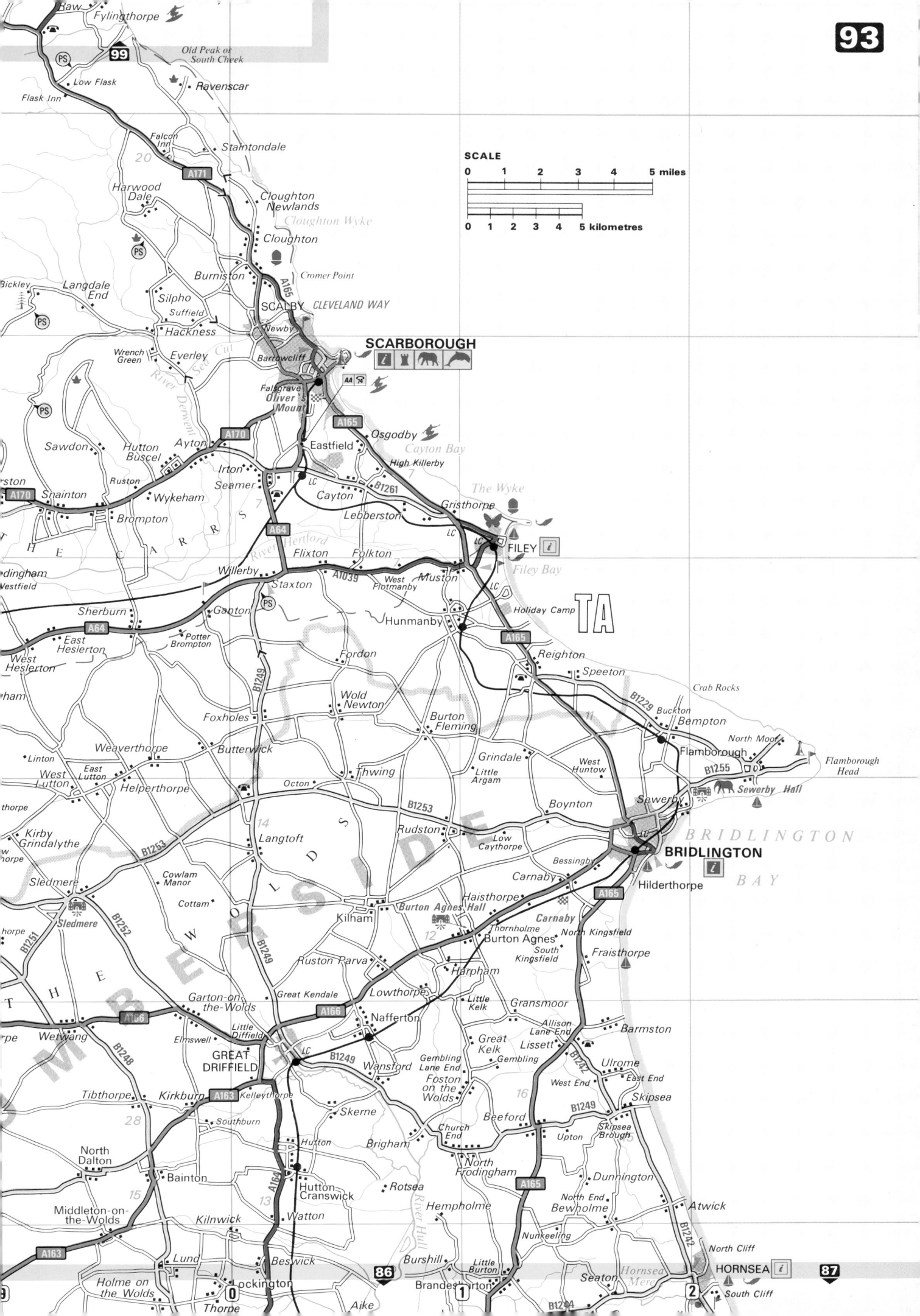
Fylingthorpe
99
Old Peak or South Cheek
Low Flask
Ravenscar
Flask Inn
Falcon Inn
Staintondale
A171
Harwood Dale
Cloughton Newlands
Cloughton Wyke
Cloughton
Cromer Point
Burniston
A165
Langdale End
Silpho
Suffield
SCALBY
CLEVELAND WAY
Hackness
Newby
SCARBOROUGH
Wrench Green
Everley
Sea Cut
River Derwent
Barrowcliff
Falsgrave
Oliver's Mount
A170
Osgodby
Cayton Bay
Sawdon
Hutton Buscel
Ayton
Eastfield
High Killerby
Irton
Seamer
Ruston
Wykeham
Snainton
B1261
Cayton
The Wyke
Gristhorpe
Lebberston
Brompton
A64
River Hertford
Flixton
Folkton
FILEY
Filey Bay
Willerby
A1039
West Flotmanby
Muston
Staxton
Sherburn
Ganton
Holiday Camp
TA
Hunmanby
A165
East Heslerton
Potter Brompton
West Heslerton
Reighton
Fordon
Speeton
Crab Rocks
B1249
B1229
Buckton
Bempton
Wold Newton
Foxholes
Burton Fleming
North Moor
Flamborough
Flamborough Head
Weaverthorpe
Butterwick
Grindale
Little Argam
West Huntow
B1255
Linton
West Lutton
East Lutton
Helperthorpe
Thwing
Octon
Sewerby Hall
Sewerby
B1253
Boynton
Kirby Grindalythe
Langtoft
Rudston
Low Caythorpe
BRIDLINGTON BAY
BRIDLINGTON
Bessingby
Hilderthorpe
Cowlam Manor
Carnaby
Sledmere
Cottam
A165
Haisthorpe
Kilham
Burton Agnes Hall
Carnaby
B1252
B1251
Thornholme
Burton Agnes
North Kingsfield
South Kingsfield
Fraisthorpe
Ruston Parva
Harpham
Great Kendale
Lowthorpe
Little Kelk
Gransmoor
Garton-on-the-Wolds
A166
Nafferton
Allison Lane End
Barmston
Wetwang
Elmswell
Little Driffield
Great Kelk
Lissett
B1248
GREAT DRIFFIELD
B1249
Gembling Lane End
Gembling
Ulrome
B1242
Wansford
East End
West End
Foston on the Wolds
Skipsea
Tibthorpe
Kirkburn
A163
Kelleythorpe
Skerne
Southburn
Beeford
B1249
Church End
Upton
Skipsea Brough
North Dalton
Hutton
Brigham
North Frodingham
Bainton
A164
Hutton Cranswick
Rotsea
A165
Dunnington
Middleton-on-the-Wolds
Watton
Hempholme
North End
Bewholme
Atwick
Kilnwick
River Hull
Nunkeeling
A163
Lund
Beswick
Burshill
Little Burton
North Cliff
86
Hornsea Mere
HORNSEA
87
Holme on the Wolds
Lockington
Brandesburton
Seaton
South Cliff
Thorpe
Aike
B1244
SCALE
0 1 2 3 4 5 miles
0 1 2 3 4 5 kilometres

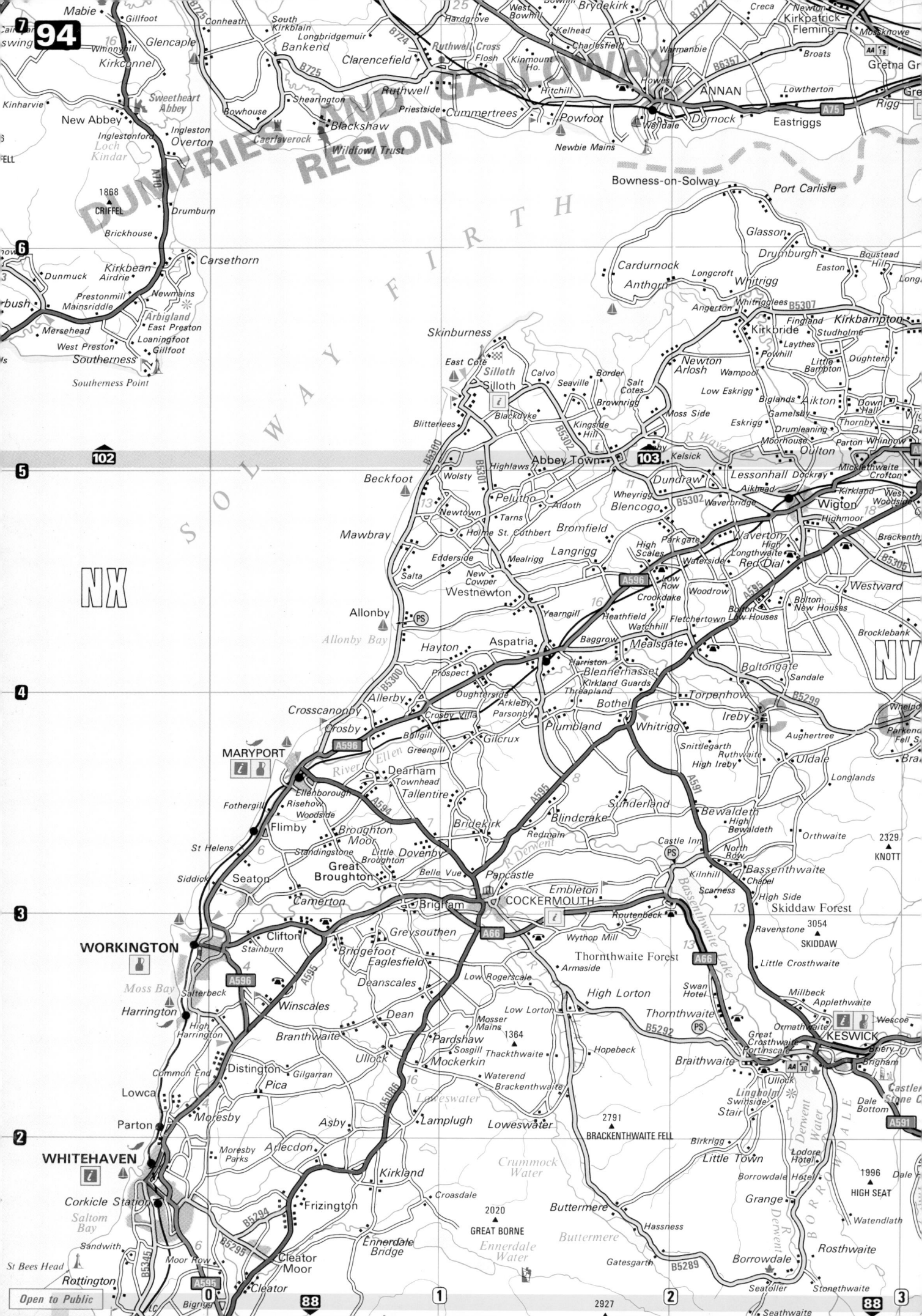
DUMFRIES AND GALLOWAY REGION
SOLWAY FIRTH
NX
NY
Mabie
Gillfoot
Conheath
South Kirkblain
Longbridgemuir
Bankend
Hardgrove
West Bowhill
Brydekirk
Creca
Newton
Kirkpatrick-Fleming
Mossknowe
Glencaple
Kirkconnel
Clarencefield
Ruthwell Cross
Flesh
Kinmount Ho.
Kelhead
Charlesfield
Warmanbie
Broats
Gretna Gr
Sweetheart Abbey
Ruthwell
Hitchill
Howes
ANNAN
Lowtherton
Rigg
Kinharvie
New Abbey
Shearington
Bowhouse
Priestside
Cummertrees
Powfoot
Welldale
Dornock
Eastriggs
Inglestonford
Ingleston
Overton
Caerlaverock
Blackshaw
Wildfowl Trust
Newbie Mains
Loch Kindar
1868
CRIFFEL
Drumburn
Brickhouse
Bowness-on-Solway
Port Carlisle
Carsethorn
Dunmuck
Kirkbean
Airdrie
Prestonmill
Mainsriddle
Newmains
Arbigland
East Preston
Mersehead
West Preston
Loaningfoot
Gillfoot
Southerness
Southerness Point
Glasson
Drumburgh
Boustead Hill
Cardurnock
Easton
Anthorn
Longcroft
Whitrigg
Whitrigglees
Angerton
Fingland
Kirkbampton
Kirkbride
Studholme
Laythes
Powhill
Oughterby
Little Bampton
Skinburness
East Cote
Silloth
Calvo
Seaville
Border
Salt Cotes
Newton Arlosh
Wampool
Low Eskrigg
Biglands
Aikton
Brownrigg
Moss Side
Gamelsby
Down Hall
Blitterlees
Blackdyke
Kingside Hill
Eskrigg
Drumleaning
Thornby
Moorhouse
Parton
Whinnow
Oulton
Kelsick
102
103
Highlaws
Abbey Town
Beckfoot
Wolsty
Dundraw
Lessonhall
Dockray
Micklethwaite
Crofton
Aikhead
Kirkland
West Woodside
Pelutho
Wheyrigg
Blencogo
Waverbridge
Wigton
Highmoor
Aldoth
Newtown
Tarns
Holme St. Cuthbert
Bromfield
Mawbray
Parkgate
Waverton
High Scales
High Longthwaite
Brackenthwaite
Edderside
Mealrigg
Langrigg
Waterside
Red Dial
Salta
New Cowper
Low Row
Woodrow
Westward
Westnewton
Crookdake
Bolton
New Houses
Allonby
Yearngill
Heathfield
Watchhill
Fletchertown
Bolton Low Houses
Brocklebank
Allonby Bay
Hayton
Aspatria
Baggrow
Mealsgate
Harriston
Blennerhasset
Boltongate
Sandale
Prospect
Kirkland Guards
Threapland
Allerby
Oughterside
Arkleby
Parsonby
Bothel
Torpenhow
Crosscanonby
Crosby Villa
Ireby
Crosby
Plumbland
Whitrigg
Aughertree
Bullgill
Gilcrux
Greengill
Snittlegarth
Ruthwaite
High Ireby
Uldale
MARYPORT
River Ellen
Dearham
Townhead
Tallentire
Longlands
Ellenborough
Risehow
Fothergill
Woodside
Sunderland
Flimby
Broughton Moor
Bridekirk
Blindcrake
Bewaldeth
High Bewaldeth
St Helens
Standingstone
Little Broughton
Dovenby
Redmain
Castle Inn
Orthwaite
2329
KNOTT
North Row
Siddick
Seaton
Great Broughton
Belle Vue
R Derwent
Papcastle
Kilnhill
Bassenthwaite
Chapel
Embleton
Scarness
High Side
Skiddaw Forest
Camerton
Brigham
COCKERMOUTH
Routenbeck
Bassenthwaite Lake
WORKINGTON
Clifton
Stainburn
Greysouthen
Wythop Mill
Ravenstone
3054
SKIDDAW
Bridgefoot
Eaglesfield
Thornthwaite Forest
Armaside
Little Crosthwaite
Moss Bay
Salterbeck
Low Rogerscale
Deanscales
High Lorton
Swan Hotel
Millbeck
Applethwaite
Harrington
Winscales
Low Lorton
Thornthwaite
Wescoe
High Harrington
Dean
Mosser Mains
Ormathwaite
Branthwaite
Pardshaw
1364
B5292
KESWICK
Sosgill
Thackthwaite
Hopebeck
Great Crosthwaite
Portinscale
Briery
Brigham
Common End
Distington
Ullock
Mockerkin
Braithwaite
Gilgarran
Waterend
Brackenthwaite
Ullock
Castlerigg Stone Circle
Pica
Lowca
Loweswater
Lingholm
Swinside
Dale Bottom
Stair
Derwent Water
BORROWDALE
Moresby
Asby
Lamplugh
Loweswater
2791
BRACKENTHWAITE FELL
Parton
Birkrigg
WHITEHAVEN
Moresby Parks
Arlecdon
Little Town
Lodore Hotel
Crummock Water
Kirkland
1996
HIGH SEAT
Dale
Borrowdale Hotel
Corkickle Station
Croasdale
Grange
Saltom Bay
Frizington
2020
GREAT BORNE
Buttermere
Watendlath
Hassness
Buttermere
Sandwith
Ennerdale Bridge
Ennerdale Water
Rosthwaite
St Bees Head
Moor Row
Cleator Moor
Gatesgarth
Borrowdale
Rottington
Cleator
Seatoller
Stonethwaite
Bigrigg
2927
Seathwaite
Open to Public
A75
A710
B725
B724
B722
B6357
B5307
B5302
B5300
B5301
B5305
B5299
A596
A595
A594
A591
A66
A5086
B5294
B5295
B5345
B5289
88
88
0
1
2
3
4
5
6
7

95
109
Spadeadam
Wileysike Ho.
Whiteside
Crofthead
Shank Castle
Longtown
Prior Rigg
Boltonfellend
Kirkcambeck
Lees Hill
West Hill
Kingbridge Ford Br
B6318
Gilsland Spa
Gilsland
Hadrian's Wall
104
Edges Gr
A6071
Kirklington
Hethersgill
Nickies Hill
Triermain
Birdoswald
Hetherside
Skitby
Sandysike
Smithfield
Scare
Greenhead
Justicetown
Westlinton
Walton
Banks
Upper Denton
Haltwhistle
Melkridge
A69
A7
Scalebyhill
Scaleby
Lanercost Priory
New Angerton
Todhills
Barclose
Newtown
Burtholme
Temon
Plenmeller
Blackford
Longpark
Laversdale
Irthington
Oldwall
Crooked Holme
Brampton
Low Row
Kellah
Park
CARLISLE (CROSBY)
Harker
Walby
Wallhead
Crosbymoor
Milton
Kirkhouse
A689
Rowfoot
High Crindledike
Low Crosby
Coanwood
Cargo
B6264
Geltside
Coalfell
Midgeholme
Houghton
High Crosby
Edmond Castle
Hallbankgate
Tindale
Wolf Hills
Kingstown
Newby East
Low
Geltbridge
Farlam
Lambley
Stonehouse
Linstock
Little Corby
Hayton
Halton Lea Gate
Grinsdale
Warwick Bridge
Talkin
Forest Head
CARLISLE
Corby Hill
Warwick
Stainton
Stanwix
How
Fenton
Castle Carrock
Eals
Belle Vue
Little Orton
Scotby
Burnrigg
Heads Nook
Faugh
Harraby
Wetheral
Knarsdale
Morton
Great Corby
Corby Castle
B6413
Upperby
Cumwhinton
Slaggyford
Carleton
Newby Cross
Cummersdale
Carlisle
Cumwhitton
Durdar
Brisco
Golden Fleece
A595
Cardewlees
Barhaugh
Dalston
103
Cotehill
River Eden
Hornsbygate
Hornsby
Cumrew
Ayle
Ratten Row
Scalesceugh
Burthwaite
Kirkhaugh
Green Head
Wreay
A6
Newbiggin
NORTHUMBERLAND
Buckabank
Bridge End
Cumdivock
Unthank
Holmwrangle
Hawksdale
Foulbridge
Croglin
Blagill
Broomfield
Raughton
South Tynedale Railway
Alston
Gaitsgill
Towngate
Ainstable
Low Hesket
Aiketgate
B5299
Raughton Head
Raise
Scale Houses
Mellguards
Armathwaite
Skiprigg
Southwaite
Bayles
Stockdalewath
Nunclose
High Hesket
Ruckcroft
Nether Welton
Renwick
Gilderdale Forest
Dale
Thetwaite
Old Town
Scales
Haresceugh
Leadgate
Baronwood
Ivegill
20
A686
Staffield
High Bankhill
Busk
Low Braithwaite
Middlesceugh
Hartside Cross
Kirkoswald
Park Head
96
Garrigill
Churchtown
Limekiln Nook
Sowerby Row
Thomas Close
Calthwaite
Unthank
Lazonby
Gamblesby
Newlands
Morton
Fieldhead
Hewer Hill
Hutton End
Glassonby
West
Southernby
B6413
B6412
B5305
Brockleymoor
Great Salkeld
Melmerby
Plumpton
Millhouse
Little Salkeld
Haltcliff Bridge
New Rent
Salkeld Dykes
Hunsonby
Lamonby
Unthank
Skelton
Shire
Row
Heggle Lane
Plumpton Head
Ellonby
Hutton-in-the-Forest
Winskill
Ousby
2930
CROSS FELL
Langwathby
Johnby
Little Blencow
Catterlen
Laithes
Townhead
Hutton Roof
Scale
Skirwith
Milburn Forest
Edenhall
Kirkland
Blencow
Newton Reigny
Bowscale
R. Eden
M6
Blencarn
PENRITH
Greystoke
B5288
Gill
Culgaith
Milburn
Berrier
Newbiggin
Motherby
Eamont Bridge
723
Penruddock
Newbiggin
A66
17
992
Stainton
Scales
Yanwath
Knock
Sockbridge
Clifton
Temple Sowerby
Hutton
Dacre
Tirril
Troutbeck
Barton
Thackthwaite
Sparket
Celleron
Melkinthorpe
Dufton
Wallthwaite
Soulby
Kirkby Thore
River Eamont
Town End
A5091
B5320
Long Marton
Keisley
Wreay
Pooley Bridge
Askham
Cliburn
Matterdale End
Bennet Head
Lowther
Morland
Bolton
Brampton
Hackthorpe
Thornythwaite
Longthwaite
Great Strickland
Crackenthorpe
High Row
Ulcat Row
Helton
Watermillock
Kings Meaburn
Dockray
Newby Head
Newby
APPLEBY-IN-WESTMORLAND
Whale
PS
A592
Colby
Dowthwaitehead
Ullswater
Low Knipe
High Knipe
Howtown
Little Strickland
Sleagill
Sandwick
B6542
Coupland
Burrells
Great Ormside
2201
Bampton
Martindale
LOADPOT HILL
Bampton Grange
Reagill
Hoff
Little Ormside
27
Glenridding
Ullswater Hotel
Rosgill
Maulds Meaburn
Burnbanks
Sandford
3116
563
Red Tarn
Patterdale
Haweswater Reservoir
Shap
Drybeck
Bridgend
Crosby Ravensworth
2634
Keld
Hotel
Great Asby
Hartsop
4
5
89
39
6
7
Brothersw

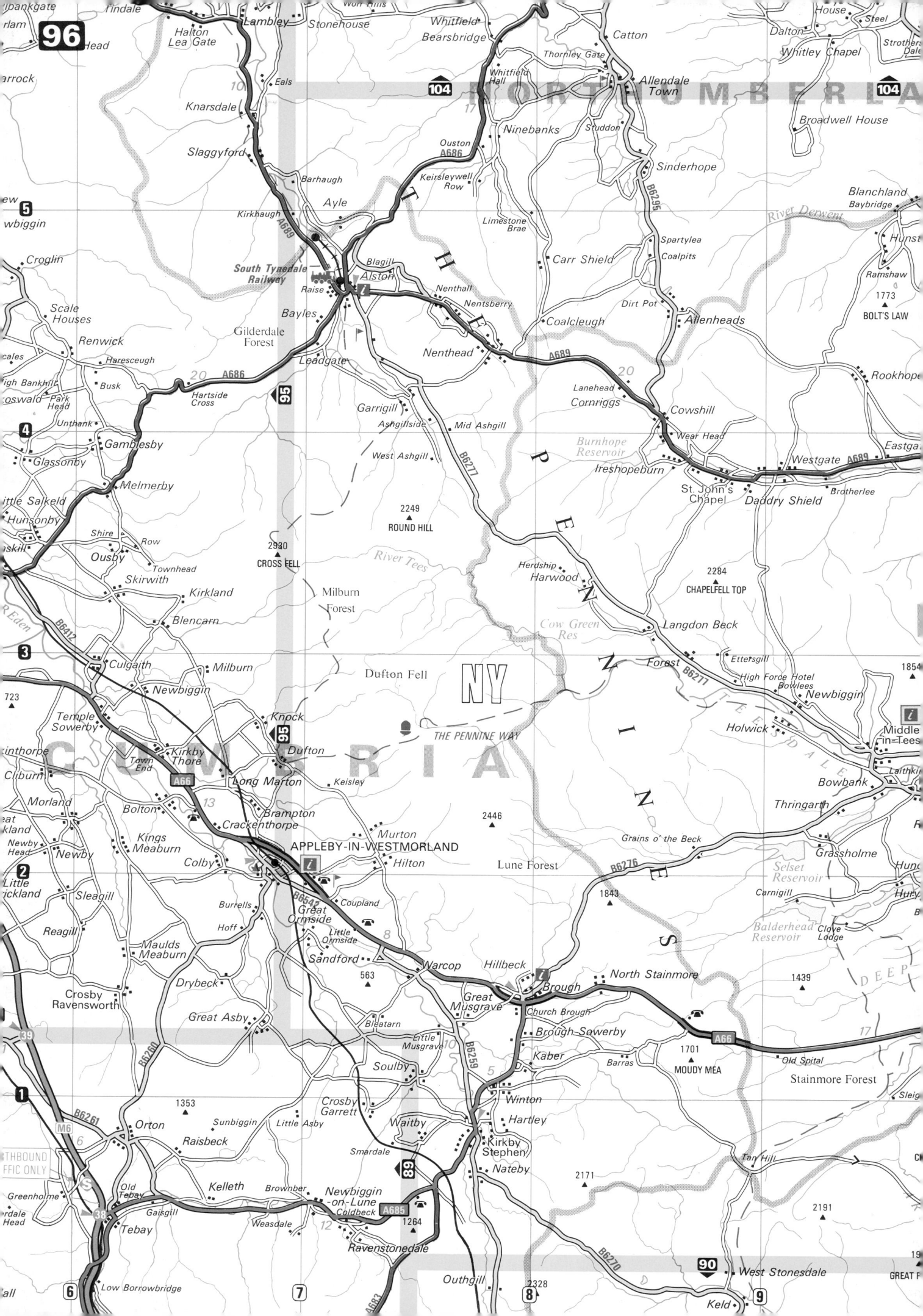

96
104
95
89
90
NORTHUMBERLAND
CUMBRIA
NY
THE PENNINES
Lambley
Stonehouse
Whitfield
Bearsbridge
Catton
Allendale Town
Halton Lea Gate
Eals
Knarsdale
Slaggyford
Ninebanks
Studdon
Sinderhope
Broadwell House
Whitley Chapel
Dalton
Ouston
A686
Keirsleywell Row
Barhaugh
Ayle
Kirkhaugh
A689
B6295
Limestone Brae
Spartylea
Coalpits
Carr Shield
Blanchland
Baybridge
River Derwent
South Tynedale Railway
Blagill
Alston
Raise
Nenthall
Nentsberry
Dirt Pot
Allenheads
Coalcleugh
Ramshaw
1773
BOLT'S LAW
Croglin
Scale Houses
Renwick
Gilderdale Forest
Bayles
Nenthead
Leadgate
Harescuegh
Busk
Park Head
Hartside Cross
Garrigill
Ashgillside
Mid Ashgill
Lanehead
Cornriggs
Cowshill
Wear Head
Rookhope
Unthank
Gamblesby
Glassonby
Melmerby
West Ashgill
B6277
Burnhope Reservoir
Ireshopeburn
Westgate
Eastgate
St. John's Chapel
Daddry Shield
Brotherlee
2249
ROUND HILL
Hunsonby
Shire
Row
Ousby
Townhead
2930
CROSS FELL
River Tees
Herdship
Harwood
2284
CHAPELFELL TOP
Skirwith
Kirkland
Milburn Forest
Blencarn
B6412
Cow Green Res
Langdon Beck
Culgaith
Milburn
Dufton Fell
Forest
Ettersgill
High Force Hotel
Bowlees
Newbiggin
1854
Newbiggin
723
Temple Sowerby
Knock
THE PENNINE WAY
Holwick
TEESDALE
Middleton-in-Teesdale
Kirkby Thore
Town End
Dufton
Cliburn
Long Marton
A66
Keisley
Laithkirk
Bowbank
Morland
Bolton
Brampton
Crackenthorpe
2446
Thringarth
Kings Meaburn
Newby Head
Newby
Murton
APPLEBY-IN-WESTMORLAND
Grains o' the Beck
Grassholme
Colby
Hilton
Lune Forest
B6276
Selset Reservoir
Little Strickland
Sleagill
B6542
Burrells
Coupland
1843
Carnigill
Great Ormside
Hoff
Little Ormside
Reagill
Balderhead Reservoir
Clove Lodge
Maulds Meaburn
Sandford
Warcop
Hillbeck
563
North Stainmore
1439
Drybeck
Crosby Ravensworth
Great Musgrave
Brough
DEEPDALE
Church Brough
Great Asby
Bleatarn
Brough Sowerby
A66
Little Musgrave
B6259
Kaber
Barras
1701
MOODY MEA
Old Spital
Stainmore Forest
Soulby
B6260
Winton
1353
Crosby Garrett
Hartley
B6261
Orton
Sunbiggin
Little Asby
Waitby
Kirkby Stephen
M6
Raisbeck
Smardale
Nateby
Tan Hill
2171
Greenholme
Old Tebay
Kelleth
Brownber
Newbiggin-on-Lune
Coldbeck
A685
1264
2191
Gaisgill
Tebay
Weasdale
Ravenstonedale
B6270
Outhgill
2328
West Stonesdale
Low Borrowbridge
A683
Keld

97
Hindley
New Ridley
Healey
Apperley Dene
Chopwell
High Spen
Highfield
ROWLAND'S GILL
Sunniside
Street Gate
Lamesley
Wrekenton
Springwell
Usworth
Castletown
Burnopfield
Byermoor
Marley Hill
Whittonstall
B6309
Hamsterley
Sheep Hill
Kibblesworth
Birtley
WASHINGTON
Wildfowl Trust
South Hylton
Penshaw
Minsteracres
Newlands
High Westwood
105
Hobson
Open-air Museum
Offerton
Barleyhill
Kiln Pit Hill
Ebchester
B6310
Tantobie
Hill Top
Tanfield
Tanfield Lea
High Urpeth
Ouston
Portobello
North Biddick
Shotleyfield
Shotley Bridge
Medomsley
Dipton
Pontop
STANLEY
Beamish
Pelton
Fatfield
Herrington
High Newport
A68
Snods Edge
B6278
Benfieldside
Bridgehill
Blackhill
Harelaw
Oxhill
West Pelton
South Moor
Perkinsville
Grange Villa
Pelton Fell
New Herrington
Shiney Row
Silksworth
New Silksworth
Carterway Heads
CONSETT
Catchgate
Leadgate
B6168
ANNFIELD PLAIN
Craghead
CHESTER-LE-STREET
Philadelphia
Newbottle
Bournmoor
HOUGHTON LE SPRING
River Wear
Crookhall
Iveston
A693
New Lambton
Dubmire
Muggleswick
Allensford
A692
Castleside
Templetown
Delves
Greencroft Hall
Maiden Law
Holmside
B6532
Waldridge
Chester Moor
Great Lumley
Fencehouses
Colliery Row
Warden Law
HETTON-LE-HOLE
Knitsley
Rowley
Ornsby Hill
Edmondsley
Nettlesworth
Healeyfield
Newbiggin
Burnhope
Lanchester
Plawsworth
Finchale Priory
East Rainton
Leamside
Murton
B6296
Sacriston
Kimblesworth
Witton Gilbert
West Rainton
Low Moorsley
High Moorsley
Easington Lane
A691
Pity Me
A167
Framwellgate Moor
A690
Pittington
South Hetton
Waskerley
Butsfield
Langley Park
Hallgarth
High Haswell
Carrville
Littletown
Esh
Bearpark
Cornsay
Quebec
Cornsay Colliery
Gilesgate Moor
Sherburn Hill
Haswell
Satley
B6302
Esh Winning
Ushaw Moor
Broom
B1283
Sherburn
Haswell Plough
Shotton Colliery
1694
COLLIER LAW
A68
B6301
Waterhouses
New Brancepeth
DURHAM
Byers Garth
A181
Shadforth
Ludworth
Crawleyside
High Stoop
Inkerman
East Hedleyhope
Langley Moor
Shincliffe
Running Waters
Old Cassop
Thornley
Wheatley Hill
Stanhope
TOW LAW
Dan's Castle
BRANDON
A177
Bowburn
Cassop Colliery
Old Quarrington
Shittlehope
Sunniside
Wolsingham
Brancepeth
Sunderland Bridge
Quarrington Hill
Wingate
Frosterley
B6297
Upper Town
Thornley
Billy Row
Oakenshaw
Croxdale
Hett
Coxhoe
Deaf Hill
A689
Bridge End
Roddymoor
CROOK
WILLINGTON
A690
NZ
Tudhoe
Standalon
Kelloe
Town Kelloe
Trimdon Grange
Trimdon Colliery
White Kirkley
River Wear
Craigside
Page Bank
A167
Cooksons Green
Helmington Row
Sunny Brow
Todhills
Byers Green
B6291
Garmondsway
Fir Tree
Rumby Hill
Lane Ends
Newfield
Mount Pleasant
Cornforth
Trimdon
St. John's
Dryderdale
Howden-le-Wear
North Bitchburn
Middlestone
SPENNYMOOR
Witton le Wear
Hunwick
Middlestone Moor
North Close
Ferryhill
Fishburn
Bedburn
High Grange
Binchester Blocks
Kirk Merrington
Mainsforth
Bishop Middleham
Low Redford
Toronto
A688
Hamsterley
Diddridge
Escomb
Leasingthorne
Chilton
Sedgefield
HAMSTERLEY FOREST
Witton Park
Low Etherley
B6282
BISHOP AUCKLAND
Coundon
A689
Emms Hill
High Etherley
Rushyford
Bradbury
Tindale Crescent
South Church
A1(M)
Morley
Toft Hill
St Helen Auckland
Coundon Grange
Sedgefield
Woodland
South Side
Howle
Butterknowle
High Lands
Oaks
West Auckland
Eldon
Middridge
Mordon
Shotton
Low Lands
Evenwood
SHILDON
Copley
B6282
Foxton
Hill Top
Eggleston
Cockfield
Esperley Lane Ends
Evenwood Gate
Bildershaw
Royal Oak
Redworth
NEWTON AYCLIFFE
Elstob
Stillington
Burnt Houses
Old Stillington
Wackerfield
Houghton Bank
Aycliffe
Whitton
B6279
Raby Castle
Hilton
Morton Tinmouth
Bolam
Heighington
Great Stainton
Kinninvie
Staindrop
Ingleton
Cross Lanes
Brafferton
Bishopton
B6278
Killerby
Walworth Gate
Denton
Coatham Mundeville
Little Stainton
Whinny Hill
Cotherstone
Langton
Stainton
Summerhouse
Beaumont Hill
Barmpton
West Newbiggin
STOCKTON-ON
Cleatlam
South Cleatlam
Headlam
Walworth
Low Walworth
Harrowgate Village
Great Burdon
Little Newsham
Gainford
B6275
B6279
Sadberge
B6277
A1150
Startforth
BARNARD CASTLE
A67
Winston
Archdeacon Newton
High Coniscliffe
Westwick
Moor Row
Carlbury
A66
Longnewton
A688
Whorlton
Piercebridge
Low Coniscliffe
B6280
Urlay Nook
River Tees
High Close
Cliffe
DARLINGTON
Boldron
Eggleston Abbey
Ovington
Manfield
A67
Oak Tree
Wycliffe
Caldwell
Cleasby
A1157
Eastbourne
A66
Cross Lanes
Greta Bridge
Eppleby
Lucy Cross
Middleton St George
TEES-SIDE
Bowes
Brignall
Hutton Magna
A66(M)
Blackwell
Middleton One Row
Gilmonby
726
Lane Head
Forcett
B6274
Stapleton
Hurworth-on-Tees
Low Dinsdale
River Greta
Scargill
West Layton
East Layton
Aldbrough St John
Neasham
Low Worsall
Thwaite
A1(M)
Barningham
Newsham
Newton Morrell
Croft-on-Tees
Eryholme
High Worsall
Melsonby
Barton
Girsby
Dalton
Ravensworth
A66
Dalton-on-Tees
Sockburn
B1264
Gayles
A167
Croft Autodrome
Low Entercommon
Hornby
Kirby Hill
Whashton
Middleton Tyas
High Entercommon
Whashton Green
Gilling West
Scotch Corner
Great Smeaton
NORTH YORKSHIRE
Aske Hall
Moulton
Helwith
1046
Skeeby
North Cowton
Langthwaite
Washfold
90
91
East Cowton
Birkby
Booze
Hurst
A1
B1263
Atley Hill
Arkle Town
River Swale
Uckerby
Skelton
1
RICHMOND
2
Citadilla
3
Forest
Catterick
Scorton
Hutton Bonville
Deighton

98
Street Gate
Wrekenton
Castletown
Monkwearmouth
Roker
SUNDERLAND
Springwell
A1(M)
Usworth
A1231
Kibblesworth
Birtley
Wildfowl Trust
South Hylton
Pennywell
WASHINGTON
Offerton
Hendon
105
Open-air Museum
High Urpeth
Ouston
Portobello
North Biddick
Penshaw
A183
A690
High Newport
Tunstall
Beamish
A693
Pelton
A195
Fatfield
Herrington
Ryhope
West Pelton
Perkinsville
Grange Villa
Pelton Fell
River Wear
New Herrington
Silksworth
New Silksworth
South Moor
Shiney Row
A183
Philadelphia
Newbottle
CHESTER-LE-STREET
Bournmoor
HOUGHTON LE SPRING
A19
A1018
New Lambton
High Dubmire
5
Waldridge
Chester Moor
B1284
Fencehouses
Colliery Row
Warden Law
Seaton
SEAHAM
Great Lumley
97
Edmondsley
Nettlesworth
East Rainton
HETTON-LE-HOLE
Parkside
Dalton-le-Dale
Murton
Sacriston
Plawsworth
Finchale Priory
Leamside
Cold Hesledon
Kimblesworth
A182
B1285
Witton Gilbert
Pity Me
A1(M)
West Rainton
Low Moorsley
High Moorsley
Easington Lane
Hawthorn
PS
A167
Framwellgate Moor
A690
Pittington
Langley Park
South Hetton
Beacon Point
Bearpark
Hallgarth
High Haswell
Littletown
B1432
Easington Colliery
Carrville
Easington
Ushaw Moor
Broom
Gilesgate Moor
Sherburn Hill
B1283
Haswell
Little Thorpe
Horden Point
Sherburn
Byers Garth
Haswell Plough
Shotton Colliery
A1086
Horden
Brancepeth
DURHAM
Shadforth
A181
Ludworth
B1280
PETERLEE
Langley Moor
Shincliffe
Running Waters
Old Cassop
Thornley
4
BRANDON
A1050
A177
Wheatley Hill
Shotton
The Castle
Blackhall Colliery
Bowburn
Old Quarrington
Cassop Colliery
Wellfield
B1281
Hesleden
Sunderland Bridge
Quarrington Hill
Wingate
Castle Eden
PS
Croxdale
Hett
Coxhoe
Deaf Hill
Station Town
Monk Hesleden
Town Kelloe
Kelloe
Trimdon Colliery
Hart Station
A660
Tudhoe
Trimdon Grange
Hutton Henry
WILLINGTON
Page Bank
Standalon
Sheraton
A167
Cookson's Green
Todhills
Byers Green
B6291
Garmondsway
South Wingate
A179
Hart
A1086
Mount Pleasant
Cornforth
Trimdon
A19
SPENNYMOOR
A177
Naisberry
High Throston
A179
HARTLEPOOL
Middlestone Moor
Ferryhill
Hurworth Burn
North Close
Elwick
Hartlepool Bay
Binchester Blocks
Middlestone
Kirk Merrington
Bishop Middleham
Fishburn
Mainsforth
B1278
A688
Leasingthorne
97
High Stotford
Dalton Piercy
Coundon
Chilton
Butterwick
Three Gates
Brierton
Seaton Carew
3
BISHOP AUCKLAND
A689
Sedgefield
Embleton
Low Stotford
Rushyford
A689
Tees Bay
South Church
Coundon Grange
Bradbury
A1(M)
Sedgefield
A689
Greatham
Eldon
Middridge
A167
Thorpe Larches
Grindon
A178
SHILDON
Mordon
Shotton
Wolviston
Newton Bewley
Coatham
Warrenby
Fulthorpe
Foxton
Cowpen Bewley
Royal Oak
Redworth
NEWTON AYCLIFFE
Elstob
Stillington
Thorpe Thewles
Billingham
Dorman
Houghton Bank
Old Stillington
A1185
Haverton Hill
Kirkleatham
Heighington
Aycliffe
Whitton
A177
Carlton
Port Clarence
Great Stainton
Norton
Toll
Grangetown
Cross Lanes
Brafferton
Bishopton
Roseworth
A19
Lazenby
Walworth Gate
PS
Redmarshall
South Bank
2
Denton
Coatham Mundeville
Little Stainton
Whinny Hill
A1027
North Ormesby
A1085
Eston
Beaumont Hill
Barmpton
West Newbiggin
STOCKTON-ON-TEES
R Tees
MIDDLESBROUGH
Lackenby
Walworth
A68
East Hartburn
B1380
Normanby
Low Walworth
Harrowgate Village
Great Burdon
Sadberge
Acklam
B6275
B6279
Archdeacon Newton
A1150
Elton
A172
A174
Carlbury
High Coniscliffe
A66
A135
Thornaby-on-Tees
Marton
Ormesby
GUISBOROUGH
Low Coniscliffe
Longnewton
A171
Cliffe
B6280
Pinchinthorpe
DARLINGTON
Urlay Nook
Nunthorpe
Manfield
A67
Oak Tree
A67
Eaglescliffe
Thornton
Hemlington
Hutton
Newton under Roseberry
Cleasby
A1150
Eastbourne
TEES-SIDE
Stainton
A66(M)
A66
Middleton St George
PS
Aislaby
Egglescliffe
High Leven
A1044
Maltby
Newby
1051
Blackwell
Middleton One Row
97
Yarm
Hilton
Langbaurgh
A173
Stapleton
Hurworth-on-Tees
Low Dinsdale
A19
Tanton
Great Ayton
Captain Cook Monument
Neasham
Low Worsall
A67
Middleton-on-Leven
Little Ayton
1
A1(M)
Seamer
Newton Morrell
Croft-on-Tees
Eryholme
Kirklevington
Easby
Barton
High Worsall
Stokesley
Girsby
Crathorne
Tame Bridge
Braworth
R Leven
Dalton-on-Tees
Sockburn
B1264
Picton
Hutton Rudby
Rudby
Sexhow
Kirkby
B1257
Middleton Tyas
Croft Autodrome
A167
Low Entercommon
Hornby
A172
Great Busby
Ingleby Greenhow
High Entercommon
Appleton Wiske
Enterpen
Great Broughton
Moulton
Great Smeaton
13
Carlton
Clay Bank
North Cowton
NORTH YORK
Potto
1427
PS
East Cowton
Rounton
East Rounton
Faceby
91
West Lees
Whorlton
Urra
A1
Uckerby
Birkby
B1263
Atley Hill
Welbury
Swainby
1490
Citadilla
Catterick Bridge
Forest
3
Hutton Bonville
Deighton
4
Ingleby Cross
Ingleby Arncliffe
5
Seave Green
Scorton
6

SCALE

0 1 2 3 4 5 miles

0 1 2 3 4 5 kilometres

shes

MARSKE-BY-THE-SEA

SALTBURN-BY-THE-SEA

New Brotton

New Skelton

Upleatham

BROTTON

Skinningrove

Boulby

Carlin How

LOFTUS

Street Houses

Cowbar

Staithes

SKELTON

North Skelton

Kilton

East Loftus

Easington

Dalehouse

Port Mulgrave

Boosbeck

Kilton Thorpe

Liverton Mines

Hinderwell

Runswick

Margrove Park

Lingdale

Liverton

Handale

Roxby

Newton Mulgrave

CLEVELAND WAY

Goldsborough

harlton

Stanghow

Borrowby

Ellerby

ND WAY

Moorsholm

B1266

A174

Lythe

A171

Scaling

Gerrick

Scaling Dam

Mickleby

West Barnby

East Barnby

Sandsend

Open to Public

WHITBY

Saltwick Bay

Commondale

Ugthorpe

Hutton Mulgrave

Raithwaite

Dunsley

Newholm

Selly Hill

Ruswarp

Danby

Stonegate

Houlsyke

Lealholm Side

Lealholm

Aislaby

Briggswath

Sneaton

Stainsacre

Hawsker

Castleton

Ainthorpe

Sleights

Iburndale

Ugglebarnby

Ness Point or North Cheek

Westerdale

The Green

Egton

Grosmont

Sneatonthorpe

Raw

Robin Hood's Bay

Low Garth

Glaisdale

Fylingthorpe

Danby Botton

Street

Egton Bridge

Esk Valley

Green End

A169

Littlebeck

B1416

IRE

92

7

Ralph Cross

Beck Hole

8

Goathland

9

Old Peak or South Cheek

93

Low Flask

Rave0car

Flask Inn

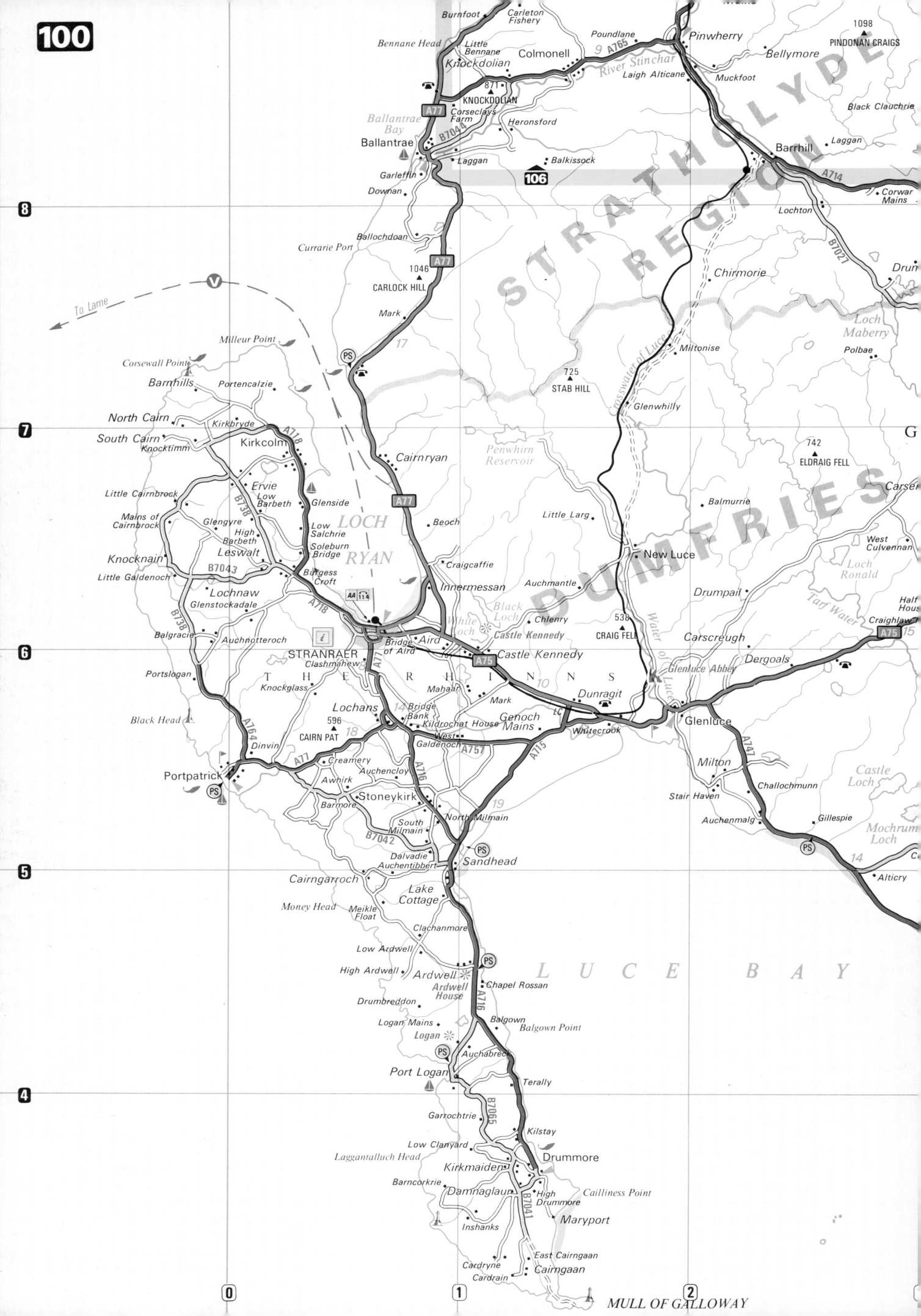

Burnfoot
Carleton Fishery
Bennane Head
Little Bennane
Knockdolian
Colmonell
Poundlane
A765
Pinwherry
Bellymore
1098
PINDONAN CRAIGS
River Stinchar
Laigh Alticane
Muckfoot
871
KNOCKDOLIAN
A77
Corseclays Farm
Heronsford
Black Clauchrie
Ballantrae Bay
B7044
Ballantrae
Laggan
Balkissock
106
Barrhill
Laggan
A714
Garleffin
Downan
Corwar Mains
Lochton
STRATHCLYDE REGION
Ballochdoan
Currarie Port
B7027
1046
CARLOCK HILL
Chirmorie
To Larne
Mark
Loch Maberry
Milleur Point
Miltonise
Polbae
Corsewall Point
725
STAB HILL
Barnhills
Portencalzie
Crosswater of Luce
Glenwhilly
North Cairn
Kirkbryde
A718
South Cairn
Knocktimm
Kirkcolm
Cairnryan
Penwhirn Reservoir
742
ELDRAIG FELL
Ervie
Little Cairnbrock
Low Barbeth
Glenside
A77
Balmurrie
B738
Mains of Cairnbrock
Glengyre
Low Salchrie
LOCH RYAN
Beoch
Little Larg
DUMFRIES
High Barbeth
Soleburn Bridge
West Culvennan
Knocknain
Leswalt
New Luce
B7043
Craigcaffie
Little Galdenoch
Burgess Croft
Loch Ronald
Lochnaw
Innermessan
Auchmantle
Drumpail
Half House
Glenstockadale
A718
Black Loch
Tarf Water
White Loch
Chlenry
538
Craighlaw
Balgracie
Auchnotteroch
Castle Kennedy
CRAIG FELL
Water of Luce
A75
Bridge of Aird
Aird
Carscreugh
STRANRAER
Castle Kennedy
Dergoals
Clashmahew
A75
Glenluce Abbey
Portslogan
THE RHINNS
Knockglass
Mahaar
Mark
Dunragit
Lochans
Bridge Bank
Genoch Mains
Black Head
596
Kildrochat House
Whitecrook
Glenluce
CAIRN PAT
West
Galdenoch
A757
A115
A747
Dinvin
A764
A77
Creamery
Auchencloy
Milton
Portpatrick
A716
Castle Loch
Awhirk
Challochmunn
Stair Haven
Stoneykirk
Barmore
North Milmain
Auchenmalg
Gillespie
South Milmain
B7042
Mochrum Loch
Dalvadie
Auchentibbert
Sandhead
Alticry
Cairngarroch
Lake Cottage
Money Head
Meikle Float
Clachanmore
Low Ardwell
LUCE BAY
High Ardwell
Ardwell
Ardwell House
Chapel Rossan
Drumbreddon
A716
Logan Mains
Balgown
Balgown Point
Logan
Auchabreck
Port Logan
Terally
Garrochtrie
B7065
Kilstay
Low Clanyard
Drummore
Laggantalluch Head
Kirkmaiden
Barncorkrie
Damnaglaur
High Drummore
Cailliness Point
B7041
Maryport
Inshanks
East Cairngaan
Cardryne
Cairngaan
Cardrain
MULL OF GALLOWAY
0
1
2
8
7
6
5
4

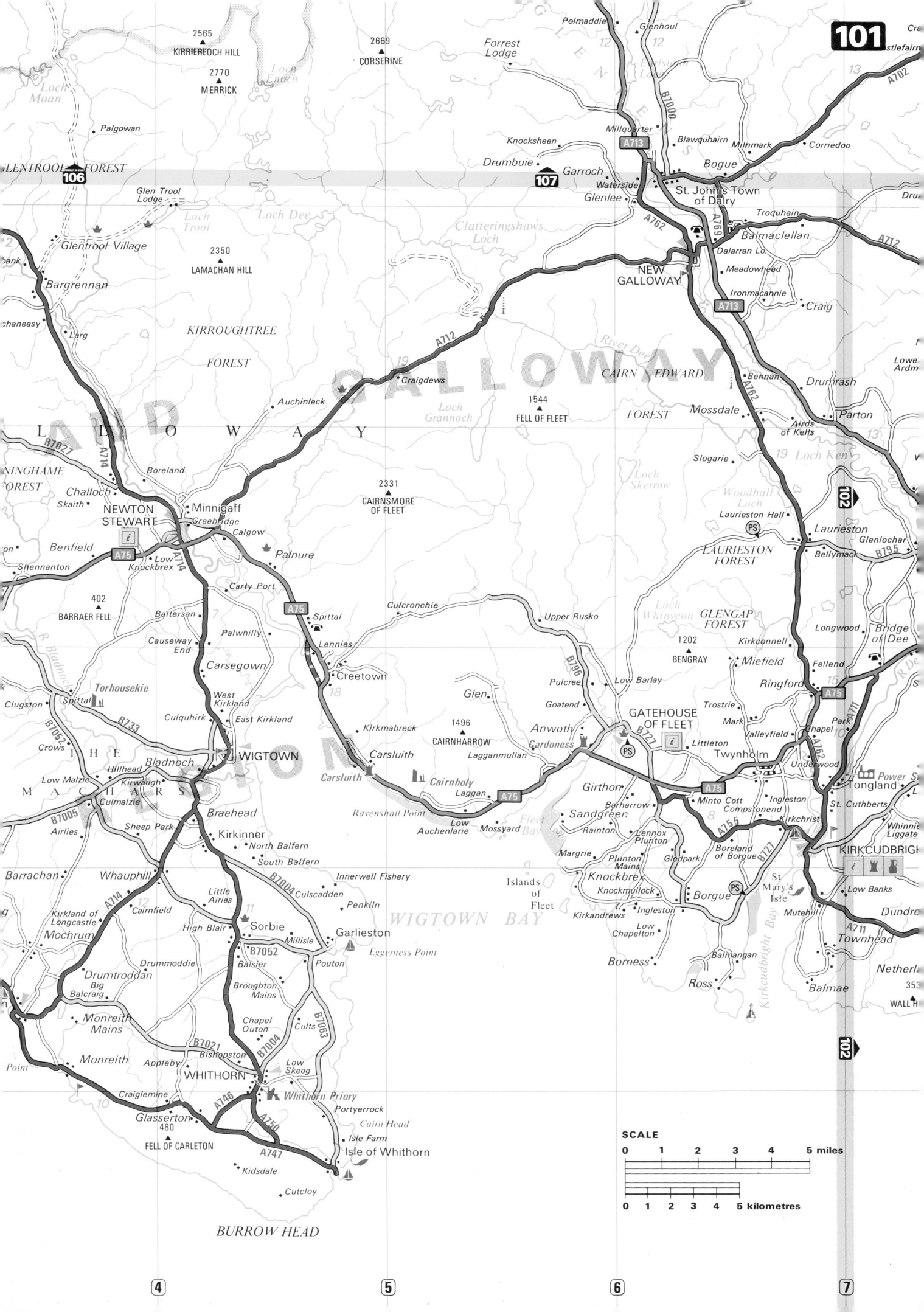
101
KIRRIEREOCH HILL
2565
CORSERINE
2669
MERRICK
2770
Loch Moan
Loch Enoch
Palgowan
GLENTROOL FOREST
106
Glen Trool Lodge
Loch Trool
Loch Dee
Glentrool Village
LAMACHAN HILL
2350
Bargrennan
Larg
KIRROUGHTREE FOREST
Forrest Lodge
Polmaddie
Glenhoul
Earlstoun Loch
Millquarter
Knocksheen
Drumbuie
107
Garroch
Waterside
Glenlee
Blawquhairn
Milnmark
Corriedoo
Bogue
St. John's Town of Dalry
Troquhain
Balmaclellan
Dalarran Lo.
Meadowhead
Ironmacannie
Craig
NEW GALLOWAY
Clatteringshaws Loch
A713
A762
A769
A712
A702
B7000
GALLOWAY
Craigdews
Auchinleck
Loch Grannoch
FELL OF FLEET
1544
CAIRN EDWARD FOREST
River Dee
Bennan
Drumrash
Parton
Mossdale
Airds of Kelts
Loch Ken
Slogarie
Loch Skerrow
Woodhall Loch
Laurieston Hall
Laurieston
Glenlochar
Bellymack
B795
LAURIESTON FOREST
Lowe Ardm
102
GALLOWAY
B7027
A714
NINGHAME FOREST
Boreland
Challoch
Skaith
NEWTON STEWART
Minnigaff
Greebridge
Calgow
Palnure
CAIRNSMORE OF FLEET
2331
Benfield
Shennanton
A75
Low Knockbrex
Carty Port
BARRAER FELL
402
Baltersan
Palwhilly
Causeway End
Carsegown
Spittal
Lennies
Culcronchie
Upper Rusko
Creetown
Torhousekie
Clugston
Spittal
West Kirkland
East Kirkland
Culquhirk
B733
B7052
Crows
R. Bladnoch
Bladnoch
WIGTOWN
THE MACHARS
Hillhead
Kirwaugh
Low Malzie
Culmalzie
B7005
Airlies
Sheep Park
Braehead
Kirkinner
North Balfern
South Balfern
Kirkmabreck
Carsluith
Carsluith
Glen
CAIRNHARROW
1496
Lagganmullan
Cairnholy
Laggan
Ravenshall Point
Low Auchenlarie
Mossyard
Fleet Bay
Pulcree
Low Barlay
Goatend
Anwoth
Cardoness
GATEHOUSE OF FLEET
B796
B727
Littleton
Twynholm
Loch Whinyeon
GLENGAP FOREST
BENGRAY
1202
Kirkconnell
Miefield
Ringford
Trostrie
Mark
Valleyfield
Chapel
Underwood
Longwood
Bridge of Dee
Fellend
Park
A711
Power St.
Tongland
St. Cuthberts
Girthon
Barharrow
Sandgreen
Rainton
Minto Cott
Compstonend
Ingleston
Kirkchrist
Lennox Plunton
Plunton Mains
Margrie
Gledpark
Boreland of Borgue
A755
B727
KIRKCUDBRIGHT
Whinnie Liggate
Knockbrex
Knockmullock
Islands of Fleet
Borgue
St Mary's Isle
Low Banks
Kirkandrews
Ingleston
Low Chapelton
Mutehill
Dundre
A711
Townhead
Borness
Balmangan
Ross
Kirkcudbright Bay
Netherl
Balmae
WALL H
353
Barrachan
Whauphill
Innerwell Fishery
Culscadden
B7004
Little Airies
Kirkland of Longcastle
Cairnfield
Penkiln
WIGTOWN BAY
Mochrum
High Blair
Sorbie
Millisle
Garlieston
Eggerness Point
B7052
Drummoddie
Balsier
Pouton
Drumtroddan
Big Balcraig
Broughton Mains
Monreith Mains
Chapel Outon
Cults
B7063
B7021
Bishopston
Monreith
Appleby
WHITHORN
Low Skeog
Point
Whithorn Priory
Craiglemine
Portyerrock
Cairn Head
A746
A750
Glasserton
480
FELL OF CARLETON
A747
Isle Farm
Isle of Whithorn
Kidsdale
Cutcloy
BURROW HEAD
SCALE
0 1 2 3 4 5 miles
0 1 2 3 4 5 kilometres
4
5
6
7

DUMFRIES
CASTLE DOUGLAS
DALBEATTIE
KIRKCUDBRIGHT
MARYPORT
LOCHMA
NX
DUMFRIES AND GALLOWAY REGION
SOLWAY
Dunscore
Holywood
Lochfoot
Kirkpatrick Durham
Springholm
New Abbey
Kirkbean
Southerness
Colvend
Rockcliffe
Kippford or Scaur
Palnackie
Auchencairn
Dundrennan
Dundrennan Abbey
Tongland
Crossmichael
Laurieston
Corsock
Shawhead
Terregles
Mabie
Beeswing
Kirkgunzeon
Caulkerbush
Carsethorn
Glencaple
Collin
Amisfield Town
Tinwald
Locharbriggs
Flimby
Crosby
Seaton
Great Broughton
1417 BOGRIE HILL
787 STEILSTON HILL
1256 LONG FELL
1868 CRIFFEL
1283 BENGAIRN
353 WALL HILL
Hestan Island
Southerness Point
Abbey Head
Balcary Point
SCALE
0 1 2 3 4 5 miles
0 1 2 3 4 5 kilometres

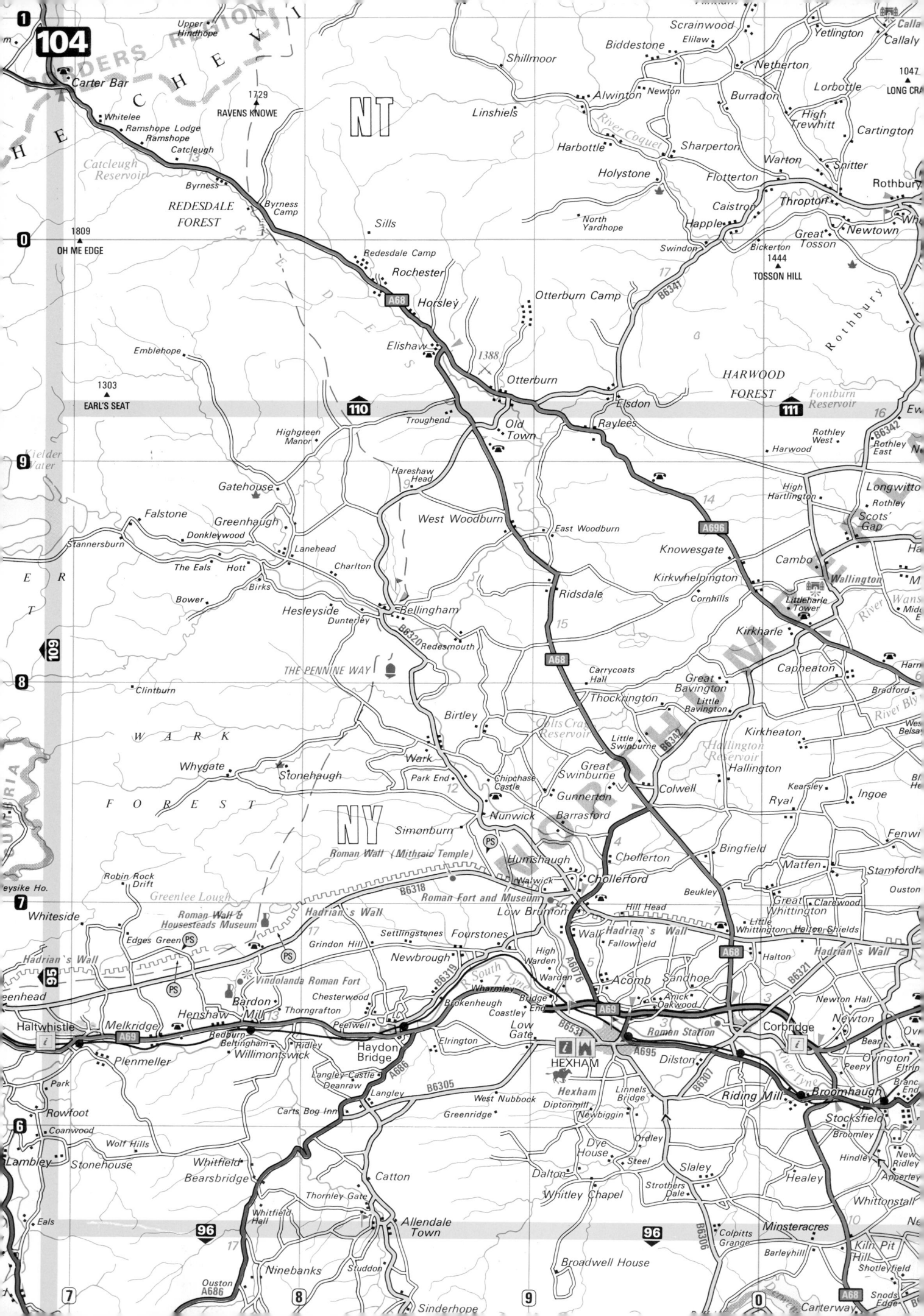
104
Carter Bar
Upper Hindhope
BORDERS REGION
THE CHEVIOT
1729
RAVENS KNOWE
NT
Whitelee
Ramshope Lodge
Ramshope
Catcleugh
Catcleugh Reservoir
Byrness
REDESDALE FOREST
Byrness Camp
1809
OH ME EDGE
Sills
Redesdale Camp
Rochester
Horsley
A68
Otterburn Camp
Elishaw
1388
Otterburn
Emblehope
1303
EARL'S SEAT
110
Troughend
Old Town
Elsdon
Raylees
HARWOOD FOREST
111
Fontburn Reservoir
Highgreen Manor
Kielder Water
Hareshaw Head
West Woodburn
East Woodburn
Gatehouse
Falstone
Greenhaugh
Donkleywood
Stannersburn
Lanehead
Charlton
The Eals
Hott
Birks
Bower
Hesleyside
Dunterley
Bellingham
Ridsdale
B6320
Redesmouth
109
THE PENNINE WAY
Clintburn
Birtley
Carrycoats Hall
Thockrington
Colt Crag Reservoir
WARK FOREST
Whygate
Stonehaugh
Wark
Park End
Chipchase Castle
Great Swinburne
Gunnerton
Nunwick
Barrasford
NY
Simonburn
Roman Wall (Mithraic Temple)
Humshaugh
Walwick
Chollerford
Chollerton
NORTHUMBERLAND
Robin Rock Drift
Greenlee Lough
B6318
Roman Fort and Museum
Low Brunton
Whiteside
Roman Wall & Housesteads Museum
Hadrian's Wall
Edges Green
Grindon Hill
Settlingstones
Fourstones
Newbrough
High Warden
Warden
Vindolanda Roman Fort
Chesterwood
B6319
South Tyne
Wharmley
Bardon Mill
Thorngrafton
Henshaw
Brokenheugh
Coastley
Bridge End
Haltwhistle
Melkridge
A69
Redburn
Beltingham
Ridley
Willimontswick
Peelwell
Haydon Bridge
Elrington
Low Gate
HEXHAM
Hexham
Plenmeller
Park
Langley Castle
Deanraw
A686
Langley
B6305
West Nubbock
Carts Bog Inn
Greenridge
Diptonmill
Newbiggin
Rowfoot
Coanwood
Wolf Hills
Lambley
Stonehouse
Whitfield
Bearsbridge
Catton
Thornley Gate
Whitfield Hall
Allendale Town
Eals
96
Ninebanks
Studdon
Ouston
Sinderhope
Dye House
Ordley
Steel
Dalton
Whitley Chapel
Slaley
Strothers Dale
Colpitts Grange
Broadwell House
B6306
Scrainwood
Elilaw
Biddestone
Shillmoor
Yetlington
Callaly
Netherton
1047
LONG CRAG
Lorbottle
Alwinton
Newton
Burradon
Linshiels
High Trewhitt
Cartington
River Coquet
Harbottle
Sharperton
Warton
Snitter
Holystone
Flotterton
Rothbury
Caistron
Thropton
North Yardhope
Happle
Newtown
Swindon
Bickerton
Great Tosson
1444
TOSSON HILL
B6341
Rothbury
Rothley West
Rothley East
B6342
Harwood
High Hartlington
Longwitton
Rothley
Scots' Gap
A696
Knowesgate
Cambo
Kirkwhelpington
Wallington
Cornhills
Littleharle Tower
Kirkharle
Capheaton
Great Bavington
Little Bavington
Bradford
River Blyth
Kirkheaton
Little Swinburne
Hallington Reservoir
Hallington
Colwell
Kearsley
Ryal
Ingoe
Bingfield
Matfen
Stamfordham
Beukley
Great Whittington
Clarewood
Ouston
Hill Head
Little Whittington
Halton Shields
Wall
Fallowfield
Halton
A6079
Acomb
Sandhoe
Anick
Oakwood
B6321
Newton Hall
Newton
B6531
Roman Station
Corbridge
A695
Dilston
River Tyne
Ovington
Peepy
Linnels Bridge
B6307
Riding Mill
Broomhaugh
Stocksfield
Broomley
Hindley
New Ridley
Apperley
Healey
Whittonstall
Minsteracres
Kiln Pit Hill
Barleyhill
Shotleyfield
Snods Edge
Carterway
7
8
9
0
1
6

NU

NZ

Alnmouth Bay

Hall
Banks
High Buston
Shilbottle
Low Buston
Eastfield Hall
Birling
Warkworth
Hermitage
Guyzance
Gloster Hill
AMBLE
Coquet Island
Hauxley
North Togston
Togston
Radcliffe
Acklington
Broomhill
South Broomhill
Red Row
Chevington Drift
East Chevington
West Chevington
Druridge Bay
Druridge
Hemscott Hills
Widdrington
Cresswell
Widdrington Station
Ellington
Ulgham
Lynemouth
Beacon Point
ASHINGTON
Woodhorn
NEWBIGGIN-BY-THE-SEA
Woodhorne Demesne
Pegswood
Bothal
Sheepwash
Hirst
MORPETH
Guide Post
North Seaton
North Seaton Colliery
Choppington
Stakeford
Scotland Gate
West Sleekburn
Cambois
Hepscott
Clifton
Netherton Colliery
Nedderton
East Sleekburn
BEDLINGTON
BLYTH
Bebside
Cowpen
New Delaval
Newsham
East Hartford
Stannington
Plessey Checks
Nelson Village
Shotton
Cramlington
New Hartley
Seaton Sluice
Hartley
New Horton Grange
East Cramlington
Seaton
SEATON DELAVAL
Open to Public
Brenkley
Seaton Burn
Annitsford
Seghill
East Holywell
Earsdon
WHITLEY BAY
Monkseaton
Cullercoats
Ponteland
Mason
Dinnington
Dudley
Burradon
Shiremoor
Murton
Hazelrigg
Wide Open
New York
Backworth
Killingworth
West Moor
Prestwick
High Callerton
Black Callerton
NEWCASTLE (WOOLSINGTON)
Woolsington
Kenton Bank Foot
LONGBENTON
TYNEMOUTH
North Shields
GOSFORTH
South Gosforth
Willington
SOUTH SHIELDS
NEWCASTLE UPON TYNE
WALLSEND
Jesmond
Heaton
Town Moor
JARROW
Westoe
Harton
Marsden Bay
Throckley
Walbottle
NEWBURN
Elswick
Walker
Byker
HEBBURN
Monkton
Pelaw
Marsden
Whitburn Colliery
Whitburn
Open to Public
Dunston
Low Team
FELLING
Boldon Colliery
West Boldon
Cleadon
East Boldon
Fulwell
WHICKHAM
GATESHEAD
Low Fell
Wrekenton
BOLDON
Southwick
Roker
Street Gate
Springwell
Castletown
Seaburn
Monkwearmouth
Sunniside
Lamesley
Usworth
South Hylton
Pennywell
SUNDERLAND
Birtley
WASHINGTON
Offerton
Hendon
Open-air Museum
Portobello
North Biddick
Penshaw
STANLEY
Beamish
Ouston
Pelton
Fatfield
Herrington
High Newport
Tunstall
New Silksworth
Ryhope

Bergen Stavanger Summer only
Goteborg Summer only
Esbjerg Summer only

SCALE
0 1 2 3 4 5 miles
0 1 2 3 4 5 kilometres

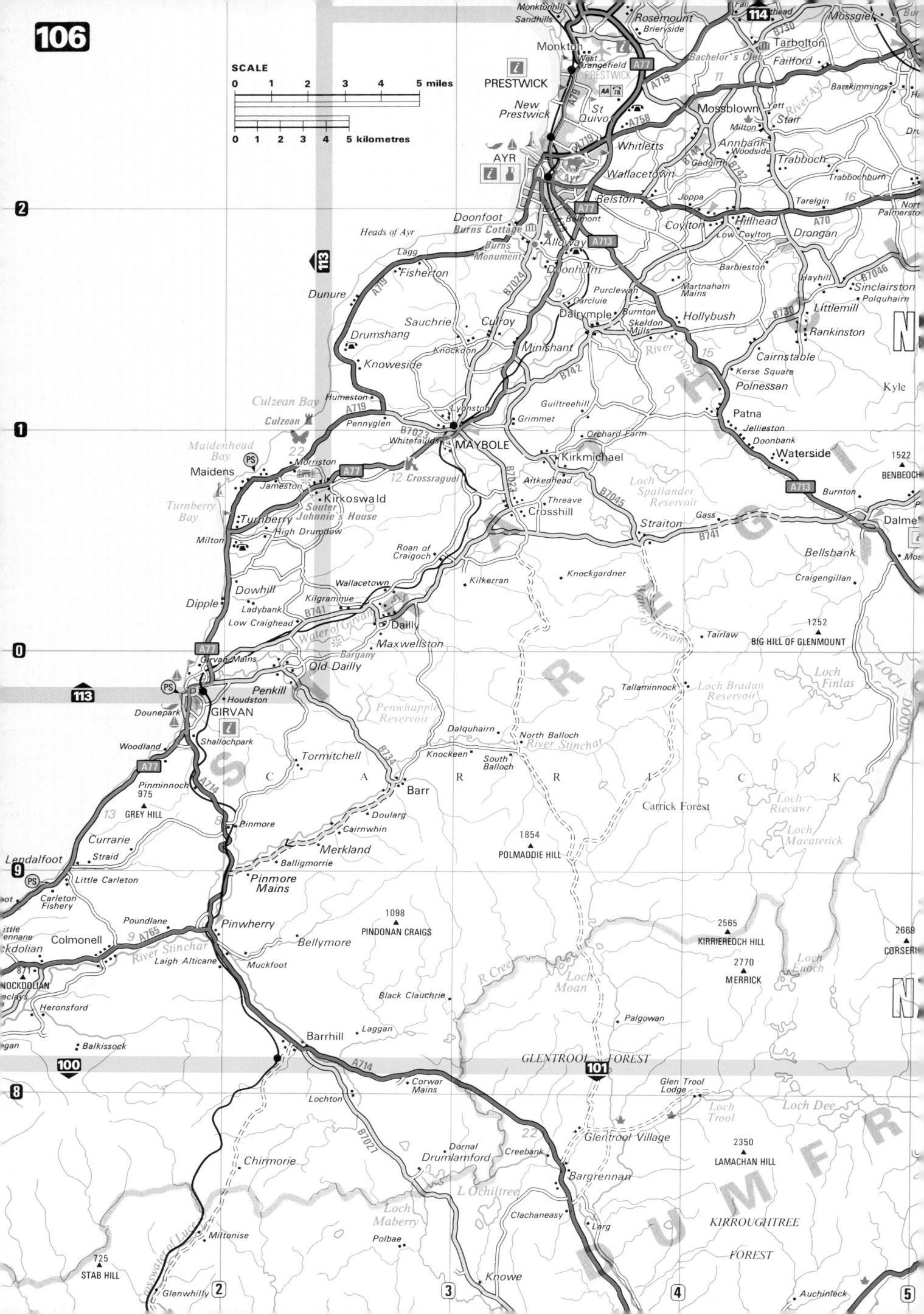

SCALE

0 1 2 3 4 5 miles

0 1 2 3 4 5 kilometres

Monktonhill
Sandhills
Rosemount
Brierside
114
Mossgiel
Monkton
West
Orangefield
PRESTWICK
A77
Bachelor's Club
Tarbolton
Failford
New
Prestwick
St Quivox
AA 78
Mossblown
Milton
Starr
Yett
Barskimmings
River Ayr
Whitletts
Annbank
Woodside
Trabboch
Gadgirth
Trabbochburn
AYR
Wallacetown
Joppa
Tarelgin
River Ayr
Belston
Coylton
Hillhead
A70
Palmersto
Heads of Ayr
Lagg
Doonfoot
Burns Cottage
Belmont
A77
Low Coylton
Drongan
B7046
Alloway
A713
Barbieston
Hayhill
Sinclairston
Burns
Monument
Doonholm
Purclewan
Martnaham
Mains
Polquhairn
Fisherton
Carcluie
Burnton
Skeldon
Mills
Hollybush
Littlemill
Dunure
Sauchrie
Culroy
Dalrymple
River Doon
Rankinston
Drumshang
Knockdon
Minishant
B730
Cairnstable
Knoweside
B42
Kerse Square
Humeston
Guiltreehill
Polnessan
Kyle
Culzean Bay
A719
Lyonston
Grimmet
Patna
Pennyglen
B7023
Orchard Farm
Jellieston
Waterside
Culzean
Whitefaulds
MAYBOLE
Doonbank
Maidenhead
Bay
22
Morriston
A77
Kirkmichael
Loch
Spallander
Reservoir
A713
Burnton
1522
BENBEOCH
PS
Jameston
12 Crossraguel
Aitkenhead
B7045
Gass
Maidens
Kirkoswald
Threave
Straiton
B741
Dalme
Turnberry
Bay
Souter
Johnnie's House
Crosshill
Bellsbank
Turnberry
High Drumdow
Roan of
Craigoch
Milton
Wallacetown
Kilkerran
Knockgardner
Craigengillan
Dowhill
Kilgrammie
1252
Dipple
Ladybank
B741
Water of Girvan
BIG HILL OF GLENMOUNT
Dailly
Tairlaw
Low Craighead
Maxwellston
Tallaminnock
Loch Bradan
Reservoir
Loch Finlas
Girvan Mains
Bargany
Old Dailly
Penwhapple
Reservoir
PS
Penkill
LOCH DOON
113
Houdston
GIRVAN
Dounepark
Shallochpark
Dalquhairn
North Balloch
River Stinchar
Woodland
Tormitchell
Knockeen
South
Balloch
Carrick Forest
Loch
Riecawr
A77
C   A   R   R   I   C   K
Pinminnoch
975
Barr
Loch
Macaterick
13 GREY HILL
Pinmore
Doularg
1854
Currarie
Straid
Cairnwhin
POLMADDIE HILL
Lendalfoot
Merkland
2565
KIRRIEREOCH HILL
PS
Little Carleton
Balligmorrie
2669
CORSERI
Pinmore
Mains
1098
Carleton
Fishery
Poundlane
PINDONAN CRAIGS
2770
MERRICK
ennane
Colmonell
A765
Pinwherry
Bellymore
Loch
Enoch
kdolian
B871
River Stinchar
Laigh Alticane
Loch
Moan
NOCKDOLIAN
Muckfoot
clays
Heronsford
Black Clauchrie
Palgowan
Balkissock
Laggan
GLENTROOL   FOREST
N
100
Barrhill
101
Glen Trool
Lodge
Loch Dee
8
A714
Corwar
Mains
Loch
Trool
Lochton
B7027
Glentrool Village
2350
LAMACHAN HILL
Chirmorie
Dornal
Drumlamford
Creebank
Bargrennan
KIRROUGHTREE
L Ochiltree
Clachaneasy
Larg
FOREST
Loch
Maberry
Polbae
725
STAB HILL
2
Glenwhilly
3
Knowe
4
Auchinleck
5

N

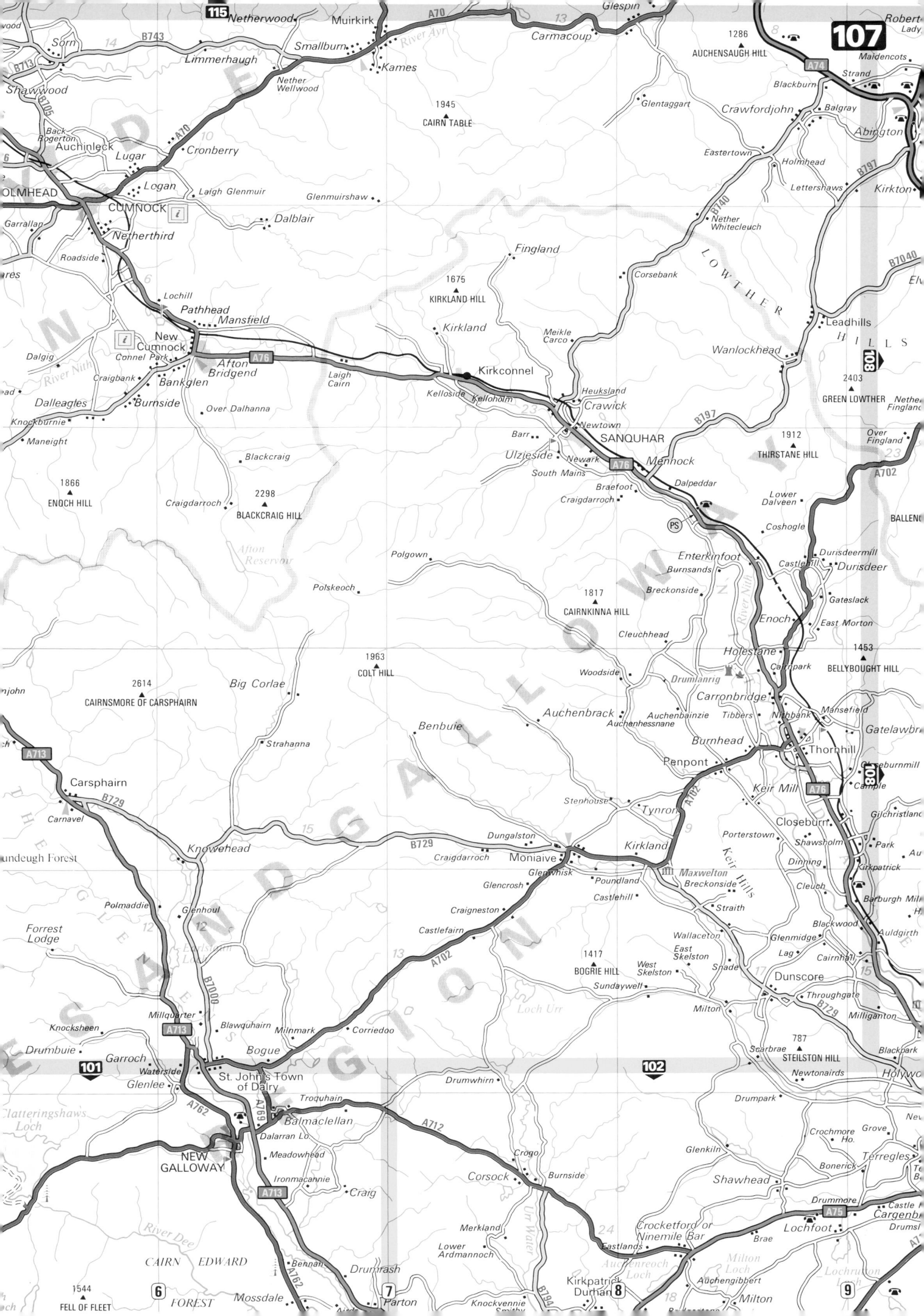
115
Netherwood
Muirkirk
A70
Glespin
13
Carmacoup
Sorn
14
B743
Smallburn
River Ayr
Kames
1286
AUCHENSAUGH HILL
8
A74
Maidencots
Strand
Blackburn
B713
Limmerhaugh
Nether Wellwood
Shawwood
B705
1945
CAIRN TABLE
Glentaggart
Crawfordjohn
Balgray
Abington
A70
10
Back Rogerton
Auchinleck
Lugar
Cronberry
Eastertown
Holmhead
B797
Logan
Laigh Glenmuir
Lettershaws
Kirkton
CUMNOCK
Glenmuirshaw
Garrallan
Dalblair
B740
Nether Whitecleuch
Netherthird
Roadside
Fingland
L O W T H E R
B7040
Corsebank
6
1675
KIRKLAND HILL
Lochill
Pathhead
Mansfield
Leadhills
New Cumnock
Connel Park
Kirkland
Meikle Carco
H I L L S
Dalgig
Afton Bridgend
A76
Wanlockhead
108
River Nith
Craigbank
Bankglen
Laigh Cairn
Kirkconnel
2403
GREEN LOWTHER
Dalleagles
Burnside
Kelloside
Kelloholm
Heuksland
Crawick
Over Dalhanna
23
Knockburnie
Newtown
B797
Maneight
Barr
SANQUHAR
1912
Over Fingland
Ulzieside
Newark
A76
Mennock
THIRSTANE HILL
23
Blackcraig
South Mains
A702
Braefoot
Dalpeddar
1866
ENOCH HILL
Craigdarroch
2298
BLACKCRAIG HILL
Craigdarroch
Lower Dalveen
PS
Coshogle
Afton Reservoir
Polgown
Enterkinfoot
Durisdeermill
Burnsands
Castlehill
Durisdeer
Polskeoch
1817
Breckonside
CAIRNKINNA HILL
Gateslack
River Nith
Enoch
East Morton
Cleuchhead
1963
COLT HILL
Holestane
1453
Carronpark
BELLYBOUGHT HILL
2614
CAIRNSMORE OF CARSPHAIRN
Big Corlae
Woodside
Drumlanrig
Carronbridge
Auchenbrack
Auchenbainzie
Tibbers
Nithbank
Mansefield
Auchenhessnane
Gatelawbr
Benbuie
Strahanna
Burnhead
Thornhill
A713
Penpont
108
Carsphairn
Keir Mill
A76
B729
A702
Stenhouse
Tynron
Carnavel
Closeburn
15
Dungalston
9
Porterstown
Knowehead
B729
Kirkland
Shawsholm
Park
Craigdarroch
Moniaive
Keir Hills
Glenwhisk
Dinning
Kirkpatrick
Poundland
Maxwelton
Breckonside
Glencrosh
Cleuch
Polmaddie
Castlehill
Barburgh Mill
Craigneston
Straith
Glenhoul
12
12
Blackwood
Forrest Lodge
Castlefairn
Wallaceton
Auldgirth
Glenmidge
East Skelston
Lag
13
A702
1417
Cairnhall
BOGRIE HILL
West Skelston
Snade
17
15
Dunscore
Sundaywell
Loch Urr
B7000
Throughgate
Milton
B729
Millquarter
Milligantou
Knocksheen
A713
Blawquhairn
Milnmark
Corriedoo
787
Drumbuie
Bogue
Scarbrae
STEILSTON HILL
Blackpark
Garroch
101
102
Newtonairds
Holywo
Waterside
St. John's Town of Dalry
Glenlee
Drumwhirn
A762
Troquhain
Drumpark
Clatteringshaws Loch
A769
Balmaclellan
A712
Dalarran Lo.
Crochmore Ho.
Grove
Meadowhead
Crogo
Glenkiln
NEW GALLOWAY
Terregles
Bonerick
Ironmacannie
Corsock
Burnside
Shawhead
A713
Craig
Drummore
A75
Castle
Cargenbr
River Dee
Merkland
Urr Water
24
Crocketford or Ninemile Bar
Lochfoot
Brae
Lower Ardmannoch
Eastlands
CAIRN EDWARD
Bennan
Auchenreoch Loch
Milton Loch
A762
Drumrash
Auchengibbert
Lochrutton Loch
1544
FELL OF FLEET
6
FOREST
Mossdale
7
Parton
Knockvennie
B794
Kirkpatrick Durham
8
18
Milton
9
G A L L O W A Y
D U M F R I E S   A N D   G A L L O W A Y   R E G I O N

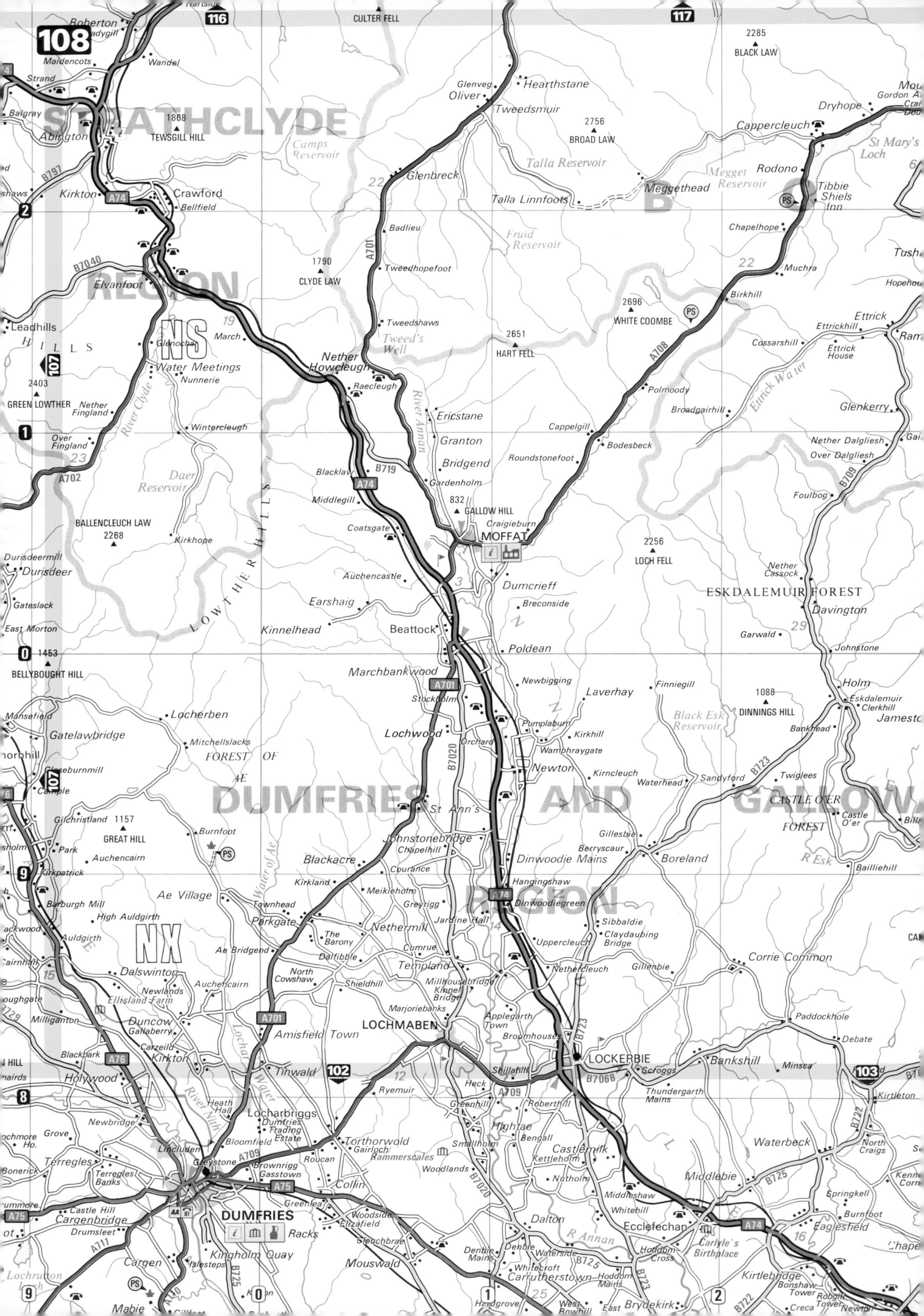

116
117
CULTER FELL
STRATHCLYDE REGION
DUMFRIES AND GALLOWAY REGION
NS
NX
Roberton
Wandel
Strand
Abington
TEWSGILL HILL
1868
Crawford
Bellfield
Kirkton
Elvanfoot
Leadhills
LOWTHER HILLS
GREEN LOWTHER
2403
Glenochar
Water Meetings
Nunnerie
Daer Reservoir
BALLENCLEUCH LAW
2268
Kirkhope
Durisdeer
Durisdeermill
Gateslack
East Morton
BELLYBOUGHT HILL
1453
Camps Reservoir
Glenveg
Oliver
Hearthstane
Tweedsmuir
Glenbreck
BROAD LAW
2756
BLACK LAW
2285
Talla Reservoir
Talla Linnfoots
Meggethead
Megget Reservoir
Rodono
Cappercleuch
Dryhope
St Mary's Loch
Tibbie Shiels Inn
Chapelhope
Badlieu
Fruid Reservoir
Tweedhopefoot
CLYDE LAW
1790
Tweedshaws
Tweed's Well
Nether Howcleugh
Raecleugh
HART FELL
2651
WHITE COOMBE
2696
Birkhill
Muchra
Polmoody
Ettrick Water
Ettrick
Ettrickhill
Cossarshill
Ettrick House
Broadgairhill
Glenkerry
Ericstane
Granton
Bridgend
Gardenholm
River Annan
Capelgill
Bodesbeck
Roundstonefoot
GALLOW HILL
832
Craigieburn
MOFFAT
Blacklaw
Middlegill
Coatsgate
Auchencastle
Earshaig
Kinnelhead
Beattock
Dumcrieff
Breconside
Poldean
LOCH FELL
2256
ESKDALEMUIR FOREST
Davington
Nether Cassock
Nether Dalgliesh
Over Dalgliesh
Foulbog
Garwald
Johnstone
Holm
Eskdalemuir
Clerkhill
Bankhead
DINNINGS HILL
1088
Black Esk Reservoir
Finniegill
Laverhay
Newbigging
Marchbankwood
Stockholm
Lochwood
Orchard
Pumplaburn
Kirkhill
Wamphraygate
Newton
Kirncleuch
Waterhead
Sandyford
Twiglees
CASTLE O'ER FOREST
Castle O'er
Locherben
Mitchellslacks
FOREST OF AE
Gatelawbridge
Closeburnmill
Gilchristland
GREAT HILL
1157
Burnfoot
Park
Auchencairn
Kirkpatrick
Ae Village
Water of Ae
St Ann's
Johnstonebridge
Chapelhill
Courance
Blackacre
Kirkland
Meikleholm
Greyrigg
Dinwoodie Mains
Berryscaur
Gillesbie
Boreland
Bailliehill
Hangingshaw
Dinwoodiegreen
Sibbaldie
Claydaubing Bridge
Uppercleuch
Barburgh Mill
High Auldgirth
Auldgirth
Townhead
Parkgate
The Barony
Nethermill
Jardine Hall
Cumrue
Dalfibble
Templand
Ae Bridgend
Dalswinton
Newlands
Ellisland Farm
Auchencairn
North Cowshaw
Shieldhill
Millhousebridge
Kinnel Bridge
Marjoriebanks
Applegarth Town
Netherdcleuch
Gillenbie
Corrie Common
Paddockhole
Debate
Milligantoun
Duncow
Gallaberry
Carzeild
Kirkton
Blackpark
Holywood
Amisfield Town
LOCHMABEN
Broomhouses
LOCKERBIE
Scroggs
Bankshill
Minsca
Thundergarth Mains
Kirtleton
Tinwald
Ryemuir
Shillahill
Heck
Greenhill
Roberthill
Hightae
Bengall
Smallholm
Castlemilk
Kettleholm
Nutholm
Waterbeck
North Craigs
Middlebie
Springkell
Burnfoot
Eaglesfield
River Nith
Lochar Water
Heath Hall
Locharbriggs
Dumfries Trading Estate
Newbridge
Grove
Lincluden
Bloomfield
Torthorwold
Gairloch
Rammerscales
Woodlands
Terregles
Terregles Banks
Greystone
Brownrigg
Gasstown
Roucan
Collin
Castle Hill
Cargenbridge
Drumsleet
DUMFRIES
Greenlea
Woodside
Elizafield
Racks
Middleshaw
Whitehill
Ecclefechan
Carlyle's Birthplace
Hoddom Cross
Dalton
R Annan
Dentie Mains
Denbie
Waterside
Whitecroft
Carrutherstown
Hoddom Mains
Kirtlebridge
Bonshaw Tower
Robgill Tower
Cargen
Islesteps
Kingholm Quay
Gleuchbrae
Mouswald
Lochrutton
Mabie
Hardgrove
West Rowhill
East Brydekirk
Creca
Newton
A74
A701
A702
A708
A709
A711
A75
A76
B719
B7020
B7040
B7068
B709
B722
B723
B725
B729
B797
102
103
107

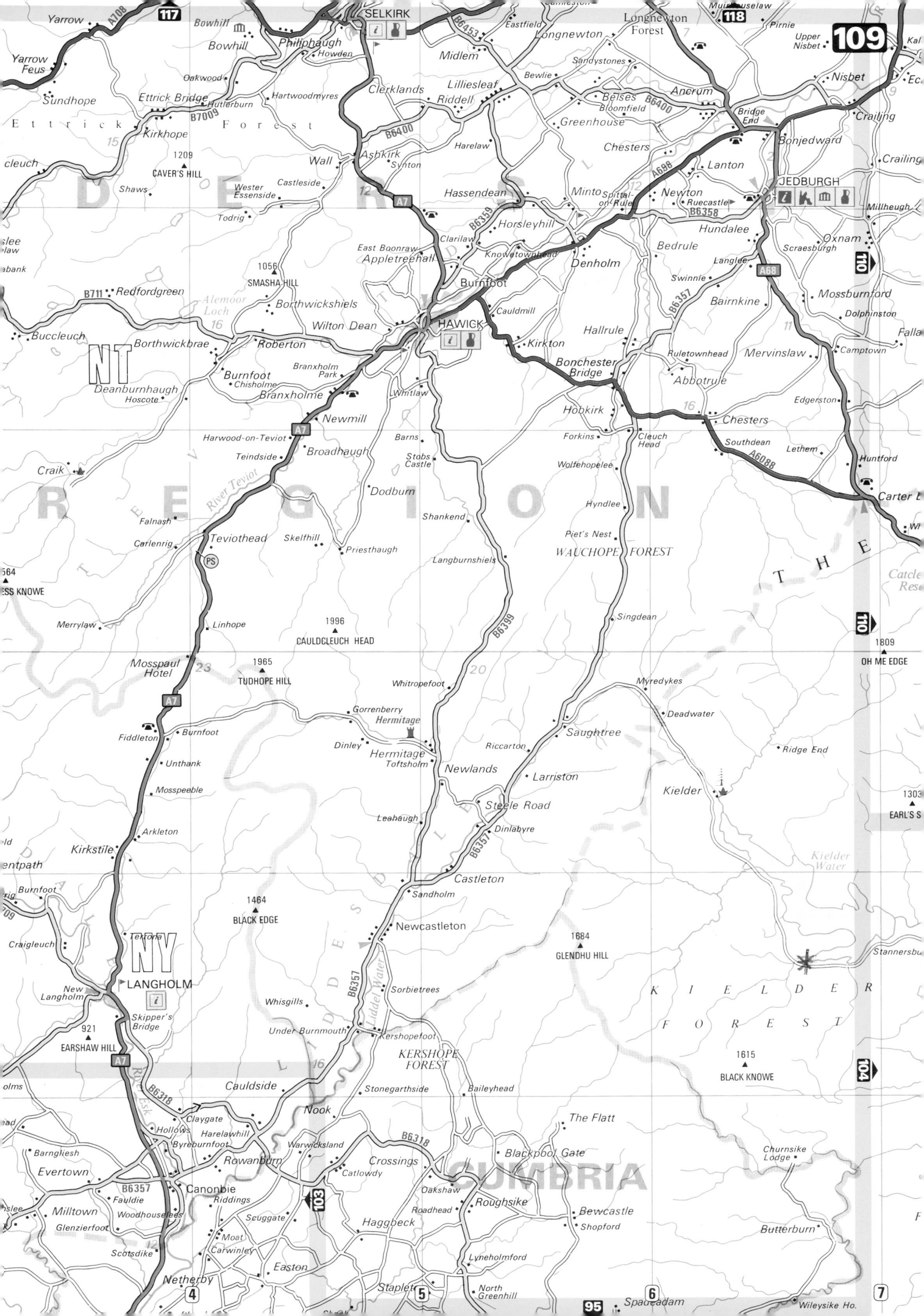
109
117
118
110
104
103
95
SELKIRK
HAWICK
JEDBURGH
LANGHOLM
Philiphaugh
Bowhill
Ettrick Bridge
Ettrick Forest
Kirkhope
Midlem
Lilliesleaf
Riddell
Clerklands
Ashkirk
Wall
Longnewton
Ancrum
Nisbet
Crailing
Bonjedward
Lanton
Newton
Minto
Denholm
Hassendean
Horsleyhill
Appletreehall
Burnfoot
Bedrule
Hundalee
Oxnam
Swinnie
Bairnkine
Mossburnford
Hallrule
Kirkton
Bonchester Bridge
Abbotrule
Hobkirk
Chesters
Camptown
Edgerston
Southdean
Huntford
Carter Bar
Roberton
Borthwickbrae
Branxholme
Newmill
Broadhaugh
Teviothead
Mosspaul Hotel
Fiddleton
Hermitage
Newlands
Saughtree
Steele Road
Castleton
Newcastleton
Kielder
Kielder Water
Kielder Forest
Wauchope Forest
Kershope Forest
Canonbie
Rowanburn
Crossings
Roughsike
Bewcastle
Haggbeck
Easton
Netherby
CUMBRIA
BORDERS REGION
NT
NY
1996 CAULDCLEUCH HEAD
1965 TUDHOPE HILL
1464 BLACK EDGE
1684 GLENDHU HILL
1615 BLACK KNOWE
921 EARSHAW HILL
1209 CAVER'S HILL
1056 SMASHA HILL
1809 OH ME EDGE
A7
A68
A698
A6088
B6357
B6399
B6318
B6400
B6358
B6359
B7009
B711
4
5
6
7

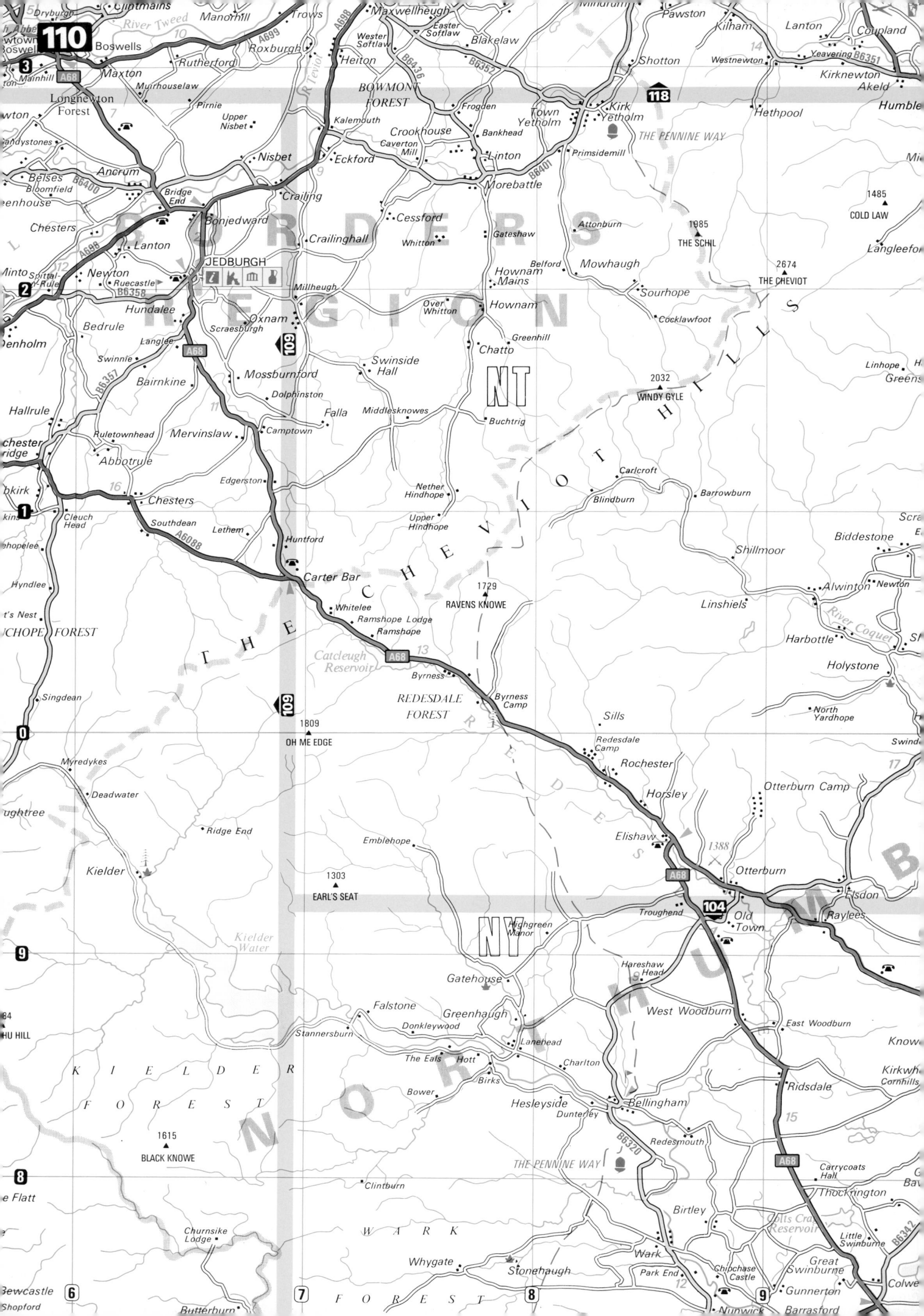
110
118
109
104
BORDERS REGION
THE CHEVIOT HILLS
NORTHUMB
NT
NY
JEDBURGH
Dryburgh
Clintmains
Manorhill
Trows
Maxwellheugh
Pawston
Kilham
Lanton
Coupland
Boswells
Roxburgh
Rutherford
Maxton
Muirhouselaw
Mainhill
Longnewton Forest
Pirnie
Upper Nisbet
Heiton
Wester Softlaw
Easter Softlaw
Blakelaw
BOWMONT FOREST
Kalemouth
Crookhouse
Caverton Mill
Frogden
Bankhead
Town Yetholm
Kirk Yetholm
Shotton
Westnewton
Yeavering
Kirknewton
Akeld
Humble
Hethpool
THE PENNINE WAY
Primsidemill
Linton
Morebattle
Eckford
Nisbet
Ancrum
Belses
Bloomfield
Bridge End
Crailing
Cessford
Whitton
Gateshaw
Attonburn
1985
THE SCHIL
1485
COLD LAW
Langleeford
Chesters
Bonjedward
Crailinghall
Lanton
Minto
Spittal-on-Rule
Newton
Ruecastle
Millheugh
Hownam Mains
Belford
Mowhaugh
Sourhope
2674
THE CHEVIOT
Cocklawfoot
Over Whitton
Hownam
Hundalee
Bedrule
Oxnam
Scraesburgh
Denholm
Langlee
Swinnie
Bairnkine
Mossburnford
Dolphinston
Swinside Hall
Chatto
Greenhill
2032
WINDY GYLE
Linhope
Hallrule
Falla
Middleknowes
Buchtrig
Ruletownhead
Mervinslaw
Camptown
Abbotrule
Edgerston
Carlcroft
Blindburn
Barrowburn
Chesters
Nether Hindhope
Upper Hindhope
Cleuch Head
Southdean
Lethem
Huntford
Biddestone
Shillmoor
Hyndlee
Carter Bar
Whitelee
1729
RAVENS KNOWE
Alwinton
Newton
Linshiels
River Coquet
Ramshope Lodge
Ramshope
Harbottle
Catcleugh Reservoir
Byrness
Holystone
REDESDALE FOREST
Byrness Camp
Singdean
1809
OH ME EDGE
Sills
North Yardhope
Redesdale Camp
Rochester
Myredykes
Deadwater
Horsley
Otterburn Camp
Ridge End
Elishaw
Emblehope
Kielder
1303
EARL'S SEAT
1388
Otterburn
Elsdon
Troughend
Old Town
Raylees
Highgreen Manor
Kielder Water
Gatehouse
Hareshaw Head
Falstone
Greenhaugh
West Woodburn
East Woodburn
Donkleywood
Stannersburn
Lanehead
The Eals
Hott
Charlton
Birks
Ridsdale
Bower
KIELDER FOREST
Hesleyside
Bellingham
Dunterley
1615
BLACK KNOWE
Redesmouth
THE PENNINE WAY
Carrycoats Hall
Clintburn
Thockrington
Birtley
Colts Crag Reservoir
Churnsike Lodge
WARK FOREST
Little Swinburne
Whygate
Stonehaugh
Wark
Great Swinburne
Park End
Chipchase Castle
Gunnerton
Bewcastle
Shopford
Butterburn
Nunwick
Barrasford
A68
A698
A699
A6088
B6436
B6352
B6351
B6401
B6400
B6358
B6357
B6320
B6342
River Tweed
R Teviot
REDE
3
2
1
0
9
8
6
7
8
9

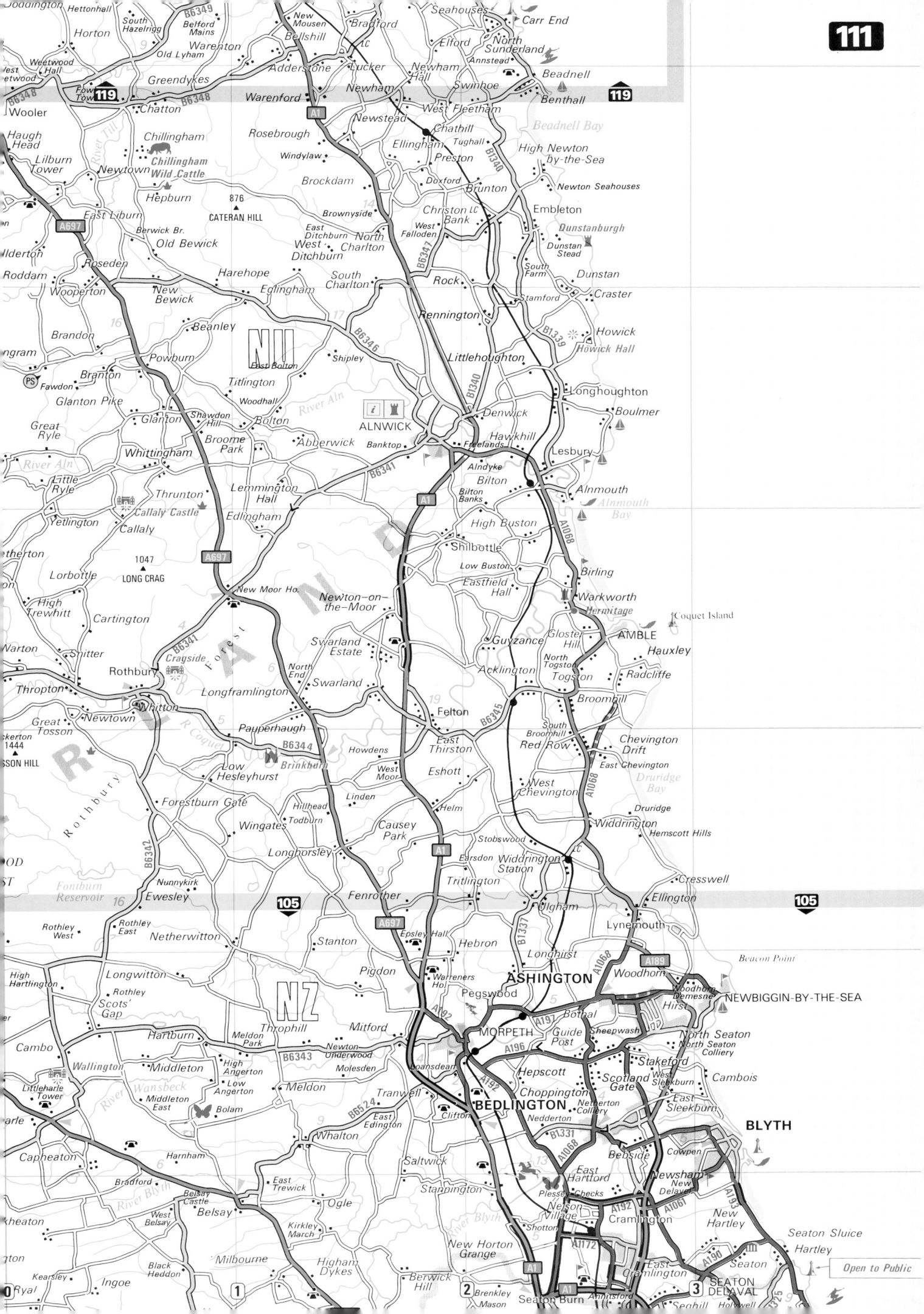

111
Hettonhall
Horton
South Hazelrigg
Belford Mains
Warenton
Old Lyham
Weetwood Hall
Greendykes
Fowberry Tower
119
Chatton
Wooler
Adderstone
Lucker
New Mousen
Bellshill
Bradford
Seahouses
Carr End
North Sunderland
Elford
Annstead
Beadnell
Benthall
Newham
Newham Hall
Swinhoe
Warenford
West Fleetham
Newstead
Chathill
Tughall
Beadnell Bay
High Newton by-the-Sea
Newton Seahouses
Ellingham
Preston
Doxford
Brunton
Embleton
Christon Bank
West Falloden
Dunstanburgh
Dunstan Stead
South Farm
Dunstan
Craster
Stamford
Rock
Rennington
Howick
Howick Hall
Littlehoughton
Longhoughton
Boulmer
Denwick
Hawkhill
Freelands
Lesbury
Aldyke
Bilton
Bilton Banks
Alnmouth
Alnmouth Bay
High Buston
Shilbottle
Low Buston
Birling
Eastfield Hall
Warkworth
Hermitage
Coquet Island
AMBLE
Hauxley
Guyzance
Gloster Hill
North Togston
Togston
Radcliffe
Acklington
Broomhill
South Broomhill
Chevington Drift
East Chevington
Red Row
West Chevington
Druridge Bay
Druridge
Widdrington
Hemscott Hills
Widdrington Station
Cresswell
Ellington
105
Lynemouth
Beacon Point
Woodhorn
Woodhorn Demesne
NEWBIGGIN-BY-THE-SEA
Hirst
ASHINGTON
Longhirst
Ulgham
Tritlington
Stobswood
Earsdon
Felton
East Thirston
Eshott
Helm
Causey Park
Swarland
Swarland Estate
North End
Newton-on-the-Moor
Howdens
West Moor
Linden
Hillhead
Todburn
Longhorsley
Wingates
Fenrother
Chillingham
Chillingham Wild Cattle
Haugh Head
Lilburn Tower
Newtown
Hepburn
876
CATERAN HILL
East Lilburn
Berwick Br.
Old Bewick
Rosebrough
Windylaw
Brockdam
Brownyside
East Ditchburn
West Ditchburn
North Charlton
South Charlton
Roseden
Roddam
Wooperton
Harehope
New Bewick
Eglingham
Beanley
Brandon
Powburn
Branton
Fawdon
Shipley
NU
East Bolton
Titlington
Woodhall
River Aln
ALNWICK
Banktop
Glanton Pike
Glanton
Shawdon Hill
Bolton
Great Ryle
Broome Park
Abberwick
Whittingham
Little Ryle
Thrunton
Lemmington Hall
Callaly Castle
Callaly
Edlingham
Yetlington
1047
LONG CRAG
Lorbottle
New Moor Ho.
High Trewhitt
Cartington
Snitter
Crayside
Rothbury
Thropton
Whitton
Great Tosson
Newtown
Longframlington
Pauperhaugh
Brinkburn
Low Hesleyhurst
Forestburn Gate
Rothbury
Fontburn Reservoir
Nunnykirk
Ewesley
Rothley West
Rothley East
Netherwitton
Stanton
Epsley Hall
Hebron
High Hartlington
Longwitton
Rothley
Scots' Gap
Pigdon
Warreners Ho.
Pegswood
NZ
Throphill
Mitford
Bothal
MORPETH
Guide Post
Sheepwash
North Seaton
North Seaton Colliery
Stakeford
Cambois
Cambo
Hartburn
Meldon Park
Newton Underwood
Molesden
Wallington
Middleton
High Angerton
Low Angerton
Meldon
Loansdean
Hepscott
Scotland Gate
West Sleekburn
East Sleekburn
Choppington
BEDLINGTON
Netherton Colliery
Nedderton
Littleharle Tower
Middleton East
Bolam
Tranwell
Clifton
East Edington
Whalton
Bebside
Cowpen
BLYTH
Capheaton
Harnham
Saltwick
East Hartford
Newsham
New Delaval
Bradford
East Trewick
Belsay Castle
Belsay
West Belsay
Ogle
Stannington
Plessey Checks
Nelson Village
Cramlington
New Hartley
Seaton Sluice
Hartley
Shotton
Kirkley March
New Horton Grange
Milbourne
Higham Dykes
Berwick Hill
East Cramlington
Seaton
Open to Public
SEATON DELAVAL
Black Heddon
Kearsley
Ingoe
Ryal
Brenkley
Mason
Seaton Burn
Annitsford
Seghill
Holywell

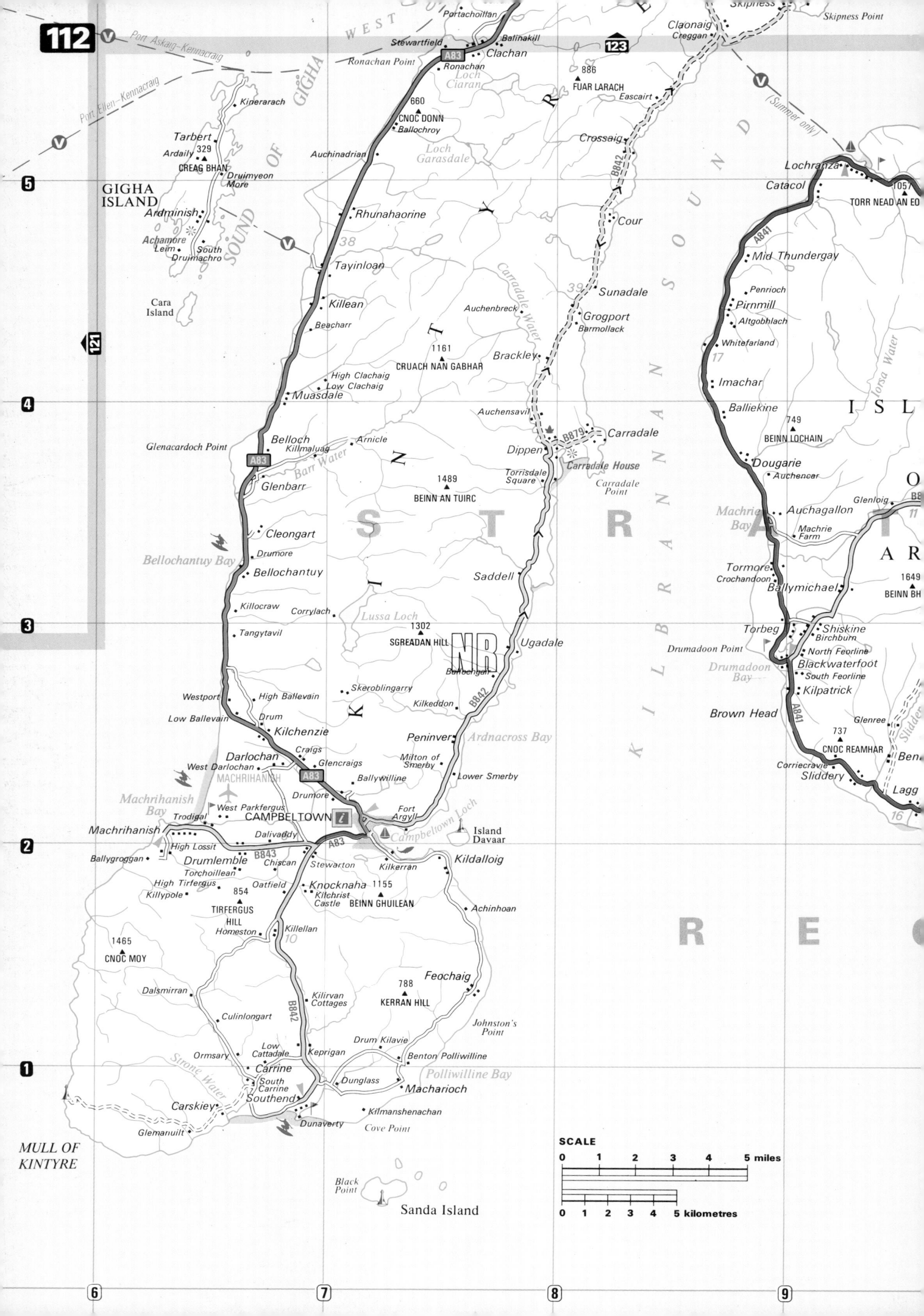

GIGHA ISLAND
Kinerarach
Tarbert
Ardaily
329
CREAG BHAN
Druimyeon More
Ardminish
Achamore
Leim
South Druimachro
Cara Island
SOUND OF GIGHA
Port Askaig–Kennacraig
Port Ellen–Kennacraig
Portachoillan
Stewartfield
Balinakill
Clachan
Ronachan Point
Ronachan
Loch Ciaran
660
CNOC DONN
Ballochroy
Auchinadrian
Loch Garasdale
Rhunahaorine
Tayinloan
Killean
Beacharr
High Clachaig
Low Clachaig
Muasdale
Glenacardoch Point
Belloch
Killmaluag
Arnicle
Barr Water
Glenbarr
Cleongart
Bellochantuy Bay
Drumore
Bellochantuy
Killocraw
Corrylach
Tangytavil
Lussa Loch
1302
SGREADAN HILL
NR
Westport
High Ballevain
Low Ballevain
Drum
Kilchenzie
Skeroblingarry
Kilkeddon
Darlochan
West Darlochan
MACHRIHANISH
Craigs
Glencraigs
Ballywilline
Machrihanish Bay
Trodigal
West Parkfergus
CAMPBELTOWN
Drumore
Machrihanish
Dalivaddy
High Lossit
Ballygroggan
Drumlemble
Chiscan
Stewarton
Kilkerran
Torchoillean
High Tirfergus
Killypole
854
TIRFERGUS HILL
Oatfield
Knocknaha
Kilchrist Castle
1155
BEINN GHUILEAN
Homeston
Killellan
1465
CNOC MOY
Dalsmirran
Kilirvan Cottages
Culinlongart
788
KERRAN HILL
Feochaig
Johnston's Point
Ormsary
Low Cattadale
Keprigan
Drum Kilavie
Benton Polliwilline
Carrine
South Carrine
Southend
Strone Water
Dunglass
Machariooch
Polliwilline Bay
Carskiey
Dunaverty
Kilmanshenachan
Glemanuilt
Cove Point
MULL OF KINTYRE
Black Point
Sanda Island
Island Davaar
Campbeltown Loch
Kildalloig
Achinhoan
Fort Argyll
Lower Smerby
Milton of Smerby
Peninver
Ardnacross Bay
Ballochgair
Ugadale
Saddell
1489
BEINN AN TUIRC
1161
CRUACH NAN GABHAR
Auchenbreck
Carradale Water
Brackley
Auchensavil
Carradale
Dippen
Carradale House
Carradale Point
Torrisdale Square
Sunadale
Grogport
Barmollack
Cour
Crossaig
Eascairt
886
FUAR LARACH
Claonaig
Creggan
Skipness
Skipness Point
KINTYRE
KILBRANNAN SOUND
STRATHCLYDE
WEST LOCH TARBERT
(Summer only)
Lochranza
Catacol
1057
TORR NEAD AN EO
Mid Thundergay
Penrioch
Pirnmill
Altgobhlach
Whitefarland
Imachar
Iorsa Water
Balliekine
749
BEINN LOCHAIN
Dougarie
Auchencar
Machrie Bay
Auchagallon
Glenloig
Machrie Farm
Tormore
Crochandoon
Ballymichael
1649
BEINN BH
Torbeg
Shiskine
Birchburn
Drumadoon Point
North Feorline
Drumadoon Bay
Blackwaterfoot
South Feorline
Kilpatrick
Brown Head
Glenree
737
CNOC REAMHAR
Corriecravie
Sliddery
Lagg
A83
B842
B843
B879
A841
SCALE
0 1 2 3 4 5 miles
0 1 2 3 4 5 kilometres

123
121

Ardscalpsie Point
Kingarth
Bruchag
GREAT CUMBRAE ISLAND
Ferry
Ballochmartin
A760
Blairpark
Glengarth
East Loch
Lochhead
123
Quochag
Kerrytonlia
Kilchattan Bay
Upper Kirkton
MILLPORT
A78
Kelburn
Muirhead Reservoir
Whitehill
Kerse
East Kerse
Largizean
Kilchattan
Mid Kirkton
New Town
Fairlie
Camphill Reservoir
North Hourat
Kilbirnie
South Camphill
Kilbirnie Loch
Beith
B777
Gateside
ND OF BUTE
Dunagoil
The Tan
Fairlie Roads
South Hourat
Glengarnock
South Garrochty
Garroch
LITTLE CUMBRAE ISLAND
Poteath
Longbar
Barrmill
Campbelton
North Kilrusken
South Kilrusken
Crosbie
Pitcon Mains
The Den
Drakemyre
B706
Highfield
Portencross
B7048
B781
Giffordland
Dalry
Burnhouse
West Kilbride
Munnoch
B780
B707
Auchenmade
Seamill
A737
Auchentiber
Auchenskeith
High C
Sannox
Dalgarven
Crossgates
B780
A78
B778
A736
Corrie
KILWINNING
B785
North Fergushill
Torranyard
A738
Eglinton Castle
Montgreenan
South Fergushill
ARDROSSAN
STEVENSTON
Cunninghamhead
A841
SALTCOATS
A78
B7080
Perceton
Girdle Toll
Brodick-Ardrossan
IRVINE
Knockentib
Bankhead
Brodick
Springside
B7081
Brodick Bay
114
Dreghorn
Fullarton
A71
Crosshouse
Irvine Bay
Drybridge
Gatehead
Strathwhillan
Brodick
North Corrygills
South Corrygills
CLYDE
A759
Kilnfold
Dundonald
Clauchlands Point
Barassie
Collenan
Bogend
Margnaheglish
FIRTH
Loans
Symington
Lamlash
Lamlash Bay
Monamore Bridge
HOLY ISLAND
A759
TROON
Cordon
A841
A78
NS
Monktonhill
Sandhills
Rosen
503
Auchencairn
Kingscross
Monkton
Knockenkelly
West Orangefield
A77
PRESTWICK
Whiting Bay
Whiting Bay
AA 78
Largymore
New Prestwick
A79
St Quivox
A758
Largybeg
Dippin Head
A719
Whitletts
Dippin
Auchenhew
AYR
Ayr
Wallacetow
Kildonan
Belston
Sound of Pladda
A77
Pladda
Doonfoot
Belmont
Burns Cottage
Heads of Ayr
Burns Monument
Alloway
A713
Lagg
106
Fisherton
Doonholm
A719
B7024
Dunure
Purclewan
Carcluie
Burnton
Dalrymple
Skeldon Mills
Sauchrie
Culroy
Drumshang
Knockdon
Minishant
ION
Knoweside
B742
Culzean Bay
Humeston
A719
Guiltreehill
Culzean
Lyonston
Grimmet
Pennyglen
Orchard Farm
B7023
Whitefaulds
MAYBOLE
Maidenhead Bay
Kirkmichael
PS
Morriston
Maidens
A77
Crossraguel
Aitkenhead
Jameston
B7023
Loch Spallander
Kirkoswald
Turnberry Bay
Souter Johnnie's House
Threave
B7045
Crosshill
Turnberry
High Drumdow
Milton
Roan of Craigoch
Kilkerran
Knockgardner
Dowhill
Wallacetown
Kilgrammie
Dipple
Ladybank
B741
Low Craighead
Dailly
Water of Girvan
AILSA CRAIG
110
Maxwellston
Bargany
A77
Mains
Old Dailly
0
1
2
3

114
Sandbank
Ardnadam
Strone
KILCREGGAN
DUNOON
Kirn
GOUROCK
GREENOCK
PORT GLASGOW
Cardross
Renton
Alexandria
Jamestown
Bonhill
DUMBARTON
Milton
Bowling
Old Kilpatrick
ERSKINE
RENFREW
Bullwood
Inverkip
Wemyss Bay
Innellan
Toward
Skelmorlie
ROTHESAY
Ascog
Kerrycroy
LARGS
Kilmacolm
Bridge of Weir
Houston
Kilbarchan
Elderslie
JOHNSTONE
Howwood
Lochwinnoch
GREAT CUMBRAE ISLAND
MILLPORT
LITTLE CUMBRAE ISLAND
Fairlie
Kilbirnie
Beith
Glengarnock
Dalry
West Kilbride
Seamill
Portencross
ARDROSSAN
SALTCOATS
STEVENSTON
KILWINNING
IRVINE
Dreghorn
Dunlop
STEWARTON
Kilmaurs
KILMARNOCK
Riccarton
Hurlford
Dundonald
Barassie
Loans
Symington
TROON
Monkton
PRESTWICK
New Prestwick
St Quivox
Tarbolton
Mossblown
Annbank
Irvine Bay
IRISH LAW
BEINN RUADH
124
123
113
106
1
2
3
4

116
DUNIPACE
DENNY
Stenhousemuir
Larbert
Carron
Skinflats
GRANGEMOUTH
BO'NESS
Grangepans
Crombie
Charlestown
Limekilns
Carriden
Muirhouses
Blackness
Camelon
FALKIRK
Head of Muir
Dennyloanhead
Bonnybridge
High Bonnybridge
Longcroft
Banknock
High Banton
Banton
KILSYTH
TOMTAIN
1487
Castlecary
Kelvinhead
Greenhill
Glen Village
Reddingmuirhead
Redding
Westquarter
Polmont
Brightons
Rumford
Shieldhill
Maddiston
California
Lauriston
Inveravon
Kinneil
Borrowstoun
Champany
Hopetoun
LINLITHGOW
Linlithgow Palace
Philpstoun
Old Philpstoun
Burnside
Bridgend
Three Miletown
Winchburgh
Whitecross
Union Canal
Loan
Cockleroy
Torphichen
Torphichen Preceptory
Wester Ochiltree
Ecclesmachan
Uphall
Dechmont
Broxburn
126
Uphall Station
Pumpherston
Cairnpapple Hill
Drumcross
BATHGATE
Belvedere
Boghall
LIVINGSTON
Mid Calder
Livingston Village
Seafield
Oakbank
Bellsquarry
Polbeth
Corston
West Calder
Auchinstarry
Croy
Dullatur
CUMBERNAULD
Eastfield
Condorrat
Luggiebank
Jawcraig
Slamannan
Crossburn
Avonbridge
Greyrigg
Standburn
Binniehill
Babbithill
Westfield
Balmuir
Limerigg
High Limerigg
125
Annathill
Riggend
Greengairs
Wattston
Longriggend
Marnock
Glenboig
Brackenhurst
Stand
Airdriehill
Glenmavis
Caldercruix
Hillend Reservoir
Blackridge
Woodend
ARMADALE
Bathville
Whiteside
Westrigg
Plains
Hillend
Forestfield
AIRDRIE
Coatdyke
Craigneuk
Old Monkland
Calderbank
Gartness
Chapelhall
Bentfoot
Eastfield
Harthill
WHITBURN
East Whitburn
Blackburn
Stoneyburn
Longridge
Mossend
Loganlea
Addiewell
Kirk of Shotts
Salsburgh
Newhouse
Birkenshaw
Viewpark
Mossend
Holytown
Bellshill
New Stevenston
Newarthill
Carfin
Cleland
Shotts
Hartwood
Dykehead
Stane
Fauldhouse
Greenburn
Breich
West Mains
West Torphin
East Torphin
Harburnhead
Wester Causewayend
Baad's Mill
North Cobbinshaw
Cobbinshaw Loch
South Cobbinshaw
Woolfords Cottages
Woolfords
Tarbrax
South Tarbrax
Headlesscross
Allanbank
Bellside
Bonkle
Allanton
MOTHERWELL
Craigneuk
115
Newmains
Morningside
WISHAW
Shieldmuir
Netherton
Waterloo
Bogside
Wildmanbridge
NS
Climpy
1029
HARE HILL
Forth
Wilsontown
Tashieburn
Rootpark
Stobwood
Auchengray
Ferniegair
Allanton
Eddlewood
Meikle Earnock
Overtown
Larkhall
Law
Castlehill
Carluke
Westertown
Yieldshields
Braehead
Quarter
Millheugh
Garrion Tower
Dalserf
Ashgill
Rosebank
Roadmeetings
West Mains
Struthernill
Birkenshaw
Swinhill
Stonehouse
Netherburn
Kilcadzow
Harelaw
Braidwood
High Brownmuir Heads
Glassford
Draffan
Crossford
Cartland
West End
Carstairs
Carnwath
Kame-end
Newbigging
Walston
Wester Walston
Anston
Dunsyre
Dolphinton
Hazelbank
Nemphlar
Ravenstruther
Carstairs Junction
Bankhead
Blackwood
Auchenheath
Burnfoot
Kirkmuirhill
Kirkfieldbank
Greenrig
LANARK
Bankhead
New Lanark
Hyndford Bridge
Pettinain
Greenshields
Libberton
Elsrickle
Sandford
Bonanhill
Boghead
Burnbrae
Deadwaters
Cauldcoats
Dillarburn
Millhill
Grangehall
Whitecastle
Candyburn
Brocketsbrae
Townfoot of Netherton
Hillhead
Shieldhill
Meadowflat
Lesmahagow
Hawksland
Millmoor
Harleyholm
Warrenhill
Quothquan
Newtown of Covington
BIGGAR
Skirling
Spittal
Cambuswallace
New Trows
Auchlochan
Eastertown
Douglas Water
Drumalbin
Eastend
Thankerton
Stockbriggs
Eastfield
Causewayend
St. John's Kirk
Symington
Wolfclyde
Cumberhead
Bellfield
Coalburn
1711
NUTBERRY HILL
Braehead
Rigside
2320
TINTO
Tinto Hills
Coulter
Bankend
Happendon
Uddington
Wiston
River Clyde
Glenholm
Greenhill
Douglas Castle
Douglas West
New Mains
Newton
Loanhead
Culteralters
Waterhead
Douglas
Lamington
Burnfoot
Glenbuck
Hazelside
Glespin
Hartside
2455
CULTER FELL
Glencotho
108
River Ayr
Carmacoup
1286
AUCHENSAUGH HILL
Roberton
Ladygill
Maidencots
Wandel
Strand
M9
M876
M80
M8
M74
A9
A80
A803
A73
A89
A8
A71
A72
A721
A723
A726
A70
A74
A702
A704
A706
A801
A899
A904
B7066
B7015
B7016
B7055
B7056
B7010
B7008
B803
B8048
B825
B8028
B8084
B792
B9080
B715
B7018

117
FIRTH OF FORTH
Hillend
St. Colme
Dalgety Bay
INVERKEITHING
North Queensferry
Inchkeith
Dirleton
Gullane Bay
Aberlady Bay
Aberlady
Luffness
Myreton Motor Museum
Mungoswells
Gosford Bay
Spittal
Ballencrieff
Athelstaneford
Longniddry
West Garleton
Huntington
Dalmeny House
Cramond Island
Granton
Dalmeny
Cramond
Lauriston Castle
Leith
EDINBURGH
COCKENZIE AND PORT SETON
PRESTONPANS
Dalmeny Rows
Cramond Bridge
Davidson's Mains
Warriston
Seton Mains
Elvingston
Turnhouse
Kirkliston
Ingliston
EDINBURGH (TURNHOUSE)
ARTHUR'S SEAT
Duddingston
Portobello
MUSSELBURGH
Fisherrow
Pinkie House
TRANENT
Gladsmuir
Gogar
Corstorphine
Morningside
Newcraighall
Inveresk
Wallyford
Macmerry
Suntrap
126
Craiglockhart
Craigmillar
Liberton
Danderhall
Elphinstone
127
New Winton
Samuelston
Bolton
New Town
Long Hermiston
Juniper Green
Colinton
Millerhill
Whitecraig
Ormiston
Easter Pencaitland
Pencaitland
Gilmerton
Crossgatehall
Dalkeith Park
Cousland
East Saltoun
Bankrugg
Currie
Torphin
Kinleith
Fairmilehead
Kaimes
LASSWADE
DALKEITH
West Saltoun
Newmills
Balerno
Malleny
Straiton
Hillend
LOANHEAD
Eskbank
Newbattle
Mayfield
Peaston Bank
Peaston
Marvingston
Malleny Mills
Boghall
BONNYRIGG
Chesterhill
Gilchriston
Woodhouselee
Easter Howgate
Bilston
Polton
Pathhead
Kidlaw
Long Newton
Threipmuir Reservoir
1636
BLACK HILL
Milton Bridge
Roslin
Rosslyn
Newtongrange
Newtonloan
Dewartown
Upper Keith
Humbie
Rosewell
Newlandrig
Crichton
Crichton Dean
Fala Dam
Blegbie
Gourlaw
Aikendean
Arniston Engine
Auchendinny
Crichton
Gorebridge
Saughland
Fala
Silverburn
PENICUIK
Newbigging
Carrington
Borthwick
North Middleton
Tynehead
Soutra Mains
670
CRIB LAW
Pomathorn
River North Esk
NT
Temple
Middleton
Howgate
Mount Lothian
Yorkston
Gilston
Carlops
Leadburn
Falahill
Craigburn
Heriot Ho.
Hillhouse
Whim
Heriot
Crookston Mains
Oxton
Netherhowden
Carfrae
Cowdenburn
Gladhouse Reservoir
MOORFOOT HILLS
West Linton
Waterheads
Brockhouse
Blackburn
Halmyre Mains
Fountainhall
Trabrown
Romannobridge
1570
WETHER LAW
Damside
River South Esk
Bankhouse
Torquhan
Whitlaw
LAUDER
Mountain Cross
Eddleston
Cathpair
Watherston
Killochyett
Blyth Bridge
Wormiston
Stow
Stagehall
Castlecraig
Drochil
1975
DUNSLAIR HEIGHTS
2163
WINDLESTRAW LAW
Lugate
Threepwood
BORDERS REGION
Lyne
Westerhappre
Hallyne
PEEBLES
Ferniehirst
Bow
HEIGHTS
Colquhar
Glentress
Bowland
Neidpath
Kings Muir
1648
LEE PEN
Kailzie
Kirkburn
Cardrona
Walkerburn
Holylee
Blackhaugh
Torwoodlee Mains
Buckholm
Stobo
Kirkton Manor
Scottish Textiles Museum
Clovenfords
GALASHIELS
CARDRONA FOREST
INNERLEITHEN
1389
MEIGLE HILL
Bridgend
Castlehill
Traquair
ELIBANK AND TRAQUAIR FOREST
Peel
Caddonfoot
Abbotsford
Bellspool
Dawyck House
River Tweed
Traquair
Boleside
Drumelzier
Glenrath
Kirkhouse
The Rink
Posso
Glen House
Fairnilee
Newhall
Ovenscloss
Lindean
2417
PYKESTONE HILL
Langhaugh
Broadmeadows
Yarrowford
Bridgelands
Linglie
108
109
SELKIRK
Yarrow
Bowhill
2285
BLACK LAW
Bowhill
Philiphaugh
Howden
2
3
4
5
Yarrow Feus
Midlem
118
A921
A90
A902
A720
A8
A1
A199
A71
A68
A6094
A7
A702
A70
A703
A766
A6093
A6137
A198
A1348
B1348
B1377
B1343
B1345
B6414
B6371
B6355
B6368
B6372
B6458
B7007
B709
B7059
A72
B7062
B710
B6362
B7060
A708
A6091
B6453
A697
B9085
B7003
B6369

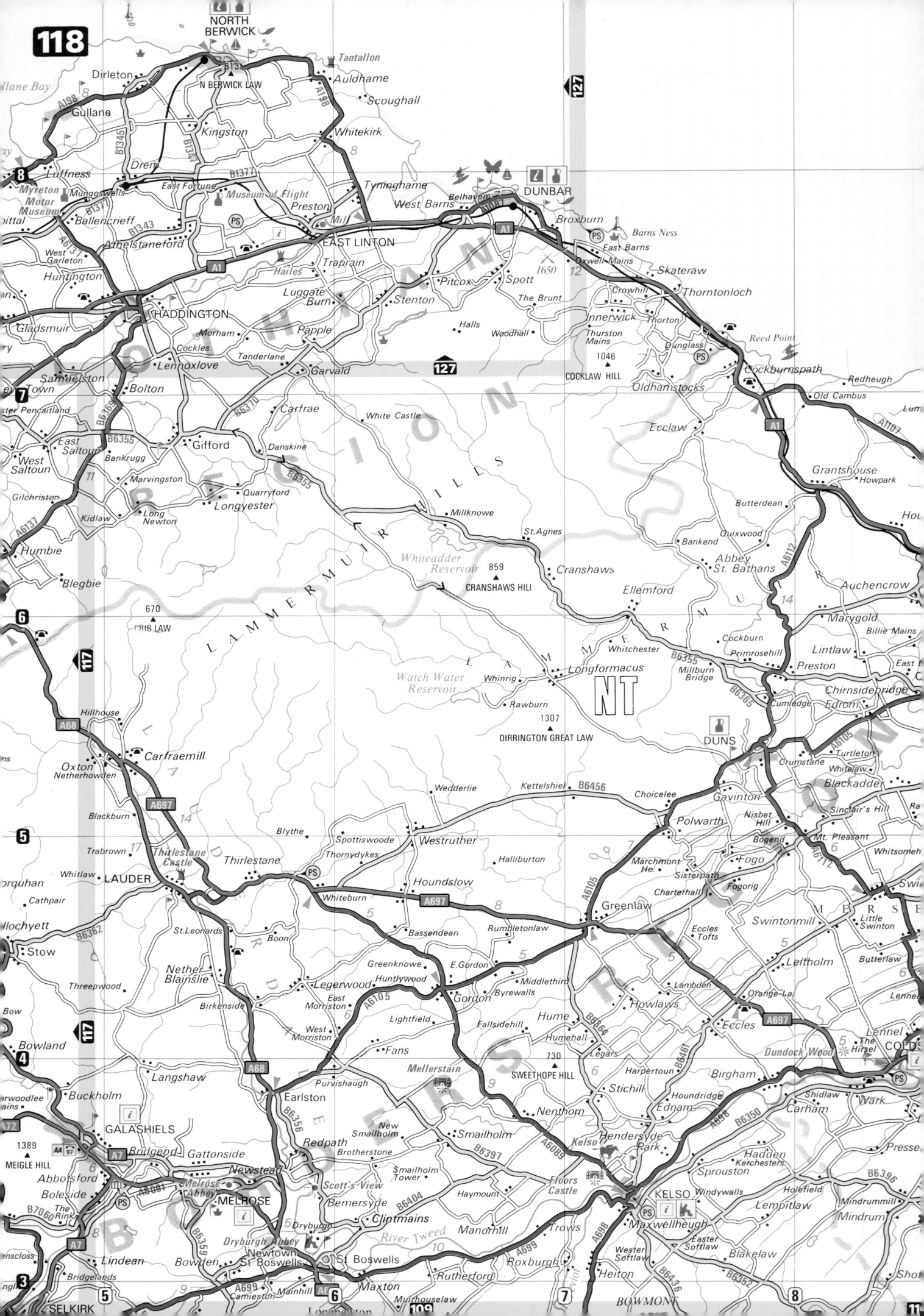
NORTH BERWICK
N BERWICK LAW
Dirleton
Gullane
Tantallon
Auldhame
Scoughall
Whitekirk
Kingston
Drem
Luffness
Myreton Motor Museum
Mungoswells
East Fortune
Museum of Flight
Tyninghame
West Barns
Belhaven
DUNBAR
Preston
Ballencrieff
Athelstaneford
EAST LINTON
Broxburn
Barns Ness
East Barns
Oxwell Mains
Skateraw
Thorntonloch
West Garleton
Huntington
Hailes
Traprain
Pitcox
Spott
The Brunt
Crowhill
Innerwick
Thorton
Thurston Mains
Dunglass
Reed Point
Luggate Burn
Stenton
Halls
Woodhall
HADDINGTON
Gladsmuir
Morham
Papple
Cockles
Lennoxlove
Tanderlane
Garvald
COCKLAW HILL
Oldhamstocks
Cockburnspath
Redheugh
Old Cambus
Samuelston
Bolton
Pencaitland
Carfrae
White Castle
Ecclaw
East Saltoun
West Saltoun
Bankrugg
Gifford
Danskine
Grantshouse
Howpark
Marvingston
Quarryford
Longyester
Long Newton
Gilchriston
Kidlaw
Milknowe
Butterdean
St.Agnes
Quixwood
Bankend
Humbie
Whiteadder Reservoir
CRANSHAWS HILL
Cranshaws
Abbey St. Bathans
Auchencrow
Blegbie
Ellemford
CRIB LAW
LAMMERMUIR HILLS
Marygold
Billie Mains
Cockburn
Whitchester
Primrosehill
Lintlaw
Millburn Bridge
Watch Water Reservoir
Whinrig
Longformacus
Preston
NT
Rawburn
DIRRINGTON GREAT LAW
Cumledge
Chirnsidebridge
Edrom
Hillhouse
DUNS
Turtleton
Crumstane
Whitelaw
Carfraemill
Oxton
Netherhowden
Wedderlie
Kettelshiel
Choicelee
Blackadder
Gavinton
Blackburn
Polwarth
Nisbet Hill
Sinclair's Hill
Blythe
Spottiswoode
Westruther
Bogend
Mt. Pleasant
Trabrown
Thirlestane Castle
Thornydykes
Thirlestane
Halliburton
Marchmont Ho.
Fogo
Whitsome
Whitlaw
LAUDER
Houndslow
Sisterpath
Fogorig
Cathpair
Whiteburn
Charterhall
Greenlaw
Swintonmill
Little Swinton
St.Leonards
Bassendean
Rumbletonlaw
Eccles Tofts
Stow
Boon
Greenknowe
E.Gordon
Leitholm
Butterlaw
Nether Blainslie
Huntlywood
Middlethird
Threepwood
Legerwood
Gordon
Byrewalls
Lambden
Howlaws
Orange Lane
Birkenside
East Morriston
Bow
Lightfield
Hume
Eccles
Fallsidehill
Humehall
West Morriston
Bowland
Fans
SWEETHOPE HILL
Legars
Lennel
The Hirsel
Dundock Wood
Langshaw
Mellerstain
Harpertoun
Bingham
Purvishaugh
Stichill
Buckholm
Earlston
Hendersyde Park
Houndridge
Ednam
Shidlaw
Wark
Carham
GALASHIELS
Nenthorn
New Smailholm
Smailholm
MEIGLE HILL
Bridgend
Gattonside
Redpath
Brotherstone
Kelso
Hadden
Kerchesters
Presse
Sprouston
Abbotsford
Newstead
Smailholm Tower
Boleside
Melrose Abbey
MELROSE
Scott's View
Haymount
Floors Castle
KELSO
Windywalls
Holefield
Mindrummill
Lempitlaw
Mindrum
Bemersyde
Clintmains
The Rink
Dryburgh
Dryburgh Abbey
River Tweed
Manorhill
Trows
Maxwellheugh
Easter Softlaw
Wester Softlaw
Blakelaw
Lindean
Bowden
Newtown St Boswells
St Boswells
Roxburgh
Bridgelands
Camieston
Mainhill
Maxton
Rutherford
Heiton
SELKIRK
Muirhouselaw
BOWMONT
LOTHIAN REGION
BORDERS REGION
MERSE

SCALE

| 0 | 1 | 2 | 3 | 4 | 5 miles |

| 0 | 1 | 2 | 3 | 4 | 5 kilometres |

ST ABB'S HEAD

Northfield

St Abbs

ham

Whitecross

Acredale

Cairncross — EYEMOUTH

Biglawburn *Gunsgreenhill*

Reston A1

Ayton *Burnmouth*

Prenderguest
usewaybank

Whiterig

Edington

B6355

Foulden *Lamberton*

Clappers A1

ugh *1333* *Conundrum*

Foulden A6105 *Meadowhill*
Newton

Indykes *Hutton* *High Letham*

Paxton BERWICK-UPON-TWEED

Hutton Mains B6461

Sunwick *Tweedmouth*

egatehead *Spittal*

Loanend

me *Fishwick* *East Ord*

B6461

Horndean *Horncliffe* *West Longridge* *Borewell*

13 *Thorntonpark* *Murton*

ykirk *Thornton* *Unthank* *Scremerston*

Norham *Newburn*

Shoreswood *West* *Cheswick*
Allerdean

West *Shoresdean*
Newbiggin

kirk *Grindon* *Ancroft Ho.* *Goswick*
Ho.

15 *Shellacres* *Grindonrigg* *Felkington* *New* *Haggerston*
Haggerston

Twizel Bridge *Berrington* *Beal*
th Park

ngton *Duddo* *West Mains* *Fenhamhill*

Castle *Bowsden* *Kentstone* *Fenham*
Heaton

hill *Etal* *Kyloe* *Fenwick*
eed

relees *Crookham* *Heatherslaw Mill* B6353 *Lowick* *Buckton*

Branxton *The Lady Waterford Hall* *Brownridge* *Elwick*
Ford

1513 *Kimmerston* *Smeafield* *Ross*

14 *Holburn* *Low Middleton*
Flodden

Howtel A697 *Detchant* *Middleton* *Easington* *Budle*

B6352 *Milfield* *Nesbit* *Hetton Steads* *Belford* *Waren*
Mill

ton *Fenton* *Hettonlaw* *North* *Sionside* *Glororum*
Town *Hazelrigg*

Lanton *Doddington* *Hettonhall* *South* B6349 *New*
Hazelrigg *Mousen*

14 *Coupland* *Newtown* *Horton* *Belford* *Bellshill*
Mains

Yeavering B6351 *Warenton*

newton *Kirknewton* *Weetwood* *9* *Old Lyham*
Akeld *Hall*

9 *Bendor* *West* *Greendykes*
wood

NU

CAUSEWAY
FLOODED
AT HIGH TIDE

HOLY ISLAND

Holy *Castle Point*
Island *Lindisfarne Priory*

Burrows Hole

Staple *Inner* FARNE ISLANDS
Sound *Sound*

Bamburgh
Budle *Bamburgh*
Bay

Spindlestone *Burton* B1340
tc B1342

Open to Public

Bradford *Seahouses*
Elford

Adderstone *Lucker* *North* *Annstead*
Sunderland

Newham *Newham* *Beadnell*
Hall *inhoe*

Warenford *Benthall*

NORTHUMBERLAND

B6461

A698

B6525

A1

A167

9 *0* *1* *2* *111*

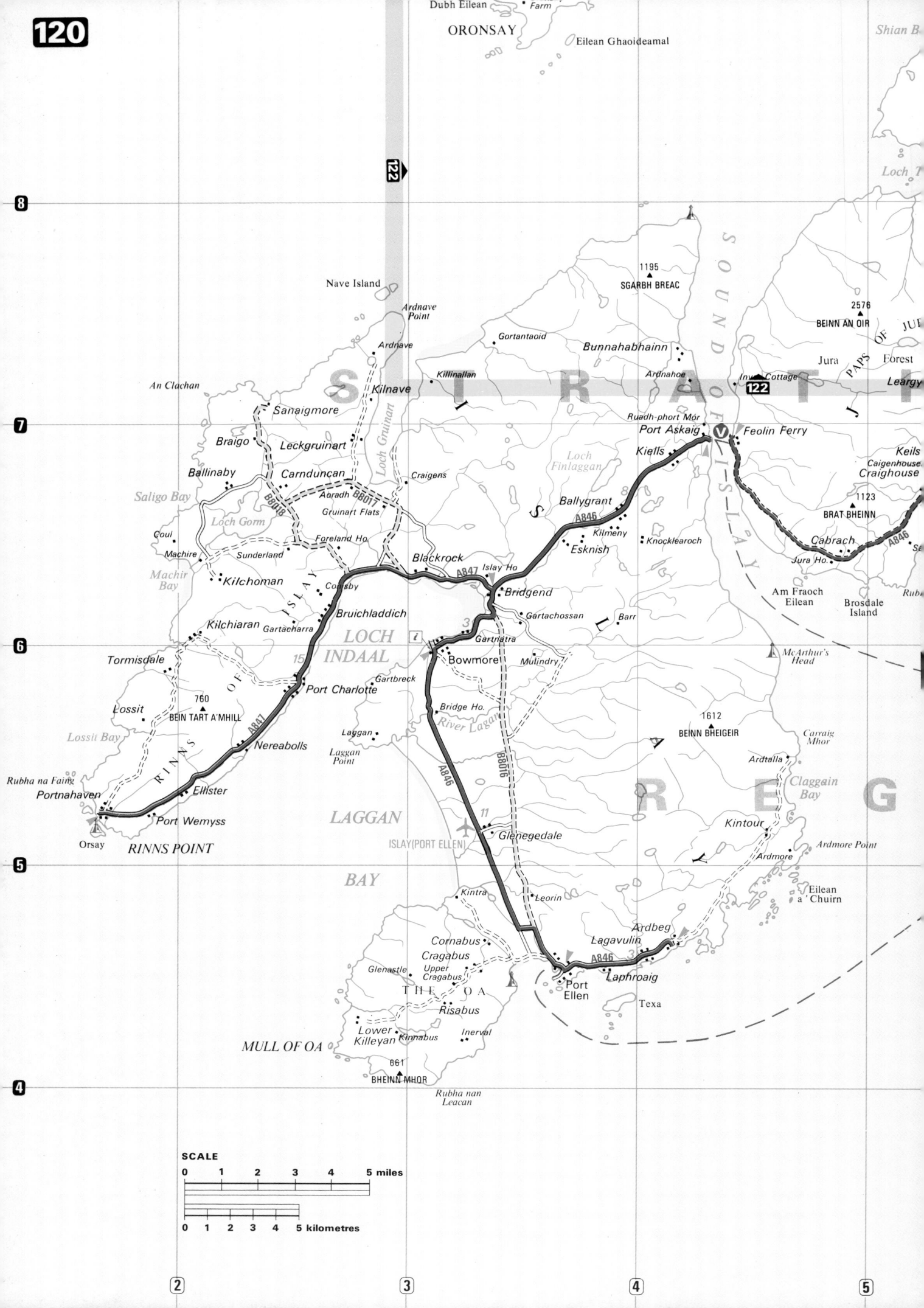

Dubh Eilean   • Farm

ORONSAY

○ Eilean Ghaoideamal

Shian B

122

8

Nave Island

Ardnave
Point

1195
▲
SGARBH BREAC

2576
▲
BEINN AN OIR

An Clachan

Ardnave

Gortantaoid

Bunnahabhainn

Jura Forest

S T R A T H

Kilnave

Killinallan

Ardnahoe

Inver Cottage
122

Leargy

7

Sanaigmore

Ruadh-phort Mór

Port Askaig ⱽ Feolin Ferry

Keils

Braigo

Leckgruinart

Kiells

Caigenhouse
Craighouse

Ballinaby

Carnduncan

Craigens

Ballygrant

1123
▲
BRAT BHEINN

Saligo Bay

B8018

Aoradh B8017

Loch
Finlaggan

A846

Kilmeny

Knocklearoch

Cabrach

A846

Loch Gorm

Gruinart Flats

S

Esknish

Jura Ho.

Coul

Foreland Ho.

Blackrock

Islay Ho.

Am Fraoch
Eilean

Brosdale
Island

Ru

Machire

Sunderland

A847

Bridgend

Gartachossan

Barr

6

Machir
Bay

Kilchoman

Conisby

Bruichladdich

L

Gartnatra

McArthur's
Head

Tormisdale

Kilchiaran Gartacharra

LOCH
INDAAL ⓘ Bowmore

Mulindry

Port Charlotte

Gartbreck

1612
▲
BEINN BHEIGEIR

Carraig
Mhor

Lossit

760
▲
BEIN TART A'MHILL

A847

Bridge Ho.

River Lagan

Ardtalla

Claggain
Bay

Lossit Bay

R
I
N
N
S

15

Laggan

Nereabolls

Laggan
Point

B8016

A846

A
Y

Kintour

Rubha na Faing

Portnahaven

Ellister

11

Glenegedale

Ardmore Point

Ardmore

Orsay

Port Wemyss

ISLAY(PORT ELLEN)

5

RINNS POINT

Eilean
a 'Chuirn

LAGGAN

Kintra

Leorin

Ardbeg

Lagavulin

BAY

Cornabus
Cragabus

Glenastle

Upper
Cragabus

A846

Laphroaig

Port
Ellen

Texa

T H E   O A

Risabus

Inerval

Lower
Killeyan Kinnabus

MULL OF OA

661
▲
BHEINN MHOR

Rubha nan
Leacan

4

SCALE

0   1   2   3   4   5 miles

0 1 2 3 4 5 kilometres

②   ③   ④   ⑤

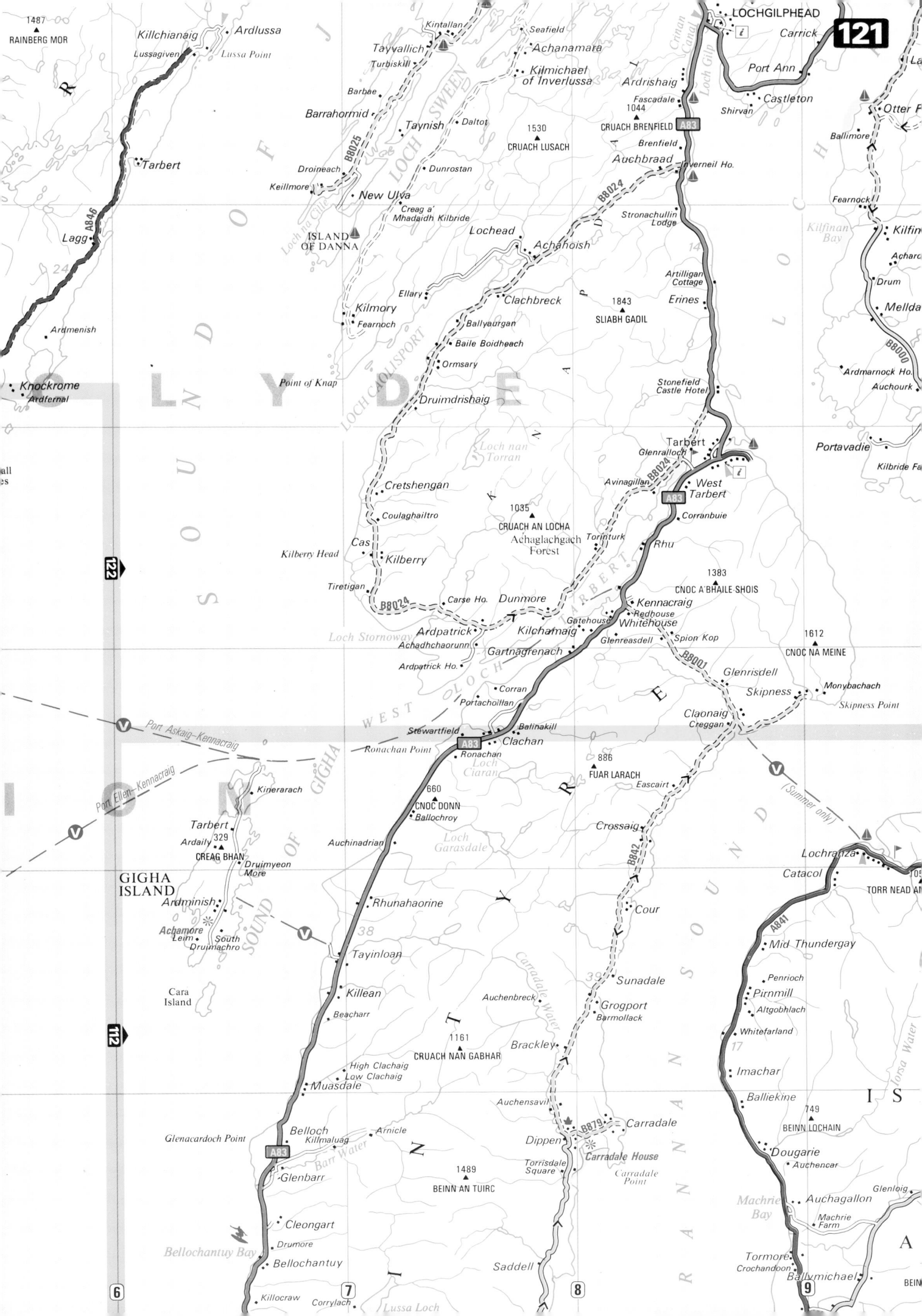

1487
RAINBERG MOR

Killchianaig • Ardlussa

Lussagiven • Lussa Point

Kintallan
Tayvallich
Turbiskill
• Seafield
• Achanamara
• Kilmichael
of Inverlussa
Ardrishaig
Fascadale
1044
CRUACH BRENFIELD A83
Carrick
Port Ann
Castleton
Shirvan
Otter F
La
Barbae
Barrahormid
Taynish • Daltot
1530
CRUACH LUSACH
Brenfield
Auchbraad Inverneil Ho.
Ballimore
Fearnock
Droineach
Keillmore
B8025
New Ulva • Dunrostan
Creag a'
Mhadaidh Kilbride
Lochhead
Achahoish
Stronachullin
Lodge
14
Tarbert

Lagg
A846

Ardmenish

Knockrome
Ardfernal

24

ISLAND
OF DANNA

Loch na Cille

LOCH SWEEN

Kilmory
Fearnoch

Ellary
Clachbreck
Ballyaurgan
• Baile Boidheach
• Ormsary
Druimdrishaig

Point of Knap

Loch Caolisport

LOCH CAOLISPORT

Artilligan
Cottage
Erines
1843
SLIABH GAOIL

Stonefield
Castle Hotel

Tarbert
Glenralloch
Avinagillan
A83
West
Tarbert
i
Corranbuie

Portavadie
Kilbride Fa

Ardmarnock Ho.
Auchourk

B8000

Kilfin
Acharc
Drum
Mellda

Kilfinan
Bay

LOCH FYNE

Loch nan
Torran

Cretshengan
Coulaghailtro

Cas
Kilberry Head
• Kilberry

Tiretigan
B8024

Carse Ho. Dunmore

Ardpatrick
Achadhchaorunn
Ardpatrick Ho.

Loch Stornoway

1035
CRUACH AN LOCHA
Achaglachgach
Forest
Torinturk
Rhu

Gatehouse
Kennacraig
Redhouse
Whitehouse
Glenreasdell
Kilchamaig
Gartnagrenach

Corran
Portachoillan

1383
CNOC A'BHAILE-SHOIS

Spion Kop

Glenrisdell

Skipness

Claonaig
Creggan

1612
CNOC NA MEINE

Monybachach

Skipness Point

B8001

KILBRANNAN SOUND

122

112

Port Askaig–Kennacraig V

Port Ellen–Kennacraig V

V

Kinererach

Tarbert
Ardaily
329
CREAG BHAN

GIGHA
ISLAND

Ardminish

Achamore
Leim
South
Druimachro

Cara
Island

Druimyeon
More

Stewartfield
Ronachan Point
A83
Ronachan

Balinakill
Clachan

Loch
Ciaran

886
FUAR LARACH
Eascairt

(Summer only) V

Lochranza
Catacol

105
TORR NEAD A

Auchinadrian

660
CNOC DONN
Ballochroy

Loch
Garasdale

Crossaig

B842

Cour

A841

Mid Thundergay

Penrioch
Pirnmill
Altgobhlach

SOUND OF GIGHA

38
Rhunahaorine

Tayinloan

Killean
Beacharr

1161
CRUACH NAN GABHAR

Auchenbreck

Brackley

39
Sunadale

Grogport
Barmollack

Whitefarland

17
Imachar

Balliekine

749
BEINN LOCHAIN

High Clachaig
Low Clachaig
Muasdale

Auchensavil

Carradale Water

B879
Carradale
Dippen

Torrisdale
Square
Carradale House
Carradale
Point

Dougarie
Auchencar

Glenloig

Machrie
Bay

Machrie
Farm

IS

I S

A

Belloch
Killmaluag
Arnicle

Glenacardoch Point
A83

Glenbarr

Cleongart

Barr Water

1489
BEINN AN TUIRC

Saddell

Auchagallon

Tormore
Crochandoon
Ballymichael

Bellochantuy Bay
Bellochantuy

Drumore

Killocraw Corrylach Lussa Loch

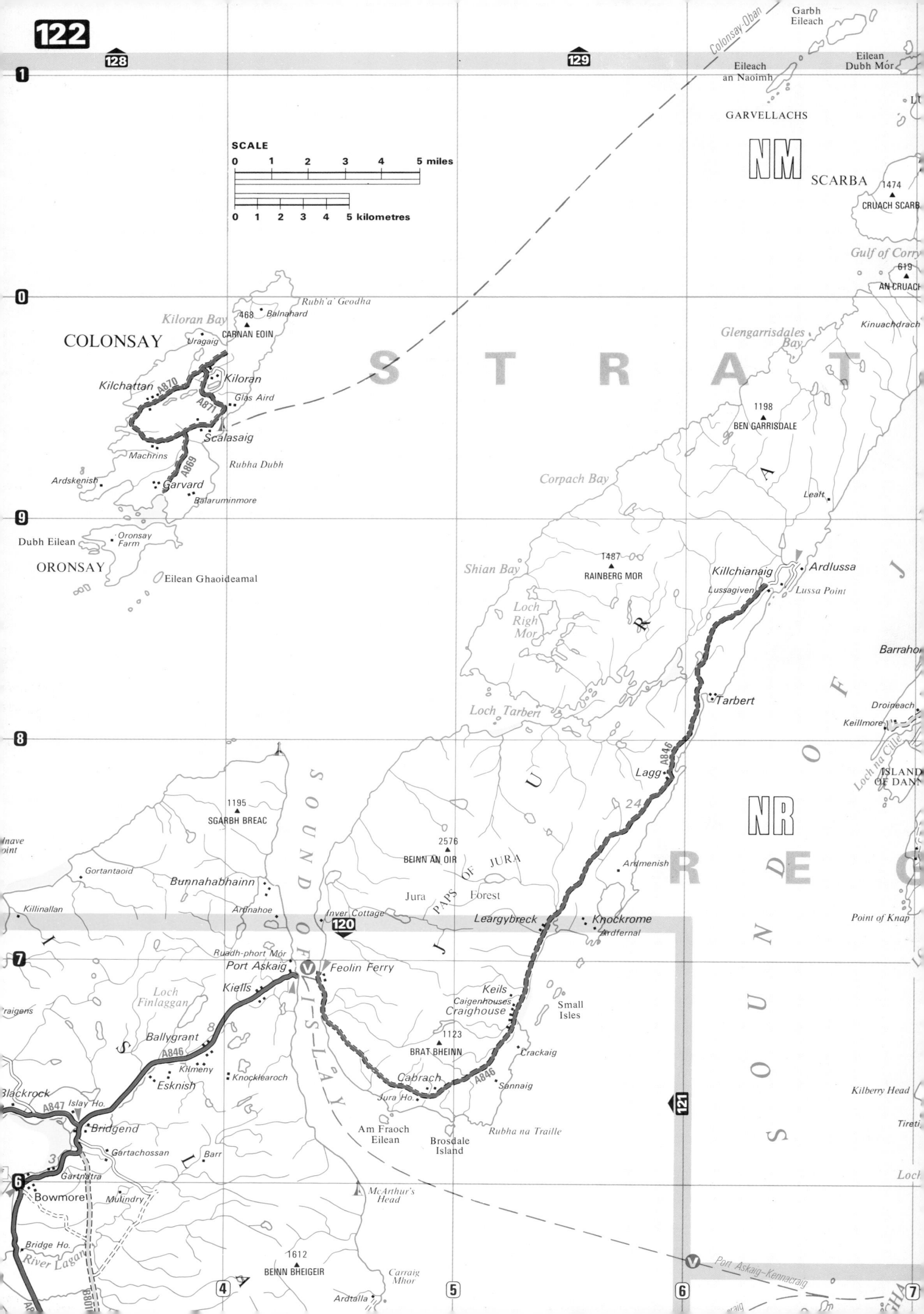

SCALE

0 1 2 3 4 5 miles

0 1 2 3 4 5 kilometres

1

128   129

Colonsay–Oban

Garbh Eileach

Eileach an Naoimh

Eilean Dubh Mór

GARVELLACHS

NM

SCARBA

1474
CRUACH SCARB

Gulf of Corry

619
AN CRUACH

0

Kiloran Bay

Rubh'a' Geodha

468   Balnahard

CARNAN EOIN

Uragaig

COLONSAY

Kiloran

Kilchattan   A870

Glas Aird

A871

Scalasaig

Machrins   A869

Ardskenish   Rubha Dubh

Garvard

Balaruminmore

9

Dubh Eilean

Oronsay Farm

ORONSAY

Eilean Ghaoideamal

S T R A T

Glengarrisdales Bay

Kinuachdrach

1198
BEN GARRISDALE

A

Corpach Bay

Lealt

1487
RAINBERG MOR

Killchianaig   Ardlussa

Lussagiven   Lussa Point

Shian Bay

Loch Righ Mor

R

Barraho

Loch Tarbert

Tarbert

Droineach

Keillmore

8

Loch na Cille

ISLAND OF DANN

NR

1195
SGARBH BREAC

U

2576
BEINN AN OIR

A846

Lagg

24

Ardmenish

NR

RE

DE

C

Inave oint

Gortantaoid

Bunnahabhainn

Ardnahoe

PAPS OF JURA

Jura   Forest

Ardfernal

Knockrome

Point of Knap

Killinallan

Inver Cottage

120

Leargybreck

7

Ruadh-phort Mór

Port Askaig

Kiells   Feolin Ferry

Keils

Caigenhouses
Craighouse

Small Isles

S O U N D   O F   I S L A Y

Loch Finlaggan

Ballygrant   A846

Kilmeny   Knocklearoch

Esknish

1123
BRAT BHEINN

Crackaig

Kilberry Head

Blackrock   A847

Islay Ho.

Cabrach   A846

Sannaig

Tireti

Bridgend

Jura Ho.

121

Gartachossan   Barr

Am Fraoch Eilean

Rubha na Traille

Loch

6

Gartnatra

Bowmore   Mulindry

Bridge Ho.

McArthur's Head

River Lagan

1612
BEINN BHEIGEIR

Ardtalla

Carraig Mhor

Port Askaig–Kennacraig

4   5   6   7

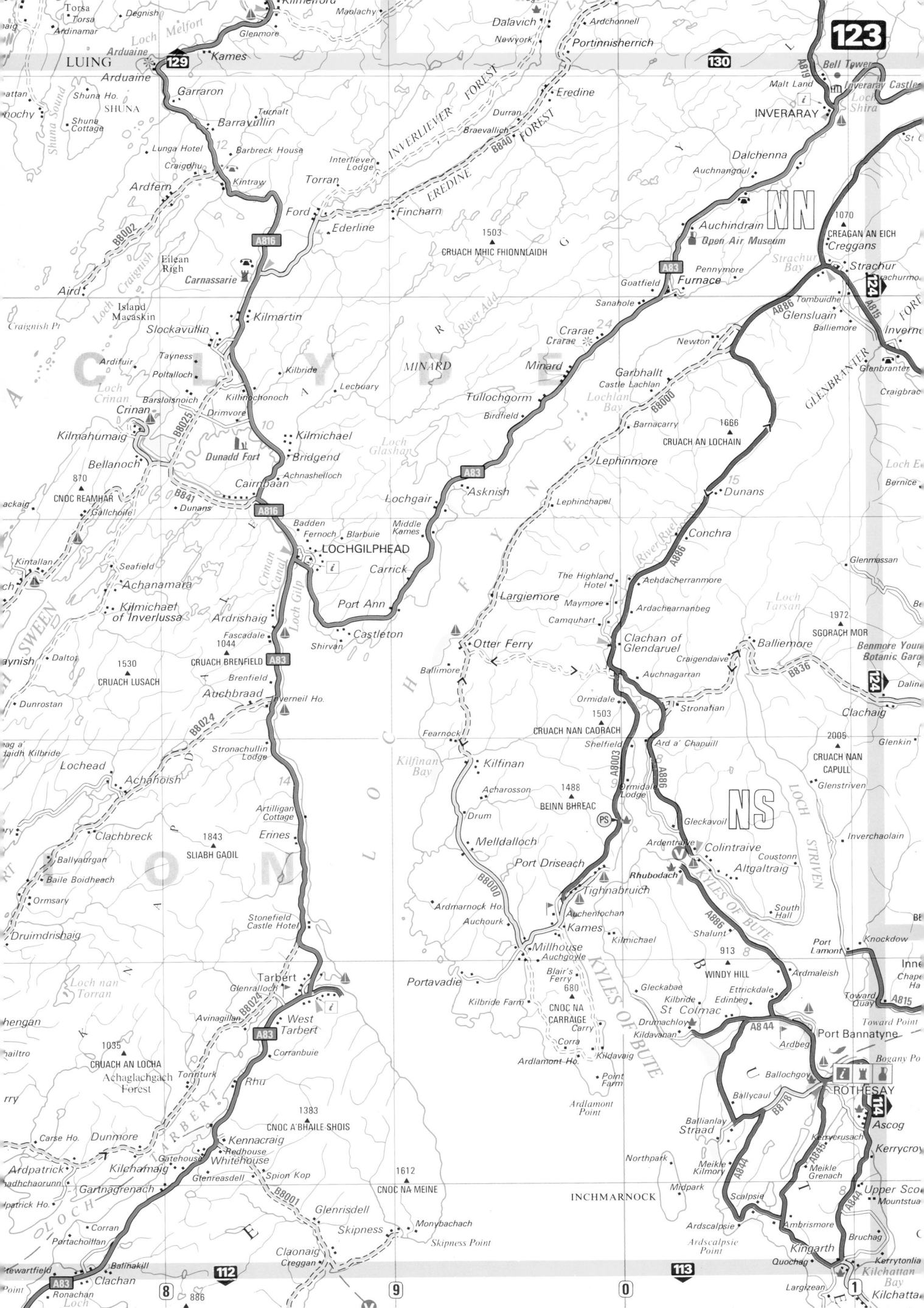
Torsa
Torsa
Degnish
Ardinamar
Loch Melfort
Kilmelford
Maolachy
Glenmore
Dalavich
Ardchonnell
Newyork
Portinnisherrich
Arduaine
LUING
Arduaine
129
Kames
130
Bell Tower
Malt Land
Inveraray Castle
INVERARAY
Loch Shira
Shuna Ho.
SHUNA
Shuna Sound
Shuna Cottage
Garraron
Turnalt
Barravullin
INVERLIEVER FOREST
Eredine
Durran
Braevallich
B840
FOREST
Lunga Hotel
Barbreck House
Craigdhu
Interliever Lodge
Torran
ERREDINE
Dalchenna
Auchnangoul
Ardfern
Kintraw
Ford
Fincharn
Ederline
NN
Auchindrain
Open Air Museum
1070
CREAGAN AN EICH
Creggans
1503
CRUACH MHIC FHIONNLAIDH
B8002
A816
Eilean Righ
Carnassarie
A83
Pennymore
Strachur Bay
Strachur
Goatfield
Furnace
124
Aird
Loch Craignish
Island Macaskin
Sanahole
Tombuidhe
Glensluain
Balliemore
A886
A815
Craignish Pt
Kilmartin
River Add
Newton
Slockavullin
Crarae
Crarae
Ardifuir
Tayness
Poltalloch
Kilbride
MINARD
Minard
Garbhallt
Castle Lachlan
GLENBRANTER
Glenbranter
Craigbrac
Loch Crinan
Crinan
Barsloisnoich
Drimvore
Kilmichonoch
Lechuary
Tullochgorm
Birdfield
Lochlan Bay
B8000
Barnacarry
1666
CRUACH AN LOCHAIN
Kilmahumaig
B8025
Kilmichael
Loch Glashan
Dunadd Fort
Bridgend
Lephinmore
Bellanoch
870
CNOC REAMHAR
Achnashelloch
Cairnbaan
B841
Dunans
A83
Asknish
Dunans
Bernice
Gallchoille
A816
Lochgair
Lephinchapel
Badden
Fernoch
Blarbuie
Middle Kames
LOCHGILPHEAD
River Ruel
Conchra
Kintallan
Seafield
Crinan Canal
Carrick
A886
Glenmassan
Achanamara
Loch Gilp
Port Ann
The Highland Hotel
Achdacherranmore
Kilmichael of Inverlussa
Largiemore
Maymore
Ardachearnanbeg
Loch Tarsan
SWEEN
Ardrishaig
Camquhart
1972
SGORACH MOR
Fascadale
1044
Castleton
Clachan of Glendaruel
Balliemore
Shirvan
Otter Ferry
Benmore Younger Botanic Garden
CRUACH BRENFIELD
A83
Craigendaive
Daltot
1530
CRUACH LUSACH
Brenfield
Ballimore
Auchnagarran
B836
124
Auchbraad
Inverneil Ho.
Ormidale
Dunrostan
1503
Stronafian
Clachaig
B8024
CRUACH NAN CAORACH
Fearnock
Shelfield
Ard a' Chapuill
2005
CRUACH NAN CAPULL
Stronachullin Lodge
Kilfinan Bay
Kilfinan
A8003
A886
Glenkin
Lochead
Achahoish
Glenstriven
Acharosson
1488
BEINN BHREAC
Ormidale Lodge
Artilligan Cottage
Drum
Gleckavoil
NS
LOCH STRIVEN
Inverchaolain
Clachbreck
1843
SLIABH GAOIL
Erines
Melldalloch
Ardentraive
Colintraive
Coustonn
Ballyaurgan
Port Driseach
Altgaltraig
Rhubodach
Baile Boidheach
B8000
Tighnabruaich
Ormsary
Ardmarnock Ho.
Auchenlochan
KYLES OF BUTE
South Hall
Stonefield Castle Hotel
Auchourk
Kames
A886
Druimdrishaig
Shalunt
Kilmichael
Port Lamont
Knockdow
Millhouse
Auchgoyle
913
WINDY HILL
Tarbert
Loch nan Torran
Glenralloch
Blair's Ferry
680
Ardmaleish
Portavadie
Ettrickdale
Edinbeg
Toward Quay
A815
B8024
Gleckabae
Kilbride
West Tarbert
Kilbride Farm
CNOC NA CARRAIGE
St Colmac
Avinagillan
Drumachloy
Toward Point
KYLES OF BUTE
Kildavanan
A844
Port Bannatyne
A83
Corry
Ardbeg
1035
Corranbuie
Corra
Kildavaig
Bogany Point
CRUACH AN LOCHA
Achaglachgach Forest
Ardlamont Ho.
Ballochgoy
Tonnturk
Rhu
Point Farm
ROTHESAY
Ballycaul
114
Ardlamont Point
B878
TARBERT
1383
CNOC A'BHAILE-SHOIS
Ballianlay
Straad
Ascog
Carse Ho.
Dunmore
Kennacraig
Redhouse
Kerrycrusach
Whitehouse
Gatehouse
Kerrycroy
Ardpatrick
Kilchamaig
Northpark
A845
Meikle Kilmory
Meikle Grenach
1612
Spion Kop
Glenreasdell
A844
Gartnagrenach
CNOC NA MEINE
INCHMARNOCK
Midpark
Upper Scoulag
Mountstuart
B8001
A844
Glenrisdell
Scalpsie
Corran
Monybachach
Ardscalpsie
Ambrismore
Bruchag
Skipness
Portachoillan
Skipness Point
Ardscalpsie Point
Claonaig
Kingarth
Balinakill
Creggan
Quochag
Kerrytonlia
Kilchattan Bay
Clachan
112
113
A83
8
9
0
1
Ronachan
886
Largizean
Kilchattan

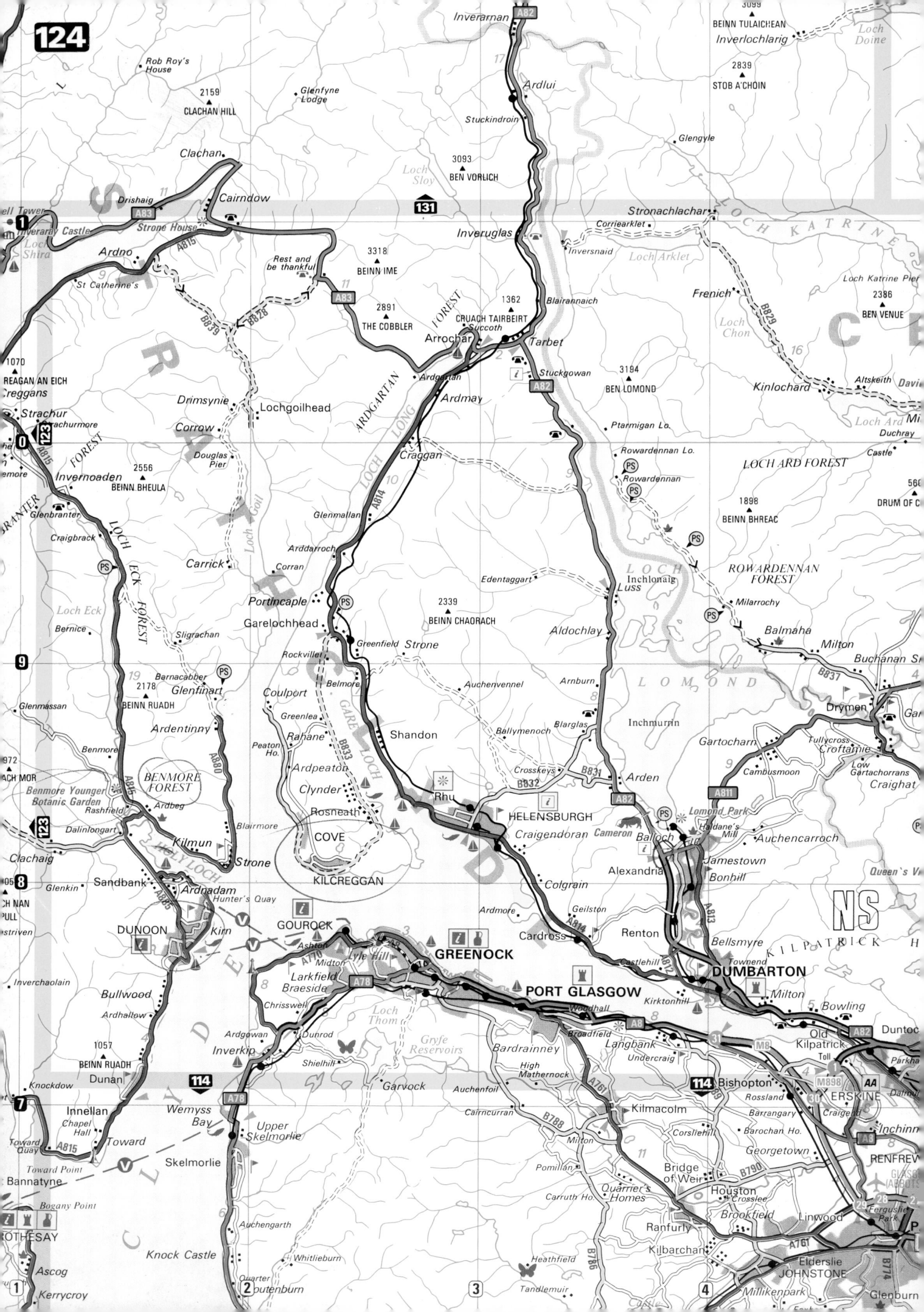

124
Inverarnan
A82
BEINN TULAICHEAN
Inverlochlarig
Loch Doine
Rob Roy's House
2159
CLACHAN HILL
Glenfyne Lodge
Ardlui
2839
STOB A'CHOIN
Stuckindroin
Glengyle
Clachan
Loch Sloy
3093
BEN VORLICH
Drishaig
Cairndow
131
Stronachlachar
LOCH KATRINE
A83
Strone House
Inveraray Castle
Loch Shira
Inveruglas
Corriearklet
Inversnaid
Loch Arklet
Ardno
A815
Rest and be thankful
3318
BEINN IME
St Catherine's
A83
2891
THE COBBLER
1362
CRUACH TAIRBEIRT
Blairannaich
Frenich
Loch Katrine Pier
2386
BEN VENUE
B839
B828
FOREST
Succoth
Arrochar
Tarbet
Loch Chon
B829
1070
BEINN REAGAN AN EICH
Creggans
Stuckgowan
A82
Ardgartan
3194
BEN LOMOND
Kinlochard
Altskeith
Drimsynie
Lochgoilhead
Ardmay
Strachur
Strachurmore
123
Corrow
ARDGARTAN
LOCH LONG
Ptarmigan Lo.
Loch Ard
Duchray
Castle
A815
FOREST
Douglas Pier
Craggan
Rowardennan Lo.
LOCH ARD FOREST
Invernoaden
2556
BEINN BHEULA
Rowardennan
Glenbranter
LOCH
A814
Loch Goil
Glenmallan
1898
BEINN BHREAC
DRUM OF CLOICH
Craigbrack
ECK
FOREST
Carrick
Arddarroch
Corran
Edentaggart
LOCH
Inchlonaig
Luss
ROWARDENNAN FOREST
Portincaple
Milarrochy
2339
BEINN CHAORACH
Loch Eck
Garelochhead
Aldochlay
Balmaha
Milton
Bernice
Sligrachan
Greenfield
Strone
Rockville
Buchanan
9
B837
Barnacabber
2178
BEINN RUADH
Glenfinart
Belmore
Auchenvennel
Arnburn
LOMOND
Coulport
Drymen
Glenmassan
Greenlea
GARE LOCH
Shandon
Ballymenoch
Blarglas
Inchmurrin
Ardentinny
Rahane
B833
Gartocharn
Tullycross
Croftamie
Benmore
Peaton Ho.
Ardpeaton
Crosskeys
B831
Cambusmoon
Low Gartachorrans
A880
BENMORE FOREST
Benmore Younger Botanic Garden
A815
Clynder
B832
Arden
Craighat
Rashfield
Ardbeg
Rhu
A81
A82
Rosneath
HELENSBURGH
Lomond Park
Dalinlongart
Blairmore
Haldane's Mill
COVE
Craigendoran
Cameron
Balloch
Auchencarroch
Kilmun
Clachaig
HOLY LOCH
Strone
Jamestown
Alexandria
Bonhill
Sandbank
KILCREGGAN
Colgrain
Queen's View
Glenkin
Ardnadam
A885
Hunter's Quay
NS
Geilston
Ardmore
DUNOON
Kirn
GOUROCK
A813
Cardross
Renton
Bellsmyre
KILPATRICK
Ashton
GREENOCK
A770
Lyle Hill
Midton
Townend
Castlehill
DUMBARTON
Inverchaolain
Larkfield
Braeside
A78
PORT GLASGOW
Milton
Bullwood
Chrisswell
Loch Thom
Kirktonhill
Woodhall
Bowling
Ardhallow
A8
Duntocher
Ardgowan
Dunrod
Gryfe Reservoirs
Broadfield
A82
Old Kilpatrick
Inverkip
Bardrainney
Langbank
M8
Undercraig
1057
BEINN RUADH
Shielhill
High Mathernock
Toll
Knockdow
Dunan
114
Garvock
Auchenfoil
A761
114
Bishopton
M898
AA
Rossland
ERSKINE
Innellan
A78
Wemyss Bay
Cairncurran
Kilmacolm
Barrangary
Craigend
Chapel Hall
Upper Skelmorlie
B788
Corslie Hill
Barochan Ho.
Inchinnan
Toward Quay
A815
Toward
Milton
A8
Skelmorlie
Georgetown
RENFREW
Toward Point
Pomillan
Bridge of Weir
B790
Bannatyne
Houston
Crosslee
GLASGOW (ABBOTSINCH)
Carruth Ho.
Quarrier's Homes
Bogany Point
Brookfield
Ferguslie Park
Linwood
ROTHESAY
Auchengarth
Ranfurly
A761
Knock Castle
Heathfield
Kilbarchan
Elderslie
B774
Ascog
Whitlieburn
B786
JOHNSTONE
Quarter
Kerrycroy
Tandlemuir
Millikenpark
Glenburn

STRATHYRE
3231
BEN VORLICH
Forest of
Glenartney
The Balloch
Culloch
Trian
Drummond
Muthill
Library
Strathyre
Kipp
Dalchruin
Tighnablair
Ochtermuthill
Auchinner
Auchnashelloch
Mill of
Drummond
Murrayfield
Strathallan
Aircraft Museum
Laggan
Runacraig
2685
BENVANE
Ardchullarie More
2072
CREAG BEINN NAN EUN
Langside
Middleton
AUCHT
Loch
Lubnaig
TAYSIDE
REGION
Garrick
Danduff
Muirtown
132
Anie
Gleneagles
Hotel
2882
Achnahard
BEN LEDI
Kilmahog
Woollen Mill
Kilmahog
CALLANDER
Braco
West Feddal
Allan Water
Blackford
Greenloaning
Millhill
Brig
o' Turk
Bochastle
Coilantogle
Upper Drumbane
Easter
Dullater
Lendrick
Invertrossachs
Nature Reserve
Menteith Hills
East Lundie
Drumvaich
Kinbuck
Ashfield
TORRIE FOREST
Kilbryde
Castle
Burn of Cambus
Lower
Auchinlay
Buchany
Motor Museum
DOUNE
Port of
Menteith
Portend
Ruskie
Ballochneck
Deanston
2364
BEN CLEUCH
Braeval
Inchmahome Priory
Doune
DUNBLANE
Pisgah
Thornhill
Meldrum
Blair
Drummond
Lake of
Menteith
Netherton
Keir
Sunnylaw
126
TILLICOUL
BRIDGE OF ALLAN
Drumbrae
ALVA
Dykehead
Cardross
Blairlogie
River Forth
REGION
Menstrie
Menstrie
Fishcross
Dasherhead
Wallace
Monument
Causewayhead
Tullibody
New Sauc
Arnprior
Kippen
Raploch
Cambuskenneth
Cauldhame
Cambus
Norwood
Keilarsbrae
Gargunnock
Buchlyvie
Auchentroig
STIRLING
ALLOA
Cambusbarron
Fallin
South
Alloa
St. Ninians
Kennet
Bannockburn Monument
Bannockburn
Mains of Throsk
Gaisland
Chartershall
1678
STRONEND
Cowie
Balfron
Harvieston
North Third
Hillhead
Dunmore
Auchenbowie
Sauchinford
Airth
Plean
Clayland
Culcreuch
Gonachan
Avenuehead
Waterslap
Killearn
Fintry
Easter
Buckieburn
Drum
Torwood
South B
Carron
Valley
Reservoir
River Carron
1897
Muirmill
Stenhousemuir
EARL'S SEAT
Dumgoyne
DUNIPACE
Carron Bridge
Carronshore
CARRON VALLEY FOREST
Stoneywood
Larbert
Carron
CAMPSIE FELLS
1487
TOMTAIN
DENNY
Head of Muir
Camelon
Dennyloanhead
FALKIRK
Netherton
Kilsyth Hills
High Banton
Braeface
Bonnybridge
Lauriston
Clachan
of Campsie
Haughhead
Colzium
Banton
Banknock
Longcroft
High
Bonnybridge
Blanefield
Strathblane
Balgrochan
Ballmalloch
KILSYTH
Haggs
Westquarter
Craigend
Castle
Lennoxtown
Queenzieburn
Kelvinhead
Castlecary
Greenhill
Glen Village
Milton of
Campsie
Auchinstarry
Dullatur
Reddingmuirhead
Mugdock
Croy
Shieldhill
Burnfoot
Blairskaith
Birdston
Eastfield
CUMBERNAULD
Jawcraig
Twechar
MILNGAVIE
Torrance
KIRKINTILLOCH
Greyrigg
Waterside
Slamannan
Crossburn
Balmore
Bardowie
Summerston
Luggiebank
Avonbridge
Mollinsburn
Condorrat
BEARSDEN
Cadder
Lenzie
Binniehill
Hillfoot
Boghead
Bridgend
Greengairs
Babbithill
Annathill
Limerigg
High Limerigg
115
116
Bishopbriggs
Auchinloch
Muirhead
Moodiesburn
Riggend
Longriggend
Temple
Maryhill
Lumloch
Marnock
Wattston
Springburn
Stepps
Glenboig
Stand
Woodend
ARMADA
Anniesland
Garnkirk
Brackenhurst
Caldercruix
Holland
Reservoir
Blackridge
Scotstoun
Partick
GLASGOW
Millerston
Gartcosh
Glenmavis
Airdriehill
Tunnel
Lochwood
Gartsherrie
Plains
Westrig
Hillend
Forestfield
COATBRIDGE
Easterhouse
AIRDRIE
Govan
Bentfoot
Shettleston
Barrachnie
Coatdyke
Craigneuk
Crookston
Baillieston
Old
Monkland
Gartness
Eastfield
Harth
Pollokshields
Calderbank
Pollok
RUTHERGLEN
Calderpark
Chapelhall
Kirk of Shotts
Carmyle
Birkenshaw
Salsburgh
Cathcart
Newton
Viewpark
Tannochside
Mossend
Newhouse

TAYSIDE
REGION
OCHIL HILLS
FIFE
FIRTH
NN
NS
133
134
125
116
117
Kirkton
Denfield
River Earn
Broom of Dalreoch
Chapelbank
Forteviot
Forgandenny
Bridge of Earn
Kintillo
Aberargie
Abernethy
NEWBURGH
Lindores
Parkhill
Kinkell Bridge
Drumtogle
Baldinnies
Glenearn
Dron
Round Tower
Glenfoot
Pitcairlie Ho.
Grange of Lindores
Strathallen Aircraft Museum
Wallfauld
Aberuthven
Dunning
Millhaugh
Shinafoot
Lumquhat
PITMEDDEN FOREST
AUCHTERARDER
Milton
Pairney
1346
CRAIG ROSSIE
Rossie Ochill
Bein Inn
Pleasance
Lochieheads
AUCHTERMUCHTY
Muirtown
Gleneagles Hotel
Path of Condie
Abbots Deuglie
Glenfarg
Newton of Balcanquhal
Arngask
Wellfield
Greenhill
Gleneagles
Blackford
Middle Rigg
Stronachie
Duncrievie
Drunzie
Gateside
Strathmiglo
Nether Urquhart
Burnside
FALKLAND
Lomond Hills
Ballo Reservoir
Middleton
Craigow
Upper Tillyrie
Mawcarse
Burleigh
Glasslie
Easter Glasslie
A823
Glendevon
River Devon
Burnfoot
Castlehill Reservoir
Dalqueich
Moors of Kinross
Milnathort
Balgedie
Easter Balgedie
Kinnesswood
Pitkevy
Carnbo
Burnbrae
KINROSS
Loch Leven
Kinross House
LOCH LEVEN
Scotlandwell
LESLIE
Yetts o'Muckhart
Drum
Coldrain
St Serfs Island
Auchmuirbridge
Walkerton
GLENROTHES
Pool o'Muckhart
Castle Campbell and Dollar Glen
Rumbling Bridge
Crook of Devon
Easter Aldie
Gairney Bank
Gairneybridge
R Leven
Kinglassie
TILLICOULTRY
ALVA
Dollarfield
DOLLAR
Gartwhinzean
Powmill
Cleish
Ballingry
Lochore
Woodend
Clunybridge
Auchterderran
Devonside
Dollarbeg
Blairingone
Wellhall
Cleish Hills
BLAIRADAM FOREST
Loch Ore
Crosshill
Cluny
Fishcross
Coalsnaughton
Hill End
Loch Glow
Glencraig
Cardenden
New Sauchie
Forest Mill
1194
KNOCK HILL
Kelty
Chapel
Keilarsbrae
Gartlove
Balgonar
LOCHGELLY
Norwood
Saline
Lassodie
Loch Fitty
Lumphinnans
Loch Gelly
Clackmannan
COWDENBEATH
South Alloa
Kennet
Cowstrandburn
Bowershall
Kilbagie
Kingseat
Hill of Beath
Auchtertool
Throsk
Dunmore
Blairhall
Carnock
Gowkhall
Townhill
Crossgates
Meadowfield
Balmule
Comrie
Oakley
Halbeath
Wellwood
Donibristle
Orrock
Airth
Kincardine
Culross Abbey
Milesmark
Cairneyhill
Fordell
Crossroads
Valleyfield
DUNFERMLINE
Newrow
Newmills
Aberdour
Waterslap
Low Valleyfield
Low Torry
Torryburn
Crossford
Drum
Dunimarle
CULROSS
South Bellsdyke
Mastertown
Hillend
BURNTISLAND
Crombie
Charlestown
St. Colme
Dalgety Bay
Carronshore
Skinflats
GRANGEMOUTH
Rosyth
Limekilns
INVERKEITHING
BO'NESS
Grangepans
Carriden
North Queensferry
FALKIRK
East Kerse Mains
Muirhouses
Blackness
Lauriston
Kinneil
Borrowstoun
Champany
Inveravon
Hopetoun
QUEENSFERRY
Dalmeny House
Cramond Island
Westquarter
Redding
Polmont
Merrylees
Dalmeny
Granton
Reddingmuirhead
Brightons
Rumford
LINLITHGOW
Philpstoun
Old Philpstoun
Newton
Woodend
Cramond
Lauriston Castle
Shieldhill
Maddiston
Whitecross
Linlithgow Palace
Burnside
Dalmeny Rows
California
Union Canal
Bridgend
Three Miletown
Cramond Bridge
Davidson's Mains
Warriston
Greyrigg
Loan
Winchburgh
Standburn
Cockleroy
Wester Ochiltree
Niddry Rows
Turnhouse
Kirkliston
EDINBURGH (TURNHOUSE)
Avonbridge
Ecclesmachan
Torphichen
Torpichen Preceptory
Newbridge
Ingliston
Babbithill
Westfield
Uphall
Corstorphine
Balmuir
Dechmont
Broxburn
Burnside
Gogar
Ratho
Suntrap
Morningside
Limerigg
Cairnpapple Hill
Drumcross
Dechmont Rd.
Uphall Station
Craiglockhart
Belvedere
BATHGATE
West Clifton
Pumpherston
Long Hermiston
Colinton
Woodend
ARMADALE
Boghall
Raw Camps
Bonnington
Juniper Green
Blackridge
Whiteside
LIVINGSTON
Wilkieston
Currie
Torphin
Fairmilehead
Bathville
Mid Calder
East Calder
Newmills
Kinleith
Westrigg
Seafield
Livingston Village
Oakbank
Kirknewton
Whelpside
Balerno
Malleny
PENTLAND HILLS
Straiton
Hillend
LOANHEAD
East Whitburn
Blackburn
Bellsquarry
Malleny Mills
Boghall
Woodhouselee
Easter Howgate
Eastfield
Harthill
WHITBURN
Mossend
Polbeth
Corston
Ainville
Threipmuir Reservoir
1636
BLACK HILL
Longridge
Stoneyburn
Water of Leith
Milton Bridge
Roslin
Loganlea
Addiewell
West Calder
Wester Causewayend
West Mains
East Torphin
Breich
A9
M90
A91
A977
A823
A985
A876
A907
A909
A921
A92
A90
M9
A904
A8
M8
A71
A70
A720
A702
A89
A899
A706
A801
B7066
B7015
B792
B8084
B8028
B825
B9080
B820
B7030
B7031
B934
B9141
B8062
B935
B996
B919
B912
B917
B914
B913
B910
B9140
B9097
B908
B921
B922
B925
B923
B9085
A912
A983
A911
A910
A906
A994
A997
A803
A905

Luthrie
Parbroath
Moonzie
Denbrae
Muirhead
A914
Hillcairnie
Dairsie or
Osnaburgh
Foodieash
South
Dron
Kincaple
Strathkinness
A91
ST. ANDREWS
Dairsie Mains
Blebocraigs
Ballone
AA 113
Brownhills
Boarhills
Boghall
Kemback
Tailabout
B939
Denhead
A915
Letham
CUPAR
Pitscottie
Prior Muir
A959
Kingsbarns
A918
Balcomie
Ladeddie
Baldinnie
Priorletham
FIFE NESS
Craighead
Ballantagar
Cupar
Muir
Bridgend
Ceres
Cameron
Reservoir
12
Stravithie
Bow Fife
Springfield
Hill of Tarvit
Priory
Dunino
134
135
LADYBANK
Craigrothie
Radernie
Peat Inn
Struthers
New
Gilston
Lathones
Kingsmuir
Lochty Private Railway
B940
East
Pitcorthie
B9171
CRAIL
Pitlessie
Balmalcolm
Coaltown of Burnturk
Kame
Woodside
NO
Backmuir
of New
Gilston
Largoward
Lochty
Carnbee
Spalefield
West Pitcorthie
Easter
Pitkierie
PS
A917
Kettlebridge
Montrave
Pratis
Wester
Newburn
B941
Arncroach
Wester
Pitkierie
Anstruther
Easter
KILRENNY
Langdyke
Kirkton of Largo
Colinsburgh
Kellie Castle
A959
Star
Bonnybank
Baintown
B921
Lundin
Links
B942
Abercrombie
B942
ANSTRUTHER
MARKINCH
Kennoway
A915
Lower
Largo
Dunotter
6
6
PITTENWEEM
Balcurvie
Scoonie
A917
Kilconquhar
ST. MONANS
A911
LEVEN
Drumeldrie
LARGO
BAY
Milton of
Balgonie
Windygates
Innerleven
EARLSFERRY
ELIE
Isle of May
Coaltown of
Balgonie
METHIL
Sauchar Point
A955
BUCKHAVEN
Coaltown of
Wemyss
East
Wemyss
A915
West
Wemyss
Dysart
OF FORTH
CALDY
NORTH
BERWICK
Tantallon
Auldhame
Scoughall
keith
Dirleton
N BERWICK LAW
A198
A198
Whitekirk
NT
Gullane
Gullane Bay
B1345
Kingston
8
Aberlady Bay
Luffness
B1347
Drem
B1377
Tyninghame
DUNBA
Aberlady
Myreton
Motor
Museum
Mungoswells
East Fortune
Museum of Flight
Preston
West Barns
Belhaven
Gosford Bay
Spittal
Ballencrieff
B1343
Mill
A1087
Longniddry
B1348
A6137
West
Garleton
Athelstaneford
PS
EAST LINTON
A1
Luggate
Burn
Stenton
Pitcox
Spott
1650
COCKENZIE AND
PORT SETON
Seton Mains
Huntington
Hailes
Traprain
The Brun
DINBURGH
A198
Elvingston
HADDINGTON
Morham
Papple
Halis
Woodhall
Portobello
1745
A1
Gladsmuir
Cockles
Tanderlane
PRESTONPANS
MUSSELBURGH
TRANENT
Macmerry
Samuelston
Lennoxlove
Garvald
118
Inveresk
Wallyford
New
Winton
Bolton
117
B6369
B6370
Elphinstone
New Town
Carfrae
White Castle
SWADE
A6094
Ormiston
A6093
Easter Pencaitland
B6368
Danderhall
Whitecraig
B6414
Pencaitland
B6355
Gifford
Danskine
Millerhill
AA 91
Crossgatehall
Cousland
Peaston
Bank
West
Saltoun
East
Saltoun
Bankrugg
Marvingston
Quarryford
Longyester
A7
DALKEITH
Peaston
Gilchriston
Millknowe
Eskbank
Newbattle
Peaston
Kidlaw
Long
Newton
BONNYRIGG
Mayfield
Chesterhill
A68
Upper
Keith
Humbie
St.Agnes
Newtongrange
Pathhead
A6137
Newtonloan
Newlandrig
Dewartown
Fala
Dam
B704
Crichton
A6137
Blegbie
Whiteadder
Reservoir
859
oswell
Arniston
Engine
Crichton
Dean
CRANSHAWS HILL
3
4
5
6

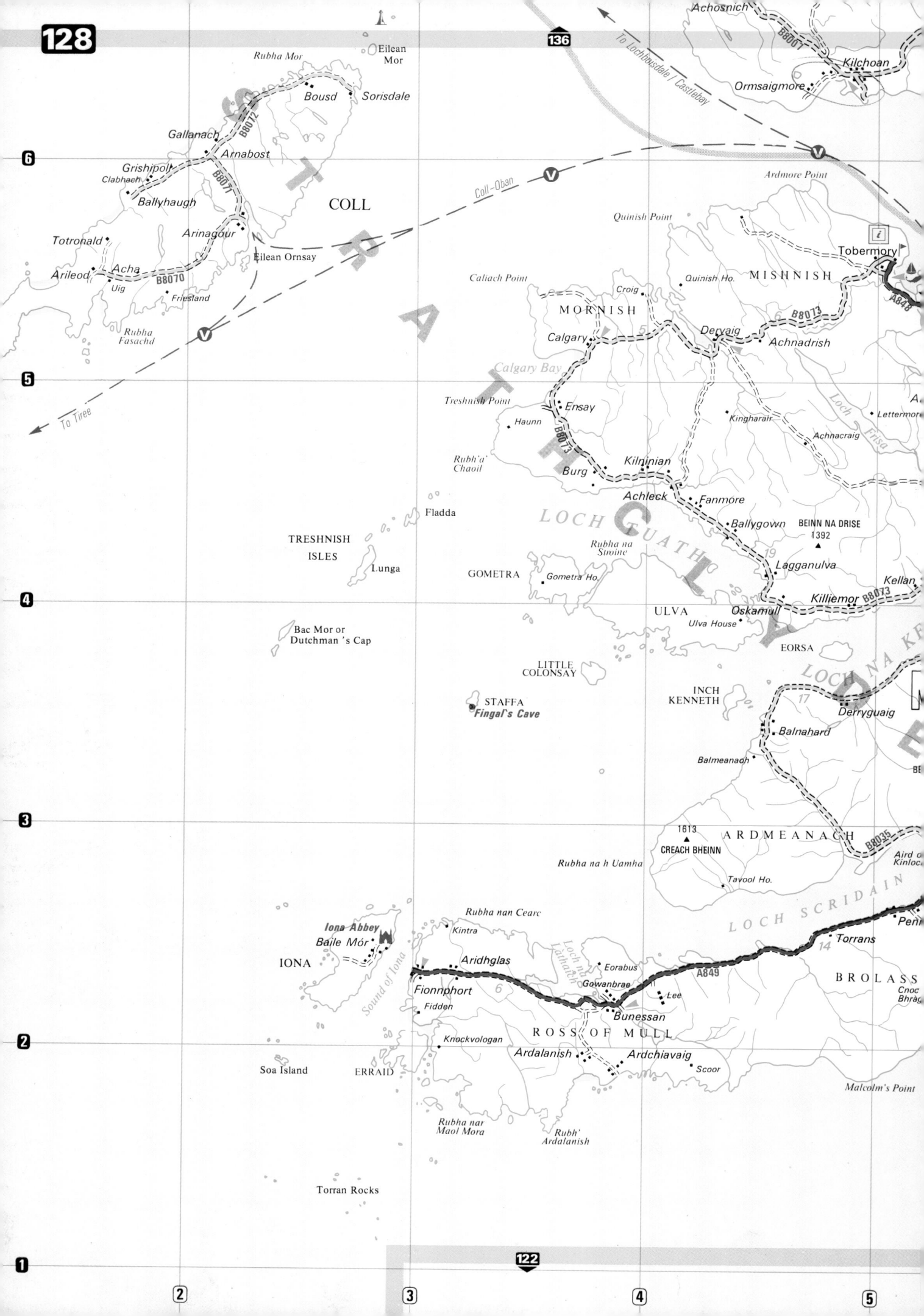

136

To Lochboisdale / Castlebay

Achosnich

B8007

Kilchoan

Ormsaigmore

Rubha Mor

Eilean
Mor

Bousd   Sorisdale

Gallanach

B8072

Arnabost

Grishipoll

B8071

Clabhach

COLL

Ballyhaugh

Arinagour

Totronald

B8070

Acha

Eilean Ornsay

Arileod

Uig

Friesland

Coll–Oban

Ardmore Point

Quinish Point

Tobermory

i

MISHNISH

A848

Caliach Point

Quinish Ho.

Croig

MORNISH

Calgary

Dervaig

B8073

Achnadrish

Rubha
Fasachd

To Tiree

Calgary Bay

Treshnish Point

Ensay

B8073

Haunn

Kingharair

Achnacraig

Lettermore

Loch Frisa

Rubh'a'
Chaoil

Kilninian

Burg

Achleck

Fanmore

LOCH TUATH

Ballygown

BEINN NA DRISE
1392

TRESHNISH
ISLES

Fladda

Rubha na
Stroine

19

Lagganulva

Lunga

GOMETRA

Gometra Ho.

ULVA

Oskamull

Killiemor

B8073

Kellan

Bac Mor or
Dutchman 's Cap

Ulva House

EORSA

LOCH NA KE

LITTLE
COLONSAY

INCH
KENNETH

17

Derryguaig

STAFFA
Fingal`s Cave

Balnahard

Balmeanach

1613

ARDMEANACH

B8035

CREACH BHEINN

Aird o
Kinloc

Rubha na h Uamha

Tavool Ho.

LOCH SCRIDAIN

Iona Abbey

Baile Mór

Rubha nan Cearc

IONA

Kintra

Loch na
Lathaich

Pen

Torrans

14

Aridhglas

Eorabus

A849

BROLASS

Sound of Iona

Fionnphort

6

Gowanbrae

Lee

Cnoc
Bhrag

Fidden

Bunessan

Knockvologan

ROSS OF MULL

Soa Island

ERRAID

Ardalanish

Ardchiavaig

Scoor

Malcolm's Point

Rubha nar
Maol Mora

Rubh'
Ardalanish

Torran Rocks

2   3   4   5

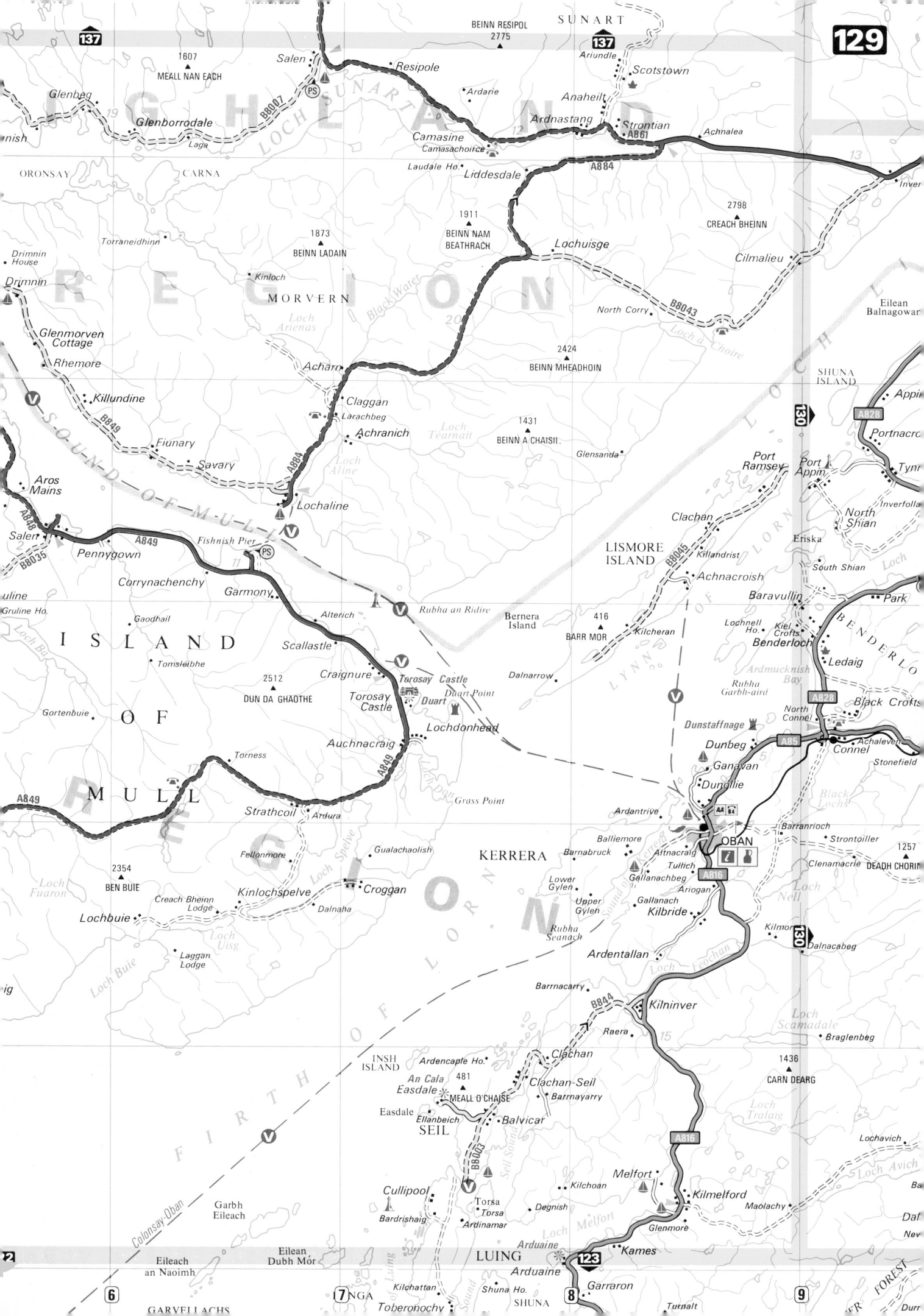
137
SUNART
BEINN RESIPOL 2775
1607
MEALL NAN EACH
Salen
Resipole
Ariundle
Scotstown
Glenbeg
Ardarie
Anaheilt
Glenborrodale
B8007
LOCH SUNART
Ardnastang
Strontian
A861
Achnalea
Laga
Camasine
Camasachoirce
ORONSAY
CARNA
Laudale Ho.
Liddesdale
A884
Inver
1911
BEINN NAM BEATHRACH
2798
CREACH BHEINN
1873
BEINN LADAIN
Torraneidhinn
Lochuisge
Cilmalieu
Drimnin House
Kinloch
Drimnin
MORVERN
Black Water
Loch Arienas
North Corry
B8043
Loch a' Choire
Eilean Balnagowan
Glenmorven Cottage
2424
BEINN MHEADHOIN
Rhemore
Acharn
SHUNA ISLAND
Killundine
Claggan
Larachbeg
Appin
A828
Achranich
Loch Tearnait
1431
BEINN A CHAISIL
Portnacroish
Loch Aline
Glensanda
Fiunary
B849
Savary
Port Ramsey
Port Appin
Tynribbie
Aros Mains
SOUND OF MULL
Lochaline
Inverfolla
A848
North Shian
Clachan
Salen
A849
Fishnish Pier
Eriska
Pennygown
LISMORE ISLAND
B8045
Killandrist
B8035
South Shian
Corrynachenchy
Achnacroish
Garmony
Loch
Baravullin
Park
Gruline Ho.
Alterich
Rubha an Ridire
Bernera Island
416
BARR MOR
Lochnell Ho.
Kiel Crofts
Gaodhail
Kilcheran
Benderloch
BENDERLOCH
ISLAND
Scallastle
Ledaig
Tomsleibhe
Craignure
Torosay Castle
Dalnarrow
LYNN OF LORN
Ardmucknish Bay
2512
DUN DA GHAOTHE
Torosay Castle
Duart
Duart Point
Rubha Garbh-aird
A828
Black Crofts
Gortenbuie
OF
Lochdonhead
North Connel
Dunstaffnage
Auchnacraig
Dunbeg
A85
Connel
Achaleven
Torness
Ganavan
Stonefield
Dunollie
Loch Don
Black Lochs
A849
MULL
Grass Point
Strathcoil
Ardura
Ardantrive
Barranrioch
Balliemore
OBAN
Strontoiller
Gualachaolish
KERRERA
Barnabruck
Altnacraig
1257
Fellonmore
Tullich
Clenamacrie
DEADH CHORIN
2354
BEN BUIE
Gallanachbeg
A816
Loch Fuaron
Lower Gylen
Ariogan
Loch Nell
Creach Bheinn Lodge
Kinlochspelve
Croggan
Upper Gylen
Gallanach
Kilbride
Dalnaha
Loch Spelve
Lochbuie
Rubha Seanach
Kilmore
130
Dalnacabeg
Loch Uisg
Ardentallan
Loch Feochan
Laggan Lodge
Loch Buie
Barnacarry
B844
Kilninver
Loch Scamadale
Raera
Braglenbeg
INSH ISLAND
Clachan
Ardencaple Ho.
1436
CARN DEARG
An Cala
481
Clachan-Seil
Easdale
MEALL O'CHAISE
Barnayarry
FIRTH OF LORN
Loch Tralaig
Easdale
Ellanbeich
Balvicar
SEIL
A816
Lochavich
B8003
Seil Sound
Loch Avich
Cullipool
Melfort
Kilchoan
Kilmelford
Garbh Eileach
Torsa
Torsa
Degnish
Maolachy
Colonsay-Oban
Bardrishaig
Ardinamar
Loch Melfort
Glenmore
Arduaine
Eilean Dubh Mor
Kames
Eileach an Naoimh
LUING
123
Arduaine
Luing
Kilchattan
Shuna Ho.
Garraron
6
LUNGA
7
8
9
Toberonochy
SHUNA
Turnalt
GARVELLACHS
FOREST

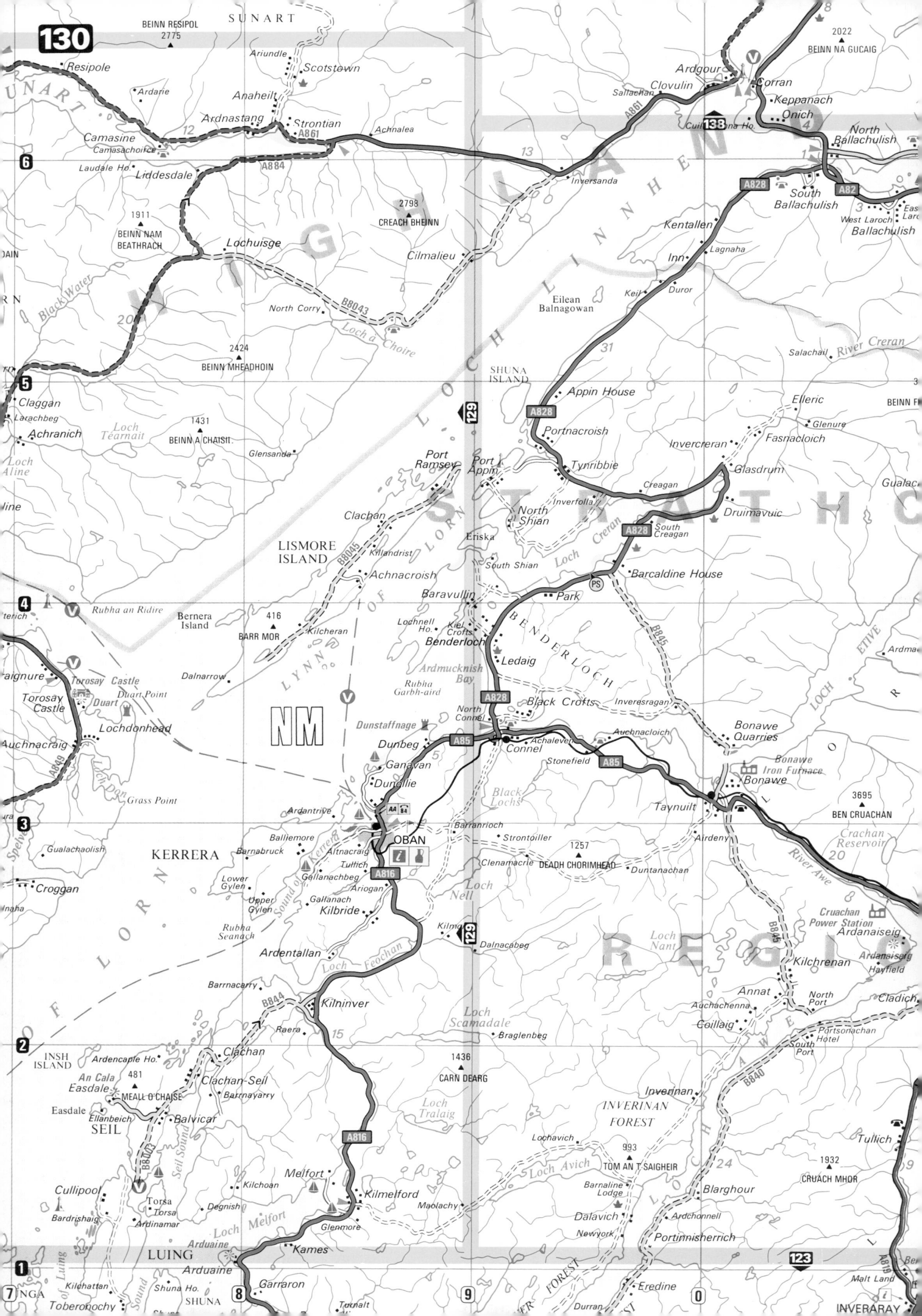

BEINN RESIPOL
2775
SUNART
Resipole
Ardarie
Ariundle
Scotstown
Anaheilt
Ardnastang
Strontian
Achnalea
A861
Camasine
Camasachoirce
12
6
Laudale Ho.
Liddesdale
A884
13
Ardgour
Clovulin
Sallachan
Corran
Keppanach
Onich
138
North Ballachulish
2022
BEINN NA GUCAIG
Inversanda
A828
South Ballachulish
A82
West Laroch
Ballachulish
2798
CREACH BHEINN
1911
BEINN NAM BEATHRACH
Lochuisge
Cilmalieu
Kentallen
Inn
Lagnaha
Keil
Duror
Black Water
North Corry
B8043
Loch a' Choire
Eilean Balnagowan
2424
BEINN MHEADHOIN
31
Salachail
River Creran
SHUNA ISLAND
5
Claggan
Larachbeg
Achranich
Loch Tearnait
1431
BEINN A' CHAISIL
Glensanda
Loch Aline
Appin House
Portnacroish
Elleric
Glenure
Fasnacloich
Invercreran
Glasdrum
Tynribbie
Port Ramsey
Port Appin
Creagan
Inverfolla
North Shian
Druimavuic
Clachan
LISMORE ISLAND
B8045
Killandrist
Achnacroish
Eriska
South Shian
Loch Creran
South Creagan
Barcaldine House
PS
Park
Baravullin
4
Rubha an Ridire
Bernera Island
416
BARR MOR
Kilcheran
Lochnell Ho.
Kiel Crofts
Benderloch
Ledaig
BENDERLOCH
B845
Craignure
Torosay Castle
Duart Castle
Duart Point
Dalnarrow
LYNN OF LORN
Ardmucknish Bay
Rubha Garbh-aird
A828
Black Crofts
Inveresragan
LOCH ETIVE
Ardmaddy
NM
Dunstaffnage
North Connel
Lochdonhead
Auchnacraig
A849
Loch Don
Grass Point
Dunbeg
A85
Connel
Achaleven
Auchnacloich
Bonawe Quarries
Stonefield
Ganavan
Dunollie
Black Lochs
Bonawe Iron Furnace
Bonawe
Taynuilt
3695
BEN CRUACHAN
3
Ardantrive
AA
Barranrioch
Strontoiller
Airdeny
Crachan Reservoir
Gualachaolish
KERRERA
Balliemore
Barnabruck
OBAN
1257
DEADH CHORIMHEAD
Clenamacrie
Duntanachan
River Awe
20
Altnacraig
Tullich
Gallanachbeg
A816
Croggan
Lower Gylen
Upper Gylen
Ariogan
Gallanach
Sound of Kerrera
Kilbride
Loch Nell
Cruachan Power Station
Ardanaiseig
Rubha Seanach
Kilmore
129
Dalnacabeg
Loch Nant
Ardentallan
Loch Feochan
Kilchrenan
Hayfield
Barrnacarry
B844
Kilninver
Annat
North Port
Cladich
Auchachenna
Coillaig
Raera
15
Loch Scamadale
Braglenbeg
2
INSH ISLAND
Ardencaple Ho.
Clachan
1436
CARN DEARG
Portsonachan Hotel
South Port
B840
An Cala
Easdale
481
MEALL O'CHAISE
Clachan-Seil
Barrnayarry
Inverinan
INVERINAN FOREST
Easdale
Ellanbeich
SEIL
Balvicar
Loch Tralaig
A816
Lochavich
993
TOM AN T SAIGHEIR
Tullich
1932
CRUACH MHOR
B8003
Seil Sound
Melfort
Kilchoan
Loch Avich
Barnaline Lodge
Blarghour
24
Cullipool
Torsa
Degnish
Kilmelford
Maolachy
Dalavich
Ardchonnell
Bardrishaig
Ardinamar
Loch Melfort
Glenmore
Newyork
Portinnisherrich
Arduaine
Kames
LUING
Arduaine
123
A819
1
Kilchattan
Shuna Ho.
SHUNA
Garraron
Eredine
Malt Land
7
Toberonochy
Sound of Luing
8
Tunnalt
9
Durran
0
INVERARAY

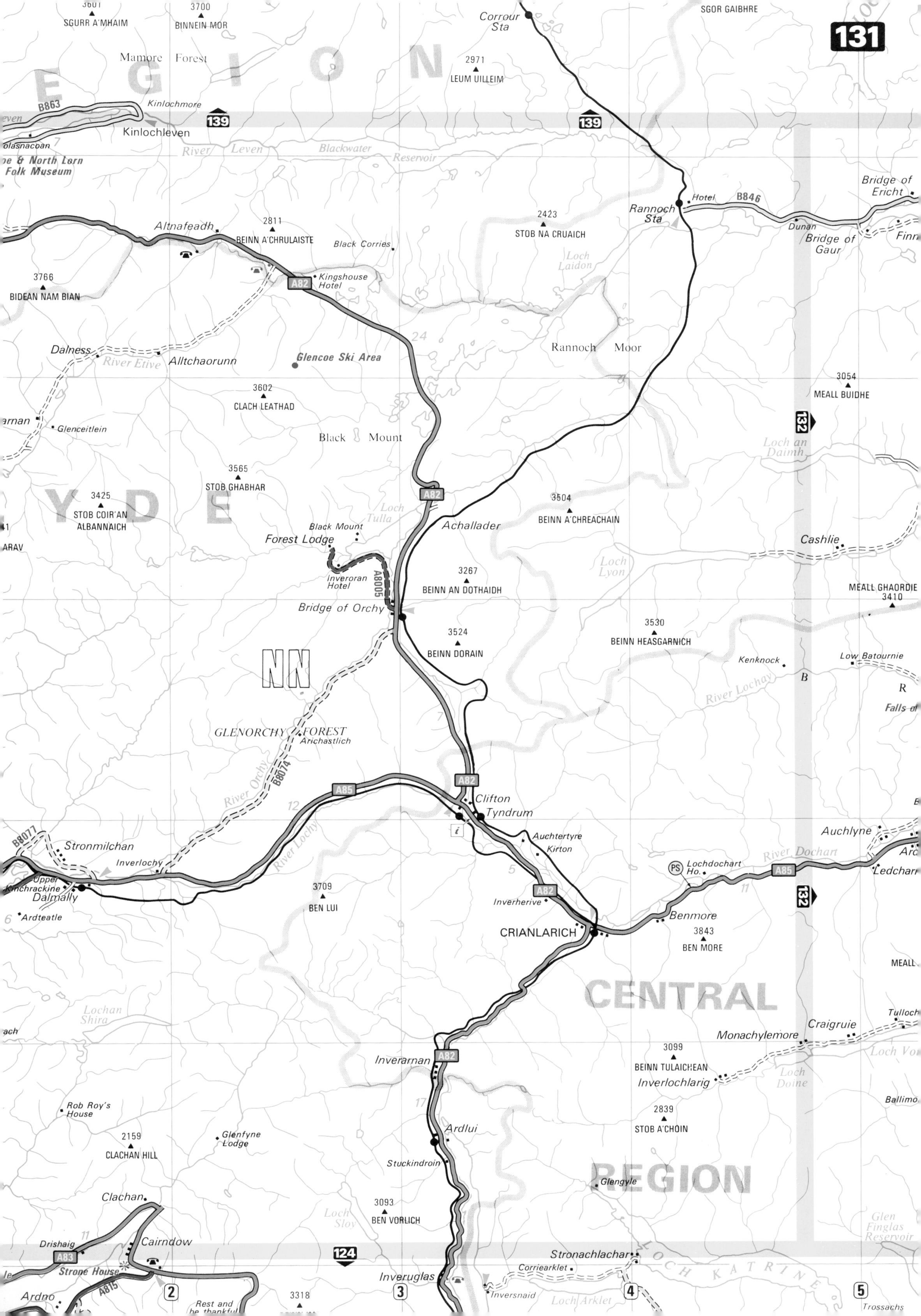

SGURR A'MHAIM
3601

BINNEIN MOR
3700

SGOR GAIBHRE

Corrour Sta

Mamore Forest

EGION

2971
LEUM UILLEIM

B863

139

Kinlochmore

Kinlochleven

139

Rannoch Sta

Hotel B846

Bridge of Ericht

River Leven   Blackwater   Reservoir

olasnacoan

7

oe & North Lorn
Folk Museum

2423
STOB NA CRUAICH

Dunan

Bridge of Gaur

Finn

Altnafeadh

2811
BEINN A'CHRULAISTE

Black Corries

Loch Laidon

A82
Kingshouse Hotel

3766
BIDEAN NAM BIAN

Rannoch   Moor

3054
MEALL BUIDHE

Dalness

Alltchaorunn

24

Glencoe Ski Area

River Etive

132

arnan

Glenceitlein

3602
CLACH LEATHAD

Black   Mount

Loch an Daimh

3565
STOB GHABHAR

3504
BEINN A'CHREACHAIN

Cashlie

YDE

3425
STOB COIR'AN ALBANNAICH

Black Mount

Loch Tulla

Achallader

Loch Lyon

MEALL GHAORDIE
3410

41

Forest Lodge

ARAV

Inveroran Hotel

A8005

3267
BEINN AN DOTHAIDH

3530
BEINN HEASGARNICH

Kenknock

Low Batournie

Bridge of Orchy

NN

3524
BEINN DORAIN

River Lochay

B

R

Falls of

GLENORCHY   FOREST

Arichastlich

B8074

River Orchy

12

A85

A82

Clifton
Tyndrum

Auchtertyre
Kirton

Auchlyne

River Dochart

Ard

B8077

Stronmilchan

Inverlochy

i

5

PS
Lochdochart Ho.

A85

132

Ledchar

Upper Kinchrackine

3709
BEN LUI

A82
Inverherive

11

Dalmally

6   Ardteatle

CRIANLARICH

Benmore

3843
BEN MORE

MEALL

Lochan Shira

CENTRAL

Monachylemore

Craigruie

ach

Inverarnan

A82

3099
BEINN TULAICHEAN

Inverlochlarig

Loch Doine

Tulloch

Ballimo

Rob Roy's House

2159
CLACHAN HILL

Glenfyne Lodge

Ardlui

2839
STOB A'CHOIN

Loch Vo

Clachan

Stuckindroin

REGION

Glengyle

Glen Finglas Reservoir

Drishaig

Cairndow

3093
BEN VORLICH

Loch Sloy

Stronachlachar

A83

Strone House

A815

124

Inveruglas

Corriearklet

LOCH KATRINE

Ardno

2

Rest and he thankful

3318

3

Inversnaid

Loch Arklet

4

5

Trossachs

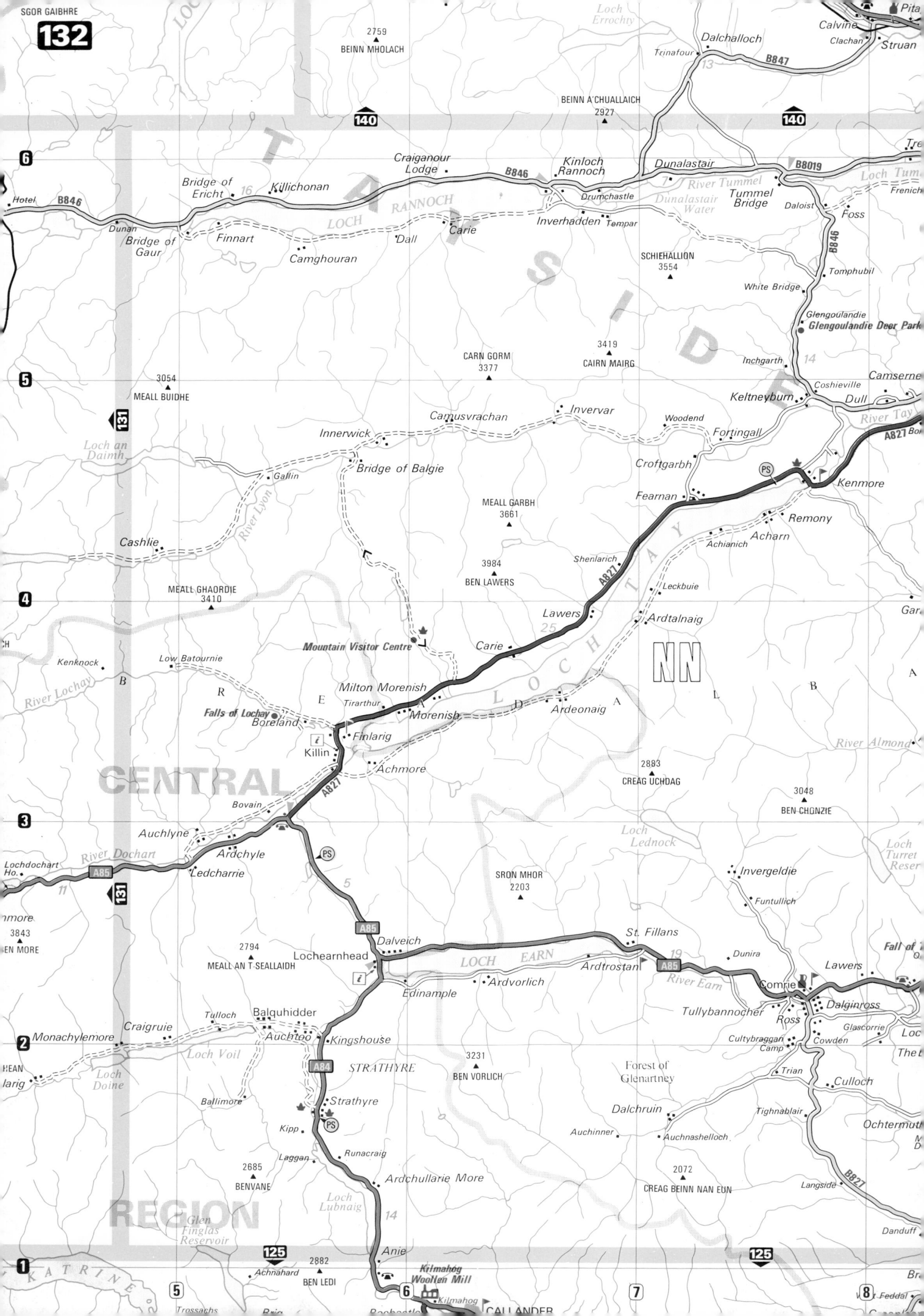
PERTHSIDE
Loch Errochy
Dalchalloch
Trinafour
Calvine
Clachan
Struan
B847
BEINN MHOLACH 2759
BEINN A'CHUALLAICH 2927
140
Craiganour Lodge
Kinloch Rannoch
Dunalastair
B8019
Loch Tummel
River Tummel
Tummel Bridge
Dunalastair Water
Drumchastle
Inverhadden
Tempar
Daloist
Foss
Frenich
Hotel
B846
Dunan
Bridge of Gaur
Bridge of Ericht
Killichonan
LOCH RANNOCH
Finnart
Camghouran
Dall
Carie
SCHIEHALLION 3554
Tomphubil
White Bridge
Glengoulandie
Glengoulandie Deer Park
Inchgarth
Coshieville
Camserney
Keltneyburn
Dull
River Tay
CARN GORM 3377
CAIRN MAIRG 3419
MEALL BUIDHE 3054
131
Loch an Daimh
Camusvrachan
Invervar
Innerwick
Woodend
Fortingall
Bridge of Balgie
Gallin
River Lyon
Croftgarbh
A827
Kenmore
Fearnan
MEALL GARBH 3661
Remony
Acharn
Achianich
Cashlie
Shenlarich
BEN LAWERS 3984
MEALL GHAORDIE 3410
Leckbuie
Lawers
Ardtalnaig
LOCH TAY
Mountain Visitor Centre
Carie
Kenknock
Low Batournie
River Lochay
BREADALBANE
NN
Milton Morenish
Tirarthur
Morenish
Ardeonaig
Falls of Lochay
Boreland
Finlarig
Killin
Achmore
River Almond
CENTRAL REGION
CREAG UCHDAG 2883
BEN CHONZIE 3048
Bovain
Auchlyne
Loch Lednock
River Dochart
Ardchyle
Lochdochart Ho.
A85
Ledcharrie
Invergeldie
Loch Turret Reservoir
SRON MHOR 2203
Funtullich
BEN MORE 3843
A85
Dalveich
St. Fillans
Fall of
MEALL AN T-SEALLAIDH 2794
Lochearnhead
LOCH EARN
Ardtrostan
Dunira
Lawers
Edinample
Ardvorlich
River Earn
Comrie
Tullybannocher
Dalginross
Ross
Balquhidder
Tulloch
Craigruie
Monachylemore
Auchtoo
Kingshouse
Loch Voil
Glascorrie
Cultybraggan Camp
Cowden
BEN VORLICH 3231
A84
STRATHYRE
Forest of Glenartney
Trian
Culloch
Loch Doine
Ballimore
Strathyre
Dalchruin
Tighnablair
Ochtermuthill
Kipp
Auchinner
Auchnashelloch
BENVANE 2685
Laggan
Runacraig
Ardchullarie More
CREAG BEINN NAN EUN 2072
Langside
B827
Loch Lubnaig
Glen Finglas Reservoir
Danduff
125
Anie
BEN LEDI 2882
Achnahard
Kilmahog Woollen Mill
Kilmahog
CALLANDER
LOCH KATRINE
Trossachs
Feddal

Blair Castle
Middlebridge
Old Bridge of Tilt
Bridge of Tilt
Blair Atholl
Aldclune
A9
Killiecrankie
BEN VRACKIE
2760
Balavoulin
Visitor Centre
Tummel Forest Centre
B8019
Queen's View
Faskally Wayside Centre
Moulin
Kinnaird
PITLOCHRY
Port na-Craig
Dunavourd
East Haugh
Dalcapon
Loch Derculich
Mains of Killichangie
Ballechin
A827
Logierait
Tulliemet House
Tulliemet
Ballinluig
Derculich
Edradynate
Grandtully
Balnaguard
Balmacneil
Kindallachan
Guay
Dowally
Kincraigie
Dalguise
B898
Dalmarnock
Inchmagranachan
1747
GRANDTULLY HILL
Loch Skiach
Loch Kennard
A826
MEALL UAINE
Tarvie
Straloch
Dalnavaid
River Ardle
Enochdhu
Balvarran
141
A924
2092
CREAG DHUBA
Williamston
Kirkmichael
STRATHARDLE
B950
Mains of Soilzarie
Milton
A93
Ballintuim
Persie Mains
1573
BLACKCRAIG HILL
Whitehouse
Netherton
Heatheryhaugh
Bridge of Cally
Rochallie
River Ericht
Riemore Lodge
Riechip
Middleton
Butterstone
Achalader
134
BLAIRGOWRIE
Lornty
A923
Forneth
Clunie
Wester Essendy
Kinloch
B947
Craigie
Concraigie
Snaigow Ho.
Easter Essendy
Carsie
Kirkton of Lethendy
Spoutwells
Dunkeld
Little Dunkeld
Inver
Birnam
A984
Spittalfield
Ballinlick
Trochrie
Laganallachy
A822
Milton
Cablea
Loch Freuchie
Amulree
River Braan
Corrymuckloch
Presnerb
Forter
B951
Clackavoid
Folda
Broughanreid
Backwater Reservoir
Kirkton of Glenisla
Blacklunans
Bridge of Brewlands
Bellaty
Wester Peathaugh
Easter Peathaugh
Forest of Alyth
Scruschloch
Middleton
Bridge of Craigisla
Dykehead
Tullymurdoch
Bamff
Gauldswell
Tullyfergus
ALYTH
New Alyth
Bonnington
Westfields of Rattray
A926
East Rattray
Aberbothrie
RATTRAY
Welltown
Rosemount
Arthurstone
Muirton of Ardblair
Wester Myreriggs
A94
Delvine
Caputh
Meikleour
Wester Banchory
COUPAR ANGUS
Little Keithick
Markethill
Kettins
Gellyburn
Murthly
Kinclaven
Layston
Woodside
Campmuir
Muir of Thorn
Ardoch
Balmains
B867
B9099
Cargill
Burrelton
Waterloo
Nether Obney
Obney
Tullybeagles Lodge
Bankfoot
Airntully
Balholmie
Gallowhill
Strelitz
East Kinnochtry
West Kinnochtry
Whitefield
Dundriven
NO
Gauls
West Tofts
Redstone
Saucher
1236
KING'S SEAT
Glenshee
2045
MEALL NAN CAORAICH
2188
MEALL REAMHAR
Stanley
Wolfhill
Dunsinnan
Kinrossie
Collace
Kirkton of Collace
Guildtown
Logiealmond Lodge
STRATHORD FOREST
Abernyte
Southfield
B953
Bandirran
St. Martin's
Chapelhill
Harrietfield
B8063
Millhaugh
Moneydie
Downhill
Newmiln
Colen
Colenden
Luncarty
Scones Lethendy
PERTH(SCONE)
Balbeggie
Craigdallie
Kinaird
Rait
River Almond
Tulchan
Buchanty
Dalcrue
Redgorton
Pitcairngreen
Scone Palace
Balboughty
Old Scone
New Scone
Kilspindie
Busby
Lawgrove
Almondbank
Keillour
Wester Keillour
Monzie
A85
Huntingtower
Perth
Methven
Braegrum
Oliverburn
Bridgend
Pitroddie
Inchmichael
Fowlis Wester
Gilmerton
Tibbermore
PERTH
Kinfauns
Hole of Clien
Glendoick
Glencarse
Milton of Cultoquhey
New Fowlis
Tomaknock
CRIEFF
Easter Cultmalundie
Wester Cultmalundie
Madderty
Clathymore
Milltown of Aberdalgie
Scoonieburn
M85
Elcho
Chapelhill
Leetown
Findo Gask
St. David's
Clathy
B9112
Aberdalgie
Craigend
Tarsappie
Pitfour Castle
B8062
Upper Cairnie
A9
M90
Rhynd
Inchyra
Fingask
Innerpeffray Library
Kirkton
Denfield
Forteviot
Forgandenny
NEWBURGH
B935
River Earn
Broom of Dalreoch
Chapelbank
Bridge of Earn
Kintillo
Aberargie
Abernethy
A913
A983
Glenearn
Kinkell Bridge
Drumtogle
B9141
Baldinnies
Dron
Round Tower
Glenfoot
Pitcairlie Ho.
Strathallan Aircraft Museum
Wallfauld
Aberuthven
Murrayfield
Middleton
Dunning
PITMEDDEN FOREST
A823
AUCHTERARDER
A824
Strathfoot
Millhaugh
B8062
Bein Inn
A912
Pleasance
Milton
Pairney
1346
CRAIG ROSSIE
Rossie Orchill
Newton of Balcanquhal
AUCHTERMUCHTY
Murtown
Gleneagles Hotel
Path of Condie
Abbots Deuglie
Glenfarg
126
Wellfield
Arngask
LC
Greenhill
Gleneagles
Duncrievie
Gateside
Strathmiglo
Blackford
Middle Rigg
Drunzie
Nether
B936
9
0
1
2

Tillyarblet
Inchbare
Marykirk
Ecclesgreig
Johnshaven
Shortside
Bush
Milton Ness
Lochside
Craigo
Pert
Auchnacree
Kirkton of Menmuir
Tigerton
Knowehead
Newtonmill
Keithock
Logie Pert
North Craigo
Logie
Morphie
St Cyrus
Pathhead
Shandford
Mains of Balhall
Belliehill
Little Keithock
Goynd
Ogil
Easter Ogil
Balquharn
Lochty
West Muir
Little Brechin
Cookston
Trinity
Mains of Pitforthie
Muirton of Ballochy
Hillside
Fern
Craigend of Careston
Barrelwell
Careston
BRECHIN
Dun
Kirkhill
Meikle Coull
Marcus Mill
A94
A935
A92
143
Tannadice
R South Esk
Blairie Mill
Burghill
Balwyllo
MONTROSE
Montrose Basin
Scurdie Ness
Murthill
Netherton
New Forebank
Haughs of Kinnaird
Barnhead
Milton of Finavon
Finavon
Crosston
B9134
Mains of Melgund
West Drums
Middle Drums
Bonnyton
Maryton
Ferryden
Foreside of Cairn
Battledykes
Oathlaw
Henwellburn
Aberlemno
Muirside of Melgund
A933
Farnell
A934
Carcary
Kirkton of Craig
Fishtown of Usan
HILL OF FINAVON
751
Pitkennedy
Westerton
Burnside
Dubton
Boddin
Carse Gray
Clochtow
Lunanhead
Turin
Pickerton
Bolshan
Hawkhill
Braehead
Lunan
A926
FORFAR
Reswallie
B9113
Balgavies
Glasterlaw
Kinnell
LUNAN BAY
A932
Burnside
Guthrie
Inverkeilor
Redcastle
A94
Teuchatcroft
Hillend
Dunnichen
Millden
Pitmuies
Friockheim
Boysack
Kingsmuir
Bowriefauld
Letham
Balmuir
Legaston
Chapelton
B965
Cauldcots
Cotton of Inchock
North Mains
South Mains
A929
Craignathro
Lowrie Moor
B9128
Idvies
Burnton
Boghead
Craichie
Leysmill
Cononsyth
Letham Grange
Drunkendub
Spittalburn
Tulloes
Colliston
Mosston
Marywell
Whigstreet
Muirheads
Redford
Mill of Inverarity
B9127
Greystone
Auchmithie
Windyhills
Ashbrook
B961
Kirkbuddo
Carmyllie
St Vigeans
Hatton
Burnside of Kirkbuddo
Hayshead
Cliffburn
The Deil's Heid
Denhead of Arbirlot
B9127
Newton of Arbirlot
Carrot
B978
Hayhillock
Easter Knox
Rosefield
Arbirlot
ARBROATH
Bonnington
Smiddy
Balcathie
Wormiehills
West Denside
Monikie
Kirkton of Monikie
West Balmirmer
Craigend
East Balmirmer
Affleck
North Kingennie
East Denside
B9128
Muirdrum
Craigton
Salmond's Muir
Wellbank
East Scryne
Newbigging
Upper Victoria
West Scryne
Panbride
East Haven
Kellas
Westhall
Templehall
Clayholes
Murroes
South Kingennie
Drumsturdy
Barry
West Haven
Burnside of Duntrune
Ethiebeaton
Mains of Ardestie
CARNOUSTIE
B961
Baldovie
Lucknow
Buddon
Grange of Monifieth
Barnhill
MONIFIETH
A930
BUDDON NESS
DUNDEE
Broughty Ferry
TAYPORT
NEWPORT ON-TAY
Kirktonbarns
B945
TENTSMUIR FOREST
A92
Craigie
Rhynd
Carrick
Leuchars
Comerton
Milton
A919
ST ANDREWS BAY
Guardbridge
R Eden
Kincaple
A91
ST. ANDREWS
Strathkinness
Brownhills
B939
Ballone
A915
Boarhills
Boghall
Denhead
Prior Muir
A959
Ladeddie
Kingsbarns
Priorletham
Cameron Reservoir
Baldinnie
Stravithie
A918
Dunino
B940
127
Radernie
Balcomie
Craighead
Peat Inn
Kingsmuir
FIFE NESS
Lathones
Lochty Private Railway
B940
East
5
6
7
8
SCALE
0
1
2
3
4
5 miles
0
1
2
3
4
5 kilometres

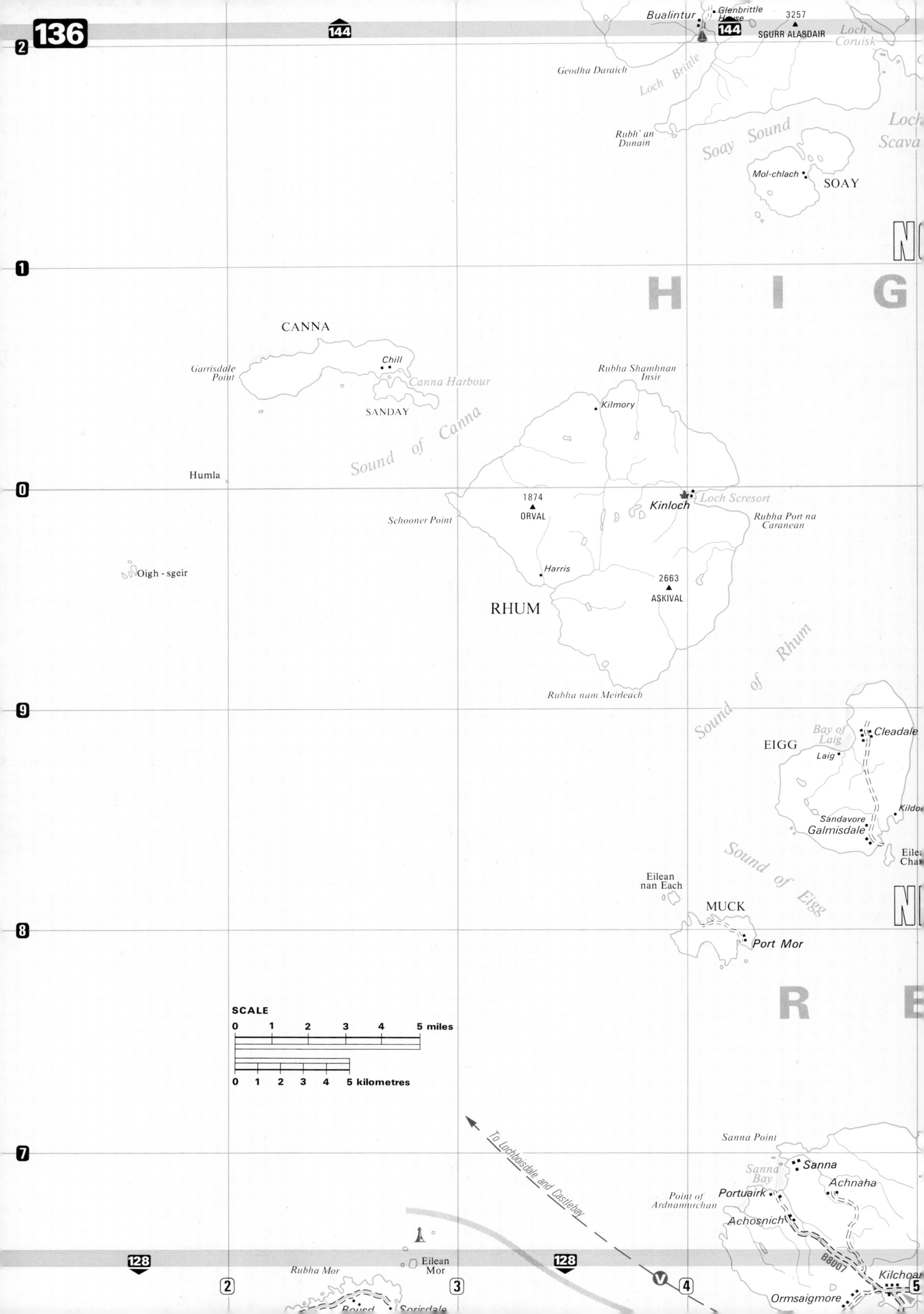

Bualintur
Glenbrittle House
3257
144
SGURR ALASDAIR
Loch Coruisk

Geodha Daraich

Loch Brittle

Loch Scava

Rubh' an Dunain

Soay Sound

Mol-chlach
SOAY

H I G

CANNA

Chill

Garrisdale Point

Canna Harbour

SANDAY

Rubha Shamhnan Insir

Kilmory

Sound of Canna

Humla

1874
ORVAL

Schooner Point

Kinloch
Loch Scresort

Rubha Port na Caranean

Oigh - sgeir

Harris

2663
ASKIVAL

RHUM

Sound of Rhum

Rubha nam Meirleach

Bay of Laig
Cleadale

EIGG

Laig

Kildo

Sandavore
Galmisdale

Eilea
Cha

Eilean nan Each

Sound of Eigg

MUCK

N

Port Mor

R

E

SCALE

0   1   2   3   4   5 miles

0   1   2   3   4   5 kilometres

To Lochboisdale and Castlebay

Sanna Point

Sanna Bay
Sanna

Achnaha

Point of Ardnamurchan

Portuairk

Achosnich

Rubha Mor

Eilean Mor

V
4

B8007

Kilchoa

Ormsaigmore

Rousd
Sorisdale

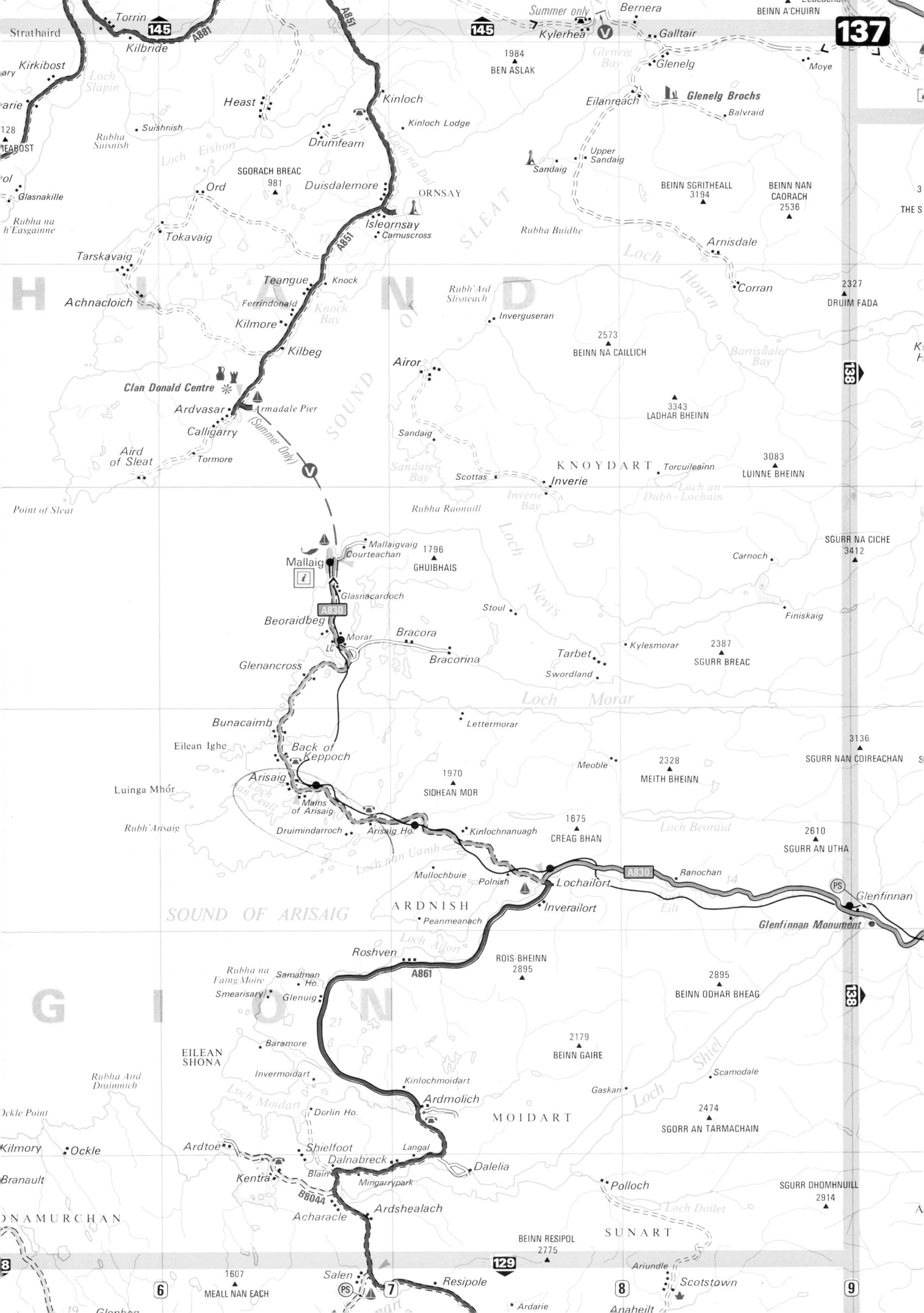
Strathaird
Torrin
Kilbride
A881
A851
Kirkibost
Loch Slapin
Heast
Suishnish
Rubha Suisnish
Loch Eishort
Kinloch
Kinloch Lodge
Drumfearn
SGORACH BREAC
981
Ord
Duisdalemore
ORNSAY
Glasnakille
Rubha na h'Easgainne
Tokavaig
Isleornsay
Camuscross
Tarskavaig
Teangue
Knock
Achnacloich
Ferrindonald
Knock Bay
Kilmore
Kilbeg
Clan Donald Centre
Ardvasar
Armadale Pier
Calligarry
(Summer Only)
Aird of Sleat
Tormore
Point of Sleat
Summer only
Kylerhea
Bernera
Galltair
BEINN A'CHUIRN
1984
BEN ASLAK
Glenelg Bay
Glenelg
Moye
Eilanreach
Glenelg Brochs
Balvraid
Upper Sandaig
Sandaig
BEINN SGRITHEALL
3194
BEINN NAN CAORACH
2536
THE S
SLEAT
Rubha Buidhe
Arnisdale
Loch Hourn
Corran
2327
DRUIM FADA
H L A N D
Rubh' Ard Slisneach
Inverguseran
SOUND OF SLEAT
2573
BEINN NA CAILLICH
Barrisdale Bay
Airor
3343
LADHAR BHEINN
Sandaig
Sandaig Bay
Scottas
KNOYDART
Inverie
Inverie Bay
Torcuileainn
3083
LUINNE BHEINN
Loch an Dubh-Lochain
Rubha Raonuill
Loch Nevis
Mallaigvaig
Courteachan
1796
GHUIBHAIS
Mallaig
SGURR NA CICHE
3412
Carnoch
Glasnacardoch
A830
Beoraidbeg
Stoul
Finiskaig
Morar
Bracora
Bracorina
LC
Kylesmorar
2387
SGURR BREAC
Tarbet
Swordland
Glenancross
Loch Morar
Lettermorar
Bunacaimb
Eilean Ighe
Back of Keppoch
Meoble
2328
MEITH BHEINN
3136
SGURR NAN COIREACHAN
Arisaig
Loch nan Ceall
1970
SIDHEAN MOR
Luinga Mhór
Mains of Arisaig
Rubh' Arisaig
Druimindarroch
Arisaig Ho.
Kinlochnanuagh
1675
CREAG BHAN
Loch Beoraid
2610
SGURR AN UTHA
Loch nan Uamh
Mullochbuie
Polnish
Lochailort
Ranochan
Loch Eilt
Glenfinnan
Glenfinnan Monument
SOUND OF ARISAIG
ARDNISH
Peanmeanach
Inveraliort
Loch Ailort
Roshven
A861
ROIS-BHEINN
2895
Rubha na Faing Moire
Samalman Ho.
Smearisary
Glenuig
2895
BEINN ODHAR BHEAG
G I O N
Baramore
EILEAN SHONA
2179
BEINN GAIRE
Rubha Aird Druimnich
Invermoidart
Kinlochmoidart
Loch Shiel
Scamodale
Gaskan
Loch Moidart
Ardmolich
Dorlin Ho.
MOIDART
2474
SGORR AN TARMACHAIN
Ockle Point
Kilmory
Ockle
Ardtoe
Shielfoot
Langal
Dalnabreck
Dalelia
Branault
Kentra
Blain
Mingarrypark
Polloch
SGURR DHOMHNUILL
2914
B8044
Acharacle
Ardshealach
Loch Doilet
ARDNAMURCHAN
SUNART
BEINN RESIPOL
2775
Ariundle
1607
MEALL NAN EACH
Salen
Resipole
Scotstown
Ardarie
Anaheilt
145
138
129
6
7
8
9

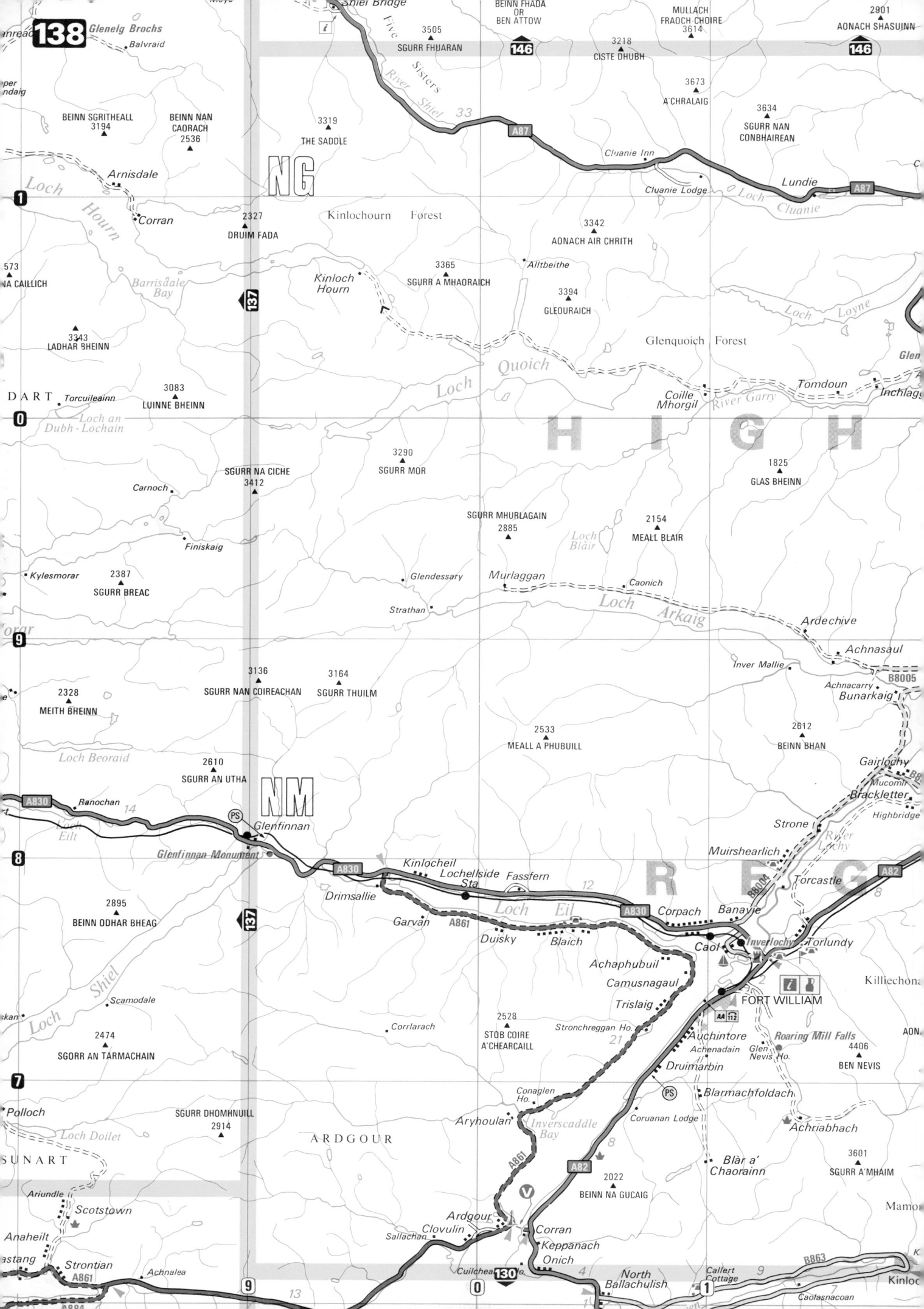

138
Glenelg Brochs
Balvraid
Shiel Bridge
Five Sisters
River Shiel
3505
SGURR FHUARAN
146
BEINN FHADA OR BEN ATTOW
3218
CISTE DHUBH
MULLACH FRAOCH CHOIRE
3614
2901
AONACH SHASUINN
3673
A'CHRALAIG
3634
SGURR NAN CONBHAIREAN
BEINN SGRITHEALL
3194
BEINN NAN CAORACH
2536
3319
THE SADDLE
A87
Cluanie Inn
Cluanie Lodge
Loch Cluanie
Lundie
NG
Arnisdale
Loch Hourn
Corran
2327
DRUIM FADA
Kinlochourn Forest
3342
AONACH AIR CHRITH
Alltbeithe
3365
SGURR A MHAORAICH
Kinloch Hourn
3394
GLEOURAICH
Barrisdale Bay
137
3343
LADHAR BHEINN
Loch Loyne
Glenquoich Forest
Loch Quoich
Tomdoun
Inchlaggan
Coille Mhorgil
River Garry
DART
Torcuileainn
3083
LUINNE BHEINN
Loch an Dubh-Lochain
HIGH
3290
SGURR MOR
1825
GLAS BHEINN
SGURR NA CICHE
3412
Carnoch
SGURR MHURLAGAIN
2885
2154
MEALL BLAIR
Loch Blàir
Finiskaig
Kylesmorar
2387
SGURR BREAC
Glendessary
Murlaggan
Caonich
Strathan
Loch Arkaig
Ardechive
Achnasaul
Inver Mallie
Achnacarry
Bunarkaig
B8005
3136
SGURR NAN COIREACHAN
3164
SGURR THUILM
2328
MEITH BHEINN
2533
MEALL A PHUBUILL
2612
BEINN BHAN
Loch Beoraid
2610
SGURR AN UTHA
Gairlochy
Mucomir
Bracklettter
Highbridge
A830
Ranochan
Loch Eilt
NM
PS
Glenfinnan
Glenfinnan Monument
Strone
River Lochy
Muirshearlich
Kinlocheil
Lochellside Sta
Fassfern
Torcastle
A82
REG
Drimsallie
Loch Eil
B8004
Corpach
Banavie
2895
BEINN ODHAR BHEAG
Garvan
A861
Duisky
Blaich
Caol
Inverlochy
Torlundy
Achaphubuil
Camusnagaul
Killiechonate
Loch Shiel
Scamodale
FORT WILLIAM
Trislaig
2528
STOB COIRE A'CHEARCAILL
Corrlarach
Stronchreggan Ho.
Auchintore
Achenadain
Roaring Mill Falls
Glen Nevis Ho.
4406
BEN NEVIS
2474
SGORR AN TARMACHAIN
Druimarbin
Conaglen Ho.
Blarmachfoldach
Polloch
SGURR DHOMHNUILL
2914
Aryhoulan
Inverscaddle Bay
Coruanan Lodge
Achriabhach
Loch Doilet
ARDGOUR
SUNART
A82
Blàr a' Chaorainn
3601
SGURR A'MHAIM
2022
BEINN NA GUCAIG
Ariundle
Scotstown
Ardgour
Clovulin
Sallachan
Corran
Keppanach
Onich
Anaheilt
Strontian
Achnalea
Cuilchea
130
North Ballachulish
Callert Cottage
B863
Caolasnacoan
Kinloch
1
0
9
8
7

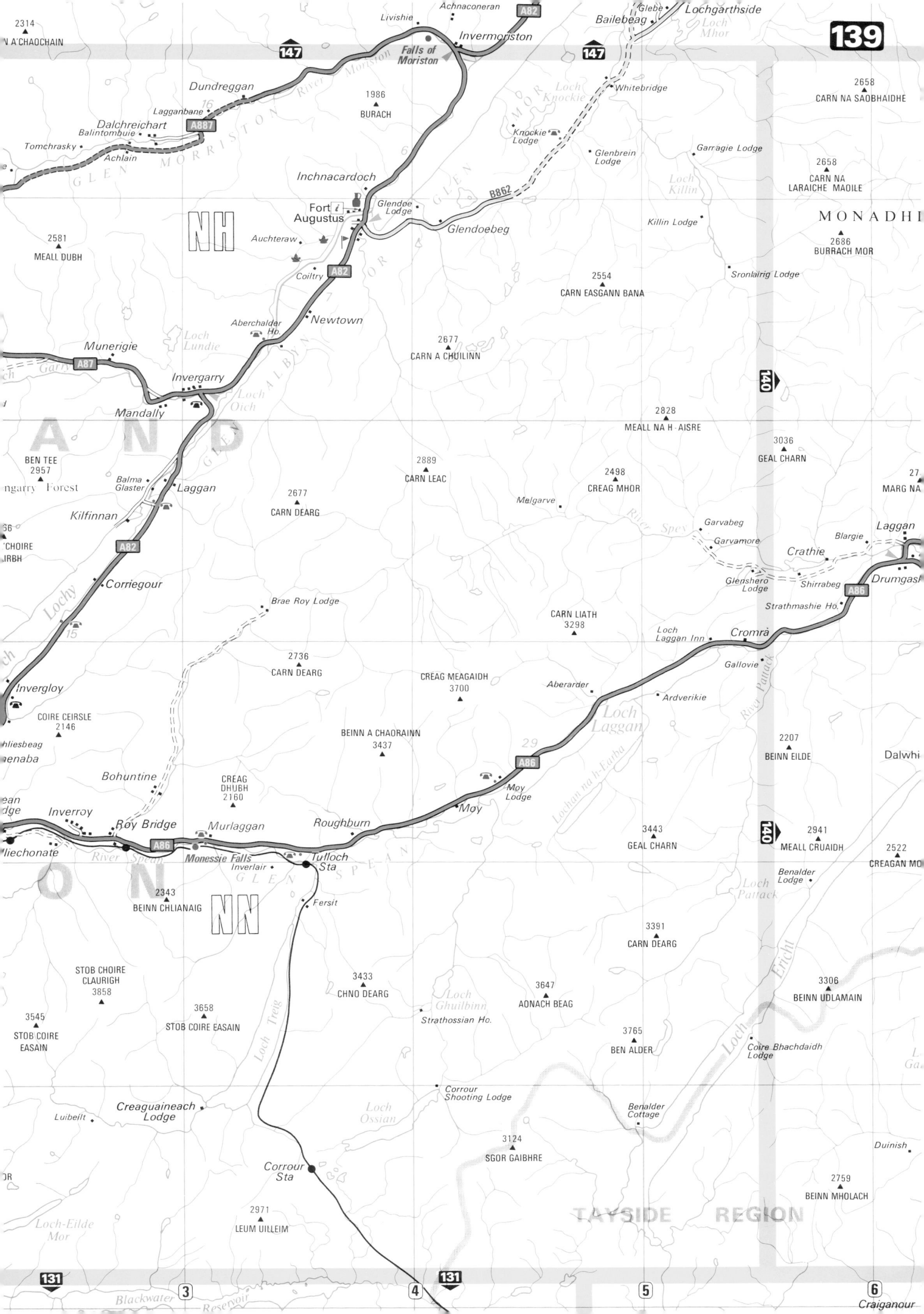

139
Achnaconeran
Livishie
Invermoriston
Falls of Moriston
Glebe
Lochgarthside
Bailebeag
Loch Mhor
147
A82
2314
A'CHAOCHAIN
Dundreggan
1986
BURACH
Whitebridge
Loch Knockie
2658
CARN NA SAOBHAIDHE
Lagganbane
A887
Dalchreichart
Balintombuie
Tomchrasky
Achlain
GLEN MORRISTON
River Moriston
Knockie Lodge
Glenbrein Lodge
Garragie Lodge
2658
CARN NA LARAICHE MAOILE
Inchnacardoch
Loch Killin
B862
Fort Augustus
Glendoe Lodge
Glendoebeg
MONADHI
NH
2581
MEALL DUBH
Auchteraw
Killin Lodge
2686
BURRACH MOR
Coiltry
2554
CARN EASGANN BANA
Sronlairig Lodge
Newtown
Aberchalder Ho.
Loch Lundie
2677
CARN A CHUILINN
Munerigie
A87
Invergarry
140
Mandally
Loch Oich
2828
MEALL NA H-AISRE
GLEN
3036
GEAL CHARN
BEN TEE
2957
Balma Glaster
Laggan
Forest
2889
CARN LEAC
2498
CREAG MHOR
27
MARG NA
2677
CARN DEARG
Melgarve
Kilfinnan
River Spey
Garvabeg
Garvamore
Laggan
Blargie
Crathie
A82
Corriegour
Glenshero Lodge
Shirrabeg
A86
Drumgask
Brae Roy Lodge
Strathmashie Ho.
Lochy
CARN LIATH
3298
Loch Laggan Inn
Cromra
2736
CARN DEARG
CREAG MEAGAIDH
3700
Gallovie
Aberarder
Invergloy
Ardverikie
Loch Laggan
River Pattack
COIRE CEIRSLE
2146
BEINN A CHAORAINN
3437
2207
BEINN EILDE
Dalwhi
Bohuntine
CREAG DHUBH
2160
Moy Lodge
Lochan na h-Earba
Moy
Inverroy
Roy Bridge
Murlaggan
Roughburn
3443
GEAL CHARN
2941
MEALL CRUAIDH
2522
CREAGAN MO
River Spean
Monessie Falls
Tulloch Sta
Inverlair
GLEN SPEAN
Benalder Lodge
Loch Pattack
2343
BEINN CHLIANAIG
Fersit
NN
3391
CARN DEARG
STOB CHOIRE CLAURIGH
3858
3433
CHNO DEARG
3647
AONACH BEAG
3306
BEINN UDLAMAIN
Loch Ericht
3658
STOB COIRE EASAIN
Loch Ghuilbinn
Strathossian Ho.
3545
STOB COIRE EASAIN
Loch Treig
3765
BEN ALDER
Coire Bhachdaidh Lodge
Corrour Shooting Lodge
Creaguaineach Lodge
Luibeilt
Loch Ossian
Benalder Cottage
Duinish
3124
SGOR GAIBHRE
Corrour Sta
2759
BEINN MHOLACH
2971
LEUM UILLEIM
TAYSIDE REGION
Loch-Eilde Mor
131
Blackwater Reservoir
3
4
5
6
Craiganour

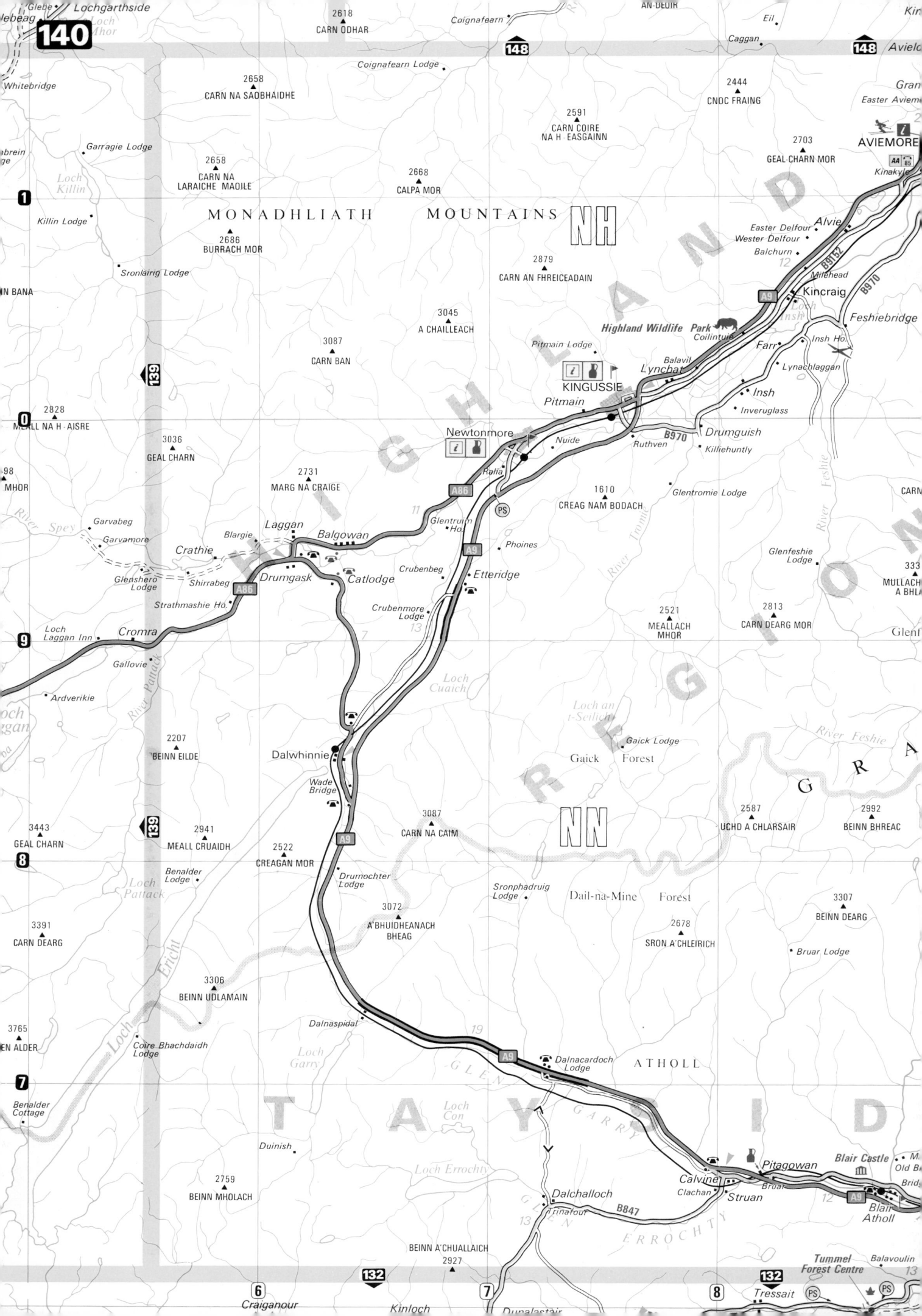

140
148
139
132
MONADHLIATH MOUNTAINS
NH
NN
HIGHLAND REGION
TAYSIDE
GRAMPIAN
Lochgarthside
Whitebridge
CARN ODHAR
CARN NA SAOBHAIDHE
Coignafearn
Coignafearn Lodge
Caggan
CNOC FRAING
CARN COIRE NA H-EASGAINN
AVIEMORE
GEAL-CHARN MOR
Garragie Lodge
CARN NA LARAICHE MAOILE
CALPA MOR
Loch Killin
Killin Lodge
BURRACH MOR
Sronlairig Lodge
CARN AN FHREICEADAIN
A CHAILLEACH
CARN BAN
Highland Wildlife Park
Kincraig
Feshiebridge
Alvie
Easter Delfour
Wester Delfour
Balchurn
Milehead
Coilintuie
Pitmain Lodge
KINGUSSIE
Lynchat
Balavil
Pitmain
Farr
Insh
Lynachlaggan
Inveruglass
Drumguish
Killiehuntly
Ruthven
Nuide
Newtonmore
Ralia
MEALL NA H-AISRE
GEAL CHARN
MARG NA CRAIGE
CREAG NAM BODACH
Glentromie Lodge
River Spey
Garvabeg
Garvamore
Laggan
Balgowan
Glentruim Ho.
Phoines
Crathie
Blargie
Drumgask
Catlodge
Crubenbeg
Etteridge
Glenfeshie Lodge
Glenshero Lodge
Shirrabeg
Strathmashie Ho.
Crubenmore Lodge
MEALLACH MHOR
CARN DEARG MOR
MULLACH A BHL
Loch Laggan Inn
Cromra
Gallovie
Ardverikie
River Pattack
Loch Cuaich
Loch an t-Seilich
Gaick Lodge
Gaick Forest
River Feshie
BEINN EILDE
Dalwhinnie
Wade Bridge
CARN NA CAIM
UCHD A CHLARSAIR
BEINN BHREAC
GEAL CHARN
MEALL CRUAIDH
CREAGAN MOR
Benalder Lodge
Loch Pattack
Drumochter Lodge
Sronphadruig Lodge
Dail-na-Mine Forest
BEINN DEARG
A'BHUIDHEANACH BHEAG
SRON A'CHLEIRICH
CARN DEARG
Bruar Lodge
River Ericht
BEINN UDLAMAIN
Dalnaspidal
Loch Garry
Loch Ericht
Coire Bhachdaidh Lodge
Dalnacardoch Lodge
ATHOLL
Glen Garry
Benalder Cottage
Loch Con
Duinish
Loch Errochty
Blair Castle
Pitagowan
Calvine
Clachan
Struan
Bruar
Blair Atholl
BEINN MHOLACH
Dalchalloch
Trinafour
Glen Errochty
BEINN A'CHUALLAICH
Tummel Forest Centre
Balavoulin
Tressait
Craiganour
Kinloch
A9
A86
B970
B9152
B847

Boat of Garten
Street of Kincardine
Strathspey Railway
Aundorach
Forest Lodge
149
Straanruie
Auchgourish
Lynamer
Milton
Pityoulish
B970
Dorback Lodge
Tomintoul
Delnabo
Auchnahchan
Alltachbeg
149
2159
MOSS HILL
Ladder
2257
CARN NA FARRAIDH
Badnafrave
Blairnamarrow
PS
2356
THE SOCACH
2692
GEAL CHARN
2636
CARN BHEADHAIR
2654
MEALL A BHUACHAILLE
Coylumbridge
Glenmore Lodge
PS
Loch Morlich
Lochgrue
Illochgrue
2332
CRAIG VEANN
2600
CARN EALASAID
A939
Cock Bridge
Milltown
Garchory
B973
Inverernan
Colnabaichin
Tornahaish
NJ
2431
RIG GARVOUN
River Avon
Lagganauld
Delnadamph Lodge
Corgarff
Greenbank
Corgarff
2435
MAM SUIM
2366
CASTLE HILL
Cairngorm Ski Area
4084
CAIRN GORM
Faindouran Lodge
Glen Avon
2338
THE BRUACH
2294
CARN LEAC SAIGHDEIR
2721
BROWN COW HILL
Loch Avon
3621
STOB AN T-SLUICHD
BEN AVON
3843
Lochbuilg Lodge
Corndavon Lodge
3553
BEINN O'CHAORRAINN
CAIRNGORM
MOUNTAINS
4248
BRAERIACH
4296
BEN MACDUI
3556
CARN EAS
CULARDOCH
2953
142
Rinloan
Torbeg
GEALLAIG HILL
2438
B976
GRAMPIAN
MOUNTAINS
4241
CAIRN TOUL
3051
BEINN BHREAC
Coilacriech
Bush Lawsie
A93
Balmoral Castle
Crathie
Mains
Tullochcoy
B976
2029
MEALL GORM
Inver
Easter Balmoral
Balnacroft
Derry Lodge
Luibeg
BRAEMAR
Braemar Castle
Khantore
Bovaglie
3795
BEINN BHROTAIN
River Dee
2666
SGOR MOR
Allanaquoich
Braemar
Keiloch
1969
CREAG NAN GALL
Linn of Dee
Claybokie
Muir
Inverey
Tomintoul
Balintuim
A93
Auchallater
Balmoral Forest
GRAMPIAN
REGION
2676
CARN LIATH
3791
LOCHNAGAR
2827
CONACHCRAIG
Allt-na-giubhsaich
Clunie Water
Loch Callater
Loch Muick
Spittal of Glenmuick
3300
CARN AN SGARSOCH
3014
CARN BHAC
Glen Clunie Lodge
2908
SGOR MOR
Glas-allt Shiel
3268
BROAD CAIRN
142
3340
CARN AN TUIRC
Fealar Lodge
NO
Glenshee Ski Area
3059
THE CAIRNWELL
3504
GLAS MAOL
Moulzie
3449
GLAS TULAICHEAN
A93
Acharn
Braedownie
2954
FINALTY HILL
Loch Loch
River South Esk
3673
BEINN A GHLO
3108
DRIESH
Glenlochsie
2846
MEALL A CHOIRE BHUIDHE
Dalmunzie Ho.
Tulchan
CARN LIATH
3197
Auchavan
Spittal of Glenshee
Slochnacraig
Dalhenzean
REGION
2428
BADENDUN HILL
2600
MEALL UAINE
Runtaleave
Presnerb
Cormuir
BEN VRACKIE
2760
Tarvie
Straloch
Dalnavaid
Forter
Folda
Killiecrankie
A93
Clackavoid
B951
Enochdhu
Glenhead Farm
Balvarran
Broughanreid
A924
2092
CREAG DHUBA
133
0
1
Blacklunans
Bridge of Brewlands
2
Kirkton of Glenisla
134
Backwater Reservoir
3
Williamston
PS

Ladder
2159
MOSS HILL
Rinmore
Glencuie
Kildrummy
Kildrummy
Milltown
150
Upper Balfour
Bithnie
Scotsmill
Bridge of Alford
Montgarrie
Auchintoul
Ardgathen
Alford
Rorandle
Gateside
150
Belnacraig
Kirkton of Glenbuchat
Glenbuchat
Mains of Glenbuchat
2356
THE SOCACH
Upper Drumallachie
Mill of Brux
Asloun
Meikle Endovie
Whitehouse
Wellhouse
Pitmunie
Todlachie
A97
A980
Bellabeg
Forbestown
Glenkindie
Sinnahard
Drybrae
Little Lynturk
Strathdon
Roughpark
Towie
Milltown of Towie
Ley
Kirkton
Newton
Inverernan Ho.
Waterside
Heugh-Head
Boultenstone
Milton of Cushnie
Muir of Fowlis
Bridgend
Tillyfourie
Meikle Ley
B973
Garchory
Waulkmill
Rowanbush
Milltown
Leochel-Cushnie
Craigievar Castle
NJ
Colnabaichin
Birkford
Hillockhead
2031
PRESSENDYE
Confunderland
Kintocher
Nether Shie
Corgarff
Tornahaish
Rinalloch
Milton of Tolmauds
Bankhead
B993
Easter Davoch
Waulkmill
GRAMPIAN REGION
Migvie
Clashmarket
Douneside
2294
CARN LEAC SAIGHDEIR
2456
CAIRN MONA GOWAN
Crossroads
Tornaveen
Coldstone
Coynach
B9119
Craskins
Findrack Ho.
Easter Tornaveen
Drumlasie
Netherton
Corrachree
Stonyford
Lumphanan
2861
MORVEN
Logie Coldstone
Tarland
Titaboutie
Sundayswells Croft
Strathmore
Coull
Cairnbeathie
Milltown of Lumphanan
Glenfenzie
B9094
Milton of Auchinhove
Wester Beltie
Milton of Logie
Bridgend
Auchlossan
Torphins
Mill of Gellan
Tilly-neckle
141
Ordie
Lochhead
Westerton
Mid Beltie
Rinloan
Lary
Slug of Dess Falls
Leyton
Balnagowan
Torbeg
Candacraig
Boghead
Heugh-head
Mains of Easter Beltie
GEALLAIG HILL
2438
A939
McEwan Galleries
Cambus o' May
A93
24
Kincardine O'Neil
Tillydrine Ho.
B976
Milton of Tullich
Aboyne
Birsemore
Backhill of Trustach
Culsh
Turnerhall
Glascorn
Dinnet
B976
Tillycairn
Burnroot
B993
Coilacriech
Birse
Potarch
Bridge of Cannie
River Dee
Pannanich Wells Hotel
Deecastle
Millfield
Crathie
Bridge of Gairn
Greystone
1742
Marywell
R Dee
Mains
BLACK CRAIG
Ballogie
Littlemill
B976
BALLATER
1017
TOM'S CAIRN
Balnacroft
Birkhall
Bridgend Cottages
1724
CARNFERG
Berrysloch
Camlet
Khantore
THE COYLES OF MUICK
Baulds
Tillygarmond
Finzean
Feughside
Bovaglie
1956
Alltcailleach
Water of Tanar
Percie
Whitestone
Drumhead
B976
1969
CREAG NAN GALL
Aucholzie
2293
CAIRN LEUCHAN
2058
CLACHAN YELL
Ballochan
Greendams
River Muick
2025
PETER HILL
Water of Aven
Forest
Scolly's Cross
2827
CONACHCRAIG
3080
MOUNT KEEN
2433
HILL OF CAT
Glendye Lodge
Allt-na-giubhsaich
2141
HILL OF SAUGHS
Spittal of Glenmuick
2554
MOUNT BATTOCK
B974
Loch Muick
Glenmark
Shinfur
Allt Shiel
141
Auchronie
2731
EASTER BALLOCH
Kirkton
Tarfside
The Retreat
1488
CAIRN O'MOUNT
Loch Lee
Mid Cairncross
GLEN ESK
Millden Lodge
NO
Moulzie
TAYSIDE
River North Esk
Fasque
Fasque
Acharn
Braedownie
2424
CRUYS
2273
WEST KNOCK
Thaneston
2941
BEN TIRRAN
Auchmull
Mains of Balnakettle
3108
DRIESH
Clova
2224
HILL OF WIRREN
River South Esk
West Burnside
Dalbog
Woodtown
Meikle Strath
B955
Wheen
Hunthill Lodge
FINBRACKS
2478
Witton
Gannachy
Rottal
Balfield
Edzell
Sauchieburn
Edzell
West Water
Bridgend
Lightnie
Dunlappie
Luthermuir
Runtaleave
Balnaboth
B955
B966
Cormuir
Pitcarity
1676
Tillyarblet
REGION
Inchmill
HILL OF COUTERNACH
Inchbare
Glenmoy
Kirkton of Menmuir
Tigerton
A94
Auchnacree
Knowehead
Newtonmill
Pert
Glencally
Redheugh
Keithock
Glenhead Farm
Shandford
Mains of Balhall
Belliehill
Little Keithock
Easter Lednathie
Goynd
Ogil
Balquharn
Lochty
Little Brechin
Trinity
Muirton of Ballochy
Backwater Reservoir
134
Horiehaugh
Glenquiech
Easter Ogil
Fern
135
West Muir
Cookston
Mains of Pitforthie
Dykehead
Newmill of Inshewan
Careston
Barrelwell
Artithol
Craigend
BRECHIN
3
4
5
6
1
0
9
8
7

143
151
Balbithan
Grantlodge
Dalmadilly
Clovenstone
Pictillum
Burgh Muir
Balbithan
Mill of Fintray
Highlands
Kinmundy
Whitecairns
Braehead
Belhelvie
Balmedie
Monymusk
Kemnay
KINTORE
Wester Fintray
Hatton of Fintray
Cothall
Milton of Potterton
Gourdieburn
West Hatton
Cottown
Kinaldie
Old Goval
Parkhill Ho.
Locheye
Blackdog
Craigearn
Overton
Lauchintilly
Castle Fraser
Leylodge
Aquherton
Cairntradlin
Blackburn
Mains of Dyce
Dyce
Dubford
Mundurno
Glascoforest
Stoneywood
Causewayend
Newton of Murcar
Achath
Lyne of Skene
Clinterty
Craibstone
Denmore
South Denmore
Bankhead
Roadside
Burnseat
East Auchronie
Little Mill of Clinterty
Bridge of Don
To Lerwick
West Kinnernie
Dunecht
Skene Ho.
Millbuie
Auchinclech
Bucksburn
Kirkton of Skene
Gullymoss
Northfield
Old Aberdeen
Loch of Skene
Gairloch
Westhill
Mastrick
Marionburgh
Kingsford
Parkhead
Kittybrewster
ABERDEEN
Balblair
Echt
Garlogie
Elrick
Kingswells
Jessiefield
South Kirkton
Carnie
Mill of Echt
Tillioch
Landerberry
Cullerlie
Blacktop
Mannofield
Torry
Easter Ord
Redhill
Templefold
Nether Contlaw
Ruthrieston
Kincorth
Nigg
Benthoul
Little Eddieston
Cults
Bieldside
Cullerlie
Hardgate
Craigton
Milltown of Cullerlie
Forest Cottage
River Dee
Banchory Devenick
South Damhead
South Loirston
Souter Head
Cove Bay
Hattonburn
Burnhead
Drum Castle
Peterculter
Milltimber
Hirn
Mains of Drum
Kingcausie
Brigg of Blair
Charlestown
Auchlunies
Hare Ness
Drumfrennie
Myrebird
Bruckleboq
Park
Upper Park
Parkhead
Kirkton of Maryculter
Causeyport
Marywell
Upper Lochton
The Neuk
Ley
Crathes Castle
Craiglug
Hillside
Cairnwell
Findon
Portlethen
Ashentilly
Muirskie
Mill of Monquich
Stranog
East Rothnick
Auchlee
Cairngrassie
Woodlands
Kirkton of Durris
Crathes
Deebank
Denside
Cammachmore
Downies
Bridge of Feugh
Crossroads
Upper Burnhaugh
South Brachmont
Burnside
Netherley
Elsick Ho.
Windyedge
Newtonhill
Borrowfield
Cookney
Stranathro
Mill of Cammie
West Mulloch
Blairdrynes
Lochton
Craiggiecat
Muchalls Castle
Muchalls
Bridge of Muchalls
Cortins
Doonie Point
Midtown
1232
MONGOUR
Union Cottage
Mowtie
Glithno
Logie
New Mains of Ury
1754
Mergie
Rickarton
1052
HILL OF TRUSTA
Swanley
Cheyne
Redcloak
Garron Point
LEACHIE HILL
1289
Kirktown of Fetteresso
Elfhill
Tewel
STONEHAVEN
Glaslaw
Dunnottar
Dunnottar Mains
Tannachie
Goosecruives
Milton of Dillavaird
New Mill
Pitdrichie
Mains of Dillavaird
Glenfarquhar Lodge
Drumlithie
Fiddes
Barras
Mill of Uras
Crawton
Glenbervie
Galloquhine
Auchenblae
Candy
Pitforthie
Mondynes
Roadside of Catterline
Catterline
Brownmuir
Roadside of Kinneff
Todhead Point
East Cairnbeg
Cairnton
Balfeith
Parkneuk
West Cairnbeg
Townhead
Fordoun
Pittarrow
Redmyre
Allardice
Kinneff
Arbuthnott
Scotston
Bent
Mains of Haulkerton
INVERBERVIE
Bervie Bay
Tulloch
West Burnside
LAURENCEKIRK
Burnton
Mains of Benholm
Redford
Forth
Gourdon
Tullo' of Benholm
West Balhagarty
Benholm
Mains of Newton
Dykelands
Mains of Brotherton
Muirhead
Marykirk
Ecclesgreig
Johnshaven
Shortside
Bush
Lochside
Milton Ness
Craigo
St Cyrus
Morphie
Pathhead
Logie
135
7
8
9
0
SCALE
0 1 2 3 4 5 miles
0 1 2 3 4 5 kilometres

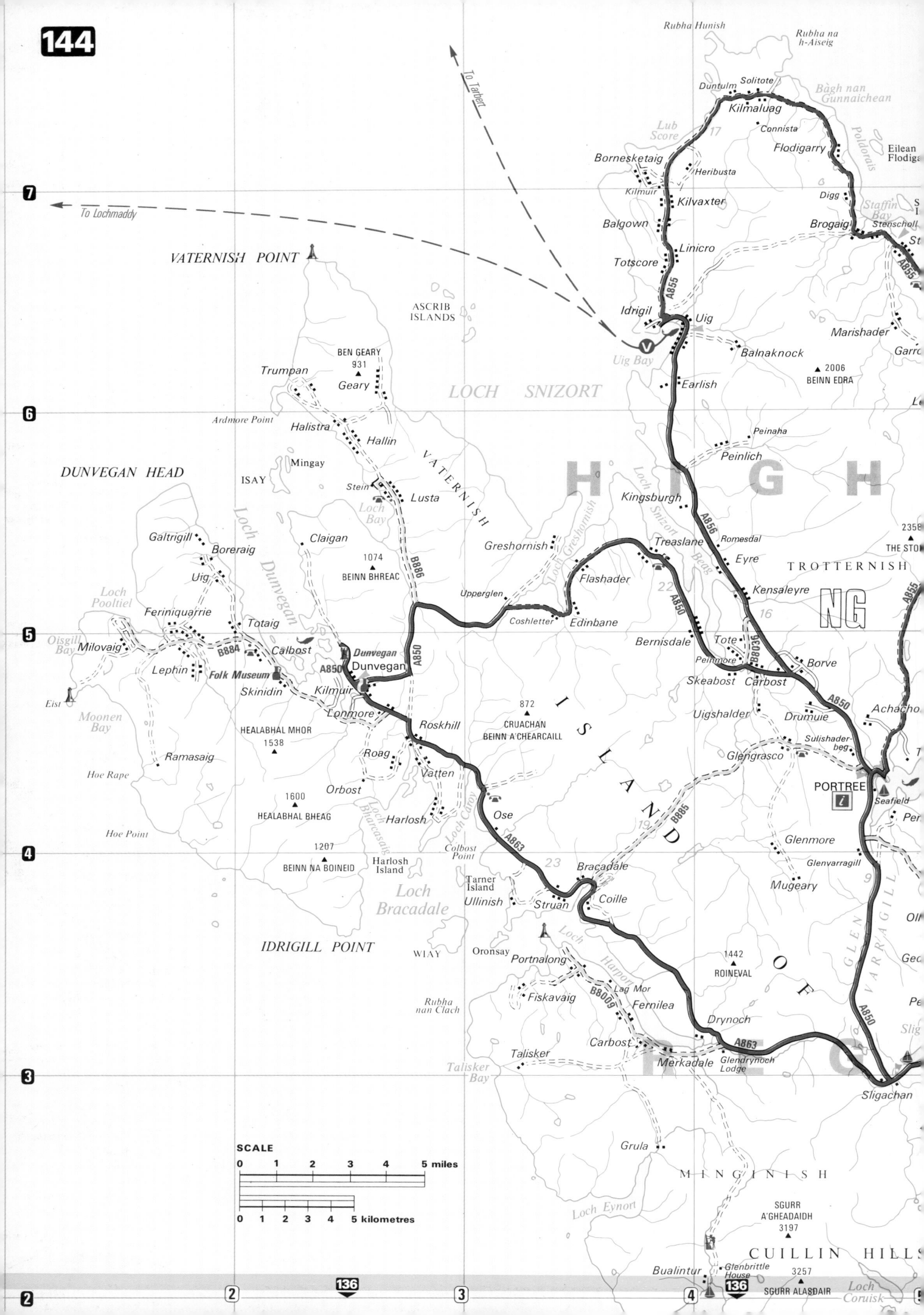
To Tarbert
To Lochmaddy
VATERNISH POINT
ASCRIB ISLANDS
BEN GEARY 931
Trumpan
Geary
Ardmore Point
Halistra
Hallin
Mingay
ISAY
DUNVEGAN HEAD
Stein
Lusta
VATERNISH
Loch Bay
Claigan
1074 BEINN BHREAC
B886
Galtrigill
Boreraig
Uig
Loch Dunvegan
Loch Pooltiel
Feriniquarrie
Totaig
Oisgill Bay
Milovaig
B884
Calbost
Dunvegan
A850
Lephin
Folk Museum
Skinidin
Kilmuir
Eist
Moonen Bay
Lonmore
Roskhill
HEALABHAL MHOR 1538
Ramasaig
Roag
Hoe Rape
Vatten
Orbost
1600 HEALABHAL BHEAG
Loch Bharcasaig
Harlosh
Ose
Loch Caroy
Hoe Point
1207 BEINN NA BOINEID
Harlosh Island
Colbost Point
A863
Tarner Island
Loch Bracadale
Ullinish
Struan
IDRIGILL POINT
WIAY
Oronsay
Portnalong
Rubha nan Clach
Fiskavaig
B8009
Talisker
Talisker Bay
Carbost
Rubha Hunish
Rubha na h-Aiseig
Duntulm
Solitote
Kilmaluag
Bàgh nan Gunnaichean
Lub Score
Connista
Flodigarry
Poldorais
Eilean Flodiga
Bornesketaig
Heribusta
Kilmuir
Kilvaxter
Digg
Staffin Bay
Balgown
Brogaig
Stenscholl
Linicro
Totscore
A855
Idrigil
Uig
Uig Bay
Balnaknock
Marishader
LOCH SNIZORT
Earlish
2006 BEINN EDRA
Peinaha
Peinlich
HIGH
Kingsburgh
Loch Snizort Beag
A856
Greshornish
Loch Greshornish
Treaslane
Romesdal
Eyre
TROTTERNISH
2358 THE STO
Flashader
Upperglen
A850
Kensaleyre
NG
Coshletter
Edinbane
B8036
Bernisdale
Tote
Peinmore
Borve
Skeabost
Carbost
872 CRUACHAN BEINN A'CHEARCAILL
ISLAND
Uigshalder
Drumuie
Achachork
Sulishader-beg
Glengrasco
PORTREE
Seafield
B885
Glenmore
Glenvarragill
Bracadale
Mugeary
Coille
GLEN VARRAGILL
OF
Loch Harport
1442 ROINEVAL
Lag Mor
Fernilea
Drynoch
A863
Merkadale
Glendrynoch Lodge
Sligachan
Grula
MINGINISH
Loch Eynort
SGURR A'GHEADAIDH 3197
CUILLIN HILLS
Bualintur
Glenbrittle House
3257 SGURR ALASDAIR
Loch Coruisk
SCALE
0 1 2 3 4 5 miles
0 1 2 3 4 5 kilometres
7
6
5
4
3
2
2
3
4
136
136

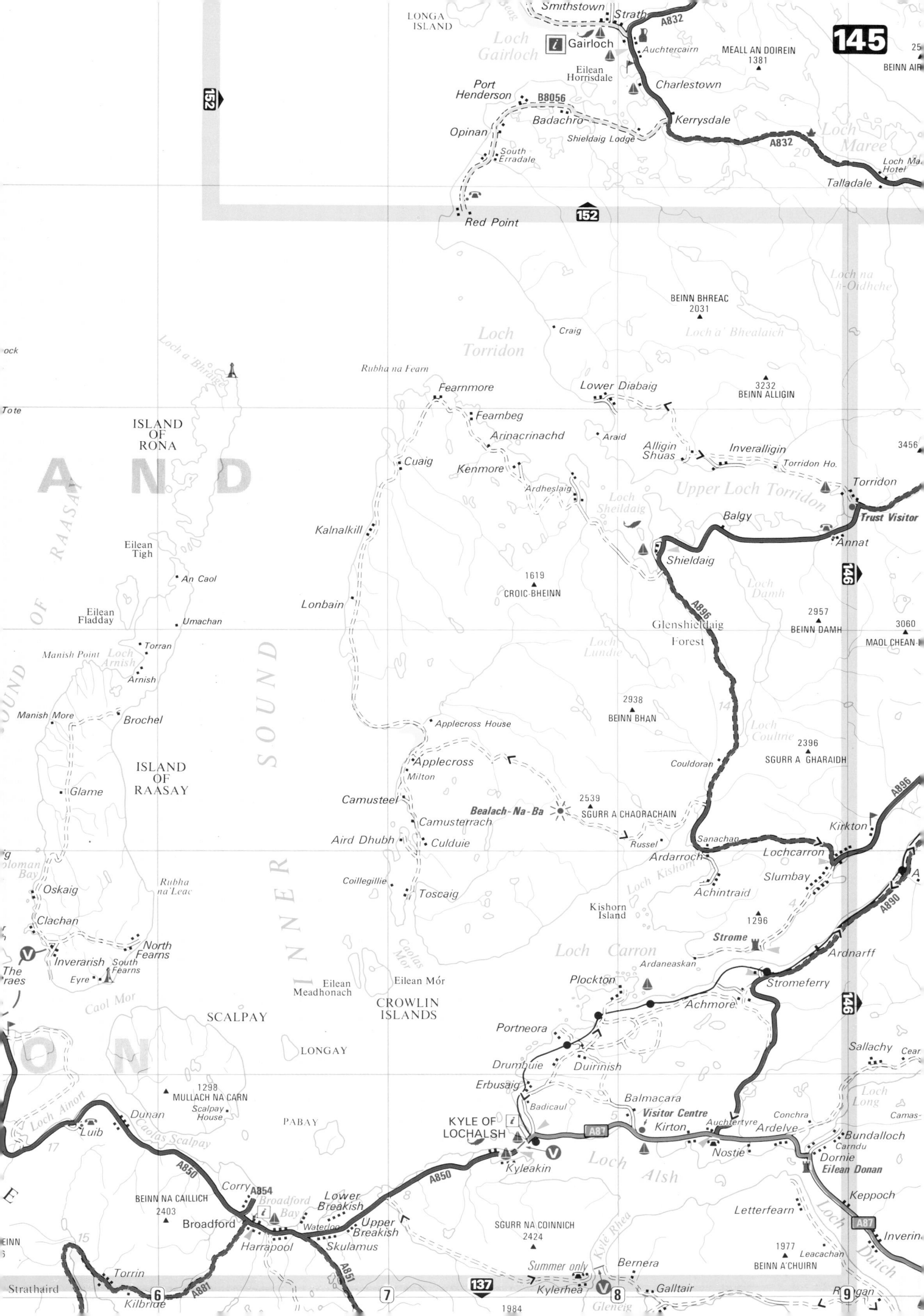
LONGA ISLAND
Smithstown
Strath
A832
Loch Gairloch
Gairloch
Auchtercairn
MEALL AN DOIREIN 1381
BEINN AIR
Eilean Horrisdale
Charlestown
Port Henderson
B8056
Badachro
Kerrysdale
Loch Maree
Opinan
Shieldaig Lodge
A832
South Erradale
Loch Maree Hotel
Talladale
152
Red Point
152
Loch na h-Oidhche
BEINN BHREAC 2031
Loch Torridon
Craig
Loch a' Bhealaich
Loch a' Bhràige
Rubha na Fearn
Fearnmore
Lower Diabaig
3232 BEINN ALLIGIN
Tote
ISLAND OF RONA
Fearnbeg
Arinacrinachd
Araid
Alligin Shuas
Inveralligin
3456
Cuaig
Kenmore
Torridon Ho.
Torridon
Ardheslaig
Upper Loch Torridon
Loch Sheildaig
Trust Visitor
RAASAY
Balgy
Annat
Kalnakill
Eilean Tigh
Shieldaig
An Caol
1619 CROIC-BHEINN
146
Loch Damh
Lonbain
Eilean Fladday
Umachan
A896
2957 BEINN DAMH
3060 MAOL CHEAN-
Glenshieldaig Forest
Torran
Loch Lundie
Manish Point
Loch Arnish
Arnish
SOUND
2938 BEINN BHAN
Manish More
Brochel
Applecross House
Loch Coultrie
2396 SGURR A' GHARAIDH
ISLAND OF RAASAY
Applecross
Couldoran
Milton
Glame
2539 SGURR A' CHAORACHAIN
A896
Camusteel
Bealach-Na-Ba
Camusterrach
Kirkton
Aird Dhubh
Culduie
Russel
Sanachan
Ardarroch
Lochcarron
Rubha na' Leac
Loch Kishorn
Oskaig
Coillegillie
Toscaig
Slumbay
Achintraid
Kishorn Island
1296
A890
Clachan
Strome
North Fearns
Loch Carron
Ardnarff
Inverarish
South Fearns
Caolas Mòr
Ardaneaskan
The Braes
Eyre
Eilean Meadhonach
Eilean Mór
Plockton
Stromeferry
Caol Mor
CROWLIN ISLANDS
Achmore
146
SCALPAY
Portneora
LONGAY
Sallachy
Drumbuie
Duirinish
1298 MULLACH NA CARN
Erbusaig
Loch Long
Scalpay House
Badicaul
Balmacara
Visitor Centre
Conchra
Camas-
Loch Ainort
Dunan
PABAY
KYLE OF LOCHALSH
A87
Kirton
Auchtertyre
Ardelve
Bundalloch
Luib
Caolas Scalpay
Carndu
Nostie
Dornie
Eilean Donan
A850
Kyleakin
Loch Alsh
Corry
A854
A850
Broadford Bay
Lower Breakish
Keppoch
BEINN NA CAILLICH 2403
Letterfearn
Loch Duich
Broadford
Waterloo
Upper Breakish
SGURR NA COINNICH 2424
A87
Inverinate
Harrapool
Skulamus
1977 BEINN A'CHUIRN
Leacachan
Kyle Rhea
A851
Summer only
Bernera
Torrin
Strathaird
A881
6
7
137
Kylerhea
8
Galltair
9
Kilbride
1984
Glenelg

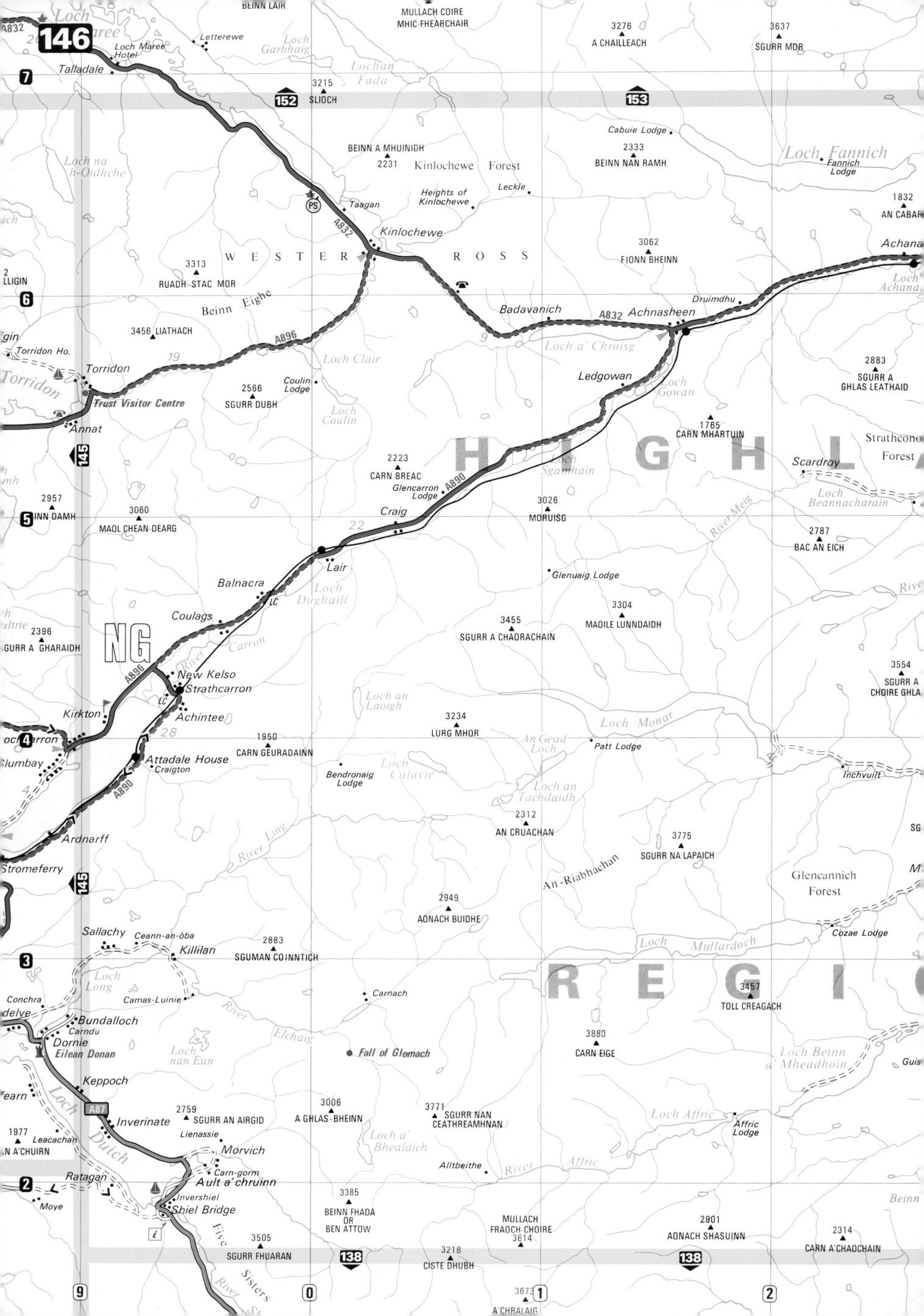

146
152
153
138
138
145
145
Loch Maree
Loch Maree Hotel
Letterewe
Talladale
BEINN LAIR
MULLACH COIRE MHIC-FHEARCHAIR
3276
A CHAILLEACH
3637
SGURR MOR
Loch Garbhaig
Lochan Fada
3215
SLIOCH
Cabuie Lodge
Loch Fannich
Fannich Lodge
BEINN A MHUINIDH
2231
Kinlochewe Forest
2333
BEINN NAN RAMH
Loch na h-Oidhche
Heights of Kinlochewe
Leckie
Taagan
A832
Kinlochewe
1832
AN CABAR
Achanalt
Loch Achanalt
3313
RUADH-STAC MOR
WESTER ROSS
3062
FIONN BHEINN
LIGIN
Beinn Eighe
Badavanich
A832
Achnasheen
Druimdhu
3456
LIATHACH
A896
Loch a' Chroisg
Torridon Ho.
Torridon
Loch Clair
Ledgowan
Loch Gowan
2883
SGURR A GHLAS LEATHAID
Trust Visitor Centre
2566
SGURR DUBH
Coulin Lodge
Loch Coulin
Annat
1765
CARN MHARTUIN
HIGHLAND
Strathconon Forest
2223
CARN BREAC
Glencarron Lodge
A890
Loch Sgamhain
Scardroy
Loch Beannacharain
2957
3060
MAOL CHEAN-DEARG
Craig
3026
MORUISG
River Meig
2787
BAC AN EICH
Lair
Glenuaig Lodge
Balnacra
Loch Dughaill
LC
3304
MAOILE LUNNDAIDH
Coulags
3455
SGURR A CHAORACHAIN
2396
NG
River Carron
A896
New Kelso
Strathcarron
LC
3554
SGURR A CHOIRE GHLAS
Kirkton
Achintee
Loch an Laoigh
3234
LURG MHOR
Loch Monar
Lochcarron
1950
CARN GEURADAINN
An Gead Loch
Patt Lodge
Slumbay
Attadale House
Craigton
Bendronaig Lodge
Loch Calavie
Loch an Tachdaidh
Inchvuilt
A890
2312
AN CRUACHAN
3775
SGURR NA LAPAICH
Ardnarff
River Ling
An Riabhachan
Glencannich Forest
Stromeferry
2949
AONACH BUIDHE
Sallachy
Ceann-an-òba
Killilan
2883
SGUMAN COINNTICH
Loch Mullardoch
Cozae Lodge
REGION
Loch Long
3457
TOLL CREAGACH
Conchra
Camas-Luinie
Carnach
River Elchaig
Bundalloch
Carndu
Dornie
Eilean Donan
Loch nan Eun
Fall of Glomach
3880
CARN EIGE
Loch Beinn a' Mheadhoin
Keppoch
Loch Duich
A87
3006
A GHLAS-BHEINN
3771
SGURR NAN CEATHREAMHNAN
Loch Affric
Affric Lodge
2759
SGURR AN AIRGID
Inverinate
1977
Leacachan
Lienassie
Morvich
Loch a' Bhealaich
Alltbeithe
River Affric
Ratagan
Carn-gorm
Ault a' chruinn
Moye
Invershiel
Shiel Bridge
3385
BEINN FHADA OR BEN ATTOW
MULLACH FRAOCH-CHOIRE
3614
2901
AONACH SHASUINN
2314
CARN A'CHAOCHAIN
Five Sisters
3505
SGURR FHUARAN
3218
CISTE DHUBH
3673
A'CHRALAIG
9
0
1
2
7
6
5
4
3
2

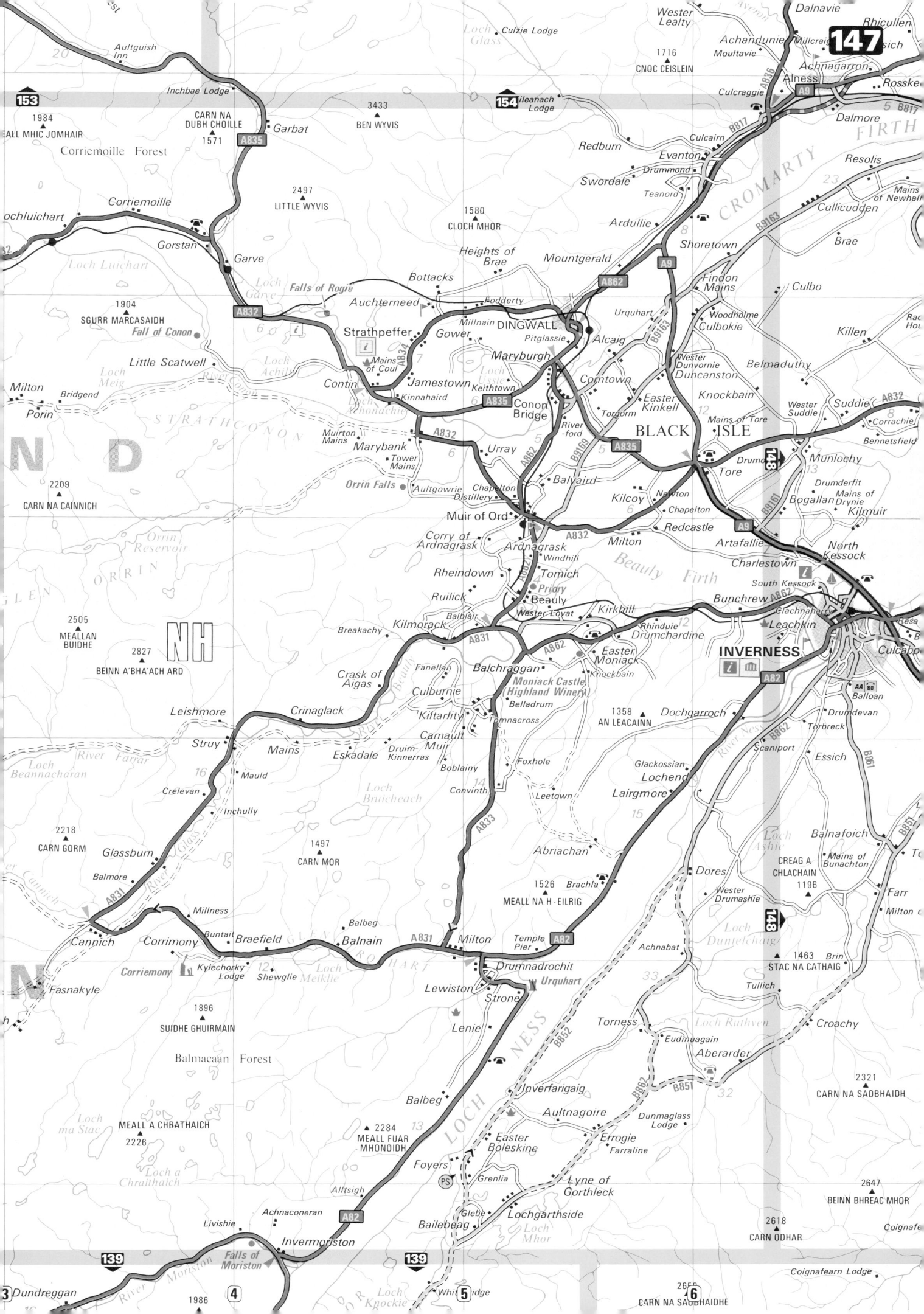
Aultguish Inn
Loch Glass
Culzie Lodge
Wester Lealty
Dalnavie
Rhicullen
Achandunie
Millcraig
Moultavie
1716
CNOC CEISLEIN
Achnagarron
Alness
Rosskeen
Culcraggie
A836
A9
B817
Dalmore
FIRTH
153
Inchbae Lodge
3433
BEN WYVIS
154
Eileanach Lodge
1984
CARN NA DUBH CHOILLE
1571
Garbat
A835
Corriemoille Forest
Redburn
Culcairn
Evanton
Drummond
Swordale
Teanord
CROMARTY
Resolis
Mains of Newhall
Cullicudden
2497
LITTLE WYVIS
1580
CLOCH MHOR
Corriemoille
Lochluichart
Gorstan
Garve
Loch Luichart
Ardullie
Shoretown
B9163
Brae
Heights of Brae
Mountgerald
A862
Bottacks
Loch Garve
Falls of Rogie
Findon Mains
Culbo
1904
SGURR MARCASAIDH
Fall of Conon
A832
Auchterneed
Fodderty
Urquhart
Millnain
DINGWALL
Strathpeffer
Gower
Pitglassie
Alcaig
Woodholme
Culbokie
Killen
Little Scatwell
Loch Meig
Loch Achilty
Mains of Coul
A834
Maryburgh
Loch Ussie
Wester Dunvornie
Duncanston
Belmaduthy
Milton
Bridgend
Porin
Contin
Jamestown
Keithtown
Cornton
Kinnahaird
Loch Achonachie
Conon Bridge
Easter Kinkell
Knockbain
Wester Suddie
Suddie
Corrachie
Torgorm
BLACK ISLE
Mains of Tore
STRATHCONON
River Conon
Muirton Mains
A832
River-ford
Marybank
Urray
Drumsmittal
Tore
148
Munlochy
Bennetsfield
Tower Mains
B9169
Balvaird
Drumderfit
Mains of Drynie
Bogallan
Kilmuir
2209
CARN NA CAINNICH
Orrin Falls
Aultgowrie
Chapelton Distillery
Kilcoy
Newton
Chapelton
B9161
Muir of Ord
Redcastle
Orrin Reservoir
ORRIN
Corry of Ardnagrask
Ardnagrask
Milton
Artafallie
North Kessock
Windhill
Beauly Firth
Charlestown
Rheindown
Tomich
Priory
South Kessock
Ruilick
Beauly
Bunchrew
Clachnaharry
Balblair
Wester Lovat
Kirkhill
Leachkin
2505
MEALLAN BUIDHE
Breakachy
Kilmorack
Rhinduie
Drumchardine
NH
2827
BEINN A'BHA'ACH ARD
A831
Easter Moniack
INVERNESS
Culcabock
Crask of Aigas
Fanellan
Balchraggan
Knockbain
A82
Moniack Castle (Highland Winery)
Balloan
Culburnie
Belladrum
Leishmore
Crinaglack
Kiltarlity
Tomnacross
1358
AN LEACAINN
Dochgarroch
Drumdevan
Camault Muir
Torbreck
Struy
Mains
Eskadale
Druim-Kinnerras
B862
Scaniport
Essich
River Farrar
Loch Beannacharan
Mauld
Boblainy
Foxhole
Glackossian
Lochend
B861
Crelevan
Loch Bruicheach
Convinth
Leetown
Lairgmore
Inchully
A833
Loch Ashie
Balnafoich
2218
CARN GORM
1497
CARN MOR
Glassburn
Abriachan
Balmore
River Glass
Dores
Mains of Bunachton
CREAG A CHLACHAIN
1526
MEALL NA H-EILRIG
Brachla
1196
Wester Drumashie
Farr
River Cannich
Millness
Milton
Balbeg
Loch Duntelchaig
Cannich
Corrimony
Buntait
Braefield
Balnain
A831
Milton
Temple Pier
Achnabat
GLEN URQUHART
1463
STAC NA CATHAIG
Corriemony
Kylechorky Lodge
Shewglie
Loch Meiklie
Drumnadrochit
Urquhart
Fasnakyle
Lewiston
Strone
Tullich
1896
SUIDHE GHUIRMAIN
Lenie
Torness
Loch Ruthven
Croachy
LOCH NESS
B852
Eudinuagain
Aberarder
Balmacaan Forest
B862
B851
2321
CARN NA SAOBHAIDH
Inverfarigaig
Balbeg
Loch ma Stac
MEALL A CHRATHAICH
2226
2284
MEALL FUAR MHONOIDH
Aultnagoire
Dunmaglass Lodge
Easter Boleskine
Errogie
Farraline
Loch a Chraithaich
Foyers
Grenlia
Lyne of Gorthleck
2647
BEINN BHREAC MHOR
Alltsigh
Achnaconeran
Glebe
Lochgarthside
Livishie
A82
Bailebeag
Loch Mhor
2618
CARN ODHAR
Coignafearn
Invermoriston
Falls of Moriston
139
139
Coignafearn Lodge
Dundreggan
River Moriston
1986
4
5
Loch Knockie
Whitebridge
2658
6
CARN NA SAOBHAIDHE

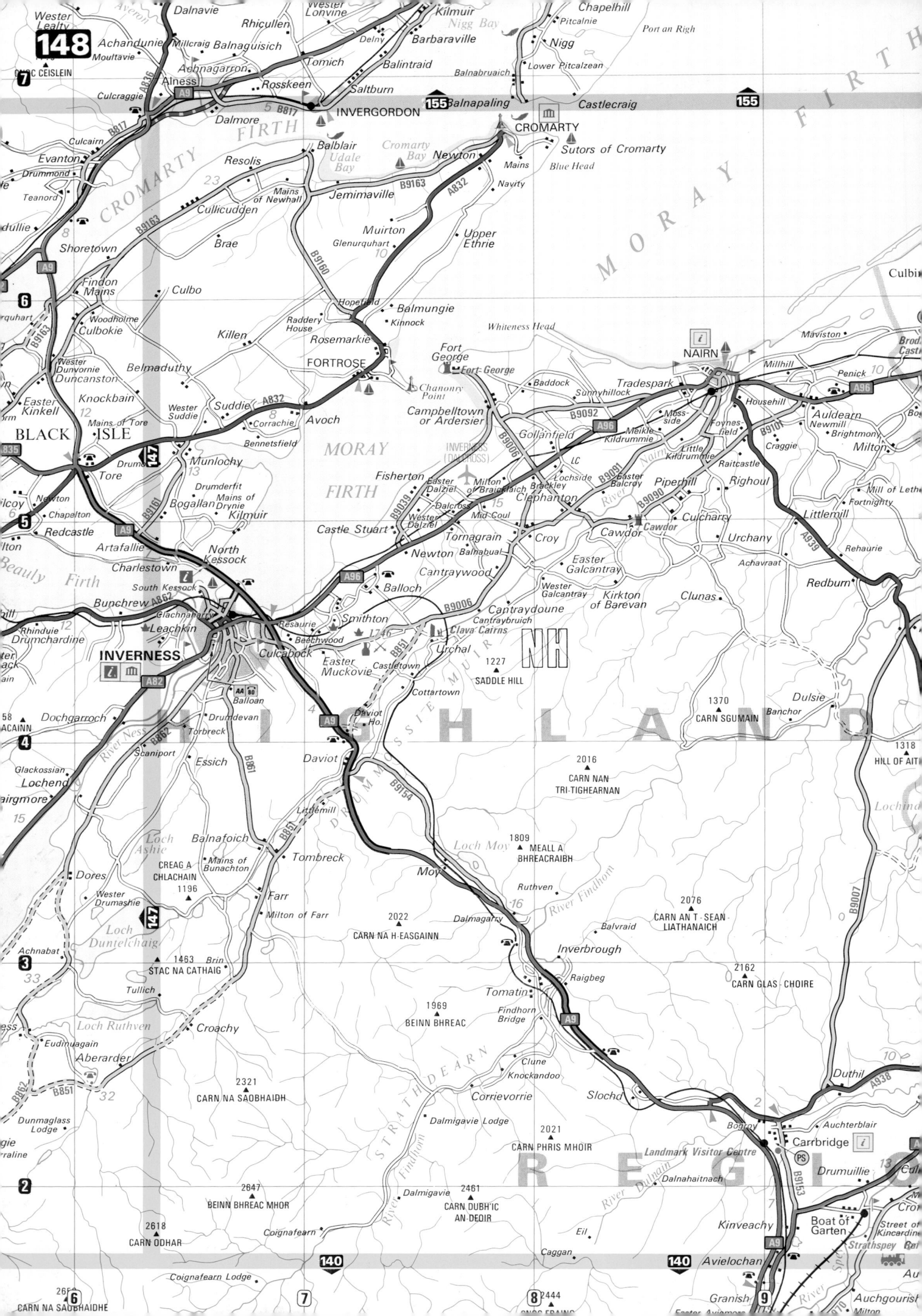
148
INVERGORDON
CROMARTY
Sutors of Cromarty
MORAY FIRTH
CROMARTY FIRTH
Black Isle
FORTROSE
Rosemarkie
Avoch
Munlochy
Fort George
NAIRN
Cawdor
Croy
INVERNESS
Culcabock
Smithton
Clava Cairns
NH
HIGHLAND REGION
Daviot
Moy
Tomatin
Slochd
Carrbridge
Landmark Visitor Centre
Boat of Garten
Dores
Alness
Evanton
Balblair
Jemimaville
Tore
North Kessock
Charlestown
Beauly Firth
Balloch
Cantraydoune
SADDLE HILL
CARN NAN TRI-TIGHEARNAN
MEALL A BHREACRAIBH
CARN NA H-EASGAINN
CARN AN T-SEAN LIATHANAICH
CARN GLAS-CHOIRE
BEINN BHREAC
CARN NA SAOBHAIDH
CARN PHRIS MHOIR
BEINN BHREAC MHOR
CARN DUBH'IC AN-DEOIR
CARN ODHAR
STAC NA CATHAIG
CARN SGUMAIN
Loch Ruthven
Loch Duntelchaig
Loch Ashie
Loch Moy
Strathdearn
Aviemore

BRANDERBURGH
Stotfield
LOSSIEMOUTH
Hopeman
B9040
Kinneddar
BURGHEAD
Burnside
Duffus
Newtown
St Aethans
Cummingston
Roseisle
Duffus
SPEY BAY
Stonewells
Kingston
Lochill
Binns
Spey Bay
College of Roseisle
B9012
Kintrae
Quarrywood
Viewfield
Garmouth
Portgordon
Findhorn
Hempriggs
Newton
Easter Calcots
B9103
Innesmill
Urquhart
Lochs Crofts
Wether Dallachy
Upper Dallachy
155
BURGHEAD BAY
Coltfield
East Grange
Newton
AA
ELGIN
Bogmoor
Newton
Auchenhalrig
Findhorn Bay
Kincorth Ho.
Kinloss
Alves
Cloves
New Elgin
Linkwood
Lhanbryde
Stynie
B9015
Braes of Enzie
Milton of Grange
Grange Hall
A96
Kilbuiack
Pittendreich
Moss of Barmuckity
Mosstodloch
Crofts of Dipple
Fochabers
Suenos Stone
Springfield
Miltonduff
Muir of Miltonduff
Wester Manbeen
Clackmarras
Longmorn Milltown
Blackburn
Dipple
A96
150
May Ho.
FORRES
Easter Lawrenceton
Easter Manbeen
Paddockhaugh
Blackhills Ho.
B9013
Orbliston
Ordiequish
Balnageith
Calfer
Pluscarden
Barnhill
Thomshill
Whitewreath
Culfoldie
Craiglug
Whiterow
Rafford
Easterton
Inchberry
Mains of Orton
Forgie
River Findhorn
B9010
Kellas
Shougle
Glenlatterach
A941
Woodside of Cairnty
Mains of Mulben
Aulthash
Mains of Craigmill
GRAMPIAN
Newlands
Garbity
Mulben
Burnsi
Branchill
Dallas
1164
PIKEY HILL
Crofts
Bridgeton
B9103
Blackhillock
Presley
CAIRN UISH
1197
ROTHES
B9015
1111
HILL OF TOWIE
Dunphail
Wester Greens
1218
MILL BUIE
PS
1546
BEN AIGAN
Tauchers
A940
Glenerney
1324
CARN NA CAILLICHE
Whiteacen
Arndilly Ho.
Dandaleith
NJ
Archiestown
B9102
Maggieknockater
B911
CARN KITTY
1712
Upper Knockando
Cardow
Ringorm
Easter Elchies
Craigellachie
Fork
A940
Distillery
Daugh of Kinermony
Midtown of Buchromb
Midthird
Knockando
Carron
Speyview
A941
ABERLOUR
Glenfiddich Distillery
Tomlea
Bridge of Derrybeg
Milltown of Edinvillie
B9014
Milltown of Auchindown
1783
LARIG HILL
Blacksboat
Marypark
A95
10
Kirktown of Mortlach
Balvenie
Dava
STRATH SPEY
Pitchroy
Distillery
Georgetown
Lettoch
Tullochallum
A920
CARN NA LOINE
1800
Ballindalloch
Bellehiglash
BEN RINNES
2759
B9009
Bridgehaugh
DUFFTOWN
1599
THE SCALP
Advie
Bridge of Avon
Dalnashaugh Inn
A941
Upper Derraid
Auchnagallin
Mains of Advie
B9008
Favillar
Aultbeg
Milltown of Laggan
Achnastank
Glenfiddich Lodge
150
Ballochford
Bridgend
Inverhar
A939
Lettoch
19
Eastertown
Camerory
Delliefure
A95
Mains of Dalvey
Craighead
Grouse Inn
Cottartown
Drumin
Glenlivet
Glen Beg
Cromdale
PS
Shenval
2561
CORRYHABBIE HILL
1872
ROUND HILL
Milltown
Auck
GRANTOWN-ON-SPEY
Auchroisk
Distillery
Minmore
Glenlivet Distillery
Auchorachan
1872
Alldunie
Cab
B9102
Dell
B9136
Aldivalloch
Craggan
Speybridge
Ballcorach
13
Wester Claggan
Pow
B970
Auchernack
Tomnavoulin
Achdregnie
Bracklach
Lynemore
Roadside of Croftbain
REGION
2065
HILL OF THREE STONES
Knockandhu
Nethy Bridge
Sliemore
Dirdhu
A939
Bridge of Brown
Auchnarrow
Gausar
Bridge of Avon
B9008
Clashnoir
Chapeltown
2073
CREAG AN EUNA
Lettoch
Laintachan
Milton of Auchriachan
Ladder Hills
Glenbuchat Lodge
Badenyon
Dell Lodge
Clachaig
Tomintoul
Delnabo
Alltachbeg
2159
MOSS HILL
Forest Lodge
Dorback Lodge
141
Bridge of Avon
141
2356
3
Belnacra
CARN NA FARRAIDH
2257
1
Badnafrave
Blairnamarrow
2
PS
Kirkton of Glenbuchat
Mains

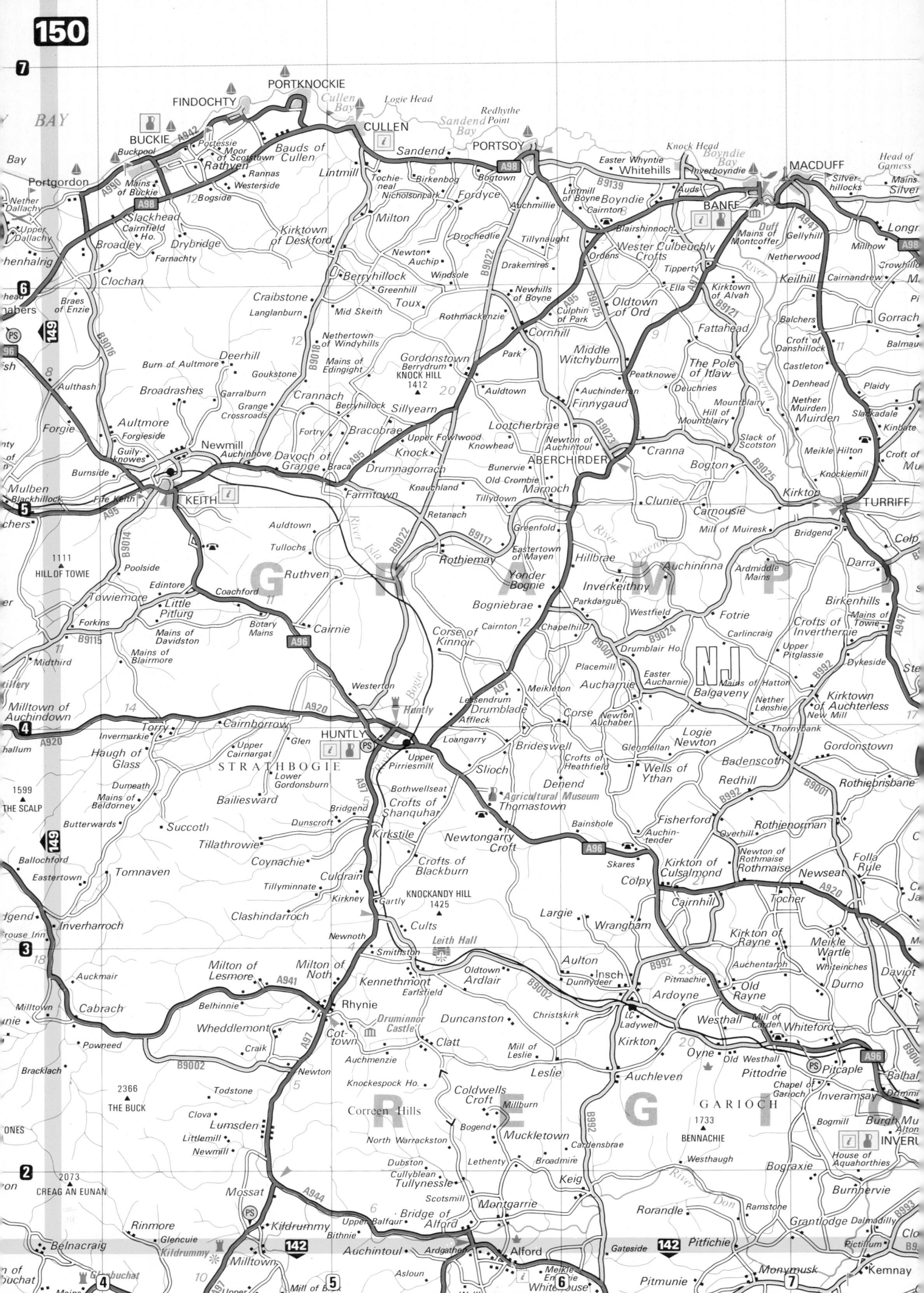

150
7
PORTKNOCKIE
FINDOCHTY
Cullen Bay
Logie Head
BAY
Redhythe Point
CULLEN
Sandend Bay
BUCKIE
A942
Portessie
Buckpool
Moor of Scotstown
Bauds of Cullen
Sandend
PORTSOY
Knock Head
Boyndie Bay
Bay
Rathven
Lintmill
Rannas
A98
Easter Whyntie
Whitehills
MACDUFF
Head of Garness
Portgordon
A990
Mains of Buckie
Westerside
Tochieneal
Birkenbog
Bogtown
B9139
Inverboyndie
Silverhillocks
Mains of Silver
Nether Dallachy
Bogside
Nicholsonpark
Fordyce
Lintmill of Boyne
Boyndie
Auds
BANFF
A98
Upper Dallachy
Slackhead
Cairnfield Ho.
Milton
Auchmillie
Cairnton
A947
Longr
Broadley
Drybridge
Kirktown of Deskford
Drochedlie
Tillynaught
Blairshinnoch
Duff Ho.
Mains of Montcoffer
Gellyhill
Millhow
henhalrig
Farnachty
Newton
Auchip
Ordens
Wester Culbeuchly
Crofts
Netherwood
Crowhillo
Clochan
B9022
Drakemires
Tipperty
River
Keilhill
Cairnandrew
6
Braes of Enzie
Windsole
Berryhillock
Greenhill
Newhills of Boyne
A95
B9025
Ella
A97
Kirktown of Alvah
Craibstone
Toux
Culphin of Park
Oldtown of Ord
B9121
Balchers
Gorrach
Langlanburn
Mid Skeith
Rothmackenzie
Cornhill
Fattahead
149
B9016
Nethertown of Windyhills
Croft of Danshillock
Balmau
Deerhill
B9018
Mains of Edingight
Gordonstown
Berrydrum
KNOCK HILL
1412
Park
Middle Witchyburn
The Pole of Itlaw
Castleton
Burn of Aultmore
Goukstone
Peatknowe
Deveron
Denhead
Aulthash
Broadrashes
Garralburn
Crannach
Auldtown
Auchinderran
Deuchries
Plaidy
Grange Crossroads
Berryhillock
Sillyearn
Finnygaud
Mountblairy
Hill of Mountblairy
Nether Muirden
Muirden
Slackadale
Kinbate
Aultmore
Forgie
Forgieside
Fortry
Bracobrae
Lootcherbrae
Guilyknowes
Newmill
Auchinhove
Upper Fowlwood
Knowhead
Newton of Auchintoul
B9023
Cranna
Slack of Scotston
Meikle Hilton
Croft of
Davoch of Grange
Knock
ABERCHIRDER
Bogton
Burnside
Drumnagorrach
Bunervie
B9025
Knockiemill
Mulben
Blackhillock
Braca
A95
Old Crombie
Marnoch
Knauchland
Fife Keith
KEITH
Farmtown
Tillydown
Clunie
Carnousie
Kirkton
TURRIFF
5
A95
Retanach
chers
Greenfold
Mill of Muiresk
Bridgend
Colp
Auldtown
River Isla
B9022
B9117
River
Deveron
B9014
Tullochs
Eastertown of Mayen
Hillbrae
Darra
1111
HILL OF TOWIE
Rothiemay
Auchininna
Ardmiddle Mains
Poolside
Ruthven
Yonder Bognie
Inverkeithny
Edintore
Coachford
Birkenhills
Towiemore
Little Pitlurg
Bogniebrae
Parkdargue
Westfield
Fotrie
Mains of Towie
Forkins
Botary Mains
Cairnie
Corse of Kinnoir
Cairnton
Chapelhill
B9024
Crofts of Inverthernie
Carlincraig
A947
B9115
Mains of Davidston
A96
B9001
Drumblair Ho.
Upper Pitglassie
Mains of Blairmore
Midthird
Placemill
NJ
Dykeside
B992
Ste
Easter Auchairnie
Mains of Hatton
Westerton
Bogie
Meikleton
Aucharnie
Balgaveny
Kirktown of Auchterless
Milltown of Auchindown
A97
Lessendrum
Drumblade
Huntly
Nether Lenshie
New Mill
14
A920
Affleck
Corse
Newton of Auchaber
4
Torry
Cairnborrow
HUNTLY
Loangarry
Thornybank
Invermarkie
A920
Upper Cairnargat
Glen
Brideswell
Logie Newton
Gordonstown
hallum
Haugh of Glass
STRATHBOGIE
PS
Upper Pirriesmill
Crofts of Heathfield
Glenmellan
Badenscoth
Slioch
Wells of Ythan
Lower Gordonsburn
Dumeath
A97
Bothwellseat
Denend
Redhill
1599
THE SCALP
Mains of Beldorney
Baillieward
Crofts of Shanquhar
Agricultural Museum
Thomastown
B992
B9001
Rothiebrisbane
Bridgend
Fisherford
Butterwards
Succoth
Dunscroft
Bainshole
Rothienorman
Auchintender
149
Tillathrowie
Kirkstile
Newtongarry Croft
Overhill
A96
Newton of Rothmaise
Ballochford
Coynachie
Crofts of Blackburn
Skares
Kirkton of Culsalmond
Rothmaise
Folla Rule
Eastertown
Tomnaven
Culdrain
Newseat
Colpy
Tillyminnate
KNOCKANDY HILL
1425
Kirkney
Tocher
A920
Cairnhill
Gartly
Largie
Clashindarroch
Inverharroch
Cults
Wrangham
Kirkton of Rayne
Newnoth
Meikle Wartle
Frouse Inn
3
Leith Hall
Smithston
Auchentarph
Whiteinches
Daviot
Aulton
Insch
B992
Milton of Lesmore
Milton of Noth
Pitmachie
A941
Kennethmont
Oldtown
Ardlair
Dunnydeer
Old Rayne
Durno
Auckmair
Earlsfield
Ardoyne
B9002
Milltown
Belhinnie
Rhynie
Cabrach
Christskirk
LC
Ladywell
Westhall
Mill of Carden
Whiteford
Wheddlemont
Druminnor Castle
Duncanston
Craik
Cottown
Clatt
Kirkton
Powneed
Mill of Leslie
Oyne
Old Westhall
A97
Auchmenzie
A96
B9002
PS
Pitcaple
Bracklach
Leslie
Pittodrie
Newton
Auchleven
Balhal
Chapel of Garioch
2366
THE BUCK
Todstone
Knockespock Ho.
Coldwells Croft
Inveramsay
Drimmi
GARIOCH
Correen Hills
Millburn
Clova
B992
1733
BENNACHIE
Bogmill
Burgh Mu
Lumsden
Bogend
Alton
ONES
Muckletown
Littlemill
North Warrackston
Cardensbrae
INVERU
Newmill
Broadmire
Westhaugh
House of Aquahorthies
Dubston
Lethenty
2
2073
CREAG AN EUNAN
Cullyblean
Keig
Tullynessle
River
Bograxie
Mossat
A944
Burnhervie
Scotsmill
Montgarrie
Don
PS
Ramstone
Rorandle
Upper Balfour
Bridge of Alford
Grantlodge
Dalmadilly
Rinmore
Kildrummy
B993
Glencuie
Bithnie
Clo
Belnacraig
Pitfichie
142
Auchintoul
Ardgathen
Alford
Gateside
142
Pictillum
Kildrummy
Milltown
Meikle Endovie
Monymusk
Kemnay
Glenbuchat
10
Asloun
Whitehouse
Pitmunie
Mains
4
A97
Upper
Mill of Bracks
5
6
Wellhouse
7
Craigearn

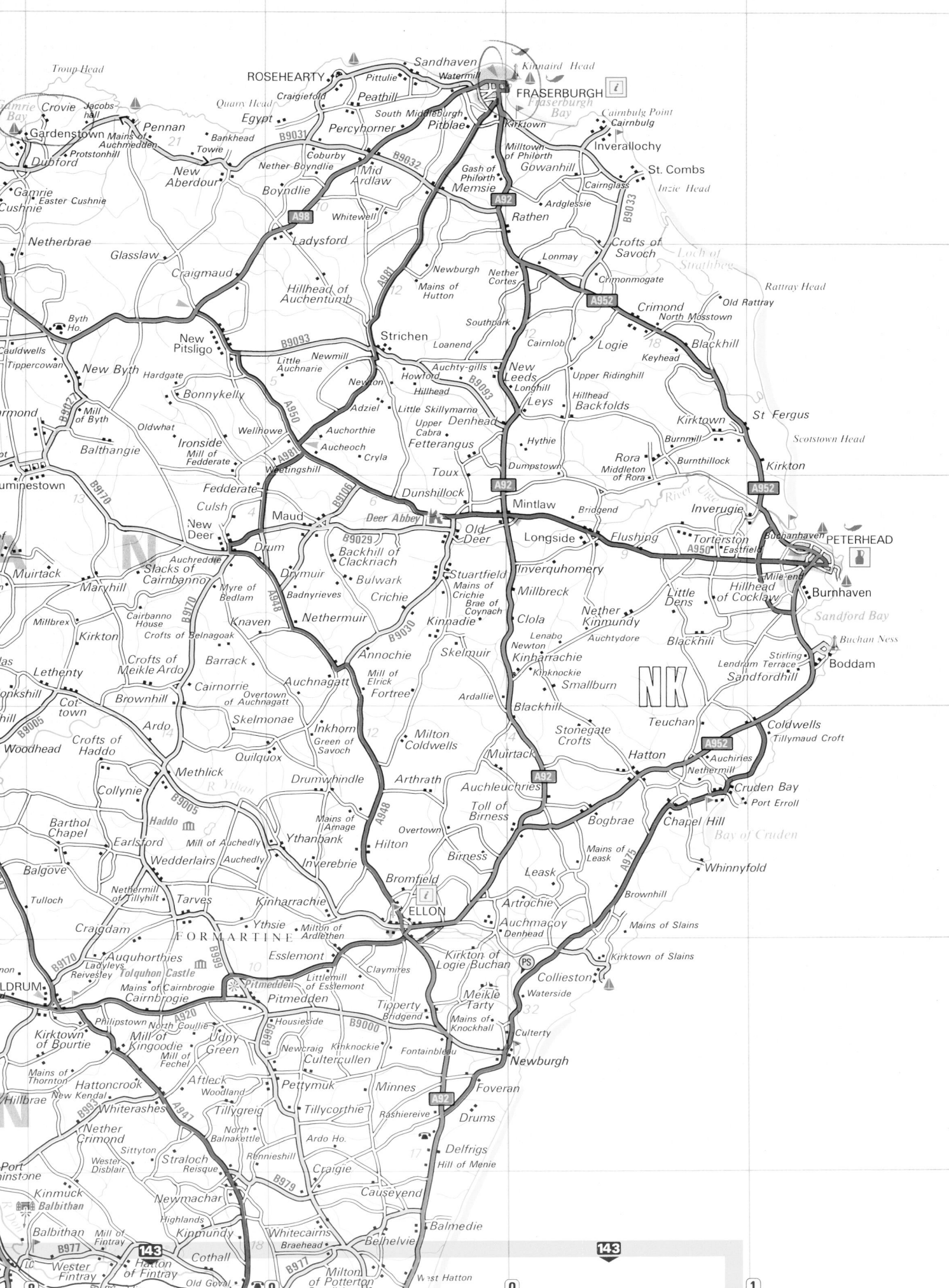

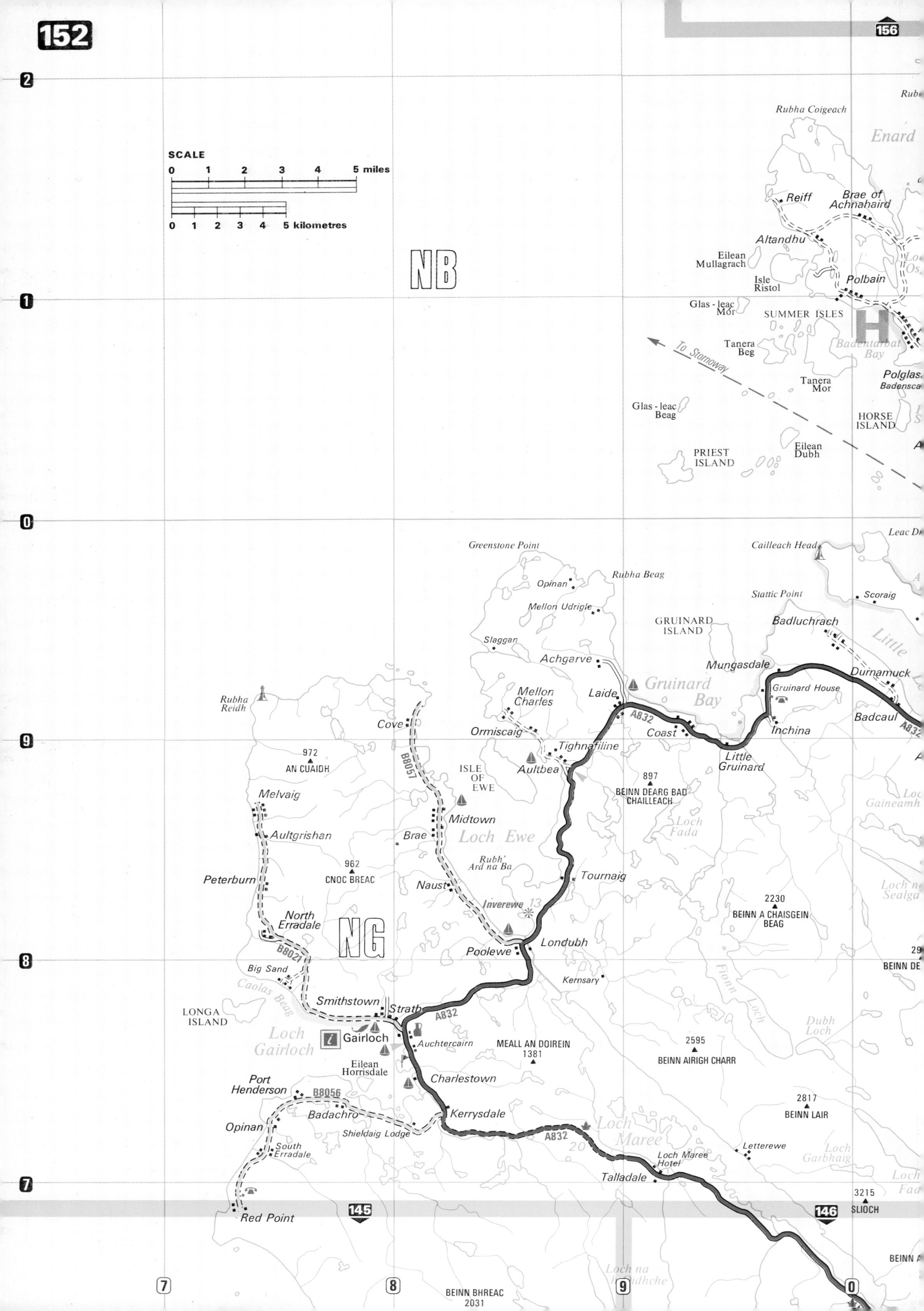

2

SCALE

0 1 2 3 4 5 miles

0 1 2 3 4 5 kilometres

NB

1

Rubha Coigeach

Reiff

Brae of Achnahaird

Altandhu

Eilean Mullagrach

Isle Ristol

Polbain

Glas - leac Mor

SUMMER ISLES

Badentarbat Bay

Polglas

Badensca

H

To Stornoway

Tanera Beg

Tanera Mor

Glas - leac Beag

Eilean Dubh

HORSE ISLAND

PRIEST ISLAND

0

Greenstone Point

Cailleach Head

Opinan

Rubha Beag

Stattic Point

Scoraig

Mellon Udrigle

GRUINARD ISLAND

Badluchrach

Slaggan

Achgarve

Mungasdale

Durnamuck

Mellon Charles

Laide

Gruinard Bay

Gruinard House

Rubha Reidh

Cove

A832

Coast

Inchina

Badcaul

A832

9

Ormiscaig

Tighnafiline

Little Gruinard

Aultbea

972

AN CUAIDH

B8057

ISLE OF EWE

897

BEINN DEARG BAD CHAILLEACH

Loch Fada

Loch Gaineamh

Melvaig

Midtown

Aultgrishan

Brae

Loch Ewe

Rubh' Ard na Ba

Tournaig

2230

BEINN A CHAISGEIN BEAG

Loch na Sealga

Peterburn

962

CNOC BREAC

Naust

Inverewe 13

NG

North Erradale

B8021

Poolewe

Londubh

8

BEINN DE

Big Sand

Kernsary

Fionn Loch

Dubh Loch

Caolas Beag

Smithstown

Strath

A832

LONGA ISLAND

Loch Gairloch

i Gairloch

Auchtercairn

MEALL AN DOIREIN 1381

2595

BEINN AIRIGH CHARR

Eilean Horrisdale

Charlestown

Port Henderson

B8056

Kerrysdale

2817

BEINN LAIR

Opinan

Badachro

Shieldaig Lodge

A832

Loch Maree

South Erradale

Loch Garbhaig

Letterewe

7

Talladale

Loch Maree Hotel

3215

SLIOCH

Red Point

145

146

BEINN

7 8 9 0

BEINN BHREAC 2031

Loch na h-Oidhche

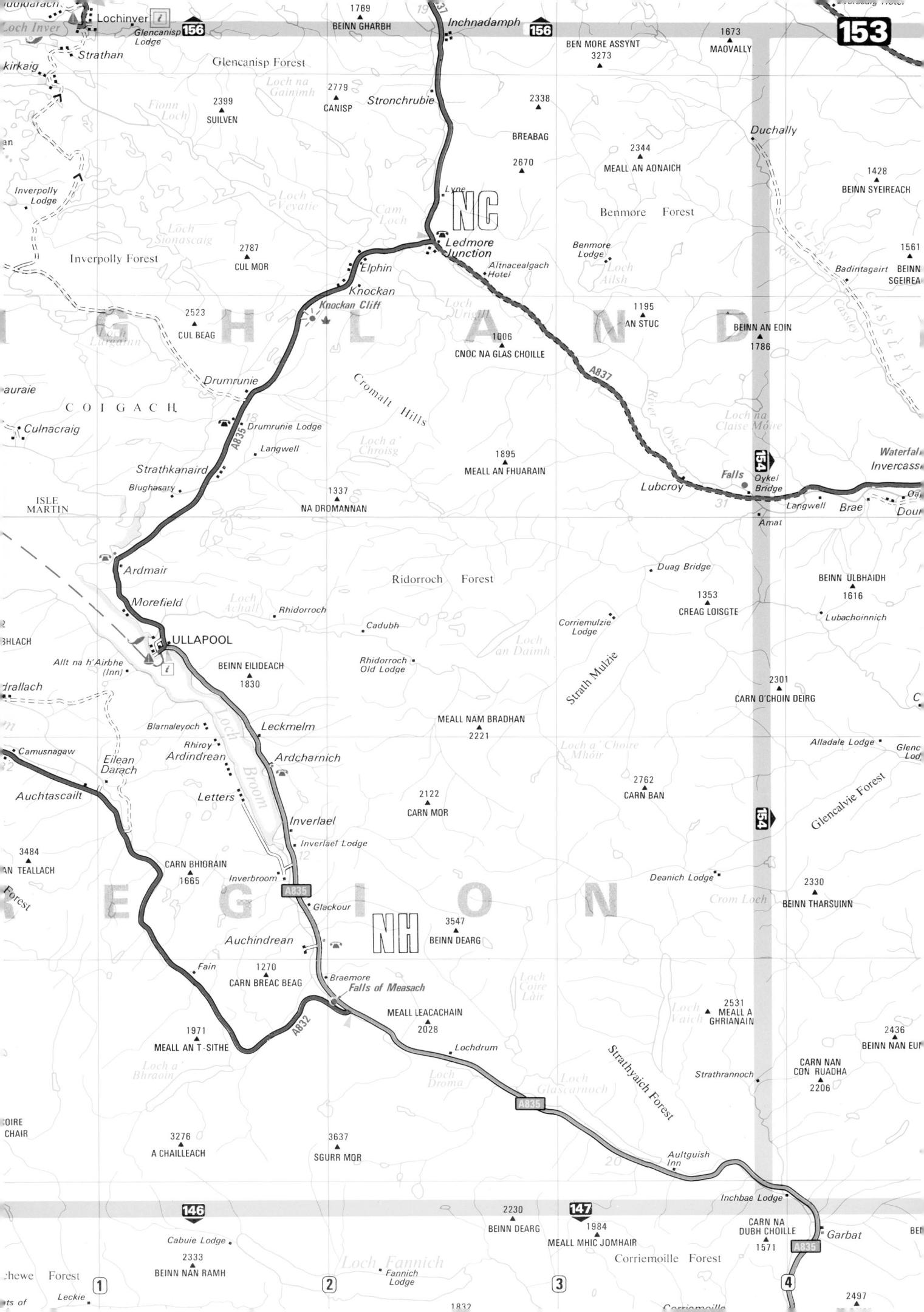

153
Lochinver
Loch Inver
Glencanisp Lodge
156
Strathan
Glencanisp Forest
1769
BEINN GHARBH
Inchnadamph
156
BEN MORE ASSYNT
3273
1673
MAOVALLY
Loch na Gainimh
2779
CANISP
Stronchrubie
2399
SUILVEN
Fionn Loch
2338
BREABAG
Duchally
2344
MEALL AN AONAICH
2670
1428
BEINN SYEIREACH
Inverpolly Lodge
Loch Veyatie
Cam Loch
Lyne
NC
Benmore Forest
Loch Sionascaig
Ledmore Junction
Benmore Lodge
Loch Ailsh
1561
Inverpolly Forest
2787
CUL MOR
Elphin
Altnacealgach Hotel
Badintagairt
BEINN SGEIREA
Knockan
Knockan Cliff
Loch Urigill
1195
AN STUC
2523
CUL BEAG
Loch Lurgainn
HIGHLAND
1006
CNOC NA GLAS CHOILLE
BEINN AN EOIN
1786
Glen Cassley
A837
Drumrunie
COIGACH
Cromalt Hills
River Oykel
Loch na Claise Mòire
Culnacraig
Drumrunie Lodge
A835
Langwell
Loch a' Chroisg
1895
MEALL AN FHUARAIN
154
Waterfall
Invercassley
Strathkanaird
Falls
Oykel Bridge
Lubcroy
Blughasary
Langwell
Brae
1337
NA DROMANNAN
Amat
ISLE MARTIN
Duag Bridge
Ardmair
Ridorroch Forest
BEINN ULBHAIDH
1616
1353
CREAG LOISGTE
Loch Achall
Morefield
Rhidorroch
Corriemulzie Lodge
Lubachoinnich
Cadubh
ULLAPOOL
Loch an Daimh
Allt na h'Airbhe (Inn)
BEINN EILIDEACH
1830
Rhidorroch Old Lodge
Strath Mulzie
2301
CARN O'CHOIN DEIRG
MEALL NAM BRADHAN
2221
Blarnaleyoch
Leckmelm
Loch a' Choire Mhòir
Alladale Lodge
Camusnagaw
Rhiroy
Ardindrean
Eilean Darach
Ardcharnich
Loch Broom
2762
CARN BAN
Glencalvie Forest
Auchtascailt
Letters
2122
CARN MOR
154
Inverlael
Inverlael Lodge
3484
CARN BHIORAIN
1665
Inverbroom
Deanich Lodge
2330
BEINN THARSUINN
Crom Loch
A835
Glackour
REGION
NH
3547
BEINN DEARG
Auchindrean
Fain
1270
CARN BREAC BEAG
Braemore
Falls of Measach
Loch Coire Làir
Loch Vaich
2531
MEALL A GHRIANAIN
MEALL LEACACHAIN
2028
A832
1971
MEALL AN T-SITHE
Lochdrum
2436
BEINN NAN EUN
Loch a' Bhraoin
Strathyaich Forest
CARN NAN CON RUADHA
2206
Loch Droma
Loch Glascarnoch
Strathrannoch
A835
3276
A CHAILLEACH
3637
SGURR MOR
Aultguish Inn
Inchbae Lodge
146
2230
BEINN DEARG
147
1984
MEALL MHIC JOMHAIR
CARN NA DUBH CHOILLE
1571
Garbat
A835
Cabuie Lodge
2333
BEINN NAN RAMH
Loch Fannich
Fannich Lodge
Corriemoille Forest
Forest
Leckie
1
2
3
4
2497
1832

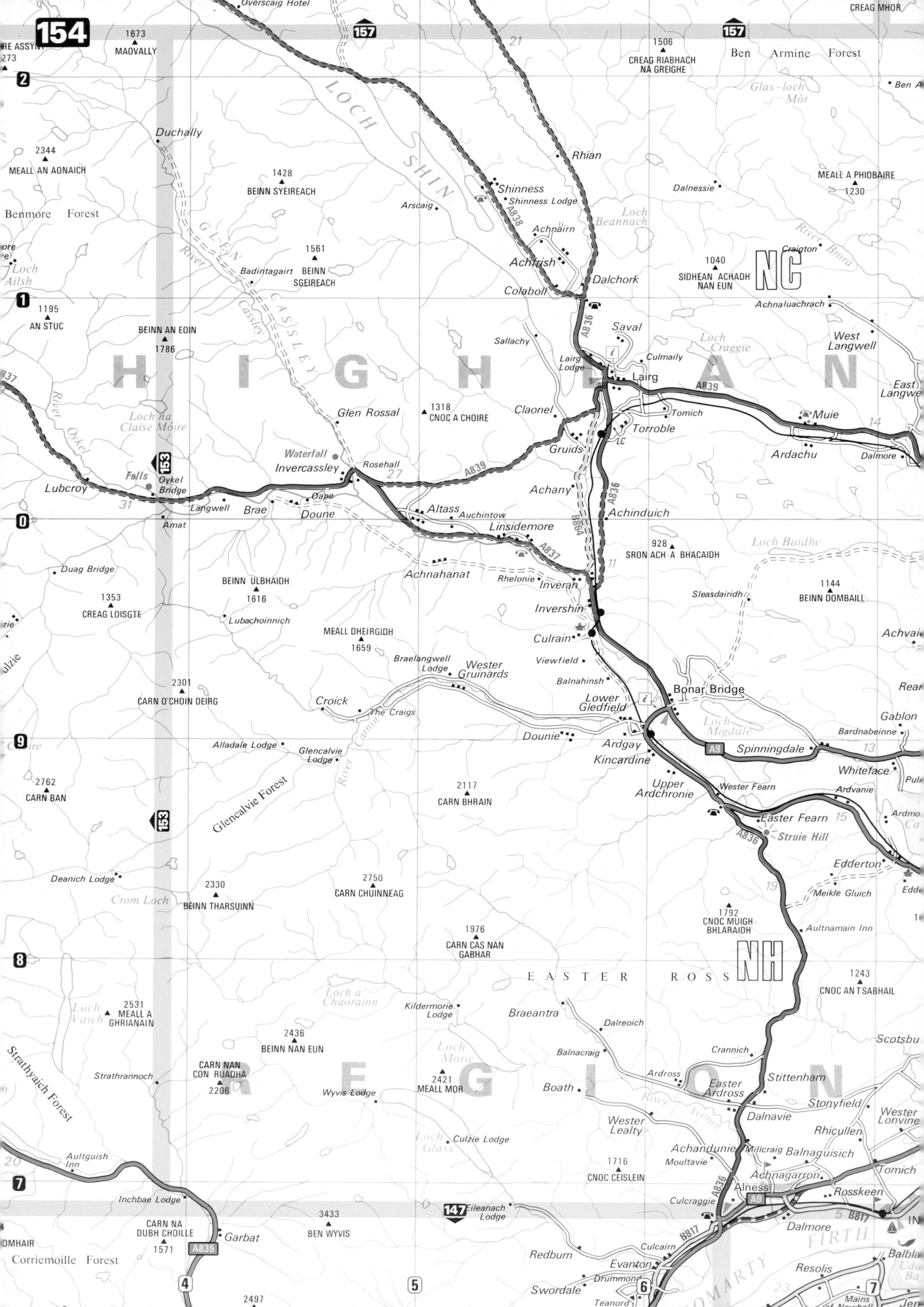

Overscaig Hotel
157
157
CREAG MHOR
1673
MAOVALLY
1506
CREAG RIABHACH NA GREIGHE
Ben Armine Forest
Ben A
Glas-loch Mór
LOCH SHIN
Duchally
2344
MEALL AN AONAICH
1428
BEINN SYEIREACH
Rhian
Shinness
Shinness Lodge
A838
Arscaig
Dalnessie
MEALL A PHIOBAIRE
1230
Loch Beannach
Benmore Forest
GLEN CASSLEY
River Cassley
1561
BEINN SGEIREACH
Badintagairt
Achnairn
Achfrish
Dalchork
Colaboll
Craigton
River Brora
1040
SIDHEAN ACHADH NAN EUN
NC
Loch Ailsh
Achnaluachrach
1195
AN STUC
BEINN AN EOIN
1786
Sallachy
A836
Saval
Loch Craggie
West Langwell
Culmaily
Lairg Lodge
HIGHLAND
Lairg
A839
East Langwe
River Oykel
Loch na Claise Móire
Glen Rossal
1318
CNOC A CHOIRE
Claonel
Tomich
Torroble
Muie
Ardachu
Dalmore
14
153
Waterfall
Invercassley
Rosehall
27
A839
Gruids
Falls
Oykel Bridge
Lubcroy
31
Langwell
Oape
Brae
Doune
Amat
Altass
Auchintow
Achany
A836
Achinduich
Linsidemore
B864
A837
928
SRON ACH-A BHACAIDH
Loch Buidhe
Duag Bridge
BEINN ULBHAIDH
1616
Achnahanat
Rhelonie
Inveran
11
Sleasdairidh
1144
BEINN DOMBAILL
1353
CREAG LOISGTE
Lubachoinnich
Invershin
MEALL DHEIRGIDH
1659
Culrain
Achvai
Braelangwell Lodge
Wester Gruinards
Viewfield
Balnahinsh
2301
CARN O'CHOIN DEIRG
Croick
The Craigs
Lower Gledfield
Bonar Bridge
Rear
Loch Migdale
Gablon
Bardnabeinne
Dounie
Ardgay
Alladale Lodge
Glencalvie Lodge
River Carron
A9
Spinningdale
13
Kincardine
Whiteface
Pul
2762
CARN BAN
2117
CARN BHRAIN
Upper Ardchronie
Wester Fearn
Ardvanie
Glencalvie Forest
153
Easter Fearn
15
A836
Struie Hill
Ardmo
Edderton
Deanich Lodge
2330
BEINN THARSUINN
Crom Loch
2750
CARN CHUINNEAG
19
Meikle Gluich
1792
CNOC MUIGH-BHLARAIDH
Aultnamain Inn
1976
CARN CAS NAN GABHAR
8
NH
EASTER ROSS
1243
CNOC AN TSABHAIL
Loch a' Chaorainn
Kildermorie Lodge
Braeantra
Dalreoich
Loch Vaich
2531
MEALL A GHRIANAIN
2436
BEINN NAN EUN
Scotsbu
Balnacraig
Crannich
Loch Morie
Strathyaich Forest
Strathrannoch
CARN NAN CON RUADHA
2206
2421
MEALL MOR
Wyvis Lodge
REGION
Boath
Ardross
Easter Ardross
Stittenham
River Alness
Stonyfield
Dalnavie
Wester Lonvine
Wester Lealty
Rhicullen
Culzie Lodge
Loch Glass
Achandunie
Millcraig
Balnaguisich
Aultguish Inn
20
1716
CNOC CEISLEIN
Moultavie
Tomich
7
Achnagarron
A836
Alness
Rosskeen
Inchbae Lodge
147
Eileanach Lodge
Culcraggie
A9
3433
BEN WYVIS
CARN NA DUBH CHOILLE
1571
Garbat
A835
Dalmore
B817
5
FIRTH
Corriemoille Forest
Redburn
Cailcairn
B817
Balbla
Evanton
Resolis
Drummond
Swordale
CROMARTY
23
4
5
6
7
2497
Teanord
Mains

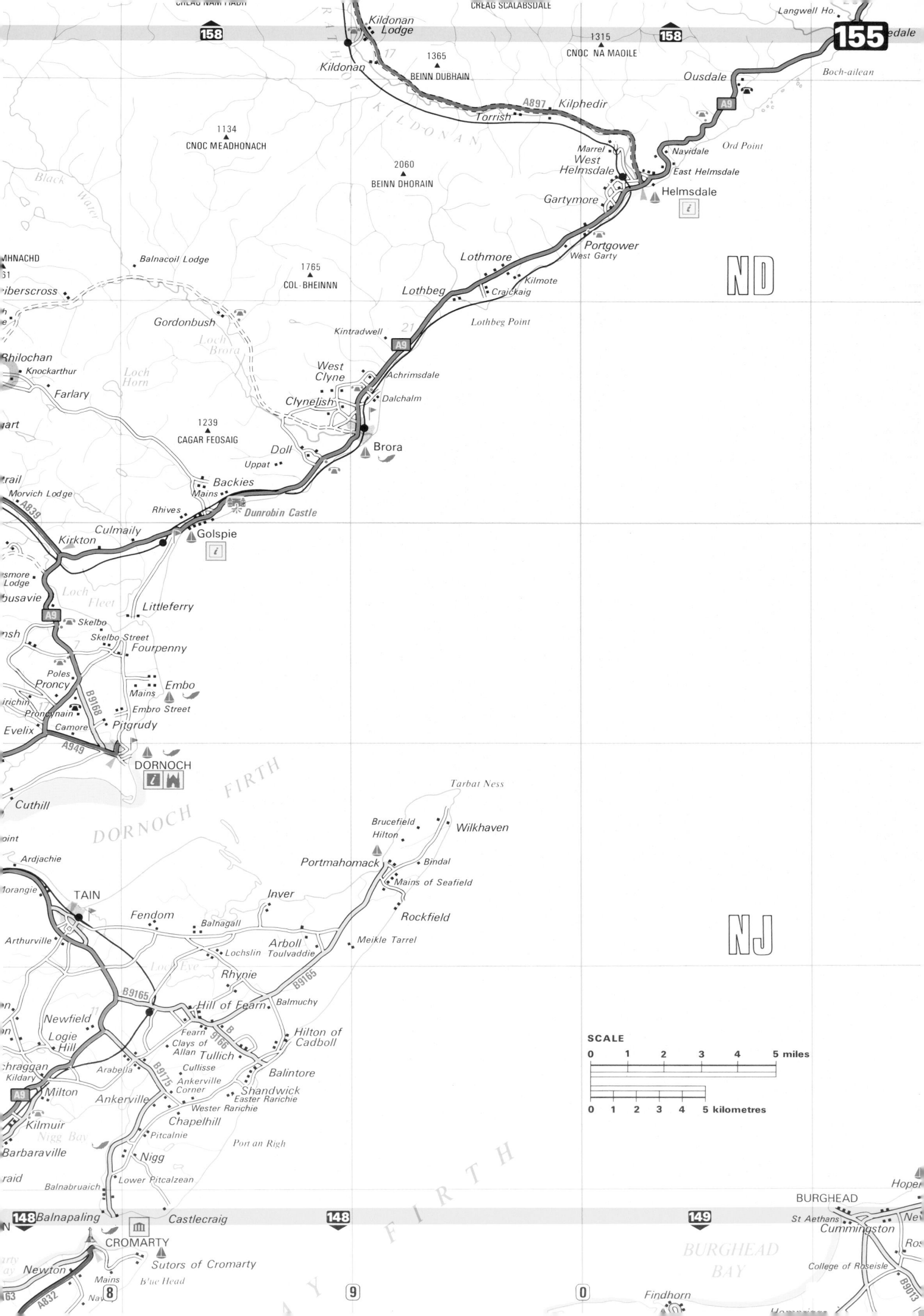

CREAG NAM FIADH
CREAG SCALABSDALE
Langwell Ho.

158   Kildonan Lodge   **158**   **155** edale
1315
CNOC NA MAOILE
17
Kildonan   Boch-ailean
1365
BEINN DUBHAIN   Ousdale
A897   Kilphedir
Torrish   A9
1134   Marrel   Navidale   Ord Point
CNOC MEADHONACH   West Helmsdale   East Helmsdale
2060   Gartymore   Helmsdale
BEINN DHORAIN   i
MHNACHD   Portgower
61   Balnacoil Lodge   Lothmore   West Garty
iberscross   1765
COL-BHEINNN   Lothbeg   Kilmote
Gordonbush   Craickaig
hilochan   21   Lothbeg Point
Knockarthur   Kintradwell   A9
Loch   West
Farlary   Loch Brora   Clyne   Achrimsdale
art   Horn   Clynelish   Dalchalm
1239
CAGAR FEOSAIG   Doll   Brora
trail   Uppat
Morvich Lodge   Backies
A839   Mains
Rhives   Dunrobin Castle
Culmaily
Kirkton   Golspie
i
smore
Lodge   Loch
usavie   Fleet   Littleferry   ND
nsh   A9   Skelbo
Skelbo Street
Fourpenny   NJ
Poles   Embo
Proncy   Mains
ririchin   Embro Street
Proncynain   Pitgrudy
Evelix   Camore
A949   Tarbat Ness
DORNOCH   Brucefield
i   Hilton   Wilkhaven
Cuthill   Portmahomack   Bindal
Ardjachie   Mains of Seafield
DORNOCH FIRTH   Inver
Morangie   TAIN   Rockfield
Arthurville   Fendom   Balnagall   Arboll   Meikle Tarrel
Lochslin   Toulvaddie
Rhynie
B9165   B9165
Newfield   Hill of Fearn   Balmuchy
Logie   Fearn   Hilton of
Hill   Clays of   Cadboll
Allan   Tullich
chraggan   Arabella   Cullisse   Balintore
Kildary   Ankerville   Shandwick
A9   Milton   Corner   Easter Rarichie
Ankerville   Wester Rarichie
Kilmuir   Chapelhill
Nigg Bay   Pitcalnie   Port an Righ
Barbaraville   Nigg
raid   Lower Pitcalzean   BURGHEAD
Balnabruaich   Hoper
148 Balnapaling   Castlecraig   **148**   **149**   St Aethans   New
CROMARTY   Cummingston
Sutors of Cromarty   BURGHEAD
Newton   B'ue Head   BAY   College of Roseisle   Ros
63   A832   Nav   Findhorn   B9013
8   9   0

SCALE
0   1   2   3   4   5 miles

0 1 2 3 4   5 kilometres

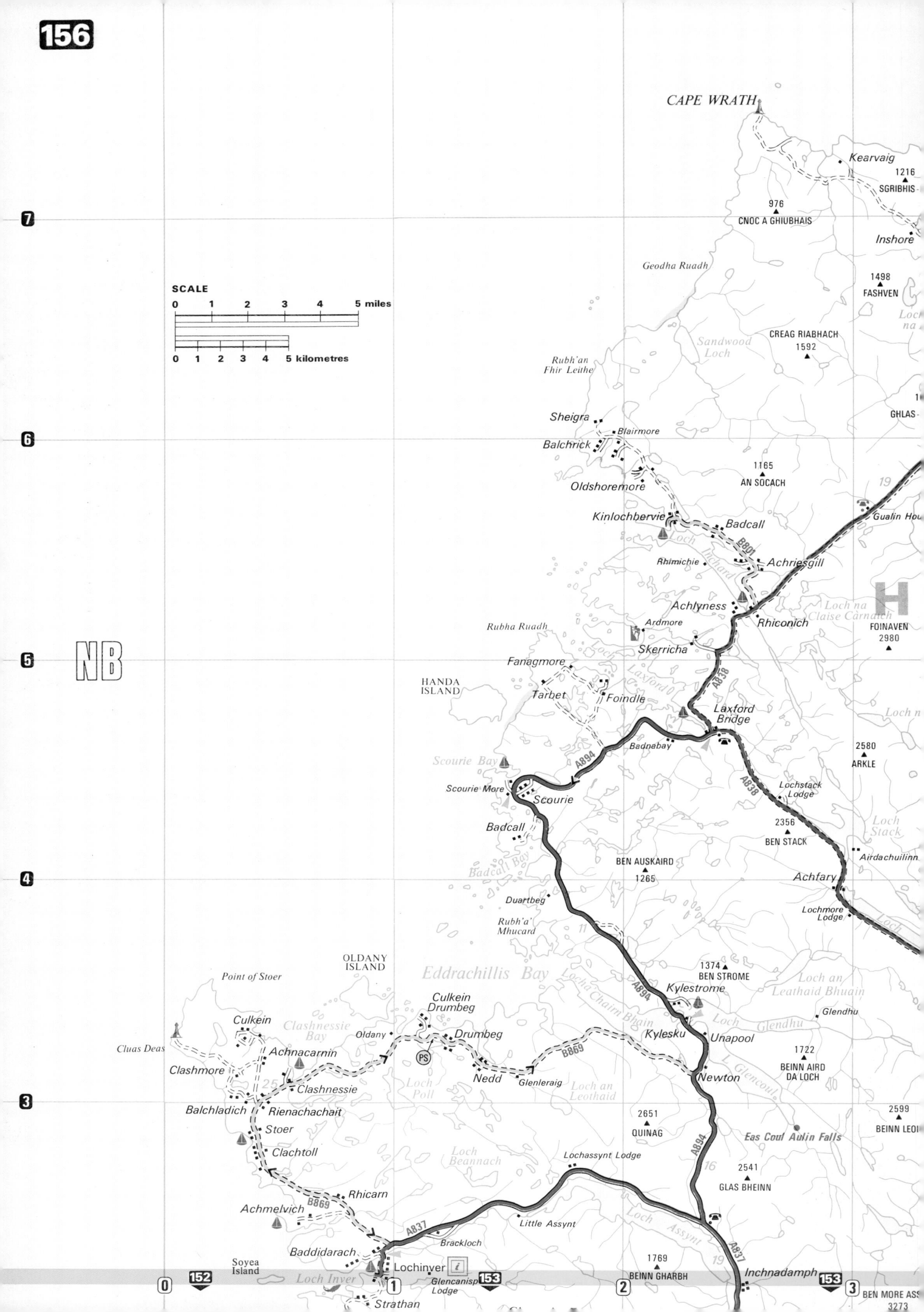
CAPE WRATH
Kearvaig
1216
SGRIBHIS
976
CNOC A GHIUBHAIS
Inshore
Geodha Ruadh
1498
FASHVEN
SCALE
0 1 2 3 4 5 miles
0 1 2 3 4 5 kilometres
Sandwood Loch
CREAG RIABHACH
1592
Rubh'an Fhir Leithe
GHLAS
Sheigra
Blairmore
Balchrick
1165
AN SOCACH
Oldshoremore
Kinlochbervie
Badcall
B801
Gualin House
Rhimichie
Loch Inchard
Achriesgill
Achlyness
Loch na Claise Càrnaich
Rhiconich
FOINAVEN
2980
Ardmore
Rubha Ruadh
Skerricha
NB
Fanagmore
Loch Laxford
A838
HANDA ISLAND
Tarbet
Foindle
Laxford Bridge
Badnabay
2580
ARKLE
Scourie Bay
A894
Scourie More
Scourie
Lochstack Lodge
Badcall
2356
BEN STACK
Loch Stack
Badcall Bay
BEN AUSKAIRD
1265
Airdachuilinn
Achfary
Duartbeg
Lochmore Lodge
Rubh'a' Mhucard
OLDANY ISLAND
Eddrachillis Bay
1374
BEN STROME
Point of Stoer
Loch a' Chàirn Bhàin
Kylestrome
Loch an Leathaid Bhuain
Culkein Drumbeg
Glendhu
Loch Glendhu
Culkein
Clashnessie Bay
Oldany
Drumbeg
Kylesku
Unapool
Cluas Deas
Achnacarnin
PS
B869
1722
BEINN AIRD DA LOCH
Clashmore
Nedd
Newton
Loch Glencoul
Clashnessie
Loch Poll
Glenleraig
Loch an Leothaid
Balchladich
Rienachachait
2651
QUINAG
2599
BEINN LEOID
Stoer
Eas Coul Aulin Falls
Clachtoll
Loch Beannach
Lochassynt Lodge
2541
GLAS BHEINN
Rhicarn
Achmelvich
Little Assynt
Loch Assynt
Brackloch
A837
Baddidarach
1769
Soyea Island
Loch Inver
Lochinver
BEINN GHARBH
Inchnadamph
Glencanisp Lodge
152
153
153
0
1
2
3
4
5
6
7
BEN MORE ASSYNT
3273
Strathan

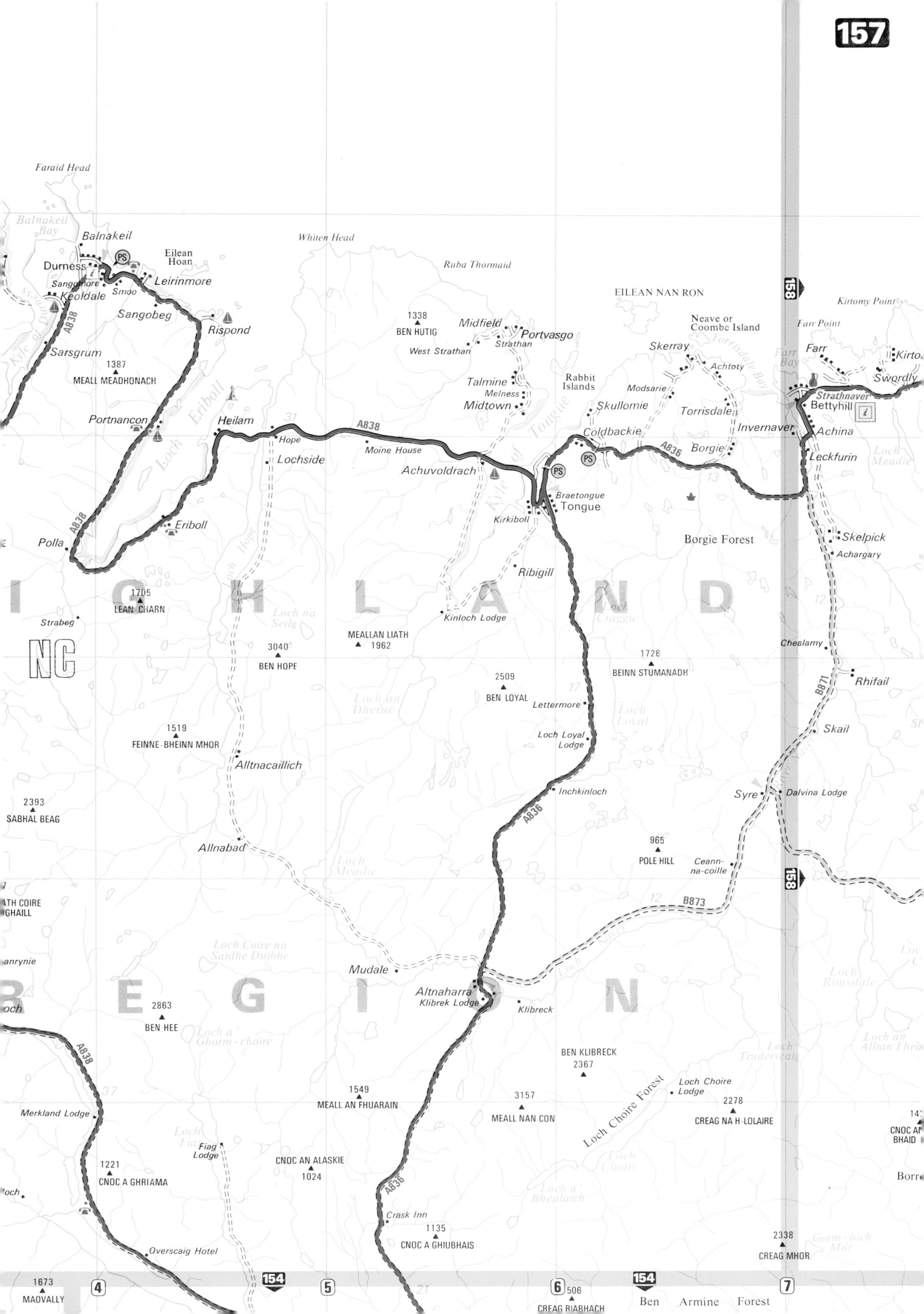

Faraid Head

Balnakeil Bay

Balnakeil

Durness PS

Eilean Hoan

Leirinmore

Sanggomore *Smoo*

Keoldale

Sangobeg

Kyle of Durness

Sarsgrum

Rispond

1387
MEALL MEADHONACH

Portnancon

A838

1705
LEAN-CHARN

Strabeg

NC

Whiten Head

Ruba Thormaid

Heilam

Hope

Lochside

Loch Hope

A838

Moine House

Achuvoldrach

1338
BEN HUTIG

Midfield

West Strathan

Strathan

Portvasgo

Talmine

Melness

Midtown

Kyle of Tongue

EILEAN NAN RON

Neave or Coombe Island

Skerray

Achtoty

Torrisdale Bay

Farr Bay

Farr Point

Farr

Strathnaver

Bettyhill

Achina

Loch Meadie

Swordly

Kirto

Kirtomy Point

158

Modsarie

Skullomie

Coldbackie

Borgie

A836

Torrisdale

Invernaver

Leckfurin

Rabbit Islands

PS PS
Braetongue
Tongue

Kirkiboll

Ribigill

MEALLAN LIATH
1962

Loch na Seilg

3040
BEN HOPE

Loch an Dherue

2509
BEN LOYAL

Kinloch Lodge

Borgie Forest

1728
BEINN STUMANADH

Skelpick

Achargary

Chealamy

B871

Rhifail

1519
FEINNE-BHEINN MHOR

Alltnacaillich

Lettermore

Loch Loyal
Lodge

Loch Loyal

Skail

2393
SABHAL BEAG

Allnabad

Inchkinloch

965
POLE HILL

Ceanna-coille

Syre

Dalvina Lodge

158

Loch Meadie

ATH COIRE GHAILL

anrynie

Loch Coire na Saidhe Duibhe

REGION

2863
BEN HEE

Loch a' Ghorm-choire

Mudale

Altnaharra
Klibrek Lodge

Klibreck

B873

Loch Rimsdale

Loch an Alltan Fhea

A838

Merkland Lodge

1549
MEALL AN FHUARAIN

BEN KLIBRECK
2367

3157
MEALL NAN CON

Loch Choire Forest

Loch Choire Lodge

2278
CREAG NA H-IOLAIRE

CNOC AI
BHAID

1221
CNOC A GHRIAMA

Fiag Lodge

CNOC AN ALASKIE
1024

A836

Crask Inn

1135
CNOC A GHIUBHAIS

Overscaig Hotel

1673
MAOVALLY

4

154

5

Borr

2338
CREAG MHOR

Gorm-loch Mor

6 506
CREAG RIABHACH

154

Ben Armine Forest

7

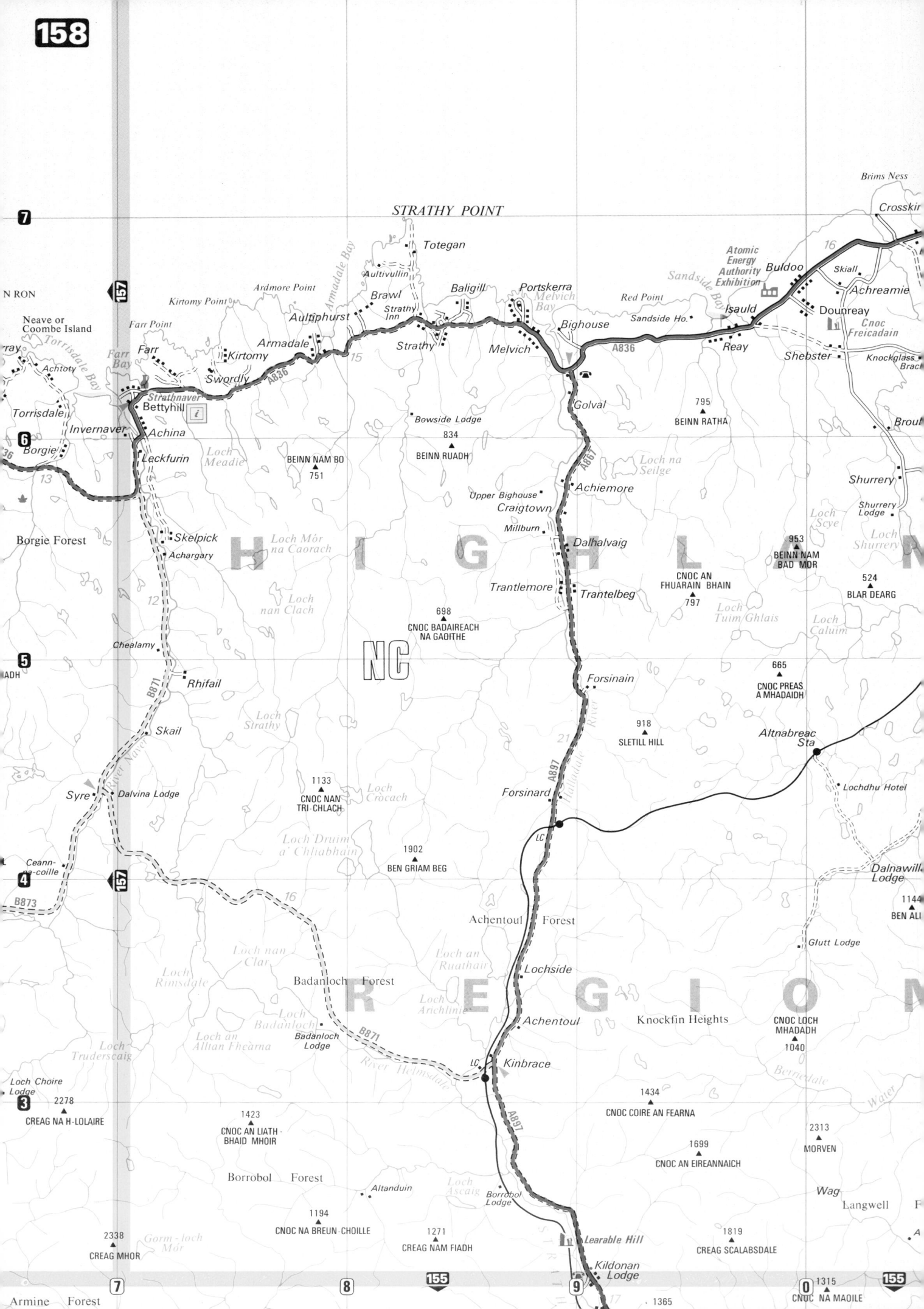

STRATHY POINT

Brims Ness

Crosskir

7

Totegan

Atomic
Energy
Authority
Exhibition

Buldoo

Skiall

Achreamie

16

N RON

157

Ardmore Point

Aultivullin

Brawl

Baligill

Portskerra

Melvich
Bay

Sandside Bay

Red Point

Isauld

Dounreay

Kirtomy Point

Strathy
Inn

Sandside Ho.

Cnoc
Freicadain

Farr Point

Aultiphurst

Bighouse

Reay

Knockglass
Brac

Armadale

Strathy

A836

Shebster

Farr
Bay

Farr

A836

15

Melvich

Golval

A836

Broul

Torrisdale Bay

Kirtomy

Swordly

Achtoty

Farr
Point

Strathnaver

Bettyhill

Bowside Lodge
834
BEINN RUADH

Loch na
Seilge

795
BEINN RATHA

Torrisdale

Invernaver

Achina

6

36

Borgie

13

Leckfurin

Loch
Meadie

BEINN NAM BO
751

Upper Bighouse

Craigtown

Achiemore

A897

Loch na
Seilge

Shurrery

Shurrery
Lodge

Loch
Scye

Loch
Shurrery

Borgie Forest

Skelpick

Achargary

H

Loch Mór
na Caorach

I

G

Loch
nan Clach

Millburn

H

Dalhalvaig

L

953
BEINN NAM
BAD MOR

524
BLAR DEARG

Chealamy

12

Trantlemore

Trantelbeg

CNOC AN
FHUARAIN BHAIN
797

Loch
Tuim Ghlais

Loch
Caluim

5

ADH

B871

Rhifail

NC

698
CNOC BADAIREACH
NA GAOITHE

665
CNOC PREAS
A MHADAIDH

Skail

Loch
Strathy

918
SLETILL HILL

Altnabreac
Sta

Syre

River Naver

Dalvina Lodge

1133
CNOC NAN
TRI-CHLACH

Loch
Crocach

Forsinain

A897

21

Lochdhu Hotel

Ceann-
na-coille

Loch Druim
a' Chliabhain

Forsinard

LC

Dalnawill
Lodge

4

B873

157

16

1902
BEN GRIAM BEG

Achentoul Forest

LC

1144
BEN ALI

Glutt Lodge

Loch nan
Clar

Loch an
Ruathair

Lochside

R

E

Loch
Rimsdale

G

I

O

N

Badanloch Forest

Loch an
Allt an Fhearna

Badanloch
Lodge

B871

River Helmsdale

Loch
Arichlinie

Achentoul

Knockfin Heights

CNOC LOCH
MHADADH
1040

Bernedale

Loch
Truderscaig

LC

Kinbrace

Loch Choire
Lodge

3

2278
CREAG NA H-LOLAIRE

1423
CNOC AN LIATH
BHAID MHOIR

A897

1434
CNOC COIRE AN FEARNA

2313
MORVEN

Borrobol Forest

Altanduin

Loch
Ascaig

Borrobol
Lodge

1699
CNOC AN EIREANNAICH

Wag

Langwell

Water

1194
CNOC NA BREUN-CHOILLE

1271
CREAG NAM FIADH

Learable Hill

1819
CREAG SCALABSDALE

2338
CREAG MHOR

Gorm-loch
Mór

Kildonan
Lodge

1315
CNOC NA MAOILE

Armine Forest

7

8

155

9

17

1365

0

155

159
Pentland Skerries
Langaton Point
Nethertown
ISLAND OF STROMA
Uppertown
DUNNET HEAD
To Stromness
Briga Head
St John's Point
Boars of Duncansby
Scarfskerry
Castle of Mey
Ham
B855
Brough
St. John Loch
Mey
Gills Bay
Kirkstyle
Huna
DUNCANSBY HEAD
The Thirl
Hunspow
Rattar
A836
Gills
John o'Groats
West Dunnet
Corsback
Barrock
Canisbay
Dunnet
Clardon Head
DUNNET BAY
Thurso Bay
West Murkle
Inkstack
Loch Heilen
Brabstermire
Skirza
Clardon
Castlehill
A9
Tofts
Millbank
Murkle
Greenland Mains
Greenland
Slickly
THURSO
Castletown
Thurdistoft
Freswick Bay
Freswick
Glengolly
Olrig Ho.
Garth
Tain
Ness Head
A882
B876
Reaster
Weydale
Alterwall
Geise
Auckengill
Hilliclay
Durran
Granton Mains
Bowermadden
Nybster
Buckies
Bower
Sortat
Lythe
B874
Achingills
Howe
Brough Head
Sordale
Bowertower
Keiss
B870
Calder Mains
Knockdee
Hastigrow
Roadside
Loch Scarmclate
Tang Head
Gillock
Halcro
Mireland
Clayock
Loch of Wester
Halkirk
LC
Kirk
North Watten
Westerloch
A882
B876
SINCLAIR'S BAY
Lynegar
Harpsdale
Banniskirk
Mains of Watten
Killimster
Loch Watten
Biggins
Castles Girnigoe & Sinclair
Noss Head
Sta
A895
Spital
Olgrinmore
Wester Watten
Watten
Killimster Mains
Reiss
Winless
Ackergillshore
Sealky Head
Ackergill
B874
Sibster
Backlass
Loch of Toftingall
Bilbster
Wick River
Papigoe
Staxigoe
raehour
Mybster
Haster
Milton
WICK
Wick Bay
Westerdale
Strath
Thuster
Acharole
Stirkoke House
Janets-town
23
ND
Old Wick
Castle of Old Wick
Newton
Loch Hempriggs
Badibster
Whiterow
Hempriggs Ho.
Tannach
Helman Head
Strathmore Lodge
446
BEINN CHAITEAG
Lochmore Cottage
Thrumster
Rangag
Camster
Sarclet
Loch Ruard
Borrowston
Achavanich
Loch of Yarrows
Loch Sand
Camster
Mains of Ulbster
Ulbster
Loch Rangag
741
COIRE NA BEINN
Whaligoe
Roster
Crofts of Benachielt
Bruan
Upper Lybste
Mid Clyth
881
CNOCAN CONACHREAG
West Clyth
Clyth
Halberry Head
Millbuie
Swiney
Houstry
Forse House
Invershore
Lybster
Land-hallow
Forse
Latheron
Smerral
Latheronwheel House
Janetstown
Balnabruich
Dunbeath
raemore
Knockally
Ramscraigs
Dunbeath Mains
SCALE
0 1 2 3 4 5 miles
0 1 2 3 4 5 kilometres
Borgue
Newport
20
Langwell Ho.
Berriedale
1
2
3
4

THE BRITISH ISLES

Scale 1:4 500 000

0   50   100   150 miles

0   50   100   150   200   250 kilometres

This map shows the major islands off the coast of Britain – all are located in their correct geographical positions. A selection of these islands, or groups of islands, is shown at a larger scale on the following pages. Airports and ferry ports serving the islands are located and named on this page, enabling journey planning decisions to be made. For example, some islands are linked to the mainland by both air and sea services, and are therefore easily and regularly accessible, while others may have no official linking service.

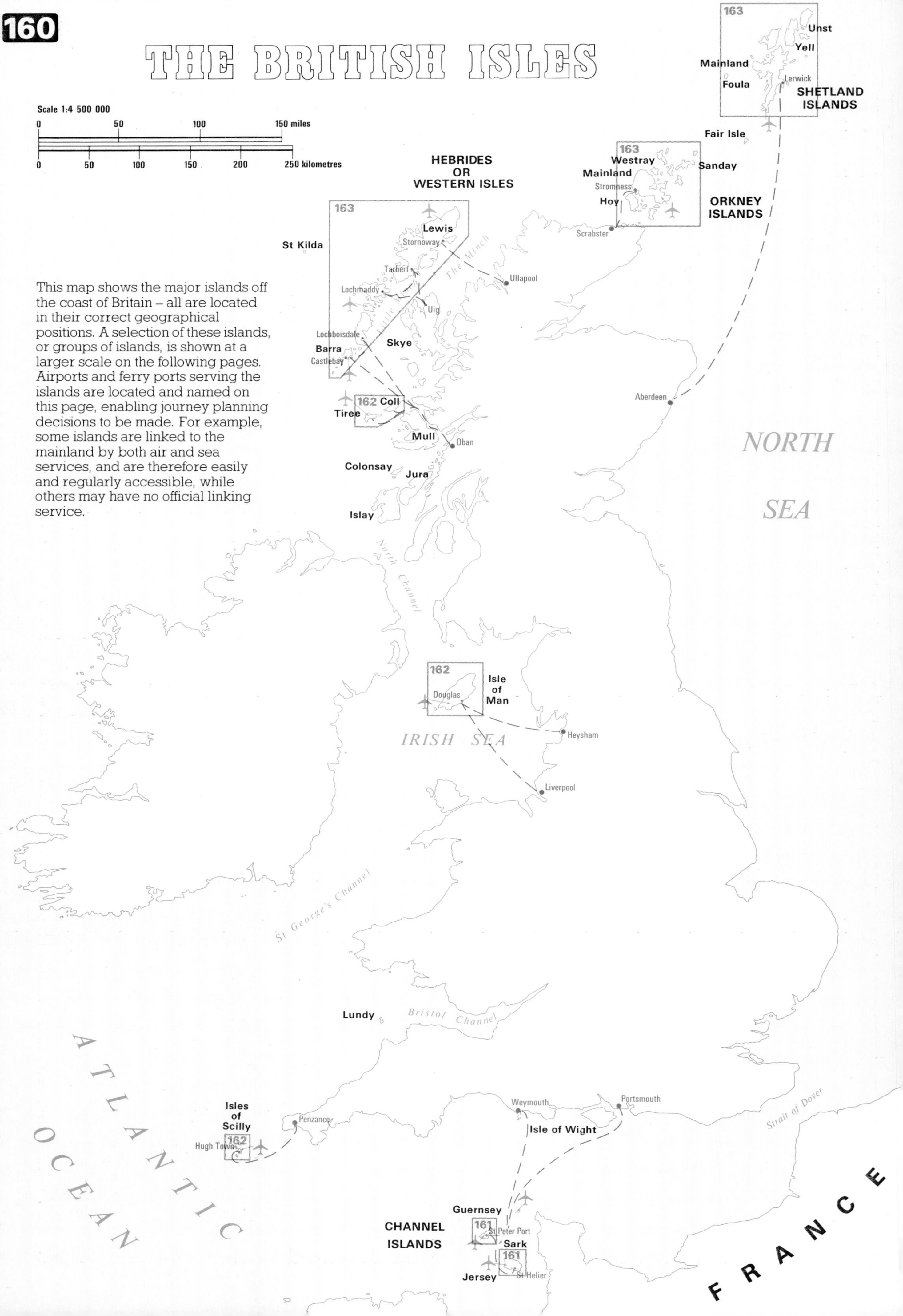

HEBRIDES OR WESTERN ISLES

163

Lewis
Stornoway
Tarbert
St Kilda
Lochmaddy
Uig
Lochboisdale
Barra
Castlebay
Skye
The Minch
Ullapool

162 **Coll**
Tiree
Mull
Oban
Colonsay
Jura
Islay
North Channel

163
Westray
Mainland
Stromness
Hoy
Scrabster
Fair Isle
Sanday
ORKNEY ISLANDS

163
Unst
Yell
Mainland
Foula
Lerwick
SHETLAND ISLANDS

Aberdeen

NORTH

SEA

162
Douglas
Isle of Man
Heysham
IRISH SEA
Liverpool

St George's Channel

Lundy
Bristol Channel

Weymouth
Portsmouth
Strait of Dover

Isles of Scilly
Penzance
Hugh Town
162

Isle of Wight

A T L A N T I C

O C E A N

Guernsey
St Peter Port
161
Sark
161
Jersey
St Helier

CHANNEL ISLANDS

F R A N C E

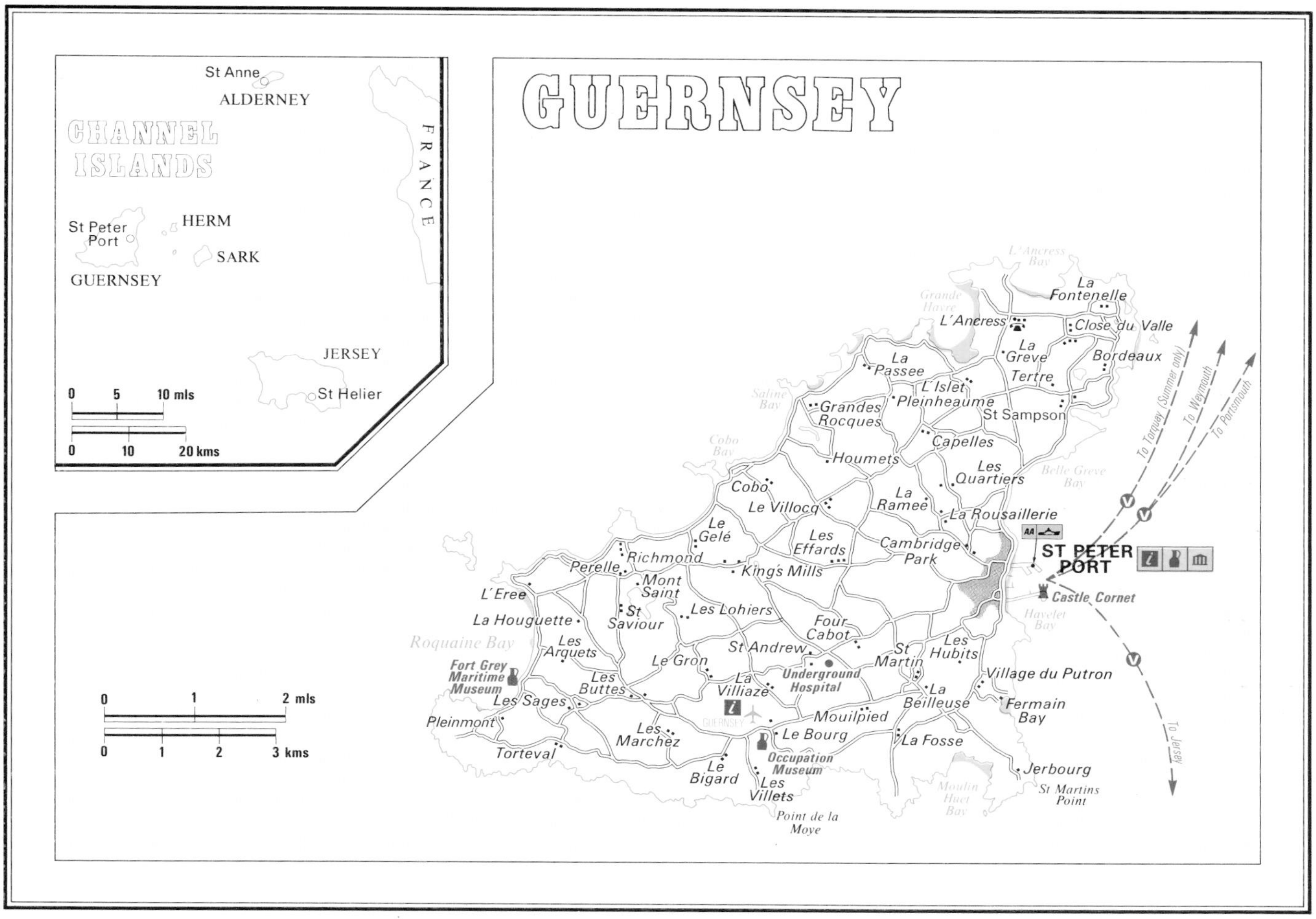

GUERNSEY

CHANNEL ISLANDS

St Anne
ALDERNEY

FRANCE

St Peter Port
HERM

SARK

GUERNSEY

JERSEY

St Helier

0 5 10 mls

0 10 20 kms

0 1 2 mls

0 1 2 3 kms

L'Ancress Bay

La Fontenelle

Grande Havre

L'Ancress

Close du Valle

Bordeaux

La Grève
Tertre

La Passee

L'Islet

Pleinheaume

St Sampson

Saline Bay

Grandes Rocques

Capelles

Les Quartiers

Belle Grève Bay

Houmets

Cobo Bay

Cobo

Le Villocq

La Ramée

La Rousaillerie

Le Gelé

Les Effards

Cambridge Park

AA

ST PETER PORT

Perelle

Richmond

King's Mills

Castle Cornet

L'Eree

Mont Saint

Les Lohiers

Havelet Bay

La Houguette

St Saviour

Four Cabot

Roquaine Bay

Les Arquets

Le Gron

St Andrew

St Martin

St Hubits

Les Hubits

Village du Putron

Fort Grey Maritime Museum

Les Buttes

La Villiaze

Underground Hospital

La Beilleuse

Fermain Bay

Les Sages

Pleinmont

Les Marchez

Le Bourg

La Fosse

Torteval

Mouilpied

GUERNSEY

Occupation Museum

Le Bigard

Les Villets

Jerbourg

St Martins Point

Moulin Huet Bay

Point de la Moye

To Torquay (Summer only)
To Weymouth
To Portsmouth

V

V

To Jersey

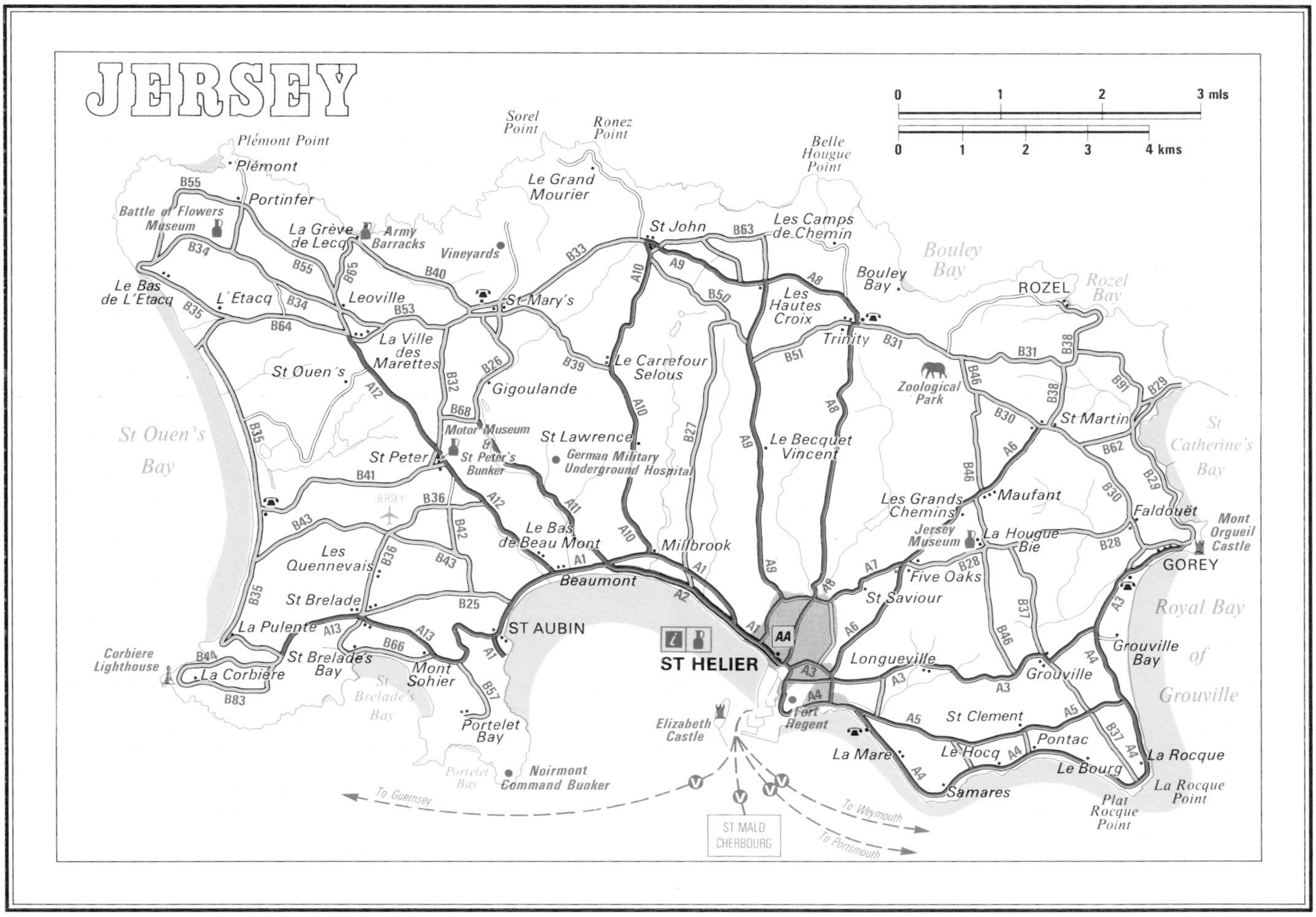

JERSEY

0 1 2 3 mls

0 1 2 3 4 kms

Plémont Point

Sorel Point

Ronez Point

Belle Hougue Point

Plémont

Portinfer

B55

Battle of Flowers Museum

La Grève de Lecq

Army Barracks

Le Grand Mourier

St John

B63

Les Camps de Chemin

Bouley Bay

Bouley Bay

Rozel Bay

B34

Vineyards

B33

A10

A9

B50

ROZEL

Le Bas de L'Etacq

B55

Leoville

B40

St Mary's

Les Hautes Croix

A8

Rozel Bay

L'Etacq

B65

B34

B53

Trinity

B31

B31

B38

B91

B29

B35

B64

La Ville des Marettes

B26

B39

Le Carrefour Selous

B51

Zoological Park

B46

B30

St Martin

St Ouen's

A12

Gigoulande

A10

B27

Le Becquet Vincent

B38

B62

B68

Motor Museum & St Peter's Bunker

St Lawrence

A8

B46

B30

Faldouët

St Ouen's Bay

B35

St Peter

German Military Underground Hospital

A9

Les Grands Chemins

Maufant

Mont Orgueil Castle

B41

JERSEY

B36

A12

Le Bas de Beau Mont

A10

A11

Millbrook

A8

Jersey Museum

La Hougue Bie

B28

B28

GOREY

B43

B42

A1

Beaumont

A9

Five Oaks

A7

B37

Royal Bay of Grouville

Les Quennevais

B36

B43

B25

A2

St Saviour

A6

Longueville

Grouville Bay

Corbiere Lighthouse

St Brelade

La Pulente

A13

B66

Mont Sohier

B57

ST AUBIN

AA

ST HELIER

AA

A3

Longueville

A3

Grouville

A4

B44

St Brelade's Bay

A13

Fort Regent

A5

St Clement

A5

A3

B37

La Rocque

B83

La Corbière

St Brelade's Bay

Portelet Bay

Elizabeth Castle

La Mare

Le Hocq

A4

Pontac

B37 A4

La Rocque Point

Portelet Bay

Noirmont Command Bunker

Samares

Le Bourg

Plat Rocque Point

To Guernsey

V

V V V

To Weymouth

ST MALO
CHERBOURG

To Portsmouth

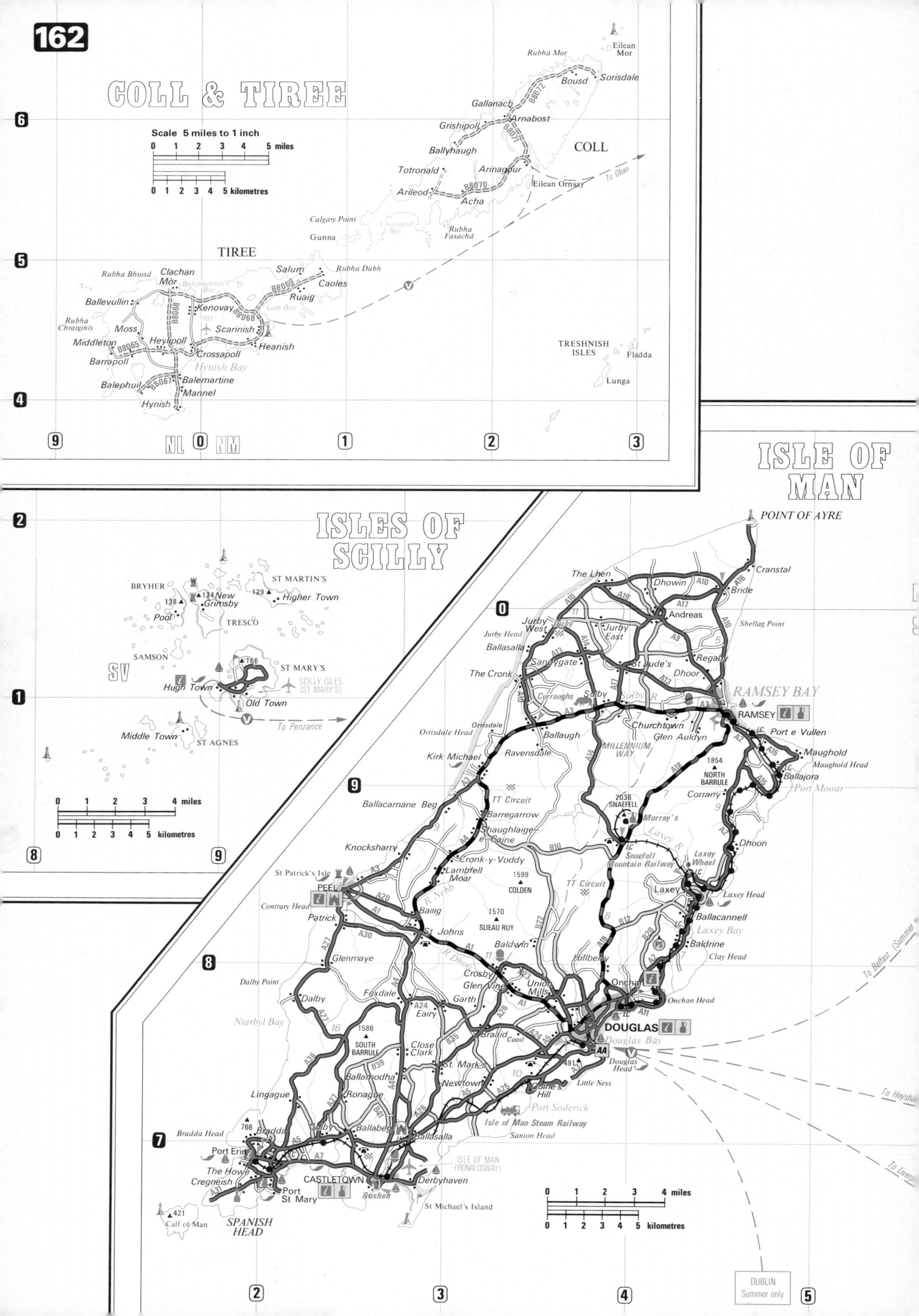
COLL & TIREE
Scale 5 miles to 1 inch
0 1 2 3 4 5 miles
0 1 2 3 4 5 kilometres
COLL
TIREE
Arnabost
Gallanach
Grishipoll
Ballyhaugh
Totronald
Arinagour
Arileod
Acha
Eilean Ornsay
To Oban
Sorisdale
Bousd
Rubha Mor
Eilean Mor
Calgary Point
Gunna
Rubha Fasachd
Clachan Mor
Rubha Bhiosd
Salum
Rubha Dubh
Caoles
Ruaig
Ballevullin
Kenovay
Scarinish
Heanish
Moss
Middleton
Heylipoll
Crossapoll
Barrapoll
Hynish Bay
Balemartine
Balephuil
Mannel
Hynish
TRESHNISH ISLES
Fladda
Lunga
ISLES OF SCILLY
BRYHER
ST MARTIN'S
Higher Town
New Grimsby
Pool
TRESCO
SAMSON
ST MARY'S
Hugh Town
Old Town
SCILLY ISLES (ST MARY'S)
To Penzance
Middle Town
ST AGNES
0 1 2 3 4 miles
0 1 2 3 4 5 kilometres
ISLE OF MAN
POINT OF AYRE
Cranstal
Bride
The Lhen
Dhowin
Andreas
Shellag Point
Jurby West
Jurby East
Jurby Head
Ballasalla
Sandygate
St Jude's
Regaby
Dhoor
The Cronk
Curraughs
Sulby
RAMSEY BAY
RAMSEY
Churchtown
Glen Auldyn
Port e Vullen
Orrisdale
Orrisdale Head
Ballaugh
Ravensdale
MILLENNIUM WAY
Maughold
Maughold Head
Kirk Michael
1854 NORTH BARRULE
Ballajora
Port Mooar
Corrany
Ballacarnane Beg
TT Circuit
2036 SNAEFELL
Murray's
Barregarrow
Shaughlaige-e-Caine
Laxey R
Dhoon
Knocksharry
Snaefell Mountain Railway
Laxey Wheel
Cronk-y-Voddy
Lambfell Moar
1599 COLDEN
St Patrick's Isle
PEEL
R Nebb
Laxey
Laxey Head
Contrary Head
Baing
1570 SLIEAU RUY
Ballacannell
Patrick
Laxey Bay
St Johns
Baldrine
Clay Head
Glenmaye
R Dhoo
Baldwin
Hillberry
Crosby
Glen Vine
Union Mills
Onchan
Onchan Head
Dalby Point
Dalby
Foxdale
Garth
Eairy
DOUGLAS
Douglas Bay
Niarbyl Bay
1586 SOUTH BARRULE
Close Clark
Braaid
Cooil
Douglas Head
St. Mark's
Ballamodha
Newtown
Quine's Hill
Little Ness
Lingague
Ronague
Port Soderick
Isle of Man Steam Railway
Santon Head
Bradda Head
766 Bradda
Colby
Ballabeg
Ballasalla
Port Erin
ISLE OF MAN (RONALDSWAY)
The Howe
Cregneish
CASTLETOWN
Derbyhaven
Port St Mary
Rushen
St Michael's Island
421 Calf of Man
SPANISH HEAD
0 1 2 3 4 miles
0 1 2 3 4 5 kilometres
To Belfast (Summer
To Heysha
To Liverp
DUBLIN Summer only

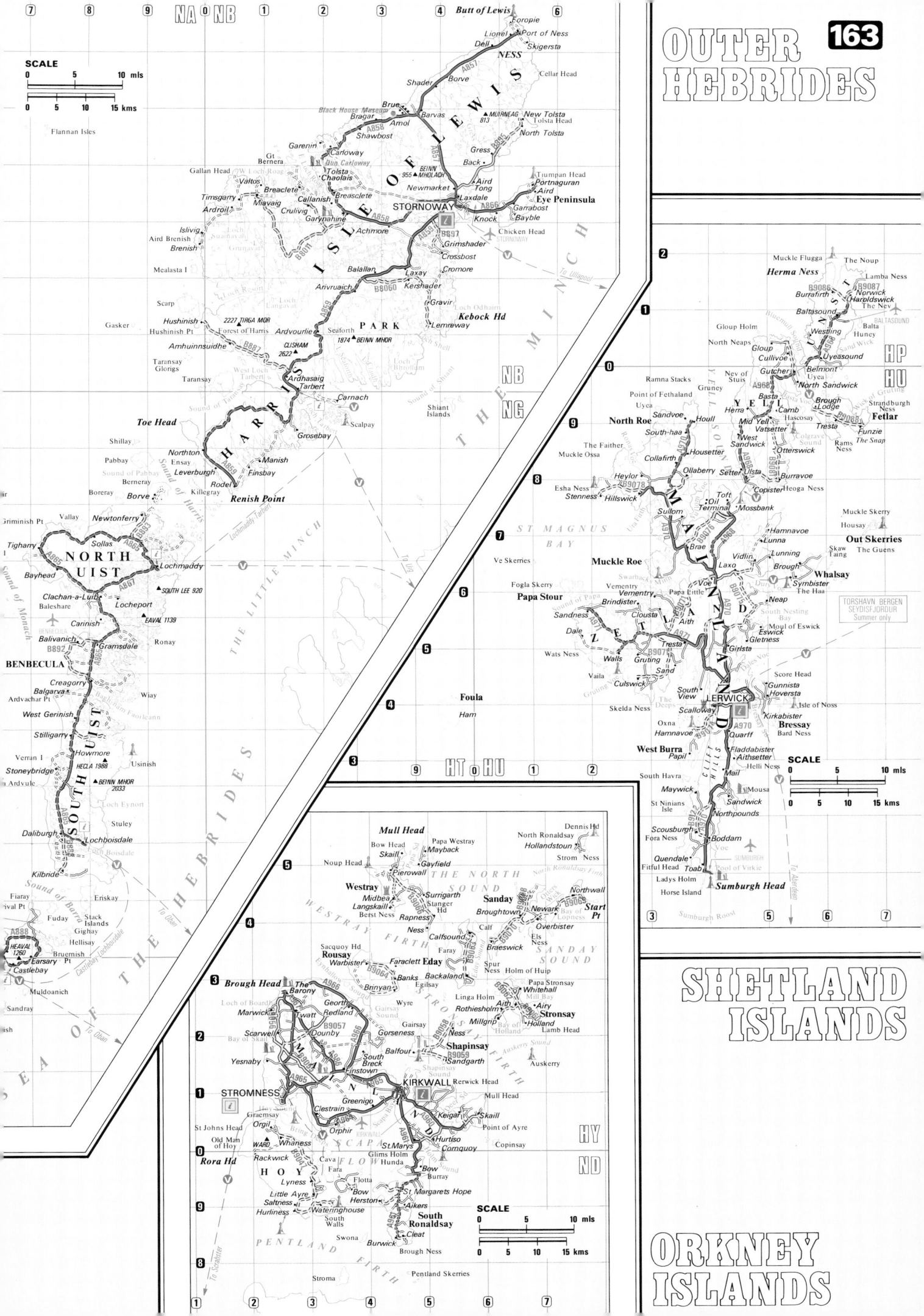
OUTER HEBRIDES
SHETLAND ISLANDS
ORKNEY ISLANDS
SCALE
0 5 10 mls
0 5 10 15 kms
Butt of Lewis
Eoropie
Lionel
Port of Ness
Dell
Skigersta
NESS
Cellar Head
Shader
Borve
Brue
Black House Museum
Bragar
Arnol
Barvas
MUIRNEAG 813
New Tolsta
Tolsta Head
North Tolsta
Shawbost
Flannan Isles
Garenin
Carloway
Dun Carloway
Gt Bernera
Gress
Back
Gallan Head
Valtos
Tolsta Chaolais
BEINN MHOLACH 955
Tiumpan Head
Portnaguran
Aird
Aird Tong
Newmarket
Eye Peninsula
Timsgarry
Breaclete
Callanish
Breasclete
STORNOWAY
Laxdale
Garrabost
Ardroil
Miavaig
Crulivig
Garynahine
Knock
Bayble
ISLE OF LEWIS
Islivig
Aird Brenish
Brenish
Achmore
Chicken Head
Grimshader
Crossbost
Mealasta I
Balallan
Laxay
Cromore
Arivruaich
Kershader
Gravir
Scarp
Loch Langavat
Loch Odhairn
Hushinish
2227 TIRGA MOR
Forest of Harris
Kebock Hd
Gasker
Hushinish Pt
Ardvourlie
Seaforth
PARK
Lemreway
CLISHAM 2622
1874 BEINN MHOR
Amhuinnsuidhe
Taransay
Glorigs
Taransay
Ardhasaig
Tarbert
Carnach
Shiant Islands
Scalpay
Toe Head
HARRIS
Grosebay
Shillay
Northton
Ensay
Manish
Pabbay
Leverburgh
Finsbay
Berneray
Rodel
Renish Point
Boreray
Borve
Killegray
Vallay
Newtonferry
Griminish Pt
Tigharry
Sollas
NORTH UIST
Lochmaddy
Bayhead
SOUTH LEE 920
Clachan-a-Luib
Baleshare
Locheport
Carinish
EAVAL 1139
Balivanich
BENBECULA
Gramsdale
Ronay
BENBECULA
Creagorry
Balgarva
Ardvachar Pt
Wiay
West Gerinish
Stilligarry
Howmore
Verran I
HECLA 1988
Usinish
Stoneybridge
Ardvule
BEINN MHOR 2033
SOUTH UIST
Stuley
Daliburgh
Lochboisdale
Kilbride
Fiaray
Eriskay
Fuday
Stack Islands
Gighay
Hellisay
HEAVAL 1260
Earsary
Bruernish Pt
Castlebay
Muldoanich
Sandray
THE MINCH
THE LITTLE MINCH
SEA OF THE HEBRIDES
Sound of Harris
Sound of Barra
Sound of Monach
To Ullapool
To Uig
To Oban
Lochmaddy-Tarbert
Castlebay-Lochboisdale
NA NB
NB NG
HT HU
HP HU
Muckle Flugga
The Noup
Herma Ness
Lamba Ness
Burrafirth
Norwick
Haroldswick
The Nev
Baltasound
UNST
Gloup Holm
Balta
Huney
North Neaps
Westing
Gloup
Cullivoe
Uyeasound
Belmont
Uyea
Nev of Stuis
Gutcher
North Sandwick
Ramna Stacks
Gruney
Point of Fethaland
Basta
Brough Lodge
Uyea
YELL
Herra
Camb
Strandburgh Ness
North Roe
Sandvoe
Houll
Mid Yell
Hascosay
Fetlar
South-haa
Vatsetter
Tresta
Funzie
The Faither
West Sandwick
The Snap
Muckle Ossa
Housetter
Otterswick
Rams Ness
Collafirth
Ollaberry
Setter
Ulsta
Burravoe
Heylor
Esha Ness
Copister
Heoga Ness
Stenness
Hillswick
Toft
Oil Terminal
Mossbank
Sullom
Muckle Skerry
Housay
ST MAGNUS BAY
Hamnavoe
Lunna
Out Skerries
Skaw Taing
The Guens
Ve Skerries
Brae
Lunning
Muckle Roe
Vidlin
Laxo
Brough
Whalsay
Fogla Skerry
Vementry
Symbister
The Haa
Papa Stour
Vementry
Voe
Papa Little
Neap
TORSHAVN BERGEN SEYDISFJORDUR Summer only
Brindister
Clousta
South Nesting
Sandness
Aith
Moul of Eswick
Eswick
Dale
Gletness
Tresta
Wats Ness
Girlsta
Walls
Gruting
Vaila
Sand
Culswick
Score Head
Gunnista
Hoversta
South View
LERWICK
Isle of Noss
Skelda Ness
Scalloway
Kirkabister
Oxna
Bressay
Hamnavoe
Quarff
Bard Ness
West Burra
Papil
Fladdabister
Aithsetter
Helli Ness
South Havra
Mail
Maywick
Mousa
St Ninians Isle
Sandwick
Northpounds
Scousburgh
Fora Ness
Boddam
Quendale
Fitful Head
Toab
Pool of Virkie
Ladys Holm
Horse Island
Sumburgh Head
Sumburgh Roost
ZETLAND
MAINLAND
To Aberdeen
Mull Head
Papa Westray
Dennis Hd
Bow Head
Mayback
North Ronaldsay
Hollandstoun
Skaill
Gayfield
Strom Ness
Noup Head
Pierowall
THE NORTH SOUND
North Ronaldsay Firth
Westray
Surrigarth
Sanday
Northwall
Midbea
Stanger Hd
Newark
Start Pt
Langskaill
Broughtown
Berst Ness
Rapness
Bay of Lopness
WESTRAY FIRTH
Calf
Overbister
Ness
Els Ness
Calfsound
Sacquoy Hd
Braeswick
Rousay
Faray
SANDAY SOUND
Faraclett
Eday
Warbister
Spur Ness
Holm of Huip
Backaland
Banks
Egilsay
Papa Stronsay
Brough Head
The Barony
Brinyan
Whitehall
Linga Holm
Loch of Boardhouse
Wyre
Georth
Rothiesholm
Aith
Airy
Marwick
Twatt
Redland
Gairsay Sound
Stronsay
Millgrip
Holland
Lamb Head
Dounby
Gairsay
Scarwell
Bay of Skaill
Gorseness
Nesss
STRONSAY FIRTH
Balfour
Shapinsay
Auskerry
Yesnaby
South Breck
Sandgarth
Finstown
Shapinsay Sound
STROMNESS
KIRKWALL
Rerwick Head
MAINLAND
Mull Head
Greenigo
Graemsay
Clestrain
Keigar
Skaill
St Johns Head
Orgil
Point of Ayre
Orphir
Old Man of Hoy
WARD
Whaness
Hurtiso
Comquoy
Copinsay
St Marys
Rora Hd
Rackwick
Cava
Glims Holm
SCAPA FLOW
Hunda
HOY
Fara
Bow
Burray
Lyness
Flotta
Little Ayre
Bow
Saltness
Herston
St Margarets Hope
Hurliness
Wateringhouse
Aikers
South Walls
South Ronaldsay
Cleat
Swona
Burwick
Brough Ness
PENTLAND FIRTH
Pentland Skerries
Stroma
To Scrabster
HY
ND

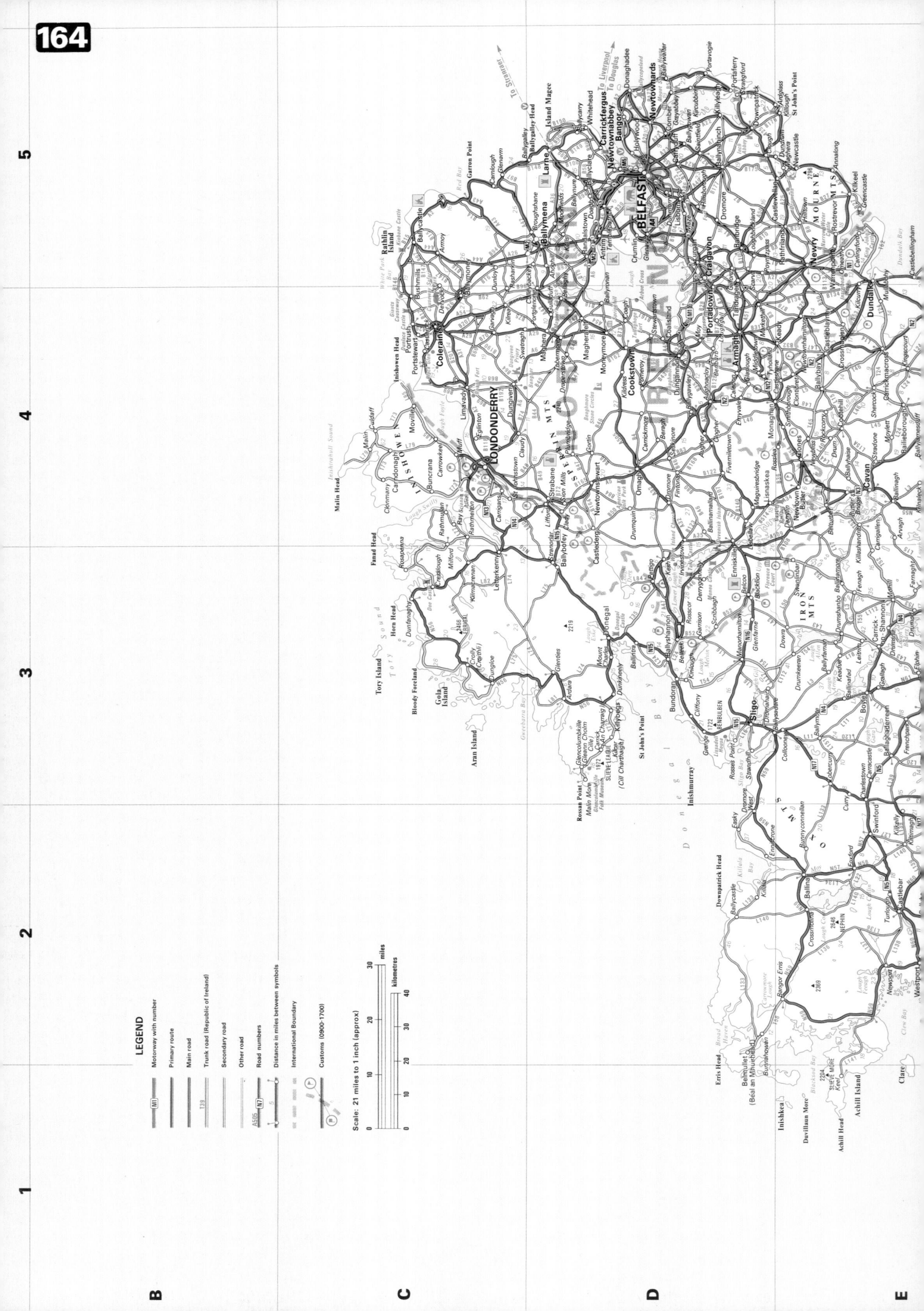
1
2
3
4
5
B
C
D
E
LEGEND
Motorway with number
Primary route
Main road
Trunk road (Republic of Ireland)
Secondary road
Other road
Road numbers
Distance in miles between symbols
International Boundary
Customs (0900-1700)
Scale: 21 miles to 1 inch (approx)
0 10 20 30 miles
0 10 20 30 40 kilometres
NORTHERN IRELAND
LONDONDERRY
BELFAST
Coleraine
Ballymena
Larne
Carrickfergus
Newtownabbey
Bangor
Newtownards
Lisburn
Craigavon
Portadown
Armagh
Newry
Dundalk
Cavan
Sligo
Donegal
Letterkenny
Strabane
Omagh
Cookstown
Dungannon
Enniskillen
Ballina
Castlebar
Westport
INISHOWEN
SPERRIN MTS
MOURNE MTS
IRON MTS
OX MTS
Donegal Bay
Malin Head
Tory Island
Bloody Foreland
Aran Island
Rathlin Island
To Stranraer
To Liverpool
To Douglas

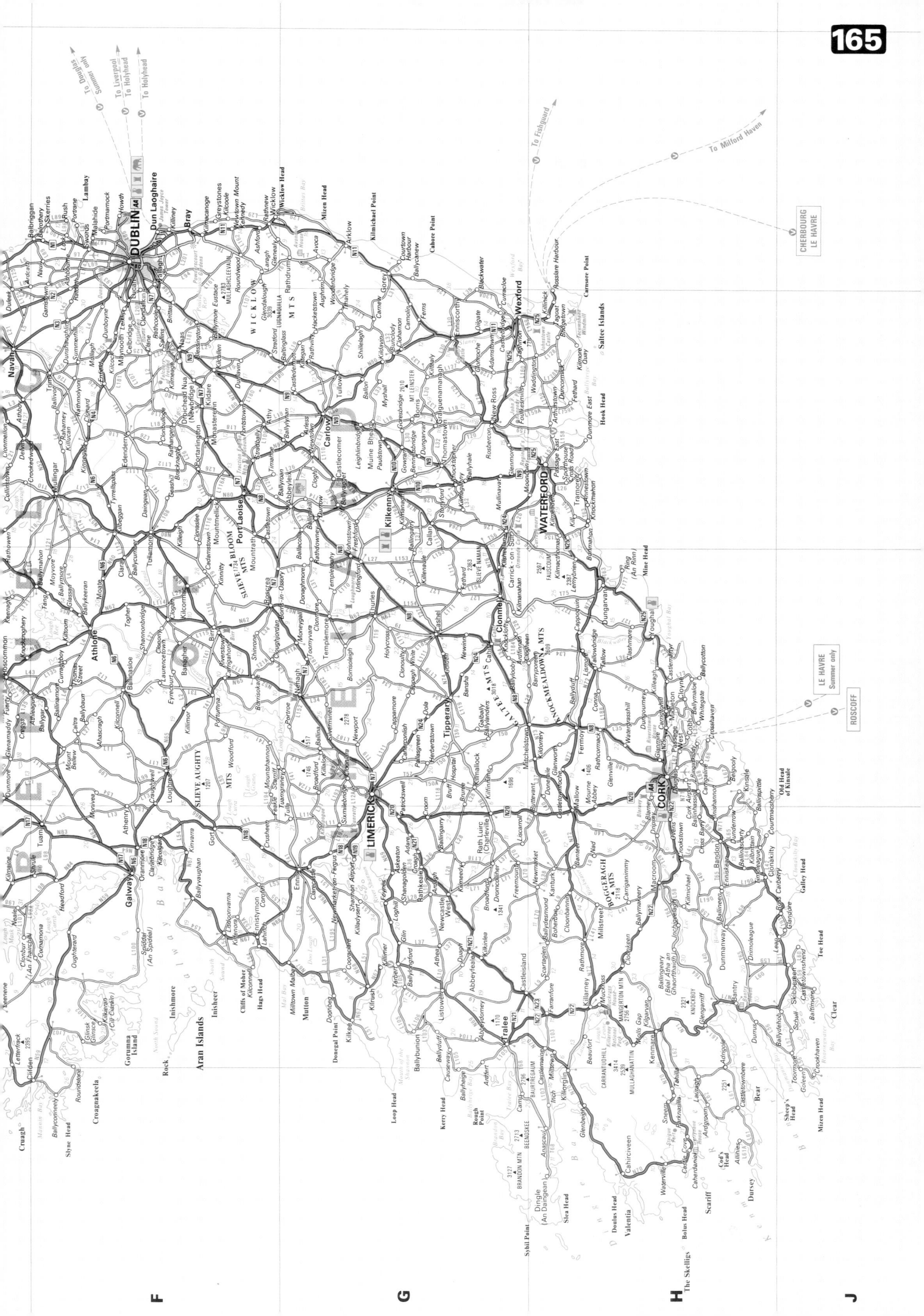
DUBLIN
CORK
LIMERICK
WATERFORD
Galway
Wexford
Kilkenny
Carlow
Tralee
Athlone
Clonmel
Tipperary
Port Laoise
Dun Laoghaire
Bray
Wicklow
Arklow
Youghal
Dungarvan
Killarney
Kenmare
Bantry
Ennis
Tuam
Navan
Mullingar
To Douglas Summer only
To Liverpool
To Holyhead
To Holyhead
To Fishguard
To Milford Haven
CHERBOURG LE HAVRE
LE HAVRE Summer only
ROSCOFF
SLIEVE AUGHTY MTS
SLIEVE BLOOM MTS
WICKLOW MTS
GALTEE MTS
KNOCKMEALDOWN MTS
BOGGERAGH MTS
Aran Islands
Saltee Islands
F
G
H
J

Inner London

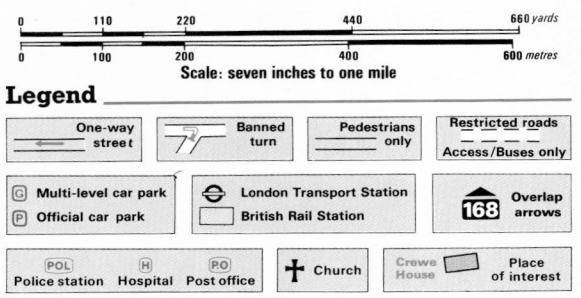

Scale bar:
0 — 110 — 220 — 440 — 660 yards
0 — 100 — 200 — 400 — 600 metres

Scale: seven inches to one mile

Legend

One—way street	Banned turn	Pedestrians only	Restricted roads Access/Buses only
Ⓖ Multi-level car park	Ⓟ Official car park	London Transport Station / British Rail Station	168 Overlap arrows
POL Police station	Ⓗ Hospital / P.O Post office	✝ Church	Crewe House / Place of interest

The one—way streets and banned turns shown on this map are in operation at time of going to press. Some of these are experimental and liable to change. Only the more important banned turns are shown, some of which operate between 7am and 7pm only, and these are sign—posted accordingly. No waiting or unilateral waiting restrictions apply to many streets. All such restrictions are indicated by official signs.

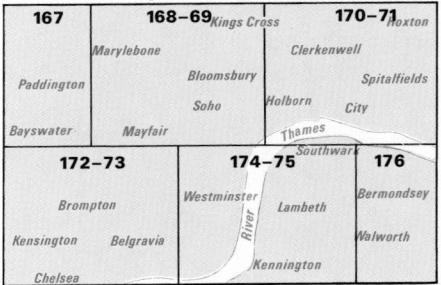

Key to Map Pages

167	168–69 Kings Cross	170–71 Hoxton
Marylebone	Clerkenwell	
Paddington	Bloomsbury	Spitalfields
	Soho	Holborn	City
Bayswater	Mayfair	Thames Southwark
172–73	174–75	176
Brompton	Westminster River	Bermondsey
Kensington	Belgravia	Lambeth	Walworth
Chelsea		Kennington	

Theatreland

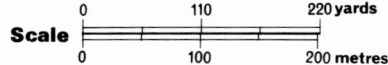

Scale:
0 — 110 — 220 yards
0 — 100 — 200 metres

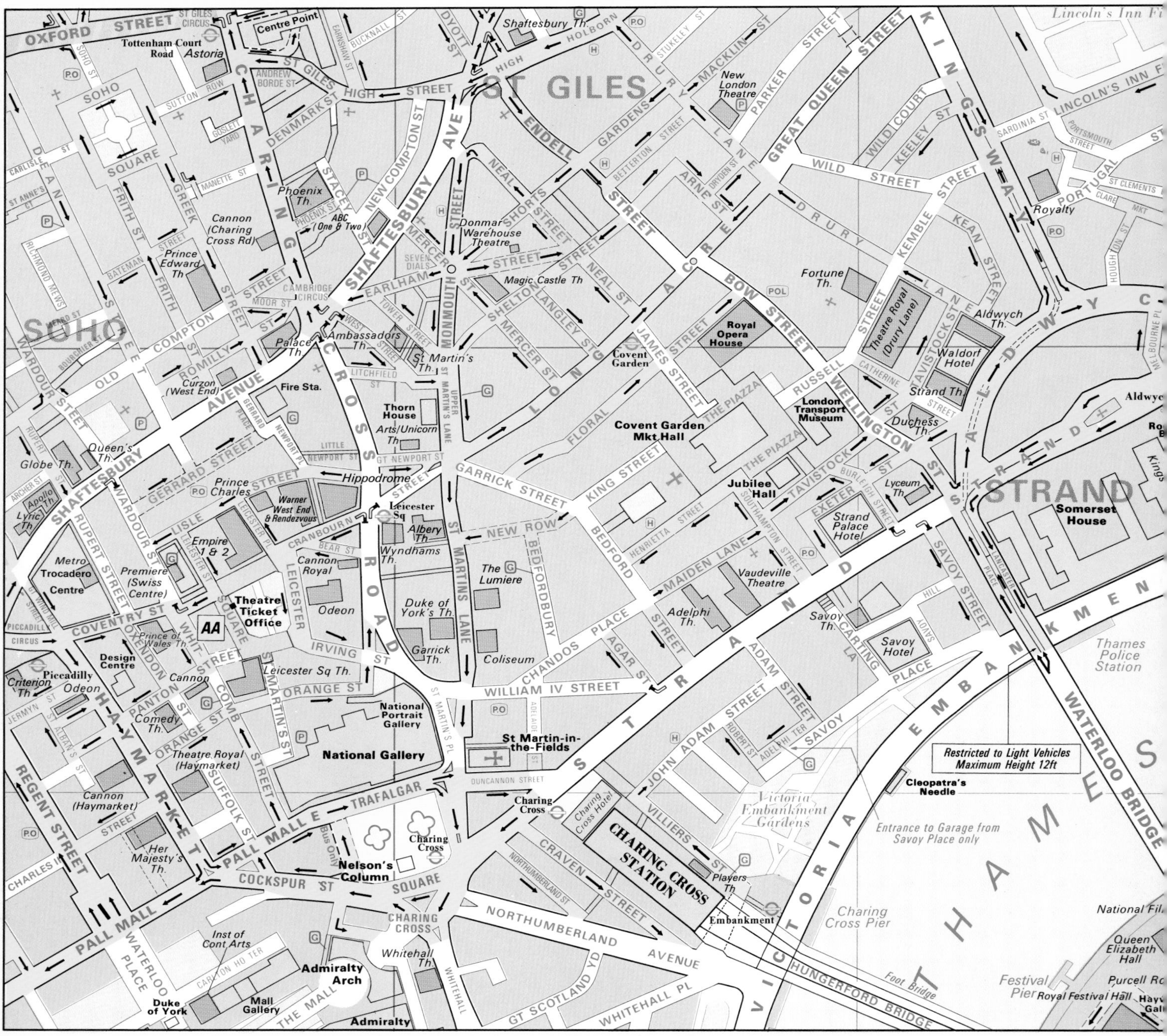

[Map of Theatreland area of Inner London showing streets, theatres, and landmarks including: Oxford Street, St Giles Circus, Tottenham Court Road, Astoria, Centre Point, Shaftesbury Th., Soho Square, Charing Cross Road, Phoenix Th., Cambridge Circus, Seven Dials, Donmar Warehouse Theatre, Magic Castle Th., New London Theatre, Great Queen Street, Drury Lane, Kingsway, Lincoln's Inn Fields, Prince Edward Th., Palace Th., Ambassadors Th., St Martin's Th., Fortune Th., Theatre Royal (Drury Lane), Aldwych Th., Waldorf Hotel, Royal Opera House, Covent Garden, Covent Garden Mkt Hall, Strand Th., Duchess Th., Lyceum Th., Queen's Th., Globe Th., Apollo Th., Lyric Th., Hippodrome, Warner West End & Rendezvous, Leicester Square, Albery Th., Wyndhams Th., Empire 1 & 2, Prince Charles, Cannon Royal, Duke of York's Th., The Lumiere, Garrick Th., Coliseum, Adelphi Th., Vaudeville Theatre, Jubilee Hall, Strand Palace Hotel, Savoy Hotel, Savoy Th., Somerset House, Strand, Metro Trocadero Centre, Premiere (Swiss Centre), Theatre Ticket Office, Odeon, Leicester Sq Th., National Portrait Gallery, National Gallery, Criterion Th., Piccadilly Odeon, Comedy Th., Design Centre, Theatre Royal (Haymarket), Her Majesty's Th., Cannon (Haymarket), Regent Street, Haymarket, Pall Mall, Trafalgar Square, Nelson's Column, Charing Cross, Charing Cross Station, Admiralty Arch, Duke of York, Mall Gallery, Whitehall Th., Victoria Embankment Gardens, Cleopatra's Needle, Charing Cross Pier, Hungerford Bridge, Waterloo Bridge, Royal Festival Hall, Queen Elizabeth Hall, Purcell Rm, National Film Theatre, Thames Police Station, Embankment]

ST JOHN'S WOOD
MAIDA VALE
ST MARYLEBONE
PADDINGTON
BAYSWATER
A
B
C
D
E
F
G
H
J
K
L
M
Maida Vale
Lord's Cricket Ground
Lord's Cricket Museum
Wellington Hosp
Public Gdns.
Winfield House
Nuffield Foundation
London Central Mosque
Ladbroke Westmereland Hotel
Boat House
HANOVER GATE
Royal College of Obstetricians & Gynaecologists
Maida Vale Hospital
Clarendon Ct Hotel
Warwick Avenue
Cockpit Theatre
Recreation Ground
Childrens Hospital
Little Venice
Fire Sta
GOODS STATION
ABC Cinema
Cannon Cine
Paddington Basin
Paddington
PADDINGTON STA
St Mary's Hosp
Gt Western Royal Hotel
Marylebone
MARYLEBONE STATION
Harewood Hotel
Western Ophthalmic Hospital
Samaritan Hospital
Edgware Road
Seymour Hall
Holiday Inn
Arabic Centre (Cinema)
Hallfield Estate
Leinster Towers Hotel
London Toy Model Museum
Central Park Hotel
Post House Hotel
Royal Lancaster Hotel
Queensway
Lancaster Gate
Fountains
Peter Pan
Entrance and Exit Underground Car
SUSSEX SQUARE
MAIDA VALE
ST JOHNS WOOD ROAD
EDGWARE ROAD
MARYLEBONE ROAD
BAYSWATER ROAD
PRINCE ALBERT RD
OUTER CIRCLE
PARK ROAD
GLOUCESTER PLACE
BAKER STREET
PRAED STREET
SUSSEX GARDENS
WESTBOURNE TERRACE
BISHOP'S BRIDGE ROAD
NORTH WHARF ROAD
HARROW ROAD
THE RING
NORTH RIDE
168
172
OXFORD STREE
Oxford Street, where specially marked,
to through traffic (except buses &
0700 hours – 1900 Monday – Satur

REGENT'S PARK
Closed between midnight & 0700
OXFORD STREET
Oxford Street, where specially marked, is closed to through traffic (except buses & taxis) 0700 hours – 1900 Monday – Saturday.
REGENT'S PARK
MARYLEBONE
MAYFAIR
Winfield House
Nuffield Foundation
Public Gdns.
Prince Albert Rd
London Central Mosque
Ladbroke Westmereland Hotel
Hanover Gate
Hanover Terrace
Kent Terr
Outer Circle
Inner Circle
Chester Road
Boat House
Boating Lake
Open Air Theatre
Queen Mary's Gardens
Regent's College
York Bridge
Royal College of Obstetricians & Gynaecologists
Royal College of Physicians
Park Road
Rossmore Road
Gloucester Place
Baker Street
Marylebone Station
Clarence Gate
Allsop Place
Madame Tussaud's
Planetarium
Lost Property Office
Royal Academy of Music
London Clinic
Park Square
Park Crescent
Portland Place
Marylebone Road
Marylebone Circus
Polytechnic of Central London
Princess Grace Hospital
Town Hall
Western Ophthalmic Hospital
Samaritan Hospital
Harewood Hotel
Cockpit Theatre
Lisson Grove
Edgware Road
Seymour Place
Dorset Square
Melcombe Street
Devonshire Street
Weymouth Street
New Cavendish Street
Harley Street
Wimpole Street
Marylebone High Street
Nat Heart Hosp
Clifton Ford Hotel
Wallace Collection
Manchester Square
Wigmore Street
Wigmore Hall
Londoner Hotel
New Mandeville Hotel
Royal Coll of Medicine
Cavendish Square
Queen Anne Street
Portman Square
Portman Intercontinental Hotel
Home House
Bryanston Court Hotel
Churchill Hotel
Montcalm Hotel
Fitzroy Nuffield Hospital
Holiday Inn
Arabic Centre (Cinema)
Seymour Hall
Connaught Square
Connaught Place
Marble Arch
Cumberland Hotel
Mount Royal Hotel
Odeon
Selfridge Hotel
(Selfridges)
Bond Street
Oxford Street
Stratford Court Hotel
South Molton Street
North Audley Street
London Marriott Hotel
Grosvenor Square
U.S. Embassy
Britannia Hotel
Grosvenor House Hotel
Claridges Hotel
Brook Street
Brook's Mews
Park Lane
Upper Brook Street
Upper Grosvenor Street
Mount Street
Library
Connaught Hotel
Berkeley Square
Bayswater Road
Hyde Park Square
Hyde Park Crescent
Speakers Corner
Cumberland Gate
Stanhope Gate
Albion Gate
The Ring
North Ride
Brook Gate
Grosvenor Gate
Entrance and Exit to Underground Car Park
Exit and Entrance to Underground Car Park
Clarendon Gate
Broad Walk
Albany Street
167
173

SOMERS TOWN
KING'S CROSS STA
ST PANCRAS STATION
EUSTON STATION
Euston
Motorail
St Pancras
BLOOMSBURY
SOHO
ST GILES
HAMPSTEAD ROAD
EUSTON ROAD
EVERSHOLT STREET
MIDLAND ROAD
GRAY'S INN ROAD
PENTONVILLE ROAD
ARGYLE STREET
SWINTON STREET
ACTON STREET
Kings Cross St Pancras
British Coachways Coach Sta
Town Hall
Elizabeth Garrett Anderson Hosp
Kennedy Hotel
National Temperance Hosp
DRUMMOND STREET
Euston Tower
Capital Radio
Thames TV
Euston Centre
Warren Street
Euston Square
University College
College Hosp
GOWER STREET
TOTTENHAM COURT ROAD
WOBURN PLACE
TAVISTOCK SQUARE
TAVISTOCK PLACE
HUNTER STREET
JUDD STREET
Percival David Foundation
Bloomsbury Theatre
Courtauld Institute Gallery
University of London
British Medical Ass
Jewish Museum
Thomas Coram Foundation
Coram's Fields Playground
BRUNSWICK SQUARE
MECKLENBURGH SQUARE
GUILFORD STREET
BERNARD STREET
Russell Square
RUSSELL SQUARE
Hospital for Sick Children
National Hospital
Royal London Homeopathic Hospital
GREAT ORMOND STREET
SOUTHAMPTON ROW
THEOBALD'S ROAD
Telecom Tower
Middlesex Hosp
Drill Hall
Building Centre
British Museum
BEDFORD SQUARE
BLOOMSBURY SQUARE
GREAT RUSSELL STREET
BLOOMSBURY WAY
NEW OXFORD STREET
HIGH HOLBORN
Holborn (Kingsway)
KINGSWAY
OXFORD STREET
Oxford Circus
REGENT STREET
St Giles Circus
Tottenham Court Road
CHARING CROSS ROAD
SHAFTESBURY AVENUE
SOHO SQUARE
Cambridge Circ
SEVEN DIALS
Covent Garden
Royal Opera House
London Transport Mus
Covent Garden Mkt Hall
THE PIAZZA
Leicester Square
LEICESTER SQUARE
Piccadilly Circus
Eros
HAYMARKET
Trocadero Centre
Museum of Mankind
Royal Academy of Arts
Royal Institute
Burlington Arcade
National Portrait Gallery
National Gallery
St Martin-in-the-fields
TRAFALGAR SQUARE
Nelson Column
Charing Cross
STRAND
Savoy Hotel
Strand Palace Hotel
Victoria Embankment Gardens
Cleopatra's Needle
Entrance to Garage from Savoy Place only
York Water Gate
WATERLOO
Palladium
Mag Court
Baths
Soho Poly
Lincoln's Inn
Freemason's Hall
Holborn Town Hall
New London Theatre
Shaftesbury Hospital
House of St Barnabas
Thorn House
Fire Sta
St James's Church
The Pipe Museum
170
174

PENTONVILLE
FINSBURY
ST PANCRAS
CLERKENWELL
HOLBORN
STRAND
Thomas Coram Foundation
Coram's Fields Playground
Royal Scot Hotel
Mount Pleasant (Postal Sorting Office)
London Records Office
Gray's Inn
Lincoln's Inn Fields
Royal Courts of Justice
London School of Economics
Somerset House
Restricted to light vehicles max. height 12ft
Entrance to Garage from Savoy Place only
Blackfriars Station
Holborn Viaduct Station
Central Markets (Smithfield)
Temple Church
Inner Temple
Middle Temple Hall
Cleopatra's Needle
Waterloo Bridge
Blackfriars Bridge
Embankment
R I V E

169
175

HOXTON
SHOREDITCH
ST LUKE'S
SPITALFIELDS
WHITECHAPEL
CITY
CITY ROAD
OLD STREET
GREAT EASTERN STREET
KINGSLAND ROAD
HACKNEY ROAD
COLUMBIA ROAD
BETHNAL GREEN ROAD
SHOREDITCH HIGH STREET
COMMERCIAL STREET
COMMERCIAL ROAD
BISHOPSGATE
MOORGATE
FINSBURY SQUARE
FINSBURY CIRCUS
LONDON WALL
CHEAPSIDE
POULTRY
CORNHILL
LEADENHALL STREET
FENCHURCH STREET
CANNON STREET
QUEEN VICTORIA STREET
THAMES STREET
UPPER THAMES STREET
LOWER THAMES STREET
EASTCHEAP
KING WILLIAM STREET
GRACECHURCH ST
THREADNEEDLE
LOMBARD STREET
HOUNDSDITCH
MIDDLESEX STREET
ALDGATE HIGH STREET
WHITECHAPEL HIGH STREET
MANSELL STREET
MINORIES
TOWER HILL
ALDERSGATE
ST MARTIN'S LE GRAND
SOUTHWARK BRIDGE
LONDON BRIDGE
CHISWELL STREET
BUNHILL ROW
WORSHIP STREET
OLD BROAD STREET
Moorfields Eye Hosp
St Matthew Hospital
Mildmay Mission Hospital
ARNOLD CIRCUS
Old Street
Wesley's House & Museum
H.A.C. HQ.
Playing Field
Exhibition Halls
Barbican Centre
The Barbican
Guildhall School of Music
St Giles
Moorgate
Ironmongers Hall
Barber Surgeons Hall
London Museum
LIVERPOOL STREET STATION
Liverpool Street
Great Eastern Hotel
Spitalfields Market
Bishopsgate Institute
Panmakers Hall
Nat. West Tower
Carpenters Hall
Drapers Hall
Stock Exchange
Bank of England
Royal Exchange
Bank
Guildhall
Clock Museum
Goldsmiths Hall
Saddlers Hall
Mercer's Hall
Grocers Hall
Bank of England Extension
St Mary le Bow
Mansion House
Temple of Mithras
St Stephen
Founders Hall
London Stone
Painter's Hall
Tallow Chandler's Hall
Skinners Hall
Innholder Hall
Vintners Hall
CANNON ST STA
Monument
The Monument
The Merchant Taylors Hall
City of London Club
Leathersellers Hall
Baltic Exch
Leadenhall Market
Lloyd's
FENCHURCH ST STATION
Clothworker's Hall
Corn Exchange
The Watermens Hall
Bakers Hall
Custom House
Fishmongers Hall
Trinity House
City of London Poly
Aldgate
Aldgate East
Aldgate Bus & Coach Sta
Camperdown House
Tower Hill
Tower of London
World Trade Centre
St Katharine Dock
Tower Pier
Tower Stairs
Queenhithe Stairs
Southwark Br Stairs
Bear Gardens Museum
THAMES
176

167
KENSINGTON GARDENS
HYDE PARK
The Serpentine
Round Pond
Kensington Palace
Peter Pan
The Long Water
Physical Energy
Serpentine Bridge
Norwegian/British Monument
Restaurant & Cafe
Serpentine Gallery
Boat House
Lido
Pier
Albert Mem
Royal Garden Hotel
Knightsbridge Barracks
KENSINGTON ROAD
Royal Albert Hall
Royal Geographical Society
Royal School of Needlework
Royal College of Music
Imperial College
City & Guilds College
Brompton Oratory
Science Museum
Geological Museum
British Museum of Natural History
Victoria and Albert Museum
Baden-Powell House
BROMPTON
SOUTH KENSINGTON
CHELSEA
CROMWELL ROAD
BROMPTON ROAD
FULHAM ROAD
KINGS ROAD
OLD BROMPTON ROAD
GLOUCESTER ROAD
QUEEN'S GATE
EXHIBITION ROAD
South Kensington
Gloucester Road
Brompton Hosp
Royal Marsden Hosp
Women's Hosp
Chelsea Fire Station
Chelsea Old Town Hall
Chelsea Cinema
ABC Cinema
CHELSEA SQUARE
THE BOLTONS
REDCLIFFE GARDENS
SLOANE AVENUE
Harrods

A
B
C
D
E
F
G
H
J
K
L
M
168
174
ST JAMES'S
GREEN PARK
HYDE PARK CORNER
CONSTITUTION HILL
(Closed to traffic on Sundays)
HORSE RIDE
THE MALL
BIRDCAGE
Buckingham Palace
Buckingham Palace Gardens
Queens Gallery
The Royal Mews
Queen Victoria Memorial
Canada Gate
St James's Park
Wellington Arch
Hyde Park Corner
Apsley House
Underpass
SERPENTINE ROAD
LOVERS' WALK
PARK LANE
PICCADILLY
PALL MALL
ST JAMES'S STREET
GROSVENOR PLACE
GROSVENOR CRESCENT
BELGRAVE SQUARE
BELGRAVIA
VICTORIA STATION
Victoria Coach Sta
VICTORIA STREET
BUCKINGHAM PALACE ROAD
BUCKINGHAM GATE
VAUXHALL BRIDGE ROAD
BELGRAVE ROAD
KING'S ROAD
SLOANE SQUARE
SLOANE STREET
LOWER SLOANE STREET
ECCLESTON STREET
EBURY STREET
EBURY BRIDGE ROAD
ELIZABETH STREET
ELIZABETH BRIDGE
ECCLESTON BRIDGE
PIMLICO ROAD
PIMLICO
WARWICK WAY
ST GEORGE'S DRIVE
LUPUS STREET
CHELSEA BRIDGE ROAD
CHELSEA EMBANKMENT
CHELSEA BRIDGE
GROSVENOR ROAD
Churchill Gardens
DOLPHIN SQUARE
Royal Hospital
Ranelagh Gardens
Chelsea Barracks
National Army Mus
Burtons Court
ROYAL HOSPITAL ROAD
Westminster Cathedral
Westminster City Hall
Westminster Children's Hosp
Apollo Victoria
London Tourist Board
Queen Mother Sports Centre
Wellington Barracks
Home Office
Guard's Chapel
St James's Palace
Clarence House
Lancaster House
Marlborough House
Schomberg House
Spencer House
Dorchester Hotel
Hilton Hotel
Inter-Continental Hotel
Londonderry House Hotel
Ritz Hotel
Goring Hotel
Royal Westminster Hotel
Grosvenor Hotel
Hyatt Carlton Tower Hotel
Sheraton Park Tower Hotel
Berkeley Hotel
Lowndes Hotel
Wilbraham Hotel
Royal Court Hotel
Blewcoat School
Caxton Hall
Royal Hort Society Old Hall

169
173
ST JAMES'S
PALL MALL
JERMYN STREET
PICCADILLY
COCKSPUR STREET
PALL MALL EAST
TRAFALGAR
Nelson Column
Charing Cross
NORTHUMBERLAND AVE
CRAVEN STREET
VILLIERS STREET
Embankment
Cleopatra's Needle
Entrance to Garage from Savoy Place only
Charing Cross Pier
Festival Pier
Hungerford Bridge (Foot)
Royal Festival Hall
Queen Eliz.
Admiralty Arch
Admiralty
Inst. of Contemporary Art
Mall Gallery
Duke of York Column
Carlton House Terrace
CARLTON GARDENS
Schomberg House
Marlborough House
St James's Palace
Clarence House
Lancaster House
Spencer House
CLEVELAND ROW
MARLBOROUGH ROAD
THE MALL
(Closed to traffic on Sundays)
Green Park
QUEENS WALK
KING STREET
ST JAMES'S STREET
Ritz Hotel
Stafford Hotel
Duke's Hotel
The Pipe Museum
Cavendish Hotel
St James's Church
PARK
Horse Guards
HORSE GUARDS ROAD
WHITEHALL
WHITEHALL PLACE
WHITEHALL CT
Royal Horseguards Hotel
HORSEGUARDS AVENUE
Banqueting House
Government Offices
Hispaniola
P.S Tattershall Castle
Jubilee Gardens
VICTORIA EMBANKMENT
DOWNING STREET
RICHMOND TERR
Cenotaph
Norman Shaw Building (MP's Offices)
County Hall
Westminster Pier
KING CHARLES STREET
PARLIAMENT STREET
CANNON ROW
Westminster
Duck Island
ST JAMES'S PARK
St James's Park Lake
Canada Gate
Queen Victoria Memorial
Buckingham Palace
Cabinet War Rooms
Queen Elizabeth II Conf Centre
GREAT GEORGE STREET
BRIDGE STREET
WESTMINSTER BR
Big Ben
BIRDCAGE WALK
OLD QUEEN ST
ANNE'S GATE
LEWISHAM ST
Central Hall
Guard's Chapel
PARLIAMENT SQUARE
Middx Guildhall
BROAD SANCTUARY
St Margaret's
ST MARGARETS ST
Westminster Hall
Houses of Parliament
LAMBETH
St Thomas's Hospital
Home Office
Wellington Barracks
BUCKINGHAM GATE
BROADWAY
TOTHILL STREET
PETTY FRANCE
St James's Park
St Ermins Hotel
Caxton Hall
CAXTON STREET
DEAN FARRAR ST
DACRE STREET
New Scotland Yard
Westminster Abbey
Dean's Yard
Jewel Tower
Ashburnham House
GREAT COLLEGE STREET
ABINGDON STREET
Victoria Tower Gardens
VICTORIA STREET
ABBEY ORCHARD ST
GREAT SMITH STREET
ST ANN'S STREET
OLD PYE STREET
Bluecoat (or Blewcoat) School
St James's Hotel
Westminster City Hall
SPENSER STREET
PALACE STREET
STAG PLACE
Rubens Hotel
BRESSENDEN PLACE
Westminster Th.
WILFRED STREET
CASTLE LANE
ARTILLERY ROW
STRUTTON GR
ST MATTHEW
GREAT PETER STREET
MARSHAM STREET
TUFTON STREET
SMITH SQUARE
St John's Concert Hall
Transport House
MILLBANK
LAMBETH BRIDGE
LAMBETH PALACE ROAD
Lambeth Palace
Tradescant Trust
OLD PARADISE
Fire Brigade Headquarters
HOWICK PLACE
Victoria Palace
Cathedral Piazza
Westminster Cathedral
AMBROSDEN AVE
THIRLEBY RD
GREYCOAT PLACE
CHADWICK ST
Grey Coat Hosp
Royal Hort Society New Hall
MONCK STREET
Goverment Buildings
ROMNEY STREET
DEAN BRADLEY ST
HORSEFERRY ROAD
Westminster Hospital
DEAN RYLE ST
THORNEY STREET
PAGE STREET
ASHLEY PLACE
CARLISLE PLACE
Apollo Victoria
MORPETH TERRACE
FRANCIS STREET
EMERY HILL ST
GREENCOAT PLACE
STILLINGTON ST
ROCHESTER ROW
Royal Hort Society Old Hall
VINCENT SQUARE
MAUNSEL STREET
ROTHERFORD ST
ELVERTON STREET
REGENCY STREET
VINCENT STREET
JOHN ISLIP STREET
Millbank Tower
WESTMINSTER
Westminster Children's Hosp
Queen Mother Sports Centre
VAUXHALL BRIDGE ROAD
GILLINGHAM
GUILDHOUSE STREET
Ecclestone Hotel
LONGMOORE STREET
TACHBROOK STREET
UPPER TACHBROOK ST
WARWICK WAY
BELGRAVE ROAD
HIDE PLACE
CHAPTER STREET
DOUGLAS STREET
Millbank Estate
ERASMUS STREET
HERRICK STREET
Tate Gallery
ATTERBURY STREET
CURETON STREET
CAUSTON ST
PONSONBY PLACE
PONSONBY TERRACE
ALBERT EMBANKMENT
RIVER THAMES
LAMBETH HIGH STREET
WHITGIFT STREET
RANDALL ROAD
BLACK PRINCE ROAD
JONATHAN STREET
GLASSHOUSE WALK
WORGAN STREET
TYERS STREET
WICKHAM STREET
VAUXHALL
CHURTON STREET
CHARLWOOD STREET
DENBIGH STREET
DENBIGH PLACE
WARWICK SQUARE
ST GEORGE'S DRIVE
MORETON STREET
MORETON PLACE
MORETON TERR
RAMPAYNE ST
DORSET PL
Pimlico
DRUMMOND GATE
BESSBOROUGH ST
BESSBOROUGH GARDENS
BESSBOROUGH PLACE
VAUXHALL BRIDGE
PIMLICO
LUPUS STREET
CLAVERTON STREET
CHICHESTER ST
ST GEORGE'S SQUARE
AYLESFORD STREET
DOLPHIN SQUARE
Churchill Gardens
CHURCHILL GARDENS ROAD
Private Road
GROSVENOR ROAD
Vauxhall
VAUXHALL STA
KENNINGTON LANE
HARLEYFORD ROAD
DURHAM STREET
VAUXHALL GROVE
GOODING
Covent Garden Flower Mkt.
A B C D E F G H J K L M

170
London Weekend T.V.
National Theatre
Gardens Museum
Southwark Cathedral
NORTH SOUTHWARK
UPPER GROUND
STAMFORD STREET
DUCHY
COIN
CORNWALL ROAD
DOON STREET
AQUINAS ST
Royal Waterloo Hosp
WATERLOO ROAD
CONCERT APPROACH
THEED STREET
WHITTLESEY STREET
ROUPELL STREET
BRAD STREET
EXTON STREET
Waterloo Station (Eastern)
WOOTTON STREET
WINDMILL WALK
GREET ST
HATFIELDS
PARIS GARDEN
COLOMBO ST
MEYMOTT STREET
JOAN
RENNIE
BLACKFRIARS ROAD
HOPTON STREET
HOLLAND STREET
SOUTHWARK STREET
BEAR LANE
PRICE'S ST
GREAT SUFFOLK ST
LAVINGTON STREET
DOLBEN
GAMBIA ST
SCORESBY ST
SUMNER STREET
ZOAR ST
EMERSON STREET
PARK STREET
SOUTHWARK BRIDGE ROAD
THRALE STREET
CLINK STREET
STONEY
Borough Market
George Inn
Guy's
EWER STREET
GUILDFORD
UNION STREET
Waterloo
WATERLOO STATION
THE CUT
Young Vic Th
Old Vic Theatre
MITRE ROAD
SHORT STREET
UFFORD ST
NELSON SQUARE
COPPERFIELD STREET
LOMAN STREET
SURREY ROW
SAWYER
POCOCK
KING'S BENCH STREET
RUSHWORTH STREET
GREAT SUFFOLK STREET
GLASSHILL ST
MINT ST
MARSHALSEA ROAD
REDCROSS WAY
NEWCOMEN
TENNIS STREET
BOROUGH HIGH STREET
LANT STREET
TOLMIN STREET
SUDREY ST
Borough
TABARD
WEBBER STREET
VALENTINE PL
CORAL STREET
GRAY ST
BARON'S PLACE
WEBBER ROW
LOWER MARSH
FRAZIER STREET
BAYLIS ROAD
PEARMAN STREET
MORLEY
GERRIDGE STREET
DODSON STREET
LANCASTER STREET
BOYFIELD STREET
SILEX STREET
JAMES STREET
LIBRARY STREET
MILCOTE ST
Liby
ST. GEORGE'S CIRCUS
Royal Eye Hosp
BOROUGH ROAD
SOUTHWARK BRIDGE ROAD
BOROUGH ROAD
TRINITY STREET
COLE STREET
GREAT DOVER STREET
PILGRIMAGE
SWAN STREET
GLOBE ST
TRINITY CH SQ
WESTMINSTER BRIDGE ROAD
Lambeth North
KENNINGTON ROAD
ST GEORGE'S ROAD
LAMBETH RD
St George's Cathedral
LONDON ROAD
ROTARY ST
KEYWORTH ST
TH DOYLE ST
South Bank Polytechnic
SOUTHWARK STREET
CAUSEWAY
NEWINGTON CAUSEWAY
AVONMOUTH ST
Crown Court
Newington Gardens
HARPER ROAD
BROCKHAM ST
DICKENS SQ
MERRICK SQ
TRINITY STREET
CARLISLE LANE
HERCULES ROAD
COSSER STREET
KING EDWARD WALK
GLADSTONE STREET
GARDEN ROW
ONTARIO ST
SKIPTON STREET
Elephant & Castle
Coronet Cinema
BATH TERRACE
ROCKINGHAM STREET
ARCH STREET
FALMOUTH ROAD
SPURGEON ST
DEVERELL
SOUTHWARK
LAMBETH ROAD
Imperial War Museum
GAYWOOD STREET
WEST SQUARE
London College of Printing
ELEPHANT & CASTLE
Metropolitan Tabernacle
Recreation Centre
ABC Cine
Shopping Centre
NEW KENT ROAD
COUNTY STREET
BROOK DRIVE
AUSTRAL ST
HAYLES STREET
ELLIOTT'S ROW
OSWIN STREET
WALCOT SQUARE
WALNUT TREE WALK
FITZALAN STREET
LAMBETH WALK
BISHOP'S TERRACE
OAKDEN STREET
ST MARY'S WALK
MONKTON
LOLLARD STREET
Lambeth Walk Open Space
LONGVILLE RD
DANTE RD
London Park Hotel
CHURCH YARD ROW
HOLYOAK ROAD
ELEPHANT ROAD
DEACON WAY
MUNTON ROAD
RODNEY PLACE
ELBA PL
BALFOUR STREET
HENSHAW ST
HEYGATE STREET
BRANDON STREET
WANSEY STREET
RODNEY ROAD
WALWORTH ROAD
BUTTS
NEWINGTON BUTTS
Draper Estate
WOOLASTON CLOSE
HOWELL WALK
HAMPTON STREET
STEEDMAN ST
WINCOTT STREET
GILBERT ROAD
DRYDEN CT
RENFREW ROAD
KNIGHT'S WALK
REEDWORTH STREET
KEMPSFORD RD
Cotton Gardens Estate
NEWINGTON
WINCHESTER CLOSE
MARLBOROUGH CLOSE
ROBERT DASHWOOD WAY
Walworth Town Hall
The Cuming Museum
CHARLESTON STREET
LARCOM STREET
TURQUAND ST
COTHAM ST
BRANDON STREET
CONTENT STREET
WADDING STREET
STEAD STREET
ORB ST
Ethelred Estate
LOLLARD ST
DISTIN ST
MARYLEE WAY
CHESTER WAY
DENNY CRES
DENNY STREET
KENNINGTON LANE
OPAL STREET
COTTINGTON CLOSE
COTTINGTON STREET
WESLEY CL
CANTERBURY PLACE
PEACOCK STREET
CRAMPTON STREET
PENTON PLACE
ILIFFE STREET
AMELIA STREET
AMELIA ST
THRUSH ST
BROWNING STREET
KING AND QUEEN STREET
MORECAMBE STREET
HOTSPUR STREET
TRACEY ST
TAVY CLOSE
WHITE HART STREET
Lambeth County Court
KENNINGTON PARK ROAD
ALBERTA STREET
AMBERGATE STREET
MANOR PLACE
OCCUPATION ROAD
BLACKWOOD ST
EAST STREET
PORTLAND STREET
CARDIGAN STREET
COURTENAY STREET
AVELINE STREET
LOUGHBOROUGH ST
CLEAVER STREET
BOWDEN ST
CLEAVER SQUARE
Kennings Estate
Kennington
KENNINGS WAY
Art School
BRAGANZA STREET
GAZA ST
TARVER ROAD
MARSHLAND CL
BURDETT CL
PASLEY CL
PENTON STREET
PENROSE STREET
PENROSE GROVE
CARTER PL
WALWORTH ROAD
SUTHERLAND WALK
CADIZ ST
LIVERPOOL GROVE
KENNINGTON
METHLEY STREET
RAVENSDON STREET
BADCOT ST
MILVERTON ST
AULTON PL
STANNARY STREET
MONTFORD PLACE
MONTFORD PL
DE LAUNE STREET
SHARSTED STREET
FAUNCE STREET
HARMSWORTH STREET
DODDINGTON GR
KENNINGTON PARK PLACE
WESTCOTT ROAD
CHAPTER ROAD
LORRIMORE SQUARE
CARTER STREET
SUTHERLAND SQUARE
MACLEOD ST
FIELDING STREET
LANGDALE CL
MERROW STREET
ARNSIDE ST
HORSLEY ST
QUEEN'S ROW
WESTMORLAND ROAD
CLAYTON STREET
Kennington Park
Kennington Park
The Oval
KENNINGTON OVAL
KENNINGTON ROAD
176

NORTH SOUTHWARK
SOUTHWARK
BERMONDSEY
WALWORTH
Southwark Cathedral
The London Dungeon
H.M.S. Belfast
Tower Pier
Southwark Crown Court
William Curtis Ecological Park
Coach & Lorry Park
Tower Bridge Museum
The Tower Hotel
London Bridge Station
Guy's Hospital
Guy's Hosp Extension
George Inn
Greenwood Theatre
London City Mission
South London College
Brewery
St John's Estate
St Saviour's Estate
Tabard Garden
Crown Court
Newington Gardens
Bermondsey Town Hall
Bricklayers Arms
Walworth Town Hall
The Cuming Museum
Coronet Cinema
Burgess Park Lake
171
175
TOOLEY STREET
ST THOMAS STREET
BOROUGH HIGH STREET
GREAT DOVER STREET
LONG LANE
TOWER BRIDGE ROAD
NEW KENT ROAD
OLD KENT ROAD
WALWORTH ROAD
EAST STREET
ALBANY ROAD
BOROUGH ROAD
UNION STREET
SOUTHWARK BRIDGE ROAD
BERMONDSEY STREET
GRANGE ROAD
ABBEY STREET
RODNEY ROAD
PORTLAND STREET

INDEX To Inner London Maps

This map employs an arbitrary system of grid reference. Pages are identified by numbers and divided into twelve squares. Each square contains a blue letter; all references give the page number first, followed by the letter of the square in which a particular street can be found. Reference for Exhibition Road is *172*E, meaning that the relevant map is on page *172* and that the street appears in the square designated E.

Key to Town Plans

ABERDEEN

DUNDEE

GLASGOW · Greenock · Paisley · EDINBURGH

NEWCASTLE · SUNDERLAND

MIDDLESBROUGH

YORK

BLACKPOOL · LEEDS · HULL

HUDDERSFIELD

MANCHESTER · LIVERPOOL · DONCASTER · SHEFFIELD

STOKE-UPON-TRENT

DERBY · NOTTINGHAM

WOLVERHAMPTON · LEICESTER · Hinkley · NORWICH

BIRMINGHAM · COVENTRY

NORTHAMPTON · CAMBRIDGE

IPSWICH · FELIXSTOWE · HARWICH

SWANSEA · Caerphilly · NEWPORT · OXFORD · SWINDON · LUTON

CARDIFF · Barry · BRISTOL · BATH · HEATHROW

GATWICK · DOVER · FOLKESTONE

SOUTHAMPTON · BRIGHTON · EASTBOURNE · PORTSMOUTH · NEWHAVEN

EXETER · BOURNEMOUTH · WEYMOUTH

PLYMOUTH · TORQUAY

Airports and Seaports

Most people who leave Britain by air or sea use the airports and seaports detailed in words and maps in these pages. The maps indicate the approach roads into each complex with information on main routes, parking and telephone numbers through which details on costs and other travel information can be quickly obtained. The hotels listed are AA-appointed, and the garages have been selected by the AA only because they provide adequate long term parking facilities.

HEATHROW AIRPORT Tel: 01-759 4321 (Airport Information)

Heathrow, one of the world's busiest international airports, lies sixteen miles west of London. The airport is situated on the Piccadilly Underground line at Heathrow Central station. It is also served by local bus and long distance coach services. For short-term parking, multi-storey car parks are sited at each of the passenger terminals Tel: 01-745 7160 & 01-745 7072. Charges for the long-term car parks on the northern perimeter road are designed to encourage their use for a stay in excess of four hours. A free coach takes passengers to and from the terminals. Commercial garages offering long-term parking facilities within easy reach of the airport include: Airways Garage Tel: 01-759 9661/4; Courtlands Car Services Tel: (0293) 771555; Cranford Hall Garage Tel: 01-759 9413, 9852 or 9555; Flyaway Car Storage Tel: 01-759 1567 or 2020; Kenning Car Hire Tel: 01-759 9701; and National Car Parks Tel: 01-759 9878. Car Hire: Avis Rent-A-Car Tel: 01-897 9321; Budget Rent-A-Car Tel: 01-759 2216; Godfrey Davis Europcar Tel: 01-897 0811/5; Hertz Rent-A-Car Tel: 01-679 1799; and Kenning Car Hire Tel: 01-759 9701. The 4-star hotels in the area are The Excelsior Tel: 01-759 6611; the Heathrow Penta Tel: 01-897 6363; the Holiday Inn Tel: (0895) 445555 and the Sheraton Tel: 01-759 2424. The 3-star hotels are the Berkeley Arms Tel: 01-897 2121; the Ariel Tel: 01-759 2552; the Post House Tel: 01-759 2323; and the Skyway Tel: 01-759 6311.

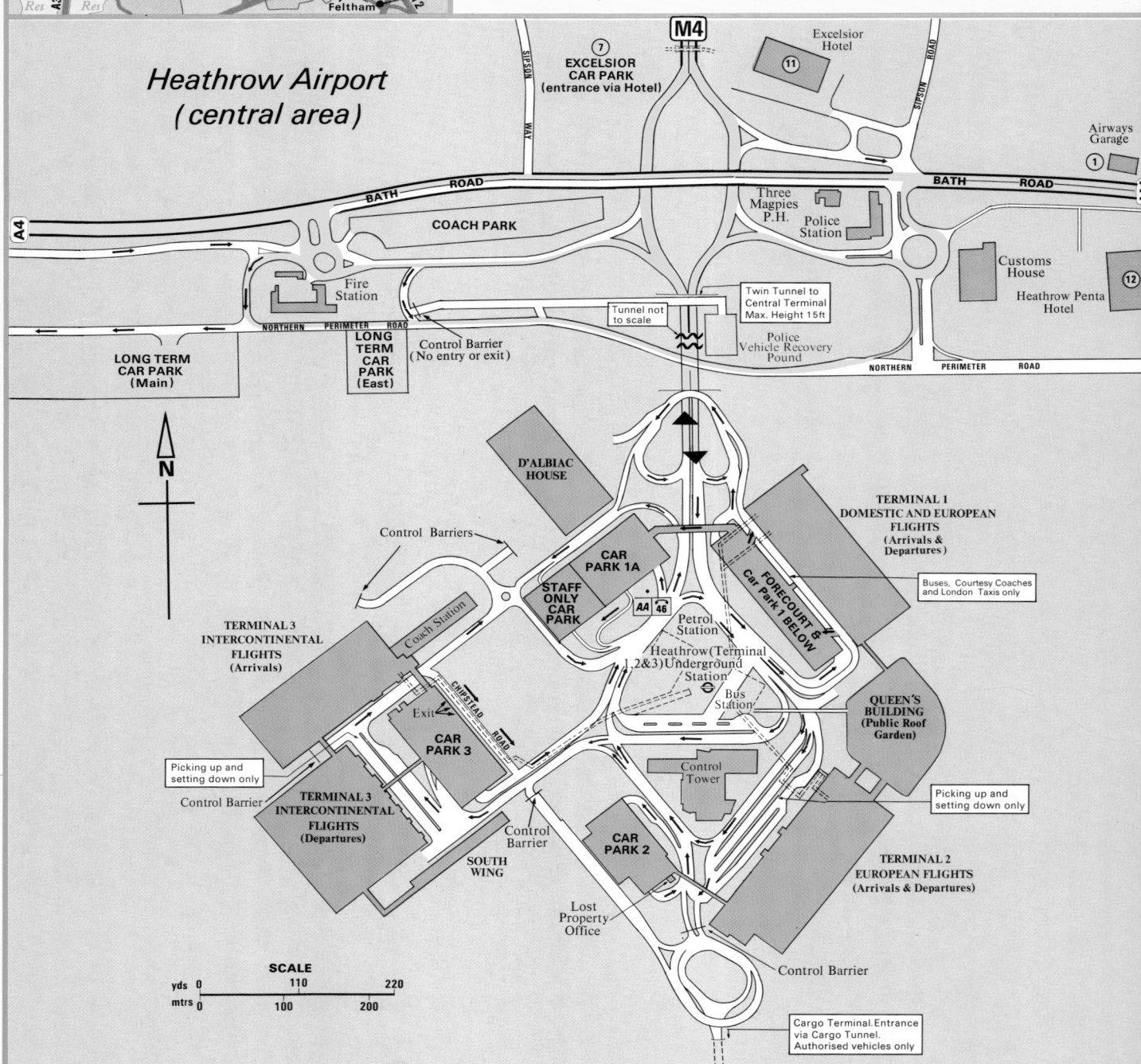

Heathrow Airport (central area)

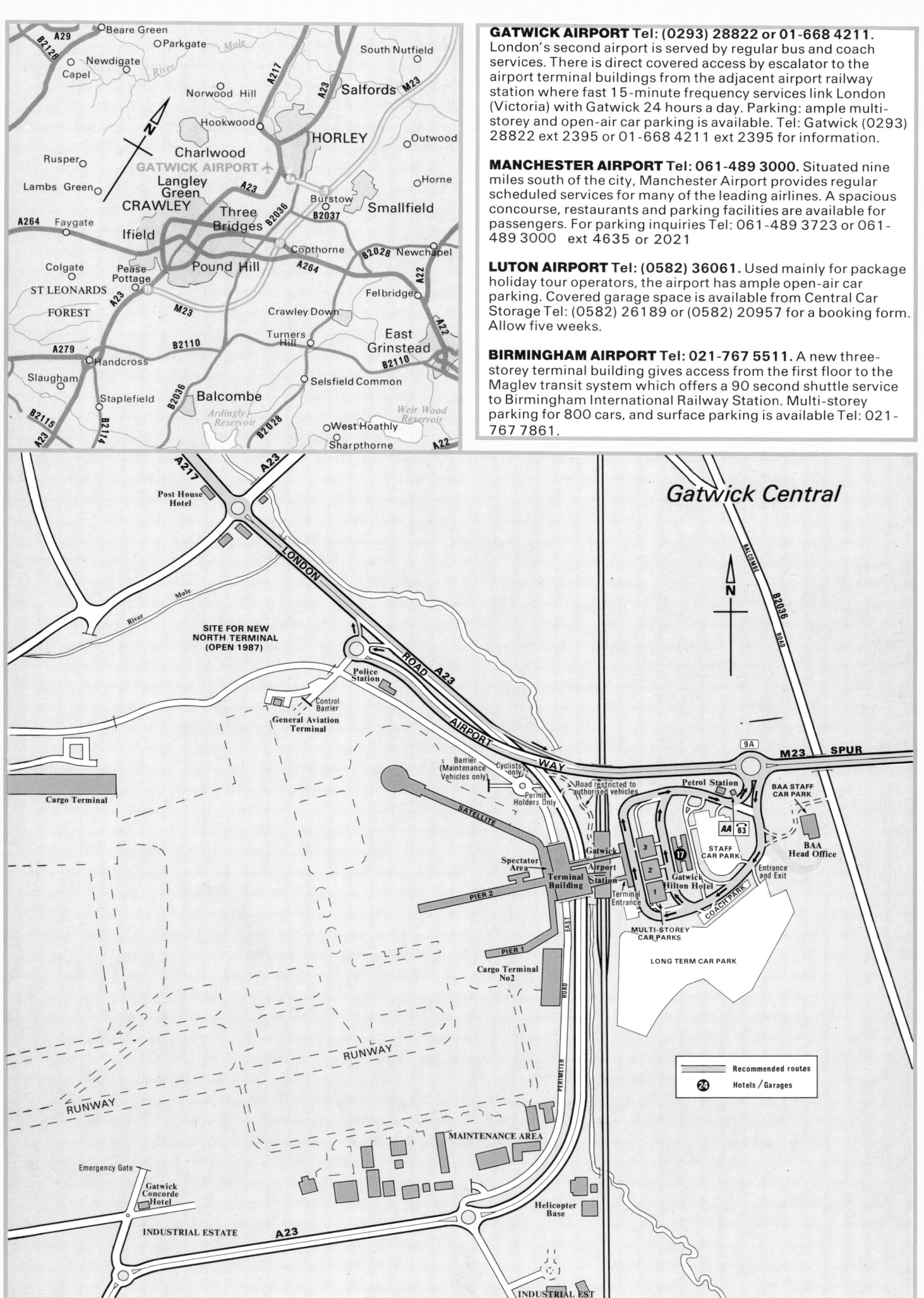

GATWICK AIRPORT Tel: (0293) 28822 or 01-668 4211.
London's second airport is served by regular bus and coach services. There is direct covered access by escalator to the airport terminal buildings from the adjacent airport railway station where fast 15-minute frequency services link London (Victoria) with Gatwick 24 hours a day. Parking: ample multi-storey and open-air car parking is available. Tel: Gatwick (0293) 28822 ext 2395 or 01-668 4211 ext 2395 for information.

MANCHESTER AIRPORT Tel: 061-489 3000. Situated nine miles south of the city, Manchester Airport provides regular scheduled services for many of the leading airlines. A spacious concourse, restaurants and parking facilities are available for passengers. For parking inquiries Tel: 061-489 3723 or 061-489 3000 ext 4635 or 2021

LUTON AIRPORT Tel: (0582) 36061. Used mainly for package holiday tour operators, the airport has ample open-air car parking. Covered garage space is available from Central Car Storage Tel: (0582) 26189 or (0582) 20957 for a booking form. Allow five weeks.

BIRMINGHAM AIRPORT Tel: 021-767 5511. A new three-storey terminal building gives access from the first floor to the Maglev transit system which offers a 90 second shuttle service to Birmingham International Railway Station. Multi-storey parking for 800 cars, and surface parking is available Tel: 021-767 7861.

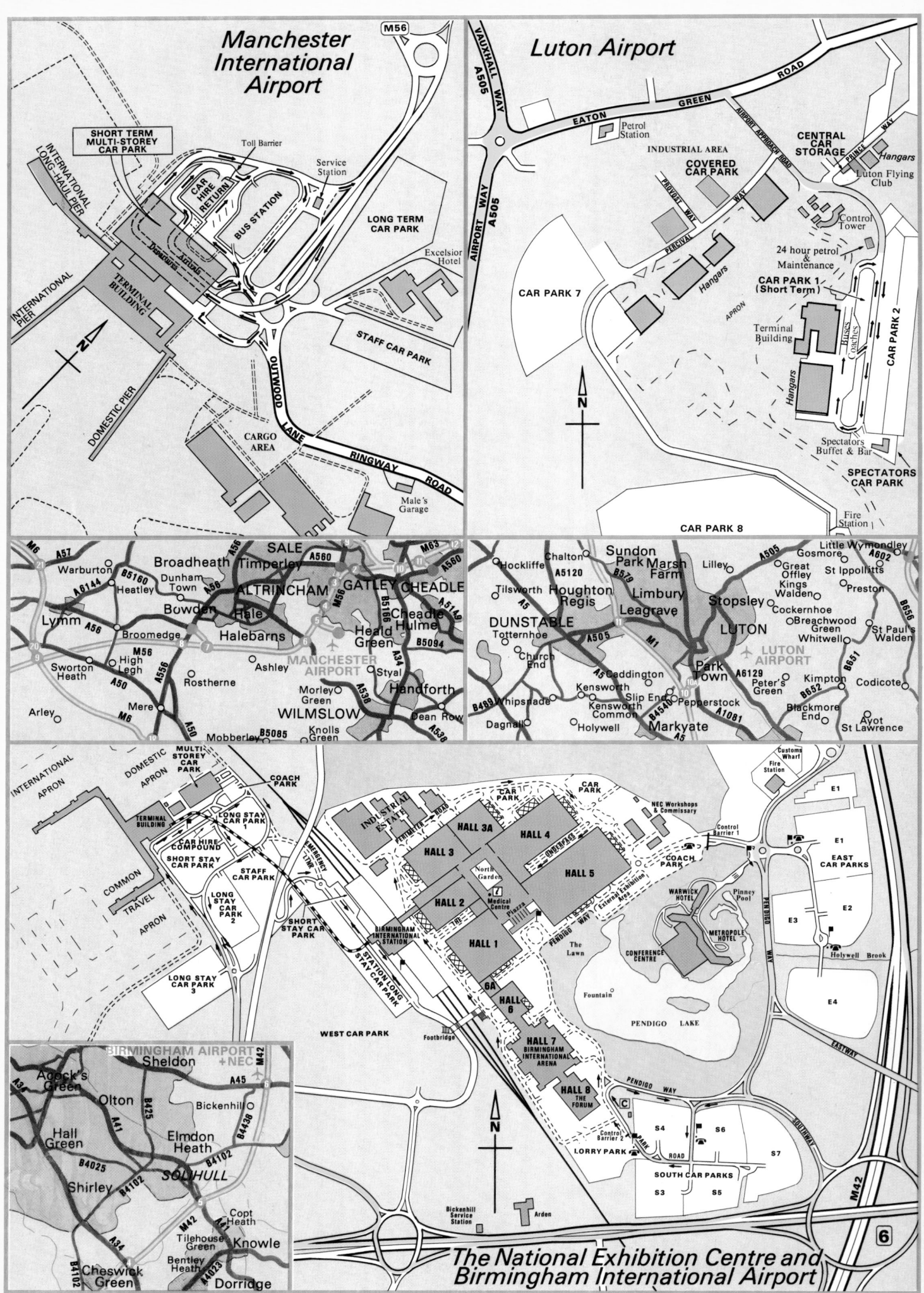

Manchester International Airport

SHORT TERM MULTI-STOREY CAR PARK

Toll Barrier

CAR HIRE RETURN

Service Station

BUS STATION

LONG TERM CAR PARK

Excelsior Hotel

INTERNATIONAL LONG-HAUL PIER

Departures

Arrivals

TERMINAL BUILDING

INTERNATIONAL PIER

DOMESTIC PIER

OUTWOOD LANE

STAFF CAR PARK

CARGO AREA

RINGWAY ROAD

Male's Garage

M56

Manchester area map

M6 A57
21
Warburton B5160
A6144 Heatley
Lymm A56
20
9 Sworton Heath
M56
A50 High Legh
M6 Mere
Arley A50
Mobberley B5085

Broadheath SALE Timperley A560
Dunham Town A56
ALTRINCHAM M56
Bowden Hale
Broomedge Halebarns
8
7 6
Ashley MANCHESTER AIRPORT
Rostherne Morley Green
Styal
WILMSLOW Knolls Green Dean Row
A538

M63 12
10 11 A560
GATLEY CHEADLE
B5166 Cheadle Hulme
Heald Green A5149
B5094
A34
Handforth
A538

Luton Airport

VAUXHALL WAY
A505 EATON GREEN ROAD
Petrol Station
INDUSTRIAL AREA
COVERED CAR PARK
AIRPORT APPROACH ROAD
CENTRAL CAR STORAGE
PRINCE WAY
Hangars
Luton Flying Club
AIRPORT WAY A505
PROVOST WAY
PERCIVAL WAY
CAR PARK 7
Hangars
APRON
Control Tower
24 hour petrol & Maintenance
CAR PARK 1 (Short Term)
Terminal Building
Buses Coaches
CAR PARK 2
Hangars
N
Spectators Buffet & Bar
SPECTATORS CAR PARK
Fire Station
CAR PARK 8

Luton area map

Hockliffe Chalton
Tilsworth A5120
A5
DUNSTABLE
Totternhoe A505
Church End
B489 Whipsnade
Dagnall
Holywell

Sundon Park Marsh Farm
Houghton Regis B579
Limbury
Leagrave
Caddington
Kensworth
Kensworth Common Slip End
Markyate A5

Lilley A505 Gosmore Little Wymondley A602
Great Offley St Ippollitts
Kings Walden Preston
Stopsley Cockernhoe Breachwood Green B656 St Paul's Walden
LUTON Whitwell
M1 LUTON AIRPORT B551
Park Town A6129 Peter's Green Kimpton B652
Pepperstock A1081 Blackmore End Codicote
Ayot St Lawrence

The National Exhibition Centre and Birmingham International Airport

INTERNATIONAL APRON
DOMESTIC APRON
MULTI-STOREY CAR PARK
COACH PARK
TERMINAL BUILDING
COMMON TRAVEL APRON
CAR HIRE COMPOUND
LONG STAY CAR PARK 1
SHORT STAY CAR PARK
STAFF CAR PARK
LONG STAY CAR PARK 2
LONG STAY CAR PARK 3
EMERGENCY

INDUSTRIAL ESTATE
PERIMETER ROAD
HALL 3A HALL 4
HALL 3
HALL 5
HALL 2
North Garden
Medical Centre
Piazza
HALL 1
6A
HALL 6
BIRMINGHAM INTERNATIONAL STATION
SHORT STAY CAR PARK
STATION LONG STAY CAR PARK
WEST CAR PARK
Footbridge
HALL 7 BIRMINGHAM INTERNATIONAL ARENA
HALL 8 THE FORUM
C
Control Barrier 2
LORRY PARK

CAR PARK
CAR PARK
NEC Workshops & Commissary
UNDERPASS
Control Barrier 1
COACH PARK
External Exhibition Area
WARWICK HOTEL
The Lawn
Fountain
PENDIGO WAY
CONFERENCE CENTRE
METROPOLE HOTEL
Pinney Pool
PENDIGO LAKE
PENDIGO WAY
PARK
SOUTHWAY
ROAD
S4 S6
S7
SOUTH CAR PARKS
S3 S5

Customs Wharf
Fire Station
E1
E1
EAST CAR PARKS
E2
PENDIGO WAY
E3
Holywell Brook
E4
EASTWAY
M42
6

Bickenhill Service Station
Arden
N

Birmingham area inset

BIRMINGHAM AIRPORT + NEC
Sheldon A45 M42 6
Acock's Green A3
Olton B425 Bickenhill
Hall Green M41
Elmdon Heath B4438
B4025 Shirley B4102 SOLIHULL
B4102
M42 Copt Heath
Tilehouse Green
Knowle
Bentley Heath
A34
Cheswick Green B4023
Dorridge

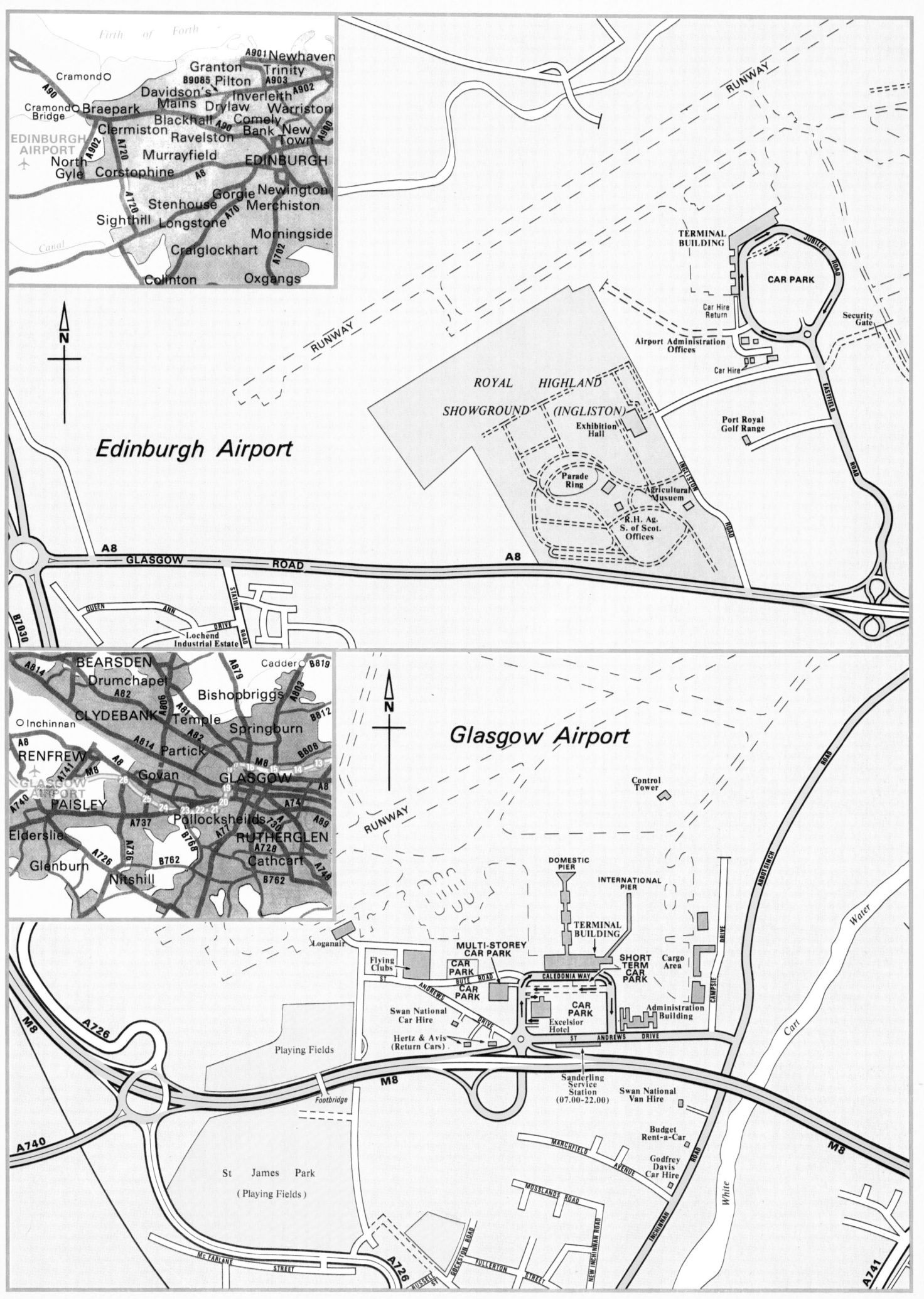

Edinburgh Airport

Firth of Forth

Cramond○
Cramond○ Bridge
Braepark
EDINBURGH AIRPORT ✈
North Gyle
A90
A902
A720
A8
Clermiston
Blackhall
Murrayfield
Corstophine

Davidson's Mains
Drylaw
Ravelston
A901 Newhaven
Granton Trinity
B9085 Pilton
A903
Inverleith
A902
Warriston
Comely
Bank New Town
A900
EDINBURGH

Stenhouse
Sighthill
A720
Longstone
A70
Gorgie
Newington
Merchiston
Craiglockhart
A702
Morningside
Colinton
Oxgangs

Canal

N

RUNWAY

RUNWAY

TERMINAL BUILDING

CAR PARK

JUBILEE ROAD

Security Gate

Car Hire Return

Airport Administration Offices

Car Hire

EASTFIELD ROAD

ROYAL HIGHLAND SHOWGROUND (INGLISTON)

Exhibition Hall

Port Royal Golf Range

INGLISTON ROAD

Parade Ring

Agricultural Museum

R.H. Ag. S. of Scot. Offices

A8
GLASGOW ROAD
A8

B7030
QUEEN ANNE DRIVE
STATION ROAD
Lochend Industrial Estate

Glasgow Airport

BEARSDEN
Drumchapel
A82
CLYDEBANK
A814
A81
Temple
A82
○ Inchinnan
RENFREW
A741
M8
A8
Govan
Partick
Cadder○ B819
A879
B812
Bishopbriggs
A803
Springburn
B808
GLASGOW
17 16 15 14 13
M8
A8
PAISLEY
A740
A737
A726
A73F
Pollockshields
B766
B762
Glenburn
Nitshill
Elderslie
26
25 24 23 22 21
20
18 19
A77
A730
RUTHERGLEN
A728
Cathcart
A749
A89
A74
B762
GLASGOW AIRPORT

N

RUNWAY

Control Tower

Loganair

DOMESTIC PIER

INTERNATIONAL PIER

ABBOTSINCH ROAD

TERMINAL BUILDING

Flying Clubs

ST

MULTI-STOREY CAR PARK

CAR PARK

BUTE ROAD

SHORT TERM CAR PARK

Cargo Area

CAMPSIE DRIVE

White Cart Water

Swan National Car Hire

ST ANDREWS DRIVE

CALEDONIA WAY

CAR PARK

Excelsior Hotel

Administration Building

Hertz & Avis (Return Cars)

ST ANDREWS DRIVE

M8

A726

Playing Fields

Footbridge

Sanderling Service Station (07.00-22.00)

Swan National Van Hire

Budget Rent-a-Car

Godfrey Davis Car Hire

MARCHFIELD AVENUE

MOSSLANDS ROAD

BRECKSTON ROAD

FULLERTON STREET

NEW INCHINNAN ROAD

INCHINNAN ROAD

M8

A740

St James Park
(Playing Fields)

McFARLANE STREET

RUSSELL ST

A726

A741

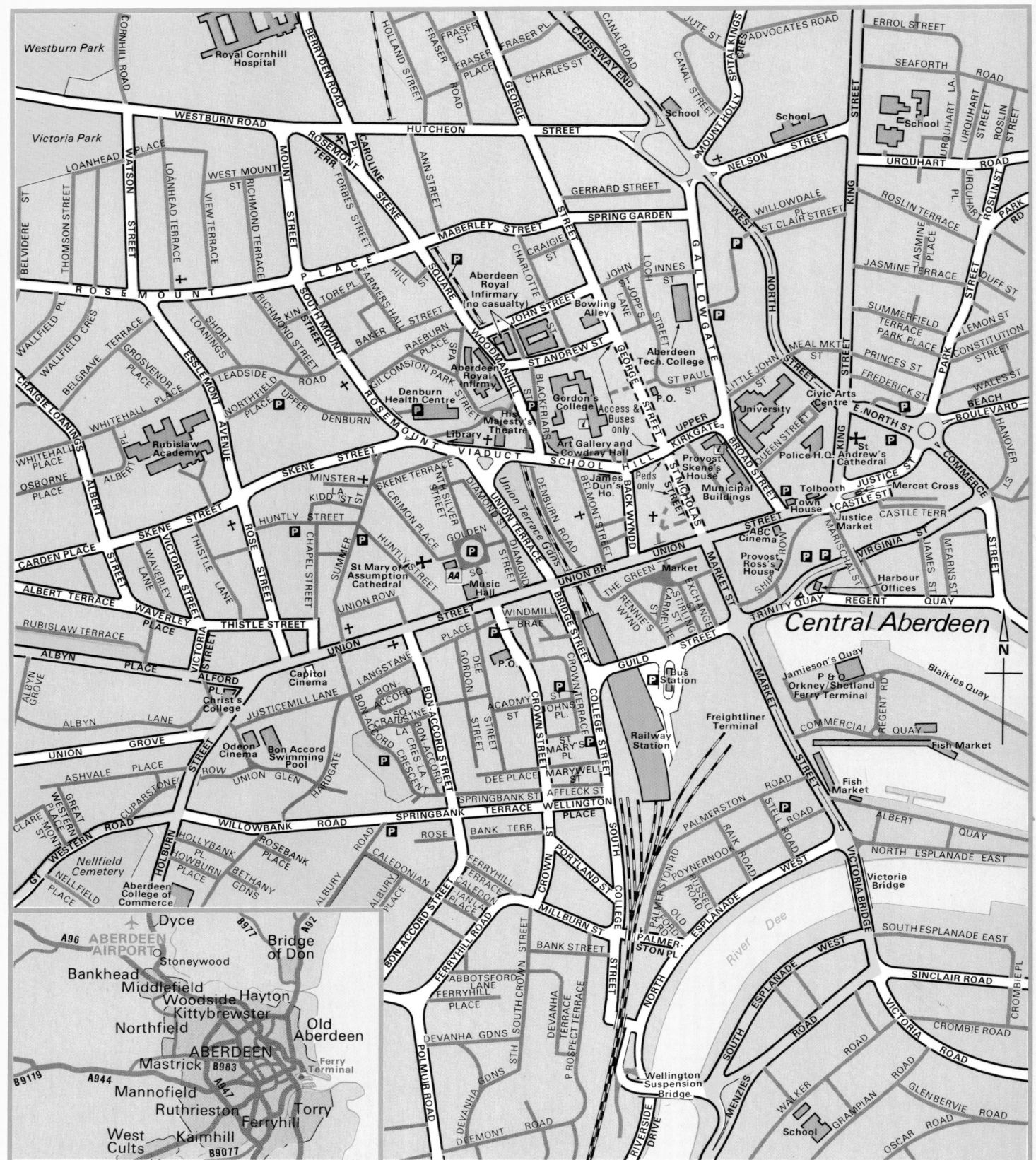

Central Aberdeen

EDINBURGH AIRPORT Tel: 031-333 1000
A regular coach service operates between Edinburgh (Waverley Bridge) seven miles away, and the airport. The service also links with Glasgow and Glasgow Airport. The airport has parking for just over 1,000 vehicles, all open air, Tel: 031-344 3197. Off the airport Alexander Latto in Seafield Road East, Edinburgh have covered parking, and collect and deliver. Tel: 031-669 5733 or 031-553 2995. The information desk is located on the main concourse. Tel: 031-333 1000 or 031-344 3136. There are also several top class hotels within easy reach of the airport, and car hire facilities are provided by Avis Tel: 031-333 1866, Godfrey Davis/Europcar Tel: 031-333 2588 and Hertz Tel: 031-333 1019.

GLASGOW AIRPORT Tel: 041-887 1111
Situated eight miles west of Glasgow, the airport is linked with Central Glasgow and Edinburgh by regular coach services. Nearly 2,000 parking spaces are available, some under cover. Tel: 041-889 2751. Open-air parking is also provided by Harvey's Garage, Porterfield Road, in Renfrew. Tel: 041-886 4009. For the disabled there is easy access to the terminal at ground level. The information desk is located on the first floor Tel: 041-887 1111 ext 4552. There is one 4-star hotel within easy reach of the airport, as well as five 3-star and two 2-star hotels. Car hire is available, from among others, Avis Tel: 041-887 2261, Hertz Tel: 041-887 2451, Godfrey Davis/Europcar Tel: 041-887 0414.

ABERDEEN AIRPORT AND HELIPORT
Tel: (0224) 722331
Situated seven miles north west of Aberdeen, the airport has its main access from the A96 which also serves for the West Heliport. Coach services operate between Aberdeen City Centre and the Main Terminal/West Heliport. Bus services from Aberdeen pass the entrance to East Heliport. There is open air parking for 900 vehicles. Tel: (0224) 722331, extension 5142. At the Heliport there is open air parking for 300 vehicles. The information desk is in the check-in area, Tel: (0224) 722331 extension 5312/3/4. There are three 4-star hotels in the airport area and car hire is available through Avis Tel: (0224) 722282, Godfrey Davis/Europcar Tel: (0224) 723404, Hertz Tel: (0224) 722373.

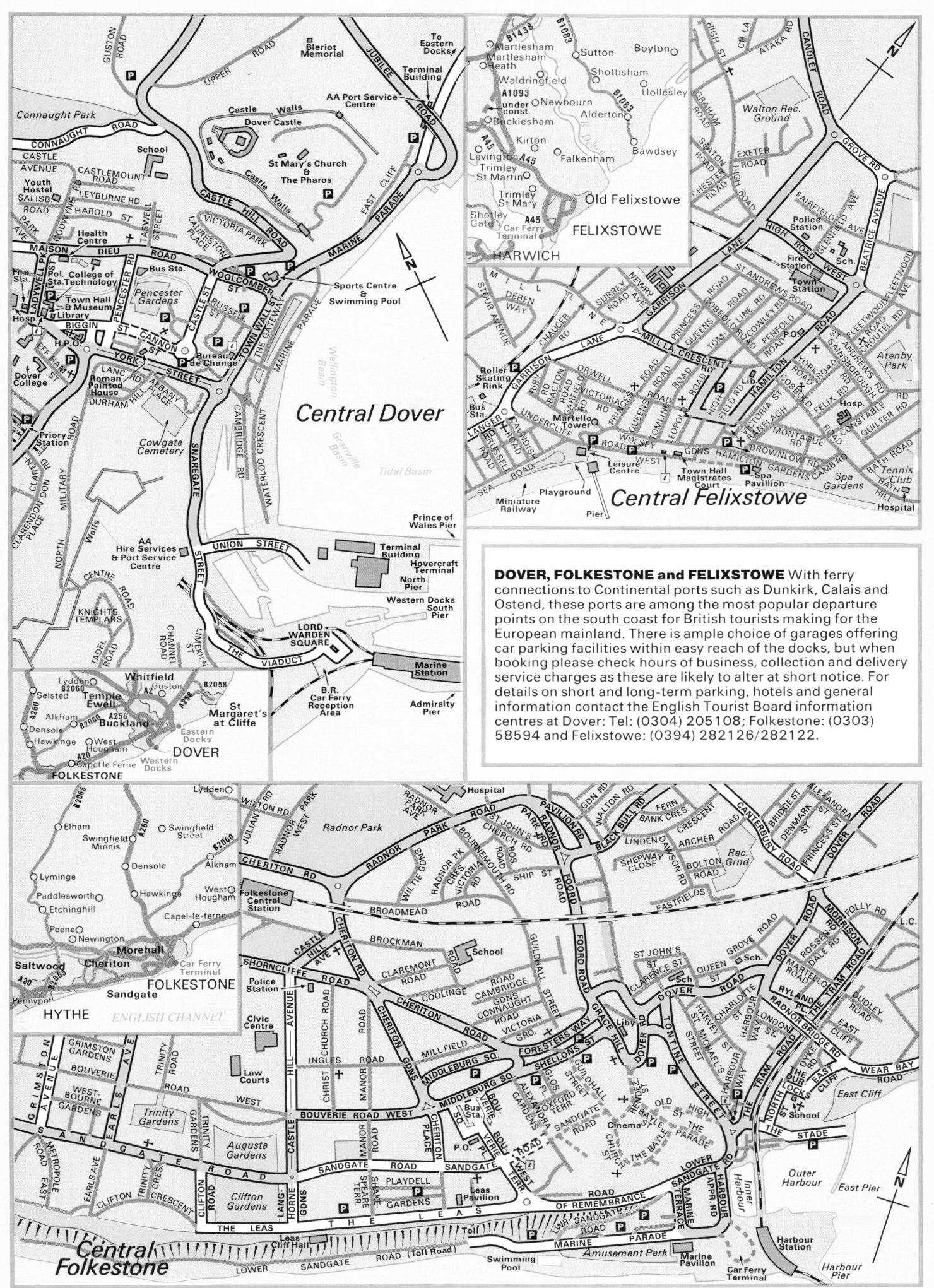

Central Dover

Connaught Park

GUSTON ROAD
UPPER ROAD
JUBILEE
Bleriot Memorial
To Eastern Docks
Terminal Building
AA Port Service Centre
Castle Walls
Dover Castle
Castle Walls
St Mary's Church & The Pharos
Sports Centre & Swimming Pool

CONNAUGHT ROAD
CASTLE AVENUE
Youth Hostel SALISB
School
CASTLEMOUNT ROAD
LEYBURNE RD
GODWYNE RD
HAROLD ST
TASWELL STREET
CASTLE HILL ROAD
LAURESTON PLACE
VICTORIA PARK
EAST CLIFF
MARINE PARADE

Health Centre
MAISON DIEU ROAD
Fire Sta.
LADYWELL PK
Pol. College of Sta.Technology
Town Hall & Museum Library
Hosp.
Bus Sta.
WOOLCOMBER ST
RUSSELL ST
CASTLE ST
TOWN WALL ST
THE GATEWAY
MARINE PARADE

Pencester Gardens
BIGGIN ST
H.P.O.
PENCESTER RD
CANNON ST
Bureau de Change
YORK STREET
Dover College
LANC RD
ALBANY PLACE
Roman Painted House
DURHAM HILL
Cowgate Cemetery
Wellington Basin
Granville Basin
Tidal Basin

EFF HAM
Priory Station
Priory Road
MILITARY ROAD
CLARENDON PLACE
North Military ROAD
KNIGHTS TEMPLARS
TADEL ROAD
CHANNEL ROAD
LIMEKILN ST
SNARGATE STREET
CAMBRIDGE RD
WATERLOO CRESCENT

Walls
AA Hire Services & Port Service Centre
UNION STREET
CENTRE ROAD
LORD WARDEN SQUARE
THE VIADUCT

Prince of Wales Pier
Terminal Building
Hovercraft Terminal
North Pier
Western Docks South Pier

B.R. Car Ferry Reception Area
Marine Station
Admiralty Pier

DOVER

Whitfield
Lydden
Selsted
B2060
Temple Ewell
Guston
A2
A256
B2058
Alkham
B2060
Densole
Buckland
A256
St Margaret's at Cliffe
Hawkinge
West Hougham
A20
Capel le Ferne
Western Docks
Eastern Docks
FOLKESTONE

Martlesham
Martlesham Heath
Waldringfield
B1438
B1083
Sutton
Boyton
Shottisham
Hollesley
A1093
under const.
Newbourn
Alderton
Bawdsey
Bucklesham
A45
Kirton
Falkenham
Levington
A45
Trimley St Martin
Trimley St Mary
A45
Shotley Gate
Car Ferry Terminal
Old Felixstowe
FELIXSTOWE
HARWICH

Central Felixstowe

HIGH ST
ATAKA RD
CANDLET ROAD
GROVE RD
Walton Rec. Ground
GRAHAM ROAD
SEATON ROAD
CHESTER ROAD
EXETER ROAD
FAIRFIELD AVE
GLENFELD AVE
BEATRICE AVENUE
Police Station
Sch.
Fire Station
Town Station
FLEETWOOD
CROUTEL RD
FELIX RD
MILL LANE
STOUR AVENUE
DEBEN WAY
SURREY RD
NEWRY AVE
GARRISON LANE
ST ANDREWS ROAD
COBBOLD ROAD
PRINCESS ROAD
QUEENS ROAD
TOM- ROAD
LINE RD
ROCOWLEY RD
PENFOLD
P.O.
YORK ROAD
COBBOLD
GAINSBOROUGH
Atenby Park
CONSTABLE RD
QUILTER RD
CHAUCER RD
RIBY
BACTON
ORWELL ROAD
FAIRFIELD ROAD
VICTORIA RD
PRINCES
QUEENS ROAD
FIELD RD
HIGH ROAD
HAMILTON ROAD
VICTORIA ST
DANELAGH
MONTAGUE RD
Lib.
Hosp.
Roller Skating Rink
Bus Sta.
Martello Tower
WOLSEY ROAD
LEOPOLD RD
BROWNLOW RD
BATH ROAD
LANGER ROAD
CAVENDISH ROAD
UNDERCLIFF ROAD WEST
GDNS
HAMILTON GARDENS CAMB- RD
Spa Gardens
SEA ROAD
Leisure Centre
Town Hall Magistrates Court
Spa Pavilion
BATH HILL
Tennis Club
Playground
Miniature Railway
Pier
Hospital

DOVER, FOLKESTONE and FELIXSTOWE With ferry connections to Continental ports such as Dunkirk, Calais and Ostend, these ports are among the most popular departure points on the south coast for British tourists making for the European mainland. There is ample choice of garages offering car parking facilities within easy reach of the docks, but when booking please check hours of business, collection and delivery service charges as these are likely to alter at short notice. For details on short and long-term parking, hotels and general information contact the English Tourist Board information centres at Dover: Tel: (0304) 205108; Folkestone: (0303) 58594 and Felixstowe: (0394) 282126/282122.

Central Folkestone

B2065
Elham
A260
Swingfield Street
Swingfield Minnis
B2060
Densole
Lyminge
Alkham
Paddlesworth
Hawkinge
West Hougham
Etchinghill
Peene
Capel-le-ferne
Newington
Morehall
Cheriton
Car Ferry Terminal
Saltwood
A20
B2065
Sandgate
FOLKESTONE
Pennypot
HYTHE
ENGLISH CHANNEL

Hospital
Radnor Park
RADNOR PARK WEST
WILTON RD
JULIAN RD
RADNOR PARK AVE
PAVILION RD
RADNOR PK GDNS
PARK RD
ST JOHN'S ROAD
RADNOR PK CRES
BOURNEMOUTH RD
VICTORIA RD
SHIP ST
CHURCH RD
RADNOR PK
FOORD RD
BLACK BULL RD
WALTON RD
GDN RD
FERN BANK CRES
LINDEN CRESCENT
CANTERBURY ROAD
DAWSON RD
ARCHER RD
SHEPWAY CLOSE
BOLTON ROAD
EASTFIELDS
BRIDGE ST
DENMARK ST
PRINCESS ST
ALEXANDRA ST
DOVER RD
FOLLY RD
L.C.
CHERITON ROAD
Folkestone Central Station
BROADMEAD ROAD
BROCKMAN ROAD
School
CLAREMONT ROAD
COOLINGE ROAD
CAMBRIDGE GDNS
CONNAUGHT RD
VICTORIA GRO.
GUILDHALL STREET
ST JOHN'S ST
CLARENCE ST
QUEEN ST
GROVE RD
Sch.
DOVER ROAD
RYLAND PL
ROSSEN DALE RD
MARTELLO RD
DUDLEY ROAD
THE TRAM ROAD
CASTLE HILL AVE
SHORNCLIFFE ROAD
Police Station
Civic Centre
CHERITON GDNS
CHERITON ROAD
MILL FIELD
FORESTERS WAY
SHELLONS ST
GRACE HILL
Liby
HARVEY ST
CHARLOTTE ST
ST MICHAEL'S ST
LONDON ST
RADNOR BRIDGE RD
EAST CLIFF
WEAR BAY ROAD
GRIMSTON GARDENS
BOUVERIE ROAD
WEST-BOURNE GARDENS
TRINITY ROAD
TRINITY GARDENS
Trinity Gardens
Law Courts
CHRIST CHURCH ROAD
INGLES ROAD
MANOR ROAD
MIDDLEBURG SQ
MIDDLEBURG SQ
BOUVERIE BOU.
Bus Sta.
OXFORD TERR
GUILDHALL STREET
GLOS ST
ALEXANDRA GARDENS
SANDGATE RD
RENDEZ
OLD ST
THE BAYLE
Cinema
CHURCH
THE DUR EAST
NORTH LOCKS
East Cliff
GRIMSTON AVENUE
METROPLE EAST
EARLS AVE
CLIFTON CRESCENT
CLIFTON GDNS
Clifton Gardens
Augusta Gardens
SANDGATE ROAD
CHERITON PLACE
P.O.
LANGHORNE GDNS
SHAKESPEARE TERR
PLAYDELL GARDENS
Leas Pavilion
BOUVERIE ROAD WEST
SANDGATE ROAD
LWR SANDGATE ROAD
ROAD OF REMEMBRANCE
MARINE TERRACE
SANDGATE APPR. RD
THE LEAS
Leas Cliff Hall
LOWER SANDGATE ROAD (Toll Road)
Toll
Swimming Pool
MARINE PARADE
Amusement Park
Marine Pavilion
Outer Harbour
East Pier
Inner Harbour
Harbour Station
Car Ferry Terminal
Harbour Pier
THE STADE
School

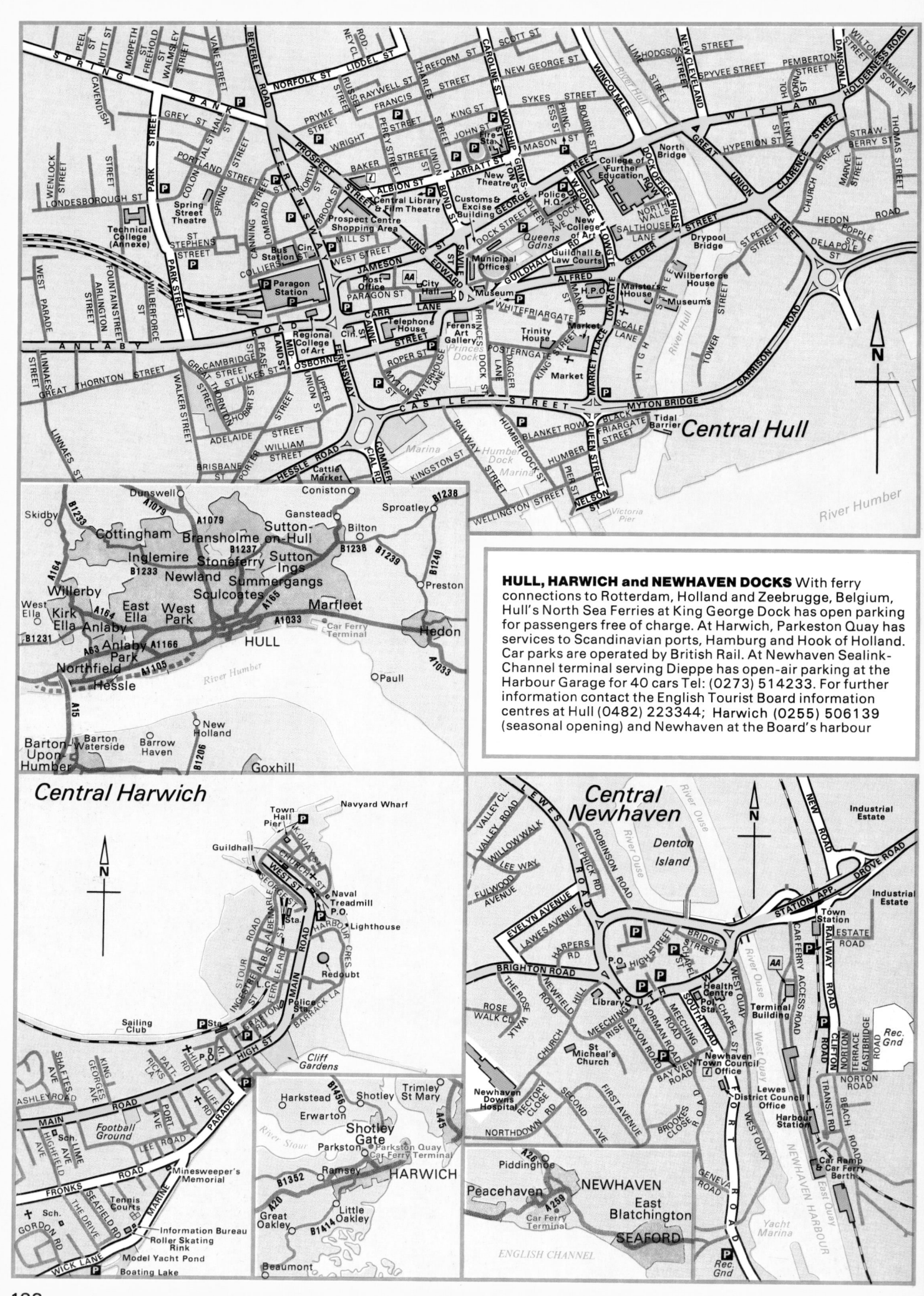

Central Hull

HULL, HARWICH and NEWHAVEN DOCKS With ferry connections to Rotterdam, Holland and Zeebrugge, Belgium, Hull's North Sea Ferries at King George Dock has open parking for passengers free of charge. At Harwich, Parkeston Quay has services to Scandinavian ports, Hamburg and Hook of Holland. Car parks are operated by British Rail. At Newhaven Sealink-Channel terminal serving Dieppe has open-air parking at the Harbour Garage for 40 cars Tel: (0273) 514233. For further information contact the English Tourist Board information centres at Hull (0482) 223344; Harwich (0255) 506139 (seasonal opening) and Newhaven at the Board's harbour

Central Harwich

Central Newhaven

188

Liverpool

The docks, serving mainly Belfast and Dublin are controlled by the Mersey Docks and Harbour Company, Tel: 051-200 2020. There is no open parking at the docks, but garages listed below are within easy reach. Britannia Garage, Brownlow Hill, Tel 051-709 7200. The National Car Parks have a multi-storey in Hanover Street, Tel: 051-709 7910, in St John's Precinct, Tel: 051-708 8442 and Duke Street, Tel: 051-709 4103. There are other multi-storey car parks run by the Liverpool City Council in the centre of Liverpool and three 4-star, two 3-star, four 2-star hotels and one 1-star hotel.

Newcastle upon Tyne

The Tyne Commission Quay, nearly nine miles east of the city, has sailings to Norway (Bergen) and to Denmark (Esbjerg) and to Sweden (Göteborg). Garage accommodation is normally available near the quay, but covered parking is scarce, particularly during the summer. Advance booking is necessary. Send applications to E J Turnbull & Son Ltd, Albion Road, North Shields, Tel: 091-257 -1201 who have a collection and delivery service. Accommodation is available in 3-star hotels at Tynemouth or Wallsend. Other hotels are in Whitley Bay

Central Newcastle Upon Tyne

Central Weymouth

Weymouth

Weymouth, which handles sailings to Cherbourg and the Channel Islands, provides garage facilities at Channel ferry car parks in King Street, Tel: (0305) 783408 just over ½ mile from the docks. It has covered accommodation for 300 cars and unlimited open spaces for parking. Coach service to and from the ferry terminal is free. Caravan Transit Service Tel: (0305) 783408 provides parking for caravanners arriving in Weymouth a day prior to shipping and on their return. This park is a few hundred yards from the seafront and the town. Weymouth has six 2-star hotels and one 1-star.

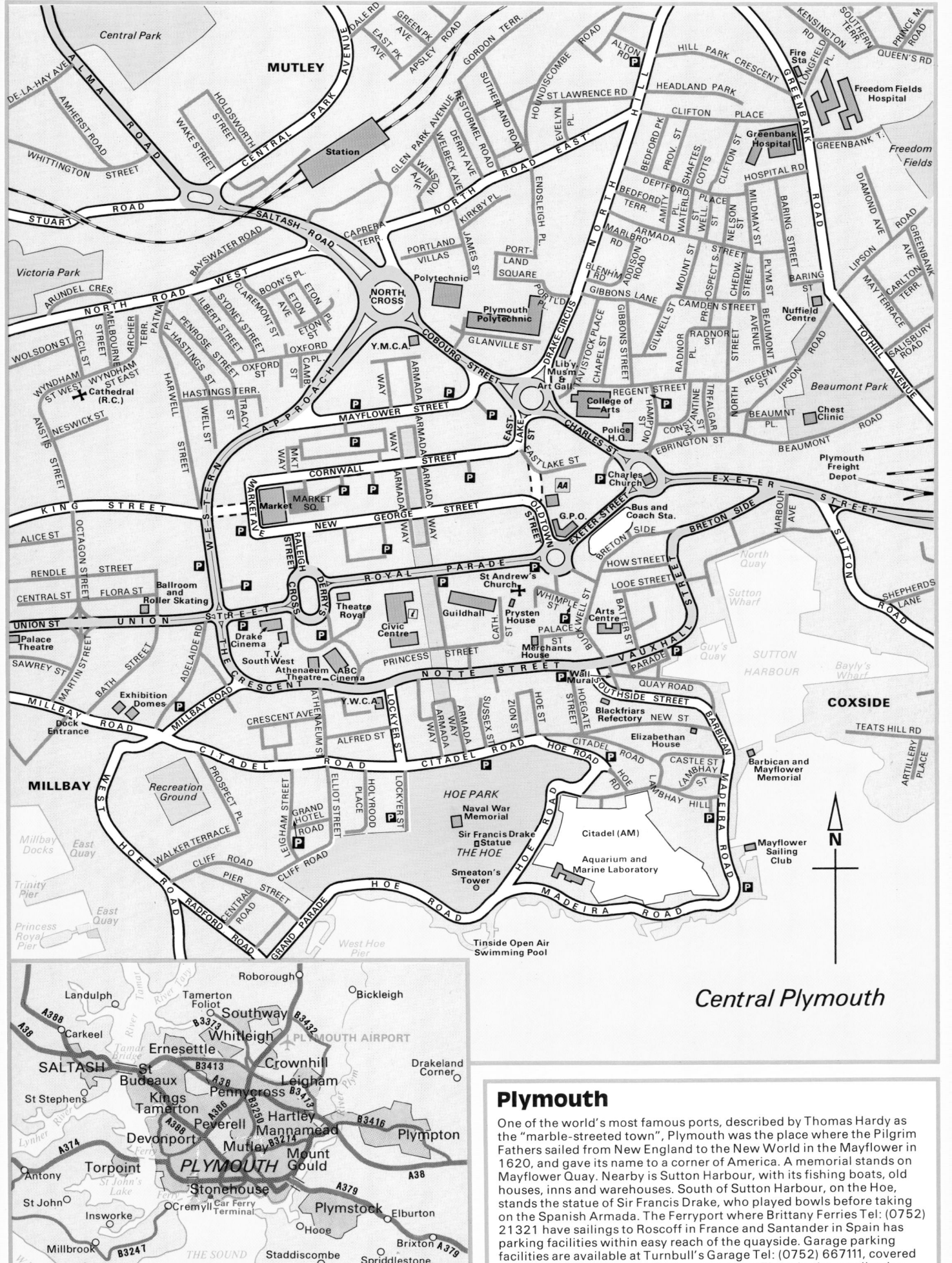

Central Plymouth

Plymouth

One of the world's most famous ports, described by Thomas Hardy as the "marble-streeted town", Plymouth was the place where the Pilgrim Fathers sailed from New England to the New World in the Mayflower in 1620, and gave its name to a corner of America. A memorial stands on Mayflower Quay. Nearby is Sutton Harbour, with its fishing boats, old houses, inns and warehouses. South of Sutton Harbour, on the Hoe, stands the statue of Sir Francis Drake, who played bowls before taking on the Spanish Armada. The Ferryport where Brittany Ferries Tel: (0752) 21321 have sailings to Roscoff in France and Santander in Spain has parking facilities within easy reach of the quayside. Garage parking facilities are available at Turnbull's Garage Tel: (0752) 667111, covered parking for 6 cars is one mile from the quay. There is also a collection and delivery service. One 4-Star, Four 3-Star, four 2-Star and three 1-star hotels are near the Ferryport.

191

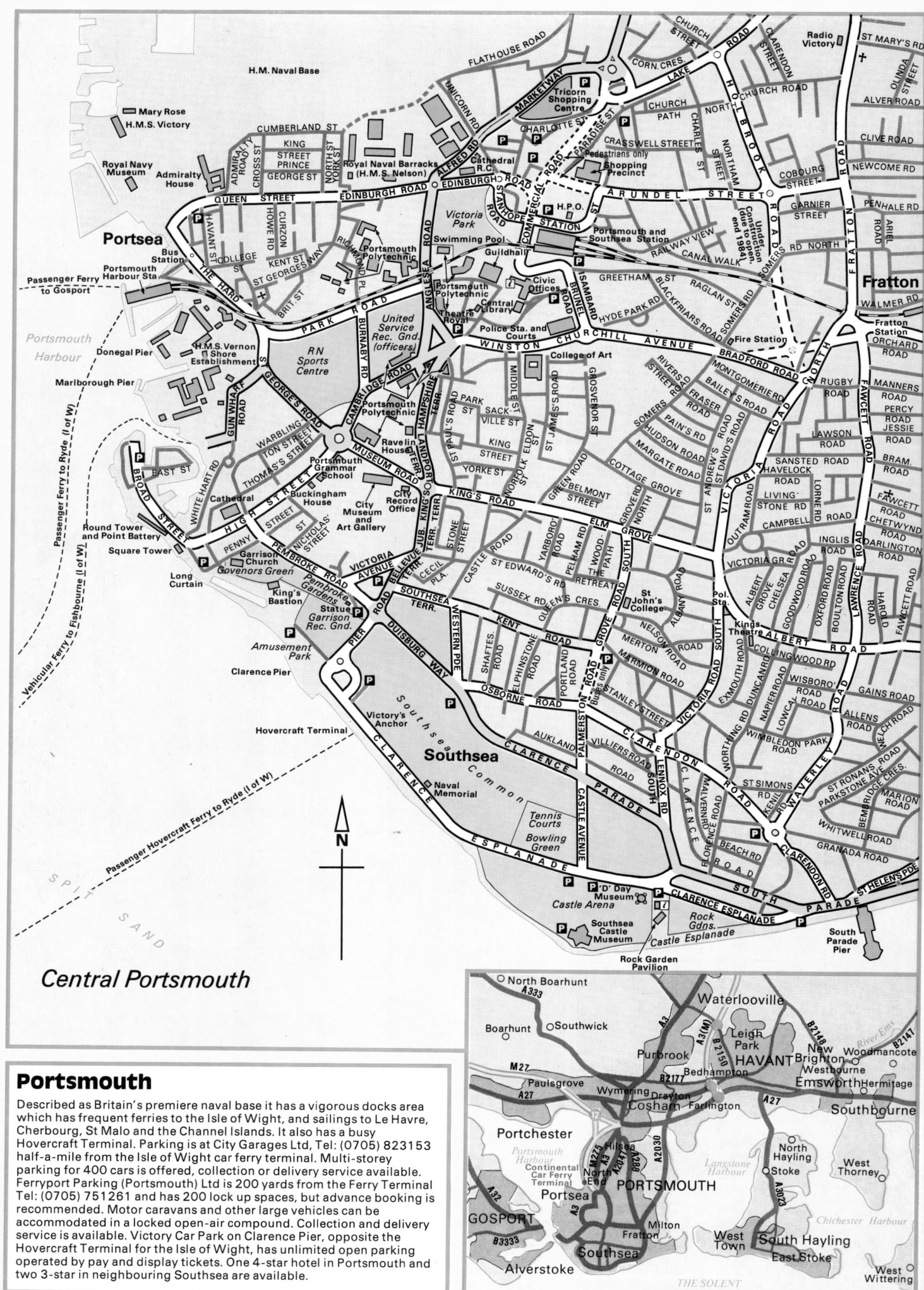

Central Portsmouth

H.M. Naval Base

Mary Rose
H.M.S. Victory

Royal Navy Museum
Admiralty House

Portsea

Bus Station

Passenger Ferry to Gosport
Portsmouth Harbour Sta.

Portsmouth Harbour

Donegal Pier

H.M.S. Vernon Shore Establishment

Marlborough Pier

Passenger Ferry to Ryde (I of W)

Vehicular Ferry to Fishbourne (I of W)

Round Tower and Point Battery
Square Tower

Long Curtain

King's Bastion

Amusement Park

Clarence Pier

Hovercraft Terminal

Passenger Hovercraft Ferry to Ryde (I of W)

SPIT SAND

Southsea

CUMBERLAND ST

ADMIRALTY ROAD
KING STREET PRINCE
GEORGE ST
NORTH ST
CROSS ST
YORK ST

Royal Naval Barracks (H.M.S. Nelson)

ALFRED RD
Cathedral R.C.
EDINBURGH ROAD

QUEEN STREET
EDINBURGH ROAD

HAVANT ST
COLLEGE ST
HOWE RD
CURZON
KENT ST
ST GEORGES WAY
RICHMOND PL
BRIT. ST

THE HARD
PARK ROAD

GEORGE'S ROAD
GUN WHARF ROAD

RN Sports Centre

BURNABY RD
CAMBRIDGE ROAD
MUSEUM ROAD

WARBLING TON STREET
THOMAS'S STREET

Portsmouth Polytechnic
United Service Rec. Gnd. (officers)

Portsmouth Polytechnic
Ravelin House

EAST ST
BROAD STREET
WHITE HART RD
HIGH STREET

Cathedral

Buckingham House
Portsmouth Grammar School

City Museum and Art Gallery
City Record Office

PENNY STREET
ST NICHOLAS'S STREET

Garrison Church
Govenors Green

PEMBROKE ROAD
Pembroke Gardens

Statue
Garrison Rec. Gnd.

VICTORIA AVENUE
PIER ROAD
SOUTHSEA TERR.

DUISBURG WAY

WESTERN PDE

Victory's Anchor

Naval Memorial

Southsea Common

CLARENCE PARADE

CASTLE AVENUE

ESPLANADE

Tennis Courts
Bowling Green

'D' Day Museum
Castle Arena
Rock Gdns.
Castle Esplanade
Southsea Castle Museum
Rock Garden Pavilion

CLARENCE ESPLANADE SOUTH PARADE

South Parade Pier

St. HELEN'S PDE

ANGLESEA ROAD
LANDPORT TERR.
HAMPSHIRE TERR.
KING'S TERR.

Victoria Park
Swimming Pool

Portsmouth Polytechnic
Theatre Royal

Civic Offices
Central Library

Police Sta. and Courts

College of Art

FLATHOUSE ROAD
UNICORN RD
MARKETWAY
PARADISE ST
CHARLOTTE ST
CRASSWELL STREETS

Tricorn Shopping Centre
Cathedral
Pedestrians only Shopping Precinct

COMMERCIAL ROAD
STANHOPE ROAD

H.P.O.
STATION

Portsmouth and Southsea Station
Guildhall

RAILWAY VIEW
CANAL WALK

Civic Offices

ISAMBARD BRUNEL ROAD

GREETHAM ST
HYDE PARK RD
BLACKFRIARS ROAD

WINSTON CHURCHILL AVENUE

BRADFORD ROAD

ST PAUL'S ROAD
PARK ST
SACK VILLE ST
MIDDLE ST
ST JAMES'S ROAD
GROSVENOR ST
GROSVENOR ST

KING STREET
YORKE ST
NORFOLK ST
ELDON ST
GREEN RD

KING'S ROAD
BELMONT STREET

CASTLE ROAD
ST EDWARD'S RD
PELHAM RD
YARBORO ROAD
WOOD PATH
GROVER D
THE RETREAT

SUSSEX RD
QUEEN'S CRES
St John's College

KENT ROAD
ELPHINSTONE ROAD
PORTLAND ROAD
MERTON ROAD
MARMION ROAD
STANLEY STREET

NELSON ROAD
ALBANY ROAD

GROVE ROAD SOUTH
PALMERSTON ROAD

SHAFTES
OSBORNE ROAD

AUKLAND ROAD
VILLIERS ROAD

LENNOX RD
CLARENCE

CLARENDON ROAD

CASTLE AVENUE

Pol. Sta.

BEACH RD

ELM GROVE
HUDSON ROAD
MARGATE ROAD
COTTAGE GROVE

SOMERS ROAD NORTH
PAIN'S RD
RIVERS STREET ROAD
FRASER ROAD
BAILEY'S ROAD

ST ANDREW'S ROAD
ST DAVID'S ROAD

VICTORIA ROAD

MONTGOMERIE RD
OUTRAM ROAD
LIVINGSTONE RD
CAMPBELL ROAD

ALBERT GROVE CHELSEA ROAD
GOODWOOD ROAD
OXFORD ROAD
BOULTON RD
COLLINGWOOD RD
EXMOUTH RD
DUNCAN RD

VICTORIA GR. ROAD
LAWRENCE ROAD

KINGS THEATRE
ALBERT ROAD

WORTHING RD
NAPIER ROAD
LOWCA ROAD
WIMBLEDON PARK ROAD

WISBORO ROAD
GAINS ROAD
ALLENS ROAD
WELCHROAD

ST SIMONS ROAD

ST RONANS ROAD
PARKSTONE AVE
BEMBRIDGE CRES.
MARION ROAD

GRANADA ROAD
WHITWELL ROAD

CHURCH STREET
CHURCH ROAD
LAKE ROAD

CORN. CRES.
CHURCH PATH
CHURCH STREET NORTH
NORTHAM STREET

CHARLES STREET

HOLBROOK ROAD

CLARENDON STREET

COBOURG STREET
GARNIER STREET

ARUNDEL STREET

SOMERS RD
RAGLAN ST

Fire Station

NORTH END
FRATTON ROAD

Radio Victory

ST MARY'S RD
ALVER ROAD
CLIVE ROAD
NEWCOME RD

GARNIER STREET
PENHALE RD
ARIEL ROAD

RD NORTH

WALMER RD

Fratton
Fratton Station
ORCHARD ROAD

MANNERS ROAD
PERCY ROAD
JESSIE ROAD

RUGBY ROAD

LAWSON ROAD

SANSTED ROAD
HAVELOCK ROAD
LORNE RD

FAWCETT ROAD
CHETWYND ROAD
DARLINGTON ROAD
INGLIS ROAD

HAROLD ROAD
FAWCETT ROAD

Underline Construction (due to open, end 1984)

N

Portsmouth

Described as Britain's premiere naval base it has a vigorous docks area which has frequent ferries to the Isle of Wight, and sailings to Le Havre, Cherbourg, St Malo and the Channel Islands. It also has a busy Hovercraft Terminal. Parking is at City Garages Ltd, Tel: (0705) 823153 half-a-mile from the Isle of Wight car ferry terminal. Multi-storey parking for 400 cars is offered, collection or delivery service available. Ferryport Parking (Portsmouth) Ltd is 200 yards from the Ferry Terminal Tel: (0705) 751261 and has 200 lock up spaces, but advance booking is recommended. Motor caravans and other large vehicles can be accommodated in a locked open-air compound. Collection and delivery service is available. Victory Car Park on Clarence Pier, opposite the Hovercraft Terminal for the Isle of Wight, has unlimited open parking operated by pay and display tickets. One 4-star hotel in Portsmouth and two 3-star in neighbouring Southsea are available.

North Boarhunt
Waterlooville
Boarhunt
Southwick
Purbrook
Leigh Park
New Brighton
Woodmancote
HAVANT
Westbourne
Emsworth Hermitage
Paulsgrove
Wymering
Drayton
Bedhampton
Cosham
Farlington
Southbourne
Portchester
Hilsea
Continental Car Ferry Terminal
North End
GOSPORT
Portsea
PORTSMOUTH
Milton
Fratton
Southsea
Stoke
North Hayling
West Thorney
West Town
South Hayling
East Stoke
West Wittering
Alverstoke
THE SOLENT
Portsmouth Harbour
Langstone Harbour
Chichester Harbour
River Ems

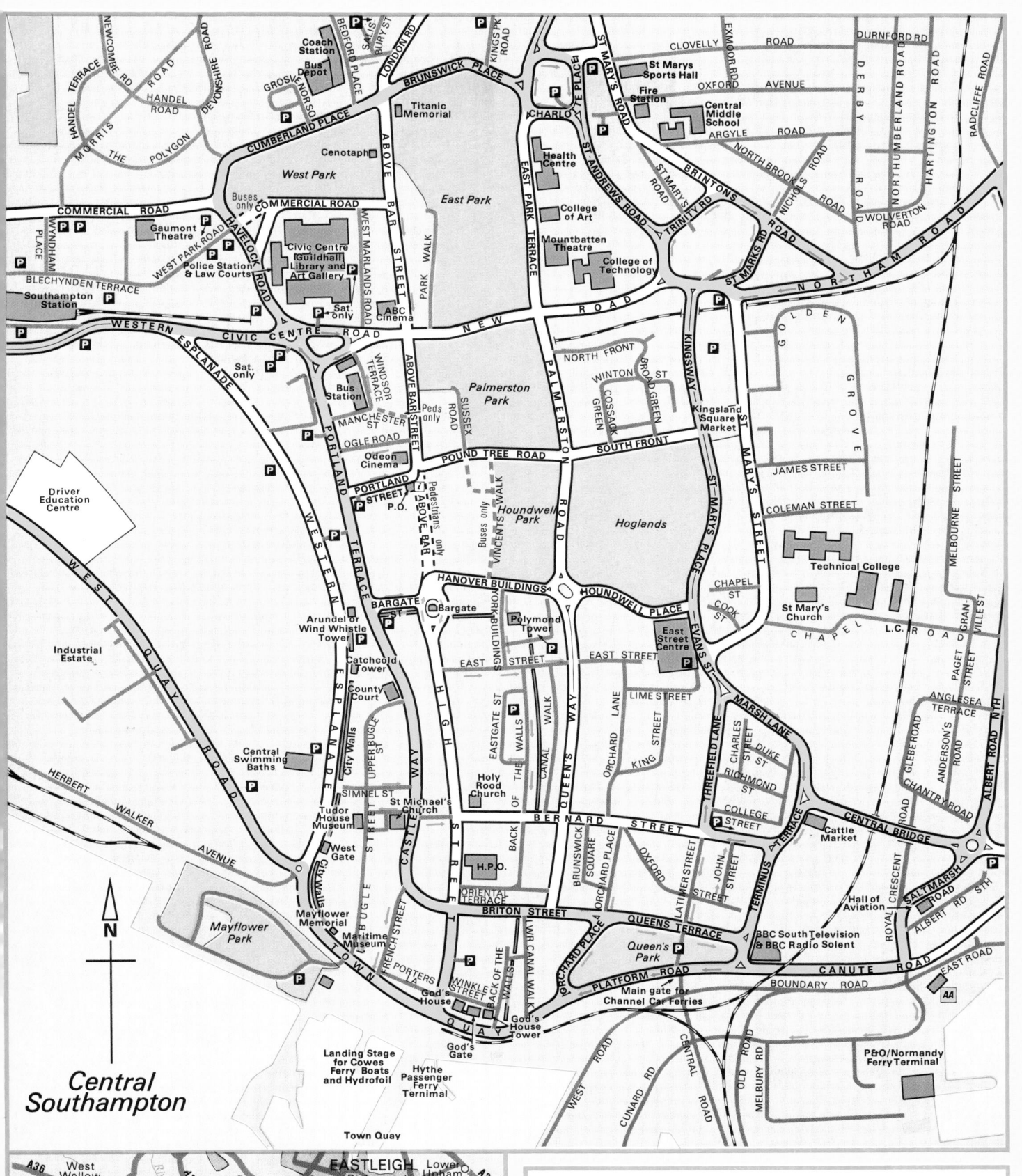

Central Southampton

N

Southampton Area

(Area map labels: West Wellow, Canada, Ower, Bramshaw, Copythorne, Cadnam, Netley Marsh, Minstead, Woodlands, Bartley, Ashurst, Lyndhurst, TOTTON, Shirley, Millbrook, SOUTHAMPTON, Marchwood, Woolston, Netley, Hythe, Hamble, Warsash, EASTLEIGH, Bishopstoke, Upton, Rownhams, Nursling, Chilworth, Swaythling, Portswood, West End, Bitterne, Sholing, Hedge End, Botley, Curdridge, Durley, Fair Oak, Horton Heath, Lower Upham, Bursledon, Lower Swanwick, Sarisbury, Park Gate, Locks Heath, Swanwick, Burridge, I.O.W. Ferry Terminal, River Test, River Itchen, Beaulieu River, River Hamble)

Roads: A36, A27, A333, A335, B3037, A3051, A334, A3025, A326, A337, A35, A31, A336, M27, M271, B3056, A3090

Southampton

Southampton has been the major port for transatlantic sailings since 1911, when it took over from Liverpool. The great ocean liners are no longer crowding the dock area, but the QE2 and the Canberra still dominate the docks skyline when they berth. The British Transport Docks Board runs the dock traffic and accommodates Andrews (Shipside Services) Ltd, garage at 10 Gate Western Docks, Tel: (0703) 228001/2/3 and 2 Gate Eastern Dock where covered or fenced compound parking is available for 1600 vehicles. It is open for all ferry departures and arrivals. A collection and delivery service is provided. There are several multi-storey car parks in the city centre area. There are a number of AA-appointed hotels within a mile or so of the dock area, and these include one 4-star, three 3-star and one 2-star hotels.

193

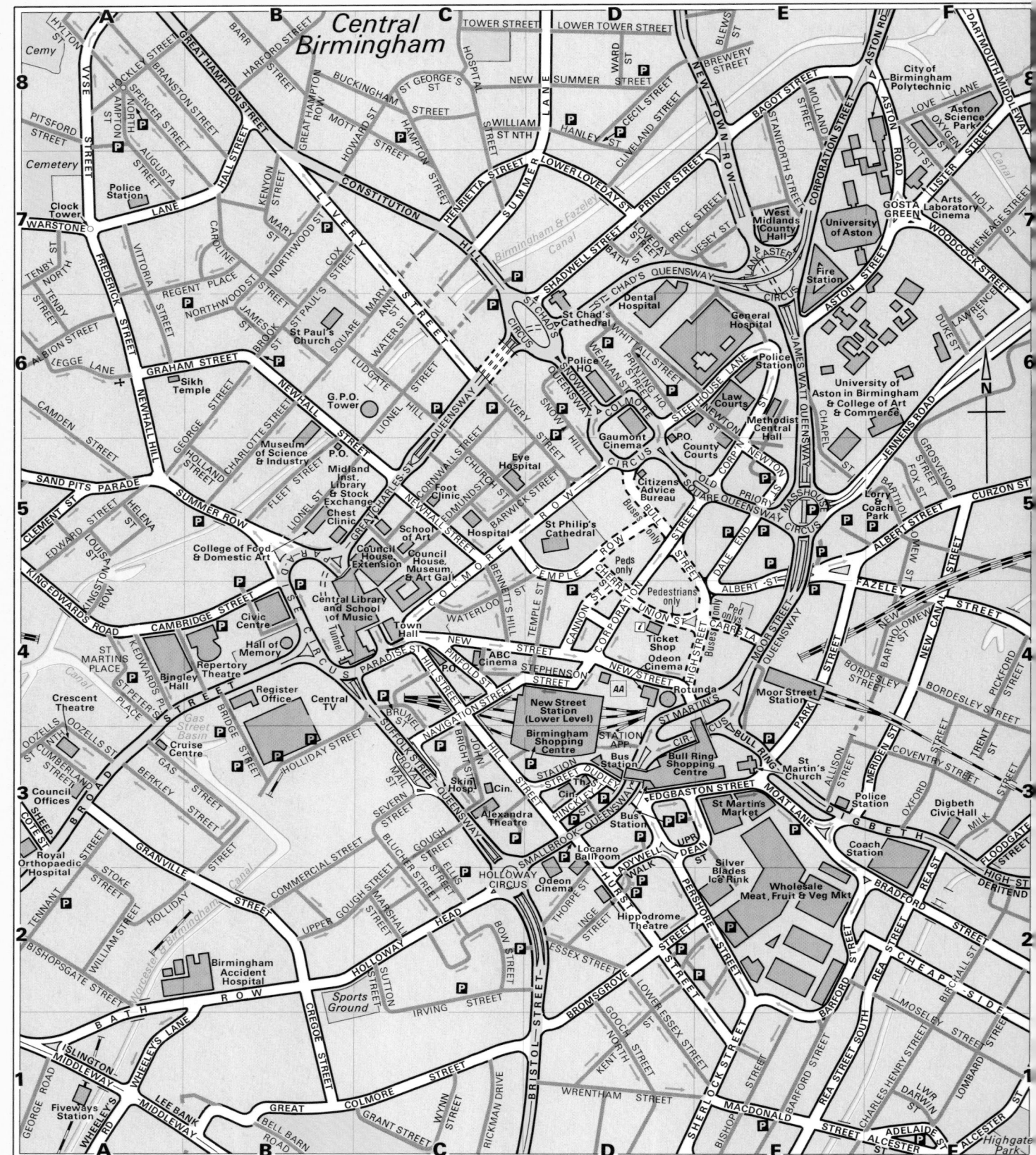

Birmingham

It is very difficult to visualise Birmingham as it was before it began the growth which eventually made it the second-largest city in England. When the Romans were in Britain it was little more than a staging post on Icknield Street. Throughout medieval times it was a sleepy agricultural centre in the middle of a heavily-forested region. Timbered houses clustered together round a green that was eventually to be called the Bull Ring. But by the 16th century, although still a tiny and unimportant village by today's standards, it had begun to gain a reputation as a manufacturing centre. Tens of thousands of sword blades were made here during the Civil War. Throughout the 18th century more and more land was built on. In 1770 the Birmingham Canal was completed, making trade very much easier and increasing the town's development dramatically. All of that pales into near insignificance compared with what happened in the 19th century. Birmingham was not represented in Parliament until 1832 and had no town council until 1838. Yet by 1889 it had already been made a city, and after only another 20 years it had become the second largest city in England. Many of Birmingham's most imposing public buildings date from the 19th century, when the city was growing so rapidly. Surprisingly, the city has more miles of waterway than Venice.

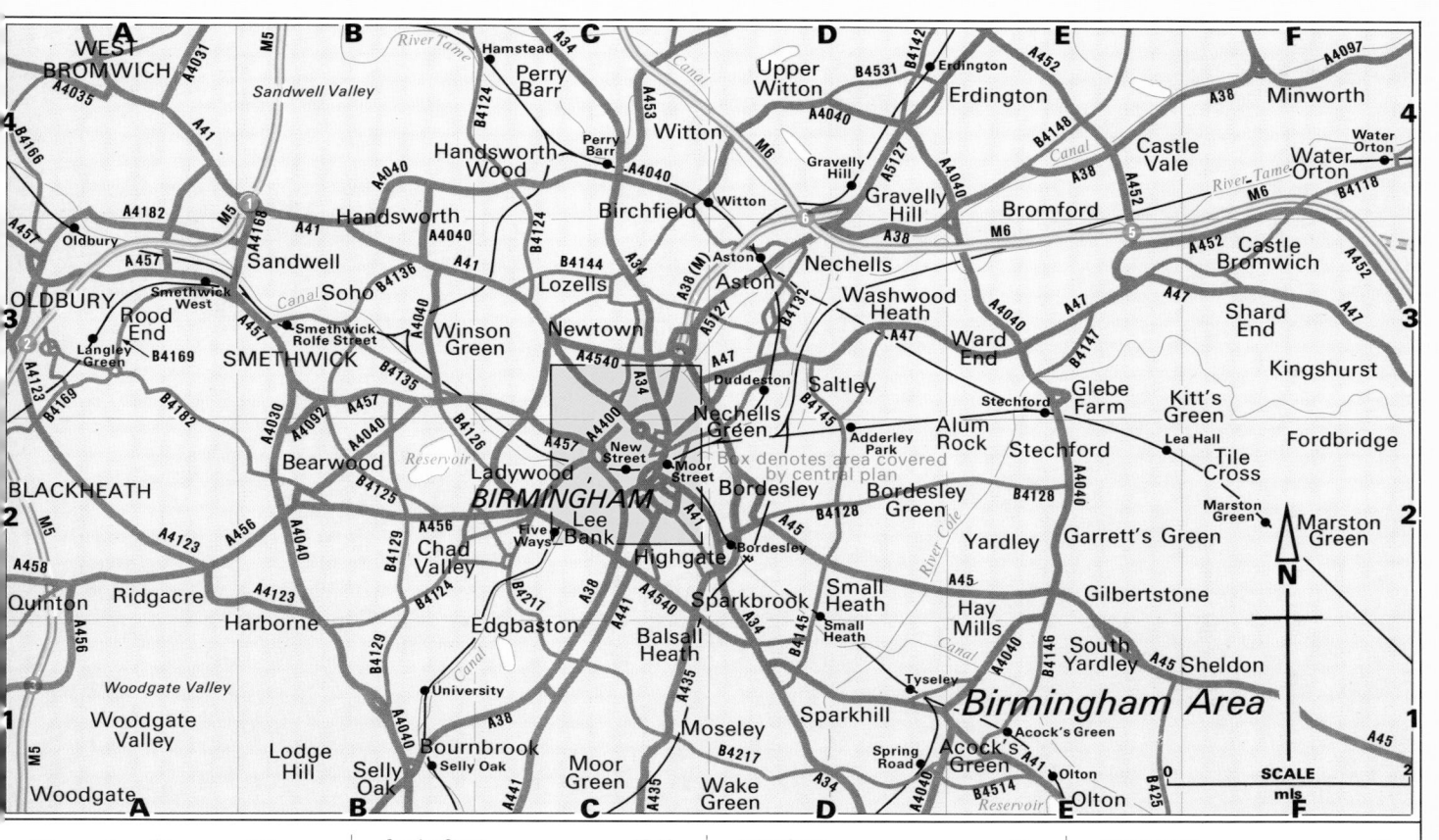

Key to Town Plan and Area Plan

Town Plan

AA Recommended roads
Restricted roads
Other roads
Buildings of interest   Station
AA Service Centre   AA
Car Parks   P
Parks and open spaces
One Way Streets

Area Plan

A roads
B roads
Locations   Meer End ○

Street Index with Grid Reference

Birmingham

Adelaide Street	F1
Albert Street	E4-E5-F5
Albion Street	A6
Alcester Street	F1
Allison Street	E3
Aston Road	E8-F8-F7
Aston Street	E6-E7-F7
Augusta Street	A7-A8
Bagot Street	E8
Barford Street	E1-E2-F2
Barr Street	B8
Bartholomew Street	F4-F5
Barwick Street	C5-D5
Bath Row	A1-A2-B2
Bath Street	D7
Bell Barn Road	B1
Bennett's Hill	C4-C5
Berkley Street	A3-B3
Birchall Street	F1-F2
Bishop Street	E1
Bishopsgate Street	A2
Blews Street	E8
Blucher Street	C2-C3
Bordesley Street	E4-F4-F3
Bow Street	C2
Bradford Street	E3-E2-F2
Branston Street	A8-B8-B7
Brewery Street	E8
Bridge Street	B3-B4
Bristol Street	C1-D1-D2-C2
Broad Street	A2-A3-A4-B4
Bromsgrove Street	D1-D2-E2
Brook Street	B6
Brunel Street	C3-C4
Buckingham Street	B8-C8
Bull Ring	E3
Bull Street	D5-E5-E4
Cambridge Street	A4-B4-B5
Camden Street	A5-A6
Cannon Street	D4
Caroline Street	B6-B7
Carrs Street	E4
Cecil Street	D8
Chapel Street	E5-E6
Charles Henry Street	F1
Charlotte Street	B5-B6
Cheapside	F1-F2
Cherry Street	D4-D5
Church Street	C6-C5-D5
Clement Street	A5
Cliveland Street	D7-D8-E8
Colmore Circus	D5-D6
Colmore Row	C4-C5-D5
Commercial Street	B2-B3-C3
Constitution Hill	B7-C7
Cornwall Street	C5-C6
Corporation Street	D4-D5-E5-E6-E7-E8
Coventry Street	E3-F3
Cox Street	B7
Cregoe Street	B1-B2
Cumberland Street	A3
Curzon Street	F5
Dale End	E4-E5
Dartmouth Middleway	F7-F8
Digbeth	E3-F3
Dudley Street	D3
Duke Street	F6
Edgbaston Street	D3-E3
Edmund Street	C5-D5
Edward Street	A5
Ellis Street	C2-C3
Essex Street	D2
Fazeley Street	E5-E4-F4
Fleet Street	B5
Floodgate Street	F3
Fox Street	F5
Frederick Street	A6-A7
Gas Street	A3-B3
George Road	A1
George Street	A5-B5-B6
Gooch Street North	D1-D2
Gosta Green	F7
Gough Street	C3
Graham Street	A6-B6
Grant Street	C1
Granville Street	A3-A2-B2
Great Charles St Queensway	B5-C5-C6
Great Colmore Street	B1-C1-D1
Great Hampton Row	B8
Great Hampton Street	A8-B8
Grosvenor Street	F5-F6
Hall Street	B7-B8
Hampton Street	C7-C8
Hanley Street	D7-D8
Helena Street	A5
Heneage Street	F7
Henrietta Street	C7-D7
High Street	D4-E4
High Street Deritend	F2-F3
Hill Street	C4-C3-D3
Hinckley Street	D3
Hockley Street	A8-B8
Holland Street	B5
Holliday Street	A2-B2-B3-C3-C4
Holloway Circus	C2-C3-D3-D2
Holloway Head	B2-C2
Holt Street	F7-F8
Hospital Street	C7-C8
Howard Street	B7-C7-C8
Hurst Street	D3-D2-E2-E1
Hylton Street	A8
Inge Street	D2
Irving Street	C2-D2
Islington Middleway	A1
James Street	B6
James Watt Queensway	E5-E6
Jennens Road	E5-F5-F6
John Bright Street	C3-C4
Kent Street	D1-D2
Kenyon Street	B7
King Edward's Place	A4
King Edward's Road	A4-A5
Kingston Row	A4
Ladywell Walk	D2-D3
Lancaster Circus	E6-E7
Lawrence Street	F6-F7
Lee Bank Middleway	A1-B1
Legge Lane	A6
Lionel Street	B5-C5-C6
Lister Street	F7-F8
Livery Street	B7-C7-C6-D6-D5
Lombard Street	F1-F2
Louisa Street	A5
Love Lane	F8
Loveday Street	D7
Lower Darwin Street	F1
Lower Essex Street	D2-D1-E1
Lower Loveday Street	D7
Lower Tower Street	D8
Ludgate Hill	B6-C6
Macdonald Street	E1-F1
Marshall Street	C2
Mary Street	B7
Mary Ann Street	C6-C7
Masshouse Circus	E5
Meriden Street	E3-F3
Milk Street	F3
Moat Lane	E3
Molland Street	E8
Moor Street Queensway	E4-E5
Moseley Street	E2-F2-F1
Mott Street	B8-C8-C7
Navigation Street	C3-C4
New Street	C4-D4
New Bartholomew Street	F4
New Canal Street	F4-F5
Newhall Hill	A5-A6
Newhall Street	B6-B5-C5
New Summer Street	C8-D8
Newton Street	E5
New Town Row	D8-E8-E7
Northampton Street	A8
Northwood Street	B6-B7
Old Square	D5-E5
Oozells Street	A3-A4
Oozells Street North	A3-A4
Oxford Street	F3-F4
Oxygen Street	F7-F8
Paradise Circus	B4-B5
Paradise Street	C4
Park Street	E3-E4
Pershore Street	D3-D2-E2
Pickford Street	F4
Pinfold Street	C4
Pitsford Street	A8
Price Street	D7-E7
Princip Street	D7-E7-E8
Printing House Street	D6
Priory Queensway	E5
Rea Street	E2-F2-F3
Rea Street South	E1-F1-F2
Regent Place	A7-B7
Rickman Drive	C1
Royal Mail Street	C3
St Chad's Circus	C7-C6-D6
St Chad's Queensway	D6-D7-E7
St George's Street	C8
St Martin's Circus	D3-D4-E4-E3
St Martin's Place	A4
St Paul's Square	B7-B6-C6
St Peter's Place	A4
Sand Pits Parade	A5
Severn Street	C3
Shadwell Street	D6-D7
Sheepcote Street	A3
Sherlock Street	D1-E1-E2
Smallbrook Queensway	C3-D3
Snow Hill	D5-D6
Snow Hill Queensway	D6
Spencer Street	A8-A7-B7
Staniforth Street	E7-E8
Station Approach	D3
Station Street	D3
Steelhouse Lane	D6-E6
Stephenson Street	C4-D4
Stoke Street	A2-A3
Suffolk Street Queensway	B4-C4-C3
Summer Row	A5-B5
Summer Lane	C7-D7-D8
Sutton Street	C2
Temple Row	C5-D5
Temple Street	D4-D5
Tenby Street	A6-A7
Tenby Street North	A7
Tennant Street	A2-A3
Thorpe Street	D2-D3
Tower Street	C8-D8
Trent Street	F3-F4
Union Street	D4
Upper Dean Street	D3-E3
Upper Gough Street	B2-C2-C3
Vesey Street	D7-E7
Vittoria Street	A6-A7
Vyse Street	A7-A8
Ward Street	D8
Warford Street	B8
Warstone Lane	A7-B7
Water Street	C6
Waterloo Street	C4-C5-D5
Weaman Street	D6
Wheeley's Lane	A1-B1-B2
Wheeley's Road	A1
Whittall Street	D6-E6
William Street	A2
William Street North	C8-D8
Woodcock Street	F6-F7
Wrentham Street	D1-E1
Wynn Street	C1

195

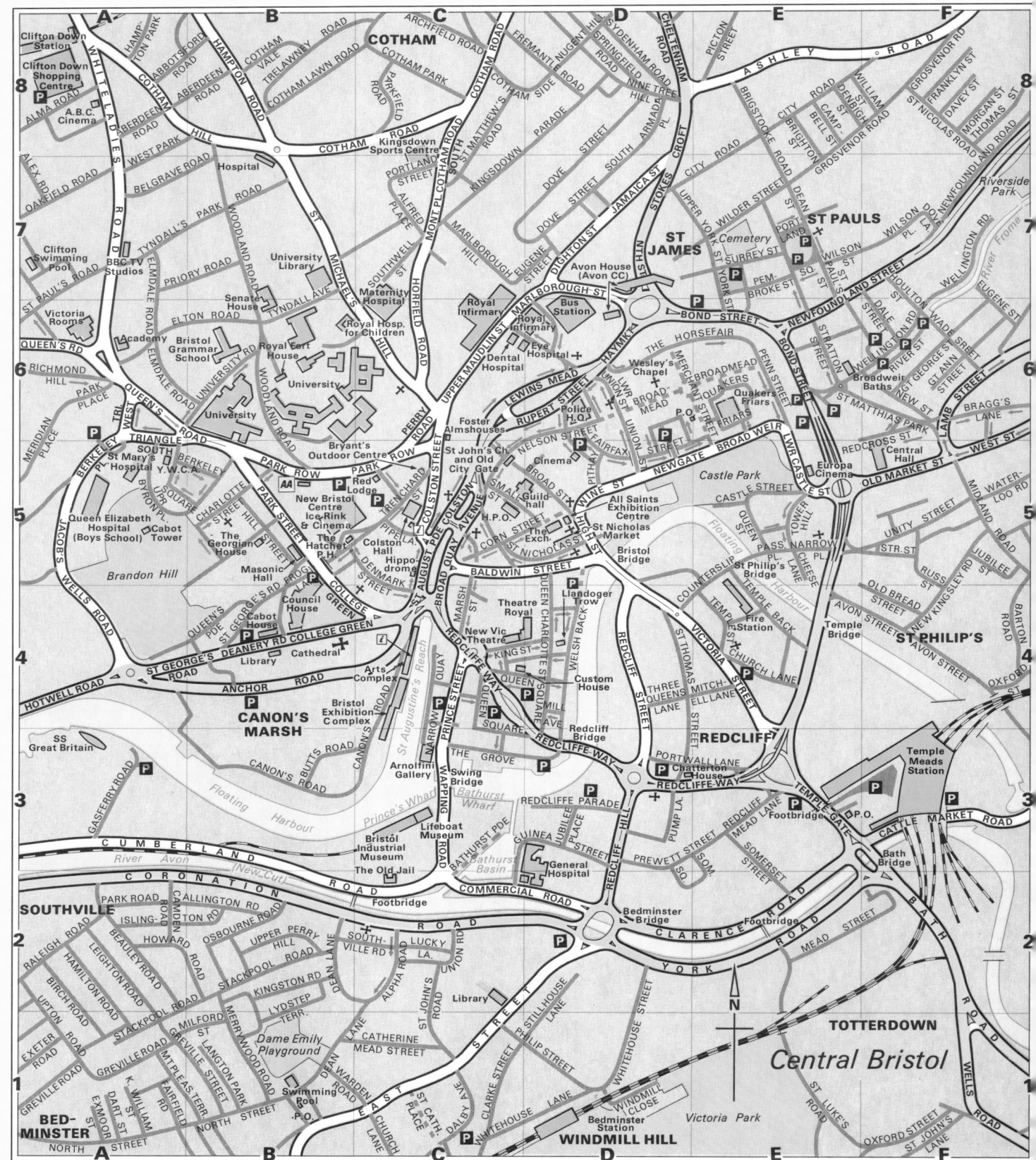

Bristol

One of Britain's most historic seaports, Bristol retains many of its visible links with the past, despite terrible damage inflicted during bombing raids in World War II. Most imposing is the cathedral, founded as an abbey church in 1140. Perhaps even more famous than the cathedral is the Church of St Mary Redcliffe. Ranking among the finest churches in the country, it owes much of its splendour to 14th- and 15th-century merchants who bestowed huge sums of money on it.

The merchant families brought wealth to the whole of Bristol, and their trading links with the world are continued in today's modern aerospace and technological industries. Much of the best of Bristol can be seen in the area of the Floating Harbour – an arm of the Avon. Several of the old warehouses have been converted into museums, galleries and exhibition centres. Among them are genuinely picturesque old pubs, the best-known of which is the Llandoger Trow. It is a timbered 17th-century house, the finest of its kind in Bristol. Further up the same street – King Street – is the Theatre Royal, built in 1766 and the oldest theatre in the country. In Corn Street, the heart of the business area, is a magnificent 18th-century corn exchange. In front of it are the four pillars known as the 'nails', on which merchants used to make cash transactions, hence 'to pay on the nail'.

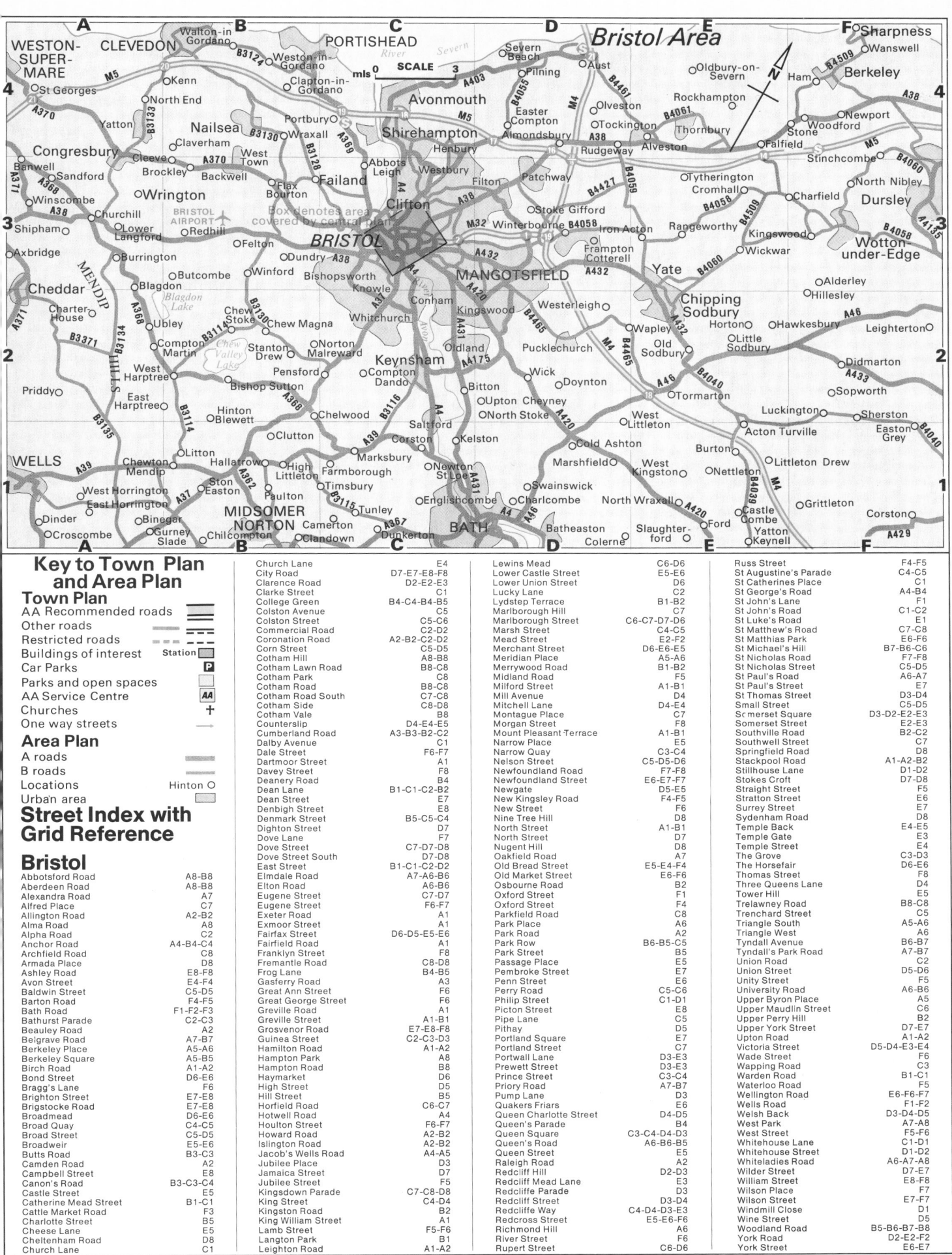

Key to Town Plan and Area Plan

Town Plan
AA Recommended roads
Other roads
Restricted roads
Buildings of interest — Station
Car Parks — P
Parks and open spaces
AA Service Centre — AA
Churches — +
One way streets

Area Plan
A roads
B roads
Locations — Hinton O
Urban area

Street Index with Grid Reference

Bristol

Street	Grid Ref
Abbotsford Road	A8-B8
Aberdeen Road	A8-B8
Alexandra Road	A7
Alfred Place	C7
Allington Road	A2-B2
Alma Road	A8
Alpha Road	C2
Anchor Road	A4-B4-C4
Archfield Road	C8
Armada Place	D8
Ashley Road	E8-F8
Avon Street	E4-F4
Baldwin Street	C5-D5
Barton Road	F4-F5
Bath Road	F1-F2-F3
Bathurst Parade	C2-C3
Beauley Road	A2
Belgrave Road	A7-B7
Berkeley Place	A5-A6
Berkeley Square	A5-B5
Birch Road	A1-A2
Bond Street	D6-E6
Bragg's Lane	F6
Brighton Street	E7-E8
Brigstocke Road	E7-E8
Broadmead	D6-E6
Broad Quay	C4-C5
Broad Street	C5-D5
Broadweir	E5-E6
Butts Road	B3-C3
Camden Road	A2
Campbell Street	E8
Canon's Road	B3-C3-C4
Castle Street	E5
Catherine Mead Street	B1-C1
Cattle Market Road	F3
Charlotte Street	B5
Cheese Lane	E5
Cheltenham Road	D8
Church Lane	C1
Church Lane	E4
City Road	D7-E7-E8-F8
Clarence Road	D2-E2-E3
Clarke Street	C1
College Green	B4-C4-B4-B5
Colston Avenue	C5
Colston Street	C5-C6
Commercial Road	C2-D2
Coronation Road	A2-B2-C2-D2
Corn Street	C5-D5
Cotham Hill	A8-B8
Cotham Lawn Road	B8-C8
Cotham Park	C8
Cotham Road	B8-C8
Cotham Road South	C7-C8
Cotham Side	C8-D8
Cotham Vale	B8
Countership	D4-E4-E5
Cumberland Road	A3-B3-B2-C2
Dalby Avenue	C1
Dale Street	F6-F7
Dartmoor Street	A1
Davey Street	F8
Deanery Road	B4
Dean Lane	B1-C1-B2
Dean Street	E7
Denbigh Street	E8
Denmark Street	B5-C5-C4
Dighton Street	D7
Dove Lane	F7
Dove Street	C7-D7-D8
Dove Street South	D7-D8
East Street	B1-C1-C2-D2
Elmdale Road	A7-A6-B6
Elton Road	A6-B6
Eugene Street	C7-D7
Eugene Street	F6-F7
Exeter Road	A1
Exmoor Street	A1
Fairfax Street	D6-D5-E5-E6
Fairfield Road	A1
Franklyn Street	F8
Fremantle Road	C8-D8
Frog Lane	B4-B5
Gasferry Road	A3
Great Ann Street	F6
Great George Street	F6
Greville Road	A1
Greville Street	A1-B1
Grosvenor Road	E7-E8-F8
Guinea Street	C2-C3-D3
Hamilton Road	A1-A2
Hampton Park	A8
Hampton Road	B8
Haymarket	D6
High Street	D5
Hill Street	B5
Horfield Road	C6-C7
Hotwell Road	A4
Houlton Street	F6-F7
Howard Road	A2-B2
Islington Road	A2-B2
Jacob's Wells Road	A4-A5
Jubilee Place	D3
Jamaica Street	D7
Jubilee Street	F5
Kingsdown Parade	C7-C8-D8
King Street	C4-D4
Kingston Road	B2
King William Street	A1
Lamb Street	F5-F6
Langton Park	B1
Leighton Road	A1-A2
Lewins Mead	C6-D6
Lower Castle Street	E5-E6
Lower Union Street	D6
Lucky Lane	C2
Lydstep Terrace	B1-B2
Marlborough Hill	C7
Marlborough Street	C6-C7-D7-D6
Marsh Street	C4-C5
Mead Street	E2-F2
Merchant Street	D6-E6-E5
Meridian Place	A5-A6
Merryward Road	B1-B2
Midland Road	F5
Milford Street	A1-B1
Mill Avenue	D4
Mitchell Lane	D4-E4
Montague Place	C7
Morgan Street	F8
Mount Pleasant Terrace	A1-B1
Narrow Place	E5
Narrow Quay	C3-C4
Nelson Street	C5-D5-D6
Newfoundland Road	F7-F8
Newfoundland Street	E6-E7-F7
Newgate	D5-E5
New Kingsley Road	F4-F5
New Street	F6
Nine Tree Hill	D8
North Street	A1-B1
North Street	D7
Nugent Hill	D8
Oakfield Road	A7
Old Bread Street	E5-E4-F4
Old Market Street	E6-F6
Osbourne Road	B2
Oxford Street	F1
Oxford Street	F4
Parkfield Road	C8
Park Place	A6
Park Road	A2
Park Row	B6-B5-C5
Park Street	B5
Passage Place	E5
Pembroke Street	E7
Penn Street	E6
Perry Road	C5-C6
Philip Street	C1-D1
Picton Street	E8
Pipe Lane	C5
Pithay	D5
Portland Square	E7
Portland Street	C7
Portwall Lane	D3-E3
Prewett Street	D3-E3
Prince Street	C3-C4
Priory Road	A7-B7
Pump Lane	D3
Quakers Friars	E6
Queen Charlotte Street	D4-D5
Queen's Parade	B4
Queen Square	C3-C4-D4-D3
Queen's Road	A6-B6-B5
Queen Street	E5
Raleigh Road	A2
Redcliff Mead Lane	E3
Redcliffe Parade	D3
Redcliff Street	D3-D4
Redcliffe Way	C4-D4-D3-E3
Redcross Street	E5-E6-F6
Richmond Hill	A6
River Street	F6
Rupert Street	C6-D6
Russ Street	F4-F5
St Augustine's Parade	C4-C5
St Catherines Place	C1
St George's Road	A4-B4
St John's Lane	F1
St John's Road	C1-C2
St Luke's Road	E1
St Matthew's Road	C7-C8
St Matthias Park	E6-F6
St Michael's Hill	B7-B6-C6
St Nicholas Road	F7-F8
St Nicholas Street	C5-D5
St Paul's Road	A6-A7
St Paul's Street	E7
St Thomas Street	D3-D4
Small Street	C5-D5
Somerset Square	D3-D2-E2-E3
Somerset Street	E2-E3
Southville Road	B2-C2
Southwell Street	C7
Springfield Road	D8
Stackpool Road	A1-A2-B2
Stillhouse Lane	D1-D2
Stokes Croft	D7-D8
Straight Street	F5
Stratton Street	E6
Surrey Street	E7
Sydenham Road	D8
Temple Back	E4-E5
Temple Gate	E3
Temple Street	E4
The Grove	C3-D3
The Horsefair	D6-E6
Thomas Street	F8
Three Queens Lane	D4
Tower Hill	E5
Trelawney Road	B8-C8
Trenchard Street	C5
Triangle South	A5-A6
Triangle West	A6
Tyndall Avenue	B6-B7
Tyndall's Park Road	A7-B7
Union Road	C2
Union Street	D5-D6
Unity Street	F5
University Road	A6-B6
Upper Byron Place	A5
Upper Maudlin Street	C6
Upper Perry Hill	B2
Upper York Street	D7-E7
Upton Road	A1-A2
Victoria Street	D5-D4-E3-E4
Wade Street	F6
Wapping Road	C3
Warden Road	B1-C1
Waterloo Road	F5
Wellington Road	E6-F6-F7
Wells Road	F1-F2
Welsh Back	D3-D4-D5
West Park	A7-A8
West Street	F5-F6
Whitehouse Lane	C1-D1
Whitehouse Street	D1-D2
Whiteladies Road	A6-A7-A8
Wilder Street	D7-E7
William Street	E8-F8
Wilson Place	F7
Wilson Street	E7-F7
Windmill Close	D1
Wine Street	D5
Woodland Road	B5-B6-B7-B8
York Road	D2-E2-F2
York Street	E6-E7

197

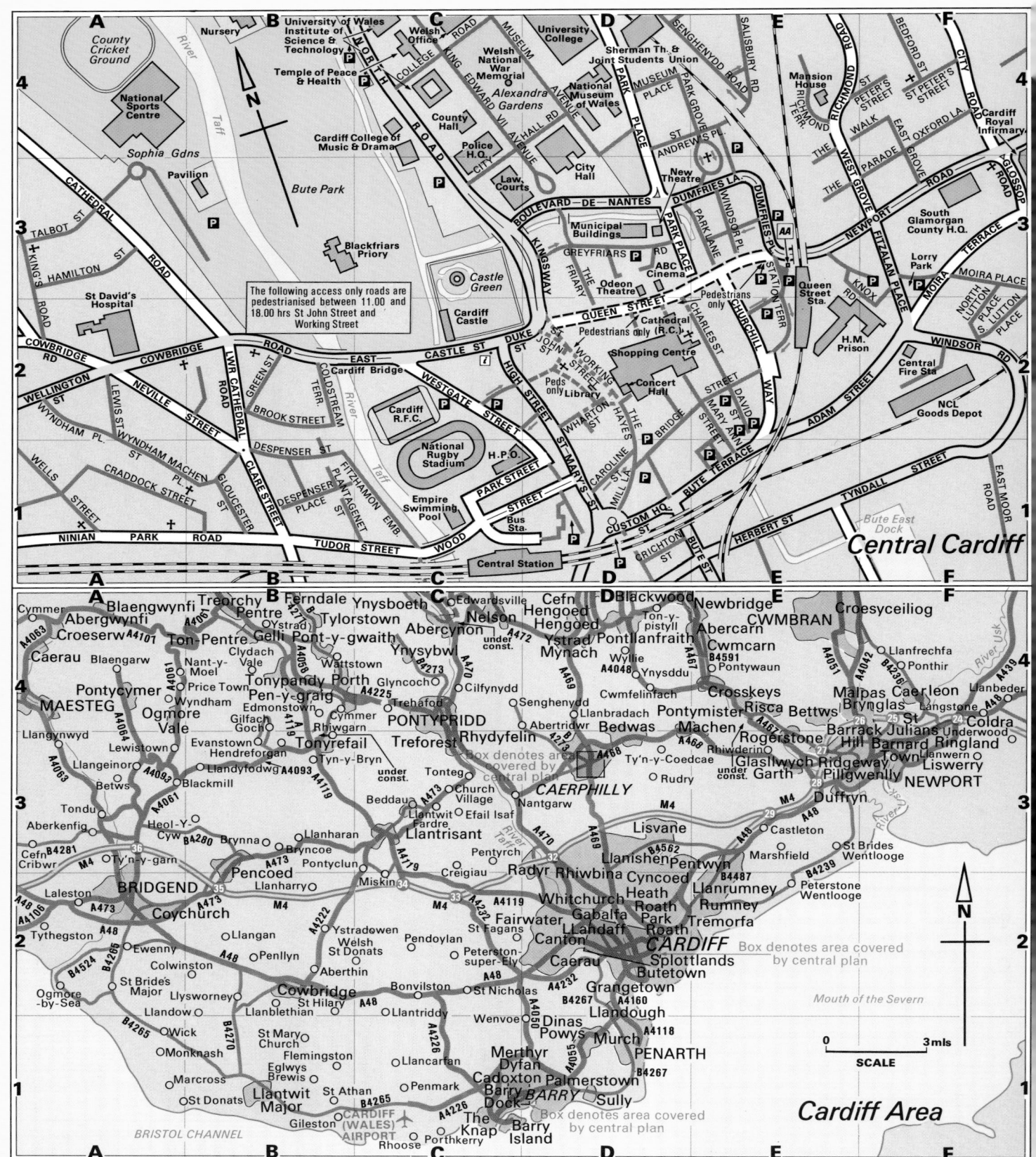

Central Cardiff

(Map grid references A–F horizontally, 1–4 vertically)

County Cricket Ground
National Sports Centre
Sophia Gdns
Pavilion
CATHEDRAL ROAD
Talbot St
King's
Hamilton
St David's Hospital
COWBRIDGE RD
WELLINGTON ST
LEWIS ST
NEVILLE STREET
WYNDHAM PL
WYNDHAM ST
MACHEN PL
WELLS ST
CRADDOCK STREET
GLOUCESTER ST
CLARE STREET
LWR CATHEDRAL ROAD
BROOK STREET
DESPENSER ST
DESPENSER PLACE
FITZHAMON EMB
PLANTAGENET ST
NINIAN PARK ROAD
TUDOR STREET

River Taff
Nursery
University of Wales Institute of Science & Technology
Temple of Peace & Health
Cardiff College of Music & Drama
Bute Park
NORTH ROAD
COLLEGE RD
Welsh Office
County Hall
Police H.Q.
Blackfriars Priory
Castle Green
Cardiff Castle
COLDSTREAM TERR
GREEN ST
Cardiff Bridge
WESTGATE STREET
Cardiff R.F.C.
National Rugby Stadium
Empire Swimming Pool
H.P.O.
Bus Sta.
WOOD STREET
Central Station

KING EDWARD VII AVENUE
HALL RD
Welsh National War Memorial
Alexandra Gardens
Law Courts
City Hall
BOULEVARD – DE – NANTES
Municipal Buildings
GREYFRIARS RD
The Friary
QUEEN STREET
KINGSWAY
CASTLE ST
DUKE ST
HIGH STREET
JOHN ST
WORKING STREET
ST MARY'S ST
WHARTON ST
THE HAYES
CAROLINE ST
MILL LA
ST MARY ST
CUSTOM HQ
CRICHTON ST

Museum
University College
Sherman Th. & Joint Students Union
National Museum of Wales
PARK PLACE
MUSEUM PLACE
PARK GROVE
ST ANDREWS PL
New Theatre
Odeon Theatre
ABC Cinema
Pedestrians only (R.C.)
Cathedral
Shopping Centre
Concert Hall
Library
Peds only
THE BRIDGE
MARY ANN STREET
DAVID STREET
BUTE TERRACE
ADAM STREET
HERBERT ST

SENGHENYDD ROAD
SALISBURY RD
DUMFRIES LA
DUMFRIES PL
PARK LANE
WINDSOR PL
STATION TERR
CHARLES ST
CHURCHILL WAY
Queen Street Sta.
KNOX RD
H.M. Prison
STATION TERRACE
TYNDALL STREET

RICHMOND ROAD
Mansion House
PETER'S ST
ST PETER'S STREET
THE WALK
WEST GROVE
THE PARADE
NEWPORT ROAD
FITZALAN PLACE
Lorry Park
MOIRA TERR
Cardiff Royal Infirmary
EAST OXFORD LA
GLOSSOP ROAD
South Glamorgan County H.Q.
MOIRA PLACE
NORTH LUTON PL
SOUTH LUTON PL
WINDSOR RD
Central Fire Sta.
NCL Goods Depot
EAST MOOR ROAD
Bute East Dock
CITY ROAD
BEDFORD ST

The following access only roads are pedestrianised between 11.00 and 18.00 hrs St John Street and Working Street

Cardiff Area

(Map grid references A–F horizontally, 1–4 vertically)

Cymmer
Blaengwynfi
Abergwynfi
Croeserw
Caerau
Pontycymer
MAESTEG
Ogmore Vale
Llangynwyd
Llangeinor
Betws
Tondu
Aberkenfig
Cefn Cribwr
Ty'n-y-garn
Laleston
BRIDGEND
Coychurch
Tythegston
Ewenny
Colwinston
St Bride's Major
Llysworney
Llandow
Wick
Monknash
Marcross
St Donats
Llantwit Major
Ogmore-by-Sea
Treorchy
Pentre
Ton-Pentre
Gelli
Clydach Vale
Nant-y-Moel
Blaengarw
Price Town
Wyndham
Gilfach Goch
Evanstown
Hendreforgan
Lewistown
Llandyfodwg
Blackmill
Heol-Y-Cyw
Brynna
Bryncoe
Pencoed
Llanharry
Llangan
Ystradowen
Welsh St Donats
Cowbridge
St Hilary
Llanblethian
St Mary Church
Flemingston
Eglwys Brewis
St Athan
Gileston
Ferndale
Ynysboeth
Tylorstown
Ystrad
Pont-y-gwaith
Tonypandy
Porth
Wattstown
Pen-y-graig
Trehafod
Cymmer
Rhiwgarn
Tonyrefail
Tyn-y-Bryn
Beddau
Llantwit Fardre
Efail Isaf
Church Village
Llanharan
Pontyclun
Miskin
Creigiau
Pentyrch
Pendoylan
Peterston-super-Ely
Bonvilston
St Nicholas
Llantriddy
Wenvoe
Dinas Powys
Merthyr Dyfan
Cadoxton
Barry Dock
The Knap
Porthkerry
Rhoose
BARRY
Barry Island
Sully
Palmerstown
Murch
PENARTH
Edwardsville
Nelson
Abercynon
Ynysybwl
Glyncoch
Cilfynydd
PONTYPRIDD
Treforest
Rhydyfelin
Tonteg
Nantgarw
Radyr
St Fagans
Fairwater
Canton
Caerau
Llandaff
Grangetown
Butetown
Splottlands
CARDIFF
Llandough
Cefn Hengoed
Hengoed
Ton-y-pistyll
Ystrad Mynach
Wyllie
Ynysddu
Llanbradach
Senghenydd
Abertridwr
Bedwas
Rudry
Ty'n-y-Coedcae
CAERPHILLY
Nantgarw
Rhiwderin
Lisvane
Llanishen
Cyncoed
Pentwyn
Whitchurch
Gabalfa
Heath
Roath Park
Roath
Tremorfa
Rhiwbina
Blackwood
Newbridge
Pontllanfraith
Cwmfelinfach
Crosskeys
Risca
Machen
Glaslwych
Garth
Llanrumney
Marshfield
Castleton
St Brides Wentlooge
Peterstone Wentlooge
Croesyceiliog
CWMBRAN
Abercarn
Cwmcarn
Pontywaun
Pontymister
Rogerstone
Ridgeway
Duffryn
Llanfrechfa
Ponthir
Malpas
Bryn glas
Barrack Julians Hill
Underwood
Caerleon
Langstone
Llanbeder
Coldra
Bettws
Barnard
Ringland
Liswerry
Pillgwenlly
Llanwern
NEWPORT

River Usk
River Rhymney
River Ebbw
River Taff
River Ely

BRISTOL CHANNEL
Mouth of the Severn

Box denotes area covered by central plan

0   3 mls
SCALE

Cardiff

Strategically important to both the Romans and the Normans, Cardiff slipped from prominence in medieval times and remained a quiet market town in a remote area until it was transformed – almost overnight – by the effects of the Industrial Revolution. The valleys of South Wales were a principal source of iron and coal – raw materials which helped to change the shape and course of

the 19th-century world. Cardiff became a teeming export centre; by the end of the 19th century it was the largest coal-exporting city in the world.

Close to the castle – an exciting place with features from Roman times to the 19th century – is the city's civic centre – a fine concourse of buildings dating largely from the early part of the 20th century. Among them is the National Museum of Wales – a superb collection of art and antiquities from Wales and around the world.

Barry has sandy beaches, landscaped gardens and parks, entertainment arcades and funfairs. Like Cardiff it grew as a result of the demand for coal and steel, but now its dock complex is involved in the petrochemical and oil industries.

Caerphilly is famous for two things – a castle and cheese. The cheese is no longer made here, but the 13th-century castle, slighted by Cromwell, still looms above its moat. No castle in Britain – except Windsor – is larger.

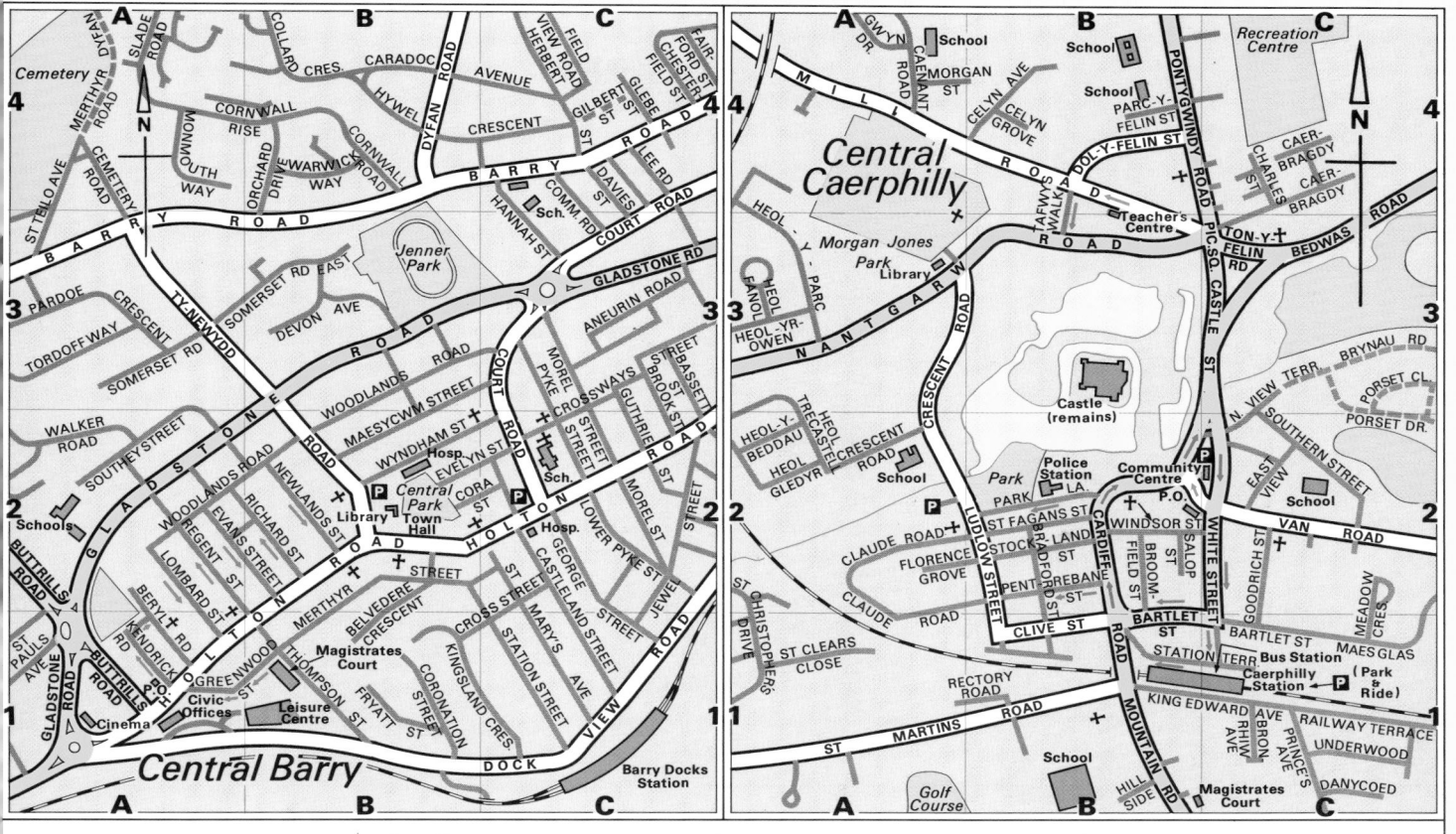

LEGEND

Town Plan
AA recommended route
Restricted roads
Other roads
Buildings of interest   Cinema ▪
Car parks   P
Parks and open spaces
One way streets

Area Plan
A roads
B roads
Locations   Glyncoch ○
Urban area

Street Index with Grid Reference

Cardiff

Adam Street	E1-E2-F2
Bedford Street	F4
Boulevard de Nantes	C3-D3
Bridge Street	D1-D2-E2
Brook Street	B2
Bute Street	D1-E1
Bute Terrace	D1-E1
Caroline Street	D1
Castle Street	C2
Cathedral Street	A4-A3-B3-B2-A2
Charles Street	D2-E2
Churchill Way	E2-E3
City Hall Road	C3-C4-D4
City Road	F4
Clare Street	B1
Coldstream Terrace	B2
College Road	C4
Cowbridge Road	A2
Cowbridge Road East	A2-B2-C2
Craddock Street	A1-B1
Crichton Street	D1
Custom House Street	D1
David Street	E2
Despenser Place	B1
Despenser Street	B1
Duke Street	C2-D2
Dumfries Lane	D3-E3
Dumfries Place	E3
East Grove	F4-F3
East Moor Road	F1
Fitzalan Place	F3-F2
Fitzhamon Embankment	B1-C1
Glossop Road	F3
Gloucester Street	B1
Green Street	B2
Greyfriars Road	D3
Hamilton Street	A3
Herbert Street	E1
High Street	C2-D2
King Edward VII Avenue	C4-D4-D3-C3
King's Road	A2-A3
Kingsway	C3-D3-D2
Knox Road	E3-F3-F2
Lewis Street	A2
Lower Cathedral Road	B1-B2
Machen Place	A1-B1
Mary Ann Street	E1-E2
Mill Lane	D1
Moira Place	F3
Moira Terrace	F2-F3
Museum Avenue	C4-D4
Museum Place	D4
Neville Street	A2-B2-B1
Newport Road	E3-F3-F4
Ninian Park Road	A1-B1
North Lutton Place	F2-F3
North Road	B4-C4-C3
Oxford Lane	F4
Park Grove	D4-E4
Park Lane	D3-E3
Park Place	D4-D3-E3
Park Street	C1-D1
Plantagenet Street	B1-C1
Queen Street	D2-D3
Richmond Road	E4
Richmond Terrace	E4
St Andrew's Place	D4-E4
St John Street	D2
St Mary's Street	D1-D2
St Peter's Street	E4-F4
Salisbury Road	E4
Senghenydd Road	D4-E4
South Lutton Place	F2-F3
Station Terrace	E2-E3
The Friary	D2-D3
The Hayes	D1-D2
The Parade	E3-F3-F4
The Walk	E3-E4-F4
Talbot Street	A3
Tudor Street	B1-C1
Tyndall Street	E1-F1
Wellington Street	A2
Wells Street	A1
Westgate Street	C2-D2-D1
West Grove	E4-E3-F3
Wharton Street	D2
Windsor Place	E3
Windsor Road	F2
Wood Street	C1-D1
Working Street	D2
Wyndham Place	A2
Wyndham Street	A1-A2

Barry

Aneurin Road	C3
Barry Road	A3-A4-B3-B4-C4
Bassett Street	C2-C3
Belvedere Crescent	B1-B2
Beryl Road	A1-A2
Brook Street	C2-C3
Buttrills Road	A1-A2
Caradoc Avenue	B4-C4
Castleland Street	C1-C2
Cemetery Road	A3-A4
Chesterfield Street	C4
Collard Crescent	B4
Commercial Road	C3-C4
Cora Street	B2-C2
Cornwall Rise	A3-A4
Cornwall Road	B4
Coronation Street	B1
Cross Street	B1-C1-C2
Crossways Street	C2-C3
Court Road	C2-C3-C4
Davies Street	C3-C4
Devon Avenue	B3
Dock View Road	B1-C1-C2
Dyfan Road	B4
Evans Street	A2-B2
Evelyn Street	B2-C2
Fairford Street	C4
Field View Road	C4
Fryatt Street	B1
George Street	C1-C2
Gilbert Street	C4
Gladstone Road	A1-A2-B2-B3-C3
Glebe Street	C4
Greenwood Street	A1-B1
Guthrie Street	C3-C2
Hannah Street	C4-C3
Herbert Street	C4
Holton Road	A1-B1-B2-C2
Hywell Crescent	B4-C4
Jewel Street	C1-C2
Kendrick Road	A1
Kingsland Crescent	B1-C1
Lee Road	C4
Lombard Street	A1-A2
Lower Pyke Street	C2
Maesycwm Street	B2-B3-C3
Merthyr Dyfan Road	A4
Merthyr Street	B1-B2-C2
Monmouth Way	A4
Morel Street	C2-C3
Newlands Street	B2
Orchard Drive	B3-B4
Pardoe Crescent	A3
Pyke Street	C3-C2
Regent Street	A2-B2
Richard Street	A2-B2
St Mary's Avenue	C1-C2
St Pauls Avenue	A1
St Teilo Avenue	A3-A4
Slade Road	A4
Somerset Road	A3
Somerset Road East	A3-B3
Southey Street	A2-A3
Station Street	C1
Thomson Street	B1
Tordoff Way	A3
Ty-Newydd Road	A3-B3-B2
Walker Road	A2
Warwick Way	B4
Woodlands Road	A2-B2-B3-C3
Wyndham Street	B2-C2

Caerphilly

Bartlet Street	B2-B1-C1
Bedwas Road	C3-C4
Bradford Street	B1-B2
Broomfield Street	B2
Bronrhiw Avenue	C1
Brynau Road	C3
Caenant Road	A4
Caer Bragdy	C4
Cardiff Road	B1-B2
Castle Street	C3
Celyn Avenue	B4
Celyn Grove	B4
Charles Street	C4
Claude Road	A1-A2-B2
Clive Street	B1-B2
Crescent Rod	A2-A3-B3
Danycoed	C1
Dol-y-Felen Street	B4
East View	C2
Florence Grove	A2-B2
Goodrich Street	C1-C2
Gwyn Drive	A4
Heol Fanal	A3
Heol Gledyr	A2
Heol Trecastell	A2-A3
Hillside	B1
Heol-y-Beddau	A2
Heol-yr-Owen	A3
King Edward Avenue	B1-C1
Ludlow Street	A2-B2-B1
Maes Glas	C1
Meadow Crescent	C1-C2
Mill Road	A4-B4-B3
Morgan Street	A4-B4
Mountain Road	B1
Nantgarw Road	A3-B3
North View Terrace	C2-C3
Parc-y-Felin Street	B4
Park Lane	B2
Pentrebone Street	B2
Piccadilly Square	C3
Pontygwindy Road	B4-C4
Porset Close	C3
Porset Drive	C2-C3
Prince's Avenue	C1
Railway Terrace	C1
Rectory Road	A1-B1
St Christopher's Drive	A1-A2
St Clears Close	A1
St Fagans Street	B2
St Martins Road	A1-B1
Salop Street	B2
Southern Street	C2-C3
Station Terrace	B1-C1
Stockland Street	B2
Tafwy Walk	B3-B4
Ton-y-Felin Road	C3
Underwood	C1
Van Road	C2
White Street	C2
Windsor Street	B2

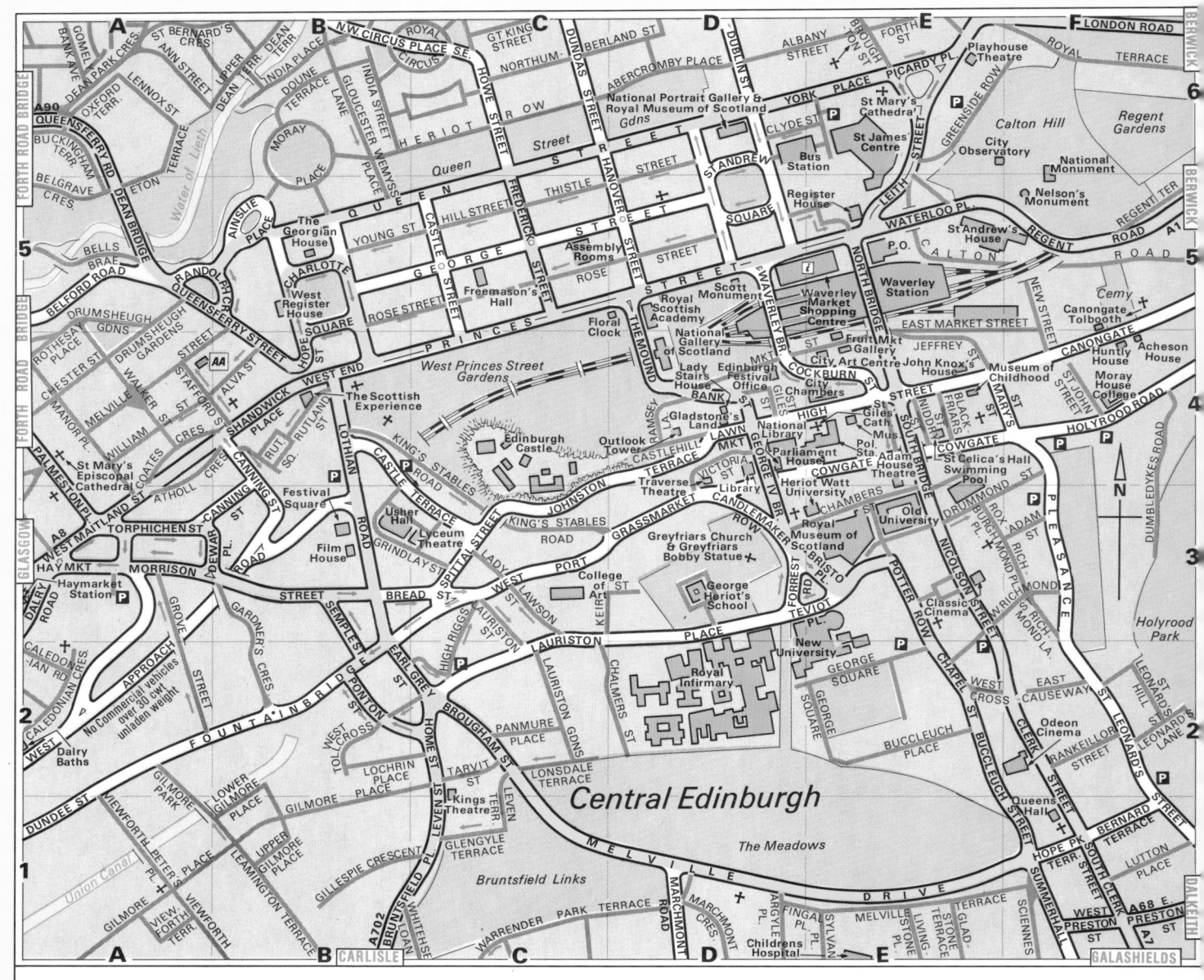

Key to Town Plan and Area Plan

Town Plan
A A Recommended roads ▬▬▬
Other roads ═══
Restricted roads ┅┅
Buildings of interest **Gallery** ▬
Car Parks **P**
Parks and open spaces ▬
A A Service Centre **AA**
Churches ✝

Area Plan
A roads ▬▬▬
B roads ▬▬▬
Locations Newcraighall ○
Urban area ▬

Street Index with Grid Reference

Edinburgh

Edinburgh

Scotland's ancient capital, dubbed the "Athens of the North", is one of the most splendid cities in the whole of Europe. Its buildings, its history and its cultural life give it an international importance which is celebrated every year in its world-famous festival. The whole city is overshadowed by the craggy castle which seems to grow out of the rock itself. There has been a fortress here since the 7th

century and most of the great figures of Scottish history have been associated with it. The old town grew up around the base of Castle Rock within the boundaries of the defensive King's Wall and, unable to spread outwards, grew upwards in a maze of tenements. However, during the 18th century new prosperity from the shipping trade resulted in the building of the New Town and the regular, spacious layout of the Georgian development makes a striking contrast with the old

hotch-potch of streets. Princes Street is the main east-west thoroughfare with excellent shops on one side and Princes Street Gardens with their famous floral clock on the south side.

As befits such a splendid capital city there are numerous museums and art galleries packed with priceless treasures. Among these are the famous picture gallery in 16th-century Holyroodhouse, the present Royal Palace, and the fascinating and unusual Museum of Childhood.

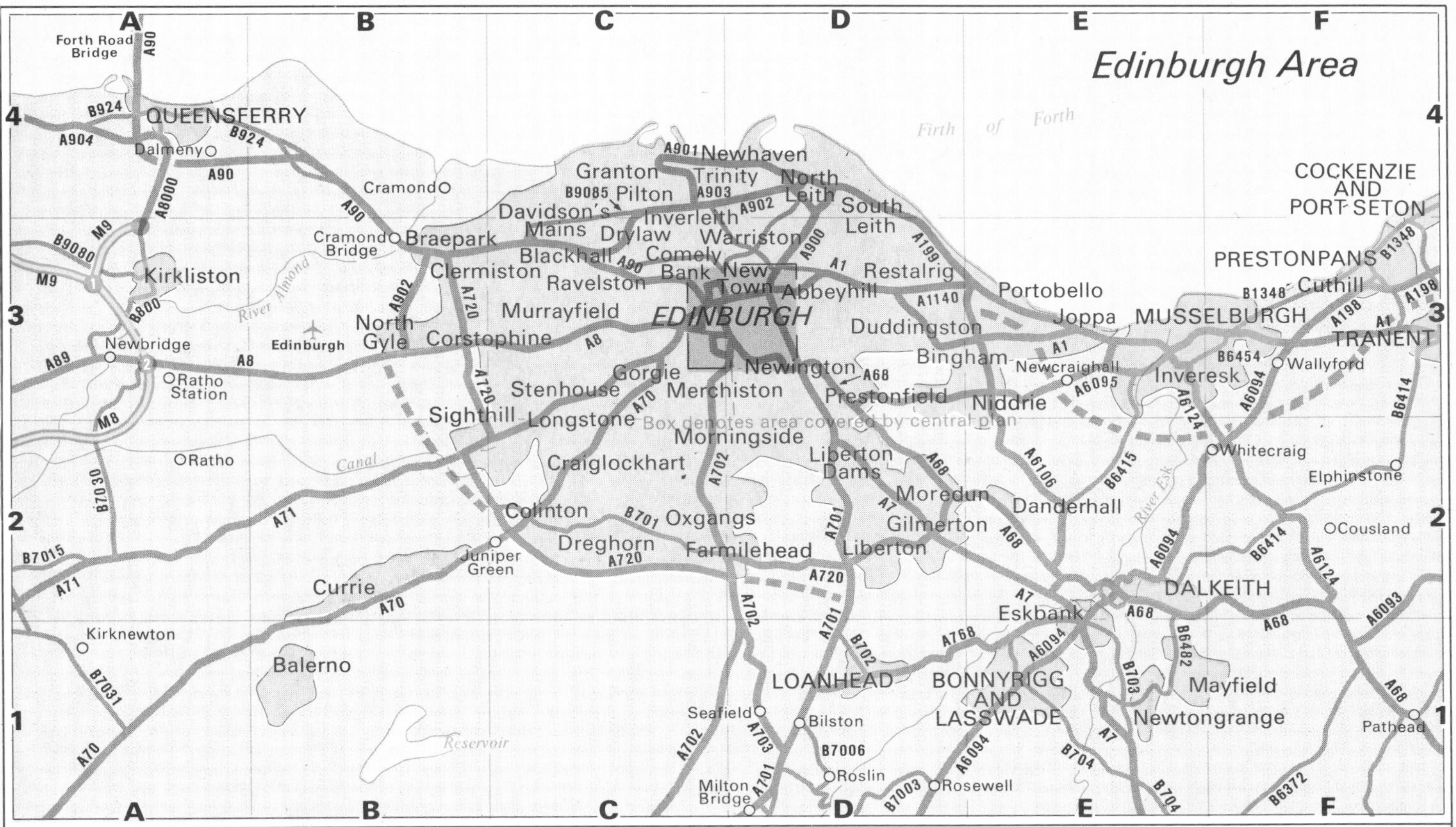

Edinburgh Area

(Map of the Edinburgh area showing grid references A–F horizontally and 1–4 vertically, with place names including Queensferry, Kirkliston, Balerno, Currie, Ratho, Newbridge, Corstorphine, Edinburgh, Portobello, Musselburgh, Tranent, Prestonpans, Cockenzie and Port Seton, Dalkeith, Loanhead, Bonnyrigg and Lasswade, Newtongrange, and numerous roads including A90, A71, A720, A68, A1, etc.)

Earl Grey Street	B2-C2	India Street	B6
East Cross Causeway	F2	Jeffrey Street	E4
East Market Street	E5-E4-F4-F5	Johnston Terrace	C3-C4-D4
East Preston Street	F1	Kier Street	C3-D3
Eton Terrace	A5-A6	King's Stables Road	B4-C4-C3
Fingal Place	D1-E1	Lady Lawson Street	C3
Forrest Road	D3	Lauriston Gardens	C2
Fountain Bridge	A2-B2-B3-C3	Lauriston Place	C2-C3-D3
Frederick Street	C5	Lauriston Street	C2-C3
Forth Street	E6	Lawn Market	D4
Gardeners Crescent	B2-B3	Leamington Terrace	A1-B1
George IV Bridge	D3-D4	Leith Street	E5-E6
George Square	E2	Lennox Street	A6
George Street	B5-C5-D5	Leven Street	C1-C2
Gillespie Crescent	B1-C1	Leven Terrace	C1-C2
Gilmore Park	A1-A2	Livingtone Place	E1
Gilmore Place	A1-B1-B2-C2	Lochrin Place	B2-C2
Gladstone Terrace	E1	London Road	F6
Glengyle Terrace	C1	Lonsdale Terrace	C2
Gloucester Lane	B6	Lothian Road	B3-B4
Grass Market	D3	Lower Gilmore Place	B1-B2
Great King Street	C6	Lutton Place	F1
Greenside Row	E6-F6	Manor Place	A4
Grindley Street	B3-C3	Marchmont Crescent	D1
Grove Street	A2-A3	Marchmont Road	D1
Hanover Street	C6-D6-D5	Market Street	D4-E4
Hay Market	A3	Melville Drive	C2-C1-D1-E1-F1
Heriot Row	B6-C6	Melville Street	A4-B4-B5
High Riggs	C2-C3	Melville Terrace	E1-F1
High Street	D4-E4	Moray Place	B5-B6
Hill Street	C5	Morriston Street	A3-B3
Holyrood Road	F4	New Street	F4-F5
Home Street	C2	Nicolson Street	E3-E2-F2
Hope Park Terrace	F1	Niddry Street	E4
Hope Street	B4	North Bridge	E4-E5
Howe Street	C6	North West Circus Place	B6
India Place	B6	Northumberland Street	C6-D6
Oxford Terrace	A6	South Bridge	E3-E4
Palmerston Place	A3-A4	South Clerk Street	F1
Panmure Place	C2	South East Circus Place	C6
Picardy Place	E6	Spittal Street	C3
Pleasance	F3-F4	Stafford Street	A4-B4
Ponton Street	B2-C2	Summerhall	F1
Potter Row	E2-E3	Sylvan Place	E1
Princes Street	B4-C4-C5-D5-E5	The Mound	D4-D5
Queen Street	B5-C5-C6-D6	Tarvit Street	C2
Queensferry Road	A5-A6	Teviot Place	D3-E3
Queensferry Street	A5-B5-B4	Thistle Street	C5-D5-D6
Ramsey Lane	D4	Torphichen Street	A3
Randolph Crescent	A5-B5	Upper Dean Terrace	B6
Rankeillor Street	F2	Upper Gilmore Place	B1
Regent Road	E5-F5	Victoria Street	D4
Regent Terrace	F5	Viewforth	A1-B1
Richmond Lane	F2-F3	Viewforth Terrace	A1
Richmond Place	E3-F3	Walker Street	A4-A5
Rose Street	B5-C5-D5	Warrender Park Terrace	C1-D1
Rothesay Place	A4-A5	Waterloo Place	E5
Roxbury Place	E3	Waverley Bridge	D4-D5
Royal Circus	B6-C6	Wemyss Place	B5-B6
Royal Terrace	E6-F6	West Approach Road	A2-A3-B3
Rutland Square	B4	West Cross-Causeway	E2
Rutland Street	B4	West End	B4
St Andrew Square	D5-D6	West Maitland Street	A3-A4
St Bernard's Crescent	A6-B6	West Port	C3
St Giles Street	D4	West Preston Street	F1
St John Street	F4	West Richmond Street	E3-F3
St Leonards Hill	F2	West Tollcross	B2
St Leonards Lane	F2	Whitehouse Loan	B1-C1
St Leonard's Street	F1-F2	William Street	A4
St Mary's Street	E4-F4	York Place	D6-E6
St Peter Place	A1	Young Street	B5-C5
Sciennes	F1		
Semples Street	B2-B3		
Shandwick Place	B4		

EDINBURGH
Holyrood Palace orginated as a guest house for the Abbey of Holyrood in the 16th century, but most of the present building was built for Charles II. Mary Queen of Scots was one of its most famous inhabitants.

Glasgow

Although much of Glasgow is distinctly Victorian in character, its roots go back very many centuries. Best link with the past is the cathedral; founded in the 6th century, it has features from many succeeding centuries, including an exceptional 13th- century crypt. Nearby is Provand's Lordship, the city's oldest house. It dates from 1471 and is now a museum. Two much larger museums are to

be found a little out of the centre – the Art Gallery and Museum contains one of the finest collections of paintings in Britain, while the Hunterian Museum, attached to the University, covers geology, archaeology, ethnography and more general subjects. On Glasgow Green is People's Palace – a museum of city life. Most imposing of the Victorian buildings are the City Chambers and City Hall which was built in 1841 as a concert hall but now houses the Scottish National Orchestra.

Paisley is famous for the lovely fabric pattern to which it gives its name. It was taken from fabrics brought from the Near East in the early 19th century, and its manufacture, along with the production of thread, is still important.

Greenock has been an important port and shipbuilding centre since as early as the 16th century. Its most famous son is James Watt, the inventor of steam power, born here in 1736. The town has numerous memorials to the great man.

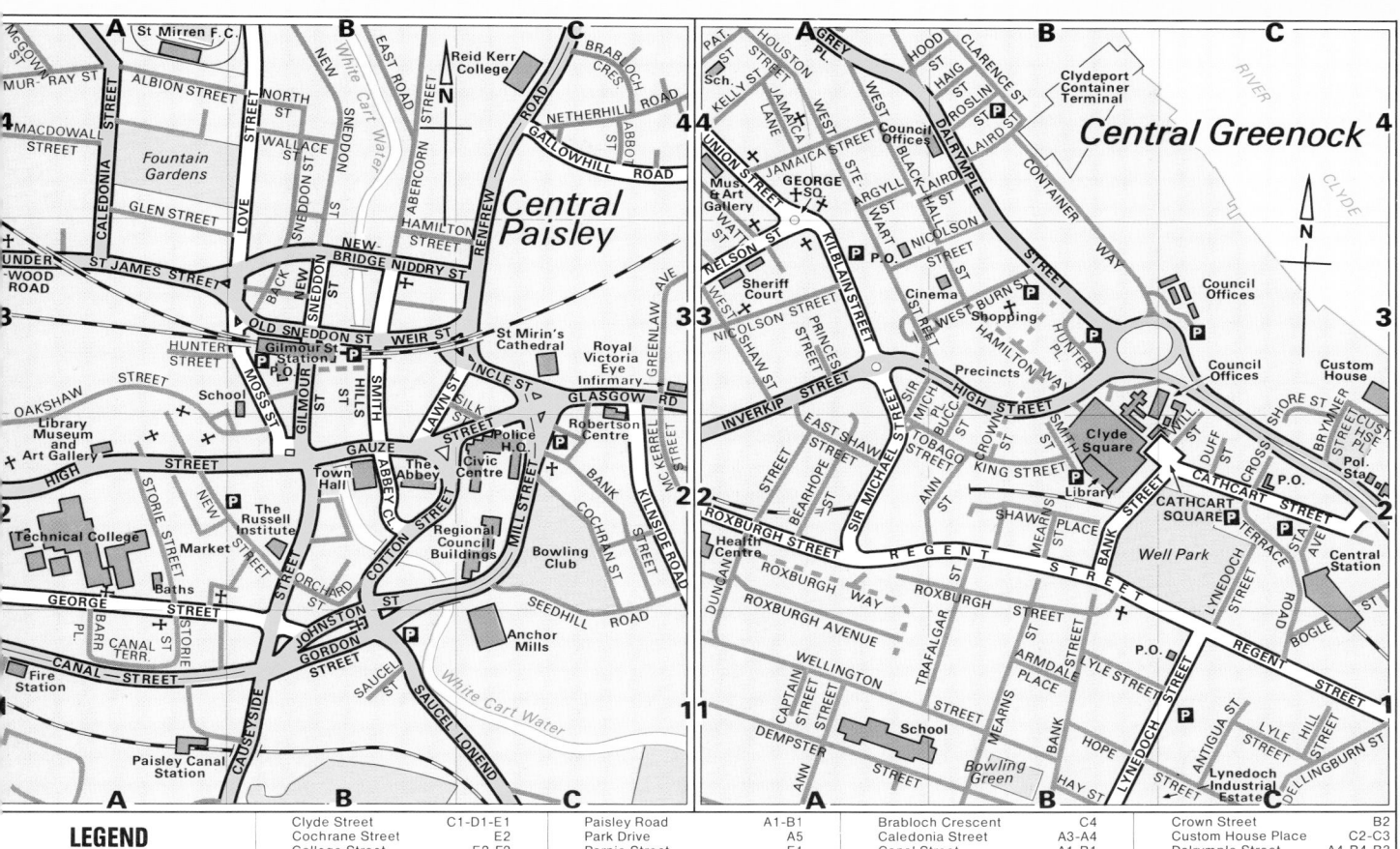

St Mirren F.C.

Central Paisley

Central Greenock

LEGEND

Town Plan
AA recommended route
Restricted roads
Other roads
Buildings of interest — Station
Car parks — P
Parks and open spaces
One way streets

Area Plan
A roads
B roads
Locations — Garvock ○
Urban area

Street Index with grid reference

Glasgow

Albion Street	E1-E2
Anderston Quay	A2-A1-B1
Argyle Arcade	D2
Argyle Street	A3-A2-B2-C2-D2-D1-E1
Arlington Street	A5
Ashley Street	A5
Baird Street	E4-E5-F5-F4
Bath Street	B4-C4-C3-D3
Bell Street	E2-E1-F1
Berkeley Street	A4
Blythswood Square	B3-C3
Blythswood Street	C2-C3
Bothwell Street	B3-C3-C2
Bridgegate	D1-E1
Bridge Street	C1
Broomielaw	B1-C1
Brown Street	B1-B2
Brunswick Street	E2
Buccleuch Street	B4-C4
Buchannan Street	D3-D4
Cadogan Street	B2-C2
Calgary Street	E4-E5-E4
Canal Street	D5-E5
Candleriggs	E1-E2
Cambridge Street	C4
Carlton Place	C1-D1
Carnarvon Street	A5-B5
Carrick Street	B1-B2
Castle Street	F3
Cathedral Street	D3-E3-F3
Cheapside Street	A1-A2
Clyde Place	B1-C1

Clyde Street	C1-D1-E1
Cochrane Street	E2
College Street	E2-F2
Collins Street	F3
Commerce Street	C1
Cowcaddens Road	C4-D4-E4
Craighall Road	C5-D5
Dalhousie Street	C4
Dobbies Loan	C5-D5-E5-E4-D4
Dobbies Loan Place	E4
Douglas Street	B3-C3
Duke Street	F2
Dunblane Street	D4-D5
Dundas Street	D3
Dundasvale Road	C4-D4
Elderslie Street	A3-A4
Elmbank Street	B3-B4
Gallowgate	E1-F1
Garscube Road	C4-C5
Garnet Street	B4
George V Bridge	C1
George Square	D3-E3-E2-D2
George Street	E3-E2-F2
Glasgow Bridge	C1
Glassford Street	E2
Glebe Court	F4
Glenmavis Street	C5-C4-D4
Grafton Place	E3
Grant Street	A5-B5
Granville Street	A3-A4
Great Dovenhill	F1
Great Western Road	A5-B5
High Street	E1-E2-F2-F3
Hill Street	B4-C4
Holland Street	B3-B4
Holm Street	C2
Hope Street	C2-C3-C4-D4
Howard Street	C1-D1
Hutcheson Street	E1-E2
Hyde Park Street	A1-A2
Ingram Street	D2-E2-F2
Jamaica Street	C1-C2-D2
James Watt Street	B1-B2-C2
John Street	E3
Kennedy Street	E4-F4
Kent Road	A3-A4
Kent Street	F1
King Street	E1
Kingston Bridge	B1
Kingston Street	B1-C1
Kyle Street	E4
Lancefield Street	A1-A2
Lister Street	F4
London Road	E1-F1
Lyndoch Place	A5
Lyndoch Street	A4-A5
McAlpine Street	B1-B2
McAslin Court	B4
Maitland Street	C5-D5-D4
Maryhill Road	B5
Maxwell Street	D1-D2
Miller Street	D2
Milton Street	D4-D5
Mitchell Street	D2
Moncur Street	F1
Montrose Street	E2-E3
North Street	A3-A4
North Frederick Street	E3
North Hannover Street	D3-E3-E4
North Wallace Street	E4
Old Wynd	E1
Osborne Street	E1
Oswald Street	C1-C2

Paisley Road	A1-B1
Park Drive	A5
Parnie Street	E1
Pinkston Drive	F5
Pinkston Road	F5
Pitt Street	B2-B3-B4
Port Dundas Road	D4-D5
Queen Street	D2
Renfield Street	D4-D3-C3-C2-D2
Renfrew Street	B4-C4-D4
Richmond Street	E3-E2-F2
Robertson Street	C1-C2
Rose Street	C3-C4
Ross Street	F1
Rottenrow	F3
St Andrew's Square	E1-F1
St Enoch Square	D1-D2
St George's Road	A4-B4-B5
St James Road	E3-F3
St Mungo Avenue	E3-E4-F4
St Vincent Place	D2-D3
St Vincent Street	A3-B3-C3-D3-D2
Saltmarket	E1
Sandyford Place	A4
Sauchiehall Street	A4-B4-C4-C3-D3
Scott Street	B4-C4
Shaftesbury Street	A3
Shamrock Street	B5-C5-C4
Spoutmouth	F1
Springfield Quay	A1
Steel Street	E1
Stirling Road	F3
Stockwell Street	D1-E1
Taylor Place	F4
Taylor Street	F3
Trongate	E1
Turnbull Street	E1
Union Street	C2-D2
Virginia Street	D2-E2
Warroch Street	A1-A2
Washington Street	B1-B2
Waterloo Street	B2-C2
Weaver Street	F3
Wellington Street	C2-C3
West Street	B1
West Campbell Street	C2-C3
West George Street	B3-C3-D3
West Graham Street	B5-C5-C4
West Nile Street	D3-D4
West Prince's Street	A5-B5
West Regent Street	B3-C3-D3
Westend Park Street	A5
Windmill Croft Quay	B1
Woodlands Road	A4-A5
Woodside Place	A4
Woodside Terrace	A4
York Street	C1-C2

Paisley

Abbey Close	B2
Abbot Street	C4
Abercorn Street	B3-B4
Albion Street	A4-B4
Back Sneddon Street	B3-B4
Bank Street	C2
Barr Place	A1

Brabloch Crescent	C4
Caledonia Street	A3-A4
Canal Street	A1-B1
Canal Terrace	A1
Causeyside Street	A1-B1-B2
Cochran Street	C2
Cotton Street	B2
East Road	B4
Gallowhill Road	C4
Gauze Street	B2-C2-C3
George Street	A1-B1-B2-A2
Gilmour Street	B2-B3
Glasgow Road	C3
Glen Street	A4-A3-B3
Gordon Street	B1
Greenlaw Avenue	C3
Hamilton Street	B3-C3
High Street	A2-B2
Hunter Street	A3-B3
Incle Street	C3
Johnston Street	B1-B2
Kilnside Road	C2-C3
Lawn Street	B2-B3-C3
Love Street	B3-B4
Macdowall Street	A4
McGown Street	A4
McKerrel Street	C2-C3
Mill Street	C2
Moss Street	B2-B3
Murray Street	A4
Netherhill Road	C4
Newbridge	B3
New Sneddon Street	B3-B4
New Street	A2-B2
Niddry Street	B3-C3
North Street	B4
Oakshaw Street	A2-A3-B2
Old Sneddon Street	B3
Orchard Street	B2
Renfrew Road	C3-C4
St James Street	A3
Saucel Lonend	B1-C1
Saucel Street	B1
Seedhill Road	C1-C2
Silk Street	B3-C3-C2
Smith Hills Street	B2-B3
Storie Street	A1-A2
Underwood Road	A3
Wallace Street	B4
Weir Street	B3-C3

Greenock

Ann Street	A1
Ann Street	A2-B2
Antigua Street	C1
Argyll Street	A4
Armdale Place	B1
Bank Street	B1-B2-C2
Bearhope Street	A2
Bogle Street	C1-C2
Brymner Street	C2-C3
Buccleugh	B2-B3
Captain Street	A1
Cathcart Square	B2-C2
Cathcart Street	C2
Clarence Street	B4
Container Way	B3-B4
Cross Shore Street	C2-C3

Crown Street	B2
Custom House Place	C2-C3
Dalrymple Street	A4-B4-B3
Dellingburn Street	C1
Dempster Street	A1-B1
Duff Street	C2
Duncan Street	A1-A2
East Shaw Street	A2-A3
George Square	A3-A4
Grey Place	A4
Haig Street	B4
Hamilton Way	B3
Hay Street	B1
High Street	A3-B3-B2
Hill Street	C1
Hood Street	A4-B4
Hope Street	B1-C1
Houston Street	A4
Hunter Place	B3
Inverkip Street	A2-A3
Jamaica Lane	A4
Jamaica Street	A4
Kelly Street	A4
Kilblain Street	A3
King Street	B2
Laird Street	A4-B4
Lyle Street	B1-C1
Lynedoch Street	B1-C1-C2
Mearns Street	B1-B2
Nelson Street	A3
Nicolson Street	A3-B3
Patrick Street	A4
Princes Street	A3
Regent Street	A2-B2-C2-C1
Roslin Street	B2
Roxburgh Avenue	A1-A2
Roxburgh Street	A2-B2-B1
Roxburgh Way	A1-A2
Shaw Place	B2
Sir Michael Place	A2-A3
Sir Michael Street	A2-A3
Smith Street	B2
Station Avenue	C2
Terrace Road	C1-C2
Tobago Street	A2-B2
Trafalgar Street	A1-B1-B2
Union Street	A4
Watt Street	A3-A4
Wellington Street	A1-B1
West Blackhall Street	A4-A3-B3
West Burn Street	A3-B3
West Shaw Street	A3
West Stewart Street	A4-A3-B3
William Street	C2-C3

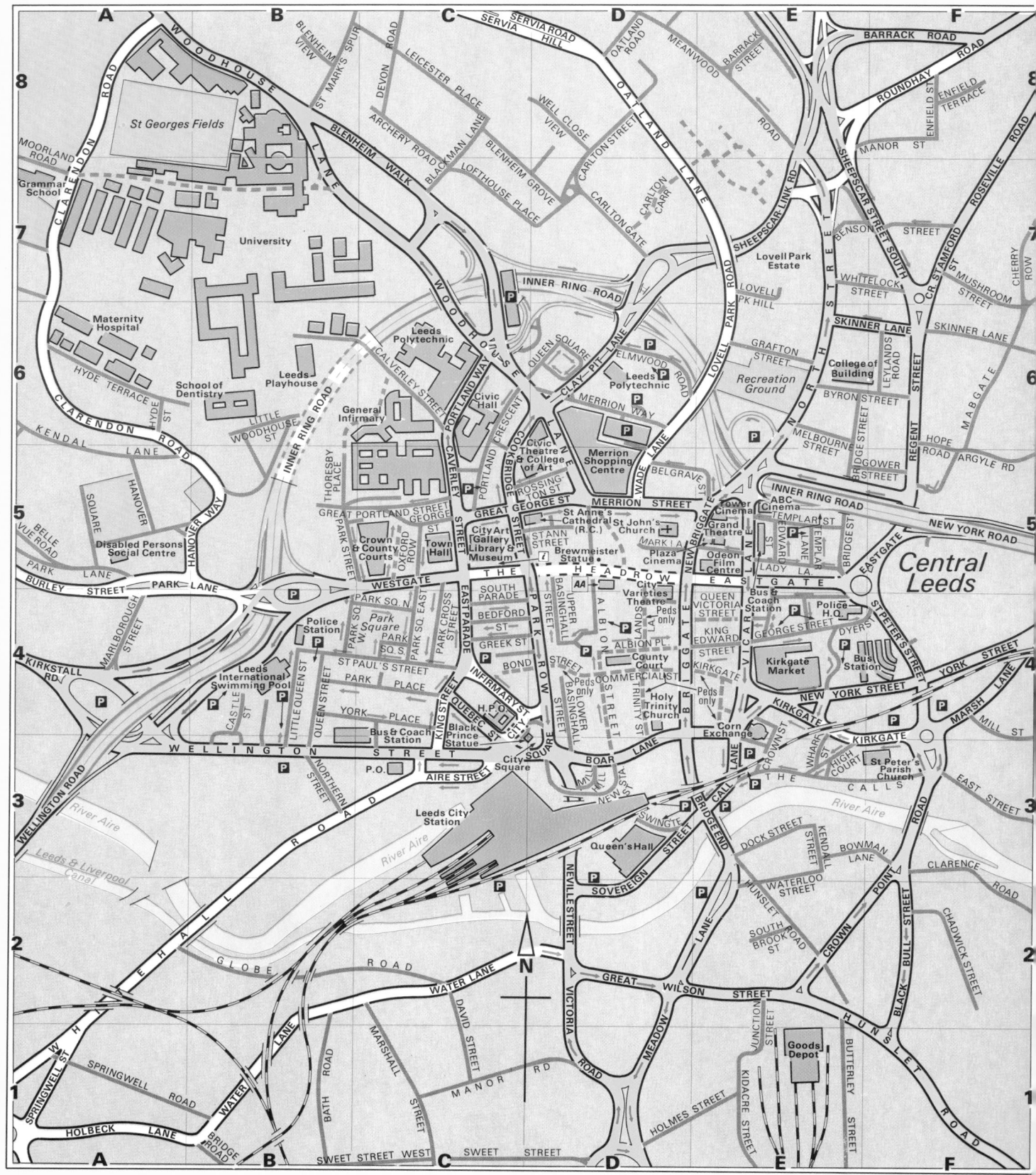

Leeds

In the centre of Leeds is its town hall – a
monumental piece of architecture with a 225ft
clock-tower. It was opened by Queen Victoria in
1858, and has been a kind of mascot for the city
ever since. It exudes civic pride; such buildings
could only have been created in the heyday of
Victorian prosperity and confidence. Leeds' staple
industry has always been the wool trade, but it
only became a boom town towards the end of the
18th century, when textile mills were introduced.
Today, the wool trade and ready-made clothing
(Mr Hepworth and Mr Burton began their work
here) are still important, though industries like
paper, leather, furniture and electrical equipment
are prominent.

Across Calverley Street from the town hall is
the City Art Gallery, Library and Museum. Its
collections include sculpture by Henry Moore, who
was a student at Leeds School of Art. Nearby is the
Headrow, Leeds' foremost shopping thoroughfare.
On it is the City Varieties Theatre, venue for many
years of the famous television programme 'The
Good Old Days'. Off the Headrow are several
shopping arcades, of which Leeds has many
handsome examples. Leeds has a good number of
interesting churches; perhaps the finest is St
John's, unusual in that it dates from 1634, a time
when few churches were built.

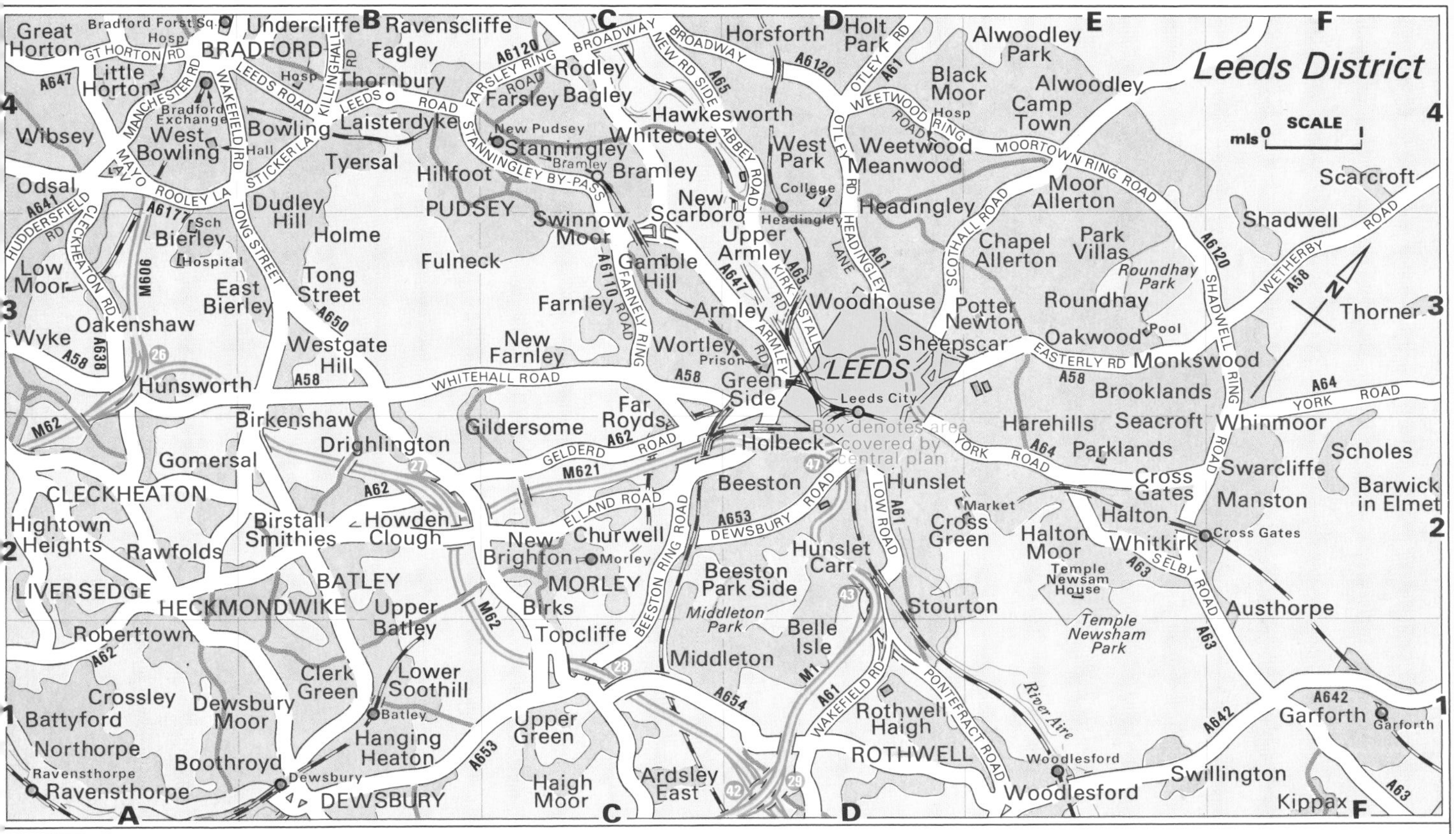

Leeds District

(District map of Leeds and surrounding areas, with SCALE in miles)

LEGEND

Town Plan
AA Recommended roads
Other roads
Restricted roads
Buildings of interset — Museum
AA Service Centre — AA
Parks and open spaces
Car Parks — P
Churches — +
One way streets

District Plan
A roads
B roads
Stations — Kirkgate
Urban area
Buildings of interest — Hospital

Street Index with Grid Reference

Leeds

Street	Grid
Aire Street	C3
Albion Place	D4
Albion Street	D3-D4-D5
Archery Road	C7-C8
Argyle Road	F5
Barrack Road	E8-F8
Barrack Street	E8
Bath Road	B1-B2
Bedford Street	C4
Belgrave Street	D5-E5
Belle Vue Road	A5
Benson Street	E7-F7
Black Bull Street	F1-F2-F3
Blackman Lane	C7-C8
Blenheim Grove	C8-C7-D7
Blenheim View	B8
Blenheim Walk	B8-C8-C7
Boar Lane	D3-D4
Bond Street	C4-D4
Bowman Lane	E3-F3
Bridge End	D3-E3
Bridge Road	B1
Bridge Street	E5-E6
Briggate	D3-D4-D5
Burley Street	A4-A5
Butterley Street	E1-E2
Byron Street	E6-F6
Call Lane	E3
Calverley Street	C5-C6
Carlton Carr	D7
Carlton Gate	D7
Carlton Street	D7-D8
Castle Street	B3-B4
Chadwick Street	F2
Chapeltown Road	E8
Cherry Row	F7
City Square	C3-C4-D4-D3
Clarence Road	F2-F3
Clarendon Road	A8-A7-A6-A5-B5
Clay Pit Lane	D6
Commercial Street	D4
Cookbridge Street	C5-C6-D6
Cross Stamford Street	F6-F7
Crown Street	E3-E4
Crown Point Road	E2-F2-F3
David Street	C1-C2
Devon Road	C8
Dock Street	E3
Dyer Street	E4-F4
East Parade	C4-C5
East Street	F3
Eastgate	E5-F5
Edward Street	E5
Elmwood Road	D6
Enfield Street	F8
Enfield Terrace	F8
George Street	C5
George Street	E4
Globe Road	A2-B2-C2
Gower Street	E5-F5
Grafton Street	E6
Great George Street	C5-D5
Great Portland Street	B5-C5
Great Wilson Street	D2-E2
Greek Street	C4-D4
Hanover Square	A5
Hanover Way	A5-B5
High Court	E3
Holbeck Lane	A1-B1
Holmes Street	D1-E1
Hope Road	F5-F6
Hunslett Road	E3-E2-E1-F1-F2
Hyde Street	A6
Hyde Terrace	A6
Infirmary Street	C4-D4
Inner Ring Road	B5-B6-C6-C7-D7-D6-E6-E5-F5
Junction Street	E1-E2
Kendal Lane	A5-A6
Kendal Street	E3
Kidacre Street	E1
King Street	C3-C4
King Edward Street	D4-E4
Kirkgate	E4-E3-F3-F4
Kirkstall Road	A4
Lady Lane	E5
Lands Lane	D4-D5
Leicester Place	C8
Leylands Road	F6
Lisbon Street	B3-B4
Little Queen Street	B3-B4
Little Woodhouse Street	B6
Lofthouse Place	C7-D7
Lovell Park Hill	E7
Lovell Park Road	D6-E6-E7
Lower Basinghall Street	D3-D4
Mabgate	F6
Manor Road	C1-D1
Manor Street	E8-F8
Mark Lane	D5
Marlborough Street	A4
Marsh Lane	F4
Marshall Street	C1-C2
Meadow Lane	D1-D2-E2-E3
Meanwood Road	D8-E8
Melbourne Street	E6
Merrion Street	D5-E5
Merrion Way	E6
Mill Hill	D3
Mill Street	F4
Moorland Road	A7-A8
Mushroom Street	F6-F7
Neville Street	D2-D3
New Briggate	D5-E5
New Station Street	D3
New York Road	E4-F4
New York Street	E5-E6-E7
North Street	B3
Northern Street	B3
Oatland Lane	D8-D7-E7
Oatland Road	D8
Oxford Row	C5
Park Cross Street	C4-C5
Park Lane	A5-B5-B4
Park Place	B4-C4
Park Row	C4-C5-D5-D4
Park Square East	C4
Park Square North	B4-C4
Park Square South	C4
Park Square West	B4
Park Street	B5-C5
Portland Crescent	C5-C6
Portland Way	C6
Quebec Street	C3-C4
Queen Street	B3-B4
Queen Square	C6-D6
Queen Victoria Street	D4-E4
Regent Street	F5-F6
Roseville Road	F7-F8
Rossington Street	C5-D5
Roundhay Road	E8-F8
St Ann Street	C5-D5
St Mark's Spur	B8-C8
St Paul's Street	B4-C4
St Peter's Street	E4-F4
Servia Hill	C8-D8
Servia Road	C8-D8
Sheepscar Link Road	E7-E8
Sheepscar Street North	E8
Sheepscar Street South	E8-E7-F7
Skinner Lane	E6-F6
South Brook Street	C4
South Parade	C4
Sovereign Street	D2-D3-E3
Springwell Road	A1-B1
Springwell Street	A1
Sweet Street	C1-D1
Sweet Street West	B1-C1
Swinegate	D3
The Calls	E3-F3
The Headrow	C5-D5
Templar Lane	E5
Templar Street	E5
Thoresby Place	B5-B6
Trinity Street	D4
Upper Basinghall Street	D4-D5
Vicar Lane	E4-E5
Victoria Road	D1-D2
Wade Lane	D5-D6
Water Lane	B1-B2-C2-D2
Waterloo Street	E2-E3
Well Close View	D8
Wellington Road	A3
Wellington Street	A3-B3-C3
Westgate	B4-B5-C5-C4
Wharf Street	E3-E4
Whitehall Road	A1-A2-B2-B3-C3
Whitelock Street	E7-F7
Woodhouse Lane	A8-B8-B7-C7-C6-D6-D5
York Place	B4-C4
York Street	F4

LEEDS
Offices now occupy the handsome twin-towered Civic Hall which stands in Calverley Street in front of the new buildings of Leeds Polytechnic. This area of the city – the commercial centre – has been extensively redeveloped

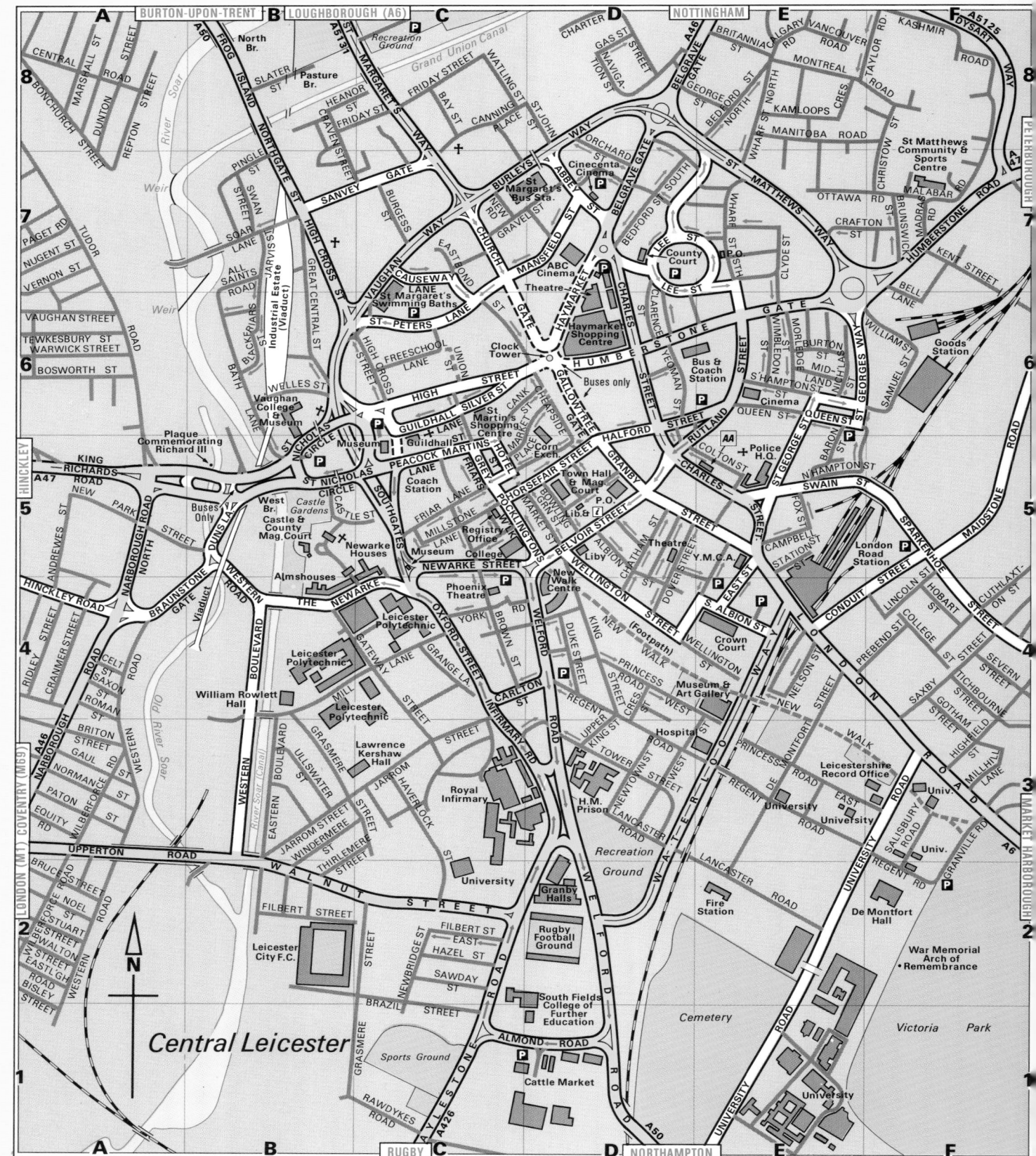

Leicester

A regional capital in Roman times, Leicester has retained many buildings from its eventful and distinguished past. Today the city is a thriving modern place, a centre for industry and commerce, serving much of the Midlands. Among the most outstanding monuments from the past is the Jewry Wall, a great bastion of Roman masonry. Close by are remains of the Roman baths and

several other contemporary buildings. Attached is a museum covering all periods from prehistoric times to 1500. Numerous other museums include the Wygston's House Museum of Costume, with displays covering the period 1769 to 1924; Newarke House, with collections showing changing social conditions in Leicester through four hundred years; and Leicestershire Museum and Art Gallery, with collections of drawings, paintings, ceramics, geology and natural history.

The medieval Guildhall has many features of interest, including a great hall, library and police cells. Leicester's castle, although remodelled in the 17th century, retains a 12th-century great hall. The Church of St Mary de Castro, across the road from the castle, has features going back at least as far as Norman times; while St Nicholas's Church is even older, with Roman and Saxon foundations. St Martin's Cathedral dates mainly from the 13th to 15th centuries and has a notable Bishop's throne.

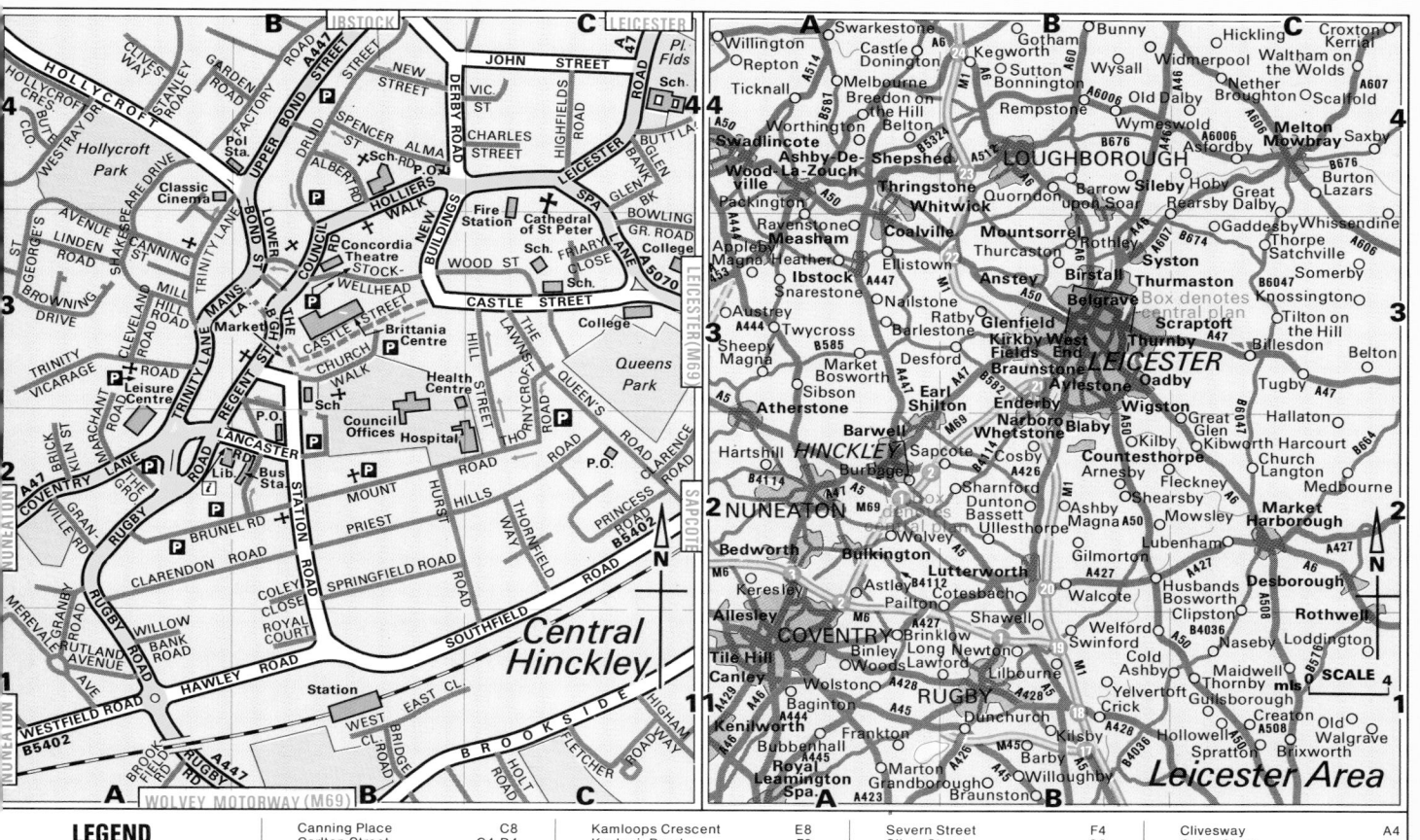

LEGEND

Town Plan

AA Recommended route	
Restricted roads	
Other roads	
Buildings of interest	
Car parks	P
Parks and open spaces	

Area Plan

A roads	
B roads	
Locations	Creaton ○
Urban area	

Street Index with Grid Reference

Leicester

Abbey Street	D7
Albion Street	D4-D5
All Saints Road	B7
Almond Road	C1-D1
Andrewes Street	A4-A5
Aylestone Road	C1-C2
Baron Street	E5-E6
Bath Lane	B5-B6
Bay Street	C8
Bedford Street North	E8
Bedford Street South	D7
Belgrave Gate	D7-D8-E8
Bell Lane	F6-F7
Belvoir Street	D5
Bisley Street	A1-A2
Blackfriars Street	B6
Bonchurch Street	A7-A8
Bosworth Street	A6
Bowling Green Street	D5
Braunstone Gate	A4-B4-B5
Brazil Street	C1-C2
Britannia Street	E8
Briton Street	A3
Brown Street	C4
Bruce Street	A2
Brunswick Street	F7
Burgess Street	C7
Burleys Way	C7-D7-D8
Burton Street	E6
Calgary Road	E8
Campbell Street	E5
Cank Street	C6-D6
Canning Place	C8
Carlton Street	C4-D4
Castle Street	B5-C5
Celt Street	A4
Central Road	A8
Charles Street	D7-D6-D5-E5
Charter Street	D8
Chatham Street	D4-D5
Cheapside	D5-D6
Christow Street	F7-F8
Church Gate	C7-C6-D6
Clarence Street	D6-D7
Clyde Street	E6-E7
College Street	F4
Colton Street	D5-E5
Conduit Street	E4-F4-F5
Crafton Street	E7-F7
Cranmer Street	A4
Craven Street	B7-B8
Crescent Street	D4
Cuthlaxton Street	F4-F5
De Montfort Street	E3-E4
Dover Street	D4-D5
Duke Street	D4
Duns Lane	B5
Dunton Street	A8
Dysart Way	F7-F8
East Bond Street	C6-C7-D6
East Street	E4-E5
Eastern Boulevard	B3-B4
Eastleigh Road	A2
Equity Road	A3
Filbert Street	B2-C2
Filbert Street East	C2
Fox Street	E5
Freeschool Lane	C6
Friar Lane	C5
Friday Street	B8-C8
Frog Island	B8
Gallowtree Gate	D6
Gas Street	D8
Gateway Street	B4-C4-C3
Gaul Street	A3
George Street	D8-E8
Gotham Street	F3-F4
Granby Street	D5-E5
Grange Lane	C4
Granville Road	F2-F3
Grasmere Street	B4-B3-C3-C2-C1-B1
Gravel Street	C7-D7
Great Central Street	B6-B7
Greyfriars	C5
Guildhall Lane	C5
Halford Street	D5-D6-E6
Haverlock Street	C2-C3
Haymarket	D6-D7
Hazel Street	C2
Heanor Street	B8-C8
High Cross Street	B7-B6-C6
Highfield Street	F3
High Street	C6-D6
Hinckley Road	A4
Hobart Street	F4
Horsefair Street	C5-D5
Hotel Street	C5
Humberstone Gate	D6-E6
Humberstone Road	F7
Infirmary Road	C4-C3-D3
Jarrom Street	B3-C3
Jarvis Street	B7
Kamloops Crescent	E8
Kashmir Road	F8
Kent Street	F7
King Richards Road	A5
King Street	D4-D5
Lancaster Road	D3-E3-E2
Lee Street	D6-D7-E7
Lincoln Street	F4-F5
London Road	E5-E4-F4-F3
Madras Road	F7
Maidstone Road	F5-F6
Malabar Road	F7
Manitoba Road	E8-F8
Mansfield Street	C7-D7
Market Place	C5-C6-D6
Market Street	D5
Marshall Street	A8
Midland Street	E6
Mill Hill Lane	F3
Mill Lane	B4-C4
Millstone Lane	C5
Morledge Street	E6
Montreal Road	E8-F8
Narborough Road	B3-A4
Narborough Road North	A4-A5
Navigation Street	D8
Nelson Street	E4
Newarke Street	C5
Newbridge Street	C2
New Park Street	A5-B5
New Road	C7
Newtown Street	D3
New Walk	D4-E4-E3-F3
Nicholas Street	E6
Noel Street	A2
Northampton Street	E5
Northgate Street	B7-B8
Norman Street	A3
Nugent Street	A7
Orchard Street	D7-D8
Ottawa Road	E7-F7
Oxford Street	C4
Paget Road	A7
Paton Street	A3
Peacock Lane	C5
Pingle Street	B7
Pocklingtons Walk	C5-D5
Prebend Street	E4-F4
Princess Road East	E3-F3
Princess Road West	D4-E4
Queen Street	E6
Rawdykes Road	B1-C1
Regent Street	E6
Regent Road	D4-D3-E3-F3-F2
Repton Street	A7-A8
Ridley Street	A4
Roman Street	A4
Rutland Street	D5-E5-E6
St George Street	E5-E6
St Georges Way	E6-F6
St John Street	D8
St Margaret's Way	B8-C8-C7
St Martins	C5
St Mathews Way	E7
St Nicholas Circle	B6-B5-C5
St Peters Lane	C6
Salisbury Road	F2-F3
Samuel Stuart	F6
Sanvey Gate	B7-C7
Sawday Street	C2
Saxby Street	F4
Saxon Street	A4
Severn Street	F4
Silver Street	C6
Slater Street	B8
Soar Lane	B7
South Albion Street	E4
Southampton Street	E6
Southgates	C5
Sparkenhoe Street	F4-F5
Station Street	E5
Stuart Street	A2
Swain Street	E5-F5
Swan Street	B7
The Newarke	B4-C4
Taylor Road	E8-F8
Tewkesbury Street	A6
Thirlemere Street	B2-B3-C3
Tichbourne Street	F3-F4
Tower Street	D3
Tudor Road	A5-A6-A7-A8
Ullswater Street	B3
Union Street	C6
University Road	E1-E2-E3-F3
Upper King Street	D3-D4
Upperton Road	A3-B3-B2
Vancouver Road	E8
Vaughan Way	C6-C7
Vaughan Street	A6
Vernon Street	A6-A7
Walnut Street	B3-B2-C2
Walton Street	A2
Warwick Street	A4
Waterloo Way	D2-D3-E3-E4
Watling Street	C8
Welford Road	D1-D2-D3-D4
Welles Street	B6
Wellington Street	D4-E4-D5
Western Boulevard	B3-B4
Western Road	A1-A2-A3-A4-B4-B5
West Street	D3-E3-E4
Wharf Street North	E7-E8
Wharf Street South	E7
Wilberforce Road	A2-A3
William Street	F6
Wimbledon Street	E6
Windermere Street	B2-B3-C3
Yeoman Street	D6
York Road	C4

Hinckley

Albert Road	B4
Alma Road	B4
Bowling Green Road	C3
Brick Kiln Street	A2
Bridge Road	B1
Brookfield Road	A1
Brookside	B1-C1
Browning Drive	A3
Brunel Road	A2-B2
Bute Close	A4
Butt Lane	C4
Canning Street	A3
Castle Street	B3-C3
Charles Street	C4
Church Walk	B3
Clarence Road	C2
Clarendon Road	A2-B2
Cleveland Road	A3
Clivesway	A4
Coley Close	B2
Council Road	B3
Coventry Lane	A2
Derby Road	B4
Druid Street	B3-B4
East Close	B1-C1
Factory Road	A4-B4
Fletcher Road	C1
Friary Close	C3
Garden Road	A4-B4
Glen Bank	C4
Granby Road	A1-A2
Granville Road	A2
Hawley Road	A1-B1
Higham Way	C1
Highfields Road	C4
Hill Street	C2-C3
Holliers Walk	B3-B4
Hollycroft	A4
Hollycroft Crescent	A4
Holt Road	C1
Hurst Road	B2-C1-C2
John Street	C4
Lancaster Road	A2-B2
Leicester Road	C4
Linden Road	A3
Lower Bond Street	B3-B4
Mansion Lane	A3-B3
Marchant Road	A2-A3
Merevale Avenue	A1
Mill Hill Road	A3
Mount Road	B2-C2
New Buildings	B3-B4
New Street	B4
Priest Hills Road	B2-C2
Princess Road	C2
Queens Road	C2-C3
Regent Street	A2-B2-A3-A3
Royal Court	B1
Rugby Road	A2-A1-B1
Rutland Avenue	A1
St George's Avenue	A3-A4
Shakespeare Drive	A3-A4
Southfield Road	B1-C1-C2
Spa Lane	C3-C4
Spencer Street	B4
Springfield Road	B2
Stanley Road	A4
Station Road	B1-B2
Stockwellhead	B3
The Borough	B3
The Grove	A2
The Lawns	C3
Thornfield Way	C2
Thornycroft Road	C2-C3
Trinity Lane	A2-A3-A4-B4
Trinity Vicarage Road	A3
Upper Bond Street	B4
Victoria Street	C4
West Close	B1
Westray Drive	A4
Westfield Road	A1
Willow Bank Road	A1
Wood Street	B3-C3

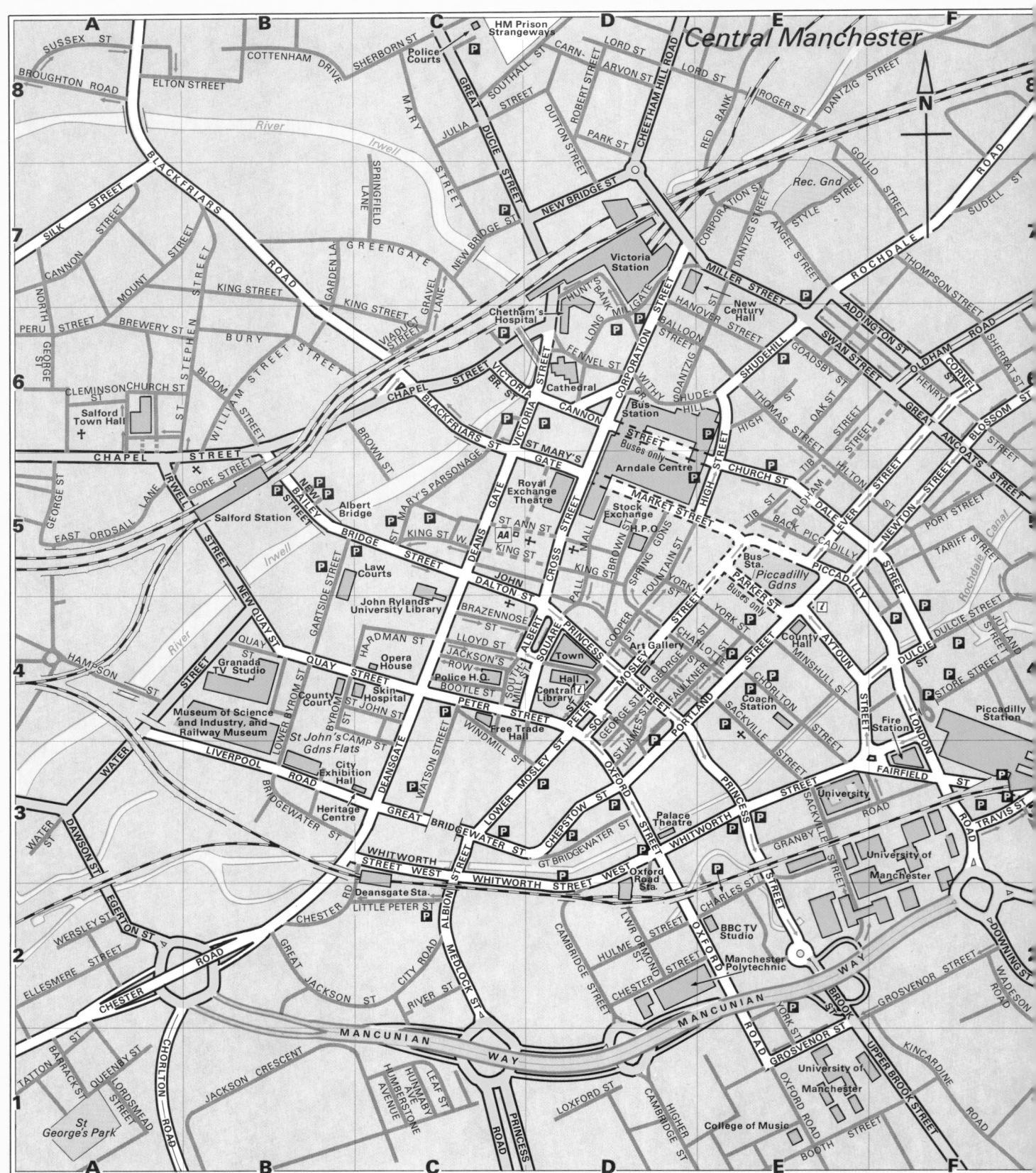

Manchester

The gigantic conurbation called Greater Manchester covers a staggering 60 square miles, reinforcing Manchester's claim to be Britain's second city. Commerce and industry are vital aspects of the city's character, but it is also an important cultural centre – the Halle Orchestra has its home at the Free Trade Hall (a venue for many concerts besides classical music), there are several theatres, a library (the John Rylands) which houses one of the most important collections of books in the world, and a number of museums and galleries, including the Whitworth Gallery with its lovely watercolours.

Like many great cities it suffered badly during the bombing raids of World War II, but some older buildings remain, including the town hall, a huge building designed in Gothic style by Alfred Waterhouse and opened in 1877. Manchester Cathedral dates mainly from the 15th century and is noted for its fine tower and outstanding carved woodwork. Nearby is Chetham's Hospital, also 15th-century and now housing a music school. Much new development has taken place, and more is planned. Shopping precincts cater for the vast population, and huge hotels have provided services up to international standards. On the edge of the city is the Belle Vue centre, a large entertainments complex including concert and exhibition facilities, and a speedway stadium.

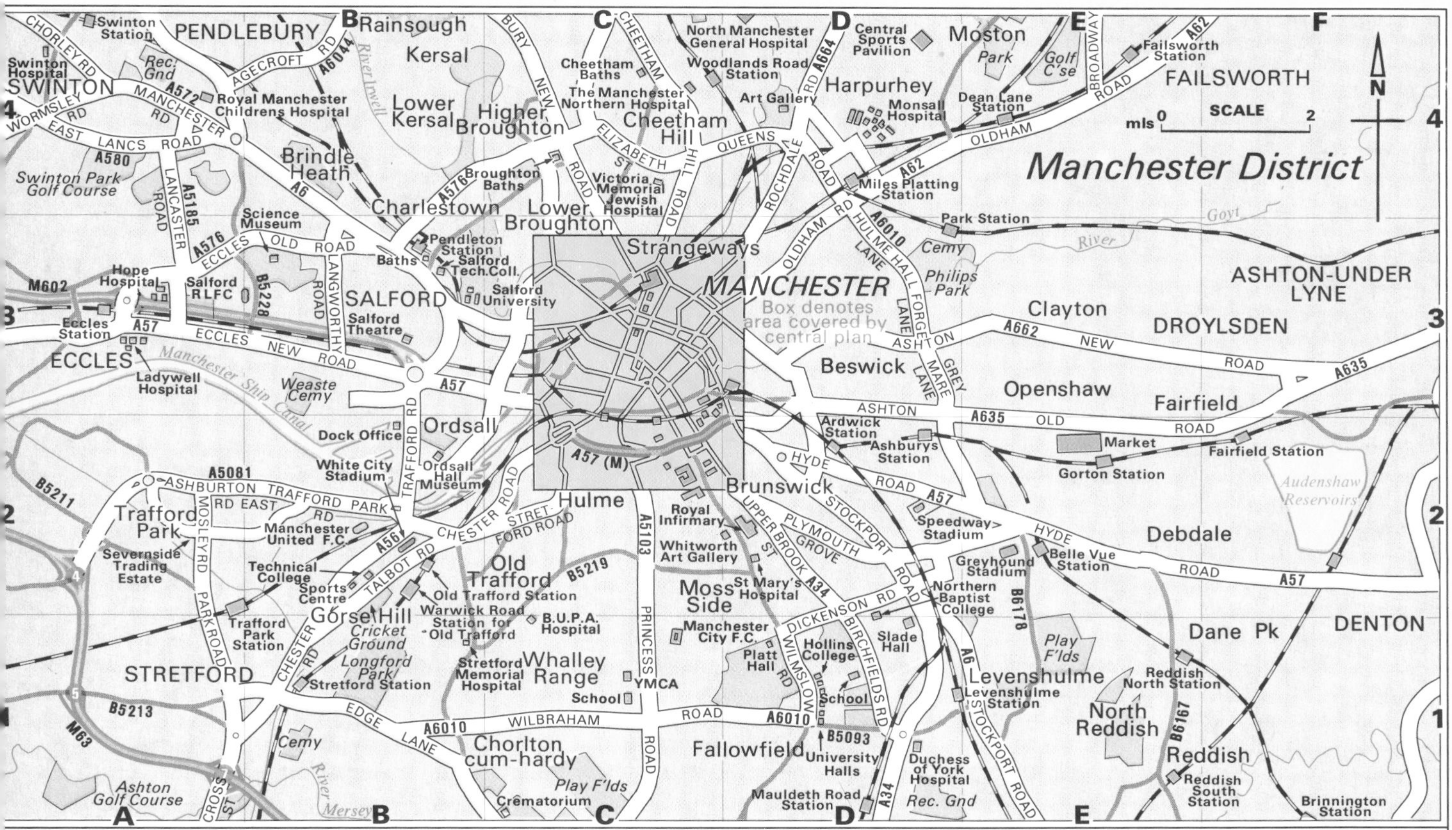

Manchester District Map

Map labels (geographic):

PENDLEBURY · Swinton Station · Rainsough · Kersal · North Manchester General Hospital · Woodlands Road Station · Central Sports Pavilion · Moston Park · Golf C'se · Failsworth Station

Swinton Hospital · Rec. Gnd · Agecroft · Lower Kersal · Higher Broughton · Cheetham Baths · The Manchester Northern Hospital · Art Gallery · Harpurhey · Dean Lane Station · Monsall Hospital · FAILSWORTH

SWINTON · Wormsley Rd · East Lancs Road · Royal Manchester Childrens Hospital · Brindle Heath · Charlestown · Cheetham Hill · Queens · Miles Platting Station · *Manchester District* · SCALE mls 0 .. 2 · N

Swinton Park Golf Course · Science Museum · Baths · Pendleton Station · Salford Tech. Coll. · Salford University · Victoria Memorial Jewish Hospital · Lower Broughton · Strangeways · *MANCHESTER* · Park Station · Cemy · ASHTON-UNDER-LYNE

Hope Hospital · Eccles Station · Salford RLFC · Salford Theatre · SALFORD · Box denotes area covered by central plan · Philips Park · Clayton · DROYLSDEN

ECCLES · M602 · Ladywell Hospital · Weaste Cemy · Dock Office · Ordsall · Ordsall Hall Museum · White City Stadium · A57(M) · Strangeways · Beswick · Openshaw · Fairfield · Market · Fairfield Station

Trafford Park · Ashburton Trafford Park Rd East · Manchester United F.C. · Technical College · Sports Centre · Hulme · Royal Infirmary · Whitworth Art Gallery · Upper Brook St · Plymouth Grove · Ardwick Station · Ashburys Station · Gorton Station · Debdale · Audenshaw Reservoirs

Severnside Trading Estate · Trafford Park Station · Gorse Hill · Old Trafford · Old Trafford Station · Warwick Road Station for Old Trafford · B.U.P.A. Hospital · Moss Side · St Mary's Hospital · Manchester City F.C. · Platt Hall · Hollins College · Slade Hall · Northern Baptist College · Greyhound Stadium · Belle Vue Station · Speedway Stadium · Dane Pk · DENTON

STRETFORD · Longford Park · Stretford Station · Cricket Ground · Stretford Memorial Hospital · Whalley Range · School · YMCA · School · Levenshulme · Levenshulme Station · North Reddish · Reddish North Station

Ashton Golf Course · Cemy · Chorlton cum-hardy · Play F'lds · Crematorium · Wilbraham Road · Fallowfield · University Halls · Mauldeth Road Station · Duchess of York Hospital · Rec. Gnd · Reddish · Reddish South Station · Brinnington Station

MANCHESTER
The Barton Swing Bridge carries the Bridgewater Canal over the Manchester Ship Canal, which links Manchester with the sea nearly 40 miles away. Completed in 1894, the canal is navigable by vessels up to 15,000 tons.

INDEX TO ATLAS

This index contains over 25,000 entries.
All towns and large villages are included, as are locally important settlements.

To locate a place in the atlas, first look up the name of the town or village required in the index. Turn to the page number indicated in *italic* type, and find the location using the last four numbers. Taking **Hythe (Kent)** . . . . . *29* **TR 1635** as our example, take the first figure of the reference, 1, which refers to the number along the bottom of the page. The second figure, 6, tells you the distance to move in tenths to the right of this numbered line. A vertical line through this point is the first half of the reference. The third figure, 3, refers to the number on the lefthand side of the page. Finally, the fourth figure, 5, indicates the distance to move in tenths above this numbered line. A horizontal line drawn through this point to intersect with the first line gives the precise location of the place in question. (For an explanation of the double letters, ie TR, in the reference, see the national grid page.)

Street plans of towns included within the index on the pages shown:

212

Aughton (Lancs.) Barton St. David

Aughton (Lancs.) 82 SD 3804
Aughton (Lancs.) 89 SD 5467
Aughton (S Yorks.) 78 SK 4586
Aughton (Wilts.) 23 SU 2356
Aughton Park 82 SD 4106
Auldearn 148 NH 9155
Aulden 47 SO 4654
Auldgirth 107 NX 9287
Auldhame 127 NT 5984
Auldhouse 115 NS 6250
Ault-a-Chruinn 146 NG 9420
Aultbea 152 NG 8789
Aultgowrie 146 NH 4852
Aultgrishan 152 NG 7485
Aultguish Inn 152 NH 3571
Aultiphurst 158 NC 8065
Aultmore (Grampn.) 150 NJ 4053
Aultnagoire 147 NH 5423
Aultnamain Inn 153 NH 6782
Aulton 150 NJ 6028
Aundorach 141 NH 9716
Aunk 9 ST 0400
Aunsby 67 TF 0438
Auquhorthies 151 NJ 8329
Aust 35 ST 5789
Austerfield 79 SK 6594
Austonley 84 SE 1207
Austrey 65 SK 2906
Authorpe 81 TF 4080
Authorpe Row 81 TF 5373
Avebury 23 SU 0969
Aveley 27 TQ 5680
Avening 36 ST 8797
Averham 79 SK 7654
Aveton Gifford 6 SX 6947
Avielochan 140 NH 9016
Aviemore 140 NH 8912
Avington 24 SU 3767
Avoch 148 NH 6955
Avon 12 SZ 1498
Avon Dassett 54 SP 4150
Avonbridge 126 NS 9072
Avonmouth 35 ST 5177
Avonwick 6 SX 7158
Awbridge 13 SU 3323
Awkley 35 ST 5885
Awliscombe 9 ST 1301
Awre 36 SO 7008
Awsworth 78 SK 4843
Axbridge 21 ST 4254
Axford (Hants.) 24 SU 6043
Axford (Wilts.) 23 SU 2369
Axminster 9 SY 2998
Axmouth 9 SY 2591
Aycliffe 97 NZ 2822
Aylburton 35 SO 6101
Aylburton Common 35 SO 6002
Ayle 96 NY 7149
Aylesbeare 9 SY 0391
Aylesbury 39 SP 8213
Aylesby 87 TA 2007
Aylescott 8 SS 6116
Aylesford 28 TQ 7359
Aylesham 29 TR 2352
Aylestone 66 SK 5701
Aylmerton 71 TG 1839
Aylsham 71 TG 1926
Aylton 52 SO 6537
Aymestrey 51 SO 4265
Aynho 38 SP 5133
Ayot St. Lawrence 40 TL 1916
Ayot St. Peter 40 TL 2115
Ayr 106 NS 3321
Aysgarth 90 SE 0088
Ayside 89 SD 3983
Ayston 67 SK 8601
Aythorpe Roding 41 TL 5815
Ayton (Berwick.) 119 NT 9260
Ayton (N Yorks.) 93 SE 9884
Azerley 91 SE 2574

B

Babbacombe 7 SX 9265
Babbinswood 63 SJ 3329
Babbs Green 41 TL 3916
Babcary 21 ST 5628
Babel 45 SN 8235
Babell 74 SJ 1574
Babeny 6 SX 6774
Babicaul 144 NG 7628
Babraham 57 TL 5150
Babworth 79 SK 6880
Bachau 72 SH 4383
Back 163 NB 4840
Back of Keppoch 137 NM 6587
Backaland 163 HY 5630
Backbarrow 89 SD 3584
Backfolds 151 NK 0353
Backford 75 SJ 3971
Backhill 151 NJ 7840
Backhill of Clackriach 151 NJ 9347
Backhill of Trustach 142 NO 6397
Backies 155 NC 8302
Backlass 159 ND 2254
Backmuir of New Gilston 127 NO 4308
Backwell 21 ST 4868
Backworth 105 NZ 2972
Bacon End 42 TL 6018
Baconsthorpe 70 TG 1237
Bacton (Here & W) 47 SO 3732
Bacton (Norf.) 71 TG 3434
Bacton (Suff.) 58 TM 0466
Bacup 83 SD 8622
Badachro 152 NG 7873
Badavanich 146 NH 1258
Badbury 37 SU 1980
Badby 54 SP 5559
Badcall (Highld.) 156 NC 1541
Badcall (Highld.) 156 NC 2355
Badcaul 152 NH 0191
Baddeley Green 76 SJ 9250
Baddesley Clinton 53 SP 2172
Baddesley Ensor 65 SP 2798
Baddidarach 156 NC 0923
Badenscoth 150 NJ 7038
Badenyon 149 NJ 3419
Badger 64 SO 7699
Badgers Mount 27 TQ 4962
Badgeworth (Glos.) 36 SO 9019
Badgworth (Somer.) 21 ST 3952
Badibster 159 ND 2549
Badicaul 144 NG 7628
Badingham 59 TM 3067
Badlesmere 28 TR 0154
Badluarach 152 NG 9994
Badminton 36 ST 8082
Badninsh 155 NH 7695
Badrallach 153 NH 0691
Badsey 53 SP 0743
Badshot Lea 25 SU 8648
Badsworth 85 SE 4614
Badwell Ash 58 TL 9969
Bagby 91 SE 4680
Bage, The 47 SO 3243
Bagendon 37 SP 0006
Bagginswood 52 SO 6881
Bagillt 74 SJ 2175
Baginton 53 SP 3474
Baglan 33 SS 7493
Bagley 63 SJ 4027
Bagnall 76 SJ 9250
Bagshot (Surrey) 25 SU 9163
Bagshot (Wilts.) 23 SU 3165
Bagshot Heath 25 SU 9262
Bagthorpe (Norf.) 69 TF 7932
Bagthorpe (Notts.) 78 SK 4751
Bagworth 66 SK 4408
Bagwy Llydiart 47 SO 4427
Baildon 84 SE 1539
Baile Mor 128 NM 2824
Bailebeag 147 NH 5018
Bailiesward 150 NJ 4738
Baillieston 115 NS 6764
Bainbridge 90 SD 9390
Bainton (Cambs.) 68 TF 0906
Bairnkine 109 NT 6515
Baker Street 27 TQ 6381
Baker's End 41 TL 3917
Bakewell 77 SK 2168
Bala 62 SH 9236
Balallan 163 NB 2720
Balbeg 147 NH 4924
Balbeggie 134 NO 1629
Balbithan 151 NJ 7917
Balblair 148 NH 7066
Balchladich 156 NC 0330
Balchraggan 147 NH 5343
Balchrick 156 NC 1960
Balcombe 15 TQ 3130
Balcombe Lane 15 TQ 3132
Balcomie 127 NO 6310
Balcurvie 127 NO 3400
Baldersby 91 SE 3578
Balderstone 83 SD 6332
Balderton 79 SK 8151
Baldhu 3 SW 7743
Baldinnie 135 NO 4311
Baldock 41 TL 2434
Baldrine 162 SC 4281
Baldwin 162 SC 3581
Baldwin's Gate 64 SJ 7939
Baldwinholme 103 NY 3351
Bale 70 TG 0136
Balemartine 162 NL 9841
Balephuil 162 NL 9640
Balerno 117 NT 1666
Balfield 142 NO 5468
Balfour 163 HY 4716
Balfron 125 NS 5488
Balgarva 163 NF 7647
Balgaveny 150 NJ 6640
Balgavies 135 NO 5351
Balgedie 126 NO 1603
Balgonar 126 NT 0395
Balgove 151 NJ 8133
Balgowan 140 NN 6394
Balgown 144 NG 3868
Balgray 134 NO 4138
Balgrochan 125 NS 6278
Balgy 145 NG 8456
Balhalgardy 150 NJ 7623
Balhary 134 NO 2646
Baligill 158 NC 8566
Balintore (Highld.) 155 NH 8675
Balintore (Tays.) 134 NO 2859
Balintraid 155 NH 7370
Balivanich 163 NF 7755
Balkeerie 134 NO 3244
Balkholme 86 SE 7828
Ball 63 SJ 3026
Ball Hill 24 SU 4263
Ball's Green 36 ST 8699
Ballabeg 162 SC 2470
Ballacannell 162 SC 4382
Ballacarnane Beg 162 SC 3088
Ballachulish 130 NN 0758
Ballajora 162 SC 4790
Ballamodha 162 SC 2773
Ballantrae 100 NX 0882
Ballards Gore 42 TQ 9092
Ballasalla (I. of M.) 162 SC 2870
Ballater 142 NO 3695
Ballaugh 162 SC 3493
Ballchraggan 155 NH 7775
Ballechin 147 NN 9353
Ballencrieff 127 NT 4878
Ballevullin 162 NL 9546
Ballhill 18 SS 2625
Ballidon 77 SK 2055
Balliekine 112 NR 8739
Ballig 162 SC 2882
Ballinaby 120 NR 2267
Ballindean 134 NO 2529
Ballinger Common 39 SP 9103
Ballingham 47 SO 5731
Ballingry 126 NT 1797
Ballinluig 133 NN 9852
Ballintuim 133 NO 1054
Balloch (Highld.) 148 NH 7346
Balloch (Strath.) 124 NS 3981
Balloch (Tays.) 132 NN 8419
Balloch (Tays.) 134 NO 3557
Ballochan 142 NO 5290
Balls Cross 14 SU 9826
Balls Green 16 TQ 4936
Ballsalla (I. of M.) 162 SC 3497
Ballygown 128 NM 4343
Ballygrant 120 NR 3966
Ballyhaugh 162 NM 1758
Ballymichael 112 NR 9231
Balmacara 145 NG 8028
Balmaclellan 101 NX 6578
Balmacneil 133 NN 9850
Balmae 101 NX 6845
Balmaha 124 NS 4290
Balmalcolm 127 NO 3108
Balmedie 151 NJ 9617
Balmerino 134 NO 3525
Balmerlawn 13 SU 3003
Balmore 125 NS 6073
Balmullo 134 NO 4220
Balmungie 148 NH 7359
Balnabruaich 154 NH 7970
Balnacra 146 NG 9746
Balnageith 148 NJ 0257
Balnaguard 133 NN 9451
Balnaguisich 154 NH 6771
Balnahard 128 NM 4534
Balnain 147 NH 4430
Balnakeil 157 NC 3968
Balnaknock 144 NG 4162
Balnapaling 148 NH 7969
Balquhidder 132 NN 5320
Balsall 53 SP 2376
Balsall Common 53 SP 2377
Balsall Street 53 SP 2276
Balscote 54 SP 3841
Balsham 57 TL 5850
Baltasound (Unst) 163 HP 6208
Balterley 76 SJ 7550
Balthangie 151 NJ 8351
Baltonsborough 21 ST 5434
Balvaird 147 NH 5452
Balvicar 129 NM 7616
Balvraid 136 NG 8516
Bamber Bridge 82 SD 5526
Bamber's Green 41 TL 5723
Bamburgh 119 NU 1834
Bamford 77 SK 2083
Bamfurlong 36 SO 9021
Bampton (Cumbr.) 95 NY 5118
Bampton (Devon.) 8 SS 9522
Bampton (Oxon.) 37 SP 3103
Bampton Grange 95 NY 5218
Banavie 138 NN 1177
Banbury 54 SP 4540
Banc-y-ffordd 44 SN 4037
Bancffosfelem 32 SN 4811
Banchory 143 NO 6995
Banchory-Devenick 143 NJ 9101
Bancycapel 44 SN 4215
Bancyfelin 44 SN 3218
Banff 150 NJ 6863
Bangor 73 SH 5872
Bangor-is-y-coed 63 SJ 3945
Bangors 5 SX 2099
Banham 58 TM 0688
Bank 13 SU 2807
Bank Lane 83 SD 8016
Bank Newton 83 SD 9152
Bank Street 51 SO 6362
Bankend (Dumf & G) 102 NY 0268
Bankend (Strath.) 115 NS 8033
Bankfoot 133 NO 0635
Bankglen 107 NS 5912
Bankhead (Grampn.) 142 NJ 6608
Bankhead (Grampn.) 143 NJ 8910
Banknock 125 NS 7779
Banks (Cumbr.) 95 NY 5664
Banks (Lancs.) 82 SD 3820
Banks (Orkneys) 163 HY 4331
Bankshill 108 NY 1981
Banningham 71 TG 2129
Bannister Green 42 TL 6920
Bannockburn 125 NS 8190
Banstead 26 TQ 2559
Bantham 6 SX 6643
Banton 125 NS 7479
Banwell 21 ST 3959
Bapchild 28 TQ 9363
Bapton 22 ST 9938
Bar Hill 56 TL 3864
Barassie 114 NS 3232
Baravullin 129 NM 9040
Barbaraville 155 NH 7471
Barber Booth 77 SK 1184
Barbon 89 SD 6282
Barbrook 19 SS 7147
Barby 54 SP 5470
Barcaldine 130 NM 9743
Barcheston 53 SP 2639
Barcombe 16 TQ 4214
Barcombe Cross 16 TQ 4216
Barden 91 SE 1493
Bardfield Saling 42 TL 6826
Bardney 80 TF 1169
Bardon 66 SK 4613
Bardon Mill 104 NY 7764
Bardowie 125 NS 5873
Bardrainney 124 NS 3372
Bardsea 88 SD 3074
Bardsey 85 SE 3643
Bardsley 83 SD 9201
Bardwell 58 TL 9473
Barewood 47 SO 3856
Barford (Norf.) 70 TG 1107
Barford (Warw.) 53 SP 2660
Barford St John 38 SP 4333
Barford St. Martin 23 SU 0531
Barford St. Michael 38 SP 4332
Barfreston 29 TR 2650
Bargoed 34 SO 1500
Bargrennan 101 NX 3476
Barham (Cambs.) 56 TL 1375
Barham (Kent) 29 TR 2050
Barham (Suff.) 58 TM 1451
Barholm 68 TF 0811
Barkby 66 SK 6310
Barkby Thorpe 66 SK 6309
Barkestone-le-Vale 67 SK 7734
Barkham 25 SU 7866
Barking (Gtr London) 27 TQ 4785
Barking (Suff.) 58 TM 0653
Barking Tye 58 TM 0652
Barkingside 27 TQ 4489
Barkisland 84 SE 0419
Barkston (Lincs.) 67 SK 9241
Barkston (N Yorks.) 85 SE 4936
Barkway 41 TL 3835
Barlaston 64 SJ 8938
Barlavington 14 SU 9716
Barlborough 78 SK 4777
Barlby 85 SE 6334
Barlestone 66 SK 4205
Barley (Herts.) 56 TL 4038
Barley (Lancs.) 83 SD 8240
Barleythorpe 67 SK 8409
Barling 42 TQ 9289
Barlings 80 TF 0774
Barlow (Derby.) 78 SK 3474
Barlow (N Yorks.) 85 SE 6428
Barlow (Tyne and Wear) 105 NZ 1560
Barmby Moor 92 SE 7748
Barmby on the Marsh 86 SE 6828
Barmer 70 TF 8133
Barmouth 61 SH 6115
Barmpton 98 NZ 3118
Barmston 93 TA 1659
Barnack 68 TF 0705
Barnacle 54 SP 3884
Barnard Castle 97 NZ 0516
Barnard Gate 38 SP 4010
Barnardiston 57 TL 7148
Barnburgh 85 SE 4803
Barnby 59 TM 4789
Barnby Dun 85 SE 6109
Barnby Moor 79 SK 6684
Barnby in the Willows 79 SK 8552
Barnes 26 TQ 2276
Barnes Street 27 TQ 6447
Barnet 26 TQ 2496
Barnetby le Wold 87 TA 0509
Barney 70 TF 9932
Barnham (Suff.) 58 TL 8779
Barnham (W Susx) 14 SU 9604
Barnham Broom 70 TG 0807
Barnhead 135 NO 6657
Barnhill 149 NJ 1457
Barnhills 100 NW 9871
Barningham (Durham) 97 NZ 0810
Barningham (Suff.) 58 TL 9676
Barnoldby le Beck 87 TA 2303
Barnoldswick 83 SD 8746
Barns Green 15 TQ 1227
Barnsley (Glos.) 37 SP 0705
Barnsley (S Yorks.) 85 SE 3406
Barnstaple 19 SS 5533
Barnston (Essex) 42 TL 6519
Barnston (Mers.) 74 SJ 2783
Barnt Green 53 SP 0073
Barnton 75 SJ 6374
Barnwell All Saints 55 TL 0584
Barnwell St Andrew 55 TL 0585
Barnwood 36 SO 8518
Baron's Cross 47 SO 4758
Barony, The 163 HY 2328
Barr 106 NX 2794
Barrachan 101 NX 3649
Barrack (Grampn) 151 NJ 8942
Barrahormid 122 NR 7385
Barrapoll 162 NL 9542
Barras (Cumb.) 96 NY 8412
Barras (Grampn.) 143 NO 8580
Barrasford 104 NY 9273
Barravullin 123 NM 8307
Barregarrow 162 SC 3288
Barrhead 115 NS 5058
Barrhill (Strath.) 106 NX 2382
Barrington (Cambs.) 56 TL 3949
Barrington (Somer.) 10 ST 3918
Barripper 2 SW 6338
Barrmill 114 NS 3651
Barrock 159 ND 2571
Barrow (Glos.) 36 SO 8824
Barrow (Lancs.) 83 SD 7338
Barrow (Leic.) 67 SK 8815
Barrow (Salop) 51 SJ 6500
Barrow (Somer.) 22 ST 7231
Barrow (Suff.) 57 TL 7663
Barrow Common 21 ST 5467
Barrow Gurney 21 ST 5267
Barrow Street 22 ST 8330
Barrow upon Humber 87 TA 0721
Barrow upon Soar 66 SK 5717
Barrow upon Trent 66 SK 3528
Barrow-in-Furness 88 SD 1969
Barroway Drove 69 TF 5703
Barrowby 67 SK 8736
Barrowden 67 SK 9400
Barrowford 83 SD 8538
Barry (S Glam.) 20 ST 1168
Barry (Tays) 135 NO 5334
Barry Island 20 ST 1166
Barsby 66 SK 6911
Barsham 59 TM 3989
Barston 53 SP 2078
Bartestree 47 SO 5641
Barthol Chapel 151 NJ 8134
Barthomley 76 SJ 7652
Bartley 13 SU 3012
Bartlow 57 TL 5845
Barton (Avon) 21 ST 3956
Barton (Cambs.) 56 TL 4055
Barton (Ches.) 75 SJ 4454
Barton (Devon.) 7 SX 9067
Barton (Glos.) 37 SP 0925
Barton (Lancs.) 82 SD 5136
Barton (N Yorks.) 97 NZ 2208
Barton (Warw.) 53 SP 1051
Barton Bendish 69 TF 7105
Barton End 36 ST 8497
Barton Hartshorn 38 SP 6431
Barton Mills 57 TL 7273
Barton Seagrave 55 SP 8877
Barton St. David 21 ST 5431

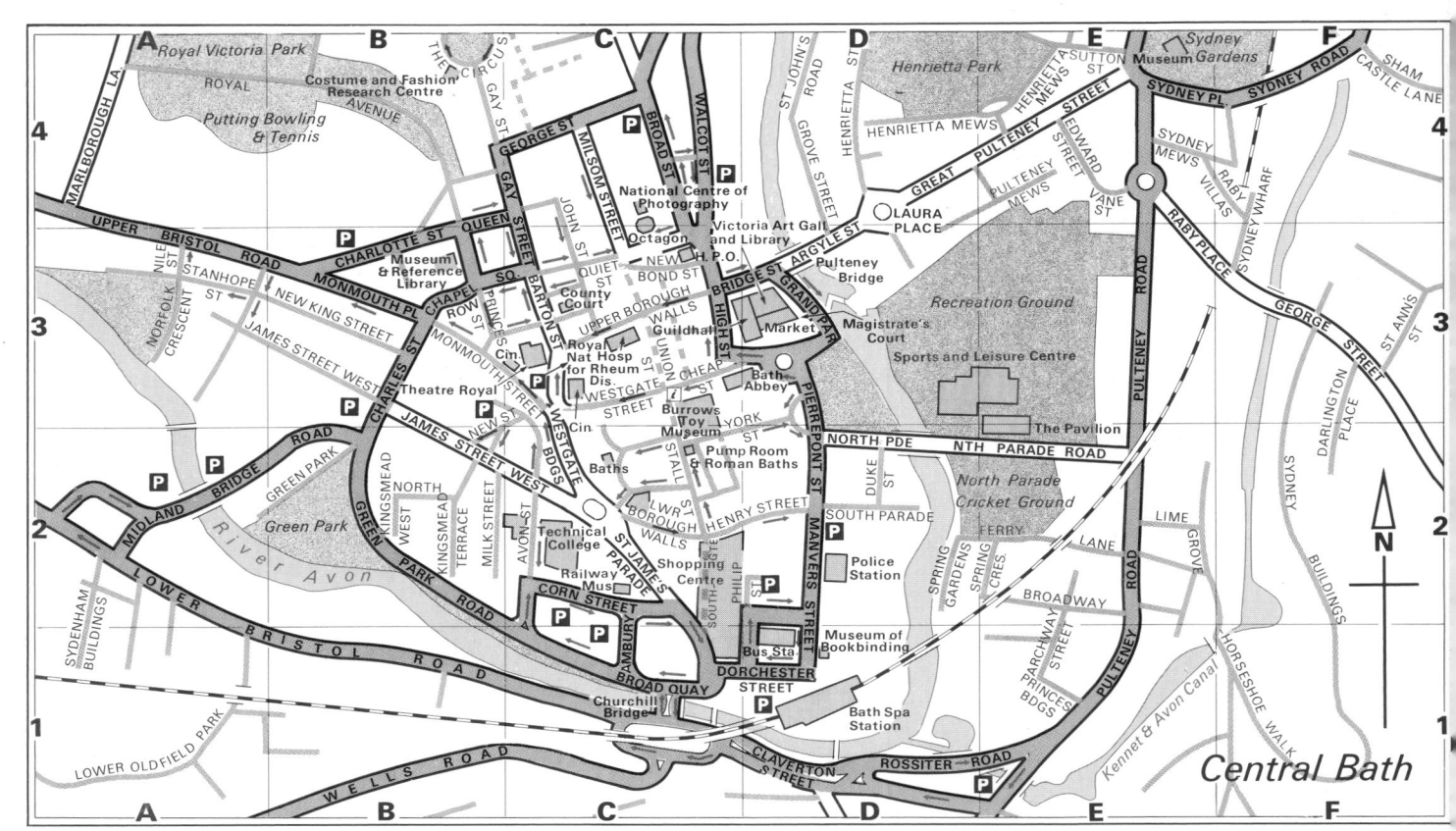

Central Bath

Blashford

Bottisham

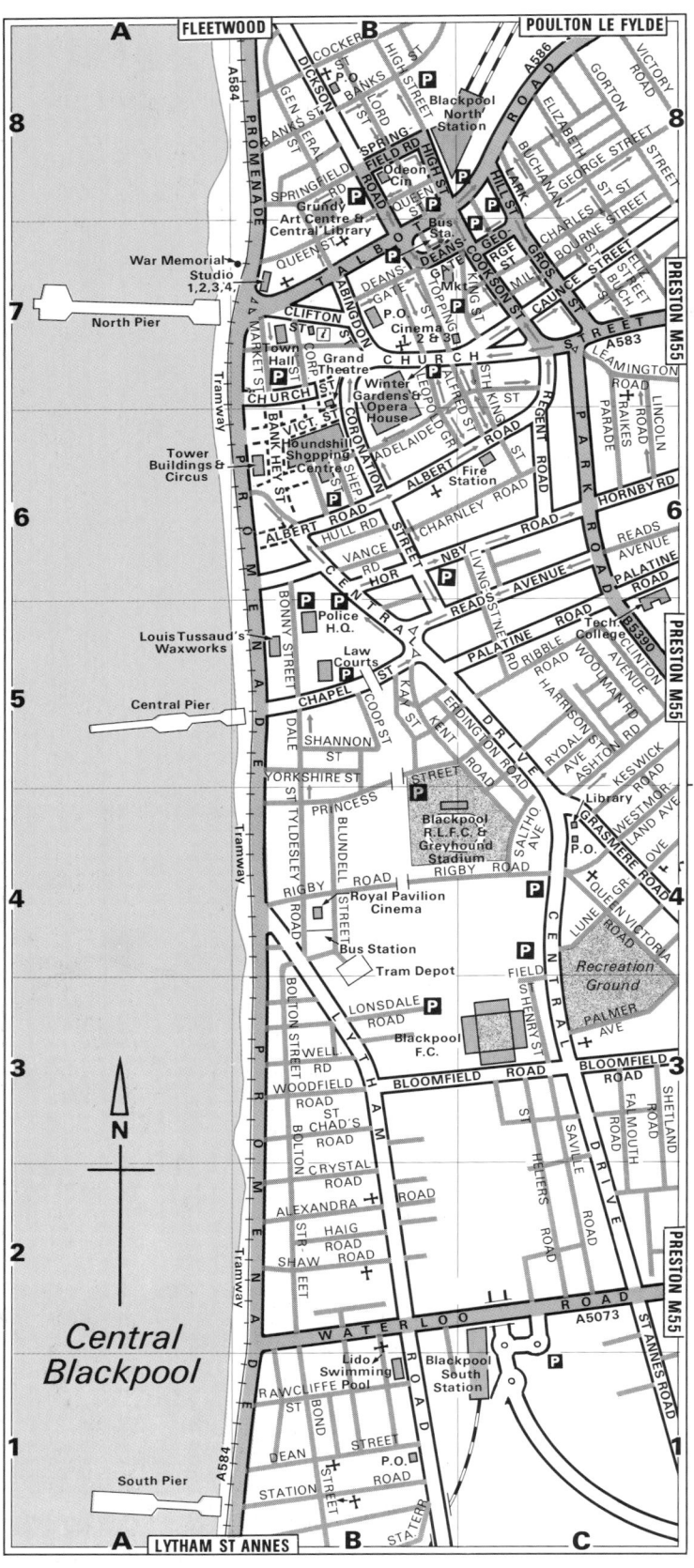

Central Blackpool

FLEETWOOD · POULTON LE FYLDE · LYTHAM ST ANNES

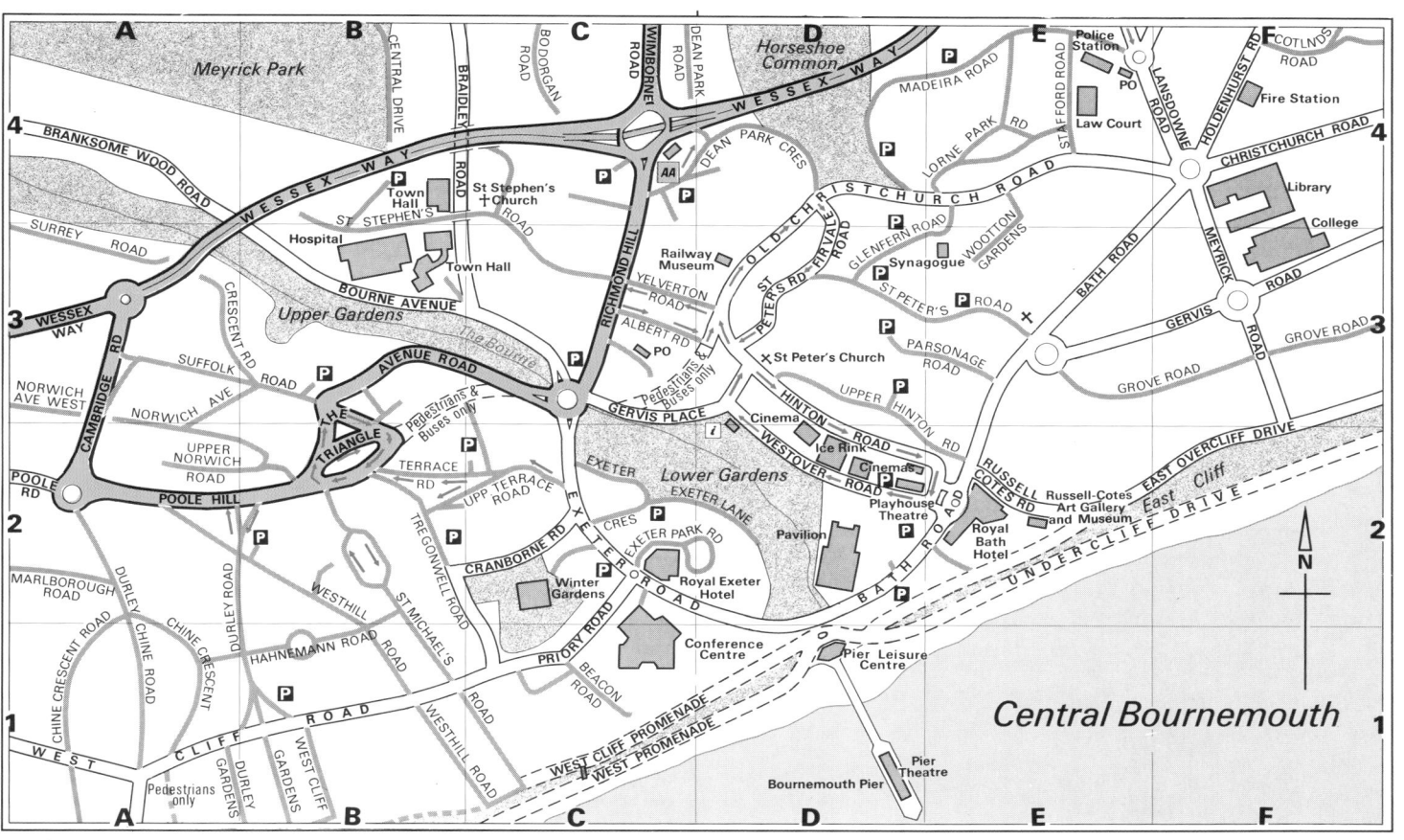

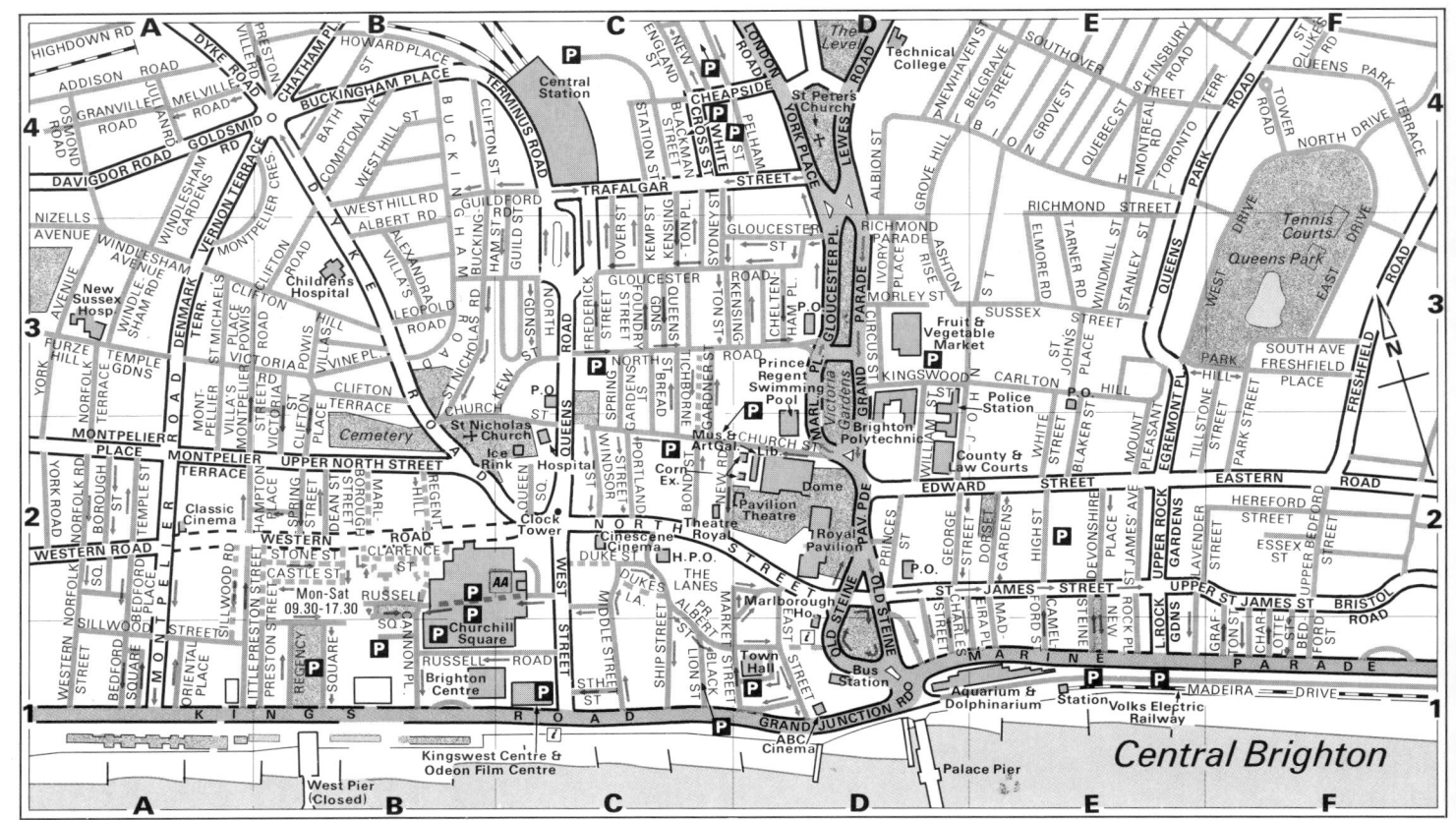

Central Brighton

Brandon (Durham) ...97.. NZ 2439	Breasclete ...163.. NB 2135	Bridge of Avon ...149.. NJ 1835	Brightons ...126.. NS 9277
Brandon (Lincs.) ...79.. SK 9048	Breaston ...66.. SK 4533	Bridge of Avon ...148.. NJ 1419	Brightwalton ...24.. SU 4278
Brandon (Northum.) ...111.. NU 0417	Brechfa ...45.. SN 5230	Bridge of Balgie ...132.. NN 5746	Brightwell (Oxon.) ...38.. SU 5790
Brandon (Suff.) ...57.. TL 7886	Brechin ...135.. NO 5960	Bridge of Brewlands ...134.. NO 1962	Brightwell (Suff.) ...59.. TM 2543
Brandon (Warw.) ...54.. SP 4076	Breckles ...70.. TL 9594	Bridge of Cally ...134.. NO 1351	Brightwell Baldwin ...38.. SU 6594
Brandon Bank ...57.. TL 6289	Breckrey ...144.. NG 5061	Bridge of Canny ...142.. NO 6597	Brignall ...97.. NZ 0712
Brandon Creek ...69.. TL 6091	Brecon ...46.. SO 0428	Bridge of Craigisla ...134.. NO 2553	Brigsley ...87.. TA 2501
Brandon Parva ...70.. TG 0708	Bredbury ...76.. SJ 9292	Bridge of Dee ...102.. NX 7360	Brigsteer ...89.. SD 4889
Brandsby ...92.. SE 5872	Brede ...17.. TQ 8218	Bridge of Don ...143.. NJ 9409	Brigstock ...55.. SP 9485
Brane ...2.. SW 4028	Bredenbury ...47.. SO 6058	Bridge of Dye ...142.. NO 6585	Brill ...38.. SP 6513
Branksome ...12.. SZ 0393	Bredfield ...59.. TM 2653	Bridge of Earn ...133.. NO 1318	Brilley ...46.. SO 2549
Bransbury ...24.. SU 4242	Bredgar ...28.. TQ 8860	Bridge of Ericht ...132.. NN 5358	Brimfield ...51.. SO 5267
Bransby ...79.. SK 8979	Bredhurst ...28.. TQ 7962	Bridge of Feugh ...143.. NO 7094	Brimington ...78.. SK 4073
Branscombe ...9.. SY 1988	Bredon ...52.. SO 9236	Bridge of Forss ...158.. ND 0568	Brimley ...7.. SX 7977
Bransford ...52.. SO 7952	Bredon's Hardwick ...52.. SO 9035	Bridge of Gairn ...142.. NO 3597	Brimpsfield ...36.. SO 9312
Bransgore ...12.. SZ 1897	Bredon's Norton ...52.. SO 9339	Bridge of Gaur ...132.. NN 5056	Brimpton ...24.. SU 5564
Bransley ...52.. SO 6574	Bredwardine ...47.. SO 3344	Bridge of Muchalls ...143.. NO 8991	Brimscombe ...36.. SO 8702
Branson's Cross ...53.. SP 0870	Breedon on the Hill ...66.. SK 4022	Bridge of Orchy ...131.. NN 2939	Brimstage ...77.. SJ 2982
Branston (Leic.) ...67.. SK 8029	Breich ...116.. NS 9560	Bridge of Weir ...114.. NS 3865	Brind ...86.. SE 7430
Branston (Lincs.) ...80.. TF 0167	Breighton ...86.. SE 7033	Bridgefoot ...94.. NY 0529	Brindister ...163.. HU 2857
Branston (Staffs.) ...65.. SK 2221	Breinton ...47.. SO 4739	Bridgehouse Gate ...91.. SE 1565	Brindle ...83.. SD 5924
Branston Booths ...80.. TF 0669	Bremhill ...22.. ST 9873	Bridgemary ...13.. SU 5702	Brindley Ford ...76.. SJ 8754
Branstone ...13.. SZ 5583	Bremley ...19.. SS 8128	Bridgend (Borders) ...118.. NT 5235	Brindley Heath ...65.. SJ 9914
Brant Broughton ...79.. SK 9154	Brenchley ...16.. TQ 6741	Bridgend (Cumbr.) ...95.. NY 4014	Brineton ...64.. SJ 8013
Brantham ...43.. TM 1034	Brendon (Devon) ...19.. SS 7648	Bridgend (Devon) ...6.. SX 5547	Bringhurst ...67.. SP 8492
Branthwaite (Cumbr.) ...94.. NY 0525	Brendon (Devon) ...18.. SS 3607	Bridgend (Dumf & G) ...108.. NT 0708	Brington ...56.. TL 0875
Branthwaite (Cumbr.) ...94.. NY 2937	Brenish ...163.. NA 9926	Bridgend (Fife.) ...134.. NO 3911	Briningham ...70.. TG 0334
Brantingham ...86.. SE 9429	Brent ...26.. TQ 2084	Bridgend (Grampn.) ...149.. NJ 3731	Brinkhill ...81.. TF 3773
Branton (Northum.) ...111.. NU 0416	Brent Eleigh ...58.. TL 9447	Bridgend (Islay) ...120.. NR 3362	Brinkley ...57.. TL 6254
Branton (S. Yorks.) ...85.. SE 6401	Brent Knoll ...21.. ST 3350	Bridgend (Lothian) ...126.. NT 0475	Brinklow ...54.. SP 4379
Branxholm Park ...109.. NT 4612	Brent Pelham ...41.. TL 4330	Bridgend (Mid Glam.) ...33.. SS 9079	Brinkworth ...37.. SU 0184
Branxholme ...109.. NT 4611	Brentford ...26.. TQ 1778	Bridgend (Strath.) ...123.. NR 8592	Brinscall ...83.. SD 6321
Branxton ...119.. NT 8937	Brentingby ...67.. SK 7818	Bridgend (Strath.) ...125.. NS 6970	Brinsley ...78.. SK 4548
Brassey Green ...75.. SJ 5261	Brentwood ...27.. TQ 5993	Bridgend (Tays.) ...134.. NO 1224	Brinsop ...47.. SO 4344
Brassington ...77.. SK 2354	Brenzett ...17.. TR 0027	Bridgend (Tays.) ...142.. NO 5368	Brinsworth ...78.. SK 4190
Brasted ...27.. TQ 4755	Brereton ...65.. SK 0516	Bridgend of Lintrathen ...134.. NO 2854	Brinton ...70.. TG 0335
Brasted Chart ...27.. TQ 4653	Brereton Green ...76.. SJ 7764	Bridgerule ...18.. SS 2803	Brinyan ...163.. HY 4327
Brathens ...143.. NO 6798	Brereton Heath ...76.. SJ 8064	Bridges ...51.. SO 3996	Brisco ...102.. NY 4252
Bratoft ...81.. TF 4765	Bressingham ...58.. TM 0780	Bridgetown (Corn.) ...5.. SX 3489	Brisley ...70.. TF 9421
Brattleby ...80.. SK 9480	Bretby ...65.. SK 2923	Bridgetown (Somer.) ...20.. SS 9233	Brislington ...35.. ST 6170
Bratton ...22.. ST 9152	Bretford ...54.. SP 4277	Bridgeyate ...22.. ST 6873	Brissenden Green ...28.. TQ 9339
Bratton Clovelly ...5.. SX 4691	Bretforton ...53.. SP 0943	Bridgham ...58.. TL 9686	Bristol ...35.. ST 5872
Bratton Fleming ...19.. SS 6437	Bretherton ...82.. SD 4720	Bridgnorth ...64.. SO 7193	Briston ...70.. TG 0632
Bratton Seymour ...22.. ST 6729	Brettenham (Norf) ...58.. TL 9383	Bridgtown ...65.. SJ 9808	Britannia ...83.. SD 8821
Braughing ...41.. TL 3925	Brettenham (Suff.) ...58.. TL 9653	Bridgwater ...21.. ST 3037	Britford British Legion Village ...28.. TQ 7257
Braunston (Leic.) ...67.. SK 8306	Bretton ...75.. SJ 3563	Bridlington ...93.. TA 1766	Brithdir ...61.. SH 7618
Braunston (Northants.) ...54.. SP 5366	Brewham ...22.. ST 7136	Bridport ...10.. SY 4692	Briton Ferry ...33.. SS 7394
Braunstone ...66.. SK 5502	Brewood ...64.. SJ 8808	Bridstow ...47.. SO 5824	Britwell Salome ...38.. SU 6792
Braunton ...19.. SS 4836	Briantspuddle ...11.. SY 8193	Brierfield ...83.. SD 8436	Brixham ...7.. SX 9255
Brawby ...92.. SE 7378	Brick End ...41.. TL 5725	Brierley (Glos.) ...47.. SO 6215	Brixton ...6.. SX 5452
Brawl ...158.. NC 8066	Bricket Wood ...40.. TL 1301	Brierley (Here & W) ...47.. SO 4956	Brixton Deverill ...22.. ST 8638
Brawlbin ...159.. ND 0757	Bricklehampton ...52.. SO 9842	Brierley (S Yorks.) ...85.. SE 4011	Brixworth ...55.. SP 7470
Bray ...25.. SU 9079	Bride ...162.. NX 4501	Brierley Hill ...64.. SO 9187	Brize Norton ...37.. SP 2907
Bray Shop ...5.. SX 3374	Bridekirk ...94.. NY 1133	Brig o'Turk ...125.. NN 5306	Broad Alley ...52.. SO 8867
Braybrooke ...55.. SP 7684	Bridell ...31.. SN 1742	Brigg ...86.. TA 0007	Broad Blunsdon ...37.. SU 1490
Brayford ...19.. SS 6834	Bridestowe ...5.. SX 5189	Briggate ...71.. TG 3127	Broad Campden ...53.. SP 1537
Braystones ...88.. NY 0105	Brideswell ...150.. NJ 5739	Briggswath ...99.. NZ 8708	Broad Chalke ...23.. SU 0325
Brayton ...85.. SE 6030	Bridford ...8.. SX 8186	Brigham (Cumbr.) ...94.. NY 0830	Broad Green (Essex) ...42.. TL 8723
Brazacott ...5.. SX 2691	Bridge ...29.. TR 1854	Brigham (Humbs.) ...93.. TA 0753	Broad Green (Here & W) ...52.. SO 7656
Breachwood Green ...40.. TL 1522	Bridge End (Durham) ...97.. NZ 0336	Brighouse ...84.. SE 1423	Broad Haven ...30.. SM 8613
Breaclete ...163.. NB 1537	Bridge End (Lincs.) ...68.. TF 1436	Brighstone ...13.. SZ 4282	Broad Hill (Cambs.) ...57.. TL 5976
Breadsall ...66.. SK 3639	Bridge End (Northum.) ...104.. NY 9166	Bright's Hill ...36.. SO 7020	Broad Hinton ...23.. SU 1076
Breadstone ...36.. SO 7000	Bridge Green ...58.. TL 4636	Brightgate ...77.. SK 2659	Broad Laying ...24.. SU 4362
Breage ...2.. SW 6128	Bridge Reeve ...8.. SS 6613	Brighthampton ...38.. SP 3803	Broad Marston ...53.. SP 1346
Bream ...35.. SO 6005	Bridge Sollers ...47.. SO 4142	Brightling ...16.. TQ 6821	Broad Oak (Cumbr.) ...88.. SD 1194
Bream's Meend ...35.. SO 5905	Bridge Street ...58.. TL 8749	Brightlingsea ...43.. TM 0816	Broad Oak (E Susx) ...17.. TQ 8320
Breamore ...12.. SU 1517	Bridge Trafford ...75.. SJ 4471	Brighton (Corn.) ...3.. SW 9054	Broad Oak (Here & W) ...47.. SO 4421
Brean ...21.. ST 2955	Bridge of Alford ...150.. NJ 5617	Brighton (E Susx) ...15.. TQ 3105	Broad Street (Kent) ...28.. TQ 8356
Brearton ...91.. SE 3260	Bridge of Allan ...125.. NS 7897		Broad Street (Kent) ...29.. TR 1140

Broad Town Burston (Norf.)

Broad Town 37 SU 0977
Broadbottom 76 SJ 9993
Broadbridge 14 SU 8105
Broadbridge Heath 15 TQ 1431
Broadclyst 9 SX 9897
Broadford 145 NG 6423
Broadford Bridge 15 TQ 0921
Broadhaugh 109 NT 4509
Broadheath (Gtr Mches.) 76 SJ 7689
Broadheath (Here & W) 52 SO 6665
Broadheath (Here & W) 52 SO 8156
Broadhembury 9 ST 1004
Broadhempston 7 SX 8066
Broadland Row 17 TQ 8319
Broadley (Grampn.) 150 NJ 4161
Broadley (Gtr Mches.) 83 SD 8716
Broadley Common 41 TL 4207
Broadmayne 11 SY 7286
Broadmeadows 117 NT 4130
Broadmere 24 SU 6247
Broadmoor 31 SN 0905
Broadnymett 8 SS 7001
Broadoak 36 SO 6912
Broadoak (Dorset) 10 SY 4496
Broadoak (E Susx) 16 TQ 6022
Broadoak (Kent) 29 TR 1661
Broadrashes 150 NJ 4354
Broadstairs 29 TR 3967
Broadstone 35 SO 5003
Broadstone (Dorset) 12 SZ 0095
Broadstone (Salop) 51 SO 5389
Broadwas 52 SO 7555
Broadwater 15 TQ 1504
Broadway (Here & W) 53 SP 0937
Broadway (Somer.) 9 ST 3215
Broadwell (Glos.) 37 SP 2027
Broadwell (Oxon.) 37 SP 2503
Broadwell (Warw.) 54 SP 4565
Broadwell Lane End 35 SO 5811
Broadwey 10 SY 6683
Broadwindsor 10 ST 4302
Broadwood-Kelly 8 SS 6105
Broadwoodwidger 5 SX 4089
Brochel 145 NG 5848
Brock 82 SD 5140
Brock's Green 24 SU 5061
Brockbridge 13 SU 6118
Brockdam 111 NU 1624
Brockdish 59 TM 2179
Brockenhurst 13 SU 2902
Brocketsbrae 116 NS 8239
Brockford Green 58 TM 1265
Brockford Street 58 TM 1166
Brockhall 54 SP 6362
Brockham 26 TQ 2049
Brockhampton (Glou.) 37 SP 0423
Brockhampton (Here & W) 47 SO 5932
Brockholes 84 SE 1411
Brocklesby 87 TA 1311
Brockley 21 ST 4666
Brockley Green (Suff.) 58 TL 8254
Brockley Green (Suff.) 57 TL 7246
Brockleymoor 95 NY 4957
Brockton 64 SJ 8131
Brockton (Salop) 51 SJ 3104
Brockton (Salop) 64 SJ 7103
Brockton (Salop) 51 SO 3285
Brockton (Salop) 51 SO 5793
Brockweir 35 SO 5301
Brockwood Park 13 SU 6226
Brockworth 36 SO 8916
Brocton 64 SJ 9619
Brodick 113 NS 0136
Brodle 147 NH 9857
Brodsworth 85 SE 5007
Brogaig 144 NG 4768
Brogborough 55 SP 9638
Broken Cross (Ches.) 76 SJ 6872
Broken Cross (Ches.) 76 SJ 8973
Brokenborough 36 ST 9189
Brokenheugh 104 NY 8666
Bromborough 75 SJ 3582
Brome 58 TM 1376
Brome Street 58 TM 1576
Bromeswell 59 TM 3050
Bromfield (Cumb.) 94 NY 1746
Bromfield (Salop) 51 SO 4876
Bromham (Beds.) 55 TL 0051
Bromham (Wilts.) 22 ST 9665
Bromley (Gtr London) 27 TQ 4365
Bromley Common 27 TQ 4266
Bromley Green 28 TQ 9936
Brompton (Kent) 28 TQ 7668
Brompton (N Yorks) 93 SE 9482
Brompton (N Yorks.) 91 SE 3796
Brompton Ralph 20 ST 0832
Brompton Regis 20 SS 9531
Brompton-on-Swale 91 SE 2199
Bromsash 36 SO 6424
Bromsberrow 52 SO 7434
Bromsberrow Heath 52 SO 7332
Bromsgrove 52 SO 9570
Bromstead Heath 64 SJ 7917
Bromyard 52 SO 6554
Bromyard Downs 52 SO 6655
Bronaber 61 SH 7131
Bronant 48 SN 6467
Brongest 44 SN 3245
Bronington 63 SJ 4839
Bronllys 46 SO 1435
Bronwydd Arms 44 SN 4124
Bronygarth 62 SJ 2636
Brook (Hants.) 12 SU 2713
Brook (Hants.) 23 SU 3428
Brook (I. of W.) 13 SZ 3983
Brook (Kent) 29 TR 0644
Brook (Surrey) 25 SU 9338
Brook (Surrey) 15 TQ 0545
Brook End 56 TL 0763
Brook Hill 12 SU 2714
Brook Street 27 TQ 5792
Brook Street 15 TQ 3026
Brook Street 28 TQ 9334
Brooke (Leic.) 67 SK 8405
Brooke (Norf.) 71 TM 2999
Brookend 36 SO 6802
Brookfield 114 NS 4164
Brookhouse 89 SD 5464
Brookhouse Green 76 SJ 8061
Brookland 17 TQ 9825
Brookmans Park 41 TL 2404
Brooks 50 SO 1499
Brooks Green 15 TQ 1225
Brooksby 66 SK 6716
Brookthorpe 36 SO 8312
Brookville 69 TL 7396
Brookwood 25 SU 9557
Broom (Beds.) 56 TL 1743
Broom (Warw.) 53 SP 0953
Broom Hill (Dorset) 12 SU 0302
Broome (Here & W) 52 SO 9078
Broome (Norf.) 71 TM 3591
Broome (Salop) 51 SO 3981
Broome Green 52 SO 7132
Broome Park 111 NU 1213
Broomedge 76 SJ 7085
Broomer's Corner 15 TQ 1221
Broomfield (Essex) 42 TL 7010
Broomfield (Grampn.) 151 NJ 9532
Broomfield (Kent) 28 TQ 8452
Broomfield (Kent) 29 TR 2066
Broomfield (Somer.) 20 ST 2231
Broomfleet 86 SE 8727
Broomhaugh 105 NZ 0261
Broomhill (Northum.) 111 NU 2400
Brora 155 NC 9003
Broseley 51 SJ 6701
Brotherhouse Bar 68 TF 2615
Brotherlee 96 NY 9338
Brothertoft 81 TF 2746
Brotherton 85 SE 4825
Brotton 99 NZ 6819
Broubster 158 ND 0360
Brough (Cumbr.) 96 NY 7914
Brough (Derby.) 77 SK 1882
Brough (Highld.) 159 ND 2273
Brough (Humbs.) 86 SE 9326
Brough (Notts.) 79 SK 8358
Brough (Shetld.) 163 HU 5141
Brough Lodge 163 HU 5894
Brough Sowerby 96 NY 7912
Broughall 63 SJ 5641
Broughton (Borders) 117 NT 1136
Broughton (Bucks.) 55 SP 8940
Broughton (Cambs.) 56 TL 2878
Broughton (Clwyd) 74 SJ 3363
Broughton (Gtr Mches.) 83 SD 8201
Broughton (Hants.) 23 SU 3132
Broughton (Humbs.) 86 SE 9508
Broughton (Lancs.) 82 SD 5234
Broughton (Mid Glam.) 33 SS 9271
Broughton (N Yorks) 92 SE 7673
Broughton (N Yorks.) 83 SD 9451
Broughton (Northants.) 55 SP 8375
Broughton (Oxon.) 54 SP 4238
Broughton Astley 66 SP 5292
Broughton Beck 88 SD 2882
Broughton Gifford 22 ST 8763
Broughton Green 52 SO 9560
Broughton Hackett 52 SO 9254
Broughton Hill 67 SK 7123
Broughton Mills 88 SD 2290
Broughton Moor 94 NY 0533
Broughton Poggs 37 SP 2303
Broughton in Furness 88 SD 2187
Broughtown 163 HY 6540
Broughty Ferry 135 NO 4630
Brown Candover 24 SU 5839
Brown Edge 76 SJ 9053
Brown Heath 75 SJ 4564
Brownhill (Grampn.) 151 NJ 8640
Brownhills (W Mids) 65 SK 0405
Browninghill Green 24 SU 5859
Brownlow Heath 76 SJ 8360
Brownmuir 143 NO 7477
Brownston 6 SX 6952
Browston Green 71 TG 4901
Broxbourne 41 TL 3707
Broxburn (Lothian) 126 NT 0872
Broxburn (Lothian) 127 NT 6977
Broxted 41 TL 5727
Broxton 75 SJ 4854
Broxwood 47 SO 3654
Bruan 159 ND 3039
Bruar 139 NN 8366
Bruera 75 SJ 4360
Bruichladdich 120 NR 2661
Bruisyard 59 TM 3266
Bruisyard Street 59 TM 3365
Brund 77 SK 1061
Brundall 71 TG 3208
Brundish 59 TM 2669
Brundish Street 59 TM 2671
Bruntingthorpe 66 SP 6090
Brunton (Fife) 134 NO 3220
Brunton (Northum.) 111 NU 2024
Brunton (Wilts.) 23 SU 2456
Brushford 20 SS 9225
Brushford Barton 8 SS 6707
Bruton 22 ST 6834
Bryanston 11 ST 8706
Brydekirk 103 NY 1870
Brymbo 74 SJ 2953
Bryn (Gtr Mches.) 82 SD 5600
Bryn (Salop) 50 SO 2985
Bryn (W Glam.) 33 SS 8192
Bryn Du 72 SH 3472
Bryn Gates 83 SD 5901
Bryn Golau 33 SS 9988
Bryn Saith Marchog 62 SJ 0750
Bryn-Mawr 60 SH 2433
Bryn-coch 33 SS 7499
Bryn-henllan 30 SN 0139
Bryn-y-maen (Clwyd) 73 SH 8376
Brynamman 45 SN 7114
Brynberian 31 SN 1035
Bryncae 33 SS 9983
Bryncethin 33 SS 9184
Bryncir 60 SH 4641
Bryncroes 60 SH 2231
Bryncrug 48 SH 6003
Bryneglwys 62 SJ 1447
Brynford 74 SJ 1774
Bryngwran 72 SH 3477
Bryngwyn (Gwent) 35 SO 3909
Bryngwyn (Powys) 46 SO 1849
Brynhoffnant 44 SN 3351
Brynithel 34 SO 2101
Brynmawr 34 SO 1911
Brynmenyn 33 SS 9084
Brynna 33 SS 9883
Brynrefail (Gwynedd) 72 SH 4786
Brynrefail (Gwynedd) 72 SH 5663
Brynsadler 34 ST 0380
Brynsiencyn 72 SH 4867
Brynteg 72 SH 4982
Bualintur 144 NG 4020
Bubbenhall 54 SP 3672
Bubwith 86 SE 7136
Buccleuch 109 NT 3214
Buchanan Smithy 124 NS 4789
Buchanty 133 NN 9328
Buchlyvie 125 NS 5793
Buck's Cross 18 SS 3422
Buck's Mills 18 SS 3523
Buckabank 95 NY 3749
Buckden (Cambs.) 56 TL 1967
Buckden (N Yorks.) 90 SD 9477
Buckenham 71 TG 3505
Buckerell 9 ST 1200
Buckfast 6 SX 7367
Buckfastleigh 6 SX 7466
Buckhaven 127 NT 3598
Buckholm 117 NT 4838
Buckhorn Weston 22 ST 7524
Buckhurst Hill 27 TQ 4193
Buckie 150 NJ 4265
Buckingham 38 SP 6933
Buckland (Bucks.) 39 SP 8812
Buckland (Devon.) 6 SX 6743
Buckland (Glos.) 53 SP 0836
Buckland (Herts.) 41 TL 3533
Buckland (Kent) 29 TR 2942
Buckland (Oxon.) 37 SU 3497
Buckland (Surrey) 26 TQ 2250
Buckland Brewer 18 SS 4120
Buckland Common 39 SP 9306
Buckland Dinham 22 ST 7550
Buckland Filleigh 18 SS 4609
Buckland Monachorum 5 SX 4868
Buckland Newton 10 ST 6905
Buckland Ripers 10 SY 6482
Buckland St. Mary 9 ST 2713
Buckland in the Moor 6 SX 7273
Buckland-Tout-Saints 7 SX 7546
Bucklebury 24 SU 5570
Bucklerheads 135 NO 4636
Bucklers Hard 13 SZ 4099
Bucklesham 59 TM 2442
Buckley 74 SJ 2764
Bucklow Hill 76 SJ 7282
Buckminster 67 SK 8722
Bucknall (Lincs.) 80 TF 1668
Bucknall (Staffs.) 76 SJ 9147
Bucknell (Oxon.) 38 SP 5525
Bucknell (Salop) 51 SO 3574
Bucks Green 15 TQ 0732
Bucks Hill 40 TL 0500
Bucks Horn Oak 25 SU 8142
Bucksburn 143 NJ 8909
Buckton 93 TA 1872
Buckton (Here & W) 51 SO 3873
Buckton (Northum.) 119 NU 0838
Buckworth 56 TL 1476
Budbrooke 53 SP 2565
Budby 79 SK 6169
Bude 18 SS 2006
Budge's Shop 5 SX 3259
Budlake 9 SS 9700
Budle 119 NU 1534
Budleigh Salterton 9 SY 0682
Budock Water 3 SW 7832
Buerton 76 SJ 6843
Bugbrooke 54 SP 6757
Bugle 4 SX 0158
Bugthorpe 92 SE 7757
Buildwas 51 SJ 6404
Builth Road 46 SO 0253
Builth Wells 46 SO 0451
Bulbourne 39 SP 9313
Bulbridge 23 SU 0930
Bulby 67 TF 0526
Buldoo 158 NC 9967
Bulford 23 SU 1643
Bulford Barracks 23 SU 1843
Bulkeley 75 SJ 5254
Bulkington (Warw.) 54 SP 3986
Bulkington (Wilts.) 22 ST 9458
Bulkworthy 18 SS 3914
Bull Bay 72 SH 4395
Bulley 36 SO 7519
Bullgill 94 NY 0938
Bullinghope 47 SO 5137
Bullwood 124 NS 1674
Bulmer (Essex) 58 TL 8440
Bulmer (N Yorks.) 92 SE 6967
Bulmer Tye 58 TL 8438
Bulphan 27 TQ 6385
Bulstone 9 SY 1789
Bulverhythe 17 TQ 7809
Bulwark 151 NJ 9447
Bulwell 78 SK 5345
Bulwick 67 SP 9694
Bumble's Green 41 TL 4005
Bunacaimb 137 NM 6588
Bunarkaig 138 NN 1887
Bunbury 75 SJ 5658
Bunchrew 147 NH 6145
Buncton 15 TQ 1413
Bundalloch 146 NG 8927
Bunessan 128 NM 3821
Bungay 59 TM 3389
Bunnahabhainn 122 NR 4173
Bunny 66 SK 5829
Buntingford 41 TL 3629
Bunwell 70 TM 1293
Burbage (Derby.) 77 SK 0472
Burbage (Leic.) 66 SP 4492
Burbage (Wilts.) 23 SU 2261
Burchett's Green 25 SU 8381
Burcombe (Wilts.) 23 SU 0630
Burcot (Here & W) 52 SO 9871
Burcot (Oxon.) 38 SU 5595
Burdale 92 SE 8762
Bures 42 TL 9034
Burford 37 SP 2512
Burg 128 NM 3745
Burgates 14 SU 7728
Burgess Hill 15 TQ 3118
Burgh (Suff.) 59 TM 2251
Burgh Castle 71 TG 4805
Burgh Heath 26 TQ 2458
Burgh Le Marsh 81 TF 5065
Burgh Muir 150 NJ 7622
Burgh St. Margaret 71 TG 4413
Burgh St. Peter 71 TM 4693
Burgh by Sands 103 NY 3259
Burgh next Aylsham 71 TG 2125
Burgh on Bain 80 TF 2186
Burghclere 24 SU 4660
Burghead 155 NJ 1168
Burghfield 24 SU 6668
Burghfield Common 24 SU 6466
Burghfield Hill 24 SU 6567
Burghill 47 SO 4744
Burghwallis 85 SE 5312
Burham 28 TQ 7262
Buriton 14 SU 7320
Burland 75 SJ 6153
Burlawn 4 SW 9970
Burleigh (Berks.) 25 SU 9070
Burleigh (Glos.) 36 SO 8602
Burlescombe 9 ST 0716
Burleston 11 SY 7794
Burley (Hants.) 12 SU 2103
Burley (Leic.) 67 SK 8810
Burley Gate 47 SO 5947
Burley Lawn 12 SU 2103
Burley Street 12 SU 2004
Burley Woodhead 84 SE 1544
Burley in Wharfdale 84 SE 1646
Burleydam 63 SJ 6042
Burlingjobb 46 SO 2558
Burlton 63 SJ 4526
Burmarsh 29 TR 1032
Burn 85 SE 5928
Burn of Cambus 125 NN 7203
Burnage 76 SJ 8692
Burnaston 65 SK 2832
Burnbanks 95 NY 5116
Burnbrae 114 NS 7243
Burnby 86 SE 8346
Burnedge 83 SD 9110
Burneside 89 SD 5095
Burneston 91 SE 3084
Burnett 22 ST 6665
Burnfoot (Borders) 109 NT 4113
Burnfoot (Borders) 109 NT 5116
Burnfoot (Dumf & G) 108 NX 9792
Burnfoot (Strath.) 124 NS 6776
Burnfoot (Tays.) 126 NN 9804
Burnham (Berks. — Bucks.) 25 SU 9382
Burnham (Humbs.) 87 TA 0517
Burnham Beeches 39 SU 9585
Burnham Deepdale 69 TF 8044
Burnham Green 41 TL 2616
Burnham Market 70 TF 8342
Burnham Norton 70 TF 8243
Burnham Overy 70 TF 8442
Burnham Thorpe 70 TF 8541
Burnham-on-Crouch 42 TQ 9496
Burnham-on-Sea 21 ST 3049
Burnhaven 151 NK 1244
Burnhead 107 NX 8595
Burnhervie 150 NJ 7319
Burnhill Green 64 SJ 7800
Burnhope 97 NZ 1948
Burnhouse 114 NS 3850
Burniston 93 TA 0193
Burnley 83 SD 8332
Burnmouth 119 NT 9560
Burnopfield 105 NZ 1756
Burnsall 90 SE 0363
Burnside (Fife.) 126 NO 1607
Burnside (Lothian) 126 NT 0971
Burnside (Strath) 107 NS 5912
Burnside (Tays.) 135 NO 5050
Burnside of Duntrune 135 NO 4434
Burnt Fen 57 TL 6085
Burnt Heath 43 TM 0627
Burnt Houses 97 NZ 1223
Burnt Yates 91 SE 2461
Burntcommon 26 TQ 0454
Burntisland 126 NT 2385
Burntwood 65 SK 0609
Burpham (Surrey) 26 TQ 0151
Burpham (W. Susx.) 15 TQ 0408
Burra Firth (Unst.) 163 HP 6113
Burradon (Northum.) 111 NT 9806
Burradon (Tyne and Wear) 105 NZ 2772
Burras 2 SW 6734
Burraton 5 SX 4067
Burravoe (Shetld.) 163 HU 3666
Burravoe (Yell.) 163 HU 5280
Burrells 95 NY 6818
Burrelton 134 NO 1936
Burridge 13 SU 5110
Burrill 91 SE 2387
Burringham 86 SE 8309
Burrington (Avon) 21 ST 4759
Burrington (Devon.) 8 SS 6316
Burrington (Here & W) 51 SO 4472
Burrough Green 57 TL 6355
Burrough on the Hill 67 SK 7510
Burrow Bridge 21 ST 3530
Burrowhill 25 SU 9763
Burry Port 32 SN 4400
Burrygreen 32 SS 4591
Burscough 82 SD 4310
Burscough Bridge 82 SD 4411
Bursea 86 SE 8033
Burshill 93 TA 0948
Bursledon 13 SU 4809
Burslem 76 SJ 8749
Burstall 58 TM 0944
Burstock 10 ST 4202
Burston 8 SS 7102
Burston (Norf.) 58 TM 1383

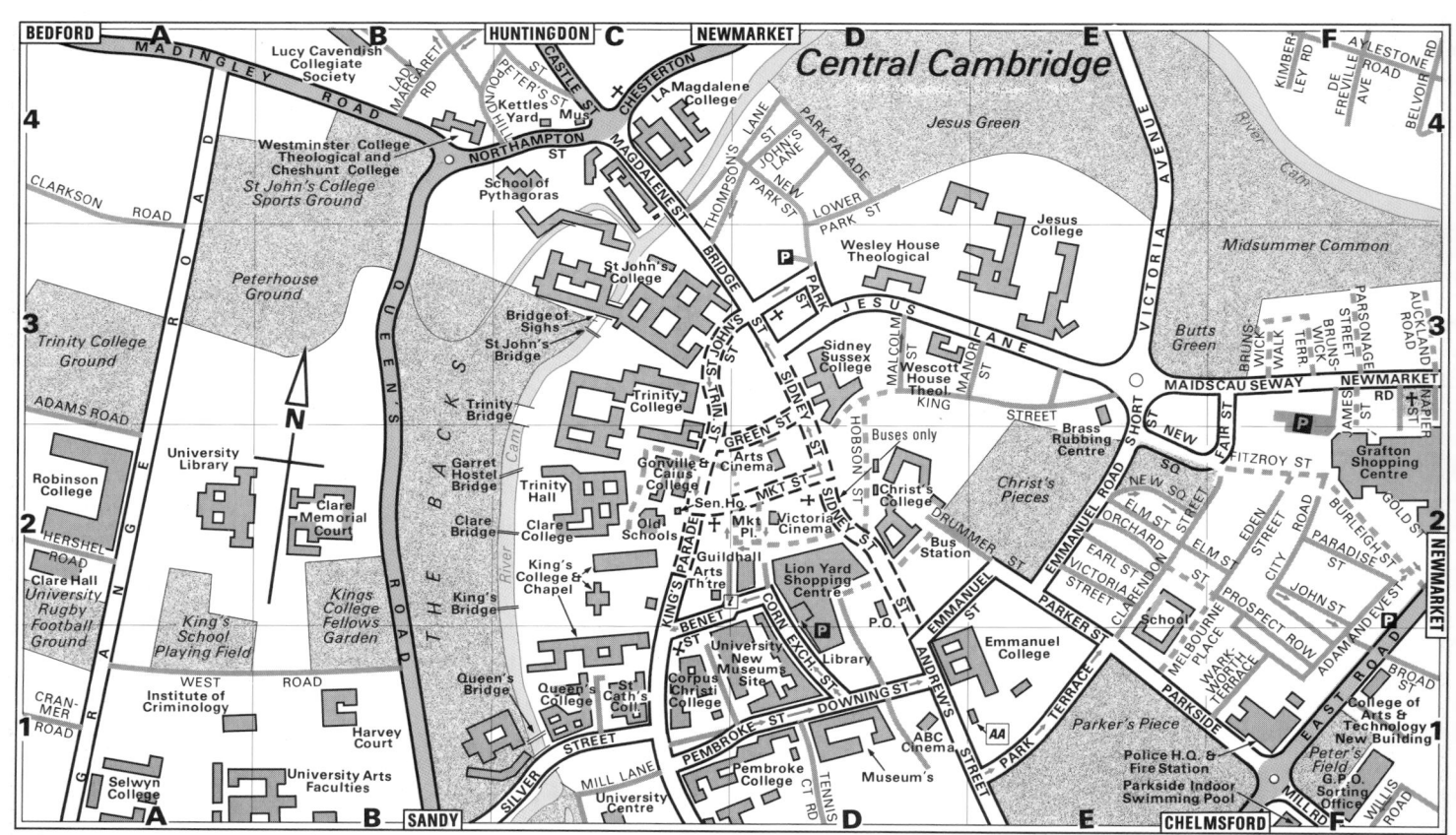

Charlinch Cleverton

Charlinch 20 ST 2337
Charlton (Gtr London) 27 TQ 4278
Charlton (Hants.) 24 SU 3547
Charlton (Here & W) 53 SP 0045
Charlton (Northants.) 38 SP 5236
Charlton (Northum.) 104 NY 8285
Charlton (Salop.) 63 SJ 5911
Charlton (Somer.) 21 ST 2827
Charlton (W Susx.) 14 SU 8812
Charlton (Wilts.) 11 ST 9021
Charlton (Wilts.) 36 ST 9688
Charlton (Wilts.) 23 SU 1155
Charlton (Wilts.) 23 SU 1723
Charlton Abbots 37 SP 0324
Charlton Adam 21 ST 5328
Charlton Horethorne 10 ST 6623
Charlton Kings 36 SO 9620
Charlton Mackrell 21 ST 5228
Charlton Marshall 11 ST 8903
Charlton Musgrove 22 ST 7229
Charlton-on-Otmoor 38 SP 5615
Charlwood 15 TQ 2441
Charminster 10 SY 6792
Charmouth 10 SY 3693
Charndon 38 SP 6724
Charney Bassett 38 SU 3894
Charnock Richard 82 SD 5415
Charsfield 59 TM 2556
Chart Sutton 28 TQ 8049
Charter Alley 24 SU 5957
Charterhouse 21 ST 4955
Chartershall 125 NS 7990
Charterville Allotments 37 SP 3110
Chartham 29 TR 1054
Chartham Hatch 29 TR 1056
Chartridge 39 SP 9303
Charwelton 54 SP 5455
Chase Terrace 65 SK 0409
Chasetown 65 SK 0408
Chastleton 37 SP 2429
Chatburn 83 SD 7644
Chatcull 64 SJ 7934
Chatham 28 TQ 7567
Chatham Green 42 TL 7115
Chathill 111 NU 1826
Chattenden 28 TQ 7672
Chatteris 56 TL 3986
Chattisham 58 TM 0942
Chatto 110 NT 7718
Chatton 111 NU 0528
Chawleigh 8 SS 7112
Chawston 56 TL 1556
Chawton 24 SU 7037
Chaxhill 36 SO 7314
Cheadle (Gtd Mches.) 76 SJ 8788
Cheadle (Staffs.) 76 SK 0043
Cheadle Hulme 76 SJ 8686
Cheam 26 TQ 2463
Chearsley 39 SP 7110
Chebsey 64 SJ 8528
Checkendon 38 SU 6682
Checkley (Ches.) 76 SJ 7245
Checkley (Staffs.) 65 SK 0237
Chedburgh 57 TL 7957
Cheddar 21 ST 4553
Cheddington 39 SP 9217
Cheddleton 76 SJ 9651
Cheddon Fitzpaine 20 ST 2327
Chedgrave 71 TM 3699
Chedington 10 ST 4805
Chediston 59 TM 3577
Chediston Green 59 TM 3578
Chedworth 37 SP 0511
Chedzoy 21 ST 3337
Cheesden 83 SD 8216
Cheesemaris Green 28 TR 0338
Cheetham Hill 83 SD 8401
Cheldon 8 SS 7313
Chelford 76 SJ 8174
Chellaston 66 SK 3830
Chellington 55 SP 9656
Chelmarsh 64 SO 7187
Chelmondiston 59 TM 2037
Chelmorton 77 SK 1169
Chelmsford 42 TL 7006
Chelsfield 27 TQ 4864
Chelsworth 58 TL 9748
Cheltenham 36 SO 9422
Chelveston 55 SP 9969
Chelvey 21 ST 4668
Chelwood 21 ST 6361
Chelwood Gate 16 TQ 4130
Chelworth 36 ST 9694
Chelworth Lower Green 37 SU 0892
Chelworth Upper Green 37 SU 0892
Cheney Longville 51 SO 4184
Chenies 26 TQ 0198
Chepstow 35 ST 5393
Cherhill 23 SU 0370
Cherington (Glos.) 36 ST 9098
Cheriton (Devon.) 19 SS 7346
Cheriton (Devon.) 9 ST 1001
Cheriton (Hants.) 13 SU 5828
Cheriton (Kent) 29 TR 2036
Cheriton (W Glam.) 32 SS 4593
Cheriton Bishop 8 SX 7793
Cheriton Fitzpaine 8 SS 8606
Cherrington 63 SJ 6619
Cherry Burton 86 SE 9842
Cherry Hinton 57 TL 4857
Cherry Willingham 80 TF 0173
Chertsey 26 TQ 0466
Cheselbourne 11 SY 7699
Chesham 39 SP 9601
Chesham Bois 39 SU 9698
Cheshunt 41 TL 3502
Cheslyn Hay 64 SJ 9707
Chessington 26 TQ 1863
Chester 75 SJ 4066
Chester-le-Street 97 NZ 2751
Chesterblade 22 ST 6641
Chesterfield (Derby.) 78 SK 3871
Chesterfield (Staffs.) 65 SK 1005
Chesters (Borders) 109 NT 6210
Chesters (Borders) 109 NT 6123
Chesterton (Cambs.) 68 TL 1295
Chesterton (Cambs.) 57 TL 4660
Chesterton (Oxon.) 38 SP 5621
Chesterton (Salop) 64 SO 7897
Chesterton (Staffs.) 76 SJ 8249
Chesterton Green 54 SP 3558
Chesterwood 104 NY 8365
Chestfield 29 TR 1365
Cheswardine 64 SJ 7129
Cheswick 119 NU 0346
Cheswick Green 53 SP 1275
Chetnole 10 ST 6008
Chettiscombe 8 SS 9614
Chettisham 57 TL 5483
Chettle 11 ST 9513
Chetton 51 SO 6690
Chetwode 38 SP 6429
Chetwynd Aston 64 SJ 7517
Cheveley 57 TL 6760
Chevening 27 TQ 4857
Chevington 57 TL 7860
Chevington Drift 111 NZ 2699
Chevithorne 8 SS 9715
Chew Magna 21 ST 5763
Chew Stoke 21 ST 5561
Chewton Keynsham 22 ST 6566
Chewton Mendip 21 ST 5952
Chicheley 55 SP 9046
Chichester 14 SU 8605
Chickerell 10 SY 6480
Chicklade 22 ST 9134
Chidden 14 SU 6517
Chiddingfold 25 SU 9635
Chiddingly 16 TQ 5414
Chiddingstone 16 TQ 5045
Chiddingstone Causeway 16 TQ 5147
Chideock 10 SY 4292
Chidgley 20 ST 0436
Chidham 14 SU 7803
Chidswell 84 SE 2623
Chieveley 24 SU 4773
Chignall Smealy 42 TL 6611
Chignall St. James 42 TL 6709
Chigwell 27 TQ 4493
Chigwell Row 27 TQ 4693
Chilbolton 24 SU 3939
Chilcomb (Hants.) 13 SU 5028
Chilcombe (Dorset) 10 SY 5291
Chilcompton 21 ST 6452
Chilcote 65 SK 2811
Child Okeford 11 ST 8312
Child's Ercall 63 SJ 6625
Childer Thornton 75 SJ 3677
Childrey 38 SU 3687
Childswickham 53 SP 0738
Childwall 75 SJ 4089
Chilfrome 10 SY 5898
Chilgrove 14 SU 8314
Chilham 29 TR 0753
Chilla 18 SS 4402
Chillaton 5 SX 4381
Chillenden 29 TR 2753
Chillerton 13 SZ 4883
Chillesford 59 TM 3852
Chillingham 111 NU 0625
Chillington (Devon.) 7 SX 7942
Chillington (Somer.) 10 ST 3811
Chilmark 22 ST 9632
Chilson 37 SP 3119
Chilsworthy (Corn.) 5 SX 4172
Chilsworthy (Devon.) 18 SS 3206
Chilthorne Domer 10 ST 5219
Chiltington 16 TQ 3815
Chilton (Bucks.) 38 SP 6811
Chilton (Devon) 8 SS 8603
Chilton (Durham) 98 NZ 3031
Chilton (Oxon.) 38 SU 4885
Chilton Candover 24 SU 5940
Chilton Cantelo 10 ST 5621
Chilton Foliat 23 SU 3170
Chilton Polden 21 ST 3739
Chilton Street 57 TL 7547
Chilton Trinity 21 ST 2939
Chilworth (Hants) 13 SU 4018
Chilworth (Surrey) 15 TQ 0246
Chimney 38 SP 3500
Chineham 24 SU 6554
Chingford 27 TQ 3893
Chinley 77 SK 0382
Chinnor 39 SP 7500
Chipnall 64 SJ 7231
Chippenham (Cambs.) 57 TL 6669
Chippenham (Wilts.) 22 ST 9173
Chipperfield 40 TL 0401
Chipping (Herts.) 41 TL 3532
Chipping (Lancs.) 83 SD 6243
Chipping Campden 53 SP 1539
Chipping Hill 42 TL 8215
Chipping Norton 37 SP 3127
Chipping Ongar 41 TL 5502
Chipping Sodbury 36 ST 7282
Chipping Warden 54 SP 4948
Chipstable 20 ST 0427
Chipstead (Kent) 27 TQ 5055
Chipstead (Surrey) 26 TQ 2756
Chirbury 50 SO 2598
Chirk 62 SJ 2937
Chirmorie 100 NX 2076
Chirnside 119 NT 8756
Chirnsidebridge 118 NT 8556
Chirton 23 SU 0757
Chisbury 23 SU 2766
Chiselborough 10 ST 4614
Chiseldon 37 SU 1879
Chislehampton 38 SU 5999
Chislehurst 27 TQ 4470
Chislet 29 TR 2264
Chiswellgreen 40 TL 1303
Chiswick 26 TQ 2077
Chisworth 76 SJ 9991
Chithurst 14 SU 8423
Chittering 57 TL 4970
Chitterne 22 ST 9843
Chittlehamholt 8 SS 6420
Chittlehampton 19 SS 6325
Chittoe 22 ST 9666
Chivelstone 7 SX 7838
Chivenor 19 SS 5034
Chobham 25 SU 9761
Cholderton 23 SU 2242
Cholesbury 39 SP 9307
Chollerford 104 NY 9170
Chollerton 104 NY 9372
Cholsey 38 SU 5886
Cholstrey 47 SO 4659
Chop Gate 92 SE 5699
Choppington 105 NZ 2583
Chopwell 105 NZ 1158
Chorley (Ches.) 63 SJ 5650
Chorley (Lancs.) 82 SD 5817
Chorley (Salop) 52 SO 6983
Chorley (Staffs.) 65 SK 0711
Chorleywood 26 TQ 0396
Chorlton 76 SJ 7250
Chorlton Lane 63 SJ 4547
Chorlton-cum-Hardy 76 SJ 8093
Chowley 75 SJ 4756
Chrishall 57 TL 4439
Christchurch (Cambs.) 69 TL 4996
Christchurch (Dorset) 12 SZ 1593
Christchurch (Glos.) 47 SO 5713
Christian Malford 36 ST 9678
Christleton 75 SJ 4365
Christmas Common 39 SU 7193
Christon 21 ST 3956
Christon Bank 111 NU 2122
Christow 8 SX 8385
Chudleigh 7 SX 8679
Chudleigh Knighton 7 SX 8477
Chulmleigh 8 SS 6814
Chunal 77 SK 0391
Church 83 SD 7428
Church Brampton 55 SP 7165
Church Broughton 65 SK 2033
Church Crookham 25 SU 8152
Church Eaton 64 SJ 8417
Church End (Beds.) 39 SP 9921
Church End (Beds.) 56 TL 1937
Church End (Beds.) 56 TL 1059
Church End (Cambs.) 68 TF 3909
Church End (Cambs.) 57 TL 4857
Church End (Cambs.) 56 TL 3669
Church End (Essex) 57 TL 5841
Church End (Hants.) 24 SU 6756
Church End (Warw.) 65 SP 2892
Church End (Warw.) 65 SP 2490
Church End (Wilts.) 37 SU 0278
Church Enstone 38 SP 3825
Church Fenton 85 SE 5136
Church Green 9 SY 1796
Church Gresley 65 SK 2918
Church Hanborough 38 SP 4212
Church Hill 75 SJ 6464
Church Knowle 11 SY 9481
Church Langton 67 SP 7293
Church Lawford 54 SP 4476
Church Lawton 76 SJ 8255
Church Leigh 65 SK 0235
Church Lench 53 SP 0251
Church Minshull 75 SJ 6660
Church Norton 14 SZ 8695
Church Preen 51 SO 5398
Church Pulverbatch 51 SJ 4303
Church Stoke 50 SO 2694
Church Stowe (Northants.) 54 SP 6357
Church Street 28 TQ 7174
Church Stretton 51 SO 4593
Church Town 26 TQ 3551
Church Village 34 ST 0886
Church Warsop 78 SK 5668
Churcham 36 SO 7618
Churchdown 36 SO 8819
Churchend (Essex) 42 TL 6323
Churchend (Essex) 43 TR 0092
Churchgate Street 41 TL 4811
Churchill (Avon) 21 ST 4359
Churchill (Devon) 9 ST 2901
Churchill (Here & W) 52 SO 8779
Churchill (Oxon.) 37 SP 2824
Churchill Green 21 ST 4360
Churchingford 9 ST 2112
Churchover 54 SP 5080
Churchstanton 9 ST 1914
Churchstow (Devon.) 6 SX 7145
Churchtown (Cumbr.) 95 NY 3742
Churchtown (Devon) 19 SS 6744
Churchtown (I. of M.) 162 SC 4294
Churchtown (Lancs.) 82 SD 4842
Churchtown (Mers.) 82 SD 3618
Churston Ferrers 7 SX 9056
Churt 25 SU 8538
Churton 75 SJ 4156
Churwell 84 SE 2729
Chwilog 60 SH 4338
Chyandour 2 SW 4731
Cilan Uchaf 60 SH 2923
Cilcain 74 SJ 1765
Cilcennin 44 SN 5160
Cilcewydd 50 SJ 2333
Cilfor 61 SH 6237
Cilfrew 33 SN 7600
Cilfynydd 34 ST 0892
Cilgerran 31 SN 1943
Cilgwyn 45 SN 7430
Ciliau-Aeron 44 SN 5058
Cilmaengwyn 33 SN 7406
Cilmalieu 129 NM 8955
Cilmery 46 SO 0051
Cilrhedyn 44 SN 2734
Cilsan 45 SN 5922
Ciltalgarth 61 SH 8840
Cilybebyll 33 SN 7404
Cilycwm 45 SN 7540
Cinderford 36 SO 6513
Cirencester 37 SP 0201
City Dulas 72 SH 4687
City, The 39 SU 7797
Clachaig 124 NS 1181
Clachan (Lismore Island) 129 NM 8543
Clachan (North Uist) 163 NF 8163
Clachan (Raasay) 145 NG 5436
Clachan (Strath.) 131 NN 1813
Clachan (Strath.) 129 NM 7819
Clachan (Strath.) 112 NR 7656
Clachan Mor 162 NL 9847
Clachan of Campsie 125 NS 6179
Clachan of Glendaruel 123 NR 9984
Clachan-Seil 129 NM 7718
Clachbreck 123 NR 7675
Clachnaharry 147 NH 6546
Clachtoll 156 NC 0427
Clackavoid 141 NO 1463
Clackmannan 126 NS 9191
Clacton-on-Sea 43 TM 1715
Cladich 130 NN 0921
Cladswell 53 SP 0458
Claggan 129 NM 7049
Claigan 144 NG 2354
Claines 52 SO 8559
Clandown 22 ST 6955
Clanfield (Hants.) 14 SU 6916
Clanfield (Oxon.) 37 SP 2801
Clannaborough Barton 8 SS 7402
Clanville 23 SU 3148
Claonaig 123 NR 8656
Claonel 154 NC 5604
Clapgate (Dorset) 12 SU 0102
Clapgate (Herts.) 41 TL 4424
Clapham (Beds.) 55 TL 0252
Clapham (Devon) 8 SX 8986
Clapham (Gtd London) 26 TQ 2875
Clapham (N Yorks.) 89 SD 7469
Clapham (W Susx) 15 TQ 0906
Clappers 119 NT 9455
Clappersgate 88 NY 3603
Clapton 21 ST 6453
Clapton (Somer.) 10 ST 4106
Clapton-in-Gordano 35 ST 4774
Clapton-on-the-Hill (Glos.) 37 SP 1617
Clapworthy 19 SS 6724
Clarach 48 SN 6084
Clarbeston 30 SN 0421
Clarbeston Road 30 SN 0121
Clarborough 79 SK 7383
Clardon 159 ND 1468
Clare 57 TL 7645
Clarebrand 102 NX 7666
Clarencefield 102 NY 0968
Clark's Green 15 TQ 1739
Clarkston 115 NS 5757
Clashindarroch 150 NJ 4832
Clashmore 155 NH 7489
Clashnessie 156 NC 0530
Clatt 150 NJ 5426
Clatter 49 SN 9994
Clatworthy 20 ST 0530
Claughton (Lancs.) 82 SD 5242
Claughton (Lancs.) 89 SD 5666
Claunie Inn 137 NH 0712
Claverdon 53 SP 1964
Claverham 21 ST 4566
Clavering 41 TL 4832
Claverley 64 SO 7993
Claverton 22 ST 7864
Clawdd-newydd 62 SJ 0852
Clawthorpe 89 SD 5377
Clawton 5 SX 3599
Claxby (Lincs.) 80 TF 1194
Claxby (Lincs.) 81 TF 4571
Claxton (N Yorks.) 92 SE 6960
Claxton (Norf.) 71 TG 3303
Clay Common 59 TM 4781
Clay Coton 54 SP 5977
Clay Cross 78 SK 3963
Clay End 41 TL 3025
Claybokie 141 NO 0889
Claybrooke Magna 54 SP 4988
Claydon (Oxon.) 54 SP 4550
Claydon (Suff.) 58 TM 1350
Claygate (Kent) 28 TQ 7144
Claygate (Surrey) 26 TQ 1563
Claygate Cross 27 TQ 6155
Clayhanger (Devon.) 9 ST 0223
Clayhanger (W Mids.) 65 SK 0404
Clayhidon 9 ST 1615
Clayhill (E. Susx.) 17 TQ 8423
Clayhill (Hants) 13 SU 3007
Clayhithe 57 TL 5064
Claypits 36 SO 7606
Claypole 79 SK 8449
Clayton (S Yorks.) 85 SE 4507
Clayton (Staffs.) 76 SJ 8443
Clayton (W Susx.) 15 TQ 3014
Clayton (W Yorks.) 84 SE 1131
Clayton Green 82 SD 5723
Clayton West 84 SE 2511
Clayton-le-Moors 83 SD 7431
Clayton-le-Woods 82 SD 5722
Clayworth 79 SK 7288
Cleadale 136 NM 4789
Cleadon 105 NZ 3862
Clearbrook 5 SX 5265
Clearwell 35 SO 5708
Cleasby 97 NZ 2713
Cleat 163 ND 4585
Cleatlam 97 NZ 1118
Cleator 94 NY 0113
Cleator Moor 94 NY 0214
Cleckheaton 84 SE 1825
Clee St. Margaret 51 SO 5684
Cleedownton 51 SO 5880
Cleehill 51 SO 5975
Cleethorpes 87 TA 3008
Cleeton St. Mary 51 SO 6178
Cleeve 21 ST 4566
Cleeve Hill 36 SO 9827
Cleeve Prior 53 SP 0849
Clehonger 47 SO 4637
Cleish 126 NT 0998
Cleland 115 NS 7958
Clench Common 23 SU 1765
Clenchwarton 69 TF 5820
Clent 52 SO 9179
Cleobury Mortimer 52 SO 6775
Cleobury North 51 SO 6187
Cleongart 112 NR 6734
Clephanton 148 NH 8450
Clerklands 109 NT 5024
Clestran 163 HY 3107
Clevancy 23 SU 0475
Clevedon 35 ST 4071
Cleveleys 82 SD 3142
Cleverton 36 ST 9785

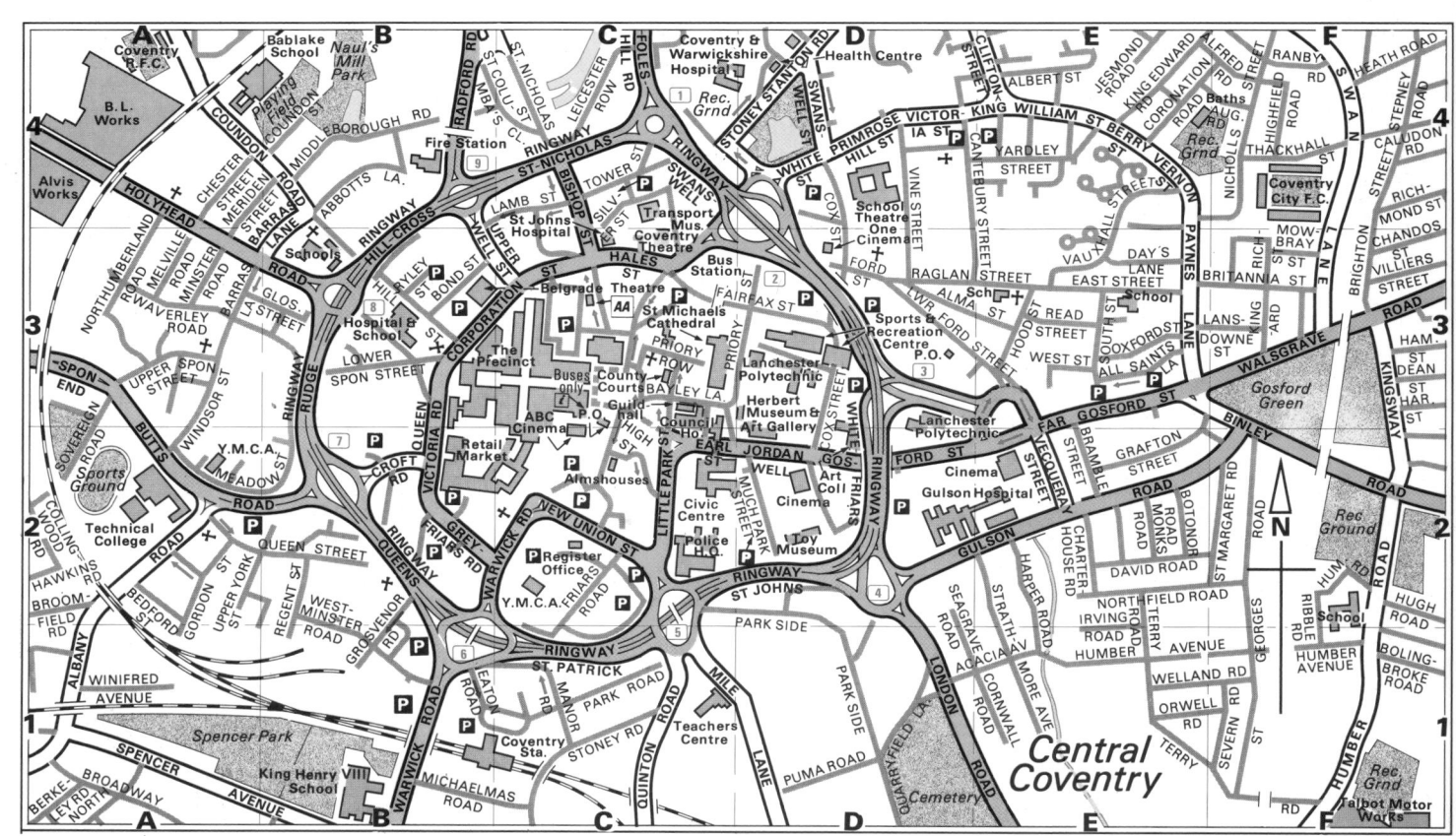

Central Coventry

Craven Arms Dalton-on-Tees

Craven Arms 51 SO 4382
Crawcrook 105 NZ 1363
Crawford 108 NS 9520
Crawfordjohn 107 NS 8823
Crawick 107 NS 7710
Crawley (Hants.) 24 SU 4234
Crawley (Oxon.) 37 SP 3312
Crawley (W Susx.) 15 TQ 2636
Crawley Down 15 TQ 3437
Crawleyside 97 NY 9940
Crawshawbooth 83 SD 8125
Crawton 143 NO 8779
Cray (N Yorks.) 90 SD 9479
Cray's Pond 24 SU 6380
Crayford 27 TQ 5175
Crayke 92 SE 5670
Crays Hill 42 TQ 7192
Craze Lowman 8 SS 9814
Creacombe 8 SS 8119
Creagorry 163 NF 7948
Creaton 54 SP 7071
Creca 102 NY 2371
Credenhill 47 SO 4543
Crediton 8 SS 8300
Creech Heathfield 20 ST 2827
Creech St. Michael 20 ST 2725
Creed 3 SW 9347
Creedy Park 8 SS 8302
Creekmouth 27 TQ 4581
Creeting Bottoms 58 TM 1157
Creeting St. Mary 58 TM 0956
Creeton 67 TF 0120
Creetown 101 NX 4758
Creggans 123 NN 0802
Cregneish 162 SC 1967
Cregrina 46 SO 1252
Creich (Fife.) 134 NO 3221
Creigiau 34 ST 0881
Cremyll 6 SX 4553
Cressage 51 SJ 5904
Cressbrook 77 SK 1673
Cresselly 30 SN 0606
Cressing 42 TL 7920
Cresswell (Dyfed) 30 SN 0506
Cresswell (Northum.) 111 NZ 2993
Cresswell (Staffs.) 64 SJ 9739
Creswell (Derby.) 78 SK 5274
Cretingham 59 TM 2260
Cretshengan 123 NR 7268
Crew Green 63 SJ 3215
Crewe (Ches.) 75 SJ 4253
Crewe (Ches.) 76 SJ 7055
Crewkerne 10 ST 4409
Crews Hill 41 TL 3100
Crianlarich 131 NN 3825
Cribbs Causeway 35 ST 5780
Cribyn 45 SN 5251
Criccieth 60 SH 4938
Crich 78 SK 3554
Crichie 151 NJ 9544
Crichton 117 NT 3862
Crick 35 ST 4890
Crick (Northants.) 54 SP 5872
Crickadarn 46 SO 0942
Cricket St. Thomas 10 ST 3708
Crickheath 62 SJ 2923
Crickhowell 46 SO 2118
Cricklade 37 SU 0993
Cridling Stubbs 85 SE 5221
Crieff 133 NN 8621
Criggion 62 SJ 2915
Crigglestone 85 SE 3116
Crimble 83 SD 8612
Crimond 151 NK 0556
Crimplesham 69 TF 6503
Crinaglack 147 NH 4240
Crinan 123 NR 7894
Cringleford 71 TG 1905
Crinow 31 SN 1214
Cripp's Corner 17 TQ 7821
Cripplesease 2 SW 5036
Cripplestyle 12 SU 0912
Croachy 148 NH 6527
Croasdale 94 NY 0917
Crockenhill 27 TQ 5067
Crocker End 38 SU 7086
Crocker's Ash 47 SO 5316
Crockerhill 14 SU 9207
Crockernwell 8 SX 7592
Crockerton 22 ST 8642
Crocketford or Ninemile Bar 102 NX 8272
Crockey Hill 85 SE 6246
Crockham Hill 27 TQ 4450
Crockleford Heath 43 TM 0426
Croes-lan 44 SN 3844
Croes-y-mwyalch 35 ST 3092
Croeserw 33 SS 8695
Croesgoch 30 SM 8330
Croesyceiliog (Gwent) 44 SN 4016
Croesyceiliog (Gwent) 35 ST 3196
Croesywaun 72 SH 5159
Croft (Ches.) 75 SJ 6393
Croft (Leic.) 66 SP 5195
Croft (Lincs.) 81 TF 5162
Croft-on-Tees 97 NZ 2909
Croftamie 124 NS 4786
Croftgarbh 132 NN 7348
Crofton (W. Yorks.) 85 SE 3717
Crofton (Wilts.) 23 SU 2562
Crofts of Benachielt 159 ND 1739
Crofts of Blackburn 150 NJ 5433
Crofts of Haddo 151 NJ 8337
Crofts of Inverthernie 150 NJ 7344
Crofts of Meikle Ardo 151 NJ 8542
Crofts of Savoch 151 NK 0561
Crofts of Shanquhar 150 NJ 5536
Crofty 32 SS 5295
Crogen 62 SJ 0237
Croggan 129 NM 7027
Croglin 95 NY 5747
Croick 154 NH 4591
Cromarty 148 NH 7867
Crombie 125 NT 0585
Cromblet 150 NJ 7836
Cromdale 149 NJ 0728
Cromer (Herts.) 41 TL 2928
Cromer (Norf.) 71 TG 2142
Cromford 77 SK 2956
Cromhall 36 ST 6990
Cromhall Common 36 ST 6989
Cromore 163 NB 4021
Cromra 139 NN 5489
Cromwell 79 SK 7961
Cronberry 107 NS 6022
Crondall 25 SU 7948
Cronk, The 162 SC 3495
Cronk-y-Voddy 162 SC 3086
Cronton 75 SJ 4988
Crook (Cumbr.) 89 SD 4695
Crook (Durham) 97 NZ 1635
Crook of Devon 126 NO 0300
Crooked End 47 SO 6217
Crookham (Berks.) 24 SU 5364
Crookham (Northum.) 119 NT 9138
Crookham Village 25 SU 7952
Crookhouse 110 NT 7627
Crooklands 89 SD 5383
Cropredy 54 SP 4646
Cropston 66 SK 5511
Cropthorne 53 SO 9944
Cropton 92 SE 7589
Cropwell Bishop 66 SK 6835
Cropwell Butler 66 SK 6837
Crosby (Cumbr.) 94 NY 0738
Crosby (I. of M.) 162 SC 3279
Crosby (Mers.) 82 SJ 3099
Crosby Garrett 89 NY 7309
Crosby Ravensworth 95 NY 6214
Crosby Villa 94 NY 0939
Croscombe 21 ST 5844
Cross (Somerset) 21 ST 4154
Cross Ash 47 SO 4019
Cross Bush 15 TQ 0306
Cross End 55 TL 0658
Cross Foxes Hotel 61 SH 7616
Cross Green (Devon.) 5 SX 3888
Cross Green (Staffs.) 64 SJ 9105
Cross Green (Suff.) 58 TL 9952
Cross Hands 45 SN 5612
Cross Hills 84 SE 0145
Cross Houses (Salop) 51 SJ 5307
Cross Inn (Dyfed) 44 SN 3957
Cross Inn (Dyfed) 48 SN 5464
Cross Inn (Dyfed) 45 SN 7725
Cross Inn (Mid Glam.) 34 ST 0583
Cross Lane Head 64 SO 7095
Cross Lanes (Clwyd) 63 SJ 3746
Cross Lanes (Dorset) 11 ST 7602
Cross Lanes (N Yorks.) 92 SE 5264
Cross Roads 5 SX 4586
Cross Street 59 TM 1876
Cross in Hand 16 TQ 5621
Cross of Jackston 150 NJ 7432
Crossaig 112 NR 8351
Crossapoll 162 NL 9943
Crossbost 163 NB 3924
Crosscanonby 94 NY 0739
Crossdale Street 71 TG 2239
Crossens 82 SD 3719
Crossford (Fife.) 126 NT 0686
Crossford (Strath.) 116 NS 8246
Crossgates (Fife.) 126 NT 1488
Crossgates (Powys) 50 SO 0865
Crossgill 89 SD 5562
Crosshill (Fife.) 126 NT 1796
Crosshill (Strath.) 106 NS 3206
Crosshouse (Strath.) 114 NS 3938
Crossings 109 NY 5177
Crosskeys (Gwent) 34 ST 2292
Crosskirk 158 ND 0370
Crosslanes (Salop.) 63 SJ 3218
Crosslee 109 NT 3018
Crossmichael 102 NX 7267
Crossmoor 82 SD 4438
Crosspost 15 TQ 2522
Crossway (Gwent) 47 SO 4419
Crossway (Here & W) 47 SO 6130
Crossway (Powys) 46 SO 0557
Crossway Green 52 SO 8368
Crossways 11 SY 7688
Crosswell 31 SN 1236
Crosthwaite 89 SD 4491
Croston 82 SD 4818
Crostwick 71 TG 2515
Crostwight 71 TG 3329
Crouch Hill 10 ST 7010
Crouchers 14 SU 8401
Croucheston 23 SU 0625
Croughton 38 SP 5433
Crovie 151 NJ 8065
Crow 12 SU 1603
Crow Hill 47 SO 6326
Crow's Nest 5 SX 2669
Crowan 2 SW 6434
Crowborough 16 TQ 5130
Crowcombe 20 ST 1336
Crowe Green 52 SO 9256
Crowell 39 SU 7499
Crowfield (Northants.) 54 SP 6141
Crowfield (Suff.) 58 TM 1557
Crowhurst (E Susx) 17 TQ 7512
Crowhurst (Surrey) 16 TQ 3947
Crowhurst Lane End 27 TQ 3848
Crowland 68 TF 2310
Crowlas 2 SW 5133
Crowle (Here & W) 52 SO 9256
Crowle (Humbs.) 86 SE 7713
Crowmarsh Gifford 38 SU 6189
Crown Corner 59 TM 2570
Crownhill 5 SX 4857
Crownthorpe 70 TG 0803
Crowntown 2 SW 6331
Crows-an-Wra 2 SW 3927
Crowthorn School 83 SD 7518
Crowthorne 25 SU 8464
Crowton 75 SJ 5774
Croxall 65 SK 1913
Croxdale 97 NZ 2636
Croxden 65 SK 0639
Croxley Green 26 TQ 0795
Croxton 70 TF 9831
Croxton (Cambs.) 56 TL 2459
Croxton (Humbs.) 87 TA 0912
Croxton (Norf.) 58 TL 8786
Croxton (Staffs.) 64 SJ 7832
Croxton Kerrial 67 SK 8329
Croy (Highld.) 148 NH 7949
Croy (Strath.) 125 NS 7275
Croyde 18 SS 4439
Croyde Bay 18 SS 4339
Croydon (Cambs.) 56 TL 3149
Croydon (Gtr London) 26 TQ 3365
Cruckmeole 51 SJ 4309
Cruckton 63 SJ 4210
Cruden Bay 151 NK 0936
Crudgington 63 SJ 6317
Crudwell 36 ST 9592
Crug 50 SO 1872
Crugmeer 4 SW 9076
Crugybar 45 SN 6537
Crulivig 163 NB 1733
Crumlin 34 ST 2198
Crundale (Dyfed.) 30 SM 9718
Crundale (Kent) 29 TR 0749
Crunwear 31 SN 1810
Cruwys Morchard 8 SS 8712
Crux Easton 24 SU 4256
Crwbin 44 SN 4713
Crymmych 31 SN 1833
Crynant 33 SN 7095
Crystal Palace 26 TQ 3470
Cuaig 145 NG 7057
Cubbington 54 SP 3368
Cubert 3 SW 7857
Cubley 84 SE 2401
Cublington 39 SP 8422
Cuckfield 15 TQ 3024
Cucklington 22 ST 7527
Cuckney 78 SK 5671
Cuckoo's Corner 25 SU 7441
Cuddesdon 38 SP 5902
Cuddington (Bucks.) 39 SP 7311
Cuddington (Ches.) 75 SJ 5971
Cuddington Heath 63 SJ 4646
Cuddy Hill 82 SD 4937
Cudham 27 TQ 4459
Cudliptown 5 SX 5278
Cudworth (S Yorks.) 85 SE 3808
Cudworth (Somer.) 10 ST 3810
Cuffley 41 TL 3002
Culbo 148 NH 6360
Culbokie 147 NH 6059
Culburnie 147 NH 4941
Culcabock 148 NH 6844
Culcharry 148 NH 8650
Culcheth 75 SJ 6594
Culdrain 150 NJ 5133
Culduie 145 NG 7140
Culford 58 TL 8370
Culgaith 95 NY 6129
Culham 38 SU 5095
Culkein 156 NC 0333
Culkein Drumbeg 156 NC 1133
Culkerton 36 ST 9296
Cullachie 148 NH 9720
Cullen 150 NJ 5166
Cullercoats 105 NZ 3571
Cullerlie 143 NJ 7603
Cullicudden 148 NH 6564
Cullingworth 84 SE 0636
Cullipool 129 NM 7313
Cullivoe 163 HP 5402
Culloch 132 NN 7818
Cullompton 9 ST 0207
Culmaily 155 NH 8099
Culmington 51 SO 4982
Culmstock 9 ST 1013
Culnacraig 153 NC 0603
Culnaknock 144 NG 5263
Culrain 154 NH 5794
Culross 126 NS 9885
Culroy 106 NS 3114
Culsh (Grampn.) 151 NJ 8848
Culsh (Grampn.) 142 NO 3598
Culswick 163 HU 2745
Cultercullen 151 NJ 9124
Cults (Grampn.) 150 NJ 5331
Cults (Grampn.) 143 NJ 8903
Culverlane 7 SX 7460
Culverstone Green 27 TQ 6363
Culverthorpe 67 TF 0240
Culworth 54 SP 5447
Cumbernauld 125 NS 7676
Cumberworth 81 TF 5073
Cuminestown 151 NJ 8050
Cummersdale 103 NY 3952
Cummertrees 103 NY 1366
Cummingston 149 NJ 1368
Cumnock 107 NS 5619
Cumnor 38 SP 4604
Cumrew 95 NY 5550
Cumwhinton 95 NY 4552
Cumwhitton 95 NY 5052
Cundall (N Yorks.) 91 SE 4272
Cunninghamhead 114 NS 3741
Cupar 134 NO 3714
Cupar Muir 134 NO 3613
Curbar 77 SK 2574
Curbridge (Hants.) 13 SU 5211
Curbridge (Oxon.) 37 SP 3208
Curdridge 13 SU 5313
Curdworth 65 SP 1892
Curland 9 ST 2716
Currarie 106 NX 1693
Curridge 24 SU 4972
Currie 117 NT 1867
Curry Mallet 9 ST 3221
Curry Rivel 21 ST 3824
Curtisden Green 28 TQ 7440
Curtisknowle 6 SX 7353
Cury 2 SW 6721
Cushnie 151 NJ 7962
Cushuish 20 ST 1930
Cusop 46 SO 2341
Cutcombe 20 SS 9239
Cuthill (Highld.) 155 NH 7587
Cutiau 61 SH 6317
Cutnall Green 52 SO 8768
Cutsdean 37 SP 0830
Cutthorpe 78 SK 3473
Cuxham 38 SU 6695
Cuxton 28 TQ 7166
Cuxwold 87 TA 1701
Cwm (Clwyd) 74 SJ 0677
Cwm (Gwent) 34 SO 1805
Cwm (W Glam.) 32 SS 6895
Cwm Irfon 49 SN 8549
Cwm-Cewydd 61 SH 8713
Cwm-Llinau 49 SH 8407
Cwm-y-glo 72 SH 5562
Cwmafan 33 SS 7892
Cwmaman 32 SS 9999
Cwmann 45 SN 5747
Cwmbach (Dyfed) 44 SN 2525
Cwmbach (Mid Glam.) 34 SO 0201
Cwmbelan 49 SN 9481
Cwmbran 34 ST 2894
Cwmcarn 34 ST 2293
Cwmcarvan 35 SO 4707
Cwmcoy 44 SN 2941
Cwmdare 33 SN 9803
Cwmdu (Dyfed) 45 SN 6330
Cwmdu (Powys) 46 SO 1823
Cwmduad 44 SN 3731
Cwmfelin 33 SS 8889
Cwmfelin Boeth 31 SN 1919
Cwmfelin Mynach 44 SN 2324
Cwmfelinfach 34 ST 1891
Cwmffrwd 44 SN 4217
Cwmgorse 32 SN 7110
Cwmgwrach 33 SN 8605
Cwmisfael 44 SN 4915
Cwmllynfell 33 SN 7413
Cwmparc 33 SS 9496
Cwmpengraig 44 SN 3436
Cwmpennar 34 SO 0400
Cwmsychpant 44 SN 4746
Cwmtillery 34 SO 2105
Cwmyoy 47 SO 2923
Cwmystwyth 49 SN 7873
Cwn-y-glo 45 SN 5513
Cwrt-newydd 44 SN 4847
Cwrt-y-gollen 46 SO 2317
Cyffylliog 74 SJ 0557
Cylibebyll 33 SN 7404
Cymmer (Mid Glam.) 34 ST 0290
Cymmer (W Glam.) 62 SS 8696
Cynghardy 45 SN 8139
Cynonville 33 SS 8295
Cynwyd 62 SJ 0541
Cynwyl Elfed 44 SN 3727

D

Daccombe 7 SX 9068
Dacre (Cumbr.) 95 NY 4526
Dacre (N Yorks.) 91 SE 1960
Dacre Banks 91 SE 1961
Daddry Shield 96 NY 8937
Dadford 54 SP 6638
Dadlington 66 SP 4098
Dafen 32 SN 5201
Daffy Green 70 TF 9609
Dagenham 27 TQ 5084
Daglingworth 37 SO 9905
Dagnall 39 SP 9916
Dailly 106 NS 2701
Dairsie or Osnaburgh 134 NO 4117
Dalavich 130 NM 9612
Dalbeattie 102 NX 8361
Dalblair 107 NS 6419
Dalbog 142 NO 5871
Dalby 162 SC 2178
Dalcapon 133 NN 9755
Dalchalloch 140 NN 7264
Dalchalm 154 NC 9106
Dalchenna 123 NN 0706
Dalchork 154 NC 5711
Dalchreichart 139 NH 2912
Dalchruin 132 NN 7316
Dalcross 148 NH 7748
Dalderby 80 TF 2465
Dale (Derby.) 66 SK 4338
Dale (Dyfed) 30 SM 8005
Dale (Shetld.) 163 HU 1852
Dalelia 137 NM 7369
Dalgarven 114 NS 2945
Dalgety Bay 126 NT 1683
Dalginross 132 NN 7721
Dalguise 133 NN 9947
Dalhalvaig 158 NC 8954
Dalham 57 TL 7261
Daliburgh 163 NF 7421
Dalkeith 117 NT 3367
Dall 132 NN 5956
Dallas 149 NJ 1252
Dalleagles 107 NS 5710
Dallinghoo 59 TM 2654
Dallington 16 TQ 6519
Dalmally 131 NN 1527
Dalmary 125 NS 5195
Dalmellington 106 NS 4705
Dalmeny 126 NT 1477
Dalmeny Rows 126 NT 1478
Dalmore (Highld.) 148 NH 6668
Dalnabreck 137 NM 7069
Dalnavie 154 NH 6483
Dalnawillan Lodge 158 ND 0341
Dalness 131 NN 1751
Dalqueich 126 NO 0704
Dalry 114 NS 2949
Dalrymple 106 NS 3514
Dalserf 115 NS 7950
Dalston 103 NY 3750
Dalswinton 108 NX 9385
Dalton (Dumf & G) 103 NY 1173
Dalton (Lancs.) 82 SD 4907
Dalton (N Yorks.) 97 NZ 1108
Dalton (N Yorks.) 91 SE 4376
Dalton (N Yorks.) 78 SK 4593
Dalton (Northum.) 104 NY 9158
Dalton (Northum.) 105 NZ 1172
Dalton Piercy 98 NZ 4631
Dalton in Furness 88 SD 2374
Dalton-le-Dale 98 NZ 4047
Dalton-on-Tees 97 NZ 2908

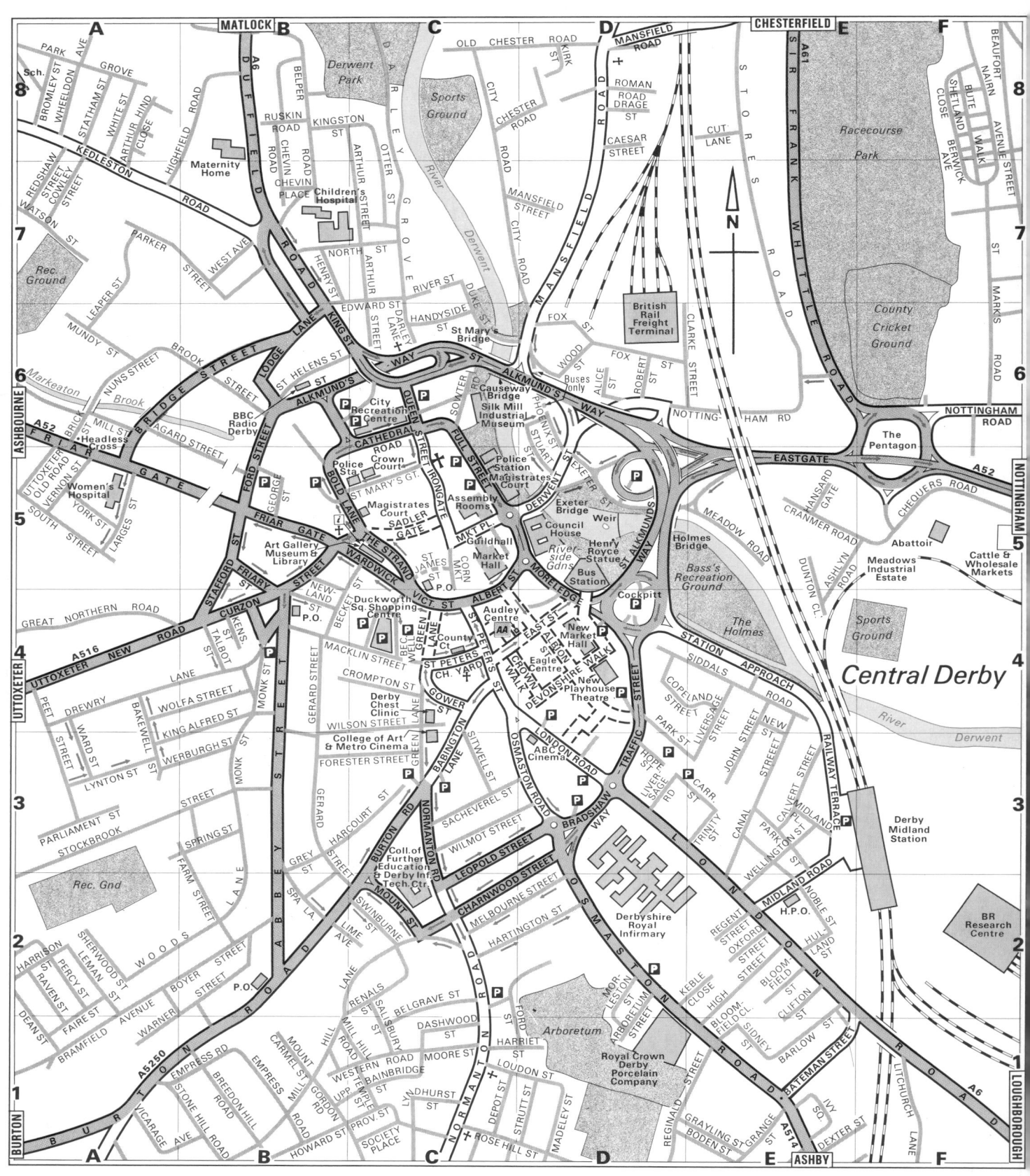

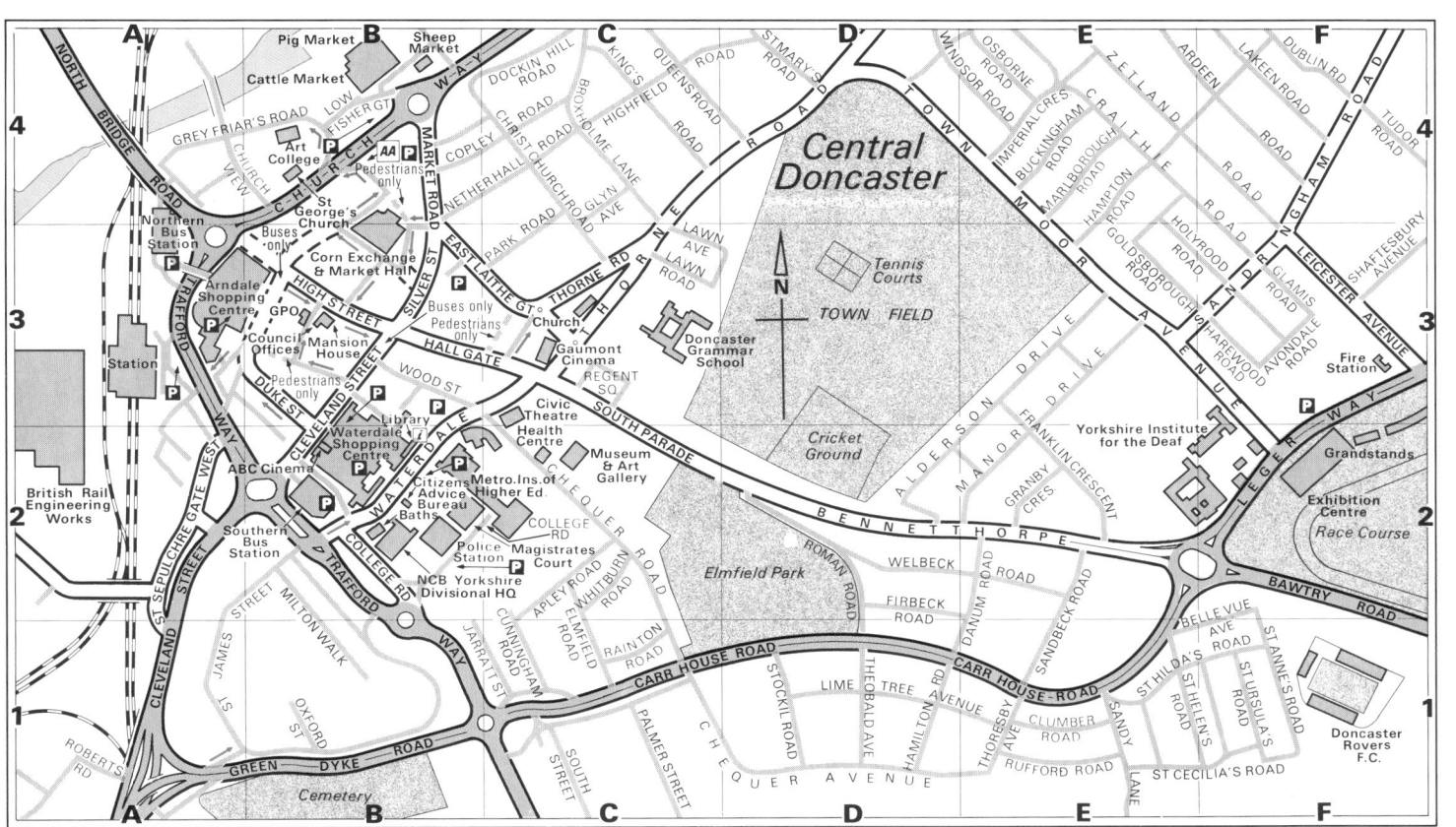

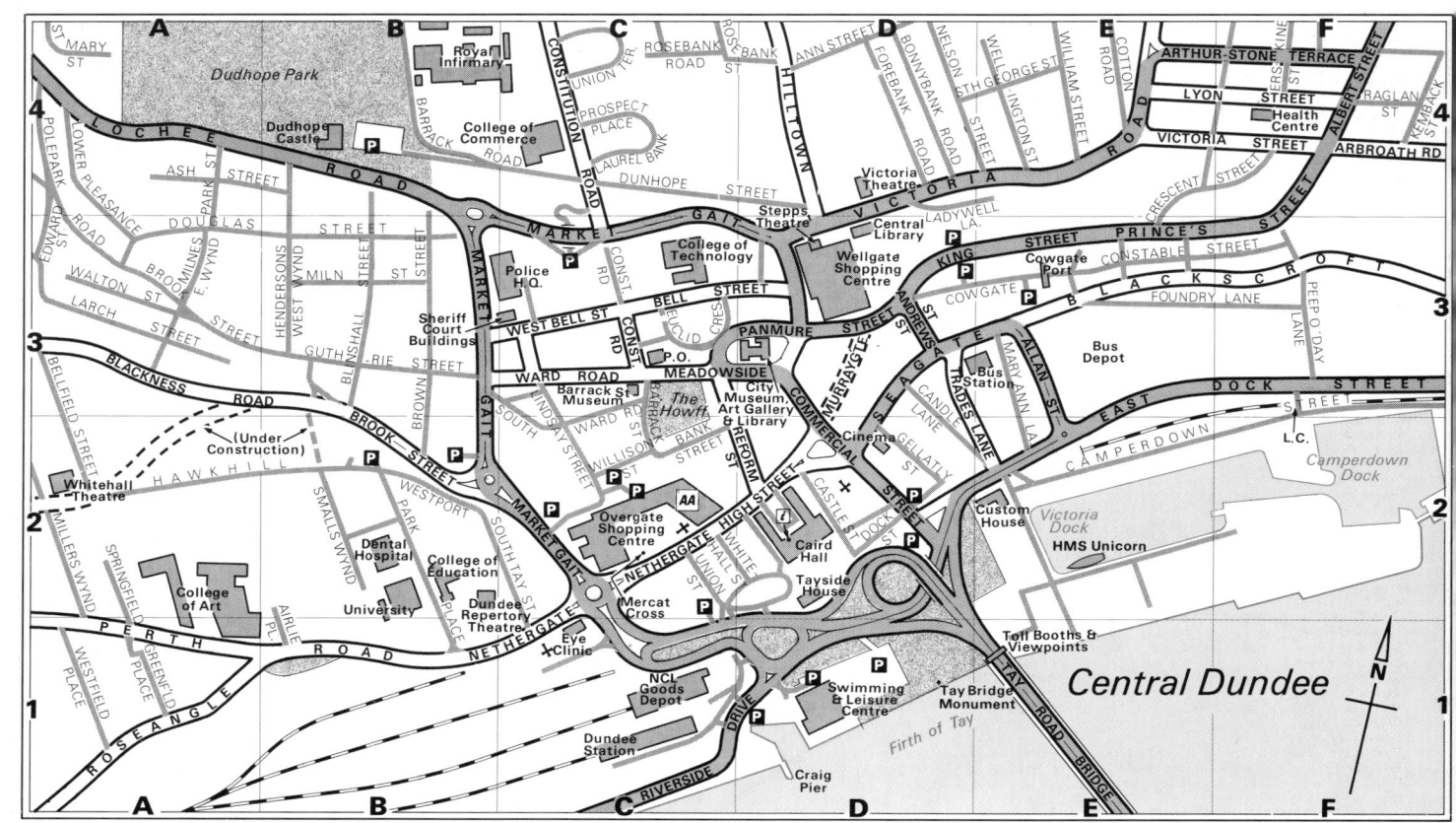

Dunkirk (Avon) Edge

Dunkirk (Avon) 36 ST 7886
Dunkirk (Kent) 29 TR 0758
Dunlappie 142 NO 5967
Dunley 52 SO 7869
Dunlop 114 NS 4049
Dunmere Bridge 4 SX 0467
Dunmore (Central.) 126 NS 8989
Dunmore (Strath.) 123 NR 7961
Dunnet 159 ND 2171
Dunnichen 135 NO 5048
Dunning 133 NO 0114
Dunnington (Humbs.) 93 TA 1551
Dunnington (N. Yorks.) 92 SE 6652
Dunnington (Warw.) 53 SP 0653
Dunnockshaw 83 SD 8127
Dunollie 129 NM 8532
Dunoon 124 NS 1777
Dunphail 148 NJ 0148
Dunragit 100 NX 1557
Duns 118 NT 7853
Duns Tew 38 SP 4528
Dunsby 68 TF 1026
Dunscore 102 NX 8684
Dunscroft 85 SE 6409
Dunsdale 98 NZ 6119
Dunsden Green 25 SU 7477
Dunsfold 14 TQ 0036
Dunsfold Green 14 TQ 0037
Dunsford 8 SX 8089
Dunshelt 134 NO 2410
Dunshillock 151 NJ 9848
Dunsley 99 NZ 8511
Dunsmore 39 SP 8605
Dunsop Bridge 83 SD 6549
Dunstable 40 TL 0221
Dunstall 65 SK 1920
Dunstall Green 57 TL 7460
Dunstan 111 NU 2419
Dunster 20 SS 9943
Dunston (Lincs.) 80 TF 0663
Dunston (Norf.) 71 TG 2302
Dunston (Staffs.) 64 SJ 9217
Dunston (Tyne and Wear) 105 NZ 2263
Dunstone (Devon) 6 SX 5951
Dunstone (Devon) 6 SX 7175
Dunsville 85 SE 6407
Dunswell 87 TA 0735
Dunsyre 116 NT 0748
Dunterton 5 SX 3779
Duntisbourne Abbots 36 SO 9707
Duntisbourne Rouse 36 SO 9805
Dunsish 10 ST 6906
Duntocher 124 NS 4972
Dunton (Beds.) 56 TL 2344
Dunton (Bucks.) 39 SP 8224
Dunton (Norf.) 70 TF 8730
Dunton Bassett 66 SP 5490
Dunton Green 27 TQ 5157
Dunton Wayletts 27 TQ 6590
Duntulm 143 NG 4275
Dunure 106 NS 2515
Dunvant 32 SS 5993
Dunvegan 144 NG 2548
Dunwich 59 TM 4770
Durdar 103 NY 4051
Durham 97 NZ 2742
Durisdeer 107 NS 8903
Durisdeermill 106 NS 8804
Durleigh 20 ST 2736
Durley (Hants.) 13 SU 5115
Durley (Wilts.) 23 SU 2364
Durley Street 13 SU 5217
Durnamuck 152 NH 0192
Durness 157 NC 4067
Durno 150 NJ 7128
Durran 159 ND 1863
Durrington (W Susx.) 15 TQ 1105
Durrington (Wilts.) 23 SU 1544
Dursley 36 ST 7597
Dursley Cross 36 SO 6920
Durston 21 ST 2828
Durweston 11 ST 8508
Duston 55 SP 7261
Duthil 148 NH 9324
Dutlas 50 SO 2077
Duton Hill 42 TL 6026
Dutson 5 SX 3485
Dutton 75 SJ 5779
Duxford 57 TL 4846
Dwygyfylchi 73 SH 7377
Dwyran 72 SH 4466
Dyce 143 NJ 8812
Dye House 104 NY 9458
Dyffryn 33 SS 8593
Dyffryn Ardudwy 61 SH 5822
Dyffryn Castell 49 SN 7781
Dyffryn Ceidrych 45 SN 7025
Dyffryn Cellwen 33 SN 8509
Dyke (Devon.) 18 SS 3123
Dyke (Grampn.) 149 NH 9858
Dyke (Lincs.) 68 TF 1022
Dykehead (Central) 125 NS 5997
Dykehead (Strath.) 116 NS 8759
Dykehead (Tays.) 134 NO 3860
Dykends 134 NO 2557
Dylife 49 SN 8594
Dymchurch 17 TR 1029
Dymock 36 SO 6931
Dyrham 22 ST 7375
Dysart 127 NT 3093
Dyserth 74 SJ 0579

E

Eagland Hill 82 SD 4345
Eagle 79 SK 8767
Eaglescliffe 98 NZ 4215
Eaglesfield (Cumbr.) 94 NY 0928
Eaglesfield (Dumf & G) 103 NY 2374
Eaglesham 115 NS 5751
Eaglethorpe 68 TL 0791
Eairy 162 SC 2977
Eakring 79 SK 6762
Ealand 86 SE 7811
Ealing 26 TQ 1781
Eals 95 NY 6856
Eamont Bridge 95 NY 5228
Earby 83 SD 9046
Eardington 64 SO 7290
Eardisland 47 SO 4158
Eardisley 47 SO 3149
Eardiston (Here & W) 52 SO 6968
Eardiston (Salop) 63 SJ 3725
Earith 56 TL 3875
Earl Shilton 66 SP 4697
Earl Soham 59 TM 2363
Earl Sterndale 77 SK 0967
Earl Stonham 58 TM 1158
Earl's Croome 52 SO 8642
Earl's Green 58 TM 0366
Earl's Seat (Central) (mt.) 125 NS 5783
Earl's Seat (Northum.) 110 NY 7192
Earle 110 NT 9826
Earlestown 75 SJ 5795
Earley 25 SU 7571
Earlish 144 NG 3861
Earls Barton 55 SP 8563
Earls Colne 42 TL 8528
Earlsdon 53 SP 3177
Earlsferry 127 NO 4800
Earlsford 151 NJ 8334
Earlston (Borders) 118 NT 5738
Earlston (Strath.) 114 NS 4035
Earlswood 53 SP 1174
Earlswood Common 35 ST 4595
Earnley 14 SZ 8196
Earsdon 105 NZ 3272
Earshaig 108 NT 0402
Earsham 59 TM 3289
Earswick 92 SE 6157
Eartham 14 SU 9309
Easby 98 NZ 5708
Easdale (Strath.) 129 NM 7317
Easebourne 14 SU 8922
Easenhall 54 SP 4679
Eashing 25 SU 9443
Easington (Bucks.) 38 SP 6810
Easington (Cleve.) 99 NZ 7418
Easington (Durham) 98 NZ 4143
Easington (Humbs.) 87 TA 3919
Easington (Northum.) 119 NU 1234
Easington (Oxon.) 38 SU 6697
Easington Lane 98 NZ 3646
Easingwold 92 SE 5269
Easole Street 29 TR 2652
Eassie 133 NO 3547
Eassie and Nevay 134 NO 3345
East Aberthaw 20 ST 0367
East Allington 7 SX 7648
East Anstey 19 SS 8626
East Anton 24 SU 3647
East Ashling 14 SU 8207
East Auchronie 143 NJ 8309
East Barkwith 80 TF 1681
East Barming 28 TQ 7254
East Barnby 99 NZ 8212
East Barnet 26 TQ 2794
East Barsham 70 TF 9133
East Beckham 70 TG 1640
East Bedfont 26 TQ 1074
East Bergholt 43 TM 0734
East Bilney 70 TF 9519
East Blatchington 16 TQ 4800
East Boldon 105 NZ 3762
East Boldre 13 SU 3700
East Bradenham 70 TF 9208
East Brent 21 ST 3452
East Bridgford 79 SK 6943
East Buckland 19 SS 6731
East Budleigh 9 SY 0684
East Burton 11 SY 8386
East Cairnbeg 143 NO 7076
East Calder 116 NT 0867
East Carleton (Norf.) 71 TG 1802
East Carlton (Northants.) 55 SP 8389
East Carlton (W. Yorks.) 84 SE 2243
East Challow 38 SU 3988
East Charleton 7 SX 7642
East Chiltington 15 TQ 3715
East Chinnock 10 ST 4913
East Chisenbury 23 SU 1352
East Cholderton 23 SU 2945
East Clandon 26 TQ 0651
East Claydon 39 SP 7325
East Combe (Somer.) 20 ST 1631
East Compton 21 ST 6141
East Cottingwith 86 SE 7042
East Coulston 22 ST 9454
East Cowes 13 SZ 5095
East Cowton 98 NZ 3103
East Cramlington 105 NZ 2876
East Creech 11 SY 9282
East Dean (E Susx.) 16 TV 5597
East Dean (Hants.) 23 SU 2726
East Dean (W Susx.) 14 SU 9013
East Dereham 70 TF 9913
East Down 19 SS 5941
East Drayton 79 SK 7775
East Dundry 21 ST 5766
East End (Avon) 35 ST 4770
East End (Dorset) 11 SY 9998
East End (Hants) 14 SU 6524
East End (Hants.) 24 SU 4161
East End (Hants.) 13 SZ 3697
East End (Herts.) 41 TL 4527
East End (Kent) 28 TQ 8335
East End (Oxon.) 38 SP 3914
East Everleigh 23 SU 2053
East Farleigh 28 TQ 7353
East Farndon 55 SP 7185
East Ferry 86 SK 8199
East Garston 24 SU 3676
East Ginge 38 SU 4486
East Goscote 66 SK 6413
East Grafton 23 SU 2560
East Grange 148 NJ 0962
East Green 59 TM 4065
East Grimstead 23 SU 2227
East Grinstead 16 TQ 3938
East Guldeford 17 TQ 9321
East Haddon 54 SP 6668
East Hagbourne 38 SU 5388
East Halton 87 TA 1419
East Ham (Gtr London) 27 TQ 4283
East Hanney 38 SU 4192
East Hanningfield 42 TL 7601
East Hardwick 85 SE 4618
East Harling 58 TL 9986
East Harlsey 91 SE 4299
East Harptree 21 ST 5655
East Hartford 105 NZ 2679
East Harting 14 SU 7919
East Hatley 56 TL 2850
East Hauxwell 91 SE 1693
East Heckington 80 TF 1944
East Hedleyhope 97 NZ 1540
East Hendred 38 SU 4588
East Heslerton 93 SE 9276
East Hewish 21 ST 3964
East Hoathly 16 TQ 5216
East Holme 11 SY 8986
East Horndon 27 TQ 6389
East Horrington 21 ST 5846
East Horsley 26 TQ 0952
East Huntspill 21 ST 3444
East Hyde 40 TL 1317
East Ilsley 24 SU 4981
East Kennett 23 SU 1167
East Keswick 85 SE 3544
East Kilbride 115 NS 6354
East Kirkby 81 TF 3362
East Knighton 11 SY 8185
East Knoyle 22 ST 8830
East Lambrook 10 ST 4319
East Lamington 155 NH 7578
East Langdon 29 TR 3346
East Langton 67 SP 7292
East Langwell 154 NC 7206
East Lavington 14 SU 9416
East Layton 97 NZ 1609
East Leake 66 SK 5526
East Leigh 6 SX 6852
East Leigh (Devon.) 8 SS 6905
East Lexham 70 TF 8617
East Lilburn 111 NU 0423
East Linton 127 NT 5977
East Looe 5 SX 2553
East Lound 86 SK 7899
East Lulworth 11 SY 8581
East Mains 143 NO 6797
East Malling 27 TQ 7057
East March 135 NO 4436
East Marden 14 SU 8014
East Markham 79 SK 7472
East Marton 83 SD 9050
East Meon 14 SU 6822
East Mersea 43 TM 0414
East Molesey 26 TQ 1568
East Morden 11 SY 9194
East Morton 84 SE 1042
East Norton 67 SK 7800
East Oakley 24 SU 5749
East Ogwell 7 SX 8370
East Ord 119 NT 9851
East Panson 5 SX 3692
East Peckham 27 TQ 6649
East Pennard 21 ST 5937
East Perry 56 TL 1467
East Poringland 71 TG 2701
East Portlemouth 7 SX 7438
East Prawle 7 SX 7736
East Preston 15 TQ 0702
East Putford 18 SS 3616
East Quantoxhead 20 ST 1343
East Rainton 98 NZ 3347
East Ravendale 87 TF 2399
East Raynham 70 TF 8825
East Rudham 70 TF 8228
East Runton 71 TG 1942
East Ruston 71 TG 3427
East Saltoun 117 NT 4767
East Shefford 24 SU 3974
East Sleekburn 105 NZ 2785
East Stoke (Dorset) 11 SY 8787
East Stoke (Notts.) 79 SK 7549
East Stour 11 ST 8022
East Stourmouth 29 TR 2662
East Stratton 24 SU 5440
East Studdal 29 TR 3149
East Taphouse 4 SX 1863
East Thirston 111 NZ 1999
East Tilbury 27 TQ 6877
East Tisted 24 ST 7032
East Torrington 80 TF 1483
East Tuddenham 70 TG 0811
East Tytherley 23 SU 2929
East Tytherton 22 ST 9674
East Village 8 SS 8405
East Wall 51 SO 5293
East Walton 69 TF 7416
East Wellow 13 SU 3020
East Wemyss 127 NT 3396
East Whitburn 116 NS 9665
East Wickham 27 TQ 4576
East Williamston 31 SN 0905
East Winch 69 TF 6916
East Wittering 14 SZ 7996
East Witton 91 SE 1486
East Woodhay 24 SU 4061
East Woodlands 22 ST 7843
East Worldham 25 SU 7538
East Wretham 70 TL 9190
Eastbourne 16 TV 6199
Eastbridge 59 TM 4566
Eastburn 84 SE 0244
Eastbury (Berks.) 23 SU 3477
Eastbury (Gtr London) 26 TQ 0991
Eastby 90 SE 0154
Eastchurch 28 TQ 9871
Eastcombe (Glos.) 36 SO 8804
Eastcote (Gtr London) 26 TQ 1188
Eastcote (Northants) 54 SP 6854
Eastcote (W Mids) 53 SP 1979
Eastcott (Corn.) 18 SS 2515
Eastcott (Wilts.) 23 SU 0255
Eastcourt 36 ST 9792
Eastend (Essex) 42 TQ 9492
Easter Ardross 154 NH 6373
Easter Balmoral 141 NO 2693
Easter Boleskine 147 NH 5122
Easter Compton 35 ST 5782
Easter Davoch 142 NJ 4607
Easter Fearn 154 NH 6387
Easter Galcantray 148 NH 8147
Easter Kinkell 147 NH 5756
Easter Lednathie 142 NO 3363
Easter Moniack 147 NH 5543
Easter Muckovie 148 NH 7044
Easter Ord 143 NJ 8304
Easter Stanhope 117 NT 1229
Eastergate 14 SU 9405
Eastern Green 53 SP 2780
Easterton 23 SU 0154
Eastertown 21 ST 3454
Eastfield (N Yorks.) 93 TA 0484
Eastfield (Strath.) 125 NS 7574
Eastfield (Strath.) 116 NS 8964
Eastfield Hall 111 NU 2206
Eastgate (Durham) 96 NY 9538
Eastgate (Norf.) 70 TG 1423
Eastham (Mers.) 75 SJ 3580
Easthampstead 25 SU 8667
Easthope 51 SO 5695
Easthorpe 42 TL 9121
Eastington (Devon) 8 SS 7409
Eastington (Glos.) 36 SO 7705
Eastington (Glos.) 37 SP 1213
Eastleach Martin 37 SP 1905
Eastleach Turville 37 SP 1905
Eastleigh (Devon) 19 SS 4827
Eastleigh (Hants.) 13 SU 4518
Eastling 28 TQ 9656
Eastney 14 SZ 6698
Eastnor 52 SO 7337
Eastoft 86 SE 8016
Eastoke 14 SZ 7398
Easton (Cambs.) 56 TL 1371
Easton (Cumbr) 102 NY 2859
Easton (Cumbr.) 103 NY 4372
Easton (Devon.) 8 SX 7288
Easton (Dorset) 10 SY 6871
Easton (Hants.) 24 SU 5132
Easton (I. of W.) 13 SZ 3485
Easton (Lincs.) 67 SK 9226
Easton (Norf.) 70 TG 1311
Easton (Somer.) 21 ST 5147
Easton (Suff.) 59 TM 2858
Easton Grey 36 ST 8787
Easton Maudit 55 SP 8858
Easton Royal 23 SU 2060
Easton on the Hill 67 TF 0004
Easton-in-Gordano 35 ST 5175
Eastrea 68 TL 2997
Eastriggs 103 NY 2465
Eastrington 86 SE 7929
Eastry 29 TR 3155
Eastville 81 TF 4057
Eastwell 67 SK 7728
Eastwick 41 TL 4311
Eastwood (Essex) 42 TQ 8588
Eastwood (Notts.) 78 SK 4646
Eastwood (W Yorks.) 84 SD 9625
Eathorpe 54 SP 3969
Eaton (Ches.) 75 SJ 5763
Eaton (Ches.) 76 SJ 8765
Eaton (Leic.) 67 SK 7929
Eaton (Norf.) 71 TG 2006
Eaton (Notts.) 79 SK 7077
Eaton (Oxon.) 38 SP 4403
Eaton (Salop) 51 SO 3789
Eaton (Salop) 51 SO 4989
Eaton Bishop 47 SO 4439
Eaton Bray 39 SP 9720
Eaton Constantine 51 SJ 5906
Eaton Hall 75 SJ 4262
Eaton Hastings 37 SU 2698
Eaton Socon 56 TL 1658
Eaton upon Tern 63 SJ 6523
Eaves Green 53 SP 2682
Ebberston 93 SE 8983
Ebbesborne Wake 22 ST 9824
Ebblake 12 SU 1008
Ebbw Vale (Gwent) 34 ST 2094
Ebchester 97 NZ 1055
Ebford 9 SX 9887
Ebnal 63 SJ 4948
Ebrington 53 SP 1840
Ecchinswell 24 SU 5059
Ecclaw 118 NT 7568
Ecclefechan 103 NY 1974
Eccles (Borders) 118 NT 7641
Eccles (Gtr Mches) 76 SJ 7798
Eccles (Kent) 28 TQ 7260
Eccles Green 47 SO 3748
Eccles Road 70 TM 0190
Eccles on Sea 71 TG 4028
Ecclesfield 78 SK 3393
Eccleshall 64 SJ 8329
Ecclesmachan 126 NT 0573
Eccleston (Ches.) 75 SJ 4162
Eccleston (Lancs.) 82 SD 5216
Eccleston (Mers.) 75 SJ 4895
Eccup 84 SE 2842
Echt 143 NJ 7305
Eckford 110 NT 7125
Eckington (Derby) 78 SK 4379
Eckington (Here & W) 52 SO 9241
Ecton 55 SP 8263
Edale 77 SK 1285
Eday Aerodrome 163 HY 5634
Edburton 15 TQ 2311
Edderton 154 NH 7184
Eddleston 117 NT 2447
Edenbridge 16 TQ 4446
Edenfield 83 SD 8019
Edenhall 95 NY 5632
Edenham 67 TF 0621
Edensor 77 SK 2469
Edenthorpe 85 SE 6206
Ederline 123 NM 8702
Edern 60 SH 2739
Edgarley 21 ST 5138
Edgbaston 53 SP 0684
Edgcott (Bucks) 38 SP 6722
Edgcott (Somer) 19 SS 8438
Edge 51 SJ 3908

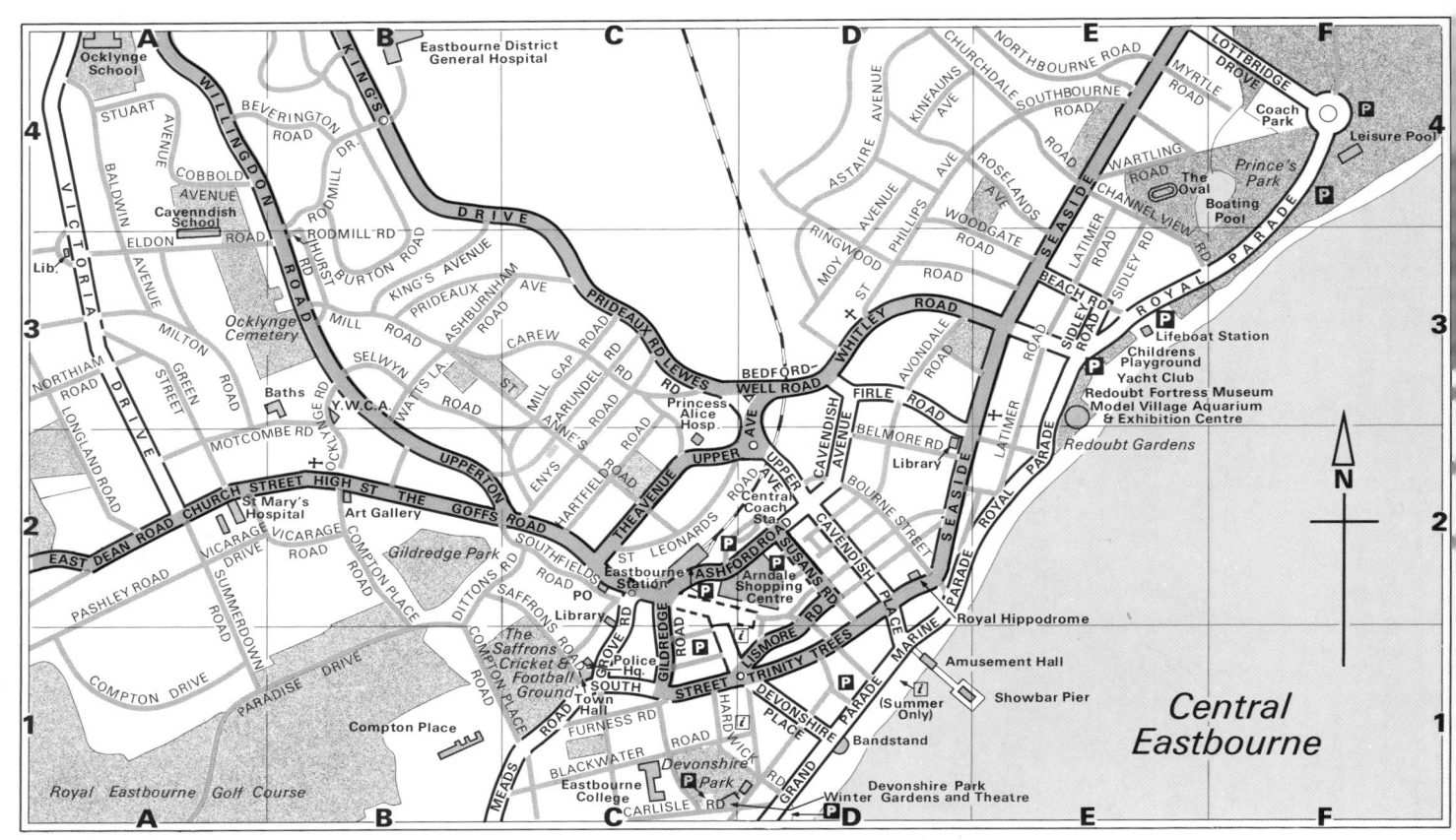

Central
Eastbourne

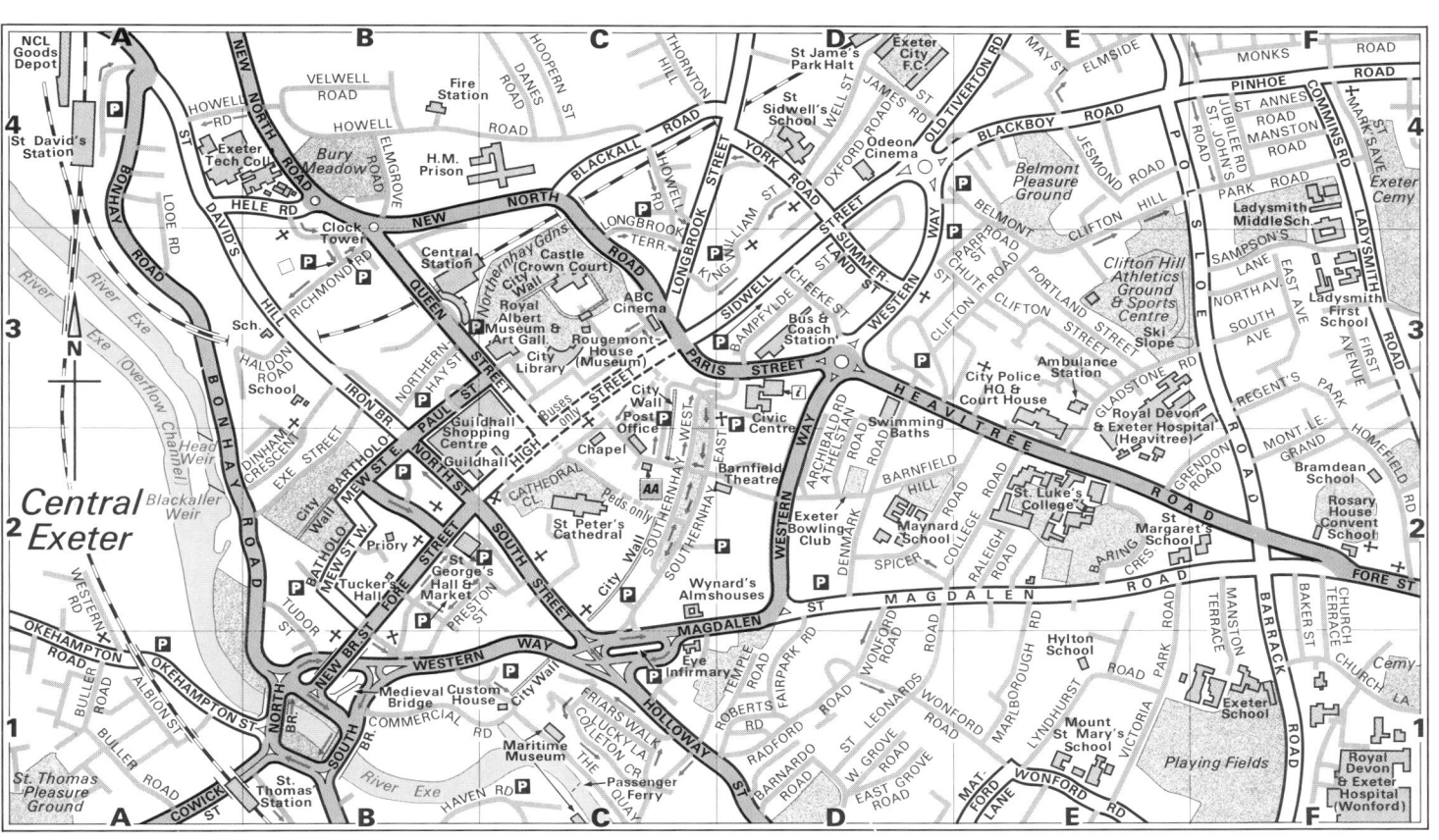

Central Exeter

234

Harthill (S Yorks.) High Callerton

Harthill (S Yorks.) 78 SK 4980
Hartington 77 SK 1360
Hartland 18 SS 2624
Hartland Quay 18 SS 2224
Hartlebury 52 SO 8470
Hartlepool 98 NZ 5032
Hartley (Cumbr.) 96 NY 7808
Hartley (Kent) 27 TQ 6166
Hartley (Kent) 28 TQ 7634
Hartley (Northum.) 105 NZ 3475
Hartley Wespall 24 SU 6958
Hartley Wintney 25 SU 7756
Hartlip 28 TQ 8364
Hartoft End 92 SE 7592
Harton (N Yorks.) 92 SE 7061
Harton (Salop) 51 SO 4888
Harton (Tyne and Wear) 105 NZ 3864
Hartpury 36 SO 7924
Hartshead 84 SE 1822
Hartshill 65 SP 3293
Hartshorne 65 SK 3221
Hartsop 95 NY 4013
Hartwell 55 SP 7850
Hartwood 116 NS 8459
Harvel 27 TQ 6563
Harvington (Here & W) 53 SP 0548
Harvington (Here & W) 52 SO 8774
Harvington Cross 53 SP 0549
Harwell (Notts.) 79 SK 6891
Harwell (Oxon.) 38 SU 4989
Harwich 43 TM 2431
Harwood (Durham) 96 NY 8133
Harwood (Gtr Mches.) 83 SD 7411
Harwood Dale 93 SE 9595
Harworth 79 SK 6291
Hasbury 52 SO 9583
Hascombe 14 TQ 0039
Haselbech 54 SP 7177
Haselbury Plucknett 10 ST 4711
Haseley 53 SP 2368
Haseley Knob 53 SP 2371
Haselor 53 SP 1257
Hasfield 36 SO 8227
Hasguard 30 SM 8509
Haskayne 82 SD 3507
Hasketon 59 TM 2550
Hasland 78 SK 3969
Haslemere 25 SU 9032
Haslingden 83 SD 7823
Haslingden Grane 83 SD 7523
Haslingfield 56 TL 4052
Haslington 76 SJ 7355
Hassall 76 SJ 7657
Hassall Green 76 SJ 7758
Hassell Street 29 TR 0946
Hassendean 109 NT 5420
Hassingham 71 TG 3605
Hassocks 15 TQ 3015
Hassop 77 SK 2272
Hastigrow 159 ND 2661
Hastingleigh 29 TR 0945
Hastings 17 TQ 8009
Hastingwood 41 TL 4807
Hastoe 39 SP 9209
Haswell 98 NZ 3743
Hatch (Beds.) 56 TL 1547
Hatch (Hants.) 24 SU 6752
Hatch (Wilts.) 22 ST 9228
Hatch Beauchamp 9 ST 3020
Hatch End 26 TQ 1391
Hatchet Gate 13 SU 3701
Hatching Green 40 TL 1313
Hatchmere 75 SJ 5571
Hatcliffe 87 TA 2100
Hatfield (Here & W) 47 SO 5859
Hatfield (Here & W) 52 SO 8750
Hatfield (Herts.) 41 TL 2309
Hatfield (S Yorks.) 85 SE 6609
Hatfield Broad Oak 41 TL 5516
Hatfield Heath 41 TL 5215
Hatfield Peverel 42 TL 7911
Hatfield Woodhouse 86 SE 6708
Hatford 37 SU 3394
Hatherden 23 SU 3450
Hatherleigh 19 SS 5404
Hathern 66 SK 5022
Hatherop 37 SP 1505
Hathersage 77 SK 2381
Hatherton (Ches.) 76 SJ 6847
Hatherton (Staffs.) 64 SJ 9610
Hatley St. George 56 TL 2851
Hatt 5 SX 3961
Hattingley 24 SU 6437
Hatton (Ches.) 75 SJ 5982
Hatton (Derby.) 65 SK 2130
Hatton (Grampn.) 151 NK 0537
Hatton (Gtr London) 26 TQ 1075
Hatton (Lincs.) 80 TF 1776
Hatton (Salop) 51 SO 4690
Hatton (Warw.) 53 SP 2367
Hatton Heath 75 SJ 4561
Hatton of Fintray 143 NJ 8316
Hattoncrook 151 NJ 8424
Haugh Head 111 NU 0026
Haugh of Glass 150 NJ 4339
Haugh of Urr 102 NX 8066
Haugham 81 TF 3381
Haughley 58 TM 0262
Haughley Green 58 TM 0364
Haughton (Notts.) 79 SK 6772
Haughton (Salop) 63 SJ 3727
Haughton (Salop) 63 SJ 5516
Haughton (Salop) 51 SO 6795
Haughton (Salop) 64 SJ 7408
Haughton (Staffs.) 64 SJ 8620
Haughton Green 76 SJ 9393
Haughton Moss 75 SJ 5756
Haultwick 41 TL 3423
Haunton 65 SK 2411
Hauxley 111 NU 2703
Hauxton 57 TL 4352
Havant 14 SU 7106
Haven 47 SO 4054
Haven Bank 80 TF 2352
Havenhouse Station 81 TF 5259
Havenstreet 13 SZ 5690
Haverfordwest 30 SM 9515
Haverhill 57 TL 6745
Haverigg 88 SD 1578
Havering 27 TQ 5587
Havering's Grove 27 TQ 6594
Havering-atte-Bower 27 TQ 5193
Haversham 55 SP 8343
Haverthwaite 88 SD 3483
Havyatt 21 ST 5338
Hawarden 74 SJ 3165
Hawbridge 52 SO 9048
Hawen 44 SN 3446
Hawes 90 SD 8789
Hawford 52 SO 8460
Hawick 109 NT 5014
Hawkchurch 9 ST 3400
Hawkedon 57 TL 7952
Hawkenbury 28 TQ 8044
Hawkeridge 22 ST 8653
Hawkerland 9 SY 0588
Hawkes End 53 SP 2983
Hawkesbury (Avon) 36 ST 7687
Hawkesbury (W. Mids) 54 SP 3684
Hawkesbury Upton 36 ST 7786
Hawkhill 111 NU 2212
Hawkhurst 28 TQ 7630
Hawkinge 29 TR 2139
Hawkley 14 SU 7429
Hawkridge 19 SS 8630
Hawkshaw 83 SD 7615
Hawkshead 88 SD 3598
Hawkswick 90 SD 9570
Hawksworth (Notts.) 79 SK 7543
Hawksworth (W Yorks.) 84 SE 1641
Hawkwell 42 TQ 8691
Hawley (Hants.) 25 SU 8558
Hawley (Kent) 27 TQ 5571
Hawling 37 SP 0623
Hawnby 92 SE 5389
Haworth 84 SE 0337
Hawsker 99 NZ 9207
Hawstead 58 TL 8559
Hawthorn (Durham) 98 NZ 4145
Hawthorn (Hants.) 24 SU 6733
Hawthorn (Mid. Glam.) 34 ST 0987
Hawthorn Hill (Berks.) 25 SU 8873
Hawthorn Hill (Lincs.) 80 TF 2155
Hawton 79 SK 7851
Haxby 92 SE 6057
Haxey 86 SK 7699
Hay-on-Wye 46 SO 2342
Haybridge 21 ST 5346
Haydock 75 SJ 5696
Haydon (Dorset) 10 ST 6615
Haydon (Somer.) 9 ST 2523
Haydon Bridge 96 NY 8464
Haydon Wick 37 SU 1388
Haye 5 SX 3570
Hayes (Gtr London) 26 TQ 0980
Hayes (Gtr London) 27 TQ 4165
Hayfield 77 SK 0386
Hayhillock 135 NO 5242
Hayle 2 SW 5537
Hayley Green 52 SO 9482
Hayling Island 14 SU 7201
Haynes 56 TL 0841
Hayscastle 30 SM 8925
Hayscastle Cross 30 SM 9125
Hayton (Cumbr.) 94 NY 1041
Hayton (Cumbr.) 95 NY 5057
Hayton (Humbs.) 86 SE 8145
Hayton (Notts.) 79 SK 7284
Hayton's Bent 51 SO 5280
Haytor Vale 7 SX 7677
Haytown 18 SS 3814
Haywards Heath 15 TQ 3324
Haywood Oaks 79 SK 6055
Hazel Grove 76 SJ 9287
Hazelbank 116 NS 8344
Hazelbury Bryan 11 ST 7408
Hazeleigh 42 TL 8203
Hazeley 25 SU 7459
Hazelslade 65 SK 0212
Hazelton Walls 134 NO 3321
Hazelwood 78 SK 3245
Hazlemere 39 SU 8895
Hazlerigg 105 NZ 2472
Hazleton 37 SP 0718
Heacham 69 TF 6737
Head of Muir 125 NS 8080
Headbourne Worthy 24 SU 4831
Headcorn 28 TQ 8344
Headington 38 SP 5407
Headlam 97 NZ 1818
Headley (Hants.) 24 SU 5162
Headley (Hants.) 25 SU 8236
Headley (Surrey) 26 TQ 2054
Headley Down 25 SU 8435
Headon 79 SK 7476
Heads 114 NS 7248
Heads Nook 95 NY 4955
Heage 78 SK 3650
Healaugh (N Yorks.) 90 SE 0198
Healaugh (N Yorks.) 85 SE 4947
Heale 19 SS 6446
Healey (Lancs.) 83 SD 8817
Healey (N Yorks.) 91 SE 1780
Healey (Northum.) 104 NZ 0158
Healeyfield 97 NZ 0648
Healing 87 TA 2110
Heamoor 2 SW 4631
Heanish 162 NM 0343
Heanor 78 SK 4346
Heanton Punchardon 19 SS 5035
Heapham 79 SK 8788
Hearn 25 SU 8337
Hearthstane 108 NT 1125
Heasley Mill 19 SS 7332
Heast 137 NG 6417
Heath 78 SK 4467
Heath End (Hants.) 24 SU 5762
Heath End (Hants.) 24 SU 4162
Heath Hayes 65 SK 0110
Heath Hill 64 SJ 7614
Heath House 21 ST 4146
Heath and Reach 39 SP 9228
Heathcote 77 SK 1460
Heather 66 SK 3910
Heatherside 102 NY 4366
Heathfield (Devon.) 7 SX 8376
Heathfield (E Susx) 16 TQ 5821
Heathfield (Somer.) 20 ST 1526
Heathhall 101 NX 9879
Heathrow Airport — London 26 TQ 0775
Heathton 64 SO 8192
Heatley 76 SJ 7088
Heaton (Lancs.) 89 SD 4460
Heaton (Staffs.) 76 SJ 9462
Heaton (Tyne and Wear) 105 NZ 2665
Heatons Bridge 82 SD 4011
Heaverham 27 TQ 5758
Hebburn 105 NZ 3265
Hebden 90 SE 0263
Hebden Bridge 84 SD 9927
Hebden Green 75 SJ 6365
Hebron (Dyfed) 31 SN 1827
Hebron (Northum.) 105 NZ 1989
Heck 102 NY 1080
Heckfield 25 SU 7260
Heckfield Green 59 TM 1875
Heckington 80 TF 1444
Heckmondwike 84 SE 2123
Heddington 22 ST 9966
Heddington Wick 22 ST 9866
Heddon-on-the-Wall 105 NZ 1366
Hedenham 71 TM 3193
Hedge End 13 SU 4812
Hedgerley 39 SU 9787
Hedging 21 ST 3029
Hedley on the Hill 105 NZ 0759
Hednesford 65 SK 0012
Hedon 87 TA 1828
Hedsor 39 SU 9187
Hegdon Hill 47 SO 5854
Heighington (Durham) 97 NZ 2522
Heighington (Lincs.) 80 TF 0269
Heightington 52 SO 7671
Heights of Brae 147 NH 5161
Heilam 157 NC 4560
Heiton 118 NT 7130
Hele (Devon) 7 SX 7470
Hele (Devon.) 19 SS 5347
Hele (Devon.) 9 SS 9902
Hele (Somer.) 20 ST 1824
Helensburgh 124 NS 2982
Helford 3 SW 7526
Helford Passage 3 SW 7527
Helhoughton 70 TF 8626
Helions Bumpstead 57 TL 6541
Hell Corner 24 SU 3864
Helland 4 SX 0770
Hellesdon 71 TG 2010
Hellidon 54 SP 5158
Hellifield 90 SD 8556
Hellingly 16 TQ 5812
Hellington 71 TG 3103
Helm 110 NZ 1997
Helmdon 54 SP 5843
Helmingham 59 TM 1857
Helmington Row 97 NZ 1835
Helmsdale 155 ND 0215
Helmshore 83 SD 7821
Helmsley 92 SE 6183
Helperby 91 SE 4369
Helperthorpe 93 SE 9570
Helpringham 68 TF 1340
Helpston 68 TF 1205
Helsby 75 SJ 4875
Helston 2 SW 6527
Helstone 4 SX 0881
Helton 95 NY 5122
Hemblington 71 TG 3411
Hemel Hempstead 40 TL 0506
Hemerdon 6 SX 5657
Hemingbrough 86 SE 6730
Hemingby 80 TF 2374
Hemingford Abbots 56 TL 2870
Hemingford Grey 56 TL 2970
Hemingstone 58 TM 1453
Hemington (Northants.) 56 TL 0985
Hemington (Somer.) 22 ST 7253
Hemley 59 TM 2842
Hemlington 98 NZ 5013
Hempholme 93 TA 0850
Hempnall 71 TM 2494
Hempnall Green 71 TM 2593
Hempriggs 149 NJ 1064
Hempstead (Essex) 57 TL 6338
Hempstead (Norf.) 71 TG 4028
Hempsted (Glos) 36 SO 8117
Hempstead (Norf.) 70 TG 1037
Hempton (Norf.) 70 TF 9129
Hempton (Oxon.) 38 SP 4431
Hemsby 71 TG 4917
Hemswell 79 SK 9290
Hemsworth 85 SE 4213
Hemyock 9 ST 1313
Henbury (Avon) 35 ST 5478
Hendersyde Park 118 NT 7435
Hendomen 50 SO 2198
Hendon (Gtr London) 26 TQ 2389
Hendon (Tyne and Wear) 105 NZ 4055
Hendy 32 SN 5804
Heneglwys 72 SH 4276
Henfield 15 TQ 2116
Hengoed (Mid Glam.) 34 ST 1495
Hengoed (Powys) 46 SO 2253
Hengoed (Salop) 62 SJ 2833
Hengrave 58 TL 8268
Henham 41 TL 5428
Heniarth 50 SJ 1108
Henlade 20 ST 2624
Henley (Dorset) 10 ST 6904
Henley (Glos.) 36 SO 9016
Henley (Salop) 51 SO 5476
Henley (Somer.) 21 ST 4232
Henley (Suff.) 58 TM 1551
Henley (W Susx) 14 SU 8926
Henley Park 25 SU 9352
Henley on Thames 25 SU 7682
Henley's Down 16 TQ 7312
Henley-in-Arden 53 SP 1465
Henllan (Clwyd) 74 SJ 0268
Henllan (Dyfed) 44 SN 3540
Henllan Amgoed 31 SN 1820
Henllys 34 ST 2693
Henlow 56 TL 1738
Henlow Camp 56 TL 1636
Hennock 7 SX 8380
Henny Street 58 TL 8738
Henry's Moat (Castell Hendre) 30 SN 0427
Henryd 73 SH 7674
Hensall 85 SE 5923
Henshaw 104 NY 7664
Henstead 59 TM 4986
Hensting 13 SU 4922
Henstridge 11 ST 7219
Henstridge Marsh 11 ST 7420
Henton (Oxon.) 39 SP 7602
Henton (Somer.) 21 ST 4845
Henwick 52 SO 8354
Henwood 5 SX 2673
Heol Senni 46 SN 9223
Heol-y-Cyw 33 SS 9484
Hepburn 111 NU 0724
Hepple 110 NT 9800
Hepscott 105 NZ 2284
Heptonstall 84 SD 9827
Hepworth (Suff.) 58 TL 9874
Hepworth (W Yorks.) 84 SE 1606
Herbrandston 30 SM 8707
Hereford 47 SO 5040
Hergest 46 SO 2655
Heriot 117 NT 3952
Hermitage (Berks.) 24 SU 5072
Hermitage (Borders) 109 NY 5095
Hermitage (Dorset.) 10 ST 6306
Hermitage (Hants.) 14 SU 7505
Hermon (Dyfed) 44 SN 2032
Hermon (Dyfed) 44 SN 3630
Hermon (Gwyn.) 72 SH 3868
Herne 29 TR 1866
Herne Bay 29 TR 1768
Herne Pound 27 TQ 6654
Herner 19 SS 5926
Hernhill 29 TR 0660
Herodsfoot 5 SX 2160
Herongate 27 TQ 6391
Heronsgate 26 TQ 0294
Herra Hu 163 HU 4693
Herriard 24 SU 6645
Herringfleet 71 TM 4797
Herringswell 57 TL 7170
Herrington 98 NZ 3553
Hersden 29 TR 1961
Hersham (Corn.) 18 SS 2507
Hersham (Surrey) 26 TQ 1164
Herstmonceux 16 TQ 6312
Herston 163 ND 4291
Hertford 41 TL 3212
Hertford Heath 41 TL 3510
Hertingfordbury 41 TL 3112
Hesket Newmarket 95 NY 3438
Hesketh Bank 82 SD 4323
Hesketh Lane 83 SD 6141
Hesleden 98 NZ 4438
Hesleyside 104 NY 8183
Heslington 92 SE 6250
Hessay 92 SE 5253
Hessenford 5 SX 3057
Hessett 58 TL 9361
Hessle 87 TA 0326
Hest Bank 89 SD 4566
Heston 26 TQ 1277
Heswall 74 SJ 2682
Hethe 38 SP 5929
Hethelpit Cross 36 SO 7729
Hethersett 70 TG 1505
Hethersgill 95 NY 4767
Hethpool 110 NT 8928
Hett 97 NZ 2836
Hetton 90 SD 9658
Hetton-le-Hole 98 NZ 3548
Heugh 105 NZ 0873
Heugh-Head 142 NJ 3711
Heveningham 59 TM 3372
Hever 16 TQ 4744
Heversham 89 SD 4983
Hevingham 71 TG 2021
Hewelsfield 35 SO 5602
Hewish (Avon) 21 ST 4064
Hewish (Somer.) 10 ST 4108
Hexham 104 NY 9364
Hextable 27 TQ 5170
Hexton 40 TL 1030
Hexworthy 6 SX 6572
Hey 83 SD 8843
Heybridge (Essex) 42 TL 8508
Heybridge (Essex) 27 TQ 6498
Heybridge Basin 42 TL 8707
Heybrook Bay 6 SX 4948
Heydon (Cambs.) 56 TL 4340
Heydon (Norf.) 70 TG 1127
Heydour 67 TF 0039
Heylipoll 162 NL 9643
Heylor 163 HU 2881
Heysham 89 SD 4161
Heyshott 14 SU 8918
Heytesbury 22 ST 9242
Heythrop 38 SP 3527
Heywood (Gtr Mches.) 83 SD 8510
Heywood (Wilts.) 22 ST 8753
Hibaldstow 86 SE 9702
Hickleton 85 SE 4805
Hickling (Norf.) 71 TG 4124
Hickling (Notts.) 66 SK 6929
Hickling Green 71 TG 4023
Hickling Heath 71 TG 4022
Hickstead 15 TQ 2620
Hidcote Boyce 53 SP 1742
High Ackworth 85 SE 4317
High Bankhill 95 NY 5643
High Beach 27 TQ 4097
High Bentham 89 SD 6669
High Bickington 8 SS 5920
High Birkwith 90 SD 8076
High Blantyre 115 NS 6756
High Bonnybridge 125 NS 8378
High Bray 19 SS 6934
High Bullen 19 SS 5320
High Buston 111 NU 2308
High Callerton 105 NZ 1670

High Catton

Horseman's Green

High Catton	92	SE 7153
High Cogges	38	SP 3709
High Coniscliffe	97	NZ 2215
High Crindledike	102	NY 3861
High Cross (Hants.)	14	SU 7126
High Cross (Herts.)	41	TL 3618
High Cross Bank	65	SK 3018
High Easter	42	TL 6214
High Eggborough	85	SE 5722
High Ellington	91	SE 1983
High Ercall	63	SJ 5917
High Etherley	97	NZ 1628
High Force Hotel	96	NY 8829
High Garrett	42	TL 7726
High Grange	97	NZ 1731
High Green (Norf.)	70	TG 1305
High Green (S Yorks.)	85	SK 3397
High Green (Salop)	52	SO 7082
High Green (W. Yorks.)	84	SE 2014
High Halden	28	TQ 9037
High Halstow	28	TQ 7875
High Ham	21	ST 4231
High Harrington	94	NY 0125
High Hatton	63	SJ 6024
High Hesket	95	NY 4744
High Hoyland	84	SE 2710
High Hunsley	86	SE 9535
High Hurstwood	16	TQ 4926
High Kelling	70	TG 1039
High Land	97	NZ 1225
High Lane (Gtr Mches.)	76	SJ 9585
High Lane (Here & W)	52	SO 6760
High Laver	41	TL 5208
High Legh	76	SJ 7084
High Leven	98	NZ 4512
High Littleton	21	ST 6458
High Lorton	94	NY 1625
High Marishes	92	SE 8178
High Melton	85	SE 5001
High Newton	89	SD 4082
High Newtown-by-the-Sea	111	NU 2325
High Nibthwaite	88	SD 2990
High Offley	64	SJ 7826
High Ongar	41	TL 5603
High Onn	64	SJ 8216
High Post	23	SU 1536
High Roding	42	TL 6017
High Salvington	15	TQ 1206
High Shaw	90	SD 8791
High Spen	105	NZ 1359
High Street (Corn.)	3	SW 9753
High Street (Suff.)	59	TM 4355
High Street Green	58	TM 0055
High Toynton	81	TF 2869
High Trewhitt	111	NU 0105
High Westwood	105	NZ 1256
High Worsall	98	NZ 3809
High Wray	89	SD 3799
High Wych	41	TL 4614
High Wycombe	39	SU 8593
Higham (Derby.)	78	SK 3959
Higham (Kent)	28	TQ 7171
Higham (Lancs.)	83	SD 8036
Higham (Suff.)	57	TL 7465
Higham (Suff.)	43	TM 0335
Higham Dykes	105	NZ 1375
Higham Ferrers	55	SP 9669
Higham Gobion	40	TL 1033
Higham on the Hill	66	SP 3895
Highampton	19	SS 4804
Highbridge (Highld.)	137	NN 1982
Highbridge (Somer.)	21	ST 3147
Highbrook	15	TQ 3630
Highburton	84	SE 1813
Highbury	22	ST 6849
Highclere	24	SU 4360
Highcliffe	12	SZ 2193
Higher Ansty	11	ST 7603
Higher Ballam	82	SD 3630
Higher Bartle	82	SD 5033
Higher Bockhampton	11	SY 7292
Higher Chillington	10	ST 3910
Higher Gabwell	7	SX 9169
Higher Penwortham	82	SD 5128
Higher Prestacott	5	SX 3896
Higher Tale	9	ST 0601
Higher Town	162	SV 9314
Higher Walreddon	5	SX 4771
Higher Walton (Ches.)	75	SJ 5985
Higher Walton (Lancs.)	82	SD 5727
Higher Wych	63	SJ 4943
Highfield (Strath.)	114	NS 3050
Highfield (Tyne and Wear)	105	NZ 1459
Highfields	56	TL 3559
Highleadon	36	SO 7623
Highleigh	14	SZ 8498
Highley	52	SO 7483
Highmoor (Cumbr.)	94	NY 2647
Highmoor (Oxon.)	38	SU 7085
Highmoor Cross	38	SU 7084
Highmoor Hill	35	ST 4689
Highnam	36	SO 7919
Highnam Green	36	SO 7920
Highsted	28	TQ 9161
Highstreet Green	25	SU 9834
Hightown (Ches.)	76	SJ 8762
Hightown (Mers.)	82	SD 2903
Highway	23	SU 0474
Highweek	7	SX 8472
Highworth	37	SU 2092
Hilborough (Norf.)	70	TF 8200
Hildenborough	27	TQ 5648
Hildersham	57	TL 5448
Hilderstone	64	SJ 9434
Hilderthorpe	93	TA 1765
Hilgay	69	TL 6298
Hill (Avon)	35	ST 6495
Hill (Devon)	19	SS 6926
Hill Brow	14	SU 7926
Hill Chorlton	64	SJ 8039
Hill Common	20	ST 1525
Hill Cottages	92	SE 7198
Hill Dyke	81	TF 3447
Hill End (Durham)	97	NZ 0135
Hill End (Fife.)	126	NT 0495
Hill Head (Hants.)	13	SU 5402
Hill Ridware	65	SK 0718
Hill Row	57	TL 4475
Hill Side	52	SO 7561
Hill Top (Durham)	97	NZ 0024
Hill Top (Hants.)	13	SU 4002
Hill Top (W Yorks.)	85	SE 3315
Hill of Fearn	155	NH 8377
Hill, The	88	SD 1783
Hillam	85	SE 5028
Hillbeck	96	NY 7915
Hillberry	162	SC 3879
Hillborough (Kent)	29	TR 2168
Hillbrae (Grampn.)	150	NJ 6047
Hillbrae (Grampn.)	151	NJ 7923
Hillend (Fife.)	126	NT 1483
Hillersland	47	SO 5614
Hillesden	38	SP 6828
Hillesley	36	ST 7689
Hillfarrance	20	ST 1624
Hillfoot	124	NS 5672
Hillhead (Devon.)	7	SX 9053
Hillhead (Strath.)	106	NS 4219
Hillhead of Auchentumb	151	NJ 9258
Hillhead of Cocklaw	151	NK 0844
Hilliard's Cross	65	SK 1412
Hilliclay	159	ND 1764
Hillingdon	26	TQ 0882
Hillington	69	TF 7225
Hillis Corner	13	SZ 4793
Hillmorton	54	SP 5374
Hillockhead	142	NJ 3809
Hillpound	13	SU 5715
Hillside (Devon)	6	SX 7060
Hillside (Grampn.)	143	NO 9298
Hillside (Tays.)	143	NO 7061
Hillstreet	13	SU 3415
Hillswick	163	HU 2877
Hilmarton	23	SU 0175
Hilperton	22	ST 8759
Hilsea	14	SU 6503
Hilton (Cambs.)	56	TL 2966
Hilton (Cleve.)	98	NZ 4611
Hilton (Cumbr.)	96	NY 7320
Hilton (Derby.)	65	SK 2430
Hilton (Dorset)	11	ST 7802
Hilton (Durham)	97	NZ 1621
Hilton (Grampn.)	151	NJ 9434
Hilton (Salop)	64	SO 7795
Hilton of Cadboll	155	NH 8776
Himbleton	52	SO 9458
Himley	64	SO 8891
Hincaster	89	SD 5148
Hinckley	66	SP 4294
Hinderclay	58	TM 0276
Hinderwell	99	NZ 7916
Hindford	63	SJ 3333
Hindhead	25	SU 8736
Hindley	83	SD 6104
Hindley Green	83	SD 6403
Hindlip	52	SO 8758
Hindolveston	70	TG 0329
Hindon	22	ST 9032
Hindringham	70	TF 9836
Hingham	70	TG 0202
Hinstock	64	SJ 6926
Hintlesham	58	TM 0843
Hinton (Avon)	22	ST 7376
Hinton (Hants.)	12	SZ 2095
Hinton (Here & W)	47	SO 3338
Hinton (Northants.)	54	SP 5352
Hinton (Salop)	51	SJ 4008
Hinton Ampner	13	SU 5927
Hinton Blewett	21	ST 5956
Hinton Charterhouse	22	ST 7758
Hinton Marsh	13	SU 5827
Hinton Martell	12	SU 0106
Hinton Parva	37	SU 2283
Hinton St. George	10	ST 4212
Hinton St. Mary	11	ST 7816
Hinton Waldrist	38	SU 3799
Hinton on the Green	53	SP 0204
Hinton-in-the-Hedges	54	SP 5537
Hints (Salop)	51	SO 6175
Hints (Staffs.)	65	SK 1503
Hinwick	55	SP 9361
Hinxhill	28	TR 0442
Hinxton	57	TL 4945
Hinxworth	56	TL 2340
Hipperholme	84	SE 1225
Hipswell	91	SE 1898
Hirn	143	NJ 7300
Hirnant (Powys)	62	SJ 0423
Hirnant (Powys)	49	SN 8869
Hirst	105	NZ 2787
Hirst Courtney	85	SE 6124
Hirwaun	33	SN 9505
Hiscott	19	SS 5426
Histon	57	TL 4363
Hitcham	58	TL 9851
Hitchin	40	TL 1829
Hither Green	27	TQ 3874
Hittisleigh	8	SX 7395
Hixon	65	SK 0026
Hoaden	29	TR 2759
Hoaldalbert	47	SO 3923
Hoar Cross	65	SK 1223
Hoarwithy	47	SO 5429
Hoath	29	TR 2064
Hobarris	51	SO 3078
Hobbs Cross	27	TQ 4799
Hobkirk	109	NT 5810
Hobson	105	NZ 1755
Hoby	66	SK 6617
Hockering	70	TG 0713
Hockerton	79	SK 7156
Hockley	42	TQ 8293
Hockley Heath	53	SP 1572
Hockliffe	39	SP 9726
Hockwold cum Wilton	57	TL 7288
Hockworthy	9	ST 0319
Hoddesdon	41	TL 3709
Hoddlesdon	83	SD 7122
Hodgeston	30	SS 0399
Hodnet	63	SJ 6128
Hodsall Street	27	TQ 6262
Hodthorpe	78	SK 5476
Hoe (Hants.)	13	SU 5617
Hoe (Norf.)	70	TF 9916
Hoe Gate	13	SU 6213
Hoff	95	NY 6717
Hoggeston	39	SP 8025
Hoghton	83	SD 6125
Hognaston	77	SK 2350
Hogrill's End	65	SP 2291
Hogsthorpe	81	TF 5372
Holbeach	68	TF 3625
Holbeach Bank	68	TF 3627
Holbeach Drove	68	TF 3212
Holbeach Hurn	68	TF 3927
Holbeach St. Johns	68	TF 3418
Holbeach St. Marks	68	TF 3731
Holbeach St. Matthew	68	TF 4132
Holbeck	78	SK 5473
Holberrow Green	53	SP 0259
Holbeton	6	SX 6150
Holbrook (Derby)	78	SK 3645
Holbrook (Suff.)	59	TM 1636
Holburn	119	NU 0436
Holbury	13	SU 4303
Holcombe (Devon.)	7	SX 9574
Holcombe (Somer.)	22	ST 6649
Holcombe Brook	83	SD 7715
Holcombe Burnell Barton	8	SX 8591
Holcombe Rogus	9	ST 0519
Holcot	55	SP 7969
Holden	83	SD 7749
Holdenby	54	SP 6967
Holder's Green	42	TL 6328
Holdgate	51	SO 5589
Holdingham	80	TF 0547
Holdsworth	84	SE 0829
Hole Street	15	TQ 1414
Hole-in-the-Wall	47	SO 6228
Holemoor	18	SS 4205
Holestane	107	NX 8799
Holford	20	ST 1541
Holker	88	SD 3577
Holkham	70	TF 8944
Hollacombe (Devon)	18	SS 3702
Hollacombe (Devon)	8	SS 8000
Holland (Papa Westray)	163	HY 4851
Holland (Stronsay)	163	HY 6622
Holland Fen	80	TF 2349
Holland-on-Sea	43	TM 2016
Hollandstoun	163	HY 7553
Hollesley	59	TM 3544
Hollingbourne	28	TQ 8455
Hollington (Derby)	65	SK 2239
Hollington (E Susx.)	17	TQ 7911
Hollington (Staffs.)	65	SK 0538
Hollingworth	84	SK 0096
Hollins	83	SD 8108
Hollins Green	76	SJ 6990
Hollinsclough	77	SK 0666
Hollinswood	64	SJ 6909
Hollinwood	63	SJ 5236
Hollocombe	8	SS 6311
Holloway	78	SK 3256
Hollowell	54	SP 6972
Holly End	69	TF 4906
Hollybush (Gwent)	34	SO 1603
Hollybush (Here & W)	52	SO 7636
Hollybush (Strath.)	106	NS 3914
Hollym	87	TA 3425
Hollywood	53	SP 0777
Holm (Dumf & G)	108	NY 2598
Holmacott	19	SS 5028
Holmbridge	84	SE 1106
Holmbury St. Mary	15	TQ 1144
Holme (Cambs.)	56	TL 1987
Holme (Cumbr.)	89	SD 5278
Holme (Notts.)	79	SK 8059
Holme (W Yorks.)	84	SE 1005
Holme Chapel	83	SD 8728
Holme Hale	70	TF 8807
Holme Lacy	47	SO 5535
Holme Marsh	47	SO 3354
Holme next the Sea	69	TF 7043
Holme on the Wolds	86	SE 9646
Holme upon Spalding Moor	86	SE 8138
Holmer	47	SO 5042
Holmer Green	39	SU 9097
Holmes Chapel	76	SJ 7667
Holmesfield	78	SK 3277
Holmeswood	82	SD 4316
Holmewood	78	SK 4365
Holmfirth	84	SE 1408
Holmhead	107	NS 5620
Holmpton	87	TA 3623
Holmrook	88	SD 0799
Holne	6	SX 7069
Holnest	10	ST 6509
Holsworthy	18	SS 3403
Holsworthy Beacon	18	SS 3508
Holt (Clwyd)	75	SJ 4053
Holt (Dorset)	12	SU 0203
Holt (Hants.)	25	SU 7354
Holt (Here & W)	52	SO 8262
Holt (Norf.)	70	TG 0738
Holt (Wilts.)	22	ST 8661
Holt End	53	SP 0769
Holt Heath (Dorset)	12	SU 0504
Holt Heath (Here & W)	52	SO 8163
Holtby	92	SE 6754
Holton (Oxon.)	38	SP 6006
Holton (Somer.)	22	ST 6826
Holton (Suff.)	59	TM 4077
Holton Heath	11	SY 9491
Holton St. Mary	58	TM 0537
Holton cum Beckering	80	TF 1181
Holton le Clay	87	TA 2802
Holton le Moor	87	TF 0797
Holtye	16	TQ 4539
Holwell (Dorset)	10	ST 7010
Holwell (Herts.)	40	TL 1633
Holwell (Leic.)	67	SK 7323
Holwell (Oxon)	37	SP 2309
Holwell (Somer.)	22	ST 7345
Holwick	96	NY 9026
Holworth	11	SY 7683
Holy Cross	52	SO 9279
Holy Green	52	SO 8541
Holy Island	119	NU 1543
Holybourne	25	SU 7341
Holyhead	72	SH 2482
Holymoorside	78	SK 3369
Holyport	25	SU 8977
Holystone	110	NT 9502
Holytown	115	NS 7760
Holywell (Cambs.)	56	TL 3370
Holywell (Clwyd)	74	SJ 1875
Holywell (Corn.)	3	SW 7658
Holywell (Dorset)	10	ST 5904
Holywell Green	84	SE 0918
Holywell Lake	9	ST 1020
Holywell Row	57	TL 7077
Holywood	102	NX 9480
Hom Green	47	SO 5822
Homer	51	SJ 6101
Homersfield	59	TM 2885
Homington	23	SU 1226
Honey Hill	29	TR 1161
Honey Tye	42	TL 9535
Honeyborough	30	SM 9506
Honeybourne	53	SP 1144
Honeychurch	8	SS 6202
Honeystreet	23	SU 1061
Honiley	53	SP 2472
Honing	71	TG 3227
Honingham	70	TG 1011
Honington (Lincs.)	80	SK 9443
Honington (Suff.)	58	TL 9174
Honington (Warw.)	53	SP 2642
Honiton	9	ST 1600
Honley	84	SE 1311
Hoo (Kent)	28	TQ 7872
Hoo Green	59	TM 2559
Hoo Meavy	5	SX 5265
Hooe (Devon.)	6	SX 5052
Hooe (E Susx)	16	TQ 6809
Hook (Dyfed)	30	SM 9811
Hook (Hants.)	25	SU 7254
Hook (Humbs.)	86	SE 7525
Hook (Surrey)	26	TQ 1764
Hook (Wilts.)	37	SU 0784
Hook Green	16	TQ 6535
Hook Norton	38	SP 3533
Hooke (Dorset)	10	ST 5300
Hookgate	64	SJ 7435
Hookway	8	SX 8598
Hookwood	15	TQ 2643
Hoole	75	SJ 4367
Hooley	26	TQ 2856
Hooley bridge	83	SD 8511
Hooton	75	SJ 3679
Hooton Levitt	78	SK 5291
Hooton Pagnell	85	SE 4808
Hooton Roberts	85	SK 4897
Hop Pole	68	TF 1813
Hope (Clwyd)	74	SJ 3058
Hope (Derby.)	77	SK 1783
Hope (Devon.)	6	SX 6740
Hope (Powys)	50	SJ 2507
Hope (Salop)	51	SJ 3401
Hope (Staffs.)	77	SK 1254
Hope Bagot	51	SO 5874
Hope Bowdler	51	SO 4792
Hope Mansell	47	SO 6219
Hope under Dinmore	47	SO 5052
Hopeman	155	NJ 1469
Hopesay	51	SO 3883
Hopstone	64	SO 7894
Hopton (Salop)	63	SJ 5926
Hopton (Staffs.)	64	SJ 9426
Hopton (Suff.)	58	TL 9979
Hopton Cangeford	51	SO 5480
Hopton Castle	51	SO 3678
Hopton Wafers	51	SO 6476
Hopton on Sea	71	TG 5200
Hoptonheath	51	SO 3877
Hopwas	65	SK 1705
Hopwood	53	SP 0375
Horam	16	TQ 5717
Horbling	68	TF 1135
Horbury	84	SE 2918
Horden	98	NZ 4441
Horderley	51	SO 4086
Hordle	12	SZ 2795
Hordley	63	SJ 3730
Horeb	44	SN 3942
Horham	59	TM 2172
Horiehaugh	142	NO 4163
Horkesley Heath	43	TL 9829
Horkstow	86	SE 9818
Horley (Oxon.)	54	SP 4143
Horley (Surrey)	15	TQ 2843
Horn Hill	26	TQ 0292
Hornblotton Green	21	ST 5833
Hornby (Lancs.)	89	SD 5868
Hornby (N Yorks.)	98	NZ 3605
Hornby (N Yorks.)	91	SE 2293
Horncastle	81	TF 2669
Hornchurch	27	TQ 5487
Horncliffe	119	NT 9249
Horndean	14	SU 7013
Horndon	5	SX 5080
Horndon on the Hill	27	TQ 6683
Horne	15	TQ 3344
Horning	71	TG 3417
Horninghold	67	SP 8097
Horninglow	65	SK 2324
Horningsea	57	TL 4962
Horningsham	22	ST 8241
Horningtoft	70	TF 9323
Horns Cross	18	SS 3823
Hornsby	95	NY 5150
Hornsea	93	TA 2047
Hornsey	26	TQ 3089
Hornton	54	SP 3945
Horrabridge	5	SX 5169
Horringer	58	TL 8261
Horrocksford	83	SD 7444
Horsebridge (Devon)	5	SX 4074
Horsebridge (E Susx)	16	TQ 5711
Horsebridge (Hants.)	23	SU 3430
Horsebridge (Staffs.)	76	SJ 9553
Horsebrook	64	SJ 8810
Horsehay	51	SJ 6707
Horseheath	57	TL 6147
Horsehouse	90	SE 0481
Horsell	25	SU 9959
Horseman's Green	63	SJ 4441

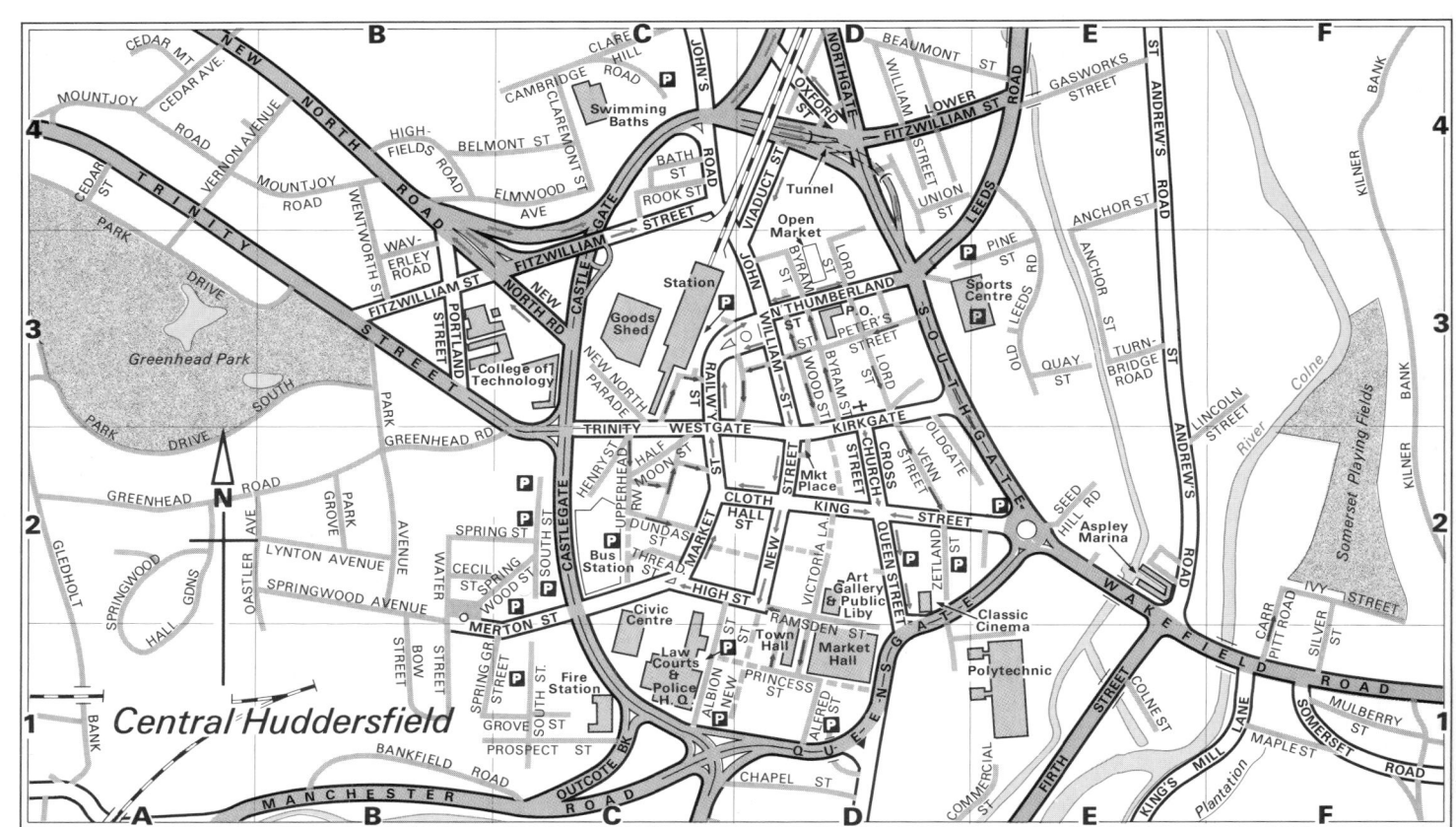

Central Huddersfield

Horseway	56	TL 4287
Horsey (Norf.)	71	TG 4523
Horsey (Somer.)	21	ST 3239
Horsey Corner	71	TG 4523
Horsford	71	TG 1916
Horsforth	84	SE 2337
Horsham (Here & W)	52	SO 7357
Horsham (W Susx)	15	TQ 1730
Horsham St. Faith	71	TG 2114
Horsington (Lincs.)	80	TF 1868
Horsington (Somer.)	22	ST 7023
Horsley (Derby.)	78	SK 3744
Horsley (Glos.)	36	ST 8398
Horsley (Northum.)	110	NY 8496
Horsley (Northum.)	105	NZ 0966
Horsley Cross	43	TM 1227
Horsley Woodhouse	78	SK 3945
Horsleycross Street	43	TM 1228
Horsleyhill	109	NT 5319
Horsmonden	16	TQ 7040
Horspath	38	SP 5704
Horstead	71	TG 2619
Horsted Keynes	16	TQ 3828
Horton (Avon)	36	ST 7684
Horton (Berks.)	26	TQ 0175
Horton (Bucks.)	39	SP 9219
Horton (Dorset)	12	SU 0307
Horton (Lancs.)	83	SD 8550
Horton (Northants.)	55	SP 8254
Horton (Northum.)	119	NU 0230
Horton (Somer.)	9	ST 3214
Horton (Staffs.)	76	SJ 9457
Horton (W Glam.)	32	SS 4785
Horton (Wilts.)	23	SU 0463
Horton Cross	9	ST 3315
Horton Green	63	SJ 4549
Horton Heath (Dorset)	12	SU 0606
Horton Heath (Hants.)	13	SU 4916
Horton Kirby	27	TQ 5668
Horton in Ribblesdale	90	SD 8172
Horwich	83	SD 6311
Horwood	19	SS 5027
Hoscar	82	SD 4712
Hose	67	SK 7329
Hoses	88	SD 2393
Hosh	133	NN 8523
Hotham	86	SE 8934
Hothfield	28	TQ 9644
Hoton	66	SK 5722
Hough	76	SJ 7151
Hough Green	75	SJ 4885
Hough-on-the-Hill	79	SK 9246
Hougham	79	SK 8844
Houghton (Cambs.)	56	TL 2871
Houghton (Cumbr.)	103	NY 4159
Houghton (Dyfed)	30	SM 9807
Houghton (Hants.)	23	SU 3331
Houghton (W Susx)	14	TQ 0111
Houghton Conquest	55	TL 0441
Houghton Green	17	TQ 9222
Houghton Regis	40	TL 0224
Houghton St. Giles	70	TF 9235
Houghton le Spring	98	NZ 3450
Houghton on the Hill	66	SK 6703
Houll	163	HU 3792
Houlsyke	99	NZ 7308
Houmets (Guernsey)	161	ZZ 9999
Hound Green	25	SU 7259
Houndslow	118	NT 6347
Houndwood	118	NT 8464

Hounslow	26	TQ 1276
Hounslow Green	42	TL 6518
Housetter	163	HU 3784
Houston	114	NS 4067
Houstry	159	ND 1534
Hove	15	TQ 2805
Hoveringham	79	SK 6946
Hoversta	163	HU 4940
Hoveton	71	TG 3018
Hovingham	92	SE 6675
How	95	NY 5056
How Caple	47	SO 6030
Howden	86	SE 7428
Howden-le-Wear	97	NZ 1633
Howe (Cumbr.)	89	SD 4588
Howe (Highld.)	159	ND 3062
Howe (Norf.)	71	TM 2799
Howe Green	42	TL 7403
Howe Street (Essex)	42	TL 6914
Howe Street (Essex)	42	TL 6934
Howe of Teuchar	151	NJ 7947
Howe, The	162	SC 1967
Howell	80	TF 1346
Howes	102	NY 1967
Howey	46	SO 0558
Howgate	117	NT 2457
Howick	111	NU 2517
Howlaws	118	NT 7242
Howle	64	SJ 6823
Howle Hill	47	SO 6020
Howlett End	41	TL 5834
Howley	9	ST 2609
Howmore	163	NF 7636
Hownam	110	NT 7719
Hownam Mains	110	NT 7820
Howsham (Humbs.)	86	TA 0404
Howsham (N Yorks.)	92	SE 7362
Howton	47	SO 4129
Howtown	95	NY 4419
Howwood	114	NS 3960
Hoxne	59	TM 1877
Hoylake	74	SJ 2189
Hoyland Nether	85	SE 3600
Hoyland Swaine	84	SE 2604
Hubberholme	90	SD 9278
Hubbert's Bridge	81	TF 2643
Huby (N. Yorks.)	92	SE 5665
Huby (N. Yorks.)	84	SE 2747
Hucclecote	36	SO 8717
Hucking	28	TQ 8358
Hucknall	78	SK 5349
Huddersfield	84	SE 1416
Huddington	52	SO 9457
Hudscott	19	SS 6525
Hudswell	91	NZ 1400
Huggate	93	SE 8855
Hugh Town	162	SV 9010
Hughenden Valley	39	SU 8695
Hughley	51	SO 5697
Hugmore	63	SJ 3752
Huish (Devon.)	19	SS 5311
Huish (Wilts.)	23	SU 1463
Huish Champflower	20	ST 0429
Huish Episcopi	21	ST 4226
Hulcott	39	SP 8516
Hulland	77	SK 2447
Hulland Ward	77	SK 2547
Hullavington	36	ST 8982
Hullbridge	42	TQ 8194
Hulme End	77	SK 1059

Hulme Walfield	76	SJ 8465
Hulver Street	59	TM 4686
Humber Court	47	SO 5356
Humberston	87	TA 3105
Humberstone	66	SK 6206
Humbie	117	NT 4562
Humbleton (Humbs.)	87	TA 2234
Humbleton (Northum.)	110	NT 9728
Humby	67	TF 0032
Hume	118	NT 7041
Humshaugh	104	NY 9171
Huna	159	ND 3573
Huncoat	83	SD 7730
Huncote	66	SP 5197
Hundalee	109	NT 6418
Hunderthwaite	96	NY 9821
Hundleby	81	TF 3966
Hundleton	30	SM 9600
Hundon	57	TL 7348
Hundred Acres	13	SU 5911
Hundred End	82	SD 4122
Hundred House	46	SO 1154
Hundred, The	51	SO 5264
Hungarton	66	SK 6807
Hungerford	20	ST 0440
Hungerford (Berks.)	23	SU 3368
Hungerford (Hants.)	12	SU 1612
Hungerford Newtown	24	SU 3571
Hungerstone	47	SO 4435
Hunmanby	93	TA 0977
Hunningham	54	SP 3768
Hunnington	52	SO 9681
Hunsdon	41	TL 4114
Hunsingore	91	SE 4253
Hunsonby	95	NY 5835
Hunspow	159	ND 2172
Hunstanton	69	TF 6741
Hunstanworth	96	NY 9449
Hunston (W Susx)	14	SU 8601
Hunstrete	21	ST 6462
Hunt End	53	SP 0364
Hunt's Corner	58	TM 0588
Hunt's Cross	75	SJ 4385
Hunters Lodge Inn	123	?
Hunters Quay	123	NS 1879
Huntingdon (Cambs.)	56	TL 2371
Huntingdon (Salop)	51	SJ 6507
Huntingfield	59	TM 3374
Huntington (Ches.)	75	SJ 4164
Huntington (Here & W)	46	SO 2553
Huntington (Lothian)	127	NT 4875
Huntington (N Yorks.)	92	SE 6156
Huntington (Staffs)	76	SJ 9713
Huntingtower	133	NO 0725
Huntley	36	SO 7219
Huntly	150	NJ 5339
Hunton (Kent)	28	TQ 7149
Hunton (N Yorks.)	91	SE 1892
Huntsham	9	ST 0020
Huntspill	21	ST 3045
Huntworth	21	ST 3134
Hunwick	97	NZ 1832
Hunworth	70	TG 0635
Hurdcott	23	SU 1633
Hurdsfield	76	SJ 9274
Hurley (Berks.)	39	SU 8283
Hurley (Warw.)	65	SP 2495
Hurley Common	65	SP 2396
Hurlford	114	NS 4536
Hurliness	163	ND 2888

Hurn	12	SZ 1296
Hursley	13	SU 4225
Hurst (Berks.)	25	SU 7972
Hurst (Gtr Mches.)	83	SD 9400
Hurst (N. Yorks.)	90	NZ 0402
Hurst (Somer.)	10	ST 4518
Hurst Green (E Susx)	16	TQ 7327
Hurst Green (Lancs.)	82	SD 6838
Hurst Green (Surrey)	27	TQ 3951
Hurstbourne Priors	24	SU 4346
Hurstbourne Tarrant	24	SU 3853
Hurstpierpoint	15	TQ 2816
Hurstway Common	47	SO 2949
Hurtiso	163	HY 5001
Hurtmore	25	SU 9545
Hurworth-on-Tees	97	NZ 3010
Hury	96	NY 9619
Husbands Bosworth	54	SP 6484
Husborne Crawley	39	SP 9535
Husinish	163	NA 9812
Husthwaite	92	SE 5175
Hut Green	85	SE 5623
Huthwaite	78	SK 4659
Huttoft	81	TF 5176
Hutton (Avon)	21	ST 3458
Hutton (Borders)	119	NT 9053
Hutton (Cumbr.)	95	NY 4326
Hutton (Essex)	27	TQ 6394
Hutton (Lancs.)	82	SD 4926
Hutton (N Yorks.)	92	SE 7667
Hutton Bonville	91	NZ 3300
Hutton Buscel	93	SE 9784
Hutton Conyers	91	SE 3273
Hutton Cranswick	93	TA 0252
Hutton End	95	NY 4538
Hutton Henry	98	NZ 4236
Hutton Magna	97	NZ 1212
Hutton Roof (Cumbr.)	95	NY 3734
Hutton Roof (Cumbr.)	89	SD 5777
Hutton Rudby	98	NZ 4606
Hutton Sessay	91	SE 4776
Hutton Wandesley	92	SE 5050
Hutton-le-Hole	92	SE 7090
Huxley	75	SJ 5061
Huyton	75	SJ 4490
Hycemoor	88	SD 0989
Hyde (Glos.)	36	SO 8801
Hyde (Gtr. Mches.)	76	SJ 9294
Hyde (Hants.)	12	SU 1612
Hyde Heath	39	SP 9300
Hydestile	25	SU 9740
Hyndford Bridge	115	NS 9242
Hynish	162	NL 9839
Hyssington	51	SO 3194
Hythe (Hants.)	13	SU 4207
Hythe (Kent)	29	TR 1635
Hythe End	26	TQ 0172

Ibberton	11	ST 7807
Ible	77	SK 2457
Ibsley	12	SU 1509
Ibstock	66	SK 4010
Ibstone	39	SU 7593

238

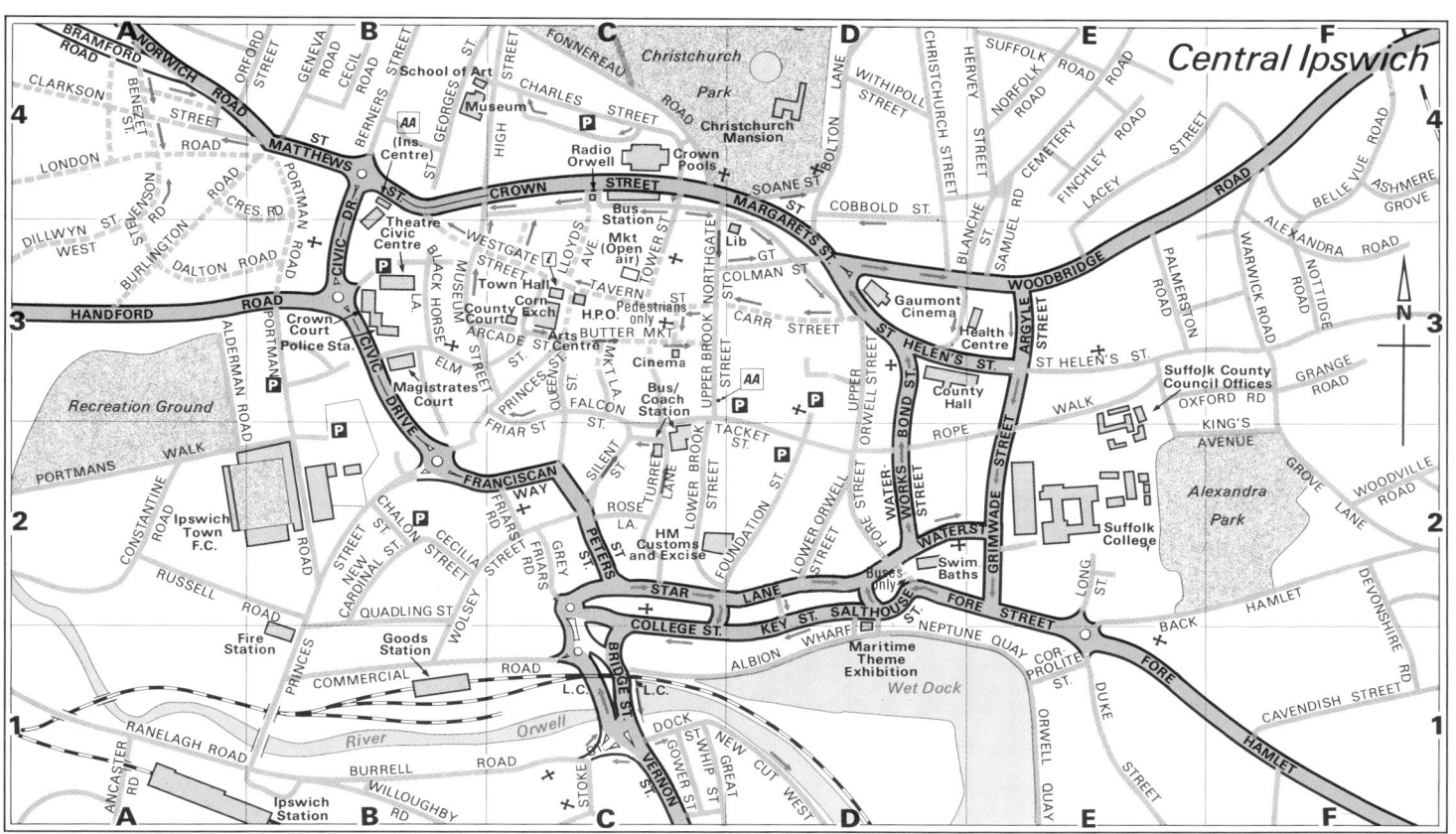

Central Ipswich

J

K

Kaber 96 NY 7911
Kaimes (Lothian) 117 NT 2767
Kalnalkill 145 NG 6857
Kames (Strath.) 129 NM 8211
Kames (Strath.) 123 NR 9771
Kames (Strath.) 107 NS 6926
Kea 3 SW 8042
Keadby 86 SE 8311
Keal 81 TF 3763
Keal Cotes 81 TF 3661
Kearsley 83 SD 7504
Kearstwick 89 SD 6079
Kearton 90 SD 9999
Kearvaig 166 NC 2874
Keasden 89 SD 7266
Keddington (Lincs.) 81 TF 3388
Kedington (Suff.) 57 TL 7046
Kedleston 65 SK 2941
Keelby 87 TA 1610
Keele 76 SJ 8045
Keele University 76 SJ 8144
Keeley Green 55 TL 0046
Keeston 30 SM 9019
Keevil 22 ST 9157
Kegworth 66 SK 4826
Kehelland 2 SW 6241
Keig 150 NJ 6119
Keigar 163 HY 5506
Keighley 84 SE 0641
Keilarsbrae 126 NS 8993
Keilhill 150 NJ 7259
Keillor 134 NO 2640
Keillour 133 NN 9725
Keils 120 NR 5268
Keinton Mandeville 21 ST 5430
Keir Mill 107 NX 8593
Keisby 67 TF 0328
Keiss 159 ND 3461
Keith 150 NJ 4350
Keithock 142 NO 6063
Kelbrook 83 SD 9044
Kelby 67 TF 0041
Keld (Cumbr.) 95 NY 5514
Keld (N Yorks.) 90 NY 8901
Kelfield 85 SE 5938
Kelham 79 SK 7755
Kellan 128 NM 5342
Kellas (Grampn.) 149 NJ 1654
Kellas (Tays.) 135 NO 4535
Kellaton 7 SX 8039
Kelleth 89 NY 6605
Kelleythorpe 93 TA 0156
Kelling 70 TG 0942
Kellington 85 SE 5524
Kelloe 98 NZ 3435
Kelly 5 SX 3981
Kelly Bray 5 SX 3571
Kelmarsh 55 SP 7379
Kelmscot 37 SU 2499
Kelsale 59 TM 3865
Kelsall 75 SJ 5268
Kelshall 56 TL 3236
Kelsick 102 NY 1950
Kelso 118 NT 7333
Kelstedge 78 SK 3363
Kelstern 80 TF 2590
Kelston 22 ST 6966
Keltneyburn (Tays.) 132 NN 7749
Kelton Hill or Rhonehouse 102 NX 7459
Kelty 126 NT 1494
Kelvedon 42 TL 8618
Kelvedon Hatch 27 TQ 5698
Kelynack 2 SW 3729
Kemback 134 NO 4115
Kemberton 64 SJ 7204
Kemble 37 ST 9897
Kemerton 52 SO 9437
Kemnay 143 NJ 7315
Kemp Town 15 TQ 3303
Kempley 36 SO 6729
Kempley Green 36 SO 6728
Kempsey 52 SO 8549
Kempsford 37 SU 1596
Kempston 55 TL 0347
Kempston Hardwick 55 TL 0244
Kempton 51 SO 3582
Kemsing 27 TQ 5558
Kenardington 28 TQ 9732
Kenchester 47 SO 4343
Kencot 37 SP 2504
Kendal 89 SD 5192
Kendleshire 36 ST 6679
Kenfig 33 SS 8081
Kenfig Hill 33 SS 8483
Kenilworth 53 SP 2872
Kenley (Gtr London) 26 TQ 3259
Kenley (Salop) 51 SJ 5600
Kenmore (Highld.) 145 NG 7557
Kenmore (Tays.) 132 NN 7745
Kenn (Avon) 21 ST 4168
Kenn (Devon.) 8 SX 9285
Kennack Sands 2 SW 7316
Kennacraig 123 NR 8262
Kennerleigh 8 SS 8107
Kennet 126 NS 9291
Kennethmont 150 NJ 5328
Kennett 57 TL 7068
Kennett End 57 TL 7066
Kennford 8 SX 9186
Kenninghall 58 TM 0386
Kennington (Kent) 28 TR 0245
Kennington (Oxon) 38 SP 5202
Kennoway 127 NO 3402
Kennyhill 57 TL 6680
Kennythorpe 92 SE 7865
Kenovay 162 NL 9946
Kensaleyre 144 NG 4251
Kensington and Chelsea 26 TQ 2778
Kensworth 40 TL 0318
Kensworth Common 40 TL 0317
Kent's Green 36 SO 7423
Kent's Oak 23 SU 3224
Kentallen 130 NN 0057
Kentchurch 47 SO 4125
Kentford 57 TL 7066
Kentisbeare 9 ST 0608
Kentisbury 19 SS 6144
Kentisbury Ford 19 SS 6242
Kentmere 89 NY 4504
Kenton (Devon.) 8 SX 9583
Kenton (Gtr London) 26 TQ 1688
Kenton (Suff.) 59 TM 1965
Kenton Bank Foot 105 NZ 2169
Kentra 137 NM 6568
Kents Bank 89 SD 3975
Kenwick 63 SJ 4230
Kenwyn 3 SW 8145
Kenyon 75 SJ 6295
Keoldale 157 NC 3866
Keppanach 138 NN 0262
Keppoch 146 NG 9621
Kepwick 91 SE 4690
Keresley 53 SP 3182
Kernborough 7 SX 7941
Kerne Bridge 47 SO 5819
Kerridge 76 SJ 9376
Kerris 2 SW 4427
Kerry 50 SO 1490
Kerry's Gate 47 SO 3933
Kerrycroy 114 NS 1061
Kerrysdale 152 NG 8373
Kersall 79 SK 7162
Kersbrook 9 SY 0683
Kersey 58 TM 0044
Kersey Upland 58 TL 9942
Kershader 163 NB 3419
Kershopefoot 108 NY 4883
Kersoe 53 SO 9939
Kerswell 9 ST 0806
Kerswell Green 52 SO 8646
Kesgrave 59 TM 2245
Kessingland 59 TM 5286
Kessingland Beach 59 TM 5385
Kestle 3 SW 9845
Kestle Mill 3 SW 8459
Keston 27 TQ 4164
Keswick (Cumbr.) 94 NY 2723
Keswick (Norf.) 71 TG 2004
Keswick (Norf.) 71 TG 3533
Ketsby 81 TF 3776
Kettering 55 SP 8778
Ketteringham 70 TG 1503
Kettins 134 NO 2338
Kettlebaston 58 TL 9650
Kettlebridge 127 NO 3007
Kettlebrook 65 SK 2103
Kettleburgh 59 TM 2660
Kettleshulme 76 SJ 9879
Kettlesing Bottom 91 SE 2257
Kettlestone 70 TF 9631
Kettlethorpe 79 SK 8475
Kettlewell 90 SD 9772
Ketton 67 SK 9704
Kew 26 TQ 1877
Kewstoke 21 ST 3363
Kexbrough 84 SE 3009
Kexby (Lincs.) 79 SK 8785
Kexby (N Yorks.) 92 SE 7050
Key Green 76 SJ 8963
Key Street 28 TQ 8864
Keyham 66 SK 6606
Keyhaven 13 SZ 3091
Keymer 15 TQ 3115
Keyningham 87 TA 2425
Keynsham 22 ST 6568
Keysoe 56 TL 0763
Keysoe Row 56 TL 0861
Keyston 55 TL 0475
Keyworth 66 SK 6130
Kibblesworth 105 NZ 2456
Kibworth Beauchamp 66 SP 6893
Kibworth Harcourt 66 SP 6894
Kidbrooke 27 TQ 4076
Kiddemore Green 64 SJ 8509
Kidderminster 52 SO 8376
Kiddington 38 SP 4122
Kidlington 38 SP 4913
Kidmore End 24 SU 6979
Kidsgrove 76 SJ 8354
Kidstones 90 SD 9581
Kidwelly 32 SN 4106
Kielder 109 NY 6293
Kiells 120 NR 4168
Kilbarchan 114 NS 4063
Kilbeg 137 NG 6506
Kilberry 123 NR 7164
Kilbirnie 114 NS 3154
Kilbride (S. Uist) 163 NF 7514
Kilbride (Skye) 137 NG 5820
Kilbride (Strath.) 129 NM 8525
Kilburn (Derby.) 78 SK 3845
Kilburn (N Yorks.) 92 SE 5179
Kilby 66 SP 6295
Kilcadzow 116 NS 8848
Kilchamaig 123 NR 8363
Kilchattan (Bute) 113 NS 1054
Kilchattan (Colonsay) 122 NR 3795
Kilchenzie 112 NR 6725
Kilchiaran 120 NR 2060
Kilchoan 128 NM 4963
Kilchoman 120 NR 2163
Kilchrenan 130 NN 0322
Kilconquhar 135 NO 4802
Kilcot 36 SO 6925
Kilcoy 147 NH 5751
Kilcreggan 124 NS 2380
Kildale 99 NZ 6009
Kildalloig 112 NR 7518
Kildonan (Highld.) 155 NC 9121
Kildonan (Island of Arran) 113 NS 0321
Kildonan Lodge 158 NC 9122
Kildrummy 150 NJ 4617
Kildwick 84 SE 0145
Kilfinan 123 NR 9378
Kilfinnan 139 NN 2795
Kilgetty 31 SN 1207
Kilgwrrwg Common 35 ST 4797
Kilham (Humbs.) 93 TA 0564
Kilham (Northumb.) 119 NT 8832
Kilkenny 37 SP 0119
Kilkhampton 18 SS 2511
Killamarsh 78 SK 4680
Killay 32 SS 6092
Killchianaig 122 NR 6486
Killean 112 NR 6944
Killearn 125 NS 5286
Killen 148 NH 6758
Killerby 97 NZ 1919
Killichonan 132 NN 5458
Killichronan 129 NM 5441
Killiechanate 139 NN 2481
Killiecrankie 141 NN 9162
Killiemore 128 NM 4740
Killilan 146 NG 9430
Killimster 159 ND 3156
Killin 132 NN 5732
Killinghall 91 SE 2858
Killington 89 SD 6188
Killochyett 117 NT 4545
Killundine 129 NM 5849
Kilmacolm 114 NS 3569
Kilmahogg 124 NN 6208
Kilmahumaig 123 NR 7893
Kilmaluag 144 NG 4374
Kilmany 134 NO 3821
Kilmarie 137 NG 5417
Kilmarnock 114 NS 4237
Kilmartin 123 NR 8398
Kilmaurs 114 NS 4141
Kilmelford 129 NM 8413
Kilmersdon 22 ST 6952
Kilmeston 13 SU 5825
Kilmichael Glassary 123 NR 8593
Kilmichael of Inverlussa 123 NR 7785
Kilmington (Devon.) 9 SY 2798
Kilmington (Wilts.) 22 ST 7736
Kilmorack 147 NH 4944
Kilmore (Island of Skye) 137 NG 6507
Kilmory (Highld.) 137 NM 5270
Kilmory (Island of Arran) 112 NR 9621
Kilmory (Strath.) 122 NR 7075
Kilmuir (Highld.) 148 NH 6749
Kilmuir (Highld.) 155 NH 7573
Kilmuir (Highld.) 144 NG 3870
Kilmuir (Island of Skye) 144 NG 2547
Kilmun 124 NS 1781
Kiln Green 47 SO 6019
Kiln Pit Hill 97 NZ 0454
Kilnave 120 NR 2871
Kilndown 16 TQ 7035
Kilnhill 94 NY 2333
Kilnhurst 85 SK 4697
Kilninian 128 NM 3945
Kilninver 129 NM 8221
Kilnsea 87 TA 4015
Kilnsey 90 SD 9767
Kilnwick 93 SE 9949
Kiloran 122 NR 3996
Kilpatrick 112 NR 9027
Kilpeck 47 SO 4430
Kilphedir 155 NC 9818
Kilpin 86 SE 7726
Kilrenny 127 NO 5705
Kilsby 54 SP 5671
Kilspindie 134 NO 2225
Kilsyth 125 NS 7178
Kiltarlity 147 NH 5041
Kilton 20 ST 1644
Kilvaxter 144 NG 3869
Kilve 20 ST 1443
Kilvington 67 SK 8042
Kilwinning 114 NS 3043
Kimberley (Norf.) 70 TG 0704
Kimberley (Notts.) 78 SK 4944
Kimble 39 SP 8206
Kimble Wick 39 SP 8007
Kimblesworth 97 NZ 2547
Kimbolton (Cambs.) 56 TL 0967
Kimbolton (Here & W) 51 SO 5261
Kimcote 54 SP 5888
Kimmeridge 11 SY 9179
Kimmerston 119 NT 9535
Kimpton (Hants.) 23 SU 2746
Kimpton (Herts.) 40 TL 1718
Kinbrace 158 NC 8631
Kinbuck 125 NN 7905
Kincaple 135 NO 4518
Kincardine (Fife.) 126 NS 9387
Kincardine (Highld.) 154 NH 6089
Kincardine O'Neil 142 NO 5999
Kinclaven 134 NO 1538
Kincraig 140 NH 8305
Kincraigie 133 NN 9849
Kindallachan 133 NN 9950
Kineton (Glos.) 37 SP 0926
Kineton (Warw.) 53 SP 3351
Kinfauns 134 NO 1622
King Sterndale 77 SK 0972
King's Acre 47 SO 4741
King's Bromley 65 SK 1216
King's Cliffe 67 TL 0097
King's Coughton 53 SP 0858
King's Heath 53 SP 0781
King's Lynn 69 TF 6220
King's Mills (Guernsey) 161 ZZ 9999
King's Newton 66 SK 3926
King's Norton (Leic.) 66 SK 6800
King's Norton (W Mids) 53 SP 0579
King's Nympton 8 SS 6819
King's Pyon 47 SO 4350
King's Somborne 24 SU 3631
King's Stag 11 ST 7210
King's Stanley 36 SO 8103
King's Sutton 54 SP 5036
King's Walden 40 TL 1623
Kingarth 123 NS 0956
Kingcoed 35 SO 4205
Kingham 37 SP 2523
Kingholm Quay 102 NX 9773
Kinghorn 126 NT 2686
Kinglassie 126 NT 2298
Kingoodie 134 NO 3329
Kings Bridge 32 SS 5997
Kings Caple 47 SO 5628
Kings Langley 40 TL 0702
Kings Meaburn 95 NY 6221
Kings Muir (Borders) 117 NT 2539
Kings Ripton 56 TL 2576
Kings Worthy 24 SU 4932
Kingsand 6 SX 4350
Kingsbarns 135 NO 5912
Kingsbridge (Devon.) 6 SX 7344
Kingsbridge (Somer.) 20 SS 9837
Kingsburgh 144 NG 3955
Kingsbury (Gtr London) 26 TQ 1989
Kingsbury (Warw.) 65 SP 2196
Kingsbury Episcopi 10 ST 4320
Kingsclere 24 SU 5258
Kingscote 36 ST 8196
Kingscott 19 SS 5318
Kingscross 113 NS 0428
Kingsdon 21 ST 5126
Kingsdown 29 TR 3748
Kingseat 126 NT 1290
Kingsey 39 SP 7406
Kingsfold 15 TQ 1636
Kingsford 52 SO 8281
Kingshall Street 58 TL 9161
Kingsheanton 19 SS 5537
Kingshouse 132 NN 5620
Kingskerswell 7 SX 8767
Kingskettle 127 NO 3008
Kingsland 51 SO 4461
Kingsley (Ches) 75 SJ 5474
Kingsley (Hants.) 25 SU 7838
Kingsley (Staffs.) 76 SK 0047
Kingsley Green 25 SU 8930
Kingsmead 13 SU 5813
Kingsmuir (Fife) 127 NO 5409
Kingsmuir (Tays.) 135 NO 4849
Kingsnorth 28 TR 0039
Kingstanding 65 SP 0794
Kingsteignton 7 SX 8773
Kingsthorne 47 SO 4932
Kingsthorpe 55 SP 7563
Kingston (Cambs.) 56 TL 3455
Kingston (Devon.) 6 SX 6347
Kingston (Dorset) 11 ST 7509
Kingston (Dorset) 11 SY 9579
Kingston (Grampn.) 149 NJ 3365
Kingston (Hants.) 12 SU 1401
Kingston (I. of W.) 13 SZ 4781
Kingston (Kent) 29 TR 1951
Kingston (Lothian) 127 NT 5482
Kingston Bagpuize 38 SU 4098
Kingston Blount 39 SU 7399
Kingston Deverill 22 ST 8436
Kingston Lisle 37 SU 3287
Kingston Maurward 11 SY 7290
Kingston Russell 10 SY 5891
Kingston Seymour 21 ST 3966
Kingston St. Mary 20 ST 2229
Kingston by Sea 15 TQ 2205
Kingston near Lewes 16 TQ 3908
Kingston on Soar 66 SK 5027
Kingston upon Hull 87 TA 0929
Kingston upon Thames 26 TQ 1869
Kingstone (Here & W) 47 SO 4235
Kingstone (Somer.) 10 ST 3713
Kingstone (Staffs.) 65 SK 0629
Kingstown 103 NY 3959
Kingswear 7 SX 8851
Kingswells 143 NJ 8606
Kingswinford 64 SO 8888
Kingswood (Avon) 35 ST 6473
Kingswood (Bucks) 38 SP 6819
Kingswood (Glos.) 36 ST 7491
Kingswood (Kent) 28 TQ 8351
Kingswood (Powys) 50 SJ 2402
Kingswood (Surrey) 26 TQ 2455
Kingswood (Warw.) 53 SP 1871
Kingswood Common 47 SO 2953
Kingswood Common 64 SJ 8302
Kingthorpe 80 TF 1275
Kington (Avon) 35 ST 6190
Kington (Here & W) 46 SO 2956
Kington (Here & W) 53 SO 9955
Kington Langley 22 ST 9276
Kington Magna 11 ST 7622
Kington St. Michael 22 ST 9077
Kingussie 140 NH 7500
Kingweston 21 ST 5230
Kinharrachie (Grampn.) 151 NJ 9231
Kinharrachie (Grampn.) 151 NK 0142
Kinkell Bridge 133 NN 9316
Kinlet 52 SO 7280
Kinloch (Fife.) 134 NO 2812
Kinloch (Highld.) 157 NC 3434
Kinloch (Rhum) 136 NM 4099
Kinloch (Skye) 137 NG 6916
Kinloch (Tays.) 134 NO 1444
Kinloch (Tays.) 134 NO 2644
Kinloch Hourn 138 NG 9407
Kinloch Rannoch 132 NN 6658
Kinlochard 124 NN 4502
Kinlochbervie 156 NC 2156
Kinlocheil 138 NM 9779
Kinlochewe 146 NH 0261
Kinlochleven 131 NN 1861
Kinlochmoidart 136 NM 7174
Kinlochspelve 129 NM 6526
Kinlock 134 NO 2713
Kinloss 149 NJ 0661
Kinmel Bay 74 SH 9881
Kinmuck 151 NJ 8119
Kinmundy 151 NJ 8817
Kinnadie 151 NJ 9643
Kinnahaird 146 NH 4755
Kinnaird 134 NO 2428
Kinneff 143 NO 8574
Kinnelhead 108 NT 0201
Kinnell 135 NO 6050
Kinnerley 63 SJ 3321
Kinnersley (Here & W) 47 SO 3449
Kinnersley (Here & W) 52 SO 8743
Kinnerton (Ches.) 74 SJ 3361
Kinnerton (Powys) 50 SO 2463
Kinnesswood 126 NO 1702
Kinninvie 97 NZ 0521
Kinnordy 134 NO 3654
Kinoulton 66 SK 6730
Kinross 126 NO 1102
Kinrossie 134 NO 1832

Kinsham (Here & W) Lapley

Kinsham (Here & W) 51 SO 3664
Kinsham (Here & W) 52 SO 9335
Kinsley 85 SE 4114
Kinson 12 SZ 0696
Kintbury 24 SU 3866
Kintessack 149 NJ 0060
Kintillo 133 NO 1317
Kintocher 142 NJ 5709
Kinton 63 SJ 3619
Kintore 143 NJ 7916
Kintour 120 NR 4752
Kinveachy 148 NH 9118
Kinver 52 SO 8483
Kippax 85 SE 4130
Kippen 125 NS 6594
Kippford or Scaur 102 NX 8355
Kirbister (Orkney) 163 HY 3607
Kirby Bedon 71 TG 2705
Kirby Bellars 67 SK 7117
Kirby Cane 71 TM 3794
Kirby Cross 43 TM 2120
Kirby Grindalythe 93 SE 9067
Kirby Hill (N Yorks.) 97 NZ 1306
Kirby Hill (N Yorks.) 91 SE 3868
Kirby Knowle 91 SE 4687
Kirby Misperton 92 SE 7779
Kirby Muxloe 66 SK 5104
Kirby Row 71 TM 3792
Kirby Sigston 91 SE 4194
Kirby Underdale 92 SE 8158
Kirby Wiske 91 SE 3784
Kirby le Soken 43 TM 2222
Kirdford 15 TQ 0226
Kirk 159 ND 2859
Kirk Bramwith 85 SE 6111
Kirk Deighton 91 SE 3950
Kirk Ella 87 TA 0129
Kirk Hallam 66 SK 4540
Kirk Hammerton 91 SE 4655
Kirk Ireton 77 SK 2650
Kirk Langley 65 SK 2838
Kirk Merrington 97 NZ 2631
Kirk Michael (I. of M.) 162 SC 3190
Kirk Sandall 85 SE 6007
Kirk Smeaton 85 SE 5116
Kirk Yetholm 110 NT 8227
Kirk of Shotts 116 NS 8462
Kirkandrews upon Eden 103 NY 3558
Kirkbampton 103 NY 3056
Kirkbean 102 NX 9859
Kirkbride 103 NY 2356
Kirkbuddo 135 NO 5043
Kirkburn (Humbs.) 93 SE 9855
Kirkburton 84 SE 1912
Kirkby (Lincs.) 80 TF 0692
Kirkby (Mers.) 82 SJ 4098
Kirkby (N Yorks.) 98 NZ 5306
Kirkby Fleetham 91 SE 2984
Kirkby Green 80 TF 0857
Kirkby Lonsdale 89 SD 6178
Kirkby Malham 90 SD 8960
Kirkby Mallory 66 SK 4500
Kirkby Malzeard 91 SE 2374
Kirkby Overblow 91 SE 3249
Kirkby Stephen 96 NY 7708
Kirkby Thore 95 NY 6325
Kirkby Underwood 68 TF 0727
Kirkby in Ashfield 78 SK 5056
Kirkby la Thorpe 80 TF 0946
Kirkby on Bain 80 TF 2362
Kirkbymoorside 92 SE 6986
Kirkcaldy 127 NT 2791
Kirkcambeck 95 NY 5368
Kirkcarswell 102 NX 7549
Kirkcolm 100 NX 0268
Kirkconnel 107 NS 7312
Kirkconnel 102 NX 9868
Kirkcowan 101 NX 3260
Kirkcudbright 101 NX 6851
Kirkfieldbank 116 NS 8643
Kirkgunzeon 102 NX 8666
Kirkham (Lancs.) 82 SD 4231
Kirkham (N Yorks.) 92 SE 7365
Kirkhamgate 84 SE 2922
Kirkharle 105 NZ 0182
Kirkheaton (Northum.) 104 NZ 0177
Kirkheaton (W Yorks.) 84 SE 1817
Kirkhill (Highld.) 147 NH 5545
Kirkhill (Tays.) 135 NO 6860
Kirkhope (Borders) 109 NT 3823
Kirkhouse 117 NT 3233
Kirkibost (Island of Skye) 137 NG 5417
Kirkinch 134 NO 3144
Kirkinner 101 NX 4251
Kirkintilloch 125 NS 6573
Kirkland (Cumbr.) 94 NY 0718
Kirkland (Cumbr.) 95 NY 6432
Kirkland (Dumf & G) 107 NS 7214
Kirkland (Dumf & G) 107 NX 8090
Kirkleatham 98 NZ 5921
Kirklevington 98 NZ 4309
Kirkley 71 TM 5491
Kirkleyditch 76 SJ 8778
Kirklington (N Yorks.) 91 SE 3181
Kirklington (Notts.) 79 SK 6757
Kirklinton 103 NY 4366
Kirkliston 126 NT 1274
Kirkmaiden 100 NX 1236
Kirkmichael (Strath.) 106 NS 3408
Kirkmichael (Tays.) 133 NO 0860
Kirkmuirhill 115 NS 7943
Kirknewton (Lothian) 117 NT 1166
Kirknewton (Northum.) 119 NT 9130
Kirkoswald (Cumbr.) 95 NY 5541
Kirkoswald (Strath.) 106 NS 2407
Kirkpatrick Durham 102 NX 7870
Kirkpatrick-Fleming 103 NY 2770
Kirksanton 88 SD 1380
Kirkstall 84 SE 2635
Kirkstead Bridge 80 TF 1762
Kirkstile (Dumf & G) 109 NY 3690
Kirkstile (Grampn.) 145 NJ 5235
Kirkstone Pass Inn 89 NY 4108
Kirkstyle 158 ND 3473
Kirkton (Borders) 109 NT 5413
Kirkton (Dumf & G) 108 NX 9781
Kirkton (Fife.) 134 NO 3625
Kirkton (Grampn.) 142 NJ 6112
Kirkton (Grampn.) 150 NJ 6425
Kirkton (Grampn.) 150 NJ 6950
Kirkton (Grampn.) 151 NJ 8243
Kirkton (Grampn.) 151 NK 1050
Kirkton (Highld.) 146 NG 9141
Kirkton (Highld.) 155 NH 7998
Kirkton (Strath.) 108 NS 9422
Kirkton (Tays.) 133 NN 9618
Kirkton (Tays.) 135 NO 4246
Kirkton Manor 117 NT 2137
Kirkton of Airlie 134 NO 3151
Kirkton of Auchterhouse 134 NO 3338
Kirkton of Barevan 148 NH 8347
Kirkton of Collace 134 NO 1931
Kirkton of Craig 135 NO 7055
Kirkton of Durris 143 NO 7796
Kirkton of Glenbuchat 142 NJ 3715
Kirkton of Glenisla 134 NO 2160
Kirkton of Kingoldrum 134 NO 3354
Kirkton of Largo 127 NO 4203
Kirkton of Lethendy 133 NO 1241
Kirkton of Logie Buchan 151 NJ 9829
Kirkton of Maryculter 143 NO 8599
Kirkton of Menmuir 142 NO 5364
Kirkton of Monikie 135 NO 5138
Kirkton of Rayne 150 NJ 6930
Kirkton of Skene 143 NJ 8007
Kirkton of Strathmartine 134 NO 3735
Kirkton of Tealing 134 NO 4037
Kirktown 151 NK 0952
Kirktown of Auchterless 150 NJ 7141
Kirktown of Bourtie 151 NJ 8024
Kirktown of Deskford 150 NJ 5061
Kirktown of Fetteresso 143 NO 8585
Kirkwall 163 HY 4410
Kirkwhelpington 104 NY 9984
Kirmington 87 TA 1011
Kirmond le Mire 80 TF 1892
Kirn 124 NS 1878
Kirriemuir 134 NO 3854
Kirstead Green 71 TM 2997
Kirtlebridge 103 NY 2372
Kirtleton 102 NY 2780
Kirtling 57 TL 6857
Kirtling Green 57 TL 6855
Kirtlington 38 SP 4919
Kirtomy 158 NC 7463
Kirton (Highld.) 145 NG 8327
Kirton (Lincs.) 68 TF 3038
Kirton (Notts.) 79 SK 6869
Kirton (Suff.) 59 TM 2739
Kirton End 68 TF 2840
Kirton Holme 68 TF 2642
Kirton in Lindsey 86 SK 9398
Kislingbury 54 SP 6959
Kite Green 53 SP 1666
Kites Hardwick 54 SP 4668
Kittisford 9 ST 0822
Kittle 32 SS 5789
Kittybrewster 143 NJ 9208
Kitwood 24 SU 6633
Kiveton Park 78 SK 4982
Knaith 79 SK 8284
Knap Corner 22 ST 8023
Knaphill 25 SU 9658
Knapp (Somer.) 21 ST 3025
Knapp (Tays.) 134 NO 2831
Knapton (N Yorks.) 92 SE 5652
Knapton (N Yorks.) 92 SE 8775
Knapton (Norf.) 71 TG 3034
Knapwell 56 TL 3362
Knaresborough 91 SE 3557
Knarsdale 95 NY 6752
Knaven 151 NJ 8943
Knayton 91 SE 4387
Knebworth 41 TL 2520
Kneesall 79 SK 7064
Kneesworth 56 TL 3444
Kneeton 79 SK 7146
Knelston 32 SS 4689
Knightacott 19 SS 6439
Knightcote 54 SP 3954
Knightley 64 SJ 8125
Knighton (Devon.) 6 SX 5249
Knighton (Leic.) 66 SK 6001
Knighton (Powys) 50 SO 2872
Knighton (Somer.) 20 ST 1944
Knighton (Staffs.) 64 SJ 7240
Knighton (Staffs.) 64 SJ 7427
Knightwick 52 SO 7355
Knill 50 SO 2960
Knipton 67 SK 8231
Knitsley 97 NZ 1148
Kniveton 77 SK 2050
Knock (Cumbr.) 95 NY 6826
Knock (Grampn.) 150 NJ 5452
Knock (Island of Mull) 129 NM 5438
Knock (Isle of Lewis) 163 NB 4931
Knock Castle 114 NS 1863
Knockally 159 ND 1428
Knockan 153 NC 1528
Knockando 149 NJ 1941
Knockbain (Highld.) 147 NH 6255
Knockbain (Highld.) 147 NH 5543
Knockbrex 101 NX 5849
Knockdee 159 ND 1761
Knockdolian 106 NX 1285
Knockdown 36 ST 8388
Knockenkelly 113 NS 0426
Knockentiber 114 NS 3939
Knockholt 27 TQ 4658
Knockholt Pound 27 TQ 4859
Knockin 63 SJ 3322
Knocknaha 112 NR 6817
Knocknain 100 NW 9855
Knockrome 122 NR 5571
Knocksharry 162 SC 2785
Knodishall 59 TM 4261
Knole 21 ST 4825
Knolls Green 76 SJ 8079
Knolton 63 SJ 3738
Knook 22 ST 9341
Knossington 67 SK 8008
Knott End-on-Sea 82 SD 3548
Knotting 55 TL 0063
Knotting Green 55 TL 0062
Knottingley 85 SE 5023
Knotty Green 39 SU 9392
Knowbury 51 SO 5774
Knowe 101 NX 3171
Knowehead 107 NX 6090
Knowesgate 104 NY 9885
Knoweside 106 NS 2512
Knowl Green 57 TL 7841
Knowl Hill 25 SU 8279
Knowle (Avon) 35 ST 6170
Knowle (Devon) 9 SY 0482
Knowle (Devon) 9 ST 0006
Knowle (Devon.) 19 SS 4938
Knowle (Devon.) 8 SS 7801
Knowle (Somer.) 21 ST 3439
Knowle (W Mids) 53 SP 1876
Knowle Cross 9 SY 0397
Knowle Green 83 SD 6337
Knowlton 29 TR 2853
Knowsley 75 SJ 4395
Knowstone 8 SS 8223
Knox 91 SE 2958
Knox Bridge 28 TQ 7940
Knucklas 50 SO 2574
Knuston 55 SP 9366
Knutsford 76 SJ 7578
Knypersley 76 SJ 8856
Krumlin 84 SE 0519
Kuggar 2 SW 7216
Kyle of Lochalsh 145 NG 7627
Kyleakin 145 NG 7526
Kylerhea 137 NG 7820
Kylesku 157 NC 2334
Kylestrome 156 NC 2234
Kyloe 119 NU 0540
Kymin 35 SO 5212
Kynnersley 63 SJ 6716
Kyre Park 51 SO 6263

L

L'Ancress (Guernsey) 161 ZZ 9999
L'Eree (Guernsey) 161 ZZ 9999
L'Etacq (Jersey) 161 ZZ 9999
L'Gele (Guernsey) 161 ZZ 9999
L'Gran (Guernsey) 161 ZZ 9999
L'Islet Pleinheaume (Guernsey) 161 ZZ 9999
La Beilleuse (Guernsey) 161 ZZ 9999
La Corbiere (Jersey) 161 ZZ 9999
La Fontenelle (Guernsey) 161 ZZ 9999
La Fosse (Guernsey) 161 ZZ 9999
La Greve (Guernsey) 161 ZZ 9999
La Greve de Lecq (Jersey) 161 ZZ 9999
La Hougue Bie 161 ZZ 9999
La Houguette (Guernsey) 161 ZZ 9999
La Mare (Jersey) 161 ZZ 9999
La Passee (Guernsey) 161 ZZ 9999
La Pulente (Jersey) 161 ZZ 9999
La Rammee (Guernsey) 161 ZZ 9999
La Rocque (Jersey) 161 ZZ 9999
La Rousaillerie (Guernsey) 161 ZZ 9999
La Villacq (Guernsey) 161 ZZ 9999
La Ville des Marettes (Jersey) 161 ZZ 9999
La Villiage (Guernsey) 161 ZZ 9999
Laceby 87 TA 2106
Lacey Green 39 SP 8200
Lach Dennis 76 SJ 7071
Lackford 57 TL 7970
Lacock 22 ST 9168
Ladbroke 54 SP 4158
Laddingford 16 TQ 6948
Lade Bank 81 TF 3954
Ladock 3 SW 8950
Lady Hall 88 SD 1986
Ladybank (Fife.) 127 NO 3009
Ladycross 5 SX 3288
Ladykirk 119 NT 8847
Ladysford 151 NJ 9060
Ladywood 52 SO 8761
Lagavulin 120 NR 4045
Lagg (Island of Arran) 112 NR 9521
Lagg (Jura) 122 NR 5978
Laggan (Highld.) 140 NN 2997
Laggan (Highld.) 139 NN 6194
Lagganulva 128 NM 4541
Laide 152 NG 8992
Laindon 27 TQ 6889
Lair 146 NH 0148
Lairg 154 NC 5806
Laithes 95 NY 4633
Lake (Devon) 18 SS 4402
Lake (Devon) 19 SS 5531
Lake (I.O.W.) 13 SZ 5983
Lake (Wilts) 23 SU 1239
Lake Cottage 100 NX 0949
Lake Side 89 SD 3787
Lakenham 71 TG 2307
Lakenheath 57 TL 7182
Lakenheath Halt 57 TL 7387
Lakesend 69 TL 5196
Laleham 26 TQ 0568
Laleston 33 SS 8779
Lamanva 3 SW 7631
Lamarsh 42 TL 8935
Lamas 71 TG 2423
Lamberhurst 16 TQ 6735
Lamberton 119 NT 9657
Lambeth 26 TQ 3078
Lambfell Moar 162 SC 2984
Lambley (Northum.) 95 NY 6758
Lambley (Notts.) 79 SK 6245
Lambourn 37 SU 3278
Lambourne End 27 TQ 4894
Lambs Green 15 TQ 2136
Lambston 30 SM 9016
Lamerton 5 SX 4476
Lamesley 105 NZ 2557
Lamington (Highld.) 155 NH 7577
Lamington (Strath.) 116 NS 9730
Lamlash 113 NS 0231
Lamonby 95 NY 4135
Lamorick 4 SX 0364
Lamorna 2 SW 4524
Lamorran 3 SW 8741
Lampeter 45 SN 5748
Lampeter-Velfrey 31 SN 1514
Lamphey 30 SN 0100
Lamplugh 94 NY 0820
Lamport 55 SP 7574
Lamyatt 22 ST 6535
Lana (Corn.) 5 SX 3496
Lana (Devon) 18 SS 3007
Lanark 116 NS 8843
Lancaster 89 SD 4761
Lanchester 97 NZ 1647
Lancing 15 TQ 1804
Landbeach 57 TL 4765
Landcross 18 SS 4524
Landerberry 143 NJ 7404
Landewednack 2 SW 7012
Landford 12 SU 2519
Landford Manor 12 SU 2620
Landimore 32 SS 4693
Landkey 19 SS 5931
Landrake 5 SX 3760
Landscove 7 SX 7766
Landshipping 30 SN 0211
Landulph 5 SX 4261
Landwade 57 TL 6268
Landywood 65 SJ 9806
Lane 3 SW 8260
Lane End (Bucks.) 39 SU 8091
Lane End (Cumbr.) 88 SD 1093
Lane End (Hants.) 13 SU 5525
Lane End (Wilts.) 22 ST 8145
Lane Head 97 NZ 1212
Laneast 5 SX 2283
Laneham 79 SK 8076
Lanehead (Durham) 96 NY 8442
Lanehead (Northum.) 104 NY 7986
Lanes 3 SW 9040
Laneshaw Bridge 83 SD 9240
Langar 67 SK 7234
Langbank 124 NS 3873
Langbar 90 SE 0951
Langcliffe 90 SD 8264
Langdale End 93 SE 9391
Langdon 4 SX 2092
Langdon Beck 96 NY 8732
Langdon Hills 27 TQ 6786
Langdyke 127 NO 3304
Langenhoe 43 TM 0018
Langford (Beds.) 56 TL 1841
Langford (Devon.) 9 ST 0203
Langford (Essex) 42 TL 8408
Langford (Notts.) 79 SK 8258
Langford (Oxon.) 37 SP 2402
Langford Budville 9 ST 1122
Langford End 56 TL 1654
Langford Green 9 ST 0302
Langham (Essex) 43 TM 0233
Langham (Leic.) 67 SK 8411
Langham (Norf.) 70 TG 0041
Langham (Suff.) 58 TL 9769
Langho 83 SD 7034
Langholm 109 NY 3684
Langleeford 110 NT 9623
Langley (Berks.) 26 TQ 0078
Langley (Ches.) 76 SJ 9471
Langley (Essex) 41 TL 4435
Langley (Hants.) 13 SU 4400
Langley (Herts.) 40 TL 2122
Langley (Kent) 28 TQ 8051
Langley (Northum.) 104 NY 8362
Langley (Somer.) 20 ST 0828
Langley (W Susx) 14 SU 8029
Langley (Warw.) 53 SP 1962
Langley Burrell 22 ST 9275
Langley Castle 104 NY 8463
Langley Marsh 20 ST 0729
Langley Mill 78 SK 4447
Langley Moor 97 NZ 2541
Langley Park 97 NZ 2144
Langley Street 71 TG 3601
Langney 16 TQ 6302
Langold 78 SK 5887
Langore 5 SX 3086
Langport 21 ST 4226
Langrick 81 TF 2648
Langridge 22 ST 7369
Langrigg 94 NY 1645
Langrish 14 SU 7023
Langsett 84 SE 2100
Langshaw 118 NT 5139
Langskaill 163 HY 4443
Langstone 14 SU 7104
Langthorne 91 SE 2491
Langthorpe 91 SE 3867
Langthwaite 97 NZ 0002
Langtoft (Humbs.) 93 TA 0166
Langtoft (Lincs.) 68 TF 1212
Langton (Durham) 97 NZ 1719
Langton (Lincs.) 80 TF 2368
Langton (Lincs.) 81 TF 3970
Langton (N Yorks.) 92 SE 7967
Langton Green (Kent) 16 TQ 5439
Langton Green (Suff.) 58 TM 1474
Langton Herring 10 SY 6182
Langton Matravers 11 SY 9978
Langton by Wragby 80 TF 1476
Langtree 18 SS 4415
Langwathby 95 NY 5733
Langwith 78 SK 5269
Langworth 80 TF 0676
Lanieth 3 SW 9752
Lanivet 4 SX 0364
Lank 4 SX 0875
Lanlivery 4 SX 0759
Lanner 2 SW 7139
Lanreath 4 SX 1756
Lansallos 4 SX 1751
Lansdown 22 ST 7268
Lanteglos 4 SX 0882
Lanteglos Highway 4 SX 1453
Lanton (Borders) 109 NT 6221
Lanton (Northum.) 119 NT 9231
Lapford 8 SS 7308
Laphroaig 120 NR 3845
Lapley 64 SJ 8713

Place	Page	Grid ref.
Llanynys	74	SJ 1062
Llanyre	50	SO 0462
Llanystumdwy	60	SH 4738
Llanywern	46	SO 1028
Llawhaden	30	SN 0717
Llawnt	62	SJ 2430
Llawryglyn	49	SN 9291
Llay	74	SJ 3255
Llechcynfarwy	72	SH 3881
Llechfaen	46	SO 0828
Llechryd (Dyfed)	44	SN 2243
Llechryd (Mid Glam.)	34	SO 1009
Llechrydau	62	SJ 2234
Lledrod (Clwyd)	62	SJ 2229
Lledrod (Dyfed)	48	SN 6470
Llidiadnenog	45	SN 5437
Llidiardau	60	SH 1929
Llidiart-y-parc	62	SJ 1243
Llithfaen	60	SH 3543
Lloiney	50	SO 2475
Llong	74	SJ 2562
Llowes	46	SO 1941
Llwydcoed	32	SN 9905
Llwydiarth	62	SJ 0315
Llwyn	50	SO 2880
Llwyn-y-Groes	45	SN 5956
Llwyncelyn	44	SN 4459
Llwyndafydd	44	SN 3755
Llwynderw	50	SJ 2004
Llwyndrynys	60	SH 3741
Llwyngwril	48	SH 5909
Llwynhendy	32	SS 5599
Llwynmawr	62	SJ 2236
Llwynypia	33	SS 9993
Llynclys	62	SJ 2924
Llynfaes	72	SH 4178
Llys-y-fran	30	SN 0424
Llysfaen	73	SH 8977
Llyswen (Dyfed)	48	SN 4661
Llyswen (Powys)	46	SO 1337
Llysworney	33	SS 9674
Llywel	45	SN 8630
Loan	126	NS 9575
Loanend	119	NT 9450
Loanhead	117	NT 2765
Loans	114	NS 3431
Lobb	18	SS 4637
Lobhillcross	5	SX 4686
Loch Katrine Pier	123	NN 4907
Loch Laggan Inn	138	NN 5390
Loch Lubnaig	132	NN 5713
Loch Maree Hotel	151	NG 9271
Loch Skiach	133	NN 9547
Lochailort (Highld.)	137	NM 7682
Lochaline (Highld.)	129	NM 6744
Lochans	100	NX 0656
Locharbriggs	102	NX 9980
Lochawe (Strath.)	130	NN 1227
Lochboisdale (S. Uist)	163	NF 7820
Lochbuie (Strath.)	163	NM 6125
Lochcarron (Highld.)	145	NG 9039
Lochdonhead	129	NM 7333
Lochead	123	NR 7778
Lochearnhead	132	NN 5823
Lochee	134	NO 3631
Lochend (Highld.)	147	NH 5937
Locheport (N. Uist)	163	NF 8563
Locherben	108	NX 9797
Lochfoot	102	NX 8973
Lochgair	123	NR 9290
Lochgarthside	147	NH 5219
Lochgelly	126	NT 1893
Lochgilphead	123	NR 8687
Lochgoilhead	124	NN 1901
Lochhill	149	NJ 2964
Lochinver	156	NC 0922
Lochlane	132	NN 8320
Lochluichart	147	NH 3262
Lochmaben	108	NY 0882
Lochmaddy	163	NF 9169
Lochnaw	100	NW 9962
Lochore	126	NT 1796
Lochranza (Island of Arran)	112	NR 9350
Lochs Crofts	148	NJ 3163
Lochside (Grampn.)	143	NO 7464
Lochside (Highland.)	158	NC 8735
Lochside (Highld.)	157	NC 4858
Lochside (Highld.)	148	NH 8253
Lochslin	154	NH 8481
Lochton	143	NO 7592
Lochuisge	129	NM 7856
Lochwinnoch	114	NS 3558
Lochwood (Dumf & G)	108	NY 0896
Lochwood (Strath.)	115	NS 6966
Lockengate	4	SX 0361
Lockerbie	108	NY 1381
Lockeridge	23	SU 1467
Lockerley	23	SU 2925
Locking	21	ST 3659
Lockington (Humbs.)	86	SE 9947
Lockington (Leic.)	66	SK 4628
Lockleywood	64	SJ 6828
Locks Heath	13	SU 5207
Lockton	92	SE 8489
Loddington (Leic.)	67	SK 7802
Loddington (Northants.)	55	SP 8178
Loddiswell	6	SX 7148
Loddon	71	TM 3698
Lode	57	TL 5362
Loders	10	SY 4994
Lodge Green	53	SP 2583
Lodsworth	14	SU 9223
Lofthouse (N Yorks.)	90	SE 1073
Lofthouse (W Yorks.)	85	SE 3325
Loftus	99	NZ 7118
Logan	107	NS 5820
Loggerheads	64	SJ 7336
Loggie	151	NH 1491
Logie (Fife)	134	NO 4020
Logie (Grampn.)	151	NK 0356
Logie (Tays.)	143	NO 6963
Logie Coldstone	142	NJ 4304
Logie Hill	155	NH 7776
Logie Newton	150	NJ 6638
Logie Pert	142	NO 6664
Logierait	133	NN 9752
Login	31	SN 1623
Lolworth	56	TL 3664
Lonbain	145	NG 6853
Londesborough	86	SE 8645
London	26	TQ 3281
London Apprentice	4	SX 0050
London Colney	40	TL 1603
Londonderry	91	SE 3087
Londonthorpe	67	SK 9537
Londubh	152	NG 8680
Long Ashton	35	ST 5470
Long Bank	52	SO 7574
Long Bennington	79	SK 8344
Long Bredy	10	SY 5690
Long Buckby	54	SP 6267
Long Clawson	67	SK 7227
Long Common	13	SU 5014
Long Compton (Staffs.)	64	SJ 8522
Long Compton (Warw.)	53	SP 2832
Long Crendon	38	SP 6908
Long Crichel	11	ST 9710
Long Ditton	26	TQ 1666
Long Drax	86	SE 6528
Long Duckmanton	78	SK 4371
Long Eaton	66	SK 4933
Long Green	52	SO 8433
Long Hanborough	38	SP 4114
Long Hermiston	117	NT 1770
Long Itchington	54	SP 4165
Long Lane	63	SJ 6215
Long Lawford	54	SP 4775
Long Load	10	ST 4623
Long Marston (Herts.)	39	SP 8915
Long Marston (N Yorks.)	92	SE 5051
Long Marston (Warw.)	53	SP 1548
Long Marton	95	NY 6624
Long Meadowend	51	SO 4081
Long Melford	58	TL 8646
Long Newnton (Glos.)	35	ST 9092
Long Preston	90	SD 8357
Long Riston	87	TA 1242
Long Stratton	71	TM 1992
Long Street (Bucks.)	55	SP 7946
Long Sutton (Hants.)	25	SU 7347
Long Sutton (Lincs.)	69	TF 4322
Long Sutton (Somer.)	21	ST 4625
Long Thurlow	58	TM 0168
Long Whatton	66	SK 4723
Long Wittenham	38	SU 5493
Longbenton	105	NZ 2668
Longborough	37	SP 1729
Longbridge (W Mids)	53	SP 0178
Longbridge (Warw.)	53	SP 2662
Longbridge Deverill	22	ST 8640
Longburgh	102	NY 3159
Longburton	10	ST 6412
Longcliffe	77	SK 2255
Longcombe	7	SX 8359
Longcot	37	SU 2790
Longcroft	125	NS 7979
Longden	51	SJ 4306
Longden Common	51	SJ 4404
Longdon (Here & W)	52	SO 8336
Longdon (Staffs.)	65	SK 0714
Longdon Heath	52	SO 8338
Longdon upon Tern	63	SJ 6215
Longdown	8	SX 8691
Longdowns	3	SW 7434
Longfield	27	TQ 6069
Longfield Hill	27	TQ 6268
Longford (Derby.)	65	SK 2137
Longford (Glos.)	36	SO 8320
Longford (Gtr London)	26	TQ 0576
Longford (Salop)	63	SJ 6433
Longford (Salop)	64	SJ 7218
Longford (W Mids.)	54	SP 3583
Longforgan	134	NO 3129
Longformacus	118	NT 6957
Longframlington	111	NU 1201
Longham (Dorset)	12	SZ 0697
Longham (Norf.)	70	TF 9415
Longhirst	105	NZ 2289
Longhope	36	SO 6819
Longhorsley	111	NZ 1494
Longhoughton	111	NU 2414
Longlands	94	NY 2736
Longley Green	52	SO 7350
Longmanhill	150	NJ 7462
Longmoor Camp	25	SU 7930
Longmorn	149	NJ 2358
Longnewton (Bord)	109	NT 5827
Longnewton (Cleve.)	98	NZ 3816
Longney	36	SO 7612
Longniddry	127	NT 4476
Longnor (Salop)	51	SJ 4800
Longnor (Staffs.)	77	SK 0864
Longparish	24	SU 4344
Longridge (Lancs.)	83	SD 6037
Longridge (Lothian)	116	NS 9462
Longriggend	116	NS 8270
Longrock	2	SW 4931
Longsdon	76	SJ 9554
Longshaw Common	82	SD 5302
Longside	151	NK 0347
Longslow	63	SJ 6535
Longstanton	56	TL 4066
Longstock	24	SU 3536
Longstone Wells	19	SS 7634
Longstowe	56	TL 3054
Longstreet (Wilts.)	23	SU 1451
Longthorpe	68	TL 1698
Longthwaite	95	NY 4323
Longton (Lancs.)	82	SD 4725
Longton (Staffs.)	64	SJ 9043
Longtown (Cumbr.)	102	NY 3768
Longtown (Here & W)	47	SO 3228
Longueville (Jersey)	161	ZZ 9999
Longville in the Dale	51	SO 5393
Longwick	39	SP 7805
Longwitton	105	NZ 0788
Longwood	51	SJ 6007
Longworth	38	SU 3899
Longyester	118	NT 5465
Lonmore	144	NG 2646
Loose	28	TQ 7552
Loosley Row	39	SP 8100
Lootcherbrae	150	NJ 6054
Lopcombe Corner	23	SU 2435
Lopen	10	ST 4214
Loppington	63	SJ 4629
Lorbottle	111	NU 0306
Lornty	134	NO 1746
Loscoe	78	SK 4247
Lossiemouth	155	NJ 2370
Lossit	120	NR 1856
Lostock Gralam	76	SJ 6976
Lostock Green	76	SJ 6975
Lostock Junction	83	SD 6708
Lostwithiel	4	SX 1059
Lothbeg	155	NC 9410
Lothersdale	84	SD 9545
Lothmore	155	NC 9611
Loudwater	39	SU 8990
Loughborough	66	SK 5319
Loughor	32	SS 5898
Loughton (Bucks.)	55	SP 8337
Loughton (Essex)	27	TQ 4296
Loughton (Salop)	51	SO 6183
Lound (Lincs.)	67	TF 0618
Lound (Notts.)	79	SK 6986
Lound (Suff.)	71	TM 5099
Lount	66	SK 3819
Louth	81	TF 3287
Lovaton	5	SX 5466
Love Clough	83	SD 8126
Lover	12	SU 2120
Loversall	85	SK 5798
Loves Green	42	TL 6404
Loveston	30	SN 0808
Lovington	21	ST 5931
Low Ackworth	85	SE 4517
Low Borrowbridge	89	NY 6101
Low Bradfield	77	SK 2691
Low Bradley	90	SE 0048
Low Braithwaite	95	NY 4242
Low Brunton	104	NY 9269
Low Burnham	86	SE 7702
Low Catton	92	SE 7053
Low Crosby	102	NY 4459
Low Dinsdale	98	NZ 3411
Low Eggborough	85	SE 5522
Low Fell	105	NZ 2660
Low Gate	104	NY 9064
Low Green	91	SE 2059
Low Ham	21	ST 4329
Low Hesket	95	NY 4646
Low Hesleyhurst	111	NZ 0997
Low Knipe	95	NY 5210
Low Laithe	91	SE 1963
Low Lorton	94	NY 1524
Low Mill	92	SE 6795
Low Moor	83	SD 7241
Low Redford	97	NZ 0731
Low Row (Cumbr.)	95	NY 5863
Low Row (N Yorks.)	90	SD 9897
Low Santon	86	SE 9312
Low Street	71	TG 3424
Low Torry	126	NT 0086
Low Worsall	97	NZ 3909
Lowbands	36	SO 7731
Lowca	94	NX 9821
Lowdham	79	SK 6646
Lower Aisholt	20	ST 2035
Lower Ansty	11	ST 7603
Lower Ashton	8	SX 8484
Lower Assendon	39	SU 7484
Lower Beeding	15	TQ 2227
Lower Benefield	55	SP 9888
Lower Bentham	89	SD 6469
Lower Beobridge	64	SO 7891
Lower Boddington	54	SP 4752
Lower Brailes	53	SP 3139
Lower Breakish	145	NG 6725
Lower Bullingham	47	SO 5038
Lower Bullington	24	SU 4541
Lower Burgate	12	SU 1515
Lower Cam	36	SO 7401
Lower Chapel	46	SO 0235
Lower Chicksgrove	22	ST 9730
Lower Chute	23	SU 3153
Lower Common	34	SU 6344
Lower Cwmtwrch	33	SN 7710
Lower Darwen	83	SD 6824
Lower Dean	55	TL 0569
Lower Dicker	16	TQ 5511
Lower Down	51	SO 3384
Lower Dunsforth	91	SE 4464
Lower Elsted	14	SU 8320
Lower Farringdon	24	SU 7035
Lower Fittleworth	14	TQ 0118
Lower Frankton	63	SJ 3732
Lower Froyle	25	SU 7544
Lower Gabwell	7	SX 9169
Lower Gledfield	154	NH 5990
Lower Godney	21	ST 4742
Lower Green	70	TF 9837
Lower Greenbank	82	SD 5254
Lower Grove Common	47	SO 5525
Lower Halstow	28	TQ 8567
Lower Hardres	29	TR 1453
Lower Hergest	46	SO 2755
Lower Heyford	38	SP 4824
Lower Higham	28	TQ 7172
Lower Holbrook	43	TM 1735
Lower Hordley	63	SJ 3929
Lower Horncroft	14	TQ 0017
Lower Killeyan	120	NR 2743
Lower Kingswood	26	TQ 2453
Lower Knapp	21	ST 3025
Lower Langford	21	ST 4660
Lower Largo	127	NO 4102
Lower Lemington	53	SP 2134
Lower Llanfadog	49	SN 9366
Lower Lovacott	19	SS 5227
Lower Loxhore	19	SS 6137
Lower Lydbrook	47	SO 5916
Lower Lye	51	SO 4067
Lower Machen	34	ST 2288
Lower Maes-coed	47	SO 3431
Lower Mayland	42	TL 9101
Lower Moor	52	SO 9847
Lower Morton	35	ST 6491
Lower Nazeing	41	TL 3906
Lower Penarth	20	ST 1869
Lower Penn	64	SO 8696
Lower Pennington	13	SZ 3193
Lower Peover	76	SJ 7474
Lower Quinton	53	SP 1847
Lower Shelton	55	SP 9942
Lower Shiplake	25	SU 7779
Lower Shuckburgh	54	SP 4862
Lower Slaughter	37	SP 1622
Lower Soudley	36	SO 6609
Lower Stanton St. Quintin	36	ST 9180
Lower Stow Bedon	70	TL 9694
Lower Street (Dorset)	11	SY 8399
Lower Street (Norf.)	71	TG 2635
Lower Sundon	40	TL 0526
Lower Swanwick	13	SU 4909
Lower Swell	37	SP 1725
Lower Tale	9	ST 0601
Lower Tean	65	SK 0138
Lower Thurlton	71	TM 4299
Lower Town	2	SW 6629
Lower Tysoe	53	SP 3445
Lower Upham	13	SU 5219
Lower Vexford	20	ST 1135
Lower Weare	21	ST 4053
Lower Welsdon	47	SO 2950
Lower Westmancote	52	SO 9337
Lower Whatley	22	ST 7347
Lower Wield	24	SU 6340
Lower Willingdon	16	TQ 5803
Lower Winchendon	39	SP 7312
Lower Woodend	39	SU 8187
Lower Woodford	23	SU 1235
Lowertown	5	SX 4584
Lowesby	67	SK 7207
Lowestoft	71	TM 5493
Lowestoft End	71	TM 5394
Loweswater	94	NY 1420
Lowfield Heath	15	TQ 2740
Lowgill (Lancs.)	89	SD 6564
Lowick (Cumbr.)	88	SD 2985
Lowick (Northants.)	55	SP 9781
Lowick (Northum.)	119	NU 0139
Lownie Moor	135	NO 4848
Lowsonford	53	SP 1867
Lowthorpe	93	TA 0860
Lowton	75	SJ 6197
Lowton Common	75	SJ 6397
Loxbeare	8	SS 9116
Loxhill	14	TQ 0037
Loxhore	19	SS 6138
Loxley	53	SP 2553
Loxton	21	ST 3755
Loxwood	15	TQ 0431
Lubenham	54	SP 7087
Luberoy	153	NC 3602
Luccombe	20	SS 9144
Luccombe Village	13	SZ 5880
Lucker	119	NU 1530
Luckett	5	SX 3873
Luckington	36	ST 8383
Lucklawhill	135	NO 4222
Luckwell Bridge	20	SS 9038
Lucton	51	SO 4364
Ludborough	87	TF 2995
Ludbrook	6	SX 6554
Ludchurch	31	SN 1411
Luddenden	84	SE 0425
Luddenden Foot	84	SE 0425
Luddesdown	27	TQ 6766
Luddington	86	SE 8216
Ludford (Lincs.)	80	TF 1989
Ludford (Salop)	51	SO 5173
Ludgershall (Bucks.)	38	SP 6617
Ludgershall (Wilts.)	23	SU 2650
Ludgvan	2	SW 5033
Ludham	71	TG 3818
Ludham Bridge	71	TG 3717
Ludlow	51	SO 5175
Ludwell	11	ST 9122
Ludworth	98	NZ 3641
Luffincott	5	SX 3394
Lufflands	18	SS 3209
Luffness	127	NT 4780
Lugar	107	NS 5821
Luggate Burn	127	NT 6075
Luggiebank	125	NS 7672
Lugton	114	NS 4152
Lugwardine	47	SO 5441
Luib	145	NG 5628
Lulham	47	SO 4041
Lullington (Derby.)	65	SK 2513
Lullington (Somer.)	22	ST 7851
Lulsgate Bottom	21	ST 5065
Lulsley	52	SO 7455
Lulworth Camp	11	SY 8381
Lumb (Lancs.)	83	SD 8424
Lumb (W Yorks)	84	SE 0221
Lumbutts	84	SD 9623
Lumby	85	SE 4830
Lumloch	115	NS 6369
Lumphanan	142	NJ 5804
Lumphinnans	126	NT 1692
Lumsden	150	NJ 4722
Lunan	135	NO 6851
Lunanhead	135	NO 4752
Luncarty	133	NO 0929
Lund (Humbs.)	93	SE 9648
Lund (N Yorks.)	85	SE 6532
Lundie (Highld)	138	NH 1311
Lundie (Tays.)	134	NO 2836
Lundin Links	127	NO 4002
Lunna	163	HU 4969
Lunning	163	HU 5066
Lunsford's Cross	16	TQ 7210
Lunt	82	SD 3401
Luntley	47	SO 3955
Luppitt	9	ST 1606
Lupton	89	SD 5581
Lurgashall	14	SU 9326
Lurgmore	147	NH 5937
Lurley	8	SS 9214
Lusby	81	TF 3367
Luss	124	NS 3592
Lusta	144	NG 2756
Lustleigh	8	SX 7881
Luston	47	SO 4863
Luthermuir	142	NO 6568
Luthrie	142	NO 3219

Luton (Beds.) Melbury Sampford

Luton (Beds.) 40 TL 0821
Luton (Devon) 7 SX 9076
Luton (Kent) 28 TQ 7766
Lutterworth 54 SP 5484
Lutton (Devon.) 6 SX 5959
Lutton (Lincs.) 69 TF 4325
Lutton (Northants.) 56 TL 1187
Lutworthy 8 SS 7615
Luxborough 20 SS 9738
Luxulyan 4 SX 0458
Lybster 159 ND 2435
Lydbury North 51 SO 3486
Lydcott 19 SS 6936
Lydd 17 TR 0421
Lydd-on-Sea 17 TR 0819
Lydden 29 TR 2645
Lyddington 67 SP 8797
Lydeard St. Lawrence 20 ST 1232
Lydford (Devon.) 5 SX 5084
Lydford (Somer.) 21 ST 5731
Lydgate (Gtr. Mches.) 84 SD 9516
Lydgate (W. Yorks) 83 SD 9225
Lydham 51 SO 3391
Lydiard Green 37 SU 0885
Lydiard Millicent 37 SU 0986
Lydiate 82 SD 3604
Lydlinch 11 ST 7413
Lydney 35 SO 6203
Lydstep 31 SS 0898
Lye 52 SO 9284
Lye Green 39 SP 9703
Lye Green 16 TQ 5034
Lye's Green 22 ST 8246
Lyford 38 SU 3994
Lymbridge Green 29 TR 1243
Lyme Regis 9 SY 3492
Lyminge 29 TR 1641
Lymington 13 SZ 3295
Lyminster 15 TQ 0204
Lymm 75 SJ 6786
Lymore 13 SZ 2992
Lympne 29 TR 1235
Lympsham 21 ST 3454
Lympstone 9 SX 9984
Lynbridge 19 SS 7248
Lynch 20 SS 9047
Lynchat 140 NH 7801
Lyndhurst 13 SU 2907
Lyndon 67 SK 9004
Lyne 26 TQ 0166
Lyne of Gorthleck 147 NH 5420
Lyne of Skene 143 NJ 7610
Lyneal 63 SJ 4433
Lynegar 159 ND 2357
Lyneham (Oxon.) 37 SP 2720
Lyneham (Wilts.) 37 SU 0179
Lynemouth 105 NZ 2991
Lyness 163 ND 3094
Lyng (Norf.) 70 TG 0617
Lyng (Somer.) 21 ST 3328
Lynmouth 19 SS 7249
Lynsted 28 TQ 9461
Lynstone 18 SS 2005
Lynton 19 SS 7149
Lyon's Gate 10 ST 6605
Lyonshall 47 SO 3356
Lytchett Matravers 11 SY 9495
Lytchett Minster 11 SY 9593
Lyth 159 ND 2763
Lytham 82 SD 3727
Lytham St. Anne's 82 SD 3427
Lythe 99 NZ 8413

M

Mabe Burnthouse 3 SW 7634
Mabie 102 NX 9570
Mablethorpe 81 TF 5085
Macclesfield 76 SJ 9173
Macclesfield Forest 76 SJ 9772
Macduff 150 NJ 7064
Mace Green 58 TM 1041
Macharioch 112 NR 7309
Machen 34 ST 2189
Machrihanish 112 NR 6220
Machynlleth 49 SH 7401
Mackerel's Common 14 TQ 0128
Mackworth 65 SK 3137
Macmerry 127 NT 4372
Madderty 133 NN 9522
Maddiston 126 NS 9476
Madehurst 14 SU 9810
Madeley (Salop) 64 SJ 6904
Madeley (Staffs.) 76 SJ 7744
Madeley Heath 76 SJ 7845
Madingley 56 TL 3960
Madley 47 SO 4138
Madresfield 52 SO 8047
Madron 2 SW 4532
Maen-y-groes 44 SN 3858
Maenaddwyn 72 SH 4684
Maenclochog 30 SN 0827
Maendy 34 ST 0176
Maenporth 3 SW 7829
Maentwrog 61 SH 6640
Maer 64 SJ 7938
Maerdy (Clwyd) 62 SJ 0144
Maerdy (Mid Glam.) 33 SS 9798
Maes-glas 35 ST 2985
Maes-y-cwmmer 34 ST 1794
Maesbrook 63 SJ 3121
Maesbury Marsh 63 SJ 3125
Maesgwynne 44 SN 2024
Maeshafn 74 SJ 2061
Maesllyn 44 SN 3644
Maesmynis 46 SO 0148
Maesteg 33 SS 8591
Maesybont 45 SN 5616
Maesycwmmer 34 ST 1594
Magdalen Laver 41 TL 5108
Maggieknockater 149 NJ 3145
Magham Down 16 TQ 6111
Maghull 82 SD 3702
Magor 35 ST 4287
Maiden Bradley 22 ST 8038
Maiden Head 21 ST 5666
Maiden Law 97 NZ 1749
Maiden Newton 10 SY 5997
Maidencombe 7 SX 9268
Maidenhayne 9 SY 2795
Maidenhead 25 SU 8881
Maidens 113 NS 2107
Maidenwell 4 SX 1470
Maidford 38 SP 6052
Maids' Moreton 38 SP 7035
Maidstone 28 TQ 7656
Maidwell 55 SP 7477
Mail 163 HU 4328
Mains 147 NH 4239
Mains of Ardestie 135 NO 5034
Mains of Balhall 142 NO 5163
Mains of Ballindarg 134 NO 4051
Mains of Cairnbarrow 150 NJ 4643
Mains of Dalvey 149 NJ 1132
Mains of Dillavaird 142 NO 7482
Mains of Drum 143 NO 8099
Mains of Thornton 143 NO 6871
Mains of Throsk 125 NS 8690
Mainsforth 98 NZ 3232
Mainstone 50 SO 2687
Maisemore 36 SO 8121
Major's Green 53 SP 1077
Malborough 6 SX 7039
Malden 26 TQ 2166
Maldon 42 TL 8506
Malham 90 SD 9062
Mallaig 137 NM 6796
Mallaigvaig 136 NM 6997
Malleny Mills 117 NT 1665
Malltraeth 72 SH 4069
Mallwyd 61 SH 8612
Malmesbury 36 ST 9387
Malmsmead 19 SS 7947
Malpas (Ches.) 63 SJ 4847
Malpas (Cornwall) 3 SW 8442
Maltby (Cleve.) 98 NZ 4613
Maltby (Lincs.) 81 TF 3084
Maltby (S Yorks.) 78 SK 5392
Maltby le Marsh 81 TF 4681
Maltman's Hill 28 TQ 9043
Malton 92 SE 7871
Malvern Link 52 SO 7848
Malvern Wells 52 SO 7742
Mamble 52 SO 6871
Mamhilad 35 SO 3003
Manaccan 3 SW 7625
Manafon 50 SJ 1102
Manaton 8 SX 7481
Manby 81 TF 3986
Mancetter 65 SP 3196
Manchester 76 SJ 8397
Mancot 74 SJ 3267
Mandally 139 NH 2900
Manea 57 TL 4789
Manfield 97 NZ 2213
Mangotsfield 36 ST 6676
Manish (Harris) 163 NG 1089
Manish (Isle of Lewis) 163 NA 9513
Mankinholes 84 SD 9523
Manley 75 SJ 5071
Manmoel 34 SO 1703
Mannel 162 NL 9840
Manning's Heath 15 TQ 2028
Manningford Bohune 23 SU 1357
Manningford Bruce 23 SU 1359
Mannington 12 SU 0605
Manningtree 43 TM 1031
Mannofield 143 NJ 9104
Manorbier 30 SS 0698
Manorhill 118 NT 6632
Manorowen 30 SM 9336
Mansefield 106 NX 8996
Mansell Gamage 47 SO 3944
Mansell Lacy 47 SO 4245
Mansergh 89 SD 6082
Mansfield (Notts.) 78 SK 5361
Mansfield (Strath.) 107 NS 6214
Mansfield Woodhouse 78 SK 5363
Mansriggs 88 SD 2880
Manston (Dorset) 11 ST 8115
Manston (Kent) 29 TR 3466
Manswood 11 ST 9708
Manthorpe (Lincs.) 68 TF 0616
Manthorpe (Lincs.) 67 SK 9237
Manton (Humbs.) 86 SE 9302
Manton (Leic.) 67 SK 8704
Manton (Wilts.) 23 SU 1768
Manuden 41 TL 4926
Maperton 22 ST 6726
Maple Cross 26 TQ 0392
Maplebeck 79 SK 7160
Mapledurham 24 SU 6776
Mapledurwell 24 SU 6851
Maplehurst 15 TQ 1924
Mapleton 77 SK 1748
Mapperley 78 SK 4343
Mapperton 10 SY 5099
Mappleborough Green 53 SP 0866
Mappleton 87 TA 2244
Mappowder 11 ST 7105
Marazion 2 SW 5130
Marbury 63 SJ 5545
March 68 TL 4197
Marcham 38 SU 4596
Marchamley 63 SJ 5929
Marchbankwood 108 NY 0899
Marchington 65 SK 1330
Marchington Woodlands 65 SK 1128
Marchros 60 SH 3126
Marchwiel 63 SJ 3547
Marchwood 13 SU 3810
Marcross 20 SS 9269
Marden (Here & W) 47 SO 5247
Marden (Kent) 28 TQ 7444
Marden (Wilts.) 23 SU 0857
Marden Thorn 28 TQ 7643
Mardy 47 SO 3016
Mare Green 21 ST 3326
Marefield 67 SK 7408
Mareham le Fen 81 TF 2761
Mareham on the Hill 81 TF 2867
Marehill 15 TQ 0618
Maresfield 16 TQ 4624
Marfleet 87 TA 1329
Marford 75 SJ 3556
Margam 33 SS 7887
Margaret Marsh 11 ST 8218
Margaret Roding 41 TL 5912
Margaretting 42 TL 6601
Margate 29 TR 3670
Margnaheglish 113 NS 0331
Marham 69 TF 7110
Marhamchurch 18 SS 2203
Marholm 68 TF 1402
Marian-glas 72 SH 5084
Mariansleigh 8 SS 7422
Marishader 144 NG 4963
Maristow 5 SX 4764
Mark 21 ST 3747
Mark Causeway 21 ST 3547
Mark Cross 16 TQ 5831
Markbeech 16 TQ 4842
Markby 81 TF 4878
Market Bosworth 66 SK 4003
Market Deeping 68 TF 1310
Market Drayton 63 SJ 6734
Market Harborough 55 SP 7387
Market Lavington 22 SU 0154
Market Overton 67 SK 8816
Market Rasen 80 TF 1089
Market Stainton 80 TF 2279
Market Weighton 86 SE 8741
Market Weston 58 TL 9877
Markethill 134 NO 2239
Markfield 66 SK 4810
Markham 34 SO 1601
Markinch 127 NO 2901
Markington 91 SE 2864
Marks Tey 42 TL 9123
Marksbury 22 ST 6662
Markwell 5 SX 3658
Markyate 40 TL 0616
Marl Bank 52 SO 7840
Marlborough 23 SU 1869
Marlbrook (Here & W) 47 SO 5054
Marlbrook (Here & W) 52 SO 9874
Marlcliff 53 SP 0950
Marldon 7 SX 8663
Marlesford 59 TM 3258
Marley Green 63 SJ 5745
Marley Hill 105 NZ 2058
Marlingford 70 TG 1208
Marloes 30 SM 7908
Marlow 39 SU 8587
Marlpit Hill 16 TQ 4447
Marnhull 11 ST 7718
Marnoch 150 NJ 5950
Marple 76 SJ 9588
Marr 85 SE 5105
Marrick 90 SE 0798
Marros 31 SN 2008
Marsden 84 SE 0411
Marsett 90 SD 9086
Marsh 9 ST 2410
Marsh Baldon 38 SU 5699
Marsh Gibbon 38 SP 6423
Marsh Green (Devon.) 9 SY 0493
Marsh Green (Kent) 16 TQ 4344
Marsh Green (Salop) 63 SJ 6014
Marsh Lane 35 SO 5807
Marsh Street 20 SS 9944
Marsh, The 50 SO 3197
Marshall's Heath 40 TL 1515
Marsham 71 TG 1924
Marshaw 82 SD 5853
Marshborough 29 TR 2958
Marshbrook 51 SO 4389
Marshchapel 87 TF 3598
Marshfield (Avon) 22 ST 7773
Marshfield (Gwent) 34 ST 2582
Marshgate 4 SX 1592
Marshside 82 SD 3419
Marshwood 10 SY 3899
Marske 90 NZ 1000
Marske-by-the-Sea 99 NZ 6322
Marston (Ches.) 75 SJ 6474
Marston (Here & W) 47 SO 3657
Marston (Lincs.) 79 SK 8943
Marston (Oxon.) 38 SP 5208
Marston (Staffs.) 64 SJ 8314
Marston (Staffs.) 64 SJ 9227
Marston (Warw.) 65 SP 2095
Marston (Wilts.) 22 ST 9656
Marston Doles 54 SP 4658
Marston Green 53 SP 1685
Marston Jabbet 54 SP 3888
Marston Magna 10 ST 5922
Marston Meysey 37 SU 1297
Marston Montgomery 65 SK 1338
Marston Moretaine 55 SP 9941
Marston St. Lawrence 54 SP 5342
Marston Trussell 54 SP 6986
Marston on Dove 65 SK 2329
Marstow 47 SO 5519
Marsworth 39 SP 9214
Marten 23 SU 2860
Marthall 76 SJ 8076
Martham 71 TG 4518
Martin (Hants.) 12 SU 0719
Martin (Lincs.) 80 TF 1259
Martin Dales 80 TF 1761
Martin Drove End 12 SU 0420
Martin Drove End 12 SU 0521
Martin Hussingtree 52 SO 8860
Martindale 95 NY 4319
Martinhoe 19 SS 6648
Martinscroft 75 SJ 6589
Martinstown 10 SY 6488
Martlesham 59 TM 2547
Martletwy 30 SN 0310
Martley 52 SO 7559
Martock 10 ST 4619
Marton (Ches.) 76 SJ 8468
Marton (Cleve.) 98 NZ 5115
Marton (Lincs.) 79 SK 8381
Marton (N Yorks.) 91 SE 4162
Marton (N Yorks.) 92 SE 7383
Marton (Salop) 50 SJ 2802
Marton (Warw.) 54 SP 4069
Marton Abbey 92 SE 5868
Marton-Le Moor 91 SE 3771
Martyr Worthy 24 SU 5132
Martyr's Green 26 TQ 0857
Marwick 163 HY 2325
Marwood 19 SS 5437
Mary Tavy 5 SX 5079
Marybank 147 NH 4753
Maryburgh 147 NH 5456
Maryfield 6 SX 4256
Marygold 118 NT 8160
Maryhill 151 NJ 8245
Marykirk 143 NO 6865
Marylebone 82 SD 5807
Marypark 149 NJ 1938
Maryport (Cumbr.) 94 NY 0336
Maryport (Dumf & G) 100 NX 1434
Marystow 5 SX 4382
Maryton 135 NO 6856
Marywell (Grampn.) 142 NO 5896
Marywell (Tays.) 135 NO 6544
Masham 91 SE 2280
Mashbury 42 TL 6511
Masongill 89 SD 6675
Mastrick 143 NJ 9007
Matching 41 TL 5212
Matching Green 41 TL 5311
Matching Tye 41 TL 5111
Matfen 104 NZ 0371
Matfield 16 TQ 6541
Mathern 35 ST 5291
Mathon 52 SO 7345
Mathry 30 SM 8832
Matlaske 70 TG 1534
Matlock 78 SK 3060
Matlock Bath 77 SK 2958
Matterdale End 95 NY 3923
Mattersey 79 SK 6889
Mattingley 25 SU 7357
Mattishall 70 TG 0510
Mattishall Burgh 70 TG 0511
Mauchline 106 NS 4927
Maud 151 NJ 9247
Maufant (Jersey) 161 ZZ 9999
Maugersbury 37 SP 1925
Maughold 162 SC 4991
Maulden 55 TL 0538
Maulds Meaburn 95 NY 6216
Maunby 91 SE 3486
Maund Bryan 47 SO 5550
Maundown 20 ST 0528
Mautby 71 TG 4712
Mavesyn Ridware 65 SK 0817
Mavis Enderby 81 TF 3666
Maw Green 65 SP 0197
Mawbray 94 NY 0846
Mawdesley 82 SD 4914
Mawgan 2 SW 7024
Mawgan Cross 2 SW 6924
Mawgan Porth 3 SW 8467
Mawla 2 SW 7045
Mawnan 3 SW 7827
Mawnan Smith 3 SW 7728
Maxey 68 TF 1208
Maxstoke 65 SP 2386
Maxted Street 29 TR 1244
Maxton 118 NT 6129
Maxwellheugh 118 NT 7333
Maxwellston 106 NS 2600
Maxworthy 5 SX 2593
Mayback 163 HY 5053
Maybole 106 NS 3009
Mayfield (E Susx) 16 TQ 5827
Mayfield (Lothian) 117 NT 3564
Mayfield (Staffs.) 77 SK 1545
Mayford 25 SU 9956
Maylandsea 42 TL 9002
Maynard's Green 16 TQ 5818
Maypole (Gwent.) 47 SO 4716
Maypole (Kent) 29 TR 2064
Maypole Green 71 TM 4195
Maypole Green 59 TM 2767
Maywick 163 HU 3824
Mead 18 SS 2217
Meadgate 22 ST 6758
Meadle 39 SP 8005
Meadowtown 51 SJ 3101
Meadwell 5 SX 4081
Meal Bank 89 SD 5495
Mealsgate 94 NY 2141
Mearbeck 90 SD 8160
Meare 21 ST 4541
Meare Green 9 ST 2922
Mears Ashby 55 SP 8366
Measham 65 SK 3312
Meathop 89 SD 4380
Meaux 87 TA 0939
Meavy 5 SX 5467
Medbourne 67 SP 8093
Medburn 105 NZ 1470
Meddon 18 SS 2717
Medmenham 39 SU 8084
Medomsley 97 NZ 1354
Medstead 24 SU 6537
Meer End 53 SP 2474
Meerbrook 76 SJ 9860
Meesden 41 TL 4432
Meeth 19 SS 5408
Meeting House Hill 71 TG 3028
Meggethead 108 NT 1722
Meidrim 44 SN 2820
Meifod 62 SJ 1513
Meigle 134 NO 2844
Meikle Earnock 115 NS 7253
Meikle Strath 142 NO 6471
Meikle Tarty 151 NJ 9928
Meikle Wartle 150 NJ 7230
Meikleour 134 NO 1539
Meinciau 32 SN 4610
Meir 64 SJ 9342
Melbourn (Cambs.) 56 TL 3844
Melbourne (Derby.) 66 SK 3825
Melbourne (Humbs.) 86 SE 7543
Melbury Abbas 11 ST 8820
Melbury Bubb 10 ST 5906
Melbury Osmond 10 ST 5707
Melbury Sampford 10 ST 5705

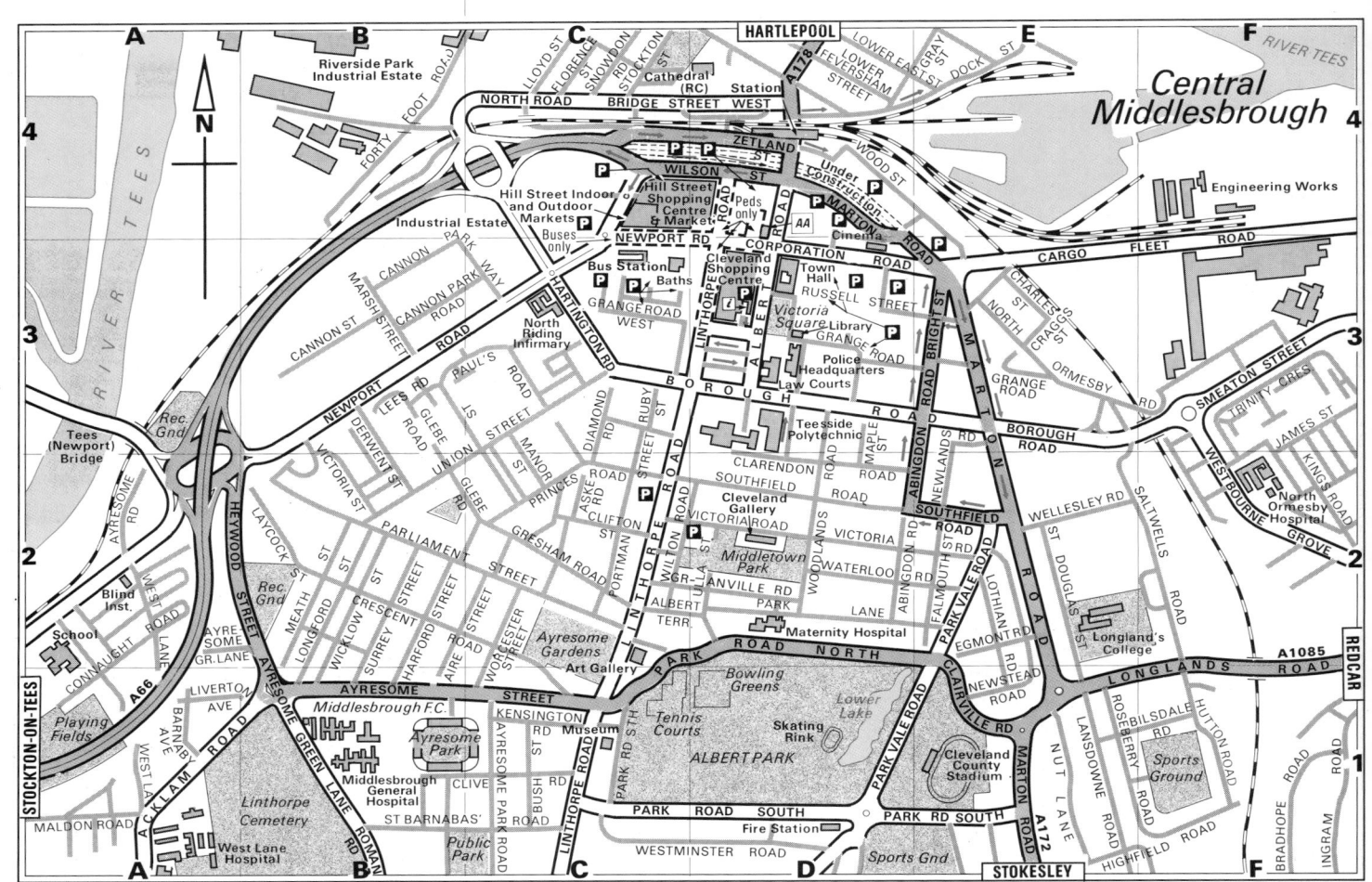

Mile Elm — Mundham (Norf.)

Name	Page	Grid ref.
Mile Elm	22	ST 9968
Mile End (Essex)	43	TL 9827
Mile End (Glos)	35	SO 5911
Milebrook	51	SO 3172
Milebush	28	TQ 7546
Mileham	70	TF 9119
Miles Hope	51	SO 5664
Milesmark	126	NT 0688
Milfield	119	NT 9333
Milford (Derby.)	78	SK 3445
Milford (Devon)	18	SS 2322
Milford (Powys)	50	SO 0991
Milford (Staffs.)	64	SJ 9721
Milford (Surrey)	25	SU 9442
Milford Haven (Dyfed)	30	SM 9006
Milford on Sea	13	SZ 2891
Milkwall	35	SO 5809
Mill Bank	84	SE 0321
Mill Common	59	TM 4081
Mill End (Bucks.)	39	SU 7885
Mill End (Herts.)	41	TL 3332
Mill Green (Essex)	42	TL 6400
Mill Green (Norf.)	58	TM 1384
Mill Green (Suff.)	58	TL 9542
Mill Hill (Essex)	42	TQ 8293
Mill Hill (Gtr London)	26	TQ 2292
Mill Lane	25	SU 7850
Mill Side	89	SD 4584
Mill Street (Norf.)	70	TG 0118
Mill Street (Norf.)	70	TG 0517
Mill of Cammie	142	NO 6993
Mill of Kingoodie	151	NJ 8425
Milland	14	SU 8228
Milland Marsh	14	SU 8326
Millbreck	151	NK 0045
Millbridge	25	SU 8542
Millbrook (Beds.)	55	TL 0138
Millbrook (Corn.)	6	SX 4252
Millbrook (Hants.)	13	SU 4012
Millbrook (Jersey)	161	ZZ 9999
Millbrook Station	55	TL 0141
Millburn (Strath.)	114	NS 4429
Millcorner	17	TQ 8223
Miller's Dale	77	SK 1373
Millerhill	117	NT 3269
Millgreen (Salop)	63	SJ 6727
Millgrip	163	HY 6123
Millhalf	46	SO 2748
Millhayes	9	ST 2303
Millheugh	115	NS 7551
Millholme	89	SD 5690
Millhouse (Cumbr.)	95	NY 3637
Millhouse (Strath.)	123	NR 9570
Millhouse Green	84	SE 2203
Millhousebridge	107	NY 1185
Millikenpark	114	NS 4162
Millington	92	SE 8351
Millmeece	64	SJ 8333
Millnain	146	NH 5059
Millom	88	SD 1780
Millpool	4	SX 1170
Millport	113	NS 1655
Millthrop	89	SD 6691
Milltimber	143	NJ 8501
Millton of Auchriachan	149	NJ 1718
Milltown (Derby.)	78	SK 3561
Milltown (Devon.)	19	SS 5539
Milltown (Dumf & G)	103	NY 3375
Milltown (Grampn.)	142	NJ 4616
Milltown of Aberdalgie	133	NO 0720
Milltown of Auchindown	149	NJ 3540
Milltown of Campfield	142	NJ 6400
Milltown of Craigston	151	NJ 7655
Milltown of Edinvillie	149	NJ 2369
Milltown of Towie	142	NJ 4612
Milnathort	126	NO 1204
Milngavie	125	NS 5574
Milnrow	83	SD 9212
Milnthorpe	89	SD 4981
Milovaig	144	NG 1550
Milson	51	SO 6372
Milstead	28	TQ 9058
Milston	23	SU 1645
Milton (Cambs.)	57	TL 4762
Milton (Central)	124	NN 5001
Milton (Central)	124	NN 5102
Milton (Central)	124	NS 4490
Milton (Cumbr.)	95	NY 5560
Milton (Derby.)	65	SK 3126
Milton (Dumf & G)	100	NX 2154
Milton (Dumf & G)	102	NX 8470
Milton (Dyfed)	30	SN 0302
Milton (Grampn.)	150	NJ 5163
Milton (Highld.)	159	ND 3451
Milton (Highld.)	147	NH 3055
Milton (Highld.)	147	NH 4930
Milton (Highld.)	147	NH 5749
Milton (Highld.)	155	NH 7674
Milton (Highld.)	148	NH 9553
Milton (Highld.)	144	NG 7144
Milton (Oxon.)	38	SP 4535
Milton (Oxon.)	38	SU 4892
Milton (Somer.)	10	ST 4621
Milton (Staffs.)	76	SJ 9050
Milton (Strath.)	124	NS 4274
Milton (Tays.)	133	NN 9138
Milton (Tays.)	134	NO 3843
Milton Abbas	11	ST 8001
Milton Abbot	5	SX 4079
Milton Bridge	117	NT 2363
Milton Bryan	39	SP 9730
Milton Clevedon	22	ST 6637
Milton Coldwells	151	NJ 9538
Milton Combe	5	SX 4866
Milton Common	38	SP 6503
Milton Damerel	18	SS 3810
Milton Ernest	55	TL 0156
Milton Green	75	SJ 4558
Milton Hill	38	SU 4790
Milton Hill	7	SX 9278
Milton Keynes	55	SP 8738
Milton Lilbourne	23	SU 1860
Milton Malsor	55	SP 7355
Milton Morenish	132	NN 6135
Milton Regis	28	TQ 9064
Milton of Auchinhove	142	NJ 5503
Milton of Balgonie	127	NO 3100
Milton of Campsie	125	NS 6576
Milton of Cushnie	142	NJ 5111
Milton of Dillavaird	143	NO 7381
Milton of Lesmore	150	NJ 4628
Milton of North	150	NJ 5028
Milton of Potterton	143	NJ 9415
Milton of Tullich	142	NO 3897
Milton on Stour	22	ST 7928
Milton-under-Wychwood	37	SP 2618
Miltonduff	149	NJ 1760
Milverton	20	ST 1225
Milwich	64	SJ 9632
Milwr	74	SJ 1974
Minard	123	NR 9796
Minchinhampton	36	SO 8600
Mindrum	118	NT 8432
Minehead	20	SS 9746
Minera	62	SJ 2651
Minety	37	SU 0290
Minety Lower Moor	37	SU 0291
Minffordd	61	SH 5938
Miningsby	87	TF 3264
Minions	5	SX 2671
Minishant	106	NS 3314
Minllyn	61	SH 8614
Minmore	148	NJ 1929
Minnes	151	NJ 9423
Minnigaff	101	NX 4166
Minnonie	150	NJ 7861
Minskip	91	SE 3864
Minstead	13	SU 2811
Minsted	14	SU 8521
Minster (Kent)	28	TQ 9573
Minster (Kent)	29	TR 3164
Minster Lovell	37	SP 3111
Minsteracres	104	NZ 0255
Minsterley	51	SJ 3705
Minsterworth	36	SO 7717
Minterne Magna	10	ST 6504
Minting	80	TF 1873
Mintlaw	151	NK 0048
Minto	109	NT 5620
Minton	51	SO 4290
Minwear	30	SN 0413
Minworth	65	SP 1592
Mireland	159	ND 3160
Mirfield	84	SE 2019
Miserden	36	SO 9308
Miskin (Mid Glam)	34	ST 0481
Miskin (Mid Glam)	34	ST 0498
Misson	79	SK 6895
Misterton (Leic.)	54	SP 5584
Misterton (Notts.)	79	SK 7694
Misterton (Somer.)	10	ST 4508
Mistley	43	TM 1231
Mitcham	26	TQ 2868
Mitchel Troy	35	SO 4910
Mitcheldean	36	SO 6618
Mitchell	3	SW 8554
Mitchellslacks	107	NX 9796
Mitcheltroy Common	35	SO 4909
Mitford	105	NZ 1786
Mithian	3	SW 7450
Mitton	64	SJ 8815
Mixbury	38	SP 6033
Moat	102	NY 4274
Moats Tye	58	TM 0455
Mobberley	76	SJ 7880
Mobberley	65	SK 0041
Moccas	47	SO 3542
Mochdre (Clwyd)	73	SH 8278
Mochdre (Powys)	50	SO 0788
Mochrum	101	NX 3446
Mockbeggar	12	SU 1609
Mockerkin	94	NY 0823
Modbury	6	SX 6551
Moddershall	64	SJ 9236
Moelfre (Clwyd)	62	SJ 1828
Moelfre (Gwyn.)	72	SH 5186
Moffat	108	NT 0805
Mogerhanger	56	TL 1349
Mogworthy	8	SS 8517
Moira	65	SK 3216
Molash	28	TR 0251
Mold	74	SJ 2363
Molehill Green	41	TL 5624
Molehill Green	42	TL 7120
Molescroft	86	TA 0140
Molesworth	55	TL 0775
Molland	19	SS 8028
Mollington (Ches.)	75	SJ 3870
Mollington (Northants.)	54	SP 4347
Mollinsburn	125	NS 7171
Monachty	48	SN 5062
Monachylemore	131	NN 4719
Mondynes	143	NO 7879
Monewden	59	TM 2358
Moneydie	133	NO 0629
Moniaive	107	NX 7791
Monifieth	135	NO 5033
Monikie	135	NO 4938
Monimail	134	NO 2914
Monington	31	SN 1344
Monk Fryston	85	SE 5029
Monk Sherborne	24	SU 6056
Monk Soham	59	TM 2165
Monk Street	42	TL 6128
Monk's Gate	15	TQ 2027
Monken Hadley	26	TQ 2497
Monkhide	47	SO 6144
Monkhopton	51	SO 6293
Monkland	47	SO 4557
Monkleigh	18	SS 4520
Monknash	33	SS 9270
Monkokehampton	19	SS 5805
Monks Eleigh	58	TL 9647
Monks Kirby	54	SP 4683
Monks' Heath	76	SJ 8873
Monkshill	151	NJ 7941
Monksilver	20	ST 0737
Monkswood	35	SO 3403
Monkton (Devon.)	9	ST 1803
Monkton (Kent)	29	TR 2865
Monkton (Strath.)	106	NS 3527
Monkton (Tyne and Wear)	105	NZ 3463
Monkton Combe	22	ST 7761
Monkton Deverill	22	ST 8537
Monkton Farleigh	22	ST 8065
Monkton Heathfield	20	ST 2526
Monkton Up Wimborne	12	SU 0113
Monkwood	24	SU 6730
Monmouth	47	SO 5113
Monnington on Wye	47	SO 3743
Monreith	101	NX 3641
Monreith Mains	101	NX 3643
Mont Saint (Guernsey)	161	ZZ 9999
Mont Sohier (Jersey)	161	ZZ 9999
Montacute	10	ST 4916
Montford	63	SJ 4114
Montford Bridge	63	SJ 4215
Montgarrie	150	NJ 5717
Montgomery	50	SO 2296
Montgreenan	114	NS 3343
Montrave	127	NO 3706
Montrose	135	NO 7157
Monxton	23	SU 3144
Monyash	77	SK 1566
Monymusk	143	NJ 6815
Monzie	133	NN 8725
Moonzie	134	NO 3317
Moor Crichel	11	ST 9908
Moor Monkton	92	SE 5056
Moor Nook	83	SD 6537
Moor Row (Cumbr)	94	NY 0014
Moor Row (Durham)	97	NZ 1515
Moor, The	17	TQ 7529
Moorby	81	TF 2964
Moorcock Inn	90	SD 8092
Moorcot	47	SO 3555
Moordown	12	SZ 0994
Moore	75	SJ 5584
Moorend	36	SO 7303
Moorends	86	SE 6915
Moorhall	78	SK 3175
Moorhampton	47	SO 3846
Moorhouse (Cumbr.)	103	NY 3356
Moorhouse (Notts.)	79	SK 7566
Moorlinch	21	ST 3936
Moorsholm	99	NZ 6814
Moorside	84	SD 9507
Moortown (I. of W.)	13	SZ 4283
Moortown (Lincs.)	87	TF 0699
Morangie	154	NH 7784
Morar	136	NM 6893
Morborne	68	TL 1391
Morchard Bishop	8	SS 7607
Morcombelake	10	SY 4093
Morcott	67	SK 9200
Morda	62	SJ 2827
Morden (Dorset)	11	SY 9195
Morden (Gtr London)	26	TQ 2567
Mordiford	47	SO 5637
Mordon	98	NZ 3326
More	51	SO 3491
Morebath	20	SS 9525
Morebattle	110	NT 7724
Morecambe	89	SD 4364
Morefield	153	NH 1195
Moreleigh	7	SX 7652
Morenish	132	NN 6035
Moresby	94	NX 9821
Moresby Parks	94	NY 0019
Morestead	13	SU 5125
Moreton (Dorset)	11	SY 8089
Moreton (Essex)	41	TL 5307
Moreton (Mers.)	74	SJ 2689
Moreton (Oxon.)	38	SP 6904
Moreton Corbet	63	SJ 5523
Moreton Jeffries	47	SO 6048
Moreton Morrell	53	SP 3155
Moreton Paddox	53	SP 3054
Moreton Pinkney	54	SP 5749
Moreton Say	63	SJ 6234
Moreton Valence	36	SO 7809
Moreton on Lugg	47	SO 5045
Moreton-in-Marsh	37	SP 2032
Moretonhampstead	8	SX 7586
Morfa Bychan	61	SH 5437
Morfa Glas	33	SN 8606
Morfa Nefyn	60	SH 2840
Morgan's Vale	12	SU 1921
Morland	95	NY 6022
Morley (Derby.)	66	SK 3941
Morley (Durham)	97	NZ 1227
Morley (W Yorks.)	84	SE 2627
Morley Green	76	SJ 8282
Morley St. Botolph	70	TM 0799
Mornick	5	SX 3172
Morningside	126	NT 2471
Morningthorpe	71	TM 2192
Morpeth	105	NZ 2085
Morphie	143	NO 7164
Morrey	65	SK 1218
Morriston (Strath)	112	NS 2308
Morriston (W Glam)	32	SS 6698
Morston	70	TG 0043
Mortehoe	18	SS 4545
Morthen	78	SK 4789
Mortimer	24	SU 6564
Mortimer West End	24	SU 6363
Mortimer's Cross	51	SO 4263
Mortlake	26	TQ 2075
Morton (Avon)	35	ST 6491
Morton (Derby.)	78	SK 4060
Morton (I of W)	13	SZ 6086
Morton (Lincs.)	79	SK 8091
Morton (Lincs.)	68	TF 0924
Morton (Norf.)	70	TG 1217
Morton (Salop)	62	SJ 2824
Morton Bagot	53	SP 1164
Morton-on-Swale	91	SE 3292
Morvah	2	SW 4035
Morval	5	SX 2556
Morvich	146	NG 9621
Morville	51	SO 6694
Morville Heath	64	SO 6893
Morwenstow	18	SS 2015
Mosborough	78	SK 4281
Moscow	114	NS 4840
Mosedale	95	NY 3532
Moseley (Here & W)	52	SO 8159
Moseley (W Mids)	53	SP 0883
Moss (Clwyd)	63	SJ 3052
Moss (S Yorks.)	85	SE 5914
Moss (Tiree)	162	NL 9644
Moss Bank	75	SJ 5198
Moss Side	82	SD 3830
Moss of Barmuckity	149	NJ 2461
Mossat	150	NJ 4719
Mossbank (Shetld.)	163	HU 4475
Mossblown	106	NS 4024
Mossbrow	76	SJ 7088
Mossburnford	109	NT 6616
Mossdale	101	NX 6571
Mossend	115	NS 7460
Mossgiel	106	NS 4828
Mosside	135	NO 4252
Mossley	84	SD 9702
Mosstodloch	149	NJ 3361
Mosston	135	NO 5444
Mosterton	10	ST 4505
Mostyn	74	SJ 1680
Motcombe	22	ST 8425
Motherby	95	NY 4328
Mothercombe	6	SX 6047
Motherwell	115	NS 7557
Mottingham	27	TQ 4272
Mottisfont	23	SU 3226
Mottistone	13	SZ 4083
Mottram in Longdendale	84	SJ 9995
Mouilpied (Guernsey)	161	ZZ 9999
Mouldsworth	75	SJ 5171
Moulin	133	NN 9459
Moulsecoomb	15	TQ 3307
Moulsford	38	SU 5984
Moulsoe	55	SP 9041
Moulton (Ches.)	75	SJ 6569
Moulton (Lincs.)	68	TF 3023
Moulton (N Yorks.)	97	NZ 2303
Moulton (Northants.)	55	SP 7866
Moulton (Suff.)	57	TL 6964
Moulton Chapel	68	TF 2918
Moulton Eaugate	68	TF 3016
Moulton Seas End	68	TF 3227
Moulton St Mary	71	TG 3907
Mount (Corn.)	3	SW 7856
Mount (Corn.)	4	SX 1467
Mount Bures	42	TL 9032
Mount Hawke	2	SW 7147
Mount Pleasant (Here & W)	53	SP 0064
Mount Pleasant (Suff.)	59	TM 5077
Mount Pleasant (Suff.)	57	TL 7347
Mountain Ash	34	ST 0498
Mountain Cross	117	NT 1446
Mountain Water	30	SM 9224
Mountbenger	108	NT 3125
Mountfield	16	TQ 7320
Mountgerald	147	NH 5661
Mountjoy	3	SW 8760
Mountnessing	27	TQ 6297
Mounton	35	ST 5193
Mountsorrel	66	SK 5814
Mousehole	2	SW 4626
Mouswald	102	NY 0672
Mow Cop	76	SJ 8557
Mowhaugh	110	NT 8120
Mowsley	54	SP 6489
Mowtie	143	NO 8388
Moy (Highld)	148	NH 7635
Moy (Highld.)	139	NN 4282
Moyles Court	12	SU 1607
Moylgrove	31	SN 1244
Muasdale	112	NR 6840
Much Birch	47	SO 5030
Much Cowarne	47	SO 6147
Much Dewchurch	47	SO 4831
Much Hadham	41	TL 4319
Much Hoole	82	SD 4723
Much Marcle	52	SO 6533
Much Wenlock	51	SO 6199
Muchalls	143	NO 9091
Muchelney	21	ST 4224
Muchlarnick	5	SX 2156
Muchrachd	146	NH 2734
Mucking	27	TQ 6881
Mucklestone	64	SJ 7237
Muckleton	63	SJ 5821
Muckletown	150	NJ 5621
Muckton	81	TF 3781
Mudale	156	NC 5336
Muddiford	19	SS 5638
Muddles Green	16	TQ 5413
Mudeford	12	SZ 1892
Mudford	10	ST 5719
Mudgley	21	ST 4445
Mugdock	125	NS 5576
Mugeary	144	NG 4438
Mugginton	77	SK 2843
Muggleswick	97	NZ 0450
Muie	154	NC 6704
Muir	141	NO 0689
Muir of Fowlis	142	NJ 5612
Muir of Ord	147	NH 5250
Muirdrum	135	NO 5637
Muirhead (Fife.)	127	NO 2805
Muirhead (Strath.)	115	NS 6869
Muirhead (Tays.)	134	NO 3434
Muirhouses	126	NT 0180
Muirkirk	107	NS 6927
Muirshearlich	138	NN 1380
Muirskie	143	NO 8295
Muirtack (Grampn.)	151	NJ 8146
Muirtack (Grampn.)	151	NJ 9937
Muirton	148	NH 7463
Muirton of Ardblair	134	NO 1743
Muirton of Ballochy	142	NO 6462
Muirtown	133	NN 9211
Muiryfold	150	NJ 7651
Muker	90	SD 9198
Mulbarton	71	TG 1901
Mulben	149	NJ 3450
Mullacott Cross	19	SS 5144
Mullion	2	SW 6719
Mumbles, The	32	SS 6287
Mumby	81	TF 5174
Munderfield Row	52	SO 6451
Munderfield Stocks	52	SO 6550
Munderno	143	NJ 9614
Mundesley	71	TG 3136
Mundford	69	TL 8093
Mundham (Norf.)	71	TM 3298

Mundon Hill

Newton (Cumbr.)

Place	Page	Grid ref.
Mundon Hill	42	TL 8702
Mundorno	143	NJ 9413
Munerigie	139	NH 2602
Mungasdale	152	NG 9895
Mungrisdale	95	NY 3630
Munlochy	148	NH 6453
Munsley	52	SO 6640
Munslow	51	SO 5187
Munslow Aston	51	SO 5086
Murchington	8	SX 6888
Murcott	38	SP 5815
Murkle	159	ND 1668
Murlaggan (Highld.)	138	NN 0193
Murlaggan (Highld.)	139	NN 3181
Murrow	68	TF 3707
Mursley	39	SP 8128
Murthill	135	NO 4657
Murthly	133	NO 0938
Murton (Cumbr.)	96	NY 7221
Murton (Durham)	98	NZ 3947
Murton (N Yorks.)	92	SE 6452
Murton (Northum.)	119	NT 9748
Musbury	9	SY 2794
Muscoates	92	SE 6880
Musselburgh	127	NT 3472
Muston (Leic.)	67	SK 8237
Muston (N Yorks.)	93	TA 0979
Mustow Green	52	SO 8774
Mutford	59	TM 4888
Muthill	133	NN 8616
Mutterton	9	ST 0304
Mybster	159	ND 1652
Myddfai	45	SN 7730
Myddle	63	SJ 4623
Mydroilyn	44	SN 4555
Mylor	3	SW 8135
Mylor Bridge	3	SW 8036
Mynachlog-ddu	31	SN 1430
Myndtown	51	SO 3889
Mynytho	60	SH 3031
Myrebird	143	NO 7498
Mytchett	25	SU 8855
Mytholm	84	SD 9827
Mytholmroyd	84	SE 0125
Myton-on-Swale	91	SE 4366

N

Place	Page	Grid ref.
Naburn	85	SE 5945
Nackington	29	TR 1554
Nacton	59	TM 2240
Nafferton	93	TA 0559
Nailbridge	36	SO 6516
Nailsbourne	20	ST 2128
Nailsea	35	ST 4670
Nailstone	66	SK 4107
Nailsworth	36	ST 8499
Nairn	148	NH 8756
Nalderswood	15	TQ 2345
Nancegollan	2	SW 6632
Nancledra	2	SW 4936
Nanhoron	60	SH 2831
Nannau	61	SH 7420
Nannerch	74	SJ 1669
Nanpantan	66	SK 5017
Nanpean	3	SW 9556
Nanstallon	4	SX 0367
Nant Peris	73	SH 6159
Nant-ddu	46	SO 0015
Nant-glas	49	SN 9965
Nant-y-Bwch	34	SO 1210
Nant-y-derry	35	SO 3306
Nant-y-moel	33	SS 9393
Nanternis	44	SN 3756
Nantgaredig	44	SN 4921
Nantgarw	34	ST 1285
Nantglyn	74	SJ 0061
Nantlle	72	SH 5053
Nantmawr	62	SJ 2424
Nantmel	50	SO 0366
Nantmor	61	SH 6046
Nantwich	63	SJ 6552
Nantyffyllon	33	SS 8492
Nantyglo	34	SO 1910
Naphill	39	SU 8496
Napleton	52	SO 8548
Napton	54	SP 4661
Napton on the Hill	54	SP 4661
Narberth	31	SN 1114
Narborough (Leic.)	66	SP 5497
Narborough (Norf.)	69	TF 7413
Nasareth	60	SH 4749
Naseby	54	SP 6878
Nash (Bucks.)	39	SP 7734
Nash (Gwent)	35	ST 3483
Nash (Here & W)	51	SO 3062
Nash (Salop)	51	SO 6071
Nash Lee	39	SP 8408
Nassington	67	TL 0696
Nasty	41	TL 3624
Natcott	18	SS 2723
Nateby (Cumbr.)	96	NY 7706
Nateby (Lancs.)	82	SD 4644
Natland	89	SD 5289
Naughton	58	TM 0249
Naunton (Glos.)	37	SP 1123
Naunton (Here & W)	52	SO 8739
Naunton Beauchamp	52	SO 9652
Naust	152	NG 8283
Navenby	80	SK 9857
Navestock	27	TQ 5397
Navestock Side	27	TQ 5697
Nawton	92	SE 6584
Nayland	43	TL 9734
Nazeing	41	TL 4106
Neacroft	12	SZ 1897
Neal's Green	53	SP 3384
Neap	163	HU 5060
Near Cotton	77	SK 0646
Near Sawrey	89	SD 3795
Neasham	98	NZ 3210
Neath	33	SS 7597
Neatham	25	SU 7440
Neatishead	71	TG 3421
Nebo (Dyfed)	48	SN 5465
Nebo (Gwyn.)	60	SH 4750
Nebo (Gwyn.)	73	SH 8356
Nebo (Gwyn.)	72	SH 4690
Necton	70	TF 8709
Nedd	156	NC 1332
Nedderton	105	NZ 2482
Nedging Tye	58	TM 0149
Needham	59	TM 2281
Needham Market	58	TM 0855
Needingworth	56	TL 3472
Neen Savage	52	SO 6777
Neen Sollars	52	SO 6572
Neenton	51	SO 6487
Nefyn	60	SH 3040
Neilston	114	NS 4657
Nelson (Lancs.)	83	SD 8737
Nelson (Mid Glam.)	34	ST 1195
Nelson Village	105	NZ 2577
Nemphlar	116	NS 8544
Nempnett Thrubwell	21	ST 5360
Nenthall	96	NY 7546
Nenthead	96	NY 7743
Nenthorn	118	NT 6837
Neopardy	8	SX 7998
Nercwys	74	SJ 2260
Nereabolls	120	NR 2255
Nerston	115	NS 6457
Nesbit	119	NT 9833
Ness (Ches.)	74	SJ 3075
Ness (N Yorks.)	92	SE 6878
Ness (Shapinsay) (Ork.)	163	HY 5423
Ness (Westray) (Ork.)	163	HY 5039
Nesscliffe	63	SJ 3819
Neston (Ches.)	74	SJ 2877
Neston (Wilts.)	22	ST 8667
Nether Alderley	76	SJ 8476
Nether Blainslie	118	NT 5443
Nether Broughton	66	SK 6925
Nether Burrow	89	SD 6174
Nether Cassock	107	NT 2404
Nether Cerne	10	SY 6698
Nether Compton	10	ST 5917
Nether Contlaw	143	NJ 8402
Nether Crimond	151	NJ 8222
Nether Dallachy	149	NJ 3663
Nether Dallachy	148	NJ 3664
Nether Exe	8	SS 9300
Nether Handwick	134	NO 3641
Nether Haugh	85	SK 4196
Nether Heyford	54	SP 6658
Nether Howeclevch	108	NT 0312
Nether Kellet	89	SD 5067
Nether Kinmundy	151	NK 0444
Nether Kirkton	114	NS 4757
Nether Langwith	78	SK 5371
Nether Muirden	150	NJ 7055
Nether Padley	77	SK 2478
Nether Poppleton	92	SE 5654
Nether Silton	91	SE 4592
Nether Skyborry	50	SO 2774
Nether Stowey	20	ST 1939
Nether Urquhart	126	NO 1808
Nether Wallop	23	SU 3036
Nether Wasdale	88	NY 1204
Nether Welton	95	NY 3645
Nether Westcote	37	SP 2220
Nether Whitacre	65	SP 2393
Nether Worton	38	SP 4230
Netheravon	23	SU 1448
Netherbrae	151	NJ 7959
Netherburn	115	NS 7947
Netherbury	10	SY 4799
Netherby	103	NY 3971
Nethercote	54	SP 5164
Netherend	35	SO 5900
Netherfield	16	TQ 7018
Netherhampton	23	SU 1029
Netherlaw	102	NX 7445
Netherley	143	NO 8593
Nethermill	108	NY 0487
Nethermuir	151	NJ 9143
Netherplace	115	NS 5155
Netherseal	65	SK 2813
Netherstreet	22	ST 9764
Netherthird	107	NS 5818
Netherthong	84	SE 1309
Netherton (Central)	125	NS 5579
Netherton (Devon.)	7	SX 8971
Netherton (Here & W)	53	SO 9941
Netherton (Northum.)	111	NT 9907
Netherton (Salop)	52	SO 7382
Netherton (Tays.)	134	NO 1452
Netherton (Tays.)	135	NO 5457
Netherton (W Yorks.)	84	SE 2716
Netherton (W. Yorks)	84	SE 1313
Nethertown (Cumbr.)	88	NX 9807
Nethertown (Highld.)	159	ND 3578
Nethertown (Staffs.)	65	SK 1017
Netherwitton	105	NZ 1090
Netherwood	107	NS 6727
Nethy Bridge	149	NJ 0020
Netley	13	SU 4508
Netley Marsh	13	SU 3312
Nettlebed	38	SU 7086
Nettlebridge	21	ST 6448
Nettlecombe	10	SY 5195
Nettleden	40	TL 0210
Nettleham	80	TF 0075
Nettlestead	27	TQ 6852
Nettlestead Green	27	TQ 6850
Nettlestone	13	SZ 6290
Nettlesworth	97	NZ 2648
Nettleton (Lincs.)	87	TF 0075
Nettleton (Lincs.)	87	TA 1000
Nettleton (Wilts.)	36	ST 8178
Netton	23	SU 1236
Neuk, The	143	NO 7397
Nevendon	42	TQ 7390
Nevern	30	SN 0840
New Abbey	102	NX 9665
New Aberdour	151	NJ 8863
New Addington	27	TQ 3863
New Alresford	24	SU 5832
New Alyth	134	NO 2447
New Annesley	78	SK 5153
New Arram	87	TA 0345
New Ash Green	27	TQ 6065
New Barn	27	TQ 6168
New Bewick	111	NU 0620
New Bolingbroke	81	TF 3058
New Brancepeth	97	NZ 2342
New Brighton (Clwyd)	74	SJ 2565
New Brighton (Hants.)	14	SU 7407
New Brighton (Mers.)	74	SJ 3093
New Brinsley	78	SK 4550
New Buckenham	70	TM 0890
New Byth	151	NJ 8254
New Clipstone	78	SK 5863
New Costessey	71	TG 1710
New Cross	48	SN 6376
New Cumnock	107	NS 6113
New Deer	151	NJ 8846
New Delph	84	SD 9806
New Duston	55	SP 7162
New Earswick	92	SE 6155
New Edlington	85	SK 5399
New Elgin	148	NJ 2362
New Ellerby	87	TA 1639
New Eltham	27	TQ 4573
New End	53	SP 0560
New Farnley	84	SE 2431
New Ferry	74	SJ 3385
New Fryston	85	SE 4526
New Galloway	101	NX 6377
New Gilston	127	NO 4207
New Grimsby	162	SV 8914
New Hainford	71	TG 2118
New Hartley	105	NZ 3076
New Haw	26	TQ 0563
New Hedges	31	SN 1302
New Holland	87	TA 0724
New Houghton (Derby.)	78	SK 5065
New Houghton (Norf.)	69	TF 7827
New Houses	90	SD 8073
New Hutton	89	SD 5691
New Hythe	28	TQ 7159
New Inn (Devon)	18	SS 4408
New Inn (Dyfed)	44	SN 4736
New Inn (Gwent)	35	SO 4800
New Inn (Gwent)	35	ST 3099
New Inn (N Yorks.)	90	SD 8072
New Invention	50	SO 2976
New Kelso	146	NG 9442
New Lanark	116	NS 8742
New Lane	82	SD 4212
New Leake	81	TF 4057
New Leeds	151	NJ 9954
New Longton	82	SD 5125
New Luce	100	NX 1764
New Mains of Ury	143	NO 8787
New Marske	99	NZ 6221
New Marton	63	SJ 3334
New Mill (Corn.)	2	SW 4534
New Mill (Herts.)	39	SP 9212
New Mill (W Yorks.)	84	SE 1608
New Mill (Wilts.)	23	SU 1862
New Mills (Corn.)	3	SW 8952
New Mills (Derby.)	76	SK 0085
New Mills (Powys)	50	SJ 0901
New Milton	12	SZ 2495
New Moat	30	SN 0625
New Ollerton	79	SK 6568
New Pitsligo	151	NJ 8855
New Polzeath	4	SW 9379
New Prestwick	106	NS 3424
New Quay (Dyfed)	44	SN 3859
New Rackheath	71	TG 2812
New Radnor	50	SO 2161
New Rent	95	NY 4536
New Ridley	104	NZ 0659
New Romney	17	TR 0624
New Rossington	85	SK 6198
New Sauchie	126	NS 8993
New Scone	134	NO 1325
New Silksworth	98	NZ 3853
New Stevenston	115	NS 7659
New Tolsta	163	NB 5349
New Town (Glos.)	53	SP 0432
New Town (Lothian)	117	NT 4470
New Tredegar	34	SO 1403
New Tupton	78	SK 3966
New Ulva	122	NR 7080
New Walsoken	69	TF 4709
New Waltham	87	TA 2804
New Wimpole	56	TL 3450
New Winton	117	NT 4271
New Yatt	38	SP 3713
New York (Lincs.)	80	TF 2455
New York (Tyne and Wear)	105	NZ 3270
Newark (Cambs.)	68	TF 2100
Newark (Dunf. and Galwy.)	106	NS 7908
Newark (Ork.)	163	HY 7242
Newark-on-Trent	79	SK 7953
Newarthill	115	NS 7859
Newbald	86	SE 9136
Newbattle	116	NT 3456
Newbiggin (Cumbr.)	95	NY 5649
Newbiggin (Cumbr.)	95	NY 6228
Newbiggin (Cumbr.)	95	NY 4728
Newbiggin (Cumbr.)	88	SD 2669
Newbiggin (Durham)	96	NY 9127
Newbiggin (N Yorks.)	90	SD 9591
Newbiggin (N. Yorks.)	90	SD 9985
Newbiggin (Northum.)	104	NY 9461
Newbiggin-by-the-Sea	105	NZ 3187
Newbiggin-on-Lune	89	NY 7005
Newbigging (Strath.)	116	NT 0145
Newbigging (Tays.)	134	NO 2841
Newbigging (Tays.)	134	NO 4237
Newbigging (Tays.)	135	NO 4936
Newbold (Derby)	78	SK 3773
Newbold (Leic.)	66	SK 4018
Newbold Pacey	53	SP 2957
Newbold Verdon	66	SK 4403
Newbold on Avon	54	SP 4877
Newbold on Stour	53	SP 2446
Newborough (Cambs.)	68	TF 2006
Newborough (Gwyn.)	72	SH 4265
Newborough (Staffs.)	65	SK 1325
Newbottle	54	SP 5236
Newbourn	59	TM 2743
Newbridge (Clwyd)	62	SJ 2841
Newbridge (Corn.)	2	SW 4231
Newbridge (Dunf. and Galwy.)	101	NX 9579
Newbridge (Gwent)	34	ST 2197
Newbridge (Hants.)	13	SU 2915
Newbridge (I. of W.)	13	SZ 4187
Newbridge (Lothian)	126	NT 1272
Newbridge (Oxon.)	38	SP 4001
Newbridge Green	52	SO 8439
Newbridge on Wye	46	SO 0158
Newbridge-on-Usk	35	ST 3894
Newbrough	104	NY 8767
Newbuildings	8	SS 7903
Newburgh (Fife)	134	NO 2318
Newburgh (Grampn.)	151	NJ 9925
Newburgh (Lancs.)	82	SD 4810
Newburn	105	NZ 1765
Newbury	24	SU 4666
Newby (Cumbr.)	95	NY 5921
Newby (N Yorks.)	98	NZ 5012
Newby (N Yorks.)	89	SD 7269
Newby Bridge	89	SD 3686
Newby East	95	NY 4758
Newby West	103	NY 3653
Newby Wiske	91	SE 3687
Newcastle (Gwent)	47	SO 4417
Newcastle (Salop)	50	SO 2482
Newcastle Emlyn	44	SN 3040
Newcastle upon Tyne	105	NZ 2464
Newcastle-under-Lyme	76	SJ 8445
Newcastleton	109	NY 4887
Newchapel (Dyfed)	44	SN 2239
Newchapel (Staffs.)	76	SJ 8654
Newchapel (Surrey)	15	TQ 3642
Newchurch (Dyfed)	44	SN 3724
Newchurch (Gwent)	35	ST 4597
Newchurch (I. of W.)	13	SZ 5585
Newchurch (Kent)	29	TR 0531
Newchurch (Powys)	46	SO 2150
Newchurch in Pendle	83	SD 8239
Newcott	9	ST 2309
Newcraighall	126	NT 3272
Newdigate	15	TQ 2042
Newell Green	25	SU 8771
Newenden	17	TQ 8327
Newent	36	SO 7226
Newfield (Durham)	97	NZ 2033
Newfield (Highld.)	155	NH 7877
Newfound	24	SU 5851
Newgale	30	SM 8422
Newgate	70	TG 0443
Newgate Street	41	TL 3005
Newhall (Ches.)	63	SJ 6045
Newhall (Derby.)	65	SK 2821
Newham (Gtr London)	27	TQ 4082
Newham (Northum.)	119	NU 1728
Newham Hall	119	NU 1729
Newhaven	16	TQ 4401
Newhaven Hotel	77	SK 1660
Newhay	84	SD 9515
Newholm	99	NZ 8610
Newhouse	115	NS 7961
Newick	16	TQ 4121
Newingreen	29	TR 1236
Newington (Kent)	28	TQ 8665
Newington (Kent)	29	TR 1737
Newington (Notts.)	79	SK 6693
Newington (Oxon.)	38	SU 6196
Newland (Glos.)	35	SO 5509
Newland (Here & W)	52	SO 7948
Newland (N Yorks.)	86	SE 6824
Newlandrig	117	NT 3662
Newlands (Borders)	108	NY 5294
Newlands (Grampn.)	149	NJ 3051
Newlands (Northum.)	104	NZ 0955
Newlands of Geise	159	ND 0865
Newlyn	2	SW 4628
Newlyn East	3	SW 8256
Newmachar	151	NJ 8819
Newmains	116	NS 8256
Newman's Green	58	TL 8844
Newmarket (Isle of Lewis)	163	NB 4235
Newmarket (Suff.)	57	TL 6463
Newmill (Borders)	109	NT 4510
Newmill (Grampn.)	150	NJ 4352
Newmill of Inshewan	135	NO 4260
Newmillerdam	85	SE 3215
Newmills (Fife)	125	NT 0286
Newmills (Lothian)	117	NT 1667
Newmiln	133	NO 1230
Newmilns	115	NS 5337
Newnham (Glos.)	36	SO 6911
Newnham (Hants)	24	SU 7054
Newnham (Herts.)	56	TL 2437
Newnham (Kent)	28	TQ 9557
Newnham (Northants.)	54	SP 5859
Newnham Bridge	51	SO 6469
Newport (Devon)	19	SS 5631
Newport (Dyfed)	30	SN 0639
Newport (Essex)	41	TL 5234
Newport (Glos.)	36	ST 7097
Newport (Gwent)	35	ST 3187
Newport (Highld.)	159	ND 1224
Newport (Humbs)	86	SE 8530
Newport (I. of W.)	13	SZ 4989
Newport (Norf.)	71	TG 5017
Newport (Salop)	64	SJ 7419
Newport Pagnell	55	SP 8743
Newport-on-Tay	135	NO 4228
Newpound Common	15	TQ 0627
Newquay (Corn.)	3	SW 8161
Newsbank	76	SJ 8366
Newseat (Grampn.)	150	NJ 7033
Newsham (Lancs.)	82	SD 5136
Newsham (N Yorks.)	97	NZ 1010
Newsham (Northum.)	105	NZ 3079
Newsholme (Humbs.)	86	SE 7229
Newsholme (Lancs.)	83	SD 8451
Newstead (Borders)	118	NT 5634
Newstead (Northum.)	111	NU 1526
Newstead (Notts.)	78	SK 5252
Newthorpe	85	SE 4632
Newtimber Place	15	TQ 2613
Newton (Borders)	109	NT 6020
Newton (Cambs.)	68	TF 4314
Newton (Cambs.)	57	TL 4349
Newton (Ches.)	75	SJ 5059
Newton (Ches.)	75	SJ 5274
Newton (Cumbr.)	88	SD 2371

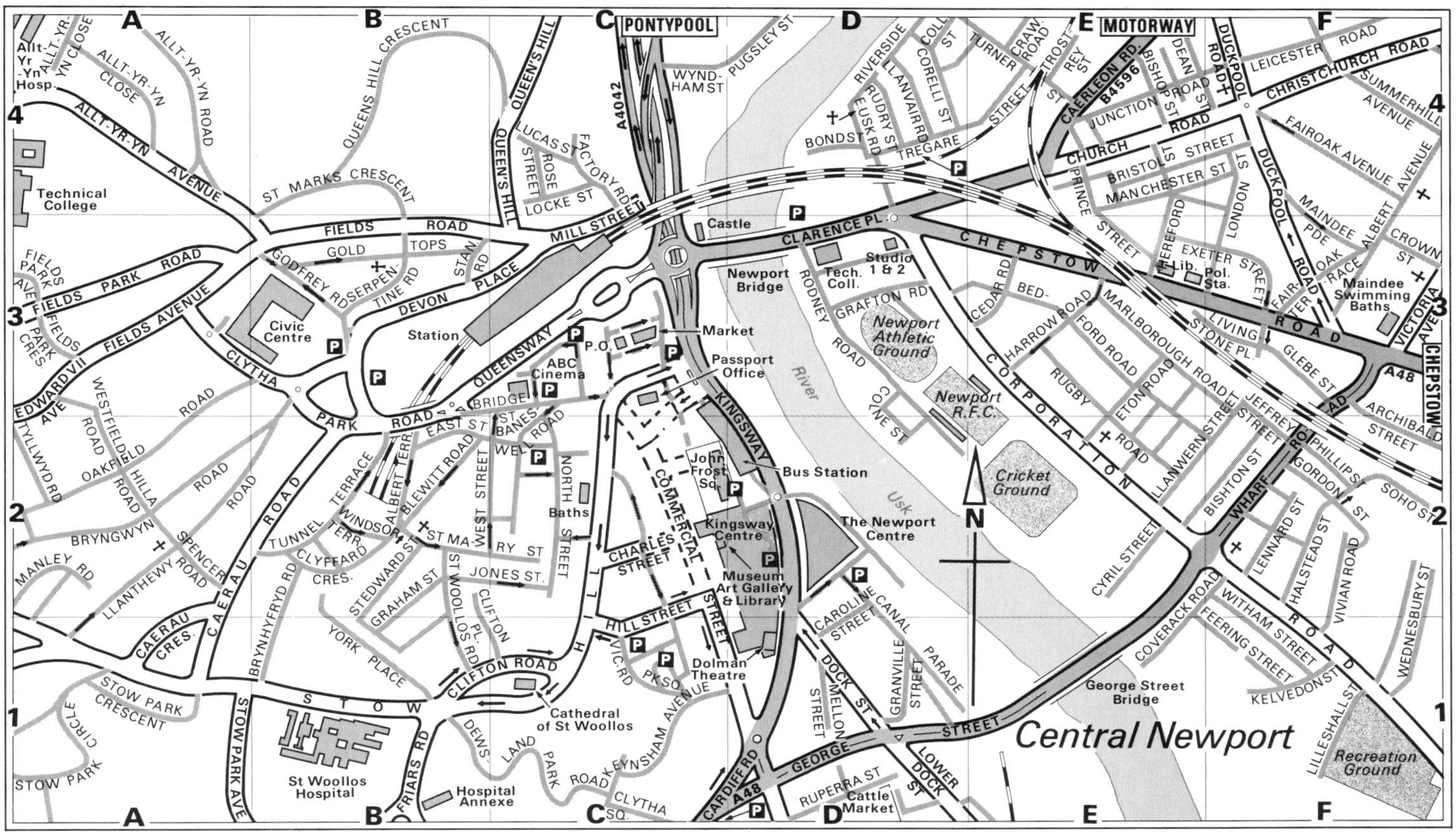

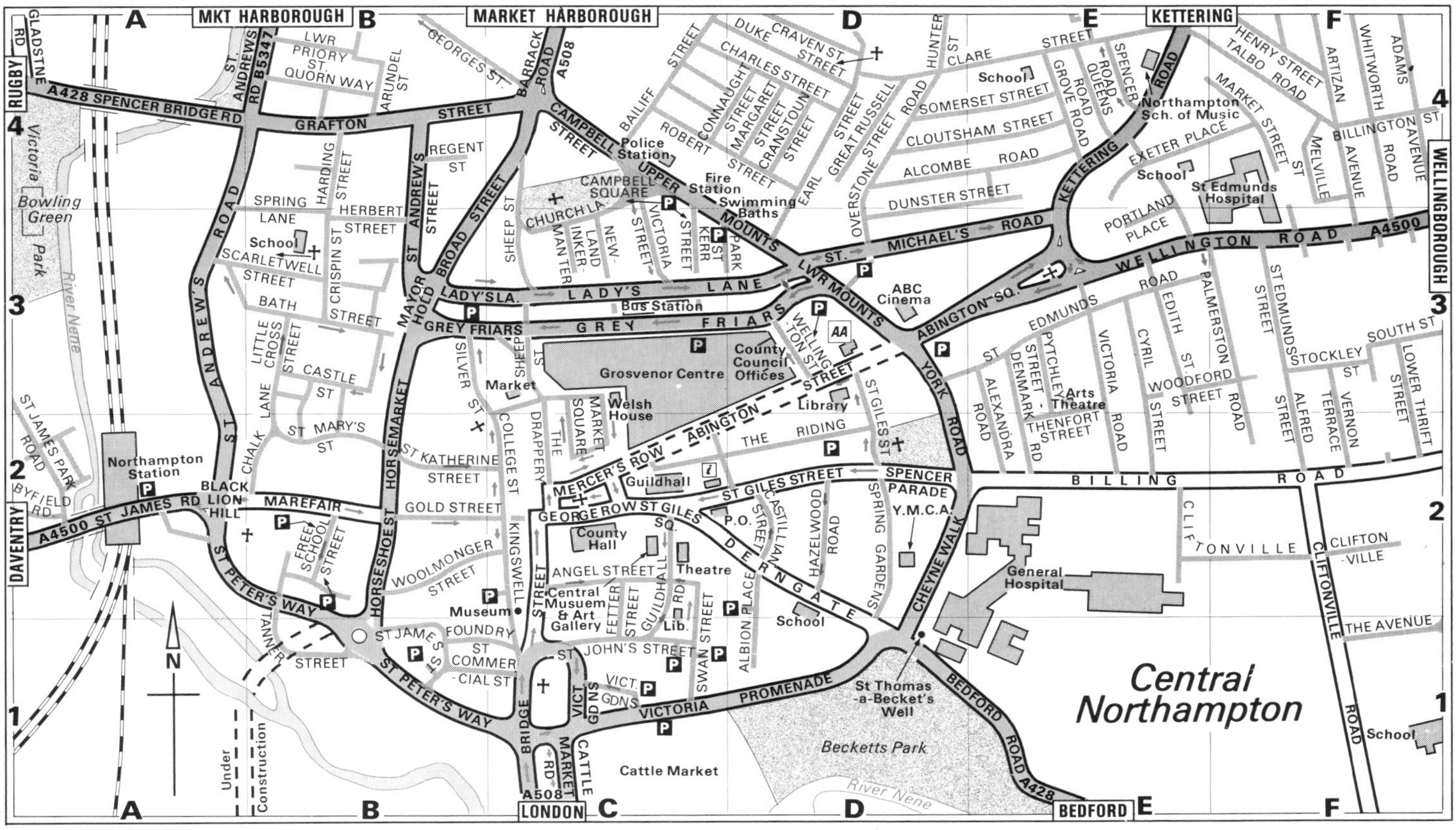

Central Newport

Central Northampton

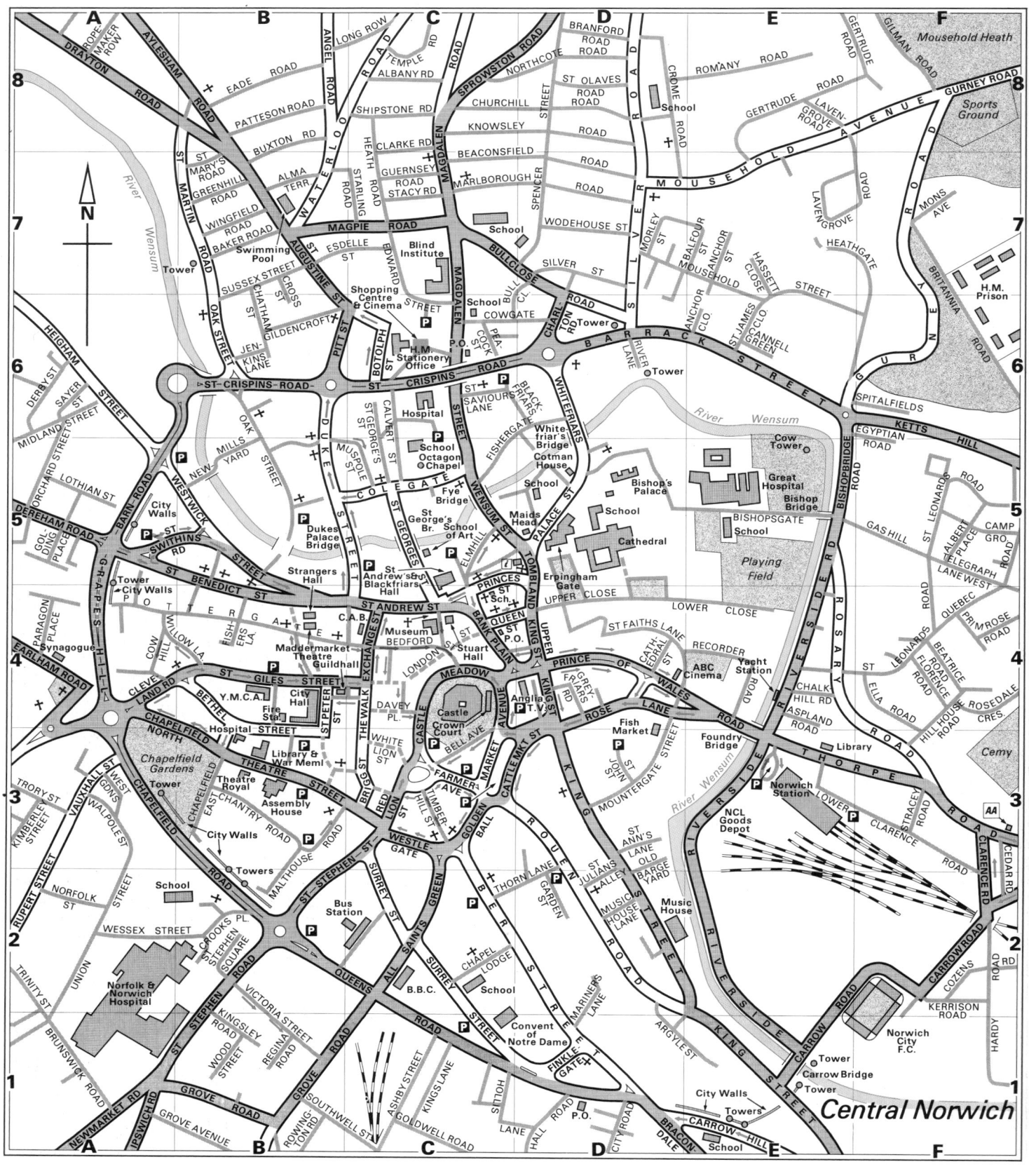

Central Norwich

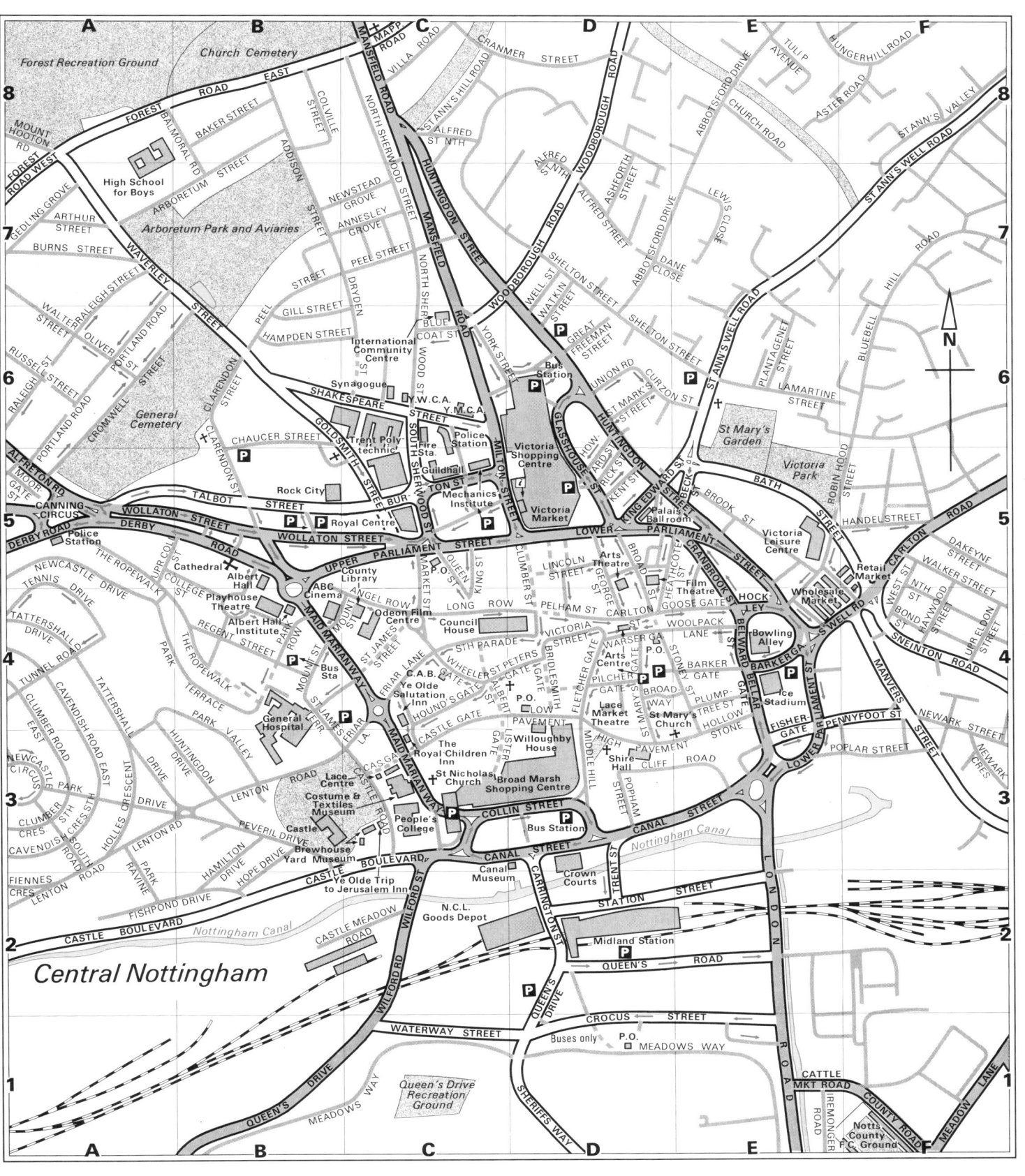

Central Nottingham

Norris Green Organford

Norris Green 5 SX 4169
Norris Hill 65 SK 3216
North Ashton 82 SD 5401
North Aston 38 SP 4728
North Baddesley 13 SU 4020
North Ballchulish 130 NN 0560
North Barrow 21 ST 6029
North Barsham 70 TF 9135
North Benfleet 42 TQ 7590
North Berwick 127 NT 5485
North Bitchburn 97 NZ 1733
North Boarhunt 13 SU 6010
North Bovey 8 SX 7483
North Bradley 22 ST 8554
North Brentor 5 SX 4781
North Buckland 18 SS 4740
North Burlingham 71 TG 3610
North Cadbury 21 ST 6327
North Cairn 100 NW 9770
North Carlton 80 SK 9477
North Cave 86 SE 8832
North Cerney 37 SP 0208
North Charford 12 SU 1919
North Charlton 111 NU 1622
North Cheriton 22 ST 6825
North Chideock 10 SY 4294
North Cliffe 86 SE 8737
North Clifton 79 SK 8272
North Close 97 NZ 2633
North Connell 129 NM 9135
North Cotes 87 TA 3400
North Country 2 SW 6944
North Cove 59 TM 4689
North Cowton 97 NZ 2803
North Crawley 55 SP 9244
North Cray 27 TQ 4972
North Creake 70 TF 8538
North Curry 21 ST 3125
North Dalton 93 SE 9352
North Darley 5 SX 2773
North Deighton 91 SE 3851
North Duffield 86 SE 6837
North Elkington 81 TF 2890
North Elmham 70 TF 9820
North End (Avon) 21 ST 4167
North End (Berks.) 24 SU 4063
North End (Essex) 42 TL 6618
North End (Hants.) 14 SU 6502
North End (Hants.) 13 SU 5829
North End (Hants.) 12 SU 1016
North End (Humbs.) 87 TA 1023
North End (Norf.) 70 TM 0092
North End (W Susx) 15 TQ 1209
North End (W. Susx.) 14 SU 9804
North Erradale 152 NG 7481
North Fambridge 42 TQ 8597
North Fearns 145 NG 5835
North Ferriby 86 SE 9826
North Frodingham 93 TA 1053
North Green 59 TM 2288
North Grimston 92 SE 8467
North Hayling 14 SU 7203
North Heasley 19 SS 7333
North Heath 15 TQ 0621
North Hill 5 SX 2776
North Hillingdon 26 TQ 0884
North Hinksey 38 SP 4806
North Holmwood 15 TQ 1646
North Huish 6 SX 7156
North Hykeham 80 SK 9465
North Kelsey 86 TA 0401
North Kessock 148 NH 6548
North Killingholme 87 TA 1417
North Kilvington 91 SE 4285
North Kilworth 54 SP 6183
North Kingennie 135 NO 4736
North Kyme 80 TF 1452
North Lee (Bucks.) 39 SP 8309
North Leigh (Oxon.) 38 SP 3813
North Leverton with Habblesthorpe 79 SK 7882
North Littleton 53 SP 0847
North Lopham 58 TM 0383
North Luffenham 67 SK 9303
North Marden 14 SU 8015
North Marston 39 SP 7722
North Middleton 117 NT 3559
North Molton 19 SS 7329
North Moor 93 TA 2471
North Moreton 38 SU 5689
North Mundham 14 SU 8702
North Muskham 79 SK 7958
North Newington 54 SP 4139
North Newnton 23 SU 1257
North Newton 21 ST 2931
North Nibley 36 ST 7396
North Oakley 24 SU 5354
North Ockendon 27 TQ 5984
North Ormsby 81 TF 2893
North Otterington 91 SE 3589
North Owersby 80 TF 0594
North Perrott 10 ST 4709
North Petherton 21 ST 2832
North Petherwin 5 SX 2889
North Pickenham 70 TF 8606
North Piddle 52 SO 9654
North Poorton 10 SY 5197
North Queensferry 126 NT 1380
North Radworthy 19 SS 7534
North Rigton 91 SE 2749
North Rode 76 SJ 8866
North Runcton 69 TF 6416
North Sandwick 163 HU 5598
North Scale 88 SD 1769
North Scarle 79 SK 8466
North Seaton 105 NZ 2986
North Shian 130 NM 9143
North Shields 105 NZ 3468
North Shoebury 42 TQ 9286
North Side 68 TL 2799
North Skirlaugh 87 TA 1540
North Somercotes 87 TF 4296
North Stainley 91 SE 2876
North Stainmore 96 NY 8215
North Stifford 27 TQ 6080
North Stoke (Avon) 22 ST 7068
North Stoke (Oxon.) 38 SU 6186
North Stoke (W Susx) 15 TQ 0211
North Street (Berks.) 24 SU 6372
North Street (Hants.) 24 SU 6433
North Street (Kent) 28 TR 0158
North Sunderland 119 NU 2131
North Tamerton 5 SX 3197
North Tawton 8 SS 6601
North Thoresby 87 TF 2998
North Tidworth 23 SU 2248
North Tolsta 163 NB 5347
North Town 19 SS 5109
North Tuddenham 70 TG 0413
North Walsham 71 TG 2730
North Waltham 24 SU 5546
North Warnborough 25 SU 7351
North Watten 159 ND 2458
North Weald Basset 41 TL 4904
North Weston 35 ST 4674
North Whilborough 7 SX 8766
North Wick (Avon) 21 ST 5865
North Widcombe 21 ST 5758
North Willingham 80 TF 1688
North Wingfield 78 SK 4064
North Witham 67 SK 9221
North Wootton (Dorset) 10 ST 6614
North Wootton (Norf.) 69 TF 6424
North Wootton (Somer.) 21 ST 5641
North Wraxall 22 ST 8174
North Wroughton 37 SU 1581
Northacre 70 TL 9598
Northall 39 SP 9620
Northall Green 70 TF 9915
Northallerton 91 SE 3793
Northam (Devon.) 18 SS 4429
Northam (Hants.) 13 SU 4312
Northampton 55 SP 7561
Northaw 41 TL 2802
Northay 9 ST 2811
Northborough 68 TF 1508
Northbourne 29 TR 3352
Northbrook 24 SU 5139
Northchapel 14 SU 9529
Northchurch 39 SP 9708
Northcott (Corn.) 18 SS 2109
Northcott (Devon) 5 SX 3392
Northcott (Devon) 9 ST 0912
Northcott (Devon) 9 ST 1109
Northend (Avon) 22 ST 7867
Northend (Bucks.) 39 SU 7392
Northend (Warw.) 54 SP 3852
Northfield (Borders) 119 NT 9167
Northfield (Grampn.) 143 NJ 9008
Northfield (W Mids.) 53 SP 0179
Northfleet 27 TQ 6274
Northiam 17 TQ 8324
Northill 56 TL 1446
Northington 24 SU 5637
Northlands 81 TF 3453
Northleach 37 SP 1114
Northleigh (Devon.) 9 SY 1995
Northlew 5 SX 5099
Northmoor 38 SP 4202
Northmoor Green or Moorland 21 ST 3332
Northmuir 134 NO 3855
Northney 14 SU 7305
Northolt 26 TQ 1285
Northop 74 SJ 2468
Northop Hall 74 SJ 2767
Northorpe (Lincs.) 86 SK 8996
Northorpe (Lincs.) 68 TF 0917
Northover 21 ST 5223
Northowram 84 SE 1127
Northrepps 71 TG 2439
Northton 163 NF 9889
Northwall 163 HY 7545
Northway 52 SO 9234
Northwich 75 SJ 6573
Northwick (Avon) 35 ST 5586
Northwold 69 TL 7596
Northwood (Gtr London) 26 TQ 1090
Northwood (I. of W.) 13 SZ 4992
Northwood (Salop) 63 SJ 4633
Northwood Green 36 SO 7216
Norton (Ches.) 75 SJ 5581
Norton (Cleve.) 98 NZ 4421
Norton (Glos.) 36 SO 8624
Norton (Gwent) 47 SO 4420
Norton (Here & W) 52 SO 8750
Norton (Here & W) 53 SP 0447
Norton (Herts.) 40 TL 2234
Norton (I. of W.) 13 SZ 3489
Norton (N Yorks.) 92 SE 7971
Norton (Northants.) 54 SP 6063
Norton (Notts.) 78 SK 5772
Norton (Powys) 51 SO 3067
Norton (S Yorks.) 85 SE 5415
Norton (S Yorks.) 78 SK 3581
Norton (Salop) 51 SJ 5609
Norton (Salop) 64 SJ 7200
Norton (Salop) 51 SO 4581
Norton (Salop) 51 SO 6382
Norton (Suff.) 58 TL 9565
Norton (W Susx) 14 SU 9306
Norton (Wilts.) 36 ST 8884
Norton Bavant 22 ST 9043
Norton Bridge 64 SJ 8629
Norton Canes 65 SK 0108
Norton Canon 47 SO 3847
Norton Corner 70 TG 0928
Norton Disney 79 SK 8859
Norton Ferris 22 ST 7936
Norton Fitzwarren 20 ST 1925
Norton Green 13 SZ 3388
Norton Hawkfield 21 ST 5964
Norton Heath 42 TL 6004
Norton Hill 22 ST 6753
Norton Lindsey 53 SP 2263
Norton Malreward 21 ST 6065
Norton St. Philip 22 ST 7755
Norton Subcourse 71 TM 4098
Norton Wood 47 SO 3648
Norton in Hales 64 SJ 7038
Norton in the Moors 76 SJ 8951
Norton sub Hamdon 10 ST 4615
Norton-Juxta-Twycross 65 SK 3207
Norton-le-Clay 91 SE 4071
Norwell 79 SK 7661
Norwell Woodhouse 79 SK 7462
Norwich 71 TG 2308
Norwick (Unst) 163 HP 6414
Norwood Green (Gtr. London) 26 TQ 1378
Norwood Green (W. Yorks) 84 SE 1427
Norwood Hill 15 TQ 2443
Noseley 67 SP 7398
Noss Mayo 6 SX 5447
Nosterfield 91 SE 2780
Nosterfield End 57 TL 6344
Nostie 145 NG 8527
Notgrove 37 SP 1020
Nottage 33 SS 8278
Nottingham (Dorset) 10 SY 6582
Nottingham (Notts) 66 SK 5741
Notton (W Yorks.) 85 SE 3413
Notton (Wilts.) 22 ST 9169
Nounsley 42 TL 7910
Noutard's Green 52 SO 7966
Nox 63 SJ 4010
Nuffield 38 SU 6687
Nun Monkton 92 SE 5057
Nunburnholme 92 SE 8548
Nuneaton 66 SP 3592
Nuneham Courtenay 38 SU 5599
Nunney 22 ST 7345
Nunney Catch 22 ST 7344
Nunnington 92 SE 6679
Nunthorpe 98 NZ 5313
Nunton (Wilts.) 23 SU 1525
Nunwick 104 NY 8774
Nursling 13 SU 3615
Nursted 14 SU 7621
Nutbourne 15 TQ 0718
Nutbourne Common 15 TQ 0718
Nutfield 26 TQ 3150
Nuthall 78 SK 5144
Nuthampstead 41 TL 4134
Nuthurst 15 TQ 1926
Nutley (E. Susx.) 16 TQ 4427
Nutley (Hants.) 24 SU 6144
Nutwell 85 SE 6303
Nybster 159 ND 3663
Nyetimber 14 SZ 8998
Nyewood 14 SU 8021
Nymet Rowland 8 SS 7108
Nymet Tracey 8 SS 7200
Nympsfield 36 SO 8000
Nynehead 9 ST 1422
Nyton 14 SU 9305

Oad Street 28 TQ 8762
Oadby 66 SK 6200
Oak Hill 59 TM 3645
Oakamoor 77 SK 0544
Oakbank 116 NT 0866
Oakdale 34 ST 1898
Oake 20 ST 1525
Oaken 64 SJ 8502
Oakenclough 82 SD 5447
Oakengates 64 SJ 7010
Oakenshaw (Durham) 97 NZ 2036
Oakenshaw (W Yorks.) 84 SE 1727
Oakford (Devon.) 8 SS 9021
Oakford (Dyfed) 44 SN 4557
Oakgrove 76 SJ 9169
Oakham 67 SK 8509
Oakhanger 25 SU 7635
Oakhill 21 ST 6347
Oakington 56 TL 4164
Oaklands 73 SH 8158
Oakle Street 36 SO 7517
Oakley (Beds.) 55 TL 0153
Oakley (Bucks.) 38 SP 6412
Oakley (Fife.) 126 NT 0289
Oakley (Hants.) 24 SU 5650
Oakley (Suff.) 58 TM 1678
Oakley Green 25 SU 9376
Oakleypark 49 SN 9886
Oakridge 36 SO 9103
Oaks 51 SJ 4204
Oaksey 36 ST 9893
Oakthorpe 65 SK 3213
Oakwood 104 NY 9566
Oakwoodhill 15 TQ 1337
Oakworth 84 SE 0238
Oare (Kent) 28 TR 0062
Oare (Somer.) 19 SS 8047
Oare (Wilts.) 23 SU 1563
Oasby 67 TF 0039
Oathlaw 135 NO 4756
Oban 129 NM 8630
Obney 133 NO 0336
Oborne 10 ST 6518
Obthorpe 68 TF 0915
Occlestone Green 76 SJ 6962
Occold 58 TM 1570
Ochiltree 107 NS 5121
Ochtermuthill 132 NN 8216
Ockbrook 66 SK 4235
Ockham 26 TQ 0756
Ockle 137 NM 5570
Ockley 15 TQ 1640
Ocle Pychard 47 SO 5946
Odcombe 10 ST 5015
Odd Down 22 ST 7462
Oddingley 52 SO 9159
Oddington (Glos.) 37 SP 2225
Oddington (Oxon.) 38 SP 5514
Odell 55 SP 9658
Odham 18 SS 4703
Odiham 25 SU 7350
Odsey 56 TL 2938
Odstock 23 SU 1426
Odstone 66 SK 3907
Offchurch 54 SP 3565
Offenham 53 SP 0546
Offham (E Susx) 16 TQ 4012
Offham (Kent) 27 TQ 6557
Offord Cluny 56 TL 2267
Offord Darcy 56 TL 2266
Offton 58 TM 0649
Offwell 9 SY 1999
Ogbourne Maizey 23 SU 1871
Ogbourne St. Andrew 23 SU 1872
Ogbourne St. George 23 SU 2074
Ogil 142 NO 4561
Ogle 105 NZ 1378
Ogmore 33 SS 8877
Ogmore Vale 33 SS 9490
Ogmore-by-Sea 33 SS 8674
Okeford Fitzpaine 11 ST 8010
Okehampton 5 SX 5895
Okehampton Camp 5 SX 5893
Olchard 7 SX 8776
Old 55 SP 7873
Old Aberdeen 143 NJ 9408
Old Alresford 24 SU 5834
Old Basing 24 SU 6652
Old Bewick 111 NU 0621
Old Bolingbroke 81 TF 3564
Old Brampton 78 SK 3371
Old Bridge of Urr 102 NX 7767
Old Buckenham 70 TM 0691
Old Burghclere 24 SU 4657
Old Byland 92 SE 5486
Old Church Stoke 50 SO 2894
Old Cleeve 20 ST 0342
Old Colwyn 73 SH 8678
Old Coulsdon 26 TQ 3057
Old Dailly 106 NX 2299
Old Dalby 66 SK 6723
Old Deer 151 NJ 9747
Old Down 35 ST 6187
Old Felixstowe 43 TM 3135
Old Fletton 68 TL 1997
Old Hall Green 41 TL 3622
Old Heath 43 TM 0122
Old Hunstanton 69 TF 6842
Old Hutton 89 SD 5688
Old Kea 3 SW 8441
Old Kilpatrick 124 NS 4673
Old Knebworth 40 TL 2320
Old Leake 81 TF 4050
Old Malton 92 SE 7972
Old Milton 12 SZ 2494
Old Milverton 53 SP 2967
Old Monkland 115 NS 7163
Old Montsale 43 TR 0197
Old Newton 58 TM 0662
Old Philpstoun 126 NT 0577
Old Radnor 46 SO 2559
Old Rayne 150 NJ 6728
Old Romney 17 TR 0325
Old Scone 133 NO 1226
Old Shoreham 15 TQ 2006
Old Sodbury 36 ST 7581
Old Somerby 67 SK 9633
Old Town (Cumbr.) 89 SD 5983
Old Town (Northum.) 104 NY 8891
Old Town (Scilly Isles) 162 SV 9110
Old Warden 56 TL 1343
Old Weston 56 TL 0977
Old Windsor 25 SU 9874
Old Wives Lees 29 TR 0755
Old Woking 26 TQ 0256
Oldberrow 53 SP 1165
Oldborough 8 SS 7706
Oldbury (Salop) 64 SO 7092
Oldbury (W Mids.) 64 SO 9889
Oldbury (Warw.) 65 SP 3194
Oldbury-on-Severn 35 ST 6092
Oldcastle 47 SO 3224
Oldcotes 78 SK 5888
Oldcroft 35 SO 6406
Oldfield 52 SO 8464
Oldford 22 ST 7849
Oldham 83 SD 9305
Oldhamstocks 118 NT 7470
Oldhurst 56 TL 3077
Oldland 22 ST 6771
Oldmeldrum 151 NJ 8027
Oldmill 5 SX 3673
Oldpark 64 SJ 6909
Oldshore 156 NC 2059
Oldstead 92 SE 5280
Oldtown of Ord 150 NJ 6259
Oldwalls 32 SS 4891
Oldways End 19 SS 8624
Olgrinmore 159 ND 0955
Oliver 108 NT 0924
Oliver's Battery 13 SU 4527
Ollaberry 163 HU 3680
Ollach 144 NG 5137
Ollerton (Ches.) 76 SJ 7776
Ollerton (Notts.) 79 SK 6567
Ollerton (Salop) 63 SJ 6425
Olmarch 45 SN 6255
Olney 55 SP 8851
Olton 53 SP 1282
Olveston 35 ST 6007
Ombersley 52 SO 8463
Ompton 79 SK 6865
Onchan 162 SC 4078
Onecote 77 SK 0555
Onen 47 SO 4314
Ongar Hill 69 TF 5724
Ongar Street 51 SO 3967
Onibury 51 SO 4579
Onich 138 NN 0261
Onllwyn 33 SN 8310
Onneley 64 SJ 7542
Onslow Village 25 SU 9849
Opinan (Highld.) 152 NG 7472
Orbost 144 NG 2644
Orby 81 TF 4967
Orchard 11 ST 8216
Orchard Portman 21 ST 2421
Orcheston 23 SU 0545
Orcop 47 SO 4726
Orcop Hill 47 SO 4728
Ordhead 143 NJ 6610
Ordie 142 NJ 4502
Ordiequish 149 NJ 3357
Ore 17 TQ 8311
Oreham Common 15 TQ 2214
Oreton 52 SO 6580
Orford (Ches.) 75 SJ 6090
Orford (Suff.) 59 TM 4250
Organford 11 SY 9392

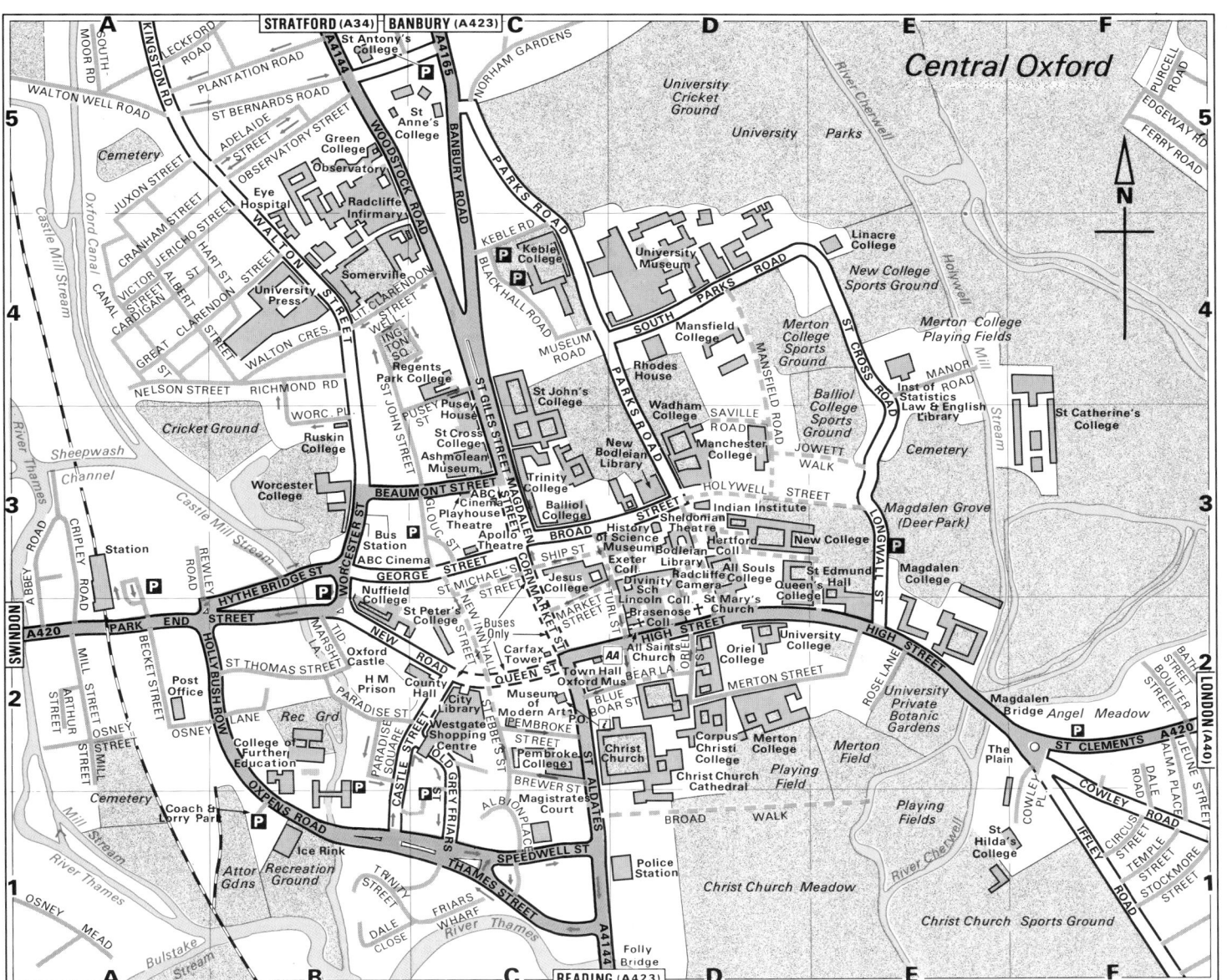

Central Oxford

Packington Pilley (Hants.)

P

Place	Page	Grid ref.
Packington	66	SK 3614
Padanaram	135	NO 4251
Padanaram	134	NO 4352
Padbury	39	SP 7130
Paddington	26	TQ 2482
Paddlesworth	29	TR 1939
Paddock Wood	16	TQ 6645
Paddockhaugh	149	NJ 2058
Paddockhole	107	NY 2384
Paddolgreen	63	SJ 5032
Paddon	18	SS 3509
Padeswood	74	SJ 2761
Padiham	83	SD 7933
Padstow	4	SW 9175
Padworth	24	SU 6166
Padworth Common	24	SU 6264
Pagham	14	SZ 8897
Paglesham	42	TQ 9292
Paignton	7	SX 8960
Pailton	54	SP 4781
Paincastle	46	SO 1646
Painshawfield	104	NZ 0660
Painswick	36	SO 8609
Painter's Forstal	28	TQ 9958
Paisley	114	NS 4864
Pakefield	71	TM 5390
Pakenham	58	TL 9267
Pale	62	SH 9836
Pale Green	57	TL 6542
Palestine	23	SU 2640
Paley Street	25	SU 8776
Palgrave	58	TM 1178
Palmerstown	20	ST 1369
Palnackie	102	NX 8257
Palnure	101	NX 4563
Palterton	78	SK 4768
Pamber End	24	SU 6158
Pamber Green	24	SU 6059
Pamber Heath	24	SU 6162
Pamington	52	SO 9333
Pamphill	11	ST 9900
Pampisford	57	TL 4948
Panborough	21	ST 4745
Panbride	135	NO 5635
Pancrasweek	18	SS 2905
Pancross	20	ST 0469
Pandy (Clwyd)	62	SJ 1935
Pandy (Gwent)	47	SO 3322
Pandy (Powys)	49	SH 9004
Pandy (Powys.)	48	SH 6202
Pandy Tudur	73	SH 8564
Panfield	42	TL 7325
Pangbourne	24	SU 6376
Pannal	91	SE 3051
Pannanich Wells Hotel	141	NO 3997
Pant	62	SJ 2722
Pant Mawr	49	SN 8482
Pant-glas (Gwyn.)	60	SH 4747
Pant-pastynog	74	SJ 0461
Pant-y-dwr	49	SN 9875
Pant-y-ffridd	50	SJ 1502
Pant-y-gog	33	SS 9090
Pant-yr-awel	33	SS 9287
Pantglas (Powys)	49	SN 7898
Pantglas Hall	45	SN 5526
Pantgwyn	44	SN 2446
Panton	80	TF 1778
Pantperthog	49	SH 7504
Pantside	34	ST 2297
Pantyffynnon	32	SN 6210
Pantygasseg	34	SO 2501
Panxworth	71	TG 3413
Papcastle	94	NY 1231
Papil	163	HU 3631
Papple	127	NT 5972
Papplewick	78	SK 5451
Papworth Everard	56	TL 2862
Papworth St. Agnes	56	TL 2664
Par	4	SX 0653
Parbold	82	SD 4911
Parbrook	21	ST 5736
Parc Seymour	35	ST 4091
Parcllyn	44	SN 2451
Pardown	24	SU 5848
Pardshaw	94	NY 0924
Parham	59	TM 3060
Park (Grampn.)	143	NO 7798
Park (Strath.)	130	NM 9340
Park Corner	38	SU 6988
Park Gate	52	SO 9871
Park Gate	52	SO 9371
Park Gate (Hants.)	13	SU 5108
Park Mill	84	SE 2611
Parkend (Glos.)	35	SO 6108
Parkeston	43	TM 2332
Parkgate (Ches.)	74	SJ 2778
Parkgate (Ches.)	76	SJ 7874
Parkgate (Dumf & G)	108	NY 0288
Parkgate (Surrey)	15	TQ 2043
Parkham	18	SS 3821
Parkham Ash	18	SS 3620
Parkhouse	35	SO 5002
Parkhurst	13	SZ 4991
Parkmill	32	SS 5489
Parkneuk	143	NO 7976
Parkstone	12	SZ 0491
Parley Common	12	SZ 0999
Parley Cross	12	SZ 0898
Parracombe	19	SS 6744
Parrog	30	SN 0439
Parson Drove	68	TF 3708
Parsonby	94	NY 1438
Partick	115	NS 5567
Partington	76	SJ 7191
Partney	81	TF 4168
Parton (Cumbr.)	94	NX 9720
Parton (Dumf & G)	102	NX 6970
Partridge Green	15	TQ 1919
Parwich	77	SK 1854
Passenham	55	SP 7839
Paston	71	TG 3235
Patchacott	5	SX 4798
Patcham	15	TQ 3009
Patching	15	TQ 0806
Patchole	19	SS 6142
Patchway	35	ST 6082
Pateley Bridge	91	SE 1565
Path of Condie	133	NO 0711
Pathe	21	ST 3730
Pathhead (Lothian)	117	NT 3964
Pathhead (Strath.)	107	NS 6114
Pathlow	53	SP 1758
Patmore Heath	41	TL 4526
Patna	106	NS 4110
Patney	23	SU 0758
Patrick	162	SC 2482
Patrick Brompton	91	SE 2290
Patrington	87	TA 3122
Patrington Haven	87	TA 3021
Patrixbourne	29	TR 1855
Patterdale	95	NY 3915
Pattingham	64	SO 8299
Pattishall	54	SP 6654
Paul	2	SW 4627
Paulerspury	55	SP 7145
Paull	87	TA 1626
Paulton	21	ST 6456
Pauperhaugh	111	NZ 1099
Pavenham	55	SP 9955
Pawlett	21	ST 2942
Pawston	118	NT 8532
Paxford	53	SP 1837
Paxton	119	NT 9352
Payhembury	9	ST 0801
Paythorne	83	SD 8251
Peacehaven	16	TQ 4101
Peachley	52	SO 8057
Peak Dale	77	SK 0976
Peak Forest	77	SK 1179
Peakirk	68	TF 1606
Pearsie	134	NO 3659
Pease Pottage	15	TQ 2633
Peasedown St. John	22	ST 7057
Peasemore	24	SU 4576
Peasenhall	59	TM 3569
Peaslake	15	TQ 0844
Peasmarsh (E. Susx.)	17	TQ 8822
Peasmarsh (Surrey)	25	SU 9946
Peaston Bank	117	NT 4466
Peat Inn	127	NO 4509
Peathill (Grampn.)	151	NJ 9365
Peatling Magna	66	SP 5992
Peatling Parva	54	SP 5889
Peaton	51	SO 5385
Pebmarsh	42	TL 8533
Pebworth	53	SP 1347
Pecket Well	84	SD 9929
Peckforton	75	SJ 5356
Peckleton	66	SK 4701
Pedmore	52	SO 9182
Pedwell	21	ST 4236
Peebles	117	NT 2540
Peel	162	SC 2484
Pegswood	105	NZ 2287
Pegwell Bay	29	TR 3563
Peinchorran	144	NG 5233
Peinlich	144	NG 4158
Peinmore	143	NG 4248
Pelaw	105	NZ 2962
Peldon	43	TL 9816
Pelsall	65	SK 0103
Pelton	97	NZ 2553
Pelutho	94	NY 1249
Pelynt	4	SX 2055
Pemberton	32	SS 5300
Pembrey	32	SN 4201
Pembridge	47	SO 3858
Pembroke	30	SM 9901
Pembroke Dock	30	SM 9603
Pembury	16	TQ 6240
Pen-Sarn (Gwyn.)	60	SH 4344
Pen-Sarn (Gwyn.)	61	SH 5728
Pen-Yr-Heolgerrig	34	SO 3006
Pen-bont Rhydybeddau	48	SN 6783
Pen-ffordd	30	SN 0722
Pen-isa'r-cwm	62	SJ 0018
Pen-llyn (Gwyn.)	72	SH 3482
Pen-lon	72	SH 4364
Pen-twyn (Gwent)	35	SO 5209
Pen-twyn (Gwent)	34	SO 2603
Pen-twyn (Gwent)	34	SO 2000
Pen-y-Clawdd	35	SO 4507
Pen-y-Gwryd Hotel	73	SH 6556
Pen-y-bont (Clwyd)	62	SJ 2123
Pen-y-bryn (Dyfed)	31	SN 1742
Pen-y-bryn (Gwynedd)	61	SH 6919
Pen-y-cae (Powys)	45	SN 8413
Pen-y-cefn	74	SJ 1175
Pen-y-coedcae	34	ST 0587
Pen-y-cwn	30	SM 8523
Pen-y-garn (Dyfed)	45	SN 5731
Pen-y-garn (Dyfed)	48	SN 6285
Pen-y-graig	60	SH 2033
Pen-y-graig	60	SH 2033
Pen-y-groeslon	60	SH 2131
Pen-y-stryt	62	SJ 2051
Penallt	35	SO 5210
Penally	31	SS 1199
Penalt	47	SO 5629
Penant	48	SN 5163
Penare	3	SW 9940
Penarth	34	ST 1871
Penblewan Cross	31	SN 1216
Penbryn	44	SN 2952
Pencader	44	SN 4436
Pencaitland	117	NT 4468
Pencarnisiog	72	SH 3573
Pencarreg	45	SN 5345
Pencelli	46	SO 0925
Penclawdd	32	SS 5495
Pencoed (Mid Glam.)	33	SS 9581
Pencombe	47	SO 5952
Pencoyd	47	SO 5126
Pencraig (Here & W)	47	SO 5722
Pencraig (Powys)	62	SJ 0427
Pendeen	2	SW 3834
Penderyn	33	SN 9408
Pendine	31	SN 2308
Pendlebury	83	SD 7802
Pendleton	83	SD 7539
Pendock	52	SO 7832
Pendoggett	4	SX 0279
Pendomer	10	ST 5210
Pendoylan	34	ST 0676
Penegoes	49	SH 7701
Penelewey	3	SW 8140
Pengam	34	ST 1797
Penge	26	TQ 3570
Pengorffwysfa	72	SH 4692
Pengover Green	5	SX 2864
Pengwern	74	SJ 0176
Penhallow	3	SW 7651
Penhalvean	2	SW 7037
Penhow	35	ST 4290
Penhurst	16	TQ 6916
Peniarth	48	SH 6105
Penicuik	117	NT 2359
Peniel	44	SN 4323
Penifiler	144	NG 4841
Peninver	112	NR 7524
Penisar Waun	72	SH 5564
Penistone	84	SE 2402
Penjerrick	3	SW 7730
Penketh	75	SJ 5687
Penkill	113	NX 2398
Penkridge	64	SJ 9214
Penley	63	SJ 4139
Penllergaer	32	SS 6199
Penllyn (S Glam.)	33	SS 9776
Penmachno	61	SH 7950
Penmaen (Gwent)	34	ST 1897
Penmaen (W. Glam)	32	SS 5288
Penmaenmawr	73	SH 7176
Penmaenpool	61	SH 6918
Penmark	20	ST 0568
Penmon	73	SH 6381
Penmorfa	61	SH 5440
Penmynydd	72	SH 5174
Penn	39	SU 9193
Penn Street	39	SU 9296
Pennal	48	SH 7000
Pennan	151	NJ 8465
Pennant	49	SN 8897
Pennant-Melangell	62	SJ 0226
Pennard	32	SS 5688
Pennerley	51	SO 3599
Pennington	88	SD 2577
Pennsylvania	22	ST 7473
Penny Bridge	88	SD 3082
Pennycross	128	NM 5025
Pennygown	129	NM 6042
Pennymoor	8	SS 8611
Penparc	44	SN 2148
Penparcau	48	SN 5980
Penpedairheal	34	ST 1397
Penpedairheol	35	SO 3303
Penperlleni	35	SO 3204
Penpethy	4	SX 0886
Penpillick	4	SX 0756
Penpol	3	SW 8139
Penpoll	4	SX 1454
Penponds	2	SW 6439
Penpont (Dumf & G)	107	NX 8494
Penpont (Powys)	46	SN 9728
Penrherber	44	SN 2839
Penrhiw	44	SN 2440
Penrhiwceiber	34	ST 0597
Penrhiwllan	44	SN 3742
Penrhiwpal	44	SN 3445
Penrhos (Gwent)	35	SO 4111
Penrhos (Gwyn.)	72	SH 2781
Penrhos (Gwyn.)	60	SH 3433
Penrhos (Powys)	33	SN 8011
Penrhyn Bay	73	SH 8281
Penrhyn-side	73	SH 8181
Penrhyncoch	48	SN 6484
Penrhyndeudraeth	61	SH 6139
Penrhys	34	ST 0095
Penrice	32	SS 4988
Penrith	95	NY 5130
Penrose	4	SW 8770
Penruddock	95	NY 4227
Penryn	3	SW 7834
Pensarn (Clwyd)	73	SH 9478
Pensax	52	SO 7269
Pensby	74	SJ 2683
Penselwood	22	ST 7531
Pensford	21	ST 6163
Pensham	52	SO 9444
Penshaw	98	NZ 3253
Penshurst	16	TQ 5243
Penshurst Station	16	TQ 5247
Pensilva	5	SX 2969
Pentewan	4	SX 0147
Pentir	73	SH 5767
Pentire	3	SW 7961
Pentlepoir	31	SN 1105
Pentlow	58	TL 8144
Pentney	69	TF 7213
Penton Grafton	23	SU 3247
Penton Mewsey	23	SU 3247
Pentraeth	72	SH 5278
Pentre (Clwyd)	74	SJ 0862
Pentre (Clwyd)	62	SJ 2840
Pentre (Mid Glam)	33	SS 9797
Pentre (Powys)	50	SO 0686
Pentre (Powys)	50	SO 2466
Pentre (Powys)	50	SO 2791
Pentre (Powys)	62	SJ 1413
Pentre (Salop)	63	SJ 3617
Pentre Berw	72	SH 4772
Pentre Halkyn	74	SJ 2072
Pentre Meyrick	33	SS 9675
Pentre ty gwyn	45	SN 8135
Pentre'r-felin	46	SN 9130
Pentre-Cagal	44	SN 3340
Pentre-Dolau-Honddu	46	SN 9943
Pentre-Gwenlais	45	SN 6116
Pentre-bach (Powys)	46	SN 9033
Pentre-bont	61	SH 7351
Pentre-celyn (Clwyd)	74	SJ 1453
Pentre-cwrt	44	SN 3938
Pentre-dwr	32	SS 6996
Pentre-llyn	48	SN 6174
Pentre-tafarn-y-fedw	73	SH 8162
Pentrebach (Mid Glam.)	34	SO 0604
Pentrebeirdd	62	SJ 1913
Pentrefelin (Gwyndd)	61	SH 5239
Pentrefelin (Gwyndd)	72	SH 4391
Pentrefoelas	61	SH 8751
Pentregat	44	SN 3551
Pentregof	72	SH 3703
Pentrich	78	SK 3852
Pentridge	12	SU 0317
Pentyrch	34	ST 1082
Penuwch	48	SN 5962
Penwithick	4	SX 0256
Penybanc	45	SN 6124
Penybont (Powys)	50	SO 1164
Penybontfawr	62	SJ 0824
Penybryn	34	ST 1395
Penycae (Clwyd)	62	SJ 2745
Penyffordd	74	SJ 3061
Penygarnedd	62	SJ 1023
Penygraig	33	SS 9991
Penygraigwen	72	SH 4488
Penygroes (Dyfed)	45	SN 5813
Penygroes (Gwyn.)	72	SH 4753
Penysarn	72	SH 4690
Penywaun	33	SN 9704
Penzance	2	SW 4730
Peopleton	52	SO 9350
Peover Heath	76	SJ 7973
Peper Harow	25	SU 9344
Peplow	63	SJ 6324
Pepperstock	40	TL 0817
Percie	142	NO 5991
Percyhorner	151	NJ 9565
Perelle (Guernsey)	161	ZZ 9999
Perivale	26	TQ 1682
Perkin's Beach	51	SJ 3600
Perran Wharf	3	SW 7738
Perranarworthal	3	SW 7738
Perranporth	3	SW 7554
Perranuthnoe	2	SW 5329
Perranwell	3	SW 7752
Perranzabuloe	3	SW 7752
Perrott's Brook	37	SP 0106
Perry Barr	65	SP 0791
Perry Green (Essex)	42	TL 8021
Perry Green (Herts.)	41	TL 4317
Perry Green (Somer.)	20	ST 2738
Perry Street	9	ST 3405
Pershore	52	SO 9446
Pert	142	NO 6565
Pertenhall	56	TL 0865
Perth	133	NO 1123
Perthcelyn	34	ST 0595
Perthy	63	SJ 3633
Perton	64	SO 8598
Peter Tavy	5	SX 5177
Peter's Green	40	TL 1419
Peterborough	68	TL 1999
Peterburn	152	NG 7384
Peterchurch	47	SO 3438
Peterculter	143	NJ 8400
Peterhead	151	NK 1346
Peterlee	98	NZ 4440
Peters Marland	18	SS 4713
Petersfield	14	SU 7423
Peterston-super Ely	34	ST 0876
Peterstone Wentlooge	34	ST 2680
Peterstow	47	SO 5624
Petham	29	TR 1251
Petrockstow	19	SS 5109
Pett	17	TQ 8714
Pettaugh	58	TM 1659
Petteridge	16	TQ 6641
Pettinain	116	NS 9542
Pettistree	59	TM 2954
Petton (Devon.)	20	ST 0024
Petton (Salop)	63	SJ 4326
Petts Wood	27	TQ 4467
Petty	150	NJ 7636
Pettycur	126	NT 2686
Pettymuk	151	NJ 9024
Petworth	14	SU 9721
Pevensey	16	TQ 6405
Pevensey Bay	16	TQ 6504
Pewsey	23	SU 1761
Pheasant's Hill	39	SU 7887
Philham	18	SS 2522
Philiphaugh	109	NT 4427
Phillack	2	SW 5539
Philleigh	3	SW 8639
Philpstoun	126	NT 0577
Phocle Green	47	SO 6225
Phoenix Green	25	SU 7655
Pic Corner	51	SO 6461
Pica	94	NY 0222
Piccotts End	40	TL 0509
Pickering	92	SE 7983
Picket Piece	24	SU 3947
Picket Post	12	SU 1905
Pickford Green	53	SP 2781
Pickhill	91	SE 3483
Picklescott	51	SO 4399
Pickmere	76	SJ 6876
Pickwell (Devon.)	18	SS 4540
Pickwell (Leic.)	67	SK 7811
Pickwick	22	ST 8670
Pickworth (Leic.)	67	SK 9913
Pickworth (Lincs.)	67	TF 0433
Picton (Ches.)	75	SJ 4371
Picton (N Yorks.)	98	NZ 4107
Piddinghoe	16	TQ 4303
Piddington (Northants.)	55	SP 8054
Piddington (Oxon.)	38	SP 6317
Piddlehinton	10	SY 7197
Piddletrenthide	10	SY 7099
Pidley	56	TL 3377
Piercebridge	97	NZ 2115
Pierowall	163	HY 4348
Pigdon	105	NZ 1588
Pikehall	77	SK 1959
Pilford	12	SU 0301
Pilgrims Hatch	27	TQ 5895
Pilham	79	SK 8693
Pill	35	ST 5275
Pillaton	5	SX 3664
Pillerton Hersey	53	SP 2948
Pillerton Priors	53	SP 2947
Pilleth	50	SO 2568
Pilley (Hants.)	13	SZ 3398

Pucklechurch Ridgewell

Pucklechurch 22 ST 6976
Puckrup 52 SO 8836
Puddington (Ches.) 74 SJ 3273
Puddington (Devon) 8 SS 8310
Puddledock 70 TM 0592
Puddletown 11 SY 7594
Pudleston 47 SO 5659
Pudsey 84 SE 2232
Pulborough 15 TQ 0418
Puleston 64 SJ 7322
Pulford 75 SJ 3758
Pulham 10 ST 7008
Pulham Market 59 TM 1986
Pulham St. Mary 59 TM 2185
Pulloxhill 40 TL 0634
Pumpherston 116 NT 0669
Pumsaint 45 SN 6540
Puncheston 30 SN 0029
Puncknowle 10 SY 5388
Punnett's Town 16 TQ 6220
Purbrook 14 SU 6707
Purfleet 27 TQ 5578
Puriton 21 ST 3241
Purleigh 42 TL 8301
Purley (Berks.) 24 SU 6676
Purley (Gtr Lon.) 26 TQ 3161
Purlogue 50 SO 2877
Purlpit 22 ST 8766
Purls Bridge 57 TL 4787
Purse Caundle 10 ST 6917
Purslow 51 SO 3680
Purston Jaglin 85 SE 4319
Purtington 10 ST 3808
Purton (Glos.) 36 SO 6605
Purton (Glos.) 36 SO 6904
Purton (Wilts.) 37 SU 0887
Purton Stoke 37 SU 0890
Pury End 54 SP 7045
Pusey 38 SU 3596
Putley 47 SO 6437
Putney 26 TQ 2274
Putsborough 18 SS 4540
Puttenham (Herts.) 39 SP 8814
Puttenham (Surrey) 25 SU 9347
Puxton 21 ST 4063
Pwll 32 SN 4801
Pwll Trap 44 SN 2616
Pwll-glas 74 SJ 1154
Pwll-y-glaw 33 SS 7993
Pwllcrochan 30 SM 9202
Pwlldefaid 60 SH 1526
Pwllgloyw 46 SO 0233
Pwllheli 60 SH 3735
Pwllmeyric 35 ST 5192
Pye Corner (Gwent) 35 ST 3485
Pye Corner (Herts.) 41 TL 4512
Pye Green 65 SJ 9814
Pye Hill 21 ST 6137
Pyecombe 15 TQ 2912
Pyle (I. of W.) 13 SZ 4879
Pyle (Mid Glam.) 33 SS 8282
Pylle 21 ST 6038
Pymore (Cambs.) 57 TL 4986
Pymore (Dorset) 10 SY 4694
Pyrford 26 TQ 0458
Pyrton 38 SU 6895
Pytchley 55 SP 8574
Pyworthy 18 SS 3102

Q

Quabbs 50 SO 2080
Quadring 68 TF 2233
Quainton 39 SP 7420
Quaker's Yard 34 ST 0996
Quarff 163 HU 4235
Quarley 23 SU 2743
Quarndon 65 SK 3340
Quarrier's Homes 114 NS 3666
Quarrington 80 TF 0544
Quarrington Hill 98 NZ 3337
Quarry Bank (W Mids.) 52 SO 9386
Quarrybank (Ches.) 75 SJ 5465
Quarrywood 149 NJ 1864
Quarter 115 NS 7251
Quatford 64 SO 7390
Quatt 64 SO 7588
Quebec 97 NZ 1743
Quedgeley 36 SO 8114
Queen Adelaide 57 TL 5681
Queen Camel 21 ST 5924
Queen Charlton 21 ST 6366
Queen's Bower 13 SZ 5784
Queen's Head 63 SJ 3426
Queenborough 28 TQ 9172
Queensbury 84 SE 1030
Queensferry (Clwyd) 74 SJ 3168
Queensferry (Lothian) 126 NT 1278
Queenzieburn 125 NS 6977
Quemerford 22 SU 0169
Quendale 163 HU 3713
Quendon 41 TL 5130
Queniborough 66 SK 6412
Quenington 37 SP 1404
Quernmore 89 SD 5160
Quethiock 5 SX 3164
Quidenham 58 TM 0287
Quidhampton (Hants) 24 SU 5150
Quidhampton (Wilts.) 23 SU 1030
Quilquox 151 NJ 9038
Quina Brook 63 SJ 5232
Quine's Hill 162 SC 3473
Quinton 55 SP 7754
Quintrell Downs 3 SW 8460
Quoditch 5 SX 4097
Quoig 132 NN 8222
Quorndon 66 SK 5616
Quothquan 116 NS 9939

R

Raby 74 SJ 3179
Rachub 73 SH 6268
Rackenford 8 SS 8418
Rackham 15 TQ 0514
Rackheath 71 TG 2814
Racks 102 NY 0374
Rackwick (Hoy) 163 ND 1999
Radbourne 65 SK 2836
Radcliffe (Gtr Mches) 83 SD 7806
Radcliffe (Northum.) 111 NU 2602
Radcliffe on Trent 66 SK 6439
Radclive 38 SP 6734
Radcot 37 SU 2899
Radernie 127 NO 4609
Radford 53 SP 0054
Radford Semele 54 SP 3464
Radlett 40 TL 1600
Radley 38 SU 5398
Radnage 39 SU 7897
Radstock 22 ST 6854
Radstone 54 SP 5840
Radway 54 SP 3648
Radway Green 76 SJ 7754
Radwell 41 TL 2335
Radwinter 57 TL 6037
Radyr 34 ST 1380
Rafford 149 NJ 0656
Ragdale 66 SK 6619
Raglan 35 SO 4107
Ragnall 79 SK 8073
Rahane 124 NS 2386
Rainford 82 SD 4700
Rainham (Gtr London) 27 TQ 5282
Rainham (Kent) 28 TQ 8165
Rainhill 75 SJ 4990
Rainhill Stoops 75 SJ 5090
Rainow 76 SJ 9575
Rainton 91 SE 3775
Rainworth 79 SK 5958
Raisbeck 89 NY 6407
Raise 96 NY 7146
Rait 134 NO 2226
Raithby (Lincs.) 81 TF 3084
Raithby (Lincs.) 81 TF 3767
Rake 14 SU 8027
Ralph Cross 92 NZ 6702
Ram Hill 36 ST 6779
Ram Lane 28 TQ 9646
Ramasaig 144 NG 1644
Rame (Corn.) 2 SW 7233
Rame (Corn.) 6 SX 4249
Rampisham 10 ST 5502
Rampside 88 SD 2366
Rampton (Cambs.) 56 TL 4268
Rampton (Notts.) 79 SK 7978
Ramsbottom 83 SD 7916
Ramsbury 23 SU 2771
Ramscraigs 159 ND 1427
Ramsdean 14 SU 7021
Ramsdell 24 SU 5957
Ramsden (Here & W) 52 SO 9246
Ramsden (Oxon.) 38 SP 3515
Ramsden Bellhouse 42 TQ 7194
Ramsden Heath 42 TQ 7195
Ramsey (Cambs.) 56 TL 2885
Ramsey (Essex) 43 TM 2130
Ramsey (I. of M.) 162 SC 4594
Ramsey Forty Foot 56 TL 3187
Ramsey Island 42 TL 9506
Ramsey Mereside 56 TL 2889
Ramsey St. Mary's 56 TL 2588
Ramseycleuch 108 NT 2715
Ramsgate 29 TR 3865
Ramsgill 91 SE 1170
Ramshorn 77 SK 0845
Ramsnest Common 25 SU 9433
Ranby 79 SK 6480
Rand 80 TF 1078
Randwick 36 SO 8206
Ranfurly 114 NS 3865
Rangemore 65 SK 1822
Rangeworthy 36 ST 6886
Rankinston 106 NS 4514
Ranskill 79 SK 6587
Ranton 64 SJ 8524
Ranworth 71 TG 3514
Rapness 163 HY 5141
Rascarrel 102 NX 7948
Rashwood 52 SO 9164
Raskelf 91 SE 4971
Rassau 34 SO 1411
Rastrick 84 SE 1321
Ratagan 146 NG 9220
Ratby 66 SK 5105
Ratcliffe Culey 65 SP 3299
Ratcliffe on Soar 66 SK 4928
Ratcliffe on the Wreake 66 SK 6314
Rathen 151 NK 0060
Rathillet 134 NO 3620
Rathmell 90 SD 8059
Ratho 117 NT 1370
Rathven 150 NJ 4465
Ratlake 13 SU 4123
Ratley (Hants.) 13 SU 3223
Ratley (Warw.) 54 SP 3847
Ratlinghope 51 SO 4096
Rattar 159 ND 2672
Ratten Row 82 SD 4241
Rattery 6 SX 7361
Rattlesden 58 TL 9758
Rattray 134 NO 1745
Rauceby 80 TF 0146
Raughton Head 95 NY 3745
Raunds 55 SP 9972
Ravenfield 78 SK 4895
Ravenglass 88 SD 0896
Raveningham 71 TM 3996
Ravenscar 93 NZ 9801
Ravensdale 162 SC 3592
Ravensden 55 TL 0754
Ravenshead 78 SK 5654
Ravensmoor 63 SJ 6250
Ravensthorpe (Northants.) 54 SP 6670
Ravensthorpe (W Yorks.) 84 SE 2220
Ravenstone (Bucks.) 55 SP 8450
Ravenstone (Leic.) 66 SK 4013
Ravenstonedale 89 NY 7203
Ravenstruther 116 NS 9245
Ravensworth 97 NZ 1407
Raw 99 NZ 9305
Rawcliffe (Humbs.) 86 SE 6822
Rawcliffe (N Yorks.) 92 SE 5855
Rawcliffe Bridge 86 SE 6921
Rawdon 84 SE 2139
Rawmarsh 85 SK 4396
Rawreth 42 TQ 7793
Rawridge 9 ST 2006
Rawtenstall 83 SD 8122
Raydon 58 TM 0438
Raylees 104 NY 9291
Rayleigh 42 TQ 8090
Raymond's Hill 9 SY 3396
Rayne 42 TL 7222
Reach 57 TL 5666
Read 83 SD 7634
Reading 24 SU 7272
Reading Street 28 TQ 9230
Reagill 95 NY 6017
Rearquhar 154 NH 7492
Rearsby 66 SK 6514
Rease Heath 75 SJ 6454
Reaster 159 ND 2565
Reay 158 NC 9664
Reculver 29 TR 2269
Red Dial 94 NY 2545
Red Hill 53 SP 1355
Red Rock 82 SD 5809
Red Roses 31 SN 2012
Red Row 111 NZ 2599
Red Street 76 SJ 8251
Red Wharf 72 SH 5280
Red Wharf Bay (Gwyn.) 72 SH 5281
Redberth 30 SN 0804
Redbourn 40 TL 1012
Redbourne 86 SK 9699
Redbridge 27 TQ 4389
Redbrook (Clwyd) 63 SJ 5141
Redbrook (Glos.) 35 SO 5309
Redbrook Street 28 TQ 9336
Redburn (Highld.) 147 NH 5767
Redburn (Highld.) 148 NH 9447
Redcar 99 NZ 6024
Redcastle (Highld.) 147 NH 5849
Redcastle (Tays.) 135 NO 6850
Redcliff Bay 35 ST 4475
Redding 126 NS 9178
Reddingmuirhead 126 NS 9177
Reddish 76 SJ 8993
Redditch 53 SP 0468
Rede 57 TL 8055
Redenhall 59 TM 2684
Redesdale Camp 109 NY 8399
Redesmouth 104 NY 8782
Redford 135 NO 5644
Redfordgreen 109 NT 3616
Redgrave 58 TM 0478
Redheugh 142 NO 4463
Redhill (Avon) 21 ST 4962
Redhill (Grampn.) 150 NJ 6837
Redhill (Grampn.) 143 NJ 7704
Redhill (Surrey) 26 TQ 2850
Redisham 59 TM 4084
Redland (Avon) 35 ST 5875
Redland (Orkney) 163 HY 3724
Redlingfield 59 TM 1871
Redlynch (Somer.) 22 ST 6933
Redlynch (Wilts.) 12 SU 2020
Redmain 94 NY 1434
Redmarley D'Abitot 36 SO 7531
Redmarshall 98 NZ 3821
Redmile 67 SK 7935
Redmire 90 SE 0491
Redmoor 4 SX 0761
Rednal 63 SJ 3628
Redpath 118 NT 5835
Redpoint (Highld.) 145 NG 7368
Redruth 2 SW 6941
Redwick (Avon) 35 ST 5485
Redwick (Gwent) 35 ST 4184
Redworth 97 NZ 2423
Reed 56 TL 3636
Reed End 56 TL 3436
Reedham 71 TG 4201
Reedness 86 SE 7922
Reedy 8 SX 8189
Reepham (Lincs.) 80 TF 0373
Reepham (Norf.) 70 TG 1023
Reeth 90 SE 0499
Regaby 162 SC 4397
Reiff 152 NB 9614
Reigate 26 TQ 2550
Reighton 93 TA 1275
Reiss 159 ND 3354
Rejerrah 3 SW 8055
Releath 2 SW 6633
Relubbus 2 SW 5632
Relugas 149 NH 9948
Remenham 39 SU 7784
Remenham Hill 39 SU 7883
Rempstone 66 SK 5724
Rendcomb 37 SP 0109
Rendham 59 TM 3564
Renfrew 114 NS 4967
Renhold 56 TL 0953
Renishaw 78 SK 4477
Rennington 111 NU 2118
Renton 124 NS 3878
Renwick 95 NY 5943
Repps 71 TG 4116
Repton 65 SK 3026
Resaurie 147 NH 7145
Resipole 129 NM 7264
Resolis 148 NH 6765
Resolven 33 SN 8202
Reston 119 NT 8861
Reswallie 135 NO 5051
Retew 3 SW 9256
Retford 79 SK 7080
Rettendon 42 TQ 7698
Rettendon Place 42 TQ 7797
Revesby 81 TF 2961
Rew 7 SX 7570
Rewe 8 SX 9499
Rexon Cross 5 SX 4188
Reydon 59 TM 4977
Reymerston 70 TG 0206
Reynalton 31 SN 0909
Reynoldston 32 SS 4890
Rezare 5 SX 3677
Rhadyr 35 SO 3601
Rhandirmwyn 45 SN 7843
Rhayader 49 SN 9668
Rhedyn 60 SH 3032
Rheindown 147 NH 5147
Rhemore 129 NM 5750
Rhes-y-cae 74 SJ 1870
Rhewl (Clwyd) 74 SJ 1060
Rhewl (Clwyd) 62 SJ 1744
Rhian 154 NC 5717
Rhicarn 156 NC 0725
Rhiconich 156 NC 2552
Rhicullen 154 NH 6971
Rhifail 158 NC 7349
Rhigos 33 SN 9205
Rhilochan 155 NC 7407
Rhiwbina 34 ST 1681
Rhiwbryfdir 67 SH 6946
Rhiwderyn 34 ST 2587
Rhiwlas (Clwyd) 62 SJ 1931
Rhiwlas (Gwyn.) 73 SH 5765
Rhiwlas (Gwyn.) 62 SH 9237
Rhod-mad 48 SN 5875
Rhodes Minnis 29 TR 1542
Rhodesia 78 SK 5680
Rhodiad 30 SM 7627
Rhonehouse or Kelton Hill 102 NX 7459
Rhoose 20 ST 0666
Rhos (Dyfed) 44 SN 3835
Rhos (W Glam.) 33 SN 7303
Rhos Lligwy 72 SH 4986
Rhos-fawr 60 SH 3838
Rhos-on-Sea 73 SH 8480
Rhos-y-gwaliau 62 SH 9434
Rhos-y-llan 60 SH 2337
RhosMaen 45 SN 6323
Rhosaman 45 SN 7214
Rhoscefnhir 72 SH 5276
Rhoscolyn 72 SH 2675
Rhoscrowther 30 SM 9002
Rhosesmor 74 SJ 2168
Rhosgadfan 72 SH 5057
Rhosgoch 46 SO 1847
Rhosgoch (Gwyn.) 72 SH 4189
Rhoslan 60 SH 4841
Rhoslefain 48 SH 5705
Rhosllanerchrugog 62 SJ 2946
Rhosmeirch 72 SH 4677
Rhosneigr 72 SH 3172
Rhosnesni 63 SJ 3451
Rhossili 32 SS 4188
Rhosson 30 SM 7225
Rhostryfan 72 SH 4958
Rhostyllen 63 SJ 3148
Rhosybol 72 SH 4288
Rhosymedre 62 SJ 2842
Rhu (Strath.) 123 NR 8264
Rhu (Strath.) 124 NS 2783
Rhuallt 74 SJ 0774
Rhubodach 122 NS 0374
Rhuddlan 74 SJ 0277
Rhulen 46 SO 1349
Rhunahaorine 112 NR 7048
Rhyd (Gwyn.) 61 SH 6341
Rhyd (Powys) 49 SH 9801
Rhyd-Ddu 61 SH 5652
Rhyd-lydan 61 SH 8950
Rhyd-y-clafdy 60 SH 3235
Rhyd-y-meirch 35 SO 3107
Rhyd-yr-onnen 48 SH 6102
Rhydargaeau 44 SN 4326
Rhydcymerau 45 SN 5738
Rhydd 52 SO 8345
Rhydding 33 SS 7498
Rhydlewis 45 SN 3447
Rhydlios 60 SH 1830
Rhydowen 44 SN 4445
Rhydrosser 48 SN 5667
Rhydspence 46 SO 2447
Rhydtalog 74 SJ 2354
Rhydwyn 72 SH 3188
Rhydycroesau 62 SJ 2330
Rhydyfelin (Dyfed) 48 SN 5979
Rhydyfelin (Mid Glam.) 34 ST 0988
Rhydyfro 32 SN 7105
Rhydymain 61 SH 7922
Rhydymwyn 74 SJ 2066
Rhyl 74 SJ 0181
Rhymney 34 SO 1107
Rhynd 134 NO 1520
Rhynie (Grampn.) 150 NJ 4927
Rhynie (Highld.) 155 NH 8578
Ribbesford 52 SO 7874
Ribbleton 82 SD 5630
Ribchester 83 SD 6435
Ribigill 157 NC 5854
Riby 87 TA 1807
Riccall 85 SE 6237
Riccarton (Border) 108 NY 5596
Riccarton (Strath.) 114 NS 4235
Richards Castle 51 SO 4969
Richmond 91 NZ 1701
Richmond (Guernsey) 161 ZZ 9999
Richmond upon Thames 26 TQ 1874
Rickarton 143 NO 8188
Rickford 21 ST 4859
Rickham 7 SX 7437
Rickinghall Inferior 58 TM 0475
Rickinghall Superior 58 TM 0475
Rickling 41 TL 4931
Rickling Green 41 TL 5029
Rickmansworth 26 TQ 0594
Riddell 109 NT 5124
Riddlecombe 8 SS 6013
Riddlesden 84 SE 0742
Ridge (Dorset) 11 SY 9386
Ridge (Herts.) 40 TL 2100
Ridge (Wilts.) 22 ST 9531
Ridge Lane 65 SP 2994
Ridgebourne 50 SO 0560
Ridgehill (Avon) 21 ST 5362
Ridgemont 55 SP 9736
Ridgeway Cross 52 SO 7147
Ridgewell 57 TL 7340

Ridgewood Salwarpe

Ridgewood 16 TQ 4719
Riding Mill 104 NZ 0161
Ridley Green 75 SJ 5655
Ridlington (Leic.) 67 SK 8402
Ridlington (Norf.) 71 TG 3430
Ridsdale 104 NY 9084
Riechip 133 NO 0647
Rienachachait 156 NC 0530
Rievaulx 92 SE 5785
Rigg 103 NY 2966
Riggend 115 NS 7670
Righoul 148 NH 8851
Rigsby 81 TF 4375
Rigside 116 NS 8734
Riley Green 83 SD 6225
Rileyhill 65 SK 1115
Rilla Mill 5 SX 2973
Rillaton 5 SX 2973
Rillington 92 SE 8574
Rimington 83 SD 8045
Rimpton 10 ST 6021
Rimswell 87 TA 3128
Rinaston 30 SM 9825
Ring O'Bells 82 SD 4610
Ring's End 68 TF 3902
Ringford 101 NX 6857
Ringland 70 TG 1313
Ringmer 16 TQ 4412
Ringmore 6 SX 6545
Ringorm 149 NJ 2644
Ringsfield 59 TM 4088
Ringsfield Corner 59 TM 4187
Ringshall (Bucks.) 39 SP 9814
Ringshall (Suff.) 58 TM 0452
Ringshall Stocks 58 TM 0551
Ringstead (Norf.) 69 TF 7040
Ringstead (Northants.) 55 SP 9875
Ringwood 12 SU 1405
Ringwould 29 TR 3648
Rinmore 150 NJ 4118
Rinsey 2 SW 5927
Ripe 16 TQ 5010
Ripley (Derby.) 78 SK 3950
Ripley (Hants.) 12 SZ 1698
Ripley (N. Yorks.) 91 SE 2860
Ripley (Surrey) 26 TQ 0556
Riplingham 86 SE 9631
Ripon 91 SE 3171
Rippingale 68 TF 0927
Ripple (Here & W) 52 SO 8737
Ripple (Kent) 29 TR 3550
Ripponden 84 SE 0319
Risabus 120 NR 3143
Risbury 47 SO 5455
Risby (Suff.) 57 TL 7966
Risca 34 ST 2391
Rise 87 TA 1541
Risegate 68 TF 2029
Riseley (Beds.) 55 TL 0463
Riseley (Berks.) 25 SU 7263
Rishangles 58 TM 1568
Rishton 83 SD 7229
Rishworth 84 SE 0317
Risley (Chesh.) 75 SJ 6492
Risley (Derby.) 66 SK 4635
Risplith 91 SE 2467
Rispond 157 NC 4565
Rivar 23 SU 3161
Rivenhall End 42 TL 8316
River 14 SU 9322
River Bank 57 TL 5368
Riverhead 27 TQ 5156
Rivington 83 SD 6214
Roa Island 88 SD 2364
Roachhill 8 SS 8422
Roade 55 SP 7551
Roadmeetings 116 NS 8649
Roadside 159 ND 1560
Roadside of Kinneff 143 NO 8476
Roadwater 20 ST 0238
Roag 144 NG 2744
Roast Green 41 TL 4532
Roath 34 ST 1978
Roberton (Borders) 109 NT 4314
Roberton (Strath.) 108 NS 9428
Robertsbridge 16 TQ 7323
Roberttown 84 SE 1922
Robeston Cross 30 SM 8809
Robeston Wathen 30 SN 0815
Robin Hood's Bay 99 NZ 9505
Roborough 19 SS 5717
Roby 75 SJ 4291
Roby Mill 82 SD 5106
Rocester 65 SK 1039
Roch 30 SM 8821
Rochdale 83 SD 8913
Roche 4 SW 9860
Rochester (Kent) 28 TQ 7467
Rochester (Northum.) 110 NY 8397
Rochford (Essex) 42 TQ 8790
Rochford (Here & W) 51 SO 6268
Rock (Corn.) 4 SW 9475
Rock (Here & W) 52 SO 7371
Rock (Northum.) 111 NU 2020
Rock Ferry 74 SJ 3386
Rockbeare 9 SY 0195
Rockbourne 12 SU 1118
Rockcliffe (Cumbr.) 103 NY 3561
Rockcliffe (Dumf & G) 102 NX 8553
Rockcliffe Cross 102 NY 3463
Rockfield (Gwent) 47 SO 4814
Rockfield (Highld.) 155 NH 9282
Rockford (Devon) 19 SS 7547
Rockford (Hants.) 12 SU 1608
Rockhampton 36 ST 6593
Rockingham 67 SP 8691
Rockland All Saints 70 TL 9896
Rockland St. Mary 71 TG 3104
Rockland St. Peter 70 TL 9897
Rockley 23 SU 1571
Rockwell End 39 SU 7988
Rockwell Green 20 ST 1220
Rodbourne 36 ST 9383
Rodbridge Corner 58 TL 8643
Rodd 51 SO 3162
Roddam 111 NU 0220
Rodden 10 SY 6184
Roddymoor 97 NZ 1436
Rode 22 ST 8053
Rode Heath (Ches.) 76 SJ 8056
Rodeheath (Ches.) 76 SJ 8766
Rodel 163 NG 0483
Roden 63 SJ 5716
Rodhuish 20 ST 0139
Rodington 63 SJ 5814
Rodley 36 SO 7411
Rodmarton 36 ST 9397
Rodmell 16 TQ 4106
Rodmersham 28 TQ 9261
Rodney Stoke 21 ST 4849
Rodono 108 NT 2323
Rodsley 65 SK 2040
Rodway 20 ST 2540
Roe Green 41 TL 3133
Roecliffe 91 SE 3765
Roehampton 26 TQ 2373
Roewen 73 SH 7571
Roffey 15 TQ 1931
Rogart 155 NC 7303
Rogate 14 SU 8023
Rogerstone 34 ST 2688
Rogerton 115 NS 6256
Rogiet 35 ST 4587
Roker 105 NZ 4059
Rollesby 71 TG 4415
Rolleston (Leic.) 67 SK 7300
Rolleston (Notts.) 79 SK 7452
Rolleston (Staffs.) 65 SK 2327
Rolston 87 TA 2145
Rolvenden 28 TQ 8431
Rolvenden Layne 28 TQ 8530
Romaldkirk 96 NY 9921
Romanby 91 SE 3693
Romannobridge 117 NT 1547
Romansleigh 8 SS 7220
Romford 27 TQ 5188
Romiley 76 SJ 9390
Romsey 13 SU 3521
Romsley (Here & W) 52 SO 9679
Romsley (Salop) 52 SO 7883
Romsley Hill 52 SO 9678
Ronague 162 SC 2472
Rookhope 96 NY 9342
Rookley 13 SZ 5084
Rooks Bridge 21 ST 3752
Roos 87 TA 2830
Rootpark 116 NS 9554
Ropley 24 SU 6431
Ropley Dean 24 SU 6331
Ropsley 67 SK 9834
Rora 151 NK 0650
Rorandle 150 NJ 6518
Rorrington 51 SJ 3000
Rose 3 SW 7754
Rose Ash 8 SS 7821
Roseacre 82 SD 4336
Rosebank 116 NS 8049
Rosebrough 111 NU 1326
Rosebush 30 SN 0729
Rosedale Abbey 92 SE 7296
Roseden 111 NU 0321
Rosehearty 151 NJ 9367
Rosehill 63 SJ 6630
Roseisle 149 NJ 1367
Rosemarket 30 SM 9508
Rosemarkie 148 NH 7357
Rosemary Lane 9 ST 1514
Rosemount (Strath.) 106 NS 3729
Rosemount (Tays) 134 NO 2043
Rosenannon 3 SW 9566
Rosewell 117 NT 2862
Roseworthy 2 SW 6139
Rosgill 95 NY 5316
Roshven 137 NM 7078
Roskhill 144 NG 2745
Rosley 95 NY 3245
Roslin 117 NT 2663
Rosliston 65 SK 2416
Rosneath 124 NS 2583
Ross (Dumf & G) 101 NX 6444
Ross (Northum.) 119 NU 1336
Ross (Tays.) 132 NN 7621
Ross-on-Wye 46 SO 6024
Rossett 75 SJ 3657
Rossie Orchill 133 NO 0813
Rossington 85 SK 6298
Rosskeen 154 NH 6869
Roster 159 ND 2639
Rostherne 76 SJ 7483
Rosthwaite 94 NY 2514
Roston 65 SK 1241
Rosudgeon 2 SW 5529
Rosyth 126 NT 1183
Rothbury 111 NU 0601
Rotherby 66 SK 6716
Rotherfield 16 TQ 5529
Rotherfield Greys 25 SU 7282
Rotherfield Peppard 24 SU 7081
Rotherham 78 SK 4492
Rothersthorpe 54 SP 7156
Rotherwick 24 SU 7156
Rothes 149 NJ 2749
Rothesay 123 NS 0864
Rothiebrisbane 150 NJ 7437
Rothiemay 105 NJ 5447
Rothienorman 150 NJ 7235
Rothiesholm 163 HY 6123
Rothley 66 SK 5812
Rothley Plain 66 SK 5713
Rothmaise 150 NJ 6832
Rothwell (Lincs.) 87 TF 1599
Rothwell (Northants.) 55 SP 8181
Rothwell (W Yorks.) 85 SE 3428
Rotsea 93 TA 0651
Rottal 142 NO 3769
Rottingdean 15 TQ 3602
Rottington 94 NX 9613
Roud 13 SZ 5280
Rough Close 64 SJ 9239
Rougham 70 TF 8320
Rougham Green 58 TL 9061
Roughburn 139 NN 3781
Roughlee 83 SD 8440
Roughley 65 SP 1399
Roughpark 141 NJ 3412
Roughsike 109 NY 5275
Roughton (Lincs.) 80 TF 2364
Roughton (Norf.) 71 TG 2136
Roughton (Salop) 64 SO 7594
Roundham 10 ST 4209
Roundhay 85 SE 3235
Roundsbush 42 TL 8501
Roundstreet Common 15 TQ 0528
Roundway 22 SU 0163
Roundyhill 133 NO 3852
Rounton 98 NZ 4103
Rous Lench 53 SP 0153
Rousdon 9 SY 2990
Routenburn 114 NS 1961
Routh 87 TA 0842
Row (Corn.) 4 SX 0976
Row (Cumbr.) 89 SD 4589
Row (Cumbr.) 95 NY 6335
Row Heath 43 TM 1519
Rowanburn 103 NY 4177
Rowberrow 21 ST 4558
Rowde 22 ST 9762
Rowden 8 SX 6498
Rowfoot 104 NY 6860
Rowhedge 43 TM 0221
Rowhook 15 TQ 1234
Rowington 53 SP 2069
Rowland 77 SK 2072
Rowland's Castle 14 SU 7310
Rowland's Gill 105 NZ 1658
Rowledge 25 SU 8243
Rowley (Durham) 97 NZ 0848
Rowley (Humbs.) 86 SE 9732
Rowley (Salop) 51 SJ 3006
Rowley Regis 64 SO 9787
Rowlstone 47 SO 3727
Rowly 15 TQ 0441
Rowner 13 SU 5801
Rowney Green 53 SP 0471
Rownhams 13 SU 3816
Rowsham 39 SP 8518
Rowsley 77 SK 2566
Rowston 80 TF 0856
Rowton (Ches.) 75 SJ 4464
Rowton (Salop) 63 SJ 6119
Roxburgh 118 NT 6930
Roxby (Humbs.) 86 SE 9217
Roxby (N Yorks) 99 NZ 7616
Roxton 56 TL 1554
Roxwell 42 TL 6408
Roy Bridge 139 NN 2781
Royal Lemington Spa 53 SP 3166
Royal Tunbridge Wells 16 TQ 5839
Roydon (Essex) 41 TL 4009
Roydon (Norf.) 69 TF 7022
Roydon (Norf.) 58 TM 0980
Royston (Herts.) 56 TL 3541
Royston (S Yorks.) 85 SE 3611
Royton 83 SD 9207
Rozel (Jersey) 161 ZZ 9999
Ruabon 63 SJ 3043
Ruaig 162 NM 0647
Ruan Lanihorne 3 SW 8942
Ruan Major 2 SW 7016
Ruan Minor 2 SW 7115
Ruardean 47 SO 6117
Ruardean Hill 47 SO 6317
Ruardean Woodside 47 SO 6216
Rubery 52 SO 9777
Ruckcroft 95 NY 5344
Ruckhall Common 47 SO 4539
Ruckinge 28 TR 0233
Ruckland 81 TF 3378
Ruckley 51 SJ 5300
Ruddington 66 SK 5733
Rudge 22 ST 8252
Rudgeway 35 ST 6286
Rudgwick 15 TQ 0934
Rudhall 47 SO 6225
Rudley Green 42 TL 8303
Rudry 34 ST 1986
Rudston 93 TA 0967
Rudway Barton 8 SS 9301
Rudyard 76 SJ 9557
Rufford 82 SD 4515
Rufforth 92 SE 5251
Rugby 54 SP 5075
Rugeley 65 SK 0418
Ruilick 147 NH 5046
Ruishton 20 ST 2624
Ruislip 26 TQ 0987
Rumbling Bridge 126 NT 0199
Rumburgh 59 TM 3581
Rumford 4 SW 8970
Rumney 34 ST 2179
Runcorn 75 SJ 5182
Runcton 14 SU 8802
Runcton Holme 69 TF 6109
Runfold 25 SU 8747
Runhall 70 TG 0507
Runham 71 TG 4610
Runnington 9 ST 1121
Runswick 99 NZ 8016
Runtaleave 141 NO 2867
Runwell 42 TQ 7494
Rush Green 27 TQ 5187
Rushall (Here & W) 47 SO 6434
Rushall (Norf.) 59 TM 1982
Rushall (W Mids.) 65 SK 0201
Rushall (Wilts.) 23 SU 1255
Rushbrooke 58 TL 8961
Rushbury 51 SO 5191
Rushden (Herts.) 41 TL 3031
Rushden (Northants.) 55 SP 9566
Rushford (Devon) 5 SX 4476
Rushford (Norf.) 58 TL 9281
Rushlake Green 16 TQ 6218
Rushmere 59 TM 4987
Rushmere St. Andrew 59 TM 2046
Rushmoor 25 SU 8740
Rushock 52 SO 8871
Rusholme 76 SJ 8494
Rushton (Ches.) 75 SJ 5863
Rushton (Northants) 55 SP 8483
Rushton (Salop) 51 SJ 6008
Rushton Spencer 76 SJ 9363
Rushwick 52 SO 8353
Rushyford 97 NZ 2828
Ruskie 125 NN 6200
Ruskington 80 TF 0850
Rusland 88 SD 3488
Rusper 15 TQ 2037
Ruspidge 36 SO 6512
Russ Hill 15 TQ 2240
Russell's Water 38 SU 7089
Rusthall 16 TQ 5639
Rustington 15 TQ 0502
Ruston Parva 93 TA 0661
Ruswarp 99 NZ 8809
Rutherford 118 NT 6530
Rutherglen 115 NS 6161
Ruthernbridge 4 SX 0166
Ruthin 74 SJ 1257
Ruthrieston 143 NJ 9204
Ruthven (Grampn.) 150 NJ 5046
Ruthven (Tays.) 134 NO 2848
Ruthvoes 3 SW 9360

S

Ruthwaite 94 NY 2436
Ruthwell 103 NY 1067
Ruyton-XI-Towns 63 SJ 3922
Ryal 104 NZ 0174
Ryal Fold 83 SD 6621
Ryall (Dorset) 10 SY 4094
Ryall (Here & W) 52 SO 8540
Ryarsh 27 TQ 6659
Rydal 89 NY 3606
Ryde 13 SZ 5992
Rye 17 TQ 9220
Rye Court 52 SO 7735
Rye Foreign 17 TQ 8822
Rye Harbour 17 TQ 9419
Rye Street 52 SO 7835
Ryhall 67 TF 0311
Ryhill 85 SE 3814
Ryhope 98 NZ 4152
Rylstone 90 SD 9758
Ryme Intrinseca 10 ST 5810
Ryther 85 SE 5539
Ryton (Glos.) 36 SO 7232
Ryton (N Yorks.) 92 SE 7975
Ryton (Salop) 64 SJ 7502
Ryton (Tyne and Wear) 105 NZ 1564
Ryton-on-Dunsmore 54 SP 3874
Sabden 83 SD 7737
Sacombe 41 TL 3419
Sacriston 97 NZ 2447
Sadberge 98 NZ 3416
Saddell 112 NR 7832
Saddington 66 SP 6591
Saddle Bow 69 TF 6015
Saffron Walden 57 TL 5438
Sageston 30 SN 0502
Saham Hills 70 TF 9003
Saham Toney 70 TF 9002
Saighton 75 SJ 4462
Saint Hill (Devon) 9 ST 0908
Saint Hill (W. Susx.) 16 TQ 3835
Saintbury 53 SP 1139
Salcombe 6 SX 7338
Salcombe Regis 9 SY 1488
Salcott 42 TL 9413
Sale 76 SJ 7990
Sale Green 52 SO 9358
Saleby 81 TF 4578
Salehurst 17 TQ 7424
Salem (Dyfed) 45 SN 6226
Salem (Dyfed) 48 SN 6684
Salem (Gwyn.) 72 SH 5456
Salen (Highld.) 129 NM 6864
Salen (Island of Mull) 129 NM 5743
Sales Point 43 TM 0209
Salesbury 83 SD 6732
Salford (Beds.) 55 SP 9339
Salford (Gtr Mches.) 76 SJ 7796
Salford (Oxon.) 37 SP 2828
Salford Priors 53 SP 0751
Salfords 15 TQ 2846
Salhouse 71 TG 3114
Saline 126 NT 0292
Salisbury 23 SU 1429
Salkeld Dykes 95 NY 5536
Sall 70 TG 1024
Sallachy (Highld.) 146 NG 9130
Salmonby 81 TF 3273
Salmond's Muir 135 NO 5837
Salperton 37 SP 0720
Salph End 56 TL 0752
Salsburgh 116 NS 8262
Salt 64 SJ 9527
Saltash 5 SX 4258
Saltburn 154 NH 7269
Saltburn-by-the-Sea 99 NZ 6621
Saltby 67 SK 8426
Saltcoats 113 NS 2441
Saltdean 16 TQ 3802
Salter 89 SD 6063
Salterbeck 94 NY 0025
Salterforth 83 SD 8845
Saltergate Inn 92 SE 8595
Salters Lode 69 TF 5801
Salterswall 75 SJ 6267
Salterton 23 SU 1236
Saltfleet 81 TF 4593
Saltfleetby All Saints 81 TF 4590
Saltfleetby St. Clements 81 TF 4591
Saltfleetby St. Peter 81 TF 4389
Saltford 22 ST 6867
Salthouse 70 TG 0743
Saltmarshe 86 SE 7824
Saltness 163 ND 2790
Saltney 75 SJ 3864
Salton 92 SE 7180
Saltrens 18 SS 4522
Saltwick 105 NZ 1780
Saltwood 29 TR 1536
Salum 162 NM 0748
Salwarpe 52 SO 8762

258

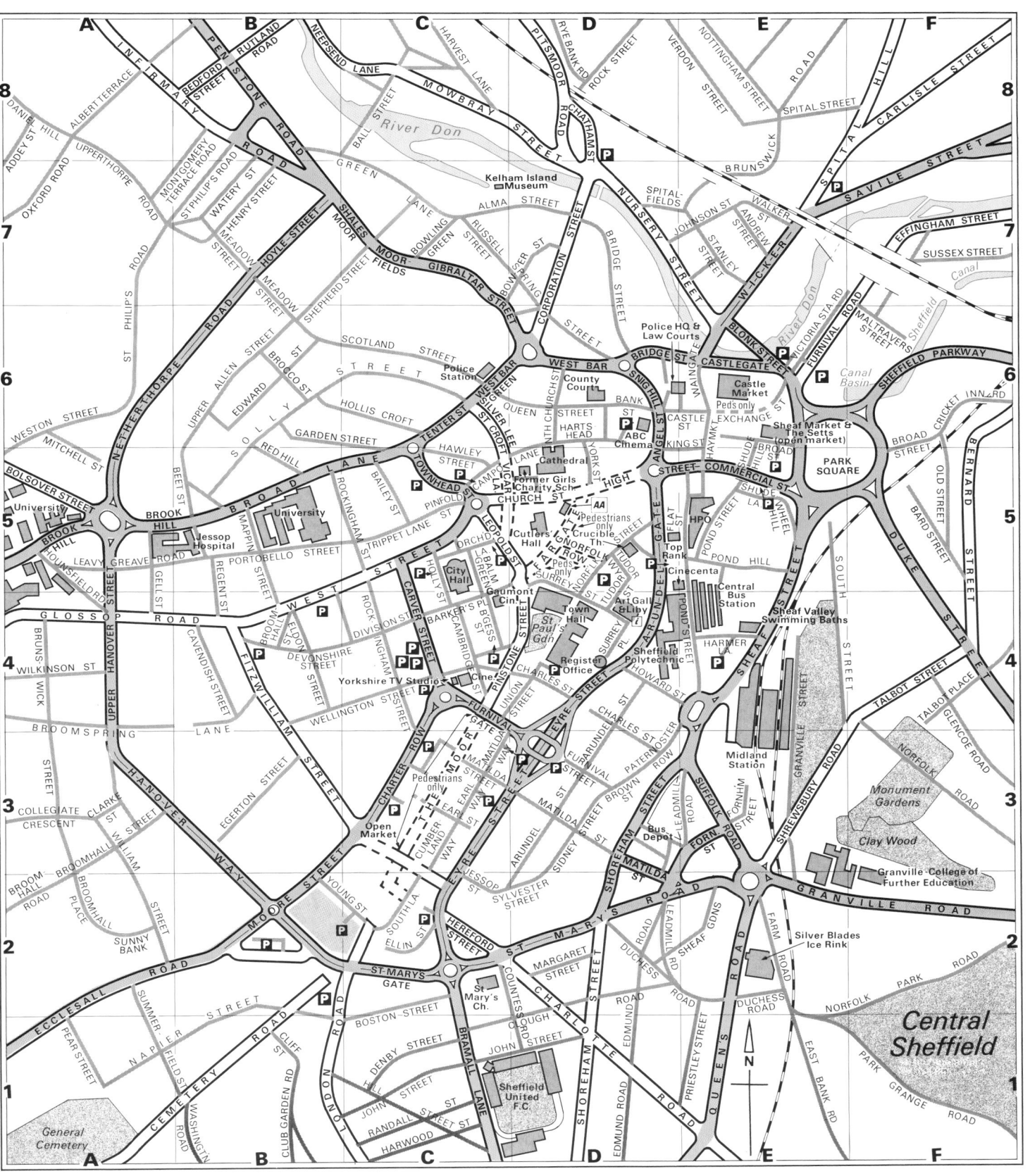

Central Sheffield

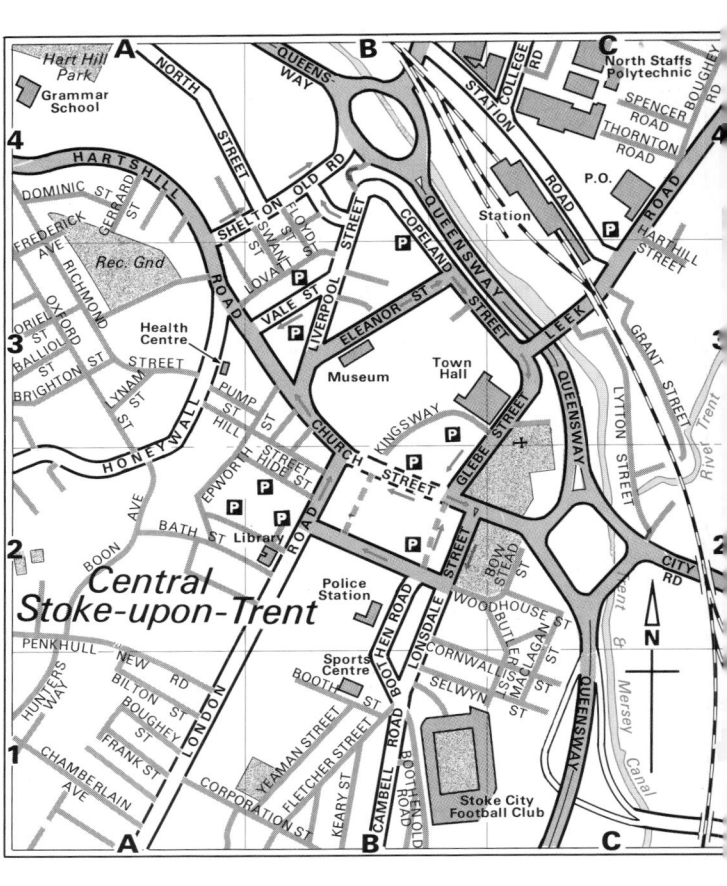

Central Stoke-upon-Trent

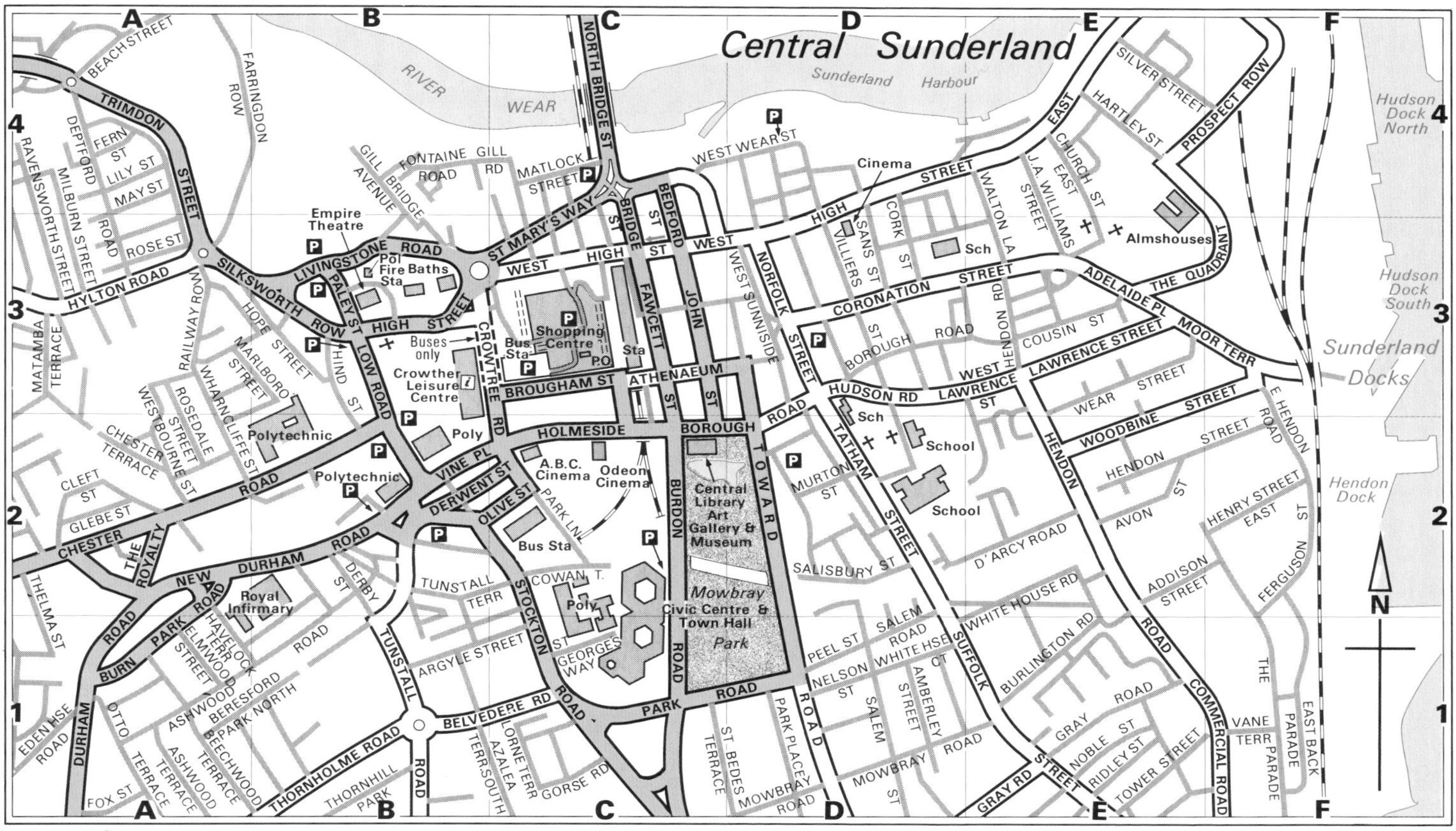

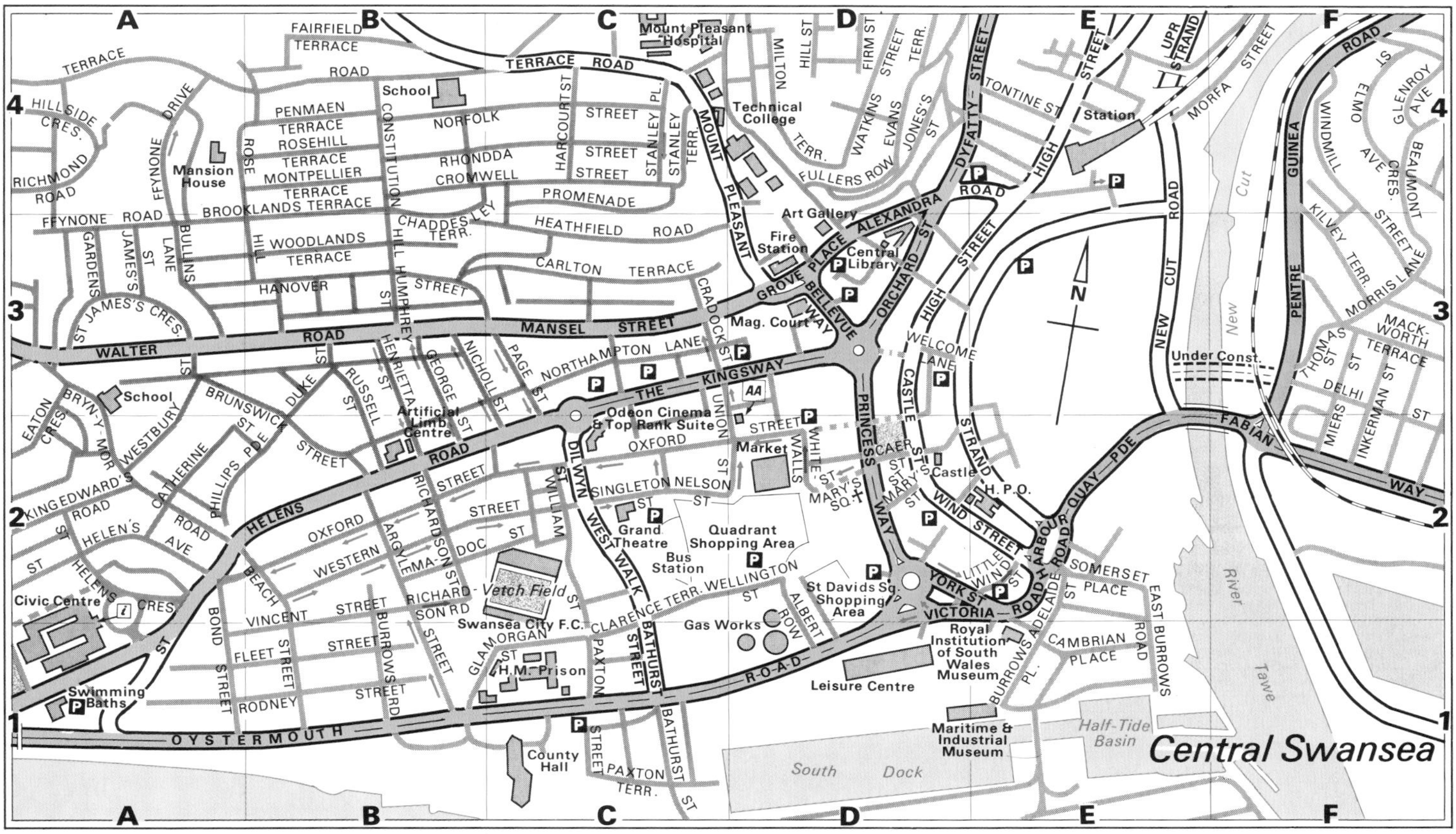

Central Sunderland

Central Swansea

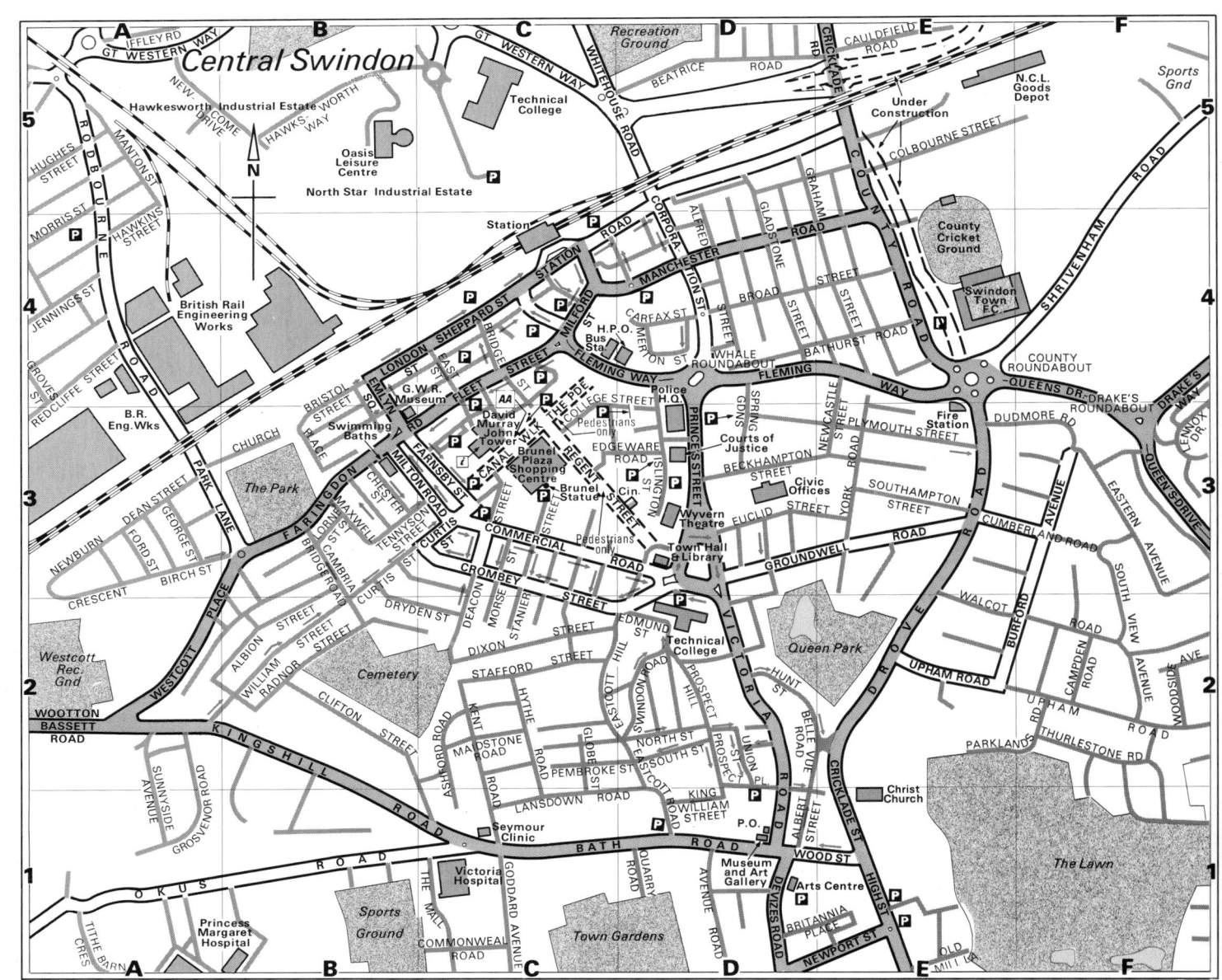

Swaton Thorpe in Balne

Swaton 68 TF 1337
Swavesey 56 TL 3668
Sway 12 SZ 2798
Swayfield 67 SK 9822
Swaythling 13 SU 4315
Sweetham 8 SX 8799
Sweets 4 SX 1595
Sweetshouse 4 SX 0861
Swefling 59 TM 3463
Swepstone 66 SK 3610
Swerford 38 SP 3731
Swettenham 76 SJ 8067
Swffryd 34 ST 2299
Swilland 59 TM 1853
Swillington 85 SE 3830
Swimbridge 19 SS 6230
Swinbrook 37 SP 2812
Swinderby 79 SK 8662
Swindon (Glos.) 36 SO 9325
Swindon (Staffs.) 64 SO 8690
Swindon (Wilts.) 37 SU 1484
Swine 87 TA 1335
Swinefleet 86 SE 7621
Swineford 22 ST 6968
Swineshead (Beds.) 55 TL 0565
Swineshead (Lincs.) 68 TF 2340
Swineshead Bridge 68 TF 2142
Swiney 159 ND 2335
Swinford (Leic.) 54 SP 5679
Swinford (Oxon.) 38 SP 4408
Swingfield Minnis 29 TR 2142
Swinhill 115 NS 7748
Swinhoe 119 NU 2028
Swinhope 87 TF 2196
Swinithwaite 90 SE 0489
Swinscoe 77 SK 1347
Swinside Hall 110 NT 7216
Swinstead 67 TF 0122
Swinton (Borders) 118 NT 8447
Swinton (Gtr Mches.) 83 SD 7701
Swinton (N Yorks.) 91 SE 2179
Swinton (N Yorks.) 92 SE 7573
Swinton (S Yorks.) 85 SK 4499
Swintonmill 118 NT 8145
Swithland 66 SK 5413
Swordale 147 NH 5765
Swordly 158 NC 7363
Sworton Heath 76 SJ 6884
Swyddffynnon 48 SN 6966
Swynnerton 64 SJ 8435
Swyre 10 SY 5288
Syde 36 SO 9411
Sydenham (Gtr London) 26 TQ 3571
Sydenham (Oxon.) 39 SP 7301
Sydenham Damerel 5 SX 4075
Sydenhurst 25 SU 9534
Syderstone 70 TF 8332
Sydling St. Nicholas 10 SY 6399
Sydmonton 24 SU 4857
Syerston 79 SK 7447
Syke 83 SD 8915
Sykehouse 85 SE 6216
Sykes 83 SD 6251
Syleham 59 TM 2178
Sylen 32 SN 5107
Symbister 163 HU 5362
Symington (Strath.) 114 NS 3831
Symington (Strath.) 116 NS 9935
Symonds Yat 47 SO 5516
Symondsbury 10 SY 4493
Synod Inn 44 SN 4054
Syre 157 NC 6843
Syreford 37 SP 0320
Syresham 54 SP 6241
Syston (Leic.) 66 SK 6211
Syston (Lincs.) 67 SK 9240
Sytchampton 52 SO 8466
Sywell 55 SP 8267

T

Tackley 38 SP 4720
Tacolneston 70 TM 1395
Tadcaster 85 SE 4843
Tadden 11 ST 9801
Taddington (Derby) 77 SK 1471
Taddington (Glos.) 37 SP 0831
Taddiport 19 SS 4818
Tadley 24 SU 6060
Tadlow 56 TL 2847
Tadmarton 54 SP 3937
Tadworth 26 TQ 2356
Tafarn-y-Gelyn 74 SJ 1861
Tafarnaubach 34 SO 1110
Taff Merthyr Garden Village 34 ST 1198
Taff's Well 34 ST 1283
Tafolwern 49 SH 8902
Tai'n-lon 60 SH 4450
Tai'r Bull 46 SN 9926
Tai-bach (Clwyd) 62 SJ 1528
Taibach (W Glam.) 33 SS 7789
Tain (Highld.) 159 ND 2266
Tain (Highld.) 155 NH 7782
Takeley 41 TL 5521
Takeley Street 41 TL 5421
Tal-y-Bont (Gwyn.) 73 SH 7668
Tal-y-bont (Gwyn.) 61 SH 5921
Tal-y-bont (Gwyn.) 73 SH 6070
Tal-y-cafn 73 SH 7971
Tal-y-llyn (Gwyn.) 48 SH 7109
Talachddu 46 SO 0733
Talacre 74 SJ 1284
Talaton 9 SY 0699
Talbenny 30 SM 8412
Talerddig 49 SH 9300
Talgarreg 44 SN 4251
Talgarth 46 SO 1534
Taliesin 48 SN 6591
Talisker 144 NG 3230
Talke 76 SJ 8253
Talkin 95 NY 5557
Talla Linnfoots 108 NT 1421
Talladale 152 NG 9270
Tallentire 94 NY 1035
Talley 45 SN 6332
Tallington 68 TF 0908
Talmine 157 NC 5862
Talog 44 SN 3325
Talsarn 45 SN 5456
Talsarnau 61 SH 6135
Talskiddy 3 SW 9165
Talwrn 72 SH 4876
Talybont (Dyfed) 48 SN 6589
Talybont-on-Usk 46 SO 1122
Talysarn 72 SH 4852
Talywern 49 SH 8200
Tamerton Foliot 5 SX 4761
Tamworth 65 SK 2004
Tan Hill 96 NY 8907
Tan-lan 73 SH 7963
Tan-y-fron 73 SH 9564
Tan-y-groes 44 SN 2849
Tandridge 27 TQ 3750
Tanfield 97 NZ 1855
Tangley 23 SU 3352
Tangmere 14 SU 9006
Tankersley 85 SK 3499
Tankerton 29 TR 1267
Tannach 159 ND 3247
Tannachie 142 NO 7884
Tannadice 135 NO 4758
Tannington 59 TM 2467
Tansley 78 SK 3259
Tansor 67 TL 0590
Tantobie 97 NZ 1754
Tanton 98 NZ 5210
Tanworth in Arden 53 SP 1170
Tanygrisiau 61 SH 6845
Taplow 25 SU 9182
Tarbert (Gigha) 112 NR 6553
Tarbert (Harris) 163 NB 1500
Tarbert (Jura) 122 NR 6082
Tarbert (Strath.) 123 NR 8668
Tarbet (Highld.) 156 NC 1648
Tarbet (Highld.) 137 NM 7992
Tarbet (Strath.) 124 NN 3104
Tarbock Green 75 SJ 4687
Tarbolton 106 NS 4327
Tarbrax 116 NT 0255
Tardebigge 53 SO 9969
Tarfside 142 NO 4979
Tarland 142 NJ 4804
Tarleton 82 SD 4420
Tarlscough 82 SD 4313
Tarlton 36 ST 9599
Tarnbrook 82 SD 5855
Tarnside 89 SD 4391
Tarporley 75 SJ 5562
Tarr 20 ST 1030
Tarrant Crawford 11 ST 9203
Tarrant Gunville 11 ST 9212
Tarrant Hinton 11 ST 9310
Tarrant Keynston 11 ST 9204
Tarrant Launceston 11 ST 9409
Tarrant Monkton 11 ST 9408
Tarrant Rawston 11 ST 9306
Tarrant Rushton 11 ST 9305
Tarring Neville 16 TQ 4404
Tarrington 47 SO 6140
Tarsappie 134 NO 1220
Tarskavaig 137 NG 5810
Tarves 151 NJ 8631
Tarvie 141 NO 0264
Tarvin 75 SJ 4867
Tasburgh 71 TM 2096
Tasley 64 SO 6994
Taston 38 SP 3521
Tatenhill 65 SK 2022
Tathwell 81 TF 3282
Tatsfield 27 TQ 4156
Tattenhall 75 SJ 4858
Tatterford 70 TF 8628
Tattersett 70 TF 8429
Tattershall 80 TF 2157
Tattershall Bridge 80 TF 1956
Tattershall Thorpe 80 TF 2159
Tattingstone 58 TM 1337
Tatworth 9 ST 3205
Tauchers 149 NJ 3850
Taunton 20 ST 2324
Taverham 70 TG 1513
Tavernspite 31 SN 1812
Tavistock 5 SX 4774
Taw green 8 SX 6497
Tawstock 19 SS 5529
Taxal 76 SK 0079
Tayinloan 112 NR 6945
Taynish 123 NR 7283
Taynton (Glos.) 36 SO 7221
Taynton (Oxon.) 37 SP 2313
Taynuilt 130 NN 0031
Tayport 135 NO 4528
Tayvallich 123 NR 7386
Tealby 80 TF 1590
Teangue 137 NG 6609
Teanord 146 NH 5965
Tebay 89 NY 6104
Tebworth 39 SP 9926
Tedburn St. Mary 8 SX 8194
Teddington (Glos.) 52 SO 9632
Teddington (Gtr London) 26 TQ 1671
Tedstone Delamere 52 SO 6958
Tedstone Wafre 52 SO 6759
Teeton 54 SP 6970
Teffont Evias 22 ST 9831
Teffont Magna 22 ST 9832
Tegryn 44 SN 2233
Teigh 67 SK 8616
Teign Village 7 SX 8381
Teigngrace 7 SX 8474
Teignmouth 7 SX 9473
Telford 64 SJ 6909
Tellisford 22 ST 8055
Telscombe 16 TQ 4003
Telscombe Cliffs 16 TQ 3901
Templand 108 NY 0886
Temple (Corn.) 4 SX 1473
Temple (Lothian) 117 NT 3158
Temple (Strath.) 115 NS 5469
Temple Balsall 53 SP 2075
Temple Bar 45 SN 5354
Temple Cloud 21 ST 6157
Temple Ewell 29 TR 2844
Temple Grafton 53 SP 1254
Temple Guiting 37 SP 0928
Temple Hirst 85 SE 6025
Temple Normanton 78 SK 4167
Temple Sowerby 95 NY 6127
Templecombe 10 ST 7022
Templeton (Devon.) 8 SS 8813
Templeton (Dyfed) 31 SN 1111
Templeton Bridge 8 SS 8714
Tempsford 56 TL 1653
Ten Mile Bank 69 TL 6097
Tenbury Wells 51 SO 5968
Tenby 31 SN 1300
Tendring 43 TM 1424
Tendring Green 43 TM 1425
Tendring Heath 43 TM 1326
Tenterden 28 TQ 8833
Terling 42 TL 7715
Ternhill 63 SJ 6332
Terregles 102 NX 9377
Terrington 92 SE 6670
Terrington St. Clement 69 TF 5520
Terrington St. John 69 TF 5416
Teston 27 TQ 7053
Testwood 13 SU 3514
Tetbury 36 ST 8993
Tetbury Upton 36 ST 8795
Tetchill 63 SJ 3832
Tetcott 5 SX 3396
Tetford 81 TF 3374
Tetney 87 TA 3101
Tetney Lock 87 TA 3402
Tetsworth 38 SP 6802
Tettenhall 64 SJ 8801
Teversal 78 SK 4861
Teversham 57 TL 4958
Teviothead 109 NT 4005
Tewin 41 TL 2714
Tewkesbury 52 SO 8933
Teynham 28 TQ 9663
Thackthwaite 94 NY 1524
Thakeham 15 TQ 1017
Thame 38 SP 7006
Thames Ditton 26 TQ 1567
Thames Haven 42 TQ 7581
Thamesmead 27 TQ 4779
Thaneston 142 NO 6375
Thanington 29 TR 1356
Thankerton 116 NS 9737
Tharston 71 TM 1894
Thatcham 24 SU 5167
Thatto Heath 75 SJ 5093
Thaxted 42 TL 6131
The Arms 70 TL 8797
The Bank 51 SO 6199
The Bourne 52 SO 9756
The Bratch 64 SO 8693
The Bryn 35 SO 3309
The City 39 SU 7896
The Common 37 SU 0285
The Common 11 ST 7810
The Crossways 47 SO 3538
The Den 114 NS 3251
The Fence 35 SO 5405
The Grove 52 SO 8640
The Haven 15 TQ 0830
The Haw 36 SO 8427
The Ling 71 TM 3098
The Narth 35 SO 5206
The Pole of Itlaw 150 NJ 6857
The Reddings 36 SO 9021
The Sands 25 SU 8846
The Sheet 51 SO 5374
The Shoe 22 ST 8074
The Smeeth 69 TF 5209
The Smithies 51 SO 6897
The Stocks 17 TQ 9127
The Straits 25 SU 7839
The Vale 15 TQ 1207
Theakston 91 SE 3085
Thealby 86 SE 8917
Theale (Berks.) 24 SU 6371
Theale (Somer.) 21 ST 4646
Thearne 87 TA 0736
Theberton 59 TM 4365
Thedden Grange 24 SU 6839
Theddingworth 54 SP 6685
Theddlethorpe All Saints 81 TF 4688
Theddlethorpe St. Helen 81 TF 4788
Thelbridge Barton 8 SS 7812
Thelbridge Cross 8 SS 7812
Thelnetham 58 TM 0178
Thelveton 58 TM 1681
Thelwall 75 SJ 6587
Themelthorpe 70 TG 0524
Thenford 54 SP 5141
Therfield 56 TL 3337
Thetford 58 TL 8783
Thetwaite 94 NY 3744
Theydon Bois 27 TQ 4598
Thickwood 22 ST 8272
Thimble End 53 SP 1394
Thimbleby (Linc.) 80 TF 2369
Thimbleby (N Yorks.) 91 SE 4495
Thirkleby 91 SE 4778
Thirlby 91 SE 4884
Thirlestane 118 NT 5647
Thirn 91 SE 2185
Thirsk 91 SE 4282
Thistleton (Lancs.) 82 SD 4037
Thistleton (Leics.) 67 SK 9118
Thistley Green 57 TL 6776
Thixendale 92 SE 8461
Thockrington 104 NY 9579
Tholomas Drove 68 TF 4006
Tholthorpe 91 SE 4766
Thomas Chapel 31 SN 1008
Thomastown (Grampn.) 150 NJ 5737
Thomastown (Mid Glam.) 34 ST 0086
Thompson 70 TL 9296
Thomshill 149 NJ 2157
Thong 27 TQ 6770
Thongsbridge 84 SE 1510
Thongsleigh 8 SS 9011
Thoralby 90 SE 0086
Thoresby 79 SK 6371
Thoresway 87 TF 1696
Thorganby (Lincs.) 87 TF 2097
Thorganby (N Yorks.) 86 SE 6841
Thorgill 92 SE 7096
Thorington 59 TM 4274
Thorington Street 43 TM 0135
Thorlby 90 SD 9652
Thorley 41 TL 4719
Thorley Street 13 SZ 3788
Thormanby 91 SE 4974
Thornaby-on-Tees 98 NZ 4518
Thornage 70 TG 0436
Thornborough (Bucks.) 39 SP 7433
Thornborough (N Yorks.) 91 SE 2979
Thornbury 84 SE 2033
Thornbury (Avon) 36 ST 6390
Thornbury (Devon.) 18 SS 4008
Thornbury (Here & W) 47 SO 6159
Thornby (Cumbr.) 102 NY 2952
Thornby (Northants.) 54 SP 6675
Thorncliff 76 SK 0158
Thorncombe 10 ST 3703
Thorncombe Street 14 TQ 0042
Thorncross 13 SZ 4381
Thorndon 58 TM 1469
Thorndon Cross 5 SX 5293
Thorne 86 SE 6813
Thorne St. Margaret 9 ST 0920
Thornehillhead 18 SS 4116
Thorner 85 SE 3740
Thorney (Cambs.) 68 TF 2804
Thorney (Notts.) 79 SK 8572
Thorney (Somer.) 10 ST 4222
Thorney Hill 12 SZ 2099
Thorney Island 14 SU 7503
Thorney Toll 68 TF 3404
Thornfalcon 20 ST 2723
Thornford 10 ST 6013
Thorngrafton 104 NY 7966
Thorngrove 21 ST 3632
Thorngumbald 87 TA 2026
Thornham 69 TF 7343
Thornham Magna 58 TM 1071
Thornham Parva 58 TM 1072
Thornhaugh 67 TF 0600
Thornhill (Central) 125 NS 6699
Thornhill (Cumbr.) 88 NY 0109
Thornhill (Derby.) 77 SK 1983
Thornhill (Dumf & G) 107 NX 8795
Thornhill (Hants.) 13 SU 4612
Thornhill (Mid Glam.) 34 ST 1584
Thornhill (W Yorks.) 84 SE 2418
Thornhill (Wilts.) 37 SU 0778
Thornholme 93 TA 1164
Thornicombe 11 ST 8703
Thornley (Durham) 97 NZ 1137
Thornley (Durham) 98 NZ 3639
Thornley Gate 104 NY 8356
Thornliebank 115 NS 5459
Thorns 57 TL 7455
Thornthwaite (Cumbr.) 94 NY 2225
Thornthwaite (N Yorks.) 91 SE 1858
Thornton 98 NZ 4713
Thornton (Bucks.) 39 SP 7535
Thornton (Fife.) 126 NT 2897
Thornton (Humbs.) 86 SE 7545
Thornton (Lancs.) 82 SD 3342
Thornton (Leic.) 66 SK 4607
Thornton (Lincs.) 80 TF 2467
Thornton (Mers.) 82 SD 3300
Thornton (Northum.) 119 NT 9547
Thornton (Tays.) 134 NO 3946
Thornton (W Yorks.) 84 SE 1032
Thornton Curtis 87 TA 0817
Thornton Dale 92 SE 8383
Thornton Hough 74 SJ 3080
Thornton Rust 90 SD 9788
Thornton Steward 91 SE 1787
Thornton Watlass 91 SE 2385
Thornton le Moor (Lincs.) 86 TF 0496
Thornton-in-Craven 83 SD 9048
Thornton-le-Beans 91 SE 3990
Thornton-le-Clay 92 SE 6875
Thornton-le-Moor (N Yorks.) 91 SE 3988
Thornton-le-Moors 75 SJ 4474
Thorntonhall 115 NS 5955
Thorntonloch 118 NT 7574
Thorntonpark 119 NT 9448
Thornwood Common 41 TL 4705
Thoroton 67 SK 7642
Thorp Arch 85 SE 4346
Thorpe (Derby.) 77 SK 1550
Thorpe (Humbs.) 86 SE 9946
Thorpe (Lincs.) 81 TF 4982
Thorpe (N Yorks.) 86 SE 0161
Thorpe (Norf) 71 TM 4398
Thorpe (Notts.) 77 SK 7649
Thorpe (Surrey) 26 TQ 0268
Thorpe Abbotts 59 TM 1979
Thorpe Acre 66 SK 5120
Thorpe Arnold 67 SK 7620
Thorpe Audlin 85 SE 4715
Thorpe Bassett 92 SE 8573
Thorpe Bay 42 TQ 9284
Thorpe Constantine 65 SK 2608
Thorpe End Garden Village 71 TG 2811
Thorpe Green (Essex) 43 TM 1723
Thorpe Green (Suff.) 58 TL 9354
Thorpe Hesley 85 SK 3796
Thorpe Langton 67 SP 7492
Thorpe Larches 98 NZ 3862
Thorpe Malsor 55 SP 8379
Thorpe Mandeville 54 SP 5345
Thorpe Market 71 TG 2436
Thorpe Morieux 58 TL 9453
Thorpe Salvin 78 SK 5281
Thorpe Satchville 67 SK 7311
Thorpe St. Andrew 71 TG 2609
Thorpe St. Peter 81 TF 4861
Thorpe Thewless 98 NZ 4023
Thorpe Underwood (N. Yorks.) 91 SE 4659
Thorpe Underwood (Northants.) 55 SP 7880
Thorpe Waterville 55 TL 0281
Thorpe Willoughby 85 SE 5731
Thorpe by Water 67 SP 8996
Thorpe in Balne 85 SE 5910

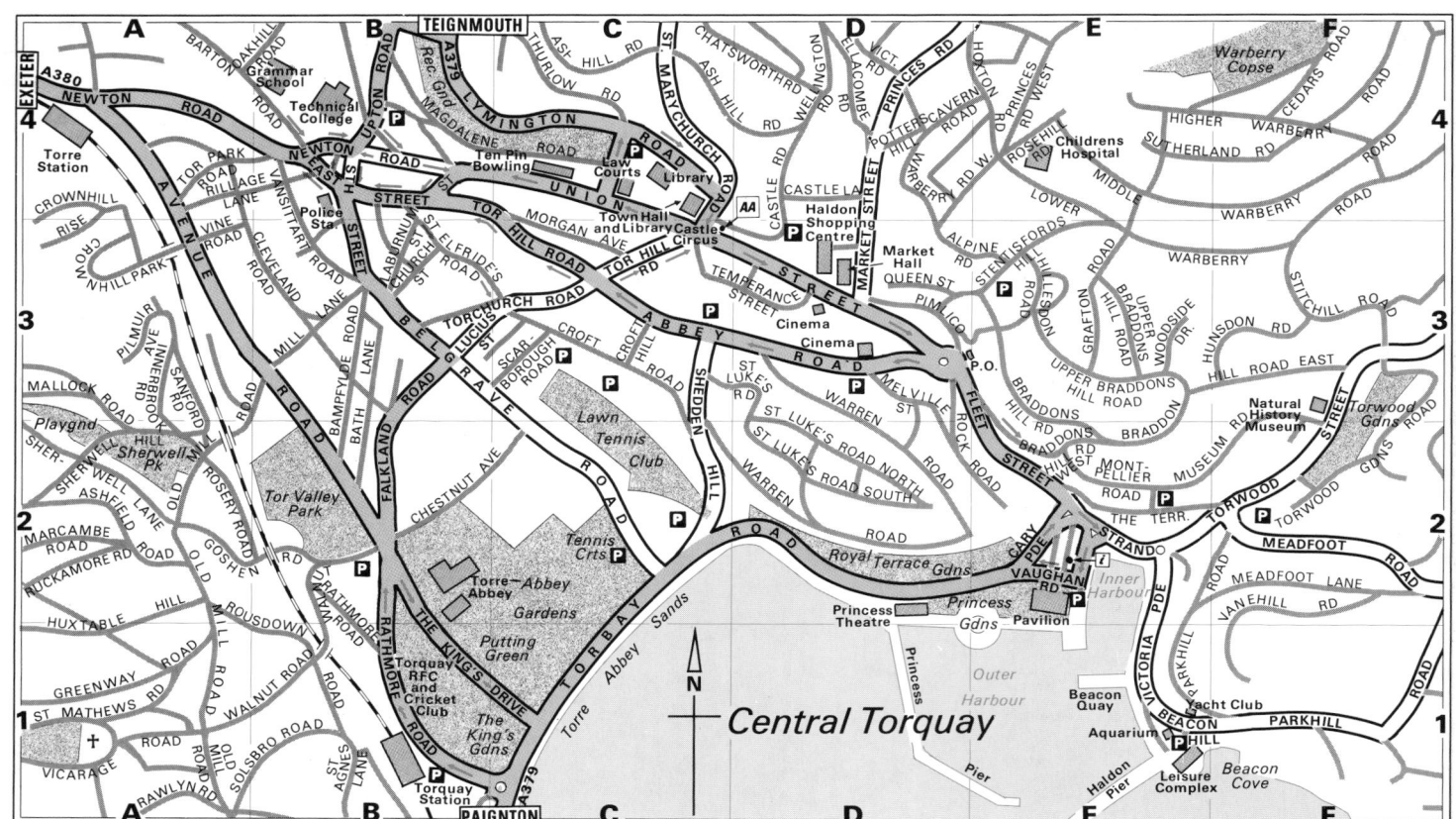

Tondu Tytherington (Avon)

Tondu 33 SS 8984
Tonfanau 48 SH 5604
Tong (Isle of Lewis) 163 NB 4436
Tong (Salop) 64 SJ 7907
Tong Norton 64 SJ 7908
Tonge 66 SK 4123
Tongham 25 SU 8848
Tongland 102 NX 6953
Tongue 157 NC 5957
Tongue End 68 TF 1518
Tongwynlais 34 ST 1581
Tonmawr 33 SS 8096
Tonna 33 SS 7798
Tonwell 41 TL 3317
Tonypandy 33 SS 9992
Tonyrefail 34 ST 0188
Toot Baldon 38 SP 5600
Toot Hill (Essex) 41 TL 5102
Toot Hill (Hants.) 13 SU 3718
Toothill 37 SU 1283
Topcliffe 91 SE 3976
Topcroft 71 TM 2693
Topcroft Street 71 TM 2692
Toppesfield 57 TL 7337
Toppings 83 SD 7213
Toprow 70 TM 1698
Topsham 8 SX 9788
Torbay 7 SX 8962
Torbeg 112 NR 8929
Torbryan 7 SX 8266
Torcastle 138 NN 1378
Torcross 7 SX 8242
Tore 147 NH 6052
Torksey 79 SK 8378
Torlundy 138 NN 1477
Tormarton 36 ST 7678
Tormisdale 120 NR 1858
Tormitchell 106 NX 2394
Tormore 112 NR 8932
Tornagrain 148 NH 7649
Tornahaish 142 NJ 2908
Tornaveen 142 NJ 6106
Torness 147 NH 5727
Toronto 97 NZ 1930
Torpenhow 94 NY 2039
Torphichen 126 NS 9672
Torphins 142 NJ 6202
Torpoint 6 SX 4355
Torquay 7 SX 9164
Torquhan 117 NT 4447
Torr 6 SX 5751
Torran (Strath.) 123 NM 8704
Torrance 125 NS 6174
Torrans 128 NM 4827
Torranyard 113 NS 3644
Torre 20 ST 0439
Torridon 146 NG 9055
Torrin 145 NG 5720
Torrisdale 157 NC 6761
Torrish 155 NC 9718
Torrisholme 89 SD 4464
Torroble 154 NC 5904
Torry (Grampn.) 150 NJ 4339
Torry (Grampn.) 143 NJ 9404
Torryburn 126 NT 0286
Torrylin 112 NR 9621
Tortan 52 SO 8472
Torterston 151 NK 0747
Torteval (Guernsey) 161 ZZ 9999
Torthorwald 102 NY 0378
Tortington 14 TQ 0005
Tortworth 36 ST 6992
Torvaig 149 NG 4944
Torver 88 SD 2894
Torwood 125 NS 8484
Torworth 79 SK 6586
Toscaig 145 NG 7138
Toseland 56 TL 2362
Tosside 90 SD 7655
Tostock 58 TL 9563
Totaig 144 NG 2050
Tote 144 NG 4149
Totegan 158 NC 8268
Totford 24 SU 5738
Totland 13 SZ 3286
Totley 78 SK 3179
Totnell 10 ST 6208
Totnes 7 SX 8060
Toton 66 SK 5034
Totscore 144 NG 3866
Tottenham 26 TQ 3491
Tottenhill 69 TF 6310
Totteridge 26 TQ 2494
Totternhoe 39 SP 9921
Tottington 83 SD 7712
Totton 13 SU 3513
Tournaig 152 NG 8783
Toux (Grampn.) 150 NJ 5458
Toux (Grampn.) 151 NJ 9850
Tovil 28 TQ 7554
Tow Law 97 NZ 1139
Toward 114 NS 1368
Towcester 54 SP 6948
Towednack 2 SW 4838
Tower Hamlets 26 TQ 3582
Towersey 39 SP 7305
Towie 142 NJ 4412
Towiemore 150 NJ 3945
Town End (Cambs.) 68 TL 4195
Town End (Cumbr.) 89 SD 4483
Town Street 57 TL 7786
Town Yetholm 110 NT 8127
Towngate 95 NY 5347
Townhead (Cumbr.) 95 NY 6334
Townhead (Cumbr.) 94 NY 0836
Townhead (Dumf & G) 102 NX 6946
Townhead of Greenlaw 102 NX 7465
Townhill 126 NT 1089
Townlake 5 SX 4074
Towns End 24 SU 5658
Townshend 2 SW 5932
Townwell 36 ST 6990
Towthorpe 92 SE 6258
Towthorpe 93 SE 9062
Towton 85 SE 4839
Towyn (Clwyd) 74 SH 9779
Toy's Hill 27 TQ 4751
Toynton All Saints 81 TF 3964
Toynton Fen Side 81 TF 3961
Toynton St. Peter 81 TF 4063
Trabboch 106 NS 4321
Traboe 3 SW 7421
Tradespark (Highld.) 148 NH 8656
Trallong 46 SN 9629
Tranent 127 NT 4072
Trantlebeg 158 NC 9054
Trantlemore 158 NC 8853
Tranwell 105 NZ 1883
Trapp 45 SN 6519
Traprain 127 NT 5975
Traquair 117 NT 3334
Traveller's Rest 19 SS 6027
Trawden 83 SD 9138
Trawsfynydd 61 SH 7035
Tre Gagle 35 SO 5208
Tre Gibbon 33 SN 9905
Tre'r-ddol 48 SN 6592
Tre-groes 44 SN 4044
Trealaw 33 SS 9992
Treales 82 SD 4432
Trearddur Bay 58 SH 2478
Treaslane 144 NG 3953
Trebanos 32 SN 7103
Trebartha 5 SX 2677
Trebarwith 4 SX 0585
Trebetherick 4 SW 9377
Treborough 20 ST 0036
Trebudannon 3 SW 8961
Trebullett 5 SX 3278
Treburley 5 SX 3477
Trebursye Oak 5 SX 3084
Trecastle 45 SN 8729
Trecott 8 SS 6300
Trecwyn 30 SM 9632
Trecynon 33 SN 9903
Tredavoe 2 SW 4528
Treddiog 30 SM 8928
Tredegar 34 SO 1409
Tredington (Glos.) 36 SO 9029
Tredington (Warw.) 53 SP 2543
Tredinnick (Corn.) 4 SW 9270
Tredinnick (Corn.) 5 SX 2357
Tredomen 46 SO 1231
Tredrizzick 4 SW 9576
Tredunnock 35 ST 3795
Treen 2 SW 3923
Treeton 78 SK 4387
Trefdraeth 72 SH 4070
Trefecca 46 SO 1431
Trefeglwys 49 SN 9690
Trefenter 48 SN 6068
Treffgarne 30 SM 9523
Treffgarne Owen 30 SM 8625
Treffynnon 30 SM 8428
Trefil 46 SO 1212
Trefilan 45 SN 5457
Treflach Wood 62 SJ 2625
Trefnannau 62 SJ 2015
Trefnant 74 SJ 0570
Trefonen 62 SJ 2526
Trefor 72 SH 3779
Trefriw 73 SH 7763
Tregadillett 5 SX 2983
Tregaian 72 SH 4579
Tregare 35 SO 4110
Tregaron 45 SN 6759
Tregarth 73 SH 6067
Tregeare 5 SX 2486
Tregeiriog 62 SJ 1733
Tregele 72 SH 3592
Tregidden 3 SW 7523
Treglemais 30 SM 8229
Tregole 4 SX 1998
Tregonetha 3 SW 9563
Tregony 3 SW 9244
Tregoodwell 4 SX 1183
Tregoyd 46 SO 1937
Tregrehan Mills 4 SX 0554
Tregurrian 3 SW 8465
Tregynon 50 SO 0998
Trehafod 34 ST 0491
Trehan 5 SX 4058
Treharris 34 ST 1097
Treherbert (Dyfed) 45 SN 5846
Treherbert (Mid Glam.) 33 SS 9398
Trehunist 5 SX 3163
Trekenner 5 SX 3478
Treknow 4 SX 0586
Trelawnyd 74 SJ 0879
Trelech 44 SN 2830
Trelech a'r Betws 44 SN 3026
Treleddyd-fawr 30 SM 7528
Trelewis 34 ST 1197
Treligga 4 SX 0484
Trelights 4 SW 9879
Trelill 4 SX 0477
Trelissick 3 SW 8339
Trelleck 35 SO 5005
Trelleck Grange 35 SO 4901
Trelogan 74 SJ 1180
Trelystan 50 SJ 2603
Tremadog 61 SH 5640
Tremail 4 SX 1686
Tremain 44 SN 2348
Tremaine 5 SX 2388
Tremar 5 SX 2568
Trematon 5 SX 3959
Tremeirchion 74 SJ 0773
Tremethick Cross 2 SW 4430
Trenance 4 SW 8567
Trenarren 4 SX 0348
Trench 64 SJ 6913
Treneglos 5 SX 2088
Trenewan 4 SX 1753
Trent 10 ST 5918
Trentham 64 SJ 8640
Trentishoe 19 SS 6448
Treoes 33 SS 9478
Treorchy 33 SS 9596
Trequite 4 SX 0276
Trerhyngyll 34 ST 0077
Trerulefoot 5 SX 3258
Tresaith 44 SN 2751
Trescott 64 SO 8497
Trescowe 2 SW 5731
Tresham 36 ST 7991
Tresillian 3 SW 8646
Treskinnick Cross 5 SX 2098
Tresmeer 5 SX 2387
Tresparrett 4 SX 1491
Tressait 132 NN 8160
Tresta (Fetlar) 163 HU 6190
Tresta (Shetld.) 163 HU 3650
Treswell 79 SK 7779
Trethevey 4 SX 0789
Trethomas 34 ST 1889
Trethurgy 4 SX 0355
Tretio 30 SM 7828
Tretire 47 SO 5124
Tretower 46 SO 1821
Treuddyn 74 SJ 2458
Trevalga 4 SX 0889
Trevalyn 75 SJ 3856
Trevanson 4 SW 9772
Trevarren 3 SW 9160
Trevarrian 3 SW 8466
Trevarrick 3 SW 9843
Treveighan 4 SX 0779
Trevellas 2 SW 7452
Trevelmond 4 SX 2063
Treveor 3 SW 9841
Treverva 3 SW 7631
Trevethin 35 SO 2802
Trevia 4 SX 0983
Trevigro 5 SX 3369
Trevine 30 SM 8432
Treviscoe 3 SW 9455
Trevone 4 SW 8975
Trevor 60 SH 3746
Trewalder 4 SX 0782
Trewarmett 4 SX 0686
Trewarthenick 3 SW 9044
Trewassa 4 SX 1486
Trewellard 2 SW 3733
Trewennack 2 SW 6828
Trewidland 5 SX 2560
Trewint (Corn.) 4 SX 1897
Trewint (Corn.) 5 SX 2180
Trewint (Corn.) 5 SX 2963
Trewithian 3 SW 8737
Trewoon 4 SW 9952
Treworga 3 SW 8940
Treworthal 3 SW 8838
Treyarnon 4 SW 8673
Treyford 14 SU 8218
Triangle (Glos.) 35 SO 5401
Triangle (W Yorks.) 84 SE 0422
Trickett's Cross 12 SU 0801
Trimdon 98 NZ 3634
Trimdon Colliery 98 NZ 3835
Trimdon Grange 98 NZ 3735
Trimingham 71 TG 2738
Trimley 59 TM 2736
Trimley Heath 59 TM 2737
Trimpley 52 SO 7978
Trimsaran 32 SN 4504
Trimstone 19 SS 5043
Trinafour 139 NN 7365
Trinant 34 SO 2000
Tring 39 SP 9211
Trinity (Devon) 9 SS 9905
Trinity (Jersey) 161 ZZ 9999
Trinity (Tayside) 142 NO 6061
Triscombe 20 ST 1535
Trislaig 138 NN 0874
Trispen 3 SW 8450
Tritlington 111 NZ 2092
Trochrie 133 NN 9740
Troedrhiwfuwch 34 SO 1204
Troedyraur 44 SN 3245
Troedyrharn 46 SO 0630
Troedyrhiw 34 SO 0702
Trofarth 73 SH 8571
Troon (Corn.) 2 SW 6638
Troon (Strath.) 114 NS 3230
Trossachs Hotel 124 NN 5297
Troston 58 TL 8972
Trottiscliffe 27 TQ 6460
Trotton 14 SU 8322
Troutbeck 89 NY 4002
Troutbeck Bridge 89 NY 4000
Trow Green 35 SO 5706
Trowbridge 22 ST 8557
Trowle Common 22 ST 8358
Trows 118 NT 6932
Trowse Newton 71 TG 2406
Trudoxhill 22 ST 7443
Trull 9 ST 2122
Trumpan 144 NG 2261
Trumpet 52 SO 6539
Trumpington 57 TL 4455
Trunch 71 TG 2834
Truro 3 SW 8244
Trusham 8 SX 8582
Trusley 65 SK 2535
Trusthorpe 81 TF 5183
Trysull 64 SO 8494
Tubney 38 SU 4498
Tuckenhay 7 SX 8156
Tuckhill 64 SO 7887
Tuckingmill 22 ST 9329
Tuddenham (Suff.) 57 TL 7371
Tuddenham (Suff.) 59 TM 1948
Tudeley 16 TQ 6245
Tudhoe 97 NZ 2635
Tudweiloig 60 SH 2336
Tuesley 25 SU 9642
Tuffley 36 SO 8315
Tufton (Dyfed) 30 SN 0428
Tufton (Hants.) 24 SU 4546
Tugby 67 SK 7601
Tugford 51 SO 5587
Tughall 110 NU 2227
Tullibody 125 NS 8595
Tullich (Highld.) 155 NH 8576
Tullich (Strath.) 130 NN 0815
Tullich Muir 155 NH 7373
Tulliemet 133 NN 9952
Tulloch (Grampn.) 142 NO 7671
Tullochcoy 141 NO 2397
Tullochgorm 123 NR 9695
Tulloes 135 NO 5145
Tullybannocher 132 NN 7521
Tullyfergus 134 NO 2149
Tullynessle 150 NJ 5519
Tumble 32 SN 5411
Tumbler's Green 42 TL 8025
Tumby 80 TF 2359
Tumby Woodside 81 TF 2657
Tummel Bridge 132 NN 7659
Tunley 22 ST 6959
Tunnel Hill 52 SO 8440
Tunstall (Humbs.) 87 TA 3032
Tunstall (Kent) 28 TQ 8961
Tunstall (Lancs.) 89 SD 6073
Tunstall (N Yorks.) 91 SE 2195
Tunstall (Norf.) 71 TG 4107
Tunstall (Staffs.) 76 SJ 8551
Tunstall (Suff.) 59 TM 3655
Tunstead 71 TG 3022
Tunstead Milton 77 SK 0279
Tunworth 24 SU 6748
Tupsley 47 SO 5340
Tur Langton 67 SP 7194
Turgis Green 24 SU 6959
Turin 135 NO 5352
Turkdean 37 SP 1017
Turleigh 22 ST 8060
Turnastone 47 SO 3536
Turnberry 113 NS 2005
Turnditch 77 SK 2946
Turner's Green 53 SP 1969
Turner's Hill 15 TQ 3435
Turners Puddle 11 SY 8394
Turnworth 11 ST 8107
Turriff 150 NJ 7249
Turton Bottoms 83 SD 7315
Turvey 55 SP 9452
Turville 39 SU 7691
Turville Heath 39 SU 7391
Turweston 54 SP 6037
Tutbury 65 SK 2129
Tutnall 53 SO 9870
Tutshill 35 ST 5394
Tuttington 71 TG 2227
Tuxford 79 SK 7370
Twatt (Orkney) 163 HY 2624
Twechar 125 NS 6975
Tweedmouth 119 NT 9952
Tweedsmuir 108 NT 1024
Twelveheads 3 SW 7642
Twemlow Green 76 SJ 7868
Twenty 68 TF 1520
Twerton 22 ST 7263
Twickenham 26 TQ 1473
Twigworth 36 SO 8421
Twineham 15 TQ 2519
Twinhoe 22 ST 7359
Twinstead 58 TL 8637
Twiss Green 75 SJ 6595
Twiston 83 SD 8243
Twitchen (Devon.) 19 SS 7830
Twitchen (Salop) 51 SO 3679
Twizel Bridge 118 NT 8943
Two Bridges 6 SX 6075
Two Dales 77 SK 2762
Two Gates 65 SK 2101
Two Mile Oak Cross 7 SX 8467
Twycross (Leic.) 65 SK 3305
Twyford (Berks.) 25 SU 7975
Twyford (Bucks.) 38 SP 6626
Twyford (Derby.) 65 SK 3228
Twyford (Hants.) 13 SU 4724
Twyford (Leics.) 67 SK 7210
Twyford (Norf.) 70 TG 0124
Twyford Common 47 SO 5135
Twyn-y-Sheriff 35 SO 4005
Twynholm 101 NX 6654
Twyning 52 SO 8936
Twyning Green 52 SO 9037
Twynllanan 45 SN 7524
Twynmynydd 45 SN 6614
Twywell 55 SP 9578
Ty Calch 72 SH 4271
Ty Rhiw 34 ST 1283
Ty'n-dwr 62 SJ 2342
Ty'n-y-bryn 33 SS 9987
Ty'n-y-groes 73 SH 7771
Ty'n-y-maes 73 SH 6364
Ty-hen 60 SH 1731
Ty-mawr 62 SH 9047
Ty-nant (Clwyd) 62 SH 9944
Ty-nant (Gwyn.) 62 SH 9026
Ty-uchaf 62 SH 9922
Tyberton 47 SO 3739
Tyburn 65 SP 1490
Tycroes 32 SN 6010
Tycrwyn 62 SJ 1018
Tydd Gote 69 TF 4518
Tydd St. Giles 69 TF 4216
Tydd St. Mary 69 TF 4418
Tye 14 SU 7302
Tye Green (Essex) 41 TL 5935
Tye Green (Essex) 42 TL 7820
Tyes Cross 16 TQ 3832
Tyldesley 83 SD 6902
Tyler Hill 29 TR 1460
Tyler's Green (Essex) 41 TL 5005
Tylers Green (Bucks.) 39 SU 9094
Tylorstown 34 ST 0195
Tylwch 49 SN 9780
Tyn-y-ffridd 62 SJ 1230
Tyn-y-graig 46 SO 0149
Tynant 34 ST 0684
Tyndrum 131 NN 3330
Tyneham 11 SY 8880
Tynehead 117 NT 3960
Tynemouth (Tyne and Wear) 105 NZ 3468
Tynewydd 33 SS 9399
Tyninghame 127 NT 6179
Tynribbie 130 NM 9446
Tynron 107 NX 8093
Tynygongl 72 SH 5182
Tynygraig 48 SN 6969
Tyringham 55 SP 8547
Tythecott 18 SS 4117
Tythegston 33 SS 8578
Tytherington (Avon) 36 ST 6788

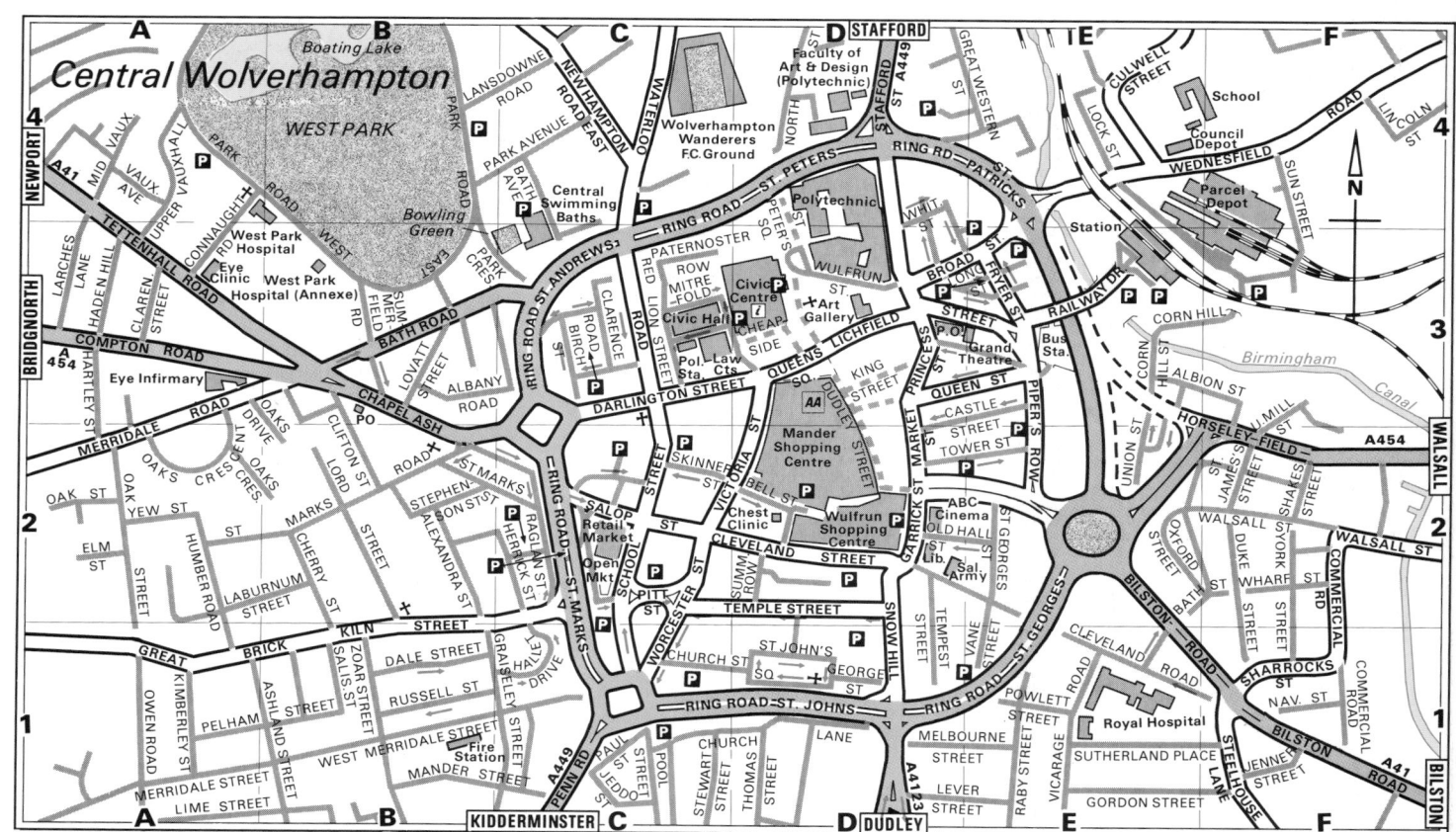

Whitchurch (Oxon) Wolverton (Wilts)

Place	Page	Grid ref.
Whitchurch (Oxon)	24	SU 6377
Whitchurch (S Glam)	34	ST 1680
Whitchurch (Salop)	63	SJ 5441
Whitchurch Canonicorum	10	SY 3995
Whitchurch Hill	24	SU 6478
Whitcott Keysett	50	SO 2782
White Chapel	82	SD 5542
White Colne	42	TL 8629
White Coppice	83	SD 6119
White Court	42	TL 7421
White End	52	SO 7833
White Lackington	10	SY 7198
White Ladies Aston	52	SO 9252
White Notley	42	TL 7818
White Pit	81	TF 3777
White Post Inn	79	SK 6356
White Roding	41	TL 5613
White Stone	47	SO 5642
White Waltham	25	SU 8577
Whiteacen	149	NJ 2647
Whiteacre Heath	65	SP 2192
Whitebridge	138	NH 4915
Whitebrook	35	SO 5306
Whitecairns	151	NJ 9218
Whitechurch	31	SN 1436
Whitecliffe	35	SO 5610
Whitecraig (Lothian)	117	NT 3570
Whitecroft	35	SO 6106
Whitecross (Central)	126	NS 9676
Whitecross (Corn)	4	SW 9672
Whiteface	154	NH 7189
Whitefield (Gtr Mches.)	83	SD 8005
Whitefield (Tays)	134	NO 1734
Whiteford	150	NJ 7126
Whitegate	75	SJ 6269
Whitehall (Hants)	25	SU 7452
Whitehall (Orkney)	163	HY 6528
Whitehall (W. Susx)	15	TQ 1321
Whitehaven	94	NX 9718
Whitehill (Hants.)	25	SU 7934
Whitehill (Strath.)	114	NS 2656
Whitehills	150	NJ 6565
Whitehouse (Grampn.)	142	NJ 6214
Whitehouse (Strath)	123	NR 8161
Whitekirk	127	NT 5981
Whitelackington	10	ST 3815
Whiteley Bank	13	SZ 5581
Whiteley Green	76	SJ 9278
Whiteley Village	26	TQ 0962
Whitemans Green	15	TQ 3025
Whitemire	149	NH 9854
Whitemoor	3	SW 9757
Whiteparish	23	SU 2423
Whiterashes	151	NJ 8523
Whiterow (Grampian)	148	NJ 0256
Whiterow (Highland)	159	ND 3548
Whiteshill	36	SO 8307
Whiteside (Lothian)	116	NS 9667
Whiteside (Northum)	95	NY 7169
Whitesmith	16	TQ 5214
Whitestaunton	9	ST 2810
Whitestone	8	SX 8694
Whitewall Corner	92	SE 7970
Whiteway	36	SO 9110
Whitewell	83	SD 6546
Whiteworks	6	SX 6171
Whitewreath	149	NJ 2356
Whitfield (Avon)	36	ST 6791
Whitfield (Kent)	29	TR 3146
Whitfield (Northants)	54	SP 6039
Whitfield (Northum)	104	NY 7758
Whitford (Clwyd)	74	SJ 1477
Whitford (Devon)	9	SY 2595
Whitgift	86	SE 8022
Whitgreave	64	SJ 8928
Whithorn	101	NX 4440
Whiting Bay (Island of Arran)	113	NS 0425
Whitington	69	TL 7199
Whitland	44	SN 1916
Whitletts	106	NS 3622
Whitley (Berks)	25	SU 7170
Whitley (Ches.)	75	SJ 6178
Whitley (N Yorks)	85	SE 5521
Whitley (Wilts)	22	ST 8866
Whitley Bay	105	NZ 3577
Whitley Bridge	85	SE 5622
Whitley Chapel	104	NY 9257
Whitley Row	27	TQ 5052
Whitlock's End	53	SP 1076
Whitminster	36	SO 7708
Whitmore	64	SJ 8041
Whitnage	9	ST 0215
Whitnash	53	SP 3263
Whitney	46	SO 2647
Whitrigg (Cumbr.)	94	NY 2038
Whitrigg (Cumbr.)	103	NY 2257
Whitsbury	12	SU 1218
Whitsome	119	NT 8650
Whitson	35	ST 3783
Whitstable	29	TR 1166
Whitstone	5	SX 2698
Whittingham	111	NU 0611
Whittingslow	51	SO 4288
Whittington (Derby)	78	SK 3975
Whittington (Glos.)	37	SP 0120
Whittington (Here & W)	52	SO 8582
Whittington (Here & W)	52	SO 8752
Whittington (Lancs.)	89	SD 5976
Whittington (Salop)	63	SJ 3230
Whittington (Staffs.)	65	SK 1508
Whittle-le-Woods	82	SD 5822
Whittlebury	54	SP 6943
Whittlesey	68	TL 2797
Whittlesford	57	TL 4748
Whitton (Clev.)	98	NZ 3822
Whitton (Humbs.)	86	SE 9034
Whitton (Northum.)	111	NU 0501
Whitton (Powys)	51	SO 2667
Whitton (Salop)	50	SO 5772
Whitton (Suff.)	58	TM 1447
Whittonditch	23	SU 2872
Whittonstall	104	NZ 0757
Whitwell (Derby.)	78	SK 5276
Whitwell (Herts.)	40	TL 1821
Whitwell (I of W.)	13	SZ 5277
Whitwell (Leic.)	67	SK 9208
Whitwell (N Yorks.)	91	SE 2899
Whitwell Street	70	TG 1022
Whitwell-on-the-Hill	92	SE 7265
Whitwick	66	SK 4316
Whitwood	85	SE 4124
Whitworth	83	SD 8818
Whixall	63	SJ 5034
Whixley	91	SE 4457
Whorlton (Durham)	97	NZ 1014
Whorlton (N Yorks.)	97	NZ 4802
Whygate	104	NY 7675
Whyle	51	SO 5560
Whyteleafe	26	TQ 3358
Wibdon	35	ST 5797
Wibtoft	54	SP 4787
Wichenford	52	SO 7860
Wichling	28	TQ 9256
Wick (Avon)	22	ST 7072
Wick (Devon)	9	ST 1604
Wick (Dorset)	12	SZ 1591
Wick (Here & W)	52	SO 9645
Wick (Highld.)	159	ND 3650
Wick (S Glam.)	33	SS 9272
Wick (W Susx)	15	TQ 0203
Wick (Wilts.)	12	SU 1621
Wick Rissington	37	SP 1821
Wick St. Lawrence	21	ST 3665
Wicken (Cambs.)	57	TL 5770
Wicken (Northants.)	55	SP 7439
Wicken Bonhunt	41	TL 5033
Wickenby	80	TF 0882
Wickersley	78	SK 4891
Wickford	42	TQ 7593
Wickham (Berks.)	24	SU 3971
Wickham (Hants.)	13	SU 5711
Wickham Bishops	42	TL 8412
Wickham Market	59	TM 3056
Wickham Skeith	58	TM 0969
Wickham St. Paul	58	TL 8336
Wickham Street (Suff.)	57	TL 7554
Wickham Street (Suff.)	58	TM 0869
Wickhambreaux	29	TR 2158
Wickhambrook	57	TL 7454
Wickhamford	53	SP 0642
Wickhampton	71	TG 4205
Wicklewood	70	TF 0702
Wickmere	71	TG 1733
Wickwar	36	ST 7288
Widdington	41	TL 5331
Widdrington	111	NZ 2595
Widdrington Station	111	NZ 2594
Wide Open	105	NZ 2472
Widecombe in the Moor	6	SX 7176
Widegates	5	SX 2857
Widemouth Bay	18	SS 1902
Widford (Essex)	42	TL 6905
Widford (Herts.)	41	TL 4115
Widham	37	SU 0988
Widmerpool	66	SK 6327
Widnes	75	SJ 5185
Wigan	82	SD 5805
Wiggaton	9	SY 1093
Wiggenhall St. Germans	69	TF 5914
Wiggenhall St. Mary Magdalen	69	TF 5911
Wiggenhall St. Mary the Virgin	69	TF 5814
Wiggens Green	57	TL 6642
Wigginton (Herts.)	39	SP 9410
Wigginton (N Yorks.)	92	SE 5958
Wigginton (Oxon.)	38	SP 3833
Wigginton (Staffs.)	65	SK 2106
Wigglesworth	90	SD 8056
Wiggonby	103	NY 2953
Wiggonholt	15	TQ 0616
Wigham	8	SS 7508
Wighill	85	SE 4746
Wighton	70	TF 9339
Wigley	13	SU 3217
Wigmore (Here & W)	51	SO 4169
Wigmore (Kent)	28	TQ 8063
Wigsley	79	SK 8570
Wigsthorpe	55	TL 0482
Wigston	66	SP 6099
Wigthorpe	79	SK 5983
Wigtoft	68	TF 2636
Wigton	94	NY 2548
Wigtown	101	NX 4355
Wigtwizzle	77	SK 2495
Wike	85	SE 3342
Wilbarston	55	SP 8188
Wilberfoss	92	SE 7350
Wilburton	57	TL 4875
Wilby (Norf.)	58	TM 0389
Wilby (Northants.)	55	SP 8666
Wilby (Suff.)	59	TM 2472
Wilcot	23	SU 1461
Wilcott	63	SJ 3718
Wildboarclough	76	SJ 9868
Wilden (Beds)	56	TL 0955
Wilden (Here & W)	52	SO 8272
Wildhern	24	SU 3550
Wildhill	41	TL 2606
Wildsworth	86	SK 8097
Wilford	66	SK 5637
Wilkesley	63	SJ 6241
Wilkhaven	155	NH 9486
Wilkieston	117	NT 1168
Willand	9	ST 0310
Willaston (Ches.)	74	SJ 3277
Willaston (Ches.)	75	SJ 6752
Willenhall (W Mids.)	64	SO 9698
Willenhall (W Mids.)	54	SP 3676
Willerby (Humbs.)	86	TA 0230
Willerby (N Yorks.)	93	TA 0079
Willersey	53	SP 1039
Willersley	47	SO 3147
Willesborough	28	TR 0441
Willesden	26	TQ 2284
Willesley	36	ST 8588
Willett	20	ST 1033
Willey (Salop)	51	SO 6799
Willey (Warw.)	54	SP 4984
Willey Green	25	SU 9451
Williamscot	54	SP 4745
Williamstown	34	ST 0090
Willian	40	TL 2230
Willimontswick	104	NY 7763
Willingale	41	TL 5907
Willingdon	16	TQ 5902
Willingham (Cambs)	56	TL 4070
Willingham by Stow	79	SK 8784
Willington (Beds.)	56	TL 1150
Willington (Derby.)	65	SK 2928
Willington (Durham)	97	NZ 1935
Willington (Tyne and Wear)	105	NZ 3167
Willington (Warw.)	53	SP 2638
Willington Corner	75	SJ 5367
Willisham Tye	58	TM 0750
Willitoft	86	SE 7434
Williton	20	ST 0740
Willoughby (Lincs.)	81	TF 4772
Willoughby (Warw.)	54	SP 5167
Willoughby Waterleys	66	SP 5792
Willoughby-on-the-Wolds	66	SK 6325
Willoughton	79	SK 9293
Willows Green	42	TL 7119
Willsbridge	22	ST 6670
Wilmcote	53	SP 1658
Wilmington (Avon)	22	ST 6962
Wilmington (Devon.)	9	SY 2199
Wilmington (E Susx)	16	TQ 5404
Wilmington (Kent)	27	TQ 5372
Wilmslow	76	SJ 8480
Wilnecote	65	SK 2201
Wilpshire	83	SD 6832
Wilsden	84	SE 0935
Wilsford (Lincs.)	80	TF 0043
Wilsford (Wilts.)	23	SU 1057
Wilsford (Wilts.)	23	SU 1339
Wilshamstead	55	TL 0643
Wilsill	91	SE 1864
Wilson (Here & W)	47	SO 5523
Wilson (Leics)	66	SK 4024
Wilsthorpe	68	TF 0913
Wilstone	39	SP 9014
Wilton (Cleve.)	98	NZ 5819
Wilton (Cumbr)	88	NY 0411
Wilton (Here & W)	47	SO 5824
Wilton (N Yorks.)	92	SE 8582
Wilton (Wilts.)	23	SU 0931
Wilton (Wilts.)	23	SU 2661
Wilton Dean (Borders)	109	NT 4914
Wimbish	57	TL 5936
Wimbish Green	42	TL 6035
Wimbledon	26	TQ 2470
Wimblington	68	TL 4192
Wimborne Minster	12	SZ 0199
Wimborne St. Giles	12	SU 0212
Wimbotsham	69	TF 6205
Wimpstone	53	SP 2148
Wincanton	22	ST 7128
Wincham	75	SJ 6675
Winchburgh	126	NT 0874
Winchcombe	37	SP 0228
Winchelsea	17	TQ 9017
Winchelsea Beach	17	TQ 9115
Winchester	13	SU 4829
Winchfield	25	SU 7654
Winchmore Hill (Bucks.)	39	SU 9394
Winchmore Hill (Gtr London)	26	TQ 3195
Wincle	76	SJ 9565
Windermere (Cumbr.)	89	SD 4198
Winderton	53	SP 3240
Windhill	146	NH 5348
Windlesham	25	SU 9363
Windley	78	SK 3045
Windmill	4	SW 8975
Windmill Hill (E Susx)	16	TQ 6412
Windmill Hill (Somer.)	9	ST 3116
Windrush	37	SP 1913
Windsor	25	SU 9676
Windygates	127	NO 3400
Wineham	15	TQ 2320
Winestead	87	TA 2924
Winfarthing	58	TM 1085
Winford (Avon)	21	ST 5364
Winford (IOW)	13	SZ 5684
Winforton	47	SO 2947
Winfrith Newburgh	11	SY 8084
Wing (Bucks.)	39	SP 8822
Wing (Leic.)	67	SK 8903
Wingate (Durham)	98	NZ 4036
Wingates (Gtr Mches.)	83	SD 6507
Wingates (Northum.)	111	NZ 0995
Wingerworth	78	SK 3867
Wingfield (Beds.)	39	SP 9926
Wingfield (Suff.)	59	TM 2276
Wingfield (Wilts.)	22	ST 8256
Wingham	29	TR 2457
Wingmore	29	TR 1846
Wingrave	39	SP 8719
Winkburn	79	SK 7158
Winkfield	25	SU 9072
Winkfield Row	25	SU 9071
Winkhill	77	SK 0651
Winkleigh	8	SS 6308
Winksley	91	SE 2471
Winkton	12	SZ 1696
Winlaton Mill	105	NZ 1862
Winless	159	ND 3054
Winmarleigh	82	SD 4748
Winnall Common	47	SO 4534
Winnersh	25	SU 7870
Winscales	94	NY 0226
Winscombe	21	ST 4157
Winsford (Ches.)	75	SJ 6566
Winsford (Somer.)	20	SS 9034
Winsham	10	ST 3706
Winshill	65	SK 2623
Winskill	95	NY 5835
Winslade	24	SU 6547
Winsley	22	ST 7960
Winslow	39	SP 7627
Winson	37	SP 0908
Winster (Cumbr.)	89	SD 4193
Winster (Derby.)	77	SK 2460
Winston (Durham)	97	NZ 1416
Winston (Suff.)	59	TM 1861
Winstone	36	SO 9609
Winswell	19	SS 4913
Winterborne Came	10	SY 7088
Winterborne Clenston	11	ST 8302
Winterborne Herringston	10	SY 6887
Winterborne Houghton	11	ST 8104
Winterborne Kingston	11	SY 8697
Winterborne Monkton (Dorset)	10	SY 6787
Winterborne Stickland	11	ST 8304
Winterborne Whitechurch	11	SY 8399
Winterborne Zelston	11	SY 8997
Winterbourne (Avon)	36	ST 6480
Winterbourne (Berks)	24	SU 4572
Winterbourne Abbas	10	SY 6190
Winterbourne Bassett	23	SU 1074
Winterbourne Dauntsey	23	SU 1734
Winterbourne Earls	23	SU 1633
Winterbourne Gunner	23	SU 1735
Winterbourne Monkton (Wilts.)	23	SU 0972
Winterbourne Steepleton	10	SY 6289
Winterbourne Stoke	23	SU 0740
Winterburn	90	SD 9358
Winteringham	86	SE 9222
Winterley	76	SJ 7457
Wintersett	85	SE 3815
Winterton	86	SE 9218
Winterton-on-Sea	71	TG 4919
Winthorpe (Lincs.)	81	TF 5665
Winthorpe (Notts.)	79	SK 8156
Winton (Cumbr.)	96	NY 7810
Winton (Dorset)	12	SZ 0894
Wintringham	93	SE 8873
Winwick (Cambs.)	56	TL 1080
Winwick (Ches.)	75	SJ 6092
Winwick (Northants.)	54	SP 6273
Wirksworth	77	SK 2854
Wirswall	63	SJ 5444
Wisbech	69	TF 4609
Wisbech St. Mary	68	TF 4208
Wisborough Green	15	TQ 0526
Wiseman's Bridge	31	SN 1406
Wiseton	79	SK 7189
Wishaw (Strath.)	116	NS 7954
Wishaw (Warw.)	65	SP 1794
Wisley	26	TQ 0659
Wispington	80	TF 2071
Wissett	59	TM 3679
Wistanstow	51	SO 4385
Wistanswick	63	SJ 6629
Wistaston	76	SJ 6853
Wiston (Dyfed)	30	SN 0218
Wiston (Strath.)	116	NS 9531
Wiston (W Susx)	15	TQ 1512
Wistow (Cambs.)	56	TL 2781
Wistow (N Yorks.)	85	SE 5835
Wiswell	83	SD 7437
Witcham	57	TL 4680
Witchampton	11	ST 9806
Witchford	57	TL 5078
Withacott	18	SS 4315
Witham	42	TL 8114
Witham Friary	22	ST 7440
Witham on the Hill	67	TF 0516
Withcall	81	TF 2883
Witherenden Hill	16	TQ 6426
Witheridge	8	SS 8014
Witherley	65	SP 3297
Withern	81	TF 4382
Withernsea	87	TA 3328
Withernwick	87	TA 1940
Withersdale Street	59	TM 2781
Withersfield	57	TL 6547
Witherslack	89	SD 4384
Withiel	4	SW 9965
Withiel Florey	20	SS 9832
Withies	47	SO 5642
Withington (Ches.)	76	SJ 8170
Withington (Glos.)	37	SP 0315
Withington (Gtr Mches.)	76	SJ 8392
Withington (Here & W)	47	SO 5643
Withington (Salop)	63	SJ 5713
Withington Green	76	SJ 8071
Withleigh	8	SS 9012
Withnell	83	SD 6322
Withybrook	54	SP 4384
Withycombe	20	ST 0141
Withyham	16	TQ 4935
Withypool	19	SS 8435
Withywood	21	ST 5667
Witley	25	SU 9439
Witnesham	59	TM 1850
Witney	38	SP 3509
Wittering	67	TF 0502
Wittersham	17	TQ 8927
Wittingslow	51	SO 4388
Witton	71	TG 3331
Witton Gilbert	97	NZ 2345
Witton Park	97	NZ 1730
Witton le Wear	97	NZ 1431
Wiveliscombe	20	ST 0827
Wivelsfield	15	TQ 3420
Wivelsfield Green	15	TQ 3519
Wivelsfield Station	15	TQ 3120
Wivenhoe	43	TM 0321
Wivenhoe Cross	43	TM 0423
Wiveton	70	TG 0343
Wix	43	TM 1628
Wixford	53	SP 0854
Wixoe	57	TL 7142
Woburn	39	SP 9433
Woburn Sands	55	SP 9235
Wokefield Park	24	SU 6765
Woking	26	TQ 0058
Wokingham	25	SU 8068
Wold Newton (Humbs.)	93	TA 0473
Wold Newton (Humbs.)	87	TF 2496
Woldingham	27	TQ 3755
Wolf's Castle	30	SM 9627
Wolferlow	52	SO 6661
Wolferton	69	TF 6528
Wolfhill	134	NO 1533
Wolfsdale	30	SM 9321
Wollaston (Northants.)	55	SP 9062
Wollaston (Salop)	63	SJ 3212
Wollerton	63	SJ 6229
Wolsingham	97	NZ 0737
Wolston	54	SP 4175
Wolvercote	38	SP 4809
Wolverhampton	64	SO 9198
Wolverley (Here & W)	52	SO 8279
Wolverley (Salop)	63	SJ 4631
Wolverton (Bucks.)	55	SP 8141
Wolverton (Hants.)	24	SU 5557
Wolverton (Warw.)	53	SP 2062
Wolverton (Wilts)	22	ST 7831

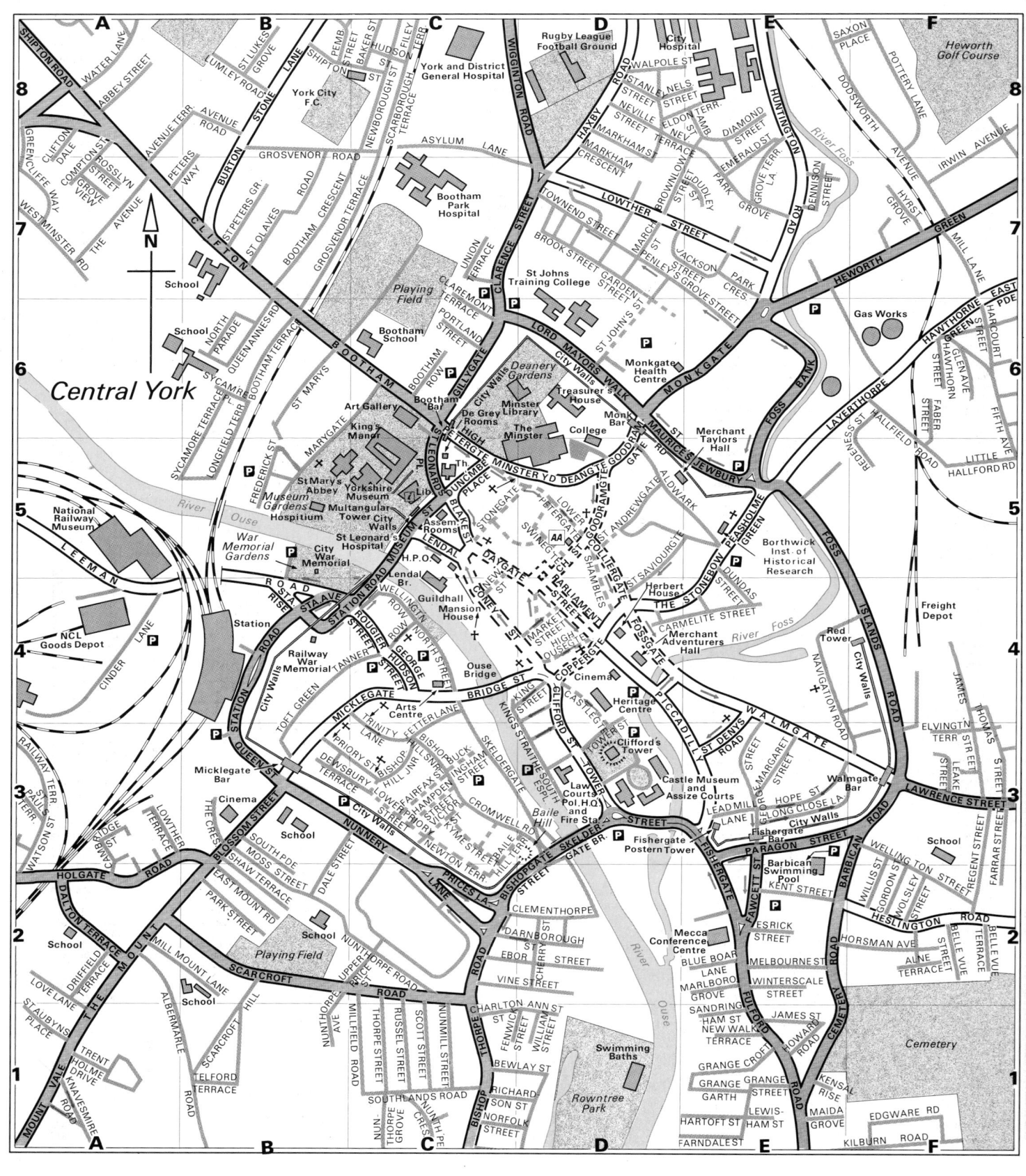

Central York

Woodham Zouch

Woodham 26 TQ 0462
Woodham Ferrers 42 TQ 7999
Woodham Mortimer 42 TL 8205
Woodham Walter 42 TL 8006
Woodhaven 135 NO 4127
Woodhead (Grampn.) 151 NJ 7938
Woodhill 21 ST 3527
Woodhorn 105 NZ 2988
Woodhouse (Leic.) 66 SK 5315
Woodhouse (S Yorks.) 78 SK 4184
Woodhouse Down 35 ST 6184
Woodhouse Eaves 66 SK 5214
Woodhouselee 117 NT 2364
Woodhurst 56 TL 3176
Woodingdean 15 TQ 3605
Woodland (Devon) 7 SX 7968
Woodland (Durham) 97 NZ 0726
Woodland Head 8 SX 7796
Woodlands (Dorset) 12 SU 0508
Woodlands (Grampn.) 143 NO 7895
Woodlands (Hants.) 13 SU 3111
Woodlands Park 25 SU 8578
Woodlands St Mary 23 SU 3375
Woodleigh 6 SX 7348
Woodlesford 85 SE 3629
Woodley (Berks) 25 SU 7773
Woodley (Gtr. Mches) 76 SJ 9492
Woodmancote (Glos) 36 ST 7798
Woodmancote (Glos) 36 SO 9727
Woodmancote (Glos.) 37 SP 0008
Woodmancote (Here & W) 52 SO 9042
Woodmancote (W Sussx) 15 TQ 2314
Woodmancote (W Susx) 14 SU 7707
Woodmancott 24 SU 5642
Woodmansey 87 TA 0537
Woodmansterne 26 TQ 2760
Woodminton 12 SU 0122
Woodnesborough 29 TR 3156
Woodnewton 67 TL 0394
Woodplumpton 82 SD 4934
Woodrising 70 TF 9803
Woodrow 52 SO 8875
Woodseaves (Salop) 64 SJ 6830
Woodseaves (Staffs.) 64 SJ 7925
Woodsend 23 SU 2275
Woodsetts 78 SK 5483
Woodsford 11 SY 7690
Woodside (Berks.) 25 SU 9371
Woodside (Herts.) 41 TL 2506
Woodside (Tays.) 134 NO 2037
Woodstock (Dyfed) 30 SN 0225
Woodstock (Oxon) 38 SP 4416
Woodthorpe (Derby.) 78 SK 4574
Woodthorpe (Leic.) 66 SK 5417
Woodton 71 TM 2894
Woodtown (Devon) 19 SS 4926
Woodtown (Devon) 18 SS 4123
Woodvale 82 SD 2911
Woodville 65 SK 3119
Woodyates 12 SU 0219
Woofferton 51 SO 5168
Wookey 21 ST 5145
Wookey Hole 21 ST 5347
Wool 11 SY 8486
Woolacombe 18 SS 4543
Woolage Green 29 TR 2449
Woolaston 35 ST 5999
Woolaston Common 35 SO 5801
Woolavington 21 ST 3441
Woolbeding 14 SU 8722
Wooler 111 NT 9928
Woolfardisworthy (Devon) 18 SS 3321
Woolfardisworthy (Devon) 8 SS 8208
Woolhampton 24 SU 5766
Woolhope 47 SO 6135
Woolland 11 ST 7706
Woollard 21 ST 6364
Woollaton 18 SS 4712
Woolley (Cambs.) 56 TL 1474
Woolley (Corn) 18 SS 2516
Woolley (W Yorks.) 85 SE 3113
Woolmer Green 41 TL 2518
Woolmere Green 52 SO 9663
Woolpack Inn 88 NY 1901
Woolpit 58 TL 9762
Woolridge 36 SO 8023
Woolscott 54 SP 4968
Woolsgrove 8 SS 7902
Woolsington 105 NZ 1970
Woolstaston 51 SO 4498
Woolsthorpe (Lincs.) 67 SK 8334
Woolsthorpe (Lincs.) 67 SK 9224
Woolston (Ches.) 75 SJ 6589
Woolston (Corn) 5 SX 2968
Woolston (Devon) 6 SX 7141
Woolston (Hants.) 13 SU 4410
Woolston (Salop) 63 SJ 3224
Woolston (Salop) 51 SO 4287
Woolston (Somer) 22 ST 6528
Woolston Green 7 SX 7765
Woolstone (Glos) 36 SO 9530
Woolstone (Oxon.) 37 SU 2987
Woolton 75 SJ 4286
Woolton Hill 24 SU 4261
Woolvers Hill 21 ST 3860
Woolverstone 59 TM 1838
Woolverton 22 ST 7853
Woolwich 27 TQ 4478
Woonton 47 SO 3552
Wooperton 111 NU 0420
Woore 64 SJ 7242
Wooton 51 SO 4677
Wootten Green 59 TM 2373
Wootton (Beds.) 55 TL 0045
Wootton (Hants.) 12 SZ 2498
Wootton (Humbs.) 87 TA 0815
Wootton (Kent) 29 TR 2246
Wootton (Northants.) 55 SP 7656
Wootton (Oxon.) 38 SP 4319
Wootton (Oxon.) 38 SP 4701
Wootton (Staffs.) 64 SJ 8227
Wootton (Staffs.) 77 SK 1045
Wootton Bassett 37 SU 0682
Wootton Bridge 13 SZ 5491
Wootton Common 13 SZ 5390
Wootton Courtenay 20 SS 9343
Wootton Fitzpaine 10 SY 3695
Wootton Rivers 23 SU 1962
Wootton St. Lawrence 24 SU 5953
Wootton Wawen 53 SP 1563
Worcester 52 SO 8555
Worcester Park 26 TQ 2266
Wordsley 52 SO 8887
Worfield 64 SO 7595
Workhouse Green 58 TL 8937
Workhouse Hill 43 TL 9931
Workington 92 NX 9928
Worksop 78 SK 5879
Worlaby 86 TA 0113
World's End (Berks.) 24 SU 4876
Worlds End (Hants) 13 SU 6312
Worle 21 ST 3562
Worleston 75 SJ 6856
Worlingham 59 TM 4489
Worlington (Devon.) 8 SS 7713
Worlington (Suff.) 57 TL 6973
Worlingworth 59 TM 2368
Wormald Green 91 SE 3065
Wormbridge 47 SO 4230
Wormegay 69 TF 6611
Wormelow Tump 47 SO 4930
Wormhill 77 SK 1274
Wormiehills 135 NO 6239
Wormingford 42 TL 9332
Worminghall 38 SP 6408
Wormington 53 SP 0336
Worminster 21 ST 5742
Wormit 134 NO 3925
Wormleighton 54 SP 4453
Wormley (Herts) 41 TL 3605
Wormley (Surrey) 25 SU 9438
Wormshill 28 TQ 8857
Wormsley 47 SO 4248
Worplesdon 25 SU 9753
Worrall 78 SK 3092
Worsbrough 85 SE 3503
Worsley 83 SD 7400
Worstead 71 TG 3026
Worsthorne 83 SD 8732
Worston (Devon) 6 SX 5952
Worston (Lancs) 83 SD 7642
Worswell 6 SX 5447
Worth (Kent) 29 TR 3356
Worth (Somer) 21 ST 5145
Worth (W Susx) 15 TQ 3036
Worth Abbey 15 TQ 3234
Worth Matravers 11 SY 9777
Wortham 58 TM 0777
Worthen 51 SJ 3204
Worthenbury 63 SJ 4146
Worthing (Norf.) 70 TF 9919
Worthing (W Susx) 15 TQ 1402
Worthington 66 SK 4020
Wortley (Glos) 36 ST 7691
Wortley (S. Yorks) 84 SK 3099
Worton (N. Yorks) 90 SD 9590
Worton (Wilts) 22 ST 9757
Wortwell 59 TM 2784
Wotherton 50 SJ 2800
Wotter 5 SX 5562
Wotton 15 TQ 1247
Wotton Under Edge 36 ST 7593
Wotton Underwood 38 SP 6815
Wouldham 28 TQ 7164
Wrabness 43 TM 1731
Wrafton 19 SS 4935
Wragby 80 TF 1378
Wramplingham 70 TG 1106
Wrangaton 6 SX 6757
Wrangham 150 NJ 6331
Wrangle 81 TF 4250
Wrangway 9 ST 1217
Wrantage 9 ST 3022
Wrawby 86 TA 0108
Wraxall (Avon) 35 ST 4872
Wraxall (Somer.) 21 ST 5936
Wray 89 SD 6067
Wraysbury 26 TQ 0173
Wrayton 89 SD 6172
Wrea Green 82 SD 3931
Wreay (Cumbr.) 95 NY 4349
Wreay (Cumbr.) 95 NY 4423
Wrecclesham 25 SU 8245
Wrekenton 105 NZ 2758
Wrelton 92 SE 7686
Wrenbury 63 SJ 5947
Wreningham 70 TM 1699
Wrentham 59 TM 4982
Wrentnall 51 SJ 4203
Wressing 9 ST 0508
Wressle 86 SE 7031
Wrestlingworth 56 TL 2547
Wretton 69 TF 6800
Wrexham 63 SJ 3349
Wribbenhall 52 SO 7975
Wrightington Bar 82 SD 5313
Wrinehill 76 SJ 7546
Wrington 21 ST 4662
Writhlington 22 ST 7054
Writtle 42 TL 6606
Wrockwardine 63 SJ 6212
Wroot 86 SE 7102
Wrotham 27 TQ 6159
Wrotham Heath 27 TQ 6258
Wroughton 37 SU 1480
Wroxall (I. of W.) 13 SZ 5579
Wroxall (Warw.) 53 SP 2271
Wroxeter 51 SJ 5608
Wroxham 71 TG 3017
Wroxton 54 SP 4141
Wyaston 65 SK 1842
Wyatt's Green 27 TQ 5999
Wyberton 68 TF 3240
Wyboston 56 TL 1656
Wybunbury 76 SJ 6949
Wych Cross 16 TQ 4231
Wychbold 52 SO 9166
Wyche 52 SO 7643
Wychnor 65 SK 1716
Wyck 25 SU 7539
Wycoller 83 SD 9339
Wycombe Marsh 39 SU 8992
Wyddial 41 TL 3731
Wye 29 TR 0546
Wyfordby 67 SK 7918
Wyke (Dorset) 22 ST 7926
Wyke (Salop) 51 SJ 6402
Wyke (Somer) 8 SX 8799
Wyke (W Yorks.) 84 SE 1526
Wyke Champflower 22 ST 6634
Wyke Regis 10 SY 6677
Wyke, The (Salop) 64 SJ 7306
Wykeham (N Yorks.) 93 SE 9683
Wyken 64 SO 7694
Wykey 63 SJ 3925
Wylam 105 NZ 1164
Wylde Green 65 SP 1293
Wyllie 34 ST 1794
Wylye 22 SU 0037
Wymering 13 SU 6405
Wymeswold 66 SK 6023
Wymington 55 SP 9564
Wymondham (Leic.) 67 SK 8518
Wymondham (Norf.) 70 TG 1101
Wymondley 40 TL 2128
Wyndham 33 SS 9391
Wynds Point 52 SO 7640
Wynford Eagle 10 SY 5895
Wynne's Green 47 SO 6047
Wyre Piddle 52 SO 9647
Wysall 66 SK 6027
Wythall 53 SP 0775
Wytham 38 SP 4708
Wyton (Cambs) 56 TL 2772
Wyton (Humbs) 87 TA 1833
Wyverstone 58 TM 0468
Wyverstone Street 58 TM 0367

Y Fan 49 SN 9487
Y Ffor 60 SH 3939
Y Rhiw 60 SH 2228
Y-Ffrith 74 SJ 0483
Yaddlethorpe 86 SE 8806
Yafford 13 SZ 4581
Yafforth 91 SE 3494
Yalberton 7 SX 8658
Yalding 27 TQ 7050
Yanworth 37 SP 0713
Yapham 92 SE 7851
Yapton 14 SU 9703
Yarbridge 13 SZ 6086
Yarburgh 81 TF 3493
Yarcombe 9 ST 2408
Yarde 20 ST 0538
Yardley 53 SP 1385
Yardley Gobion 55 SP 7644
Yardley Hastings 55 SP 8656
Yardro 46 SO 2258
Yarford 20 ST 2029
Yarkhill 47 SO 6042
Yarlet 64 SJ 9129
Yarley 21 ST 5045
Yarlington 22 ST 6529
Yarm 98 NZ 4111
Yarmouth 13 SZ 3589
Yarnacott 19 SS 6230
Yarnbrook 22 ST 8654
Yarnfield 64 SJ 8632
Yarnscombe 19 SS 5523
Yarnton 38 SP 4711
Yarpole 51 SO 4665
Yarrow (Borders) 109 NT 3527
Yarrow (Somer) 21 ST 3747
Yarrow Feus 109 NT 3325
Yarrowford 116 NT 4030
Yarwell 67 TL 0697
Yate 36 ST 7082
Yateley 25 SU 8160
Yatesbury 23 SU 0671
Yattendon 24 SU 5474
Yatton (Avon) 21 ST 4265
Yatton (Here & W) 51 SO 4367
Yatton (Here & W) 47 SO 6330
Yatton Keynell 22 ST 8676
Yaverland 13 SZ 6185
Yawl 9 SY 3194
Yaxham 70 TG 0010
Yaxley (Cambs.) 68 TL 1892
Yaxley (Suff.) 58 TM 1173
Yazor 47 SO 4046
Yeading 26 TQ 1182
Yeadon 84 SE 2040
Yealand Conyers 89 SD 5074
Yealand Redmayne 89 SD 5075
Yealmpton 6 SX 5751
Yearsley 92 SE 5874
Yeaton 63 SJ 4319
Yeaveley 65 SK 1840
Yedingham 93 SE 8979
Yelford 38 SP 3504
Yelling 56 TL 2562
Yelvertoft 54 SP 5975
Yelverton (Devon) 5 SX 5267
Yelverton (Norf.) 71 TG 2901
Yenston 10 ST 7120
Yeo Park 6 SX 5852
Yeoford 8 SX 7898
Yeolmbridge 5 SX 3187
Yeovil 10 ST 5515
Yeovil Marsh 10 ST 5418
Yeovilton 10 ST 5422
Yerbeston 30 SN 0609
Yesnaby 163 HY 2215
Yetlington 111 NU 0209
Yetminster 10 ST 5910
Yettington 9 SY 0585
Yetts o'Muckhart 126 NO 0001
Yielden 55 TL 0167
Yieldshields 116 NS 8750
Yiewsley 26 TQ 0680
Ynysboeth 34 ST 0696
Ynysddu 34 ST 1892
Ynyshir 34 ST 0292
Ynyslas 48 SN 6092
Ynysmaerdy 34 ST 0384
Ynysmeudwy 32 SN 7305
Ynyswen 45 SN 8313
Ynysybwl 34 ST 0594
Ynysymaengwyn 48 SH 5902
Yockenthwaite 90 SD 9079
Yockleton 63 SJ 3910
Yokefleet 86 SE 8124
Yoker 115 NS 5168
Yonder Bognie 150 NJ 5946
Yondertown 6 SX 5958
York 92 SE 6052
Yorkletts 29 TR 0963
Yorkley 35 SO 6306
Yorton 63 SJ 4923
Youlgreave 77 SK 2164
Youlstone 18 SS 2715
Youlthorpe 92 SE 7655
Youlton 91 SE 4863
Young's End 42 TL 7319
Yoxall 65 SK 1419
Yoxford 59 TM 3968
Ysbyty Ifan 61 SH 8448
Ysbyty Ystwyth 48 SN 7371
Ysceifiog 74 SJ 1571
Ysgubor-y-coed 48 SN 6895
Ystalyfera 33 SN 7608
Ystrad 33 SS 9796
Ystrad Aeron 45 SN 5256
Ystrad Meurig 48 SN 7067
Ystrad Mynach 34 ST 1493
Ystradfelte 46 SN 9313
Ystradgynlais 33 SN 7910
Ystradowen (Dyfed) 33 SN 7512
Ystradowen (S Glam.) 34 ST 0177
Ythanbank 151 NJ 9034
Ythsie 151 NJ 8830

Z

Zeal Monachorum 8 SS 7103
Zeals 22 ST 7731
Zelah 3 SW 8051
Zennor 2 SW 4538
Zouch 66 SK 5023

Index To Ireland

The map for Ireland employs an arbitrary system of grid reference. Each entry is identified by the page number, and is followed by a letter on the left-hand side of the map and by a number at the top. The entry can be located in the square where the lettered and numbered sections converge, e.g., Londonderry is to be found in the square marked by the dissecting blue lines of C4.

ACKNOWLEDGEMENTS

Daily Telegraph Colour Library *2/3 Satellite Image, 4/5 Satellite Image, 4 NOAA8, 4 Meteosat 2;* Meteorological Office Bracknell *4 Hercules Weather Aircraft Crown Copyright permission by HMSO;* Satellite Receiving Station Dundee University *5 Weather Satellite Image;* National Remote Sensing Centre RAE Farnborough *6/7 South Coast Satellite Image;* Austin Rover Group *6 Montego production line;* The Ford Motor Company *6 Model T Ford;* The Mansell Collection *7 Thomas Telford;* Sefton Photo Library Manchester *7 Blackstone Edge;* E A Bowness *7 Hardknott Pass;* The Post Office *7 Stamps;* AA Harry Williams *7 flap Tarr Steps, 14 Stonehenge, 15 Exmoor, 17 Grand Western Canal, 24/25 Sugar Loaf, Viewpoint, slopes of Sugar Loaf, River Usk; 34/35 Ben Lomond; 30/31, Farlington Marshes;* AA Colin Molyneux *7 flap Humber Bridge, 19 Tan Hill, 26/27 Kidderminster;* Sealand Aerial Photography *8/9 M25 Junction M3;* AA Picture Library *9 Swindon, Gantry signs, 11 Telephone boxes, Gantry signs, Rubbish, 13 Road signs, 16 Pontcysyllte, 23 Blackpool Tower, 32/33 Knaresborough, 36/37 Puffin Island, Conway, 38/39 Cobbler;* AA Archive Library *9 Traffic Lights;* Transport and Road Research Laboratory Crown copyright *10 flap Spaghetti Junction;* Spectrum Colour Library *10/11 M23 Motorway;* Ian Beames Ardea London *10 Kestrel;* E A James Nature Photographers Ltd *10 Ragwort;* Reflecting Roadstuds Ltd *11 Percy Shaw;* AA Martyn J Adelman *12/13 A322 Bagshot, 19 Bealach Na Ba' 26/27 Clent Hills, 28/29 Central Forest Park, Stoke, 30/31 Portsdown Hill, 32/33 Sutton Bank, Thirsk, Glider, 34/35 Cockleroy, 38/39 Lyle Hill, Cross of Lorraine;* AA John Wyand *12 Toll charges, 14 Westbury, 21 Corton;* Mary Evans Picture Library *12 Toll gates, 16 Harvest Mouse, 243 Engraving;* QT Associates *Design and artwork, 13 chart;* HMSO *13 Highway Code;* Richard Draper and Anne Winterbottom *illustrations on pages 14/15, 16/17, 18/19, 20/21, 22/23;* S & O Mathews *20 Biddenden Maids;* AA Sarah King *15 Wastwater;* Geoffrey Wright *15 Pennine Way;* AA T. Wood *17 Wicken Fen, Fenland Nr. Ramsey;* Museum of English Rural Life, Reading University *17 Water Can;* Chris Mylne Nature Photographers Ltd *18 Wild Cat;* L H Brown Nature Photographers Ltd *18 Ptarmigan;* Doc Rowe Centre for English Cultural Tradition Sheffield University *21 Abbots Bromley, Burry Man, Druids;* Picture by courtesy of the Hull Daily Mail *22 Holderness;* National Railway Museum York *23 Skegness;* BBC Hulton Picture Library *23 Bathing Machine;* AA Richard Surman *23 Lindisfarne, 26/27 Herefordshire Beacon, 28/29 Mow Cop;* West Air Photography *23 St Michaels Mount;* KAG Design *Retouching;* Bob Johnson *40 Barbury Castle viewpoint;* AA Bowater *33/35 Forth Bridges;* AA Robert Eames *36/37 Gt. Orme's Head;* AA Richard Newton *26/27 Dudley Castle, 28/29 City Museum;* Robin Fletcher *30/31 Portsmouth;* Brian Colquoun & Partners *10 sectional motorway surface diagram;* Roger Thomas, *text and research;* Gwen Manchester, North Wales Tourism Council, *Gt. Orme's Head viewpoint text;* Nature Conservancy Council; British Waterways Board; English Tourist Board; British Tourist Authority.

London's Orbital Routes

When the M25 is complete it will form a circular motorway route round London, apart from the section between junctions 2 and 31, linked by the Dartford Tunnel. This map shows the latest available information on the progress of the orbital route. All junctions are shown, with their exit signs, as appear at the actual junctions. The map also shows the North and South Circular roads and the Inner Ring Road. By using this map you can plan your route into or around the capital to be much less stressful; driving on motorways and trunk roads invariably saves time and frayed nerves.

LEGEND

Symbol	Meaning
M25	London Orbital Motorway
28	Junction (number indicated) on London Orbital Motorway
8/7	Motorway interchange showing junction numbers for both motorways
5	Junction with restricted access and exits (number indicated) on London Orbital Motorway
▭▭▭	London Orbital Motorway (under construction)
A10 Hertford 10 Enfield 3 / **25** / **A10** Enfield 3 Hertford 10	Exit signs showing road numbers and important destinations (distances are AA figures and do not appear on the actual signs)
10	Mileages between junctions
M4	Other motorways
3	Junction (number indicated) on other motorways
2	Junction with restricted access and exits (number indicated) on other motorways
S	Service area
A501	North & South Circular Roads and Inner Ring Road
A406 A12	Dual carriageway
A414	Primary route
A4020	A road
B2039	B road
= = = = = = =	Projected road

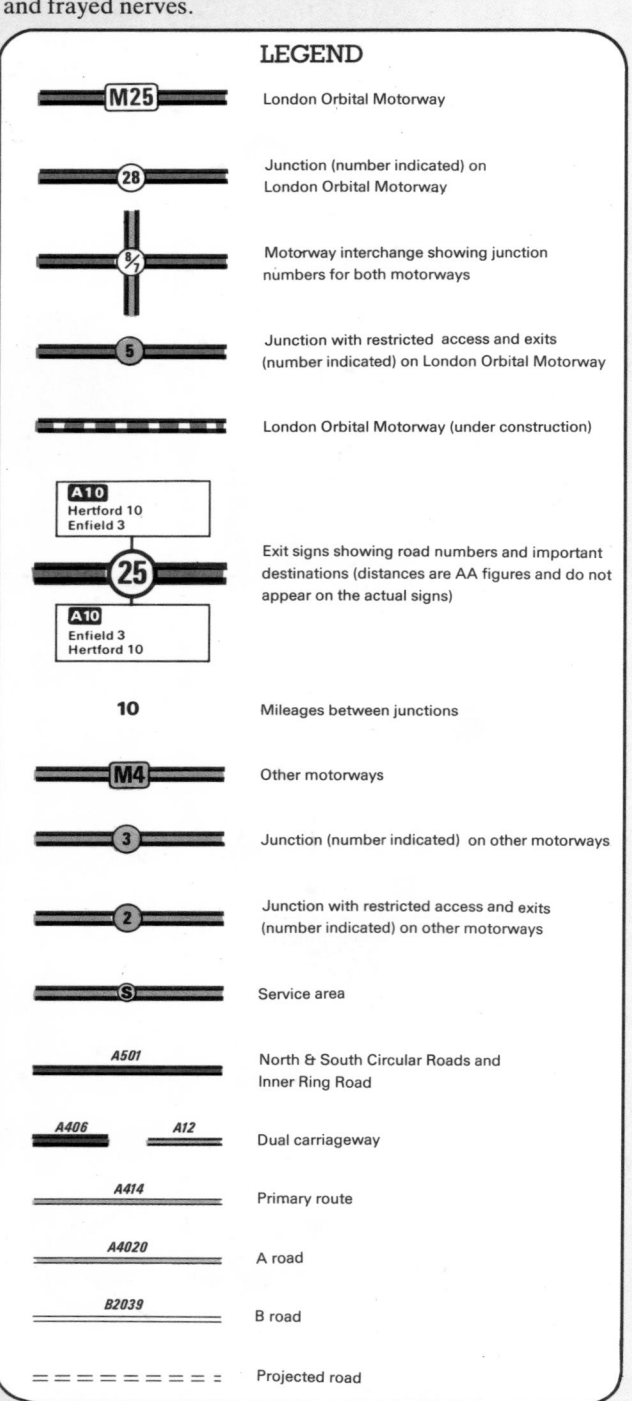

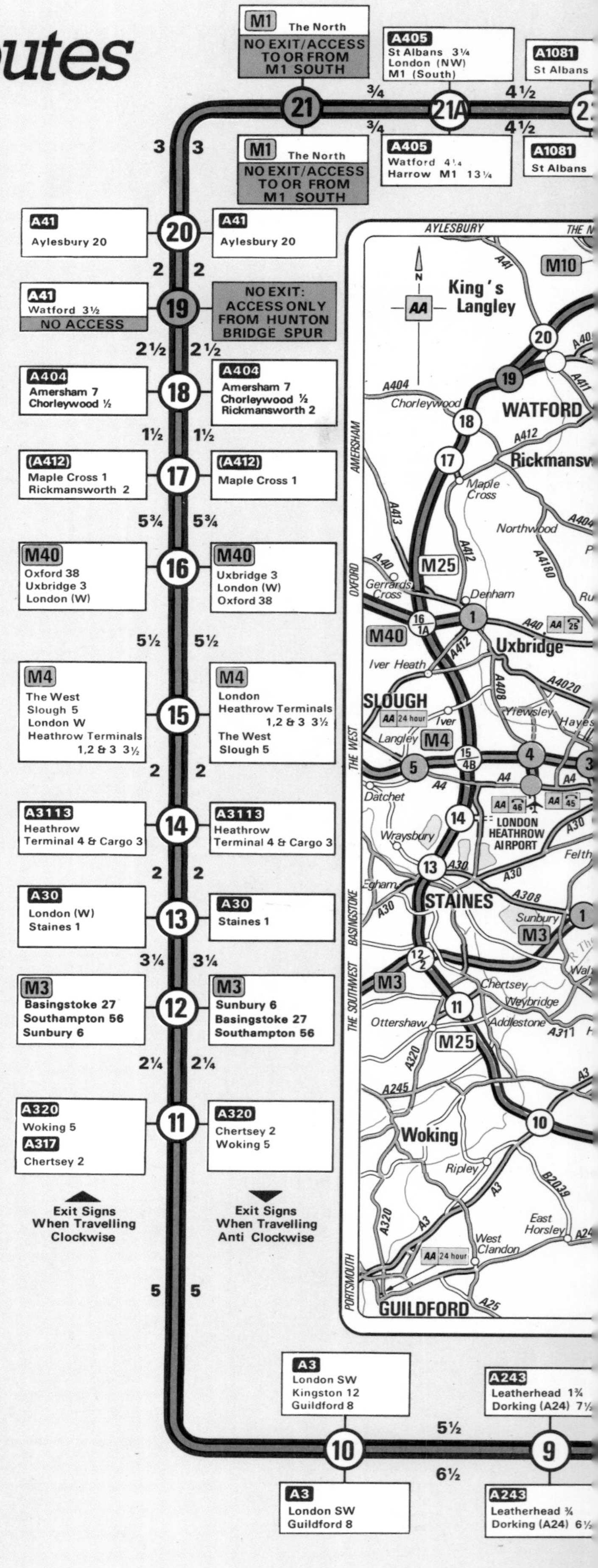

Exit Signs When Travelling Clockwise ▲

Exit Signs When Travelling Anti Clockwise ▼

Clockwise exit signs (left column)

21 — M1 The North NO EXIT/ACCESS TO OR FROM M1 SOUTH

20 — A41 Aylesbury 20

19 — A41 Watford 3½ NO ACCESS

18 — A404 Amersham 7 Chorleywood ½

17 — (A412) Maple Cross 1 Rickmansworth 2

16 — M40 Oxford 38 Uxbridge 3 London (W)

15 — M4 The West Slough 5 London W Heathrow Terminals 1,2 & 3 3½

14 — A3113 Heathrow Terminal 4 & Cargo 3

13 — A30 London (W) Staines 1

12 — M3 Basingstoke 27 Southampton 56 Sunbury 6

11 — A320 Woking 5 / A317 Chertsey 2

10 — A3 London SW Guildford 8

Anti-clockwise exit signs (right column)

21A — A405 St Albans 3¼ London (NW) M1 (South)

21 — A405 Watford 4¼ Harrow M1 13¼

A1081 St Albans

20 — A41 Aylesbury 20

19 — NO EXIT: ACCESS ONLY FROM HUNTON BRIDGE SPUR

M1 The North NO EXIT/ACCESS TO OR FROM M1 SOUTH

18 — A404 Amersham 7 Chorleywood ½ Rickmansworth 2

17 — (A412) Maple Cross 1

16 — M40 Uxbridge 3 London (W) Oxford 38

15 — M4 London Heathrow Terminals 1,2 & 3 3½ The West Slough 5

14 — A3113 Heathrow Terminal 4 & Cargo 3

13 — A30 Staines 1

12 — M3 Sunbury 6 Basingstoke 27 Southampton 56

11 — A320 Chertsey 2 Woking 5

9 — A243 Leatherhead 1¾ Dorking (A24) 7½

9 — A243 Leatherhead ¾ Dorking (A24) 6½

10 — A3 London SW Guildford 8

Mileages between junctions

3 · ¾ · 4½ · 3 · ¾ · 4½ · 2 · 2½ · 1½ · 5¾ · 5½ · 2 · 2 · 2 · 3¼ · 2¼ · 5 · 5½ · 6½

Top right signs

A405 St Albans 3¼ London (NW) M1 (South)

A1081 St Albans

A405 Watford 4¼ Harrow M1 13¼

A1081 St Albans